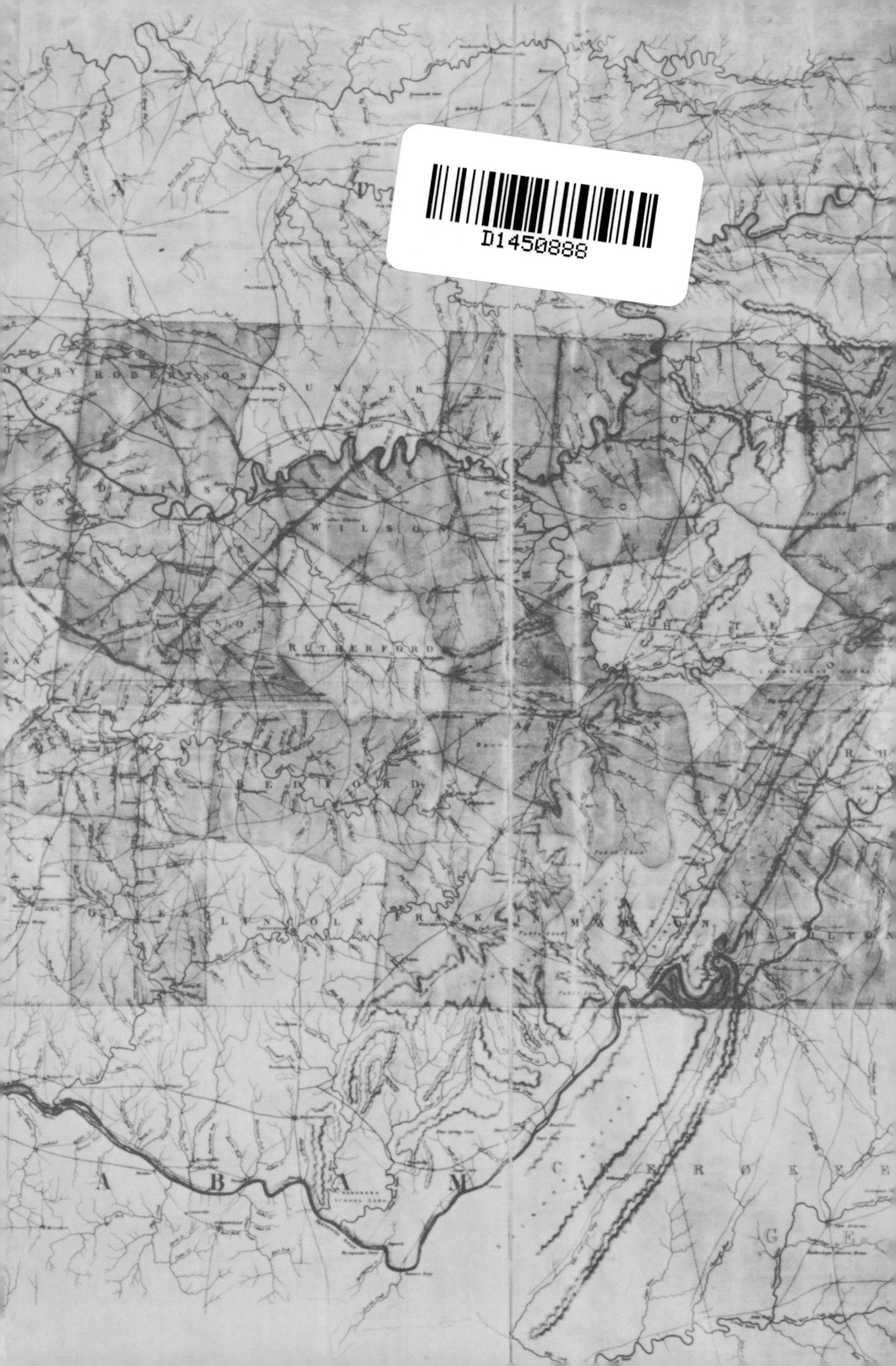
ROBERTSON
SUMNER
WILSON
RUTHERFORD
BEDFORD
LINCOLN
HAMILTON
CHEROKEE SCHOOL LAND

Volume Five of the correspondence covers three years of Polk's career, 1839–1841, during which period he completes his second term as Speaker of the U.S. House of Representatives, conducts a colorful and successful race for the governorship of Tennessee, fights for passage of his legislative program, seeks the 1840 vice-presidential nomination of the Democratic party, directs Van Buren's presidential campaign in Tennessee, and loses his bid for reelection as governor in 1841.

Polk's letters demonstrate that his two gubernatorial races attracted considerable national attention. In 1839 he ran as much against Henry Clay as Newton Cannon, the incumbent Whig governor. Polk's stunning victory signaled that Clay might have difficulty carrying the western states and thus probably hurt the Kentuckian's chances for winning the Whig presidential nomination in 1840. The gubernatorial election of 1841 proved just as colorful and arduous as that of 1839. Whig divisions at the national level almost gave Polk another upset victory; despite his loss he remained the overwhelming favorite and active leader of the Old Democracy in Tennessee. Polk's political letters illustrate much of the enthusiasm and spontaneity of politics at the state and local levels, which frequently involved as many as 85 percent of the eligible voters. Letters relating to the governor's official duties often pallor in comparison to the high drama of mass rallies, stump oratory, and partisan journalism.

Although family concerns surface with less frequency than previously, this volume does include two interesting series of letters in which James and Sarah inform one another of campaign activities. These personal exchanges reveal that Polk's wife played an active part in his political career by serving as his informal campaign coordinator. Letters to and from his large family connection tell of street fights, bank embezzlement, runaway slaves, financial distress, and many other diverse topics that reflect the variety and richness of that larger collection of over 2,400 letters from which the editors have selected 688 items for inclusion in Volume Five.

The Polk Project is sponsored jointly by Vanderbilt University, the National Historical Publications and Records Commission, the Tennessee Historical Commission, and the

Correspondence of James K. Polk

VOLUME V, 1839–1841

JAMES K. POLK

Engraving by J. B. Forrest
for the U.S. Democratic Review, *1844.*

Correspondence of
JAMES K. POLK

Volume V
1839-1841

WAYNE CUTLER
Editor

EARL J. SMITH
CARESE M. PARKER
Associate Editors

1979
Vanderbilt University Press
Nashville

Library of Congress Cataloging in Publication Data (Revised)

Polk, James Knox, Pres. U.S., 1795–1849.
Correspondence of James K. Polk.

Vol. 5 edited by W. Cutler.
CONTENTS: v. 1. 1817–1832.—v. 2. 1833–1834.—v. 3. 1835–1836.—v. 4. 1837–1838.—v. 5. 1839–1841.
1. Polk, James Knox, Pres. U.S., 1795–1849. 2. Tennessee—Politics and government—To 1865—Sources. 3. United States—Politics and government—1845–1849—Sources. 4. Presidents—United States—Correspondence. 5. Tennessee—Governors—Correspondence. I. Weaver, Herbert, ed. II. Cutler, Wayne, 1938–
III. Title.
E417.A4 1969 973.6′1′0924 75–84005
ISBN 0–8265–1208–9

Printed in the United States of America
by Kingsport Press, Inc., Kingsport, Tennessee

Sponsored by

Vanderbilt University

The National Historical Publications and Records Commission

The Tennessee Historical Commission

The Polk Memorial Association

To

Herbert Weaver

Paul H. Bergeron and Kermit L. Hall

PREFACE

Writing to Andrew Jackson Donelson from Washington on January 3, 1839, Speaker Polk looked ahead to his forthcoming gubernatorial contest and gave directions for placing J. George Harris in the editorial chair of the *Nashville Union.* Donelson must supply Harris with information "in regard to the local politics of the State"; but on national questions the new editor would need no instruction. Polk's selection of a New Englander as his chief campaign polemicist signaled the direction of his political strategy for returning Tennessee to the Old Democracy. Local and state issues generally must give way to those of national consequence, for the gubernatorial and congressional races were part of the continuing partisan struggle for national supremacy. Democrats in Arkansas and Whigs in Massachusetts could afford to concentrate on local issues precisely because their electorates were decidedly of one mind on national questions. But in Tennessee no such consensus could be effected.

In each of Polk's three gubernatorial races the results would prove exceedingly close. In 1839 he received 51 percent of the vote; in 1841 he lost with 48.5 percent; and in 1843 he failed with 48.2 percent. National questions dominated all three contests and engendered a high level of voter participation. According to estimates made by Brian G. Walton, "The Second Party System in Tennessee," *East Tennessee Historical Society's Publications,* No. 43 (1971), p. 19, over 85 percent of the eligible adult white males voted in each of the three elections. Anticipating very close decisions, Polk and his opponents left little to chance and took no voter for granted; thus the intensity of party organizational efforts reinforced a popular notion that what happened in Tennessee elections really mattered.

In the 1839 campaign Polk successfully made Henry Clay's 1840 presidential prospects the central issue. Although Martin Van Buren enjoyed no great personal appeal among Tennesseans, Clay commanded even less. The Kentucky Whig bore the indelible stain of having bargained away the presidency in 1824. In that one piece of power brokerage he had violated the very essence of popular rule and had cast his lot with resurgent Federalism. That Tennessee's favorite son, Andrew Jackson, had been injured by the bargain further compromised Clay's standing with the Tennessee electorate. Polk also attacked Clay's previous support of such consolidationist measures as protective tariffs, internal improvements, and a national bank. The Whig gubernatorial candidate, incumbent Governor Newton Cannon, tried to deflect Polk's attacks on Clay by dismissing national questions all together and running on his record of success in launching the state's 1838 internal improvements program. That stratagem failed because Cannon would neither disavow Clay nor administer the improvements program with that measure of liberality thought desirable by many Whig contractors. Polk picked the right approach and mounted one of the most aggressive campaigns ever waged in Tennessee's often turbulent political history.

While completing his final session as House Speaker, Polk kept one eye on his official duties and the other on Tennessee political movements. The third and final session of the Twenty-fifth Congress proved singularly unproductive, for effective control of the House had passed to the Whigs when in 1838 Sergeant S. Prentiss and Thomas J. Word of Mississippi took their much disputed seats. Even the formality of the House's adopting a resolution of thanks to its Speaker gave rise to Whig charges that Polk had been unduly partisan. S. S. Southworth, a Whig reporter for several eastern newspapers, thought the accusations against the Speaker unwarranted and credited him with having been "dignified, impartial and upright" in presiding over the House. Although official duties held Polk in Washington City until March 4, he prepared himself and his lieutenants for the campaign in Tennessee.

Having lost all but three of Tennessee's thirteen congressional races in 1837, Democrats paid special heed to their selection of congressional candidates. In Middle Tennessee Polk's home district required particular attention when A. O. P. Nicholson withdrew from the race and opened the door to factional rivalries. Skillful management avoided schism and gave the preference to Harvey M. Watterson of Bedford County. Robert M. Burton accepted the party's call to run against John Bell in the heavily Whig district of Nashville. Cave Johnson, another experienced, but reluctant leader, ran for his old seat in the Clarksville district. In the Pulaski district Polk prevented a three-man race by placing Aaron V. Brown's fellow Democrat, Andrew A. Kincannon, in a lucrative position with the federal Indian office. William G. Childress, cousin of Sarah Childress Polk, led the Democrats in the Franklin-Murfreesboro district, which was a Whig stronghold. William B. Trousdale decided to make a second effort at ousting William B. Campbell from his Gallatin-Carthage seat. Incumbent Hopkins L. Turney of the Mountain District faced nominal opposition from Anthony Dibrell. Thus in Middle Tennessee Polk's party ran but one incumbent in the seven congressional races; without strong candidates for Congress Polk's chances of winning large majorities in the state's traditionally Democratic section would be extremely slight. No one understood better than Polk the difficulty of offsetting Whig majorities in East and West Tennessee. He had little reason to hope for victories by Burton, Childress, or Trousdale, but Whig majorities in those districts might be reduced. Thus determined efforts in the Whig districts might aid his bid for the governorship.

Of the four East Tennessee districts Polk could count on only that of Abraham McClellan from Sullivan County. Democrats in the Knoxville district chose not to contest the reelection of Joseph L. Williams. Joseph Powell agreed to challenge incumbent William B. Carter of Carter County, and Julius W. Blackwell undertook his first political race to run against incumbent William Stone. In the Western District William C. Dunlap and Stephen C. Pavatt raised the party standard against two very popular Whigs, Christopher H. Williams and John W. Crockett. As was the case in Middle Tennessee, Democrats in East and West Tennessee faced very poor prospects for reversing the Whig triumph of 1837.

The General Assembly elections of 1839 also were thought to be vital to the gubernatorial race, but Polk left to each congressional candidate the arrangement of Assembly candidates and campaigns within his district. No other party structure could serve those functions, for party members elected to the Assembly were thrown together but for a few months every other year. Even when Democrats controlled the executive branch of the state government, the party structure remained diffused; the number of placemen was never so large as to allow centralization of state political power. The Old Democracy found its political center at the county level, where court-day meetings were held to choose candidates for the legislature and to appoint committees to manage election campaigns. Coordination of candidate selection and campaign finance seldom extended above the level of the congressional district. Much depended upon the congressional elections, for failure at that level often left the party vulnerable to factional discord and division. By pressing strong local leaders into the 1839 election Polk laid the foundations for his party's revival in Tennessee.

During the four months of intensive campaigning prior to the August election Polk permitted himself only two days' rest at his home in Columbia. Never before in Tennessee history had a candidate for governor given himself so completely to the rigors of the saddle and the stump. Arriving home from Washington City on March 23, Polk spent almost a week preparing an "Address to the People of Tennessee," of which ten thousand copies were ordered for statewide distribution. In his twenty-eight page pamphlet he set forth a brief history of U.S. political parties and explained his personal views on both national and state issues. Armed with his position paper and two weeks' preparation, Polk launched his first tour on April 8. He visited several counties in Middle Tennessee and on April 21 crossed the Cumberland Mountain into East Tennessee, where he delivered at least one speech in every county. Governor Cannon traveled with Polk through Middle Tennessee, but declined to accompany his opponent into East Tennessee. Polk wrote Sarah regularly during his trip, informed her of his reception at each appointment, and frequently requested her aid in handling his incoming correspondence. Indeed, she in Columbia and Postmaster Robert Armstrong in Nashville served informally as his campaign coordinators. On May 20 he reached Johnson County and on the day following turned westward taking the northern tier of counties on his return to Middle Tennessee. He spoke in Gallatin on June 12 and arrived in Columbia on June 17. Two days later he set out for the Western District, where he campaigned through the first week of July. During the next two weeks of the contest Polk attended meetings in Middle Tennessee. With but ten days remaining he adjusted his schedule, followed Cannon into East Tennessee, and ended the campaign on August 1 at Knoxville.

Polk won his first race for governor by a scant 2,116 votes. He received 51 percent of the 106,008 votes cast in that contest. His 4,403-vote majority in Middle Tennessee offset his 361-vote loss in East Tennessee and his 1,926-deficit in the Western District. The 1839 race for the governorship drew over 20,000 more voters than did the 1837 contest. In the Assembly elections Democrats gained a 14-to-11 advantage in the Senate and a 42-to-33 majority in the House. Although Democrats did not win but six of Tennessee's thirteen congressional races, their gain of three seats signaled that the Democracy in Tennessee had recovered much of its former support. In all quarters Polk's friends attributed the electoral triumph to the governor-elect's personal exertions and partisan orthodoxy.

Polk's dramatic reversal of his party's fortunes in Tennessee encouraged many southern Democrats in their efforts to drop Vice-President Richard M. Johnson from the 1840 ticket. Johnson's southern adversaries argued that his private indiscretions and abolitionist sympathies would defeat efforts to unite behind the president. Polk, by way of contrast, had demonstrated great personal integrity in risking his political career for the "redemption" of Tennessee; his success in healing party schisms had commended his example to the Democracy in all sections of the country.

Tennessee Democrats needed no outside encouragement to excite their hopes for placing Polk on the 1840 ticket. As though by prearrangement, friendly editors throughout the state followed their election reports with calls for Polk's selection as the party's candidate for the vice-presidency. Democrats in North Alabama took up the idea and honored Polk with dinners at Courtland and Huntsville. Shortly after the governor-elect's inauguration on October 14, Samuel H. Laughlin introduced a resolution in the Tennessee Senate recommending a Van Buren–Polk ticket for 1840.

Polk's formal entry into the race for the vice-presidential nomination evoked words of caution from confidants in both Arkansas and Alabama. Archibald Yell urged him to defer to Thomas H. Benton's ambitions to succeed Van Buren four years hence; Polk was young enough to wait. Joshua Martin echoed Yell's advice and assured Polk that his turn would come. For his part the young Tennessee governor took one election at a time and sought to avert an almost certain Whig triumph in the South, for the party there could not carry the burden of both Van Buren and Johnson. Having denounced the Whigs for trying to force the 1836 presidential election into the U.S. House, Polk felt obliged to oppose those in his own party who for reasons of expediency would send the 1840 vice-presidential election to the U.S. Senate. The Senate's choice for vice-president in 1837 had proved sufficiently embarrassing to warrant the trouble of holding a national nominating convention and forcing the party to make a responsible decision.

According to Cave Johnson's testimony, Polk did not view his vice-presidential candidacy as a stepping-stone to the 1844 presidential nomination. In the fall of 1839 Polk favored Benton's claims to succeed Van Buren. Cave Johnson so informed one of Benton's backers, William Allen of Ohio. Of course, Polk's denial of aspirations for the succession was not the same as a pledge to back Benton or to remove himself from all future consideration. Polk needed the support of Benton, as well as of Calhoun, if he were to force Van Buren's selection of a running mate agreeable to the party in all sections of the country. The unexpected Whig nomination of William H. Harrison for president aborted efforts to detach Benton from his support of Vice-President Johnson, whose western ties and military record were judged necessary offsets to the Whig selection of a westerner to head their ticket. Although Polk received

Calhoun's endorsement, he failed to convince the South Carolinian of the necessity of a national convention. Thomas Ritchie of Virginia also supported Polk's candidacy, but balked at sending a delegation. Van Buren let it be known that New York would prefer Polk in the Electoral College or in a Senate election, but would take neutral ground in the national convention, which met in Baltimore on May 5, 1840. Without the votes of South Carolina, Virginia, and New York, Polk's lieutenants saw no possibility of winning the nomination and acceded to Van Buren's wishes that the convention drop the vice-presidential question.

Polk left the possibility open for a consensus nomination at the state level, but declared emphatically his intention to withdraw his candidacy should it be sponsored by only a minority of his party. Party leaders in the North and West ignored Polk's threat to leave Van Buren without a running mate in the South. True to his word, Polk took his name out of the contest and with no little embarrassment fought to carry his own state for Van Buren. The Whig party in Tennessee won a 12,000-vote majority and reduced the Democracy to a state of near total despondency.

In his inaugural address Polk launched his term as governor with a brief declaration of his anti-consolidationist political principles. At some greater length a week later he detailed in a legislative message his agenda of business to be considered by the General Assembly. Two questions figured most prominently in his analysis, both of which tested fully the new governor's resolve to put theory into practice. During his first week in office Tennessee bankers had learned of a severe financial crisis in the eastern money markets and had suspended specie payments indefinitely. Believing that the banks ought to meet their obligations to the full extent of their resources and fearing that suspension would lead to excessive issues of bank notes, the governor called for a prompt resumption of specie payments, a six-month ban on bank dividends, and an end to the issuance of bank notes in denominations of under ten dollars. Justifying his hard-money approach to political economy, Polk argued that Tennesseans must look to their own industry and resources to carry them through hard times. Depreciating the circulating medium would only inflate prices, fuel speculation, and postpone the contraction of trade that must follow periods of borrowed prosperity. Government-controlled economies were, in Polk's day, the rule rather than the exception; but then so were despotic governments. Mercantilism might render the country greater wealth, but it almost certainly would curb the sphere of individual freedom. Polk's political creed, however, could not be implemented without legislative action against the banking industry, for the state government long since had chartered its way into the economic order. Democratic members of the legislature split over the governor's banking proposals, and with Democratic assistance a Whig minority succeeded in blocking all efforts at effective banking reform. Whig editors across Tennessee taunted the governor that perhaps a want of genuine devotion to party principles accounted for the apostacy of his friends in the legislature. His detractors, however, produced no evidence that he had sabotaged his own banking program.

Polk's recommendations for maintaining and improving control over the state's internal improvements system met with even less support from Democratic legislators. The governor had urged the legislature to raise the interest level payable on internal improvements bonds from 5 to 6 percent. His object was to enable the Bank of Tennessee to secure bond purchases in specie or sterling equivalencies. Additional bond sales would reduce the scarcity of coin in the state. By funding in specie the state's half of the internal improvements capitalization he would diminish pressures occasioned by his hard-money banking reforms. Having lost control of the Bank of Tennessee and having opposed a forced specie resumption, Whig legislators scuttled the internal improvements program that they had begun in 1838. Numerous Democrats joined the Whigs in ending the state's subscription to new ventures and in creating a board of commissioners to review the application of funds previously subscribed. Polk's reform program had called for a public works board, but credit for that minor reform went to the Whigs. Faced with worsening economic conditions and trimming Democrats, Polk failed to enact the two principal proposals in his legislative program. That the governor had played a more active legislative role than most of his predecessors made his failures all the more visible. Yet his deep sense of duty and his penchant for consistency did not allow him to take a more expedient course of action.

Polk attended to his executive duties, such as they were, with efficiency and ease. A small cadre of five officials, which included the secretary of state, comptroller, treasurer, attorney-general, and school superintendent, managed the state's business and answered for it directly to the legislature. Although the 1834 Constitution charged the governor with responsibility for enforcing the laws faithfully, it gave the chief magistrate almost no powers. He had authority to grant pardons, commute sentences, require reports from executive departments, fill vacancies in state offices (between legislative sessions), call special sessions of the General Assembly, sign commissions, and head the state's army, navy, or militia, if not pressed into active federal service. Having no power to remove state officials or to veto legislation, the governor held the reins of state government but very loosely. Polk found that the authority to report and recommend state needs to the legislature often amounted to little more than noble pleading.

In his capacity as party leader Polk demonstrated a greater measure of influence. For example, Democratic legislators deferred to the governor's wish to elect Felix Grundy to the U.S. Senate in the fall of 1839. In that particular instance the governor's strategy worked because it produced agreement and avoided factional splits. In the spring of 1841 Polk received conflicting advice on the question of calling a special session of the General Assembly to fill vacancies in both U.S. Senate seats. Without such action Tennessee would be without senatorial representation in the special session of Congress scheduled to meet in the summer. The governor chose to leave the seats vacant, and Democratic aspirants for the U.S. Senate accepted the decision without complaint. Nor did any Democrat rise to challenge the governor's decision to run for a second term, for none had an equal claim or prospect of election.

With some fifteen months remaining of his two-year term, Polk announced his bid for reelection at a party rally in Knoxville on July 4, 1840. As a declared candidate for office the governor felt free to travel the state and encourage party workers to action in the coming presidential election. Almost with reckless abandon he risked his personal prestige in a race that really was not his own. To be certain the governor wanted a Van Buren victory, but in all probability he yielded to party pleas for assistance because above all he loved a good scrap and suffered boredom rather badly. He was a zealous partisan with an unbounded passion for political action. Whig editors seized on his intrusion into the presidential campaign and argued that electing presidents was not one of the duties for which Tennesseans paid their governor $2,000 a year in salary. Polk dismissed the complaint and urged his fellow citizens to ignore the "trickery and flummery" of Whig promises, which included the establishment of a federal government as innocent and heroic as their western nominee of log-cabin, hard cider, and raccoon-hat fame. Searching hard for an issue, Polk cited Harrison's support of a "white slave" law in Ohio, his alleged connections with abolitionists, and his campaign committee's refusal to let the candidate speak or write for himself. Unfortunately for the governor, the viable issues in Tennessee remained that of corruption and hard times under Van Buren's administration. The fusion of those two issues, plus Polk's rejection as his party's candidate for vice-president, probably would have brought the Whigs victory without their resort to campaign mummery. Polk's distain for their refusal to discuss substantive issues only intensified his determination to win reelection in 1841.

Thus for the third successive year Polk reached out to the voters of

Tennessee, explained his party's political principles, and urged them to reject Whig claims upon the cause of popular sovereignty. Knowing that Polk would mount an issue-oriented campaign and believing that the electorate would respond better to a "man of the people" candidate, Whig leaders chose a good storyteller, James C. Jones, to run against the sober-minded governor. Jones probably did not win many votes with his country humor; nor, on the other hand, did he lose so many as to defeat himself. At the beginning of the campaign he enjoyed the advantages of a novel approach to campaigning and a greater measure of party support. However, Whig divisions in Washington between Clay and Tyler brought serious issues into focus and cracked the facade of Whig unity in Tennessee. By mid-July Polk had gained the initiative by attacking Clay's management of both the Congress and the acting president's cabinet. For the first time the governor's party awakened to the possibility of winning the election, but its revival came too late. Polk did succeed in reducing the Whig majority of 1840 by some nine thousand votes. Democrats quickly claimed a moral victory for their candidate. Having done better than anyone dared hope, Polk retained the loyalty and affection of the party faithful, who admired his fidelity to principle and courage in battle. Ex-governor Polk did not stand alone in his defeat.

This Volume

Polk's correspondence continues to reflect his heavy involvement in Democratic party politics at both the state and national levels. Although family concerns surface with less frequency, this volume does include two interesting series of letters in which James and Sarah inform one another of campaign activities. Exchanges between Polk and other members of his large family connection tell of William H. Polk's conviction for assaulting Richard H. Hayes, Samuel W. Polk's illness and death, James Walker's discovery of bank embezzlement, Silas M. Caldwell's recovery of Polk's runaway slaves, Ezekiel P. McNeal's efforts to sell Polk lands in the Western District, William G. Childress' unsuccessful race for Congress, and Edwin F. Polk's refutation of charges of Toryism against Ezekiel Polk. These and many other topics indicate the diversity and richness of that larger collection of over 2,400 letters from which the editors have selected 688 items for inclusion in the present volume. Space limitations would permit no more than a sampling of the governor's official correspondence, which for the most part dealt with pardons, bond issues, applications and recommendations for office, and commissions for civil and military office.

Continuing under the assumption that their primary responsibility is to assemble and make available the significant correspondence of James K. Polk, the editors have made no important changes in the editorial procedures adopted for the first four volumes. Selectivity has been necessary, but otherwise the editors have continued in their efforts to reproduce the correspondence in a form as faithful to the original text of each letter as possible; original spelling, punctuation, capitalization, and grammar have been preserved except when slight alterations have been required for the sake of clarity. Lowercase letters at the beginning of sentences have been converted to capitals. When it has been impossible at other places to determine whether the writer intended a capital or a lowercase letter, current style has been followed. Commas and semicolons have been inserted sparingly in sentences that lack clarity or are deficient in punctuation. Superfluous dashes have generally been deleted, and those that appeared at the ends of sentences have been converted to appropriate punctuation marks. Words unintentionally repeated by the writers have been deleted. These minor changes have been made silently, without editorial indications of where they occur. Letters that were particularly difficult to decipher or those written by semiliterate persons have been given special attention, and that fact is indicated in the footnotes. Reliance on the ever-useful *sic* has been severely limited.

As all the letters printed are either to or from James K. Polk, his name will seldom be included in the headings that appear above the documents. Regardless of their position in the original manuscript, the salutation, provenance, and date will ordinarily appear on a single line just below the heading. Except in rare instances, complimentary closings have been omitted. An unnumbered note at the end of each letter or summary gives the document's classification, repository designation, place of address, authorial notations, endorsements, and notice of previous publication.

Numbered annotations follow the unnumbered note. Ordinarily a brief explanation or identification is given upon the first mention of a person or special subject. Later appearances of such persons or subjects are not usually accompanied by editorial comment. To identify everything is, of course, impossible; some items have been identified only tentatively. The editors thought that these tracings, however slight in some cases, might prove useful to the researcher. The names of some persons are marked "not identified further" either for want of sources or for lack of textual clarity as to which of two or more persons by the same name was intended. Unusual cases of the latter kind have been explained briefly. The index will be helpful in sorting references in which only a surname is given and in finding the location of the original explanation or identification.

The annotations often have been assembled from several sources. Frequently the sources are so obvious as to need no identification. These considerations, coupled with a desire to insure that the footnotes do not overwhelm the presentation of the textual material, have persuaded the editors to forego the citation of sources in footnotes.

Acknowledgments

The dedication of this volume to Herbert Weaver, Paul H. Bergeron, and Kermit L. Hall is but a small tribute to that excellence of historical scholarship and editing which they brought to the first four volumes of Polk's correspondence. In a substantive way their work continues and blends with that of the present editor, who acknowledges with thanks the sustaining contributions made by his editorial predecessors. Of similar magnitude are his debts to Earl J. Smith and Carese M. Parker, without whose associated labors volume five would have remained greatly unfinished.

Together we take this occasion to express our appreciation to the talented and helpful staffs of the Vanderbilt University Library, the Tennessee State Library and Archives, the National Archives and Records Service, and the Library of Congress. For their generous sponsorship of the Polk Project special thanks go to the members of the National Historical Publications and Records Commission and its staff, headed by Frank G. Burke; to members of the Tennessee Historical Commission and its staff, directed by Herbert L. Harper; and to members of the Polk Memorial Association and its Auxiliary. We also single out the kind assistance of John W. Poindexter, Jane C. Tinsley, Gary G. Gore, and Estelle K. Leach in shepherding this volume through the intricacies of manufacture and distribution. Leta R. Cutler, our staff assistant, merits the highest of praise for rendering our efforts decipherable to the typographers.

It is the editor's particular pleasure to say "thank you" to the history faculty and general officers of Vanderbilt University for including the Polk Project in their long-range program of research and publication. No project could hope to be associated with a group of scholars more supportive than are they in maintaining high standards of scholarship and collegiality.

WAYNE CUTLER

Nashville, Tennessee
July 1979

CONTENTS

1840

1841

SYMBOLS

Document Classifications

ADS	Autograph Document Signed
ADS, copy	Autograph Document Signed, copied by writer
AE	Autograph Endorsement
AEI	Autograph Endorsement Initialed
AES	Autograph Endorsement Signed
AEs	Autograph Endorsements
AL	Autograph Letter
AL, draft	Autograph Letter, drafted by writer
AL, fragment	Autograph Letter, fragment
ALI	Autograph Letter Initialed
ALS	Autograph Letter Signed
ALS, draft	Autograph Letter Signed, drafted by writer
ALsS	Autograph Letters Signed
Copy	Copy, not by writer; authorship attributed
DS	Document Signed
EI	Endorsement Initialed
L	Letter, penned and signed by person other than the writer; authorship attributed
LS	Letter Signed
PL	Printed Letter; authorship attributed

Repository Designations

A	Alabama Archives and Department of History
CU	University of California Library, Berkeley
DLC	Library of Congress
DLC–AJ	Library of Congress, Andrew Jackson Papers
DLC–AJD	Library of Congress, Andrew Jackson Donelson Papers

DLC–GWC	Library of Congress, George Washington Campbell Papers
DLC–JKP	Library of Congress, James K. Polk Papers
DLC–MVB	Library of Congress, Martin Van Buren Papers
DNA	National Archives
MH	Harvard University Library
MHi	Massachusetts Historical Society
MoHi	Missouri State Historical Society
NBuHi	Buffalo Historical Society
NhHi	New Hampshire Historical Society
NHi	New-York Historical Society
NHpR	Franklin D. Roosevelt Library, Hyde Park
NjMoHP	Morristown National Historical Park
NjP	Princeton University Library
NN–A	New York Public Library-Astor Collection
NNPM	Pierpont Morgan Library, New York
PHi	Historical Society of Pennsylvania
PP	Free Library of Philadelphia
T	Tennessee State Library
T–JKP	Tennessee State Library, James K. Polk Papers
THi–JKP	Tennessee Historical Society, James K. Polk Papers
TU	University of Tennessee, Knoxville

Published Sources

ETHSP	*East Tennessee Historical Society's Publications*
THM	*Tennessee Historical Magazine*
THQ	*Tennessee Historical Quarterly*

CHRONOLOGY

1795	November 2	Born in Mecklenburg County, North Carolina
1806	Fall	Moved to Maury County, Tennessee
1812	Fall	Underwent major surgery by Dr. Ephraim McDowell in Danville, Kentucky
1813	July	Began study under Robert Henderson at Zion Church Academy
1816	January	Entered University of North Carolina as a sophomore
1818	June	Graduated from University of North Carolina
	Fall	Began reading law in office of Felix Grundy
1819	September	Elected clerk of the senate of Tennessee General Assembly
1820	June	Admitted to the bar
1823	August	Elected to the lower house of Tennessee General Assembly
1824	January 1	Married to Sarah Childress of Murfreesboro
1825	August	Elected to United States House of Representatives
1827	August	Re-elected to House of Representatives
	November 5	Death of his father, Samuel Polk
1829	August	Re-elected to House of Representatives
1831	January 21	Death of his brother Franklin, aged 28
	April 12	Death of his brother Marshall, aged 26
	August	Re-elected to House of Representatives
	September 28	Death of his brother John, aged 24
1833	August	Re-elected to House of Representatives
	December	Became chairman, Ways and Means Committee
1834	June	Defeated by John Bell for Speaker of the House
1835	August	Re-elected to House of Representatives
	December 7	Elected Speaker of the House over John Bell

1836	August 6	Death of his sister Naomi, wife of Adlai O. Harris
1837	August	Re-elected to House of Representatives
	September 4	Re-elected Speaker of the House
1839	August	Elected Governor of Tennessee over Newton Cannon
1841	August	Defeated in gubernatorial election by James C. Jones
1843	August	Defeated in gubernatorial election by James C. Jones
1844	May	Nominated for the presidency at Democratic National Convention
	November	Elected President of the United States over Henry Clay
1845	March 4	Inaugurated as President of the United States
1849	March 4	Yielded office to his successor, Zachary Taylor
	June 15	Died in Nashville

Correspondence of James K. Polk

VOLUME V, 1839–1841

1839

FROM WILLIAM H. POLK[1]

Dear Brother, Columbia Tennessee Jany 2d 1839

I received some days ago your letter under cover to Dr. Hays.[2] The suggestions contained in it I have adhered to. I have consulted my Counsel,[3] on the course you suggested to me, to endeavor to suppress and put an end to the prosecution before the *Grand Jury*. They had determined to make the effort and have no doubt of its success, if the *Grand Jury* are in possession of the *entire facts*—they will use all exertion to have them properly *charged* by the Judge and have no doubt but what the *Solicitor* (Thomas)[4] will furnish the Grand Jury with all the evidence. I of course consulted them, as if the propriety of stifling the prosecution before the Grand Jury had occurred to my own mind and not, as having received suggestions on the subject from you or any one else. None of the family know that Dr. Hays or myself have received letters *from you*. Nor shall they know it. On the reception of your letter, I immediately wrote to Dr. Dickinson,[5] in reference to giving Mr. Foster[6] a statement of the facts, in such a way, as to induce him, to advise *his friends*. I received in answer a letter from Dr. Dickinson in which he said he had anticipated the necessity of placing the *facts* in Mr. Foster's possession and had written to him a fiew days before he received my letter. I also wrote Dr. D. to employ Mr. Fletcher.[7] He seen Mr. Fletcher and he requested him to say to me, as a friend that he considered "my case *a very plain one*"; and he thought any foreign assistance would be prejudicial to me, as it would evince too much anxiety on my part, and lead to the inference that I was highly fearful of the *result*. And by all means for me to have the Trial over the first Court. He at the same time told Dr. D. "that it was probably against his interest that he had given the advice which he had and that if I still desired his services, he would cheerfully render me any assistance in his power." Knowing this to be Mr. Fletcher's opinion, I have determined *not to employ him.*

I received this evening your letter of the 22d. Dec.[8] I have been very careful, in having all the evidence ascertained—and by who such facts could be proven by. Dr. Hays is doing this. You need have no fears. The case shall be managed carefully and with dilligence by my Counsel, if it is in my power to urge them to it. Public opinion is running in my favour. I have in a great measure withdrawn myself from society—go into the Town very seldom and will by no act of mine give my *enimies* the least pretext for an acquisation [accusation] of any character so as to prejudice the public mind against me. I think I will employ Jonas E. Thomas,[9] as his assistance will be important in the selection of a Jury.

In your letter to Mr. Walker[10] you say that Mr. Foster is of the impression that I am condemned for shooting *buck shot* instead of a *single ball.* I am not condemed in public estimation for this. I did not know with what weapon I was to be attacked—all the information I had from Mr. Hayes was that he intended to attack me *on sight.* I was in total ingnorance, as to what weapon he intended to use—whether it was a rifle, a shot gun, or a *single ball pistol.* The pistol which I shot belonged to Mark Pillow[11]—it was one of a pair which he *loaned me last summer.* I had never shot it with *buck shot.* It was impossible for me to know any advantage if I had it. I armed myself, so as to make the most effective defence I could. He had been enquiering for buck shot all over Town on Saturday—this if I *needed* any *justification* would be sufficient. One of the Pistols on his person was loaded with *buck shot,* I understand, & probably all the others were so loaded, if they had been examined. If I had known Mr. Hayes intended to shoot a single ball, I would have shot one. So far from knowing that—I did not even know the weapon he *intended using.* The substance of the affair of Munday is as follows. I had been home to my dinner in the country. When I came in Town, in walking by Herndons Corner I was hailed [by M]ark[12] Pillow to stop. I did so. We were engaged in conversation. We had not been there more than five minutes before Hayes left his office, walked up the pavement until nearly opposite—where he turned and advanced on me very rapidly, and when within about 20 paces he called on me "to stand and *defend myself.*" Suiting the action to the word he drew & fired. I occupied my position, making no movement until he addressed me. I then drew and fired as soon as I could—there was not more than a seconds difference in the report of the two pistols. The result being ascertained, I immediately dlivered myself up to the legal authorities. My whole conduct on Munday morning & evening was particularly guarded, with a view to a *clear justification,* should I prove fortunate in the affray. I did not go on the side of the street, on which his office is, for I did not wish to appear as bullying him into the attack. The first Munday in January the Court commences. From the present state of public opinion, my Counsel think it best to have the *trial* the first Court. I will write again in a fiew days. My Love to Sister Sarah.

WILL HAWKINS POLK

ALS. DLC–JKP. Addressed to Washington.

1. William H. Polk, oldest surviving brother of James K. Polk, attended the University of North Carolina and the University of Nashville; he opened a legal practice in Columbia in 1839. On December 3, 1838, William duelled with Richard Hightower Hayes and wounded his adversary in the head. Young Hayes died the following day. See John B. Hays to Polk, December 4, 1838.

2. Polk's letters to his brother and to John B. Hays have not been found. A Columbia physician, Hays was the husband of Ophelia Clarissa Polk, James K. and William H. Polk's youngest sister, and a brother of Andrew Hays of Nashville. Richard H. Hayes, who was killed by William H. Polk, was of a different family. The son of Oliver B. and Sarah C. Hightower Hayes of Nashville, Richard Hayes moved to Columbia in 1838 and practiced law with A. O. P. Nicholson.

3. William Polk's attorneys of record are not identified further. Gideon J. Pillow and Samuel D. Frierson took evidence for William Polk from witnesses present at the shooting. It is possible that these two friends of the family later served as defense attorneys in the case. Circuit court records do not name the defendant's attorneys.

4. Edmund Dillahunty and James H. Thomas. A prominent Columbia lawyer, Dillahunty was from 1836 until 1851 judge of the Eighth Judicial Circuit, which held jurisdiction in the case. Thomas served as district attorney, 1836–42, and prosecuted the state's case against William H. Polk. Later a law partner of James K. Polk, Thomas served as a Democrat in Congress, 1847–51 and 1859–61.

5. William G. Dickinson, a prominent surgeon in Franklin, was the father of William H. Polk's wife, Belinda.

6. Robert C. Foster, Jr., son of Robert C. Foster, Sr., and brother of Ephraim H. Foster, practiced law in Williamson County, where Dickinson resided. A Whig, Robert Foster, Jr., sat for three terms in the Tennessee House, 1829–31, 1833–35 and 1839–41, and for one term in the Senate, 1841–43, during which service he presided as Speaker.

7. Thomas H. Fletcher, an early and prominent criminal lawyer in Nashville, shared a mercantile business with Andrew Hynes, but lost heavily in the Panic of 1819. He represented Franklin County in the Tennessee House for one term, 1825–27, and served as secretary of state from 1830 until 1832.

8. Letter not found.

9. Thomas, a successful lawyer and farmer, represented Maury County in

the Tennessee House, 1835–41, and sat for Maury and Giles counties in the Senate, 1845–47. William H. Polk defeated him in the congressional election of 1851.

10. Letter not found. James Walker, a prosperous Columbia businessman, was the husband of Jane Maria Polk, sister of James K. and William H. Polk.

11. Probably Marcus L. Pillow, son of William Pillow of Maury County. Marcus attended Columbia College with James H. Thomas and later removed to Texas.

12. Manuscript mutilated.

FROM ALFRED BALCH[1]

Dear Sir, Washington 3d January, 39

During the pending session of Congress I think you ought to prepare a strong and well considered circular to the people of Ten and let it precede your return in March. This address should sustain the admn of the federal Govt because you will find that your claims will call out the two great parties of the state upon national politics. Cannon is a Bank man—a Federal man—and a Clay man.[2] I wish sincerely that Rives may not be made a man of straw of, as poor old White was, and enter in his proper person into the canvass for the Presidency.[3] That the Federal leaders in our state wish it ardently I have not had a doubt since May last and as I then stated to the President. If he does not take this suicidal step, it will be only because he believes that his selfish views will not be promoted by it. You ought to have very copious lists of persons Every where in the state to whom to send your circular. I am advised that there is a strong disposition in Wilson County, in our friends, to make a rally and try to beat in upon the immense majority for the Feds there, the vote of the county being exceedingly heavy and our number *comparatively* small. Wm Masterson[4] & others of Lebanon and its vicinity might furnish you with lists which should include Federalists as well as Democrats.

Campbell[5] of course is working in his District with all his might against you & counts on large Majorities in Smith & Jackson, quite strong counties for Cannon. Can you not paralize his efforts in some degree in those quarters? The truth [is] the election for Govr is going to be a very hot one. Your plan of operations is perfectly plain. Your play will be to make friends by conciliation where you are weak and move Heaven and Earth to push up your majorities to the greatest possible extent where you are strong. Cave Johnson[6] will I hope take the field for Congress. His interest and yours will go together. The same between

Childress and Gentry. Also in Shield's District Brown will take your interest.[7] In Turneys[8] District you may calculate on a heavy majority as well as in your own. In McClellands[9] you will have some of a majority. What I most fear is Stones and Williams's Districts for Carters will not go very much against you.[10] But in Stones and Williams's Districts the people go mightily in masses, and Stone & Williams may see that their own fall is bound up with that of Cannon. These heavy majorities in particular spots are hard to over come. As to the Western District the vote there will be very large, perhaps twenty five of thirty thousand votes. Cannon was Salting his Cattle in those parts seven years before he became a candidate for Gov and as he is a pretty cunning fellow he may retain his strength there notwithstanding all that you and your friends may be able to do. I take it that your shot should be fired mainly at Stones and Williams's Districts in the East—at Wilson [County]—at Campbells District and at the whole Western District. Your friends will take care of your interest in the balance of the state. Some good *bold* and talking friends should be secured in every one of the towns.

A. Balch

P.S. I think that Woodbury should request that a committee be appointed to examine into his official conduct.[11] I have so said to him. An innocent man *always* gains by investigation and under the persecutions of his enemies. Woodbury wants and needs *boldness.*

ALS. DLC–JKP. Probably addressed locally.

1. Balch, a Nashville lawyer, was an important political strategist, although never a candidate for elective office.

2. Newton Cannon, a Williamson County planter and supporter of Henry Clay, lost his race for the governorship in 1827, but won bids for that office in 1835 and 1837.

3. William C. Rives and Hugh L. White. A Democratic senator from Virginia, Rives opposed the Independent Treasury plan and subsequently went into the Whig party. Senator White had been a regular Democrat and administration supporter until 1836, when he ran for president against Van Buren. White carried but two states, Tennessee and Georgia.

4. In 1838 William Masterson married Maria Grundy, daughter of Felix and Nancy Ann Rodgers Grundy; three years later Masterson became postmaster at Green Hill in Wilson County.

5. William B. Campbell, a lawyer from Carthage, served in the U.S. House, 1837–43; he had served previously in the Tennessee House, 1835–36.

6. One of Polk's closest friends and political allies, Cave Johnson practiced law in Clarksville and served in the U.S. House as a Democrat, 1829–37 and 1839–45. Polk appointed him postmaster general in 1845.

7. William G. Childress, Meredith P. Gentry, Ebenezer J. Shields, and

Aaron V. Brown. Childress and Gentry were opponents in the 1839 congressional races, as were Shields and Brown. A resident of Williamson County and cousin of Sarah Polk, Childress had served as a Democratic member of the Tennessee House, 1835–37; he ran unsuccessfully for the U.S. House in 1839. Gentry practiced law in Williamson County; served as a Whig in the Tennessee House; 1835–39; and sat in the U.S. House, 1839–43 and 1845–53. Gentry ran unsuccessfully for governor in 1853 on the American party ticket. Shields, a Pulaski lawyer and ally of John Bell and Hugh L. White, served in the U.S. House, 1835–39, but lost his bid for reelection in 1839. Brown, also from Pulaski, was Polk's long-time friend and former law partner. He served in the Tennessee Senate and House, 1821–33, in the U.S. House, 1839–45, and in the governorship, 1845–47. From 1857 until his death in 1859 Brown was postmaster general under James Buchanan.

8. A lawyer from Winchester, Hopkins L. Turney served four terms in the Tennessee House, 1825–37, three in the U.S. House, 1837–43, and one in the U.S. Senate, 1845–51. He was Polk's close friend and spokesman in the Mountain District.

9. Abraham McClellan, a farmer from Sullivan County, served many years in the Tennessee House and Senate before going to the U.S. House as a Democrat, 1837–43.

10. William Stone, Joseph L. Williams, and William B. Carter. Stone and Williams represented Tennessee's Fourth and Third Congressional districts, respectively. An old war hero, General Stone ran as the Whig candidate in 1837, lost the election to incumbent James Standifer, but one month later won a special election occasioned by Standifer's death. Stone lost his race for reelection in 1839. Williams, a lawyer from Knoxville and the son of former Senator John Williams, sat in the U.S. House, 1837–43. Carter, a Whig, represented the First Congressional District, 1835–41. Carter had presided over Tennessee's Constitutional Convention of 1834.

11. Levi Woodbury was secretary of the treasury, 1834–41. Earlier he had served as governor of New Hampshire, Democratic senator from that state, and secretary of the navy. After heading the Treasury Department, Woodbury returned to the Senate and served there until appointed to the United States Supreme Court in 1846. Woodbury had come under political attack when it was discovered that Samuel Swartwout, customs collector for the port of New York City, had stolen over a million dollars in Treasury funds and had fled abroad.

TO ANDREW JACKSON DONELSON[1]

My Dear Sir Washington City Jany 3rd 1839

The calls upon my time have been so constant, that I have not written to you (though I have frequently intended it) since the Session of Congress opened. You will probably have learned from Genl.

Armstrong or Mr Smith, that Mr J. G. Harris late of New Bedford,[2] and more recently of Boston Mass. has accepted Mr Smith's terms, and agreed to go out forthwith and take charge of the Editorial Department of the *Union.*[3] Mr Harris is very highly recommended by Mr Bancroft, Mr Green of the Boston Post, Mr Jarvis,[4] & many other of our leading friends at the North, as being a man of a high order of talents, and extensive political information, sound in all his opinions, and withal possessing experience as an Editor. He was for five years the Editor of a daily paper at New Bedford, and more recently of the "Bay-State Democrat." I have no doubt he will fully meet the expectations of our friends. He will leave Boston for Nashville in about ten days, taking this City in his way. I will give him a letter to you, and also to the Genl.[5] Our friends should treat him kindly on his first arrival, and as far as practicable make his situation agreeable to him. He will need information in regard to the local politics of the State. Upon all the great questions which now divide the country, he will need none. His acceptance of Mr Smith's terms is unconditional and absolute, and nothing but death or want of health, will prevent him, from being at Nashville before the last of January. There must be no failure on Mr Smith's part, to put him, at once, at the head of the Editorial Department of his paper.

I have but little time this morning to say any thing, of the undercurrents, and political movements here. Mr Rives you see, no longer occupies an equivocal position, but has taken ground distinctly and openly with the opposition. He is doubtless looking first to his reelection to the Senate by Whig votes, and then I fear will bend an easy ear to the Southern Whigs, who may wish to induce him, to play the part that White did, of a *Southern Sectional candidate,* for the Presidency, not with the slightest hope of electing him, but with the hope of draining off the Southern vote from Mr V.B., defeating an election by the people, and casting the election into the House to be bargained for. Clay, despairing of the vote of the South, may be willing to see him play the part of a *Southern Sectional* candidate. These are my conjectures, growing out of the "signs of the times" here. A few weeks will more fully develope the causes of the opposition and especially of the Southern portion of it. Webster is manifestly forming the views of Genl. Harrison, and no doubt seems to be entertained that he has made up his mind to run for the Vice Presidency on Harrison's ticket. This has produced much trouble in the Whig camp. Clay it is said, is resolved not to yield his pretensions. It is his last chance. It is "much or nothing" with him. They are in trouble and confusion, and likely to continue so; and "*so mote it be.*"[6] I have not a remaining doubt of Mr V.B.s election. The late result in New York,[7] has not discouraged our friends, but on the contrary, they are perfectly confident that the "Empire State" will be with us, in the great contest of 1840. In all other quarters things are looking well.

I will write to the General soon. Let me hear from you.

JAMES K. POLK

ALS. DLC–AJD. Addressed to Nashville and marked "private."

1. A nephew of Rachel Jackson, Donelson was a graduate of West Point and studied law at Transylvania University. In 1823 he was admitted to the bar. He served as confidential secretary to Andrew Jackson, 1824–28, and as his private secretary while Jackson was president, 1829–37. He later guided U.S. negotiations for the annexation of Texas and was minister to Prussia.

2. Robert Armstrong, Joel M. Smith, and J. George Harris. Armstrong served as postmaster of Nashville, 1829–45, and as commander of Tennessee militia called to fight in the Seminole War; he ran unsuccessfully for governor in 1837 and coordinated Polk's campaign for that office in 1839. Smith, part owner of the Democratic *Nashville Union*, had been searching for a new editor for some months. Before becoming editor of the *Nashville Union*, Harris had been associated with the New London *Political Observer* (Conn.), the *New Bedford Daily Gazette* (Mass.), and the Boston *Bay State Democrat*. More recently he had been associate editor of Charles G. Greene's Boston *Morning Post*.

3. Started in 1835 by Medicus A. Long, the *Nashville Union* was the leading Democratic newspaper in Tennessee.

4. George Bancroft, Charles G. Greene, and Leonard Jarvis. Historian and diplomat, Bancroft published his pro-Jackson *A History of the United States* between 1831 and 1840. In 1844 he was influential in the nomination of Polk to the presidency and subsequently served as his secretary of the navy. In 1831 Greene founded the Democratic Boston *Morning Post*, which prospered under his leadership for nearly half a century. Jarvis, a Democrat, was a representative from Maine, 1829–37, after which he served as navy agent for the port of Boston, 1838–41.

5. Andrew Jackson.

6. An archaic verbal auxiliary, *mote* has been replaced by the use of *may* or *might*.

7. The Panic of 1837 dealt a serious blow to the Albany Regency; Van Buren's home party divided between conservative or bank Democrats and hard money advocates. In November 1838, New York Whigs won the governorship and majority control in both houses of the legislature.

FROM J. G. M. RAMSEY[1]

Mecklenburg, Tennessee. January 5, 1839

Ramsey acknowledges receipt of Polk's letter of December 13, 1838,[2] and expresses satisfaction with its statements on internal improvements in Tennessee. He advises that he will use the letter "as will seem on the whole best." The author notes that Democrats in the area are bringing out candidates for the legislature, including Baker in Jefferson County, Wheeler in Campbell County, and Lyon in Knox County.[3] Ramsey complains that Kendall made an unfortunate choice in choosing Crozier's successor as postmaster of Knoxville.[4] He has assured friends that Polk was not consulted on the appointment. He requests confirmation that his assurances were true.

ALS. DLC–JKP. Addressed to Washington.

1. Physician, author, railroad promoter, and banker in the Knoxville area, he wrote *The Annals of Tennessee to the End of the Eighteenth Century.*
2. Letter not found.
3. John Baker, John E. Wheeler, and Thomas C. Lyon. Baker has not been identified further. Originally a blacksmith, Wheeler became a lawyer; he served in the Tennessee Senate, 1839–41. Lyon, a Knoxville attorney, became U.S. district attorney in 1845.
4. Amos Kendall and John Crozier. Former newspaperman and member of Andrew Jackson's "Kitchen Cabinet," Kendall had become postmaster general in 1835. John Crozier, wealthy businessman and planter, served as Knoxville's postmaster from 1804 until his death in the fall of 1838. Lewis P. Roberts, Knoxville merchant and political advisor to Polk, succeeded Crozier as postmaster on December 3, 1838.

FROM JOEL M. SMITH

Nashville, Tennessee. January 5, 1839

Smith says that Polk's letter of December 27,[1] addressed jointly to himself and Armstrong, is in hand and that Harris' acceptance of the editorship of the *Nashville Union* is good news. The author observes that Cunningham's services will be terminated on the first of February.[2]

ALS. DLC–JKP. Addressed to Washington.

1. Polk's letter to Smith and Robert Armstrong has not been found.
2. Joshua Cunningham came to the *Nashville Union* from the Democratic Louisville *Public Advertiser*. Succeeding John O. Bradford, he served as editor of the *Union* from November 30, 1837, until February 1, 1839, when he was succeeded by Jeremiah George Harris.

FROM JAMES W. HALE[1]

Greeneville, Tennessee, January 6, 1839

Hale expresses hope that the enclosed list of names will answer Polk's purposes.[2] The author reports that the chief objection to Polk's candidacy is that he discusses "no question of policy except those of the Federal government." Hale says that the complaint arises not from the degree of attention paid national issues, but from differences of opinion on the issues themselves.

ALS. DLC–JKP. Addressed to Washington.

1. An attorney in Greene County.

2. List not found. Polk wanted to frank public documents to as many potential supporters as possible.

FROM SAMUEL A. WARNER[1]

Dresden, Tennessee. January 6, 1839

Warner reminds Polk of their conversation of the previous fall in which the two discussed the local *Tennessee Patriot,*[2] of which Warner is a part owner. He notes that the editor is trying to improve the publication and that any federal printing patronage given the newspaper "would be thankfully received, promptly and well attended to."

ALS. DLC–JKP. Addressed to Washington. AE on the cover states that this letter was answered on January 21, 1839; Polk's reply has not been found.

1. Samuel A. Warner was one of the earliest members of the Dresden bar.

2. The Dresden *Tennessee Patriot* was Weakley County's first newspaper; its initial issue, edited by Jesse Leigh, appeared on December 21, 1838.

FROM M. D. COOPER & CO.[1]

Sir New Orleans Jany 7th 183[9][2]

Your favour of the 23rd Ult is just arrived and contents duly noted.[3] None of your Cotton has at yet arrived and the prospect for an early rise in the Yalabusha river somewhat gloomy.[4] We send you a Price sheet giving a succinct statement of the market.

The resumption of specie payments by the banks curtailing their ability to grant the usual facilities in purchasing bills, through which medium nearly all the heavy mercantile operations of this city are transacted, has somewhat contracted the cotton operations for the last week, but the stock is very light, holders firm, and the certainty of the shortness of the crop every day more clearly developed which confirms a belief in the stability of present prices, and a prospect for an advance during the season.

Should you want any funds before your cotton arrives, you may draw on us at 30 days after sight, and the draft shall be honored. Drafts on

New York and Philadelphia 1/2 prct premium for Bank checks, out door checks par.

M D Cooper & Co

LS. DLC–JKP. Addressed to Washington. AE on the cover states that this letter was answered on January 25, 1839; Polk's reply has not been found.

1. Matthew D. Cooper probably moved to Maury County prior to 1830. A successful cotton dealer and merchant, he was for some time a partner with Madison Caruthers in a commission merchant business operating through New Orleans.

2. Year identified through content analysis.

3. Letter not found.

4. Polk owned a plantation near Coffeeville, in Yalobusha County, Mississippi.

FROM JOHN B. HAYS

Wednesday night

Dear Sir Columbia [January 9, 1839][1]

As yet no prosecutor has appeared. Nor has there been any action by the Grand Jury. Though O. B. Hays came in the stage tonight.[2] On tomorrow night I will write again, if there is any action in the matter. At any rate on the next night. There is no excitement. I am rather disposed to think that there will be no prosecution by the friends, Though William will have it before the G. Jury. Fletcher thinks that there had better be no other than the local lawyers. If it goes to trial Nicholson[3] will appear to assist in selecting the Jury.

Saml. is, I think, declining.[4]

On to day it has been ascertained, certainly, that Nicholson & Cahal[5] have become partners in the practice of the law, Each agreeing to decline politics entirely. Of course the "party party" and the "no party party" are in a ferment, Nicholson giving as an excuse to his friends, his embarrassments &c. I think that they will not be satisfied with him, for doing it at this time without having consulted some of them. They of course are in confusion. Half a dozen spoken of. Dr. Greenfield[6] thinks that a man of talents ought to be selected, with money enough to go through the campaign, But has no wish to run, if the friends should select another than himself. Dr. Thomas will not consider himself well treated if he is not selected.[7] There is certainly no head to the party. And I view it as a loss to you. I hope that you are as great a man as G______,[8] in not leaving any thing, in confidence, in writing to appear in judgement against you.

If you wish to communicate any thing to any person in the district, if I can serve you by acting in the strictest confidence, you can communicate through me without any fears, untill your things can be got in train again. I will confer personally or hand any communication to any one, unless there is some one of your political friends that you can sufficiently confide in. I think that suggestions that might be made by you, would be attended to. E. Frierson has been thought of, Waterson spoken of. &c.[9] If I have any thing worthy of communicating, I will write. But I think that you had better write, to some of your political friends &c.

J. B. Hays

ALS. DLC–JKP. Addressed to Washington.

1. Erroneously dated "Decr 9th"; month and year identified through content analysis. This letter bears a postmark dated January 11.

2. Oliver B. Hayes. On January 11 the Maury grand jury rejected the presentment for a murder indictment against William H. Polk. The following day, the jury indicted him for assault and battery. See James Walker to Polk, December 10, 1838.

3. A. O. P. Nicholson was graduated from the University of North Carolina, studied law, and practiced his profession in Maury County. In 1838 he shared a legal practice with the ill-fated Richard H. Hayes. A Democrat, Nicholson served in the Tennessee House, 1833–37, and sat in the Senate, 1843–45. He was a presidential elector on the Democratic ticket of Martin Van Buren and Richard M. Johnson, and in 1840 was appointed by Polk to the U.S. Senate to fill the vacancy caused by the death of Felix Grundy.

4. Samuel W. Polk, the youngest brother of James K. Polk, was graduated from Yale College in August, 1838. He contracted tuberculosis while in New Haven, eventually returned to his home in Maury County, and died there on February 24, 1839, at twenty-one years of age.

5. Terry H. Cahal, member of the Tennessee Senate, 1835–36 and 1837–39, practiced law in Columbia and identified politically with John Bell's "no-party" coalition, which had supported Hugh L. White for president in 1836. A Whig presidential elector for Harrison and Tyler in 1840, Cahal ran an unsuccessful race for Congress in 1841.

6. Gerrard T. Greenfield was born in Maryland and migrated to Tennessee. A physician and farmer in Maury County, he was considered one of the state's most skilled medical practitioners.

7. Born in North Carolina, Isaac J. Thomas migrated to Maury County in 1814, practiced medicine there for thirty years, and represented Maury County in the Tennessee House, 1825–27. He was the father of James H. Thomas.

8. Probably a reference to Felix Grundy.

9. Erwin J. Frierson and Harvey M. Watterson. A graduate of the University of North Carolina, Frierson studied law at the office of James K. Polk in Columbia and practiced law at Shelbyville, Bedford County. He was attor-

ney general of the Eighth Judicial Circuit, 1827–36, and judge of the Bedford County Court, 1848. A Democrat, he served in the Tennessee House, 1845–47. Watterson had a long career in law and journalism. He practiced law at Shelbyville until 1831, when he established and edited the *Western Freeman.* He served in the Tennessee House, 1835–37, and was elected as a Democrat to the U.S. House of Representatives, 1839–43. He was elected to the Tennessee Senate, 1845–47, during which term he served as Speaker. For four years, 1847–51, he was proprietor and editor of the Nashville *Daily Union.* In 1851 he became editor of the *Washington Union.*

FROM WILLIAM C. DUNLAP[1]

Bolivar, Tennessee. January 10, 1839

Dunlap informs Polk that the local Democratic candidates for the 1839 election have not been chosen yet. Coe cannot beat Williams if Graham runs also.[2] Graham will not yield to Coe but probably would to Dunlap. Dunlap agrees to run "if that is the only alternative." Cannon has campaigned in the District lately, but lost votes there. Polk will certainly win in the District.

ALS. DLC–JKP. Addressed to Washington.

1. A lawyer from Bolivar, William C. Dunlap served as a Democratic congressman, 1833–37. He held a circuit judgeship in Tennessee, 1840–49, and served several terms in the Tennessee House and Senate in the 1850's.

2. Levin H. Coe and Christopher Harris Williams; Graham is not identified further. Coe was a popular lawyer from Somerville and a Democratic member of the Tennessee Senate, 1837–41; he served as Speaker during the latter part of his second term. Williams was a lawyer from Lexington, Tennessee, and a Whig congressman, 1837–43 and 1849–53. He was the grandfather of John Sharp Williams. Dunlap ran and lost his race for Congress.

FROM PENDLETON G. GAINES[1]

Memphis, Tennessee. January 10, 1839

Gaines informs Polk that a new Democratic newspaper, the *Western World and Memphis Banner of the Constitution,*[2] has been established at Memphis. Gaines requests that Polk try to secure for it a contract to print the public laws. Gaines is running for the legislature from Shelby County.

ALS. DLC–JKP. Addressed to Washington.

1. Trained in law, Pendleton G. Gaines became editor of the Memphis *Gazette,* a Democratic newspaper which he edited from 1834 until its termination in 1838. He was elected to the Tennessee House in 1839 and served one term.

2. This newspaper was published by Solon Borland until 1840, when its ownership changed hands and its name became the *Memphis Appeal*.

FROM ROBERT ARMSTRONG

Dear Sir Nashville 11th Jay [1839][1]

We are all in confusion about Nicholsons declineing a canvass in your old District and entering in to partnership with Cahal. I fear it is too true and I assure you we regret it here. I have no doubt he has been as beseechd by Caruthers[2] Cahal & Co. Williamson Smith[3] is now here and both him and Laughlin[4] promises to write you to night.

I have the same thoughts about Carroll[5] and his running as when I last wrote you. He expects an appointment from the Government. Unless he *now* runs he deserves nothing and no expectations ought to be held out to him. He could beat Bell[6] but is not willing to try it. He would sooner be in the Land business.

You must write us immediately. Will Kincannon[7] do or who can be taken up in that District. I have the thing fixed from bringing out Carroll in a few days. He cannot get over it unless he bolts entirely and the push will be made next week when Burton[8] comes down to the Supream Court and the old Genl comes down to attend the Trial of his Boys.[9] All is arranged and he cannot get over it. Our Candidates for the Legislature will be got out, but I assure you it is hard work to get along with such materials.

I have written Genl Wallace[10] and hope something may be done there in relation to the establishment of a paper. Smith is well satisfied with the reports of Mr Harris and the prospect of a change. I have no doubt he will be well received and our friends will rejoice that other hands have hold of the Editorial Dept. of the Union.

Write me often, let me know what is to be done with your old District and who must take the field, we must never give up. The prospect never was better, and our party more certain of success than at this time. The news is good from every quarter but *Simms, Ewing & Nicholson* declining *show* what the course of those opposed to us are persueing.[11]

R. ARMSTRONG

ALS. DLC–JKP. Addressed to Washington and marked "Private."

1. Year identified through content analysis.

2. Robert L. Caruthers, a Whig lawyer in Lebanon, had served Wilson County in the Tennessee House, 1835–37, and was elected to the U.S. House of Representatives, 1841–43.

3. A Columbia lawyer, Smith served out the unfinished term of Terry H. Cahal in the Tennessee Senate, 1836–37, and represented Maury County in that body, 1839–41.

4. Editor of the *Nashville Union*, 1835–37, Samuel H. Laughlin resided in McMinnville where he practiced law, farmed, and worked in behalf of Polk and the Democratic party. He represented Warren and Franklin counties in the Tennessee Senate, 1839–43, and Warren, Cannon, Coffee, and DeKalb counties in that body, 1843–45.

5. William Carroll was governor of Tennessee, 1821–27 and 1829–35. His health became a political liability, and he lost the governorship to Newton Cannon in 1835.

6. John Bell, Speaker of the U.S. House of Representatives, 1834–35, led Hugh Lawson White's presidential bid in 1836. Since the Speakership contests of 1834 and 1835, Bell and Polk had been bitter enemies.

7. Andrew A. Kincannon, a resident of Lincoln County, was a lawyer. A perennial candidate, he was running for Congress.

8. A lawyer in Lebanon, Robert M. Burton represented Wilson County in the Tennessee House, 1827–29, and in the Constitutional Convention of 1834. He ran unsuccessfully for Congress in 1839.

9. Reference is to Andrew Jackson. See Jackson to Polk, February 11, 1839.

10. William Wallace, a native of Sevier County and prominent railroad promoter, served as sheriff of Blount County, 1820–42, and sat in the Tennessee House, 1853–55.

11. Simms, Andrew Ewing, A. O. P. Nicholson. Simms is not identified further. A Nashville lawyer, Ewing was elected as a Democrat to one term in the U.S. House, 1849–51; in 1839 he was partner in a legal practice with his brother, Edwin H. Ewing, a Whig.

FROM SOLON BORLAND[1]

Memphis, Tennessee. January 11, 1839

Borland states that he has bought the Memphis *Gazette* and established the *Western World*, through which he pledges to support the Democracy and the present administration. He solicits Polk's aid in obtaining appointment as printer of the public laws. Borland further states that he needs a thousand or fifteen hundred subscriptions from wealthy party members who can distribute the paper throughout the District. Only then can the paper operate without loss and the District be won for the Democratic party.

ALS. DLC–JKP. Addressed to Washington.

1. Borland, a physician, published the *Western World and Memphis Banner of the Constitution* until 1840. During the Mexican War he served as a major in Archibald Yell's Arkansas Volunteer Cavalry. In 1848 the Arkansas legislature sent Borland to the U.S. Senate; in 1853 he resigned to become

minister to Nicaragua. During the Civil War he rose to the rank of brigadier general in the Confederate service.

FROM PHILIP B. GLENN[1]

Covington, Tennessee. January 11, 1839

Glenn reports that Polk's speech at Covington the previous fall[2] has strengthened the Democrats' spirits and encouraged their efforts. Resumption of specie payments has silenced most Whig demands for a national bank. Kit,[3] however, is committed irrevocably to supporting such a bank. Democratic party prospects are good.

ALS. DLC–JKP. Addressed to Washington.

1. A lawyer from Covington, Glenn served as a Democrat in the Tennessee House, 1837–41 and 1843–47.

2. Polk had spoken at Covington on October 4, 1838, while touring the Western District.

3. Christopher H. Williams.

FROM JOHN B. HAYS

Dear Sir, Columbia Jany 11th (Friday evening) 1839

Contrary to my expec[ta]tions, on yesterday morning the Revd. O. B. Hays had the case sent before the G. Jury.[1] The whole matter from the whipping on Friday evening till the finale on monday evening, was fully investigated, the state's witnesses alone, being before them. They returned a verdict of "not a true bill." Whether there will be another suit, of any kind is not yet known. If there should be I will inform you. At any rate I will write in a day or two.

Nicholson's withdrawal is very far from being pleasing to the Democracy. They will from this quarter almost entirely petition E. Frierson. They have not confidence in any other, particularly those in Bedford that are anxious to run.

John B. Hays

ALS. DLC–JKP. Addressed to Washington.

1. Oliver B. Hayes. See William H. Polk to Polk, January 2, 1839; and John B. Hays to Polk, January 9, 1839.

FROM SAMUEL H. LAUGHLIN

City Hotel, Nashville, Tenn.
Dear Sir, January 11, 1839

On entering the public room in this establishment early this morning, Mr. McIntosh[1] one of the proprietors pointed out to me in much surprise an editorial paragraph in the Banner, which the carrier had just left in the barroom, stating that Messrs. Nicholson and Cahal had just entered into a partnership in the practice of law, and had agreed mutually to withdraw from politics—Nicholson from the field as a candidate for Congress, and Cahal not to become a candidate. I will cut out and enclose the article.[2]

Now, it does seem to me that there must be some great mistake in the matter. I saw Nicholson here last week, and heard not a word of such a movement. Cahal was also here, having just come from Sumner where I understood he and his family had been on a visit. Mr. McIntosh says that he heard Dr. Hoggatt, Cahal's brother in law, and Sam Yerger[3] now of Pulaski, talking this morning, and they stated to each other, that Nicholson and Cahal were mutually affraid of each other—that Nicholson was somewhat embarrassed in his affairs, and feared that a hard contest would do him great injury by adding to his embarrassments, and that the compromise grew out of this state of things. I am totally in the dark and so much astonished, that I do not know what to think. I hope the whole is a *mistake*, a thing *talked of* but not concluded. The paper was printed before day light this morning. Sam Yerger arrived here in the stage yesterday evening from Pulaski and Columbia, and perhaps brought the news.

If a little pecuniary trouble ought to drive a man from the field, I ought not only to have left the field long ago, but to have hung myself in despair. While Nicholson may be slightly embarrassed, I have been ruined, having spent more than two years of time, and more money, and incurred more debts, than three year's hard work and hard living afterwards, will enable me to replace and pay—and as yet, denied the receipt of one cent of the accruing proceeds of the debts and earnings I left in the business I was engaged in.[4] In this respect my usage has been more than hard—but I can't give up my principles, my friendships and feelings on this account. An occurrence however has just taken place which admonishes me that I am not done working for others—at least if I can be made responsible to their demands—or ought to be so responsible. Mr. Cave Johnson has written me that he must and will look to me personally for the money he advanced to Long, every cent of which was paid to take up the Bill which Mr. Kezer accepted for the purchase of presses from Guilford of Cincinnati, and which presses were burnt up in Parson Green's house.[5] Yourself, Maj. Donelson, and Mr. Grundy transferred to, and released me from similar liabilities, and Maj. Donelson made a similar transfer for Mr. Johnson, but not being fully satisfied with his authority himself, I destroyed it to reliieve him in the presence of Gen. Armstrong, being fully satisfied that Mr. Johnson would be as liberal in his dealing with me as others. This being the case—if I am bound—I ought to go to work. From Nesbet or Smith,[6] I have never received the first cent. I have not only been cruelly used here, but grossly misrepresented, and misunderstood. Cunningham, I understand, cannot stand Smith, or Smith cannot stand him, and he is likely to quit. These are things intimated to me, for I enter into no counsels about Union matters. It will be well if the establishment can get another who will do as well.

I wrote Mr. Turney a day or two ago; and will write again when any new thing occurs. The Court is now meeting, so I must conclude. Make my respects to Mrs. Polk. Her friends at Murfreesboro were well a few days ago.

S. H. LAUGHLIN

P.S. I also enclose the Whig account of this morning.[7] Our friends are in astonishment. I have seen Armstrong. We can't conceive what has led to it. Gen. Jackson will be in town next Tuesday. His health, I understand, is good.

ALS. DLC–JKP. Addressed to Washington.

1. Probably John McIntosh, a friend of Polk and timekeeper at the Tennessee State Prison in the mid 1830's.

2. Nashville *Republican Banner,* January 11, 1839. Shadrack Nye and Allen A. Hall, strong adherents of John Bell, published the *Banner* from 1837 until 1841. Enclosure not found.

3. Hoggatt is not further identified. Sam Yerger was a brother of George S. Yerger, Tennessee's first attorney general.

4. Laughlin had edited the *Nashville Union* from its beginning in March 1835 until July 1837.

5. Medicus A. Long, Timothy Kezer, Nathan Guilford, and Alexander Little Page Green. Long published several newspapers in the 1830's, including the *Nashville Union,* 1835–36. Kezer, a Nashville merchant and hatmaker, was Laughlin's son-in-law. Guilford led the fight for free schools in Ohio; he also established a publishing house to advance his educational projects. Green, a leading Methodist minister in Nashville and Davidson County, was instru-

mental in locating the Southern Methodist Publishing House in Nashville. Details about the purchase of the presses and the fire have not been found.

6. Robert Nesbit bought Laughlin's interest in the *Union* in July 1837 but remained in the business only a short time before selling out to Joel M. Smith.

7. Reference is to a brief notice of Nicholson and Cahal's forming a law partnership. The second *Nashville Whig*, edited by C. C. Norvell, began publication in January 1838.

FROM JABEZ JACKSON[1]

Washington City. January 12, 1839

Jackson requests an explanation of remarks Polk had made to him privately about their differences.[2] The author reminds Polk of his unkept promise to discuss these matters further when the Speaker had spare time. Jackson explains that his letter's "harsh" language had been occasioned by great irritability arising from his illness. He expresses regret for his indiscretion.

ALS. DLC–JKP. Addressed locally.

1. A Georgia Democrat, Jackson served in the U.S. House, 1835–39, after which he returned to private life.

2. Jackson and Polk had differed on the question of paying Jackson's salary during his absence the last sixteen days of the previous session. See Jackson to Polk, July 14, 1838.

FROM THOMAS P. MOORE[1]

Dr Polk Columbus Mi Jan 12. 1839

All will go right here; a democratic senator will certainly be elected, if an election be had at all. In my transit through Ten. coming at my leisure, I think I could perceive that you were "going ahead." What effect the N.Y. election produced I know not. A L Martin[2] says none. I saw many of your people last week at our land sales & I hope we done you some good. Spare *nothing*, you fight for a glorious cause, & may win imperishable honors. The defaulters (their defaulters I know all about them) are used by your most unscrupulous Federal press. At Memphis &c &c. Let documentary proof of the real character of the defaulters correct this & promptly.[3]

My daughter[4] an idolized child returned with Mr Kendall. I have told her if she could accompany Mrs P. to Maysville or Louisville to do so provided she could do it without occasioning the slightest inconvenience.

I shall return in a few weeks. I go tomorrow to Pontotoc. Regards to Mrs. P.

T. P. MOORE

ALS. DLC–JKP. Addressed to Washington.

1. A Democrat from Mercer County, Kentucky, Moore sat in the U.S. House, 1823–29; served as minister to Columbia, 1829–33; and ran unsuccessfully for Congress in 1833.

2. Andrew L. Martin, an able criminal lawyer at Jackson, served in the Tennessee House, 1829–31 and 1835–39. A White supporter and former nullifier, Martin had returned to the ranks of the Democratic party by 1839.

3. Reference is probably to Samuel Swartwout's defalcation in New York; see Alfred Balch to Polk, January 3, 1839. The Memphis *Enquirer* was "Federalist," i.e. "Whig," in its political orientation.

4. Not further identified.

FROM JOHN B. HAYS

Dear Sir Columbia Sunday morning Jany 13 [1839][1]

On yesterday O. B. Hays[2] had a bill sent to the G Jury for assault & battery. A "true bill" was found. He will evidently push the matter, as far as he possibly can. William[3] will evidently have it continued.

I have spoken to Herndon to intimate to Hays, the certainty of William's prosecuting Hightower for aiding and abetting in this matter.[4] That may stop farther proceedings. After trying the case for murder, and failing in it, their trying it, in another shape, has and will change the sympathies of the public.

On the subject of "Buckshot" in your last.[5] Had there been an agreement on the subject of weapons or a meeting equally, it would have been improper to have used but one ball. Hays[6] had been endeavoring on Saturday to procure "Buckshot" from a person, whom he told at the same time, that he would shoot Wm. down, on sight, like a dog. It was also known that he had all sorts of weapons. Consequently it made it necessary that Wm. should also arm himself properly. I did not ask the person who examined,[7] but I suppose that his pistols were charged with Buckshot. I have not heard him censured for loading with them.

E. Frierson is the person, whom the Republicans wish to run, from this county. He has not been heard from. They fear that he will not consent. He has been written to by several, that if he will not, they wish him not to refuse at present until the matter can be cooly considered, and a substantial and popular person can be selected. The friends here wish Bedford [County] to supply the candidate. They will probably act by convention if Frierson does not run.

Various conjectures as to the cause of Nicholson's declining. He evidently has lost the confidence of his friends.

J.B.H.

ALI. DLC–JKP. Addressed to Washington.

1. Year identified through content analysis.
2. Oliver B. Hayes.
3. William H. Polk.
4. Joseph C. Herndon, Oliver B. Hayes, William H. Polk, and Richard R. Hightower. Herndon was a Columbia lawyer who had rented Polk's home at one time. A Franklin physician, Hightower was a brother of Oliver B. Hayes' wife Sarah Hightower Hayes; he was therefore an uncle of Richard Hightower Hayes. See John B. Hays to Polk, December 4, 1838.
5. Letter not found.
6. Richard Hightower Hayes.
7. Not identified further.

FROM EZEKIEL P. McNEAL[1]

Dear Sir Bolivar Jany 13 1839

I am in recpt of your[s] of 23d Ultimo,[2] and so soon as Mr Thos Dodson[3] makes the collections alluded to and pays the same over, I will add all the collections that I can make on a/c of rents or purchase & remit you a check.[4] The bonds for rents last year amount to about $500—none of which has been paid. I have the promises of men to be relied on for $200.00 in time to remit you and I hope to collect more. I sent you by this mail the 2d number of the "Bolivar Sentinel"[5] & the 1st number of the [Memphis] "Western World." The Memphis Gazette after a suspension of 2 months published on the 23d December her last Will & Testament, and gave up the ghost. The friends of that paper in & about Memphis, adopted various expedients to keep it a going. We were applied to for aid and J C McLemore wrote us (B & McN)[6] that you desired us to make some advances. Knowing as I did something about the manner in which the Gazette was conducted, & the persons who had charge of it I was confident that it would be a useless waste of means to bestow them, on that paper, so long as it remained, under the same managers. The with-holding of aid, has I think resulted more favorably than to have granted them.

Solon Borland, the talented proprietor & Editor of the Western World, bought the Gazette office, & has commenced his labours in good earnest. His paper takes well and I have no doubt will be liberally patronized and sustained. Borland you will percive is of the States Rights or nullyfing order of politicians but now with us to the fullest extent. All who are acquainted with him award him talents far above mediocracy. His first sheet promises well.

I regret that it is not in my power to give you all the inform[a]tion desired relative to our Candidats. They are very tardy in comeing out. I have not heard from *Coe* for some weeks. He is the man that we wish to run for Congress. P. G Gaines is not announced but will run for Shelby County. His prospects are said to be good, no opposition candidate for that County. S Macklin & Williamson[7] for Fayette Co. M. will succeed. In this County, Crisp or Neely,[8] the latter unless he runs for the Senate, which his friends desire, he being the most available candidate we could start. In McNairy, Maclin Cross[9] tis said will run, if so, successfully. In this County either Crisp or Neely *can* succeed against any opposition that may come. In Madison our friends have not as yet got out any Candidate. The Whigs of that County will run Lyon the Sheriff, a popular man, though rather on the Davy Crockett order.[10] Conner of Brownville, our Candidate for senator in Counties north of Hatchie, is opposed by John B Ashe of the same town.[11] We look for success in that contest. There is but little saying at present about Candidats & politics. The time is near at hand when the work must commence in good earnest, although we are somewhat slow & lethargic in our movements. You may rest assured that the District will do her duty, and elect her proportion of the *right stripe* for the next *Legislature* of Tennessee.

Governor Cannon was moving about through the District whilst you were in it last fall. He has again been through it this winter. He was here about 3 weeks since. His arrival at this place made no stir. In fact more than half the citzens never knew he was here until he had been gone several days. I am told he is very particular in telling that he is not in favor of Clay, nor never was a Clay man. His warm friends say he is a Clay man. How their contradictory statements will work, time alone will develop but if I was permitted to prophesy I should say most disastriously.

Your prospects in the District I should say are fully as good, in fact better than when you were here in the fall. The general opinion is that you will in the *whole* District get a handsome majority.

E P McNeal

ALS. DLC–JKP. Addressed to Washington.

1. A first cousin to Polk, McNeal was a Bolivar merchant and farmer. He handled Polk's business interests in Hardeman County.

2. Letter not found.

3. On past occasions Dodson held Polk's power of attorney and cared for Polk's legal affairs in the Western District.

4. On February 2, 1839, McNeal informed Polk that collections totaled $255 and that a check on an eastern bank would be purchased and the funds remitted through the Bank of Tennessee's Nashville office. ALS. DLC–JKP.

5. Probably started in early 1839, the Bolivar *Sentinel* was a Democratic newspaper. No copies of this paper have survived.

6. John C. McLemore, John H. Bills, and Ezekiel Polk McNeal. A wealthy land jobber who owned lands throughout Tennessee, McLemore was formerly surveyor general of Tennessee. Bills married Prudence Tate McNeal, sister of Ezekiel P. McNeal. Bills and McNeal ran a general store in Bolivar.

7. Sackfield Maclin and James M. Williamson. A Democrat, Maclin represented Fayette, Hardeman, and Shelby counties in the Tennessee Senate for one term, 1841–43. Formerly a resident of North Carolina and a member of that state's House of Commons, 1834–36, Williamson moved in 1838 to Somerville in Tennessee's Fayette County and took up the practice of law. He served in the Tennessee Senate from 1845 until 1847.

8. Elihu C. Crisp and Rufus P. Neely. Born in South Carolina, Crisp moved to Hardeman County sometime prior to 1835. He held several county offices: surveyor, 1835–36; circuit court clerk, 1836–62; and sometime chairman of the county court. A Democrat, he defeated Edward D. Tarver for a seat in the Tennessee House in 1837 and served one term. Rufus Neely moved to Hardeman County in 1823 with his grandfather, Ezekiel Polk. Neely held several local offices and represented Hardeman County as a Democrat in the Tennessee House for one term, 1839–41.

9. Maclin Cross, an early settler of McNairy County was both merchant and lawyer. Circuit court clerk from 1824 until 1826, he became one of the principal leaders of the Democratic party in West Tennessee.

10. James S. Lyon and David Crockett. A wealthy planter and horse breeder, Lyon held several county posts, including that of sheriff. He served as a Whig in the Tennessee House from 1839 until 1841. Crockett engaged variously in frontier political and military activities. Moving frequently from place to place, he served two terms as a Democrat in the U.S. House, 1827–31; during his third and final term in Congress, 1833–35, he sided with those who opposed Jackson's administration.

11. Probably William Conner and John B. Ashe. Conner settled in Haywood County in the early 1820's. Surviving financially the panic of 1837, he became a leading merchant in Brownsville in the 1840's. Ashe, who was a member of a prominent political family in North Carolina, practiced law in Brownsville and served as a Whig in the Tennessee Senate for two terms, 1839–43.

FROM LEWIS P. ROBERTS

My dear Sir Knoxville Jany 15th [18]39

Your esteemed favor came to hand in due course of mail,[1] and I am gratifyed at the news that it contains, viz that the administration is still looking forward with bright hopes, and pleasing anticipations to the future. Also of your prospects as regards your election in Tennessee. My utmost exertions will be used in your behalf, and I will try and give you six hundred votes in Knox County if possible. Your prospects I think must brighten and continue to do so, untill the election, and when you come into the state & mix among the "bone & sinue" of the cuntry I have no fear of the result.

I have some fear of the administration relative to the New York defalcation. The opposition are doing their utmost, attempting to render the administration odious, in the eyes of the people.[2] I hope they will miss their object, and fail in their attempts. Why dont Hamer or Frank Thomas, use up, that *scoundrel* Wise.[3] Either of them are able. He deserves a severe castigation, and would to God he would recieve one. Wise is evidently the great man of the Whigs, at all events he figures the largest, he has the impudence of the evil one, and I suppose is esteemed by the Whigs as the "Saviour of the Country." I hope for the best, and pray with all my heart, that the administration will sustain itself in defiance of all the opposition that can be brought against it. Mr Van Buren has had a difficult road to tread, ever since he came into office, diserted by pretended friends, and abused by open enemys—his publick acts mystefyed and all sorts of calumly that genious could invent or mercinary editors manufacture have been heaped upon him. Yet notwithstanding all this, aided by all the talents, wealth and influence of the aristocracy, he has boldly made his way, bidding defiance, to the combined elements, and riding the storm in tryumph.

Ramsey[4] has made an attack on the administration in consequence of my appointment to the office of post master. He abuses the Post office department without mercy. His principal object is to affect your election. He is understood here, by every person. He will die of his own insignificance, and that shortly I hope. A rejoinder was sent him, with the request that he would publish it, but he had not the spirit or magnanimity to do so. I had an idea of sending it to the Union—but upon reflection, considering the family afflictions that we have suffered, declined doing so, and besides it would give him a decided advantage as he would publish anything he pleased without giving you an opportunity of replying. Upon the whole—his attack is so well understood, that a [. . .][5] would be unnecessary.

Politics as yet, has not been agitated but by very few of the people, not much said in regard to any of the election, but I suppose we will have some warm work before the season closes. I think Genl Wallace, will give Jo Williams a race for Congress. Wallace has considerable tact, but not much talents, but would make a respectable member of Congress.

Williams is not as popular as he was some time since, and I do not think that he would be hard to beat. Time will tell &c.

I find the post office will not suit me, and am compelled to rent a room in the city Hotel which makes it very inconvenient, for me, as the store is a full square from it, and from unavoidable circumstances I will be compelled to resign. I will hold on till the Quarter ends, in the mean time would suggest that my friend R. B. Reynolds[6] sh[ould] receive the appointment. He can attend to it without any trouble, as he can always be there, as it is his boarding house. I will write you more fully in my next on the subject.

In my next I will give you a more full history of partys, &c in this state. Excuse this scrall, as I am in haste & pressed for time. Present my respects to Mrs. P. . . .

L P Roberts

ALS. DLC–JKP. Addressed to Washington.

1. Letter not found.

2. See Alfred Balch to Polk, January 3, 1839.

3. Thomas L. Hamer, Francis Thomas, and Henry A. Wise. All three were congressmen at this time. Hamer of Ohio, a lawyer and Democrat, served in the U.S. House, 1833–39; commissioned a brigadier general in the Mexican War, he died in the service in 1846. Thomas, a leading lawyer from western Maryland, served as a Democratic congressman, 1831–41. Wise, a lawyer from Virginia, sat in Congress, 1833–44; originally a Democrat, he broke with Jackson over the Bank issue and became an ardent Whig. He subsequently served as governor of Virginia, 1856–60.

4. William B. A. Ramsey, member of a prominent East Tennessee family, was owner and editor of the *Knoxville Register,* a leading Whig paper. Also interested in railroads, steamboats, and banks, Ramsey served as Tennessee's secretary of state, 1847–55.

5. Word omitted by author.

6. Robert B. Reynolds, a Knoxville lawyer, was a nephew of Governor John Reynolds of Illinois.

FROM JOSEPH H. TALBOT[1]

Dear Sir Jackson Jany. 19th 1839

I recd yours[2] covering a copy of the bill introduced in the Senate by Mr. Foster and return the same to you with proposed amendments.[3]

In the first section strike out the words included in *Black lines* from the word counties down to the word compose and insert *That the counties of Hardin Perry Benton Henry and all the counties west of them in the State of Tennessee shall* (you will observe I at first by mistake struck out the inacting clause). In the 3d Section strike out the words "in April" and insert *in July and January* and add an S to the termination of the previous word Monday in the 3d and fifth lines. This will give us two terms, which by this law is proposed to be given to the Court at Nashville.

The above time, has been agreed upon by a large majority of the bar in this Section of country, for whose benifit, the court is established. If it be determined to give us but one court in the year, let the time be the *first Monday in January*. The time fixed upon in the bill, is the time of the sitting of the [Tennessee] Supreme Court, and both courts sitting at the same time, would be very inconvenient. I learn that Mr. Foster consulted the *Gentlemen of Nashville*[4] as to the time of sitting of *this* court. He may look upon them as his constituents and alone interested. But we of this off cast district claim the priviledge of being heard and our convenience consulted. In the sixth line after the word "October" insert the words *and April*, the same insertion after the word "October" in the 8th line. With these alterations the three last lines of the section from the words "and writs" in the 9th line may be *expunged* entirely. You will observe however if we get but one term and that 1st Monday in January the rule days must be the 1st Mondays in *July* instead of October as in the bill.

The whole of the proviso in the 4th Section ought to be stricken out,[5] for the simple reason, that it will be doing injustice to the Marsall of this district. It is an unusual provision and partakes of a degree of favouritism towards the Marshall of Middle Tennessee that ought not to be found in any law. It also increases *the costs to parties in paying milage from Nashville*. Personally I like S B Marshall better than R J Chester,[6] "but let Justice be done though the heavens fall."[7]

The whole of the 7th Section may be stricken out. If it be the general law (of which I am not advised) that counterparts of writs may issue to bring defendants together who reside in different districts, there is no use for this Section. If it be not the *general* law, why should it be different in this case. I suspect this is another provision dictated at Nashville. If Mr. Foster should get possession of a note for collection upon a man in this district it will only be necessary to make a *ficticious indorsement* to some body in Nashville, and thereby give to that court the whole jurisdiction of this country in actions of debt and assumpsit upon notes and bills.

The bar of Nashvill have oposed the establishment of this court for years, and after all hope was distroyed to do so by direct means, they resorted to strategem, the first attempt at which they succeeded, in imposing upon poor Crocket[8] by making this a Court of concurrent jurisdiction, with the court at Nashville, and the last Section of this act is a similar attempt. We have to rely upon you and Mr. Turney to protect us in this war. Mr. Crocket and Mr. Williams are too indifferent about it, or too much disposed to please Messrs Bell and Foster.

As the duties of the district Judge will by this act be increased it would be well to give him some additional salary, say two hundred dollars (provided he holds the Court and not without).

No New[s]. Democracy & the Independent Treasury are in the ascendent. I write in great haste from a pressure of business but I hope you will be able to decipher this scrawl.

JOS H. TALBOT

ALS. DLC–JKP. Probably addressed to Washington.

1. Talbot, a Madison County lawyer, succeeded his brother Eli as clerk of the Chancery Court of Williamson County in 1832, served several years as clerk of the Tennessee Supreme Court, and in 1838 became the first U.S. district attorney for the newly formed West Tennessee court. The following year he was succeeded by Henry W. McCorry, who served until 1849.

2. See Polk to Talbot, December 27, 1838.

3. A Nashville lawyer and one of the founders of the Whig party in Tennessee, Ephraim H. Foster served in the Tennessee House, 1827–31 and 1835–37; he was Speaker during his last two terms. Appointed to the U.S. Senate upon the resignation of Felix Grundy, Foster served from September 17, 1838, and was reelected for the term beginning March 4, 1839. He resigned, however, in November before Congress met, rather than follow instructions sent to him by the new Tennessee legislature. Grundy filled the vacancy until his death in December 1840. A. O. P. Nicholson served an interim appointment until the 1841–42 legislative session ended. Failing to hold an election, the legislature left the seat vacant until 1843, when Foster was chosen to complete his original term. Talbot's suggestions were unavailing; Foster's bill on the federal judiciary in Tennessee already had received Van Buren's signature on January 18, 1839. Talbot's enclosure not found.

4. Reference probably is to members of the Nashville bar.

5. The fourth section's proviso gave the marshal of the Middle Tennessee district power to collect executions and serve all process on circuit court judgments previously rendered or pending, regardless of whether the enforcement was to be in Middle or West Tennessee.

6. Samuel B. Marshall and Robert J. Chester. Marshall served at Nashville as U.S. marshal for Middle Tennessee, 1831–41. His wife, Jane Childress Marshall, had important family connections, including George C. Childress, Morgan W. Brown, Benjamin Litton, and John Catron. Chester, an old friend of Andrew Jackson, moved to Madison County after the Panic of 1819. He was a contractor, land speculator, lumberman, postmaster of

Jackson, 1825–33, and West Tennessee marshal, 1838–49. Chester County, Tennessee, was named in his honor.

7. Legal maxim attributed to William Watson, *Ten Quodlibeticall Questions Concerning Religion and State*, published in 1601.

8. John Wesley Crockett, son of David Crockett of Alamo fame, practiced law in Paris, Tennessee. He was elected as a Whig to Congress for two terms, 1837–41.

FROM WILLIAM S. HAYNES[1]

Shelbyville, Tennessee. January 20, 1839

Haynes warns that dissension may hurt Democrats in the congressional contest. Although Harvey M. Watterson was selected to replace Nicholson by a "full conference" of leading Maury County politicians, Dr. Kincaid has determined to run on the "fence" between Watterson and Col. Webster, the Whig candidate.[2] Watterson will win that race, but Democratic candidates for the Tennessee House may lose if friends of Kincaid and Webster unite. E. J. Frierson was the Democrats' first choice for Congress, but he declined to run because of Kincaid's candidacy.

ALS. DLC–JKP. Addressed to Washington.

1. Born in Virginia, Haynes came to Tennessee in 1838 and became editor of the *Weekly Times*, a Democratic newspaper in Murfreesboro. By January 1839 he was editing the *Western Star* in Shelbyville.

2. Joseph A. Kincaid and Jonathan Webster. A physician and a political veteran in Bedford County, Kincaid consistently opposed the Polk–Van Buren faction. He had served three terms in the Tennessee House and had been a delegate to the 1834 Constitutional Convention. A large landholder in Bedford County, Webster served numerous terms in both houses of the Tennessee legislature, 1813 to 1837; he won election as presiding officer of the Senate, 1835–37. Although he had supported Polk for many years, Webster ran as a Whig in 1839.

FROM M. D. COOPER & CO.

New Orleans, Louisiana. January 21, 1839

Cooper & Co. reports that Chisholm & Minter[1] of Troy have stored 33 bales of cotton received from Polk's plantation. Having insured all of the cotton against fire and river damage, the company expects to receive the shipment in a few days. Cooper further states that "fair lots of cotton are scarce" and command fair prices.

LS. DLC–JKP. Addressed to Washington.

1. One of the partners in the firm of Chisholm & Minter of Troy, Mississippi, was James Minter; Chisholm has not been identified.

FROM THOMAS J. READ & SON[1]

Louisville, Kentucky. January 22, 1839

The company sends an itemized bill totaling $482.89 for supplies ordered November 4, 1838. These goods have been shipped this day to Vicksburg, Mississippi, with instructions to reship them to Chisolm & Minter of Troy, Mississippi. George W. Bratton[2] has been advised also.

LS. DLC–JKP. Addressed to Washington. AE on the cover indicates that on February 3, 1839, Polk sent his note for $600 to Samuel P. Walker to cover this bill.

1. A staunch Jacksonian, Thomas J. Read moved from Nashville to Louisville in 1835 and became a wealthy commission merchant.

2. From January 1837 until his death in July 1839, Bratton served as overseer of Polk's plantation in Yalobusha County, Mississippi.

FROM HILLARY LANGTRY[1]

Dear Sir Columbia 24th Jany 1839

I returned here a few days since after an absence of nearly two months endeavouring to dispose of our Steam property,[2] and was much surprised to hear the change effected in the political prospects of our district by the withdrawal, I will not say defection, of A. O. P. N[icholson] who acted without consultation with any of his political friends, and has thereby I think resigned all his future political prospects so far as they may depend on the party with which he acted. In the mean time we have several in the field all from Bedford, Say Jno Webster, H Waterson & Dr. Kincaid, not one of whom so far as I can learn will be heartily supported by this constituency, whose eyes are turned on E J Frierson, whose activity habits and modesty aided by the influence of his relations (& good whigs) has so far prevented him from giving a favourable response to applications. In this county there are two or three spoken of (or either wish to be so), Dr. Thomas, B. Martin and some say Dr Greenfield.[3] In the mean time our people are perfectly placid waiting for some concerted and united action and so soon as a selection can be made by a sufficient number in whom they have confidence I have no doubt whoever may be selected will obtain a general support. Genl Pillow[4] has been mentioned and called on but has declined. E. J. Thomas[5] is the only one here I can think of whose selection would insure the support of a heavy majority should we protract the nomination to any late period, but nothing but want of unanimity in the selection can defeat us much as the present circumstances are embarrassing. Something should be done soon and efficiently and several of our tried friends are absent who could give tone to public feeling. I write so poorly on politics I had better Stop whilst I have room to subscribe myself as ever your continued friend & well wisher.

H. LANGTRY

ALS. DLC–JKP. Probably addressed to Washington.

1. A Columbia merchant of Irish descent, Langtry was involved in local internal improvements. Having been a director of the Columbia Railroad Company in 1834, he now had interests in steam navigation on the Duck River.

2. Though he disposed of his steam property, Langtry's interest must have continued, as he was among those appointed to sell subscriptions in the Duck River Steam Navigation Company upon its incorporation in January 1840.

3. Isaac J. Thomas, Barkly Martin, and Gerrard T. Greenfield. A lawyer and politician, Martin served as a Democrat in the Tennessee House, 1839–41, 1847–49, and 1851–53, and sat in the Senate, 1841–43. He was elected to the U.S. House of Representatives and served from 1845 until 1847.

4. A Columbia lawyer and general in the militia, Gideon J. Pillow played a key role at the 1844 Democratic presidential convention. He served as a general officer in the Mexican War and commanded a Confederate brigade during the Civil War.

5. Reference is to Jonas E. Thomas, who represented Maury County in the Tennessee House, 1835–51.

FROM DAVID A. STREET[1]

Jackson, Tennessee. January 24, 1839

Street requests that Polk forward him political news and says that he will reciprocate Polk's kindness. He notes that Martin and Chalmers have moved to Holly Springs, Mississippi, and that Sheppard has taken residence in Franklin, Tennessee.[2]

ALS. DLC–JKP. Addressed to Washington.

1. Street, a nullifier and former White supporter, edited the Jackson *District Telegraph and State Sentinel* from March 1838 until early 1839.

2. Andrew L. Martin, Joseph W. Chalmers, and Benjamin H. Sheppard. Chalmers, a Democrat, represented Mississippi in the U.S. Senate, 1845–47.

Sheppard and James L. Talbot, nephew of Joseph H. Talbot, assumed management of the Jackson *Truth Teller* in early 1837 and changed its name to that of the Jackson *District Telegraph and State Sentinel*. Sheppard later served as U.S. marshal in Middle Tennessee.

FROM J. GEORGE HARRIS

My Dear Sir, Nashville Tenn Jan. 25, 1839

Here I am. Arr. this morning at day-light per steamboat, ten days from Wheeling Va. & thirteen days from Washington—*pretty entirely* jaded. I have slept but little in stage and steamboat, and must have a few days rest before taking the ed. chair of "the Union." It is quite rainy to-day and I have delivered only a few of my letters—say those to Mr Smith and yours to Genl Armstrong. If pleasant to-morrow I shall deliver the remainder. I find Mr. Smith to be a gentleman—all you represented him to be—and have determined with him to commence my labors on the 1st of Feb. when the paper will be enlarged, and, I hope, *improved*.

I think I shall like Nashville. In appearance it is more like our New England cities than any one I have seen west of the mountains. With its inhabitants I have yet to form an acquaintance.

I perceive that the Banner is pub. Mr. Bell's Speech *in extenso*.[1] I think I shall pub a few critical notes as an *offset* or *antidote* (rather than as a *reply*) in my first nos.[2]

Bear me in remembrance to your mess and be good enough to tell Mrs. Catron that her package to Miss Marshall is now safe in the City Hotel at Nashville and will be delivered to-morrow.[3] Do write me frankly & freely. I have already made my private arrangement at the P.O. as you desired.

J G Harris

Monday morn. Before mailing my letters this morn I have broken open this to say that "the Old Chief"[4] arrived in town last evening & has taken lodging at the Inn. I just received two letters from you, each covering letters directed to me at Boston from some of my friends in Mass. I am sorry Mr Hoyt, my agent at Boston,[5] troubles you with them. He does so without my order—but you may depend that he is a gentleman in whom I repose all confidence and a fast friend of ours. I have written him to send my letters directly to me and not trouble you with them. I hope you will commence writing me as soon as you can conveniently. Let me know of the primary movements of parties in the House &c. JGH.

ALS. DLC–JKP. Addressed to Washington.

1. The Nashville *Republican Banner* of January 25, 26, and 28, 1839, carried John Bell's speech, delivered in the U.S. House of Representatives on December 26, 1838; Bell's comments were very critical of Van Buren's 1838 State of the Union message.

2. Harris' response has not been found.

3. The Polks and Catrons were staying at Jonathan Elliot's boarding house, located on Pennsylvania Avenue. Harris' reference to "Miss Marshall" probably is to one of Matilda Childress Catron's nieces; her sister, Jane, was married to Samuel B. Marshall of Nashville.

4. Andrew Jackson.

5. Hoyt is not identified further.

FROM ALFRED BALCH

Dear Sir, Washington 26th Jany 39

I have a letter from a friend in Tennessee who says "Johnson *can beat Cheatham*[1] *if he will offer* but he is pausing and hesitating and speaks of leaving Clarksville." I wish that you would write in the most pressing manner and urge Johnson by all means to offer. Your own election is much connected with Johnsons becoming a candidate and if Cheatham can be beaten it will add one vote to our strength here and even one vote will be most material with reference to the speakership on which Bells heart is fixed.

Kincannon ought to be disposed of and Brown pressed heavily by our friends. The backing out of Nicholson has left your District rather destitute. But Frierson is a clever fellow & will carry a heavy vote in Bedford since Bedford will feel honored by his nomination. I do not know but Friersons offering will take a larger vote in Bedford for you whilst your own residence in Maury will carry you ahead there to the same extent as if Nicholson were in the field. Be sure to write to Johnson. Bell & Campbell are invincible in their Districts and you have much to fear from the majorities in them unless you can bring them down by your own efforts.

A B.

PS In my opinion the majority now against you in Wilson, Davidson, Smith & Jackson is at the least 3000 votes. But I do not doubt that this majority may be materially lessened by your own exertions and those of your friends there. Duncans[2] is a capital ad captandum[3] speech. It ought to be sent to every part of the country.[4]

ALI. DLC–JKP. Addressed locally and marked "Private."

1. Richard Cheatham was a prominent merchant and farmer in Springfield. He represented Robertson County in the Tennessee House, 1825–33, and won election as a Whig to the U.S. House of Representatives, 1837–39. As Alfred Balch predicted, Cheatham's race for reelection against Cave Johnson was unsuccessful.

2. Alexander Duncan, Democratic representative from Ohio, addressed the U.S. House of Representatives on January 17, 1839, on the mode for raising a committee to inquire into the defalcations of Samuel Swartwout. If chosen by the House, the committee would reflect Whig thinking, minimize Swartwout's frauds, and blame Treasury Secretary Levi Woodbury for the scandal. More generally, Duncan argued that the present government was an administration of the people, that its recommendations for economy should be supported, and that money should not be wasted by printing voluminous documents detailing unsettled accounts of government officials.

3. The Latin phrase *ad captandum* comes from the verb *capio* and translates "winning" or "captivating."

4. Last two sentences of the postscript are written in the left margin.

FROM WILLIAM H. POLK

Dear Brother Columbia Jany 26th 1839

Since writing you last nothing has transpired of any importance. You are I presume informed of the determination of my difficulty. The Jury refused to find a true Bill. I was afterwards prosecuted for an Assault & Battery. I deemed it most prudent to continue that case to the next term. I did not do this, in the fear of any serious consequences resulting from it, beyond punishment in a pecuniary form, but the agitated state of public feeling, I feared might operate upon the Judge,[1] when the affair was so fresh, in the infliction of the damages. There was another consideration which prompted me to this course. The public mind seemed to be shocked and indignant at the vindictive course which Mr O B Hayes was pursuing in relation to the affair. The public look upon it as gross injustice to the memory of his Son, in pursuing a course which his Son disdained to resort to for redress, in prosecuting me for the very *act* for which I jeopardized my life. It disarmed the public of all sympathy for a bereaved Parent, and awakened the disgust of many of those who cared nothing for him, farther than to show him attention, to operate to my disadvantage. The decision of the Jury stamps *falsehood* upon the thousand exaggerated accounts which were afloat, and public judgement is no longer swayed by designing men, discoloring the facts of the case. They have the decision of the Grand Jury, which will condemn all unjust reports. "Justice will be done."

Since I wrote you, I have entirely disembarrassed myself with regard to my pecuniary matters, by the sale of my *plantation,* on which I lived. I sold it for Ten thousand seven hundred dollars—four thousand in *Cash,* the ballance in one, two & three years. It was purchased, 100 Acres for Bishop Otey by a fiew Gentlemen, the other portion by David Looney.[2] The Cash I immediately appropriated to the liquidation of my *Bank debt* (you say that was right!) or "well *Sarah* the fellows getting to have some sense at last."

Brother Samuel is not near as well as when you left home. He is evidently on the decline. It is with difficulty that he can now walk across the room. Dr Hays is of the opinion that he cannot recover. He does not I believe apprehend any immediate danger, but thinks the disease is perminently settled on him. I hope though, that he may be mistaken. His cough is not worse than it was when he arrived home. He has been much better for the last fiew days, apparently.

Kincaid & Watterson & Webster of Bedford Cty. are all Candidates for Congress. The Shelbyville paper[3] has hoisted the name of Watterson. The Democrat[4] has not as yet, made any preference. It waits the settlement of the matter at the Marshall Cty Court, which comes on the first or second Monday of next month. Jonas E Thomas is willing to run if he is the choice of the party, but will in no event run so as to create a division. There is nothing new. Give my love to Sister Sarah. All Mr Walkers family are well.

WILL HAWKINS POLK

ALS. DLC–JKP. Addressed to Washington.

1. Edmund Dillahunty.

2. James H. Otey and David Looney. An educator and rector of the Episcopal Church in Franklin, Otey was consecrated as the first Protestant Episcopal bishop in Tennessee in 1834. Looney was a son of Abraham Looney, a wealthy Columbia merchant, and a son-in-law of Patrick Maguire, another well-to-do Columbia merchant. He owned interest in an iron works in Wayne County.

3. Probably the Shelbyville *Western Star,* edited in 1839 by William S. Haynes.

4. Established as a weekly Jackson paper in 1835 by Chesley P. Bynum and Ewin Cameron, the Columbia *Tennessee Democrat* was edited by James H. Thompson by 1838.

FROM JOHN W. CHILDRESS[1]

Murfreesboro, Tennessee. January 27, [1839][2]

Childress reports that county candidates have not yet begun to campaign. Yoakum appears to be more popular than previously thought and will run Ready a good race.[3]

ALS. DLC–JKP. Addressed to Washington.

1. A younger brother of Sarah Polk, Childress lived in Murfreesboro where he practiced law. Married in 1831 to Sarah Williams, he was the father of six children.

2. Erroneously dated "1838"; year identified through content analysis.

3. Henderson K. Yoakum and Charles Ready. Graduated from the U.S. Military Academy in 1832, Yoakum resigned from the service the following year and moved to Murfreesboro. He held the post of town mayor, 1837–43, and won election as a Democrat to the Tennessee Senate, 1839–41. Ready, a member of the Murfreesboro bar, frequently was mentioned as a candidate for office by the anti-Jackson forces and was elected as a Whig to the Tennessee House for one term, 1835–37. He later served in the U.S. House as a Whig, 1853–59.

FROM RICHARD M. WOODS[1]

Sir, Greeneville 28 January 1839

Will you be good enough to bear with me, while I dictate to you. I think it would be of advantage to the Republican cause, and add something to your success, if you will take a range through the first Congressional District as you return from Congress, (viz) be sure to commence at Taylorsville, Johnson County, Elizabethton, Jonesborough, Greeneville, New Port, Sevierville and Dandridge. The reasons why I think so, is, that in our District, it is now most likely that we will not have a republican Candidate, for Congress, and we will need help very much in the commencement of the comeing contest. It is with us here death or victory the next race. August next redeems this state from the odium of Federal Whiggery or stamps it with lasting infamy and disgrace, for having deserted the Democratic Standard and renounced its first principals. Genls Carter and Arnold[2] will I fear be our only candidates, both Clay and Cannon men, and Bank men, and Anty Subtreasury men and any thing but republicans. We are at present in rather a desperate fix, politically, in this District without a head, we have no prominant leader, like sheep in the mountains without a shepherd. In old Greene we will tell well for you, at the Ballot Box, if we get no back set this spring. These are my reasons for thinking that we will need help most this spring rather than later in the season. A good start is excellent in a race. I have advised with some of my friends on this subject, who have written you before this I expect. A Democratic Republican News Paper printed at Knoxville, would be of great advantage to our cause in this end of the State. Friend Gifford[3] has now gone west to try to make the arrangement, and procure funds to purchase the Press &c for that purpose, but I fear he will not succeed. Our Mountain Counties on the northern range see very little news, but the Knoxville Register,[4] which is rank poison. The United States Attorney Genl. for the Eastern District of Tennessee, J A McKenney,[5] is now on the track in oposition to Col McClellan. He opened his battery in the mountains perhaps at Jacksborough a few days since.

I would have been much pleased to have seen you and heard you, as you went on to the City, but had it not in my power.

R. M. Woods

ALS. DLC–JKP. Addressed to Washington. AE on the cover states that this letter was answered on February 7, 1839; Polk's reply has not been found.

1. Appointed U.S. marshal for East Tennessee in 1838, Woods held that job at least until 1843. He also served as sheriff of Greene County, 1826–1840 and a trustee of Tusculum Academy.

2. William B. Carter and Thomas D. Arnold. Formerly from Knoxville and now from Greene County, Arnold was a lawyer and a bitter opponent of Jackson and Polk. He served as a Whig in the U.S. House, 1831–33 and 1841–43.

3. Lawson Gifford helped establish the Jonesboro *Tennessee Sentinel* in 1835. He also assisted in founding the Knoxville *Argus*, a Democratic newspaper edited by E. G. Eastman and first published on June 27, 1839.

4. An influential opposition newspaper in East Tennessee, the *Knoxville Register* was established by Frederick S. Heiskell in 1816. William B. A. Ramsey took over the editorship in 1836, purchased the paper soon thereafter, and backed Hugh L. White for president.

5. John A. McKinney, Rogersville merchant and U.S. attorney for the Eastern District of Tennessee, 1829–41, lost this congressional race to Democrat Abraham McClellan.

FROM WILLIAM E. OWEN[1]

Dear Sir Brownsville 29 Jany 1839

The people in this section of the Country are very anxious to have a mail coach on this route either from Jackson through this place to Randolph or to Branch from Huntingdon via Trenton, Cherryville, Brownsville, Wesley, Covington, to Randolph. Do see what can be done. We have no faith in our Representative.[2] I will not trouble him on the subject. Our County Court have appropriated one thousand dollars for Bridges to be made on the Wesley Road across the sluys[3] on the Hatchee bottom which is susceptable of being made the best crossing in said bottom. At any rate the mail as now carried ought to go by Wesley from here instead of Durhamsville on to Covington.

You see we have opposition to Majr. Conner in this District. Jno. P. Perkins and Mathew D Anderson[4] are candidates for a seat in the H of Representative. You know Mr Perkins, he is a Son of Col N. T. Perkins of Williamson. He is and will be opposed to any and every thing Jackson ever did. He will not be hard to beat by a Democrat who is a pretty clever fellow. As for Mr. Anderson I know not much of him. He is not very popular. He was elected a Major in this Regmt last Summer and has thereby assumed some consequence. We will try and get some one who belongs to the Democratic party to come out. We have been urging Mr. Edwin J Taliaferro[5] for some time but he as yet hangs back and I think has some what injured his popularity by it. The Democratic side is evidently gaining ground and if the principles as laid down in your speech[6] when you were here are discussd, as they should be, the State of Tennessee will be as she was when Jackson was elected President. I had left Brownsville before Mr Bell arrived and was not there when he made his speech, but this I know, he done no good for his side. I was told he said he had not changed since his first political career commenced. There is no man who know more of John Bell than I do. We commenced our career in the Town of Franklin in the same year (1816), was friendly, and very intimate and I am satisfied no man in the County was of more service to him in all his elections than I was when he opposed Mr. Grundy.[7] I was a candidate for the Legislature and had he have avowed the same principles then as he does at this time he would not have recd. two hundred votes in the County of Williamson. If there ever was a case of being bought I think Mr. B one. He has been bought by his *Wife*[8] but I am truly sorry for my friend Foster. He was a member of the Legislature in 1827 when the Resolutions of *A. V. Brown* was presented. Mr. Foster approved and advocated the Resolutions and I think there were not more than four members in the H of R who voted against them.[9] I am also sorry for Judge White for the people now see (all who are disposed to do Justice) he is acting the part of the spoild child as did Mr Clay before him. They have both in their turn gone against their party and principles and [are] now in the ranks of those they once violently opposed.

Since I saw you I have been appointed Post Master here. In my letter to Mr. Kendall I refered him to all and any Gentlemen from Ten. who might be at Washington. If you were instrumental in geting the appointment please accept of my thanks. Should the Deptmt need an agent to superintend any Business I should be very glad to be employed, for the emoluments of this office is very small and I should be much pleased to be engaged in attending to any matters of the Deptmt in this or the adjoining States.

I should be glad to hear from you at any time you may have the leisure and any thing I can do for you shall be attended to. Should you think it necessary to write to me do not use your Frank but write me as Post Master. I will give you my reason when I see you. On all Public Documents use your own Frank.

I have been urging our friend Huntsman[10] to run against Crockett. I think he is stronger than Martin. I can do much for him. We have been members together, and to Huntsman belongs the Credit of Feriting out the bad management of the Old State Bank [. . .]ish was Cashr.[11]

I could beat Perkins in this county but [. . .][12] be impossible for me to run. I am too *poor*. Give my respects to Mr. Grundy.

Wm. E. Owen

ALS. DLC–JKP. Addressed to Washington.

1. Owen operated a general merchandise store in Franklin in the 1820's. He was elected mayor of Franklin, 1823–27, and was appointed Williamson County agent for the Bank of the State of Tennessee in 1824. He represented Williamson County in the Tennessee House, 1827–31, and later removed to Brownsville, where he was a pioneer merchant and postmaster, 1838–41.

2. John W. Crockett.

3. Incorrect spelling of "slues" or "sloughs."

4. Born in Knox county, Perkins moved to Haywood County, which he represented in the Tennessee House, 1839–43. He was a son of Nicholas T. Perkins of Williamson County. Anderson is not further identified.

5. Not further identified.

6. Polk last spoke in Brownsville on October 3, 1838.

7. Bell defeated Grundy for Congress in 1826.

8. Jane Bell, daughter of Andrew Erwin of Bedford County, was married first to Thomas Yeatman, wealthy Nashville merchant, banker, and ironmaster. Widowed with four children in 1833, she married Bell in 1835.

9. On October 18, 1827, Aaron V. Brown of Giles County offered a resolution in the Tennessee Senate favoring the election of Andrew Jackson as president and proposing a constitutional amendment to provide for the direct election of the president by the people.

10. Born in Virginia, Adam Huntsman had moved to Overton County by 1809, where he practiced law and speculated in land on a large scale until 1821.

He sat for that county in the Tennessee Senate, 1815–21, and later represented Madison County in that body, 1827–31. A Democrat, he had defeated David Crockett for a term in the U.S. House of Representatives, 1835–37. However, Huntsman did not run against John W. Crockett in 1839.

11. In 1819 Tennesseans experienced financial panic, as did citizens of other western states. So disastrous were its effects, the legislature established the Bank of the State of Tennessee the following year, with a capital stock of $1,000,000, to relieve the distress and improve state revenues. With the main office at Nashville, a branch at Knoxville, and agencies in each county in the state formed prior to 1819, the Bank seemed to function efficiently. However, as capital was distributed over the state, large amounts were lost by defalcations of county agents. In 1832, Joel Parrish, cashier of the main bank at Nashville, was discovered to have permitted overdrafts amounting to $80,000, the greater part of which was lost. In the following year, the legislature abolished the Bank and deposited its funds in the newly incorporated Union Bank. Huntsman's part in exposing mismanagement in the Bank has not been ascertained.

12. Manuscript mutilated.

FROM JABEZ JACKSON

D Sir [Washington City. January 30, 1839][1]

In your communication with Mr Johnson[2] please to bear in mind, and say to him, that I ask compensation *only for the 16 days before the adjournment*—for I have withdrawn any claim to compensation for the time I was sick *after the 9 July,* though I was ill several weeks.[3]

J.J.

ALI. DLC–JKP. Probably addressed locally. AE on the cover reads: "Hon. Jabez Jackson. Written immediately after interview on the 30th Janry. 1839."

1. Dated from Polk's endorsement.
2. Joseph Johnson, representative from Virginia, 1823–27, 1835–41, and 1845–47, was chairman of the House committee on accounts, which reviewed Jackson's compensation claims.
3. See Jabez Jackson to Polk, January 12, 1839.

FROM SAMUEL W. POLK

Dear Brother, Columbia Ten. Jany [30, 1839][1]

I can write but very brief letter to you at this time. My health has very rapidly declined since you left us. My cough has increased daily almost. All I can do for it is to use such medicine as will cause it to be easy of expectoration. My strength has failed me. I can scarcely cross the room and back again. Of recovery I have little hope; *but do hope* that I shall see you and my dear Sister once more. The Drs (Dickinson & Hays) say they have seen apparently worse cases recover.[2]

I wish you, dear brother, would order for me, in Philadelphia or any other place a carriage worth from $700 to 800, and if possible have it land at Nashville by the 1st or 15th of April. Should I survive the winter I will be in need of a long suitable carriage for a sick person to travel in. I should dislike to borrow for fear of accident. I suppose if you cannot find time to leave the City, some member from Phil will be going into the city and can order it.[3] If Mr Walker cannot furnish you the means to pay for it, the sum can be remitted through some merchant going from Columbia this spring to Phil.

All well. My best love to sister and respects to Dr. Sewall.[4]

S W Polk

ALS. DLC–JKP. Addressed to Washington.

1. The day of the month is taken from the postmark of the letter; the year is identified through content analysis.

2. Samuel Polk died of tuberculosis on February 24, 1839.

3. James K. Polk had purchased his carriage from a Philadelphia coach maker, Lyman Knowles. Knowles and Company formerly conducted their business in Boston.

4. Thomas Sewell, a Washington physician, attended Samuel during the spring and summer of 1838.

TO AMOS KENDALL

Sir. Washington City January 31 1839

I have the honor to present for your consideration, the enclosed petitions[1] numerously signed by citizens of Madison, Henderson, Maury and other Counties in Tennessee, praying for the establishment of a line of two horse stages from Mount Pleasant, in Maury County by the way of Perryville and Lexington, to Jackson.[2] I regard the route as an important one, and hope it may be in the power of the Department to grant the prayer of the petitioners. During the past year, I had the honor in a letter,[3] addressed to the Department strongly to urge the establishment of a line of four horse post coaches from McMinnville, by the way of *Shelbyville Lewisburg, Columbia, Mt. Pleasant,* and thence over the route prayed for by the petitioners, to Jackson. For the considerations and reasons, which induced the application at that time, I beg leave to refer you to that letter.

The opinions and views therein expressed, have not been changed, but on the contrary, I am the more impressed with the importance of the route. For reasons assigned in your answer,[4] that application was declined. Mount Pleasant is situated on the main stage route, from Nashville to Tuscumbia Alabama, and thence to New Orleans. The mail is at present carried from Mt. Pleasant to Jackson, on horseback.

The increased expense of putting a line of two horse stages on the route, would be small, whilst the facilities afforded to the section of Country in which the petitioners reside would be considerable. Referring you to my letter of last year I have only to repeat the request, that the prayer of the petitioners (if the means of the Department will permit it) may be granted.

James K. Polk

Copy. DLC–JKP. Addressed locally and marked "Copy."

1. Petitions not found.

2. Construction of the new Columbia Central Turnpike may have occasioned local demands for stagecoach service between Columbia and Jackson. The turnpike ran from Columbia through Mt. Pleasant to Clifton, a village on the Tennessee River. Selah R. Hobbie, first assistant postmaster general, wrote Polk on February 12, 1839, that the service was declined. LS. DLC–JKP.

3. See Polk and Hopkins L. Turney to Amos Kendall, March 29, 1838.

4. See Amos Kendall to Polk and Hopkins L. Turney, May 12, 1838, for the reply.

FROM ERWIN J. FRIERSON

Dear Sir Shelbyville Tenn. Feby. the 1st 1839

You will have heard before this reaches you that our affairs are in such a situation as to make it madness in another candidate of our party to enter the field. Kincaid & Watterson are both candidates and also old Webster. I recd. one solitary letter from Columbia, when it was known that Nicholson had withdrawn (which event took me as much by surprise as it did you) stating that my name had been spoken of by some of our friends as a candidate. This letter was from Sam Walker[1] and concluded by saying that it was thought advisable that no one should announce themselves until the different parts of the District had time to compare ideas. This letter took me by surprise, for I had no more calculation of being taken up as a candidate than Teague R Ragan.[2] On the next day I was called upon by the Editor of the Star[3] to know if he might announce me in his next paper; this I *positively* refused as I understood it to be the wish of our Columbia friends that there should be no precipitancy in the matter. I at the same time told him that I thought it doubtful whether even after deliberating I could be a candidate. The next thing I knew the Editor of the Star was gone on a mission to Columbia, and *immediately* on his return Watterson was announced as a candidate. I never knew that Watterson had any idea of running until I heard he was a candidate. I do not think that I could have been a candidate under any circumstances, but if the matter had not been hurried on with such precipitancy and we could have compared ideas with our Maury friends I would have urged it as the best policy at this crisis to have run Kincaid. He had declared as soon as Nicholsons withdrawal was known that he was in the field, and he is such a selfish animal, that we could by running him as our candidate have made him so straight as to *lean back*, and in a single handed race between him & Webster, I believe that he could have beaten Webster 1000 or 1500 votes. As it is I think it more than probable he will fly off of the helve altogether or will do us more harm than if he was an open mouthed enemy. He has already opened against what he calls the Columbia *junto*[4] and swears that he will mount anti-masonry &c &c. There has scarcely been time to see how the thing will work. The indications so far shew that Watterson is likely to be supported with more unanimity than I had anticipated, but I cannot but think that our position is a very vulnerable one if it is properly managed against us. *Our new converts wooling* each other already for an office which their enemies charged at the time was the motive to their conversion, places them in a predicament not much to be envied. I do not know what we are to do for county candidates. Warner & Dean[5] speak of not running, fearing the storm which has been raised by the Grocery law.[6] I cannot be a candidate for the Senate. The names of Swanson, H. B. Coffee & A. Boyd[7] have been mentioned, but I do not know whether they will run.

E. J. FRIERSON

ALS. DLC–JKP. Probably addressed to Washington.

1. Samuel P. Walker was the eldest son of James and Jane Maria Polk Walker, and a nephew of James K. Polk. During the 1840's he moved to Memphis where he became a prominent lawyer and judge.

2. Teague O'Regan was a hot-headed Irish officer who served James II in Ireland during the Glorious Revolution.

3. William Scott Haynes edited the Shelbyville *Western Star*.

4. A. O. P. Nicholson probably was Watterson's major advocate in Maury County. See John B. Hays to Polk, February 7, 1839.

5. Richard Warner and Thomas Dean. A farmer in the Chapel Hill neighborhood, Warner was active in the militia and local politics. A faithful Democrat, he was elected to the Tennessee House, 1833–35 and 1837–39, and served in the Senate, 1839–43 and 1845–47. Dean was a farmer in the Flat Creek community in Bedford County, where he owned large tracts of land. Also a Democrat, he had defeated Warner for a seat in the Tennessee House in 1835, but served with him in that body, 1837–39.

6. By an Act of February 5, 1836, the legislature had increased the state's licensing tax on retail merchants; in 1840 the rate was lowered.

7. Swanson, Henry B. Coffey and Aaron Boyd. Swanson is not further identified. A resident of the Wartrace community of Bedford County, Coffey served one term as a Democrat in the Tennessee House, 1839–41. Boyd lived in the Chapel Hill community of Bedford and later in Marshall County. He ran unsuccessfully for delegate to the Tennessee Constitutional Convention in 1834.

FROM LAWSON GIFFORD

Dear Col. Knoxville, Fb 4 1839

You will see from the top of my letter that I am in Knoxville. I have been down the country & have seen many of our friends, and I assure you I had no expectation of seeing so many of them marked with *Polk berries*, as I found in the counties of Knox, Blount, Monroe, McMinn & Roane. There is lots of them I assure you, and they are of the right stripe, and will cast their votes for Republican men in August.

I have been making head way here for a press[1] on your suggestions in your letter to Dr. Kenny[2] under date of 15th of Jan. last.[3] The idea is popular and it is conceded by all our friends that a paper advocating the right doctrines at this place is the most important move that can be made. That a paper here will exercise more influence in the coming contest, than any other is true. The following named counties look to Knoxville for their information, & there is no paper of our politics in any of them, although 3 or 4 of a different discription. Cocke, Jefferson, Sevier, Grainger, Hawkins, Claiborne, Campbell, Anderson, Morgan, Roane, Rhea, Bledsoe, Marion, in part, Monroe, & Blount. Voting as an aggregate not less than 20,000. Besides all the balances of the counties in East Tennessee are more or less effected in the same way. You will see, by the bye, that this statement embraces all the strong Whig counties in this part of the State, and they are the very counties in which the battle is to be fought. Our friends are very anxious that the matter should be gone into immediately, and they will subscribe money amply sufficient to pay for the office, and to keep its head above the water, for the first 12 or 18 months, until it can live itself. The matter can be managed very easily, by getting Mr. Cambreling[4] or some other of our friends to have the order for the Type, Press, &c. filled and forwarded to this place by some of his friends in New York. The notes can be forwarded to me & I will then sign them. If the Press, &c. could be bought on 12 or 18 months credit (with interest from dates) it would materially aid our cause. Their money can be made safe and will be paid over when due. You know the difficulty that the office will have to contend with; there is not a commercial house except Mr. Roberts on our side, and of course it can not expect to live by its advertising patronage, but will have to be supported by its frinds. There is an order in New York, now for printing materials for a *new Federal Whig paper*[5] to be published in this place. The paper is to be edited by John H. Crozier & Thos. Humes.[6] It is to be in operation in a short time. I know of no better plan to adopt than to get the order filled as I have suggested. You nor nobody else will be known in the matter & I give my own notes for the Press, &c. The whole will not cost more than 800 dollars (eight). I will forward the order to McClellan when I get home so that there can be no charge made on you. You will please send the gentleman[7] alluded to in your letter[8] out to Jonesboro', immediately, and I will make arrangements with him that I have no doubt will prove highly satisfactory to him and all concerned. The Prospectus will be issued in a few days. Gen. Anderson[9] is writing it now. He also gives the paper his hearty support, both as to writing and advancing money. Gen Wallace will advance almost any sum—& so will many others.

I have a long letter to write you about several things of importance, but will delay it 'till I get to Jonesboro'.

L. Gifford

[P.S.] You will please get the gentleman that you allude to in your letter as willing to come out here, to write to me to Jonesboro', immediately giving his views, &c. and let him make his way out as soon as possible.

ALS. DLC–JKP. Addressed to Washington.

1. Gifford was arranging for the publication of the Knoxville *Argus*.

2. Daniel Kenney, a Jonesboro physician and merchant, represented Greene, Hawkins, and Washington counties for one term in the Tennessee House, 1843–45.

3. Letter not found.

4. Churchill C. Cambreleng engaged in mercantile business in New York City and served as a Democrat in the U.S. House, 1821–39. Van Buren appointed him minister to Russia, 1840–41.

5. Knoxville *Times*.

6. John H. Crozier and Thomas W. Humes. Son of John Crozier, longtime Knoxville postmaster, John H. Crozier had a number of business, civic, and political interests in addition to his law practice in Knoxville. A Whig, he represented Knox County in the Tennessee House, 1837–39, and served in the U.S. House, 1845–49. Thomas W. Humes, a Knoxville merchant, became editor of the *Times* in 1839. In 1840 he was editor of the *Knoxville Register*. See Gifford to Polk, February 11, 1839.

7. Reference is not further identified.

8. Letter not found.

9. Alexander O. Anderson, a Knoxville lawyer, was superintendent of the U.S. land office in Alabama in 1836, and government agent in 1838 for removing the Indians from Alabama and Florida. He was elected as a Democrat to the U.S. Senate in place of Hugh L. White, resigned. Anderson served for two years, 1840–41.

FROM JOHN THOMSON[1]

Dear Sir

Columbus [Ohio] Feb. 4th 1839

By a letter received a few days since, from Mr Hamer, I am informed, that he and Senator Allen[2] had prepared a recommendation, had procured the Signatures of all the Democratic members in Congress from this State to it and had presented it to the President, asking for me some appointment within his gift.

The same letter says the recommendation was well, and favourably received, also assurance given by the President that so soon as a suitable situation presented I should be remembered, and the paper was sent to the War department at that time, as the most likely channel through which an appointment might soon be obtained.

Now my Dear Sir I think that was a most unfortunate reference for me, for of all the Secretaries, Mr. Poinset[3] is the only one with whom I have no acquaintance, nor he with me, as he just came into that office as I left Congress, but I presume that fact was not thought of by Messrs Allen & Hamer, nor have I since mentioned it to them.

I well remember an expression you made to me the last time we conversed together in your room which was that you never forgot nor forsook an old friend, that you considered me as such, and that if ever you had it in your power to do me a kindness you stood prepared to do it, and from that expression I am emboldened to write this short letter to you knowing that from the elevated station which you occupy you have a commanding influence with the President and a word from you in my behalf will be worth those of an host of others.

If you have time to spare from your ardious duties to the house and your own constituents, drop a line to me at your leisure in answer to this, directing to New Lisbon Ohio, which is the place of my residence, I being here only for a few days more, as a lobby for a canal that passes through our town and county.[4]

Please make my kind respects to Mrs Polk. . . .

JOHN THOMSON

ALS. DLC–JKP. Addressed to Washington.

1. A physician in New Lisbon, Ohio, Thomson served several years in the state legislature and five terms in the U.S. House, 1825–27 and 1829–37.

2. Thomas L. Hamer and William Allen. A lawyer, farmer, and stock raiser from Chillicothe, Ohio, Allen won election as a Democrat to the U.S. House, 1833–35, and sat in the U.S. Senate, 1837–49.

3. Joel R. Poinsett of South Carolina, first U.S. minister to Mexico, 1825–29, served as Van Buren's secretary of war, 1837–41.

4. New Lisbon, which became Lisbon, is in Columbiana County, Ohio. Probably Thomson was lobbying for the Sandy and Beaver Canal, designed to run between Bolivar and Beaver, Ohio. Opened by a private company in 1850, the canal was of little importance as a transport facility, as its limited water supply never permitted regular navigation.

FROM ROBERT ARMSTRONG

Dear Col [Nashville] 6 Feby [1839][1]

How Waterson[2] will be disposed of I know not. I fear our friends have been hasty and indiscrete in promiseing to support him. Williamson Smith was here a Short time since and told me Thomas was the man. I send you a letter inclosed from Long.[3] I have recd others on the Subject.

I have written Roberts at Knoxville in relation to the paper[4] and requested him to See Reynolds and Genl Wallace and get them to write me the prospects &c. What Sum can be raised there.

Carroll has deceved us. He never intended to run and you will see that he wont raise a finger for you, or in aid of your Election. The Truth is he is ready to go over any day, believes he sees the Whig[s] will surely succeed. No aid. No movement will be made by him in support of Mr Van Buren's Administration, and you must see that the Administration does nothing more for him. His Conduct now is a *withdrawal* from the party and the Int. of the Party and [is] so viewed by our friends. He could have beat Bell. So can Burton but I fear the latter is too fond of money to give up his practice. The old Genl.[5] perhaps may get him out.

From every quarter the accounts are cheering & improving. I have no help or aid in geting on but I have no fear of the State. Our New Editor[6] bids fair to render good service. Keep him advised. Cunningham has gone back to Louisville. Our cause looks better from every quarter. *See What* Swartwout done with his money. I think he loaned Hall through Danl. Jackson[7] last summer in New York 9000 or 10 Thousand Dollars and *was* to get a mortgage on Hall & Eatons Distilery and on the 60 acres of Land decreed by the Supream Court Out of the Fairfield Tract to Eatons first wife.[8] Hall Spoke to McLemore & myself to value the property, saying that Swartwout was acquainted. No deed [was] recorded. Danl. Jackson may be between them. It must have been Swartwout's advanced.

R ARMSTRONG

ALS. DLC–JKP. Probably addressed to Washington. Heading of this letter is marked "*Private*." Editorial liberties have been taken in transcribing punctuation and capitalization.

1. Year is identified through content analysis.
2. Harvey M. Watterson.
3. No letter on this subject by Medicus A. Long has been found.
4. Knoxville *Argus*.
5. Andrew Jackson.
6. J. George Harris, editor of the *Nashville Union*.
7. Allen A. Hall and Daniel Jackson. A prominent New York businessman and Democrat, Jackson was a director of the Morris Canal Bank and a government contractor for Indian supplies.
8. John H. Eaton, a strong supporter of Andrew Jackson, resigned his Senate seat in 1829 to become secretary of war in Jackson's cabinet. Washington society's refusal to accept Eaton's second wife, Peggy O'Neale, led to his resignation two years later. Eaton became governor of Florida, 1834–35, and then minister to Spain, 1836–40. Allen A. Hall and Eaton's distillery partnership is not identified further. Eaton first married Myra Lewis, daughter of William Terrell Lewis, whose estate in Davidson County was named "Fairfield."

TO BENJAMIN F. BUTLER[1]

My dear Sir, Washington City Feby 6th, 1839

Allow me to introduce to your acquaintance my brother-in-law Mr. James Walker of Tennessee, who visits New York, with a view to ascertain the State of the money market, and if practicable to negotiate the sale of certain State Stocks of Tennessee, bearing an interest of 5 and 6 per cent. If you will be so kind as to introduce him, to persons in whom he can confide, in making these negotions, you will confer a favour upon him as well as myself. Mr. Walker is a sound Democrat, and thoroughly with the administration in all its great measures, and may make suggestions to you which will show the importance of affecting the sale of these Bonds. The truth is, that our political opponents have control of much the larger proportion of these Bonds, which form the basis of a Bank of five millions chartered by the State,[2] and we suspect that they do not wish to make sale of them at this time, because they may wish to use the fact that they cannot be sold as an apology, for a *pressure* in the State, which they will seek to produce during the political contest of the present year. Mr. Walker as well as myself will be greatly obliged to you for any assistance or facilities you may afford him by introducing him to the business men of your City. He is an honable man and you may fully confide in him.

JAMES K. POLK

ALS. British Museum—Autographs Add. Mss. 26,154, folder 21. Addressed to New York City.

1. A lawyer and politician, Butler served as U.S. attorney general under Andrew Jackson, 1833–37, as well as acting secretary of war, 1836–37. A leader of the New York bar, he became U.S. attorney for the Southern District of New York and served 1838–41 and 1845–48.

2. On January 19, 1838, the legislature passed an aggressive banking, internal improvement, and education act. Introduced by Andrew L. Martin and spirited through the Assembly by A. O. P. Nicholson and Josephus C. Guild, the legislation provided that the Bank of Tennessee would have a capital of five million dollars and from profits would pay $100,000 a year for common schools and $18,000 for academies. Four million dollars in state bonds would be issued, with which the state would subscribe for half the stock of various internal improvement companies. Interest on the bonds would be six per cent per annum, payable semi-annually.

TO AZARIAH C. FLAGG[1]

Dear Sir Washington City Feby. 7th 1839

I am requested by my kinsman Mr James Walker of Tennessee, to forward to you the enclosed letter,[2] and to add my request to his, that you will, (as far as may be conveniently in your power), give him the information which he seeks. He has been referred to you, for information upon the subject to which his letter relates.[3] Will you do me the favour to enclose your answers to him, to me, that I may transmit it to him, if he shall have left before it arrives.

James K. Polk

ALS. NN–A. C. Flagg Papers. Addressed to Albany, New York.

1. A New York legislator and leader of the Albany Regency, Flagg was appointed secretary of state by DeWitt Clinton in 1826, a position which he filled for seven years. He was state comptroller of New York for nine years during the 1830's and 1840's.

2. Letter not found.

3. See Polk to B. F. Butler, February 6, 1839.

FROM JOHN B. HAYS

Dear Sir Columbia Feby 7th 1839

Your several letters on the subject of this district have been received.[1] Your suggestions, as to the proper course, had been anticipated, and every effort made to effect the object. But there has been a failure. E. Frierson will not run, though he was the first choice of the republicans of marshal[2] & this county, as well as his own. He could have been elected easily.

J. E. Thomas, I understand, wishes to resign, But still will not. He is too timid. He can be elected. He is the choice of this county & marshal decidedly. I have not seen him as yet. He is at marshal court, where there was a meeting of the people of that county on monday. There was not a decided opinion arrived at, in the matter. The nearest they came to any conclusion, was that Kincade & Waterson[3] were to run on, at present. If Waterson on viewing the matter in Maury sees that he will not probably get as many votes in Maury as Thomas can get in Bedford, there will be a convention of the District held for the purpose of organising the thing anew. I have but a confused account from marshal. Kincade does not seem to operate in any way to embarrass matters. Dr. Thomas told me that he will abide the decision of a convention. He is very anxious, But you know his strength. Pillow will not run. I could say a great deal on the above matters & the above named men, But you can conjecture all.

From the first the Democracy of this county & marshall have given a dicid[4] preferance to Frierson & Thomas. They will go in full for either. Frierson will not run. Thomas probably will. I have engaged many of his friends on his return, to urge him in the most anxious manner as I will also, when he returns. Osborn[5] sent me word that he would be here to see me the first of next week. I feel somewhat satisfied that we will succeed. My own opinion has been, that Thomas ought first to offer the thing to Frierson as the best man in Bedford, then on his refusal to come boldly forward, and swim or sink with his principles. He cannot fail to be elected. The republicans will all come to the poles for him. They will not for Waterson. Every means will be resorted to, on my part, as well as by the balance of your friends on this subject, that can be with propriety. Nicholson's influence for Waterson, is what is causing the embarrassment (I think).

Nixon Wilkes & Allen[6] are the persons that will be looked to, though they have not as yet been spoken to.

After seeing Osborn I will be able to give you a better account.

J. B. HAYS

[P.S.] Your own vote, in consequence of the declining of Nicholson, will not be diminished in this district. It may be in the state. Your friends seem to view the matter in such a way as to give them fresh feelings for you. And they will be at the poles for you.

ALS. DLC–JKP. Addressed to Washington.

1. Letters not found.
2. Marshall County, Tennessee.
3. Joseph A. Kincaid and Harvey M. Watterson.
4. Incorrect spelling of "decided."
5. James Osburn, a prominent Polk supporter in Marshall County, had raised a political furor in 1835 by divulging without permission a private letter between John Bell and Charles Cassedy. Osburn was among the commissioners appointed to lay off the town of Lewisburg in 1836; he served as foreman of the First Circuit Court jury of Marshall in that same year.
6. Wesley Nixon, Richard A. L. Wilkes, and Richard H. Allen. One of the early settlers of Mt. Pleasant and a colonel in the local militia, Nixon was the son of a Methodist minister, John Nixon. Wilkes, a colonel in the militia, took an interest in education and aided in establishing schools in Maury County. He served as a Democrat in the Tennessee House, 1845–49, and in the Senate, 1849–51. Allen, prominent in militia affairs in Giles County after the War of 1812, moved to Mt. Pleasant in the mid-1830's. He attained the rank of general in the militia in 1838; he subsequently moved to Lawrence County.

TO ANDREW JACKSON

My Dear Sir Washington City Feby 7th 1839

I saw the President last night. He intends during the months of April and May to make a tour through the southern and some of the South-

Western states, and will visit Tennessee or not as may be thought best by his friends. My settled opinion is, and I frankly so informed him, that his appearance in the state in the midst of our elections, would have a decidedly bad effect, and would probably be followed by disastrous consequences. Our opponents have already falsely charged that I was the Government candidate, selected and sent out, on a mission to revolutionize the state. The Whig presses teemed with such stuff as this during the last fall. I pronounced it to be false wherever I was. But Mr Van Buren's appearance in the state, pinding the elections, would be immediately seized upon, and heralded forth, in every corner of the state, to give colour to the charge. However prudent his conduct and conversation might be his visit, would be set down, to a desire to interfere in our elections, and control the politics of the state. The hue and cry of *dictation*, would be proclaimed from every little press, and babbling politician in the state, and in spite of all our efforts to counteract its effect, it could not fail to do much injury to our cause. Upon communicating these views to him, Mr V.B. at once said, he would not place his friends in such a situation, and we separated with the understanding, that after full conference with you and other friends, after my return home, I was to write him to New Orleans, and he would be governed in his movements by our advice. He informed me that he would so write to you. I will take a day to see & consult with you, on my return, upon this and other matters, connected with the struggle in which we are engaged. I have mixed more with the people of the state, than you have recently, and am sure I am not mistaken in my apprehensions of the effects of his appearance in the state, before our elections. If he could visit us, *after* the election, nothing would give me more pleasure, and our people I know would hail him with delight. But I will confer more fully with you upon the subject, upon my return. He is very anxious to see you, and it might be, that your health would enable you to run down in a Steam Boat and meet him at the mouth of the Cumberland & accompany him up to Louisville. This however is a mere suggestion of my own.

I am waiting anxiously to learn whether Col. Burton will take the field for Congress. He may be disinclined to engage in politics, but there are times when every citizen owes a duty to his country which he is not at liberty to disregard. He owes it to himself, to his friends & to our cause to come to our aid, in this time of our need. He will be inexcusable if he does not. We are engaged in a great contest of principle and every man should perform his part.

I became fully satisfied as I passed through *Sumner and Jackson* last fall, that if *Col. Guild,*[1] was the candidate for Congress in that District, he could be elected. Our excellent friend *Trousdale*[2] however is in the field, and I have but little hope, from his reserved manners and want of popular address, of his success. It is a matter of great delicacy to suggest to him, the propriety of giving way to *Guild*, and yet if he does not I fear the District is lost. I hope you will not fail to write the letter which I requested you, in my last[3] to write to *Cave Johnson*. I shall be detained here some days after the adjournment & there will be time for me to hear from you. I am glad to learn, from some of my friends that your health has improved, since I saw you.

JAMES K. POLK

ALS. DLC–AJ. Addressed to the Hermitage and marked "Private."

1. Josephus C. Guild, a lawyer and Democratic politician in Gallatin, served three terms in the Tennessee House, 1833–36, 1845–47, and 1851–53, and sat for one term in the Senate, 1837–39. He was a presidential elector in 1844 on the ticket of Polk and George M. Dallas. In 1878, Guild published *Old Times in Tennessee*.

2. William Trousdale, a Gallatin lawyer, won election to the Tennessee Senate, 1835–36, but resigned to serve in the Seminole War. After losing races for Congress in 1837, 1839, and 1845, he won the governorship of Tennessee and served from 1849 until 1851.

3. Reference probably is to a letter of January 29, 1839, which was answered by Jackson on February 11, 1839. Polk's letter has not been found.

FROM EZEKIEL P. McNEAL

Dear Sir Boliver, Feby 7 1839

I addressed you on the 2d Inst.[1] advising of my having Sent $255 to Nashville to be invested in an Eastern Check & remitted to you—that amt. being all the rent money that has come to my hands for rents of 1838.

I have not heard one word from Mr Thomas Dodson of Fayette County on the Subject of money. Majr. Bills[2] left last evening for Somerville & will endeavor to see or hear from Dodson. If the Sum expected from him comes to hand in time to reach you at Washington by the 4th proximo it shall be forwarded promptly. & If paid and not in time to reach you at Washington I will forward to Columbia, unless otherwise directed. Will you come direct home or traverse East Tennessee on your trip home? I shall leave for Phila. the last days of this month & *possibly* may meet you if you come home by the River.

E P MCNEAL

ALS. DLC–JKP. Addressed to Washington.

1. McNeal had advised Polk on February 2, 1839, that he had arranged for Frank Williams of Nashville to remit Polk a check for $250 on a Philadelphia or New York bank. ALS. DLC–JKP. Williams mailed the check to Polk on February 7, 1839. ALS. DLC–JKP.

2. John H. Bills, postmaster and merchant at Bolivar, was married to McNeal's sister, the former Prudence Tate McNeal.

FROM WILLIAM CARROLL

Nashville, Tennessee. February 8, 1839

Carroll writes that he has received the Speaker's letter of January 25,[1] enclosing pension papers for Captain Scoby.[2] Carroll states that the poor condition of his health will not permit him to run for Congress against Bell, but Carroll hopes that Burton will make the race. Carroll further writes that he thinks Polk's contest for the governorship will be hard, but favorable, and asks that Polk tell Judge Catron[3] that he will write as soon as health permits.

ALS. DLC–JKP. Addressed to Washington.

1. Letter not found.

2. John Scoby, not further identified.

3. John Catron of Tennessee, a strong political ally of Polk, was appointed to the U.S. Supreme Court in the last days of the Jackson administration. Catron helped the *Nashville Union* financially and served occasionally as an editorial writer.

FROM J. GEORGE HARRIS

Nashville, Tennessee. February 9, 1839

Harris writes that though he has not heard from the Speaker recently, he is sure that Polk has seen the new look of the *Nashville Union.* Harris is pleased with Nashville, though he finds his opponents, the editors of the *Banner* and the *Whig,*[1] less than honorable. He recalls that earlier in the day William H. Polk visited the *Union* office and spoke of Democratic support for Watterson's candidacy and party hopes for Burton's running against Bell. He asks that he be kept informed of movements in Congress. Alexander Duncan's address on the Swartwout defalcation,[2] as well as a note on the Erwin defalcations,[3] will be printed in the next weekly issue of the *Union.* It has been hinted, Harris notes, that Allen Hall "knows where some of Swartwout's deficits were expended."[4]

ALS. DLC–JKP. Addressed to Washington.

1. Allen A. Hall was editor of the Nashville *Republican Banner* and Caleb C. Norvell, of the *Nashville Whig*.

2. See Alfred Balch to Polk, January 26, 1839.

3. On January 17, 1838, Treasury Secretary Levi Woodbury transmitted to Congress a report on public defaulters; included were details on the related cases of Andrew and James Erwin. In 1820 Andrew owed duty bonds in excess of $58,000. Suit was ordered in 1829, and in the following year judgment was obtained in the amount of $92,635. The Treasury Department did not make recovery of the judgment, as Andrew was known to be insolvent. In 1834 a suit in equity was commenced against James Erwin for defaulting on duty bonds in excess of $2,800. See House Document No. 111, 25 Congress, 2 Session.

4. See Robert Armstrong to Polk, February 6, 1839.

FROM JESSE B. CLEMENTS[1]

Dr Sir Fayetteville Feby 11th 1839

I was in company with Col Benjamin Raynolds[2] two or three days Since and he informed me that the President had intimated to him his intention to dismiss all the approving Agents officies, alledging that they had but little to do and that it cost the Government considerable to keep them up. I understand from Col. Raynolds that the President intends to discharge that duty himself—believing that he can do So without mutch inconvenience or trouble. In this he would find that the trouble to him would be grate, but that it would be putting those who hold deeds to verry greate inconvenience, in Sending their Deeds to Washington for examining and approving by the President or any other person at Washington. You know that the office which Col. Kincannon holds in the Chocktaw Nation is that of examining and Approving Agent. Now if he Should be dismissed from that office, I am fearfull that he would return here and Still run for Congress in doing which he would of course defeat our friend Brown in this county, and if Kincannon can be held off Browns Success is certain. I am of opinion that as the case now Stands that Brown can beat Shields in this county from 1000 to 1200 votes. But Should Col. Kincannon return and be a candidate or even be hostile to Brown it might turn the Seat against us. Now if Kincannons office is to be made void, for Gods Sake have him provided for So as to keep him out of the way. And in this way our Success is certain. This is a matter that is not known here to any person except myself and Doct. Bonner.[3] Nor will it be Spoken of at all. We understand that Brown can beat Shields in all the lower Counties but Wayne which I suppose is a Strong

Whig County. I will remark to you that Some of our Strongest Whigs in this place has lately come over to you (to wit) Esqr. Lanier[4] who would not go to hear you Speake at the time you were here,[5] and Capt. Gilliland[6] who heretofore has been hostile to you on account of your politicks. These and other gentlemen have lately fallen out with our present Gov., on account of his refusing to Sign the State Bonds, for the erection of a turnpike road from Shelbyville to the Alabama line after the Stockholders has complyed with the law.[7] I give it as my opinion that old Lincoln will give you 2500 votes at the ballot Box and I know of no County in Middle Tennessee that will not give you a majority except it is Williamson & Wilson. In fact your friends here have no doubt of your Success by a very large majority in the State. I dislike verry mutch to trouble with this matter of Col. Kincannon and I would not write to you on the Subject but for the greate interest I feel in our Success as Democrats in Tennessee. I presume before this time you have become acquainted with my Brother who I took the liberty of Introducing to you by letter.[8] I am extreamely anxious to hear from him and hear how he is doing with his busin[e]ss and his prob[abi]lity of Success. We have as candidates in this County George W. Jones & Col Caruthers[9] for the Senate and old Buchannon[10] and I suppose Ira McKinny[11] for the lower Branch of the Legislature all *Democrats*. The Whigs will not start a candidate this year as [they a]ll[12] agree that one cannot be Elected. Let me hear from you soon.

J. B. Clements

ALS. DLC–JKP. Addressed to Washington.

1. Clements was elected brigadier general in the Tennessee militia in 1836. He was probably a son of Benjamin Clements, who in 1838 served as one of the state-appointed directors of the Fayetteville and Shelbyville Turnpike Company.

2. Benjamin Franklin Reynolds, a pioneer of Maury County, served four terms in the Tennessee Senate, 1819–21 and 1823–29. Appointed agent to the Chickasaws in 1830, he removed to Franklin County, Alabama, and served in that state's House of Representatives, 1839–41.

3. William Bonner, an ardent Democrat, was a wealthy surgeon in Lincoln County.

4. John Lanier was a major investor in the Fayetteville and Shelbyville Turnpike Company, which was organized in 1835.

5. Polk had spoken at Fayetteville on September 7, 1838.

6. Samuel E. Gilliland of Fayetteville was a business partner of Robert H. McEwen and treasurer of the Fayetteville and Shelbyville Turnpike Company.

7. On September 18, 1838, Newton Cannon had issued a regulatory circular stating that before state bonds could be issued to an improvements com-

pany, every subscriber in that company must pay the first installment on stock purchases in money, which was defined as the notes of chartered banks in Tennessee or the equivalent thereof in other bank notes current in the state. The law itself did not specify that every subscriber had to make good his subscription; nor did it define the term "money."

8. On December 27, 1838, Clements wrote introducing his brother, Major Ruben E. Clements, who would personally explain his business in Washington. ALS. DLC–JKP.

9. George W. Jones and James Caruthers. A native of Virginia, Jones became a saddler in Fayetteville. He served two terms in the Tennessee House, 1835–39, and sat one term in the Senate, 1839–41. A candidate for presidential elector on the Van Buren ticket in 1840, Jones won election to the U.S. House in 1843 and served until 1859. Caruthers served as a Democrat for one term in the Tennessee Senate, 1837–39. A resident of Lincoln County and a large landholder in West Tennessee, he later removed to Mississippi.

10. John Buchanan represented Giles County as a Democrat in the Tennessee House, 1835–37, 1839–43, and 1845–47.

11. Ira McKinney represented Lincoln County for one term in the Tennessee House, 1839–41.

12. Manuscript mutilated.

FROM LAWSON GIFFORD

Dear Sir Jonesborough Feb 11, 1839

I omitted to say anything to you while I was down the country in relation to the feeling of Dr Ramsay, Genl Anderson & Mr A. Crozier[1] in regard to the appointment of Post Master at Knoxville. Considerable excitement has existed in regard to that appointment and those gentlemen have all stood conspicuous, both because they are Mr. Deadericks relatives[2] and because they waited on you while you were in their town. They do not believe that you acted any other than a manly & fair course & that the little you wrote in favor of Mr. D. was done in good faith. Your enemies there have various rumors afloat such as you wrote a letter also for Roberts, and your old friend Judge White went so far as to say that politicians have private marks whereby there wishes are made known, that such things as they want are made to pass & those that they wish treated differently, are rejected. The venerable Senator may have used those private marks himself ere now.

It will be very gratifying for your friends to receive an explanation of your participation in the matter. The best defense has been made for you there that they are capable of. And that is this: That Judge Grundy's course having been run in this State, he [Grundy] did not care how matters went on here and that John Crozier[3] being De[a]dericks brother-in-law, and he (C) having voted the instructions to Grundy & against Carrol for Eph Foster, thought he [Grundy] had a fair opportunity of paying back part of the Crozier debt by having Roberts appointed over Deaderick. Those gentlemen Anderson Crozier & Ramsay are all high minded honorable gentlemen and I assure you they felt mortified in the highest degree that such charges should be made against you. Ramsay informed me that he had written to you, but that you had not yet answered his letter. He was waiting rather anxiously for your explanation.[4]

In regard to the establishment of a press at Knoxville it is considered as a matter of the greatest moment—in fact it is considered as a settler to the Governors election, and of course it will carry the State for Mr Van Buren if we succeed for Governor. There is as I stated in a former letter,[5] some fifteen counties that are entirely under the influence of the Federal presses. They take no other papers scarcely & of course, those presses give tone & influence public feeling to a great extent. I have a negotiation pending whereby I expect the Knoxville Register will fall into our hands. If that can be done the "dog is dead" with the Opposition in East Tennessee. The Register has an extensive patronage, say from 15 to 1800 Subscribers, & we might reasonably calculate on retaining half of them. That arrangement would also give us more than a fair start with "Times," the new Clay paper that is to be put in operation by Crozier & Humes. It is expected that Heiskell[6] will take charge of that paper.

A considerable amount of money can be raised for a press at Knoxville, and a fair proportion of the advertisements & job work of the town can be had, but it may be reasonably calculcated on that the paper will have to have the *real support* of many of its friends. That money will have to be advanced at any rate for the first 12 mo. to keep its expenses down.

I wrote to Col. McClellan from Knoxville that some money must be raised to the North to assist. & I have no doubt that it can be done. This movement if carried into effect, and it is gone too far in to back out from now, will emphatically be the salvation of our success in Tennessee, in fact I know of no other move half as important. McClellan is vitally interested in it, *for beat him they will if possible this time.* McKinny has commenced the canvass in earnest already, and the Bunch & Cocke party[7] in the lower counties of his District will all unite on old John A. McKinny. He runs as a Van Buren man, but is opposed to the Sub Treasury and also to *all Banks.* McClellan & him will fight before the canvass is over. I will advise you as soon as I hear from Knoxville, and if the Register cannot be bought I will immediately forward a bill to McC[le]llan to [be] handed over to some body at the North for a press & type. I will order only a sufficiency for the paper & other necessary articles, making the bill as light as possible. If no other way I will give my notes, relying on my friends to help me in this *one* time of need.

The Printer that you spoke of in your letter will go to Knoxville with me & I will leave the Sentinel in charge of a younger brother, who with Dr Kinny & our friends here, will keep it a going in most effective style.[8] The gentleman had better come out directly so as to be on the ground. I will take great pains to have our new paper circulated extensively in the lower counties. I hope the gentleman is of unimpeachable character. If not they use a "fellow up," with out mercy. Write to me at this place.

LAWSON GIFFORD

ALS. DLC–JKP. Addressed to Washington.

1. James G. M. Ramsey, Alexander O. Anderson, and Arthur R. Crozier. Crozier, son of John Crozier, was editor of the *Knoxville Standard* in 1845 and comptroller of Tennessee, 1851–55.

2. David Anderson Deaderick, an unsuccessful candidate for the Knoxville postmastership, had conducted a mercantile business with his father-in-law, John Crozier, from 1834 to 1838. Deaderick served as secretary of East Tennessee University, 1838–68, and as clerk of Knox County's Chancery Court, 1859–70. Ramsey and Deaderick married sisters of Arthur R. Crozier.

3. John H. Crozier.

4. See Ramsey to Polk, January 5, 1839. Polk's friends in Knoxville were at pains to credit Grundy with the selection of Roberts and to absolve Polk of White's charge of duplicity.

5. See Gifford to Polk, February 4, 1839.

6. Frederick S. Heiskell had published the *Knoxville Register* from 1816 until 1837, when he sold his interest in the newspaper and retired from journalism.

7. Reference is to supporters of Whig politicians Samuel Bunch and John Cocke. Bunch sat in the Tennessee Senate, 1819–25, and in the U.S. House, 1833–37; he was married to Cocke's niece, Amanda Anderson. Cocke served in the Tennessee House, 1796–99 and 1807–13; in the Senate, 1799–1801 and 1843–45; and in the U.S. House, 1819–27.

8. Polk's letter has not been found. The name of the printer of whom Polk had written is unknown. Lawson Gifford did not move to the editorship of the Knoxville *Argus*; his reference to a younger brother probably was to F. Gifford, who had been associated with the *Tennessee Sentinel* at the time of its founding in 1835. Daniel Kenney, Jonesboro physician and merchant, served in the Tennessee House, 1843–45. See Richard M. Woods to Polk, January 28, 1839.

FROM ANDREW JACKSON

My Dear Sir, Hermitage February 11th 1839

Your letter of the 29th ulto.[1] is just received & now before me. Your anxiety cannot be greater than mine upon the Subject of a candidate for Congress in this District. It is shamefull & disgracefull to the district that in a contest involving all the leading measures of mine & Mr Van Burens administration, that patriotism here should be at so low an ebb, that there was no candidate to be found, *nobly*, to Stand up & vindicate the truth.

Governor Carroll has behaved in a manner that I do not understand. Early in January I had a long & confidential conversation with him on the Subject of his comeing out forthwith, or, by an address to the people of the District, to withdraw. I set forth to him all the disadvantages of these delays to the cause, & to our candidate. He promised me that on the next Saturday (that being thursday) he would have a meeting with his friends at the post office Nashville and either announce himself or withdraw. I saw Dr Robertson, Col Weakly, Genl Armstrong & others,[2] urged them to be Sure to See him on Saturday & have his posivitive determination, & have it announcd to the people over his own signature.

I spent week before last in Nashville attending to one of the most vindictive & unjust prosecutions against three of my Negroes—the 4th being acquitted by the Grand Jury—all finally acquitted by the traverse Jury in two minutes (as I am told) after submitted to the jury, to the great mortification & disgraice of my two Nephews—Stokely & William Donelson.[3] This was a case equal to the Whigg persecution of yourself.[4] The ransaked, the drunken hords of Negroes, worthless Whig Scamps, & worthless fishermen—all would not do. Truth is mighty & ever will prevail. They swore too much—contradicted each other, and their credit was blown sky high. Four of my boys, out of from forty to one hundred negroes, all drunk & in a general riot were taken from the rest by warrant by Stockly Donelson, before one tittle of evidence was heard. It was a good Whigg court, whose negroes might have been included, if mine were not arrested, & this stre[n]gthened the prosecution by combining all the guilty against mine to convict them. But it resulted in their full acquittal, and on the minds of the jury that one of Stockly was the fellow who had done the deed.

Whilst in Nashville I was daily urging Doctor Robertson & others to see and bring Carroll out, but it appears he Shunned them. Major Donelson went down on friday to See him but failed. The Major goes down tomorrow with a full determination to have him Seen & an end put to this Shuffling. Why the Governor acts thus I am unable to Say—but mark one thing it is truly Strange conduct to me. There is Something I cannot understand. It may be he has been Speculating in Lands & is afraid of Bell exposing him, as it is believed here that Bell & brothers, with Erwin and Tom Williams,[5] are deeply engaged in Land Speculation and have become acquainted with Carrolls Speculation whilst a commissioner. Be this so or not, there is some thing we cannot understand.

Mr. Kendall when here and myself obtained a promise from Mr Burton that if Carroll did not come out, he would, but such has been the delay, Burton may now urge that he relied on Carroll & has made arrangements that will not enable him to fulfill that pledge. The conduct of Govr. Carroll has brought down upon him the Suspicions of Some of his best friends that hereafter will do him great injury should he at any future period wish to come forward in political life, should he fail to come out now.

You may Shew this confidentially to the president & Mr Grundy with my kind regards to each.

Rest assured, tho confined as I am with affliction, & disease, the great cause has not been lost sight of by me—nor will it be. I fear no consequences in a good cause. I am scarcely now able, with pain, to wield the pen. With my kind regards to your Lady & all friends in which my family joins, to Benton, & the Chief Justice.[6] I bid you farewell. Major Donelson will write you & the president from Nashville tomorrow.

ANDREW JACKSON

P.S. Our new Editor[7] you will see has Seated himself in the Editorial chair of the Nashville Union. It is believed he will fill it well. He appears to have energy & talent, and discretion, all this necessary for a good Editor. A.J.

Note, it would give me pleasure to receive from you a detailed account of the doings & final result of the Swartwout committee. If the Republican members on the committee act firmly and call before the committee, Daniel Jackson, and others [of] Swartwouts associates and those Whigg merchants who Eulogised Swartwout so much, it will be found that from eight hundred thousand dollars to one million are still in their hands—& I suspect some may be found [in] Mr. Talmages.[8] Swartwout has as [. . .][9] believe given up the bonds to the merchants and hold[s] their acknowledgement of the debts. If the truth can be elicited it will destroy the Whiggs, & pass the Subtreasury bill—*mark this.* What could Swartwout have done with a million & a quarter? It does not appear that his Speculations has amounted to $150,000. Where is the ballance of $1,150,000? *The Whiggs have it.* A.J.

ALS. DLC–JKP. Addressed to Washington and marked *"private."* Extracts from this letter have been published in John Spencer Bassett, ed., *Correspondence of Andrew Jackson* (7 vols.; Washington, D.C.: Carnegie Institution, 1926–1935), VI, pp. 4–5.

1. Letter not found.

2. Felix Robertson, Robert Weakley, and Robert Armstrong. Robertson, a son of James Robertson, practiced medicine with distinction and served as mayor of Nashville in 1818, 1827, and 1828. Weakley, formerly a surveyor, was a large landholder and an influential adviser in the Democratic party.

3. Stockley and William Donelson were sons of John Donelson, Jr., brother of Rachel Donelson Jackson. Stockley Donelson had filed a complaint against four of Jackson's slaves for killing a fellow slave in an altercation on the evening of December 29, 1838. The Davidson County grand jury returned a true bill against three of the slaves; their case went to trial in circuit court on January 28, 1839; and six days later the petit jury found them innocent.

4. Reference probably is to the indictment of William H. Polk on charges of assault and battery in the Hayes affair.

5. John Bell, James Erwin, and Thomas L. Williams. Bell had two living brothers, Thomas, a farmer near Nashville, and James, a merchant in Mississippi. Williams, chancellor for East Tennessee from 1836 to 1854, was a brother of former U.S. Senator John Williams.

6. Thomas H. Benton and Roger B. Taney. A strong supporter of Jackson and hard money, Benton represented Missouri in the U.S. Senate for thirty years. Taney of Maryland was chief justice of the U.S. Supreme Court from 1836 until his death in 1864; previously he had served in Jackson's cabinet as attorney general and as secretary of the treasury.

7. Jeremiah George Harris.

8. Nathaniel P. Tallmadge served as a U.S. senator from New York from March 4, 1833, to June 17, 1844, when he resigned to become governor of Wisconsin Territory.

9. Manuscript mutilated.

FROM GEORGE R. POWEL[1]

Rogersville, Tennessee. February 11, 1839

Powel writes about political races in Hawkins and Sullivan counties and notes that Fain and Watterson[2] are running for places in the legislature. The Democratic Party in Hawkins County is better organized now than at any period since White's defection. The opposition is forming a "Rives" press[3] under Orville Bradley,[4] though that newspaper secretly favors Clay. The Democracy is in need of a press in Rogersville or at Knoxville, but it is unlikely that one will be started in time to affect the elections in the summer.[5] Powel asks Polk to inform McClellan that he will have John A. McKinney as his opponent for reelection to Congress.

ALS. DLC–JKP. Addressed to Washington.

1. Son of Samuel Powel, George R. Powel represented Hawkins and Sullivan counties in the Tennessee House, 1835–37. He was circuit court clerk of Hawkins County, 1840–52, and clerk and master of chancery court, 1855–58.

2. Nicholas Fain and Henry Watterson. A Rogersville merchant and postmaster, 1823–39, Fain won election to the Tennessee House for two terms, 1839–43. He was the father-in-law of George R. Powel. Henry Watterson, a farmer, served as trustee of Hawkins County, 1836–40.

3. The Rogersville *East Tennessean,* edited by William Wales, first appeared in February 1839 and publicly supported William C. Rives for president. That newspaper had but a brief existence.

4. Reared in Hawkins County during its early settlement, Bradley inherited large tracts of land. He studied law under Hugh L. White, whom he supported for president in 1836. A Democrat until 1836, he served in the Tennessee House, 1833–35, and sat in the Senate, 1835–37.

5. The Knoxville *Argus,* a Democratic press, appeared in June, 1839. See Richard M. Woods to Polk, January 28, 1839.

FROM M. D. COOPER & CO.

New Orleans, Louisiana. February 12, 1839

As requested in Polk's letter of January 25, 1839,[1] Cooper & Co. encloses two drafts on New York totaling $1,600. The company acknowledges receipt of 34 bales of cotton.[2] Prices have been up as much as ¾ of a cent, and favorable accounts are expected daily from Liverpool. The balance of Polk's cotton is expected soon.

LS. DLC–JKP. Addressed to Washington. Published in John Spencer Bassett, *The Southern Plantation Overseer as Revealed in His Letters* (Northampton, Mass.: Smith College, 1925), 118.

1. Letter not found.

2. On February 2, 1839, M. D. Cooper & Co. had acknowledged receipt of the 34 bales and had promised to report later on sales and prices. LS. DLC–JKP.

FROM NATHANIEL SMITH[1]

Dr. Sir. Athens Tenn. 12 Feby 1839

The letters lately received from the present Commr. Ind. Affairs,[2] serve to confirm me, in the opinion entertained for some months past, that impressions had been made not only on the mind of that officer, but upon that of the Secry. of War, and possibly, even, of the President of the U. States highly unfavorable to me, as an officer of the Govermt. which I might consider myself up to the 26th of last month, when, as I think, I was rather unceremoniously discharged from the office of Superintendent of Cher. Emigration.[3]

True, it is, that the business connected with this employment has pretty well terminated, and I beg you to understand that I feel no mortification at the fact, of being notified, that my services were no longer necessary, but, to the *manner and tone* of that notification: for, rely on it, it is not my disposition to retain any public appointment one hour longer, than I feel that I am rendering my country or fellow Citizens some valuable services.

The paragraph to which I allude in the Commrs. Letter of the 17th Jany. stand thus: "I have further to say, that as a necessary result, of this view of the Subject of the Emigration of the Cherokees, your further services are deemed unnecessary; your duties and compensation as Superint. of Cherokee Emgration will therefore cease on the 26th Inst." Now, it might seem that in the paragraph above transcribed, there would appear nothing very exceptionable; but taken in connexion with the tone of the entire Letter, and others lately recd. from that source, I cannot avoid the conclusion, that impressions have been made upon the mind of that officer, or Secry of War, no way favorable to me, as a man, and public agent; influenced by this belief, I hope you will not consider me over sensitive, or, importunate in my demands, when I request of you, as one of my best friends, the kindness of making with as little delay as possible, the necessary inquiries & investigations, relative to the true character and extent of those malignant impressions against me, and if possible, the agents, who have accomplished this illiberal purpose.

I am of opinion, that, I need look no further in seeking for the workers against me, than, the *principal military officers*, connected with the business of Cherokee Emigration; but, in this, I may possibly be deceived; if so, I should be well satisfied to know the fact. In the Letter I had the honor to address you last autumn,[4] in which I endeavored to give you, not only an honest, but a full and correct Statement, of the Revolution in the business of Cher. Emigration, and the means and resources, employed to accomplish this great change, I probably acquainted you, in what terms of violent and vindictive deprecation, the measures of the Govermn. were denounced, by the principal military officers here stationed, not only on the subject of Indian Emigration, but upon every important point of policy, lately adopted by or suggested by the administration; occupying different ground, in Sentiment, as well as duty, I could not give my acquiescence, to such unhallowed conduct, on the part of public agents, *embarrassing the very duty they were dele-*

gated to perform. I became, I am conscious, an unpleasant, if not offensive associate in this work, for which, I have little doubt, the most illiberal misrepresentations have been made both of my public conduct, and even of my best motives. In closing this letter, already too long, I beg leave to assure you, that in the different public offices hitherto held by me, I have never in all my life felt equal anxiety to acquit myself with credit to those kind friends *(yourself among the number)* who procured me the appointment; and usefulness to my country, than I have experienced in this business.

But, it has turned out that not only have I been embarrassed, all the time, by the *counter action* of those who should have been my most faithful and efficient collaborators, by the wealthy intelligent and influential Chiefs & head men of the Cherokee nation, but, even the elements of nature appeared to conspire against me in bringing about protracted and inclement winters, and low and frozen streams, or dry and parching summers, as though to thwart the best exertions I could possibly make.

When all these things are taken into the account, and there be added, the repeated and unequivocal instructions of the Department, "to exercise no coercion, not even undue persuasion," over the movements of the Indians till the 23 May last, with continued assurances that, not only would there be no alteration or modification of the late Treaty, but that the measures of the Govermn. then in progress as to the means & mode of Removal, would be humanely, but perseveringly carried out, of which I was directed on all occasions to assure the Indians. I say, under all these conflicting circumstances it is no way miraculous that so little had been accomplished by me, in the removal of this Tribe up to the 1st of June last. I hope my Dear Sir, you will not only properly appreciate the facts within stated, for your own satisfaction, but if time will any way admit, you will so employ them with the Departments in which my standing has been sought to be shaken, as to place me on such footing, as my very humble pretensions (well known to you) may appear to entitle me and you will very greatly add to the great debt of gratitude under which I already stand to you.

If your efforts to procure me a fair and just estimation with the Departments of my country fail, I feel it a duty, not only to my family and myself, but to you Sir, and my other valued friends, to ask for a most rigid Investigation of all my public conduct, from the beginning to the termination of my duties: be assured that I should meet any tribunal that might be organized to inquire, not only unflinchingly, but with much pleasure, expecting to have it most clearly developed that, if my management of this business should be found lacking in ability, it will at least tower above the imputation of meditated corruption.

NAT SMITH

ALS. DLC–JKP. Addressed to Washington and marked *"Confidential."*

1. A brigadier general in the militia, Smith represented Grainger County in the Tennessee House, 1823–24. He was an agent to the Cherokees in the 1830's and was superintendent of Cherokee emigration, 1837–39.

2. Carey A. Harris, former resident of Williamson County, Tennessee, rose to the rank of chief clerk in the War Department; in 1836 Jackson chose Harris to head the Office of Indian Affairs, in which post he served until his resignation in early 1839.

3. Under the Treaty of New Echota, signed in December 1835, the Cherokees were to immigrate to the West within two years following the agreement's ratification. Five million dollars would be allowed the Indians for property loss and travel expense. By the spring of 1838 it was evident that these removal incentives, administered by civilian agents of the Indian Office, would prove largely ineffectual. Secretary of War Joel R. Poinsett ordered General Winfield Scott to take command of the removal program. Scott appointed Chief John Ross to lead the westward migration, every phase of which was hastened and policed by Scott's military forces.

4. Letter not found.

FROM JOHN S. YOUNG[1]

McMinnville, Tennessee. February 13, 1839

Young has received a recent message from Polk concerning an appointment for himself in the Indian Department.[2] Having served with merit under Senator Lumpkin and General Scott[3] in the Cherokee emigration for two years, Young now desires a more permanent position.[4] Young reports that Polk's course of meeting the Whigs openly and boldly during his visit to the District and East Tennessee was decidedly successful.

ALS. DLC–JKP. Addressed to Washington.

1. Born in Virginia, Young settled in Warren County, Tennessee, about the year 1830; he established a medical practice in Nashville prior to moving to the Cherokee agency at Calhoun in 1836. Young campaigned hard for Democratic candidates in 1839; the Twenty-second General Assembly rewarded his services by electing him secretary of state, a position he held for eight years.

2. This letter is the first of three extant enquiries from Young to Polk concerning an appointment in the Indian service. Having received information through Hopkins L. Turney that Polk had procured him a position, Young wrote Polk on March 23 and 31, 1839, inquiring further about the appointment. ALsS. DLC–JKP. Polk's letter to Young has not been found.

3. Wilson Lumpkin and Winfield Scott. A lawyer, planter, and politician, Lumpkin served as a commissioner under the Cherokee Treaty of 1835. When voluntary removal under the Cherokee Treaty proved unsuccessful, Scott was appointed by the War Department to take charge of the Cherokee emigration. See Nathaniel Smith to Polk, February 12, 1839.

4. Secretary of War Joel R. Poinsett wrote Polk on April 30, 1839, that for want of congressional funding Young could not be appointed disbursing agent in the Indian Department, as the Speaker had requested. ALS. DLC–JKP.

FROM SAMUEL H. LAUGHLIN

McMinnville, Tennessee. February 15, 1839

Laughlin writes that he hopes the Speaker will tour through White, Warren, and Franklin counties on his return from Washington. Polk has only to advise Laughlin and plans will be readied. Laughlin has learned from Turney that Cave Johnson has been "instructed" about his claims.[1] He expects to be sued by Johnson and asks Polk's advice. Laughlin comments upon the political situation in Bedford, Rutherford, and Williamson counties and concludes by declaring his fears that Carroll will not run for Congress. Laughlin suggests that if Carroll does not run, "he can be forced into the State Senate and made Speaker."

ALS. DLC–JKP. Addressed to Washington and marked "Private."

1. See Samuel H. Laughlin to Polk, January 11, 1839.

FROM JAMES H. THOMPSON[1]

Columbia, Tennessee. February 16, 1839

Thompson requests a subscription to Blair and Rives' *Congressional Globe* and its *Appendix*[2] for John Goddard[3] and himself. He will reimburse Polk upon the Speaker's return home. Thompson notes that Watterson has made several pleasing addresses, taking "open ground" for the administration and exposing the opposition's intentions. Samuel Polk, Thompson relates, is not expected to survive much longer.[4]

ALS. DLC–JKP. Addressed to Washington.

1. Thompson edited and published the Columbia *Tennessee Democrat* from 1838 until 1841.

2. In 1833 Francis P. Blair and John C. Rives, publishers of the Washington *Globe*, began publication of the *Congressional Globe*, which reported weekly the proceedings of each house. Selected speeches and reports were printed separately in an *Appendix* at the session's close.

3. Not identified further.

4. See John B. Hays to Polk, January 9, 1839.

FROM WILLIAM WALLACE

Maryville, Tennessee. February 16, 1839

Wallace writes that progress has been made by Gifford in establishing a Democratic newspaper in Knoxville.[1] The Knoxville Whigs are divided, and Cannon's position on internal improvements has made him unpopular with many of his party.[2] A new Whig press[3] will soon begin publication, further dividing the opposition. Wallace recommends the appointment of Henry[4] as postmaster of Louisville in place of N. Cox,[5] deceased. Cox's son[6] is also seeking the position, but the appointment of Henry would be more useful politically. Though inclined to the opposition, Henry is not committed to White. With the Democratic influence of his family, his appointment might encourage the return of White partisans in Blount County to the Democracy.

ALS. DLC–JKP. Addressed to Washington.

1. Knoxville *Argus*.
2. See Jesse B. Clements to Polk, February 11, 1839.
3. Knoxville *Times*.
4. A merchant at Louisville, John F. Henry served four terms as a Whig in the Tennessee Senate, 1843–51.
5. An early settler and merchant at Louisville, Nathaniel Cox served as postmaster from 1828 until 1839.
6. A decided Democrat, as was his father, Henry Talbot Cox was also recommended to Polk as well qualified for the office by Frederick S. Heiskell, whose letter was dated February 13, 1839. ALS. DLC–JKP. Cox received the appointment on March 2, 1839.

FROM RICHARD WARNER

Chapel Hill, Tennessee. February 16, 1839

Warner writes about candidates and electoral activities in Bedford County. He foresees that he will probably run against Barringer.[1] In order to defend the administration, Warner requests information about Barringer's politics and about federal expenditures since 1825. He advises that "considerable excitement" prevails in Shelbyville over the grocery law.[2]

ALS. DLC–JKP. Addressed to Washington.

1. A lawyer from Raleigh, North Carolina, Daniel Barringer moved in 1836 to Bedford County, where he farmed and practiced law. Having served as a Democrat in the North Carolina Commons, 1813–14 and 1819–22, and in the U.S. House, 1826–35, Barringer sought election to Congress in 1839, but lost

that bid to Harvey M. Watterson. Warner ran successfully for the Tennessee Senate against William D. Orr.

2. See Erwin J. Frierson to Polk, February 1, 1839.

FROM J. GEORGE HARRIS

Nashville, Tennessee. February 17, 1839

Harris writes that he had scarcely taken over the *Union* when the *Banner* published editorials that seemed determined to "browbeat" him and "frown" him out of the community. Harris relates that to sustain himself and to gain advantage in the campaign he has "commenced open warfare with the Banner."

ALS. DLC–JKP. Addressed to Washington.

FROM WILLIAM H. POLK

My Dear Brother Columbia Feb 17th 1839

Your letter of the 27th January[1] has been received. It grieves me that Brother Samuel's health is such as to compel me to confirm the account which you have received of his situation. He is in truly a pitiable condition, unable to gain but little sleep, on account of his *cough.* He throws up a large quantity of corruption. Since yesterday morning he has been much worse. The rapidity of his decline since yesterday is unaccountable. Dr Hays is of opinion that he cannot last but a fiew days. He is reconciled to his fate—speaks of his approaching disolution with *calmness and resignation.* I fear before you receive this that our poor Brother will be no more. It will be a melancholy farewell, to part from him *forever* who is associated with all my youthful pleasures, but it must be so, we must submit to a superior will. Dr. Hays says so rapidly is he declining, that he may not survive a day or two, and cannot linger more than a week or ten days, if he does not undergo a great change for the better, which he considers almost out of the range of possabillity. Mother[2] bears up under the affliction better than I anticipated. It is a great source of gratification to her that he has unqualifiedly placed his reliance in a superior Being. I will write you from day to day of his situation.

Prior to the reception of your letter Brother Samuel had made a disposition of his estate. I nevertheless mentioned to him the contents of your letter, with your opinion with regard to providing for Mother, giving him an opportunity, if he so desired, to make any alteration in his *will*. He told me to write to you, that he had provided *liberally* for Mother. Frierson[3] wrote his will for him. Sister Eliza[4] arrived several days ago. She will remain with us until spring. All Mr. Walkers family is well, except Ellen.[5] She presented Sam with a fine Boy a day or two ago. Give my love to Sister Sarah.

WILL. HAWKINS POLK

ALS. DLC–JKP. Addressed to Washington.

1. Letter not found.
2. Jane Knox Polk.
3. Samuel D. Frierson, a family friend and lawyer in Columbia, had been a partner of Marshall T. Polk and Jesse Egnew.
4. Lydia Eliza Polk had married Silas M. Caldwell, a physician; they lived in West Tennessee's Haywood County.
5. Eleanor Wormley had married James Walker's son, Samuel P. Walker. Their son, James, was born February 16, 1839.

FROM PHILANDER PRIESTLEY[1]

Dover, Tennessee. February 17, 1839

Priestley writes that the Whigs are attempting to gain control of the county mails before the August elections. During the previous fall they tried to change the stage route and divert the principal mails from Dover to Randolph's Furnace, located 2½ miles away.[2] Presently the Whigs are soliciting signatures for a petition favoring the removal of Hugh L. Brown as postmaster on grounds that he is not a resident of Dover. Should Brown resign, the position ought to go to John H. Petty, an active Democrat, who as assistant postmaster has been serving in Brown's place. The Whigs favor the appointment of John Kercheval.[3]

ALS. DLC–JKP. Addressed to Washington.

1. Clerk of the circuit court, 1836–40, Priestley served as one of Polk's chief operatives in Stewart County during the 1839 gubernatorial campaign.
2. Randolph Furnace, built in 1837 and fired until 1840, was owned by Cumberland Iron Works. John Bell acquired interest in the Cumberland Iron Works through his marriage to Jane Erwin Yeatman. The Works expanded its operations in the 1840's and in 1852 held assets in excess of $500,000.
3. Brown served as postmaster at Dover from February 1838 until March 1839. Petty, an innkeeper, succeeded Brown and retained the position until 1842. Kercheval owned a general store in Dover during the 1830's.

FROM WILLIAM L. S. DEARING[1]

At Home (Near Lebanon, Tenn)
February 18th 1839

My Dear Col.

I have been of late so frequently assailed with complaints of Claimants for horses lost in the late Florida Campaign, instigated I have reason to believe, by individuals prominent in the ranks of the Opposition to the Administration, and who entertain sentiments of deep hostility thereto, that I feel impelled to request your friendly aid in their adjustment at the earliest practicable period. Superadd to this the somewhat peculiar position in which I was placed, in reference to the Company I took from this County, the County you doubtless know is strongly opposed to Mr. Vanburen, in raising the Company, because I chose to rely upon the country and Mr. Vanburen, as Gov. Cannon refused to aid the Government in raising troops. I was met at the threshold with severe opposition and after having spent their venom without its taking the desired effect, the Company being raised, they indulged in many prophecies in reference to payment &c. So important did I conceive it was that the Company should go after all this ranting in order to quiet the apprehensions of the volunteers, that I went specially to see Genl. Jackson, on the subject, the good old Veteran give me his pledge that "all should be right." With this pledge in addition to my own efforts, the volunteers scouted the tales of the oppositionists and went off Cheerful & satisfied. I detail those circumstances to you in Confidence and with no other view, but to show you my position, which I hope will be sufficient to account to you & the Secretary at War[2] why I would be most particularly pleased with the earliest possible payment. I have thought it due to all parties, that I should thus unreservedly communicate to you, my sentiments & feelings in reference to the subject under review.

I observe in your Congressional proceedings that provision is made or will likely be made for the running [of] the line between the United States and Texas, also an appropriation (or a Bill for the same) of ten thousand dollars for a survey of lands West of the Mississippi for the Choctaws & other tribes. Having had much experience in this business you will confer a favour on a friend to present my claims, for one of those appointments.[3] Please let me hear from you immediately and oblige . . . .

Wm. L. S. Dearing

N.B. Address me at Lebanon Tennessee. W.L.S.D.

ALS. DLC–JKP. Addressed to Washington.

1. In December 1837 Captain Dearing led a company of volunteers from Wilson County to Florida to fight the Seminole Indians. Earlier he had spent considerable time in Mississippi and Louisiana as a surveyor.

2. Joel R. Poinsett.

3. An appropriation of $15,700, designated for implementing the Convention of 1838, received Van Buren's approval on January 11, 1839. In its general appropriation of 1839 for Indian expenses, Congress allocated $10,000 to the cost of "surveying and marking the boundaries between the Indian tribes west of the Mississippi." 5 *U.S. Stat.*, 328. Dearing failed in his bid to be appointed surveyor.

FROM WILLIAM V. PETTIT[1]

Philadelphia, Pennsylvania. February 18, 1839

Pettit writes that he has been unable to procure for Polk a copy of the Olive Branch.[2] However, he will continue efforts to find the tract,[3] as he wishes to assist Polk in "shewing up the Federal party in their true colours, in order that the people of Tennessee may understand the character of the new allies of Messrs Bell and Company . . . ."

ALS. DLC–JKP. Addressed to Washington.

1. Not further identified.

2. Mathew Carey's *Olive Branch*, published in 1814, was a plea for reconciliation among diverse political factions in America during the War of 1812.

3. Pettit wrote Polk on April 13, 1839, that he had obtained a copy of the *Olive Branch* through Charles J. Ingersoll and would forward the volume to Nashville. ALS. DLC–JKP.

FROM WILLIAM H. POLK

Dear Brother, [Columbia] Monday Night Feb 18th 1839

Brother Samuel is more comfortable this evening than he has been for several days. What I mean is, freer from bodily pain, but still rapidly declining. He is confined entirely to his Bed. Dr. Dickinson arrived this evening. He confirms Dr. Hays's opinion, that his time is very short. He may die any hour, or may linger a week.[1] He expresses a great desire to live to see you & Sister Sarah. He is comfortable in mind, and retains all the vigor of his intelect. I will write you again tomorrow. My love to Sister Sarah.

WILL HAWKINS POLK

ALS. DLC–JKP. Addressed to Washington. This letter is appended to a letter from Belinda G. D. Polk to Sarah C. Polk, February 17, 1839.

1. See John B. Hays to Polk, January 9, 1839.

FROM ROBERT B. REYNOLDS

Dear Sir, Knoxville Febry 18th 1839

I have just returned from a visit to North Alabama and have just recd your favour of the 29th ultimo & yours of Decr. 25.[1] I neglected to answer until now from a belief that I could give you more information after my return than I was prepared to do when I recd. it. I have been in about two thirds of the counties in East Tennessee since I wrote you in November[2] & I have no hesitation in saying that your majority in E.T. will not be less than 5000, & probably 10,000.

I agree with you that we labour under a great disadvantage in not having a sound Democratic paper in this town to promulgate the principles of our party & to expose federal Whiggery in its true colours. A press supporting the pure Jeffersonian faith, would no doubt wield a vast influence in the coming struggle against old fashioned federalism under a stolen name. Here, Sir, is the seat or head quarters of the federal party in E. Tennessee, and I am anxious the war should be carried in Africa. Without a press here, we cannot make the Victory complete. With one we can safely meet & conquer new born Whiggery.

I am sure we can sustain a news paper here with ease.[3] Our friends are all anxious for the erection of one here & will contribute liberally. I have seen & conversed with many of them & we have directed Lawson Gifford, a practical printer to order a press for this place & he informs us that he has done so. Gifford cannot edit a paper & we need an Editor. The editorial department will be attended to, until we can procure a gentleman of talents & character to take charge of the press as Editor & partner with Gifford &c. He must be a sound *Democrat* or we will not engage him. Can you send us one from Washington who can buffet the Storm which is brewing? It will be eventually, a profitable business as the Register is fast sinking in public estimation. We should prefer a man who was an adept in the art of printing. Gifford could then return to JonesBoro' & superintend the Sentinel.

Genl Wallace & his friends will do their duty in its support. Genl Anderson & Dr Ramsey say they will aid us but I have but little confidence in either, as they are only with us from hatred to Judge White & not from principle. Nevertheless I intend they shall serve us in the coming contest by aiding with money the press we design starting here. I do not think them simon pure democrats, altho they have talents & are professed Van Buren Polk men. Yet, they have no personal popularity.

My friends mostly reside in the country & many of them will go with me in advancing funds for our democratic sheet—& one of them says he will go if necessary $200. I will go $100 in the enterprise & I can get more money from my friends. Genl Wallace & his friends can & will do as much or even more. McClellan & his friends must lend us their aid as it will be of essential service to him in his district. I wish him to write me what he will do &c.

I will write him shortly relative to his election.

I suppose $1200 will answer for the present—$800 can be raised without trouble here. Can McC[lellan] raise the ballance. Let him see that a press is ordered & forwarded to the care of S Roberts & Son of this City.[4] I would not have the project to fail for any thing in the world. A prospectus has been written & Gifford said he would send one to Washington &c.

Our Circuit Court is now in session & I have not time to write you more at present but will do so by next mail in which I will give you the names of the candidates in the several Counties.

R B Reynolds

ALS. DLC–JKP. Addressed to Washington.

1. Letters not found.

2. See Reynolds to Polk, November 21, 1838.

3. Reference is to the establishment of the Knoxville *Argus*. See Richard M. Woods to Polk, January 28, 1839.

4. Samuel Roberts entered the Knoxville business community around 1820; he was a staunch Democrat, as was his son, Lewis P. Roberts.

FROM J. G. M. RAMSEY

My Dear Sir Mecklenburg Feb. 19. 1839

Yours of the 29th Ultimo[1] was received several days since. My new duties in organising the Branch of the S.W.R.R. Bank in Knoxville[2] & sitting it in motion have occupied me so fully till to night that I could not give an earlier reply. Your letter has set all matters right here as I hope it will elsewhere as soon as I can confirm assurances I had previously given in relation to the appointment alluded to.[3] In this county which is the head quarters of Clayism there is a strange holding off. Are they waiting for the return of Judge White? or upon the movements of the

Republicans? I cannot account for the tardy operations of the whigs. Their candidates are not yet announced. Tho our Circuit Court is over. They have some difficulty that we know nothing of. I think they have found that to run Clay will jeopardise every thing. Will they venture to run Harrison or *Rives*. This latter I think has some advocates in the conclave. But if I can divine right, It is determined from a quarter where I would expect it (indeed it is ascertained) not to mingle national politics with State legislation—but to elect sound men upon certain local improvements & state policy & leave the measures of the administration & the election of President to another time. Mark it if this is not to be the whig policy. To give every Road Co. Banking privileges, adopt the free banking system, promise each county a Rail Road or at least a bank agency, Checker out the whole State with Rail roads, have those already chartered unfinished, involve the State in millions of debt & destroy us with an unsound currency. We have as yet no candidates announced on either side. I believe we shall not wait on our part much longer. I had hoped the Register would be bought, but the arrangement can not be made. Light is all there is wanting. Your circuit through E. T. in the spring will give it. *The whole community is on the fence.* A vigorous campaign after the war commences will insure us the victory. We would have been glad to see you amongst us earlier than the time you have indicated—but you are probably right in deciding as you have. Let me hear of your appointments as soon as you can make them.

J. G. M. RAMSEY

ALS. DLC–JKP. Addressed to Washington and marked "Private."

1. Letter not found.

2. In 1837 the Tennessee legislature had granted banking privileges to the Louisville, Cincinnati and Charleston Railroad, which subsequently formed the Southwestern Railroad Bank. David Deaderick was named cashier of the Knoxville branch of this enterprise in 1839. Both the bank and its parent company, however, were terminated in 1840 at the request of the stockholders.

3. See Ramsey to Polk, January 5, 1839.

FROM ALFRED BALCH

Dear Sir, Washington 21st Feby [18]39

Shields has been engaged here in arming himself for the battle with Brown.[1] Your election is dove-tailed into that of every candidate for Congress in our state.

Shields, I am told says that he intends to charge Brown with speculating largely & profitably in the very claims which he was employed to adjudicate. If this be so I shall deeply regret it because I know that with such a sum as I could easily have commanded, I could have made in three months fifty thousand dollars but I felt myself utterly precluded by principle honor and a regard for my own character from being concerned either directly or remotely in one inch of Creek Indian land.[2]

Shields also alleges that Kilcannon was appointed to get him out of Browns way[3] and that he has obtained a document here which proves that Brown & Kilcannon were under pay by the Govt at the same time & received that pay altho it was one service that was to be paid for. You had better enquire at the Indian Bureau of Crawford[4] how this matter stands because if such payment were made it was a profligate waste of the public money & may injure Browns prospects.

A BALCH

ALS. DLC–JKP. Addressed locally.

1. Ebenezer J. Shields and Aaron V. Brown. Before entering the congressional race against Shields in 1839, Brown served as special Indian commissioner to certify contracts for the sale of Choctaw lands in Mississippi.

2. From 1836 to 1838 Balch served as special Indian commissioner to investigate alleged frauds in the sale of Creek reservation lands.

3. Andrew A. Kincannon, a perennial candidate for office, succeeded Brown as special Indian commissioner in Mississippi.

4. Thomas Hartley Crawford, a lawyer from Chambersburg, Pennsylvania, was Polk's colleague in the House of Representatives, 1829–33. He served with Balch as special Indian commissioner in the 1836 fraud investigation and subsequently as commissioner of Indian affairs from 1839 until 1845.

FROM NATHAN GAMMON[1]

Jonesboro, Tennessee. February 21, 1839

In reply to Polk's letter of February 7,[2] Gammon says that every effort is being made to bring Major McGaughey[3] into the congressional race. Thomas Anderson[4] has been suggested for that race, but he is not known well enough to win. Blair[5] is too much engaged in his mercantile pursuits to enter the contest, though he has been pressed in Sullivan County to run for the Tennessee Senate. Business obligations prevent Gammon's running, as urged by Polk. Gammon writes that candidates for the legislature have not yet declared, but Martin, Fain, and Hall are expected to do so.[6]

ALS. DLC–JKP. Addressed to Washington.

1. Gammon was a Jonesboro merchant; his father George had served in the Tennessee House, 1823–25, and Senate, 1827–29.

2. Letter not found.

3. Farmer, politician, and railroad promoter, John McGaughey served in the Tennessee House, 1827–33, and sat in the Senate, 1835–36. He was a member of the Constitutional Convention of 1834.

4. An East Tennessee physician, Thomas Von Albade Anderson was a son of Judge Joseph Anderson and brother of Alexander O., Pierce B., and Addison A. Anderson.

5. A merchant, manufacturer, and lawyer in Washington County, John Blair served as a Democrat in the U.S. House, 1823–35; he was defeated by William B. Carter in 1834. Blair represented Washington County in the Tennessee House, 1849–51.

6. Alfred Martin, Nicholas Fain, and C. W. Hall. Martin, a Washington County physician, served in the Tennessee House, 1837–41, and sat in the Senate, 1845–47. C. W. Hall is not further identified.

FROM WILLIAM H. POLK

My Dear Brother, [Columbia] Thursday Night Feb. 21st 1839

I write you again, not that any change has taken place in Brother Samuel's situation, further than a gradual decline. He manifests great anxiety to live until you & Sister Sarah reaches home. He is at this time perfectly helpless—does not possess strength sufficient to change his position in Bed—has to be lifted about like a child. Dr Hays is very attentive to him, and every thing is done in the power of mortals, to render him comfortable the short time, which we all know he has to be with us. I will write you again in a day or two. A letter will not reach Washington after this week before you leave there. I will therefore, write to you, at Wheeling, & probably at Louisville. All the family are generally well. My love to Sister Sarah.

Will Hawkins Polk

ALS. DLC–JKP. Addressed to Washington.

FROM ROBERT B. REYNOLDS

Dear Sir Knoxville Febry 21st 1839

I wrote you by the last mail[1] & gave you all the information that I possessed relative to the establishment of a Democratic paper in this

City, & I now repeat that we are determined on having a thorough going paper here in a short time.

In the several Congressional & Senatorial districts, our friends seem determined to carry the day. In Carter's district Majr McGaughey will be our candidate & will run Arnold & Carter to the dirt, if he does not beat them. McClellan I think (& so does his friends) will beat J. A. McKinney Esqr. Let McClellan get the Journals of the Convention of 1834 & he will beat him with ease. J. L. Williams will have opposition in Genl. Wallace & I think this will be a close election. Stone will have several opponents. Majr. Brown of Kingston[2] I understand will be one of them. He, I understand, professes friendship for you; yet he is a federalist & will not receive the support of the democrats. J. W. Blackwell of Athens[3] will be the democratic candidate & will be elected. I wish you would write Blackwell when you will address the people of Athens.[4] I saw him a few days ago & he says that the people of Athens are opposed to you—but that the country people, the farmers are for you & he wished to have timely notice of the time you will visit Athens—for the purpose of rallying his forces &c. In Carrigers Senatorial district[5] I have not learned who will be the candidates, but our friends claim the district. John Balch[6] it is said will be re-elected from Greene & Hawkins. Majr Porter it is said will run in the district represented by P. M. Wear in the last legislature.[7] He is a decided democrat. Col Wheeler is a candidate in Bratchers old district[8] & will no doubt be re-elected. Graves[9] is a candidate for re-election in this district & I fear he will be elected. John F. Gillespie a democrat will beat Spencer Jarnagin in the Athens district.[10] I am not informed who will run in Whitesides old district.[11]

Reps. Sullivan will elect C. W. Hall, a republican. Sullivan & Hawkins will elect Nicholas Fain over W C Kyle, a Whig.[12] Greene & Washington will elect 3 democrats viz., Martin, Campbell & Hale.[13] Carter will send a federalist.[14] Hawkins will send Critz, a V.B. man.[15] Grainger—Martin Cleaveland, V.B., against W. Williams, Whig.[16] Claiborne—all whigs in the field. Campbell, Anderson & Morgan—one Democrat & [one] whig in the field. This district sends two members. Roane—Stocton, whig, & Hembree, V.B.,[17] are the candidates. Jefferson—Col John Baker, V.B., and Carson & McFarland, feds, are out.[18] Sevier—all whigs. Blount—David McKamy, V.B., against Thompson, whig.[19] Knox—no candidates in the field for Representative—a Van Buren man will be run in this county. Monroe—James Vaughn, Democrat, against Gregory, Whig.[20] Vaughn's election certain. McMinn—James Walker, V.B.,[21] against a half dozen milk & cider opponents. Election of Walker is said to be sure. Monroe, McMinn & Bradley—Wm. Heiskell, Whig, against Col Shepherd & Col. McMillan, V.B. men.[22] Meigs & Rhea—Cowan, V.B., against Gillespie, Whig.[23] I have not learned who is the candidates in the counties of Bledsoe, Hamilton & Marion. The latter county is said to be two thirds democratic.

The cause of democracy is rapidly gaining strength in our Mountainous Region. I have had strong evidence this week, that *old Knox* will not go the Clay ticket. Your Spring campaign will no doubt open the eyes of many honest White men. Judge R. M. Anderson[24] will vote the V.B. ticket.

I fear Gifford is to inactive in getting up a Democratic paper. I have not heard from him since he left here a few weeks ago. Is there a man in Washington City who is capable of conducting a press in whom confidence can be placed that can be induced to establish himself in this town? If there is—the necessary assistance will be given him to Sustain his establishment. Let him come on.

R B Reynolds

P.S. There is a new federal paper going into operation here.[25] I wish a prospectus to be issued for a democratic Journal immediately. Please instruct Gifford what name we shall give the new paper. I propose The Argus and Commercial Advertiser.[26] R B Reynolds

ALS. DLC–JKP. Addressed to Washington.

1. See Robert B. Reynolds to Polk, February 18, 1839.

2. Thomas Brown, an early settler of Roane County and veteran of the War of 1812, served two terms in the Tennessee House, 1817–19 and 1821–23. He was an unsuccessful candidate for Congress in 1839.

3. Julius W. Blackwell won election as a Democrat to the U.S. House of Representatives in 1839 and 1843. He lost bids for reelection in 1841 and 1845.

4. Polk spoke in Athens on May 2, 1839. See Polk to Sarah Childress Polk, May 2, 1839.

5. Christian Carriger served eight terms in the Tennessee House, 1811–25 and 1831–33. He represented Carter, Sullivan, and Washington counties as a Whig in the Senate, 1837–39.

6. John T. Balch served in the Tennessee House, 1820–27, and sat in the Senate, 1837–41.

7. George M. Porter and Pleasant M. Wear. Porter, a physician in Newport, served as Cocke County clerk from 1828 until 1836. Wear represented Blount, Cocke, Jefferson, and Sevier counties in the Tennessee Senate, 1837–39. Lewis Reneau, a Whig from Sevierville, won the Senate seat in 1839.

8. John E. Wheeler and Ferrell H. Bratcher. Formerly a member of the Tennessee House, 1835–37, Bratcher served as a Whig in the Senate, where

he represented Anderson, Campbell, Claiborne, Grainger, and Morgan counties, 1837–39.

9. George Graves, a Whig, represented Knox and Roane counties in the Tennessee Senate, 1835–39.

10. John F. Gillespy and Spencer Jarnagin. A lawyer in Maryville until his removal to Madisonville in 1833, Gillespy served three terms in the Tennessee Senate, 1829–33 and 1839–41. Jarnagin studied law under Hugh L. White and practiced in Knoxville until 1837, when he removed to Athens, McMinn County, and became a leader of the Whig party. He was a presidential elector on the Whig ticket in 1840 and an unsuccessful candidate for the U.S. Senate in 1841. Two years later he was elected to the U.S. Senate and served from 1843 until 1847.

11. James A. Whiteside served in the Tennessee House, 1835–37 and 1845–49, and represented Bledsoe, Hamilton, Marion, and Rhea counties as a Whig in the Senate, 1837–39.

12. William C. Kyle, a merchant and slave trader, owned a large farm near Rogersville, Hawkins County. As Reynolds predicted, Kyle lost his bid for a seat in the legislature.

13. Alfred Martin, Brookins Campbell, and James W. Hale. Campbell served in the Tennessee House, 1835–39, 1841–43, 1845–47, and 1851–53. During the Mexican War Polk appointed him assistant quartermaster general, with the rank of major. Campbell subsequently won election to the U.S. House in 1853 and served until his death in December of that year.

14. Carter County elected Godfrey Carriger Nave, a Whig.

15. Philip Critz, a farmer, miller, and tanner, resided near Patterson's Creek in Hawkins County; he served in the Tennessee House, 1841–43 and 1859–61, and in the Senate, 1843–47.

16. Martin Cleveland and William Williams. A farmer, surveyor, tanner, and mill owner at Flat Creek, Cleveland served in the Tennessee House, 1823–25, 1835–37, and 1843–47, and sat in the Senate, 1825–27 and 1829–31. In 1839 Williams defeated Cleveland for a seat in the Tennessee House and two years later won election to the Senate, where he served one term.

17. Thomas W. Stockton and Joel Hembree. A Roane County farmer and justice of the peace, 1820–34, Stockton served three terms in the Tennessee House, 1831–37. Hembree served four terms as a Democrat in the Tennessee House, 1839–43, 1845–47, and 1849–51.

18. John Baker, James H. Carson, and McFarland. Carson represented Jefferson County four terms in the Tennessee House, 1837–41, 1843–45, and 1875–77; he served in the Tennessee Senate, 1877–79. "McFarland" reference probably is to one of the sons of Robert McFarland, Jefferson County's first sheriff. John, Robert, and Benjamin F. McFarland served in the Tennessee legislature, but none was elected in 1839.

19. David McKamy and Jesse Thompson. Although he supported Hugh L. White for the presidency in 1836, McKamy remained a Democrat; he represented Blount County four terms in the Tennessee House, 1833–37, 1839–41,

and 1849–51. Thompson represented Blount County in the Tennessee House, 1837–39.

20. James Vaughn and Few H. Gregory. A resident of Madisonville, Vaughn was sheriff of Monroe County, 1834–38. Gregory, a farmer and physician, served one term as a Democrat in the Tennessee House, 1839–41.

21. A farmer at Calhoun, Walker served in the Tennessee House, 1837–43, and sat in the Senate, 1849–51.

22. William Heiskell, Shepherd, and Joseph W. McMillin. A railroad promoter and trustee of Hiwassee College, East Tennessee University, and Hampton Sydney Academy, Heiskell served as a Whig in the Tennessee House, 1849–51; elected as a Unionist in 1865, he served one term as Speaker of that body. Colonel Shepherd is not further identified. A Democrat, McMillin served one term in the Tennessee House, 1839–41.

23. Cowan and possibly Thomas J. Gillespie. Cowan is not further identified. Gillespie represented Rhea County in the Tennessee House, 1837–39.

24. Robert M. Anderson, a native of Virginia, represented Knox and Anderson counties in the Tennessee Senate, 1831–33. An unsuccessful candidate for Congress in 1837, he was appointed in that year judge of the Twelfth Judicial Circuit and served in that post from 1837 until 1854.

25. Reference is to the Knoxville *Times*.

26. Polk's agency, if any, in selecting the name of the Knoxville *Argus* is not further identified.

TO EDWARD STANLY[1]

Sir Washington City Feby 23rd 1839

Your letter of the 16th Instant,[2] handed to me on the 19th is the same I believe, which you had delivered to me, in the first instant on the day it bears date, and which on a conference between us, was withdrawn, upon the conclusion to which we both came, that your object could be attained *in the House*. The impression at that time on my mind, and which I expressed to you was, that the interrogatory contained in your letter was of a character, which if answered by me in my official character as Speaker, it would in my judgment be proper and respectful to the House, that the answer should be given in my official place in the chair, and in the presence of the House. In this view of the subject your letter was withdrawn, in the expectation that an opportunity would be afforded you, on the next petition day (Monday) to bring the subject before the chair and the House. The course of the business on Monday, prevented this opportunity. Since your letter was returned to me, I have considered of the propriety of deciding in this form (when out of the chair and not in the presence of the House) the question which you propound. That question involves a construction of one of the rules of the House, which any member is as competent to decide as the Speaker. Whilst in the chair, and during the sitting of the House, it is the duty of the Speaker, to decide all questions of Parliamentary law, or of construction of the rules of the House, which may be raised in the course of its proceedings, and his decision is subject to an appeal to the House, and may be reversed, or overruled, if he be in error; but an opinion given by him when the House is not in Session, cannot be subject to such appeal, and no opportunity is afforded to those who may differ with him, in opinion, to have his decision overruled, if he be in error. This being the case, however well-settled my convictions may be, upon the point to which you refer, it would not in my judgment, be consistent, with official propriety or respectful to the House, either to make a decision or to repeat any former decision, upon any question of Parliamentary law or construction, in any other than in my official station, and in the presence of the House. By a reference to the Journals of the present and preceeding sessions, you will readily be able to ascertain what the action of the House and the construction of its rules have been, upon the subject to which the inquiry in your letter is directed.[3] Believing that I cannot with propriety make any decision but in my official place as Speaker, I beg leave most respectfully, to decline it, in this form;[4] assuring you at the same time that I have always been and still am ready to decide the question you propound or any other; or to repeat any former decision, I may have made, when brought up for decision in the House.

James K. Polk

ALS, draft. DLC–JKP. Addressed locally and marked "*Copy*."

1. A lawyer from North Carolina, Stanly served as a Whig in Congress, 1837–43 and 1849–53. In 1857 he ran unsuccessfully as a Republican for governor of California, and 1862–63 he served as military governor of eastern North Carolina.

2. In his letter of February 16, Stanly refers to several abolition petitions recently presented in the House. He asks if these petitions have been received officially and requests Polk's reply in writing. ALS. DLC–JKP.

3. Reference is to the "gag rule." On December 18, 1835, Speaker Polk ruled that a motion to reject a petition was unprecedented and out of order; subsequently he reconsidered and decided the House had such a right. On May 26, 1836, the House voted to table all petitions relating to the abolition of slavery. At the following session Polk held that the gag rule could not be carried forward automatically; the House readopted the rule at each session of Congress until December 3, 1844.

4. Originally intending to end his letter at this place, Polk wrote a complimentary close and signed his name. The closing and signature subsequently were crossed out and the body of the letter continued.

FROM WILLIAM H. POLK

My Dear Brother, Columbia, Feb. 24th 1839

Our poor Brother is no more.[1] He died this morning about half after four O'clock. It is gratifying to know that he manifested to the last, an entire willingness to go—his last words were in *confirmation* of christianity. He retained all his faculties to the last—requested to breath his last in his Mothers arms. He died very easy—without a struggle—without moving a muscle or distorting a feature. It is hard to realize the sad reality that he has gone to the home of his farthers. Mother is almost inconsolable. She could not bear up under the blow—but for the brilliant hopes, that he expressed of going to rest and peace. All the family are well. Give my love to Sister Sarah.

WILL. HAWKINS POLK

ALS. DLC–JKP. Addressed to Wheeling, Virginia.

1. Samuel Washington Polk died of tuberculosis.

FROM J. KNOX WALKER[1]

Dear Uncle, [Columbia. February 24, 1839][2]

Poor Sam died a few moments since, and at the request of all I hasten to drop you a few lines hoping they may reach you.[3] He died calm & happy blessing Jesus & exhorting all to meet him in the world to come.

We have been expecting him to die for a week or so & during yesterday & today he appeared to be sinking very fast—said he knew he was dying and that he was willing to go if Jesus called him. Grand ma[4] & all the family are comparatively composed & rejoicing.

J. KNOX WALKER

ALS. DLC–JKP. Addressed to Washington.

1. Joseph Knox Walker, third son of James and Jane Maria Polk Walker,

was graduated from Yale in 1838, as was his boyhood friend and relative, Samuel Washington Polk.

2. Walker noted that his hour of writing was "1/2 past 4 O'clock Sunday morning."

3. Polk was expected to depart Washington for Tennessee as soon as Congress adjourned on March 3.

4. Polk's mother, Jane Knox Polk.

FROM M. D. COOPER & CO.

New Orleans, Louisiana. February 28, 1839

Cooper & Co. encloses an invoice in the amount of $100.86 for groceries ordered by Polk.[1]

LS. DLC–JKP. Addressed to Columbia. The enclosed bill indicates that the goods were shipped on February 27 by the steamboat *Daniel Webster* and were consigned to Connor, McAlister & Co. of Nashville.

1. Polk's order not found.

FROM JAMES BROWN[1]

Oxford, Mississippi. March 1, 1839

Brown sends a grant for 274 acres of land on Muddy Creek in the 11th district.[2] Although Brown claims 54 4/5 acres as his locator's interest, he will accept 45 acres in the northeast corner as an equivalency. He states that he had anticipated such a settlement when he and J. H. Bills examined the tract for its division among the heirs of Samuel Polk.[3] Brown requests that Polk send him a deed, for the land has been sold and the purchasers want their title.[4]

ALS. DLC–JKP. Addressed to Columbia.

1. A son of Colonel Joseph Brown of Maury County, James Brown assisted Samuel Polk in surveying and locating lands in Tennessee's Western District. During the early 1830's Brown resided in Jackson and engaged in a mail contracting business with James Walker. In the 1840's Brown represented Polk's land interests in Mississippi.

2. Reference is to Polk's acreage in the southwestern part of Haywood County.

3. In 1832 Samuel Polk's location lands in the Western District were di-

vided into five equal portions and distributed by Maury County Court order to James K., William H., and Samuel W. Polk and to the estates of Franklin E. and Marshall T. Polk. Samuel Polk's will did not include John Lee Polk in the distribution of location lands.

4. On December 1, 1840, Polk prepared and signed an indenture conveying the property to Absalom and Samuel Rudd of Haywood County; across the face of Polk's copy is his endorsement, "Cancelled by making a Deed to the assignee or purchaser from the Messrs Rudd." ADS, copy. DLC–JKP.

FROM SUTHERLAND S. SOUTHWORTH[1]

Reporters Gallery No. 2 House of Reps.
Midnight [March 3][2] 1839

Sir,

I did not dream that my feelings, and least of all, my duty, as a man and an american citizen, would call on me at this late hour of the night, to address you on any subject.

But, having seen, the infirm attempt that has just been made, to deprive you of the common courtesies of life, and to hurt you with redress, I was called on, by my sense of right, to say, that I hold this attempt to which I allude, in abhorence, and the managers of it, in contempt.[3]

I have passed many years in Washington, and if my opinions are worth anything, I would say that you are the ablest man, who has ever held the responsible office of speaker of the House of Representatives.

Your course, has been dignified, impartial and upright; and to the latest day of my life, I shall recollect your administration of the affairs of this House, with veneration, respect, and admiration.

No mortal foe, can deprive you of your well earned laurels; all honest men will bear witness to your intellect and moral excellence; and I for one regret, that any political desperado should attempt to deprive you of your laurels.

Politically opposed to you, as I am, I take the greatest pleasure, in presenting to you this public and full testimonial of my respect and profound good will. Accept my assurances of profound respect . . . .

S. S. Southworth

ALS. DLC–JKP. Addressed locally.

1. Southworth served at various times as Washington correspondent for newspapers in principal eastern cities.

2. Date identified through content analysis.

3. At the evening session, March 3, 1839, Franklin Elmore of South Carolina resolved that the thanks of the House be presented to Polk "for the able, impartial, and dignified manner" in which he had presided over that body. Sergeant S. Prentiss of Mississippi said that he could not assent to the resolution and moved to amend it by striking the word "impartial." Prentiss held that Polk had not been impartial and that the House did not so consider him. Prentiss wished Polk a courteous farewell, but objected to furnishing him political capital. Elmore's resolution was passed without amendment. *Congressional Globe,* 25 Cong., 3 Sess., 250–52.

FROM JAMES N. BARKER[1]

Treasury Department First Comptrollers Office

Sir [Washington City] March 6th 1839

Your account as Speaker of the House of Representatives, agent for paying the members of said house for their mileage and compensation at the third session of the 25th Congress, has been adjusted and finally closed on the books of the Treasury.

J. N. Barker

LS. DLC–JKP. Addressed locally.

1. An ardent Jacksonian, Barker served as mayor of Philadelphia, 1819; collector of that city's port, 1829–38; and first comptroller of the treasury, 1838–41.

FROM GEORGE & ROBERT BLACKBURN & CO.[1]

Madeira, Portugal. March 7, 1839

Blackburn & Co. write that they are forwarding "one Hogshead of choice old London Particular wine." Enclosed is an invoice in the amount of $118.45.[2]

LS. DLC–JKP. Addressed to Columbia and forwarded to Nashville.

1. Not further identified.

2. Polk is billed for "One Hogshead 55 Gallons"; shipment will be routed from Madeira to New York, to the care of Messrs. Wadsworth & Smith, and from New York to New Orleans, to the care of M. D. Cooper & Co. Charges include $3.45 for insurance.

FROM M. D. COOPER & CO.

New Orleans, Louisiana. March 11, 1839

Cooper & Co. encloses Polk's account and credits it in the amount of $1,651.90 for the sale of 34 bales of cotton, which were insured at an average weight of 400 lbs each. Because total weight was overestimated,[1] insurance costs were greater. Although market prices have declined at least one cent per pound since Polk's sale, factors expect favorable rises on the European market. No further word on the balance of Polk's crop has been received. Polk's acknowledgement of receipt of $1,600 is in hand.

LS. DLC–JKP. Addressed to Columbia.

1. Polk's 34 bales weighed 13,080 lbs; gross sales receipts amounted to $1,867.68; and sundry charges totaled $215.78, including Cooper & Co.'s 2½ per cent commission.

FROM GEORGE W. BRATTON

Dr sir Miss Yallowbusha co.[1] march the 13, 1839

We are all will at present and at work as hard as we can drive. I have commenced planting of corn on monday morning and I think that I shall get nearly done panting of corn this week. If the weather holds good I can plant all of my crop in good time. I am planting a good deal more land this year than I did last year with the calculation of them hands you promised to send me when you come home and you must not fail to bring them. If you do [fail] I cannot tend my crop. The mule that julius[2] rode to tennesse is at James Walkers plantation. The produce that he sent on all come safe but one plow mule.

I want you to by me a negro woman young and likely and be sertin that she is sound on the best termes you can. Bring here down with you and I will work her on the plantation this year.

GEORGE BRATTON

L, signed by amanuensis. DLC–JKP. Addressed to Columbia. Published in Bassett, *Plantation Overseer*, 118–19.

1. Yalobusha County, Mississippi.
2. William H. Polk's slave.

FROM SAMUEL CUSHMAN[1]

Portsmouth, New Hampshire. March 13, 1839

Cushman says that the election in New Hampshire was a glorious victory for the Democratic party. John Page[2] was elected governor by a majority of five thousand votes, and Democratic majorities were returned to both houses of the state legislature. Tristram Shaw, Ira A. Eastman, Charles G. Atherton, Edmund Burke, and Jared W. Williams[3] have won election to Congress.

ALS. DLC–JKP. Addressed to Columbia.

1. In 1830 Andrew Jackson nominated Samuel Cushman to be U.S. attorney for the New Hampshire district, but the Senate rejected the appointment. In 1835 Cushman won election to the U.S. House of Representatives and served two terms.

2. John Page filled the vacancy in the U.S. Senate caused by the resignation of Isaac Hill in 1837. A Democrat, Page was elected governor of New Hampshire and served from 1840 until 1842.

3. Tristram Shaw won election to the U.S. House and served from 1839 until 1843. A graduate of Dartmouth College, Ira Eastman served two terms as a Democrat in the U.S. House, 1839–43. Also a Democrat, Charles G. Atherton served three terms in the U.S. House, 1837–43, and one term in the U.S. Senate, 1843–49. Edmund Burke, a Democrat, practiced law until 1833, when he became editor of the *New Hampshire Argus*. In 1834 the *Argus* was united with the Newport *Spectator*, which Burke edited until his election to Congress in 1839. He served three terms in the House, but did not seek reelection in 1844. He was appointed commissioner of patents by Polk and served from 1846 until 1850. Jared W. Williams, a lawyer in Lancaster, New Hampshire, won election as a Democrat to the U.S. House and served from 1837 until 1841.

FROM JOSEPH COE[1]

Somerville, Tennessee. March 14, 1839

Responding to a letter from Polk,[2] Joseph Coe writes that Dr. Wilkinson[3] signed the deed left with Coe by Polk. Coe forwarded the deed to McNeal[4] at Coffeeville for recording in the county where the property was located. Coe attributes his failure to write Polk earlier to a Whig rumor that Polk found he would be beaten for governor and that Van Buren, out of pity, had sent him to the Court of St. James, England. Coe and other Democrats are relieved to learn that the rumor was untrue and that Tennessee might be "Redeemed from Federal Bank Whig thraldom" through Polk's election. Coe informs Polk that Levin has gone to Texas, but Joseph Coe will deliver Polk's confidential letter to him upon his return.

ALS. DLC–JKP. Addressed to Columbia.

1. Joseph Coe, father of Democratic state senator Levin H. Coe, resided in Holly Springs, Mississippi.

2. Letter not found.

3. Unidentified.

4. Albert T. McNeal was a younger brother of Ezekiel P. McNeal and a first cousin of Polk.

FROM AARON V. BROWN

Dear Sir (Friday night) Pulaski March 15th [1839][1]

Your last favor was duly receivd. together with the copy of the journals, which you were good enough to forward to me.[2] I was at Lawrenceburgh Court, last monday & remaind. untill yesterday or rather the evening before. We have no candidate for the Legislature to sustain us in that County. The old Sheriff Matthews,[3] refuses to offer as he once agreed to do. Allen wont run, nor McLaren.[4] The county is clearly Democratic—but is very likely to be *given up* to the Whigs. In Wayne where I intend to be on monday next, *the powers* are against us smartly, say 2 to one. Ross I fear cant hold out against old Andy Brown.[5] *That* is the strongest *Clay* County I know of. I have not been to Hardin since Novr. But shall be there the monday after the Wayne Court. I hear there are several candidates for the assembly in that County, *all whigs.* Henry Brown & Bullock are running for the Senate, both whigs & a third Shackelford, Democrat.[6] Hardin is one of their counties.[7] In Hardin the parties *are nearly balanced.* Now if you reach home in time, how would it answer to *commence* at Wayne next Week, then to Hardin the next & thence to Perry—all circuit courts. I should like such an arrangement if suitable to yourself. I see that Leatherman[8] mislead you as to the time of the Wayne court.

Quero[9] in *confidence,* it has been *hinted* that *Prentiss*[10] was to come through *this* place & make a speech. I dont believe a word of it. But I thought it possible he might drop in about Savannah. Do you know anything that renders it probable.

You speak of hearing that I might decline. Nothing is to be feared on that score. I have been industrious through the Winter & believe that I should succeed if the election were to morrow. Still in reference to the *inertness* of some of our friends, in bringing out candidates in some of the candidates [*sic*], it would be nothing but right that I should.

I have made no reply under my own name to the Whig & the Republican Banner.[11] I have one prepared, but I feel great reluctance in going in the newspapers even in self defence. It is so long to election that I think I can take my satisfaction out of them on the stump. The Trumpet[12] replied giving the facts which the Whig says it does not pretend to controvert. [The *Whig*] let me off—reluctantly but still complains of Colo. K's having been appointed.[13] They will *mouth* about it, but I think it will do no material harm.

Your friends in Wayne & Hardin would be very glad to see you & much depends on the thumping blows we may give Mr Clay at the beginning. I think I can sustain the fact of his having abused the occupant settlers, notwithstanding his denial & his vote for the Tennessee land Bill.[14]

I do not know when we can meet, unless it be at Wayne or Hardin—as I expect the campaign to open with great activity on Shields return. No Legislative candidates *yet* in Giles on either Side.

A V Brown

ALS. DLC–JKP. Addressed to Columbia.

1. Year identified through content analysis.

2. Letter not found. On November 1, 1838, Brown had requested copies of U.S. House and Senate journals.

3. An early settler in Lawrence County, Thomas J. Matthews served as sheriff and represented Lawrence, Wayne, and Hickman counties in the Tennessee Senate as a Democrat, 1841–43.

4. Richard H. Allen. McLaren has not been identified.

5. Jesse S. Ross served as sheriff of Wayne County, 1835–37. Andrew Brown, a farmer, served in the Tennessee House as a Whig, 1835–43.

6. Henry Hill Brown, Micajah Bullock, and J. Shackleford. Brown, a resident of Henderson County and a veteran of the War of 1812, served in the Tennessee Senate, 1823–25 and 1835–41. A lawyer, Bullock represented Henderson County in the Tennessee House, 1835–37 and 1841–42; he moved to Jackson and served two additional terms in the Tennessee House, 1845–47 and 1857–59. Shackleford is not identified further.

7. Brown's senatorial district in 1839 included Henderson, Hardin, McNairy, and Perry counties.

8. Daniel Leatherman, a resident of Giles County, is not further identified.

9. *Quero*, a variant spelling of the Latin verb *quaero*, translates "I inquire."

10. A native of Maine and a graduate of Bowdoin College, Sergeant S. Prentiss settled in Mississippi and gained considerable recognition for his prowess as a trial lawyer. He successfully contested the election of John F. H.

Claiborne to Congress in 1837 and in May of the following year won the vacated seat.

11. The *Nashville Whig* and the Nashville *Republican Banner*.

12. In 1837 Brown and his friends had purchased the Pulaski *Trumpet of Liberty* and changed editorial policy from Whig to Democratic. William H. Feild became the publisher and editor. H. R. Brown, a nephew of Aaron V. Brown, also served in an editorial capacity.

13. Andrew A. Kincannon had been appointed Choctaw agent in Mississippi, replacing Brown in that position. Kincannon then withdrew in favor of Brown as the Democratic candidate for Congress.

14. The Tennessee land bill, for which Henry Clay voted in January, 1838, passed the U.S. Senate, but not the House; it would have given occupants an unconditional right to preempt at twelve and a half cents per acre public lands in the Western District of Tennessee.

FROM DANIEL KENNEY

Jonesboro, Tennessee. March 15, 1839

Kenney says that plans for a Democratic paper at Knoxville[1] are succeeding, though it may be the last of April before a press is shipped from Baltimore to Knoxville. He thinks recent legislation on the northeastern boundary[2] is a victory for the Democracy and suggests its utility to Polk in the Tennessee governor's race. Kenney awaits word on Polk's proposed movements in East Tennessee and advises Polk to publish his appointments as far in advance as possible.

ALS. DLC–JKP. Addressed to Columbia.

1. Reference is to the Knoxville *Argus*. See Richard M. Woods to Polk, January 28, 1839.

2. By Act of March 3, 1839, Congress authorized the president to protect Maine's border with Canada by raising a militia force of 50,000 troops and spending up to $10 million.

FROM CHARLES G. ATHERTON

Nashua, New Hampshire. March 16, 1839

Atherton says that the election in New Hampshire was a perfect triumph for the Democracy. Hoping to take votes from the Democratic party, the Federalists got up an abolition ticket, with Wilson for governor and Joel Eastman[1] for Congress. However, returns showed that the abolition candidates failed to encroach on Democratic support; the Whig party was identified with the abolitionist cause.

ALS. DLC–JKP. Addressed to Columbia.

1. James Wilson and Joel Eastman. A lawyer, Wilson was a member of the New Hampshire House, 1825–37, 1840, and 1846. He was an unsuccessful candidate for governor in 1835 and again in 1838, on which later occasion he was narrowly defeated by Isaac Hill. In 1839 John Page won a decisive victory over Wilson. Eastman is not identified further.

FROM SAMUEL H. LAUGHLIN

Dr Sir, McMinnville, March 19, 1839

Mr. Turney, who is now present with me, arived here, *via* Nashville and Murfreesboro', this morning on his way home. He will take the field forthwith, and will get home tomorrow to commence the campaign.

The Circuit Court at Smithville, DeKalb Co. will sit on the 2nd. Monday in April. Smithville is on the half way ground between this place and Carthage, being about 25 miles from each. From Smithville to Woodbury in Cannon is about 20 miles. From here to Woodbury is about 21 miles. And from Woodbury to Manchester in Coffee is about 25 miles, and from Manchester to Winchester about 22 miles. From Manchester to Hillsborough, which you must take in going to Winchester from Manchester, is about 8 miles. I give you these distances, in answer to your last letter.[1] In Franklin Co. they will give you a large turn out, as they will here. You *must* be at Smithville. The town is in the part of DeKalb which was formerly Warren—but it is on the Smith line, and Mr. Turney, W. B. Campbell and Gen Trousdale are expected to be there. Do write to Dr. Young, if you received his letter,[2] the reason you did not send us a *lot* of Duncans speeches[3] for *use*. His address is *Dr. J. S. Young*. He is one of our most efficient men.

From *promptings* from *without*—Nashville and elsewhere, attempts are making to give me opposition. As yet, it has failed. Rowen[4] is the man they now have in tow.

Write me forwith and to Mr. Turney. He requests to hear from you forthwith. We wish you to come round soon. We are convinced that Smithville is a most important point, and the time named, the most important.

S. H. LAUGHLIN.

P.S. We need not say to you that every thing here connected with your election, wears a favorable aspect. Your presence, however, will make that much better which is now only good. Good—better—best. We wish to see things in the *best* condition. From Smithville to Sparta is 22 miles.[5] Ridley[6] is present & presents his best wishes.

ALS. DLC–JKP. Addressed to Columbia and marked "Private."

1. Polk's letter not found.

2. Polk received John S. Young's letter of February 17, 1839, which was addressed to Washington. ALS. DLC–JKP. No reply from Polk has been found.

3. See Alfred Balch to Polk, January 26, 1839.

4. Reference probably is to Stokely D. Rowan, a Warren County lawyer.

5. The number *22* has been interlined and the number *25*, crossed out.

6. Bromfield L. Ridley, a lawyer, represented Warren County in the Tennessee House, 1835–37. He moved to Murfreesboro in 1840 and served as judge of the Chancery Court from 1840 until 1861.

TO MEDICUS A. LONG, ET AL.[1]

Gentlemen: Columbia March 23rd 1839

On my arrival at home to day, I received your letter of the 14th Instant,[2] inviting me, on behalf of my "personal and political friends," of the County of Bedford, to partake with them of a public dinner. This renewed evidence of the confidence and regard of my old friends in Bedford, I need scarcely assure you, is received by me, with feelings of the deepest gratitude. I have represented them for fourteen years in Congress, and it is a source of no ordinary gratification to me, to know, that in the discharge of the high and responsible duties, which have devolved upon me, during this long period, they have never, for a moment, withdrawn from me, their confidence, but on the contrary have given me their constant and unwavering support. Often in seasons of high political excitement, when bitterly assailed by others, my late constituents have stood by me and sustained me. To discharge my duty in a manner, to deserve the confidence they had reposed in me, has been at all times my high ambition. And now that I have retired from their service, as their Representative in Congress, to be assured of their continued approbation of my public course, is the highest and most valued testimonial, which I could receive at their hands. I beg you Gentlemen to return to my old friends in Bedford my sincere and profound acknowledgements, for the many acts of kindness both personal and political, which they have shown me, and to assure them that I shall bear them in grateful remembrance, to the latest hour of my life.

It was my intention, before the receipt of the invitation, which you have done me the honor to convey to me, to visit my old constituents in Bedford, at as early a period as I conveniently could; and it will give me pleasure to meet them, at Shelbyville, on the first Monday in April,[3] that being the day which you have designated.

Thanking you, Gentlemen, for this mark of your regard . . . .

JAMES K. POLK

ALS. DLC–JKP. Addressed to Shelbyville. AE on the cover reads, "Returned by my request, not being enabled to attend on Saturday, 6th Apl. 1839."

1. Other addressees included Preston Frazer, Thomas Dean, Wilkins Blanton, Alexander H. Coffey, and Alexander C. Yell. A brother of Granville H. and James Frazer, Preston Frazer practiced medicine in Shelbyville. Blanton is not further identified. A resident of the Wartrace community, Alexander H. Coffey was a brother of Henry B. and Benjamin B. Coffey. Alexander C. Yell was a brother of Archibald Yell, governor of Arkansas.

2. Invitation is from Medicus A. Long et al. to Polk, March 14, 1839. LS. DLC–JKP.

3. On March 28, 1839, Medicus A. Long writes that Polk's acceptance was received "at least a week later than it was expected." Long says that since preparations cannot be made by April 1, the dinner date must be changed to Saturday, April 6. ALS. DLC–JKP. As indicated on the endorsement, Polk was unable to adjust his schedule.

FROM ROBERT ARMSTRONG

Nashville, Tennessee. [March 24, 1839][1]

Armstrong informs Polk that Cannon's circular will be out in a few days; it will announce that the State of Tennessee will not issue bonds to internal improvement companies for an amount greater than the money paid in by the company or greater than the value of the work actually done.[2] Armstrong also advises Polk to campaign at Ross's Landing rather than at Dallas on his tour through Eastern Tennessee.

ALS. DLC–JKP. Addressed to Columbia.

1. Date identified through content analysis and by Armstrong's notation that he wrote on "Sunday Night."

2. Newton Cannon's circular letter of March 25, 1839, was an elaboration of an earlier policy statement governing the issuance of state internal improvements bonds; his original instructions were circulated on September 18, 1838. See Jesse B. Clements to Polk, February 11, 1839.

FROM ROBERT M. BURTON

My Dear Sir Murfreesboro. March 24th 1839

I am still at this Court where I have been for three weeks and will still be detained until perhaps the middle of next week. I am wearied out down in the mouth and home sick: I am therefore in a bad condition to reply to your letter which I had the pleasure to receive by the last mail.[1] I have not yet got my own consent to become a candidate for Congress. It is to me the most unpleasant requisition that could have been made. My political thirst had become satiated and I had hoped to be permitted to pursue the business of my profession and if I have to enter the service it will not be as a volunteer but as a drafted molitiaman who but rarely makes you know a good soldier. My District may truly be called the forlorn hope. The charge will have to be made at the point of the Bayonet with the flints stricken from the guns. I do not anticipate success but by possibility it might be so. There is a darkness of midnight error that covers the people of Wilson and I fear it cannot be dispelled. If therefore I make the sacrifice all selfish considerations will be laid aside and patriotism alone will be the incentive to action. Of my ultimate determination you shall have timely notice. I have been so much engaged in my profession that I am exceedingly deficient in political information. I will therefore need all within your power to furnish. I should desire to trail the hypocrite[2] from his first overt act of apostacy to his entire desertion. The journals of Congress will therefore be indispensable. The memorable session when he appealed so often from the decisions of the chair and when he spoke four Congressional days and then voted against his own proposition will be need[ed]—journal. Book, page, speech, vote. It must all be pointed out, all of which you can do. He will deny every thing unless the proof is at hand to be fastened on him.

On the subject of your tour to East Tenssee and your previous visit to Wilson I am some what at a loss as to the proper course. It strikes me however as the better course—that you had better visit Wilson after the people are prepared for your reception and if I Should become a Candidate, on your return might be the most favorable time. You will have to make at least five speeches in Wilson and from three to five in Davidson. If you go on through Sumner & Smith Jackson & White where Speeches ought last to be made, especialy the three last, on your return march you might speak at Woodbury in Cannon on the Thursday after the second Monday in May—I will be there at Court, then friday at Statesville and Saturday at Carter Hall[3] or Cainsville—but they are all right at Cainsville. Then on Monday 3 of May[4] at Lebanon or you may wait until the first Monday in June when the Court meets there, then at Robert Hallums[5] on Nashville road. Let me know when you expect to make your return march. I feel great confidence in your success. The cause is strong here and growing daily. Remember me to my frnd Dew[6] and tell him to do his duty in these [. . .][7] times. Every Democrat must take his napsack with his possessions—for the campaign and "let us do or die."[8]

R. M. BURTON

ALS. DLC–JKP. Addressed to Columbia.

1. Letter not found.
2. John Bell.
3. Carter Hall was probably the home of William W. Carter, postmaster of Big Springs, Tennessee.
4. Word order reversed; Burton means, "the 3 Monday of May."
5. Reference is to Robert Hallum, sheriff of Wilson County, 1847–48.
6. John H. Dew, a Wilson County lawyer, served as a Democrat in the Tennessee House, 1831–35; he moved to Columbia in 1836 and represented Maury County in the Tennessee House, 1841–43.
7. Word illegible.
8. Quotation is from Robert Burns, *Scots Wha Hae* (1794).

FROM JOHN W. CHILDRESS

Dear Sir

Murfrees Boro March 24 [1839][1]

Enclosed you will find the entire letter of Judge White to Mr Rodgers an extract of which you requested me to procure & send you.[2] Also the distances between places from this to Dandridge in Jefferson County,[3] which I obtained from Col. Yoakum and have no doubt they are correct. You will however see Yoakum at Shelbyville and can satisfy your self more fully of its correctness from him & others. He was not sufficiently conversant with the politics of persons in the route to be able to furnish a list of names to whom notices might be sent; you will therefore have to procure it from some one else. You can also learn from Yoakum the days of the Battalion muster in this County. He has a list, but I forgot to get a copy from him. I recollect However that they commence about the 11th or 12th of April at Col. Ridleys.[4] I would be glad you could arrange it so as to be at one in the lower end of the County & one in the upper, so that you might effectually put to rest the charges of Mr Ready.[5] I understand another of our candidates (Dr Gooch)[6] took occasion to abuse you in a speech yesterday. I presume they have orders from Nashville, & that is to be the plan of operations throughout the State. It should be attended to. Our candidates address the people at Fosterville next Saturday.

The Editor of the Shelbyville 'Star' has in his last paper in answer to something in the Whig paper at this place, spoken of some old tales in relation to the wife of the Editor,[7] which has excited a general indignation here against Haynes. I have no doubt Haynes is an unprincipled wretch who cares not what he says or does. I say this in order to put you on your guard. Have nothing to do with him directly or indirectly. And if our friends at Shelbyville can get rid of him without difficulty, the sooner the better. He will injure the cause wherever he goes.[8]

Tell Sarah we shall expect her on a visit when you come over. We are all in good health.

J. W. CHILDRESS

From Murf Boro to Woodbury 20 miles
Pelham 30
Manchester 18
Jasper 35
Hamilton County—Ross Landing 26
Bradly Cty—Cleaveland 32
McMinn—Calhoun 12
Athens 15
Monroe—Madisonville 15
Blount—Maryville 25
Sevier—Sevierville 30
Jefferson—Dandridge 15

ALS. DLC–JKP. Addressed to Columbia.

1. Erroneously dated "1838"; year identified through content analysis.

2. Neither Polk's request nor Childress' enclosure has been found. On September 17, 1835, White wrote to James A. Whiteside and Samuel R. Rodgers that "as to his quitting the administration and joining the opposition, the idea was fanciful. This can never happen unless the administration abandon the principles upon which the president came into power." Polk used White's letter in gubernatorial speeches to prove that the Republican friends of White in the 1836 election were not opponents of Polk's own political principles. Rodgers practiced law in Knoxville and served in the Tennessee Senate on two occasions, 1855–57 and 1865.

3. Childress listed his mileage estimates at the bottom of his second page.

4. A Revolutionary soldier, Moses Ridley owned about 2,800 acres of land in the northwest corner of Rutherford County. With his nephew, Moses R. Buchanan, he operated one of the early mills in the county. General Jackson was a frequent visitor to Ridley's plantation.

5. Charles Ready had charged Polk with arranging Andrew Kincannon's withdrawal from the congressional race in the Tenth District by procuring a federal appointment for him. Aaron V. Brown thus would have an easier race against Ebenezer Shields. Polk replied that on September 20, 1838, John M. Bell of Pulaski had written of Brown's plans to give up his commission as

Indian agent. As Kincannon was "poor and capable," Bell had urged Polk to have Kincannon appointed in Brown's place. Polk wrote to the War Department on September 22, 1838, asking for Kincannon's appointment; on October 18 Kincannon announced his candidacy for Congress.

6. John C. Gooch, a local physician since 1830, possibly ran for a state or county office; newspaper election reports do not mention Gooch's candidacy.

7. Edwin J. King, Whig editor of the Murfreesboro *Tennessee Telegraph*, married Julia Ledbetter of Rutherford County on January 11, 1837. William Scott Haynes' specific references to Mrs. King, published in the *Star* on March 22, 1839, have not been identified, as relevant issues of the Shelbyville *Western Star* have not been found.

8. According to the Nashville *Republican Banner*'s issues of April 5 and 6, 1839, a duel between King and Haynes occurred in Shelbyville on April 2. Both were injured, but neither was killed. In defense of Mrs. King, several prominent citizens of Murfreesboro and Shelbyville published a card in the Shelbyville *Advocate* on April 2, 1839, exonerating her character and condemning Haynes for his libels.

FROM WILLIAM CONNER

Haywood County, Tennessee. March 25, 1839

Conner reports on politics in the Western District. Having procured copies of Judge White's speeches of 1832 and 1834 against the Bank of the United States,[1] he has employed the arguments therein to good effect against J. B. Ashe, his Whig opponent for the Tennessee Senate. Efforts at public speaking have been more successful than either friends or enemies had expected. Conner discusses election prospects in Tipton, Lauderdale, Haywood, Madison, and Dyer counties. He concludes that both he and Polk will win, but the contest will be close in Tipton, Haywood, and Madison counties. Conner wants to know Polk's itinerary for the Western District so they can campaign together.

ALS. DLC–JKP. Addressed to Columbia.

1. Hugh L. White spoke in the Senate against the Bank of the United States on June 7 and 8, 1832, and on March 24 and 25, 1834.

FROM SAMUEL H. LAUGHLIN

McMinnville, Tennessee. March 27, 1839

Laughlin writes that since arriving home in Winchester, Turney has been very ill. Laughlin relates that he must be at Ross' Landing on business from April 15 to 17, but is determined to join Polk when he enters the Mountain

District. Therefore, Laughlin wishes to know Polk's travel plans and suggests that he be present at the land sales at the Landing on April 16. Half of the people of Ocoee District might be present that day. Polk's friends in Franklin County are also hoping for Polk's appearance at an early date. Laughlin asks Polk to make his visit when Turney can be with him.

ALS. DLC–JKP. Addressed to Columbia and marked "Private."

FROM AARON V. BROWN

Dear Sir Pulaski Friday night. 29 March 1839

I received your last from Nashville[1] on my arrival from Savannah on yesterday evening. In Laurence we have no Democratic candidate for the Legislature but I think one (Davenport)[2] will come out very shortly. We have a majority if we will take care of it. In Wayne *the odds* are fearfully against us say 2 to 1. McDougal, Gallaher & Ross[3] do their best but old Andy Brown is very popular & came out for Clay warmly in his address at Court. In Hardin there are 4 candidates for the lower house—2 Whigs & 2 Democrats—McGinnis[4] is the strong Democrat & will be elected. Alexander Hardin[5] the lawyer came out for Clay. I made good speeches in all & the work goes on rather slowly but hopefully. Write to Esqr. Harber [in] Savannah & say that the fee in the old case of the Justices of Harden county against the Old Clerk[6] is discharged & what has become of the note. He only recollects that the note has never been returned. If you destroyd it say so & if you dont know any thing only say that you have no claim for the fee. He is with us & I promised to get you to write that much *& as much more as you please.*

It is impossible that I should come to see you. Shields is here & next week being county court week & Battallion musters I must have an eye to him. I want to understand the particulars of the last day, when he tried to get up his occupant Bill—what hour it was and what chance he must have known there was of getting it thro. Where *you* were & if not *in the chair* why not, & if not how another being in your place could have prejudiced the Bill. Could you not have spoken or voted, as well in one case as the other. Shields has been trying to prejudice you with the occupants in some way on this point. But I cannot give the particulars.[7] A letter to Wright,[8] giving all the particulars & any thing shewing your wish for the success of the measure would be serviceable hereabouts. This you could do in a general letter without saying any thing about Shields statements.

What was the outline of the Bill to prevent & punish defaulters?

Where was it lost & how did S. vote upon it? Where was S on the vote of thanks?[9] What views do you intend to exhibit of the Swartwout Case? Neil S. Brown & Gordon[10] are the Giles candidates. Democrats none & who will offer doub[t]ful. Wright & Tom Martin[11] will be pressed to come [into] it, but I doubt whether either will offer. Buford & Harney[12] have declined. Wretched policy—& more Wretched indifference.

I may be here on Monday if Shields stays or we may be at Fayetteville. Where was Shields on the vote to reconsider the rejection of the graduation land Bill?[13] did he dodge? Write me often & fully.

A. V. Brown

ALS. DLC–JKP. Probably addressed to Columbia.

1. Letter not found.

2. Thomas D. Davenport, an early Giles County settler, moved to Lawrenceburg in Lawrence County about 1821, where he engaged in farming, cotton manufacturing, and brick-masonry. He was an unsuccessful Democratic candidate for Congress in 1833, but subsequently served two terms in the Tennessee House, 1835–37 and 1843–45.

3. Archibald G. McDougal, David Gallaher, and Jesse S. Ross. North Carolina born, McDougal studied law under Eleventh Circuit Judge Valentine D. Barry of Hardeman County and engaged in legal practice there for two years. In 1840 he moved to Waynesboro. An influential Democrat, he represented Hardin, Wayne, Lawrence, and Hickman counties in the Tennessee Senate, 1845–47. In 1852 McDougal moved to Savannah and represented Hardin, McNairy, and Hardeman counties in the Senate, 1857–59. Gallaher, an early Wayne County settler who resided near Shoal Creek, served as postmaster of Houston from 1837 until 1840.

4. Christopher H. McGinnis, born in Virginia and reared in North Carolina, moved to Tennessee about 1822. He opened the first hotel at Madisonville and served on the Monroe County jury in 1830. Having moved to Hardin County during the 1830's, McGinnis won election as a Democrat to the Tennessee House, 1839–47.

5. A prominent lawyer at Savannah, Alexander M. Hardin was attorney general and circuit court judge of his district.

6. Reference is probably to Samuel Harbour, a member of the Hardin County Court in 1820. The suit has not been identified.

7. On the evening of March 3, 1839, with Speaker Polk presiding, Representative William J. Graves moved that the rules of the House be suspended for purposes of taking up the Tennessee land bill, passed by the Senate. Shields voted for suspension of the rules, but the motion failed to receive the necessary two-thirds majority.

8. Archibald Wright, a Pulaski lawyer, was named a presidential elector on the Van Buren ticket in 1836. A Democrat, Wright represented Giles County in the Tennessee House, 1847–49. Isham Harris appointed him to fill a va-

cancy on the Tennessee Supreme Court in 1858. No letter from Polk to Wright has been found.

9. On February 21, 1839, the Senate passed and transmitted to the House a bill "for securing the public money in the hands of collectors and agents of the Government, and the punishment of defaulters." The House took no action on this measure; thus Shields did not vote on the question. On the resolution of thanks, Shields abstained.

10. Neil S. Brown and Thomas K. Gordon. Brown practiced law in Pulaski from 1835 until he moved to Nashville in 1847. He served as a presidential elector for White in 1836; represented Giles County in the Tennessee House, 1837–39; failed as a Whig candidate for Congress in 1843; and in 1847 won election to the governorship of Tennessee. He was appointed by Zachary Taylor as minister to Russia, 1850–53. Having joined the Know Nothing party, he was Speaker of the Tennessee House, 1855–57. Gordon, an early Giles County settler, farmed near Richland Creek. He served two terms in the Tennessee House, 1829–31 and 1835–37.

11. Archibald Wright and Thomas Martin. Martin was a Giles County businessman associated with the firm of Meredith and Martin, and later with Martin and Topp. Subsequently, he became president of the Louisville and Nashville Railroad. A Democrat and supporter of Jackson and Polk, Martin was offered a position as secretary of the treasury in Polk's administration, but the offer was declined.

12. James Buford and Harney. A successful farmer, Buford served as sheriff of Giles County, 1810–14, and represented that county as a Democrat in the Tennessee House, 1839–43. Harney is not identified.

13. On January 22, 1839, the House voted to table a bill to reduce and graduate the price of public lands. Shields voted against the motion to table; on the following day he voted for a motion to reconsider the previous day's vote.

TO SAMUEL H. LAUGHLIN

My Dear Sir Columbia March 29th 1839

I shall set out on my tour through the state in the course of a few days. I will be at Murfreesborough on Thursday the 11th of April, at Lebanon in Wilson on Saturday the 13th, at Carthage in Smith on Monday the 15th, at Sparta on Wednesday the 17th, at McMinnville on Thursday the 18th, at Winchester on Saturday the 20th and then cross the Mountain, and visit every County in East Tennessee. I must take Fentress, Overton, Jackson and Sumner on my return. Making but one speech in each County, it will take me until the 12th of June to reach Gallatin on my return, which will throw me full as late as I wish it to be, for the canvass of the balance of the state. I cannot I fear visit DeKalb—Cannon or Coffee. If I do it must be, after my return from

East Tennessee. Turney when I last saw him, was very anxious, that I should address the people at Hillsborough. I have written to him,[1] that the only opportunity I will have to do so, will be on the 19th as I pass from McMinnville to Winchester, and that if he thought it important, he might make an appointment for that day, but to have it understood in advance, that I could only remain a few hours at that place. You and he can do as you think best on the subject. I wish you, to give notice that I will be at McMinnville on the 18th and that I would be pleased to meet and address the people of Warren on that day. I hope to see you at McMinnville, when I can confer fully with you.

James K. Polk

P.S. I conclude to send you a list of my appointments,[2] in several of the Counties in East Tennessee, in which I have scarcely a personal acquaintance, in the hope, that you may have it in your power, to write to your friends—and cause the notices to be given. If you think it necessary have notices printed and forwarded to the several Counties.[3] Dr. Young of your town to whom I will write is well acquainted in that part of the state, and will I know assist you, in giving the notices. J.K.P.
I think it best *not,* to publish the appointments in the newspapers. It might have the appearance of ostentation, and more over I am wholly unapprized of Governor C.'s movements. See Mr. Ford[4] and have printed notices struck; and he may if he chooses, insert in his paper the time I will be in Warren, and the Counties immediately adjoining. I will cause the same thing to be done at Athens & Jonesborough. J.K.P.

ALS. NBuHi. Addressed to McMinnville.

1. Letter not found.
2. Enclosure not found.
3. Polk initially ended his postscript here with a brief closing and his initials, but subsequently crossed them out and appended another sentence as well as a second postscript.
4. John W. Ford, a Polk supporter, was editor of the McMinnville *Central Gazette* from 1835 until 1842; he was also postmaster at McMinnville during that same period of time.

FROM DENISON OLMSTED[1]

My Dear Sir, Yale College March 29, 1839

A slip from a newspaper containing an obituary notice of your lamented brother Samuel, brought me the first intelligence of his death. Although, from what I had previously heard, I had no reason to expect his recovery, yet it was hard to think that one who was recently present with us in all the vigor of youth, & in the prime of man hood, now lies beneath the clods of the valley, and has entered upon the solemn retributions of eternity.

Having myself parted with a wife, a sister, & a child, all bound to my heart by the strongest ties, I can enter into the feelings of your family as your dear brother breathed out his soul in the arms of his mother. Affecting and touching as the scene must have been, yet how truly consoling to witness his peace of mind in the very moment of death. Philosophy has in some few instances produced a passive resignation, but the christian religion only can inspire such hope and triumph in the hour of dissolution.

At a religious meeting of the students, I read the account of the closing scenes of your brother's life. The recital was listened to with the deepest interest, and some who knew him intimately shed tears—all appeared ready to say, let my last end be like his!

Though I have never had the pleasure to be acquainted with your honored mother, I beg you to offer her my respectful sympathies. I know there is but one adequate source of consolation for trials like hers, and of that I am assured she has experienced the unspeakable benefit.

We are admonished, my Dear Sir, when the Destroyer comes so near to us, (as Tully was at the sudden decease of his friend Crassus*), of the fallacy of our hopes and the uncertainty of our aims; but your brother's happy frame of mind in his last moments open to us sources of support & consolation of which Tully never knew. May we both be so happy as to know them. Doubtless we shall prize them as infinitely better than all the honor of this world.

DENISON OLMSTED

*O fallacem hominum spem, fragilemque fortunam, et inanes nostras contentiones. quae in medio spatio saepe franguntur, et corruunt, et ante in ipso cursu obruuntur, quam portum conspicere potuerunt.[2]

P.S. Your brother's death has been announced in our papers, so that it is generally known to his friends at the North.

ALS. DLC–JKP. Addressed to Columbia.

1. Olmsted, an instructor at Yale College, had acted as faculty adviser of Samuel W. Polk.

2. Marcus Tullius Cicero, on the death of Lucius Crassus, in *De Oratore* 3.2.7. This passage has been translated as follows: "Ah, how treacherous are men's hopes, how insecure their fortunes! How hollow are our endeavours, which often break down and come to grief in the middle of the race, or are shipwrecked in full sail before they have been able to sight the harbour!" H.

Rackham (trans.), *Cicero De Oratore,* in T. E. Page et al., eds., *Loeb Classical Library* (2 vols.; Cambridge: Harvard University Press, 1932), II, p. 7.

FROM ROBERT ARMSTRONG

Dear Sir Nashville 30h March [1839][1]

I take [a] moment to say to you That Burton *Says* he will authorize me to announce him on Monday & perhaps by the mail on Tuesday for Wednesday['s] paper. I have never laboured to effect any thing as I have this. Our County Ticket I got settled to day,

Craighead[2] Senate
Col Robt Weakley & L. P. Cheatham.[3]

I have an arrangement to make for Cheatham, I will succeed. And I will try and meet you either at Home or Murfreesboro. Wilson & Smith [counties] shall be put in a Blaze. You know how Allen of Ohio Carried that State in a Storm, and uproar.

Harris could with [but] great difficulty be kept from taking Nor[v]ell by the Nose to day. I thought it best that he should not *now,* tho the fellow deserved it. It was in relation to an Editorial in his yesterday's paper,[4] growing out of what was said by the Editor of the Shelbyville Star.[5] Write me.

R. ARMSTRONG

ALS. DLC–JKP. Addressed to Shelbyville.

1. Year identified through content analysis.
2. David Craighead, a wealthy Nashville lawyer, served as a Democrat in the Tennessee Senate, 1835–37.
3. A Nashville lawyer, Leonard P. Cheatham was a Democrat, while most of his family, including General Richard Cheatham of Robertson County, were Whigs.
4. In an editorial in the *Nashville Whig* of March 29, 1839, Caleb C. Norvell referred to J. George Harris as an irresponsible stranger and "a nobody knows who." Norvell's attack was in response to an editorial Harris wrote in the *Nashville Union* of March 27, 1839; in that editorial Harris condemned Norvell's passive submission to charges against Norvell in the Shelbyville *Western Star.* See John W. Childress to Polk, March 24, 1839.
5. William Scott Haynes.

TO J. G. M. RAMSEY

My Dear Sir Columbia March 30th 1839

I will set out in the course of a few days, on a tour through the State, and herewith transmit to you a list of the times and places, at which I would be pleased to meet and address the people.[1] I have to request the favour of yourself, Genl. Anderson and other friends, to cause the proper notices to be given: especially in *Monroe, Blount, Knox, Sevier, Jefferson, Cocke, Greene, Grainger, Claiborne, Campbell, Anderson, Roane,* and *Morgan.* I have written to my friends at Athens and Jonesborough, requesting them to give the notices in those parts of the State. I will send you by the next mail a few printed notices, and request, if you think it necessary, that you will cause others to be printed and circulated. I give you a list of the Counties, times & places &c. in East Tennessee. I shall set out from home on the 8th of April and visit a few of the Counties in Middle Tennessee before I enter East Tennessee.

Things are looking well in this part of the state, and my information from the West, is of the most encouraging character.

I have prepared an address to the people of the State, which is now ready for the press, but cannot be printed before the last of next week.[2]

James K. Polk

ALS. NhHi–Dorothy Whitney Coll. of Presidential Autographs. Addressed to Mecklenburg, Tennessee.

1. List not found.

2. A twenty-eight page pamphlet entitled "Address of James K. Polk to the People of Tennessee" was printed at Columbia and dated April 3, 1839. It was published serially in the *Nashville Union* on April 10, 12, and 15, 1839. In the address Polk presented a history of U.S. political parties and set forth his political principles on both national and state issues.

FROM JOSEPH H. TALBOT

Dear Sir Jackson April 1 1839

I learn you have by this time reached home and I presume will very shortly open the Spring Campaign. I regret nearly all our spring Courts are over. I would suggest that you commence at Hickman, from thence to Perry, thence Lexington [in] Henderson County, thence Mifflin in the corner of Henderson, so as to reach this place during our Circuit Court which commences the 4th Monday of this month. You will then want a few days rest and we can make other appointments. Perry, Henderson, this county[1] and Haywood may be considered the Hot beds of Whiggery in this country, owing to the popular men heretofore having subscribed to that faith. Marr[2] you will have learnt is our candidate for Congress in this district. I regret to say in the South[3] we have no candidate as yet. W C Dunlap I expect is the only chance. The candidates for the Legislature are generally out, and from present appearances we shall carry a majority of the members to the Legislature. Owing to the folly of Huntsman & Martin we have as yet, no candidate for the Lower house from this county. Lyon who I consider the most thorough going "whig" in all the country, has induced them to believe he will not be a "party man," and will take no side in the Senatorial election, should that subject be brought before the Legislature, but will vote as he may be *instructed.* If I can get oposition to him, I will have it, but the prospect now is dull. I hope when you are here, something may be done. If you make the appointments I suggest you had better send notices by trusty men to Hickman and Perry and I will send them to Henderson. Please let me hear from you as early as convenient. More when I see you.

Jos. H Talbot

ALS. DLC–JKP. Addressed to Columbia.

1. Madison County.

2. A lawyer and wealthy landowner, George Washington Lent Marr was attorney general for West Tennessee, 1807–9, and attorney general for the Fifth Judicial District, 1809–13. He served in Congress, 1817–19, and in the Tennessee House, 1843–45, as a Whig.

3. The congressional district south of Jackson encompassed Tipton, Shelby, Fayette, Hardeman, McNairy, Henderson, and Perry counties.

FROM JOHN H. BILLS

My dear Sir. Bolivar, T Apl. 2, 1839

I have delayed addressing you until the termination of our Circuit Court in the hope that I could be Enabled to give you the information desired as to who would be *our* Congressional & Senatorial Candidates. Even yet I am unable to do so, nor have we a Candidate of any *Creed* yet in this County for the House of Representatives. Truly we are a cold set of polititians.

Coe has just returned from Texas. I have heard nothing from him;

save only the sight of a letter from him to Gen Neely saying that he was overwhelmed with his private business & wholly disinclined to *run for any thing,* that if he Gen Neely would run for the Senate, that he Coe would at once State to the people through the "Western World" [1] that he would not run for that office & thus give the field to Neely. To which Gen Neely replied promptly that he could not consent by reason of *his* private affairs to Canvas the three Counties.[2] How matters will settle down I cannot tell, but will venture to predict that *Dunlap* will run for Congress—Coe for Senate & Neely for Rep. The Whigs manifest Equeel lethergy, they have no Senatorial Candidate, nor for the House for this County. It is wholly impossible for me to tell or Even guess what are Dunlaps prospects. That he is inclined to offer I feel assured & if he does (which will be determined at Purdy next week) I have hopes for his success and I think it quite posible Coe & Neely might have no opposition. Especially Neely.

Your friends Seem to Entertain Every Confidence of success in your Election. I trust you will have health & strength to sustain you through the Canvas. You have troubled the waters allready & before August will have the *Current* of publick opinion as it Should be & would allways have been but for the intrigues of a few individuals in and about Nashville.

JNO. H. BILLS

ALS. DLC–JKP. Delivered by "Mr. Harris."

1. *Western World and Memphis Banner of the Constitution.*
2. Fayette, Hardeman, and Shelby counties.

FROM J. GEORGE HARRIS

Dear Sir, Nashville Apl 2. 1839

I have got that pamphlet under way.[1] It will make either 24 or 32 pp. size of Benton's Speech.[2] For 10,000 copies every eight pp. will cost about $100. We can probably screw it into 24 or make it 32. Which do you think best? The first eight pp. are in type—and as Mr. Smith cannot spare the type very long from the newspaper, and I cannot get time to go to Columbia, or even to keep the type standing 3 or four days, I have ventured to put the first four to press, with the advice and consent of the Genl,[3] Donelson & McLemore, I shall send you a proof of it at Murfreesboro' on the 11th if not before at Columbia.

I find I was mistaken in supposing you would return here immediately before commencing your tour.

I have your idea of the pamphlet *clearly*, now—and shall proceed with [*it*] as speedily as possible. I wish you would send me Luke Lea's Letter,[4] as also any other document in your possession fit for the book.

As I could procure no one to spend three or four days in copying the documents for the pamphlet I have concluded to publish the matter in the Union first,[5] and then transfer the type into the pamphlet.

I shall expect a letter from you every mail until the day of the election.[6] How many pamphlets shall we print? Answer by next mail, if possible.

J GEO HARRIS

ALS. DLC–JKP. Addressed to Columbia.

1. Harris anonymously published *A Looking Glass for the Federal Whig Leaders in Tennessee, or Facts for the People*, a 24-page campaign pamphlet examining questions of national and state politics from the Democratic viewpoint. Undated, the pamphlet appeared in early June of 1839. Harris identified himself as the author of the pamphlet in the *Nashville Union* of July 1, 1839. Two other letters from Harris to Polk, dated March 25 and 26, 1839, discuss the compilation and printing of this campaign pamphlet. ALsS. DLC–JKP. Polk also received a letter from Joel M. Smith, dated April 4, 1839, in which Smith stated, "I have commenced the pamphlet you spoke of, and would be glad to know what number you wish printed." ALS. DLC–JKP. Also see Robert Armstrong to Polk, June 4, 1839.

2. Not identified.

3. Probably Robert Armstrong.

4. A Democrat, Lea served two terms in the U.S. House, 1833–37, and a partial term as Tennessee's secretary of state, 1837–39. On January 1, 1835, Lea and seven other members of the Tennessee congressional delegation wrote a letter to Cave Johnson concerning Hugh L. White's candidacy for the 1836 presidential nomination. Johnson had refused to endorse White's candidacy. For the text of that letter, see the *Nashville Union*, June 19, 1839.

5. The pamphlet was not published in the tri-weekly issues of the *Nashville Union*.

6. There is no further extant correspondence between Polk and Harris before the gubernatorial election on August 1, 1839.

FROM WILLIAM G. CHILDRESS

Dr Sir Locust Grove[1] April 3d 1839

Your favor of the 30th ult[2] has been duly recd., also the accompanying documents[3] for which I tender you my sincere thanks. On monday last Col. Gentry & myself occupied the greater portion of the day.[4] The collection was great. I had to lead the way, which generally gives an advantage to the opposition, But on this occasion turned out well. My friends claim a complete triumph, his are divided. I can assure you of one thing, I added many new members to the church.

In the morning I set out for Rutherford but will return on Sunday with the expectation of having your company at my house on Tuesday evening as also cousin Sarah. When you will be on your way to Murfreesborough, I will go with you. I am anxious that we have an interview upon the subject in which we are both engaged; my competitor will not go to Rutherford. He will remain here and attend the Williamson Musters.[5] Nothing more until I see you.

W. G. Childress

ALS. DLC–JKP. Addressed to Columbia.

1. Not identified further. Childress posted his letter at Franklin, Tennessee.

2. Letter not found.

3. Enclosures not found. In a letter to Polk, dated February 3, 1839, Childress had acknowledged receipt of extracts from the House *Journal* of 1816 and had requested a copy of the Treasury Department's 1838 budget estimates. ALS. DLC–JKP.

4. On Monday, April 1, 1839, congressional and assembly candidates addressed the people of Williamson County at Franklin.

5. The militia muster was scheduled for the second Saturday in April.

TO ROBERT B. REYNOLDS

Dear Sir Columbia April 3rd 1839

I expect to set out in the course of a few days on a visit to the Eastern part of the State, and herewith send you a list of the *times* and *places*, at which I propose to meet and address the people.[1] May I ask the favour of you, to cause the proper notices to be given in Knox and the adjoining Counties. I have written to Dr. Ramsey, and asked of him a similar favour.[2] In many of the Counties in East Tennessee, I have but a very limited personal acquaintance and must depend on yourself and other friends to give the proper notices for me. I wish you especially to cause notice to be given in *Sevier*, *Jefferson*, *Cocke*, *Grainger*, *Claiborne*, *Campbell* and *Anderson*. My object is to meet the people as generally as possible, and if deemed necessary, I wish my friends to have printed notices struck and forwarded to the several Counties. I hope to see you at Knoxville on the 8th of May.

JAMES K. POLK

ALS. NHi. Addressed to Knoxville.

1. List not found.
2. See Polk to J. G. M. Ramsey, March 30, 1839.

FROM ROBERT M. BURTON

Lebanon, Tennessee. April 4, 1839

Burton announces his decision to run for Congress. He requests that Polk campaign in the district and supply information about Bell's congressional record, Boston speech,[1] and support for Clay. Burton reports that the Democrats are gaining in Wilson County and suggests that Polk stay at Mabry's Tavern[2] when he campaigns in Lebanon. Mabry is sheriff and his influence might be enlisted to help the party's cause. In a postscript Burton urges that more copies of the *Nashville Union* be distributed free of charge in his district.

ALS. DLC–JKP. Addressed to Columbia.

1. On November 10, 1837, John Bell, a guest of honor of the Boston Whigs, delivered at Fanueil Hall a speech that was highly critical of the Van Buren administration. Bell claimed that Tennesseans were ready to unite with their New England brethren against the Democrats.
2. Sheriff from 1836 to 1839, Benjamin G. Mabry operated the Lebanon Inn, which he owned in partnership with his son, S. W. Mabry.

FROM WILLIAM ALLEN

My Dear Sir Chillicothe April 6. 1839

I find on my return, the whole Democracy, in these parts, firm and erect, nor do I think it will be possible for the enemy to shake us, in our position.

I write to enquire, how you are coming on? Will you be elected? Will it be a close contest? You must not be beaten if it be possible to avoid that disaster. You are too valuable a man to the Country and the party, to be lost.

You will see that Biddle has resigned his Presidency of the Bank.[1] The cause is as yet unknown here. Perhaps he sees that his political and cotton speculations must bring his Bank to the ground, and has thus got out of the way of its falling ruins. At all events, this is a move that will produce important consequences. Give my best respects to Mrs. Polk.

W ALLEN

ALS. DLC–JKP. Addressed to Columbia.

1. Nicholas Biddle presided over the Bank of the United States from 1822 until its dissolution in 1836. Having rechartered the bank under Pennsylvania law, he served as president until March 29, 1839.

TO SARAH C. POLK

Dear Sarah Franklin April 8th 1839

I find that I neglected to bring with me, two papers which I may need. The first is a letter from *Samuel Martin*[1] of Campbell's Station received last winter, containing inclosed a letter from governor Cannon to him. You will find it, I think, in my trunk in a file of letters in the tray of the trunk. The other paper is a statement of the votes—in the Governor's election in 1835 between Carroll and Cannon, and in 1837 between Armstrong and Cannon. This paper you will find in a bundle of papers in the top of my trunk. It was forwarded to me last winter by Danl Graham.[2] I wish you to envelope them both in strong paper, well waxed, and direct them to me at *McMinnville* where they will reach me on the 18th. In having my Addresses directed, do not fail to have the lists for Williamson and Rutherford filled. It is thought here that they will be very important for this county.

JAMES K. POLK

ALS. DLC–JKP. Addressed to Columbia.

1. Irish born, Martin first settled in Jefferson County, but then moved in 1823 to Knox County. A successful businessman and prominent Democrat, he was considered one of the most influential men in East Tennessee. Martin's letter has not been found. However, see Samuel Martin to Polk, December 3, 1838, and Polk to Samuel Martin, December 18, 1838.

2. A resident of Murfreesboro, Graham was Tennessee's secretary of state, 1818–30, and state comptroller, 1836–43. Graham's letter and enclosures have not been found.

TO SARAH C. POLK

My Dear Sarah Lebanon April 14th 1839

I requested Mary[1] to write you from Murfreesborough, and this is the first moment I have had the opportunity to do so, since I left Nashville. Cannon has accompanied me this far, but returns to day to Nashville. We addressed an immense crowd here on yesterday. He and myself got on very harmoniously, except that we differ politically. Bell attended on yesterday, and after Cannon and myself were done, and at 5½ O'Clock, took the stump in a rage of passion; attack me in his first sentence; spoke in the grove until the sun set, and adjourned to finish in the court house after supper. Before the crowd dispersed in the grove I rose and made a short reply hurling back in his teeth the assault he had made; and strange as it may seem, (being in Wilson)—during the delivery and at the close of my reply, so clearly was he put in the wrong & so complete was the victory over him, that, the shouts of applause were long and tremendous. His own friends, many of them were greatly dissatisfied & many of them disgusted at his course. After supper he commenced speaking in the Court House, and finding the effect which his violent course in the grove had produced, attempted to explain it away, and said nothing further that was personal to me or required a reply. He spoke until after 11 O'Clock at night. Burton replied in one of the happiest effects I have ever heard from any man. The day was clearly ours & our opponents knew it. Bell did more for us than I and all our friends could have done. A great revolution in public sentiment has taken place in Wilson. I have not time to give you further particulars. Col. Price[2] of this place whom you saw at Washington a year or two ago starts this morning for Nashville & Columbia & promises me to call and give you all the particulars. I am in good health & fine spirits. I go to Carthage to day.

I learned at Nashville that my boxes had gone out. If they contain Ho. Doc No. 111 and Senate Document No. 503,[3] I wish you to send them all to Genl. Armstrong at Nashville, except one copy of Doc. No. 503—which I wish you to give to Jonas E. Thomas for himself and Watterson. Our people must not hesitate longer, but go at once into the support of Watterson. I hope my Documents[4] have been sent off; send at least 6000 to Genl. Armstrong, and more if they are not wanted at Columbia; their early circulation is important. You know where I will be from day to day. Do write me often.

JAMES K. POLK

ALS. DLC–JKP. Addressed to Columbia.

1. Mary Childress, orphaned daugher of Sarah Polk's brother, Anderson, was reared by her paternal grandmother, Elizabeth Whitsitt (Mrs. Joel) Childress.

2. Virginia born, M. Andrew Price moved to Sumner County, Tennessee, and then to Lebanon, Wilson County. Price, a merchant and planter, became a stagecoach operator and held lucrative mail contracts in Middle Tennessee. He supported Hugh L. White in 1836 and served one term in the Tennessee House, 1837–39.

3. Both documents were reported by the Treasury Department during the third session of the Twenty-fifth Congress. House Document No. 111 was a list of public defaulters; Senate Document No. 503 was a statement of the amount of revenue lost by the government through nonpayment of duty bonds since 1789.

4. Reference is to Polk's "Address to the People of Tennessee" of April 3, 1839. See Polk to J. G. M. Ramsey, March 30, 1839.

TO SARAH C. POLK

My Dear Wife Sparta April 17th 1839

I met and addressed a large assemblage of the people at Carthage on Monday. I shall get a better vote in that county, than either Carroll or Armstrong did, though it is one of the weakest counties for me in the state. I stayed all night at Col. Allen's[1] and reached here last night much fatigued, having rode 45 miles. To day I shall address the people here. I learned at Nashville that my boxes had been sent out to Columbia. I wish you to send the small box directed to *Richard Alexander*[2] to Nashville and have it left with *Samuel Seay*[3] for him. I saw Mr. Alexander at Carthage and told him, I would have it sent to *Seay* for him.

I think I requested you, in my letter from Franklin,[4] to send me the statement of the votes at the two last elections for governor, which was forwarded to me last winter by *Daniel Graham*. If you have not sent it, you will find it, I think in a bundle of papers in the top of my trunk. It contains a statement of the number of votes given for each candidate in each county in the state. I shall probably not write you again until I get to Winchester.

James K. Polk

ALS. DLC–JKP. Addressed to Columbia.

1. Robert Allen, born in Virginia, moved to Carthage, Tennessee, in 1804, where he practiced law and engaged in business. He commanded a regiment of Tennessee volunteers under Jackson in the War of 1812. Having served many

years as clerk of the Smith County Court, 1804–19, Allen won election as a Democrat to the U.S. House, where he served from 1819 to 1829.

2. While in Washington Polk agreed to deliver on his return to Tennessee a small package from James M. Saunders of Warrenton, Virginia, to Richard Alexander, a resident of Carthage. The box from Saunders was delivered to Polk in Washington by Enoch Tucker. Concerning this favor Polk received two letters from Saunders, January 22, 1839, and February 4, 1839. ALsS. DLC–JKP. Polk received one letter from Tucker on February 9, 1839. ALS. DLC–JKP.

3. Manufacturer, merchant, and steamboat owner, Seay had a long business career in Nashville. He was best known as a wholesale grocer and commission merchant.

4. Polk to Sarah C. Polk, April 8, 1839.

TO SARAH C. POLK

My Dear Sarah Winchester April 20th 1839

I have not heard a syllable from you since I left home, except your note accompanying the Documents sent to me at McMinnville.[1] I met a very large assemblage of the people at McMinnville on Thursday; addressed another at Hillsborough in Coffee County on yesterday, and to day at this place I addressed a larger number of persons, than I have met [at] any other point. Governor *Cannon* joined me at McMinnville, and has been with me until this evening when he left for Nashville. My majorities in Warren, Coffee and Franklin will be very large, my friends think 4 or 5 to 1. In White, where the opposition had two years ago, a majority of nearly 3 to 1, I shall equal if not beat my opponent. The prospect thus far is most encouraging. I have had a hard week's service, addressing the people every day except one, and on that day riding 45 miles. It is the hardest week I will have.

I promised *Col. R. M. Burton* of Lebanon to write to you to forward to him some documents—viz: *The National Intelligencer*, containing an Editorial article[2] for the call of the Whig Convention at Harrisburg in Decr. next.[3] You will find it on the file for May 1838. I wish you to search among my pamphlet speeches which you will find in one of the presses among the loose papers, and send to Burton all the speeches made by *Bell*, which you may find. I believe I requested you in my letter from Sparta to send to Genl. Armstrong such copies of Senate Document No. 503. as might come on in the boxes. Do not fail to send Mr Alexander's box to Mr *Seay* of Nashville.[4] I go tomorrow to Jackson, where I will be on Monday.

James K. Polk

ALS. DLC–JKP. Addressed to Columbia.

1. Sarah C. Polk's note has not been found. See James K. Polk to Sarah C. Polk, April 8, 1839.

2. A leading Washington newspaper from 1800 until after the Civil War, the *National Intelligencer* was edited by Joseph Gales, Jr., and William W. Seaton. On April 4, 1838, the *Intelligencer* called for a national Whig convention; the editorial did not specify either date or location of the proposed meeting.

3. A Whig national nominating convention met at Harrisburg, Pennsylvania, on December 4, 1839. Committed to union and harmony, delegates nominated William Henry Harrison for president and John Tyler for vice-president.

4. See James K. Polk to Sarah C. Polk, April 14 and 17, 1839.

FROM M. D. COOPER & CO.

New Orleans, Louisiana. April 22, 1839

The company acknowledges receipt of Polk's draft in favor of Walker & Johnson[1] for the balance of funds in his account. Since Polk's additional shipment of cotton has not yet been received, the current balance is against him. If more cotton is received, Cooper & Co. will apply the proceeds of the sale to cover the draft.

LS. DLC–JKP. Addressed to Columbia.

1. Draft not found. John B. Johnson and Samuel P. Walker were proprietors of a general store in Columbia; the firm was styled "Johnson & Walker."

TO SARAH C. POLK

My Dear Wife Jasper April 22nd 1839

I write [*sic*] you from Winchester,[1] addressed to Columbia. I crossed the mountain on yesterday, and am as you will perceive in East Tennessee. If the people attend I will meet them at this place to day. Thus far on my tour the prospects are even better than I anticipated they would. I shall carry majorities, in all the Counties, (and in some of them, very large ones) in which I have been, since I left Rutherford, except in Wilson & Smith, and there, we have a decided gain. *White* has been considered a strong opposition County. In that County, I shall get at least an equal vote. Some of my friends think, a decided majority. *Tur-*

ney's re-election is beyond doubt. I shall expect to hear from you at *Athens* & Knoxville. I will write you, whenever I can get a moment's leisure to do so.

James K. Polk

ALS. DLC–JKP. Addressed to Murfreesboro.

1. See Polk to Sarah C. Polk, April 20, 1839.

TO SARAH C. POLK

My Dear Wife Ross's Landing Hamilton Cty. April 28th 1839

I have but a moment to say to you, that I am here on my tour & am in good health, though somewhat fatigued. The prospects thus far in East Tennessee, are better than I anticipated, and every where I have been my friends inform me, we are gaining ground. I have not had very large assemblages of the people to address, though I have been in thinly populated Counties. If I do not write you often you must attribute it to the fact that wherever I go, I am surrounded by company, and have scarcely a moment to do so. Say to my friends that I am much pleased with my prospects thus far.

James K. Polk

ALS. DLC–JKP. Addressed to Murfreesboro.

FROM SAMUEL H. LAUGHLIN

Dear Sir, McMinnville, April 30, 1839

Our court here did not adjourn until yesterday. So I have been confined at home, but with the daily opportunity of seeing men from every part of the county. Warren, including all within her old lines, will vote from 2500 to 3000. No man of cool sense here now pretends that Governor Cannon will get over 400 of the number. Warren proper can vote 2300—give him 300 of these, and your majority will be 1800.[1] It cannot be less. This result corresponds with Dr. Young's cooler judgment.

Turney is now in the upper counties, Overton &c. Dibrell[2] has been here within the week but returned home without going below. My candid opinion is, he will not run the race out. His paper at Sparta[3] is filled with low abuse of Turney, which does no harm and disgusts all decent men. I have advised Ford, and the Highlander at Winchester,[4] to take little or no notice of it.

I have directed Ford's last two papers to be sent you at Knoxville. I gave the imperfect account of our day here, in the haste and hurry of a few moments snatched from the confusion of the court and babbling of clients.

Dr. Rucker[5] wrote me last week, that Cannon's man Friday, who followed him here, is the Editor[6] of the Murfreesboro Telegraph; and that he had boasted after he got home, that he had *compelled* you to apologize to him on the spot for attacking from the stand here.[7] His letter to the Banner[8] is a lie from end to end, and his account in his own paper,[9] in which he states that you apologized to him is worse. On receipt of Dr. Ruckers letter I suggested the propriety of correction to Robert A. Campbell, Col. Paris, Maj. Adcock &c.[10] The result is the *card* you will find in Ford's paper of yesterday.[11] Dr. Rucker requested me to enclose you his letter. This letter and the paper you will receive,[12] will do as well or better. The signers of the card rank among our first citizens, and the number might have been incrased from 50 to 100, if it had been deemed necessary. Campbell, a lawyer, a nephew of the late Thos. Hopkins,[13] a scholler & gentleman, wrote the card. So we go.

My embrio competitor, Edmondson,[14] is gradually backing out. I have got Kincannon to manage Morford,[15] and he has managed the Dr. Ridley has assisted me; and E's retreat leaves me a month to go to Pikeville and Ross Landing, by which I shall make in Chancery fees, from occupants and Town Commissioners, fees enough to pay the expense of my campaign, and also so as to compensate for the loss of time in the fall at Nashville in some degree—if I go there.

When you reach Blountsville, or meet McClellan and my old friend Dr. Dulaney[16] of Sullivan, present them my respects. I have kinfolks in Sullivan, Pembertons and Kings. If you meet any of them, give them my good wishes. They are democrats I think, and will like to hear from me. Present my best regards to my cousin McGaughey of Greene. I wish to God he had health to run the race with Carter. He used to be a main man in helping us through with our Jackson and anti-bank resolutions in the Assembly as you well remember. At worst he has never been more than a White-republican, and never will become a Clay-federalist.

As the Spaniards say, may God preserve you a thousand years.

S. H. Laughlin

P.S. For fear of miscarriage, I send you the essentials of the notice of Cannon's man.[17]

ALS. DLC–JKP. Addressed to Knoxville.

1. The arithmetic of Laughlin's vote projection requires that this figure should be "1700."

2. A farmer and trader from White County, Anthony Dibrell ran unsuccessfully for Congress in 1839 against Hopkins L. Turney. Dibrell had been clerk of the county court from 1814 until 1835. He served as a Whig in the Tennessee House, 1845–47, and as state treasurer, 1847–55.

3. The Sparta *Jeffersonian Whig* is not further identified.

4. Launched in early 1839 and published by Henry Mabry, the Winchester *Highlander* was a Democratic newspaper.

5. A Murfreesboro physician, William R. Rucker was one of Polk's strongest supporters in Rutherford County. Rucker's wife, Susan, was Sarah Childress Polk's sister.

6. Edwin J. King, editor of the Murfreesboro *Tennessee Telegraph.*

7. Polk and Cannon had spoken at McMinnville on April 18, 1839.

8. The Nashville *Republican Banner* of April 22, 1839, carried a letter from Murfreesboro, dated April 19, which praised Cannon's speech at McMinnville and belittled Polk's performance there. The author of the letter was identified only as "C."

9. No 1839 issues of the Murfreesboro *Tennessee Telegraph* have been found.

10. Robert A. Campbell, Robert M. Paris, and Leonard Adcock. Paris and Adcock received commissions in the Tennessee militia in 1836 as colonel and major, respectively.

11. No 1839 issues of the McMinnville *Central Gazette* have been found.

12. Enclosure not found.

13. Not further identified.

14. Possibly Samuel Edmondson, brother-in-law of John S. Young.

15. Landon A. Kincannon and Josiah Furman Morford. Kincannon, a brother of Andrew A. Kincannon, was a merchant in McMinnville. Morford, a lawyer in McMinnville, served as a Whig in the Tennessee Senate, 1835–36; he was also clerk and master of chancery court for thirty-five years, beginning in 1836.

16. Elkanah R. Dulaney, a Sullivan County physician, served four terms in the Tennessee House, 1817–23, 1825–27, and 1835–39.

17. Postscript written in the left margin of the last page.

TO SARAH C. POLK

My Dear Wife Cherokee Agency April 30th 1839

My friends have made an appointment for me to meet the people at *Calhoun* near this place to day, on my way from *Cleveland* to Athens. I was yesterday in Bradley, and am now in a country, where my friends say I will carry a large majority. Our cause is gaining strength and my prospects are brightening as I proceed. I am surrounded by company, as I am at every place I stop, and have scarcely a moment to write. When I get to Athens I hope to hear from you. I will direct my next letter to you, at Columbia, as probably, you will have made your visit & returned by that time.

JAMES K. POLK

ALS. DLC–JKP. Addressed to Murfreesboro and forwarded to Columbia.

FROM GEORGE W. RICE[1]

Battle Creek, Tennessee. April 30, 1839

Rice says that Obadiah Bean,[2] leader of Polk's opposition in the southern part of Marion County, has publicly declared his support for the Democratic ticket. Having ascertained the feelings of the people since Polk addressed them,[3] Rice asserts that Polk will carry Marion County by 200 votes. He has just received fifty copies of Polk's Address.[4]

ALS. DLC–JKP. Addressed to Knoxville and forwarded to Jonesboro.

1. Rice owned land in Marion County and served as deputy clerk of the county court, 1827–30.

2. Obadiah Bean secured an early grant of land on Bean's Creek in Franklin County, but subsequently moved to Marion County, where he served as justice of the peace in 1826. By 1840 he was one of the county's larger landholders.

3. Polk addressed the people of Marion County at Jasper on April 23, 1839.

4. Reference is to Polk's "Address to the People of Tennessee." See Polk to J. G. M. Ramsey, March 30, 1839.

TO SARAH C. POLK

My Dear Wife Athens May 2nd 1839

I was glad to receive your letter of the 15th ult.[1] here last night. Since I wrote you I have addressed the people at *Calhoun* and at *Decatur* in Meigs, and find that I will have strong majorities at both places. Thompson of the Democrat[2] has treated me badly, by delaying the publication of my Addresses.[3] I fear he will not, at last publish the numbers (10,000) which I ordered. Request Saml. Walker to see that,

that number are struck, and forwarded without delay, to Genl. Armstrong for distribution. They are in great demand, and scarcely a copy in pamphlet form has reached this part of the State.

J. W. Blackwell Esqr. of this place, is the Democratic candidate for Congress, in this District. I wish you to put up in strong brown paper, bound with tape and well marked, the Journals of the House of Representatives for the Extra Session, for the 2nd or long Session of the 25th Congress, and also the Sheets of the Journal of the last Session as far as they have come on; direct them to *"J. W. Blackwell Esqr., Athens McMinn County Tennessee,"* and deposite them in the Post Office. Mr Blackwell understands, that they will come to him, through the Post Office, and will pay the Postage on them. Do not fail to attend to this immediately. Send to Mr. *Blackwell* also a copy of Senate Document No. 503, shewing the losses sustained by the Government, on duty bonds.[4] Several copies of this Document, were I think in my box of *Books*. Send to him also if you can procure it a copy of the Democrat of June 18th, 1837, containing extracts from Judge Whites speeches in the Senate, against the Bank of the U. States. You will find copies of it among my loose papers, in one of the presses. If not, it can be procured at the Democrat office.

I came here last night much fatigued, but stand my tour, much better than I anticipated I would. I wish I had my Sulky with me, but will not now order it, until my return to Middle Tennessee. Have the Sulkey horse in good condition by my return, as I will then need him. Say to my friends that I am in high spirits, and that my opinion is, that I will receive a large majority in this part of East Tennessee.

JAMES K. POLK

ALS. DLC–JKP. Addressed to Columbia.

1. Letter not found.
2. Columbia *Tennessee Democrat*.
3. See Polk to J. G. M. Ramsey, March 30, 1839.
4. See Polk to Sarah C. Polk, April 14, 1839.

FROM GEORGE W. BRATTON

Sir

May the 3rd [18]39

I will inform you that we are all well at this time. The negros is all well only maria. She has ben in bad helth since the first of march and is likly not to be able to do any Sirvice. I have the promisingist Crop that I have had since I have ben in the miss. I will finish in a few [h]ours going over the cotton the first time and I am going over my corn the third time. The mule that you sent me I can not sell it for what you give for it an I will keep it untill you come. My negros and mules is all fat and you think go ahed and I say go ahed and a good Crop i[s] the object.

Thir is a lot of negros to be sold in coffiville the first of August and for cash and I expect will be bargans to be bought and wish your asistance.

George W Bratton

L, signed by amanuensis. DLC–JKP. Addressed to Columbia. Published in Bassett, *Plantation Overseer,* 119, under date of May 31, 1839.

TO SARAH C. POLK

My Dear Wife Madisonville May 5th 1839

I received a letter from brother William on yesterday of the 22nd ult.[1] I met at Athens and at this place immense crowds of the people. The ball is in motion in this part of the state. I will carry decided majorities in the great Counties of McMinn & Monroe & all agree that our cause is rapidly on the increase. Learning from William that you had not set out to Murfreesborough, I direct this to that place. From Knoxville I will write you to Murfreesborough, & afterwards to Columbia. My health is very good, & I stand the fatigue well.

James K. Polk

ALS. DLC–JKP. Addressed to Murfreesboro and forwarded to Columbia.
1. Letter not found.

TO SARAH C. POLK

My Dear Wife Knoxville May 8th 1839

It is late at night; I am exceedingly fatigued & have only the opportunity to say, that I met & addressed between three & four hundred people here to day. The Whigs in the town did every thing in their power to prevent the people from attending. My audience was as I would have preferred it, chiefly from the country. The effect was fine, & all agree that we are gaining ground & that I will get a better vote here than was anticipated. In Blount where I met 600 or more people on Monday, it is thought my vote will be about 2 to 1. My health continues good, though I am to night more fatigued than I have been on the route. I was exceedingly gratified to receive your letter of the 28th ultimo[1] last night.

Write me often to Knoxville. Your letters will be forwarded.

JAMES K. POLK

ALS. DLC–JKP. Addressed to Columbia.

1. Letter not found.

FROM ALBERT G. HARRISON[1]

Dear Sir. Fulton [Missouri] May 10th 1839

It was but yesterday I got home which will account for the delay in answering your esteemed favor of the 5th ult.[2]

I am much astonished to learn that you have been charged with defeating the Tennessee Land bill. Nothing is more untrue. I know your sentiments on the subject well; and I do know that there was not, and has not been since I have been in Congress, a member in the whole body more sincerely and actively its friend than yourself. My position as a member of the Committee on Public Lands except during the last session enables me to speak confidently concerning the measure and your feelings towards it, and I do know most positively that at all times and upon all occasions, you was the ardent, steadfast and untiring friend of the measure. The measure having originated with the Committee on Public Lands, of which I have always been a member except last session, giving me a position calculated in all probability to have some weight with the House when it should be called up, induced you, I presume, to converse with me as often as you did on the subject, and to request me to use my exertions in behalf of the bill. I was at all times the open and avowed friend of the measure until about the close of last session, when the Hon. Mr. Yell, of Arkansas[3] and myself, with some others, being displeased with the vote given by some of your Whig colleagues on the bill to graduate the price of the Public lands, determined to pay them for their course upon the Tennessee Land bill.[4] And had the bill been taken up, I feel quite sure it would not have been passed, as Mr. Yell, myself and others, were resolved to amend it by tacking to it the general principle of graduation, applicable to all public lands. No bill at the late period of the Session to which I allude, could scarcely have succeeded under the weight of an important amendment. About this time, you came to me, and I think to Mr. Yell whose seat was adjoining mine, and pressed us in a strong & earnest manner to vote to take up the bill. We made no positive promises about it, but my opinion is that we both concluded, on your account, not to *press* the amendment with which we had threatened the bill. There were two motions made to take up the bill, one I think on Saturday night, the other on Sunday night.[5] I recollect very well that Mr. Lewis Williams,[6] a strong and decided Whig, defeated the motion on one of the occasions mentioned, and I have a faint impression that he also defeated the other. Upon both occasions you was in the chair, and put the question to the House. How I voted, or whether I voted or not, I cannot say with certainty, but presume, if I voted at all, that I voted to take up the bill, on your account, and because I am and have always been most warmly and devotedly the friend of all liberal measures respecting the public lands.

I have given you substantially my best recollections on the subject. If the Tennessee land bill, lost any friends, or the hearty and cordial support which would have been given it, it was lost through the vote of the Whig delegation from your State on the graduation bill, some, if not most whom, had voted against that measure.[7] I am not aware that it lost either friends or influence in any other way.

Remember me kindly to Mrs. Polk . . . .

A. G. Harrison

Excuse errors, blots and scratchings. I am too tired, and to tell the truth, too lazy to copy what I have written. A.G.H.

ALS. DLC–JKP. Addressed to Columbia. AE on the cover reads: "Occupant Question."

1. A lawyer, Harrison moved from his native Kentucky to Fulton, Missouri, in 1827. A Democrat, he served in the U.S. House from 1835 until his death in September 1839.

2. Letter not found.

3. Archibald Yell, a close personal and political friend of Polk, practiced law in Fayetteville, Tennessee, until his appointment as judge of the Arkansas Territory in 1832. He served in the U.S. House, 1836–39 and 1845–46. From 1840 until 1844, he was governor of Arkansas. Yell died in the Mexican War.

4. Harrison's syntax is garbled; his meaning is that they were "determined to repay them on the Tennessee Land bill."

5. On March 3, 1839, William J. Graves, representative from Kentucky, moved to suspend the rules of the House and vote on the Tennessee land bill (Senate Bill No. 173); the motion failed.

6. Lewis Williams of North Carolina served in the U.S. House from 1815 until 1842. He was the brother of John Williams, senator from Tennessee, 1815–23, and Robert Williams, representative from North Carolina, 1797–1803.

7. On January 22, 1839, the House voted to table the Senate's graduation bill; on the following day a motion to reconsider failed by a narrow vote of 99 to 98. On that final decision eight Whig and two Democratic members of the Tennessee delegation supported graduation; John Bell voted against; Christopher Williams abstained; and Speaker Polk did not vote.

TO SARAH C. POLK

My Dear Wife Dandridge May 12th 1839

Since I wrote you from Knoxville[1] I have addressed the people of Sevier & Jefferson, two of my weakest Counties in the state. At the last election Cannon received a majority of 10. to 1. in these Counties. I had a respectable crowd at Sevierville, and a decidedly favourable impression was made. At this place on yesterday the assemblage was not large, & a death in the town prevented most from attending. In both Counties their is a decided gain, and our strength is daily increasing. Carter was here on yesterday; He made a ranting, demagougacal speech, but said nothing personally offensive. He intends I am told to follow me, through his District. If he does & shall interfere with me, I shall have no difficulty in disposing of him. My information from Greene, Washington, Sullivan & Hawkins is of the most favourable character; and I now think it a reasonable calculation to say, that I will receive a majority of the votes of East Tennessee.

My health continues to be as good as usual. My horse has been taken so lame, that I am compelled to leave him, here. My friend Genl. Anderson has been so kind as to lend me his, and will send mine to me to Kingston on my return.

Tell my friends that I am somewhat fatigued but will be able to go through the campaign, and that I am in high spirits at my prospects. From Green[e]ville I will forward to you my appointments for the Counties on the Tennessee River & in the District, where I design to go, immediately on my return to Middle Tennessee.

James K. Polk

P.S. Have my sulky-horse in good condition on my return, as I will take the sulky when I get home. I will be at home a single day, on my way to the District. J.K.P.

ALS. DLC–JKP. Addressed to Columbia.

1. See Polk to Sarah C. Polk, May 8, 1839.

TO SARAH C. POLK

My Dear Wife New Port, May 13th 1839

I reached here last night in good health & expect to meet a large crowd here to day.

I had several extra copies of the Journals of the House for the 24th and 25th Congresses, put up in my boxes. I wish you to have a copy of the Journal for 1835–6 and 1836–7 strongly enveloped and addressed through the mail—to *"Col. Joseph Powell Jonesborough East Tennessee."*[1] *Col Powell* is the candidate for Congress in this District and understands that the Journals will be forwarded to him.

I have settled upon my appointments for Middle Tennessee and the Western District, & will send you a list with a view to have printed notices forwarded in a day or two. If I do not alter the arrangement, when I get to Green[e]ville, I will be in Williamson on Saturday the 15th of July, will return home the next day, and spend Monday the 17th at Columbia, and then pass on to the lower Counties.

My prospects in East Tennessee, are better than my most sanguine friends had calculated they would be & are brightening daily.

JAMES K. POLK

ALS. DLC–JKP. Addressed to Columbia.

1. A physician at Elizabethton, Joseph Powell represented Carter, Sullivan, and Washington counties in the Tennessee Senate, 1835–37; he died in 1839.

TO LEVI WOODBURY

Sir New Port East Tennessee May 13th 1839

If such a document can be conveniently furnished by your Department, I wish to obtain a statement shewing the losses sustained by the Government, under each administration, as well from defaulting public debtors as from defaulting public officers.[1] My impression is that a smaller amt. of loss was sustained under Genl. Jackson's administration, than under any other, and if the fact be so, I wish to have the official document to shew it. Mr. Toucey states it to be so, in a speech made in the House,[2] and published in the National Intelligencer of the 31st of

January 1839. Forward your answer to my residence at "*Columbia Tennessee.*" And also the same information to *Col Joseph Powell, Jonesborough Tennessee.*"

JAMES K. POLK

ALS. DLC–Papers of Levi Woodbury. Probably addressed to Washington.

1. Woodbury's reply of May 23, 1839, explains that an official document containing the requested information would require much time for preparation. He encloses an informal statement which may answer Polk's purposes. ALS. DLC–Papers of Levi Woodbury. Enclosure not found.

2. Isaac Toucey, a Connecticut Democrat, served in the U.S. House, 1835–39. He spoke on the defalcation question on January 16, 1839.

FROM JOHN W. CHILDRESS

Dear Sir MurfreesBoro May 18 1839

I have just learned from Mr G Childress,[1] who was in Franklin a few days since, that it is understood, among the friends of Mr Bell, at that place & Lebanon, that he has appointed the 12th June, and the town of Lebanon, as the time and place, of the meeting "to discuss the Bedford speech."[2] I do not know whether he has given you notice, and thought it advisable to do so myself. The rumor may however not be true. My opinion is that your friends from other counties should know it in time to be at the meeting, particularly if it takes place at Lebanon. And that you should not accept that proposition, unless you get it in time to notify your friends. It is important that you should have as many friends at the meeting as himself. However you know better than myself, about these things. The Democrats in this county seem to be very sanguine of success. I have just returned from the western District. The people there are not yet aroused. They seem to be waiting for you. The prospects are not as good as I was led to believe before my visit. I saw Sarah on my return. She was well, & will meet you at Nashville. Keeble[3] gave our whig Editor & Gov. Cannons "note taker"[4] a decent drubbing a few days since, for which, every body is well pleased.

JOHN W CHILDRESS

ALS. DLC–JKP. Addressed to Knoxville and forwarded to Rutledge.

1. George C. Childress, a Rutherford County lawyer, moved to Nashville and joined the Davidson County bar in 1828. For a short time in 1834–35 he edited the Nashville *National Banner*. Soon thereafter he went to Texas,

assisted in drafting the Texas Declaration of Independence, and served briefly as minister to the United States. Failing on several occasions to establish himself permanently in Texas, Childress resided intermittently in Nashville. He died in Texas in 1841.

2. On August 13, 1838, Polk spoke to a large crowd at Shelbyville. Assailing Bell for deserting every "public principle," Polk claimed that the Whig leader now repudiated wholly those Democratic measures embraced prior to 1835. For negotiations on the proposed Polk-Bell debate at Lebanon, see Robert M. Burton to Polk, June 5, 1839.

3. Edwin A. Keeble was editor of the Murfreesboro *Monitor*. A Democrat, he served as mayor of Murfreesboro, 1838–55, and as an elector on the Buchanan ticket in 1856. Keeble's wife, Sally, was John Bell's daughter. No 1839 issues of the *Monitor* have survived.

4. Reference is to Edwin J. King, editor of the Murfreesboro *Tennessee Telegraph*. See Samuel H. Laughlin to Polk, April 30, 1839.

TO SARAH C. POLK

My Dear Wife Elizabethton May 18th 1839

This is saturday night, and I feel more fatigued than I have done since I left home. Within the last four days, I have met and addressed not less than 11.000 people. At Green[e]ville on wednesday, there could not have been less than 1.000, and at the dinner at Jonesborough on yesterday there were estimated to be near if not quite 2.500 persons present. All the ladies of the two villages came out. In the great Counties of Greene and Washington, my majorities will be overwhelming, my friends think 3 to 1. A low calculation would be 2 to 1. In this County (Carter) the majority will be against me, though the County does not vote more than 900 strong. I go tomorrow to Taylorville in Johnson,[1] and from there will pursue my route homewards. I have waited until the last moment to learn what Governor Cannon's movements would be. Failing in this, I send you on the opposite page, a list of additional appointments,[2] and as I have not time by any possibility, to write letters to the several Counties, I must rely upon brother William and yourself, to cause printed notices to be printed and forwarded to the proper places. Have this attended to, without fail.

You will perceive that I will be in Williamson on the 15th and will spend monday the 17th at home. As Governor Cannon has been at Columbia, I think it may be expected, and might be well for me to address the people of Maury on that day. Tell brother William to consult Jonas E. Thomas Esqr. and Col. Williamson Smith on the subject, and if they think it best, let a meeting be appointed. If there is one at Columbia, it should be a County meeting. A fine barbacue would bring all the people out. My friends from Marshall if notified of it, would come down.

You can assure all my friends, that I am now satisfied, beyond doubt, that I will carry a majority in East Tennessee.

JAMES K. POLK

Wednesday	12th	June	At Smithville (in DeKalb Cty.
Thursday	13th	"	" Woodbury (in Cannon
Saturday	15th	"	" Franklin (in Williamson
Monday	17th	"	At Home
Wednesday	19th	"	" Lawrenceburg (in Lawrence
Thursday	20th		Waynesboro' (in Wayne
Friday	21st		Savannah (in Hardin
Saturday	22nd		Purdy (in McNairy
Monday	24th		Perryville (in Perry
Tuesday	25th		Lexington (in Henderson
Wednesday	26th		Mifflin (in Henderson Cty.
Friday	28th		Brownsville (in Haywood
Saturday	29th		Lauderdale C.H. (in Lauderdale Cty
Monday	1st	July	Dyersburg (in D[yer][3] Cty
Tuesday	2nd	"	Troy (in Ob[ion] Cty
Thursday	4th	"	Trenton (in Gibson
Saturday	6th	"	Huntingdon (in Carroll
Monday	8th		Benton C.H. (in Benton Cty.

ALS. DLC–JKP. Addressed to Columbia.

1. Taylorsville was the county seat; in 1885 the town's name was changed to "Mountain City."

2. Accompanying list printed following the text of this letter.

3. Manuscript mutilated.

FROM ROBERT M. BURTON

Dr Sir Lebanon May 19th 1839

I have only time to say a few words to you. I have been actively engaged in the canvass. Since I Saw [you] things are assuming a more cheering aspect. Bell is much alarmed; he stays almost constantly in this County. Next week I enter Davidson—and remain for two weeks. I have understood that an attempt is making by some here for you and

Bell to meet at this place. Let that not be done.[1] If you have to meet him, Nashville is the place. You will get a big strong vote in this County, from 12 to 15 hundred. The people express a great desire to hear you at Statesville. Wonderfull changes have been wrought there. One Speech from there will give you a majority at that place. Make an appointment for that place and another at Mount Juliet or Hallums in the lower end of this County. Write me and the matter will be attended to. Your prospects are bettering every day. Your address to the people[2] is doing wonders.

ROBERT M BURTON

ALS. DLC–JKP. Addressed to Jacksboro.

1. See John W. Childress to Polk, May 18, 1839; Robert M. Burton to Polk, June 5, 1839; and Polk to Sarah C. Polk, June 2, 1839.

2. See Polk to J. G. M. Ramsey, March 30, 1839.

FROM JAMES VAUGHN AND JOHN F. GILLESPY

Madisonville, Tennessee. May 19, 1839

Vaughn predicts that Polk will receive a majority of 500 votes in Monroe County. Recent denunciations by opponents in Knoxville and Athens have worked to Polk's advantage. Polk's address[1] has been widely circulated and well received. The prospects of other Democratic candidates are also good. Gillespy writes that Blount, McMinn, and Bradley counties will yield decided majorities for Polk. Gillespy has consented to run for the Tennessee Senate; Jarnagin has declined.

ALS. DLC–JKP. Addressed to Knoxville and forwarded to Jacksboro.

1. Reference is to Polk's "Address to the People of Tennessee," April 3, 1839. See Polk to J. G. M. Ramsey, March 30, 1839.

TO SARAH C. POLK

My Dear Wife — Sullivan County May 22nd 1839

I made a speech at Taylorsville on monday, and one at Paperville near the Va. line in this County on yesterday, and am now at the House of our old friend *McClellan*. My friends have crowded additional appointments upon me & I am required to speak to day at Blountville & tomorrow at Kingsport. I am much fatigued, but feel much better this morning than I did yesterday.

In Johnson County, contrary to my expectation, I think I shall carry a majority. All agree that my majority in Sullivan will not be less than 1000 votes. I will write you again from Kingsport.[1]

JAMES K. POLK

ALS. DLC–JKP. Addressed to Columbia.

1. See Polk to Sarah C. Polk, May 24, 1839.

FROM M. D. COOPER & CO.

Sir,

New Orleans May 23rd 1839

We received on yesterday 4 bales of Cotton upon your account. The market is exceedingly flat and prices have declined fully a cent per pound since receipt of last advices from Europe.

We will not offer them untill the market revives.[1]

M D COOPER & CO.

LS. DLC–JKP. Addressed to Columbia.

1. On June 5, 1839, M. D. Cooper & Co. wrote that Polk's account had been credited with net proceeds of $206.50 for the sale of 4 bales of cotton. LS. DLC–JKP.

TO SARAH C. POLK

My Dear Wife

Kingsport May 24th 1839

I have recovered from my fatigue. Yesterday was a glorious day here. I met 500 people, half or more from Hawkins. McKinney selected this as the point to attack me. Here was the Netherland[1] influence. Orville Bradley and his forces are up. I made my speech. McKinney replied or pretended to do so. He met none of my arguments, but exposed himself to a severe castigation and exposure. I availed myself of the advantage he had given me, & the result was, that he was routed "horse, foot & dragoon." We spoke in the church, the Rev Mr Ross[2] being one of the audience. The scene closed in the evening with a tremendous roar of laughter at McKinney's expense. He rose to respond but the people rushed out of the House the best pleased crowd I have seen in many a day. The prospect in this part of the state is most cheering. Old Sullivan is almost unanimous. Out of 1500 votes my friends are perfectly certain I will not loose 200 votes. Genl. Fain who is here tells me that a bet for a considerable sum has been made that my majority over Cannon in Hawkins will be 600 votes.

JAMES K. POLK

ALS. DLC–JKP. Addressed to Columbia.

1. Virginia born, John Netherland moved to Kingsport in 1811. He began his legal career in Franklin in 1829 and two years later returned to Sullivan County. He represented Carter, Sullivan, and Hawkins counties in the Tennessee Senate, 1833–35; backed White for president in 1836; sat for Sullivan County in the House, 1835–37; and served one term in the House for Hawkins County, 1851–53.

2. Not further identified.

FROM GEORGE M. PORTER

Dear Col. McKoysville May 24th 1839

Your address at this place on the 13th has caused much confusion in the whig ranks and many are seen daily abandoning their posts & joining the Democratic party. I could mention the *names* of some 50 or 100 individuals of this county[1] who have heretofore acted in concert with the *opposition* to the present Administration who are now *your* most warm and devoted friends. The leading men of the opposition here give you 300 or one third of the votes in the county. Many of your friends claim for you an equal division. I think myself, from the best information I can get on the subject, you will get about 400 votes, say we vote 900; which you will see is a considerable increase of the vote given Genl Armstrong at the last Election.

Of Jefferson I can say but little of my own knowledge except in the immediate vicinity of Dandridge and that part of the county south of F. Broad.[2] In these two neighbourhoods matters are going entirely well. I have no doubt it would be much to your advantage to visit this county again before August.

I have very recently seen several very intelligent gentlemen from Sevier county all of whom say that your friends in that county are very sanguine and are unwilling to put up with a divission of [that] county but claim a handsome majority.

Among other things that have become manifest since you left here is the fact that as between Vanburen & Clay this county is very decidedly in favor of Mr. V.B.—so much so in fact that the most *sagacious* whigs here are attempting to conceal the fact from the people that Mr. Clay is now & will be the most prominent Whig candidate for the presidency. Your friends here are very anxious indeed that you should get a majority in this county. They would therefore be much gratified if you could visit this county again before the election.

From some cause or other I know not what a suspicion is entertained here by some of the Whigs that there was an arrangement with you and some of your friends when here, for the removal of Majr. Roadman the Post Master at Newport—and that his place is to be filled by the appointment of Mr. Stanbury of Newport, a Democrat.[3] Believing as I do the suspicion to be unfounded I have already so expressed myself whenever the matter has been mentioned to me. Should I be mistaken in this opinion I shall sincerely regret it because I consider the removal uncalled for & the new appointment a bad one and also because I believe it would prejudice your cause very much among the people of this county. In the event that the case has been misrepresented to you by some of our friends & the suspicion is correct I would urge upon you most earnestly the propriety of letting things remain as they are till after the election.

Please write me upon this subject immediately as I feel anxious to know the truth of it.[4] Also of your prospects in other counties since you left us. I write in much haste as there is now a messenger waiting for me.

G. M. Porter

P.S. Should you conclude to address the people of this county again, it would be well for you to apprise some friend of it in advance some time & authorize them to make appointments at two or more places in the county. Porter

ALS. DLC–JKP. Addressed to Kingston.

1. Cocke County.

2. French Broad River.

3. William C. Roadman and probably John F. Stanberry. A native of Virginia, Roadman moved to Jonesboro, Tennessee, in 1808 and represented Carter and Washington counties for one term in the Tennessee Senate, 1815–17. Subsequently a farmer and businessman in Cocke County, he served as Newport's postmaster from 1837 until 1842. Stanberry was clerk of the Cocke County Court, 1839–44.

4. See George M. Porter to Polk, June 16, 1839.

FROM JAMES WALKER

Dear Sir,

Columbia May 25, 1839

I supposed when I received the enclosed letter[1] that it was mere rumor, as Bell is by every principle bound if he has designated the 12th at Lebanon to give you full and timely notice, and to make it public that the friends of both parties in other counties may know & go if they choose. I suppose there is to be no meeting on the 12th.[2] If there is, you must apprise Sam[3] and through him your friends here. Many will go if they know it in time. My own opinion is, Bell means no meeting, but I think he wants the rumor to go out that the 12th is the time agreed on & that you have failed to meet the appointment. This matter ought to be looked to, and if necessary your movements made known in the Union. I think you ought not to be later than the 20th leaving here for the lower counties and the District. All accounts from this quarter and the District are favorable. A visit to all the counties in the District I am confident will secure you a good majority. The best opinions are, that you are sure of a majority now. West Humphries[4] is just up. He is very sanguine. He says Cannon's internal improvement notions is ruining him even with the Whigs.[5] Genl. Morris[6] says he cannot go Cannon. Whig as he is, he must go in for the interest of the State, which he thinks C. is incapable of promoting. Dunlap writes in fine spirits. I shall leave home on Monday for the District—be a good deal through it. If any thing is necessary to be done here any information necessary to be given to friends, you had better write to Dr. Hays or Sam.

Rest assured, that altho William's affair is painful, the thing could not have been bettered under the circumstances. The Judge has deceived us all.[7] He fails as a Democrat & has in this I think played the demagogue. The final sentence is 6 weeks imprisonment—fine $750. It would not have done to have continued the case, with the Bowie Knife hanging over,[8] which it was pretty certain could be avoided. Nor would it have done to appeal for two reasons—the political effect would have been bad—and there is all the difference in the world between imprisonment here and the filthy jail of Nashville. Him and Belinda[9] have as good rooms and accomodations as at home—it is merely in name. The affect of his Submission to the decision of the Court has been decidedly good.

James Walker

ALS. DLC–JKP. Addressed to Kingston.

1. Walker's enclosure has not been found.

2. See Robert M. Burton to Polk, June 5, 1839.

3. Samuel P. Walker.

4. West H. Humphreys, a Somerville lawyer, was a member of the 1834 Constitutional Convention. He won election as a Democrat to the Tennessee House for one term, 1835–37. Moving to Nashville, he served as state attorney general and reporter from 1839 until 1851. Humphreys returned to the Western District in 1853 to become the first federal district judge of West Tennessee.

5. See Robert Armstrong to Polk, March 24, 1839.

6. Not identified further.

7. On May 18, 1839, William H. Polk was prosecuted on a charge of assault and battery. Andrew J. Marchbanks, judge of the Thirteenth Judicial Circuit, sentenced him to two months imprisonment and a $1000 fine. On May 24, Marchbanks reduced the sentence by two weeks and the fine by $250. See William H. Polk to Polk, January 2, 1839, and John B. Hays to Polk, January 9, 1839.

8. On May 17, 1839, William H. Polk was tried on an indictment for wearing a bowie knife concealed beneath his clothing. The jury found him "not guilty."

9. Belinda Dickinson Polk was the wife of William H. Polk.

TO SARAH C. POLK

My Dear Wife Rutledge May 28th 1839

I addressed a respectable collection of people here yesterday. McKinney again resumed his attack and was indirectly aided & assisted by the promptings of Genl Cocke. I repelled the assault and gained a great advantage over him. It was the third time that he had been foiled. He has lost ground and I have gained wherever we have met. This is one of the strongest of the opposition Counties. A decided change in our favour had been going on, for some weeks, and much was added to our strength on yesterday.

I learn by a letter from Wilson [County] and also one from your brother at Murfreesboro that *Bell* has appointed Wednesday the 12th of June to meet me in public discussion at Lebanon.[1] This was what my correspondents understood. If it be so, I must of course meet, and *will certainly do so.* I have written to Genl. Armstrong fully on the subject,[2] and urged him to let me know certainly by the time I get to Kingston. His object I understand is to discuss the subject matter contained in my Bedford speech last.[3] In the event I meet him, I will want & *must have* some documents from Home. *Brother William* or some other friend can take the Sulkey and meet me with them at Gainsborough in Jackson, on the morning of Sunday the 9th of June, when I can have time to examine them. I am to address the people at Gainsborough on the 10th, but will be there early on the 9th in the expectation of meeting the Documents I want.

I will want the Journals of the House for 1831–2, 1833–4, of all the Sessions since that date down to this time, including the Journal of the late Session in sheets as far as received.

I will want a document in manuscript which you will find in my trunk, upon the subject of the amendment of the Constitution, in relation to the election of President in 1835. The Documents to which I allude contain a letter from *Mr Berry* assistant Clerk of the House of Repts., showing my course on that subject.[4]

I will want the speeches made by Garland of Va., and *Gillet* of New York, which were republished in the Democrat in the fall of 1836—if my memory serves me.[5]

I will want the National Intelliger. which you will find among my piecemeal Newspapers in my trunk, containing *Bell's* speech in reply to Turney, upon the occasion of their fight in the House. You may find a copy of it, in pamphlet, in one of the presses. I want also *Turney's* Speech on that occasion,[6] which you will find in pamphlet in one of the presses. If not, it was republished in the Democrat. I will want also a copy of the Union or Democrat containing extracts from Bell's Hartford Speech.[7] I will want the *Globe*, containing the debate, in relation to Indian frauds, and the appointment of a committee to examine them, in the Ho. Repts. before which I gave the casting vote, at the first session I was speaker.[8] You will find it among my newspapers in the trunk, I think it is blotted with ink.

These are all that I can now remember. Possibly it might be well, to send all my newspapers, which are tied up in bundles in the trunk for the last four or five years, as possibly I may need them. There must be no failure in sending them in time. Gainsboro' is two good day's ride from Nashville.

If any that I have noted cannot be procured at Columbia, *brother William* can obtain them from Genl. Armstrong or Col. Harris at Nashville. I wish him to call at all events on Col. Harris for certain abolition newspapers,[9] which I left with him. If I can get the documents in time, you may rest perfectly assured, if I meet *Bell* in Debate, that the facts will prostrate him. *Tell William* not to make any parade about his trip to Gainsboro'—but to go off quietly. If when he gets to Nashville he should learn, that there is any mistake about Bell's having made the appointment for the 12th, of course he need not come to Gainsboro'.[10]

I have entirely recovered from my fatigue & am in fair health & spirits. The prospects in East Tennessee are much more cheering than I anticipated they would be and are brightening every day. I go to Tazewell tomorrow.

James K. Polk

P.S. Send also with the Documents, the manuscript correspondence, which you will find in a separate bundle in the trunk, between *Cave Johnson* and the Tennessee Delegation in relation to Judge White's nomination for the Presidency.[11] J.K.P.

ALS. DLC–JKP. Addressed to Columbia and marked *"Private."*

1. Polk received two letters, both dated May 10, 1839, from W. P. Sayle, Lebanon, concerning a proposed meeting with John Bell at Lebanon on June 12, 1839. ALsS. DLC–JKP. A third letter, dated May 16, 1839, from Sayle and Ramsay L. Mayson, sought to impress upon Polk the importance of the coming confrontation. LS. DLC–JKP. John W. Childress, Sarah Polk's brother, also informed Polk of a rumored meeting with Bell. See Childress to Polk, May 18, 1839.

2. Letter not found.

3. Polk spoke at Shelbyville in Bedford County on August 13, 1838. See John W. Childress to Polk, May 18, 1839.

4. On May 20, 1835, B. M. Berry forwarded to Polk a copy of George R. Gilmer's resolution to amend the constitutional procedures for electing the president and vice-president, including a proposed amendment to the resolution by Polk. ALS. DLC–JKP. Enclosure not found.

5. James Garland and Ransom H. Gillet. A Virginia Democrat, Garland served in the U.S. House from 1835 until 1841. Ransom Gillet won election as a New York Democrat to the House and served two terms, 1833–37. Their speeches have not been identified; very few issues of the Columbia *Tennessee Democrat* survive.

6. In debate on the Indian hostility appropriation bill in the House on May 31 and June 1, 1838, Hopkins L. Turney criticized John Bell's actions in Congress. In reply, Bell accused Polk and Grundy of instigating the speech and implied that the two had provided material for Turney's speech. Those remarks led to an altercation between Bell and Turney on the floor of the House. Bell struck out at Turney, and each had to be restrained. Both were forced to apologize to the House. The Washington *National Intelligencer* of June 1 and June 2, 1838, carried the proceedings of the U.S. House.

7. John Bell spoke at Hartford, Connecticut, on November 27, 1837, during his tour of the New England states. An editorial containing parts of Bell's Hartford speech appeared in the *Nashville Union* of December 28, 1837.

8. On July 4, 1836, the *Congressional Globe* published the U.S. House debate of July 1, 1836, concerning Creek land frauds, which some believed to have caused the Creek War.

9. Titles not identified.

10. See Robert M. Burton to Polk, June 5, 1839.

11. Johnson's manuscript correspondence has not been found. See Polk to John Blair et al., January 20, 1835.

FROM JAMES GILLESPY[1]

Dear Sir Maryville 30th of May 1839

I have delayed writing until Court week hopeing to hear from the different parts of this Co & also something from Sevier & Cocke. I can say but little to be *fully* relyd on. I think however you may safely calculate on a majority in this Co. Two of my sons[2] in whose opinion in such cases I have more confidence than my own say you take two thirds. I hope they may be right & it is by no means improbable they may be so. The Nashville Union has undertaken to recommend General Wallace to this District for Congress & the Athens Currier[3] has namd. the General & also others as the leading people in this Co who are in your favour which will secure you a strong vote. Now all Such S[t]atements are calculated to do much harm seldom or never any Good. Some say you will loss more than 100 votes in consequence of them. I hope that will not be the case. You had better keep yourself as free from the General as possible so as to avoid his displeasure. Should you be saying much about him or in his favour & that reach the ears of a number of such as intend voting for you, they would fly off, the prejudices in several parts of the County bein so strong against the General. Some Scattering accounts from Sevier Co give you a good divide, perhaps a majority. I wish it may be so. I have gathered nothing from Cocke Co worthy of notice. I presume you know that they are running me as a Candidate to represent this Co & I think I am geting along tolerably well so far.

JAMES GILLESPY

ALS. DLC–JKP. Addressed to Knoxville and forwarded to McMinnville and Waverly.

1. Virginia born, Gillespy migrated early to Blount County, Tennessee, where he built a mill on Pistol Creek in 1803 and engaged in farming. He served two terms in the Tennessee Senate, 1821–25, and participated in the 1834 Tennessee Constitutional Convention.

2. Although James Gillespy was the father of four sons, his reference probably was to James H. and John F. Gillespy, two sons actively engaged in politics. James H. Gillespy, a Blount County doctor and member of the Medical Society of Tennessee, owned a sawmill and gristmill, held part interest in a tavern in which the county court sometimes met, and invested in the East Tennessee and Virginia Railroad. He won election to three terms in the Tennessee House and served from 1827 until 1833.

3. The Athens *Courier*, established as a "Loco Foco" paper in 1838, was edited until 1841 by the Reverend Robert Frazier. Gibbs, the publisher, has been identified only by surname.

FROM EZEKIEL P. McNEAL

Bolivar June 1 1839

Dear Sir

We are in rcpt. of your appointments for McNairy, Perry & Henderson Counties and have sent to those Counties a Sufficient number of printed notices. Mr. James Walker of Columbia reached town this evening & advised us of your engagements up to the 8th July at Benton County. We do not wish to interfere with your arrangements but desire very much that you should address the people of Madison, Hardeman, Fayette & Shelby, or at least the three last if possible. Mr Walker is of the op[in]ion that you may be inclined to comply with the invitation from Shelby County to be at Raleigh on the 14th July. He says the invitation was forwarded to Kingston. Your visit at these counties last fall & the circulation of your *addresses* this Spring, has stired the people up, and their great anxiety to hear you [will] I have no doubt bring out greater crowds than in Counties you have not before been to. The whole ticket is safe in this county—& for the Legislature in Fayette. It will be close in Fayette for Governor and Congress—tho we claim small majorities. Coe will succeed beyond doubt. Col Dunlap has been through Perry & Hender[s]on and a part of McNairy. He is in good Spirits. The change in every County is vastly in his faver. In this County last election his majority was 120. In August, it will be 6 or 700—at the least. The chances are in his faver. The public opinion is now setting for him & will continue until the election.

Dunlap says that Williams told him that whenever you entered his Congressional District, that he would quit him & follow you so long as you remained in it. I fear he will not. God send he may do so. If he does it will elect Dunlap and increase your majority. That is one reason why we wish you to come to this and the two Counties below.[1] If you could visit us from Huntingdon, and get back in time to go through Johnsons District, you could do the cause a great deal of good in this Section of the District. If you come here give us as early notice as possible and I will see that every man in the county knows of the appointment. Should it not be conven[i]ent I will meet you in Purdy on the 22d Inst.

E. P. McNeal

ALS. DLC–JKP. Addressed to Gainsboro and forwarded to Columbia.

1. Reference is to Shelby and Fayette counties, which are west rather than south of Hardeman County.

TO SARAH C. POLK

My Dear Wife Kingston June 2nd 1839

I received your letter of the 19th at Jacksborough two days ago, and that of the 27th with its inclosure, on my arrival here to day.[1] I am distressed to learn the result of brother *William's* case.[2] The sentence is severe, but he has acted prudently in submitting without complaint. Tell him I will write to him, if I can possibly find leisure before I leave here. If not I will see him in two weeks. Since I wrote you from Rutledge I have visited the people of *Claiborne, Campbell & Anderson,* and think I shall at least divide the vote with the Governor[3] in those Counties. I have now only to address the people of this County (Roane) and Morgan, until I finish my tour in East Tennessee; and from the best computation I can make, my majority East of the Mountain will not be less than from three to five thousand votes.

I have received a letter from Col. Burton of Wilson of the 19th ult., from which I learn that he has not been consulted about the proposed meeting with *Bell* at Lebanon on the 12th and does not approve it. He thinks if we meet in discussion it should be at Nashville and not at Lebanon. I am satisfied that the whole matter has originated with hasty and indiscreet persons, who have been controlled more by their feelings than their judgments. I have written to Genl. Armstrong, Burton and to your brother[4] stating to each of them that if the 12th is the day, I will have to meet *Bell* under great disadvantages. I shall be fatigued and almost worn down by my long tour, and will not have a single day at home, to select the documents I may need. Not knowing upon what points he may touch I should be prepared upon all. Still if he has appointed the 12th my enemies shall not have it to say, that I have shrunk from the discussion, and I have said to them that I would at all hazards meet him. I have written to them to give me certain information at Gainsborough; and have requested your brother to go immediately to Nashville, see Genl. Armstrong & other friends and meet me at Gainsboro' on the 9th. Send the Journals and documents which I requested to be forwarded, in my letter from Rutledge,[5] to Genl. Armstrong, who will have them conveyed to me, if necessary. I have suggested to my friends, that I will at all events be in Wilson in the month of July, and that if *Mr Bell,* wishes me to meet him, to have the meeting postponed until some day to be agreed upon, in that month.

If I do not go to Lebanon, I will meet my appointments in DeKalb on the 12th and at Woodbury in Cannon on the 13th and will be at home on sunday the 16th. I shall not write you again before I get to Gainsboro'. It would be useless to do so, as I shall be passing through a country where the mails are only weekly, and my letters would not probably reach you, before I get home.

James K. Polk

ALS. DLC–JKP. Addressed to Columbia.

1. Sarah C. Polk's letters have not been found.

2. See James Walker to Polk, May 25, 1839.

3. Newton Cannon.

4. Polk's letters to Robert Armstrong, Robert M. Burton, and John W. Childress have not been found.

5. See Polk to Sarah C. Polk, May 28, 1839.

FROM ROBERT ARMSTRONG

Monday Morning
[Nashville] 4th June [1839][1]

Dear Sir

I have received your several letters[2] from different places and rejoice at the good news. As to the appointment made with Bell by any of our friends in Wilson I heard nothing of it *until* I receiv'd your letter. I have paid no attention to it in making your appointments for the District &c. I got Burton to call on Bell here and know if he had given the chalenge. He said if *you* fixed a day for the meeting he would try and be present but that he did not agree that it was a chalenge from *himself*. So I told Burton to have the matter put right in Wilson. To day is the Court there & him & Bell speak. You can meet him in July—it will be better on many accounts.

The Looking Glass is just out. I send two Bags up to Wilson by this mail. I will have all off in the course of this week. Burton has been here a week, and is in fine spirits and put us so. He will beat Bell in this County[3] (no doubt of it).

They have made appointments for you in Williamson for 14th & 15 June. I sent a man to Childress that he might fix any place in Williamson for 15th June. I see the Record[4] has the 14 & 15. Some of your friends will meet you, if not at Gainsboro, at Smithville. I will see you at Home on 17th. Rest assured all looks well. Pay no attention to Bell and his pack. Go on & fill your appointments. If he should give you notice at Gainsboro, just let them understand that you will meet them in *July* when your appointments are *out*. You ought to have rest and a little preparation.

The news from Virginia is cheering. Steenrod is Elected in the Wheeling Dist. & we have carried the member in the Norfolk Dist. *over* Mallory.[5] Gaining in the Legis[latur]e. All looks well. You know that all is not right about the Lebanon appointment when I assure [you] that the first I heard of it was from you in your letter a few days ago. I then got Burton to go to Bell and his reply was that *he* had made no appointment but that when call'd on he had said that he would meet you any time you or your friends would fix. This is like every thing he does and I would pay no attention to it.

R Armstrong

ALS. DLC–JKP. Addressed to Gainesboro.

1. Year identified through content analysis.
2. Letters not found.
3. Davidson County.
4. Reference is to the Franklin *Weekly Record,* edited by Henry Van Pelt.
5. Lewis Steenrod, Joel Holleman, and Francis Mallory. Steenrod, a Democrat and lawyer from Wheeling, Virginia, won election to three terms in the U.S. House, 1839–45. Holleman, a lawyer and Democrat from Burwell Bay, Virginia, served part of one term in the U.S. House, 1839–40, and several terms in the Virginia House, over which he presided as Speaker in 1844. A physician and farmer in the Norfolk area, Mallory won a seat in the U.S. House in 1837, lost his bid for reelection to Joel Holleman in 1839, regained his old seat upon Holleman's resignation in 1840, and carried his district for a second full term in 1841. From 1853 until 1859 Mallory headed the Norfolk and Petersburg Railroad Company.

TO SARAH C. POLK

My Dear Wife Kingston June 4th 1839

The mail from the West last night, brought me your letter of the 29th Ultimo,[1] but none from Nashville. I see that the Union publishes that I will be at Smithville on the 12th and at Woodbury on the 13th. I see also from the Banner a list of Governor Cannon's appointments, and that he will be with me in Overton & Jackson. I take it for granted, as none of my friends at Nashville, have written me otherwise, that the rumoured meeting with Bell at Lebanon on the 12th has been the suggestion of indiscreet & hasty friends & will not take place.[2]

I wish you to send the sulkey to meet me at Franklin on the 15th June, and I will endeavour to get home that evening. I am you know to meet the people of Williamson on the 15th. Tell *Knox Walker* I will be greatly obliged to him to accompany me on my tour to the District, & hope he will hold himself in readiness to do so.

James K. Polk

P.S. I had a fine meeting here on yesterday, and my friends think a most favourable impression was made. They are confident I will carry a majority of Roane. You may say to my friends that I am now confident of a majority of from three to five thousand in East Tennessee. If my friends in Maury have appointed a meeting for Monday the 17th I will address the people on that day. J.K.P.

ALS. DLC–JKP. Addressed to Columbia.
1. Letter not found.
2. See Robert M. Burton to Polk, June 5, 1839.

FROM ROBERT M. BURTON

Dr Sir Lebanon June 5th 1839

I have this moment recd your letter dated at Kingston.[1] I talked with Bell at Nashville. He is now trying to get out of the matter by saying he will not be considered in the light of a challenger. If he met you, he, I perceived, wished it to be understood that the Challenge came from you. I have talked with Doctr Sayle[2] and requested him to write to Bell. No notice has been given of any expected meeting here—and none is expected.[3] I want you to come in July—and am now willing for you to meet him here. Believe it when I tell you three more speeches in this county will give you a decided majority here. The Cause is most rapidly gaining. I vanquished Bell here fairly on Monday. I believe now I will best him. You have seen an account of my progress in Davidson. I was delighted. I want you to speak at Statesville Mount Juliet and Lebanon, at each of which places they will give you a public dinner. Let me hear from you at Decalb and Woodbury. But for my court I would meet you. Bell is the most unhappy man you ever saw. He sees his party must fail. In great haste.

R. M. Burton

ALS. DLC–JKP. Addressed to Gainesboro' and forwarded to Smithville.
1. Letter not found.
2. W. P. Sayle is not identified further.
3. See John W. Childress to Polk, May 18, 1839.

FROM CAVE JOHNSON

Dear Col. Clarksville June 5th [1839][1]

Our canvass has commenced with great animation. In consequence of your not coming from Gainsborough thru Sumner to this District I have made my appointments for Robertson & go there tomorrow where I shall be a week & shall be the 3rd Monday in June at Charlotte, 4th at Waverly, 1st in July at Dover, 2nd at Centreville. It will be sufficient for you to make one speech at each County seat if you are not too much exhausted. Do not miss Stewart, Montgomery & Robertson. You are looked for in the district with the greatest anxiety & will have very large crowds. *Our friends* are more active than ever before in this district & I have not the least doubt in my district & the strongest hopes of a majority in Montgomery where I was beaten 450 before. You will unite all my strength & I think more. Your election is discussed every day. Col Jordon runs agt. Turner[2] in this county with the fairest prospect—& J. W Judkins[3] agt. two or three whigs in Robertson. Give us as early notice as you can when you enter as our people will prepare you barbacue I expect every where & will *invite* Canon [Cannon].

C. JOHNSON

ALS. DLC–JKP. Addressed to Columbia.

1. Year identified through content analysis.

2. Marcenas Jordan and William K. Turner. Jordan is not identified further. A Clarksville lawyer, Turner served as attorney general for the Tenth Judicial District, 1829–36, and held the same office for the Seventh Judicial District, 1836–39. He ran an unsuccessful race for Congress on the Whig ticket in 1835, but defeated Jordan by 20 votes for a seat in the Tennessee House in 1839.

3. J. W. Judkins was a justice of the peace in Robertson County from 1840 until 1848.

FROM JOHN P. CHESTER[1]

Hon J K Polk Jonesborough June 8th 1839

It affords me a great deal of pleasure to inform you that our cause is daily increasing, and must necessarily continue so to do.

Your visit to this place has had a more powerful influence on the deluded part of our party than any thing else could that I have any knowledge of.[2] I do believe it has effected more than Genl Jackson could have done by passing through. Watch the old Govr.[3] If he makes an eastern steal, come with him and I will insure you the game.

We have just received the East Tennessean to day, and I am astonished to see the unlimited perversion of facts contained in his editorial. I do believe he can beat Brownlow the Editor of the Tennessee Whig lying and give him all trumps.[4]

The accounts from the lower counties is I am affraid too flattering, for if Powell can get anything like the vote it is stated he will, there is nothing to fear in his election. Green Moor has declined and our party have taken up Aiken.[5] He has been stumping it with Taylor,[6] but is too hard for him. Taylor told him last week after they had spoken in the upper end of this county, that he did not like that kind of speaking at all. He did not think it was necessary to meddle with national politicks at all, ie, he does not want to come out for Henry Clay, but he will have to face up.

I have been expecting those addresses you promised to send here, and I have promised a number already to furnish them with them so soon as I receive them.[7]

I hope you have got over the fatigue of your hurried campaign through this section of country, and [are] able to undertake another if the Governor should feel disposed to visit us, but that I do not expect him to do.

JOHN P CHESTER

ALS. DLC–JKP. Addressed to Columbia.

1. A Jonesboro physician and an ardent Democrat, Chester served twelve years as postmaster, 1829–37 and 1842–44.

2. Polk spoke at Jonesboro on May 17, 1839.

3. Newton Cannon.

4. William Wales and William G. Brownlow. Reared in Knoxville, Brownlow entered the ministry in 1826 as an itinerant preacher, but soon took an interest in politics. In 1839 he became editor of the Elizabethton *Tennessee Whig* and in the following year moved the newspaper to Jonesboro, where it was known as the *Jonesboro Whig and Independent.* Ten years later Brownlow again changed location and published his sheet under the title *Brownlow's Knoxville Whig.* In 1843 he sought the Whig nomination for Congress, but was defeated by Andrew Johnson.

5. Greene Moore and John A. Aiken. Moore was postmaster at Shown's Cross Roads in Carter County, 1827–36. When Johnson County was organized in 1836, he was appointed a commissioner to lay off the county seat, the original name of which was changed in 1885 from "Taylorsville" to "Mountain City." Moore operated a hotel, kept a general store, and served as postmaster in Taylorsville from 1836 until 1843. Delaware born, Aiken migrated early to Jonesboro, where he practiced law after 1810. He represented Washington County in the Tennessee House, 1827–29, and served one term for Carter, Sullivan, and Washington counties from 1839 until 1841.

6. Alfred W. Taylor, a Carter County lawyer and iron manufacturer, sat for Carter and Sullivan counties in the Tennessee House, 1833–35. He ran an unsuccessful race against John A. Aiken for the Tennessee Senate in 1839.

7. Reference is to Polk's "Address to the People of Tennessee," April 3, 1839.

FROM GEORGE W. BRATTON

Dear Sir. Miss Yallabusha June the 11 1839

Mr Bill and family is only but tolarable well.[1] We have ben sick a grate [deal] all this year. The negros is complaining, a good many of them. Maria is down and is like to be ill. Elizabeth has done nothing since Crismas. I do not think that [the complaints] are dangerous.

I have a first rate cotton Crop and the corns good but is sufering seriously for rain. Rite to me when you will be down in this cuntry.

G W Bratton

L, signed by amanuensis. DLC–JKP. Addressed to Columbia. Published in Bassett, *Plantation Overseer,* 120, under date of June 4, 1839.

1. Reference is to William H. Polk and family.

FROM J. G. M. RAMSEY

Dear Col. [Mecklenburg T. June 12. 1839][1]

Brownlow in the Elizabethton paper asserts you accused the late Col. Williams of being a Federalist &c. &c.[2] The whig papers copy it & it is being used from the stump. Genl. Jacobs[3] made the most of it on Monday at the hustings between himself & Crozier. Crozier & his friends turn it with great effect against Jacobs—for here it is well known that he & his coadjutors 10 years ago originated the same charge. Jacobs crocodile tears will avail him nothing on this subject. For during Williams life he had no bitterer reviler than his posthumous advocate. Still if we could counteract it elsewhere it would be well. In Knox County it will do little harm to you. It is well understood here.

The whigs are thrown into a panic since Monday. The canvas opened between Jacobs & Crozier on that day. He [Jacobs] began on Federal politics & his whole aim was to raise the party question. Crozier managed his card admirably, avowed his intention to vote for Polk & V.B.—would exercise his rights as a freeman & would not ask this or that man—that or the other party how or for whom he should vote—but entered into no defence of the administration & said little of Federal politics—confined his remarks to Jacobs past vociferations against Clay—gave his dinner performances in past years a review & concluded by detailing Jacobs inconsistent position. It was his first public address in town & tho the meeting was called by Jacobs friends Crozier was decidedly in the majority. J. made no reply & refused C's proposition to take the country together. A circular is spoken of. Something must be done & done soon or C. will beat him easily. I hope the V.B. editors west of the Mts. may make no (indiscreet) *boasts* of our carrying a V.B. member in Knox. It will react & injure us just now. We cannot as you know stand the party question here just now—& the moderate whig men if it is not pressed will vote for you & C. I have so written to day to the Union. Say this much to the Editor at Columbia.[4]

It is working very well & I think will so continue. Baker is said to be gaining. McKamy or Gillespie[5] will be elected in Blount & I have just heard that Dr. Porter of New Port is announced for the Senate & must beat his 3 whig opponents. *Blackwell & McClellan are safe.* Our Militia friends are concentrating on Genl. Anderson. McGhaughey[6] will probably be withdrawn & if he can be induced to do so—we will easily elect Anderson. We would like very much for you to be here the week preceeding the election. But leave it of course to your own best judgment. Capt. Polk[7] & family are here & have been for several days. Mrs. P. is threatened with a fixed disease of the lungs & may never be better. Present us kindly to Mrs. P.

J. G. M. RAMSEY

[P.S.] The Argus will issue in 2 weeks.[8]

ALS. DLC–JKP. Addressed to Columbia and marked "Not for the newspapers."

1. Place and date taken from cover as hand cancelled by the author, postmaster of Mecklenburg, Tennessee.

2. William G. Brownlow and John Williams. Born in North Carolina, Williams studied law and joined the Knox County bar in 1803. He served as a colonel under Jackson in the War of 1812. Williams went to the U.S. Senate in 1815 to fill the vacancy caused by the resignation of George W. Campbell, won election to a full term, and served until 1823. After an unsuccessful reelection bid, he was appointed by John Q. Adams to be chargé d'affaires to the Federation of Central America, 1825–26, and subsequently was elected to the Tennessee Senate, 1827–28. Williams died near Knoxville in 1837.

3. Solomon D. Jacobs, a Knoxville merchant, actively promoted internal improvements in East Tennessee. In 1837 he became president of the Hiwassee Railroad Company. He served as mayor of Knoxville, 1834–35, and represented Knox County in the Tennessee House from 1839 until 1841.

4. James H. Thompson edited the Columbia *Tennessee Democrat.*

5. John Baker, David McKamy, and James Gillespy.

6. John McGaughey.

7. William Wilson Polk, second son of Ezekiel Polk and husband of Elizabeth Dodd Polk, received his captain's commission in the Maury County

militia in 1808. He subsequently moved to the Western District and settled in Middleburg, a small village in Hardeman County. By 1840 he had removed to Phillips County, Arkansas, where he owned a large plantation.

8. The first issue of the Knoxville *Argus* appeared on June 27, 1839.

FROM LAWSON GIFFORD

Dear Sir, Cleaveland, June 16 [1839][1]

I have just made a considerable circuit thru East Tennessee, and take the liberty of giving you my opinion as to your prospects. I will commence with Johnson. In that county we will divide with the old Governor. In Carter the majority will be against us from 300 to 400. In Sullivan, Washington, Greene & Hawkins we will have a majority of from 4,500 to 5000 votes to enter Jefferson, Cocke, Grainger & Knox with; a majority so large that our enemies can never come up to us in those counties with, although, their majorities will be considerable. In Sevier county, Armstrong only got 72 votes,[2] but this time we will divide the county at least.[3] In Blount our majority will be 3 or 400, the same in Monroe, 500 for us in McMinn & not less than 500 in Bradl[e]y (this county). In Hamilton we will divide tolerably well, but our folks do not expect to carry the county. The opposition will have majorities in Bledsoe, and they may also have a very small one in Marion. In Meigs we will carry every thing before us & also in Rhea. In Roane we will divide with them. Morgan is against us. Anderson, Claiborne & Campbell are for us, which I believe are nearly all the counties in East Tennessee, except 2 or 3 & from them I have very imperfect accounts, & cannot give any thing like a correct opinion. Every thing is going on in the counties enumerated above in the very best style. Our friends are all true, and are determined to "do or die." Changes are daily taking place, and unless I am more deceived than I ever was in my life we will lick the opposition more than they ever have been. Your majority cannot be less than 3000 in East Tennessee.

As to the representatives in the next Legislature from this section, my opinion is that we will have from 16 to 20 of the 32 members—if every county does its duty.

The opposition are saying that Cannon is to be in East Tennessee before August, which I doubt, but should he be "fool hardy" enough to come you will take my advice & be found "battling by his side." In fact it will not do to let him travel over the country by himself. You will have to come & take care of him.

The new paper at Knoxville[4] will be out next week. We start with fair prospects. Dont let Cannon travel by himself.

LAWSON GIFFORD

ALS. DLC–JKP. Addressed to Columbia.

1. Cleveland, Tennessee. Year identified through content analysis.

2. Reference is to Robert Armstrong's unsuccessful race for the governorship in 1837.

3. Gifford began this sentence in the left margin and concluded it at the head of the page.

4. Knoxville *Argus*.

FROM GEORGE M. PORTER

Newport, Tennessee. June 16, 1839

Porter acknowledges receipt of Polk's letter of June 2, 1839.[1] He is glad to learn that Polk did not plan to remove Major Roadman as postmaster of Newport. The gubernatorial campaign has created political excitement seldom equaled in Cocke County. The Democrats are doing well. Col. Powell's speeches have been surprisingly effective. Carter and the other Whigs are trying to evade the issue of their support for Henry Clay. Governor Cannon is expected to campaign again in East Tennessee; Porter advises Polk to return with his rival.

ALS. DLC–JKP. Addressed to Maury County.

1. Letter not found.

FROM DANIEL KENNEY

Jonesboro, Tennessee. June 17, 1839

Kenney reports on politics in East Tennessee. Polk still is gaining ground in all counties east of the mountains. Cannon's agents are traversing the state delivering Cannon's address,[1] but Kenney doubts that the document will help Cannon's cause. If the Governor tours East Tennessee again, Polk should consider returning with him. Kenney and Blair[2] project a majority of 4,000 votes for Polk in the counties above Jefferson and Cocke. Even in the opposition strongholds of Sevier and Cocke, Polk will win. He will win easily in all the counties of upper East Tennessee except in Johnson and Carter. If Powell can get even a tolerable vote in Jefferson and Cocke, he will beat Carter in the First Congressional District. McClellan will beat McKinney badly in the Second District. Gifford has gone to Knoxville to hasten the appearance there of the new paper.[3]

ALS. DLC–JKP. Addressed to Columbia.

1. Cannon's brief campaign circular appeared in the *Nashville Whig* on May 20, 1839.

2. John Blair.

3. Knoxville *Argus*.

FROM SACKFIELD MACLIN

My dear Sir LaGrange Ten June 18th 1839

I would like much to know how ma[n]y days you can be in this county.[1] You are aware that this is the hot bed of Federalism; more so than any county in the Western District. Consequently as ma[n]y speeches as you can make here the better. The canvass in this county opened as early as February last, and it has been kept up with great warmth untill now. I have made twenty or thirty speeches, in which I discuss pretty fully all those great questions that are involved in the contest. I take hold of the *Independent Treasury* and recommend it to the people as being a *Southern measure* and the *cause* of the *people.*

The anxiety of the people of this county to see you, and to hear you discuss those great questions of national policy, is exceedingly high, and I have no hesitancy in the belief, that you will have much larger crowds than ever was seen in this county. Howevr, I am of the opinion, that we have a small majority upon the question. In Shelby you will beat Cannon. Can you make three speeches in this county?

SACKFIELD MACLIN

P.S. Write in time to have full notice given to the people. Your friends are remarcably anxious, and doing what they can. Our friends are active, and our enemies are doing nothing, and I think we will defeat them. In great haste. S. Maclin

ALS. DLC–JKP. Addressed to Purdy, in care of the postmaster.

1. Fayette County.

FROM JOHN T. MACON[1]

Sir, China Grove 20th June 1839

We have had an opportunity of conversing with many of your political friends lately and it is conceeded that never was your presence more necessary than at Raleigh on 12th July at a large concourse without distinction of parties as their seems to be many very many that are now on the fence in Shelby county and dislike to declare for Clay. It would not only do your cause good but the senators and representatives also.[2]

I would say that [there is] a great necessity also for you to meet the people at Lagrange, as much good could be done not only in that neighbourhood but in Tippo[3] & Marshall counties in Mi., as a US Senator is to be chosen in that State in place of Walker[4] and I am told by your poli[ti]cal friends in those counties that if they had notice of your coming to Lagrange that a thousand from Mi would [attend] and thereby strengthen our cause in both states. There is great necessity you may rely on it that you should attend at those places. I did expect to be at Purdy but my business will not admit of it.

Dunlap must put down that tool of Bells,[5] but his success will depend much on your coming to Raleigh & Lagrange. Then I think things will be tolerable certain in Our district.

JNO. T. MACON

P.S. Should you conclude to visit Lagrange get some friend to write to Capt James Peters[6] at Salem Mi. who is a warm Republican as well as his sons. J T M

ALS. DLC–JKP. Addressed to Purdy.

1. Formerly of Maury County, Macon moved to the Western District after 1830; his place of residence has not been identified more exactly than that of the Thirteenth Congressional District, to which he alludes in discussing William C. Dunlap's election campaign. China Grove in Gibson County was in the Twelfth Congressional District.

2. Levin H. Coe was seeking reelection as a Democrat to the state Senate; Pendleton G. Gaines was the Democratic candidate in the Tennessee House election for Shelby County.

3. Tippah County.

4. Robert J. Walker did not stand for reelection until 1841. In November 1839, the Mississippi legislature elected John Henderson to fill the seat formerly held by Thomas Hickman Williams.

5. Christopher H. Williams defeated Dunlap.

6. Not identified further.

FROM ROBERT B. REYNOLDS

Dr Sir. Knoxville June 21st 1839

I take the liberty of writing you the best information I have been able to collect as to the probable vote between yourself & Govr Cannon. I do assure you, Sir, that you have nothing to fear from the result of the election in E.T. Your majority in E. Tennessee will not be less than 3000 votes and probably more than 5000. Your gain in Grainger, Claiborne, Campbell, Anderson & Morgan is more than it is in any of the other counties in E.T. So great is the reaction in those counties that you will have majorities in each & in some of them *large* ones. You will recollect when here, we set the majority down against you in 4 of them. Equally as flattering is the accounts from above & below. Hawkins, Sullivan, Washington & Greene will give you 4000 majority. I have it on good authority that you will divide the votes in Johnson & greatly curtail the majority in Carter. In Jefferson you will reduce Cannons strength. Cocke is debateable ground. Sevier will give you one third of her votes, tho the Polkites think you will get one half.

Old Knox will do better than she did in 1837, but we concede Cannon a majority of 5 or 600. Of the other counties below, it is useless to speak as your majorities in them will certainly be large. Carter is very uneasy indeed & the race will be a close one—but the contest between McClellan & McKinney though warm is yet certain. The best informed men in that district sets down McClellans majority at 1000. McKinney acknowledged to Capt Lyon that he would be defeated. J Blackwells election is certain as that the sun rises & sets & the Feds admit it. Crozier is gaining ground in this county & will beat Jacobs with ease. The leaders have taken the alarm & are trying to stop the current that has set in for you & for Democracy, but they only add fuel to the fire.

The Looking Glass[1] is denounced in unmeasured terms by the Clay papers of this place. They fear the reward due apostacy & hence their efforts to invalidate the evidence arrayed against them in the Looking Glass. The Argus will come out amongst them in 6 or 8 days[2] (the Compositors being now at work) much to their annoyance. We will give them Looking Glasses to see themselves in—such as will let the people see them too.

I should like to hear from you & your prospects in the Western District & also at what time you can come to E.T. again & where you can address the people & what time &c. Let me know whether you will visit us again. I think it would do a vast deal of good to let the people hear you at Campbells Station & Blains XRoads & such other places as you might think best & have time to attend to.

I know it is asking much of you to again revisit old Knox, after Such hard service—yet I think your time would be usefully employed by so doing if your health & strength will allow of it.

R B Reynolds

[P.S.] Judge Grundy passed here a few days ago & we tendered him a public dinner, which he declined accepting &c.[3]

ALS. DLC–JKP. Addressed to Dyersburg and forwarded to Columbia.
1. See J. George Harris to Polk, April 2, 1839.
2. The first issue of the Knoxville *Argus* appeared on June 27, 1839.
3. Postscript written in the left margin.

FROM HOPKINS L. TURNEY

Dear Sir Livingston June the 21st 1839

Since I saw you I have been at Jamestown Fentress Co. to court, where I saw and conversed with a large potion of her Citizens—and I am well satisfied that you will beat Cannon in that county 350 votes. I cannot be mistaken in this estimate. It is less than your friends there give you. In Overton your majority will be at least 400 votes. Maj Taylor of White[1] thinks the cause is againing in his county, and that *he will be elected.* I have my fears for him. The mountain district[2] will do her duty & will give you a majority of 4000 votes. Let me hear from you If you can have time to write.

H. L. TURNEY

ALS. DLC–JKP. Addressed to Columbia.
1. Not identified further.
2. Reference is to Tennessee's Fifth Congressional District, which included Franklin, Warren, White, and Overton counties.

FROM ANDREW A. KINCANNON

Dear Col. Columbus Miss 23d June 1839

On looking over your list of appointments I see you are to address the people of Carroll County on the 6th July at Huntingdon.

Feeling as you know I must, a deep interest in the result of the canvass, in which you are ingaged, and knowing that you can tell more about the chances than any body else, I must ask of you the favour, to write me to this place, your *confidential* opinion as to the result.

Do not fail to write me & let me know the best & the worst of the case. Your political friends here, manifest a deep interest in you[r] manly undertaking, *and say to a man,* that if you succeed, or wheather you do or not, that you must be run for the Vice Presidency. They say you would help the question in this State.

Renewing as ever, the warmest friendships of my heart, for your success, I remain . . . .

ANDW. A. KINCANNON

ALS. DLC–JKP. Addressed to Huntingdon.

FROM SARAH C. POLK

Dear Husband Columbia June 25th 1839

You did not leave me any directions where to write or direct any thing to you. These letters[1] contained information I thought might be useful to you. And I have thought proper to enclose them to Majr. Bills with a request that he would send them to you. There is nothing occured since you left of importance. I have only heard from you by Genl. Pillow since you left. Why don't *Knox*[2] write to some body? I am anxious to hear from you, not political prospects only, but your *health*.

SARAH POLK

ALS. DLC–JKP. Mailed under separate cover to Bolivar, addressed to Brownsville, and forwarded to Trenton, Tennessee. Published under date of June 15, 1839, by Sarah Agnes Wallace, ed., "Letters of Mrs. James K. Polk to Her Husband," *Tennessee Historical Quarterly*, XI (June, 1952), 181–82.

1. Enclosures not found.

2. J. Knox Walker accompanied his uncle on a campaign tour through the Western District.

FROM J. G. M. RAMSEY

My Dear Sir Mecklenburg June 28. 1839

From the inclosed extract from the "Times"[1] you will see that Cannon has determined to visit E.T. & commences his circuit on the 16th July at Athens. If you are *well* employed in the other sections of the State we will only have to do the best we can for you in your absence. On the other hand if you can be spared from the West & overtake the Gov. at Sevierville or New-port or even meet him at Rogersville you will prostrate him. We cannot judge for you—but have thought it best to acquaint you with his operations. His awkward apointment of the [militia] election in the middle of our harvest is injuring him. Not one in ten of our militia has voted. Men of leisure & the towns have made the Major Genl.[2] & there is a general complaining & disaffection growing out of it. Your prospects still brighten—& we will make this oversight of the Gov. help you. I am preparing a short article on it for the "Argus"[3]—the first No. of which is out & is doing well. A good spirit prevails in E.T. & all accounts are favorable. We will elect 2 perhaps 3 to Congress & 15 or 17 to the Legislature.

If Mrs. Polk or some other friend at Columbia should in the absence of Col Polk open this & should the Col. be very distant & not conveniently reached by Mail no extra effort need be made to forward it—as I am writing to Mr. Grundy at Nashville & have requested other friends to write to several points in the Western District communicating the same intelligence. If you come to Knoxville by stage—my best horse is at your service afterwards.

J. G. M. Ramsey

[P.S.] Col. Polk can reach Newport by stage 3 times a week from Knoxville—also Greeneville, Jonesboro, Blountville & Rogersville—5 days from Nashville by stage you can over take him. It is asking too great a sacrafice of ease & comfort or I would say if you can leave Nashville by the 18 or 20 July you could do great good by coming.[4] J.G.M. Ramsey

ALS. DLC–JKP. Addressed to Columbia.

1. Enclosure not found. The Knoxville *Times* of June 28, 1839, announced Governor Cannon's return visit to East Tennessee.

2. William Brazelton, a farmer and merchant from Jefferson County, served as major-general of the East Tennessee militia, 1839–47.

3. Knoxville *Argus*.

4. Postscript written on verso.

FROM ROBERT B. REYNOLDS

Sir, Knoxville June 28. 1839

I wrote you this day to Benton Court House.[1] I enclosed you Govr Cannon's appointments for E. Ten. He opens the Campaign at Athens on the 16th July & goes all round Knoxville—I suppose from the belief that Judge White is invincible in Old Knox. He will find himself mistaken in his estimate of the firmness of her Sons. They will teach him a lesson that will last him forever.

If you can come to East Tennessee I think it would be best. I hope you will attend the Govr's appointments. It will blast all their calculations & react on their own heads. You will receive a large majty in E. Tennessee.

I think you had best meet Cannon at Athens, Madisonville, Maryville, Sevierville, & Newport; & whilst he is above in your strong counties, you had best I think make speeches at Campbell's Station, Blains XRoads, New Market & Dandridge & meet him again at Rutledge & go with him to Taz[e]well & Jacksboro' where he will be on the 1st day of August. He speaks at Newport on the 20th July & at Rutledge the 30th July. I have no doubt you could spend some time profitably by addressing the people at the places above named whilst he is wasting his ammunition in Greene, Washington, Sullivan & Hawkins. Let me hear from you early & excuse the haste which I have written you.

R B Reynolds

ALS. DLC–JKP. Addressed to Huntingdon.

1. Reynolds' first letter communicated information similar to that in the present document. ALS. DLC–JKP.

FROM ALEXANDER O. ANDERSON

Dear Colonel Knoxville June 29th 39

I recd. yours, dated in Morgan County,[1] at my return to this place, Three days since. The election of Brazleton[2] to be Major General is certain, (by several hundred votes). Tho' the returns are not complete. I was the next highest by several hundred & was beaten by the main vote of the Southern Counties being cast for McGahy & Frazier.[3] This was done a few days previous by certain representations of their strength in the upper Counties.

We shall suffer nothing, in the election of Governor, under this result. They have not polled more votes than we have, & the desire of the community is against the choice which has been made, (being made of course by a very small minority). The new *Whig* Major General having been drafted during the last war, refused to serve, & was fined fifty dollars. Besides the harvest date of the election is not satisfactory to the people—& they think a Governor ought to know when their harvests come on.

Cannon, notwithstanding his circular has appointed to visit East Tennessee & will be over by the 16th. I hope your appointments end by the 8th. I think it important, very important, you should be with him. Come if possible!!!

We are in high spirits. In the upper Counties our friends are as firm, and triumphant as ever—& we think throughout we are gaining.

The Looking Glass[4] is being put into circulation, as fast as it arrives & I think will do good.

A Anderson

P.S. I have not heard a word from Genl. Armstrong. A letter from him would help us with what we need—information! Why has he not written? A.

ALS. DLC–JKP. Addressed to Columbia.

1. Letter not found. Polk was in Morgan County on June 5, 1839.
2. William Brazelton.
3. John McGaughey and Julian Frazier. Frazier of Grainger County served as quartermaster general of the Tennessee militia during Polk's governorship. The East Tennessee militia's election for major general was held on June 25, 1839.
4. See J. George Harris to Polk, April 2, 1839.

FROM JOSEPH POWELL

Dear Col Newport Cocke Cty. June 30th 1839

I avail myself the pleasure to address you a line with regard to political movements in this Congressional District.

First with regard to the contest between yourself and Cannon—I am fully authorised to say that in the Counties of Green[e] and Washington your majority over the latter will doubtless equal the most liberal expectation of your friends. In this county your vote will be much greater than either you or myself anticipated at the time of your address in this place.[1] Your friends are sanguine in the belief that you will divide the vote equally. In Carter your vote will as a matter of course be small—though larger than I had at first anticipated. Johnson County will be about equally divided, as you have some active and influential friends engaged in discussing the questions, and in visiting all portions of the county.

I feel assured if you could revisit Jefferson County and make two or three speeches, it would not only insure for yourself and equal division of the votes—but beyond any sort of doubt secure my election. As matters now stand my chances are certainly equal. I shall beat Carter in the Counties of Johnson, Washington and Green[e]—in the latter very largly. In this county all sides acknowledge a majority for me, unless Arnold should take grounds against me. If I can secure six hundred out of eighteen in Jefferson the *Black Horse* as he is called is beaten. This victory aside from your own and Burtons, is of all others in Tennessee most important, as it would destroy Fosters most submissive *tool.*

I must implore that you will if at all possible return to Jefferson. Wm. A Harris Post Master at Panther Springs[2] would take very much pleasure in making and extensively circulating the appointments.

I have this moment been furnished with the Knoxville times[3] containing a list of appointments for Cannon—and least you should be unadvised, I will apprise you that they commence on the 16th July at Athens and continuing from day to day at Madisonville, Maryville, Sevierville, Newport, Warrensburg (corner of Green, Jefferson & Hawkins 22nd), Green[e]ville Jonesboro, Elizabethton—Blountville, Kingsport, Rogersville, Rutledge, Taswell [Tazewell] and at Jacksboro—1st Augst. And from which he considers himself (as you will perceive) entirely secure in Jefferson.

In conclusion I repeat, come to Jefferson and you make a Congressman. Accept my sincere wishes that you obtain the most signal triumph.

J. POWELL

P.S. Write me at Strawbery Plains Jefferson Cty where I shall be, about the middle of the month.

ALS. DLC–JKP. Addressed to Columbia.

1. Polk spoke at Newport on May 13, 1839.
2. Harris was postmaster from 1836 until 1840.
3. Reference is to the Knoxville *Times* of June 28, 1839.

FROM JOHN F. GILLESPY

Dear Sir, Madisonville 1st July 1839

I have been canvassing for about four weeks in the Counties of Bradl[e]y, McMinn and Monroe for the Senate of the Legislature. The excitement between you and Cannon is very high & the *question* on national politicks runs very strong. You are gaining ground rapidly in McMinn County. I think you may safely calculate on 600 majority in Bradly, 500 majority in McMinn, and 300 majority in Monroe. In Blount you will get a majority, but not as great as we had expected when I saw you. In Meigs you will as I am informed get at least ⅔. In Rhea about the same vote. In Bledsoe it is said you are gaining rapidly. I am not satisfactorily informed from other Counties in East Ten. except that the democratic Republican Van Buren Polk question is carrying every thing before it.

Gov. Cannon's friend's on this day at a public meeting of the people here gave notice that his Excellency would address them here on the 17th Instant. This is the first notice we have received of his visit to E. Ten. We have no notice as yet of any other appointments made by him. It is highly important to you & I think that you should be with him, particularly in Blackwells Congressional District. Stone and Brown are Blackwells competitors, and the prospect good for Blackwells success. Be with him if possible.

JOHN F. GILLESPY

N.B. I think I shall beat my competitors Hickey & Hurst.[1] J.F.G.

ALS. DLC–JKP. Addressed to Columbia.

1. James Hickey and Elijah Hurst. Hickey is not identified further. Hurst, a farmer and a Whig from McMinn County, served three terms in the Tennessee House, 1827–29, 1831–33, and 1835–37.

TO SARAH C. POLK

My Dear Wife Dyersburg July 1st 1839

Knox wrote to you at my request from Brownsville.[1] The most fatiguing part of the canvass has been since I left home.[2] I have been so constantly riding and in the crowd that I have had no opportunity until now to write. We had a fine day at Brownville, and there is now no doubt of a majority in Haywood which has been heretofore one of the strongest of the Whig Counties in the District. I find changes in my favour in all the Counties, through which I have passed, and without going into details—my opinion is, that my prospects in the District are as good, indeed better than I anticipated they would be. The majority West of the Tennessee will not be large either way, and the present prospects are that it will be in my favour. I found it necessary for me to visit Jackson & Paris, which will delay me some days longer in the District than I had anticipated. By my present arrangement I will be at Centerville in Hickman on *Monday the 15th July*, and will go from there to Dixon[3] without returning home. *Knox* will wish to leave me at Centerville and return home. I wish you to send my letters & particularly any from East Tennessee to meet me at Centerville on Sunday evening the 14th July. I think I will drop the Sulkey at that point and go on horseback. If brother William[4] cannot come down to Centerville, send a messenger with my letters. I do not now expect to be at home until the day of the election. Where I will be on that day I do not certainly know. If my Giles friends wish it I will be there. The Governor[5] left me at

Ripley on Saturday and has gone to the Southern Counties. He speaks of leaving the District in a few days and going to East Tennesseee.

James K. Polk

ALS. DLC–JKP. Addressed to Columbia.

1. J. Knox Walker's letter to Sarah C. Polk has not been found.
2. Polk left Columbia on June 18, 1839.
3. Reference is to Dickson County; the town of Dickson was not founded until 1868.
4. William H. Polk.
5. Newton Cannon.

FROM JAMES COWAN[1]

Dear Sir — Okachickam[2] 2d July 1839

I have been here for some two months on my farm & my place is entirely healthy, & the neighbourhood generally except the Bowel complaint, which has been very prevelent, & fatal in many instances. The Crops of Cotton are generally fine. The Corn has Suffered much for rain, but if we are blessed with it in a few days, it will be a fair Crop. The object of this Short epistle, is to inform you that your manager, *Mr Geo Bratton died* this morning with the Bowel Complaint, & perhaps the fever in addition. I learn that his wife is not expected to live. I also learn that your agent Mr McNeel[3] is absent on a visit to Ten. Under all these circumstances, I regret, that I do not know how I could Serve you agreeable to your wishes. Managers are Scarce, & good ones not to be had, & bad ones worse than none. Upon the whole, I would advise you to send some one from home, on recpt of this, for if you do not, who ever takes your farm, *now,* will want your Crop for pay. I expect to leave for Mont Holyoke Hy Conty Ten[4] in a few days, Say two, after a long absence. If I was not so Situated, I do believe I would See & do what I thot right for your Int, & that of your Blk family & take the *Responsibility*. Please be assured of my good wishes for your property, here as well as else where—& be assured that nothing would afford me more pleasure than to Serve you or any one else under Similar circumstances.

James Cowan

[P.S.] I merely write you this hasty sketch as the Stage will pass in a few moments. In the mean time, I'll Send my overseer over this way to See how matters are, & may inform you by next mail which will reach you 4 days later than this. McNeal being absent, I thot it a duty due you or any one else to give you the earliest information. J.C.

ALS. DLC–JKP. Addressed to Columbia via Holly Springs, Mississippi, and postmarked at Coffeeville, Mississippi. Published in Bassett, *Plantation Overseer*, 120–21.

1. Cowan probably moved to Henry County, Tennessee, in the late 1820's. He received appointments as commissioner of the Union Bank of Tennessee in 1831 and as postmaster of Mount Holyoke two years later. He served in the latter position through the 1850's.

2. Oakachickama, Yalobusha County, Mississippi.

3. Albert T. McNeal.

4. On July 12, 1839, Cowan wrote a similar letter while en route from Mississippi to Tennessee. ALS. DLC–JKP. Cowan's destination was Mt. Holyoke, in Henry County.

TO ROBERT B. REYNOLDS

My Dear Sir Huntingdon July 6th 1839

On reaching here last evening I received your letter of the 28th ult. and have only time to say in reply, that it will not be in my power to visit East Tennessee again before the election, nor do I think it important that I should. Before I learned that the Governor[1] would cross the mountain, which I did not learn with certainty, until the receipt of your letter, I had made appointments as you will see from the newspapers, extending up to the election. These appointments are in Counties which I have not yet visited, and even if I thought it important to go again to E. Tennessee, it is now too late to recal[l] the appointments. My friends in the East may rest assured that we will give a good account of ourselves in the West. The finest spirit is prevailing among our friends; our cause is gaining ground daily, and our majority must be a large one. I must rely upon my friends in E. Tennessee to attend to the Governor's movements when he goes over the mountain. I have not time to write to them. Will you do so, and especially to Blackwell, Powell and McClellan, to accompany him through their respective districts. I am in good health and will prosecute the canvass actively until the election. I have no doubt the leaders of the opposition will bend their whole energies to the Governor's election. My friends in the West are apprized that they will do so, and will be prepared for them at all points.

JAMES K. POLK

ALS. NHi. Addressed to Knoxville.

1. Newton Cannon.

FROM S. BELL[1]

Dr. Sir, Coffeeville Mississipp 7th July 1839

A. T. McNeal being at this time from home on a visit to Tennessee I deem it expedient to write you a few lines to acquaint you of the situation of your affairs in Mississippi. Your Overseer[2] died a few days since. Dr. Towns[3] living near him was his attending physician. 7 or 8 of your negroes have been quite sick with the same disease (Bilious Dysentery) but all have recovered or are now convaliscent save one (Caroline) & she I considered not at all dangerous. Mr. McNeal being absent I took upon myself the responsibility of riding down to your farm & employing a young man[4] to take charge of your interest until Mc[Neal's] return. The young man is recommended as one of steady and industrious habits.

You have a prospect for an abundant crop both of Corn & Cotton. The growth is large & in good order. If you wish any directions about the management of your farm, write to me & I will take great pleasure in attending to the same.

S. Bell

P.S. If you should see my old friend Cave Johnson say to him my respects & tell him that I anxiously pray his triumphant success. Yet I fear for Tennessee Democracy. What is the prospect? Bell.

ALS. DLC–JKP. Addressed to Charlotte, Tennessee, and forwarded to Columbia. Published in Bassett, *Plantation Overseer,* 121–22.

1. A local physician, not identified further.
2. George W. Bratton.
3. Not identified further.
4. Not identified further. George W. Meek declined the overseer's job in August, and John J. Garner accepted the position in September 1839.

TO SARAH C. POLK

My Dear Wife Huntingdon July 7th 1839

If I have not written to you more frequently, it is because I have been constantly riding from point to point; or surrounded by company. I have been moreover much fatigued, and until two or three days ago, did not recover entirely from my cold and hoarseness. I think I am now myself again. Cannon left me last evening for Nashville and then to East Tennessee. I shall pursue my appointments & will not be at home until after the election. You must not fail to send my letters to me to

Hickman, where I will be on the 15th. My prospects in this and Gibson Counties are better than I calculated they would be. All my information is cheering. I have given out the idea of being in Giles on the day of the election. I wrote to Mr. Walker and Genl. Armstrong on yesterday[1] to make my appointments for me, after I leave Gallatin on the 26th so as to allow me to spend the time in the strong Counties, in that region, particularly in Smith, so as to allow me to be at Sparta, on the day of the election. Do urge Mr Walker to go immediately to Nashville and make the arrangements with Armstrong & have the appointments published & notices given. In addition to what I wrote to him, you may say to him, that if my Nashville friends think it very important, they can make an appointment for the lower part of Wilson for saturday the 27th—and then I can be at Alexandria on the 29th and at two other points to be selected by my friends for tuesday and wednesday. *Rome & Lancaster* in Smith it strikes me would be proper points. From Lancaster I could reach Sparta on the day of the election.

James K. Polk

ALS. DLC–JKP. Addressed to Columbia.

1. Letters not found.

FROM JAMES WALKER

Dear Sir, Columbia July 9, 1839

I received on yesterday a letter from A. V. Brown in which he decided upon consultation that it is not advisable for you to be at Pulaski on the day of election but to be there the day before if you can. I suppose you can be there on Wednesday and his reasons seem to be good.[1] I have handed his letter to William to show you that I may be sure of your decision by Knox. I can give Martin immediate notice after Knox's return, and he will have it made public.

The letters from East Tennessee are all very encorageing. William will take them all to you. The requests are numerous & urgent for you to join Cannon and be in that end of the state at the election. I have written to Dr. Ramsey that this is impossible and given him the reasons why it is so. Things here in perfect *statu quo*. The Whigs now say, you will beat the question in this county—get from 3 to 500 Whig votes. I had not thought it was so good. Our friends in Davidson are very much excited. They are confident of a majority of 2 to 300. Armstrong says he has information he believes to be correct, that Burton will beat in Wilson.

That is almost too good to be true—but all accounts agree that our strength is rapidly increasing in Wilson, & Williamson.

You will have seen the Banner's attack on you of the 24th of June—and the reply to it.[2] I think this occurence will do good. The facts are too strong, and too plainly set forth not to have an important influence on Bell's election.

The matter is not yet decided as to the appointment at Alexandria or Lebanon. I suppose I will be advised in time to advise you at Clarksville, or that Genl Armstrong will write you himself on the subject.

Barringer and Watterson are both disgusting the people with their low vulgar ribaldry. They say what a contrast between their former Representative and the present, let who may, be elected. *But we must Suffer it to be so now.* I hope your health & strength has improved.

JAMES WALKER

ALS. DLC–JKP. Addressed to the Western District and delivered by William H. Polk.

1. On July 5, 1839, Aaron V. Brown wrote Walker that "an appointment for Colo. Polk *on the day of the election,* would do an injury in calling off from their posts, our efficient friends, & congregating them at *one point,* leaving our opponents at home to do greater mischief amongst the Whigs who did not come out." Brown asks that Walker communicate Polk's decision to Thomas Martin. ALS. DLC–JKP.

2. On June 24, 1839, Allen A. Hall, editor of the Nashville *Republican Banner,* charged that Polk had agreed to support Martin Van Buren in the late presidential contest in order to gain election over John Bell in the Speaker's race of 1835. In doing so, Polk was guilty of treachery to Hugh L. White and of desertion of Tennessee's congressional delegation, a majority of which supported White for the presidency. Four days later, J. George Harris countered in the *Nashville Union* that since 1836 Hall had changed his principles as well as his preferences for men. "He wanted office under the administration," Harris wrote of Hall, "did not get it—and then turned."

FROM ALEXANDER O. ANDERSON

Knoxville, Tennessee. July 10, 1839

Anderson urges Polk to follow Cannon to East Tennessee. Polk is now ahead of Cannon in the gubernatorial race there, but Cannon's return tour, if unaccompanied by Polk, will affect the vote.

ALS. DLC–JKP. Addressed to Columbia.

FROM JAMES WALKER

Dear Sir, Columbia July 12. 1839

I received your letter from Huntingdon[1] too late to go to Nashville & give you notice of where appointments are made for you (from Gallatin to the election) at Centreville. It was particularly necessary too for me to be at home this week out [end]. I will go to Nashville on Monday & consult with Armstrong—and give notice of the appointments in the respective neighborhoods, and advise you at Clarksville what we have concluded on. This can be certain, and it will answer every purpose.

I have replied to the letters sent to you from Dr. Ramsay, Powell, Woods &c., J F Gillispie, Gifford[2] & written the editors of the Athens[3]—giving the information that it was impossible for you to revisit East Tennessee previous to the election. And assigning the reasons, viz, that you were then 120 miles from home, had been a month in the District, and had appointments published to be in a part of Middle Tennessee (where tho very strong you had never been) up to the day of the election—that it would never do to fail in these appointments, now they were out &c. I gave the information I had of your prospects in the District & middle Tennessee.

My Judgement is that you had better send yourself a dozen or more letters to prominent men in E Ten. I know you are too much fatigued to write these letters yourself. You can write one that you think will effect good, & set Knox & William to copying as many as you want. Let Knox be here by Monday night to mail them.

Nothing very material has occured. As the day of election approaches, the Whig papers become more & more furious. As they become alarmed, they "*whistle the louder*" and endeavor to keep up the courage of the Whigs by extravagant bragging of their prospects. Both parties are making unweared exertions. All the news we get are favorable.

JAMES WALKER

ALS. DLC–JKP. Addressed to Centerville.

1. Polk's letter to Walker of July 6, 1839, has not been found.

2. See J. G. M. Ramsey to Polk, June 12 and 28, 1839; Joseph Powell to Polk, June 30, 1839; John F. Gillespy to Polk, July 1, 1839; and Lawson Gifford to Polk, June 16, 1839. On July 1, 1839, Richard M. Woods et al. urged Polk to make a return visit to East Tennessee. LS. DLC–JKP.

3. Reference is to the Athens *Courier*, edited by Robert Frazier.

TO CAVE JOHNSON, ET AL.[1]

Dear Sir Centreville July 15th 1839

At the time the appointments were made for me, to meet the people of Dickson Stewart, Montgomery and Robertson, Governor Cannon was with me, in the Western part of the State, and as I supposed intended to continue with me. A few days afterwards he left me at Huntingdon, and as I learn has gone to East Tennessee, where he has appointments to meet the people up to the day of the Election. My friends in East Tennessee are accordingly desirous that I should accompany him through that part of the State, and on my arrival here last night I received numerous letters urging me to do so.[2] I was sincerely anxious to meet the people of[3] but under the circumstances, felt that I ought to yield to the urgent calls of my friends & go immediately to East Tennessee. I have to request you to make my apology to the people for not meeting them, as I expected to have done on the and to assure them that under other circumstances, it would have given me sincere pleasure to have done so.

AL, draft. DLC–JKP. Addressed: "Hon. C. Johnson & To others in Dickson, Stewart Montgomery & Robertson," and marked "Copy."

1. Having decided to return to East Tennessee before the election, Polk probably sent copies of this letter to leading Democrats in Dickson, Stewart, Montgomery, and Robertson counties.

2. See James Walker to Polk, July 12, 1839.

3. At this place Polk canceled the words "Dickson, as well as of the Stewart, Montgomery and Robertson" and interlined the words "your County." He subsequently canceled the interlineation, probably with the intention of supplying greater specificity in each of the letter's several versions.

FROM GEORGE R. POWEL

Rogersville, Tennessee. July 24, 1839

Polk's return to East Tennessee, according to Powel, has set back the Whigs. Governor Cannon is expected to come to Rogersville on Monday[1] to attend a barbecue; Judge White has been invited. Friends have made arrangements for Polk's arrival and expect his strength to be sustained in their city.

ALS. DLC–JKP. Addressed to Cheeks X Roads.

1. July 29, 1839.

FROM N. G. FRAZIER[1]

Washington, Tennessee. July 25, 1839

Frazier is pleased to learn of Polk's following Cannon to East Tennessee. Polk will beat Cannon in McMinn County and will win by at least two to one and five to one in Rhea and Meigs counties, respectively. The Whigs have ruled out Major Brown as a congressional candidate; the race between Blackwell and Stone is now doubtful. Whig newspaper extras at Athens remind Frazier of the Coffin Handbill issued during the 1828 presidential campaign.[2]

ALS. DLC–JKP. Addressed to Jacksboro and forwarded to Knoxville.

1. Frazier was clerk of the Rhea County Court, 1836–40.

2. John Binns, editor of the Philadelphia *Democratic Press*, published a campaign handbill depicting the coffins of six soldiers whose executions Andrew Jackson had ordered during the War of 1812. The men had been charged with desertion.

FROM JOHN F. RHOTON[1]

[New Market, Tennessee] 27th July 1839[2]

Questions for Col. Polk to answer,

If you charge Henry Clay, to-day, with having "bargained and intrigued" with John Q. Adams, will you furnish the proof of that charge? If it is not susceptible of proof, will you tell the people whether or not you believe the charge? If Henry Clay had voted for Jackson, and not Adams, and Jackson had made him Secretary, would it not all have been right, fair and honest? Did not Jackson vote for the tariff of 1824—as well as Henry Clay? If it was a federal vote in Clay, was it not also in Jackson? Is it not a fact, that Van Buren, Dick Johnson, Buckannon & Wright,[3] voted for the tariff of 1828—your bill of "abominations," but that Henry Clay did not?[4] If Henry Clay was in favor of this bill of "abominations," how can you make it federalism in him and republicanism in Messrs Van Buren, Johnson, Wright & co? If being in favor of internal improvement by the general government, constitutes Henry Clay a federalist, is not Col. Polk a federalist also? What did you say on this subject in your circular to your constituents in 1825?[5] And upon the same principle, is not Van Buren a compound federalist? How did he vote touching this subject? Was Henry Clay a federalist, when he was contending side by side with president Madison, for those rights &

principles involved in the war of 1812? In whoes [*sic*] ranks was Van Buren at that time? Was Henry Clay a federalist, when he threw himself in the breach between Missouri and the United States—and by his industry & eloquence produced reconciliation & union? Was Henry Clay a federalist, when he nobly stepped forward, spiked both cannons—and hoisted the white flag of peace on the platform of the constitutions, round which South Carolina and the federal Government rallied, shook hands of friendship and buried the hatchet of death? It is desired by Col. Polk's friends that he should answer the foregoing questions—publicly—reading them all first—then take them up one by one until he shall have answered them all.

JNO. F. RHOTON

Is the speaker's chair, which under your directions, cost twenty one hundred dollars, a comfortable seat? Is not the Subtreasury when ingrafted on our System, the creation of a prerogative, and is [it] not the only one in america—and how many officers [will be] necessary to carry it out? Jno. F. Rhoton

ALS. DLC–JKP. Addressed locally.

1. John F. Rhoton was the son-in-law of Jacob Peck, an early Jefferson County settler and judge of the state Supreme Court. Rhoton is not identified further.

2. Rhoton handed Polk these questions immediately before he spoke at New Market. See Polk to Robert B. Reynolds, July 28, 1839.

3. Martin Van Buren, Richard M. Johnson, James Buchanan, and Silas Wright. Wright was Democratic senator from New York from 1833 until 1844. A strong Van Buren supporter in the 1844 election, he refused the vice-presidential nomination when Polk became the Democratic presidential candidate. Subsequently, Wright served as governor of New York from 1844 until 1846.

4. Clay was not then a member of Congress.

5. Not found.

FROM WILLIAM M. LOWRY[1]

Dr Sir Green[e]ville 28 July 1839

It would have afforded me great pleasure to have met with you at Rogersville on tomorrow, but believing I could do your cause more good by staying at home and circulating Ticketts to the different places of voting. I have never seen such efforts as are now making in this county to prejudice the minds of the people against you. Thousands of those Whig papers are now circulating gratiously amongst the people filled with the grossest misrepresentations. I was much surprised last evening at Thos D Arnold who came to town just at Dusk. I never saw a man in such a rage in my life. He called you all kinds of names from scoundrel to Liar &c. and that he would as leave tell you so at Rogersville to your face, which probably he may do. He was in a crowd that had suported him at the previous Election consisting of some 10 or 12 voters all of whom with but one exception told him that they never would support him again in their lives. He also made a charge against you pretty much in effect as follows: that you were now a citizens of Missippi & that your Only object in running for Gov was to do Van B. good. He also pronounced Van B an abolitionist. I give the above to you confidentially in order that you may see what some of our would be great men are doing. We will make the strongest pull possible for you in the county. I have just seen a Gent from the Lower counties[2] who say you will certainly get Majority in Blount, Monroe, McMin[n], Bradl[e]y Meigs, Hamilton, Rhea & Marion. We have also herd verry favourably from you at Cheeks X Roads on Friday.

WM M LOWRY

ALS. DLC–JKP. Addressed to Rogersville. AE by Polk includes notes for a speech, the time and place of which are not identified.

1. A business, personal, and political friend of Andrew Johnson, Lowry served as postmaster at Greeneville, 1843–50, and as U.S. marshal for the Eastern District of Tennessee during the years before the Civil War.

2. Not identified.

TO ROBERT B. REYNOLDS

My Dear Sir — New Market July 28th 1839

I have barely time before leaving for Rogersville, to give you a hasty account of the day here on yesterday. A large crowd attended, and the result from all I can learn was more favourable than any one anticipated it could be. One or two circumstances occurred independent of the discussion, which produced a most powerful effect, and at the close of the proceedings near night, the crowd was manifestly with us, and the day was ours. Many persons told me in person that they had not expected to support me, but would now do so, and among them leading men, of whom I may name Mr Bradshaw, who was the member of the State Convention from Jefferson.[1] The circumstances to which I allude were these.

A short time before I was to speak I receivd a list of interrogatories in writing, to be answered in my speech, signed by *Dr. John F. Rhoton,*[2] who upon inquiry I learn is the son-in-law of Judge Peck.[3] The Interrogatories denied *Clay's* bargain with Adams; requesting me if I made the charge in my speech to adduce the proof, and to state whether I believed the charge to be true; and various other silly interrogatories, embracing the newspaper slang of the times. In my speech I read and answered the interrogatories to the people, produced the proof of the bargain & stated my belief in its truth. I answered all the other interrogatories to the entire satisfaction of the people, and to the heart's content I doubt not of the person who proponded them. When I was done, by previous arrangement Judge Peck was called for to answer the Speech. He rose with voluminous notes, and indeed a book already written out. And such a speech you have not heard in many a day. He took open & bold ground for Clay; denounced Jackson & his administration, going back to the old story of his cockfighting; said that he had supported Jackson in his first election with great doubts on his mind, but in the hope that he was a reformed man; but that before two years had elapsed he had *turned* from him; that he did not attempt to prove White & Bell's consistency, but said what he blamed them for most was that they did not *turn* sooner. I cannot repeat all he said against Jackson, but may sum it up by saying, that he repeated almost every thing that his enemies had ever said against. He of course abused Van-Buren & the administration; and said that Governor Cannon had made a good Governor & that the people would show by their votes, that they condemned Jacksons course, Van-Buren's & mine. He overacted his part & produced a tremendous revulsion in the minds of his hearers. I had a fine field in reply; and did not fail to place him where he belongs with Adams, Webster & the Federalists of the North. If his speech could have been heard by the whole people of the State, fourfiths of them would be with us. There is no point in the State where I have addressed the people with so much effect. This is of course not for the public, but to place you in possession of the facts. Shew it [to][4] Genl. Anderson, to whom I wrote [at] Cheek's X Roads, mailing his letter here.[5] He will shew you my letter. In great haste.

James K. Polk

P.S. Do not fail to have the hack sent to Taz[e]well for me so as to be there on Wednesday at noon. J.K.P.

ALS. NHi. Addressed to Knoxville and marked "*Private.*"

1. Richard Bradshaw represented Jefferson County at the 1834 Constitutional Convention. He is not identified further.
2. See John F. Rhoton to Polk, July 27, 1839.

3. Jacob Peck, a native of Virginia, was an early Jefferson County settler. He practiced law from 1808 until his election in 1822 to the state Supreme Court. He served in that post until the courts were reorganized under the 1834 Constitution.
4. A tear on the margin has obliterated two words of the manuscript.
5. Letter not found.

FROM JOHN S. YOUNG

Dear Sir McMinnville 28 July 1839

At the end of three days more we make a trial of our Strength. Since the day you addressed the people at this place[1] I have made the election the subject of the most attentive enquiry and all my accounts up to the present moment are of a very satisfactory character and have brought me to the following conclusions—viz That your majority in East Tennessee will be 3000 votes and in Middle Tennessee, 2500 carrying you to the District 5,500 votes ahead. In the District altho you were very sanguine of a majority my opinion is you will be beat in the District 2500 votes, leaving you in the state a majority of 3000 votes. To this conclusion I have arrived by the most cautious calculations in which I have made the most liberal allowances to the Whigs. For instance put your Majy in Bedford at 400. This will be an increase of ½ per cent in the former vote of the state. You will get ⅔ of the increase. I think your majority in Old Warren will be 1600.

We would be most hapy to see you at our Town on your return to the West. Should you be elected Governor it is our intention to call a meeting at McMinnville and nominate you for the Vice Presidency.

John S Young

ALS. DLC–JKP. Addressed to Knoxville.

1. Polk spoke at McMinnville on April 18, 1839.

FROM ROBERT B. REYNOLDS

Dear Colonel, Knoxville July 30 [1839][1]

Our news from the lower Counties in E. Tennessee are indeed encouraging to us, and there is no doubt on my mind of your receiving a glorious majority in Judge Whites own *dominions*—indeed, Col. you have *"poached"* to[o] severely on the Judge's park.

I was rejoiced at the Victory you obtained over Judge Peck at New Market.[2] Your speech there has dampened the spirits of the Whigs in this place no little, and will no doubt teach them a lesson that will serve them the ballance of the campaign. The whigs have put on long faces in advance and which I hope they will have leave to wear the ballance of their days.

I have just returned from the Country whither I have been to raise the democracy to come out and hear you on the day of the election and I anticipate a large crowd. Many persons are anxious to here you & are now on tiptoe. I may be mistaken, but I think you will have a large audience. Many persons have declared for you and will no doubt continue to do so for the little time yet unexpired before the election.

The Extra Argus 'tis said by our friends in Blount, is doing much good to allay the excitement that the Whigs have raised in Blount about the relief bill.[3]

It will be important that you arrive here by 8 O-Clock on Thursday. The polls will be opened at 9 O-Clock and every exertion be used to Keep the people from hearing you.

I send you several numbers of the Argus. Please hand them to some friend that will hand them to the people. Let McClellan & Wheeler have them.

I hear nothing from the west since you were here, save, that McClung,[4] Judge White's nephew has returned from West Ten and reports that East Tennessee has to decid the contest. If it is left to East Tenn—there cannot be a doubt but that democracy triumphs. But I calculate with certainty on 5000 majty west of the mountains.

I have written in haste. I hope to see you going a head by 9 O Clock on Thursday in this place giving the Whigs the last *Fire* from our best field piece. Success attend all our efforts and yours particularly.

R B Reynolds

ALS. DLC–JKP. Addressed to Tazewell, Tennessee.

1. Year identified through content analysis.

2. See Polk to Robert Reynolds, July 28, 1839.

3. In the 1823 legislature Polk had voted against relinquishing debts owed the state for lands purchased in that part of East Tennessee located south of the French Broad River. Postponement of those debts had been granted first in 1811.

4. Possibly Matthew or Hugh Lawson McClung, who were sons of Margaret White McClung, wife of Charles McClung and sister of Hugh Lawson White. Charles McClung promoted the founding of Knoxville.

FROM LEWIS P. ROBERTS

My dear Sir, Knoxville July 30 '39

I write this by the boy[1] in great haste informing you that the polls will open here at 9 O-clock. There will not be many votes given in until near ten. It would be best however to be here as soon [as] possible.

We are doing the best we can, and I think are gaining ground every day. Genl. Wallace writes me that we are holding our own in Blount. We have sent him 350 extra *Argus's* to be distributed in the Coves where I think they will have a good effect.

Our regular paper comes out this morning. We will send off as many as we possibly can.

Yerger's friends say he was very much excited at the remarks in the Argus relative to his veracity.[2] His wrath has cooled of[f] & the editor of our paper[3] has not as yet received the cow skinning that Y. threatend him with. Crozier will beat Jacobs—I think without doubt. No more.

L. P. Roberts

ALS. DLC–JKP. Addressed to Tazewell, Tennessee.

1. Postmaster Roberts' messenger is not identified.

2. Reference is to George S. Yerger, who served as Tennessee's attorney general, 1831–38, and represented Davidson County in the Tennessee Senate, 1833–35. He had moved to Vicksburg, Mississippi, in 1838, but, according to an article in the Knoxville *Argus* of July 30, 1839, he had returned to Tennessee and written pro-Cannon editorials for the Knoxville *Times*. The *Argus'* earlier remarks questioning Yerger's veracity have not been found.

3. E. G. Eastman of the Knoxville *Argus*.

FROM NATHAN GAMMON

Jonesboro, Tennessee. August 2, 1839

Gammon reports election results in Washington and surrounding counties. Polk has defeated Cannon by 324 votes in Washington County. The margin would have been larger but for Democratic division over the Assembly race between Martin and Embree.[1] The decision went to Martin by 107 votes. Aiken won a seat in the state Senate. In surrounding counties Polk and the Democratic candidates have done well. McClellan has won reelection to Congress, and Fain has taken the Senate seat for Sullivan and Hawkins counties. On the other hand Carter has succeeded in his bid for reelection to Congress.

ALS. DLC–JKP. Addressed to Columbia.

1. Alfred Martin and probably Worley Embree. Embree, whose wife, Elizabeth, was the daughter of former Congressman John Blair III, served as clerk of the First Circuit Court from 1848 until 1852. For the party division in Washington County, see Alexander O. Anderson to Polk, August 6, 1839.

FROM JULIUS W. BLACKWELL

Dr. Sir. Athens Ten. Aug. 5th 1839

"We have met the enemy and they are ours" in the 4th Congressional district.[1] Never did I se[e], or heare of such exertions made by the enemy, particularly in Athens. I have never known such zeal manifested, even by the Citizens of Knoxville.

I have barely time to give you majorrities, the news papers will give you particulars, probably before this reaches you.

McMinn Co.	Polk	maj.	361
	Blackwell	do.	506
Bradley	P.	maj.	484
	B.	do.	589
Meigs	P.	do.	475
	B.	do.	531
Rhea	P.	do.	273
	B.	do.	288
Roan Co.	Can[non]	maj.	363
	Stone	do.	162
Bledso	Can.	do.	233
	S.	do.	238
Marion	Can.	do.	74
	Stone	do.	50
Hamilton	Can.	do.	187
	Stone	do.	162

One district to hear from in Bledso. A Traveller says you have a maj. in Morgan Co. of 50 votes. He could tell nothing about Congress. Gallaspie, McMillan & Walker,[2] all good and true—elected by triumphant majorrities. Your maj. in Monroe 216. You have been beat 100 in Blount. In haste.

J. W. BLACKWELL

ALS. DLC–JKP. Addressed to Columbia.

1. Quotation from Oliver H. Perry's dispatch to William H. Harrison, September 10, 1813. Perry reported on his naval victory in the battle of Lake Erie.

2. John F. Gillespy, Joseph W. McMillin, and James Walker (McMinn County).

FROM ADAM HUNTSMAN

Dr Sir Huntingdon 5th of Augt [1839] [1]

I send you the result of our election which I deem nearly accurate. I give you the majorit[i]es.

Cannons		Polks	
Haywood	75	Henry	493
Henderson	714	Weakly	455
Perry	225	Hardeman	320
McNairy	291	Benton	230
Dyer	84	Hardin	270
Fayette	70	*Obion	00
Shelby	58	Tipton	75
Carroll	788		1843
Madison	503	*majority for you unknown	
Gibson	638		
	3446		
	1843		
	1603		

We have elected 9 Democrats to 11 Whigs, a gain of 4 on our side. We have fought as well as we could.

A. Huntsman

ALS. DLC–JKP. Addressed to Columbia. Published in Emma Inman Williams, ed., "Letters of Adam Huntsman to James K. Polk," *Tennessee Historical Quarterly*, VI (1947), 344.

1. Year identified through content analysis.

FROM ROBERT B. REYNOLDS AND LEWIS P. ROBERTS

Dear Col Knoxville August 5[1839][1]

I send you all the returns that have reached me and the result is *glorious.*

	Polk	Cannon
Knox	465	1614
Jefferson	217	1509
Grainger	690	801
Roane	577	943
Rhea	433	151
Meigs	594	103
McMinn	1322	960
Monroe majty	223	
Bradley	781	300
Blount	811	911
Greene	1701	874
Washington	1119	796
Hawkins	1433	804
Sullivan	1412	250
Claiborne	782	479
Campbell 5 precincts—majty	93	
Morgan reptd majty	100	
Sevier County	151	750

Blackwell & McClellan by heavy majorities. Powell is beaten. Aiken is elected. Balch, Gillespy & Wheeler also. Cross[2] Fain & Baugh[3] from Sullivan & Hawkins. Johnson[4] Feazle[5] & Martin from Greene & Washington. McKamy of Blount. Hembree of Roane. Gregory, McMillan & Walker from Bradley McMinn & Monroe. Wan of Meigs & Rhea.[6] Bales of Claiborne.[7] All Democrats. The Feds have elected Jacobs, Nelson,[8] Carson, Williams of Grainger by 2 votes. Tunnell & R. D. Wheeler (neutrals).[9] One in Sevier, 1 in Carter & John[son], & I suppose 1 in Cocke, 1 in Bledsoe, & perhaps one in Marion & Hamilton.[10] I will write you again by next mail.[11]

R B Reynolds & L P Roberts

L, signed for both authors by Reynolds. DLC–JKP. Addressed to Columbia. Written on a four-column ledger sheet, the election returns appear in the first three columns, and the text, in the fourth and widest column.

1. Year identified through content analysis.

2. A farmer from Sullivan County, Jesse Cross served three terms in the Tennessee House, 1839–41, 1843–45, and 1847–49.

3. Michael Baugh, a silversmith, represented Hawkins County in the Tennessee House, 1839–41.

4. Andrew Johnson, seventeenth president of the United States.

5. Samuel Feazel served one term in the Tennessee House, 1839–41.

6. William Wann, first sheriff of Meigs County, 1836–39, served in the Tennessee House from 1839 until 1845.

7. Archibald Bales represented Claiborne County for one term, 1839–41.

8. Knox County lawyer and attorney general for the Fourth Judicial District of Tennessee, 1824–36, John R. Nelson served multiple terms in both the Tennessee House and Senate between 1823 and 1855.

9. William Tunnell and Richard D. Wheeler. A farmer from Anderson County, Tunnell won five terms in the Tennessee House and one in the Senate. Wheeler, a merchant and farmer, represented Campbell County in the Tennessee House from 1837 until 1845 and from 1853 until 1855.

10. Isaac A. Miller, Godfrey C. Nave, William McSween, Samuel Rankin, and William Standifer were the Whig members elected in those several counties.

11. No letter of August 6, 1839, has been found; Reynolds wrote Polk again on August 9, 1839.

FROM ALEXANDER O. ANDERSON

Dear Colonel Cheekes X Roads Augt 6th 1839

Of the vote North of the Tennessee River we have tolerably accurate information. Blount, Roane & Anderson are not heard from, except partially, & they may be considered as debateable ground.

Majorities for Polk	
Greene	827
Washington	323
Sullivan	1182
Hawkins	629
Claibourn	341
Campbell (said to be)	300[1]
Morgan (I estimate at)	160
	3762

Majorities [for] Cannon	
Knox	1148
Jefferson	1302
Cocke	392

Carter & Johnson said to be	700
Grainger	119
Sevier supposed to be	450
	4111
Deduct	3762
Cannon's majority north of the Tennessee River	349

It is not probable that Blount, Roane & Anderson will vary it materially. Cannon crossed the Tennessee River, against Armstrong with a majority of 3792. Your gain north of the Tennessee River is about 3443.

A Gentleman has reached this neighborhood from Athens who reports that you have beaten Cannon largely in Monroe, Meigs, Rhea, Bradley &c. and that your majority South of the Tennessee River is upwards of 1500—nearly 2000, with two Counties to hear from—Marion & Bledsoe, I suppose. So that if he reports correctly (and he is a man of respectability and intelligence) you have beaten Cannon in East Tennessee about 1000 votes. If your own Middle Country has done her duty, of which I have no doubt, you are elected by a very handsome majority.[2]

You will be surprised at Washington County giving way. The Legitimate majority of the Republican Party was not cast for us there, owing, as I am informed, by a gentleman of high respectability (yesterday from that section) to the uncompromising zeal with which Mr Blair & his friends sustained Mr Embree, a very bitter & fierce opponent of ours. The Gentleman whom I saw, says that our friends speak, there in very strong & significant terms of this proceeding. He also says your name was freely exchanged, at various precincts, to procure votes for Mr Embree. I deeply regret this & will not trust myself to express all I feel. But I must add, *to any man of intelligence it was perfectly apparent, that the Governor's election was every thing to us, thro' all future struggles!*

You also lost ground in Jefferson, Cocke & Greene in consequence of Powells running. You will remember my having early in the spring, confidentially intimated my fears to you upon this subject. I freely admonished our friends that this wou'd be the case, but they suffered themselves to be beguiled by the feeble hope of a gain of some two hundred in Carter & Johnson.

When our friends were preparing to contend with Carter, with much difficulty, and contrary to views of personal interest to Dr. [Thomas V.] Anderson but for the Sake of the cause, and looking specially to the election of Governor I prevailed upon him to consent to run, provided our friends shou'd take him up. His ability in speaking & writing & his familiarity with all the questions involved in the contest, and his unflinching nerve, wou'd have given to us great advantages. *But the Chapter has ended otherwise!* Still I believe we are triumphant in East Tennessee—and it is a proud day for the Democracy! We have fought the Battle manfully, cheered, in our arduous struggle, by the most masterly efforts of our favorite Leader!

It is said McClelland[3] has beaten McKinney more than 2000—and of the 9 members of the Legislature from the Counties of Greene & Hawkins upward (inclusive) the democracy have 8. There is no doubt, now, in my mind that we will have from East Tennessee a majority in the Legislature. Is it possible the Middle Country will not *improve* even upon this good news? & may not the Western District give us a majority, also, of members.

I cannot conclude without saying that the great Republican Party of this Nation owe to you higher obligations than to any other man (now acting) in the Union. Pennsylvania has justly been called the "Keystone of the Arch of the Union." Tennessee is truly the *"Keystone of the Arch* of the *Republican Party! Peculiarly so now!*

If we triumph, let us bear our new prosperity with dignity & moderation & press home with talent and energy our doctrines and our *Appeals against* Dictation! These *three things are* important.

Write me to Knoxville—always with my Christian name in full, Alexander!

A. ANDERSON

P.S. If you are elected I shall add to Toby's name and call him "Victor Toby"[4] and when he dies bury him, if not with the honors of war, at least honorably![5]

ALS. DLC–JKP. Enclosed in a second letter from Anderson to Polk of the same date. In his cover letter, addressed to Columbia, Anderson revises his estimate of Polk's majority in East Tennessee and fixes the margin of victory at 698 votes. ALS. DLC–JKP.

1. An ink mark blotted out the original number; the writer repeated the number parenthetically in the right margin.

2. The remainder of the letter was marked "Confidential."

3. Abraham McClellan.

4. Reference probably is to the horse Anderson loaned Polk during the campaign. See Polk to Sarah C. Polk, May 12, 1839.

5. The final fourteen words of the postscript were written in the left margin of the letter's first page.

FROM AARON V. BROWN

Pulaski Augst 7th 1839

Dear Sir

I either write a Book or nothing.

A V Brown

ALS. DLC–JKP. Addressed to Columbia.

FROM ABRAHAM McCLELLAN

Blountville Aug 7. 1839

Dear Col.

I write you a few lines in haste before the mail is made up. Am here waiting for the western mail to get some news respecting your election.

Your majority in my district is Something over 2000 votes. We have not heard from Campbell yet. My majr in the 4 upper counties is 1774 votes.

From what we have heard we think your majr in E. Ten will be 10 or 1500—though I fear to hear from west of the mountains. We shall have a maj. of Democrats from E. Ten in the State Legislature. We have heard that Blackwell has beaten Stone. Carter's maj is some 14 or 1500 votes &c.

We are hurried to raise the cash to pay for the Knoxville Press.[1] Please remit us the $100 as soon as possible. I hope you will write me all the news.

A. McClellan

ALS. DLC–JKP. Addressed to Columbia.

1. Reference is to the press of the Knoxville *Argus*.

FROM ROBERT B. REYNOLDS

Knoxville August 9. [18]39

Dear Colonel

Sufficient news have reached us to satisfy our minds that the Victory is yours & that you are the Governor. I own we did but half our duty in E. Tenn. We have heard from all the counties in E Tennessee but Carter & Johnson and you are 595 votes ahead. I think they have a small Majty. in E.T. but not sufficient to raise their drooping spirits. They give up the state and confess their great astonishment at the result—denounce

Cannon in unmeasured terms & say he is an old fool &c &c & that they intend to run Bell next time. Our strength in the Legislature is exactly what I anticipated—4 Senators & 13 Representatives to, 3 Whig Senators & 11 Whig Reps.

I have some notion of opposing E. Alexander[1] for Atty Genl. I think he ought to be beaten and I am willing to make any sacrifice that is honorable to defeat him.

J. W Blackwell is here. His majty. over Stone is upwards of 1350. His triumph is great. Our cause must grow & strengthen until the Clay leaders are left standing almost alone. So mote it be. I sent to Gen Armstrong to day G W. Churchwell's account of your speech here on the day of the election—& asked the Genl. to have it inserted in the Union.[2]

R B. REYNOLDS

[P.S.] Carter & Johnson gave Cannon 900 votes Majority—which gives Cannon a majority of 352 votes in E Ten. L. P. Roberts

ALS. DLC–JKP. Addressed to Columbia. Undated AES by Lewis P. Roberts appears at the bottom of the second page. AE on the cover states that this letter was answered on August 15, 1839; Polk's reply has not been found.

1. A Knoxville lawyer, Ebenezer Alexander served as attorney general for the Second Circuit in 1838 and as circuit court judge from 1844 until his death in 1857.

2. On August 16, 1839, the *Nashville Union* carried the text of a letter from Knoxville detailing Polk's remarks in that city on August 1, 1839. No attribution of the Knoxville letter was given. George W. Churchwell, a Knoxville lawyer, served in the Tennessee House as a Whig, 1835–37, but later became a Democrat.

FROM JOHN S. YOUNG

Dear Sir McMinville 9th Aug 1839

Enough has been learned to place your election beyond dispute by a majority of about 3000. Victory has perched upon your Banner. It is indeed a triumph. You now occupy ground upon which you can tread with pride and pleasure. You have realized the maxim that "Labor Vincit Omnia."[1] You now have a standing and place in the eyes of the whole nation of which you can be justly proud. Your claims to the Vice presidency on the score of policy and merit are paramount to those of any other individual and will be so viewed by the party, If the proper plan is adopted in presenting them. I have put the idea of your nomination forth here. It is received enthusiastically. The Legislature will be democratic.

It would not do to leave the matter to that body without previous action. If primary assemblies in the diferent counties would express the voice of the people it would secure a nomination by the Legislature. But how would it do to have a convention to meet at Nashville the 1st Nov. for the purpose of nominating a candidate for Vice president. You would be the choice as the proper suggestions would be made to meetings appointing delegates. Actual or implied instructions would be made by the people. In most instances members of the Legislature could act as Delegates. All movement on the subject ought to be made in anticipation of the meeting of the several Legislatures in order that Ohio and Alabama might immediately respond to it. You know I have no political aspirations. I am but a Yeoman desiring (without my name being known) to effect a measure which I view of much importance to the interests of my party. It is my wish to push my very humble efforts to the utmost, and in doing so I am backed by 2000 freemen none of whom have an opinion on this subject diferent from my own. You can write freely. Your letters shall be strictly private and in order to guard against accidents I will return them to you by each return mail.

JOHN S YOUNG

ALS. DLC–JKP. Addressed to Columbia. AE on the cover states that this letter was answered on August 15, 1839; Polk's reply has not been found.

1. "Labor overcomes all obstacles." Young's quotation is a variant of the Latin phrase, *Labor omnia vincit,* by Vergil in *Georgics* 1.

FROM LEONARD P. CHEATHAM

Dr. Sir Nashville Augt. 10th 1839

Some of the friends of Jno. McGavock[1] of Williamson request me to say it is the wish of many that he should fill one of the appointments in your Staff.[2] The County in which he lives, his *firmness* & talents besids other arguments are confirmations of the policy. We have been mild so far in our rejoicings. On yesterday we yielded to the wishes of our friends; & they mounted a polk stalk on the Cannon, drove it through town, fired as many times as we have Counties in the State, all in *good order;* & on two occasions the window glass fell from the windows by the jar. When told to raise the windows to prevent breaking, they said know, let them break, that we may put in *Polk Glass*. I think we will so manage it that we will have no dinners nor stir until the *day* of installation.

L. P. CHEATHAM

ALS. DLC–JKP. Addressed to Columbia.

1. Born in 1815, John McGavock was the son of Randal and Sarah Rodgers McGavock; he was a nephew of Nancy Ann Rodgers, wife of Felix Grundy.

2. On January 1, 1840, Polk appointed young McGavock aide-de-camp on the governor's staff with the rank of colonel in the Tennessee militia. In letters dated August 10, 1839, Robert Armstrong, James P. Grundy, and Joel M. Smith wrote recommendations in McGavock's behalf. ALsS. DLC–JKP.

FROM SAMUEL H. LAUGHLIN

My dear Sir, McMinnville, Aug 10, 1839

"The long agony is over," and Tennessee stands disenthralled, redeemed and regenerated by the universal genius of democracy. We all have reason to be thankful and proud; but you, as the hero of the achievement—the relation I sustain towards you is too sincere to admit of a word of flattery—stand on a ground so elevated in the eyes of your friends and of the country, that neither you nor those who have supported you, have anything further *at present* to wish or pray for.

I desired you, *en badinage,*[1] last winter, to present my sinc[e]re respects to the lady of the next Governor of Tennessee. Please now to perform that kind office for me in reality. Still being, as you always have been, the *modestest man,* as well as one of the most polite in the democratic *mess*, I have no doubt you will perform what I require of you in proper terms of respect.

I left our friends in Rutherford happy and Sam Rucker[2] and Sam Houston full of glory and a good dinner. Houston made a good speech to about 700 hundred hearers.[3] Sub rosa, allow me to make a suggestion. Ought not Tennessee to vote a Sword to the man of San Jacinto. Like Childe Harold, he is "a wayward wight, sore given to revel and ungodly glee,"[4] but a sword is what I think he has well earned. This will do to think about.

Our friend Dr. John S. Young, I think, ought to have something from Uncle Sam *en presente.*[5] He would, I believe, be willing to accept a temporary appointment of Post office agent anywhere in the west or south. He would also be willing I am sure, to accept a clerkship at Washington, in any Department, if the Salary was $1200 or any thing over. He has a very small family, has some means and is a frugal man. His profession in this healthy country holds out no expectation of fame or profit, and is irksome to him. He is, you know, a laborious, capable man. His aim has been an office in the Indian Department—and in that Department at Washington he would be a most useful man. If you could lend a hand in securing anything for him, immediately, I know you will do it, as far as may be proper.[6] Please consider of these matters—and do what you think right. Let me hear from you.

S. H. LAUGHLIN

ALS. DLC–JKP. Addressed to Columbia and marked "Private."

1. French phrase for "in banter" or "in jest."

2. Samuel R. Rucker, a Murfreesboro lawyer, served as mayor of that city in 1826 and represented Rutherford and Williamson counties as a Democrat in the Tennessee Senate for one term, 1827–29.

3. Sam Houston visited Andrew Jackson in the summer of 1839, spoke at McMinnville on August 3, 1839, and probably journeyed to Murfreesboro the following week. The date of Houston's Rutherford County speech is not identified.

4. Variant quotation of "in sooth he was a shameless wight, Sore given to revel and ungodly glee." Lord Byron, *Childe Harold's Pilgrimage*, canto 1, stanza 2.

5. French phrase for "at the present."

6. See John S. Young to Polk, August 25, 1839.

FROM FELIX GRUNDY

Nashville, [August][1] 12th 1839

Dear Sir,

You are Governor of Ten, thank God and the people for that. Keep the Ship right. No doubt you will. I rejoiced all day yesterday at the Hermitage over your victory.

The Old General and myself will go to Tyree's Springs[2] on Monday. I think you had better appoint John McGavock of Williamson one of your Staff. I hope you will not omit this, as the appointment will be both judicious & politic. Give my respects to Mrs. Polk.

FELIX GRUNDY

ALS. MoHi. Probably addressed to Columbia.

1. Erroneously dated "July"; month identified through content analysis.

2. A popular watering place twenty miles north of Nashville on the road to Franklin, Kentucky, the resort establishment took its name from its early proprietor, Richmond C. Tyree.

TO ANDREW JACKSON

My Dear Sir Columbia August 12th 1839

The great contest in which we have been engaged in the State, having resulted in the entire success of our principles, we can now calmly review the past and contemplate the future. That the State is now and always has been democratic in her principles I have never doubted. The causes which for a season produced an apparent departure from them, are well understood, and it requires but common prudence to guard against a similar departure hereafter. I have much to say to you, in relation to our past and present condition, but must postpone it, for a personal interview, which I hope soon to have the opportunity to have with you. There is one matter however which may require immediate attention. I take it for granted from the public pledges, which have been given, that there will be one and probably two vacancies in the Senate of the U. States. In that event I know not what Mr. Grundy's views are. It strikes me however most forcibly that having been driven from the Senate, during the temporary ascendency of our opponents, as now appears manifestly against the popular sentiment, that it would be to himself personally, "the post of honor," to return to the Senate. His place in the Cabinet[1] could be readily filled by another. It is an affair of great labour. He has discharged its duties satisfactorily to the country, and has added to his own reputation, & has no more public character to gain by remaining in it. On the other hand if he declines returning to the Senate, I apprehend indeed I know, that there will be a collision between numerous aspirants, which cannot fail greatly to weaken us, in the commencement of the new administration of the State Government. There would indeed be great difficulty in making a selection between the aspirants. If he will accept all will yield to his superior claims, and there will be perfect harmony in our ranks. In a letter to him two days ago,[2] I took the liberty to make similar suggestions to these to him, but have not yet received his answer. My brother William H. Polk who goes to Nashville to day, promises himself the pleasure of paying his respects to you at the Hermitage, and will hand you this letter in person. He can inform, you who the aspirants to the Senate now spoken of are, in the event Mr Grundy declines it, and of the embarrassing difficulties likely to be produced in our ranks by their collisions. Should a vacancy occur from East Tennessee, there would I think be but little difficulty in selecting the proper man to fill it.

[Ho]pe to have it in my power in the course [o]f[3] ten or twelve days to see you at the Hermitage.

James K. Polk

ALS. DLC–AJ. Addressed to "Hermitage" and marked "*Private.*"

1. United States attorney general.
2. Letter not found.
3. A tear on the left margin has obliterated parts of two words of the manuscript.

FROM ANDREW JACKSON

My Dr. Sir, Tyree Spr[i]ngs August 13th 1839

I am here with a few of our friends, Grundy & Armstrong for a few days, and I cannot withold my congratulations from you & my country on your election & of that of majorities in both branches of our Legislature, & the return of old democratic Tennessee to the republican fold again. It will be at least a century before she will permit herself to be again duped into her late false position by such jesuitical hypocrites & apostates as Bell White & Co. I think I may with safety say, all is well. The News from Indiana is cheering. We will have there six [to] one & probably the whole.[1] We have gained one in Kentucky perhaps two. This with the vote of alabama, if NCarolina holds her own, will give us a republican majority in Congress. Foster & White will get their walking papers & Bell will not get, as he expected, into the Senate. *Alls Well.* With kind regards to Mrs. Polk.

ANDREW JACKSON

ALS. DLC–JKP. Addressed to Columbia. AE on the cover states that this letter was answered on August 18, 1839. Published in Bassett, ed., *Jackson Correspondence*, VI, pp. 18–19.

1. Reference is to election results in Indiana's seven congressional districts.

FROM JOHN T. LEIGH[1]

Dr Sir Yala Busha County Misspi 13 Augt 1839

Mrs. Bratton (widow of your late Overseer Geo Bratton) requests me to write you to inform you of her present situation. She has had to leave your place to make room for the overseer who succeeded her husband.[2] She has removed some 8 or 10 miles off in the neighborhood of Coffeeville, is poor and in want of money to procure necessaries to live on, is anxious to know whether you will come down to your plantation this fall and at what time. She wishes to see you for the purpose of settling her husbands accounts and to obtain money to live on. She left with me a book containing some accounts—and some of her husbands papers. (I reside adjoining your plantation.) If you will inform me at what time you will be down I will send for her to my house—where I will be glad to see you.

J. T. LEIGH

[P.S.] Your crop is very fine. Direct to Oakachickama P. Office.

ALS. DLC–JKP. Addressed to Columbia. Published in Bassett, *Plantation Overseer*, 122–23.

1. Leigh owned a plantation adjacent to Polk's in Yalobusha County, Mississippi; during Polk's presidency the two neighbors corresponded frequently concerning plantation business.

2. See S. Bell to Polk, July 7, 1839.

FROM HENRY MABRY[1]

Winchester, Tennessee. August 13, 1839

Mabry congratulates Polk on his victory in the election and lauds the Mountain District, the Democratic press, and particularly the Winchester *Highlander* for contributing to that victory. Mabry suggests that Van Buren and Polk are the best Democratic candidates for president and vice-president in 1840 and that the Democratic press should promote Polk's claims aggressively. In a postscript Mabry says that he needs about two hundred dollars to sustain his newspaper and appeals for Polk's help in raising the money.

ALS. DLC–JKP. Addressed to Columbia.

1. Mabry published the Murfreesboro *Weekly Times* in 1838 and the Winchester *Highlander* in 1839.

FROM WILLIAM G. CHILDRESS

Dr Sir

Franklin August 15th 1839

The battle is over, you are triumphant & I am defeated. Yet I rejoice. As a general remark it may be said & truly so, that it is natural for man to feel a deeper & more abiding interest in his own election than that of another. In this I may be said to have been an exception. It was not to gratify that passion that prompts most of men to ask of the people high and political honours that induced me to run the race I did. The prospect before me was of that gloomy cast to forbid the idea or hope of success; but Sir a great political battle was to be fought in which was involved the great cardinal principles of this Republic. You was looked to as the captain General to bring about that revolution in Tennessee so much desired by the old Jeffersonian Republicans, for she had departed from the good old Jeffersonian Jackson Republican faith. Although you was selected to do the great work it was not supposed that you, *solitary & alone,* could perform so great a work. You must necessarily have aid. Your subaltern officers in the several districts & counties was to marshal the troops in their sphere of action in some portions of the State. The prospect of success was bright not only to you but the subalterns also. Not so in my district. Although defeat stared me in the face, it should not be & was not sufficient to prevent me from coming to the rescue. I came forward. I met the enemy. I fell in the conflict & glory in the fall. The State is again Republican. You are Governor & the Legislature democratic. The captain General has achieved the signal victory in doing which he lost some of his men. From the official reports it seems I am remembered among the *dead* & still I rejoice. I cannot complain on act [account] of my friends. Althou, they have lost me, they have grown rich in a pecuniary point of view having won all their bets of any magnitude. I never did in all my life see a people so completely cut down, as they were the morning after the election. Not a smile to be seen upon the countenance of one & upon the reception of the news of your election there was an illumination in Franklin that buried them. You are Governor. As such you have the confering of many honorary appointments. My friend John McGavock is desirous of becoming a member of your military family. He is a young man of unblemished character & high literary acquirements, well qualified to fill any station in your staff. As to his family it is unnecessary to speak as you are personally acquainted with them.

I am just from Nashville having spent two days there. I discover the federal whigs are making great preperations for another struggle. The leading feds from the different se[c]tions of middle & west Tenn are there, the elect as also the defeated. A grand caucus is said to be in session, the real object not known, many speculations upon the subject, great consternation in their ranks. Their leader John the apostate[1] is constantly in motion. He is of opinion that the country is *now* ruined. I am anxious to have a conversation with you too lengthy & tedious to commit to paper. There[fore I would] be much gratified if you would give me a [visit][2] & spend a night with me as I presume you will in a short time be at Nashville the seat of goverment. I am anxious to visit the Hermitage & would be pleased to have your company. What say you? Let me hear from you.

W. G. CHILDRESS

ALS. DLC–JKP. Addressed to Columbia. AE on the cover states that this letter was answered on August 16, 1839; Polk's reply has not been found.

1. John Bell.
2. A tear on the right margin of the manuscript has obliterated several words on two lines.

TO ANDREW JACKSON

My dear Sir: Columbia Aug 15, 1839

I thank you for your letter of the 13th. Our success in the state is cause of congratulations to the friends of such principles, not only here, but throughout the union. It has cost us a hard struggle. I have done my humble part in it, but am more than compensated by the knowledge of the fact, that the state is again in her old position. With common prudence on our part, she will remain so. I wrote you two days ago by my Brother Wm. H. Polk,[1] who expected to hand you my letter in person. I am more and more satisfied of the great importance of the suggestions therein contained. I think it probable from what I learn, if Mr G.[2] refuses to return to the Senate, that there will be at least half a dozen, probably double the number of aspirants for the place. This will sow the seeds of dissention in our ranks, and greatly embarass and weaken us.

Since writing you, I have ascertained that private business will make it necessary for me to be at Nashville, on Wednesday or Thursday of next week. I hope Mr G. may not leave for Washington before that time, as I desire much to see him. Whilst at Nashville, I will do myself the pleasure to spend a day with you at the Hermitage.

JAMES K. POLK

Copy, in unknown hand. THi–Misc. Collection. Addressed to Nashville.

1. See Polk to Andrew Jackson, August 12, 1839.
2. Felix Grundy.

FROM JOSEPH POWELL

Elizabethton, Tennessee. August 15, 1839

Powell congratulates Polk on his election. Powell says that his own defeat might have been expected because of Whig strength in the counties in the

First Congressional District. Powell's hope of success rested upon "the deep rooted prejudice" between the Arnold and Carter factions in the Whig party. Only two days before the election, however, Carter and Arnold made a "corrupt bargain," which led to Powell's defeat. Arnold endorsed Carter in this campaign in return for his promise not to run for reelection in 1841; Carter would then support Arnold for Congress.

Powell thinks that every Democratic press in the state should wage "an uncompromising war of extermination" upon Senator White and that Senator Foster will have to resign to redeem his campaign promises.[1] Powell also requests that he be appointed adjutant general for the militia in East Tennessee.

ALS. DLC–JKP. Addressed to Columbia.

1. Ephraim H. Foster had stated publicly that he would resign from the U.S. Senate if Van Buren Democrats won control of the next legislature. See John Catron to Polk, August 27, 1839.

FROM JOEL M. SMITH

Dear Sir Nashville, Augt 15 1839

When Mr Walker was last in this place I suggested the propriety of an effort being made, in Columbia, to raise a sum of money sufficient to pay for printing the "looking Glass,"[1] and not suffer the expence to fall on you. He seemed to express some fears as to the practicability of doing so under the present State of the times.

As our efforts have been crowned with such signal success, and our friends having won the Whigs money, It seems to me that there ought not to be any difficulty in raising among them a few hundred dollars to pay for extra printing which has been done during the Canvass.

In a few days, I expect either to go on myself, or send to Louisville or Cincinnatti to lay in materials for a job office, so as to be prepared to do the public printing. In order to effect this I must have money, which our friends can raise if proper exertions are made. I have done extra printing to the amt of ab[o]ut $1400 and recd only about $380. Our friends here are doing all they well can do to raise the amt. I hope Mr W will urge the matter among our friends while they are elated at our success and most likely to be in the spirit of giving. Please write me[a] line when you have leisure and believe me . . . .

J. M. SMITH

ALS. DLC–JKP. Addressed to Columbia.

1. See J. George Harris to Polk, April 2, 1839.

FROM ROBERT H. WATKINS, ET AL.[1]

Dear Sir: Courtland, Ala., 17th Aug. 1839

A meeting of Democratic Republicans, held in Courtland, on the 15th inst., have deputed us, as a committee, to communicate to you, the high estimation in which you are held, for your public services; their congratulations on the result of the late animated contest for Governor in the patriotic State of Tennessee; and also an invitation to partake of a public dinner, at such time as may suit your convenience.

It gives us much pleasure, sir, to be the organ of conveying to you, sentiments so honorable to yourself, and so sincerely and deeply felt by the Republicans of the community in which we live. It has been the lot of the brave sons of Tennessee, to have had the eyes of the American people fixed upon them, in more than one struggle with the deepest solicitude; but perhaps never with more intense interest, in the field, or at the ballot box, than during the late political contest.

This was caused by a combination of peculiar circumstances. As has been correctly remarked, "this was the first decided political struggle in that state, conducted on Federal and Republican principles." Here resided the venerable statesman of the Hermitage,[2] who was first presented to the American people, as the fittest person for the chief magistracy of the Union, by *the people of his own State*; and nobly sustained in several presidential contests; the man who had by them been used as an instrument to overturn the Federal Administration of Messrs. Adams & Clay, which (to say nothing of its suspicious commencement) was characterized throughout, by the most latitudinarian doctrines. Yet this people had, by means which you well understand, been alienated from that *man*, who did more to restore the administration of the Government to Republican principles, than any man since the days of Jefferson; and it was believed that their political leaders would succeed in transferring them to the very Federal leaders who had once cowered beneath their honest and just indignation. The contest was believed to be hopeless. But you, sir, at this juncture, when the office of Governor had been filled for one term by a gentleman of high standing and acknowledged competency,[3] dared to take issue on the great doctrines alluded to above; and the result has proven that you were not mistaken in the outset of the canvass, when you declared, "that Tennesseeans could not be Federalists."[4]

The generous self-devotion with which you have given yourself to the support of those principles held dear by the Republican party, has drawn around you the sympathies and good wishes of all who compose it:

and we will not pretend to limit your advancement in public favor, if you continue to be the same disinterested and fearless advocate of those principles.

Accept for yourself, and the Republicans by whom you have been aided in the conflict, our congratulations on the glorious result; and that the "time honored veteran" who has been pursued by slander and detraction, with so much malignity, into the very shades of private life, has *lived* to witness the re-establishment in his own state of those principles which he so fearlessly and successfully advocated.

Nothing would give us more pleasure than your acceptance of the invitation, and appointment of a day for that purpose which will best suit your engagements.

ROB'T H. WATKINS

Copy. In the *Nashville Union,* September 4, 1839.

1. Letter attributed to Watkins and four other members of the arrangements committee.

2. Andrew Jackson.

3. Newton Cannon, the incumbent governor, was serving the second of two consecutive terms.

4. Quotation not identified. Polk put forth similar arguments in his widely circulated "Address to the People of Tennessee"; see Polk to J. G. M. Ramsey, March 30, 1839.

FROM JOHN CRAMER[1]

My dear Sir. Waterford Saratoga Co. N.Y. Aug 18, 1839

I cannot permit the great and glorious results of the victory you have achieved in Tennessee, to pass off, without the emphatic expression of my joy and of my personal congratulations to yourself. So great a revolution was wholly unexpected. You must have passed through a most severe and laborious trial, and the consequences of your triumph will be deeply felt beyond the territory of your State. This event fulfills the prediction you made to me a year & an half ago, but I could hardly then indulge the hope that the prophecy would so soon become history.

The President is still at the Springs and will proceed on his tour next Tuesday. He has been enthusiastically received and is in fine health & spirits. He told me a few days since, that he felt great confidence in your success, tho your friends at home did not venture to claim it.

What may be the results of the contest here, next fall, it is impossible to say, with much certainty. That we shall be greatly the gainers admits of no doubt; but as this is not a gubernatorial election, local views will have more influence than they otherwise would. There are unfortunately so many projects of internal improvement devised and so many conflicting interests in the different sections of the State, that friends & foes will both be disappointed in results. When, however, the contest depends on general politics as it must a year hence, there can be no doubt of our complete success and we strongly hope to get the legislative power even at this time.

Among other blessings of your triumph, I have no doubt it will add at least ten years to the life of our old friend, the vetran General, who must greatly rejoice in the revolution. Please present him my personal regards when you see him, and believe me now as ever. . . .

John Cramer

P.S. Mr Clay is in this neighbourhood. He has on several occasions since his visit to this State, addressed the People; but he does not understand their genius and has generally made a failure, so far as effect is concerned. In his remarks to the People in the city of Troy, yesterday, he was compelled to allude to the recent disasters at the West; and to throw upon his party here the responsibility of the event of the Presidential election. I am fully satisfied that the leading Whigs of this State, including the Governor[2] & his cabinet will go strongly and in good faith for the nomination of Genl. Scott.[3] A decided interest is making for him in their ranks, and the appearance of Mr. Clay here, has not had a tendency to strengthen his personal influence or party. I am apprehensive, that Genl. Scott would be the most formidable candidate of the two, having no decided political character and few enemies personally. J.C.

ALS. DLC–JKP. Addressed to Columbia.

1. A lawyer and Democratic politician from Waterford, New York, Cramer sat in both houses of the state legislature and served two terms in the U.S. House, 1833–37.

2. William H. Seward, an unsuccessful gubernatorial candidate in 1834, subsequently won two terms as governor of New York and served from 1838 to 1842. He belonged successively to the Anti-Masonic, Whig, and Republican parties. After two terms in the U.S. Senate, 1848–60, Seward served as secretary of state under presidents Lincoln and Johnson.

3. Winfield Scott's effective action in completing the Cherokee Indian removal program and his restoration of peaceful relations on the Canadian border had brought him into public view as a possible candidate for the 1840 Whig presidential nomination.

FROM JOHN H. PRENTISS[1]

Dear Sir: Cooperstown, [New York] Aug 18, 1839

Permit me to congratulate you upon the result of the election in Tennessee, for it is the greatest victory ever obtained in the Union, affecting not only yourself, but the great Democratic party. The news was received in this State with the greatest possible joy. We were confident that your interviews with the People would effect a great change in their minds on political subjects, but could hardly indulge the hope that a complete revolution in the politics of the State would be accomplished. The late evidences of public opinion at the West, warrant the conclusion that Mr. Van Buren will be reelected with only the semblance of opposition.

I am happy to assure you that our prospects are flattering in this state. Mr. V.B. is winning golden opinions, and you may rely upon it the majority in our Legislature will be sound at the November election.

JNO. H. PRENTISS

ALS. DLC–JKP. Addressed to Columbia.

1. A representative from New York, Prentiss established the *Freeman's Journal* in 1808 and continued its publication until 1849. He served as postmaster of Cooperstown from 1833 until 1837, when he won election as a Democrat to the first of three terms in the U.S. House.

FROM ISAAC H. BRONSON[1]

Detroit, Michigan. August 20, 1839

Bronson sends congratulations on the Democratic victory in Tennessee and trusts that in November, New York will follow Tennessee's example and prove that his own state is not "irrevocably given over to Whig idolatry." Democrats in Michigan, where Bronson is visiting, assure him of success in the fall elections.

ALS. DLC–JKP. Addressed to Columbia.

1. A New York lawyer, Bronson won election as a Democrat to the U.S. House in 1837. Unsuccessful in his bid for reelection, he was appointed U.S. judge for the eastern district of Florida in 1840.

FROM SAMUEL H. LAUGHLIN

My dear Sir, McMinnville, Aug. 20, 1839

Your letter of the 15th instant,[1] in answer to mine of the 10th is before me. I have also seen your last letter to Dr. Young.[2] Mr. Turney is now here at our Court. About the 1st of September, proximo, large republican meetings will be held here and in Franklin. Mr. Turney and myself concur in the opinion that nominations for the Presidency and Vice Presidency had better be made in primary meetings throughout the State. The proceedings and resolutions must be conciliatory; avoiding every thing like a peremtory demand upon the concurrence of our friends abroad, they must be strictly *recommendatory*. They must distinctly embody an approval of the measures and policy of the late and present Administrations and specifically oppose a bank, and approve of the Sub Treasury. They must, as I think, instruct the members of the Legislature, in pursuance of the practice in nominating Gen. Jackson, and which was copied by the Whigs in nominating Judge White, to make a nomination. This course, or a State convention, ought to be resorted to as I humbly believe. Whichever mode is adopted, the nomination should be made on the same day the Clay national Whig convention is appointed to sit at Harrisburg. I should have been exceedingly glad if I could have met Mr. Johnson, Mr. Brown,[3] yourself and other friends at Nashville on tomorrow, but I cannot leave home. If you receive this before you leave, I would gladly receive suggestions on these subjects and other matters after you have consulted together. I hope Mr. J. or Mr. B. will write me.

As to a Senator, *vice* Foster, I wish to concur with the wishes of our party, and so as to maintain our high stand in the cabinet and legislature of the Nation. If Mr. Grundy should prefer his present station, which I should think most likely, who can we select to avoid collision among friends and aspirants? Gen. Carroll would be the choice of my constituents if a kind providence should restore his health. I should be most happy to know that such was or was likely to be his condition. Judge Campbell[4] is a veteran republican and an old and able councillor and confidential friend of Jefferson and Madison. He would take a high stand in the Senate, and do honor to the State, and his restoration to Congress would show that the republic of Tennessee, at least, was not ungrateful. These are all matters for grave consideration.

Another matter of importance. The Secretary of State in our State Administration like the Secretary of State in Washington, should be a man of the same politics of the Governor, and should enjoy his entire confidence. It will never do for it to be otherwise. I like Mr. Lea as well as any Whig in the state, with whom I have so small acquaintance, but he is a Whig, and though a moderate and modest man, yet he is a Whig and our Governor is a democrat. As a democrat, Len. Cheatham has labored and suffered in our cause.[5] How would he do? How would many others do however? I am committed to nothing, however, only that the Secretary should be a democrat. Maj. Graham I would prefer to any man in the state—I consider him as having high claims for the Senate or any other post—but we cannot spare him out of the Treasury Dept.

As Speaker of the Senate, I think it probable that Love[6] has paramount claims, but I agree to any other nomination—Aiken, Gillespie, or Coe for instance.[7] In this our party must have no split.

I wish Gen. Armstrong, or some friend would write to about half a dozen proper Senators, and as many or more representatives, to meet at Nashville about a week or ten days before the meeting of the Assembly. I will attend at the time if desired, in order to contribute my mite to our councils. Mr. Turney, of Congress, if notified, promises to attend. I hope our friends Messrs. Brown and Johnson can be induced to attend. Please mention and think of these matters. Mr. Harris might write to such gentlemen as it might be advisable to invite to a conference of the sort indicated.

I desire you, if possible, to attend the Huntsville invitation in September.[8] I[t] may do good. Let the ball be kept in motion.

S. H. LAUGHLIN

ALS. DLC–JKP. Addressed to Nashville and marked "Private & Confidential."

1. Letter not found.
2. Letter not found.
3. Cave Johnson and Aaron V. Brown.
4. Born in Scotland, George Washington Campbell immigrated with his parents to North Carolina in 1772; commenced law practice in Knoxville, Tennessee; sat as a Democrat in the U.S. House, 1803–9; became a justice of the Tennessee Supreme Court of Errors and Appeals, 1809; and served in the U.S. Senate, 1811–14. For a brief period in 1814 he held a post in Madison's cabinet as treasury secretary. After the War of 1812 Campbell returned to the U.S. Senate, 1815–18; went to Russia as Monroe's minister plenipotentiary, 1818–21; and concluded his public career as one of Jackson's appointees to the French Spoliation Claims Commission.
5. Leonard P. Cheatham had just campaigned unsuccessfully for a seat in the Tennessee House.
6. Elected Speaker of the Tennessee Senate, Thomas Love resigned as

presiding officer on December 6, 1839, because of declining health. A wealthy land owner in both North Carolina and Tennessee, Love served several terms in the North Carolina legislature before moving to Tennessee. He resided in Hawkins and Maury counties before settling in Henry County in the 1830's.

7. John A. Aiken, John F. Gillespy, and Levin H. Coe.
8. See William Smith et al. to Polk, August 29, 1839.

FROM FRANKLIN PIERCE[1]

Dear Sir

Concord N.H. Augst 20 1839

If the result of the late glorious election did not reach beyond you personally I should rejoice most sincerely in your success—but this triumphant regeneration of Tennessee is regarded by both parties as of incalculable importance in settling the great political questions now pending before the nation and the returns have been looked for with an interest and anxiety proportionate to that importance. I need not say, that your agency in this unparalleled change is duly appreciated here and that your name is upon the lips of all our friends coupled with expressions of applause & admiration. It is not a little amusing to observe the change in the tone of the Federal papers, which have been so lavish in their abuse of you for the last four years. They now say that this astounding result is to be attributed solely to your great power as a public speaker and your singular personal popularity, and really seem to derive some consolation from the belief, that this most extraordinary among political revolutions, could have been achieved under the direction of no other leader. Does such conviction probably serve to diminish Mr Bell's chagrin on the occasion? I take it not. From North Carolina & Indiana too we have intelligence surpassing the highest hopes of our most sanguine friends. Where is Conservativism? Where the boasted power and influence of that *third estate*, which assumed to hold the balance. Will it surprise you to hear James Garland and other like fair & candid politicians *re-defining* their positions, as soon as convenient after the commencement of the next session? Who will be the Democratic candidate for Speaker? If the health of John W. Jones[2] is equal to the labor of the situation, no name occurs to me upon which our friends would probably unite with more cordiality. Please to present my sincere congratulations to Cave Johnson when you see him & my kindest regards to yr Lady.

FRANKN. PIERCE

ALS. DLC–JKP. Addressed to Columbia.

1. A U.S. congressman, 1833–37, and senator, 1837–42, from New Hampshire, Pierce was the fourteenth president of the United States, 1853–57.

2. A lawyer from Chesterfield County, Virginia, Jones won election in 1835 to the U.S. House, where he served five terms. He was Speaker of that body during his last term.

FROM J. G. M. RAMSEY

My Dear Sir Mecklenburg Aug. 20. 1839

I need not tell you how sincerely I can congratulate you on the results of the late election. It is a triumph rarely enjoyed—a victory seldom won. Tennessee had been in the opinion of many of her truest friends handed over to Mr. Clay beyond redemption. Many in other States had given her up as hopelessly lost. But thanks to her democracy & her patriotism she occupies again her old position. And yet now the revolution is effected we cannot but wonder at our successes. The State patronage was industriously used in behalf of the opposition & efforts I venture to say that can never be surpassed in ingenuity or perserverance made to continue the present dynasty in power. It has all been unavailing & a most signal overthrow has followed them. Allow me to say to you without intending the least alloy of flattery that our successes have been principally owing to your own able & skillful & energetic & unequalled exertions. I am prouder of being a Tennessean in 1839 than I have ever been before. We have a Governor that is worthy of Tennessee—& Tennesseans have proved themselves worthy of their Chief magistrate. This is common sentiment I know in E.T. & I doubt not public sentiment throughout the State & elsewhere. So much so here that we can scarcely repress within prudent bounds the enthusiasm of our citizens. We wish to run you, much as we value your services to the State, upon the Democratic ticket as Vice-President of the U.S. & after the next four years as the chief magistrate of the Nation. The nomination of you as vice President at this moment as far as we are able to see its bearings would be exactly right. It will keep us organised. Secure as the state is now for Mr. V.B. it will make it still more so. It may too induce Mr. Johnston to withdraw & not embarrass our friends elsewhere about him.[1] It will especially aid us essentially in N. Carolina—where we need all the aid any of her *native* sons can give us. You are able to survey the whole ground & to see whether such a nomination can operate any where adversely. If you do not so decide by a return of Mail we will run up the Polk flag in the Argus of week after next & sink or swim stand by it.

The Whigs are utterly confounded. I think Mr. Clay will be pronounced in a short time *Unavailable*. They are evidently shy of embarking their fortunes on a ship so often pronounced un-seaworthy. A *Virginian*[2] I think is their next hope—but we can hear little—very little from them. Non comittal is now their creed. We do not know certainly what course Judge White will pursue relative to *instructions*. Some say he will not obey—& will retain his seat. As avarice is now his ruling passion perhaps he will. Others say he will not retain his seat long enough to receive instructions but will retire in disgust & resign before your inauguration. A functionary of the Govt. in his confidence gives this out as his opinion. It is all conjecture.[3]

A meeting of our L.C.&C.R.R. Co.[4] takes place at Asheville N.C. 15th Sep. It is a most important meeting. I hope Gov. C. may forget to appoint a state proxy to represent the state stock. His proxy would be I know Gen. Brazelton or some one adverse to our enterprise. If our session is prolonged till after you enter into office I will write you on the subject from Asheville where I will be a few weeks after the 15th. I find it necessary to go to the mountains a while to reestablish my health—which continues bad & has been so since the day I last saw you—& besides my official duty requires me to meet the Board of Directors & the Stockholders. Otherwise I should probably attend the 1st. Oct. at Nashville.

Did you arrive at home after your unparalled exertions & labors free of sickness? Did you find Mrs. Polk well? Say to my attentive correspondent Mr. Walker of Columbia that when his last letter arrived I was sick & before I recovered he had all the news it would have been my pleasure to have given him. Please write early in answer to the subject on the second page of this letter.[5] It meets the views of all our friends—& I think is our true policy.

J. G. M. Ramsey

ALS. DLC–JKP. Addressed to Columbia. AE on the cover states that this letter was answered on September 7, 1839; Polk's reply has not been found.

1. Vice-President Richard M. Johnson's most notorious political liability was his earlier relationship with Julia Chinn, a mulatto woman by whom he fathered two daughters.

2. Reference probably is to William H. Harrison or Winfield Scott; both were sons of the Old Dominion and were popular among Whig politicians.

3. On November 14, 1839, the Tennessee General Assembly passed resolutions instructing its senators to support the Sub-Treasury bill; unwilling to comply, White resigned his seat when the Senate took up the bill in January 1840.

4. Louisville, Cincinnati and Charleston Railroad Company.

5. Reference is to Polk's views on being advanced for the vice-presidency.

FROM DAVID A. STREET

Jackson, Tennessee. August 20, 1839

Street reports that he has sold his paper[1] and is practicing law. He wishes to use Polk as a reference in obtaining clients from among those northern and eastern merchants collecting debts in the Western District.

West Tennesseans believe that Polk has destroyed Clay politically and will have influence over the federal administration for the interests of their section. Street suggests that the "disaffected White party" should be returned to the Democratic fold, as the "balance wheel" of party politics.

ALS. DLC–JKP. Addressed to Columbia.

1. The Jackson *District Telegraph and State Sentinel.*

FROM KENNETH L. ANDERSON[1]

Shelbyville, Tennessee. August 21, 1839

Anderson congratulates Polk on his victory and insists that Polk accept an invitation to a public dinner at Shelbyville in Polk's honor.[2] Acceptance is important because Polk's old friends claim his presence as a matter of right and because the Whigs say Polk will not bother to come there until he wants votes again.

ALS. DLC–JKP. Addressed to Columbia.

1. Born in North Carolina, Anderson moved to Tennessee in 1829 and became Polk's friend and advocate in Bedford County. In 1837 Anderson moved to Texas, where he served in several governmental positions prior to his 1844 election to the vice-presidency of that Republic.

2. An invitation dated August 20, 1839, from a committee headed by William Scott Haynes asked Polk to specify a day when he could visit Shelbyville. LS. DLC–JKP.

FROM JOHN W. CHILDRESS

Murfreesboro, Tennessee. August 21, 1839

Childress replies to Polk's letter of the 16th instant[1] and states that he must attend to plantation business and will be unable to meet Polk in Nashville. A Whig meeting in Rutherford County is expected to appoint vigilance committees; the appointment of "overseers of the people" may be used by Democrats to their political advantage. Childress hopes that Colonel Crockett[2] will withdraw his announcement for the clerkship when he learns that Colonel Hill[3] is a candidate. Sam Laughlin ought not be elected Speaker of the Senate; the Democratic party's small majority in the state should not be risked on bad appointments. Childress advises that removal of the state capital from Nashville to Columbia would be politically unwise.

ALS. DLC–JKP. Addressed to Nashville and forwarded to Columbia.

1. Letter not found.

2. Granville S. Crockett, a Murfreesboro farmer, served as sheriff of Rutherford County, 1834–36. A Democrat, he won election to the Tennessee House, served from 1835 until 1837, and subsequently became clerk of that body for one term in 1839.

3. William K. Hill, a Columbia merchant and farmer, was secretary of the 1834 Constitutional Convention and served five terms as clerk of the Tennessee Senate, 1829–37 and 1839–41.

FROM ROBERT BARNWELL RHETT[1]

My Dear Sir

Aug 21 1839

Permit me to congratulate you on your glorious victory in Tennessee. If ever Man had a right to enjoy, that highest of all earthly rewards, the self satisfaction of triumphant success in accomplishing noble ends by noble means, to you such satisfaction belongs. Not only the Administration Party, but the South is deeply indebted to you. As one of her Sons accept of my thanks and congratulations for your exertions.

I enclose you a speech with this mail which I delivered to my constituents on the Subject of the Tariff.[2] May I ask of you a careful perusal of its contents on account of the Subject it discusses? However poor might be its merits in other respects, of one thing I think I can with confidence assure you. It embraces the opinions and expresses the determination of South Carolina. Looking ahead to this question, and knowing the feelings of the People of this State upon it, I have never been able to identify myself entirely with the administration Party, altho I am called by the Telescope, Prestons organ[3]—Mr Vanburens Adjutant Genl. in So Ca:—For Gods sake My Dear Sir, if possible, let us have no more strife upon this subject. We ask nothing but justice and the Constitution, and it is as certain as that the firmament is above us. South Carolina will take nothing less. A discriminating Tariff in the least degree, acknowledging the principle of protection, will be resisted by the State. And the question then is this—shall not the whole South join together and peaceably compel our rights—or shall we be divided—and this produces a deplorable oblivion, which will end God only knows where. In bringing this matter to a peaceful close you have probably in your position more power than any man in the South. You are in the South. You know the feelings of the People. You are closely associated with the Administration who are deeply indebted to you. You can approach the President with confidence, and I am sure, from what I now judge of his principles he does not differ much from us. If the matter is properly presented to him by Southern men, he cannot sacrifice us for northern interests. My position as much as I esteem him, does not authorize me to approach him on the subject; but yours does. Do write to him therefore—urge him to bring up the Subject in his message, and heal up the division in our Party, and give the South repose with her rights.

Write to me what you do, but not in the haste I am scribbling and believe me . . . .

R. Barnwell Rhett

[P.S.] Mrs. Rhett[4] joins me in remembrance to Mrs. Polk. Direct to Beaufort.

ALS. DLC–JKP. Probably addressed to Columbia.

1. An extreme advocate of states' rights and a prominent follower of John C. Calhoun, Rhett was a congressman from South Carolina from 1837 until 1849. He succeeded Calhoun in the U.S. Senate in 1850, but resigned his seat two years later. Through his newspaper, the *Charleston Mercury,* Rhett espoused the right of secession and inveighed against the South's reliance upon the Democratic party. He was at the head of those who led South Carolina out of the Union in late 1860.

2. Enclosure not found. Advocating a tariff for revenue only, Rhett wished to force the tariff issue prematurely; the compromise tariff of 1833 was not scheduled to expire until 1842.

3. William C. Preston advanced his political views in the columns of the Columbia *Telescope.* Preston, a states' rights and slavery advocate, was elected to the U.S. Senate in 1833 as a Calhoun nullifier and was reelected in 1837. Opposed to Andrew Jackson, Preston became a Whig and resigned his Senate seat in 1842 rather than follow the dictates of the South Carolina legislature.

4. Elizabeth Washington Burnet married Rhett in 1827.

FROM JOHN S. YOUNG

Dear Sir McMinnville 21 Aug 1839

Your esteemed favour of the 15 Inst has been received, its contents noted, and the letter itsself disposed of according to your wishes.[1] You will be nominated by the people of Franklin Co. on the 31st Inst and at this place on the first Monday in Sept. I have concluded not to press the idea of a convention any further. I wrote to General Anderson to day and urged him to set our friends at Work in East Tenn as soon as possible. I desire to see some action throughout the state before the Meeting of the Legislature. If the matter is managed right the people will force the Legislature to make the nomination. The matter ought to be attended to at a very early period in Lincoln, Maury, Bedford and Giles. You promised me a list of names the want of which prevents me from doing as much as I would wish.

Burton I understand is pressing his claims for the Senate in the event Foster resigns. I very much fear he will produce confusion in our ranks. I had a conversation with our Members to day. They were in favour of Carrol[l] first, next Grundy. Grundy is the man that should be elected. His talents and experience give him higher claims than any other individual. More[o]ver, the Whigs pulled us down, let us build up. Old Warren,[2] never wrong, will do what is right. Burton charges the Democracy too high damages for getting beat and he well was, because Bell was hard to shake off.

It would have afforded me much pleasure to have met you at Nashville but I am one of your poor friends and am forced to labor for my daily bread. This being the season for Physicians, I am compeled to stay at home. I expect to have the pleasure of witnessing your inauguration. In hopes soon to hear from you . . . .

JOHN S. YOUNG

ALS. DLC–JKP. Addressed to Columbia.

1. Letter not found.

2. Warren County, Tennessee.

FROM ALEXANDER O. ANDERSON

My Dear Sir, Knoxville Augt 22 1839

Your favor of the 15th Inst.[1] I had the pleasure of receiving today.

Permit me to congratulate you upon the success of our principles, & to say that you have added vastly to the high obligation which you have heretofore confered upon your Country. It has been an unparalleld victory in the annals of American politics, & will be long remembered for the important results which it must produce in favor of the great democratic party, and the permanent reestablishment of sound opinions in the heroic State of Tennessee. She has been long carried away under false pretences, and disguised colors, but you have rent the vail [veil], and the vision of the public is not only brightened, but will continue to brighten in the progress of investigation.

In the Argus of last Tuesday, I had inserted an Article headed "Review of the election for Governor—Col Polk and his unparallel[ed] triumph—The Vice Presidency."[2] The course taken in that review seemed to me the best adapted to the end proposal &c &c & to be perfectly consistent with the truth. Before this reaches Columbia, you will have seen it. I hope the scope and bearing of it will meet your approbation, as I believe it will that of the friends of correct principles throughout the State.

On the 14th Inst. Dr Anderson left home for Jonesboro', and was present, as I hear, at the celebration of the Democratic Victory, in that place. He made out a brief of the Review which he designed to have inserted in the Sentinel. I saw the brief, & think you will be pleased with it. He will take other preliminary steps, among the friends of our cause. I wrote to several of our leading men, & before he leaves they will have had a full consultation, and understanding.

Dr Ramsay yesterday read to me a letter which he had written to you.[3] I remarked to him that it was not desirable to place you in any such *delicate position, as the answer to his suggestion wou'd imply.* The Doctor was apprized of the leading views which the Argus wou'd put forth, and this *produced his punctilios &c &c—too formal by half.* But it is immaterial and I just give you *the item,* not forgetting your remark to me, once, about the political "*instinct*" of men! So, however, I suppose he has sent his letter. Albeit, things will move on to the end proposed without needing *any commitment* from you, upon paper! "Verbum sat."[4]

The Argus of next Tuesday will follow up the Subject—and I will write to some of those Gentlemen, or all of them named in your letter to me. I suppose they will be apprised by you that they can correspond with *me freely* &c &c!

The "Review" I think ought to be copied into your Nashville Union—& the Columbia paper[5] &c—and its bearing noticed.

I am not of the opinion that Judge White will resign. I presume, however, that the first movement of the legislature will be to instruct &c[6] and you *may rely upon it that is what Mr Foster means!* Read him again!

But in regard to a vacancy here the Democratic members will be I think, favorably disposed to concert. I saw Col Wheeler three days ago. He spent the night with me. He Said his mind had been disposed to obtain a conce[r]t among our friends in favor of bringing my name forward &c. Much, of course, will be done in the final disposition of this when the Legislature meet—it being the only opportunity that the members will have to confer freely with each other &c &c.

I will write you again. In the closing of this letter, however, allow me to recommend to you for the appointment which Jacobs fills on the staff of the Governor, our friend Arthur R Crozier. He is a good writer—a most determined and valuable politician, & possesses great popularity with his friends and acquaintances. We need strength here, at this central point—and this wou'd aid us vastly—and wou'd add much to our triumph—when the Federalists are rejoicing over us. I feel very solicitous for his appointment, not merely upon personal grounds, but for the good of the cause. *I understand the position of things, in the East here, and am satisfied it wou'd be one of the very best steps which cou'd be taken,* and I hope you will concur with me in opinion upon this subject. I believe that Jacobs is Quarter Master General. *I wou'd not recommend this appointment if I did not feel persuaded of its importance.* We have Unity here, but our friends need some strengthening, and whatever may give them prominence.

I expect our friend Reynolds will be a candidate for Attorney of this District. He has been good steel.

I hope you found Mrs Polk in good health. I shou'd be glad to hear from you again &c—immediately. I write freely in the *strictest confidence*—and shall dispose of your letters as requested, desiring a similar disposition be made of mine.

A Anderson

P.S. It may not be inappropriate that I shou'd add that my friend Crozier feels somewhat upon this Staff Appointment—[it] being the Same which Jacobs fills—who has just beaten him. As to Croziers course throughout the Canvass it was uncompromisingly for you. And as to his position that he wou'd abide by the will of his Constituents &c &c., [it] being the Republican doctrine—he was regulated by the belief of the friends of the Party as to what was the most judicious course. If a majority cou'd first have been obtained in the person of a popular man it wou'd soon have aided to bring them to advocate sound principles.

The political Battles of East Tennessee are very much acted upon from Knoxville. It is an important position. We need our strength mentally and numerically fostered here—and I recommend Crozier, believeing it to be, in every point of view, a most judicious appointment. If your opinions shou'd correspond with mine, upon this subject, it wou'd be very gratifying to me to hear from you to that end—and it wou'd be *more desirable to do so as soon as may be convenient &c &c.* Crozier enters with all his zeal into the movements I am making here among our leading friends touching the V.P,—and has a head to aid.

The Ball may be considered here (East Tennessee) as in actual motion—but it will ere long receive a *more formal direction!* Of course, all this is in the strictest confidence. A.A.

ALS. DLC–JKP. Addressed to Columbia and marked "*Private and confidential.*"

1. Letter not found.

2. No copy of the Knoxville *Argus*' issue of August 20 has been found. The *Nashville Union* carried Anderson's "Review" on August 30, 1839.

3. See J. G. M. Ramsey to Polk, August 20, 1839.

4. Latin phrase for "word enough."

5. No issues of the Columbia *Tennessee Democrat* for 1839 are extant.

6. See J. G. M. Ramsey to Polk, August 20, 1839.

FROM RANDOLPH D. CASEY[1]

Middleburg, Tennessee. August 22, 1839

Casey reports that many Hardeman County friends held an election celebration in Bolivar on August 13. Democrats are "holding the Whigs down" in Hardeman County. Casey has defeated Deputy Sheriff Mohondro[2] in the militia election for colonel of the 125th regiment and thereby "nip[p]ed him in the bud so deep that . . . he hardly will come out again." Casey rejoices at the election of a Democratic majority in the legislature and anticipates Foster's resignation from the U.S. Senate. It is said that Mrs. Caldwell,[3] learning that her husband had declined a wager on Polk's election, "scolded the Doct. and posted a young man off the next morning with 100$ to take the bet . . . and won it."

ALS. DLC–JKP. Addressed to Columbia.

1. Casey served as Hardeman County clerk from 1844 until 1848.

2. Not identified further.

3. Lydia Eliza Polk Caldwell, Polk's sister, was the wife of Haywood County planter and physician, Silas M. Caldwell.

FROM GEORGE W. MEEK[1]

Athens, Alabama. August 24, 1839

Meek expresses regret that in their conversation of the previous Monday evening[2] he could not accept Polk's offer. Although retained by another planter for two years, Meek would prefer to work for Polk and will take the assignment in 1841 or earlier, if released from his present commitment.[3]

ALS. DLC–JKP. Addressed to Columbia. Published in Bassett, *Plantation Overseer*, 123.

1. Meek, who was en route to Mississippi when he wrote this letter from Athens, Alabama, is not identified further.

2. August 19, 1839.

3. On August 6, 1840, Meek renewed his offer to work for Polk. ALS. DLC–JKP.

FROM JOHN E. WHEELER

Jacksboro, Tennessee. August 24, 1839

Wheeler rejoices in the Democratic victory and discusses some of its political consequences. Whigs in Knoxville are "disconsolate." It is said that White will resign from the Senate. Wheeler maintains that General Anderson is "the most efficient man" to replace White. The public offices should be filled with political friends in every instance, for the people of Tennessee have voted for political change. Only Polk could have won the state for the Democracy in 1839.

ALS. DLC–JKP. Addressed to Columbia. AE on the cover states that this letter was answered on September 5, 1839; Polk's reply has not been found.

FROM EZEKIEL P. MCNEAL

Bolivar, Tennessee. August 25, 1839

In reply to Polk's letter of the 18th instant,[1] McNeal states that by January 1, 1840, he expects to collect $782.50 in rents due Polk for 1838 and 1839. McNeal presently knows of no potential purchaser for Polk's lands near Bolivar, but suggests that for ease of sale those tracts be divided into smaller parcels. Among Polk's friends in the Western District none rejoiced more over the election victory than John T. Macon, who "went home & forthwith illuminated his whole premises, much to the mortification of one or two of his Whig neighbors."

ALS. DLC–JKP. Addressed to Columbia. AE on the cover reads: "Rents due M. T. Polk's Heirs 1st Jany. 1840—as pr within $782.50."

1. Letter not found.

FROM JOHN S. YOUNG

Dr Sir McMinnville 25 Aug 1839

Since I wrote you last[1] I have had a further conversation with our members on the subject of the election of Senator which has brought my mind to the conclusion that if Grundy (Carrol[l] being out of the way) does not accept we will have confusion in our ranks. Northcut & Hill[2] it is said would after Grundy be for Trousdale (the most irreproachoable man in the state of our party). They are personally opposed to Burton and will not sanction the idea of G. W. Campbell. Laughlin would be for Campbell and next to him Johnson or Turley.[3] So they go. How is it to be remedied? Let Grundy accept and all is quiet. The question is asked if Col Polk is placed in another situation who will be our candidate for Gov? I say Cave Johnson. Next to yourself he is the man for the people.

Our meeting will be large on Monday next. Old Warren will proclaim you to the world as the greatest force etc she has ever had except Old Hickory. I hope Anderson will put things in motion in East Tennessee. I remarked to him in my letter that the matter in East Tennessee was committed to him and to him we looked for a response from E Tenn.

John S. Young

P.S. Col Laughlin has just showed me a letter of yours,[4] from which it appears that the Col gave you his good wishes in my behalf. I had a cordial conversation with the Col in which he made many suggestions but I did not know when and what he wrote to you but I am satisfied with whatever his judgement thought best. Upon reflection I have no strong desire to have Employment connected with the Disbursement of public money. Col Laughlin suggested an agency connected with the P O Department or a situation of a Subordinate character at Washington, with either of which I would be content. I was for nearly three years in a public station which broke up all my private relations, making my late temporary employment an injury to me in a pecuniary point of view. This being the case I determined to make an effort for further favors. And if I failed I would dispose of myself in private life and indulge no further expectations. This accounts for what may seem to you great importunity on my part. Should it so turn out that I obtain employment through your kind exertions I will be thankful. You know the extent of my merit and can place my claims where you think they ought to be.[5]
JSY

ALS. DLC–JKP. Addressed to Columbia.

1. See John S. Young to Polk, August 21, 1839.

2. Woodson Northcutt and Hugh Lawson White Hill. Northcutt, a farmer, represented Warren County in the Tennessee House as a Democrat, 1833–41; he moved to Alabama and served in that state's legislature, 1845–49. Hill, a farmer, school teacher, and distiller, represented Warren County three terms in the Tennessee House as a Democrat, 1837–43; he won one term in the U.S. House, 1847–49.

3. Samuel H. Laughlin, George Washington Campbell, Cave Johnson, and probably William B. Turley. Reared and educated in Davidson County, Turley began the practice of law in Clarksville. He served as judge of the Eleventh Judicial Circuit, 1829–35, and as a justice of the Tennessee Supreme Court, 1835–50.

4. Letter not found. See Samuel H. Laughlin to Polk, August 10, 1839.

5. On September 13, 1839, Acting Secretary of War Samuel Cooper acknowledged receipt of Polk's letter of September 1, 1839 (letter not found), recommending John S. Young for an agency or clerkship in the Indian Department. Cooper explains that there are no vacant positions, but will refer the recommendation to Secretary of War Joel R. Poinsett upon his return to Washington City. Copy. DNA–RG 107, Office of the Secretary of War, Letters Sent, Vol. XXI, p. 204.

FROM MOSES DAWSON[1]

Cincinnati, Ohio. August 26, 1839

Dawson congratulates Polk on his victory and his "extraordinary exertions" in the canvass. He seeks Polk's advice on the "strength of the friends of that sensative measure in the 25th Congress"[2] and inquires whether or not this legislation will pass during the coming Congress. If its prospects are thought to be favorable, Dawson will promulgate Polk's opinion in Ohio prior to the October elections. Dawson requests an advance copy of Polk's message to the legislature[3] for publication purposes.

ALS. DLC–JKP. Addressed to Columbia.

1. An ardent Irish nationalist, Dawson was forced to flee his native land; he worked in Philadelphia before moving to Cincinnati, where he edited the *Advertiser*, a Democratic newspaper.

2. Reference probably is to the Independent Treasury bill.

3. Polk's Inaugural Address, delivered on October 14, 1839, exhibited the new governor's general political principles; his first legislative message, communicated on October 22, 1839, concentrated on the state's programs in banking and internal improvements.

TO BOLING GORDON[1]

Columbia, Tennessee. August 26, 1839

In reply to Gordon's letter of the 21st,[2] Polk acknowledges receipt of an invitation to a public dinner to be given in his honor by the Democratic-

Republican citizens of Hickman County.[3] Regretfully Polk must decline, for private and public duties require that he postpone all invitations within the state until after the meeting of the legislature. Polk asks Gordon to make the necessary explanations in Hickman County and says that he has written to Cave Johnson, urging him to attend the dinner.

ALS. T–Gordon Papers. Addressed to Nashville and marked "*Private.*"

1. Gordon, a Hickman County planter, served three terms in the Tennessee House, 1829–35, and two terms in the Senate, 1835–37 and 1843–45.
2. Letter not found.
3. See Polk to Alexander Gray et al., August 26, 1839.

TO ALEXANDER GRAY, ET AL.[1]

Columbia, Tennessee. August 26, 1839

Having received an invitation[2] from the Democratic-Republican citizens of Hickman County to be honored at a public dinner with Colonel Johnson, Polk replies that circumstances compel him to decline the honor. He expresses appreciation for Hickman County's firm support in the late election.

ALS, draft. DLC–JKP. Addressed to Centerville, Hickman County, and marked "Copy."

1. Polk addressed his letter to Gray and nine other members of the Hickman County arrangements committee.
2. Alexander Gray et al. to Polk, August 23, 1839. LS. DLC–JKP.

TO WILLIAM RICE, ET AL.[1]

Columbia, Tennessee. August 26, 1839

Polk acknowledges receipt of an invitation[2] to attend a public dinner to be given in his honor by citizens of Marion County. With regret he declines the engagement.

L, written and signed in the hand of Sarah C. Polk. DLC–JKP. Addressed to Jasper, Marion County.

1. Polk addressed his letter to Rice and four other members of the Marion County arrangements committee.
2. William Rice et al. to Polk, August 19, 1839. LS. DLC–JKP.

FROM JOHN CATRON

Dr Sir:

Nashville. Augt 27. 39

I conversd. with Mr. Craighead on renting his House—& asked the price per anm.—which he said he supposed about 600$. I think it high—& have enquired of Mr. Crockett.[1] He wishes to sell—being embarrassd. with debts. Craighead is desirous to know soon as may be, as Mr Martin, he tells me, desires to rent. He wd. prefer you as a tenant—as Mr M. has a family of children who will do harm to a house.

The Banner of this morning, has in it, enough to indicate fully the course intended by Mr Foster. Of Judge White nothing is said; and of whose intentions his party knows nothing. Depend on it, he will hold on to the last moment—for altho' he has ever pretended to great indiference for office; Still no man loves place more, or better apprehends the oblivion that wd. Swiftly over-come him by going out. So it used to be with him—& unless exceedingly changed, this much of his former self, remains. My present impression is, that Foster will be greatly weakened by continuing in the Senate and that no strong step to drive him out, *before he has to go on to Washington,* ought to be taken. The country ought to see his anxiety to hold to the office, so as to render ridicilous that chivalrous letter of his to Powel.[2] And it occurs to me furthermore, that Foster would be weakened—& his party consequently, should he remain in the Senate until after the Presidential election; of this however I have *strong* misgivings. The public sentiment does not walk on stilts—far from it; with it, the adage, that a living dog, is worth more than a dead lion,[3] holds good as a general rule; & hence it may be, that if Foster can be gotten out by means not too strong, & to his disadvantage, it will help the administration side. Great dexterity will be played off by his side—& a corresponding Skill must be used by the other—& hence I think you had better be here early in the session. One head must do the principal planing. The execution by Gillespie[4] & others will be good enough.

J. CATRON

ALS. DLC–JKP. Addressed to Columbia.

1. Possibly the residence of George Crockett, Sr. See John Catron to Polk, September 1, 1839, and David Craighead to Polk, September 3, 1839.

2. On July 4, 1839, Ephraim H. Foster advised Mathew Powell, Whig legislator from Robertson County, of his intention to resign his U.S. Senate post if a majority of the new Tennessee legislature favored the policies of the Van Buren administration. For the text of Foster's letter, see the Nashville *Republican Banner*, July 11, 1839.

3. Variant of the phrase, "A living dog is better than a dead lion." Ecclesiastes 9:4.

4. John F. Gillespy.

TO JOHN N. ESSELMAN[1]

Dear Sir Columbia Augt. 27th 1839

The "Hermitage Hickory" walking-cane which you have done me the honor to present to me, is accepted as a valued testimonial of your friendship and regard. The spot from which it was cut gives to it an additional value. It indicates not merely the personal friendship and regard of the donor, but a concurrence in the political principles of the venerated man,[2] who in his retirement, after a long and eventful life of public usefulness, inhabits "The Hermitage". Having myself long approved and sustained his political principles, your pre[se]nt is esteemed the more valuable on that account. For it I return to you my thanks.

JAMES K. POLK

ALS, draft. DLC–JKP. Addressed to Nashville and marked "Copy." AE on the cover reads: "Hermitage Hickory cane."

1. A well-known Nashville physician, Esselman was married to Anne Campbell, sister of George Washington Campbell.

2. Andrew Jackson.

TO WILLIAM S. HAYNES, ET AL.[1]

Gentlemen Columbia Augt. 27th 1839

I have had the honor to receive your letter of the 20th Instant,[2] requesting me to say on what day I can pay a visit to my old constituents and friends in the County of Bedford. I most surely assure you, that it would afford me sincere pleasure to visit once more, a people to whom I am under many and lasting obligations, for the uniform support, they have given me during a period of more than fourteen years, and to exchange with them mutual congratulations upon the continued ascendancy and triumph of the Republican principles upon which they have at all times acted. I regret however that my engagements are such as to put it out of my power to visit them at any early day, and to prevent me at the present from saying at what time I can do so. The recent political contest through which we have passed, and to which you allude derived all its importance from the fact that great public principles, were involved in the issue, and though profoundly gratified to my fellow-citizens for the distinguished honor they have conferred upon me personally, I am duly sensible that I have been but the humbler instrument in their hands through whom they have re-asserted the long cherished political principles of their fathers & of themselves. Tennessee, though for a short period, she occupied a false position, has resumed her old Station in the Republican ranks, and will I doubt not, long continue to occupy it. For the kind terms in which you have been pleased to speak of my humble efforts to affect this result, I return you my thanks and beg to assure you, that at some future period I will take pleasure in visiting my old constituents in Bedford. With assurances of personal respect and regard . . . .

James K. Polk

ALS, draft. DLC–JKP. Addressed to Shelbyville and marked "Copy."

1. Polk addressed his letter to Haynes and seven other citizens of Bedford County.

2. William Scott Haynes et al. to Polk, August 20, 1839. LS. DLC–JKP.

FROM THOMAS MAXWELL[1]

My dear Sir, Elmira Chemung Co. N.Y 27 Aug 1839

It is with joy, heartfelt & unfeigned, that I congratulate you on the result of the late election in Tennessee. "God bless her." She has restored us to hope. With the result in Tennessee & Indiana & North Carolina we can enter upon the work of regeneration in New York with renewed vigor. We hope to give a good account of the Empire State in November. When perfectly convenient, do send me the precise result in your state. Gray,[2] is rejoicing.

Th. Maxwell

ALS. DLC–JKP. Addressed to Columbia.

1. A New York lawyer, Maxwell won election as a Democrat to the U.S. House and served from 1829 until 1831. He was editor of the Elmira *Gazette*, 1834–36, and postmaster of Elmira, 1834–39.

2. Hiram Gray, a lawyer from Elmira, New York, served one term as a Democrat in the U.S. House, 1837–39. He was appointed circuit judge and vice-chancellor of New York's Sixth Judicial District in 1846 and was elected justice of the New York Supreme Court in the following year.

TO ROBERT H. WATKINS, ET AL.[1]

Gentlemen: Columbia Tenn., Aug. 28th, 1839

On my return to my residence, after an absence of some days, I had the honor to receive your letter of the 17th inst., inviting me in behalf of a "meeting of Democratic Republicans," held in Courtland, Ala. to partake with them, of a dinner, at such time as may suit my convenience." The recent political contest in Tennessee to which you have alluded, was one of principle. By a concurrence of peculiar circumstances, and by means well understood, and which it is unnecessary to reiterate, the State had for some years, been placed in a false political attitude. The mass of her people were at all times Republicans, and though for a season they were deceived and misled, the late contest in the State, furnishes but another proof of the truth of the maxim that "when reason is left free to combat error," the people will never fail, sooner or later, to arrive at correct results.[2] Though, in the canvass through which we have passed, the most extraordinary exertions were used to conceal the truth, and confuse the public mind, and though a studied system of detraction and misrepresentation of public men and measures, which may defy a parallel in any political contest ever had in any State in the Union, were resorted to, the people were honest; they were interested only in their country's welfare;—they were Republicans on *principle*, and TRUTH prevailed. The State has resumed her old position in the Republican ranks, and will, I doubt not, long continue to occupy it. In effecting this result, I have been but the humble instrument in the hands of the people, through which they have re-asserted the long cherished Republican principles of their fathers and of themselves. For the kind terms in which you have been pleased to allude to my humble "public services," and the part I have borne in common with my Republican Fellow-citizens, in redeeming the State from the Federal chains with which it was attempted to bind her, I beg to return to you my profound acknowledgments. I heartily reciprocate with you, Gentlemen, the sentiments of gratification, which you so happily express, "that the time honored veteran, (Gen. Jackson) who has been pursued by slander and detraction, with so much malignity, into the very shades of private life, has lived to witness the re-establishment, in his own State, of those principles, which he has so fearlessly and successfully advocated."

It will afford me pleasure to meet my "Democratic Republican" Fellow-citizens of Alabama, whom you represent, at Courtland, on Tuesday the 17th of Sept. next, should that be a day which will suit your convenience.

Duly impressed with the honor done me by your kind invitation, I beg that you will accept for yourselves and the Republican citizens in whose behalf you act, assurances of the high consideration and regard with which I am very respectfully . . . .

JAMES K. POLK

Copy. In the *Nashville Union*, September 4, 1839.

1. Inside address names Watkins and four other members of the arrangements committee who communicated the dinner invitation of August 17, 1839.

2. Variant quotation from Thomas Jefferson's First Inaugural Address, March 4, 1801.

TO SILAS WRIGHT

My dear Sir, Columbia Tennessee August 28, 1839

My constant attention during the whole summer to the political canvass in which I have been engaged must be my apology for neglecting until now to write you concerning the business entrusted to my care, by your letter of the 31st of March.[1] I entered upon the canvass about the 1st of April and during a period of four months was at home but two days.

I have not yet been able to see Dr Tracy[2] in person but have caused the receipt enclosed to me to be presented to him & learn from the gentleman who presented it that he has collected the sum of $187.00 only. I am not able to inform you whether the ballance of the notes in Tracy's hands are secure or when they will probably be paid. You will observe that after deducting the $170 endorsed on the receipt and paid by the Father[3] of Dr Tracy for the Doctor there will remain in his hand only $17 now collected. I expect to see Dr Tracy in the course of a few days and will then be able to inform you when the claim in his hands will probably be collected.

You have seen the result of the great political contest in which we have been engaged. The State has resumed her old position in the Republican ranks and with common prudence on our part will long continue to occupy it. It will require however continued vigilance, to retain the advantage we have gained. Our opponents are already marshalling their scattered forces for the great contest of 1840. Their leading organs have already raised the War cry for another battle. We have however possession of the field & will I doubt not be able to keep the ground we have now.

With kind respects to Mrs Wright[4] . . . .

JAMES K. POLK

Copy. DLC–JKP. Addressed to Canton, New York, and marked "Copy."

1. Letter not found.
2. Not identified further.
3. Not identified further.
4. Wright married Clarissa Moody on September 11, 1833.

FROM J. GEORGE HARRIS

My Dear Sir, Nashville Aug 29. 1839

Mr Smith starts for Columbia in the morning to confer with you upon the subject matter of his business. He tells me he is desirous of disposing of the property of the Union and closing up his business affairs in connexion with it. He has spoken to me with reference to the *successorship* and I scarcely know what to say to him. There are many weighty considerations that I find difficulty in settling in my own mind.

Perhaps no business is more hazardous than printing. Certainly none is more perplexing. The property of an establishment becomes scattered all over the country in small amounts which it is no easy matter to collect. Labor must be paid for weekly—and paper can be obtained only on short credits—while it has become too fashionable to pay newspaper bills *when convenient*. I have now in out standing debts at the North from 3 to 4 thousand dollars, due me for newspapers, which it is difficult to realize, and indeed I do not much expect ever to realize the half of them.

But I think the Union establishment offers inducements and prospects of profit, rarely seen in this country—provided the State Printing and a share of the General Government printing can be secured to it, and, I have therefore entertained the proposition of Mr. Smith favorably, though in no way definitely.

I scarcely know what to say to you on the subject. I cannot think of undertaking a business of this magnitude in a manner that will subject me to embarrassment; or, indeed, that will ever harass my mind and unfit me for a proper discharge of editorial duties at all times. Were I to take the concern upon my shoulders, the monetary concerns must be controlled entirely by a man selected for the purpose, since it would be impossible for me to edit the paper when bothered with collecting and disbursing, &c.

I confess my love of Tennessee, especially of Nashville, and would like to settle here—but you will not blame me for stepping cautiously into a business of such permanency and responsibility. That I can increase the circulation of the Union several thousands, and give it a weight of character that shall prove effective among the people I have no doubt. But I am fearful that the means required, over and above my own industry, it would be difficult for me to furnish, to say nothing of the pecuniary responsibility.

I have given the subject a good deal of thought, but as no *distinctive* propositions have been made to me, I of course have not approached to any arrangement or conclusion in the finances.

I did think of visiting Columbia on Saturday, but as Mr. Smith goes to-morrow, I think I will wait until he returns. I shall accept your kind invitation and spend a day at Columbia early next week.

Be good enough to give me a line of reply and tell me the views and feelings of Mr Smith on the subject above referred to.

J. Geo. Harris

ALS. DLC–JKP. Addressed to Columbia.

FROM WILLIAM SMITH, ET AL.[1]

Sir Huntsville, Ala. Aug., 29th, 1839

A large portion of the Democratic citizens of Madison and Limestone counties, in the State of Alabama, who approve of the measures, and support the principles of the present Administration of the General Government of these United States, viewing your whole political course as one of unwearied assiduity to serve the cause of democracy; and more especially, having seen with unfeigned pleasure, your late bold, manly, open, dignified and successful efforts, not only to maintain that Democracy unstained, but to bring it back to its true meaning, as stamped upon it by a new band of self-created Whigs—a name once dear to American freemen, but now assumed to allure the honest and unwary citizens of the United States from that policy which God and the constitution of their country have given them to promote their happiness, and the liberties of this great Republic: And, as the highest testimony of their approbation, have appointed their committee to congratulate you upon your triumphant election by the brave and watchful citizens of Tennessee, over whose State you are elected to preside for the next two years; and to solicit the pleasure of your company to partake with them of a Public Dinner.

Wm. Smith

Copy. In the *Nashville Union,* September 16, 1839.

1. Letter attributed to Smith and seven other members of the arrange-

ments committee. William Smith, a lawyer from South Carolina, served in the U.S. House, 1797–99, and in the Senate, 1816–31. Moving to Huntsville, Alabama, in 1833, he served four years in the Alabama House, 1835–39.

TO ANDREW JACKSON

My Dear Sir Columbia Tennessee August 31st 1839

I received to day, through a committee of Gentlemen from Huntsville, Alabama, an invitation to attend a Public Dinner to be given in that vicinity, and have accepted for friday the 20th of September.[1] *Judge Smith* and the other members of the committee, are exceedingly anxious that you should also accept, and will proceed from this place to the Hermitage on tomorrow in the hope that they may prevail upon you to do so. I hope, if the state of your health will possibly permit it, that you will accept. The people they say, are very anxious to see you, and think they have some claim upon you, upon the ground of a former pledge to visit them at some convenient time. Your presence I am sure would have a fine effect, in promoting the spread of sound principles. Genl. Armstrong, Majr Donelson and other friends, would accompany you if you desire it. The Committee promise, if you will consent to go, to save you the physical labour, of passing through a personal introduction to the people individually, which is generally incident to such an occasion. I hope you can by starting in time and travelling by easy stages, perform the journey without injury to your health. I will by a previous arrangement be at Courtland on the 17th[2] and am very solicitous to meet you at the Huntsville Dinner on the 20th September.

James K. Polk

ALS. DLC–AJ. Addressed to "Hermitage." AEI on the cover reads: "Col Polk—urging me to accept the invitation to Madison Alabama. I will go if I can. A.J."

1. See William Smith et al. to Polk, August 29, 1839.

2. See Robert H. Watkins et al. to Polk, August 17, 1839, and Polk to Robert H. Watkins et al., August 28, 1839.

FROM JOEL M. SMITH

Sir Nashville, Augt 31 1839

On my return home[1] I found I had been protested for $550. Nor can I get the money to take up the note so as to save my Credit. Under this state of things you can better judge of my feelings than I can describe them. Something has to be done immediately. I would therefore advise you to come in on the receipt of this & confer with our friends on what is to be done and to bring James Walker with you. I do not think Mr Harris is willing to go into the arrangement proposed.[2] If something is not done in a few days the paper will stop. I am told that Donelson will be here on tuesday and I will try and keep in town that night with the hope that you will be in.

J. M. SMITH

ALS. DLC–JKP. Addressed to Columbia. AE on the cover states that this letter was answered on September 2, 1839; Polk's reply has not been found.

1. See Joel M. Smith to Polk, August 15, 1839.
2. See J. George Harris to Polk, August 29, 1839.

TO WILLIAM SMITH, ET AL.[1]

Gentlemen: Columbia, Tenn. Aug. 31, 1839

The kind invitation which you convey to me, on the part of "the Democratic citizens of Madison and Limestone counties, in the State of Alabama, to partake with them of a public dinner," which they propose to give in that State, commands my sincere acknowledgements, for the honor done me by this mark of their regard. I can be but too sensible that no past public services of mine, could merit so high a compliment. Other and higher motives have induced it. Great and vital principles, to which you have alluded, are involved in the issues now before the country; principles which had their origin at the organization of the government, and which, through every period of our history, have agitated and divided our people. The "Party Designation," by which the advocates of opposite and conflicting political opinions and principles were formerly known, were the names they bore of *Federalists* and *Republicans*. By a recurrence to the principles which divided us in our earlier history, under these well known "party designations," it would not be difficult to demonstrate that they are the same which divide us now. Though the "party designation" of *Federalists* (that name having become unpopular) has been abandoned, and other party names, of popular import at different times assumed in its stead, yet the political principles of the leading men of the party, who give direction to its policy whether called "*National Republicans*" or "*Whigs*," are unchanged. The fraud upon the public, by which many honest men have been deceived, consists in the fact, that their *real principles* have been obscured from the public eye "by the dear magic of a name."[2] It is true that many are called "*Whigs*," at the present day, because it is a cherished and popular name of Revolutionary times, who are not "Federalists," in principle. This however cannot be said of the *leading men* who have assumed the *name*. *They* are co-laborers with the "old Federal party," to transfer the political power of the country into their hands. This was the state of things in Tennessee at the opening of the late political contest to which you allude, and the result of which is, I learn, the occasion of your proposed celebration of the triumph of Republican principles.

Tennessee, from her admission into the Union, was a Republican State. With rare and few exceptions, there was not until recently to be found within her borders, any man who ventured to avow the doctrines or to act with the Federal party. We were the most harmonious and united people in political sentiment in the Union. We were all Republicans. We were all the supporters of the Democratic doctrines of the great Jefferson. In the person of one of her favorite sons,[3] however, who had won the confidence of the State, by professing a long devotion to her principles, and who was not suspected of an intention to abandon them, or of any design to place the State, ultimately, in the false position she has lately occupied, a confiding people were, in an unsuspecting hour, unwarily seduced from the old landmarks which distinguish their principles from those of their old opponents. The people were deceived by those in whom they had been accustomed to confide, and were for a time made to believe that the leading men, whom they trusted, were still Republicans. It was against a large, and apparently overwhelming majority, composed of leading men who deceived, and a confiding people who were deceived by them, that the Democratic Republican party entered upon the late contest in the State. Free and full public discussions took place, and an enlightened and patriotic people have rendered their verdict. Tennessee has again taken her stand by the side of her sister, Alabama, and the other Republican States of the Union, and I have an abiding confidence that she will adhere to them in all future trials, when their common principles shall be assailed, or attempted to be overthrown or underminded by their Federal adversaries.

The patriotic State of which, gentlemen, you are citizens, though one of the younger members of the confederacy, furnishes a bright example of consistent adherence to principle, that is worthy of all admiration. Tennessee and Alabama are now united in political sentiment. Let no future ambitious aspirants to office, or designing demagogues, disturb or sever the union.

You attribute, gentlemen, too much of the credit due for the result of the late elections in Tennessee, to the humble agency I may have had in effecting it. I performed but the duty assigned me by my fellow citizens; a duty which I owed to them, to the State, and to my principles. To my co-laborers in the contest, and to the indomitable spirit of a free, enlightened and patriotic people, ardently attached to their ancient principles, is due much the greater part of the credit for the triumph of principle which has been achieved. Without their aid and co-operation it could not have been achieved.

The compliment of a public dinner, which you tender, is accepted, for such day in the month of September as may best suit the convenience of yourselves and those in whose behalf you act, only remarking, that by a previous engagement, I expect to be at Courtland, in your State, on the 17th of that month. Friday the 20th of September, the day you have informally suggested, or any other day in that month, will be convenient to me.

With the expression of my thanks to yourselves and the citizens in whose behalf you act, for the honor done me by your invitation and the tender to you individually of my personal respects.

JAMES K. POLK

Copy. In the *Nashville Union*, September 16, 1839.

1. Inside address names William Smith and seven other members of the arrangements committee who communicated the dinner invitation of August 29, 1839.

2. Variant quotation from Thomas Campbell's poem, *The Pleasures of Hope*, part 2, line 5 (1799).

3. Reference is to Hugh Lawson White.

FROM JOHN CATRON

Sr:

Nashville, Sepbr 1st [1839][1]

Red yrs 29 ulto[2]—will attend so far as I can to the matter to which you refer with Mr. Smith[3]—but court sits tomorrow, & cannot promise much.

Mr. Craighead's house[4] is a single H[all] with a wide passage, two parlors with folding doors—a family room back—and 4 rooms above—no office. It is the House Mr Claiborne[5] built—brick—well finished—& a very tasty House—in good repair. Stabling & kitchens good—& a gardin.

Heard from Harrodsburg Ky. Convention (Whig). Letcher nominated for Governor—& Thompson of Scott for Lt Gov.[6]

Gov. Clarke[7] died last week—what I expected. Died of intemprance.

Chilton Allen, & the Wickliffs[8] I think will bolt. Robt. Wickliff *thought* to me, last May, that if Letcher was nominated that *Tecumseh*[9] could beat him (L). Chs. Wickliff was seeking the nomination—& Letcher seemed then the favourite of Mr. Clay. Shd not be Surprised if Allen were forthwith to come out in opposition to Letcher. Think he will. This mere conjecture.

Geo. C. Childress Just returned from Phila. Says the Whigs crushed down, on hearing of your election—& declared Mr. Clay, wholly unavailable. The contest for Presdt., up, & settled, by the Ten. & Inda. elections.

600$ is the rent of Mr C.'s House. It is 100$ too much. But Mr. Martin will give it.

J. Catron

ALS. DLC–JKP. Addressed to Columbia.

1. Year identified through content analysis.
2. Letter not found.
3. Joel M. Smith wished to sell his interest in the *Nashville Union*.
4. See John Catron to Polk, August 27, 1839, and David Craighead to Polk, September 3, 1839.
5. Thomas Claiborne, a Nashville lawyer, served three terms in the Tennessee House, 1811–15 and 1831–33, and one term in the U.S. House, 1817–19.
6. The state convention of the Whig party in Kentucky met in Harrodsburg on August 26, 1839, and selected a gubernatorial ticket of Robert P. Letcher and Manlius V. Thompson. Letcher won several terms in the Kentucky legislature before winning election as a Republican and later as a Whig to the U.S. House, where he served from 1823 until 1835. Letcher carried all sections of the state in his race for the governorship against Richard French of Winchester. Thompson defeated John B. Helm of Bowling Green for the lieutenant governorship by the substantial margin of sixteen thousand votes.
7. James Clark, a circuit court judge in Kentucky from 1817 until 1824, won the governorship in 1836 and served until his death in 1839.
8. Chilton Allan, Charles A. Wickliffe, and Robert Wickliffe. A lawyer and state legislator, Allan won election to the U.S. House in 1831 and served three terms. He headed the state's Board of Internal Improvements from 1837 until 1839. Charles A. Wickliffe served several terms in the Kentucky legislature before winning election to the U.S. House, where he served five terms beginning in 1823. Elected lieutenant governor of Kentucky in 1836, he succeeded to the governorship in 1839; he also served as U.S. postmaster general from 1841 until 1845. Robert Wickliffe sat several terms in the Kentucky House for Fayette County before moving to the Senate in 1825; on most questions he sided with the anti-relief factions.
9. Richard Mentor Johnson.

FROM ARCHIBALD YELL

Waxhaws,[1] Arkansas. September 1, 1839

Yell sends congratulations on Tennessee's political regeneration and praises Polk's contribution as having "done more for the Party & Van Buren . . . than all his *Cabinet* and office holders in the U.S."

ALS. DLC–JKP. Addressed to Columbia.

1. Named after his birthplace in North Carolina, Yell's plantation was located near Fayetteville, Arkansas.

FROM JOHN S. YOUNG

Dear Sir McMinnville Sept 1. [1]839

Every preparation is made and our meeting will come off tomorrow. The meeting at Winchester is posponed until Saturday next.[1] We will appo[i]nt a committee of correspondence which will keep the *thing moving.* I have conversed with citizens of other states and found that our party elsewhere is only waiting for Tennessee to make the movement. The fact is I view the subject as one of paramount impor[tance] to the party that your name should be on the ticket as one of the most certain means of carrying the State for Mr Vanburen. It is a bold stroke of policy. Your name has become an oracle with every man that voted for you and it has strength enough to carry with it all its party associations. Add to this 10 pr cent for state pride and we have the state certain. We now occupy the inner works, having driven the enemy from them. We should not go to sleep with a treachous enemy upon our borders.

JOHN S YOUNG

ALS. DLC–JKP. Addressed to Columbia.

1. September 14, 1839.

FROM ALFRED BALCH

My Dear Sir, Sans Souci Near Nash 3d Septr, 39

I recd some days since a letter from Woodbury of which the following is an exact copy.

Dear Sir, (Private) Washington 15th August 1839

We breathe freer and deeper. All of us thank you for placing Tennessee along side of the Granite State.[1] The Hoosiers in Indiana have also come to the rescue. I am happy to inform you, that we believe North Carolina has chosen 8 to 5 friends of the administration. No other news.

May God bless you and yours
respectfully
Levi Woodbury

Alfred Balch Esqr
Nashville, Tenn.

I give you this copy to shew you how deep was the feeling of our friends at Washn. &c in our movements and how greatly they appreciate our Democratic victory. No doubt Van Buren himself never was so delighted in his life as when the joyful intelligence reached him. I *know* that his anxiety was excessive.

I called to see you twice whilst you were in Nashville but missed you. The Legislation of the Whigs in our Legislature has created two large and rickatty machines. I mean the Bank and the system of Internal improvements, the proper management of which will require all your tact and skill. You will be aware at once that a perfect understanding of the way in which both are worked and have been worked is indispensible before you *commit* yourself on these delicate topics and concerning which the people will become exceedingly Sensitive, the more especially if the system of internal improvement shall draw after it, the imposition of additional taxes! An able head of the Bank is indispensible for if that establishment gets wrong our party may be almost undone.

I perceive that an Editor attached to our party in Shelbyville[2] has announced you as a candidate for the Vice Presidency. This was ill-advised for *now* is not the exact time to stir that matter. Upon the question of the next Vice Presidency I think that I am fully advised: Wm R. King—Stephenson—Forsyth—Dick Johnson & even your old friend Felix[3] have aspirations that way. Chapman and Martin of Ala[4] held two protracted conversations with me about Kings claims. Iverson[5] also two, about the pretensions of Forsyth his father in Law.

I returned to this state by the way of Richmond & stayed four days with Ritchie[6] with whom I have corresponded constantly for 16 years. I found him full of a scheme to make Stephenson Vice President. Ritchie is however easily managed. Grundy last winter & the winter before had persons beating about to ascertain what chance he would stand to fill old Dicks place. Dr Martin[7] was active in his behalf and he is a tolerably efficient man in such matters. I have Martins confidence. The President requested me to write him when I parted from him. Then Grundy was to go north and did not intend to come here. The last of May I wrote Van Buren that we were getting Cannon Foster & Co on the hip and that your chances of victory were good & growing better hourly—that we had a great conquest in our grasp. Grundy heard the letter read & resolved to come here. He has now returned to tell the folks at Washn. that *he* did nearly all.

You are perhaps aware that Benton & myself have been brothers for nearly a quarter of a century. I do not know that he has ever entertained any sentiments on any subject that he has not communicated to me. A few days before I left Wn. we had a long political conversation touching his own prospects &c &c. and by the way if Benton lives & Van is re-elected which is already certain, he Benton will be the *hinge* on which many future important political events must turn. In the conversation to which I allude the Vice Presidency was touched on & Benton declared his decided preference for your nomination at the same time with that of Van Burens. For my own part I consider any movement in this matter premature until it is ascertained in which mode Van Burens renomination* can best be made—& as to the Vice Presidency a nomination might come most appropriately from our Legislature towards the close of the session by the Democratic members of it.

Very soon after our late victory I was asked here & from other quarters what was to become of me. One friend said to me—what notice is to be taken of you, the earliest fastest & hardest working friend of Van Buren in all Tennessee? To which I replied that I did not know, that I supposed some sort of justice would be accorded to me at last, after 15 years of labour without any other reward than a *small* commissionership! I have been looking around to see who are going to set up, of our party, to succeed Foster, who will resign, & I have asked myself whose attainments—fidelity—habits or talents are so superior to mine that I should stand back. Not knowing who will enter the lists for this prize I have not yet answered this pregnant question. One thing I *know* that Van Buren, Benton, Wright & others of our friends would be both personally & politically gratified with my elevation to a seat in the Senate. After all the disposition of this matter will depend mainly on yourself as the head of the new Dynasty—upon Cave Johnson—McClellan, Turney, & Brown. Whatever your fiat is, whether you open your mouth or not, will decide this matter. I shall practise no huckerstring in this business—if I move in it. & I do hope we shall be able to break up that miserable system of personal importunity & even servility which has heretofore marked the pursuit after office before the Legislature. Let talents have play hereafter—let true friends to our party be elected by the [. . .].[8] Let our motto be Union harmony concession—[ever]ything for the cause—nothing for men.

Let us not disgrace ourselves by permitting the whigs in the Legislature to decide a single important election by reason of divisions amongst ourselves, such divisions will do us great injury.

ALFRED BALCH

*I think that a nomination of candidates for President & Vice President in January would come best from a caucus of the members on our side of the Pennsylvania Legislature. Such a movement would have a decisive influence in every Democratic state of the Union. Benton & Buchannan[9] will see to this.

ALS. DLC–JKP. Addressed to Columbia and marked "Entirely confidential."

1. Reference is to New Hampshire.
2. William Scott Haynes edited the Shelbyville *Western Star*, a Democratic newspaper.
3. William Rufus King, Andrew Stevenson, John Forsyth, Richard Mentor Johnson, and Felix Grundy. King was U.S. Senator from Alabama from its admission into the Union in 1819 until 1844. He subsequently returned to the Senate in 1848, was elected vice-president in 1852, and died soon after his inauguration in 1853. A lawyer, Stevenson served several terms in the Virginia House of Delegates before winning election to the U.S. House, where he served from 1821 until 1834. He presided as Speaker of that body during his last four terms of service. Stevenson also served as minister to Great Britain from 1836 until 1841. John Forsyth held the post of secretary of state under both Andrew Jackson and Martin Van Buren, serving from 1834 until 1841. Previously he had won election to both houses of the U.S. Congress and to the Georgia governorship.
4. Reuben Chapman and Joshua L. Martin. Chapman was a Democratic congressman from Alabama from 1835 until his election as governor of that state in 1847. Martin's career included election to several terms in the Alabama House and appointment to various judicial posts, such as that of state solicitor in 1827, circuit court judge in 1834, and chancellor of middle Alabama in 1841. He won two terms in Congress, 1835–39, and one term as governor of Alabama, 1845–47.
5. Alfred Iverson served in both houses of the Georgia legislature, sat on the bench of the Superior Court, served one term in the U.S. House, 1847–49, and won one term in the Senate, 1855–61. He married twice; his second wife was Julia Frances Forsyth, daughter of John Forsyth.
6. Thomas Ritchie edited the Democratic *Richmond Enquirer* from 1804 until 1845.
7. Alfred Martin.
8. Mutilation of the manuscript has obliterated at least one word.
9. James Buchanan.

FROM DAVID CRAIGHEAD

Dear Sir Nashville Septr. 3rd 1839

There is a room 15 feet by 20 on the 2nd floor over the dining room which is approached by a stair Case of its own so as not to interfere with any other apartment. I have occupied this room as an office. It is both convenient and pleasant and I have not the least doubt but that for your purposes it will be found more convenient than an office under another roof. I ask for the rent of the premises 600 dollars a year. I am content, indeed it will be convenient for me, to retain possession until the middle of October.

I have no hesitation in believing that the arrangement of the dwelling and out houses will be very satisfactory. If you conclude to rent I shall be glad to hear from you that I may be able to give an answer to others.[1]

If Mrs Polk could come in It is highly probable that she and my wife could drive a trade in some articles of furniture that would be mutualy advantageous. In a house so large there are a good many things that being in places not very conspicuous do very well as they lie much better than they would if moved. I can at least assure you that Mrs C[2] will be content with a moderate price for any furniture she is disposed to part with.

David Craighead

ALS. DLC–JKP. Addressed to Columbia.

1. For two other letters to Polk on the rental of the Craighead house, see John Catron to Polk, August 27 and September 1, 1839.

2. Mary Macon Hunt Goodloe was the daughter of John Macon of Warrenton, North Carolina; she married David Craighead in 1820.

FROM ROBERT ARMSTRONG

Dear Sir Nashville 4 Septmr. [1839][1]

Col Harris goes out and will explain his views &c &c. Mr Smith will dispatch his forman to Louisville & Cincinnati by the stage tomorrow night to prepare and select additional stock for the Union office and be in readiness to do the public printing. When our friends meet we can settle down on some permanent ground in relation to the Union.[2] I am of opinion that it must be on an enlarged and improved scale. A small *little* shackling affair will do no good, such as the Union has been up to Harris taking charge of it. If properly gone into it can be the great leading paper of the South West—and it is just as easy to give it such a character as to conduct it as Smith has been doing.

The General promises to go to Alabama.[3] I will go with him but I fear it will be too much for him. I will write you if he continues determined to go. He says he will go through Murfreesboro, Shelbyville & Fayette[ville].

Yoakum, Fletcher, Smith[4] & other Democt. have been in to say *Nicholson* was here & a Successor to Foster spoken of. I fear some Trouble is brewing by the Feds on this subject. I trust our friends will manage it properly, as they must do, and every other question out of which mischief can come.

No letter from Hill for Smith.[5] Harris will give you all the news. I have been engaged with the Alabama Committee and failed to write you. No news.

R ARMSTRONG

ALS. DLC–JKP. Addressed to Columbia and delivered by J. George Harris.

1. Year identified through content analysis.
2. See J. George Harris to Polk, August 29, 1839, and Joel M. Smith to Polk, August 31, 1839.
3. See Polk to Andrew Jackson, August 31, 1839.
4. Williamson Smith.
5. Reference is probably to William K. Hill, who might have anticipated his election to the Senate clerkship and have corresponded with Joel M. Smith on the subject of the Senate's printing contracts.

FROM ISAAC FLETCHER[1]

Dear Sir, Vermont Caledonia County Lyndon Sept 4: 1839

Suffer me to congratulate you on your political success & be assured no one of your friends do it more sincerely. I have watched the political horizen in Tennessee with great solicitude, & noted its changes from time to time with much anxiety. The cevilities I have received from you at Washington interested [me] deeply in your success. The personal attack, and unprovoked abuse you received from your political enemies excited my indignation. I could not but admire your fortitude & forbearance, even beyond the indurance of northern gentlemen. You have triumphed over all political foes in a most unprecidented manner; & gives all your friends occasion of joy.

In the mean time as you will see by the public journals Mr. *Clay* has been making a northern tour. He has been in Vermont. Believe me, Dear Sir, he has gathered any thing but laurels & golden opinions, here at the North. His temperature is not calculated for a northern latitude, for New-England. Whatever his political friends may say to the contrary, could Mr. Clay have gone into every town in New-England so far as these states are concerned his political fate would have been sealed. The bearing of the man is reckless, his moral influence is bad. His manners, & conversations are those of a man, who neither fears God, or regards man. Such is the impression Mr. Clay has left to the north. There is some thing of the Puritan Spirit still left with us. It is incorporated in our very existance, and influences all our actions. We revere christianity, & hold in high respect the moral virtues, and no man can be long esteemed, who contemns religion, and disregards our moral relations. The pensioned Whigs may shout, but the yeomanry of New-England, maintain an indignant silence respecting Mr. Clay. This is ominous as the silence that preceeds the tempest.

Yesterday was the Genl. election in Vermont for State officers, Senators & Representatives to the General Assembly. The Freeman of my county & District have done above all praise. By previous arrangement the votes of this county were collected and counted at this place (Lyndon) last night. The result is triumphant thus far for the friends of the Administration. If other sections of the State have done as well, Tennessee may greet Vermont in her regener[a]cy & disenthralment. We have fourteen counties in this State. Our gain is five Representatives in the county for the Genl Assembly & over five hundred [votes] on the genl. Ticket. The Freemen of Vermont are up & on the march for political reform; if we do not conquer this year victory awates us in 1840.

ISAAC FLETCHER

ALS. DLC–JKP. Addressed to Columbia.

1. A Vermont lawyer and state legislator, Fletcher served as a Democrat for two terms in the U.S. House, 1837–41.

FROM ROBERT H. WATKINS

Dear Sir

Courtland [Alabama] 4th Sept. 1839

Your answer to our invitation to a public dinner on the 17th Inst was duly recd. and copies of it & the letter of invitation sent immediately to the Union for publication.[1] I presume that you will have seen them, before this reaches you, in that paper. We wrote immediately to Gen. Jackson and also to our old friend Col R. C. Foster Esqr. but have not yet heard from them. In the event of their acceptance of the invitation I have requested them to form a junction with you & inform us at what time you will be on the state line on the 16th Inst. I shall expect you and your company at my house on that Evening. I presume Col Foster will communicate with you on this arrangement alluded to. Please let me hear from you on the subject.

I should perhaps be doing you injustice if I did not mention to you Confidentially that the expectation is general here that you will make a public address on the great political questions & events of the day.

Permit me to assure you of the high respect & Esteem I entertain for you & with which I subscribe myself . . . .

R. H. WATKINS

P.S. Please designate what road you will travel to Lambs ferry.[2]

LS. Addressed to Columbia.

1. On September 4, 1839, the *Nashville Union* published the Courtland dinner invitation, dated August 17, 1839, and Polk's acceptance of the same, dated August 28, 1839.

2. Lamb's Ferry on the Tennessee River linked the north-south route between Rogersville and Courtland, Alabama. Roads from Pulaski and Elkton, Tennessee, to Courtland intersected at Rogersville, rather than at Lamb's Ferry.

FROM NATHAN GAMMON, ET AL.[1]

Jonesboro, Tennessee. September 5, 1839

Gammon and others recommend Pierce B. Anderson[2] for appointment as inspector general of the militia in East Tennessee. Anderson is Polk's "warm supporter and friend" and belongs "to the *right political party.*"

LS. DLC–JKP. Probably addressed to Columbia.

1. Letter signed by Gammon, Daniel Kenney, Joseph B. Gilmore, and John P. Chester. Gilmore is not identified.

2. An Athens lawyer, Anderson represented McMinn County in the Tennessee House from 1843 until 1847.

FROM SAMUEL H. LAUGHLIN

My dear Sir McMinnville, Sept. 6th. 1839

I am very much pleased to see that you have accepted of the Alabama invitations.[1] Your visit there will have a decided tendency to further matters which your friends have very much at heart, and which I need not name.[2]

You will see by the enclosed Extra Gazette[3] that we have taken our own way up in the Mountain District. Warren, in proportion to her population, gave the largest democratic vote in the late election, which gives her a fair right to make a leading movement. In doing so, she has assumed a responsibility of which all her prominent men are proud. Our Preamble and Resolutions,[4] which fell to my preparation as you may suppose, may not be cautiously drawn as they might have been, and some inaccuracies may be found in the printing—but they contain the right spirit, and no assumption but what we are willing to abide by. Since Monday, I have been every hour assisting in saving my fodder, and attending to Mrs. L.[5] who has just been confined, so that I have been unable to correct the printing, nor have I read over the copy enclosed,[6] but presume it will do—especially in substance.

From the time you were last at Nashville, I have not received a line of advice from Brown, Johnson, Armstrong, yourself, or any one; but my letters from Dr. Ramsey, and others in the East have convinced me that our movement was not premature. I can most truly say, that I have not acted by any concerted arrangement with you or those who may be esteemed your confidential friends at the seat of Government, whether the expression mean Washington or Nashville.

It is true, that on yesterday, I received a letter from Mr. A. Balch, postmarked the 4th instant, in which he makes the most favorable mention of your claims, but in which no specific action is hinted at.[7] By the by, he intreats me not to commit myself in relation to a successor of Mr. Foster. He may rest assured I will not do that. He speaks of my claims, and the propriety in case of your triumph, of my being speaker. Now, I wish it distinctly understood, that I want nothing, and will accept nothing, in anyway, which may not be clearly for the general good of our party—and unanimously esteemed so by our friends. If it was for the real good of our party, and so agreed by general consent, I might then be willing to abide things, like Phil Barbour's Virginia bride,[8] but in no other event. I cant be disappointed in not getting a thing I dont covet, and which, perhaps, I ought in no event to accept.

Let me hear from you before you leave for Alabama. I shall go to Nashville, as will Mr. Hill,[9] about 1st October, so as to be there four or five days before the meeting of the Assembly which will be on the 7th. I presume you will be present at the meeting. It has been customary.

I am truly sorry that our friends Hill and Crokett are competitors for the Clerkship.[10] I love both—and wish to serve both in any thing I can. I think they should compare notes, and whichever needs it most in reality, ought to have it. The office will add nothing to the already fair and high standing of either.

Make my respects to Mrs. P. while I remain, as ever . . . .

S. H. Laughlin

ALS. DLC–JKP. Addressed to Columbia and marked "Private."

1. See Robert H. Watkins et al. to Polk, August 17, 1839; Polk to Robert H. Watkins et al., August 28, 1839; and Polk to Andrew Jackson, August 31, 1839.

2. Reference is to the vice-presidential nomination.

3. Reference is to an extra edition of the McMinnville *Central Gazette,* a Democratic newspaper edited by John W. Ford from 1835 until about 1842. No 1839 issues of that paper have been found.

4. Democrats of Warren County met publicly on September 2, 1839, appointed Laughlin chairman of the meeting, and adopted resolutions nominating Martin Van Buren for reelection and Polk for the vice-presidency.

5. Laughlin's wife was Mary Clarke Bass Laughlin.

6. Enclosure not found.

7. See Alfred Balch to Polk, September 3, 1839.

8. Allusion not further identified.

9. Hugh L. W. Hill, not to be confused with William K. Hill mentioned in the paragraph below.

10. See John W. Childress to Polk, August 21, 1839.

FROM ARCHIBALD YELL

Waxhaws, Arkansas. September 7, 1839

Yell writes that friends have urged him to run for governor of Arkansas. He has not agreed to the race and is uncertain that he will. Polk and Yell's mutual friend A. G. Harrison may be denied the [Missouri] gubernatorial nomination; it is said that Harrison would have to resign his seat in Congress.

ALS. DLC–JKP. Addressed to Columbia.

FROM CLEMENT C. CLAY[1]

Huntsville, Alabama. September 8, 1839

Clay states that he must travel the next day to East Tennessee to attend his father, who is seriously ill.[2] Apologetic that he will be unable to meet Polk and Jackson at the Courtland and Huntsville festivities,[3] Clay extends an invitation on behalf of his wife[4] for Polk and Mrs. Polk to come "*directly to our house* and make it your Head Quarters during your stay in North Alabama."

ALS. DLC–JKP. Addressed to Columbia.

1. A lawyer and Alabama state legislator, Clay won three terms as a Democrat in the U.S. House, 1829–35; he served as governor of Alabama, 1835–37, and as U.S. Senator, 1837–1841.

2. Clay was the son of William and Rebecca Comer Clay of Grainger County, Tennessee.

3. See Robert H. Watkins et al. to Polk, August 17, 1839; Polk to Robert H. Watkins et al., August 28, 1839; William Smith et al. to Polk, August 29, 1839; and Polk to William Smith et al., August 31, 1839.

4. Susanna Claiborne Withers Clay.

FROM JULIUS W. BLACKWELL

Dear Sir, Athens Ten. Sept 9th 1839

I received by last mail yours of Aug. 26th.[1] It was too late to send any additional excuse for your not attending the dinner at Jasper.[2] I recd. two letters urging me to attend, but my business prevented me from going.

Reports were circulated in Knox & McMinn Co's that I was, or would be broke up, which has caused me to be sue'd in three cases, and caused me a great deal of trouble in other matters.[3] Every pe[r]son to whom I owed a small sum of money became very needy all at once, and called for money faster than I could collect. Having lost about $3000 by the burning of my houses in Decr. last, and being somewhat in debt in Knoxville, I was aware of the consequences when I give out my name as a candidate for congress. Hence my anxiety to settle $800 in Knoxville before I allowed my name to be announced to the publick. I failed to sittle it before I commenced the canvass, and had no time to spare afterwards, to collect money. I knew I should be moved against, to please Judge White, if for no other purpose. But the teeth of the vipers are blunted. They have bruised me considerably, but have not broken the skin, neither indeed can they. They have, however, caused me great trouble, and some cost. I find it very hard to collect money, but have five times as much owing to me, as there is wanting.

You can scarcely conceive the extent to which the Whigs of Athens have went in the late canvass, and did certainly cause you and myself to loose hundreds of votes. Imagine to yourself a little village containing the directory of a rail road & two Banks, 20 Lawyers and 19 stores, all arrayed against us, except 5 or six stores and one director—some say two—all in the very highest state of excitement, using the utmost exertion to break us down, and you may form a faint idea of what we had to encounter. In Bradley Co. the 481 as set down as your majority, agrees with the statement I saw—not official—but there are various statements of the vote, but 481 is not much out of the way. You lost considerably in Bradley, by the parade of votes from the journal on the Hiwassee land law,[4] and divers ludicrous and false charges made against you by the circulation of slips from the miscalled Patriot office in Athens.[5] They were circulated on the eve of the election, and could not be answered in time. The same cause lost us votes in Bledsoe, our papers having been stopped at some office and did not reach in time.

J. W. BLACKWELL

ALS. DLC–JKP. Addressed to Columbia.

1. Letter not found.

2. See Polk to William Rice et al., August 26, 1839.

3. Blackwell earlier had mentioned his financial difficulties in a letter to Polk of September 5, 1839. ALS. DLC–JKP.

4. See Robert B. Reynolds to Polk, July 30, 1839.

5. The Athens *Hiwassee Patriot,* a Whig newspaper edited by A. W. Elder, began publication in about 1837.

FROM JOHN W. CHILDRESS

Murfreesboro, Tennessee. September 9, 1839

Unable to accompany Polk to Courtland, Childress says that he, Fletcher, Yoakum, Keeble,[1] and, perhaps, William G. Childress will attend the meeting at Huntsville on the 20th.[2] Rutherford County Democrats had a great meeting on Saturday last. Repelling recent Whig slanders,[3] Keeble made a powerful speech and received excited applause from the crowd.

ALS. DLC–JKP. Addressed to Columbia.

1. John D. Fletcher, Henderson K. Yoakum, and Edwin A. Keeble. A farmer and Democrat, Fletcher represented Rutherford County for two terms in the Tennessee House, 1839–43, and Franklin and Lincoln counties for one term in the Senate, 1845–47.

2. See Robert H. Watkins et al. to Polk, August 17, 1839; Polk to Robert H. Watkins et al., August 28, 1839; William Smith et al. to Polk, August 29, 1839; and Polk to William Smith et al., August 31, 1839.

3. Rutherford County Whigs had accused the Democracy of frauds in the state elections and had formed vigilance committees to observe their opponents' movements. See John W. Childress to Polk, August 21, 1839.

FROM ABRAHAM McCLELLAN

My dear Sir, Blountville Ten Sept 9 1839

Yours of the 28th ult. is received.[1] I am about to start this morning for middle Tennessee and have not much time to write.

The Check which you sent, came safe to hand. I shall leave it here to be cashd, though [I] think it doubtful whether it can be done. I shall leave directions for it to be sent to me at Nashville if it cannot be cashed here. I suppose it can be there &c &c.

All of our friends in this end of the State, that I have heard from, say they will be at Nashville some day before the meeting of the Legislature.[2]

I hope we shall meet at Nashville in good health, and that every thing will be well arrangd. L. Gifford will be there to run for Printer. This matter must be well attended to. In haste.

A. McCLELLAN

ALS. DLC–JKP. Addressed to Columbia.

1. Letter and enclosure not found.

2. As required by constitutional mandate, the Tennessee legislature assembled on the first Monday of October following its election on the first Thursday of August.

FROM TURNER SAUNDERS[1]

Courtland, Alabama. September 9, 1839

Saunders offers to host Polk, Jackson, and their escort on the evening of the 16th; his brother[2] is very ill and will be unable to entertain Polk's party as previously planned. Polk's note of the 7th instant[3] has been sent to Major Watkins. Saunders will meet Polk or will send someone to conduct him when he crosses the Tennessee River.

ALS. DLC–JKP. Addressed to Columbia.

1. Saunders, son of Reverend Turner H. Saunders of Williamson County, was a member of the committee arranging Polk's September 17 speaking engagement at Courtland, Alabama. See Robert Watkins et al. to Polk, August 17, 1839.

2. James E. Saunders, member of the 1840 Alabama legislature for Lawrence County, moved to Mobile in 1842 and engaged in the mercantile business. In 1845 Polk appointed him collector of the port of Mobile, a position

which he held until 1849. Saunders married Mary F. Watkins, daughter of Robert H. Watkins.

3. Letter not found.

FROM JOHN J. GARNER[1]

Yalobusha [County], Mississippi
September the 10. 1839

Dear sir

I received a letter from you on yesterday[2] giving mee some directions how to manage your bisiness on this place which I was glad to receive; also to now what is wanting on the plantation. There was when I came here 31 yards of lincy cloth [which] was all the cloth of any cind. I wil want one hundred yards of lincy and the same of cotton cloth for sherting. Twenty one pare of socks is wanting. There is one pare here. Only twenty two pare of shews; three pare of No. 10; eight pare of 9; ten pare of 7; one pare for a little girl seven or eight yers old. If they are not a good lot of shews you had beter send more than wil shew them onst a round. I want some three or fore barrels or sacks of salt for the next year.

Our crop of cotton are cut short from the drouth which we have had to what it wold of bin when I came here. There was a prospect for a hevey crop. I think it is ingerd a third, at leaste; on the ridges near half. Our corn crop I suppose is something better than last yeare but the cuantity I cant say yet, not nowing the cuantty of acors in corn. Not so mutch as last year. When I gether it I then can give you a purty corect noledg of the cuantty. I have thirty six thousand lbs of cotton out and are ginning at this time. Wil bee able to make some bales this weak. I think owing to the drouth I can get the crop saved in a reasnoble time with the hands thats here. It ought to bee saved in time to repare the fencing a round the farm. It is so indifernt that I am pesterd to ceep the stock from destroying the crop. Your negrows are at this time helthey withe the exception of the girl Marier[3] which has bin in bad helth for some time. I think here helth improving. When I came here there was some three or fore lying up with out a cause though I have not bin pesterd cence.

It recuire a person to lern the disposition of a negrow to mange them. I wil while in your employ attend strictly to your instructions so fare as I am capible. That is for you to Judge of when you come down.

John J. Garner

ALS. DLC–JKP. Addressed to Columbia. Extensive liberty has been taken in supplying punctuation and capitalization. A variant transcription has been published in Bassett, *Plantation Overseer,* 125–26.

1. In September 1839 Garner became overseer of Polk's Mississippi plantation. Though industrious and attentive to farm business, he did not manage Polk's slaves successfully. Many ran away and on occasion threatened revolt.

2. Letter not found.

3. Variant spelling of "Maria."

FROM HARVEY M. WATTERSON

Dear Sir, Shelbiville Sept 10th 1839

Mr Knott[1] has just informed me that he saw you a few days since in Columbia, and that he learned from you, that the infamous slanders which the unprincipled and corrupt tools of Barringer, put afloat against me in my absence to the Winchester springs, had reached that town. Mark what I tell you—It has already and will continue to recoil upon their own heads with a vengeance. You have never witnessed such palpable, such bare faced villany in the trial of any cause, as was manifested in the trial of the woman, which has just terminated.[2] Illegal questions, totally irrelavant to the case in point, were asked, by the one of the Court of Enquiry, William Galbreath Esq.[3] Lewis Shappard[4] came forward without being engaged in the cause in any way, and wished to propound questions to witnesses. I was summoned by some persons (unknown to me save from suspicion) as a witness. I promptly testified to all I knew, which was nothing at all. It was evident to every body, that they were not trying the woman—but that their object was to implicate a third person. Long and Wisener[5] were counsel for the defendant. *Wisener was willing to admit illegal testimony against his own client—thinking no doubt in this way something could be drawn out that would affect my character.* Nay—he done more. He even insisted that certain questions should be answered, after the Court and Mr Frierson had decided that they were clearly illegal! Mr Long arose and indignantly remarked, that the object was not justice. It was to operate upon [an] individual out of doors—a political movement—and warned the Court against any such influences. Wisener demanded to know, if Mr Long attributed such motives to him? Mr Long looked him in the face and with great firmness, remarked "I do, Sir—I do!" Whereupon Wisener raised a chair, but before he could strike, Mr Long seized hold of it, and was about administering upon the young man, when they were separated. Wis[e]ner left the room immediately and thus terminated their difficulty for the present—and perhaps forever, as Wis[e]ner is not only an unprincipled puppy, but a most consumate coward. They involved me by the investigation in no way, manner or form. The Democrats are very much incensed at their proceedings. More excitement in town to day than I have seen for months. So far as I am concerned, rest assured, that all will be right. When I see you I will give you further particulars. In the mean time, I remain . . . .

H M Watterson

Post S—I will see you at the Huntsville Dinner on the 20th. Your friends wish to give you a dinner at Shelbyville at such time as will suit your convenience. I wish you would write to me by return of mail and specify a day. What say you to the 21st—or 23d—or 24th or 25th. HMW

ALS. DLC–JKP. Addressed to Columbia.

1. Bedford County descendents of Thomas Knott were too numerous in 1839 to allow specific assignation of this reference.

2. Case not identified further. No Bedford County Court records prior to 1848 are available; nor are there extant Shelbyville newspapers for 1839.

3. Shelbyville businessman William Galbreath was a long-time justice of the Bedford County Court; in 1848 he was chairman of that body.

4. "Shappard" is not identified further.

5. M. A. Long and William H. Wisener. Wisener owned and edited the Shelbyville *Peoples Advocate;* in 1838 he became secretary of the Shelbyville and Columbia Turnpike Company. He won multiple terms as a Whig in both houses of the Tennessee legislature during the 1840's and 1850's.

FROM THOMAS VON ALBADE ANDERSON

Dear Sir, Madisonville Monroe County Ten Sept 13th 1839

Since the late important triumph of Democratic Principles in our state, like the rest of your East Tennessee friends, I have been literally fuming & boiling over with exultation. With one heart we all join you in congratulation. The triumph is unparalleled in the history of American politics. It was a proud atchievement. The Democratic Party owe you a great debt of grattitude. Our glorious victory has been won thro' the instrumentality of your own transcendent efforts. But I have not started to write your eulogy. The future Historian will do that. The Democratic Party no doubt justly appreciate the nature & extent of your great efforts—and are sensible that your services have been as great as they have been unostentatious; and already they are preparing new honors with which to reward your untiring & faithful exertions, and distinguished merits.

I am now on my way to my residence in Jefferson, or "*little Mas-*

sachusetts" as the Whigs *familiarly & caressingly* style *Jefferson County*. I have recently travelled from Jonesboro' to Bradley, and have been in most of the intermediate counties. I find the feeling perfectly unanimous, with the Democracy in reference to bringing forward your name for the *Vice Presidency*.

The only points about which there is any difference of opinion, is as to the *time* and manner of presenting your name for that elevated station. On this subject there is great variety, & contrariety of opinion. Some are in favour of county nominations. Some in favor of a Convention of delegates from all the counties in East Tennessee, to convene at Knoxville—With the expectation that Middle, & West Tennessee will either follow or act simultaneously with us in their sections respectively. It is thought by some that the Democratic Members of the Legislature shoud nominate you and Mr Van Buren. For my own part I am too inexperienced in Political tactics to say what may be the best plan. The thing itself however is settled. It will be done in some way. It will give me great gratification to co-operate. I cannot tell how much I may be enabled to do in the coming contest. Modesty & discretion woud say on this point, make no large promises. And I will not. For I know that in very heated contests the zeal of political & personal friendship, & admiration often induces us to promise more than the well balanced & experienced mind in its calmer moods wou'd require us to fulfil. Therefore I shall only say for myself, I shall be found at my Post, & for *James K. Polk* for Vice President.

The *present* & *prospective* position of the Democratic Party requires the *union* of and exercise of all the talents, all the calm and dispassionate thought, all the sagacity & energy, all the firmness & perseverance, that can be enlisted in our cause & brought to bear upon the contest with Federalism, to meet its Protean Shapes & to resist successfully the machinations of that Macha*villian*,[1] and Piebald Party, ycleped "Whig."

It is thought that a Convention of Delegates at Knoxville wou'd have a tendency to weaken if not destroy in a great measure the influence of Judge White in the coming Presidential contest. I do not express any opinion at present but wou'd prefer a general State Convention, if we are to have any sort of Convention. I shou'd in *compliment* to Judge White be glad to have the Convention meet at Knoxville. It wou'd be gall & wormwood to him for a convention to sit at Knoxville, and nominate *Martin Van Buren* for President & *James K Polk* for Vice President.

Judge White is a potent & vindictive enemy. I am told that if he forgets any thing on setting out from home & has to turn back, he makes a *cross mark* with his foot, and *spits* as near the *centre* as possible, for *good luck!!!* Now any *man* whose superstition will exhibit him in such a frivolous light, ought to be regarded as *great* (!!) & *submitted* to as *Dictator!!* But to be more serious, Judge White has been the Bohon Upas[2] of the Republican Party in Tennessee; and I woud gladly contribute to *dig* him up, & extirpate him politically from the land. You have already withered his leaves & branches & cloven his trunk asunder. The roots only remain—and *they* will be dug up with a *Democratic mattock.* I have no doubt in the course of the present year—Tho' the Federal Whigs boldly assert that our Democratic Legislature will not *dare* to *instruct* Judge White!!! It is true Judge White's name was *once* respected—and he has himself alone to blame for his loss of public estimation. *He* has done *much* to bring upon himself public odium, and if he reflects in *honest* moments he can not but *blush* at the course he has pursued towards that venerated & illustrious man who has filled the measure of his contrys glory. Since his first attacks upon General Jackson, his carreer has been *downward.* He has continued to sink in public estimation, and History will declare him guilty of Political suicide. Judge Whites 4th of July dinner speech at Knoxville has also exceedingly lowered him in public estimation.[3] The great & discerning Public consider his effort on that occasion as the offspring of malice & a clear exhibition of his own meanness of soul, and a fair and uncontested illustration of the vulgar *puppys* of his own mind. It is believed no one was so capable of making so full a display of his whole grovelling nature as *himself.* He took the case into his own hands, made the effort and *entirely succeeded!!!* The Public Mind revolted at his whole course on that occasion, and beheld with great *pity* the vindictiveness of his spirit, and the exceeding bitterness of his soul. Miserable man! Judge Whites *considerate* friends do not justify him on that occasion; and I have no doubt if his heart since then has felt a single just or generous emotion he is by this time *ashamed* of his rampant vulgarity, so furiously, indecourously, and indiscreetly exhibited on the sacred occasion of our great National Celebration. The Public Mind has not forgotten that in his honester & better days—when *disappointed* ambition had not thrown around him her *gangrened* mouth—corroded his feelings & turned his better impulses into gall, Judge White declared often & often that "James K Polk was the right arm of the Tennessee delegation in Congress." "That James K Polk had no superior in the National Councils of his age." "That he had rather take James K Polks political prospects than those of any other man of his age in the Nation."

The Michiavelian Policy[4] of this man has also been illustrated on other occasions. The base & fraudulent transactions of his party at Rogersville was as full a public display of their arts & intrigues as they can ever make.[5] I rejoiced in the dignity, the self possession and the great abilities you displayed on that occasion. You utterly confounded your enemies—and rolled disaster & defeat into their ranks, at the very moment when they believed victory had perched upon *their* Banner. It was a great day. I never expect to see such another.

But I must close. The more I write, the more it seems I have to write. These are subjects tho' of which my heart is full. I must claim your indulgence for the loose & desultory manner in which I have thrown these scraps together. I trust you will not find your patience too seriously taxed.

THOS A ANDERSON

ALS. DLC–JKP. Addressed to Columbia.

1. An early sixteenth-century Florentine statesman, Niccolo Machiavelli espoused a political doctrine that asserted the prince's right to use unscrupulous means to achieve and sustain power.

2. The pohon upas is an Oriental tree, the latex of which is highly poisonous.

3. White's speech was sharply critical of Jackson and Polk.

4. Misspelling of "Machiavellian."

5. On July 29, 1839, Whigs in Rogersville gave a public dinner to which they had invited Cannon, White, and Polk. Although allowed to make a speech, Polk was denied opportunity to reply to charges made by his adversaries.

TO SAMUEL H. LAUGHLIN

My Dear Sir Columbia Sept. 13th 1839

I have been so much engaged in attending to my long neglected private affairs, for the last two or three weeks, as to be compelld. almost wholly to neglect my correspondence. Your letter of the 6th—with its enclosure was duly received. It is scarcely necessary for me to say, that the complimentary notice which it contains, could not but be highly gratifying. To my Democratic friends in old Warren I am under high obligations. You say truly that not the slightest intercourse either verbal or written ever took place between us on the subject. And perhaps the least I say or write on the subject the better. It strikes me that my course should be a passive one. I shall be content to leave the movements to be made for the future, to the better judgment & discretion of my friends.

I am glad to hear from you, that Mr Hill & yourself will be at

Nashville some days before the meeting of the Legistature. I hope our other Democratic friends elect, will also be there. Our members will meet you about the 1st. The only means to prevent distraction and division in our ranks, will be to adopt and act firmly upon the principle "every thing for the cause, nothing for men." Your views upon this point entirely accord with my own. I hope you may unite & act as one man in the organization of the two Houses. If you can move off smothely, you will have less difficulty, afterwards.

In regard to the Senatorial election, should a resignation take place, my opinion is, that the choice should not be hastily made, at all events not until you have fully consulted together & united upon some one man. I have some reason to suspect, that it will be the policy of our opponents to hurry the election on early in the Session & before we will have time to harmonize & unite. Their hope would be to divide us, & then if they could not elect one of their own men, to cast their votes on some minority candidate of our party, and place him under obligations to them for his election. This must be guarded against. I would not trust any man, who owed his election to their votes. He would bolt upon the first occasion when he could safely do so, or when it would be his interest. I have no doubt if you are not in too great a hurry, you can and will unite. In haste . . . .

JAMES K. POLK

P.S. I start tomorrow to the Alabama Dinners. J.K.P.

ALS. MHi. Addressed to McMinnville and marked "*Confidential.*"

FROM ARCHIBALD YELL

My Dear Sir Waxhaws Septr the 15th 1839

Yours of the 18th Ultimo[1] from Columbia was received last evening. I have learned through the Newspapers the victory we had obtained in Tennessee and have written you once or twice since.[2]

Some time since I wrote you for the Deed to Joseph Barclift of Fraklin Co. Ark. for the Fractional Q[uarte]r Contain[ing] 153 acres or thereabouts which you will find more minutely described in your patents, it being in Township 10 North [of] range 27 West I believe.[3] I am certain it is in Township 10 & that it is the only tract in that Township.

Your Br[o]the[r][4] will have to make the Deed & have it acknowledged before Some Judge or Presiding magistrate with the certificate & Seal of the Clerk & Court & then some judge to certify that he is Clerk &c, & it will be good here. Send it soon & certifyed!

I will endeavor to make sale of your Land as you desire, but I may find it [a] rather dull sale at a fare price & I am not disposed at this time to purchase your Interest at what I consider would be a fare price. I have too much wild land & there is now no markett. Too much Government Land for me to purchase & do you & myself justice. I will endeavor however to find a purchaser & will sell at a moderate price. I have had some offers for the tract in Johnson Co. It lies opposite to the Town of Pittsburgh & small vilage on the Ark. River. The land is good & the county rapidly settling & the situation a good one & must be valuable. The other near Van Buren is still more valuable but I have had no bid for it.

I am sorry to hear you have found yourself in want of funds but that is the consequence of a Campaign. I have some funds on hand for which I have no imediate use. You are more than welcome to the loan of from one to three thousand dollars if you say so. If you want it let me know & you shall have the money. I can send you Drafts on some of the Banks at Nashville or if you prefer it in the *Gold Coins* & you can get it to Tennessee, You can have that—&c.

Your Tennessee Boys here won lotts of *hats* & *boots* on your election. We live upon the Whigs here. I believe our Boys would be sorry if these Whigs get too much under par—they could get no bets.

Col McKisick is now in Tennessee & I promise he will see you & tell you all. Jas. & his wife are now with me at a Camp Meeting, at least his wife is & Jas. is at a *horse race.*[5]

We all talk about nothing else but Polk & the Tennessee elections and Rejoicing among the Tennesseans & you can beat any other man but Capt Jackson, for any thing from the Presidency down to a *Constable.* Pardon the *Simalee.*

We have had some Indian disturbances & have been in constant expectation of a fight. Our Boys are ready & willing to give them a flyer. We raised a company of Vols & they elected *me* to command it. I accepted cheerfully. We then raised a Regt of 8 companies & they voted me to Command it. That I accepted. Whinny is my Lieut. Col. John B. Dickens commands the Benton [County] volunteers. Jas McKisick & Col Hastings are his Lieuts.[6] Maj. E. D. Dickson & his *Jakesish* wife live at our place. They took Tea with me the other evng & they are your true friend and mention your visit to them last winter &c.[7]

Prsnt me to Madame & ask her if she could supply me with and old Widdow in her parts who would be willing to become a squater in Ark.[8]

A. YELL

[P.S.] a Bad pen & some abreviations in spelling![9]

ALS. DLC–JKP. Probably addressed to Columbia.

1. Letter not found.
2. See Yell to Polk, September 1 and 7, 1839.
3. On August 14, 1839, Yell had requested that a deed be prepared conveying title to land sold for Polk to Joseph G. Barclift of Ozark, Arkansas. Polk's endorsement indicates that the deed was sent on September 11, 1839. ALS. DLC–JKP. Seeking correction of an error in the deed, Barclift wrote Polk on April 1, 1840, October 4, 1840, and October 31, 1841. ALsS. DLC–JKP.
4. William H. Polk.
5. James McKisick, a good friend to both Yell and Polk, served as clerk of Bedford County, Tennessee, before moving to Arkansas about 1836. James McKisick, mentioned below as a lieutenant in the Arkansas militia, probably was the colonel's son. Young McKisick's wife is not identified further.
6. Abraham Whinney, John B. Dickson, and Joseph Hastings had removed to Arkansas from Bedford County, Tennessee. A resident in Polk's congressional district and a colonel of the Tennessee militia during the late 1820's, Whinney moved to Arkansas and served several years in the territorial legislature. Dickson represented Washington County in the Arkansas legislature. Hastings is not further identified.
7. Ephraim D. Dickson won election to Weakley County's first court and served as postmaster of Dresden from 1833 until 1836. Polk visited Dresden while on a tour of the Western District during the last week of October, 1838.
8. Yell's third wife, Maria McIllvane Ficklin Yell, had died on October 14, 1838.
9. Postscript written in the left margin of the third page.

FROM WILLIAM WALLACE

Maryville, Tennessee. September 16, 1839

Wallace rejoices in the Democratic victory in Tennessee and adds his voice to others he has heard in favor of Polk for vice-president in 1840. He thinks Polk might unify the Democratic ticket nationally and stresses the importance of party harmony.

Several factors account for Polk's defeat in Blount County. James Gillespy should not have contested McKamy for a seat in the Tennessee House; by entering the race Gillespy neutralized some of Polk's support and encouraged the opposition. Democrats were late in getting out a candidate for the Senate and left many Whig arguments unanswered. Cannon's Maryville speech, delivered shortly before the election, also went unanswered.

Wallace recommends Col. M. H. Bogle, "a firm consistent democrat," to be quartermaster general.[1]

ALS. DLC–JKP. Addressed to Columbia.

1. Bogle is not identified further.

FROM FELIX GRUNDY

Dear Sir, Washington, Sept 18th 1839

The President has not returned. I learn things are being righted in Newyork.[1] If so, all will be easy in future. I see Ellmore has resigned—so that his being Speaker is out of the question.[2] I have seen Fran. Thomas and conversed with him. He seems not to desire it—and I suspect some of our friends would very reluctantly vote for him. After all I incline to the opinion, that Jones of Virginia would be the best man, we can run. What think you of him &c? Before I left home, I heard something said, about Judge Whites resignation last fall having vacated his seat in the senate.[3] This may true. If the resignation was absolute & unconditional, I think in such a case, the Governor did not possess the power to refuse its acceptance—but this is a question, that well admits of dispute. I therefore hope the course indicated in my last[4] will be pursued. Afterwards the subject of the resignation might be investigated and acted upon.

You are at liberty to show my last and this, to Judge Catron and let him know that the Chief Justice & Justice Wayne[5] are both well. I saw them and walked in procession with them at the celebration at North Point near Baltimore.[6] Give mt best respects to Mrs. Polk.

FELIX GRUNDY

ALS. DLC–JKP. Addressed to Columbia and marked *"Confidential."*

1. New York Democrats scored gains in the November elections, but did not win control of the legislature.

2. Franklin Harper Elmore, a South Carolina lawyer and political friend of John C. Calhoun, sat in the U.S. House, 1836–39; presided over the Bank of the State of South Carolina, 1839–50; and served briefly in the U.S. Senate in 1850. Elmore did not stand for reelection to his House seat in 1839.

3. On November 8, 1838, Cannon received Hugh L. White's resignation from the U.S. Senate. Declining to accept the resignation, Cannon encouraged White to return to Washington when health permitted. White took his seat in the Senate on January 3, 1839.

4. Letter not found.

5. Roger B. Taney and James M. Wayne. Wayne, a Georgian, served in the U.S. House, 1829–35, and sat on the U.S. Supreme Court, 1835–67.

6. On September 12, 1814, the British launched an attack on Fort McHenry from North Point, which is located fourteen miles from Baltimore. Ceremonies at North Point celebrated the twenty-fifth anniversary of the British defeat.

FROM JONATHAN P. HARDWICKE[1]

Dear Sir Charlotte Sept 18th 1839

I had an interview a few days ago with J. G. Harris and A. O. P. Nicholson in which both of them Confidentially suggested your scruples upon the subject of your being at Nashville at the meeting of the Legislature. I am aware of the fact that you would be much annoyed by many of your friends that will be there for Office, and fully persuaded many more be disappointed, at not seeing you then and there. Very great exertions are made & being made by the Feds in Tenn, and especially in and about Nashvl. The Mighty Bell the Renowned Ephram[2] with all their trained bands will be brought directly into action, with their every nerve strung to the highest posible note, to effect our strength and win over some of our party to their side. And sir if we judge the future by the past we have cause for fear. At the last session we lost two from the Senate & how many from the House I dont now know.

It certainly is our policy to meet some days in advance, organize, adopt sundry strong resolutions for our future action, address our boys in a spirited and lofty tone, excite their Political pride and strengthen them in the faith.

We should never run but one man for any Office. When our friends conflict with each other which will often happen, we should among our selves assertain in an equal & fair way the strongest and drop all others, hold frequent secret meetings during the Session. Under such regulations we will not only maintain our strength, but carry every Election and important point. Great inconvenience was experienced last session for want of a convenient room to hold secret meetings. To avoid which I procured a room when last at Nashvl, for that purpose. None could be had at either of the Hotels or in the C[ourt] Ho.

Now Sir as regards your self—you have become the Capt of our band, and if any thing goes wrong you will bare the blame in the estimation of both friends & foes. It will be believed & said by many that the entire action of our party in the Legislature will be in strict accordance with your will & bidding. Hence it is my Opinion that you should be with us on Wednesday before the Commencement. And if, and I have no doubt, many will ask your influence with the Legislature for Office, but one word from you must sattisfy such when you might say any interfearance on your part would prejudice their claims. I have conversed with many friends on this subject & all think you should be with us til Satturday or Sunday, & then if you chose, to leave & return when the votes are counted. It may be some days after the meeting before we can compare & count to [the] votes. Some of the returns may not get in & others be informal.

There is great anxiety manifested by the people to be at your Inorgeration, & I would be glad that the people be notified of the day that they may attend. If you should think with us on this subject, [I] would be pleased to meet you at Nashville this day two weeks. I understand our folks will [be] there by that time.

J. P. HARDWICKE

ALS. DLC–JKP. Addressed to Columbia.

1. A tavern keeper in Charlotte, Dickson County, Hardwicke served three terms as a Democrat in the Tennessee Senate from 1837 until 1843.

2. Reference is to John Bell and Ephraim H. Foster.

FROM WILLIAM M. LOWRY

Greenville, Tennessee. September 20, 1839

Lowry sends congratulations on Polk's victory over "faction and Intrigue" in Tennessee. While in Abingdon, Virginia, Lowry heard news of Polk's victory; never was there more open disappointment than that displayed by Senator Preston and Governor Campbell.[1] Virginia will respond favorably to the McMinnville resolutions.[2] Lowry presents Andrew Johnson, who will deliver letters from friends soliciting appointments.[3]

ALS. DLC–JKP. Addressed to Nashville and forwarded to Columbia.

1. William C. Preston and David Campbell. A Virginia lawyer, Campbell served for many years as clerk of the Washington County Court, 1802–12, 1815–20, and 1824–36. He fought in the War of 1812 and in 1820 won election to the Virginia Senate, in which he served four years. Chosen governor of Virginia in 1836, he supported Whig measures during the Van Buren administration.

2. See Samuel H. Laughlin to Polk, September 6, 1839.

3. Enclosures not found.

TO THOMAS DEAN, ET AL.[1]

Gentlemen: Columbia Sept 24th 1839

When I had the honor to receive your letter which you conveyed to me at McDaniel's Spring, Al. on the 20th Instant[2] inviting me in behalf of "a meeting of the Republicans of Bedford County"—to attend a public dinner to be given at Shelbyville on the 1st of October next, in celebration of the recent triumph of Republican principles in the State, I entertained doubts whether it would be in my power to be present on that occasion. A definite answer was delayed, until my return home, & I now regret to say, that circumstances beyond my control, will deny me the pleasure which I would otherwise sincerely take, in meeting my old constituents and friends, and uniting with them in their celebration. The triumph of principle which my Republican Fellow citizens of Bedford propose to celebrate, was achieved not so much by the individual agency which you kindly attribute to me, as by the power of truth, brought to bear on the public mind. Many honest men and sound Republicans had been deceived and misled by those in whom they had been accustomed to confide; but the "sober second thought of an intelligent people["][3] enabled them to detect the deception. My old constituents of Bedford will bear me witness that I gave them timely notice many months ago of the design that was on foot, under the specious guise of a popular party name to transfer the state to the Federal ranks, and to chain her down in the wake of the Federal States. At that time those who designed stealthily to make the transfer, denied that such was their purpose or object. Many of them repudiated and rejected the idea, that they could ever be brought to the support of Mr Clay, or any man of the same political principles for the Presidency. During the pendency of the late election many of our prominent political opponents, concealed their intention to support Mr Clay & refused to take open ground for him. Since the election is over, they have come out into the open field, and have publickly taken him up as their candidate.[4] Their real position and designs can no longer be concealed, from any portion of the people, and I greatly mistake the public sentiment of the State, if a more signal overthrow, than they have yet met, does not await them, in the great contest of 1840. Sincerely regretting that I cannot be with you, I beg to tender to the company assembled, the subjoined sentiment, and to subscribe myself . . . .

JAMES K. POLK

Sentiment by J. K. Polk

The people of the County of Bedford: Always Republicans, Republicans still. In the late political contest in the State, they nobly sustained their principles.

ALS, draft. DLC–JKP. Addressed to Shelbyville and marked "Copy."

1. Addressed to Dean, Robert Matthews, E. J. Frierson, William Rucker, Preston Frazer, and "others" of the arrangements committee.

2. See Thomas Dean et al. to Polk, September 18, 1839. LS. DLC–JKP.

3. Quotation is from the letter of invitation; closing quotation marks have been supplied.

4. The following sentence was canceled in Polk's draft: "I have no hesitation in believing, if they had done so before the election, they would have lost much of the strength which they attained, by concealing this."

FROM J. GEORGE HARRIS

Nashville, Tennessee. September 24, 1839

Harris expresses pleasure that the Alabama dinners[1] were successful. Resolutions passed at a meeting of Nashville Democrats last Saturday will be published in the *Union.*[2] Burton, Johnson, and Armstrong are among the contenders for Foster's Senate seat. Johnson has written that he expects to arrive in Nashville tomorrow and hopes Polk will come next week.[3] Nashville's city elections will be held Saturday, and should the Whigs win, "Clay will probably be entertained at city expense and honored with 'city Freedom.'" Harris believes that although Hollingsworth will be defeated by Trabue, Democrats will elect a majority of the aldermen.[4]

ALS. DLC–JKP. Addressed to Columbia.

1. Reference is to Democratic meetings held in Courtland and Huntsville on September 17 and 20, 1839.

2. Submitted by Leonard P. Cheatham and adopted on September 21, 1839, the resolutions appeared in the *Nashville Union* on September 25, 1839. Supporting preemption, graduation, and an Independent Treasury, the resolutions opposed Henry Clay's proposals for a national bank, distribution of surplus revenue, and federally financed internal improvements.

3. Cave Johnson arrived in Nashville on October 3, 1839; Polk came two days later.

4. A lawyer and Democratic politician, Henry Hollingsworth served as mayor of Nashville from 1837 until his defeat in 1839 by Charles C. Trabue, the Whig candidate. The Democrats lost eleven of the twelve aldermanic races.

FROM JOEL M. SMITH

Dear Sir

Nashville, Septr 24th 1839

About three weeks since I recd. a letter from Col. Hill promising to send me some money by the next mail which I calculated on, with certainty, but it has not yet come to hand. I am sorry to trouble you with my complaints, knowing that you must have enough already on your mind without being troubled with the business of others, nor would I do so now were it not that I believe you can exercise an influence with our friends in raising money that no other person could do. My situation is a peculiar one. I have had, in order to enable me to do the Legislative work,[1] to increase my stock of materials near one thousand dollars, these materials will be here to day or tomorrow and I have not money to pay the Carriage on them much less the bill itself. This is truly a trying moment with me, and if the friends do not stand up to, and sustain me, I shall be compelled to stop my press. I am in bad health and unable to give that attention to my business as it requires, debts daily pressing upon me and no means to meet them. Let me hear from [you] soon.

J M SMITH

ALS. DLC–JKP. Addressed to Columbia.

1. See Joel M. Smith to Polk, August 15 and 31, 1839.

FROM JOHN S. YOUNG

Dear Sir McMinnville Tenn 24 Sept. 1839

Enclosed I send a letter I received from Gen Anderson.[1] It speaks for its self. We have got the ball in motion. East Tenn. will in a few days Speak in a united voice. I am astonished at the want of action amongst our friends in the West. Will not Davidson, Bedford and Maury respond to our meeting?[2]

I have resolved in doing what you may consider a rash act. Viz, to become a candidate for the office of Secretary of State, an office for which I am perhaps not qualified. As it is a matter to be settled amongst your friends it is one in which you cannot be expected to interfere. I have many things touching our late move to tell you when I see [you] which will be soon.

JNO. S YOUNG

ALS. DLC–JKP. Probably addressed to Columbia.

1. Alexander O. Anderson's letter to Young, dated September 16, 1839, notes activity on Polk's behalf in East Tennessee. A meeting at Jonesboro will nominate him for the vice-presidency. Newspapers in Knoxville and Jonesboro are supporting such a nomination. ALS. DLC–JKP.

2. See Samuel H. Laughlin to Polk, September 6, 1839.

FROM WEST H. HUMPHREYS[1]

Somerville, Tennessee. September 25, [1839][2]

Humphreys writes that La Grange, Somerville, and Jackson are "the hotbeds of Internal improvem[en]t." Citizens in these towns favor extending Tennessee's bond system further than the "interior" people will approve. Tipton, Lauderdale, and Hardeman counties' voters are "almost entirely opposed." The necessity of preserving republican principles at the national level of government transcends all differences over state or local issues; the question of internal improvements should be left "to the immediate representatives of the local interests of the state."

The "federal party" cannot gain ascendency unless there be "some convulsion in the monied affairs" of the country or division in the Democracy. Discussion of whom the Democrats might nominate following Van Buren's second term is premature and divisive. Pro-Benton articles in the *Nashville Union*[3] may lead to diminished support from the nullifiers in the coming presidential contest. Polk must work to prevent a factional split.

Humphreys complains that the last three chancellors of West Tennessee have been too partisan; they have been numbered among the "leading organizers of the federal party."[4] McCampbell[5] would make a good chancellor, for although he is a man of firm Democratic principles, he is not actively partisan. Humphreys disclaims any personal ambition for public office; his wife[6] would eschew political life; and business interest in Mississippi would suffer neglect. Noting that he has been mentioned in the press as a suitable choice for the U.S. Senate, Humphreys states that his name may be used in that regard only if the District be given a Senator and the District's legislative delegation be united in his favor. He wishes to be of assistance, but does not desire this office or that of attorney general. He has answered General Pillow's enquiries "about the office of attorney general and other matters." Humphreys writes confidentially, but authorizes Polk to show the letter to General Pillow.

ALS. DLC–JKP. Addressed to Columbia.

1. A lawyer from Somerville, West Hughes Humphreys made an unsuccessful bid for the governorship in 1835; represented Fayette and Shelby counties in the Tennessee House, 1835–37; served as state attorney general and reporter, 1839–51; and presided over the U.S. District Court for West Tennessee from 1853 until 1861, in which year he accepted the position of C.S.A. judge for Tennessee.

2. Year identified through content analysis.

3. See the *Nashville Union* of September 13, 1839.

4. Pleasant M. Miller served as chancellor of West Tennessee, 1836–37; Milton Brown, 1837–39; and George W. Gibbs, briefly in 1839.

5. Born in Virginia but reared in Knox County, Tennessee, Andrew McCampbell took residence in Jackson in 1819 and then moved to Paris about a year later. He served as chancellor of West Tennessee from 1839 until 1847.

6. Amanda Malvina Pillow, sister of Gideon J. Pillow, married West H. Humphreys in Nashville on January 1, 1839.

FROM J. G. M. RAMSEY

My Dear Sir Mecklenburg near Knoxville Sep. 26. 1839

Yours of the 7th instant reached me at Asheville.[1] My return from the meeting of the Board of Directors & also of the Stockholders of the

Charleston R.R. Co. was hastened a little by the unwelcome intelligence that met me on the way home of the dangerous illness of Mrs. Ramsey.[2] She is better the last few days & I have a leisure afternoon to devote to my unanswered letters.

So fully were we impressed with the importance & necessity & propriety of the movement I had mentioned to you that we have run up the Polk flag as V.P. in all the Democratic journals of E. T.—& are pleased to see how well it is seconded elsewhere. The restriction you placed me under as to the election five years hence shall be carefully observed. I felt myself at liberty however during our sessions at Asheville to propose you as V.P. to several delegates from the Carolinas. I have no doubt as far as I could learn that you will be well sustained in both these States. Mr. Holmes the member elect from Charleston—the successor of Mr. Legare[3] told me that if it were not for the name of Mr. Forsyth you would get all the Southern States. On my mentioning several of the reasons on which we based your claims he assented & expressed the belief that you ought to be prefered. Gov. Branch[4] passed here a few days since & is decidedly for you. This much on General politics.

You ask my views on the subject of I. I.[5] These shall relate principally to the interests of E.T. as to them I have principally devoted my attention. This section of our State you know is essentially agricultural. Bread stuffs & victualling generally form the great part of our products & for years to come these must constitute her exports. Her local position is peculiar—lying upon the tributaries of the Ohio (or Mississippi). If she aims to reach the demands of Foreign Commerce through these streams it must be by a circuitous & uncertain navigation of 3000 miles—encountering the competition of the vast & fertile grain growing regions of the great West. The value of her products is thus lost in the exportation of them. For this reason scarcely a boat from E. T. ever enters the Ohio river. My attention was early drawn to this subject & in looking into it I found that in another direction we were within 400 miles of the Atlantic Ocean & contiguous to South Atlantic States where every product of E.T. was needed & would command a ready sale & a high price. That E.T. in other words tho west of the Blue ridge was an Atlantic country—& should import from & export to Charleston & the South Atlantic sea ports—& markets. How could they be reached? By land communications—& if possible by Rail-Roads. This is the origin of our efforts in the formation of the L.C.&C.R.R. Co.[6] Kentucky has failed to cooperate in this great undertaking & the work is of course narrowed down (the better for Tennessee) to the Knoxville & Charleston Rail-Road. I have just returned from our annual meeting. The pressure in the money market—this depressed (I might say collapsed) state of all American securities in Europe &c. &c. have compelled the Co. to advance more slowly in the extension of the work Westward than was first anticipated & you will see from the proceedings of our meeting which I will send you[7] that we are limiting our efforts at the present time to the work below Columbia. Some are discouraged at the magnitude of the undertaking—especially as our old parent state North Carolina has thus far as a State done nothing but grant our Bank charter without a bonus. Her delegates however at Asheville last week assured us that when the work reached her line she would contribute liberally—especially as her own Rail Roads would be much enhanced in value by a connection with the West & our pass through the mountains would be common to & available by both states. Were I assured of the cooperation of N.C. in this great enterprise my fondest visions of the future prosperity & greatness of my native State would be fully realised. For by a connection at Knoxville of our road with the Central Rail Road (chartered & surveyed) Randolph & the Western District—Nashville or Murfreesboro & Middle Tennessee Knoxville & E.T. would be all united with Charleston & Newbern—Raleigh & Columbia. But I am free to confess to you that without this cooperation of N.C. our work cannot be completed soon. My own views are these—that our Co. has an invaluable treasure in her two charters—that let the times be as embarrassing as they may we should not abandon the work—that during the existing commercial embarrassments we should call for installments slowly—add a section at a time to the road—if it is but 10 miles a year—finish as we advance & make each mile productive & never falter till experience & estimates formed from experience demonstrate that its further extension would not be productive. The period for its completion may be prolonged & if the States in which the work is not being constructed become impatient of delay let the charter be so amended as to allow such States to Bank upon the Rail-Road instalments & state bonds issued by & paid in such states—as well as upon their Bank payments.

On this part of the subject I will only add that our Branch of the S.W.R.R. Bank at Knoxville has essentially aided in equalising exchanges & furnishing business facilities to our citizens & that to abandon the road is virtually to surrender both charters. Should Georgia succeed in completing her projected work to the Tennessee River we will have by the Hiwassee R.R.[8] & the Ten. river a connection (indirect & on account of the frequent tran-shipments inconvenient & expensive it is true) with the south—but of little avail to any of the counties east of Knoxville. That co. will ask for additional aid. As to river improvements

I confess I am sceptical. I carefully examined the result of such efforts elsewhere & find they always have failed to meet public expectation & in the Carolinas they are droped. But yet they are much the most popular works in E.T.—& public sentiment is loud in their favor & many of our members prefer that improvement to either of our roads. It is really so. As to our State Bonds I do not believe that making them Sterling will secure their sale at this time. The state of the money market abroad is the true cause of their not selling. While this continues all American securities will remain flat & unavailable.

Legislation in Tennessee at this time on Internal Improvement is a difficult & delicate task. To seem to falter in relation to our copartners in the Charleston Road—is to expose ourselves to the imputation of bad-faith on the part of North & South Carolina & to lower our public functionaries in the estimation of co-terminous States. I should not wish as a Tennessean that the proposition to abandon the work should come from us. We have individually subscribed liberally to it. Our Legislature has acted with like liberality in giving 650.000 dollars—a sum nearly sufficient to construct the road between the N.C. line & Knoxville. The proposition should come from another quarter if it come at all.

I have just learned that Genl. Hayne[9] our able President is dead. I never was discouraged about our eventual success before. He was a great & a good man.

I have to attend the meeting of the Bank Stockholders at Charleston the 20th November—& cannot for that reason visit Nashville before my return—if at all—much as I would otherwise desire to be there. I have not got a single copy of the Mecklenburg Declaration of Independence[10] left—except one which is in a frame—being on vellum. I must take a private opportunity of sending it to you. Though you will find an elegant copy on satin at the Hermitage which years ago I presented to our old friend Genl. Jackson.[11] I have no doubt he would bequeath it to you as he ought if it were suggested to him.

J. G. M. Ramsey

ALS. DLC–JKP. Addressed to Columbia and forwarded to Nashville.

1. Letter not found.

2. Peggy Barton Crozier married Ramsey in 1821.

3. Isaac E. Holmes and Hugh Swint Legaré. A Charleston lawyer, Holmes served in the South Carolina House, 1826–33. He won election as a Democrat to the U.S. House in 1839 and served in that body until 1851. Legaré, founding editor of the *Southern Review*, 1828–32, served as attorney general of South Carolina, 1830–32; went to Belgium as U.S. chargé

d'affaires, 1832–36; and sat one term in Congress as a Union Democrat, 1837–39. Appointed to Tyler's cabinet in 1841, Legaré served as attorney general until his death in 1843.

4. John Branch, governor of North Carolina, 1817–20, and U.S. senator, 1823–29, served as secretary of the navy from 1829 until his election to the U.S. House in 1831. Branch did not stand for reelection to a second term in Congress.

5. Internal Improvements.

6. Louisville, Cincinnati and Charleston Railroad Company.

7. Proceedings not found.

8. The Tennessee legislature granted a charter of incorporation to the Hiwassee Railroad Company in 1836 to construct a railroad from Knoxville through the Hiwassee District to the southern boundary of the state.

9. Robert Y. Hayne, a lawyer and Calhoun Democrat, fought in the War of 1812; began his political career in the South Carolina House, 1814–18; served as attorney general of South Carolina, 1818–22; won election to the U.S. Senate in 1823; and remained in that post until his 1832 election to the governorship of South Carolina. Chosen president of the L.C.&C.R.R. Co. in 1836, Hayne died on September 24, 1839.

10. On May 1, 1775, Thomas Polk, commanding officer of the Mecklenburg County regiment of North Carolina militia, called for the election of two representatives from each of the county's nine militia districts to assemble and consider the troubled state of the country and adopt measures to safeguard liberties. Delegates convened at Charlotte on May 19 and on the following day declared their constituents' independence.

11. Ramsey sent Jackson a copy of the Declaration in early 1824.

FROM JOHN S. YOUNG

My Dear Sir McMinnville 26 Sept 1839

I leave for Nashville on Monday next to commence my canvass for the office for which I informed you I am a candidate.[1] I am totally unknown to the Maury Representatives.[2] Would it be asking too much to ask you to say to them incidentally that you know me and that I have some standing at home. I would not for ten such offices ask you to violate the smallest feeling of delicacy you may have. I will come before the Legislature with some strength both East and West.

I have direct and late accounts from East Tenn. The whole country is in motion on the subject of the Vice-Presidency. Your speech at

Huntsville is lauded to the skies. Is C C Clay truly and sincerely desirous for you to be run. He did not convey that idea as he passed through Tennessee as I learn. I did not see him—he expressed a great wish to see me but I was absent on the day he passed.

John S. Young

ALS. DLC–JKP. Addressed to Columbia.

1. Young solicited and secured election to the post of secretary of state for Tennessee. See Young to Polk, September 24, 1839.

2. Maury County's legislative delegation included Speaker Jonas E. Thomas and Barkly Martin in the House and Williamson Smith in the Senate.

FROM ROBERT ARMSTRONG

Nashville, Tennessee. September 27, 1839[1]

Armstrong writes that he has engaged a parlor and two chambers at the City Hotel[2] and a meeting room in the Masonic Hall for friends. Armstrong cannot leave town this week, for Nashville will hold its municipal elections Saturday. This evening he is arranging ward meetings for party workers; if his plans work, the Democrats will win, even though the Whigs have money and pay the taxes for anyone who asks.

ALS. DLC–JKP. Addressed to Columbia.

1. Year identified through content analysis.

2. Presumably Armstrong reserved accommodations for the Polks, who arrived in Nashville on October 5.

FROM CAVE JOHNSON

Dear Sir, Clarksville Sept. 28th [1839][1]

I recd. your letter to day[2] & I shall go to Nashville on Wednesday next—reach there on Thursday morning but cannot remain longer than a day or two as I am preparing to leave here early in October for Washington. It is essential to the existence of our party that every selfish consideration be laid aside & act in concert & no man can do so much to effect this as yourself. I think therefore you should be at Nashville at as early a period as possible—some three or four days before the meeting of the Legislature with the view solely of producing concert of action. I wish to leave Nashville Sunday morning before they meet & besides I know I can do but little good. I see a *foolish* article in the World[3] to day in behalf of the district for Senator & calculated, if not intended to incite prejudices & arouse improper feelings among our friends.

The presence of White & Foster will require the influence of all our friends to keep things right.

It has struck me with some force, that *our friends* should go to work & do the business of the State without the slighest interference with Federal policies. Let White & Foster take their course—go on to Washington if they choose. If Foster adopts that course, he is forever disgraced. Toward the Conclusion of the Session we can instruct.

I think we ought not to make a question as to the vacancy of Whites seat tho I have no doubt it is so in reality.[4] I do not wish our party to have the semblance of Co-ercing either until it is absolutely necessary. By all means let them go on if they will. *Foster will resign* without instructions or he deceives his confidential friends in this part of the Country.

Our Legislature interfered too much before in Federal politics & I can assure you the less the better for us. And by all means let the necessity for interference be manifest before it is done. Rather let it be urged upon the Legislature by the people rather than upon the people by the Legislature.

If they get Clay to Nashville, it will be of great service to our cause.

My own opinion is to enable us to start right your presence at Nashville will be necessary several days before the meeting even if you return home & wait the notification of the Legislature.

Whig papers will abuse you, whatever course you may adopt & it will add to your strength; your presence may save us from great confusion.

I have no feeling as to the individual to be the Speaker of either house.

I have just reached home from my last court. Our cause is 1000 stronger to day than at the election.

If you should not go to Nashville I shall be pleased to hear from you there on the suggestions I have made.

C. JOHNSON

ALS. DLC–JKP. Addressed to Columbia and marked "Confidential."

1. Year identified through content analysis.
2. Letter not found.
3. Reference is to an unidentified article in the *Western World and Memphis Banner of the Constitution,* the back files of which do not survive.
4. See Felix Grundy to Polk, September 18, 1839.

FROM ROBERT ARMSTRONG

Dear Sir

Nashville 29th Septem [1839][1]

I have my quarter to close and my most reliable Clerk sick. My only object in going out was to see you and to say to you by all means you ought to be here on Wednesday.[2] I have thought a good deal on this subject and feel confident that I am right. You should return on Sunday or Monday, and get back *here* by Thursday after the meeting, when both Houses will be organized and commencing business.

R. Armstrong

ALS. DLC–JKP. Addressed to Columbia.

1. Year identified through content analysis.
2. Reference is to Wednesday, October 2, 1839.

FROM SAMUEL H. LAUGHLIN

My dear Sir, City Hotel Nashville, Sept. 30, 183[9][1]

According to my own judgment, and from consultations with Dr. Martin, of Washington, Maj. Graham, Gen. Armstrong and others of our confidential friends, I am fully persuaded of the policy as well as perfect propriety of your coming up to this city *forthwith*. Dr. Martin says he expected, and your East Tennessee friends will expect to meet you here (most of them will be on the spot in the next three days) before the commencement of the session. Great numbers of other persons, from all quarters of the State will be here in all the ensuing week, who will leave as soon as the Houses organize, and who will expect to see you—be disappointed if they do not see you—and who, for a year or two, may not have another opportunity of taking you by the hand. No person can [or] will think that you take, or can take, any part in the election of legislative officers. Let it be signified to Gov. Cannon, that you desire him to consult his own time and convenience for retiring—that you do not wish to hasten in any manner your induction into office. I wrote you before, that I thought you ought to be here,[2] and I am glad that the better judgments of our friends here concur in the opinion.

In regard to one election, I have spoken my opinion freely to all parties. We must not, in any event, elect any man Secretary of State, whose politics are not clear—who does not enjoy your entire personal confidence—and who is not of respectable qualifications; which last must include a good knowledge of men and things in the state, habits of industry, and systematic attention to business. In truth, the office has never been filled by a man of sufficient care and system, since I have lived in the state, except during the time of Maj. Graham—one man who does, and will do honor to any office confided to him. On the subject of this election, you must be consulted, and, in some way, some of us *must know your wishes*. Otherwise, your friends might act at cross purposes, and cripple you in the discharge of many of your future official duties.

If we, in all our elections, or any of them, put up a variety of sectional candidates, for the same office, and vote at random, and from personal considerations, in a scattered and divided form, we enable our adversaries to elect all the officers—not by choosing their own men, but by electing such of our men as they think will do them least harm, and thus defeat those who have the best claims on us. This, for one, I shall never consent to. For one, I am willing to take the responsibility of agreeing upon the men before hand, according to majorities of friends, upon consultation, upon compromise among sections of the State, or any other honorable mode of settling such matters; and if any of my personal friends are dropt in the arrangements, I will run the risk of making satisfactory excuses to them. Let all our friends do this, and we will have harmony, and we will show our enemies from the start that we know our rights and duties. If we go to work at random, without discipline, [we w]ill[3] show a poor militia organization.

I write in haste. Of things generally, we con[cur]. Of the Speakerships &c. Gen. Armstrong and Maj. Gra[ham] know my views, and I think approve of them.

S. H. LAUGHLIN.

ALS. DLC–JKP. Addressed to Columbia in the care of Robert Armstrong, and marked "Private."

1. Erroneously dated "1830"; year identified through content analysis.
2. See Laughlin to Polk, September 6, 1839.
3. Mutilation of the manuscript's right margin has obliterated several words.

TO SAMUEL H. LAUGHLIN AND ROBERT ARMSTRONG

My Dear Sir Columbia Oct. 1st 1839

I have this moment received your letter of yesterday.[1] My judgment was opposed to going to Nashville before the meeting of the Legislature. I have so written to Genl. Armstrong and other friends. I thought it would have the appearance of indelicacy on my part, that I could do no good by my presence, but might enable our opponents to use it to our prejudice. I had other reasons too, which I need not state. Many of my friends however think otherwise and yourself among the number. I have within the last few days, been much pressed to go up, before your meeting, and if on further consultation with my friends, it is still thought proper & important by them for me to do so, and you will so advise me by return mail, I will so arrange my matters as to leave home on friday and be in Nashville on saturday to dinner. Write me without fail by the mail of thursday. Remember you must mail your letter on the evening before, as the stage leaves Nashville before day. I have other things about which it is important I should write you, but must postpone it for the present.

James K. Polk

P.S. Shew this to Genl. Armstrong. J.K.P.

ALS. DLC–JKP. Addressed to Nashville.

1. See Samuel H. Laughlin to Polk, September 30, 183[9].

FROM BARKLY MARTIN AND SAMUEL H. LAUGHLIN

Dear Sir, Nashville 2 Oct 1839

We have seen the friends, & had general consultations in relation to the propriety of your being in Nashville as early as possible. And let me say unequivocally that all say if possible be hear by Friday Night. There can be no impropriety [in] your coming at the most early period.

Genl Jackson will be in town Saturday to dinner, and it is thought that your being hear on Friday night may in common tend to advance the *common cause.* Fail not.

B Martin

P.S.[1] I add a poscript to say, that in addition to the gentlemen named in to-day's Union as having arrived, Mr. Wheeler, Mr. Goodall, Mr. P. Walker,[2] and perhaps others, have arrived. Perfect unanimity, so far, as to Mr. Thomas in reference to Speakership. We have also agreed to have meetings (private) before Sunday night, and fix upon our officers, and then elect them by solid vote on first ballots, showing our adversaries that we understand their game of "divide & conquor," which they are already playing, and to show them that we are not in position or humor to ask help or favors in any thing we have properly a right to do. I have never seen such feelings of unanimity. The above has been my plan from first, and Messrs. Coe and Aiken cordially concur. All are agreed.

My respects are respectfully tendered to the lady whom I designated last year, as the "next Governor's wife." S. H. Laughlin

ALS. DLC–JKP. Addressed to Columbia.

1. Laughlin's postscript is marked "Private."

2. John E. Wheeler, Zachariah G. Goodall, and Pleasant B. Walker. A Democrat, Goodall represented Sumner County one term in the Tennessee House, 1839–41. Walker, a farmer, served as sheriff of Hickman County, 1832–36, and as a Democratic member of the Tennessee House, 1837–47.

FROM GEORGE W. CHURCHWELL

Knoxville, Tennessee, October 14, 1839

Churchwell solicits an appointment on Polk's staff and reports that Democrats from Knox and its adjoining counties have nominated Polk for vice-president at today's meeting which would have excited much feeling "but for a heavy dull speech."

ALS. DLC–JKP. Addressed to Nashville.

FROM JAMES WALKER

Dear Sir, Columbia Octr. 15 1839

Maj Bills makes a suggestion in relation to the interests of Marshall's children,[1] which at first I thought would not do to be thought of, but further reflection has convinced me that what he recommends would be for the interest of the children, and would afford ample means from the interest on their means to afford them good educations and free them from dependance on any one. The suggestion is this. They own near Bolivar 500 acres (I think it is) of land which a perfectly able man proposes to give $10,000 for, and the Bunker Hill tract of 0 to 400 acres, which another good man is willing to give 12 and a half dollars pr acre for. The legal interest on say $15,000, would secure $900 pr. annum, a sum sufficient for their education and support. Bills represents that the rents cannot count more than half that amount, and that the cultivation of the land by tenants will do it as much injury as the yearly rents—in fact that the land cultivated would by the time the children become of age be in gullies and entirely worn out. He thinks that instead of increasing in value, with the use that will be made of it that it will rather diminish. McNeal is an excellent agent, but no agent can prevent tenants from using up lands, when the work is so great as in that country, particularly where lands are a little uneven, as is very much the case with the Bunker Hill tract. If these views be correct, the difference would be too great not to require some consideration, $900 pr. annum, a certain cash income for 10 years at least, and cash means when of age, Sufficient for them to commence life with in addition to other valuable District lands which it would be advisable probably to lease out & *not sell*. The question then would be, in what kind of stocks the money could be invested with perfect safety. I should say not Bank Stock, for experience has proved that not a perfect safe investment. State Bonds bearing an interest of 6 pr. cent would do and I think would certainly be safe. This investment could now you know be readily made. It is however probable, that a still better & more secure investment could be made, and the money and interest undoubtedly secured, by being upon land and negroes to double the amount. This matter is worthy of consideration, and perhaps ought to be submitted to the consideration of Mr. Alexander, and other relatives on the mother's side.[2] The certain provision of good education for the children from their own property is certainly desireable. They are *no dependants*, and it is right that their means should be so used that they may be educated & supported as becomes their prospects.

Majr Bills informs me that there are plenty of men of the highest respectability who are willing to go into Court and swear that they believe a sale of the property I have mentioned, would be for the interest of the children owning the same. I have given you, Bills views, and certainly a sufficient indication of my own opinion. You must act as becomes the nearest relative of the children concerned, to be looked to & you may make any use of this letter you choose. As you can have no possible motive, but to promote the interest of Marshall's children, so far as you have the power, I make this statement to you. You may possibly be censured in any course you may think it best to take. Therefore I think it advisable for you to consult with Mr. Julius Alexander on the subject. Surely there can be no censure on any course that the intelligent and safe friends of the children may agree on. I am aware, that I have brought to your consideration a matter in which you may feel sensitiveness and much delicacy & responsibility. If Majr Bills had not convinced me of the importance of bringing the matter fully to your consideration I should not have done so.

James Walker

(private)

I intended the letter in which this is enclosed to be used in any way, your judgement may dictate. You may so use it. I have not had an opportunity of communicating to you as fully as I wished my opinions in relation to the Direction of the Bank of Tennessee. I look upon the successful administration of that Bank as a matter of much consequence to your own future political prospects, and to the success of the great Democratic party in Tennessee.

The friends of Mr. Nichol[3] say he should not be removed. They do not claim for him adequate qualification, but urge that he is now better acquainted with the business of the bank than any other person that could be put in his place. They urge further that he is a very moderate Whig.

Neither of these reasons are sufficient to justify his retention. In the first place, he has not sufficient talents, or enla[r]gement of views. In the next place, I am informed from a source I rely on, that altho, not a noisy, he is a most violent opposition man. About 12 months since he advanced Allen A. Hall $2000 to sustain the Banner—to oppose your election—not a dollar of which has yet been refunded. This is moderation with a vengeance. I need not express the opinion that it would be unsafe to retain so violent an opponent in a position where your administration could be so much affected. You have more to fear from this bank than any other thing if badly managed, or in the hands of the Whigs.

I can think of no one so well qualified to fill Nichol's place as Thomas H. Fletcher. He was selected as the Successor of Josiah Nichol[4] in the U.S. branch, on account of his talents alone, it being contrary to the usage to appoint an insolvent man even a Director.

G. W. Campbell
J W. Horton
John Waters
Sam'l R Anderson

All Democrats and good appointments.[5]

I suppose there ought to be three more Democrats. These might be found among Joseph Anderson, Frank McGavock, V. K Stephens or John B. Hall[6] is spoken well of, but I do not know him. Perhaps one of the other Democrats ought to come from the adjoining counties. Say R. P. Currin[7] from Williamson in place of N. T. Perkins.

Whigs

Jonathan Currin,[8] Rutherford, Moderate in politics, a first rate appointment.

Maj E. A White[9] Wilson,—a very clever man, and a good appointment.

Harvey Hogg[10] of Smith is I am told a good appointment.

James Woods,[11] if a Whig, would be a good appointment if he will accept. He is now in the Union Bank.

Either John W. Sanders or G. W. Martin would be good appointments from the Whig ranks. Sanders is now in the Planters bank.[12] This would leave out, W. Nichol. Col Motley. N. T. Perkins, J. W. Clay, John Shelbey & O B. Hayes[13]—all violent opposition men who never had qualifications for their stations. If you decide to put Fletcher at the head of the institution it would be very proper to hold a confidential consultation with him, that you may make the ablest directory in your power.

James Walker

ALS. DLC–JKP. Addressed to Nashville.

1. Polk's brother, Marshall Tate, died in 1831 and left his widow, Laura T. Wilson Polk, the care of their two children, Roxana Eunice Ophelia and Marshall Tate, Jr.

2. William Julius Alexander and Laura T. Wilson Polk. An 1816 graduate of the University of North Carolina and a prominent Charlotte lawyer, Alexander was a brother-in-law of Laura T. Wilson Polk.

3. William Nichol, son of Josiah Nichol, operated a steamship and commission business in Nashville and became president of the Bank of Tennessee in 1838. For two years, 1835–36, he served as mayor of Nashville.

4. An early Nashville settler and prominent businessman, Josiah Nichol served as president of the Nashville branch of the United States Bank from 1827 until his death in 1833.

5. George W. Campbell, Joseph W. Horton, John Waters, and Samuel R. Anderson were appointed directors of the Bank of Tennessee by Newton Cannon in 1838. Campbell, Horton, and Anderson were reappointed by Polk on January 25, 1840.

6. Joseph Anderson, Francis McGavock, Vernon K. Stevenson, and John B. Hall. An early Nashville settler and clerk of the Tennessee Land Office, McGavock owned a large amount of real estate in Davidson and Cheatham counties. He increased his holdings through his marriage to Amanda P. Harding, daughter of John Harding. In 1848 Stevenson became the first president of the Nashville and Chattanooga Railroad Company, a position which he held until the close of the Civil War. He was the son-in-law of John M. Bass. Anderson and Hall are not identified.

7. Robert P. Currin, an early Williamson County settler, operated a cotton-bagging manufactory in collaboration with John Sample and Hinchey Petway.

8. Jonathan Currin, a Murfreesboro merchant and businessman, was appointed a director of the Bank of Tennessee in 1838 by Newton Cannon and was reappointed by Polk on January 25, 1840.

9. A successful Lebanon merchant, Edward A. White shared a business partnership with John W. White, probably his brother.

10. Hogg served as register of Smith County from 1832 until 1842.

11. Woods was a prominent Nashville banker and commercial merchant.

12. John W. Sanders and George W. Martin are not identified further.

13. William Nichol, Benjamin F. Motley, Nicholas T. Perkins, Joseph W. Clay, John Shelby, and Oliver B. Hayes had been appointed directors of the Bank of Tennessee in 1838 by Newton Cannon. Nichol and Perkins were reappointed by Polk on January 25, 1840.

FROM FELIX GRUNDY

Dear Sir, Washington City, Oct 17th 1839

By last night's mail, I received the account of the organization of the Genrl. Assembly of Ten. I assure you it was most gratifying, to see the good republican State of Tennessee, standing sternly up to her long cherished principles. I still believe Foster will resign and not disgrace himself, as he certainly will If he holds on, after he is instructed to vote for the Independent Treasury Bill &c. Should he resign, then, I fear there will be trouble among our friends as to the successorship. And a note at the end of a letter, which I received last night from Genrl. Armstrong intimates that the last arternative may have to be resorted to[1]—respecting which, you know my feelings & wishes. White's successor should be now chosen. There should be no hesitation about it. There would then be two Senators to elect. The term of one to commence immediately; of the other, in March 1841. If the places could be changed with public approbation—every thing would be convenient & agreeable. If this is done, White will resign as sure as you live. Then the Legislature or you as the case may be, can fill the place with some person from West Ten. for the two remaining Sessions of his time. I think no one would seriously complain of this arrangement. This plan, would throw Foster's successor into East Ten—and give White's to Middle Ten. I could then remain where I am for two years and finish my political course in the Senate. My abandoning my present station at this time, might be somewhat injurious to the public, and very much so to myself individually. The feelings in your favor for the Vice-presidency is strong, and I think is growing rapidly. I have no news, but what you see in the papers. Give my respects to Mrs. Polk and write to me often.

FELIX GRUNDY

[P.S.] The foregoing suggested course, would afford Democracy the greatest triump. I Judge Mr Bell will not be Speaker, as I told old friend Gillespie[2] once. In this you must go upon faith. I have not time to shew the whys & wherefores, &c, but it will be so. Gr.

ALS. DLC–JKP. Addressed to Nashville and marked *"Confidential."*

1. Robert Armstrong's final alternative probably argued for Grundy's returning to the Senate upon Foster's resignation.
2. Probably a reference to James Gillespy of Blount County.

FROM AMOS KIRKPATRICK[1]

Meigsville, Tennessee. October 17, 1839

Kirkpatrick expresses disapproval of recent newspaper articles promoting Polk for the vice-presidency. Fearful that Polk's replacement as governor would be a Whig, Kirkpatrick worries that Tennessee Democrats would be left leaderless.

ALS. DLC–JKP. Addressed to Nashville.

1. Kirkpatrick, a Democrat, served as postmaster at Meigsville in Jackson County.

FROM WILLIAM ALLEN

My Dear Sir, Chillicothe Oct 20. 1839

Since the 10th August, until within a few days past, my attention has been so much engaged in our election affairs,[1] and I have, consequently been absent so much of the time, that I was compelled to neglect my correspondence, out of the State, altog[e]ther.

Now that the battle is over, I extend to you my hand, in congratulation, upon the result in your state, as well as in this, and other parts of the Union. You merit, for the great part you have acted in Tenn., the undivided gratitude of the whole American Democracy, and I trust, that the day is not distant, when that gratitude will be manifested towards you, in a more palpable manner, than by words. There is but one circumstance resulting from your election, that I regret, and that is, that we shall not have the pleasure of your own and your Lady's company, at Washington this winter.

On the subject of the Vice Presidency, there has been but little said, as yet, in this state. Some of the democratic papers have put up Johnson's name and resolutions have been passed at some of the meetings, opposing his course. But most of our papers have been silent on the subject, and the resolutions of approval, were nothing more than the usual matter of course declarations of the party, which could not well be omitted without also, omitting an approval of the President's course. The truth is, there is but little feeling in this state for Johnson, whilst on the other hand there is much for you, and many of our friends who say nothing, as yet, about the matter, would rather he would not run again. But as he is already, in the position, many suppose he will, of course, be the candidate, and in this fact consists his whole strength. So far, therefore, as this state is concerned, every thing will remain quiet, on the subject, until Congress shall meet, when, it is supposed the party will determine upon the question of a national Convention. At that time, I think it will be well for our friends to find some means of inducing Johnson to change his position, and accept some other situation. In that event, all the rest will be easy, for I do not think there will be the least difficulty, in presenting your name to the democracy of the Country. I am certain, that no other man named will be so acceptable to the democracy of Ohio.

I have recd. a letter from our friend, Judge Catron, on this subject. Be so good as to write to him, and inform him of the fact of my having written to you.

I wish you would write to me as soon as I get to Washington, and inform me fully, what are your particular views and wishes in every thing that relates to this matter. You will, of course, be safe, in making any suggestions that may occur to you, as to men and things there, or in the states. Please present my respects to Mrs. P.

W. ALLEN

N.B. I need not say to you that this is confidential.

ALS. DLC–JKP. Addressed to Columbia and marked "*Private.*" AE on the cover states that this letter was answered on October 28, 1839; Polk's reply has not been found.

1. Ohio Democrats won both houses of their state legislature by increased majorities.

FROM JULIUS W. BLACKWELL

Athens, Tennessee. October 20, 1839

A large meeting of the party faithful in Athens has approved the course of the present federal administration, nominated Van Buren for president, and recommended Polk for the vice-presidency. Blackwell's political enemies continue to press him and his creditors financially.[1] He must raise upwards of one thousand dollars cash with which to pay the debts of the *Courier*; if he sues his own debtors, he will injure himself politically. Having struggled almost alone to establish and sustain the *Courier*, he has come to the end of his resources and requires assistance. Blackwell notes with pleasure Democratic victories in recent elections in Maryland and Georgia.[2]

ALS. DLC–JKP. Addressed to Nashville.

1. See Blackwell to Polk, September 9, 1839.

2. Democrats won a majority of the congressional and state legislative races in Maryland and elected Charles J. McDonald governor of Georgia.

FROM JAMES WALKER

Dear Sir, Columbia Octr. 20, 1839

The bank suspension is full of consequences, and whether these consequences are to result in good or evil depends, much upon the wisdom of those who can controul events. It is very clear that this untoward event has been entirely produced by the Bank of the U.S. whether from political considerations, and reckless determination to produce another *panic*, and check the sweeping course of Democracy, or from embarrassment and dire necessity remains to be seen. It is probably both.[1] But if the movement is a political one, it must inevitably re-act upon its authors. What stronger argument could be offered in favor of the Sub Treasury, or against the creation of a mammoth Bank, *under the irresponsible controul of stockholders*, (with such powers for mischief as the late Bank of the U.S. has proven itself to possess,) than the conduct of the Banks for the last four years? The effect of the late suspension must be the prostration of the political party who controul banking power, and there is much reason to believe that it will end in the prostration of all. If the Whigs think this event is to check the growing strength of their opponents, prevent the passage of the Sub-Treasury bill, or induce the people to cry out for a National Bank, as a panecea for existing evils, I think they are widely mistaken. The effect must be to strengthen the Republican party. They do not now pretend that any action of the government has produced this suspension. Where can they lay the blame? It must rest upon the Bank of the U.S.—and her swindling post note operation.[2] But the question is, how is this thing to operate upon our interests, upon the interest and welfare of Tennessee. This is the question of immediate importance. You may be surprised that I give the opinion that it may work favorably, but there is a chance it may work most disastrously. It is very clear that the suspension is to be within a very short period universal. It cannot be helped. No single bank, nor the whole banks of no single state can stand the crash, if their paper becomes more valuable than the general currency, and of course instead of a medium of circulation, an article of trade. If the banks East, West and South, all suspend, the Union & Planter's bank[3] having suspended it will be impossible for the Bank of Tennessee to avoid a similar course, unless by producing the most severe suffering, and the entire loss of all her banking capital. This must inevitably be the result of holding on to a different course from all other banks. It is as certain, as that cause produces effect, that if the Bank of Tennessee holds out, all her specie and eastern funds will be drawn out, and a part of her paper still out without any means of immediate redemption. She can only redeem as she can make the most grinding collections. To pursue this policy will produce a state of ruin and distress among the people unparallelled in the history of the country. The Whig Directors of the Bank of Tennessee know this, and will gladly throw upon the Democratic Legislature the responsibility of holding out.[4] They know the bank cannot hold out 60 days, if all other Banks suspend and in the mean time will be utterly prostrated. It is idle to suppose that the community of brokers will hold off, and not b[u]y up her notes and send off the specie, when they can make money by it. The paper of the Bank will no longer circulate. It will be sold to the brokers & the specie drawn, as fast as the operation can be got through with. Magnanimity is not to be expected from the community on such occasions—*interest* will govern. Mr. Nichols call upon the Stock banks for $100,000 in specie must have been designed to force them into an immediate suspension. What else could have been its object? In his letter to the General Assembly of the 18th[5] he takes pains to assign good & sufficient reasons why the Bank of Tennessee should suspend. *Every word is a reason* and he then of course fixes the responsibility of a ruinous course upon the Democratic Legislature. I tell you the Whigs in the Bank of Tennessee, (Nichol at their head) know the certain result of their Bank holding out against all other Banks. They know the effect it will have on the people, and the odium of the course, when the result is seen and they are willing to witness the disaster, *upon the responsibility of a Democratic administration*, under the hope that the distress and failure occasioned, will change the popular current. Let the present directory have the responsibility of paying or suspending, and my judgement is, they will suspend in 24 hours. At all events, the responsibility ought to be on them. Let the President and Directors appointed by the Whig Governor[6] & Legislature, act on their own judgement, as to what they believe to be for the interest of the Bank and the people of the state. If they think they can hold on, let them try it upon their own responsibility, and if they say stop, I think it would be very unwise in the Legislature to force them on to destruction. All the banks of Tennessee are in a condition that makes it certain that the note holders cannot possibly loose. The principal indebtedness of the people is directly or indirectly to the Banks. The paper then must answer all home purposes as well as ever, and it is only the merchants that will Suffer the loss in exchange. It has been principally the merchants that have brought on this state of things, and their is no reason why the whole mass should suffer for their folly. Let things take their course. The agricultural interest will be benefitted by the general suspension. Cotton will now be the best and most certain medium of exchange. It must bring a better price, at least as much more as the difference of exchange. The Banks can now get out a circulation, and keep it out. If the currency is of inferior value, we shall at least have something that will pay debts, and produce exchanges of property. The great difficulty has been, that we had scarcely any currency good or bad. The country was ground down to the dust. Any change must be some relief. Our foreign debt must be paid from our Cotton crops, the price of which will be enhanced in the hands of the planters. When the foreign debt is paid, the paper of our Banks will be as good as ever again and the Banks can resume a regular business. If the bonds for Bank capital and internal improvement are made available it will throw the exchanges at once in our favor. I think it is now more desireable than ever to make our State

Securities of the best possible character. If our Cotton will now pay Eastern debts at higher prices (as it will) where are we injured. If our State Securities will pay a greater amount of Eastern debt than they otherwise would, we cannot be injured. We can pay the interest abroad with our Cotton as well as ever. I mention the advantages that will accrue to Tennessee & the South from a suspension. I do not justify it. There has been a great departure from moral principles and good faith. The Bank of the U.S. has proven itself a corrupt political instrument, or its gigantic transactions has overwhelmed it in Bankruptcy. But is it not true wisdom to make the best we can even of an acknowledged evil. This suspension must forever prostrate that mischievous bank power. For this and other benefits growing out of it, let us patiently bear the accompanying evils. I think Tennessee on the whole, will be rather benefitted. At all events we must sensibly make the best of it. If need be, I think the Legislature ought to distinctly place the responsibility on the President & Directors of the Bank, to pay or not to pay. The coin in the Bank and branches bears but a small proportion to their circulation. It is all they can rely upon. The paper of suspended banks, and bills on New Orleans, (where the Banks will all undoubtedly suspend) are not to be now relied on, as means of redemption, if the bank continues to redeem in coin at her counter, I think you will find no movement on the part of the Whigs to authorise or cause the Bank to suspend. They would willingly enough see it, and the people "*used up*" if the blame can be fairly fixed upon the Democratic majority.

I think this a very important matter, and have hastily written you what I think on the subject, if it does no good, I presume it can do no harm. Langtry feels very much concerned about [it], has called on me to talk about [it]. I asked him to give his views in writing, which I send to you.[7] Like my opinions you can take his for what it is worth.

James Walker

ALS. DLC–JKP. Addressed to Nashville.

1. In the summer of 1839 the United States Bank of Pennsylvania faced financial ruin. Having overtraded in an attempt to manipulate the price of American cotton, the bank sustained heavy losses occasioned by a countervailing retrenchment implemented by the English textile industry. The bank suspended its payment of specie on October 9, 1839.

2. Facing a critical shortage of specie reserves and seeking an excuse to suspend payments, the United States Bank of Pennsylvania sold large sums of high-interest postnotes, the proceeds of which were deposited in New York City banks. In August 1839 the U.S. Bank conducted selected specie raids on these competitor banks. Such calculated applications of pressure made good money scarce, but failed to bring on a general suspension. After its suspension, of course, the bank paid its postnote debts in uncurrent money.

3. Reference is to the Union Bank of Tennessee and the Planters' Bank of Tennessee. Established in October 1832 and based in Nashville, the Union Bank succeeded the Bank of Tennessee, which had been chartered in December 1831. The Planters' Bank, established in 1833, took as its model the Union Bank and also served the Middle Tennessee area. Both banks suspended specie payments on October 18, 1839.

4. Whig partisans controlling the bank included its president, William Nichol, and seven of its directors, among whom were T. F. Bradford, J. W. Clay, Jonathan Currin, Oliver B. Hayes, Benjamin F. Motley, Nicholas Perkins, and John Shelby.

5. On October 18, 1839, William Nichol informed the legislature that the Union and Planters' banks had suspended and that each had refused to pay considerable balances owed the Bank of Tennessee. On the following day Nichol again addressed the legislature, stating that the Bank of Tennessee's office at Nashville possessed the means of redeeming its notes, but would have to call in its loans and curtail future credits. On October 22, 1839, the Bank of Tennessee suspended.

6. Newton Cannon.

7. In a two-page memorandum, Hillary Langtry stated that he was concerned about the state government's policy on specie payments. Langtry, a director of the Bank of Tennessee's branch at Columbia, conjectured that suspension might enable planters to get crops to market and thus provide them their only measure of permanent relief.

FROM LEVI WOODBURY

Washington City. October 20, 1839

Woodbury congratulates Polk on his election to the governorship. Seldom has Woodbury known a victory to be so triumphant and gratifying. Times are troublesome in fiscal affairs; retrenchment and economy must be the order of the day.

ALS. DLC–JKP. Addressed to Nashville and marked "Private."

FROM HAMPTON C. WILLIAMS[1]

Washington City. October 21, 1839

Williams congratulates Polk on being elected governor and recalls the great degree of anxiety exhibited by Democrats in Washington City on that occasion. Tennessee's good example no doubt had "a fine effect" upon elections in Maryland, Pennsylvania, and Ohio. Sentiment for nominating Polk vice-president increases daily, and impartial judges consider him the strongest candidate. On the difficult subject of selecting Democrats to replace Foster and White in the U.S. Senate, Williams suggests that the legislature elect Grundy to succeed White in 1841. Surely White would resign; Grundy might then decline the election and remain in the cabinet; and Polk might appoint a Democrat to the vacant seat.

ALS. DLC–JKP. Addressed to Nashville.

1. Williams, an active party worker, held a clerkship in the Fourth Auditor's Office; he formerly resided in Franklin County, Tennessee.

FROM DAVID HUBBARD[1]

Dear Sir Courtland 23d Oct 1839

In accordance with the trouble I promised to give you I send you a list of members of the last Congress of the U.S.[2] I wish you would oblige me so far as to make some mark to each name by which I can distinguish, between the several classes; State right Whigs & Federal Whigs—Internal Improvement democrats & strict constructionists—also your opinion as to grades of intellect—No. 1, No. 2 & N 3 &c—also whether reserved in manner or free & communicative. Send me it to Washing at least three days before the Election of Speaker.

From some of the Southern papers of our State I discover that Lewis or Pickens[3] will one or the other be run for Speaker. I want you to let me know since the Maryland Elections[4] are over how par[ties] will be divided (without counting Mississippi) on the supposition that the N Jersey men vote for Speaker by virtue of their certificate[5] & the four Sub Treasury Whigs of Georgia[6] & Hunter of Va & Fisher of Carolina[7] vote with the Whigs.

Let me know just how it will go on this State of the case, for I fear Miss. will go against us. I have just been through six or eight Northern counties & our success in the State is not certain, nor do I think that the result in Mississippi can certainly be known in time to let the members get on to the Election of speaker.[8] A member of Congress has died in Massachusetts.[9] Is he whig or Democrat?

As much information likely to be serviceable to an inexperienced member on these subjects as you can give will be properly appreciated by . . . .

DAVID HUBBARD

ALS. DLC–JKP. Addressed to Nashville and marked "Private."

1. A lawyer, merchant, and dealer in Chickasaw lands, Hubbard served several terms in the Alabama legislature before winning election as a Democrat to the U.S. House in 1839; he again won election to the House in 1849.

Hubbard was a presidential elector on the Polk-Dallas ticket in 1844.

2. List not found.

3. Dixon H. Lewis and Francis W. Pickens. A Montgomery lawyer and member of the Alabama House, 1825–27, Lewis sat in the U.S. House from 1829 until 1844, when he resigned to fill the seat of William R. King in the U.S. Senate. In 1839 five members of the South Carolina congressional delegation ran Lewis for the speakership against Virginia's John W. Jones, nominee of the Democratic caucus and favorite of Thomas Hart Benton. Unable to elect Jones and unwilling to support Lewis, eleven Democrats, including Tennesseans Cave Johnson, Hopkins L. Turney, and Julius W. Blackwell, voted with the Whig minority to elect Robert M. T. Hunter, a nullifier from Virginia. Pickens, a South Carolina lawyer and planter, won election to Congress as a nullifier and sat from 1834 until 1843. A member of the Nashville Convention of 1850, he served as governor of South Carolina from 1860 until 1863.

4. Maryland's congressional delegation to the Twenty-sixth Congress consisted of six Democrats and two Whigs.

5. Armed with election certificates from the Whig governor of New Jersey, William Pennington, five Whigs claimed the right to attend the organization of the House. With these five votes the Whig party could control the House and choose a Whig Speaker. Upon reaching the New Jersey names on the roll of members-elect, House Clerk Hugh Garland refused to proceed; he explained that he held conflicting certifications and wished instruction. Without benefit of quorum, Speaker, or rules, members-elect heatedly debated procedural questions for ten days. At length they decided to pass over the state of New Jersey, complete the roll call, establish quorum and rules, and proceed to the election of a Speaker. Neither group of claimants voted on these questions. On March 10, 1840, the House admitted New Jersey's Democratic claimants and on July 17 awarded them their seats.

6. Only three Georgia Whigs voted for the Sub-Treasury bill: Edward J. Black, Walter T. Colquitt, and Mark A. Cooper.

7. Robert M. T. Hunter and Charles Fisher. A Virginia lawyer and member of the state legislature, Hunter served two terms in the U.S. House, 1837–1841. He was Speaker of that body from 1839 until 1841. An unsuccessful candidate for reelection in 1842, Hunter returned to the House in 1845 for one term. He won election to the U.S. Senate in 1847 and served until 1861. A Democrat, Fisher served several terms in the North Carolina legislature as well as two terms in the U.S. House, 1819–21 and 1839–41.

8. Mississippi held congressional elections in November of odd-numbered years. In 1839 Mississippi Democrats elected by general ticket Albert G. Brown and Jacob Thompson; both took their seats in Congress prior to the organization of the House.

9. James C. Alvord of Massachusetts, a Whig, died on September 27, 1839. Osmyn Baker, also a Whig, replaced Alvord, but did not take his seat until January 14, 1840.

FROM E. G. EASTMAN

Knoxville, Tennessee. October 26, 1839

Eastman urges Polk to render any assistance he can to Lonergan,[1] a firm friend and Democrat who has invested nearly a hundred thousand dollars in the Hiwassee Railroad. Eastman believes the prosperity of East Tennessee depends upon the completion of that railroad.

ALS. DLC–JKP. Addressed to Nashville.

1. Kenedy Lonergan was an Irish construction contractor on the Hiwassee Railroad, 1837–39.

FROM J. G. M. RAMSEY

Dear Sir Mecklenburg T. Oct. 26, 1839

I wrote you some time since giving you at some length as you requested my views upon Internal Improvement in East Tennessee.[1] I had intended before this time to have sent you a copy of our L.C.&C.R.R. charter[2] & was waiting to receive a printed copy of the report of the Directors to the Stockholders at their meeting in Sep. at Asheville. Our report was ordered to be printed under the care of our late President Genl. Hayne but probably in consequence of his lamented death it has not yet come to hand. I wished too to call your attention to some important suggestions in that report. I must do so from memory. One is this—to ask from all the States granting the charter an amendment of the section requiring a double track. It is unnecessary & the repeal of that clause will diminish the cost 30 per cent. The report gives a full & able statement of the progress of the work—the difficulties arising from the depression of American securities abroad & the impossibility of making sales of the Tennessee bonds belonging to the company & the consequent necessity of advancing more slowly in the construction of our road than we had anticipated, but advising constancy & perseverance. I will forward you a copy & beg in advance your particular attention to its details. Ours is a great work—& of unquestionable importance to the South & West but especially to the Carolinas & Tennessee & is indeed the favorite project of our two Atlantic partners—& sooner or later will be carried through . But as our bonds cannot be sold but at a sacrafice of 40 or 50 per cent I think the true policy of the Co. & of the States issuing them is rather to suspend temporarily operations on the road than to precipitate the sales of them at so great a loss—especially as that discount or less is not gotten by purchasers in our own state or country but by foreign capitalists or *souless* corporations at home. Yet I am not for abandoning the work as that would be to surrender our charters (which I consider an invaluable treasure to the State of Tennessee as well as the Company) & would be acting in *bad faith* to North & South Carolina each of which now holds us in the highest esteem.

I will also call your attention to the Section of our charter which provides for the representation of *State Stock*—Sect. 30: "—Any State holding stock may vote by such person as the Legislature or the Governor thereof may appoint" & our Internal Improvement & Bank law of 1837 provides that the Governor shall appoint the proxy for the State. Governor Cannon who was always adverse to our road, at the instance no doubt of Genl. Jacobs our present Senator, appointed Hugh L. McClung the State proxy to attend our last meeting at Asheville.[3] I hope you will appoint a proxy to attend the next meeting of the Co. which takes place at Columbia S.C. the 4th December 1839. The Legislature of that state is then in session & we shall apply on the spot for the alteration of the charter before mentioned. I wish I could say to you who would certainly attend if appointed; because it is important that the one appointed should attend. I can only say this however that as nearly all our stockholders live in & East of Knoxville & that as our road affects more directly our Eastern counties the selection should be made from the upper counties. The law giving our two Rail Road Companies $650,000 each, was a compromise between the upper & lower sections of E. Tennessee, & the former will of course seem to be entitled to the Representative. Who shall he be. I had a conversation with the Hon. John Blair of Jonesboro in reference to the subject. His only objection to acting was that he was not a Stockholder. The charter does not require that he should be & precedents are against his objection. If I hear as I will do in a few days whether he will attend if appointed I will so inform you in time for him to hear from Nashville.[4] For many reasons he would be a good proxy. He is a manufacturer & a merchant—a man of good sense—influence & character & would represent Tenn. well. If he says he cannot go I do not know another who is at all likely to attend but myself. As a Director of the R.R. Co. & as President of the Branch of the S.W.R.R. Bank,[5] official duty will require my attendance both at Charleston & Columbia, & many of our Stockholders have suggested to me to ask for the appointment. I say to you as frankly as I would to my brother that if you know of any competent person east of me that will certainly be at Columbia the 4th December next I would advise his appointment. If you do not know such an one & Mr. Blair should say to me he cannot go—or if you do not choose to appoint him—I cannot agree that the State stock should be unrepresented but will consent to receive the appointment & act as faithfully under it as my abilities will permit.

I shall set out for Charleston the 9th or 10th of November— will be there till the 2nd of December & after that at Columbia during the session of our Stockholders. I mention these dates & places that if you find it necessary to address me you will know where it will reach me. If it is directed to Mecklenburg T. it will be safely forwarded. If it is addressed to Columbia please endorse via Asheville N.C. If to Charleston please say, care of Mitchell King Esq. or J. G. Holmes Esq.[6]

Your Inaugural is the very thing—& will take like contagion in Carolina & elsewhere. Your views of Banks are exactly correct & tho an officer of one I endorse every word in it.[7] Our Branch at Knoxville by the way has not suspended & I hope may not. We can take up all our liabilities any time & can speak even to an "enemy at our gates."[8]

A great Whig meeting was held in town yesterday—have not heard the proceedings.[9] Our late nominating meetings have evidently stimulated them to desperation. In this county we are gaining ground but it is against wind & tide. Judge White has returned & is said to be as vindictive as ever.

Did you get the Mecklenburg Dec. of Independence from Genl. Jackson? If not I will send you the only remaining one I have. Tho a good deal the worse for age it will answer for a copy. I have thought of requesting Genl. J. to bequeath the fine Satin one I presented him with—& the reasons at length why he should do so. What do you think of it? It was accompanied by a Satin Dedication—which well deserved as it certainly was by him would not be less so by the expected legatee.

Present Mrs. Ramsey's kindest regards to Mrs. Polk with my own respects.

J. G. M. Ramsey

ALS. DLC–JKP. Addressed to Nashville.

1. See Ramsey to Polk, September 26, 1839.

2. Reference is to the charter of the Louisville, Cincinnati and Charleston Railroad Company.

3. Solomon D. Jacobs was president of the Hiwassee, a competing railroad company. In 1839 he represented Knox County in the Tennessee House, not the Senate. Hugh Lawson McClung was clerk and master of the Knox County Chancery Court, 1848–57; his father Charles conducted the early surveys of Knoxville.

4. See Ramsey to Polk, November 1, 1839.

5. Reference is to the Knoxville branch of the Southwestern Railroad Bank.

6. Polk assigned Ramsey the state's proxy to vote at the stockholder's meeting in Columbia, South Carolina. Polk's proxy commission to Ramsey has not been found. Mitchell King of South Carolina led early efforts to build a regional railroad linking Charleston to the Ohio River valley. J. G. Holmes is not identified further.

7. In his inaugural address of October 14, 1839, Polk opposed incorporation of a national bank, multiplication of state banks, and issuance of excessive amounts of bank paper.

8. Inexact translation of the Latin phrase *Intus est hostis* from Cicero, *In Catilinam* 2.5.11.

9. Knox County Whigs met in Knoxville to consider proposals for increasing the effectiveness of their party organization.

FROM WILLIAM H. POLK

Dear Brother Columbia Oct 28th 1839

Mr. Trainum[1] arrived here on yesterday. He is now with me. His account of your plantation is very encouraging. He says that thirty three Bales had been made when he arrived at the plantation, ninety one thousand pounds of Cotton had been picked, inclusive of the 33 Bales. He said they commenced bailing again the morning he left, and according to his computation they have by this time 53 Bales. He thinks you will make 130 Bales, at the *least calculation* and your Overseers opinion is that there will be more than 130.[2] Your Overseer, sends word that he will have by the 25th December, 100 Bales at Troy ready for shipping. He says your Overseer commenced in the right way, and has the negroes under fine command. Trainum is of opinion that he [Garner] will do you *full justice*. He says that he is industrious, and attentive to his business. Trainum estimates your Pork, which will be made on the plantation, at 4,500. And that Six thousand pounds will be sufficient to furnish the whole plantation. According to that account you will have to provide 1,500. The account which I give you, is the account which your overseer gave Trainum, which accords with his own observation. He says you have sixty shoats, which will do for next years use—besides many small pigs. You will make 400 Barrels of Corn. Your Cows &c are all in good order. Trainum says you were deceived in the whole negro property which you purchased of Harris.[3] Allen he says is at least 45 years old—and says he cannot perform a hands *labour*. West Harris is now in Philadelphia—he is at this time probably on his way home. I have Rented your House from Mr. Leacoq[4]—& will be bound to you for the rent. Mr. Trainum says the carry-all &c, which Dr Caldwell purchased for you, cost $41, which has to be paid the 1st of Jan'y.

WILL HAWKINS POLK

P.S. I attended to the matter with the Democrat—it will appear.[5]
W H Polk

ALS. DLC–JKP. Addressed to Nashville. Published in Bassett, *Plantation Overseer*, 127–28.

1. A resident of Maury County, Jeremiah Tranum is not identified further.
2. See John J. Garner to Polk, November 3, 1839.
3. Formerly a commissioner of Bolivar in Hardeman County, West Harris of Tipton County sold Polk four slaves on September 24, 1839; the purchase price amounted to $2,110.
4. Reference probably is to William Thomas Leacock of Maury County.
5. Reference has not been identified; no 1839 issues of the Columbia *Tennessee Democrat* have been found.

FROM JOSEPH H. TALBOT

Dear Sir Jackson October 28th 1839

On yesterday I had the pleasure to read your first message to the Legislature,[1] with which, I, in common with your friends generally am much pleased. I expected to be at Nashville during the present Session, but the times are so hard that I believe I shall have to forego that pleasure. In regard to the late suspension[2] I have a few words to say. I am glad of it, because it will show off the conservatives in their true colors. The man who *now* will advocate a connexion by the Government with the State banks, will be looked upon as a fool or knave. Mr. Rives will be driven from his position.[3] I have no doubt he will go over to the National Bank party, but the question is will his conservative friends in the Legislature of Virginia and in Congress go with him. It is likely some of them will not, but acknowledge their error and go with the administration.

I am pleased generally with your views in regard to our Banks. Now is the time for the Legislature to place the banks in their proper footing, that is, in due Subordination to the laws.

1st. That part of their charters authorizing them to charge more than six per cent interest should be altered and all the Stock banks[4] placed upon an equal footing with the State Bank in this particular.

2nd. They should all be subject to examination by a committee of the Legislature, *which should be* examind at every meeting of the Legislature.

3rd. They should be required to pay over to the State Bank in good funds all they owe on the first of Jany. next to that institution.

4th. They must resume specie payments for all Sums on or before the 2d day of Jany. 1841. This will give them the advantage of another crop. They should be required by a certain time to file in the office of the Secretary of State within a limited time their assent to the modification of their charters.

Upon their failure to comply with any one of these requisitions the Governor should be required to sue out a writ of scierie facias[5] from the Supreme Court. It is very important to have an efficient atto Genl. This man Meigs[6] will not do. The opinions he furnished Govr. Cannon, would disgrace a school boy. Genl Gibbs[7] should be suspended as chancellor, for the reason, that while he held the pro tem appointment, he attended more to politicks that his judicial duties. He took the Stump as I am informed in Obion, and used disgraceful language toward you. The Whigs may cry out proscription, but *all* parties condemned Gibbs course during the canvass. He let himself so low, that a large majority of the bar, would be gratified at his removal, provided a competent man is elected in his place.

I have no objection that Messrs Foster & White should hold on to their stations. They can do us no injury in the Senate, and we can shoot at them. I would suggest the passage of resolutions by the Legislature approving of Mr. Van Burens proposition to seperate the Banks and the Government, and not give them the *power of instructions.* I have no doubt they will hold out if they can find an apology and I have no objection that they hold on and misrepresent the feelings of the people.

JOS H. TALBOT

ALS. DLC–JKP. Addressed to Nashville.

1. Polk's legislative message of October 22, 1839, dealt primarily with banking and internal improvements. The governor stressed the following proposals: early resumption of specie payments; conversion of the Bank of Tennessee's capital stock into "sterling bonds"; proscription of small denomination bank notes; examination of branch bank locations; extension of supervisory powers over branch banks; and legislative investigation of all state chartered banks.

2. See James Walker to Polk, October 20, 1839.

3. The state banks' general suspension weakened William C. Rives' argument that state bank notes were an acceptable medium with which to pay federal taxes. Hard money advocates urged that federal taxes could be rendered uniform only if paid in specie.

4. Reference is to the Union and Planters' banks.

5. Writ of scire facias.

6. Return J. Meigs, a Davidson County lawyer, served briefly as attorney

general and court reporter for the state from early 1839 until November of that year. He became U.S. attorney for Middle Tennessee in 1841 and represented Davidson County as a Whig in the Tennessee Senate from 1847 until 1849.

7. In the early 1820's George W. Gibbs served in both houses of the legislature and in the directorship of the Nashville branch of the Bank of the State of Tennessee. By 1829 he had moved westward to Obion County; ten years later he saw brief service as chancellor of West Tennessee. Gibbs resigned as chancellor of West Tennessee a few days after Talbot's letter to Polk. George W. Gibbs to Polk, November 5, 1839. ALS. T–Governor's Papers.

FROM HOPKINS L. TURNEY

Winchester Oct the 29th 1839

Dear Sir,

In one week after I arrive at Washington I can ascertain the feelings of the democratic members of congress on the subject of our legislative nominations for President & Vice-President of the U.S. Would not some well written letters to the leading democratic papers in the different states, having for their *text* that your nomination for the Vice-Presidency, meet the entire satisfaction of the democratic party in congress, and consequently, the approbation of the party throughout the union. Would this not have a tendancy to unite the party in the support of the nominees of our legislature and to put down other aspireants, and thereby make the election safe. Let me hear from you on this subject.

I have seen and read your inaugeral. I think it contains a brief & explicit out line of the principles of our party. It containes no surplus, and is long enough. In a word it is just what it ought to be, though your speech I have no doubt was better.

I have not seen your message though it is here and I have heard it Highly spoken of. I hope you have recommended a Bankruptcy law for the banks or something of the kind.[1] This I believe is all I cear [care] for of State politics.

Joel Smith I understand is a candidate for Treasurer, not because he needs or wants the office, but mearly for the purpose of defeating the present incumbant.[2] Is it right that the *union*[3] should have every thing. Ought it not to be satisfied with the public printing. I will not trouble you further, with this disagreeable subject. The members will do as they please.

On my return home I found my Eldest daughter[4] in exceeding bad helth and as yet is no better. I fear I will not be able to leave in time to be at Washington on the 1st day of the Session.

H L Turney

ALS. DLC–JKP. Addressed to Nashville. AE on the cover states that this letter was answered on October 31, 1839; Polk's reply has not been found.

1. For the governor's recommendations on banking, see Joseph H. Talbot to Polk, October 28, 1839.

2. Miller Francis was treasurer of East Tennessee from 1827 until 1836. Under the 1834 Constitution, Francis served as treasurer of Tennessee, 1836–43. He was the father-in-law of H. L. Turney.

3. *Nashville Union*.

4. Eleanor Turney.

FROM J. G. M. RAMSEY

Mecklenburg, Tennessee. November 1, 1839

Ramsey advises that John Blair is undecided about attending the forthcoming stockholders meeting at Columbia.[1] Because of Blair's uncertainty, Ramsey suggests that he, Blair, and W. C. Roadman of Newport be named joint representatives of the state's stock. Ramsey regrets that the company's annual statement has been delayed, for he would like Polk to see the financial strength of the Southwestern Railroad Bank. The Knoxville branch has not suspended specie payments and need not suspend unless ordered to do so by the parent company.

ALS. DLC–JKP. Addressed to Nashville. AE on the cover states that this letter was answered on November 7, 1839; Polk's reply has not been found.

1. See Ramsey to Polk, October 26, 1839.

FROM JOSHUA L. MARTIN

My dear Sir

Tuskaloosa Nov 2nd 1839

I had the pleasure last night to receive your Inaugural, & respects added, for which be pleased to accept my thanks. I had read carefully, & *approved every word of it* previously. I was still greatly pleased to have it in the form sent, for my son to read & preserve for more mature years.[1]

The party is greatly your debtor, & they feel the obligation; and nothing will prevent its proper discharge, but the undue haste of friends. I see some grounds for fear arising upon that point. I allude to the effort which is being made to run you for V. Prt. I assure you that it would give me great pleasure to see you in that station, if you could be spared from that which you occupy. That however, in my humble judgt., cannot be done. The work is *splendidly done*, so far as you have gone. Go on, & finish it. Let nothing take you from the high station which you fill, untill the last, & least remains of the hope of our enemy is destroyed.

You are a young man, & need not be in haste, and let me assure you that when the proper time arrives the *White House* is yours. I ought to beg pardon for my arrogance in suggesting even, upon this subject, when you cannot need such advice. But I felt it, & said it. I never entertained a doubt of your success in the race. I knew the people of my native state needed light only, & that you could & would give it to them. Enough.

I send you my card[2] which will shew you my *whereabout, & whatabout.* I have parted company with politics forever, & shall devote myself to my profession. But still I shall not only rejoice with my party in their victories, but be ready, & lay a helping hand when necessary. Mrs. M.[3] desires to be affectionately remembered to Mrs. P. & yourself. Present my best regards to Mrs. P.

J. L. MARTIN

ALS. DLC–JKP. Addressed to Nashville.

1. Reference probably is to John Mason Martin, who was born in 1837. Following his father's example and combining a successful career in politics and law, he served in the Alabama Senate, 1871–76; taught law at the University of Alabama, 1875–86; and won election as a Democrat to the U.S. House in 1885.

2. In his printed notice, dated August 1, 1839, Martin states that he has settled in Tuscaloosa and and intends to practice law in the several courts of Alabama. Martin resided previously in Athens, Alabama.

3. Martin married twice, each time to a sister of William Mason of Limestone County, Alabama. Martin's wives are not identified further.

FROM ALEXANDER O. ANDERSON

My Dear Sir Knoxville Novr. 3 1839

Enclosed you will receive a Postscript from the Argus of today,[1] by which you will find that Mr Bell is playing off the Nashville system of Whig tactics. It is rumored here that he spoke on last Saturday at Sparta. The account given of his speech at this place is, that it was full of fury & &c. The sentiment about honesty attributed to him in the Postscript cannot be heard by any generous & high minded man without a feeling of *pity* and indignation. That it was uttered I have no doubt, from the toast which it is said immediately followed it, & which you find subjoined to the Postscript. It is said he proceeds thro' North Carolina to Washington.

It wou'd seem that personal hatred mingles its bitterness in the political spirit of our opponents. How is it possible that our friends can hesitate to avail themselves of the rights of victory, when they look at the present movements of the Federal leaders in our state? There can be no question of the absolute necessity of action in regard to the successor of Judge White. His friends here are silent as to what he will do, and I infer from this that he will hold on. Under such circumstances to leave us wholly in the hand of the enemy, in the East here, wou'd be suicidal.

The day I reached McMinnville I found our friend Dr. Young very sick of fever. He had been very bad, but thought himself, then, tolerably safe. I had, however, some apprehensions for him—but hope that by this time he may be recovering.

Dr. Young informed me that he saw Mr Alexander[2] on his way to Nashville—that he expressed much solicitude as to the choice of Senator for this section, in the event Judge White shou'd resign—Urged the propriety of Judge Powel's[3] election—& particularly objected to my being chosen. These facts Dr. Y. thought it important I shou'd know, & intended to write me, but was immediately taken sick & found himself unable to do so. I have no doubt, at the arrival of Mr Alexander, that strong efforts were made upon several of our friends, and that it may diserve some special attention. The persons upon whom an attempt was probably made I think wou'd be Mr McKamy of Blount, who voted for Alexander—Mr Hembree of Roane—also—Mr Feazel of Greene and Dr Gregory of Monroe. I mention this because, I think it most likely, if Judge White resigns, from the strong interest manifested by Mr Alexander to have me beaten, that an effort will be made by the Federalists to detach some forty of the Democrats, upon a nomination of Judge Powel. That there is reason to believe that the thing has been freely talked of, and agreed upon by the Federalists, I have no doubt, from the fact that simultaneously with this anxiety & movement of Mr Alexander the Federal presses at Athens & Rogersville[4] have both opened their batteries upon me. That vile sheet at Rogersville attacked me vindictively, & was echoed to by the Patriot at Athens—and denounced my election in the bitterest terms. Our Presses have been *purposely restrained* from noticing them. If any thing is attempted it will be by a nomination of my worthy democratic friend Judge P. with the hope of carrying, in addition to the names I have mentioned, Sullivan & Hawkins [counties]. So it is important that I left with you Judge Powel's letter to me.[5] I may be mistaken, but *I do not believe* that there will be any resignation unless some hope is entertained that I cou'd be beaten by strategem—So deep and abiding is the hatred felt toward myself. I know that no man wou'd more utterly scorn such a favor at the hands of the Federalists than Judge P. Under these circumstances a previous meeting of our friends is important, to establish absolute unity, so that no attempt at strategy (on joint Ballot) by the Federalists can possibly succeed. It wou'd do no harm to apprize Reynolds, if yet in Nashville, of the *general facts*.

Your inaugural—& your Message have a powerful effect with the people—& the Federalists *feel them* with painful mortification. In this section of the State their efforts are to be *redoubled* (literally) in 1840—and surely—surely—our friends will not leave us as naked as we were in the last [. . . .][6] fight. The Hiwassee Rail Road is of vast importance—and if the State were to take some 150 to 200 thousand Dollars more of the stock now held by Individuals, the question wou'd be settled.

I handed the Inaugural presented by you to Mrs. Anderson,[7] with which she is much pleased, & returns you her acknowledgements for your polite attention. It will occupy a place in her parlor, as worthy of the occasion, and a descendant of a revolutionary ancestor.

The nomination of Vice President has given a severe shock to the *nerves* of the unhappy Federalists. From what I have been able to learn it will increase our strength largely, here, in the great struggle that approaches. And I entertain not the slightest doubt of the action of the Democratic Party of the Nation. But our Tennessee friends must do their duty fully and ably at Washington. I shall write upon this subject shortly to Cave Johnson. With my respects to your Lady & Miss Walker[8] & best wishes for yourself . . . .

A Anderson

ALS. DLC–JKP. Addressed to Nashville and marked "*Private and Confidential.*"

1. Enclosure not found; the Knoxville *Argus* of November 3, 1839, has not been found.

2. Ebenezer Alexander was the widower of Margaret White Alexander, daughter of Hugh L. White. In 1833 Alexander married Margaret Ann Melinda McClung, youngest daughter of Charles McClung.

3. Samuel Powel served as judge of the Superior Court, 1807–9, and as judge of the First Circuit Court, 1812–13, before winning election in 1815 to the U.S. House for one term. Four years later he again became judge of the First Circuit Court, a post he held until his death in 1841.

4. References are to the Athens *Hiwassee Patriot* and the Rogersville *East Tennessean*.

5. Letter not found.

6. Word obliterated by tear in manuscript.

7. In 1825 Anderson married Eliza Rosa Deaderick, daughter of David Deaderick.

8. Reference probably is to Jane Clarissa Walker, eldest daughter of James and Jane Maria Polk Walker.

FROM JOHN J. GARNER

Dear sir Mississippi Yalobusha Cty. Nov the 3, 1839

I Take my pen in hand to say something of the affares of your plantation in yalobusha county. I shold have written to you sooner had it not bin for a hurt that I received in the wriste from the fawl of a mule. We are enjoying the best of helth at present. Bothe my famaly and the negrows are entirly helthey and I think we are getting a long verry wel a saving the crop. I have seventy fore bales of cotton packed, fifty fore of them delivered to chisholm & minter, and I think anofe picked out to make something, about one hundred, foure hundred lbs bales, and I think if the weather continues good until chrismas I can have 125 bales of cotton packed and deliverd to troy. Your crop of cotton is turning out fare, better than I thought when I came here. I wil ceep your cotton halled off as fast as I pack it. I cant say how many bales you wil make, but I think the wrise[1] of 125 bales. I have stoped picking at this time for the purpose of gethering the corne. Mr Tranum and my Self thought perhaps it wold make fore hundred Barrels of corne. I have gethered a little part of it and think wil hardley gow that mutch. I can give you a purty corect noledge in my next letter.[2] We also made an estimate of the cuantaty of porke made. We estimated it at 4,500 lbs. We thought 6000 lbs wold be little anuf to serv the plase. There is a fine chance of shotes here for the next yere if they have any attention to them. The Boy charls you sent down last spring run a way some fore weks a gow withe out any cause what ever. I think he has gaun back to tennessee where his wife is. I am pesterd withe mareners conduct stroling over the contery and corect her. She goes to sqr Mcneel[3] for portection. With them exceptions we are dwoing wel. The negrows you last sent down apere to dwo very wel. The boy Allen apere to bee weakly at this time, he says caused from a mans stobing him before you bought him. I havent yet put my hogs up to fatten. Bin weighting for rain. Put them up they wold bee in a bed of dust. If it donte rain soon I must tri them up as they are to fatten withe corn entierly. I will conclude by saying your directions[4] shall bee punctialy attended two.

John J. Garner

ALS. DLC–JKP. Addressed to Nashville. Published in Bassett, *Plantation Overseer*, 128–29.

1. Misspelling of the colloquialism, "the rise of," meaning "in excess of."
2. See Garner to Polk, November 23, 1839.
3. Albert T. McNeal.
4. Polk's directions have not been found.

FROM JOHN CATRON

Frankfort 5th Nov. [1839][1]

My Dr Sir:

For the first time, Seen yr message of 22d. On Banks very well.

P. 12: Internal improvements. The Board of works shd. be three. A prest. at a Salary of 1500$ & two others at a per diem when engaged on the public business. The Ky. plan[2] is the best in America for our State. It was framed by Welsh[3] the principal Ingineer, unrestrained: In the Fedrl. court room, the acts will be found—inquire of the Marshal. Every road Shd. be laid out by an ingineer, and he let it out, & see every foot of its construction. The Board can very well regulate all this—& they Shd. judge, after *Survey*, of the propriety of all improvements. If information is needed, Sylvester Welsh—or James T. Morehead[4] can give it. W. is the principal engineer & M. the prest of the Board.

You know we said much last winter of running Col Johnson for Gov. of K. The coarse old man has adopted another mistress—a young hearty black wench—& the thing is openly admitted.[5] He cannot get the votes of his own party, as I am assured by Tom. Moore, Doctr. Sharpe,[6] &c. I have no doubt he is the weakest man of his party of any pretension in the State. He has no friends here, that I ever meet with, for the vice Presdcy—& is actually odious. Moore assures me, that Blair & Kendal[7] now feel the same way—& if a long statement & many considerations will induce Grundy to urge Blair, Tecumseh will be droppd. by that support, thus hel have none.

Old Judge Ousley, is anxious to run for Gov agst. honest Bob Lettcher.[8] O. was an old court Judge[9]—but is a fair, honest man—& feels outraged that L. was Jobbed up in his face. O. is apparently yet in his prime of manhood, a man of high standing in all respects, & prepared to bolt from the Clay dynasty. This I have known for years. He & I, are on intimate terms. He can beat L. largely if the democrats go for him—& is anxious they do so. This is their only chance, on the Cards—for they have no available man, & must chalk out new party lines—& for the first time in many years have the opportunity afforded them. Ousley despises an intriguer & will turn out, or not let in, any politician merely because he is useful. Should it come in your way, I think you may safely give a helping hand.

I hear nothing from the Legislature. No Ten. papers come here.

J. CATRON

ALS. DLC–JKP. Addressed to Nashville.

1. Year identified through content analysis.

2. In 1835 Kentucky created a Board of Internal Improvements, which

consisted of the governor and four other members. The board employed competent surveyors, determined priorities, coordinated rivers and roads, and subscribed the state's stock in those projects. The legislature initially appropriated one million dollars for internal improvements.

3. Sylvester Welsh (or Welch) is not further identified.

4. A lawyer who served in the state legislature, Morehead won the lieutenant governorship of Kentucky in 1832; he became governor on the death of John Breathitt in 1834. Morehead presided over the state Board of Internal Improvements from 1838 until 1841, when Whigs in the legislature sent him to the U.S. Senate. He served but one term.

5. Reference is to Johnson's mistress, who is not identified further.

6. Sharpe is not further identified.

7. Francis P. Blair and Amos Kendall. A journalist and member of Jackson's "Kitchen Cabinet," Blair established the Washington *Globe* and served as its chief editor from 1830 until 1845.

8. William Owsley and Robert P. Letcher. Owsley served on the Kentucky Court of Appeals from 1812 until 1828, when he resigned to practice law in Garrard County. In 1844 he won the gubernatorial election as a Whig over Democrat, William O. Butler.

9. In 1824 advocates of relief won control of the Kentucky legislature and abolished the Court of Appeals, which had declared stay and replevy laws to be unconstitutional impingements upon the sanctity of contract. The old Court further ruled that the legislature had no power to abolish the Court of Appeals. A new Court, created by the legislature, ignored the decrees of its predecessor; thus Kentucky had two Courts sitting until 1826, when the legislature confirmed the old Court justices in their places.

FROM JOHN BLAIR

Dr Sir: Jonesboro Novr 7th 1839

I write to announce to you the entertainment afforded us today by the whigs. The Hon John Bell took this place in his route to Washington, & in pursuance to a short notice, delivered himself in the Methodist Church in a speech of near two hours. You may guess the tenor. Fearing that you may not I will say he opened with the declaration that the pillars of this fair fabric of Government were in danger from the corruption of the party in power. He excepted from the general sweep only those of our party *who were inactive*. Took your address as the text, & denounced it & the Editorial corps, who had in convention pledged themselves to support its slanderous & ill founded charges upon him & others of the whig party. Gave to the Legislature in session the most unqualified abuse I ever heard, that is, the spoils party, & felicitated himself & friends that they had given to honest spectators an exhibition of their prosecutions of the *Spoils partys motto* that to the *victor* belongs the *spoils.*[1] Went largely into the old & oft refuted charge of prodigal *expenditure* & *stealth.* Held up *Van* as an original opponent to Gl. Jackson & comeing in to his support for the loaves & fishes. Gave Jackson a passing hit, & finally whitewashed Clay from every stain denying the bargain & all & wound up with the vindication of himself from all inconsistency &c. There were but few in the auditory. Judge Powel & myself went & heard the whole budget delivered, & we both concluded that it was far below what would have been expected of John Bell. Brownlow was in the pulpit with him, & cried *Amen* when Bell said Jacksons appointing Van to be second was equally as corrupt as Adams's appointment of Clay. I could myself have wished for the whole people of the County to have been present, & I think democracy would not have suffered, even, without an advocate. He has gone to Carter & will speak there tomorrow. I cannot learn whether he is the forerunner of Clay only, or is to take the field for Governor at the next election.

(Private) Whilst writing I will say something in reference to another subject, & one which may do much for *weal* or *woe* to our party interest in this end of the State. I mean that of following in the *whig footsteps* & electing a Senator in advance of his term.[2] Some of the knowing whigs say this is determined on, & they are chuckling at the idea. I have just been from home some two weeks in the Country below, & to Knoxville. I have heard much said amongst our friends—& the universal opinion is to Harnass White with instructions, & if he will not resign, make him submit to the disgrace of disobeying—or of undoing his former mischiefs. Should he serve still, let him do so & fill the office at the proper time & with such man as would then add to the strength of the party in E Tenne. We have much to loose in this quarter by running counter to our principles & much by disregarding public opinion in the selection to be made. I pity the man who would desire to go into the office now, for fear of the decrease of our strength in the next Legislature. Should that be the case, who would be willing to remain therein. Were this the time to go into the election, I would say consult public opinion in reference to the most suitable incumbent. I have heard no other names mentioned save Judge Powel and Gl Anderson. They are both my friends & what I say to you on this subject is solely to guide to the strengthening of our interests in future contests. I do not pretend to know the sentiments of the people below Knoxville, but I do say that the people above are more united on Judge Powel as against Gl A. than I had supposed was the case. His age long standing in the party, & strict integrity are urged *una voce,* but enough on this subject as I cannot suppose the Legislature will do that for which we so loudly complained ourselves. I was this day twitted by a leading whig that the report from Nashville was that, the democratic members had pronounced Judge Powel so old that he could neither *hear* nor *urinate,* that they had left my noble self out of view because that I was on the *fence,* & had determined to go into the election & appoint Gl A. This to me was news, for I had on no occasion authorised the use of my name in that connection, and had from the first on all occasions spoken of Judge Powel as possessing the strongest claims & being in my opinion, the person on whom popular sentiment would unite. Hence I said it was a *whig invention* to give dissatisfaction. I say to you, I want no office. I have had my fill, & but for timely abandonment would have given to my children the *felicity* of being exempt from the care of property. I have in the period since I left you in public life, accumulated what would content a reasonable desire, & now can at my election empl[o]y my time as comfort may suggest.

My kind complements to your good Lady . . . .

JOHN BLAIR

ALS. DLC–JKP. Addressed to Nashville.

1. Quotation attributed to William L. Marcy in his Senate speech supporting Martin Van Buren's nomination to be U.S. minister to Great Britain. When the Senate removed its injunction of secrecy on that debate, newspapers published Marcy's reconstruction of the speech, but failed to indicate its date of delivery. The Senate debated Van Buren's nomination in executive sessions held on January 13, 24, and 25, 1832; it removed the injunction of secrecy on January 26, 1832.

2. In October of 1837 the Whig majority in the Tennessee General Assembly elected Ephraim H. Foster to succeed Felix Grundy in the U.S. Senate for the term beginning March 4, 1839.

FROM HOPKINS L. TURNEY

Dear Sir Winchester Nov the 9th 1839

I this day received your second of the 6th of this month.[1] I am gratified to hear the result of the elections for state offices before the legislature.

My daughter is no better.[2] She is in a strange condition, a lingering away, & I fear will eventually die. It is truely painful for me to leave her and I shall do so with an expectation of never seeing her again. I can be of no service to her and whether absent or presant her fate will be the same. I have therefore determind to repair to my post and discharge my duty to my constituants trusting that a kind providence may restore her to helth that I may again see her on my return home. I leave in the morning for Washington. I will travil the southern route by Charleston, from thence to Fredericktown on the rail road. I will beat our friend Brown.

William E Venable[3] of this place [is one] who is as you know a thorough democrat died in the wool. He is a perfect Gentleman, an accomplished Schollar and highly tallanted a gentleman of temperate habits, and an unblemished morral character. He desires the appointment of visitor to west Point accadamy. If it is not inconsistant with your views and feelins to others I would regard it as a great favour if you would write a letter of recommendation for him.

Present my respects to Messers Laughlin, Finch, & Howard,[4] and, in fact to the Mountain district members and say to them— their people so far as I can Learn are much pleased with them thus far. It is late and I am busy packing up. So good night.

H L Turney

ALS. DLC–JKP. Addressed to Nashville.

1. Polk's letters not found.

2. See Hopkins L. Turney to Polk, October 29, 1839.

3. A Winchester lawyer and educator, Venable represented Franklin and Lincoln counties as a Democrat in the Tennessee Senate from 1847 until 1849.

4. Samuel H. Laughlin, Thomas H. Finch, and Thomas Howard. A Franklin County farmer and local office holder, Finch won election as a Democrat to the Tennessee House in 1839. Howard represented Franklin County as a Democrat in the Tennessee House from 1839 until 1843.

FROM JOHN S. YOUNG

McMinnville, Tennessee. November 9, 1839

Because of sickness, Young may not reach Nashville before the expiration of Lea's term as secretary of state. Tennessee's nomination of Polk for vice-president is meeting a warm response from Democrats everywhere. Young regrets that there will be difficulty in selecting a U.S. senator to replace Foster, who may be the Whig candidate for governor in 1841. Anderson probably will succeed to White's U.S. Senate seat without difficulty. Young urges support for a movement already under way in the Tennessee legislature to increase the salary of the secretary of state, for the income from that office will be insufficient to support his family even in "the plainest manner."

ALS. DLC–JKP. Addressed to Nashville, "Care of Gen. Armstrong."

FROM ALEXANDER O. ANDERSON

My Dear Sir Knoxville Novr. 10th 1839

Your esteemed favors of the 4 & 5th Inst[1] were recd. yesterday, & by the return mail, in reply, I give you the latest information here upon the subject of Judge White's probable course &c. &c. The Sayings in regard to this, as emanating at different times, doubtless from himself, resemble very much the confusion in the last scenes of a farce. At the news of defeat it was Said to be given out by himself, that if he were instructed he wou'd resign, & hoped the action of the legislature wou'd be early upon the subject, if at all, and save him the trouble of a trip to Washington. In Nashville it seems his friends were left in uncertainty. At the late nightly Orgies of the Party to do homage to Mr Bell he *is said* to have pledged himself to resign if instructed. The very latest Bulletin is that *Still* "a change has come o'er the Spirit of (his) dream,"[2] and the thing is now settled that he will leave *the last of next* week for Washington, and *will take his Seat,* and continue to hold it *up to the time* when the vote shall come up upon the Independent Try question,[3] and that he will then vacate.

If this be so, there are of course various motives involved, of a mixed personal & political character. In part, unquestionably, for the gratification of his pride, and also to have an opportunity of making a rabid speech for political effect—and in which he may discharge a poisoned Parthian Shaft at old friends, and his expected Successor[4]—or as he would more classically express it to "put a Spider in our broth"[5]—and this, too, I suppose is in obedience to Mr Bell. By this course, likewise, he designs to postpone the resignation beyond the reach of the Legislature, and to cast the appointment upon you, so that he may avoid the Shame of a Legislative rebuke, by being *immediately* superceded by Legislative election—hoping that a revolution might make it impracticable hereafter. It is not difficult, however, to circumvent this flimsey strategem, as the democratic members cou'd all unite, at a proper time, before they leave, in a letter to the Governor recommending the person to be appointed, in the event of his resignation. This shou'd by all means be attended to because it wou'd carry with it, at home and abroad, the *moral force of an election over his head.* In this I have no doubt the whole Party wou'd unite with the exception of one or two—and it wou'd be keenly felt by our opponents.

The project of White's going on &c. will be the one carried out. It has the last impress of Mr Bell's restless and contriving brain. In this view, it is important that Mr Benton shou'd be correctly advised, forthwith, either directly or thro' Mr Grundy, of what are the designs of White as far as ascertained. Mr Benton or Mr Wright will I presume move upon the Independent Try question, & this shou'd be done within the first three days of the Session, and pressed to a vote as early as practicable, *taking care that White is present,* for I have no hesitation in believing that *every artifice will be resorted to in order to evade responsibility, in the tempest-driven state of the Party.* An early—very early presentation, in the Senate of the U.S. of that question *is important,* supposing these results to be pregnant—So his successor might be there in the first weeks of January, which is exceedingly desirable to Tennessee for *Several considerations.* Besides, it might be possible that White wou'd be thus called on to vote upon the Independent Try by the 13th or 14th Decr., in which event, if the Legislature shou'd happen to sit until the 1st Jany. they wou'd be ready for his resignation.

I woud suggest the propriety of forwarding two sets of Instructions, one to this place, and the other to Washington. I understand he will probably vote for every thing else. The last resolution it is Said he disregards. That is to Say he will hold on as long as he can escape the Independent Try—and will only die in the very last "long agony." In the Senate they intend to protract the Debate on this for the purposes of Capital here. Such will be the requisition of Bell upon his Party then.

Judge White, I am told, in his Speech the other night (Mr Bell's Benefit)[6] alluded directly to me. In part, "Hinc illae lachrymae."[7]

I hope the democratic Party will remain firm and united & proceed without *let or hindrance* in the election of Mr Foster's Successor. *A mistake in this wou'd be a Serious injury.*

I am anxious that a move shou'd be made abroad for a National Convention, say about the 15th Feby., if that wou'd do. I shall write to C Johnson upon this subject, so as to reach him about the time of the meeting of Congress, & press it upon his attention. The Argus will take up the subject next Tuesday week, without any thing formal &c. &c., but so speaking of the question as most likely to invite Something, and the Union I shou'd think might Copy or notice &c. &c. I shall write to Harris—and also to Genl. Armstrong. The proposition of *the day &c will come from the East.*

The Federalists are making here a desperate struggle. Their m[ach]inery is *being brought to b*[*ear*][8] and we have *now no* democratic merchant in Town except Mr Roberts.

I saw Dr. Ramsay the other day, he informs me that Mr Holmes (of So. Ca. I think. M.C) approves your nomination, and is *decidedly for suppressing all other Southern claims.*

Dr. Ramsay left yesterday (Saturday) for Charleston. He will be at Charleston at the meeting of the R.R. Co. If you know of no person *certainly* going to whom *you may confide the Representation* of the State, it *is important to confer* it *on him* forthwith, and address to Charleston.[9] Cannon's Appointment was Mr Hugh McC[l]ung. Yours will supercede it.

Our Democratic friends ought to resolve all the Branches of the St. Bks. into two, one at Jackson, & one at Knoxville! It is *the only move* "Fortiter in re."[10]

My friendly regard to Mrs. Polk & Miss Walker.[11]

A ANDERSON

ALS. DLC–JKP. Addressed to Nashville and marked "*Private & Confidential.*"

1. Letters not found.
2. Quotation from Lord Byron's *The Dream.*
3. Reference is to the Independent Treasury bill; see J. G. M. Ramsey to Polk, August 20, 1839.
4. Anderson's reference is probably to himself.
5. Quotation not identified.
6. On November 4, 1839, Knoxville Whigs honored John Bell with a dinner; White spoke in reply to a toast.
7. Latin phrase for "Hence those tears."
8. A tear in the manuscript has obliterated parts of two words.
9. Reference is to the Louisville, Cincinnati and Charleston Railroad Company. See J. G. M. Ramsey to Polk, October 26, 1839.
10. Latin phrase for "Bravely in this circumstance."
11. Reference probably is to Jane Clarissa Walker.

FROM CAVE JOHNSON

Dear Sir, Philadelphia November 10th [1839][1]

We did not reach the city until this evening & did not call by Washington. I found our friend Thomas on the cars from Baltimore to this place & we have had much conversation. He informed me that you had written him and the subject of your letter.[2] He gave me no information as to the speakership further than you had heard before we left home except that he would be gratified to have the appointment. Jones, Pickens & Banks were the only other ones he heard spoke of.[3] Bell he thinks will not be run by the Whigs. He thinks the Whigs are looking to Dawson or Garland or Hopkins.[4] I intimated Something of the Vice Presidency, with a view of ascertaining his feelings. Tho. he spoke in the kindest & most courteous terms of you, he seemed at first rather disposed to stand by the present incumbent but in the course of conversation, he made many enquiries of your *views further than that* of the *Vice Presidency* & probable opposition to Col B.[5] These enquiries gave an opportunity of expressing to him in strong terms your friendship for Col B. & that I had no doubt you would favor his pretensions & I think entirely satisfied him on that subject. He then spoke of his opposition to you at first as Speaker & the causes of it & spoke in the harshest terms of J.B.[6] and that he could have given statements that would have placed him in a dilemma from which he could not easily have escaped & finally expressed himself entirely satisfied with your nomination & that it would be a much better one than Col. R.M.J.[7]

I dined with Gov. Shanon[8] of Ohio on the way. He spoke in the warmest terms of approbation of you & your course but did not seem inclined to commit himself in any way & I could not of course press. I regretted that I did not meet Genl. L., Doct. D.—or Allen or any democratic M.C. on my rout.[9]

I shall be ever grateful for the kind part you are taking in my behalf.[10]

My wife[11] desires me to make her apologies to Mrs. P. for not calling before she left. She was most of the time in Nashville in bed. Her health has been constantly improving. I shall write you from Washington where I shall be in a few days.

C. JOHNSON

[P.S.] Write me often—every thing.

ALS. DLC–JKP. Addressed to Nashville and marked "*Private.*" AE on the cover states that this letter was answered on November 21, 1839; Polk's reply has not been found.

1. Year identified through content analysis.

2. Polk's letter to Francis Thomas has not been found.

3. John W. Jones, Francis W. Pickens, and Linn Banks. Banks, a member of the Virginia House, 1812–38, served twenty successive years as Speaker of that body. His brief career as a Democratic congressman from Virginia lasted from 1838 until 1841.

4. William C. Dawson, Rice Garland, and George W. Hopkins. Formerly a member of the Georgia House, Dawson served as a States Rights Whig in the U.S. House, 1836–41, and in the U.S. Senate, 1849–55; he made an unsuccessful bid for the Georgia governorship in 1841. Garland, a Louisiana lawyer, won election to the U.S. House as a Whig in 1834 and served until 1840, when he resigned to become judge of the Supreme Court of Louisiana. Hopkins, a conservative Democrat from Virginia, served in the Virginia House, 1833–35,

1850–51, and 1859–61; sat in the U.S. House, 1835–47 and 1857–59; and served under Polk as chargé d'affaires to Portugal, 1847–49.

5. Thomas Hart Benton.

6. John Bell.

7. Richard Mentor Johnson.

8. Wilson Shannon, an Ohio lawyer, was prosecuting attorney for that state in 1835; governor, 1838–40 and 1842–44; U.S. minister to Mexico, 1844–45; Democratic congressman from Ohio, 1853–55; and governor of the Kansas Territory, 1855–56.

9. Daniel P. Leadbetter, Alexander Duncan, and William Allen. Leadbetter, a lawyer, received a quartermaster's commission in the Ohio militia in 1831 and served two terms as a Democrat in the U.S. House, 1837–41. Duncan, a Cincinnati physician, won terms in the Ohio House and Senate, 1828–34, and served in the U.S. House, 1837–41 and 1843–45. Democrats widely acclaimed Duncan's congressional speeches for their fearless and forceful attacks on Whig principles.

10. Reference probably is to Polk's support of Johnson's bid to be elected Speaker of the U.S. House. See Johnson to Polk, November 19 and 28, 1839.

11. Elizabeth Dortch, widow of Archibald Brunson, was Cave Johnson's childhood sweetheart. She married Johnson in 1838.

TO MARTIN VAN BUREN

Dear Sir Nashville Nov. 11th 1839

I have not written to you earlier from a knowledge of the fact, that until recently you were absent from Washington, and it was uncertain when a letter would reach you. I congratulate you most sincerely upon the result of the summer and fall elections. The leading measures of your administration have been fully sustained by the people whenever they have spoken. If New York and Mississippi have rendered similar verdicts, the opposition to the administration, will scarcely be able to make a shew of resistance in the great contest of 1840. In this state the contest through which we have passed, was by far the most violent we have ever had. Judge White forgetting the dignity of his station, as well as the former character of which he boasted, descended into the political arena, and became an active partizan and brawling electioneerer. All the leading men of the party in the State, of which he is the head followed his example. They were met at every point. In the course of the canvass, it was my fortune to encounter each and all of them in public discussion. Since the election the leaders and Federal presses, have been making a desperate effort to rally their scattered forces for another battle. We have however possession of the field, and with common prudence, will I do not doubt, be able to retain the ground we have won. Mr Bell I think apprehends, now that the State is lost to his party, that his Federal friends at the North may have no sufficient motive, to select him as their candidate for Speaker, and hence the extraordinary efforts which have been made since the election, to make the impression that the State is still debateable ground and may be reclaimed. It was a selfish motive of this sort I have no doubt, which induced the delegation of Committees from Nashville and Knoxville, to visit on Mr Clay and invite him to the State. They can have no rational hope of carrying the State for him. We will have an excited and heated contest, but I have no doubt of the result. The Democratic party of the State, are in my opinion many thousands stronger now, than they were at the late election.

Resolutions of instruction to our Senators in Congress, upon all the prominent measures of your administration, have passed the Senate of our Legislature, and are now before the House, where they will pass without doubt. In that event it has been ascertained *from a source to be relied on*, that *Foster* will *resign*, and that *White* will *obey*. The old Judge has at times spoken of his fondness for retirement, and talked of resigning his seat in the Senate. I never believed him sincere, and the pertinacity with which he now holds on to his place proves that I was right. Mr *Grundy* is the only man in the State, upon whom the Democratic members of our Legislature, can be united, as *Mr Foster's* successor. Governor Carroll is in wretched health and it will not do to think of *him*. Half a dozen others of nearly equal age and claims have been spoken of, and if *Mr Grundy*, was withdrawn, a heated and violent collision between them is inevitable. The result would be that the Federalists would cast their votes, upon the man least acceptable to the Democracy and elect him. Unfortunately we have in our ranks an individual who aspires to the Senate, who would be willing to take an election from our opponents, aided by a small minority of our party, and if elected in this manner, he would I have little doubt in a very short time abandon us.[1] All the aspirants except himself, we have reason to believe, are willing to yield to *Mr Grundy*, but no one of them to either of the others. With *Mr Grundy* as our candidate, we can succeed beyond any doubt. If he is withdrawn we will as certainly be defeated. *Mr Grundy's* election too would be the most popular that could be made in the State, because it would be simply re-instating him, in the place from which he was driven, by our opponents, whilst they were temporarily in the ascendancy. It would be the severest rebuke we could give them, & would be approved by the whole Democratic party of the State. Apprehending serious difficulties in selecting a successor to *Mr Foster*, in the event of his resignation I made an earnest appeal to Mr Grundy early after the political complexion of the Legislature was known to consent to return to the Senate. He does not desire to leave the Cabinet,[2] but I believe is satisfied, that it is his duty to the State, as well as to the party, not to decline the Senatorship, if it shall be voluntarily conferred upon him. It is now settled that the party will unite upon him and elect him. The resignation and the election will probably take place, as soon as the instructing resolutions shall pass the House, which will probably be in less than a week. You would I doubt not, be pleased to retain *Mr Grundy*, in your Cabinet, yet for the sake of attaining a greater good, I have no hesitation in believing, that you would consent to dispense with his services. His place in the Cabinet will be easily filled, whereas without the use of his name as the Democratic candidate for the Senate, in the State, the party is in immanent danger of being disorganized if not for a time dissolved. In the event of his election to the Senate (which I regard as now certain) you will I know duly appreciate the necessity which induced it.

It is a matter of great importance that the next Speaker of the House, should be a supporter of your administration, and from all I learn, my opinion is, that the only sure course is, to select the candidate from the South, upon whom, the State Rights Independent Treasury men from Georgia[3] would unite.

I saw Genl. Jackson a few days ago. He is in usual health and fine spirits, and continues to take as deep an interest in public affairs, as at any former period of his life. I look for him here to day.

Wishing you entire success in consummating the measures of your administration . . . .

JAMES K. POLK

ALS. DLC–MVB. Addressed to Washington City.

1. Reference is to A. O. P. Nicholson.
2. Grundy was U.S. attorney general.
3. See David Hubbard to Polk, October 23, 1839.

FROM ALEXANDER O. ANDERSON

My dear Sir (At home) Knoxville Novr. 13th 1839

In my last[1] I omitted to say any thing upon the subject of the election of the successor of Judge White for the next Term. I found the impression existing with several (when at Nashville) that it did not commence so early as March 1841. This of course was because they did not inquire into the matter. It is unnecessary to recapitulate at length (those things having often been mentioned in conversation between us) tho the present case is not exactly parallel with that of Mr Foster—that we are to have an ocassion of a new Presidential Term, and this being the Legislature which immediately precedes the vacancy, in this respect it wou'd be sustained by all the precedents. It shou'd certainly be borne in mind that the constitutionality of the question of election cannot be touched by any judicial tribunal, and that the Legislature, & the Senate of the United States, are the only competent authorities to pass upon it, & that both, the one in its original, and the other in its appellate Character, have not only acquiesced, but may be considered as having repeatedly settled this matter. Indeed, I never considered that there was any difficulty in this particular.

As to the policy of it, under existing circumstances, I have no doubt of it, for much must depend always, upon the *moral effect* which is to be produced by a measure. The *omission* to act will be sensibly felt as a triumph on the one Side, and of *apprehension* on the other, and this loss of the tone of confidence is almost the next thing to the loss of victory. *This is a part of the secret of all successes and defeats.* But will one democratic friend not feel excited when they perceive that the course which Judge White will probably take is actually to defeat the true representation of their sentiments in the Senate of the U.S.? He goes there (if his friends speak truly) with the express design of not obeying an essential part of the Instructions of the Legislature, but of resigning when the occasion occurs, & making a *special demonstration.* Will not our friends feel the propriety of rebukeing him by every legitimate measure in their power? I do not think, upon reflection, it wou'd be prudent to pass resolutions calling upon him to resign, unless an extremity had arisen *in the Senate* in which he had *refused to obey.* That wou'd present a new state of case, and wou'd merit and justify prompt and efficient action. If a proposition was made in the Legislature to go into the election the Federalists wou'd either have to vote for it, or place themselves in an attitude of direct contradiction to former professions. I cou'd add much more—but I am aware that you will survey the whole ground.

I have, heretofore, urged the necessity of giving us strength at this place, and insisted upon the Rail Road (Hiwassee) affair[2] as being one of the proper means for interference. The position of the Banking here, also, needs counteraction—and this can only be done by a part of the Bank means of the State being placed here. I know of no method which wou'd be so decidedly advantageous to the State, as resolving all the Branches of the St. Bk. into two, & placing one of them at this place, & the other at Jackson. As an example of our position here—Mr Gifford needed, on last Tuesday, $200, to go forward into his State Contract for printing. The So. West Rail Road Bank had some Georgia paper which it designed to discount on that day—and the President Dr. Ramsey, & the Cashier David A Deaderick, both told him they were favorable to his getting it. So he placed a note on Bank for $200—endorsed by Arthur R Crozier, & myself (no objection to the goodness of the paper) but the Directory refused to discount it, while they discounted other paper to the extent of their Georgia & Alabama funds—being several thousand, I suppose. (This Bank is still paying specie. It is said will do so—& has about 60 thousand Dollars in circulation.) This paper offered by Gifford you will observe, was wholly Democratic—and I have no doubt it was the true cause why it was rejected. The impression abroad being that no Democratic paper can go, at any time, will weaken the influence of our Party—for you may rely upon it, that Knoxville exerts more control over East Tennessee, than Nashville does over Middle Tennessee. The reasons are too obvious to require deteail &c &c. But the fact is so. It is important—very important, therefore, that something shou'd be done by the Legislature. An increase of Branches will not meet the sanction of that Body, but a resolution of them into two wou'd be a wise and popular measure—equally economical and advantageous—one at Knoxville, & one at Jackson. I hope this will be done.

Cannot the Legislature advance a third of the money (or so) upon the public printing. Gifford is here, and very much in need &c &c. of some such aid. The low price of the printing wou'd justify this &c.

Be pleased to present my kindly regards to Mrs. Polk—and Miss Walker if she be [. . .].[3] Let me hear from you.

A. ANDERSON

ALS. DLC–JKP. Addressed to Nashville and marked "*Private & Confidential.*"

1. See Anderson to Polk, November 10, 1839.
2. See Anderson to Polk, December 4, 1839.
3. A tear in the manuscript has obliterated one word.

FROM JOEL R. POINSETT

Washington City. November 14, 1839

Poinsett states that a recent War Department draft on Tennessee funds in the Girard Bank of Philadelphia has been protested. The draft, amounting to $6,250, was for payment in specie of interest due in July 1839 on $250,000 in Tennessee state bonds held by the bank in trust for the Cherokee Indians. Poinsett claims that the state's agent must be instructed to pay this and future interest installments in specie or its equivalent.[1]

ALS. T–Governor's Papers. Copy in DNA–RG 107, Office of the Secretary of War, Letters Sent, Vol. XXI, pp. 204–5.

1. On November 26, 1839, Polk answered that the state's agent, the Union Bank of Tennessee, had deposited the amount of the interest payment in June last. Since that time the Union Bank has suspended specie payments; however, liability for the current exchange differential belongs to the agents of the general government, for it was they, not the state's agent, that failed to call for the funds when they were due last July 1. ALS, draft. T–Governor's Papers.

FROM ALEXANDER O. ANDERSON

My Dear Sir Knoxville Novr. 16th 1839

Within a day or two Mr Lyon, the late opponent of Mr. Reynolds for the office of District Atto., has returned to Knoxville, and I think it proper to apprize you of what he has said, as I learn thro' Arthur R. Crozier, to some of his confidential Whig friends, which leaves no doubt of the fact heretofore suggested to you of the design of the Whigs to elect a *democratic* Candidate of their own choosing, in the event of Judge White's resignation. He informs them (and one of them an intimate friend of Mr Crozier communicated it) that the matter was *sittled* in relation to the successor of Judge White, if one had to be elected, and that I wou'd be defeated—That the Whig Party wou'd unite with a few of the democrats, and take up Judge Powel or Mr Blair, either, who cou'd obtain the greatest number of democratic Votes. He speaks of it positively, & I have no doubt that a regularly planned movement is in existence upon the subject, of which the indications from Mr Alexander, to Dr Young were the *primary evidences of the plot.*[1] They seem to be resolved to dictate by strategem to the Democratic Party, and have further resolved, that come what will, their proscription of me shall be Successful & complete. Rumours are rife here of their deadly and unquenchable hatred toward me—and tho' perfectly Satisfied of the stern resistance with which their serpentine wiles will be met by the great body of our friends, I think it important you shou'd be advised, and you may rely upon it this is not mere conjecture. Having been long accustomed to be pursued by their malice I am not at all taken by surprise, even at the audacity of their present project. It is conjectured from what has transpired that they rely certainly upon the aid of Mr Gillespie, Mr McKamy, Doctor Gregory, & Mr Hembree, & count several others who they believe will be brought into the measure—or rather already spoken of as *being settled.*

You have Judge Powel's letter to me,[2] which I think it wou'd be well to confide to Col Wheeler, with the suggestion to shew it to Johnson of Greene, Martin of Washington, Cross of Sullivan, &c &c & as far to any others as may be absolutely necessary—But of all this you being sole judge.

I regret extremely to be compelled to write of any thing with which my name is connected, but I deem it due to our Party that you shou'd know the facts, which at this point indicate clearly the movements of our enemies.

Mr Crozier informs me that he will write by this mail to Genl. Armstrong of the facts &c &c, & presumes you can see the letter &c. Arthur is generally very laconic in his correspondence, but estimates the importance of this Federal move, and believes it necessary that our friends shou'd be upon their guard. In the event of any election of a successor to Judge White the Democratic Party will of course take the prudent step of a previous Convention.[3] In that case I infer Mr Fain will be prepared to settle the matter as to Judge Powel.

Since writing to you last I am induced from much we hear, to believe that it is all pretense as to Judge White's resignation— as some of his *close* friends here now give it out that he *will not resign.* And altho' I cannot see how he will avoid it, yet *so desperate, literally, have the Party become here* that they are prepared to do any thing, and Judge White is not *less Desperate.* Their present condition of feeling is more *akin to frenzy* than any thing else.

An Article was prepared for next Tuesday's Argus on the Vice Presidency, but Eastman left here on last Monday to meet his wife, & Gifford unexpectedly in the middle of the week on some urgent business to Jonesboro', and it was thought not advisable to confide the manuscript to the office in their absence, as it was by no means desirable that the printers shou'd know from whence the Editorial came. Eastman will be back on Tuesday or Wednesday, so that it will have to lay over until Tuesday week.[4] The Federalists will be touched a little, however, in the Argus of next Tuesday about their law of office &c.

It is very important that we shou'd have Laughlin's speech[5] *in extenso,* and any others which it may be found important—such as Mr Coe's &c.[6] Indeed it is to be desired that our side cou'd be generally reported in the current Party debates, from day to day. The Federal papers are endeavoring to make the most of all their members say. Be pleased to present my kind regards to Mrs Polk & Miss Walker. (Write me.)

A Anderson

ALS. DLC–JKP. Addressed to Nashville and marked "*Private & Confidential.*"

1. See Anderson to Polk, November 3, 1839.

2. Letter not found.

3. Anderson probably used the term "Convention" for the word "caucus."

4. No 1839 issues of the Knoxville *Argus* are extant.

5. On October 16, 1839, two days after Polk's inaugural ceremony, Samuel H. Laughlin introduced in the Tennessee legislature a resolution endorsing Martin Van Buren's reelection and recommending Polk's nomination for the vice-presidency.

6. On October 25, 1839, Levin H. Coe introduced "instructing resolutions" in the Tennessee Senate.

FROM EDWARD S. DWIGHT[1]

New Haven, Connecticut. November 18, 1839

As secretary of Yale College's Class of 1838, Dwight wishes to be advised of the circumstances of the death of Samuel W. Polk. Dwight requests that Polk write a letter of information or forward a newspaper obituary[2] of his brother's death.

ALS. DLC–JKP. Addressed to Columbia.

1. Dwight is not further identified.

2. Copy of a six-paragraph obituary, clipped from an unidentified Columbia newspaper, is filed with this letter.

FROM JOHN CATRON

Dr Sir: Louisville, Nov. 19th [1839][1]

By this mornings Nashville papers, it appears the instructions have passd.—and Mr Foster resigned—and Judge White's letter published.[2] The Judge said at Leabanon on his return—if God spared him hed. go to Washington the next session of Congress—but this letter will force him out. The thing now is, to keep the state to the admn.—& the means pursuing for the Vice Presdy will secure it—and hardly anything else will keep down a violent scramble. Clay & Talmadge will be run on the Whig ticket. If N.Y. had gone for the adm. Clay wd. have given way to Harrison, Scott, &c.—& probably the old game of two Elect one wd. have been played.[3] This is now assuredly ended. Col Johnson cannot get, out of the 100.000 votes of Ky., 20.000 for Gov. Albert G. Hawes[4] is greatly stronger, & no man that could be seriously thought of so weak: an admitted fact by the Col's *friends*—but *not* his foes; for they miss him, & expect in the end to use him—*sayeth Tom Moore.*

Got a letter fr. Allen of Ohio. Says he wrote you—and that at Washington shortly after the first Wednesday of Decr news comes to hand, the vice P. candidate on our side will be settled & agreed upon.[5]

Mrs. C.[6] informs Grundy will be the Senator. Nothing else will answer. For E.T. I have supposed your Judgt correct—& lent it with our frnds what of sanction my approbation woud give. Still Powel wd. be stronger in E.T. White will sink in two years. Nothing but the possn. of power can keep to him those who belong to the old John Wms party[7] real friends White has very few—& commands through the fears of the undermen. Foster is the dangerous electioneerer—and the only formidable man—of whom you must dispose in some shape.

I sat down to say, that James T. Morehead of Frankfort Ky, the Presdt. of the Board of internal improvements for Ky, desires a correspondence in reference to slacking Cumberland river—Ky owning it above & below us. I promised to write to you, & did so, but destroyed the letter fearing I might embarrass you. It may not suit your views—but, it may be that a resolution instructing the Executive to correspond &c might be passd.—of course with or through the Gov. of Ky.[8] I thought of writing to Mr. Bass but have not. It might embarrass you.

Our frd McKinley's daughter is to be married to night to Mr Churchill, the Loco member of assembly for this city.[9] His mother is a Pope—& the match decidedly good—& McKinley well pleased. I go north tomorrow.

The Cumberland can be, & in the end must be slacked. It is easily done—& the expense will not exceed that of a good Turnpike per mile. The Green river does not cost so much. Could you get the Journals of Ky of either House for the last three years, youd. learn all about it. But an Engineer, & a good one, must be employed even to examine & report. Welch[10] is one of *us*—fr. Tenn. the principal Engineer of Ky. & his frds. Steely or Snider—or Swamore, residant Eng. on the Green river, wd. answer.[11] Either [Welsh or Swamore] will be sent us if asked. The Board—that is, Morehead, can order it. They are very anxious.

J. CATRON

ALS. DLC–JKP. Addressed to Nashville.

1. Year identified through content analysis.

2. On November 14, 1839, the Tennessee legislature passed instructing resolutions, and Senator Ephraim Foster resigned on the following day. The text of his lengthy letter of resignation appeared in the Nashville *Republican Banner* on November 18, 1839. In a letter of September 5, 1839, to State Representative Solomon D. Jacobs, Senator Hugh L. White assented to the general policy of the legislature's right to "instruct" its federal senators. The

Nashville Whig of November 18, 1839, carried the text of White's letter to Jacobs.

3. Possible reference to the alleged "Corrupt Bargain" of 1825 in which John Q. Adams and Henry Clay combined to defeat Andrew Jackson's bid for the presidency.

4. A Kentucky farmer, Hawes won three terms in the U.S. House as a Jacksonian democrat and served from 1831 until 1837.

5. See William Allen to Polk, October 20, 1839. The Whig National Convention was scheduled to meet in Harrisburg, Pennsylvania, on Wednesday, December 4, 1839.

6. Matilda Childress Catron.

7. Identified as a leader of the "old Republicans" in Tennessee, John Williams had opposed that wing of the Republican party led by William Blount and John Overton; in 1824 Williams had supported William H. Crawford for the presidency.

8. Charles A. Wickliffe.

9. John McKinley and Alexander P. Churchill. McKinley began his legal career in Louisville, Kentucky; moved to Huntsville, Alabama; served several terms in the Alabama legislature, won a seat in the U.S. Senate, 1826–31; and sat for one term in the U.S. House, 1833–35. In 1837 Van Buren appointed McKinley to the U.S. Supreme Court; he resided in Louisville during his tenure on the Court. His daughter is not identified further. Churchill represented Jefferson County in the Kentucky House in 1839 and in 1850; probably he was the son of Henry and Penelope Pope Churchill.

10. Sylvester Welsh (or Welch).

11. Steely, Snider, and Swamore are not identified further.

FROM CAVE JOHNSON

Dear Sir, Washington Nov 19th [1839][1]

I recd two letters of yours on yesterday—the Pension Claim will be strictly attended to.[2] I have seen Mr. Grundy & also Mr. Blair & have had a good deal of conversation with each. Mr. G. thinks you have better prospects than any other man & Mr. B thinks that R.M.J.[3] ought not again to run & that he will be satisfied with any one the Democratic party may select but avoided an expression of opinion as to the most suitable. Both think we ought to have a National convention in the Spring, but that we had better not move on the subject until after the Harrisburgh Convention[4] & in the meantime we will consider the best mode of putting the ball in motion. B. thinks the Democratic members of C. had best have a meeting & recomend. We shall certainly have one in the Spring. I think Mr. G said that a member of the Cabinet would be in your way but I am somewhat uncertain as to the extent of the remark & in my next will explain it more fully.[5] Some effort is making in Penn. in behalf of Dallas[6] but I take it for granted we shall have a W. or S. Western man. If you could be nominated in Alabama & Mississippi & Arkansas, it [would] make you certain I think.

There seems nothing certain as to the speakership among our friends here. Mr G was of opinion that Mr Thomas or Jones would be the man if we had strength enough & that it would be more prudent for me to make no effort. He mentioned having recd your letter on the subject.[7] I never thought I had any chance, so am not disappointed. I shall be very unwilling to give a vote to P. or L.[8] I have heard such violent denunciations from that quarter that I don't see how we can consent to place either at our head. They should serve longer in the ranks. There is but one alternative that would make me vote for either—there being no other man with whom we could beat B—l.[9] I have no patience with the Hotspurs of the House, no honors to bestow on them. I hope our friends in the Legislature will be [sic] rebuke the whigs by giving a united vote for restoring Mr G to the Senate & shall so write some of my friends who spoke of my name tho I do not think Foster will resign & the old Judge[10] would like any pretence to avoid it. I heard today that Jesse Bledsoe as Senator, sent his resignation to the Gov. of Ky in a drunken frolic & the Gov. received it [but] took no steps whatever in relation to it.[11] After he became sober he wished to recall it & the Senate decided that it was a resignation & could never be recalled. I will search the precedents and send it to Coe. I am also decidedly of opinion if White does not resign a successor should be elected, placing it upon the precedent set last session. Garland & Clark are candidates for Clerkship.[12] Follensby[13] will be opposed but it is not yet certain by whom. Dorsey[14] will not probably be. The Globe will be opposed by the Metropolitan, who will probably play the same game that Allen has done.[15] The Madisonian was about expiring but G & Seaton[16] made an arrangement to keep it up until the meeting of Congress hoping they might again use the name successfully but it seems now probable, that the Metropolitan will be taken in its place.

I have taken lodgings temporarily at DeShaels,[17] on C Street near 4 & shall wait upon Brown & Watterson & try & make a mess that will be agreeable. We are anxiously expecting them.

We had a pleasant trip except two cold bitter days in the Mountains and excepting also that our servant was seduced from us in Philadelphia and we have heard nothing of him since & not likely to do so.

The Bonds given for the purchase of the Union[18] should be signed by five. Such was the understanding. I ought not to loose the other money & should have spoken on the subject when last in Nashville but had not then an opportunity.

I shall write you again soon giving you all the information I get tho you know I do not mix much with the newsmongers & I hope you will have leisure to let me know all the movements at Nashville. I am content with whatever may fall to my share, where the interests of our party is best served but I should feel mortified if some of the trimmers & shuff[l]ers should be elevated to high places to the exclusion of those who have fought the battle through from the beginning. I expected Mr. N.[19] would look to the whigs from the beginning & said so to some of my friends. Should he be run by them agt. G. it is probable he would be understood by our friends.

Mr. G. desires me to say that he will write you soon but for reasons satisfactory to him & which I think good, he will be compelled to delay a short time & in the mean time I will give you occasionally the little I know or learn.

I have been once with Benton but had no opportunity of broaching the subject. I also saw Lynn[20] & mentioned the subject. He thought well of it but carefully avoided a commitment. Lewis Williams has been here & is now on a visit to Genl Mercer.[21] Rumor says th[e] Genl has been appointed Cashier of some Bank & will resign. I also met Abbot Lawrence[22] who took his seat & returned home. It is almost certain that Morton[23] is elected Gov of Massachusetts & a majority of the Legislature with us & we have lost Michigan—a bad trade for us & disheartening one to Clay. It is by no means certain that Clay will get any state except Ky.

C. Johnson

ALS. DLC–JKP. Addressed to Nashville and marked "*Private.*" AE on the cover states that this letter was answered on November 28, 1839; Polk's reply has not been found.

1. Year identified through content analysis.
2. Letters not found; pension claim not identified.
3. Richard Mentor Johnson.
4. Reference is to the Whig National Convention, which was scheduled to meet in Harrisburg, Pennsylvania, on December 4, 1839.
5. See Cave Johnson to Polk, November 28, 1839.
6. A Philadelphia lawyer and Democrat, George M. Dallas served as mayor of Philadelphia, 1829; U.S. senator, 1831–33; minister to Russia, 1837–39; vice-president under Polk, 1845–49; and minister to Great Britain, 1856–61.
7. Letter not found.
8. Francis W. Pickens and Dixon H. Lewis.
9. John Bell.
10. Hugh Lawson White.
11. A lawyer, Bledsoe served in both houses of the Kentucky legislature

and as secretary of state in that commonwealth. He served in the U.S. Senate from March 4, 1813, until his resignation on December 24, 1814. Later he was a circuit court judge in Lexington and a professor of law at Transylvania University. Isaac Shelby was governor of Kentucky at the time of Bledsoe's resignation from the U.S. Senate.

12. Hugh A. Garland and Matthew St. Clair Clarke. A Pennsylvanian, Clarke served as clerk of the U.S. House from 1822 until 1833 and again in 1841. In 1838 and 1839, however, Clarke was defeated for the position by Garland of Virginia.

13. Joseph Follansbee was doorkeeper.

14. Roderick Dorsey was sergeant at arms.

15. The Washington *Globe*, founded in 1830 and edited by Francis P. Blair, supported the administration. The *Metropolitan* did not receive the printing contract for the U.S. House. Thomas Allen edited and published the *Madisonian*, which had been established in 1837. Initially Allen posed as a friend of the administration, but he supported Harrison in 1840.

16. Joseph Gales and William Seaton, editors of the Washington *National Intelligencer*.

17. Dashiell's boarding house in Washington.

18. *Nashville Union*.

19. A. O. P. Nicholson.

20. Lewis Fields Linn, a physician and veteran of the War of 1812, served in the Missouri Senate in 1827 and in the U.S. Senate, 1833–43.

21. Charles Fenton Mercer, a lawyer, served in the Virginia House, 1810–17, and fought in the War of 1812, rising to the rank of brigadier general. He won election to the U.S. House in 1817 and served continuously until his resignation on December 26, 1839. At various times he served as president of the Chesapeake & Ohio Canal Company, vice-president of the Virginia Colonization Society, and vice-president of the National Society of Agriculture.

22. Abbott Lawrence, a Boston importer and merchant, served as a Whig in the U.S. House, 1835–37 and 1839–40. Later he declined a cabinet position in the Taylor administration, but served as minister to Great Britain, 1849–52.

23. Marcus Morton, a lawyer, served in Congress as a Democrat from Massachusetts, 1817–21; was a judge of the state Supreme Court, 1825–40; served as governor, 1840–44; and was appointed by Polk to be collector of customs in Boston, where he served from 1845 until 1849.

FROM GEORGE F. STROTHER[1]

St. Louis, Missouri. November 20, 1839

Expressing pleasure that the Tennessee legislature has nominated Polk for the vice-presidency,[2] Strother offers his support. He thinks Polk can carry Missouri, but declines to pledge support for Van Buren.

ALS. DLC–JKP. Addressed to Nashville.

1. George French Strother, a lawyer and Democrat, served both in the Virginia House, 1806–9, and in the U.S. House, 1817–20.

2. On October 17, 1839, the Tennessee Senate adopted a resolution endorsing Van Buren for president of the United States and Polk for vice-president. The Tennessee House concurred in the resolution shortly thereafter.

FROM ALEXANDER O. ANDERSON

Home Near Knoxville
Friday morning Novr. 22d 1839

My Dear Sir,

I have the pleasure to acknowledge the receipt on Yesterday of your letters of the 14th & 17th Inst.[1]

Judge White accompanied (it is said by his family) left last week for Washington. He will meet the Instructions there. His Jacobs letter[2] will be upon him another Foster Affair,[3] and as badly recd. by his party, if it is as definite as I suppose. Without this I think it doubtful what he wou'd have done. One of his leading friends two days ago said that he wou'd obey the Instructions as to the Independent Treasury, but not as to the support of the Administration. It wou'd seem as if his letter was intended as an Appeal. But it is only an additional proof of the infatuation & desperation to which their leading men are subject.

Notwithstanding his letter his friends, the Party Clique here, are resolving and cancelling, & re-resolving—in the very midst of contradictions—and amongst which the article sent forth in their last paper at Knoxville, of this week, signed Alpha, is one of the significant signs.[4] It is intended as a feeler—and proposes to conteract the Legislative action by primary assemblies of the people. This I am well advised has been one of the embryo projects of their *Central Committee* here, at least of the confidential men of that Body. If this is attempted the Leaders of the Democracy must move in solid phalanx, & simultaneously in every part of the state, as well in its fragment Counties as in the more solid majorities. You may rely on it that a final effort is *now designed to be made* by the central power here to bring their partizans into the field by public meetings, in order to sustain Judge White, and under this whole movement to make an impression at home and abroad, that the Legislature of Tennessee have acted against public opinion, and that the recent political revolution was accidential. The *consent* of all parts of the Federal Host has not yet, as I think, been obtained to this project, from what I hear, yet withheld under motives of fear & prudence. It is probable, also, their men abroad will not give in to it, & that the thing will pass off—but the Central power here will press it. If this attempt at breaking our centre and out-flanking us at the same time, be made the whole democracy must act, & not merely talk—& must speak as with one voice. You may rest assured if they believe this project can carry with the people, the Federal power here will commence the movement at some point in East Tennessee. The first sign of this will be hailed by White as the pretence of his justification to hold on, & *respectfully wait on the popular voice*!!!! But I believe the project will fail.

If you think upon White's shewing *symptoms of resignation* at the approach of the Independent Treasury, in the Senate U.S., and the Legislature be then in Session, that thereupon it wou'd be advisable for me to go to Nashville immediately, in answer to this, give me your opinion, & I will conform to it.

I rejoice to hear of the victory in Missipi. Your letter brought me the first news. It is glorious. Can the members of Congress be in Washington in time? Will the suggestion of an express to convey the intelligence, and the commissions &c have been adopted there by our friends?

I regret deeply to hear the news from New York, & fear we have lost the State. It was this news which first suggested to the Federal Whig Central Committee here the project of Primary Assemblies to sustain White in the Senate. The result in New York does not alarm me (if it be true that we are beaten for both Branches of the Legt.). The Democracy has long shewn that it is composed of men whom difficulties animate and ill-fortune does not shock. We must all stand by our arms with a more resolved purpose.

In this state of things the question of the Vice Presidency, with the proper zeal & energy, amongst friends will be settled. Tennessee is the fifth state in the Union and it will never do, as all will at once perceive to hazard any thing in 1840 under *weak & ominous auspices*. In these times, every true Democrat will perceive that the prominent positions, such especially as the Vice Presidency, shou'd be filled by men of talent & high moral worth. Every thing which can give us an accession of mental & moral force we must "grapple to us with hooks of steel."[5] The end is that all other pretensions will be made to give way. I fear however it will hardly be practicable to obtain a Convention by Feby.—tho' I am for the earliest day—but I do not believe we will have any thing to lose even if it shou'd be later. The Argus will resume the subject. Eastman has just returned.

Every friend shou'd now act with redoubled vigor, & press his views wherever they can be brought to bear at home or abroad—*if he is for our success in 1840*!!!

Do not move in the Affair of Electors until the very last—last thing. One for each District—and one for the East and one for the West.

A Anderson

ALS. DLC–JKP. Addressed to Nashville and marked "Private & Confidential."

1. Letters not found.
2. See John Catron to Polk, November 19, 1839.
3. See John Catron to Polk, August 27, 1839.
4. The "Alpha article" probably appeared in the Knoxville *Register*, of which there are no extant issues for 1839.
5. Paraphrase of "Grapple them to thy soul with hoops of steel," from Shakespeare, *Hamlet*, act 1, scene 3.

FROM HENRY HORN[1]

My Dear Sir Philadelphia 22d Novem 1839

I have received and read with peculiar pleasure your inaugural address which you were so kind as to send me. So many of my old friends upon whose firmness and integrity I had set a high value within the last few years have changed their political creed that it is truly gratifying to me to find that I have not been mistaken in the exalted opinion I have always entertained of the character of one of them at least, who amidst all the jarring elements of party strife, the seductive arts of an insidious faction and the formidable array of state authority against him has not only maintained his own integrity but has overcome his powerful adversaries and added another state to the democratic phalanx of the union. It is indeed a source of sincere pleasure to me to recur to the first moments of my acquaintance with that distinguished individual and to have from that time to the present the perfect coincidence of sentiment and feeling which has always subsisted between us in relation to the cardinal principles upon which our republican system of government is based and the measures necessary to sustain and carry out those principles.

I rejoice that the doctrine of strict construction of the powers granted by the states to the general government openly and freely promulgated by my friend has resulted in his triumphant election by the enlightened yeomanry to the gubernatorial chair of Tennessee. It inspires me with a hope that a new era is about to open upon us and that the vile uses which have been made of our federal constitution by artful and designing demagogues will be effectually repudiated by the reversal of that system of pure democracy so justly cherished by our early patriarchs as the bulwark of our liberties and the rock of our safety.

To the loose and latitudinous constructions which have been given to the works of our revolutionary sages by modern politicians may justly be ascribed many of the evils with which we have been afflicted and the most pernicious and dangerous of these evils I believe to be the banking system. It has grown up among us to an extent that is truly alarming, boldly & insolently defying legislative enactments and threatening to trample under foot the rights of the people. These institutions must be curbed and curtailed of their power or the people must submit to an aristocracy of the most oppressive and dangerous character. Pennsylvania will never do it nor will Tennessee or I have much mistaken the character of her people—but more especially of her chief magistrate whom they have so recently and so triumphantly elected to put down the monied aristocracy. We may now I think safely felicitate ourselves upon our escape from the dangers of a national bank and upon the prospect of the establishment of an independent treasury system that shall secure the funds of the nation against the fluctuations and derangements to which they have recently been subjected by the profligacy and cupidity of state corporations. The people at large however in the respective states are still left at the mercy of these corporations who raise or depress the value of every species of property as their interests or avarice may dictate by vitiating the currency with a flood of paper which they have neither the will nor the ability to redeem when payment is demanded. Something effectual should be done to guard the people against these outrages in future. The remedy is doubtless in the hands of the states and that state which shall be a pioneer in the reform of the system and the restoration of a sound currency upon a broad metalic basis will earn the lasting gratitude of her sisters of the union, and the executive who shall be instrumental in effecting it will establish for himself the character of a public benefactor.

As a Pennsylvanian I feel anxious of course that our own state should attain the honor and distinction to which I have refered but should Tennessee take the lead of her I shall nevertheless be content consoling myself with the reflection that the good work is in good hands and that another state to which we are strongly allied in principle and in feeling will preceed us but a short time in the patriotic measure of reform. Nor shall I regret that the honor of recommending it shall have devolved upon the executive of that state since in his personal welfare and public renown I shall always feel a deep and lively interest.

HENRY HORN

ALS. DLC–JKP. Addressed to Nashville.

1. A Philadelphia hardware merchant and friend of Polk, Horn served as a Democrat in the U.S. House for one term, 1831–33.

FROM JOHN J. GARNER

Dear sir Missippi Yalobusha Cty Nov the 23, 1839

After my respects to you I wil inform you that we are all wel at presant bothe my famaly and the negrows. Phil got his hand caught in the gin a few days after I wrote to you, cut his hand very bad, but has got very near wel. I have not yet herd any thing of Charles. I have cept a lookout for him and wil continue so to dwo. The boy Allen has aperently not bin able for hard servis sence he has bin here and I believe caused from the wond which he received in the side before he came here. Mr Walker to look at him a few days a gow and he thought with my self that it wold not dwo to put him to hard work yet.[1]

I have getherd the crop of corn and agreable to the waggon I hald the corn in there is three hundred and fifty barrels of corn. Fel shorter than my self and Mr Tranum estimated. I have packed 102 bales of cotton them weighing 41,993 lbs, making 410 lbs. and somthing over to the bale, and I think there wil bee thirty bales more, twenty five at least. N.B. I think if I have luck I shal make 4500 or 5000 lbs of pork. I have forty hogs fatning and a plenty of yong hogs for the next year. I have agred with Sqr Mcneal for the next year for this place and I shold like for you to bee at your plantation as soon as convenient after chrismas as I wold like to have your advise on sertin things. Your friends here speek of this being a sickly place from some cause and speek of its beeing proper to moove the cabins to some other point convenient to the farm. I have omited stating how many bales delivered to Troy, 84 of them deliverd and three days more I will deliver the others.

JOHN J. GARNER

ALS. DLC–JKP. Addressed to Nashville. AE on the cover states that this letter was answered on December 5, 1839; Polk's reply has not been found. Published in Bassett, *Plantation Overseer*, 129–30.

1. For earlier reports to Polk on the slaves, Charles and Allen, see John J. Garner to Polk, November 3, 1839.

FROM JOSHUA L. MARTIN

My dear Sir Tuskaloosa Nov 26th 1839

I had the pleasure some days ago to receive your esteemed letter of the 13th inst.[1] A day or two previously I was honored by our friend Hon S. H. Laughlin with a communication upon the subject of my recent letter to you.[2] I feel much complimented by the notice thus taken of my crude suggestions, for they are intended simply to draw your attention to the points mentioned. I consider them, to *yourself* particularly, worthy of mature reflection.

My letter was written in great haste, & may contain much more than I, either intended to say, or ought to have said. I am gratified however to find that the spirit in which they went forth is understood by you, & as to the ballance, you will readily understand that, the whole matter was submitted to your own good judgment, & that of your better informed friends.

I did not intend to be understood as doubting for one moment, that your name would give strength to the Van Buren ticket. On the contrary I am satisfied that no name could give it more strength, & I greatly doubt whether any other would at this time give it so much. This was not the point which I intended to make. I considered that you had done enough, & I might say, suffered enough for the party, to entitle you not only to repose, but to the largest expectations at their hands & the best facilities to attain them. And I *did* think, & with all proper deference, still think that, the position which your friends are desirous you should occupy, is not the best to secure the ultimate object. I was, & still am desirous to see your elevation, & under that feeling as your friend, made the suggestions which I did. At one time I desired to see your name before the American people for V.P. at the next election, & so stated to his Honr. Justice Catron. I must candidly say to you that, at that time, I did not consider your destiny as high in this Republic as I now do. This will account for the change in my opinion.

Our friend Mr. Laughlin puts your nomination on the ground of necessity to some extent, to the triumph of the party in the next Presidential election. If I could feel the slightest fear upon that subject, I should agree with him that your name would secure that object, & that it might be proper to make the requisition of you; but a doubt has not crossed my mind upon that subject since the whigs brought Mr. Clay forward, or since his frowardness drove Harrison from the track. I think indeed there was no danger in either. Mr. C. however put the matter beyond contingency. I may be of the sanguine order, & so much so, as to impare the influence of my judgt. feeble at best, but I must be grossly mistaken in the signs of the times if there is even a cloud over any point of our political horison. *Principle is triumphant.*

I claim no credit for my continued confidence in your success here. However, I was alone upon that subject. I knew the men, & the materials upon which they were to opperate, & in this had the advantage of others. In that however, upon the subject of our *present struggle,* I am not eaqual in information, but certainly I know enough not to be mistaken, when every runner from our battle fields rends the air with the cry, *victory*, *victory*. Tennessee, N. York, Mississippi. The enemy routed horse foot & dragoons. I might have added other states, but to you of course unnecessary. I am satisfied that none of our friends will, *at this date* here of admit for one moment that our necessities require any thing of you, further than to fill as you will do, the high station which you hold, with credit to yourself, & benefit to the community.

I have been interrupted a douzen of times since I began this letter, which I am writing in my office. I have made two attempts to reply to yours before this, & have been called off. I intended when I commenced to give you some of the reasons which induced me to believe that this is not the proper time for you to run for V.P. I may do so here after, I cannot at this time, for want of space &c. I must say however that the circumstance of having a candidate in my friend Col King of this state, is not one of those reasons, nor indeed has it had the slightest influence upon me in any way. The question between you two, I know would be properly settled, & that which ought to be done is considered as done in such cases.

I shall acquiesce in whatever may be the determination of yourself, & friends in this matter. I shall with great pleasure support your name if run—and in that event, I hope your future prospects may not be injured. I fear however that you will find in your progress, *four long years* that you cannot profitably dispose of. I will in some very short time do myself the pleasure to reply to the letter of Hon. S. H. Laughlin. My professional engagements are such as to allow me but little time either for acquiring political information, or corresponding with friends upon political subjects. I devote myself to the law, & although a somewhat dry business, I prefer it to the strifes of public life. I must say before I close this subject, that your success gave me more joy, than any other political triumph. I was about to limit it. The truth is better expressed by stopping where I did. It gave me joy in a thousand ways. The *defeat* of *your enemies*, the triumph of *yourself* over them, but above all, the pleasure which I know it gave to the best man living Genl. Jackson. Enough of all this, I know you will see the points. If you meet the Old Hero, be pleased to present him my hearty congratulations &c.

Our best regards to Mrs. Polk. With the highest regard & respect . . . .

J. L. MARTIN

[P.S.] There will not be 5000 whigs in Ala. in 12 months—such is the influence of the *strong side*!!!

ALS. DLC–JKP. Addressed to Nashville and marked "*Private.*"

1. Letter not found.
2. See Joshua L. Martin to Polk, November 2, 1839.

FROM ROBERT B. REYNOLDS

Dear Govr Knoxville Nov 27th 1839

Since my return home I have been so much indisposed that I have not been able to collect any items of news worthy of communicating to you. Indeed, Sir, since the departure of Judge White, nothing of interest has occurred here that would have interested you in the least that has come to my knowledge. Every thing is quiet here amongst the people, so far as I can learn. The time has not come for action. Some men are not now able to stand the fatigue, that a warm contest would necessarily produce & others never did do service in the cause worth one groat, & are still unwilling to buffet the storms. They are still in doubt as to how E. T. will go, & are as coy & shy of the enemy as wolves are of the strong mastiff. They are unwilling to follow or profit by the example set us last summer, by one who earned a victory, which in a civil point of view, is every way equal to that, that preserved the key of the west.[1] My strength sufficiently restored, I shall lend whatever assistance my poor abilities can give the good cause. We have fought the enemy on their own ground & to say the least of it, we have stood our ground & checkmated him. We can & will defeat them in 1840.

I am rejoiced that the Hon. Mr. Grundy is again restored to his seat &c.[2] It is a triumph over his enemies, which he owed you, Sir.

Judge White will resign shortly I suppose, & I am desirous to see his appeal to the people. If it produces no better effect on the people than Foster's has,[3] or will, it will fall still born from his pen.

Who Shall be his successor, has always been a matter of deep solicitude to me—& I do hope the Legislature will not impose one upon us who will give us any additional weight to carry. My opinion is & has been that Judge Powel is the most popular & indeed I may say the safest choice that can be made. Nothing can be urged against him. Next to him stands Doct Ramsey a man of more firmness than some who have displayed a great deal of eagerness to get the seat. I do hope, Govr., that any man who has asked Whig aid or assistance may be put down. I conversed with one of the publishers of the Whig paper at Athens[4] & he admitted that that print had published an editorial to aid one of the relations of its Whig owners, to the senate, to create the impression that he was more despised by the Whigs than any man in our party. That man was then in Athens & as he has since used the same argument to me contained in that editorial, I take it for granted that he was the *author*.[5] I am opposed to all that Campbell, Vandyke, Deaderick & Co clan.[6] They are not worthy of confidence—& I repeat, we ought not to have their weight thrown on us by the selection of one, who stands so near allied to them & who is under suspicion. I think Col Frazier ought to run for Elector in 1840. He can discuss the doctrines of our party &c. Would it be right under the circumstances to place him in your staff? I shall trouble you again if any thing of interest occurs.

R. B. REYNOLDS

ALS. DLC–JKP. Addressed to Nashville.

1. Reynolds probably refers to Andrew Jackson's military victory at New Orleans in 1815.

2. On November 19, 1839, the Tennessee legislature elected Felix Grundy to the U.S. Senate seat vacated by Ephraim H. Foster. Previously Grundy had served in the Senate from 1829 until 1838.

3. See John Catron to Polk, November 19, 1839.

4. Reference probably is to A. W. Elder, nominal publisher of the Athens *Hiwassee Patriot*.

5. Reynolds probably refers to Alexander O. Anderson; see Anderson to Polk, November 3 and 16, 1839.

6. Related to the Campbells through his mother's kinship ties, Alexander O. Anderson married into the Deaderick family, which in turn was related to the Van Dykes. Among the men in this very large family connection, Thomas Jefferson Campbell, Thomas Nixon Van Dyke, and David A. Deaderick were quite active politically.

FROM CAVE JOHNSON

Dear Sir, Washington Nov. 28th [1839][1]

I intended to have written earlier but have had really nothing new. Mr. G.[2] only meant that he heard nothing from the secretaries on the subject of the V. P., only one of them (P M G)[3] objecting to the present one.[4] I am decidedly of opinion you will get the nomination—but now we talk of nothing but the orgenas[a]tion of the House. Every living member will probably be here. Mississippi members are here. Creary of Michigan[5] is on the way & if alive will be here. John Read of Mass[6] has been at deaths door. We have heard of him at N. Providence. Calhoun also sick is on the way. The city is now crowded, caucuses every day & night. The Whigs one last night & another to day. Results not known—

only [that] they have great dissention among themselves. Rumor says they wish to drop Bell & that he refuses. Our friends have a meeting to night in the Capitol. I shall not be there. I shall be engaged elsewhere. I have no hopes & of course have said nothing. Mr G is for Jones as I [t]hink. He told me frankly that he thought I would have no chance agt. Thomas or Jones & of course as is usual I am silent. He recd. last night his commission as Senator. Very lately a great difficulty has sprung up—his eligibility & I believe he is now anxiously considering that question. The Con. says he must be an "inhabitant" of the state at the time of the election.[7] Congress decided in Baileys case who was a clerk in the state department that he was not an "inhabitant" of Mass.[8] He appears wholy undecided and at a loss what to do. He is now so much occupied & will be for several days that you will not probably hear from him until after next week.[9] I should think it probable that he would decline accepting but nothing will be said of my opinion until you hear from him. In the event of his declining I hope my friends will not neglect my interest & I was glad to hear from Majr. H.[10] that you favored my pretentions as humble as they are. I should think some of our younger men ought not to be put over me but I leave all to my friends.

Brown, Hubbard, Watterson & myself are on Capitol Hill at H V Hills.[11] Rhett is with us.

So soon as the bustle gets over I shall make more enquiries into your business & in the mean[time][12] let you know all the particulars here.

C JOHNSON

[P.S.] Our delegation all here except CHW.[13] & Crocket—Judge White too!

ALS. DLC–JKP. Addressed to Nashville, marked "*private.*" AE on the cover states that this letter was answered on December 8, 1839; Polk's reply has not been found.

1. Year identified through content analysis.
2. Felix Grundy.
3. Reference is to the postmaster general, Amos Kendall.
4. See Cave Johnson to Polk, November 19, 1839.
5. Isaac Edwin Crary of Michigan served in the U.S. House from January 26, 1837, to March 3, 1841.
6. John Reed, a Massachusetts lawyer, served as a Federalist in the U.S. House, 1813–17, and as a Whig, 1821–41.
7. Reference is to article 1, section 3 of the U.S. Constitution.
8. The U.S. House resolved on March 18, 1824, that John Bailey be denied a seat in that body, as he was not a resident of the Massachusetts district from which he was elected. See Harvey M. Watterson to Polk, December 1, 1839.

9. See Felix Grundy to Polk, Robert Armstrong, and John M. Bass, December 1, 1839.
10. David Hubbard.
11. H. V. Hill's was a boarding house.
12. A tear in the manuscript has obliterated part of one word.
13. Christopher Harris Williams.

TO ROBERT A. BAKER[1]

Dear Sir Nashville Nov. 29th 1839

I have received your letter of the 22nd Instant,[2] and transmit to you by this day's mail a copy of the last Report of the Superintendant of public instruction,[3] made a few weeks since to the Legislature of this State now in Session. The Superintendant is an officer employed by the State, and receives a salary of $1500. per annum. It is his duty to collect and disburse the common school fund and generally to superintend that branch of public education. In addition to other sources of revenue applicable to this object, there is an annual appropriation of $100,000—derived from the dividends of the Bank of Tennessee which is set apart for the support of the common schools of the State. The principal of our common school fund is made by the revised constitution of the State a "perpetual fund," the interest upon which alone is annually expended. I must refer you [to] the Report of the Superintendant of Public instruction, which I herewith send to you and to the acts of our Legislature of 1835–6 and of 1837–8—establishing our system which I presume you will find among the archives of the State of Alabama, for a more full explanation of our system of common schools. The system is yet in its infancy, and is in many respects defective. In regard to our other institutions of learning, County Academies are authorized by law, and in many of the Counties they exist and are in a flourishing condition. They depend however mainly for their support, upon the tuition fees paid by the students, the public fund appropriated to this object being small. The sum of $18,000 annually derived from the dividends of the Bank of the State is distributed among the Academies. We have four Colleges, two in East and two in West Tennessee.[4] Two of them[5] are without public endowment. The College at Knoxville and the University of Nashville have been endowed by a grant of lands. This I believe contains a summary of the information which you desire to obtain. I regret that I cannot make it more full and satisfactory, and fear it will be of little use to you, in perfecting the system of public education in your state.

I have to request that you will make my kind regards to your colleagues in the Legislature and my old acquaintance and friend *Col Benj. Reynolds*, and say to him that I would be pleased to hear from him.

James K Polk

ALS, draft. DLC–JKP. Addressed to Tuscaloosa, Alabama, and marked "*Copy.*"

1. A planter from Franklin County, Alabama, Baker served five terms in the Alabama House, 1836–41; he was Speaker of that body during his last term.

2. In his letter of November 22, 1839, Baker requests information on public education in Tennessee, including the superintendent's annual report to the Tennessee legislature. The Alabama legislature, of which Baker is a member, is trying to expand and improve Alabama's system of education. ALS. DLC–JKP.

3. Enclosure not found. The text of Superintendent Robert H. McEwen's "Report on Public Instruction" was published in the *House Journal* of 1839, pp. 771–84. McEwen's "Report" was dated October 8, 1839.

4. Reference is to East Tennessee College at Knoxville, Greeneville College at Greeneville, the University of Nashville, and Jackson College at Columbia.

5. Polk canceled the words "at Greenville and Columbia."

FROM HARVEY M. WATTERSON

Dear Sir, Washington Nov. 29th 1839

I arrived here on the 23d inst. in company with Brown and Hubbard, whom I overtook at Frederick. I found no difficulty in getting up to Wheeling by water, where I chartered a Stage and came across the mountains without any accident, and with great comfort to myself.

The members are beginning to pour in rapidly. To my astonishment Judge White, or his Ghost, arrived this morning. I have not seen him, neither have I learned his intentions, or what his future movements will be. Most probably he will make the presentation of the Resolutions of Instruction from the Tennessee Legislature, the occasion to let off all his surplus *steam* against the Administration, which is to be used to blow us all up at the Presidential election of 1840. If so, he must be answered. With that view Brown, Johnson, Turney, McClellan, Blackwell and myself are going to call on Mr Grundy tomorrow, whom we have just learned, has been elected to fill Mr Foster's place. Did I say Mr Fosters place? I ask ten thousand pardons, for God forbid, that Felix Grundy should ever fill *Mr Foster's place* in the Senate of the United States. Bye the bye, Mr Benton tells a good story, which I never heard before, but which no doubt you are familiar with, in regard to a Quixotic excursion, which Foster and his friend Merrick[1] took to the Presidents at the close of the last Session of Congress. Some of our friends are of the impression, that White will not resign—but such is not my opinion. He has become, however, so totally reckless—of late years—has abandoned so many of his old professed principles—has made so many strange moves, and is now so full of "gaul and bitterness,"[2] that I shall not be greatly surprised at any course he may take. Poor man, how fallen! Once the acknowledged Cato[3] of the Senate—not without the genuine respect of either the great parties of the country. If he does raise the mad dog cry in the Senate, and endeavors to make capital to be used in our state, before he returns the trust which had been confided to him by our people, and which he disgraced by voting for Crittendons Gag Bill,[4] I want Mr Grundy to peal the "*rine*" so smooth off of him, that nothing will be left but "dry bones"![5]

After an excursion through Virginia, Mr Bell made his appearance at Brown's[6] the day before Yesterday. I have had no conversation with him, he and myself not being *acquainted*, but he looks melancholly and like something hangs heavily upon his mind. It is shrewdly suspected hereabouts, that the Whigs intend dropping him, and running Dawson of Georgia for Speaker. It is said they are to hold a Caucus tonight or tomorrow night upon the subject. Should he be dropped by his own friends, which I think not improbable, he will have enough, truly, to make him *sad*. In the event Dawson is run by the Opposition, it is thought by Turney, Gen Howard of Indiana,[7] and a few others to whom I have spoken in relation to the election of Speaker, that Cave Johnson will be our strongest man. They think he can get Hunter, Garland, and Hopkins of Va., which would secure his election. Should Mr Bell be the Whig candidate, the signs of the times are, that Mr Pickens of South Carolina, will be his opponent, or rather will receive the support of the Democratic party, with almost a certainty of success. The Democratic members are to hold a consultation on Saturday night, for the purpose of deciding this matter, as well as the course they should take in regard to Gov Penningtons Patent Right members from New Jersey.[8] On Sunday I will write to you again, and let you know what is done.

Col Johnson, Brown, Hubbard and myself, with our families, constitute a Mess—and are boarding at the old Capitol, kept by Mrs Hill.[9] It is an excellent house.

I wish you would tell Mr Harris to have my Union sent to Washington. I have not yet received the List of names in Maury and

Marshall counties you promised to forward to me. It is important I should have them.

H. M. WATTERSON

ALS. DLC–JKP. Addressed to Nashville.

1. William D. Merrick, a lawyer, served in the Maryland House, 1832–38 and 1856–57, and in the U.S. Senate as a Whig, 1838–45. Thomas Hart Benton's story about Merrick and Ephraim H. Foster is not further identified.

2. Variant quotation of Acts 8:23.

3. A Roman author and politician, Cato the Elder earned renown for being a strict judge of morals.

4. On December 21, 1838, John J. Crittenden introduced in the U.S. Senate a bill outlawing federal appointees' participation in federal or state election campaigns.

5. "Rine" is a corrupt spelling of "rind." Watterson's reference to "Dry bones" comes from Ezekiel 37:4.

6. Brown's Hotel in Washington. During the 1839–40 session John Bell resided at Mrs. Page's boardinghouse.

7. Born in South Carolina, Tilghman A. Howard practiced law in Tennessee and won one term in the Tennessee Senate, 1827–29. In 1830 he moved to Indiana and served as district attorney for Indiana, 1833–37. He went to the U.S. House in 1839, but resigned his seat the following year to make what proved to be an unsuccessful bid for the Indiana governorship. Before his death in 1844 Howard served briefly as chargé d'affaires to the Republic of Texas.

8. See David Hubbard to Polk, October 23, 1839. William Pennington, a lawyer, held the governorship from 1837 until 1843 and subsequently served as Speaker of the U.S. House from 1859 until 1861.

9. One of the larger residences on Capitol Hill, this structure temporarily housed the meetings of Congress following the Capitol's burning by the British in 1814. In 1839 H. V. Hill used the building as a boardinghouse.

FROM FELIX GRUNDY[1]

Dear Sirs, Washington, Decbr 1st 1839

I duly appreciate the difficulty in which our friends in Ten, are placed, they shall sustain no damage thro me. The first car. that leaves after the election of Speaker, carries me towards Nashville, where I expect to be nearly by the time this reaches you. Mrs Grundy must be at home. There must [be] a place secured where I can see our friends of the Legislature together on the next night after the one on which I get home. It should be private & remote so that I can talk. I can & will remove every obstacle, but to save the Constitution, I must be at home a private citizen. I shall come prepared to make every thing right instantly. If I am to take my seat in the Senate, I must not be detained. I am acting not only according to my best Judgt. but upon the safe counsel of friends here.

F GRUNDY

ALS. DLC–JKP. Addressed to Nashville and marked "*Confidential.*"
1. Addressed to Polk, Robert Armstrong, and John M. Bass.

FROM CAVE JOHNSON

Dear Sir, Washington December 1st [1839] [1]

I recd. yours of the 21st this morning.[2] We shall attend to your interests here but for a *few days* we can think or talk of nothing but the organisation & election of our officers. Several of us have been this morning with Mr. Grundy and I am authorised to say to you in strict confidence that Mr. G. has come to the Conclusion that he is not eligible[3] & most of our leading friends are of the same opinion. He is aware that difficulties may grow up at home among our friends and has therefore determined to be with you on the ground & consult with our friends there—and to do what is best. He will leave here, the *moment a Speaker is elected* perhaps *earlier* & may be with you by the time you receive this letter. And he desires me to say to you that he will expect Mrs. Grundy to be at Mrs. Bass'[4] upon his arrival. The excuse for his departure when made public here will be her indisposition & the necessity of his return. He will also be desirous of meeting *every democrat* the evening after he shall arrive. You can urge upon all *there the necessity* of not being absent from Nashville & if any are absent giving them notice to return immediately.

Our friends had a caucus last night. Jones & Lewis are the prominent men. Maine, Penn. & Alabama going for Lewis. N.Y., Virg. N.C. going for Jones. Jones had the largest number. My colleagues & Boyd[5] were for me. S.C. for Pickens—& one from Maryland for Thomas. I think Jones will get the nomination which will be finally made tomorrow morning.

We hear but little of opposition movements. Rumor says Bell & Dawson will be both run. The *Old* federalists for B. It is further understood that four or five from Geo. will under no circumstances vote for

Bell. We look upon him as a dead cock in the pit & his friends will not go for Dawson & we shall therefore beat them.

C. JOHNSON

ALS. DLC–JKP. Addressed to Nashville.

1. Year identified through content analysis.
2. Letter not found.
3. See Cave Johnson to Polk, November 28, 1839, and Felix Grundy to Polk, Robert Armstrong, and John M. Bass, December 1, 1839.
4. Malvina Grundy Bass, wife of John M. Bass, was a daughter of Felix Grundy.
5. Linn Boyd, a Democrat from Kentucky, served several terms in the U.S. House, 1835–37 and 1839–55.

FROM HARVEY M. WATTERSON

Dear Sir, Washington. Dec 1. 1839

Last night the Democratic members of the House held a "caucus" for the purpose of deciding, as I wrote you in my last,[1] upon what course it would be proper for them to take in their organization on to-morrow. After an interchange of views and some little discussion, it was *unanimously resolved*, that neither the Whig nor Democratic claimants from New jersey,[2] nor Nayler or Ingersoll of Pa,[3] should take their seats, previous to the election of a Speaker, and until their respective rights to seats, should be reported upon in the usual way, by the standing Committee of elections, and decided by those whose seats were undisputed. I do not believe there will be any backing out—any flinching—on the part of our friends. They all seem determined to march up to the work in solid column—presenting an undivided front upon all questions growing out of the main subject—an nobly resolved to resist to the very last, the gross frauds and outrages that have been committed upon the rights of the freemen of New Jersey. In doing this a *grand* row may be "kicked up"—but better that, than tamely submit to such glaring and notorious villanies, as were perpetrated in this case.

In regard to the Speaker's election, we only had a sort of trial strain, at a late hour, and after some twenty members had left. The vote stood thus: Jones of Va. 38—Lewis of Alabama 33—Johnson of Ten. 7—Thomas of Maryland 3—Pickens 2—eighty three members present. Mr Prentiss of New York then moved to adjourn until Monday morning 9 Oclock, which prevailed. The object he had in view was to have a more full attendance of members when the candidate of our party was selected. The Delgations from Pa. Maine and N Hampshire, voted for Mr. Lewis—the Delegations from New York and Va. for Mr Jones. Ohio was divided between them. Which will be finally settled upon is uncertain. My present intention is, to support the nomination of Mr. Jones, believing from what I have learned of others, that he is better qualified than Lewis, and his prospect just as fair to be elected. I don't like the idea of voting for a Nullifier, and making him the Leader of the Democratic party in the House—but anybody against Mr Bell. And if Lewis should get the nomination, I would vote most readily for him. It is said that Bell and his friends will not be "bluffed off"—and that he will be run by the Whigs. Mr Rhett of S.C. says two if not three of the Georgia members, will unite heartily with us against any National Bank Clay man. He made this Statement to the Caucus—as coming directly from *them*.

This morning Johnson, Brown, Turney and myself called upon Mr Grundy. He has come to the conclusion that he is ineligible to a seat in the Senate of the U.S. under that provision of the Constitution, which says, that no man shall be elected a Senator in Congress "who is not, *when elected*, an *inhabitant* of the State of which he is chosen."[4] There is a precedent in point, which sustains this opinion. In 1817 Mr Baley of Massachusetts[5] was appointed to a Clerkship in the Department of State. In 1823 he was elected a Representative in Congress. The question of his eligibility was raised, and the House by a vote of 155 to 25 decided against him. He went home and at the special election was again chosen. He returned and took his Seat—nobody objecting. Mr Grundy designs leaving here for Nashville in a day or two—will lay the case before his friends—and if they approve of the course he will resign. Then as in the Massachusetts case—he can be elected again, which will settle the difficulty. Of course Mr Grundy does not wish this matter spoken of—but knowing you to be one of his confidential friends—I had no hesitancy in writing you these facts, which no doubt you will receive from other sources.

It was ascertained last night, that 117 of our Democratic friends of the House, were either here then or would be here to morrow morning.

H M WATTERSON

ALS. DLC–JKP. Addressed to Nashville.

1. See Watterson to Polk, November 29, 1839.

2. See David Hubbard to Polk, October 23, 1839.

3. Charles Naylor, Whig, and Charles J. Ingersoll, Democrat, contested election results in the Fourth Congressional District of Pennsylvania. Naylor, a lawyer, won the seat and served from June 1837 to March 1841. Ingersoll,

also a lawyer, had seen previous service in Congress, 1813–15; he returned to serve four terms, 1841–49.

4. Quotation is from article 1, section 3 of the U.S. Constitution.
5. John Bailey. See Cave Johnson to Polk, November 28, 1839.

FROM HARVEY M. WATTERSON

Dear Sir Washington. Dec. 3. 1839

You will learn from the Globe[1] what was done yesterday, or rather that nothing was done at all. The House adjourned about 5 Oclock, without advancing the first step toward organization. I understand that every Democrat was in his seat—ready to discharge his duty.

Mr Jones of Virginia has been selected as the Democratic candidate for Speaker. He received in Caucus fifty votes—and Mr Lewis of Ala, forty nine.

It is understood here that a respectable portion of the whigs, do not wish to run Mr Bell, but that he and his friends, as I stated to you in my letter of the 1st inst, will not consent that his claims shall be either *definitely* or *indefinitely* postponed. Of course they will be obliged to take him up. Our friends express great confidence that they will be able to defeat him.

It is now 2 Oclock and a warm discussion is going on—upon what question—God Almighty Knows—for I am certain no member of the House does. But judging from the speeches, I should suppose there were a dozen propositions before us. We are in a *glorious* state of confusion, and when we will get out of it, this Deponent knoweth not.

H M WATTERSON

P.S. 5 Oclock—House adjourned—precisely in *Statu quo.*[2]

ALS. DLC–JKP. Addressed to Nashville.

1. Washington *Globe.*
2. Latin phrase for "in the former position."

FROM ALEXANDER O. ANDERSON

My Dear Sir At Home (near Knoxville) Decr. 4th 1839

I have just returned from my plantation on the Tennessee River, after an absence of more than a week, & had the pleasure of finding your letter of the 21st Ult.[1] at the Office.

The Opposition leaders here I think had counted very strongly on the defeat of Mr Grundy by indirection from their hands. Since his election they seem to have abandoned much hope of making any very decisive impression upon the democratic Party. Nevertheless, it is absolutely necessary to be on our guard, and whatever can be effected by the Federal Party to defeat the wishes of the majority will be done, and the gentleman to whom Judge White wrote his letter[2] will be an active Agent (if any thing be attempted) to accomplish this object.

You will have seen that Judge White has gone on—and whenever I observe any symptoms of his withdrawal from the Senate, if the Legislature is in Session, I will proceed immediately to Nashville. If you shou'd come into possession of any information, by which it will be proper to be guided advise me immediately, & I will act in conformity therewith. It is probable you will be better enabled to judge than I will. You are upon the ground, and can understand the movements which are going forward. My opinion, however, is that Judge White will make a speech upon the Independent Treasury Bill at the time he announces his withdrawal, and will I presume then send on his resignation. All this is conjecture, but I can perceive no motive for his going on without he designed to adopt some such course. Upon the receipt of this, however, advise me, & if any thing shou'd be had by way of information as to what he will do, & when, let me know specially.

Of the deep rooted hatred against me of the Whigs of East Tennessee, politically, I am fully apprized. In this respect in this quarter, I come in second only, to yourself—and consider it a special honor to be so distinguished by their ever active and untiring malice. But I do not believe they will be able to achieve any thing. They now look upon the resignation of Judge White as certain, and altho' still bent upon their purpose of ruling (even the Democrats) the election of Mr Grundy has dampened their hopes.

You will have seen in the Richmond Enquirer that Mr Ritchie has taken very high ground in favor of your inaugural.[3] This it is to be observed he has done in full view of your nomination for the Vice-Presidency, and I consider it as a decided index of his feelings, *under all the circumstances*.

From indirect sources of information I wou'd presume that the *confidential personal friend* of Mr King[4] will endeavor to bring his name forward for the Vice Presidency in the Alabama Legislature. But this will do no harm. I do not consider him as at all in the way—& with ordinary firmness & vigor among your friends, joined with prudence and judgement I look upon the question as settled. You may rely upon it that the aspect of political affairs makes it necessary to our Party abroad to take this course. The position of New York and Michigan totally postpones the pretensions of Col Johnson. It is now as I have always inculcated—*that we must carry no weights.*

Is it possible the Legislature will adjourn without something being done as to the Hiwassee Rail Road &c. &c? And can nothing be done as to the present Bank power? The whole matter is this, that we have been made to feel the magnitude of the Rail Road (Hiwassee) power here, by the Opposition, in whose hands it was, & that it may be administered without political direction it is necessary it shou'd [c]*hange*[5] *hands radically.* The Democratic Party [d]o not want it for political effect—but they object to the abuse of the power as heretofore—& they want reform—& this must be done from the President, throughout!!! and Democrats in their place!

The great Battle for Tennessee the Opposition are preparing to fight chiefly in East Tennessee, believing it the stronghold of their power! We ought to keep this in mind! *I am not mistaken!*

Very soon after my return I applied for the Mecklenberg Declaration—& have been promised it, & as soon as Dr Ramsay[6] returns from the South I shall get it—& will attend to it &c &c.

A ANDERSON

ALS. DLC–JKP. Addressed to Nashville and marked "*Private & Confidential.*"

1. Polk's letter not found.
2. See John Catron to Polk, November 19, 1839.
3. The *Richmond Enquirer* of November 15, 1839, praised Polk's legislative message of October 22, 1839; no reference in the *Enquirer* to Polk's Inaugural Address has been found.
4. James Buchanan supported William Rufus King, a personal friend, for the vice-presidential nomination in 1840. Looking ahead to the 1844 presidential nomination, Buchanan considered Polk a possible rival.
5. A tear in the manuscript has obliterated parts of two words.
6. J. G. M. Ramsey.

FROM CAVE JOHNSON

Dear Sir, Washington Dec 4th (3 oclock), [1839] [1]

In calling the House we are still at New Jersey & not likely to move any further soon. We are debating first one proposition & then another. I shall not be surprised if the opposition design to keep us in this State until the election in Massachusetts takes place in Alvords district[2] which it is said takes place on the 22nd Inst.—& besides Dennis of Maryland[3] is absent & one whig from N. York.

I met Allen to day. I commenced a conversation on the subject upon which you feel most interest.[4] He was backward at first—coy—& said that our friends in Ohio would be silent on the subject for the present and those who talked on the subject were not willing to place any man in that position, that might probably be looking to the succession. I then told him you had no such aspirations. That I heard that objection before to you & had written you on the subject & had your reply[5] & tho endorsed *private*, I felt myself at liberty to shew him. He read your letter. After looking over it, he said the idea had been suggested by the running of Forsyth for that office, who looked no doubt to the Presidency—& then said you would be strongest man that could be run in Ohio. Mr. F. would have no strength there—that R. M. J.[6] must be got rid of in some way. If we could do so peacibly, so much the better but if we could do no better the convention must settle it and nominate you. But he said we must have a further full conversation upon the subject when we had leisure & more privacy.

We shall not omit [to] do all that is right & proper in relation to this business but we now have so much confusion about the organization that we talk of nothing else. The rumor is rife that Clay will not be nominated at Harrisburgh & that Scott will. Not a word has been said, so far as I have heard of Mr. G's movement.[7]

C Johnson

ALS. DLC–JKP. Addressed to Nashville and marked "*Private.*"

1. Year identified through content analysis.
2. See David Hubbard to Polk, October 23, 1839.
3. John Dennis, a Whig from Maryland, served in the U.S. House from 1837 until 1841.
4. Reference is to Polk's vice-presidential ambitions.
5. Reference probably is to Polk's letter to Johnson, dated November 21, 1839. See Cave Johnson to Polk, December 1, 1839.
6. Richard Mentor Johnson.
7. Reference is to Felix Grundy's return to Nashville.

FROM CAVE JOHNSON

Dear Sir, [Washington City] H Rep 4 Dec. 1839

We have at length appointed J. Q Adams Chairman & adjourned until tomorrow—amidst the greatest disorder & confusion that I have ever witnessed. And Adams was literally taken up *vi et armis*[1] amidst the utmost clamor & confusion & the gallaries clapped prodigiously—

which produced motions to clear the gallaries. Amidst the confusion I moved to adjourn & was sustained. We have also adopted the rules of the House to control us, which will give us I think the power to settle sometime.

C JOHNSON

ALS. DLC–JKP. Addressed to Nashville.

1. Latin phrase meaning "by force and arms."

FROM THOMAS HART BENTON

Dear Sir, Washington City, Dec. 5. 1839

Yours of the 24th has just arrived,[1] and after talking with some of our friends, and especially with Mr. Wright, I hasten to answer it. We find great difficulty in having early action on the Independent Treasury Bill. Many of the States are but *half* represented in the Senate, and some of them cannot be until some time in January. Mr. Wright himself is trammelled by considerations of delicacy. His state will *probably* instruct him against it; and he does not wish to seem to avoid that by a hasty action, especially without a colleague.[2] It would be towards the time you mention, say middle of January before we could expect any *question* on the Bill, the initiatory steps would previously be taken. I write you *thus*, to let you see the probability of its being the end of January before you could hear of any action of ours on the Bill you mention. But before you receive this you will see Grundy who will be able to give you further views. You will find that he has had his own difficulties about his election.

I will write to you again & let you know our prospects.

The state of the H.R. you see; and I almost look upon it as providence dooming the federalists to destruction in making their leaders & party, a *party* to the New Jersey fraud.[3] Some of themselves are afraid of it; but others drive on.

Mrs. B.[4] joins me in kindest remembrance to your self & lady.

THOMAS H. BENTON

ALS. DLC–JKP. Addressed to Nashville.

1. Letter not found.

2. The New York legislature did not elect Nathaniel P. Tallmadge to a second term in the Senate until January 14, 1840.

3. See David Hubbard to Polk, October 23, 1839.

4. Elizabeth McDowell married Benton in 1821.

FROM AARON V. BROWN

Dear Sir Washington Saturday night Decr. 7, 1839

The Week has closed & no organization yet. You will see an account of the Debates, in which much more of passion than talent was displayd. I have indeed been much disappointed, in the display both as to matter & manner. Our present stage is an appeal from the decision of the chair, declaring that the N Jersey members holding the governors certificate should be counted by the tellers, on a motion to lay Mr Wise's resolution on the table.[1] That resolution proposed an organization admitting them as members. We wishd. to lay *that* on the table, in order to introduce one, directing that the *undisputed* cases should be first calld & a quorum of such being found present, that they should proceed to decide on the *disputed* cases. Duncan has the floor & making a speech for Buncomb.[2] The strength of this movement on our part consists in the unreasonableness of mens voting in *their own cases*. We are relying on the 34 rule which declares that no member shall vote on any question in which he is interested. (We adopted the rules of the house for our government.) The chairman says that *the people* of N.J. alone have an interest in the question. We reply that they have a personal, pecuniary & political interest & that therefore by *the rule*, by the universal practice in other cases & by the known reason & justice of the case they ought not to vote. But in making the count on the appeal, the same difficulty still arises. God only knows when & how it will end—not however in any probability in any violence whatever.

Bell & Dawson will both be run by the Whigs. Jones by the Democrats 1st & perhaps the 2nd Ballotting. If he cant come through in three he cant come at all & by the time they break off from Bell—our friends will probably rally on Lewis. No one here I think counts on Bell's success, but it is said, he is very unyealding in his pretentions.

We are on Capitol Hill having Mr. Calhoun with us but Pickens, Rhett & Hunter of Va. left us to day & took other quarters (some disagreement with our Land Lord).[3] They are all fine fellows & so far have acted with us very well. They are prompt & energetic in their support of the administration—but are very sensitive to any reflections on their sincerety & motives. This you know is natural enough. Mr. Calhoun is very much struck with the bold & manly message of the Governor of Virginia[4] on the refusal of the Govr. of N York[5] to give up certain persons charged with the stealing [of] sundry slaves from Virginia.[6] He thinks the administration, ought to make much out of the case & that the Legislatures ought to move in the matter every where. He suggests that the sunshine states can make such regulations (under their quarrentine laws—as will prostrate the commerce of the Northern states or rather of N York, until the Abolition governor of the State, who made the decision will be prostrated at home & abroad. Now will any suitable occasion present itself for your adverting to this subject. If so barely to state the case as it occurrd., the decision of the Govr. of N. York, & the deplorable consequence if a like decision should be made in the other free states. As to any remedy—it is too early [to] suggest any specific one—leave that to time & the suggestions of other states. The case will attract much attention—is a very strong one on our side & *a good* & happy touch, as it would work well in all the S. & S. West. You know Georgia has also a case with Maine.[7] The news here is that the Harrodsburgh convention[8] has come to a conclusion—something over 100 (perhaps 103) for Clay—77 for Harrision & 60 for Scott—Massachusetts yet to vote.

Mr Grundy's absence has not yet attracted any attention. Tell him the Secret has been well kept—& to advise us the first moment of what takes place at Home. Judge White is here. No one knows that I hear of what he intends[9]—& really it seems like no one cares. You can well immagine that in the uproar about the organization & on the partial & brief acquaintance I have formed, I have learned but little in relation to the Vice Presidency. But the proper time comeing, your friends intend to make a *strong shewing* in the case & I doubt not successfully. Ohio & Pennsylvania I think can be counted on now. Virginia & the two Carolinas also. I shall be able soon however to give you some *facts* instead of opinions.

I wish now to call your attention to another matter, which I neglected. A man is in the penitentry from Tipton by the name of Holliday for killing another I think by the name of Stone.[10] His friends have moved on Cannon for a remittance of part of the punishment—& have or will petition you also. Hollidays Brother (a very respectable man & Son in Law to Genl. Speight of Miss.) lives near my farm & desired my intercession with you.[11] I want you if the case is brought before you, to do what you can toward his relief & to write a letter, either to him or Genl. Speight assuring them that you will give a patient hearing to the petition & such decision as your official duty may require. Holliday is a very clever man & feels a great deal of anxiety about the case. He desires to get his Brother out & remove him to Mississippi. You can address him "Colo. Jno. Holliday, Columbus, care of Genl. Speight"—this will shew if I have mistaken his first name, who is intended. Speight I expect will be at Jackson having been elected to the Legislature you know.

Some six or seven years ago, winter of 1833–4, I sent you a power of Atto. & assignment of all the interest of my step mother Mrs Susan Brown in the estate of her Brother (whose name was Beard) on the Eastern shore of Maryland. Thos Wright the third was the administrator.[12] You have that assignment yet—but I fear [it] is lost in the rubbish of 5000 papers so you can [not] find it. If you can I would be glad you would enclose it to me & I will look further into the case whilst I am in these parts.

Mrs. B.[13] sends her best respects to *Mrs* Governor & congratulates her on the exchange of *Stations* & residences.

A. V. Brown

ALS. DLC–JKP. Addressed to Nashville. AE on the cover states that this letter was answered on December 18, 1839; Polk's reply has not been found.

1. Henry A. Wise offered his resolution in favor of the New Jersey Whig contestants on December 6, 1839.

2. During the Sixteenth Congress' 1819–20 session Representative Felix Walker of Waynesville, North Carolina, ignored clamorous calls for the question and continued his speech in behalf of his constituents in Buncombe County. Thereafter to speak "for Buncombe" was to speak for show or popularity.

3. Brown and Calhoun lodged at H. V. Hill's boarding house.

4. David Campbell.

5. William H. Seward.

6. Correspondence between the governors of the two states continued for more than two years without any clear resolution of the issue and without the return to Virginia of the persons charged with stealing the slaves.

7. Starting in 1837, Georgia Governor William Schley engaged in a lengthy correspondence with Governor Robert P. Dunlap of Maine about the return of a fugitive slave. Governor George R. Gilmer continued Schley's demands, but Dunlap's successor, Edward Kent, returned neither the slave nor those who had aided his flight from Georgia.

8. Reference is to the Whig National Convention, which met at Harrisburg, Pennsylvania.

9. Brown might have erred in his syntax; probably he meant to say, "No one of whom I have heard knows what he intends. . . ."

10. Convicted of killing John Stone, a tavern owner, Samuel Holliday received a commutation from Cannon on October 10, 1839.

11. John Holliday and Jesse Speight. Holliday is not identified further. Speight, Speaker of the North Carolina House in 1820, also served in the North Carolina Senate, 1823–27, and in the U.S. House, 1829–37. After moving to Mississippi, he won election to that state's Senate before serving as a Democrat in the U.S. Senate, 1845–47.

12. Susan Beard Stockell Brown, John Beard, and Thomas Wright III. Aaron Brown's efforts to collect for his stepmother a share of John Beard's

estate went back at least to November 1832. Wright practiced law in Centreville, Maryland. See Brown's letters to Polk of November 23, 1832; December 22, 1833; and January 15, 1835.

13. Sarah Burruss Brown was Aaron V. Brown's first wife.

FROM CAVE JOHNSON

Washington City. December 7, [1839][1]

Johnson reports to Polk in detail on House proceedings. Adams has taken the Chair and decided that the New Jersey delegation bearing gubernatorial certification[2] might vote on procedural motions. Adams' decision could be reversed by the House, but Johnson believes that it will be difficult to exclude the Whig delegates. House Democrats cannot agree on the Speaker's election. Jones' nomination is opposed by friends of Pickens and Lewis. Frank Thomas is most opposed to Jones. The vote will be very close, and the Democrats' only hope for control will be the support of a few discontented men who belong to neither party. Pickens and Hunter have taken quarters with these men; Rhett is quartering with members of the Georgia delegation. Since the Speaker's election will be close and the vote of the New Jersey Whigs may be decisive, necessity may force some Democrats to yield to the choice of the Whig delegation from New Jersey. Polk "will be able to guess why & wherefore" upon seeing the votes, for a man openly in opposition might be preferable to Pickens or Hunter. Reports from Harrisburg say that the Whig presidential nomination is yet uncertain.

ALS. DLC–JKP. Addressed to Nashville and marked "*private.*"

1. Year identified through content analysis.
2. See David Hubbard to Polk, October 23, 1839.

FROM CAVE JOHNSON

Dear Sir, Washington December 8th Sunday [1839][1]

I recd. your two letters of the 28th last evening.[2] Knowing the friendship of Majr. Hardwicke, so soon as I believed there was a doubt of Mr. G.s acceptance,[3] I intimated to him that another election might take place, so that he might be privately paving the way to my success & not with a view of his intimating it to any other person. I did not say so much to you because among your numerous friends who I expected would be candidates, I did not know that you favored my pretentions. Indeed I was rather inclined to think that you did not, *not from the want of friendship* but from a belief of the *necessity* of my continuing in my present position—& in truth I thought *the suggestion* of my being speaker was rather designed to turn my attention to this point for promotion, than from any hope of success. Indeed I never had the slighest hope of success—& upon my arrival here, finding Mr. G. favorable to the election of G.W.J.[4] & expressing the opinion that I ought to be elected there, I had strange thoughts for a few moments but they soon passed off. But I may suggest that the same arguments used at Nashville agt. my success, that there is danger in my district if I should be elected Senator is applied here with much more force agt. your views for the Vice Pres. You are elected to an important office—none can supply your place—we can not ever hope for one to do as well. My majority shews that there is not the slightest danger in my district—whilst your majority leaves the State in a questionable attitude at the approaching elections—& I have had to combat this notion very often here on your behalf. I did not expect you to take such a part for me but I could not but feel it a little when my prospects were destroyed by arguments of that sort from my friends. My motive always was & so expressed publicly & privately long before I left home, that I thought it due to Mr. G. *to offer* him the position from which he had been driven by the Whigs—long before I had an intimation of his wishes. Some members of the Legislature, friends, have the same in writing after I left Nashville, when I knew his opinion as communicated by you. But when I found that he thought himself inelligible, then I thought I ought not to yield my pretensions to the claims of any of the gentlemen mentioned. It was not *my wish* that he should decline, altho, I am inclined to think the position he assumed a true one. But I suppose it is all ended by his re-election. I mention these things in no spirit of unkindness & with that frankness which will always characterise my course.

Before I recd. your letters I had noticed that your nomination had not appeared in the Globe & I had a conversation with Blair on the subject. His excuse for not doing so was—that its publication at this time might have the effect of injuring him in his election as public printer & he thought he had better delay it for the present—and he talked to me in a way to induce me to believe that he was favorable to your nomination & we shall now soon take some steps to have a convention. I had a conversation with Thompson of Miss. & Cross of Arkansas,[5] both of whom regretted the course of our Legislature because your *services in Ten.* could not be dispensed with & the latter expressed the opinion that it would ultimately injure you by exciting agt. you the friends of your other competitors, who would probably have been inclined to have placed you in a still higher position at no distant time. I used all the arguments that occurred to me to shew him the propriety of their course & told him *emphatically* that if the *convention* nominated RMJ that we should be driven in Ten to run an independent ticket—that our course could not now be trusted before the people with such a weight upon our shoulders &c &c. Company came in upon us and prevented further conversation.

They have to day taken rooms with us, so that I shall have every opportunity of satisfying them. Sevier & wife[6] are in the city and are expected to take rooms here also.[7] There is none of us here who will not do all that is proper to be done. I have not heard from Allen or Benton since I wrote you. The confusion in our house keeps us in our seats & when it is to end no one knows. Nothing occurred after I wrote you yesterday except half the day spent in an effort to deny on record the decision of old Adams but it was refused by a close vote by tellers 107 to 106. Doct. Duncan was on the floor most of the day—called for the reading of the evidence on the table in behalf of the Democratic members,[8] which has not yet been read. This was objected & another debate on that—& so we adjourned until tomorrow when that question is to be settled. There is no spirit of accomodation—no chance at compromise which I attempted on yesterday and it will not be ended until the Whigs become ashamed of their course or until we all need money so much, that we will elect a speaker to give us checks. I have heard nothing further of the suspected movements to defeat the election of Jones. I shall probably know it all tomorrow. I was invited to Blairs last evening with many others with a view I suppose to the settlement of that matter but the weather was so unfavorable I did not go out. I have again slight rheumatism & fear that I shall be again prostrated.

We have heard nothing further from Harrisburgh than I wrote on yesterday.

C. JOHNSON

ALS. DLC–JKP. Addressed to Nashville. AE on the cover indicates that this letter was answered on December 17, 1839; Polk's reply has not been found.

1. Year identified through content analysis. In the date line Johnson wrote the figure eight over the figure seven.

2. Letters not found.

3. See Cave Johnson to Polk, November 28, 1839; and Felix Grundy to Polk, December 1, 1839.

4. Felix Grundy favored John W. Jones of Virginia for the House Speakership.

5. Jacob Thompson and Edward Cross. Thompson, a Mississippi Democrat, served in the U.S. House from 1839 until 1851. A native Tennessean, Cross moved to Arkansas in 1826. Having served as U.S. judge for the Arkansas Territory, 1830–36, and as U.S. surveyor general for Arkansas, 1836–38,

he won election as a Democrat to the U.S. House and served from 1839 until 1845.

6. Ambrose H. Sevier, a native Tennessean, served as delegate from the Arkansas Territory from 1828 until 1836; he won election as a Democrat to the U.S. Senate and served from 1836 until 1848. In 1827 he married Juliette Johnson, niece of Richard Mentor Johnson.

7. Johnson lodged at H. V. Hill's boarding house on Capitol Hill.

8. Reference is to the Democratic claimants in the New Jersey election contest.

FROM DAVID A. STREET

Dear Sir Jackson Ten Decr. 8th 1839

I have neglected longer than I intended to answer your letter,[1] but I hope the times and consequent press upon me will excuse both the delay and the dun. There is nothing of interest here about which to write. You have committed a false step I fear in the election of Grundy; a man against whom the state rights party have such reasons for dislike as not to regard it in any other light than a defiance of their principles. It may be true that they are weak, and can do but little towards positively elevating themselves, but I would fain believe that they have too much self esteem to remain with a party, one of whose principles it is systematically to oppress and divide them. You must remember the conversations which grew out of the difficulties here in regard to the gubernatorial nomination and that you promised to *favor* to the extent of your influence the pretentions of Mjr Martin to the Senate. Now setting aside the promise, which I cared nothing about, how does the present state of matters comport with that tenor of events which *we* were led to anticipate from your election? Can you point to one individual in our whole party that has recvd an appointment at the hands of a Legislature elected by their cooperation? And are they not as worthy in point of talents? You have elected Mr Humphreys attorney Genl. and he can tell you that we refused to sustain his nomination upon the ground that he assumed; and that so far from favoring his claims after his letter to me we should have decidedly opposed him for any office. Your organ too has essayed to call the White nomination of '36 the proceeding of a *faction*![2] You cannot believe that such is the case, when you know that it was only by an abandonment of the position that *you* held then, and assuming that which *White* held then, that you could have been elected. Then why is such conduct permitted? We as well as you deprecate Judge White's course, but you surely would not set about to prove to *us*, that ours is not the same possition we occupied in 1837?

I stated to you my candid convictions when I saw you, and time has but confirmed me in them. You may elect Mr. Pickens speaker, but what else could you do? If *he* choose to assent to the request of *his* party and become a candidate can *yours* prevent his election or the election of a federalist? You either misunderstand us, or your party is willing to deceive us: the latter *I* shall not now believe. You surely do not expect us to be satisfied with any thing short of what Mr. Calhoun demanded in his Edgefield letter?[3] Nor can you say he is selfish in those demands. For if taking the regular concatenation from Foot's resolution[4] down to the present time, the approval by your party of Hayne's speeches which were predicated of the X amendmt of the constitution and the Republican address,[5] I cannot presume what I know to be otherwise, that you can not see that while your party has changed positions *we* have stood fast upon those doctrines through all difficulty up to the present. We are not now talking to *the people.* We are stating plain matters of fact to a *man* who has the capacity to understand, and who knows himself that they are so, from experience. I know the influence that has been brought to operate upon you; and let me tell you plainly what I think, (viz) that it is entirely unworthy of you. *Verbum sat.*[6] I know that of all things this letter is the least calculated to create a popularity with the party but although I am *poor* yet when I look to the long line of ancestry who have died poor but in the service of truth and their country, I cannot consent to speak to you otherwise than in the words of truth and honest conviction. I am opposed to Grundy because I have no confidence in his political principles; and consequently I must be permitted to say nothing in *favor* of his election. I am just on the eve of starting to Alabama. I should be glad to hear from [you] by the 1st Jany. Please attend to the resolution offered by Mr. Lyon in behalf of our Female Academy.[7] It is a matter of some importance to us.

D A STREET

ALS. DLC–JKP. Addressed to Nashville.

1. Letter not found.

2. Reference probably is to the *Nashville Union.*

3. On November 3, 1837, in reply to an invitation to a public dinner planned in his honor, Calhoun wrote an exposition of his political views to the citizens of South Carolina's Edgefield District. In his remarks he urged members of the State Rights party to abandon the Whigs and join Van Buren in an effort to restrain consolidation of the general government.

4. On December 29, 1829, Samuel A. Foote of Connecticut proposed a resolution temporarily restricting the sale of public lands; his proposal occasioned an extended debate between Daniel Webster and Robert Y. Hayne over the nature of the extent of the general government's powers.

5. Reference probably is to the Kentucky and Virginia Resolutions of 1798–99, which articulated what became Republican dogmas on the compact theory of the Constitution and its related doctrines of interposition and nullification.

6. Latin phrase for "Enough said."

7. James S. Lyon's resolution in behalf of the Jackson Female Academy is not further identified.

FROM KENEDY LONERGAN

Campbell's Station, Tennessee. December 11, 1839

Lonergan writes that the Hiwassee Railroad Company desperately needs money and that without aid construction cannot continue. He has persuaded farmers and merchants in the area to supply provisions; however, additional funds must be raised within sixty days. East Tennesseans look to Polk for leadership in securing legislative relief.

ALS. DLC–JKP. Addressed to Nashville.

FROM CAVE JOHNSON

Dear Sir, [Washington City] H of Rep Dec 12th [1839][1]

We are beginning to see Land. We have had several votes yesterday on the right of the New Jersey members to take their seats & vote with us & have rejected them all & admitted Naylor & the *roll* has been this morning called in the way proposed by the Clerk[2] at the commencement & we are now likely to go *ahead*.

I saw Mr. A. of O.[3] this morning. He accords with our views & wishes entirely & has taken means to prevent if possible the Legislature of Ohio from nominating R.M.J[4] & to induce the convention of the 8th of Jany. to recomend a Convention at Baltimore in May. He thinks *if the Ohio* Legislature does not nominate all will be safe. We have concluded to have the convention suggested to the different states as soon as practicable. It is understood here. I do not know upon what authority that the Republicans in the Legislature of Va. will recomend a convention in May. Montgomery[5] will write to day to N.C. He is very decided for you & also that you must be *the Successor*. I cautioned him agt. using such expressions. We will have letters written soon to Baltimore N.Y. Phil. &c. I had also a conversation with C.C.C.[6] to day. He is of course first for K—g[7] but really for you in preference to any other. McCoy is for you. Bynum hesitates & Hawkins has yet taken no ground. I have not yet seen Conner.[8] I shall advise you occasionally of all I hear & every other movement that you may feel an interest in.

The role has been called & we have now a resolution to appoint a Co by the House to investigate the N. Jersey cases & the vote, Ayes 122 [and] Noes 82. Waddy Thompson[9] is now making a speech & having a resolution in his hand is moving her course.

C. JOHNSON

ALS. DLC–JKP. Addressed to Nashville.

1. Year identified through content analysis.
2. Hugh A. Garland of Virginia.
3. William Allen of Ohio.
4. Richard Mentor Johnson.
5. William Montgomery, a physician, won election as a North Carolina Democrat to the U.S. House in 1835 and served three terms.
6. Clement C. Clay.
7. William Rufus King.
8. James I. McKay, Jesse A. Bynum, Micajah T. Hawkins, and Henry W. Connor. McKay, a lawyer and Democrat from North Carolina, served in the U.S. House from 1831 until 1849. A lawyer and farmer, Bynum sat for several terms in the North Carolina House before going as a Democrat to the U.S. House, where he served from 1833 until 1841. A farmer, state legislator, and militiaman from North Carolina, Hawkins won election as a Democrat to the U.S. House in 1831 and served for ten years. A North Carolina planter, Connor won ten terms as a Democrat in the U.S. House and served from 1821 until 1841.
9. Waddy Thompson, Jr., a lawyer, sat in the South Carolina House before winning election to Congress in 1835; he joined the Whig party and served in the House until 1841.

FROM ARCHIBALD YELL

My Dear Sir Waxhaws Arkansas Decr the 12th 1839

The derangement of fiscal couriers in this quarter makes it imposible to arrange any money matters with our Banks. They have no Tennessee money for that is worse than our own. Nor have they any transactions with the Tennessee Banks that will enable me to effect any matter with them, and as it is a rare chance that an offer presents to send money from here to Tennessee by private conveyence I fear it will be some time before you can be accomodated with it.[1] You can make some arrangemt with the Nashville Banks by drawing on me at this place; here I have the funds to meet any draft you might see proper to draw but I only fear that our funds would not suit either you or the Banks and Tennessee money is not to be procured here. Our dealings are all another way & your money grately under *par*. Consequently scarce here; if I find any chance however to send you the money I will do so but it will be in gold.

I see E H Foster has resigned & that Grundy succeeds him. I am not sure if it would not have been better for the party to have elected Carroll or some other prominent man, Nicholson excepted, who I consider as being of but little service to our party. He is not only Burkish at heart,[2] but is not willing to risk any thing for the cause and you will find him when ever he is tried in a *Panic* that he will be found doubly at want. For such fellows I have no patience. Either Fulton or Trousdale[3] would have been of service to the party at Home for I consider that a matter now of infinate more moment to the party than in sustain[in]g Mr. Van Buren who is now able to take care of himself. Indeed you could not more effectually take care of Him than looking to your own interest in Tennessee.

I see the Legislature of Ten has Honored you with a Nomination for the Vice Presidency. I very much fear that the Vice Presidency is to give our Party some trouble at the Next election. I am well aware that *Uncle Dick*[4] is not the choice of our frinds, but the difficulty is to get rid of him without being worsted in the swap. I do not mean in the Selection we should make, for any decent man of our Party will run just as well & would be as acceptable, but the Nominee would suffer I fear more than the Party. To you I am sure I can say what I think without incuring your suspicion of my frindship.

Then I fear that you would if Nominated loose much more than you could gain by the Vice Presidency. You would incur the displeasure of the warm & personal frinds of Col Johnson who are Numerous in all the New Stats. You would create a Jelousy & hatred from King of Alabama, Forsyth, Buchannan & a strong feeling of *Rivlary* betw[ee]n *Benton* & your[se]lf. If I am not mistaken in that calculation you would find that you would be grately weakened by it—in your *Ultimate wishes*. None of those men save Benton or perhaps Buchannin desires or anticipats any thing more than the 2nd office for which they are *ripe* at all times. Those who aspire to the Presidency must see that no minor considerations defeat their main object.

You would come in at the wrong *Time* for I take it for granted that *Benton* will succeed Mr Van Buren as the Democratic Candidate & will be elected. You would go out in the middle of his 8 Years & would be out of Public view at the Succeeding Presidential election. If the Vice Presidency is therefore sought as a steping stone being in the line of "safe presiders" you should not desire it so soon by 4 years. Recollect you are only about 40 years of age, too young for the Presidency. At 52 [you] will be young enough & younger than any former President. You can & will not be looser by declining the vice Presidency at this time. You will only strengthen your[se]lf with all the *aspirants* & their particular frinds. You should cultivate the particular frindship of Johnsons & Kings frinds for they are the men who are in future to urge your pretentions to the *Presidency*. Then dont loose sight of the frindship of your Neighbors & the New States. As for Georgia she is not to be relyed upon longer than one Term; nor do I think any better of her aspirant to the *Vice Presidency*.[5] She will go off with *Calhoun* if he goes. When ever *Benton* is Nominated as the Democratic Candidate then my advice is run again for Govr. of Tennessee. Bring her farely back to the "Republican Tack" and then you will find that you will have no difficulty in either the Vice Presidency or a situation in the Cabinet infinately preferable to the Vice Presidency. It is not so much the office that a man fills that gives him Currency as the amount of Bulion he has in Circulation.[6] In 4 years you will have acquired enough to sustain your[se]lf against all the runs that may be made at you. Then I pray you do not be in too much of a hurry to commence opperations & then you will not be under the necessity to *suspend.*

The mass of the people are the same every where. There is no State in the Union Tennessee not excepted where you have more warm frinds than in Arkansas but I owe it to candor & to you to say that they will regret extremely if Col Johnson is *elbowed* off the track at the next election. Tho under different circumstances He might not be their first choice, He has however fought th[r]ough the Wars Indian & Panic and they are willing & desirous to give evidence of their continued confidence. At any other time & against any one else, you would have no difficulty. I readily infer then if here where you are as strong as anywhere there should be that feeling which I have just described it will exist in all the states where *Johnson* is strong & where King or Forsyth has frinds.

Again no man who is spoken of for the 2d office has strength enough to get up a National Convention for the purpose of a Nomination & I am sure there will be no union of concert of the dif[fer]ent aspirants for that object. Then I take it there will be no *other* nomination by a convention and that Johnson will be put on the tickett with Mr Van Buren—without some one should be so indiscreet as to run at all hazzards & that will not only ensure his defeat but it will put Him out of the way at the next Election.

Then if you should think as I do on this Subject, you should make it known in such a way as to give no offence to the other aspirants & you will strengthen yours[e]lf with the frinds of the Vice President. I have so much confidence in your discresion & forsight that I do not feel allarmed that you are to be the Sufferer by this move in Tennessee &c.

Before this you may have seen that I am a candidate for Govr of Arkansas. Judge Cross the present incumbent & my successor will again be a Candidate for Congress. He will be re-elected by an increased majority. Without a revolution in public oppinion or some unforeseen misfortune we shall both be elected.

Present my respects to your Grand Lady and tell her I say to *Her* what Dr. Linsey said to Mrs Bell when he handed her into the Carriage—When you see the old Chap present Him my kindest Respects.[7]

A. YELL

ALS. DLC–JKP. Addressed to Nashville. AE on the cover states that this letter was answered on January 8, 1840; Polk's reply has not been found.

1. See Archibald Yell to Polk, September 15, 1839.

2. Reference is to Edmund Burke, eighteenth-century British statesman, political philosopher, and Whig publicist.

3. James Fulton and William Trousdale. A prominent Fayetteville lawyer, Fulton served one term as attorney general of Tennessee's Eighth Judicial District, 1824–27.

4. Richard M. Johnson.

5. John Forsyth.

6. Probably a reference to Thomas Hart Benton, who was nicknamed "Old Bullion."

7. Philip Lindsley and Jane Erwin Yeatman Bell, wife of John Bell. Lindsley was president of the University of Nashville from 1824 until 1850; his remarks to Jane Bell are not identified further.

FROM JOHN H. BILLS

Bolivar, Tennessee. December 14, 1839

Bills urges the necessity of increasing banking capital in southwestern Tennessee; planters have taken an abundant crop to the Mississippi River, but find no money there for the purchase of their crop. Memphis ships more cotton than any other place in Tennessee and receives more goods to be forwarded to the interior than does Nashville. Yet Memphis has but one small bank, the Farmers and Merchants' Bank.[1] The legislature should authorize this bank's increasing its capital from $600,000 to $1,000,000 and establishing a branch in the interior. Bills requests support for General Neely's bill on this subject.[2]

ALS. DLC–JKP. Addressed to Nashville.

1. The Farmers and Merchants' Bank, the first bank in Memphis, received its charter in 1833; Ike Rawlings served as its first cashier.

2. On December 2, 1839, Rufus P. Neely introduced in the Tennessee House a bill to increase the capital stock of the Farmers and Merchants' Bank; the bill did not pass.

FROM HOPKINS L. TURNEY

Dear Sir. Washington city Dec the 14th 1839

It this moment occurd to me that when at Nashville I promised to keep you advised of our proseedings here. You no doubt have moore in detail the proseedings of the house than I could give in a letter. From what has taken place it is certain that neither Bell nor Dawson can be elected. The contest is now Confined to *Jones*, Lewis, & Hunter of Va. and the Nullafiers can [cause to be] elected either Jones or Hunter. By uniteing with the Democrats they will elect Jones or by uniteing with the Whigs they will elect Hunter. There are 30 democrats that will not in any event vote for Lewis. Among them are Cave Johnson, McClellan, Waterson,[1] & your humble Servant. The Whigs can elect either Jones, or Lewis, though I think they will not interfear in our fight.

Your nomination for the Vice Presidency is favourably received by our party. I have yet to find the first man who is opposed to it. I have conferd &c with our friends from Tennessee on the subject. I Suggested to you before I left home [the need] of haveing some letters written to the leading democratick papers, &c. And it meets their entire approbation. This I will have done shortly after the organisiation of the House.

Present my respects to Mrs. Polk and accept for yourself my best wishes &c.

HOP. L TURNEY

ALS. DLC–JKP. Addressed to Nashville.

1. Harvey M. Watterson.

FROM CAVE JOHNSON

Dear Sir, Washington December 16th [1839][1]

We are at last defeated & in the way I told you some two weeks since.[2] You will perceive by the voting (which I sent Coe this morning[)] that Jones recd. 113 votes—Lewis 3 (Jones, Griffin & Campbell) &

Pickens 5 *(Holmes, Sumpter, Hunter, Fisher & Rogers* [)].[3] The second ballotting was the same. The third ballotting Hubbard, Bynum & some other went to Lewis & then the cry was raised Jones has no chance—Lewis is the only man that can be elected. The nullifyers Griffin, Campbell, Fisher, Rogers, Holmes & Sumpter, professed Admn. men had no doubt determined, under the schooling of certain leaders to adhere to their men & thereby force the balance to come to them. I saw this I thought clearly, as did many more of our men & determined under no circumstances to yield to it. These men, so lately having come to our ranks could take no man of our party proper, thought too contemptibly of us for that & yet would force us to go for one of their men or elect an opposition man. I would have lost my right arm before I would have yielded to such conduct—& I was glad to find many of our men good & true, who took the same view of the matter—Drumgoole, McCoy, Conner, Frank Thomas & the other Thomas of Maryland, Banks, Turney & Blackwell & Genl. Carr & Casey[4] & we prevented the election of Lewis & thereupon, S. Carolina Dem[ocrats] (except Rhett), Fisher, & all the Whigs united on Hunter & he was elected on the 11th ballot. I rejoice at the result as we could not get a thorough friend of the adm. & the result proves that we were right. How could we trust men as our leaders, who would under any circumstances cast their votes for a whig rather than unite with us in the election of Jones. I expect they intended to rule us when they joined us—and if we are to submit to such relation from such a squad our friends must get a different sort of man from me. I am yet induced to believe that Calhoun has had no hand in the matter and disapproves of the course of his S.C. friends but is no doubt rejoiced at the Success of Hunter & it is claimed here allready as a Calhoun victory over both the parties. It will have one evil tendency [and] perhaps many more that I do not see. It will I fear make the nullifyers dissatisfied with the friends of the Administration & in that way affect the public business. Calhoun says it will not & that Hunter will give a fair support to the administration, but I cannot see how he is to do this after his election by the Whigs.

I am glad it is over and I suppose we shall now soon go to business & Hunter's course will soon develope his party predilections & satisfy us whether he deserves our support. I have heard this evening that we impracticable Democrats are to be denounced thro the Globe but I will not believe this until I see it, tho. I have heard rumors for two weeks past, that the Globe was for Pickens in order to secure the Southern votes for printer. We shall see in a few days.

The nomination of Harrison[5] makes our Southern friends believe that the slave holding states will be united except Ky. & the Whigs I understand count upon his election without them. I have heard a whisper of getting up another candidate. I have heard but little for a day or two as to the Vice presi[dency].[6] I fear my course & Turneys will do you no good as to the Vice presidency but Brown, Waterson[7] & McClelan[8] having gone for Lewis may save you from any harm.

C. JOHNSON

ALS. DLC–JKP. Addressed to Nashville and mailed under cover of Cave Johnson to Polk, December 17, 1839. ALS. DLC–JKP.

1. Year identified through content analysis.

2. See Johnson to Polk, December 7, 1839. On December 15, 1839, Johnson wrote, "I was not mistaken in the *under current* which I wrote you two or three weeks since was at work. And the States right men had nearly succeeded in getting the nomination for Lewis . . . ." ALS. DLC–JKP.

3. Levin H. Coe, John W. Jones, Dixon H. Lewis, John K. Griffin, John Campbell, Francis W. Pickens, Isaac E. Holmes, Thomas D. Sumter, Robert M. T. Hunter, Charles Fisher, and James Rogers. Johnson's reference is to the election of the House Speaker, the first ballot for which was taken on December 14, 1839. Representatives Griffin, Campbell, Sumter, and Rogers were South Carolina nullifiers; all but Griffin were Democrats.

4. George C. Dromgoole, James I. McKay, Henry W. Connor, Francis Thomas, Philip F. Thomas, Linn Banks, Hopkins L. Turney, Julius W. Blackwell, John Carr, and Zadoc Casey. Dromgoole, a lawyer and a Democrat from Virginia, served five terms in the U.S. House, 1835–41 and 1843–47. Philip Thomas of Maryland served as a Democrat in the U.S. House, 1839–41; governor of Maryland, 1848–51; comptroller of the U.S. Treasury, 1851–53; collector of the port of Baltimore, 1853–60; commissioner of patents, 1860; secretary of the treasury, 1860–61; and U.S. Senator, 1875–77. Carr of Indiana, a veteran of the Battle of Tippecanoe, rose to the rank of major general in the Indiana militia and served in the U.S. House, 1831–37 and 1839–41. Casey, lieutenant governor of Illinois in 1830, served as a Democrat in the U.S. House for ten years, 1833–43.

5. At their recent convention in Harrisburg, Pennsylvania, the Whigs had nominated William Henry Harrison for the presidency.

6. Part of this word is obliterated by the seal of the letter.

7. Harvey M. Watterson.

8. Abraham McClellan.

FROM DAVID HUBBARD

Dear Sir Washington 17th Decr 1839

You will have seen ere this that we were defeated in the election of speaker & this mainly through the Delegations from Tennessee & Maryland. You doubtless know that each of those states had candidates before us for that office & altho we had no objection to them as men, we beleived that others could unite more votes.[1] In this we were not mistaken, but our misfortune was in not being able to secure the Delegation from states having pretenders to this office & the people of the United States will wonder why they could not unite with their brether[2] who were not offering Candidates & I fear that to mortification & disappointment, will be attributed the disasters we have met. Altho we have elected [a] speaker,[3] we are yet at sea on the New Jersey case, because the whigs have again brought in a resolution to admit the whig members from that state before we elect printer & clerk & how it will end is past my knowledge.

DAVID HUBBARD

PS Your friends Brown, Waterson[4] & McLelland,[5] supported our party in the election of speaker & this I hope will free Tennessee from the bad feeling which otherwise would have prevailed upon such a disappointment as we have met.[6] David Hubbard

ALS. DLC–JKP. Addressed to Nashville and marked "private." AE on the cover states that this letter was answered on December 30, 1839.

1. Cave Johnson of Tennessee and Francis Thomas of Maryland were their states' favorite-son candidates.

2. Misspelling of "brethren."

3. Robert M. T. Hunter.

4. Harvey M. Watterson.

5. Abraham McClellan.

6. For Cave Johnson's assessment of his defection in the Speaker's election, see Johnson to Polk, December 16, 1839.

FROM J. G. M. RAMSEY

My Dear Sir　　　　Mecklenburg T Dec. 18, 1839

I returned a few days since from Charleston & Columbia S.C. whither I had gone to attend the annual meeting of the Stockholders of the S.W.R.R. Bank[1] & the adjourned meeting of the Stockholders of the L.C.&C.R.R. Co. I appeared there in the character of proxy for most of the private Stockholders in both companies from this State & having the Commission your confidence had assigned me as the representative of the State stock. You will have received before this time the printed proceedings of the Bank Meeting at Charleston & have already acted upon the report of the Principal Cashier[2] giving a statement of the concerns of the Branch at Knoxville. To that statement nothing further need be added but that the Branch has never suspended specie payments & we continue to redeem our issues whenever presented. Indeed our specie has increased & we can speak to our "enemy at our gates." That we have continued to pay specie is the more creditable to us as every other Institution in the State & any where out of it near us, has suspended some months since. Indeed I feel as the President of this Branch as much obligation to meet its liabilities as I would to take up my own were there any out against me. I believe we shall weather the storm with entire safety. I say these things in no spirit of vain boasting—for no one ought to boast that he pays his debts—but because as no friend of ours as far as I know has stated in the Legislature that ours was not among the Banks that had suspended the impression may prevail at Nashville that we have fallen into the general current. It is not so.

You will receive in a few days the proceedings of the R.R. meeting at Columbia. The principal object of the meeting was to obtain aid from the Legislature to advance the work, as the fall in the price of cotton will prevent calls upon the Stockholders from being met in time to pay a debt due from the Co in January. The opinion was prevalent at Columbia when I left that the State would make an advance upon a loan heretofore made.[3]

The subject of a union of the interests of our Co. & the Hiwassee company was very *wisely* refered by the meeting to a Committee of Tennessee Stockholders—with directions to report to the next annual meeting in September. I say wisely for certainly nothing can be more unjust—unequal & impolitic than the proposition to unite the interests of the two companies by *Legislation.*[4] Bear with me one minute while I say that S.C., N.C. & Tennessee have entered into a partnership to unite Knoxville with Charleston by a Rail Road. The good faith of the three states & of the Stockholders in each is pledged to each other to construct it. Tennessee & her citizens have contributed enough to finish the Tennessee part of the road & now when Carolina has commenced the work a bill is introduced in the Tenn. Leg. to abandon the enterprise.[5] It is bad faith to North & S. Carolina—& the good faith of a state is not to be estimated by dollars & cents. It is also unjust to our Tenn. stockholders. We have met our instalments punctually & the State has given us her bonds for $32.000 & we have carefully guarded against the expenditure of a single dollar more than was necessary to make the survey. The State bonds are secure in our vaults, $32.000 as first received, as also the individual instalments. The Tennessee Directors have determined not to construct a mile of the road—nor expend any of their funds till the road reaches our line & if it never reaches it, the bonds belong of course to the State & the instalments to our stockholders & now it is proposed in the Legislature to take these bonds & this money secure as it now is & productive (for it is so in the Bank) & to place it in the hands of those who have exhausted their own resources, State bonds & all,[6] as I am told & if the Georgia works are suspended as Gov Gilmer says they must be—these funds will be squandered & no connection at last be formed between Tennessee & her Southern sisters. It is also unjust to the upper counties of E.T. Because the taking the State bonds appropriated to a work in the upper counties & expending them in the lower is to deprive the former of all benefit intended to be secured to them by the act of 1837 giving to each the 650.000. It was a compromise between them & ought not to be violated. It is furthermore contrary to the wise policy hitherto adopted by our State in her public works—viz to take only a certain part of the expenditures in constructing them. It is in fact making the H.R. a State work & disturbing the proposition or relation that ought to exist between individual & State investment & we all know how State or U.S. works are managed. There are some prominent objections to the bill introduced in the Legislature to unite the two roads. There are others of a minor character but bearing on their face Whig management & intrigue under the pretense of building a Road to unite with a suspended one in Georgia & which if built will never pay 1 per cent. They are trying indirectly to get Banking privileges for an insolvent company. And by the amendment proposed in the bill to give the election of President of the Branch to the Tennessee Directors & allowing him to be a merchant—its Whig mover is laying a plan to put it under Whig influence & displace its present presiding officer. My *currency* sentiments & practice had given offence in high places & my banking & political principles are the true foundation of this measure. Here it is known to be so. At Nashville our friends may view it otherwise. I hope no one of them will allow Jacobs to mislead him. Mr. Gillespies constituents, some of them at least, may be in favor of the proposed union. Mr. Wheeler—Col. Aiken—Mr. Fain & indeed all the upper counties Democrats & Whigs & indirectly all the State if they want the state bonds safely & profitably invested will oppose the Union. Some of the Whigs in Knoxville affect to be in favor of it—but most of them say they will not continue stockholders to the amount they now hold in the road. It is all a humb-bug to barter away our Banking privileges for the use of the Whigs. To you I need not say my little salary has no influence in dictating these remarks. True I do not like for another to reap where I have sowed but I do object as a representative of the interests of this Co. & for a short time the guardian of the good faith

& credit & funds of the State to the proposed amalgamation—& would allow you to make use of this letter any way you might think proper but that it would be said at once that my private interest had dictated its contents & I am extremely sensitive on that subject. It may therefore remain *inter nos.*[7] I cannot believe the bill will pass. It would surprise our Carolina partners if it should & bankrupt some of our Stockholders over whose investment I have carefully watched & which is at the present perfectly secure & will remain so if undisturbed by officious legislation. The Committees appointed at Columbia are competent to arrange the Union & it ought to be left to them. If I should not find time to write to Col. Laughlin or Col. Aiken I leave it to your discretion to let them see this letter—or know some of its contents.

During my journey I passed through many of the Districts of S. Carolina & the Western part of North Carolina & was not an idle or uninterested spectator of the political movement there. When I went first to Charleston in 1828, I met with a warm hearted reception—principally because I was a Tennessean & a countryman of Jackson. My reception now was not less cordial. The estrangement of feeling which for a time existed between S.C. & T. has in a great measure given way to harmoney & identity of political sentiment.[8] Some of the older politicians affect an indifference to federal politics but much of the greater part of them are decidedly with Tennessee & the present adminstration *& will go for it & its measures.* At Charleston I met with Mr. Calhoun. His first enquiry was answered by mentioning the great revolution that had taken place last summer in Tennessee. He said it was unexpected to most people. I said it was not wholly so to me—that Tennessee never was & never would be for Mr. Clay & that she was now occupying her true position—& had been placed there mainly through your agency. He was evidently gratified in admitting the truth of all I said. In continuing the conversation I mentioned that in the primary assemblages of our people & in our Legislature you had been nominated for the Vice-presidency—that in so doing we intended no idle or unmeaning compliment to you but presented you in earnest to our *sister states* & the Union as the most fit for the station. He replied that your claims were strong & unquestioned. His friends standing at the time around us went further & said you ought & would be elected. Mr. Holmes the member elect from Charleston & the leading men of the City with whom I was thrown every day for two weeks are favorable to the ticket. I met on several occasions Mr. Cleveland formerly M.C. from Georgia now of Charleston. He is even boisterous for you & wherever I met him or his wife (who charged me to give her best regards to Mrs. P. & yourself) the party became almost a nominating Committee.[9] At Columbia where I spent several days I noticed a like feeling. Gov. Noble[10] was evidently interested in what I said on the subject & many of the members of the Legislature are for you. In taking leave of some friends in the presence of the Gov. I said to Doctor Donivant[11] "I leave Col. Polk in your care. You seem so much his friend that I shall not be surprised if you nominate him before you adjourn. He said he would as soon do it as not." I have some opportunity of knowing the sentiment of the Carolinas—& now give it as my opinion that if S.C. votes you will receive it. & are certain of N. Carolina. I have no copies left of your Inaugural to send back to my friends—it must be done. Those that had seen it pronounce it the very essence of old school Republicanism. A list of names is inclosed[12] to whom some of our friends should forward it. I wish I had a few.

At home here our cause advances. A measure which I tried to effect last spring has just been consummated. Col. Ramsey[13] has sold out the Register & retired—& I know that paper has done more for Whiggery here than all the other whig papers put together. This nucleus around which the party hung is dissolved & the fragments of it are a "chaos, rudis indigestaque moles"[14] & can never be reunited. They say here Judge White will not resign. I sometimes wish to say something of you to a *confidential* friend at Nashville & not to yourself—as some of the above remarks. Who is he?

J. G. M. RAMSEY

ALS. DLC–JKP. Addressed to Nashville.

1. The Southwestern Railroad Bank was a subsidiary of the Louisville, Cincinnati and Charleston Railroad Company.

2. David A. Deaderick.

3. In 1840 the South Carolina legislature advanced the company $600,000 on the state's stock subscription.

4. Solomon D. Jacobs' merger bill, which would have transferred unsold state bonds from the LC&C Railroad to the Hiwassee Railroad, received Whig support, but failed to reach the floor of the Tennessee House.

5. On January 25, 1840, the Tennessee legislature ended any further state subscriptions in internal improvement companies. This repeal legislation upheld the state's previous bond issuances; allowed companies the privilege of returning unsold state bonds, should directorates prefer dissolution; granted the governor visitorial powers over all active projects; and instructed the attorney general to prosecute any company official the governor suspected guilty of fraud. The law specifically exempted river improvements.

6. The Hiwassee Railroad Company had received and sold $650,000 in state bonds; the LC&C Railroad Company still held $450,000 in unsold state bonds.

7. Latin phrase for "between us."

8. Reference is to the nullification controversy of 1832–33.

9. Jesse Franklin Cleveland served as a Union Democrat in the U.S. House from 1835 until 1839; following his service in Congress he left Georgia and returned to his native state of South Carolina. Cleveland settled in Charleston and ran a mercantile establishment until his death in 1841. His wife is not identified further.

10. A graduate of Princeton College, Patrick Noble studied law under John C. Calhoun, served terms in both houses of the South Carolina legislature, and became governor in 1838.

11. Donivant is not identified further.

12. Enclosure not found.

13. William B. A. Ramsey.

14. Quotation is from Ovid's *Metamorphoses* 1.7. and may be translated, "Chaos, a rude and undigested mass."

FROM ALEXANDER O. ANDERSON

Near Knoxville (At Home)
My Dear Sir Thursday Night[1] Decr. 21st 1839

I returned home last night, after an absence of some days, & have just had the opportunity for the first time, of looking at the Bill, which it seems has passed the Senate, providing for the Union of the Charleston & Hiwassee Rail Roads.[2] I have Examined it carefully, and am extremely surprised that it appears to have met with no difficulties from any of our friends. Of all the Bills I have ever seen, when there was a vigilant eye kept by two contending Parties over the movements of each other, I have never met with one which so completely cripples the one and strengthens the other, without having awakened any apprehensions. I need not repeat to you the desperate & powerful efforts against which we have had to struggle, unaided by any advantages whatever. You were made to feel & you well understood all this in the recent efforts in which you so signally triumphed. If that Bill of *Union passes in the shape in which it is* I have no hesitation in saying, that in an unsuspecting moment the Democratic Party has sealed the *Doom of their friends in East Tennessee.* I am decidedly in favor of the Union of the two roads, but upon widely different principles, from those which are embraced by the Bill—not so far as the Question of making the [Louisville, Cincinnati &] Charleston RailRoad is concerned. That I think ought to be given up under the circumstances, but as it regards *the powers which are to grow out of the Act*—& which will be *en masse* concentrated in the hands of our enemies. They may consent to conciliate *some where to obtain certain objects,* but the impact of the Bill reaches to the actual possession of every power which will be exerted by the Bank or the Rail Road, with a view—a certainty—that every thing will be confined within the control of the Whigs. It is so designed—and a moments reflection will satisfy anyone conversant here with the state of the facts—and the state of Parties. The Bill provides for an equal share of stock by private Individuals, with that of the state. The Individual stock is now held by a large majority of the Whigs & *will be then,* so that they will give a solid phalanx of individual Directors to the Whigs. The Bank will be Whig. The Road *powers* will be Whig. The Presidents will be Whig & all the offices &c &c—and this will be added to the present machinery in this end of the state. *I entreat that our friends shall examine this matter well,* & not go forward without knowing the true condition of things.

The Act ought to provide that the stockholders of the Charleston Rail Road shall be released from their subscriptions if they see fit—& simply that the state shall subscribe the amt to the Hiwassee Rail Road, which is *unexpended,* of her stock in the Charleston rail Road—and that Individuals be *allowed* to subscribe one half of that amount *Only*—and that the state shall therupon take that increased proportion of Directors in the Hiwassee Bank & Rail Road. Nothing short of this superior power will do. Otherwise, we are *ruined politically* in East Tennessee. The state shoud retain the *Exclusive Visatorial Power.* In the same section of that Bill which provides for the transfer of the stock—it also provides that merchants may be qualified to be Presidents & Cashiers &c &c. This provision has *a particular object,* for the benefit of the most fierce of the Party, & who pursued you with untiring diligence & malignity. I cannot be mistaken—that Bill, as it now stands, will destroy us.

The Bill ought to provide that the state shall hav double the amt of the Individual stock—and directors in proportion, appointed by the Governor, every year. The Individual Directors appointed by the stock holders for the same term—&c.

Merchants should be made ineligible to the Presidency & the Chasherships.

The Bill ought specially to provide that no officer of the Rail Road or Bank—President or cashiers, or of any other grade—*(specifying the Engineers also particularly) should be concerned in any Contract in any mode whatever* & it ought to provide that every Officer—including the Presidents & Cashiers and *Engineers, should take an Oath* that they are *in no wise, nearly or remotely,* directly or indirectly, either by *writing* or *confidential verbal agreement or understanding* interested in any Contract—and that they will not be!!! This too is of the very first importance. The Bill ought to provide that a *full investigation shall be made into the concerns of the Hiwassee Rail Road &c*—and that said investigation shall be made by a Commission of three persons appointed by the Governor—& that those persons shall constitute a Committee of Inspectors from year to year, under the appointment of the Governor (to be made every year for that special occasion). It is needed. It is essential.

Further, this is the time for amending defects in the Hiwassee Charter—the Power to enter forfeitures against the stockeholders should be declared, but the power to sue abolished. It now exists. No corporate Company should possess such power. It is sufficent that the right of forfeiture should be in their hand. It is a powerful and *imperial right of itself*—but the right to sue stock holders for the recovery of subscriptions when no valuable consideration ever was created, is equally odious and despotic. By all means this should cease. It was ingrafted by a few cunning & designing lines edged into a section, the whole matter of which was irrelevant to such a claim, and hence originally passed and done without due caution. I do trust that the Democratic Party will not suffer itself to be so terribly overreached in this matter. You may depend upon it that Bill is pregnant, in its present shape, with the most alarming mischiefs to our Party, & no matter *who may advise it* as it now stands, if it passes—I repeat our Doom is fixed. Certainly, when the state has so much at stake, she ought to have not only the exclusive Visatorial Power, but she ought to have the Directory Power. I cannot sufficiently express the lively interest which I feel, except by repeating, that if that Bill passes without some such provisions as I hav named—our Doom is fixed—and *our victories turned into Defeat.*

I am anxious the Democratic Party should pass some measure for the transfer of their stock, or increases of the state stock to the Hiwassee Rail Road, but not in such a shape as to strengthen our enemies. If the Bill passes as it now is, it will create a sort of political life-Estate of power to the Federal Party in East Tennessee.

It seems to me the wisest course will be to hold it up, & not to pass it until the very last of the session—& then to pass it with the provisions I have suggested. They are for the public good.

I want nothing in the shape of power of that kind for the Democratic Party to be used politically—but it is due to themselves—to their Country, to provide against the machinations of a skilful aristocracy who if they had the power would *move with all its force upon us*, as they have done in times past.

If the Democratic Party shall move forward in this business in the way suggested, with a view to great public end, & with ample Checks &

guards, you will find the whole Federal phalanx will vote against the Bill!!!

I have conferred with some of our Confidential friends upon this subject. They think with me, & called upon me the moment I have returned home from the Cross Roads, & have great anxiety upon this subject!

So Harrison is nominated instead of Clay. I regret this as far as East Tennessee is concerned. Altho' I trust we shall be able to turn it to account and I hope the present sinuous movements of the Whigs will be more & more watched—for as things go, that Bill in its present form, to which I hav referred, might be the means of creating a desperate struggle for the Presidency in this region. Some of our friends think the nomination of Harrison more difficult to contend with here than Clay. Of this I could not at this moment (it is so recent)[3] form an opinion upon which to rely. But these apprehensions, only, should serve to increase our Caution not to trust our enemies with too much power at this moment.

We know nothing here now of the movements of Judge White—but I have little doubt he will resign in time for Legislative action—as he is irrevocably pledged, and must act pretty early in the session, after the complete organization of Congress. Of course it is impracticable that our Legislature should adjourn very soon, in the present state of business &c &c.

Brownlow in his vile sheet has attacked me fiercely, & proposes to continue his efforts. He was present at the Bell supper. Judge White then refered to me, & this degraded Editor has taken up the *hint*, and obeyed his orders. Our papers will not notice him—& one of the objects of his abuse will be lost—that of obtaining a contest. He says in the same paper[4] that Mr Blair is the only Democrat acceptable to the Whigs—and that he has "*claims on both sides.*" His allusions to me are base falsehoods in every particular.

A Anderson

ALS. DLC–JKP. Addressed to Nashville and marked "Private & Confidential."

1. In 1839 the twenty-first day of December fell on a Saturday.

2. See J. G. M. Ramsey to Polk, December 18, 1839.

3. The Whig National Convention assembled at Harrisburg, Pennsylvania, on December 4, 1839, and two days later chose William H. Harrison its presidential nominee. On the fourth and final day of the meeting the convention selected John Tyler for second place on the 1840 ticket.

4. Reference is to the Elizabethton *Tennessee Whig;* William G. Brownlow's attack on Anderson is not identified further.

FROM CAVE JOHNSON

Washington City. December[1] 21, 1839

Johnson reports on business in the House of Representatives. The new Speaker[2] does "only tolerably well"; he is "ignorant of the rules" and lacks the essential energy and power to command. The House has rejected the New Jersey Whig delegation by five votes, and Garland has defeated Clarke for clerk of the House by a narrow margin.

ALS. DLC–JKP. Addressed to Nashville.

1. Month identified through content analysis.
2. Robert M. T. Hunter.

FROM JOHN J. GARNER

Yalobusha County, Mississippi. December 25, 1839

Acknowledging Polk's letter of November 14,[1] Garner replies that Chisholm & Minter assured him that unless instructed otherwise it is their standard practice to insure all cotton and that they arranged special coverage with Polk's New Orleans commission merchants.[2] Garner has agreed with McNeal to remain as Polk's overseer for another year and apologizes for not having informed Polk earlier. All of the Negroes are well, and Charles came home on December 5. This year the farm has produced 130 bales of cotton and 3,900 pounds of pork.

ALS. DLC–JKP. Addressed to Nashville. Published in Bassett, *Plantation Overseer*, 130–31.

1. Letter not found.
2. M. D. Cooper & Company.

FROM JULIUS W. BLACKWELL

Dear Sir, Washington Decr. 30th 1839

Your esteemed favour of the 18th inst.[1] came to hand to night (monday night 9 Oclock) and I am sorry I have nothing interestin to communicate to you. I have been confined to my room for the last two days, and did not attend at the House today.

No doubt, you have learned that we have a Nullifying, Subtreasury Whig for Speaker, and that Mr. Garland is reelected Clerk, Dorsey

Sergt. at A[rm]s, and the old door keeper.[2] We have a small majority in the House, exclusive of the 5 N. Jersey members, but it is very close voting. I understand that the committees were appointed to day, and will be published in the papers tomorrow. John W. Jones at the head of the Com. of ways & means, Pickens of Foreign affairs, Thomas of Md.—Navy, Campbell of S.C.—elections, J. Q. Adams—manufactures are some that I have heard of to night, but the News Papers will probably reach you as soon as this.

Strange, it is passing strange, that an American House of Rep. should spend a month before they could organize and proceed to business. But tis' true, and I had rather see another month thrown away, than that the Gov. of N. Jersey[3] should be permitted to fource 5 members in, who were rejected by the voters of that State.

Mr. Speaker Hunter, in my humble judgment, is too young, for the important station he occupies. While you were Speaker, your friends praised, and your enemies abused you, but it is now admitted, on all sides, that Jas. K. Polk was the best presiding officer that we have had for many years, and some say the best we ever had. Now that you are out of Congress, all seem to be willing to do you Justice. I do not wish to flatter, for I dispise it, but when justice is meted out to a publick servant, tho' it[4] comes at a late period, he should know it.

We have been so much occupied with this N. Jersey question, that I have heard but little said on the subject of the V. Presidency. But I have some reason to believe, that you will be pretty generally taken up as the candidate.

Some few states seem not willing to throw aside Col. Johnson, but I do hope he may not be run. To carry him in Tennessee, is to carry a mill stone dangling around our necks. It will not do to run him in Ten. & the South generally. They will not go for him.

I have gained a character already for—*stubbornness,* because I did not vote for Dixon H. Lewis for speaker. If the issue had been brot fairly between two Nulifiers, then I would not have hesitated, but it was not made. Maj. Brown[5] pitched heavily upon the Nullifiers, in his speeches last summer, and contended that they headed the V.B. party in both Houses and I know, had I voted for Lewis, that it would have injured the cause greatly in Ten. particularly in my district.

In no part of Ten. does the prejudice of the people run higher against Nullifiers, than in the 4th Congressional District. But it will not do to reject, and throw them off. They are a great help to us at this time.

AL. DLC–JKP. Addressed to Nashville and franked "Free/J. W. Blackwell." Polk's file endorsement reads "Hon. Julius W. Blackwell."

1. Letter not found.

2. Robert M. T. Hunter, Speaker; Hugh A. Garland, clerk; Roderick Dorsey, sergeant at arms; and Joseph Follansbee, doorkeeper.

3. William Pennington.

4. Blackwell wrote "is" for "it."

5. Thomas Brown, commissioned a major in the East Tennessee Volunteer Cavalry in 1812, represented Roane County in the Tennessee House, 1817–19 and 1821–23, and served as clerk and master of the Roane Chancery Court, 1834–48. In 1839 he failed to win the Whig nomination in Tennessee's Fourth Congressional District.

TO DAVID HUBBARD

My Dear Sir Nashville Decr 30th 1839

I had the pleasure to receive your letter of the 17th three days ago, and regret as much as you can, the want of consent and harmony of action among our friends, by which you were defeated in the Speaker's election. When you had the power in your own hands, it was a *great mistake* that our friends could not & did not unite. Though much to be regretted, it cannot now be remedied. I hope however that nothing has occurred to prevent a perfect union upon the great question of the currency and the finances which divids the parties in the House as well as in the country. If you can carry the Independent Treasury measure (as I have no doubt you can if you are united) all will yet be well. I think well of Mr Hunter as a man. His principles too as far as I observed his course in the last Congress, were orthodox, and but for the fact that he owes his election mainly to our opponents, I should have confidence, that he would give to the administration a fair support. I have no idea that he can or will abandon the principles upon which he stands pledged before the country, and if he shall rise above the consideration that he was elected mainly by those who oppose his principles, and shall in the organization of the House steadily pursue them, he will add to his own reputation and you will have but little difficulty. I hope no heart-burnings whereby you may be weakened, may be permitted to exist in consequence of what has passed.

We have the Globe of the 20th and the Intelligencer of the 21st—from which I see that Governor Pennington's *"broad seal"* certificate men have again been rejected.[1] I have never known so great an outrage committed on the popular rights, as the attempt made in this instance to force men into seats as Representatives who are notoriously not entitled to them. All the special pleadings of our opponents cannot so mystify the case, as to prevent the commonest mind from understanding it. The great body of the people look to the substantial facts in the case, and care but little for ticknicalities and the alleged sanctitey of the "*Broad Seal.*" I think it probable that on saturday of the third week you elected the clerk and Printer, and possibly received the President's message.[2] If so we will get the message to night. It is looked for with much interest.

A grand Whig meeting is called here for the 4 of January, to ratify the Harrisburg nominations.[3] It is a bitter pill to some of the leaders, but they will all be whipped in. The current rumour here is that White & Foster (if the former resigns) are to head the Whig electoral ticket. They will make a desperate struggle to regain the political power of the State. Make my kind respects to your colleagues Lewis & Chapman.

James K. Polk

ALS. DLC–Blair & Rives Papers. Addressed to Washington and marked "*Private.*" Hubbard's endorsement reads as follows: "J K Polks Letter 27th [*sic*] decr 1839. Answered 21 Jany 1840—stating that party ties did not seem to bind much where petty ambition held its sway & that I feared Blair & Reeves were already marked for destruction by those who could & would not elect Lewis." Hubbard's reply has not been found.

1. On December 20, 1839, the House refused to seat the New Jersey delegation commissioned by William Pennington.

2. On December 21, 1839, the House elected Hugh A. Garland clerk and on January 30, 1840, selected Blair & Rives to serve as public printers. Martin Van Buren's Third Annual Message, dated December 2, 1839, was read in both houses of Congress on December 24, 1839.

3. See Polk to Sarah C. Polk, April 20, 1839.

FROM WILLIAM H. POLK

Columbia, Tennessee. December 30, 1839

Responding to a letter from Polk[1] concerning the escape of Charles, his slave, William H. Polk writes that he has made inquiries and has learned that Charles' family lives near Cornersville, to which place the slave might have fled. Of course, it is possible that he might have remained in the vicinity of Somerville. William H. Polk declines to purchase Reuben on a cash basis, but offers to cancel Polk's note of $1083 in exchange. Fisher, the druggist,[2] will pay $130 per annum for Reuben's hire. Campbell will be in town to close his purchase of 100 acres belonging to the estate of Brother Samuel.[3] William H.

Polk questions whether it is legal to sell the property prior to dividing it and laying off that portion left to Brother Marshall's children.[4] If no reply is received by Wednesday, the sale will be consummated as planned.

ALS. DLC–JKP. Addressed to Nashville. AE on the cover states that this letter was answered on January 1, 1840; Polk's reply has not been found. Published in Bassett, *Plantation Overseer*, 131–32.

1. Letter not found.
2. In 1838 A. B. Fisher and Thomas J. Kilpatrick, a physician from Lebanon, purchased Joseph Bretney's drug stocks and lease on Polk's building, which was located on the courthouse square next door to the Columbia Inn. See Samuel P. Walker to Polk, December 14, 1838.
3. No sale of Samuel W. Polk's lands to a purchaser with the surname Campbell has been found; Campbell is not further identified.
4. Reference is to Roxana Eunice Ophelia Polk and Marshall Tate Polk, Jr., children of Marshall Tate and Laura Wilson Polk.

FROM JAMES WALKER

Dear Sir Columbia, Dec. 30. 1839

William I presume has not written you respecting Reubin.[1] He says he does not think he can buy him, unless it is upon your two year note. Speaks of offering you $1000 for him on that note. This would be equal to about $700 cash as his hire certainly ought to be good for $150 pr. annum. I have told him if he would not take him as Cash now, he ought at least to go down to the District and turn Harry[2] into money for you which can be done, I think if there was any one to attend to it. He says he will go to Cornersville to see if any thing can be heard of your runaway negro.[3] But I think this is uncertain unless you urge him to it. I have thought a good deal about the aspect of your Cash affairs. If you get what you expect from Yell[4] with what bank accommodations you may get you can get on and relieve yourself by degrees. The difficulty is that the whole amount of your debts are pressing down upon you at once. You ought, if practicable (and I think it is) to get your debts so arranged that you could pay them in instalments, reducing about $2000 pr. an. Your plantation would supply this, pay its own expenses, and supply I presume the deficit of your expenses beyond your salary.

Unless our Democratic members, in caucus or some other way agree among themselves what is best to do in state policy, *and do it* I fear they will do a *sinking political* business. The Whigs are certainly using most adroitly, the advantages which the want of concerted action on the part of the Democratic members, gives them. They know that the country holds the Democratic party responsible for the doings of the Session. If they can manage to protract the session, and convince the people that what is done is oppressive on the mass, and important measures left unaccomplished, they will have arguments in the next canvass which it will be difficult to meet. The cause of the Whig members and the Whig press is manifestly destructive. They clearly desire that nothing shall be done to remedy the existing defects in the Bank & improvement law—that the Legislature should pursue such a harassing course towards the Banks, as to force them in self defence to oppress the country.

Thomas, has I presume, by this time introduced his system of internal improvement.[5] If he passes it I think it will give him much reputation and enable us without risque or difficulty to lay Watterson & Martin aside and be respectably represented in Congress. The effect of his Bill will be, to save the state an expenditure of from two to two and a half millions of dollars, that will otherwise be thrown away—nearly or quite half the Charters already subscribed to, will be surrendered. A compromise will be effected between the interests of East Ten, Middle T. & the District, equalizing the expenditure in each. The improvements made will pay interest. I hope it may pass, for the general interest, though I doubt whether we can under it, go on and complete our road.[6] We cannot go on and complete our road in a reasonably short time unless at least a portion of the states stock is made available. 5 pr. cent even Sterling bonds are not now available, except at a greater loss than we could bear. But if the best which can be done for general interest, is accomplished, we neither can nor will complain, but will make the best of it—if that is to surrender under the law. Our road is certainly of great importance to this section of country, and if we can possibly do so, we will go through with it. My interests at, and near the Ten. river, makes it highly important for me to *go on*—but all the Co. have not the same interest.

The Whigs have decidedly the advantage of us in the currency question. It was the currency question which enabled them to overthrow us four years ago. There is danger that it may again give us a back sett. The country is now ground down for want of a circulating medium. It is not coin that the people want, and must have. It is something that will pay debts and relieve the pressure. Unquestionably solvent bank paper will answer all desireable purposes. It is the merchants alone that suffer by the suspension and increased rates of Exchange. If Exchange is kept down, as it is, what interest can suffer by the suspension? The Whigs are goading on our party to harsh measures towards the Banks. They cry out "*you are the hard money party*—carry out your doctrines."

Knowing that as the Banks are borne on, they must bear upon their debtors, and increase the difficulties now almost insurmountable. We are the *sound currency party* and let us carry out our doctrines, but not as destructively as our opponents wickedly wish. If the banks and people are permitted to work through their difficulties in their own way, all will yet be well. When we again get out, it will be time enough to provide against the difficulties of overtrading. The country can right up, with a little more time. Why break things to pieces, to satisfy the malevolence of the Whig party? No one pretends that the banks of Tennessee are now acting imprudently. They are still straining too hard. This crop will afford great relief, even at low prices. Then why not let them alone, and allow them to allow as much indulgence to solvent debtors as they safely can. They will no doubt resume as early as it is prudent to do so, and (altho it may sound strange to those who claim to controul them,) *they are the best judges of the time.* My doctrine is to let the banks alone for the present and let them know unofficially that it is to be so. If harsh measures are adopted, forcing them to wind up, the country must be ruined—and I think Democratic ascendancy destroyed. What do men care for country—when the country ruins them. I do not think it would look well, to pass any measure approving the suspension. No action is certainly best according to my judgement. Most of the Democratic states, where there has been suspension have acted liberally and it must be the true policy under the present embarrassing state of things.

I think the Democratic party ought to have a National Convention as early as practicable. The Whigs are moving Heaven & Earth and we ought not to sleep.

James Walker

ALS. DLC–JKP. Addressed to Nashville. AE on the cover states that this letter was answered on January 3, 1840; Polk's reply has not been found. Published in Bassett, *Plantation Overseer*, 133–34.

1. See William H. Polk to Polk, December 30, 1839.
2. Harry, a slave belonging to Samuel W. Polk's estate, of which James K. Polk was executor, worked for hire as a blacksmith at Carrollton, Mississippi.
3. Reference is Polk's slave, Charles.
4. See Archibald Yell to Polk, September 15 and 16, 1839.
5. See J. G. M. Ramsey to Polk, December 18, 1839.
6. The Columbia Central Turnpike Company, incorporated by an act of the General Assembly in 1837, received $150,000 in state bonds and built approximately seventy miles of improved road from Columbia to Clifton, via Mt. Pleasant, at a reported cost of slightly more than $300,000.

FROM JOHN J. GARNER

Yalobusha County, Mississippi. December 31, 1839

In reply to Polk's inquiry of the 5th instant,[1] Garner expresses pleasure at Polk's suggestion for attaching a grist mill to the gin. Garner again assures Polk that his cotton is insured[2] and states that 132 bales will be shipped to New Orleans on the first boats unless Polk directs otherwise.

ALS. DLC–JKP. Addressed to Nashville. Published in Bassett, *Plantation Overseer*, 134–35.

1. Letter not found.
2. See John J. Garner to Polk, December 25, 1839.

1840

FROM CAVE JOHNSON

Dear Sir, Washington 1 Jany 1840

I had the pleasure of receiving two letters[1] from you within a few days, to which I have not before replied because I had nothing to write of any interest to you. Tho we have done nothing, we have been in the House more than twice as much as at any former session. We shall not take up the election of Printer earlier than the 10th & will probably elect Blair & Reeves.[2] We have spent the last two days on various propositions to suspend the rules so as to introduce resolutions on the subject of Slavery. Bell yesterday moved to suspend the rules so as to introduce a Resolution *to refer* them all to *the Com. on the District of Columbia.* Old J Q A[3] suggested that some branches of the subject would have to go to other Committees & he wished nothing more than *their reference.* Bell's making the proposition excited a good deal of sensation. Wise & he had some slight sparring. Crab complained bitterly & Campbell[4] begged him for *Gods* sake not to persist. He refused to desist as I hear, but this morning (31st) Chinn of La.[5] made the proposition & had almost two thirds for it—so I suppose B. has put him up rather than do it himself. B. & most of the Ten. Whigs voted to suspend for Chinn's resolution.

So the matter is left. Rumor says (I heard it from Pickens) that Wise & B. would *seperate,* become hostile &c &c & it is now doubted whether W. will go for Harrison. We have a variety of such rumors. Another that B. will unite himself with Col. Benton & his party upon the Tariff & all other questions hoping *thereby* to break you down in Ten. whilst you & your friends will go (judging from your inaugural) with the South, in other words for Calhoun & I shall not be surprised to learn, that such suspicions as to your course is founded on the fact, that Brown, Waterson & myself board with Calhoun.[6] But Benton & his friends entertain no such apprehensions. *My course* in relation to *the Speaker's* election, is considered by many as rather favoring Benton's pretensions. But in truth I thought of nothing, but the impolicy of yielding to a little Knot of Nullifyers, who sought to coerce us into their measures & support & if we had yielded on that instance we would have been compelled in every other. I see the letter writers to Charleston place the election upon the ground that Benton *had said no nullifyer* should be elected and therefore the S.C. delegation determined not to go in *for his man*[7] as being a movement unfavorable to Calhoun. Such is the trash upon which public opinion is founded. The Speaker[8] is evidently on the fence & has given us the principal committees—W&M,[9] Military, & Foreign affairs, but the Judiciary & the investigating Com. are given to our enemies. We do not complain much.

N.H. has proposed a convention at Baltimore, which is sanctioned at Harrisburgh for 5th of May & will I have no doubt be generally sanctioned. I think N.Y. will go for *you* in a body. Prentis[s] is open mouthed for you. Penn. are a little more cautious, tho I have but little doubt will eventually go for you. The Senators from NC seem inclined to go for K.[10] & Bynum is rather inclined to R.M.J.[11] but the balance I think decidedly for you. In the event of a Convention of which I now have no doubt I think you will be certainly nominated. *All* admit your superior qualifications & fitness in all respects, over all competitors & the opposition which you have is either a matter of policy or personal friendship for others. So high an estimate is placed upon our last Campaign, that not a doubt remains in my mind but that the nomination will be given to you. We shall use here all proper precautions on the subject. You will see that I am at the head of the Military Com. because of *my oeconomical Intrenchment* notions I suppose & as a sort of guard over the extravagance of Sec. of War.[12] I think it an unfortunate position for me & would if I could get out. It is not likely that I shall agree *with the Sec of War in any thing.* He is like all new men in office—*must do something to distinguish his adm.* I have alway voted to get rid of Genl. McComb[13] as a useless officer—always agt the military academy. The Sec's militia project[14] as far as I understand it is outrageous & his suggestion of pensioning the old officers abominable. How am I to get on? I have never seen him—but Gov Miller[15] wishes me to go up and spend an hour or two & perhaps he may convince me that oeconomy is no virtue & that we ought to have a National Guard & a splendid military establishment & that every superannuated public officer ought to be supported by the laboring classes. I shall make my bow to the Pres. to day & see the fashionable world I suppose.

We continue in better health than we usually enjoy & desire our respects to Mrs. Polk.

C Johnson

[P.S.] Ten days after Mr. G.[16] left here—it was ascertained that he was missing & the only acct. of him was that he had taken his carriage to Bladensburgh—that his carriage had returned without him. But what had become of him nobody could tell—whether robbed or murdered or killed in a duel or what had befallen him none could conjecture.

ALS. DLC–JKP. Addressed to Nashville.

1. Letters not found.
2. See Polk to David Hubbard, December 30, 1839.
3. John Quincy Adams.
4. George W. Crabb and John Campbell. Having served in the Alabama House, 1836–37, and Senate, 1837–38, Crabb won election as a Whig to the U.S. House, where he served from 1838 until 1841.
5. Thomas W. Chinn, a physician, lawyer, and planter from Louisiana, won election as a Whig to one term in the U.S. House, 1839–41.
6. Aaron V. Brown, Harvey M. Watterson, and John C. Calhoun took room and board at H. V. Hill's boarding house.
7. John W. Jones.
8. Robert M. T. Hunter.
9. House Ways and Means Committee.
10. Bedford Brown, Robert Strange, and William R. King. Brown, a planter in the vicinity of Greensboro, represented North Carolina in the U.S. Senate from 1829 until 1840. A lawyer from Fayetteville, North Carolina, Strange went to the U.S. Senate in 1836. Brown and Strange, both Democrats, resigned effective November 16, 1840, rather than accept instructions issued by the North Carolina legislature.
11. Jesse A. Bynum and Richard Menton Johnson.
12. Joel R. Poinsett.
13. Alexander Macomb, one of the first men trained at West Point, distinguished himself in the Lake Champlain region during the War of 1812. He headed the Corps of Engineers in Washington from 1821 until 1828, when he became commanding general of the U.S. army, a position which he held until his death in 1841.
14. In his annual report to Congress, dated November 30, 1839, the secretary of war proposed a plan to abolish the state militia system and establish a federal militia of one hundred thousand men in training and another hundred thousand in reserve. On March 20, 1840, the secretary submitted to Congress a plan that revised upward the age of service liability, from thirty-seven to forty-five, and that divided the new militia into ten rather than eight districts.
15. A native of Berkeley County, Virginia, John Miller served as governor of Missouri from 1825 until 1832. He won election to the U.S. House as a Van Buren Democrat and served from 1837 until 1843.
16. Felix Grundy. See Grundy to Polk et al., December 1, 1839, and John Catron to Polk, January 3, 1840.

TO WILLIAM MOORE[1]

Executive Department
Dr. Sir Nashville January 1st 1840

I have this day caused an order to be issued,[2] announcing to the militia of the State, the appointment of the Executive Staff, from which you will perceive that you have been appointed Adjutant General for the State, with the rank of Brigadier General. You are requested at an early day, to signify in writing, whether you accept or decline the same.

JAMES K. POLK

ALS. THi–JKP. Addressed to Mulberry, Lincoln County.

1. An early Lincoln County settler with large landholdings, Moore served as a Democrat in the Tennessee House, 1825–29, and sat in the Senate, 1833–37. Moore became Polk's adjutant general in January 1840.

2. The militia order has not been found; a copy of the same, dated January 1, 1840, is in T–Governors' Commission Books.

FROM JOHN CATRON

My Dr Sir: Washington, Friday eveng. Jany. 3d '40

I have been here a week—but the weather has been very cold, & congress—having not made the first move.To day in the Senate, Mr Calhoun introduced a Bill to cede the public lands to the States, when Mr Clay attacked him as an organ of the admtn. He, Mr Calhoun, having visited the Presdt, & been at the Levee 1 Jny—impugned Mr Calh's motive for the change. This drew the compromise into the aspersions—"the gentleman in his usual vein of *vanity*, & *egotism*, (said Mr. Clay) tells us he forced on us the compromise."[1] This is some of the Staple. The admn. party will go with Calhoun—the younger men heartily—the older coyly.

Have conversed with Col. Benton in regard to the contents of yours delivered thro' Mr Turney.[2] But jealousies of future asperations A. V. Brown assures me are com[mo]n with many here and that one term, & no interference on your part must be strongly certified. Now this is not from Benton, but others. Certainly Rives was overcome by Tecumseh[3] on the score of envy and apprehension. *Crockett* & Harrison, also, built on this foundation. We will try, & fortify against it. Allen of O. is warm, & thinks he can carry Ohio in the Baltimore Convention on the 5th of May— now fully determined upon. Brown & Grundy—who got here 31 ult full of health & life—of course must be your principal reliance—and Buchanan, must be quieted: that is, his alarms. Your pretensions are put on stilts, after this success for Gov.; So, as to induce the belief, that you are to be worth more than any man in the west. Indeed in the House you are so much missed—& the disparity between you & Mr. Hunter is such as to aid your character for worth to a higher price than you are aware of. The adm. has no leader, and never can be in greater need of one, & unless the session is very quiet, will lose ground in the House. Frank Thomas is cool, Brown tells me—why exactly, I dont know. I promised thro' Grundy & Benton to aid in placing him in the Van; will talk to him myself, when I learn the sore place. Between you and I, Dallas will be atty Genl. Had Gilpin[4] been, we could have relied on him—how it is with Mr. D. I dont know.

Clay is broke down—& feels it. Webster is now openly avowed by Clay's friends, to have been for Harrison, against Clay, previous to the Convention. I found it out at Phild. by accident, that the Webster delegates from Mass. were most anxious to exclude Clay, on their way to the Convention. Seeing such a Statement in a N.Y. paper—the Herald—I asked Hawes[5] if it could be true. "Surely, said He—Webster was against Clay"—stating circumstances shewing they were not even on terms [of] friendship as men. Clay looks as if he was placid & content—but it is plain enough that in debate his temper is very high.

Bell is worse broke down, than any man of his comparitive claims in his party, I have ever known, to have done no objectionable act. I am told when he came here, & made the trial for Speaker, it at once was ascertained he could to a certainty not be elected—for although he got 105—still he could only get them *once*, & on party grounds. That on learning this, he behaved very badly, & gave great offence to many of the Whigs. The truth is, he was a mere Clay man—and sunk with Mr. Clay on the occasion of the nomination, lower than his selfishness, & vindictiveness had previously sunk him. Mr. Bell today does not stand as well in the House, as Mr. H Wise, or Dnl Jenifer![6] That is, with the Whigs.

Met Judge White yesterday—conversed some. He looks utterly worn out—exceeding feeble, & voice tremilous. It was on the pavement—very cold—& it may have been that to an extent. Have not seen him to converse for 12 mo. previously. I view him as dehors[7]—& if Powel could come in his place, E.T. wd. Stand firm for the republican side for 10 years—or 20. Powel is very popular there—& just of the grade, to suit that people—with Substance, & homely plainness.

Bell & White hardly have a hope, after the nomination of Harrison, with no power to run a 3d.

We are at Elliott's—Kept by a Mrs Mount—& in your room, & Mrs. Cole's Judges to come here.[8] Not much on docket. Write me how things was at home. Regards to Madame—& self.

J. Catron

ALS. DLC–JKP. Addressed to Nashville.

1. Reference is to the tariff compromise that resolved the nullification crisis of 1832–33.

2. Polk's letter to Catron has not been found.

3. Richard Mentor Johnson.

4. A Philadelphia lawyer and Democrat, Henry D. Gilpin was U.S. attorney for eastern Pennsylvania, 1831–36; solicitor of the U.S. Treasury, 1836–40; and U.S. attorney general, 1840–41.

5. In 1835 James Gordon Bennett established the *New York Herald*, an early and successful example of the penny press. A Whig lawyer from Kentucky and a veteran of the Black Hawk War, Richard Hawes sat two terms in the U.S. House, 1837–41, and served three years as governor in Kentucky's provisional Confederate government, 1862–65.

6. Daniel Jenifer, a Maryland lawyer and Whig, served as a member of the U.S. Congress, 1831–33 and 1835–41, and as U.S. minister to Austria, 1841–45.

7. French expression for "outside."

8. During his last term in Congress Polk lodged at Elliott's, a boarding house popular with members of the Supreme Court. Those justices residing at Mrs. Coyle's boarding house have not been identified. Nor have Mrs. Mount or "Mrs. Coles" been identified further.

FROM EZEKIEL P. McNEAL

Bolivar, Tennessee. January 3, 1840

McNeal itemizes rents in the amount of $715 due the heirs of M. T. Polk. Net proceeds for the present year may amount to $540. In reply to Polk's request,[1] concerning the sale of property on Pleasant Run,[2] McNeal states that the lands ought to bring $4 per acre if sold on credit; but he adds that he does not anticipate finding a buyer. He suggests that the heirs of M. T. Polk sell all their Hardeman County lands, as interest will produce more revenue than rents and land values will decline because of soil exhaustion.[3]

ALS. DLC–JKP. Addressed to Nashville.

1. Polk's letter of December 26, 1839, has not been found.

2. Marshall T. Polk probably inherited from his father, Samuel, the property on Pleasant Run, a southwest branch of the Big Hatchee River in Hardeman County.

3. Marshall T. Polk left his two children, Roxana Eunice Ophelia and Marshall T. Polk, Jr., at least 921 additional acres in Hardeman County.

FROM WILLIAM H. POLK

Dear Brother Columbia Jan'y 3d. 1840

I received your letter[1]—the proposition which you made with regard to the purchase of Reuben I cannot acceed too. In justice to myself, I must reserve your two first payments, to meet my *necessities*. But if it would *suit you*, I am willing to give you, your price $1,000 on the note due 1842, which is the third payment. I think it the full value of Reuben. If you think otherwise, & my proposition does not suit you, we cannot trade. I estimate the value of Reuben, by the prices which negroes command in the every day transactions, in the sale & purchase of negroes. My Boy Edmund, who is as good a negro as Reuben—cost me virtually $875. I mention these things, as I do not desire to get your negro, for less than he is worth.

Please write me by Munday's mail.[2]

WILLIAM H. POLK

ALS. DLC–JKP. Addressed to Nashville.

1. Polk's letter of January 1, 1840, to William H. Polk has not been found. See William H. Polk to Polk, December 30, 1839.

2. No reply from Polk has been found.

FROM JAMES WALKER

Dr Sir, Columbia Jany 4th 1840

Maria has a wish to try Reubin for a year. I do not know but I will take him at $120, if you give me the offer.[1]

JAMES WALKER

ALS. DLC–JKP. Addressed to Nashville. AE on the cover states that this letter was answered on January 7, 1840; Polk's reply has not been found.

1. On the previous day Walker had written that he or his son, Samuel P. Walker, would try to place Reuben for hire should Polk and his brother William fail to agree on a sales price. ALS. DLC–JKP. See also William H. Polk to Polk, December 30, 1839, and January 3, 1840.

FROM MARY S. CHILDRESS[1]

Dear Uncle Murfreeboro Jan 5 [1840][2]

I came to the conclusion this morning that perhaps you might be so formal that you would not spend the evening with us on the 8 unless wee sent you an written invittation and I had some fear that you might for get the occasion entirely as you think such things of so little importance and Mah[3] says she will be quite offended if you do not come up. You have promised her a visit for some time. Now is the time to pay it and for myself I will never forgive you if you do not come up. Wee will have a large company. I have invited Judge Phillips[4] just for your benefit. Aunt Sally says she has no message for you. Uncle you must excuse this letter as it is wrote in a hury. Adieu.

M S Childress

ALS. DLC–JKP. Addressed to Nashville. AE on the cover states that this letter was answered on January 7, 1840; Polk's reply has not been found.

1. Mary S. Childress, a niece of Sarah C. Polk and John W. Childress, was the orphaned daughter of Anderson and Mary Sansom Childress.
2. Year identified by Polk's endorsement.
3. Elizabeth Whitsitt Childress, paternal grandmother and guardian of Mary S. Childress.
4. Joseph Philips, a native Tennessean, moved to Illinois following service in the War of 1812. He became secretary of the Illinois Territory in 1816 and the new state's first chief justice in 1818. Philips held that position until 1822, when he resigned and ran unsuccessfully as the pro-slavery faction's candidate for governor. He returned to Rutherford County, Tennessee, during the early 1830's.

FROM SAMUEL P. WALKER

Dear Sir Columbia Jany 7th 1840

By Saturdays mail I received your letter[1] enclosing Kilpatrick & Fishers note for $200. These gentlemen have quit business—and all their effects are in the hands of Col Dew. Dew Says they are able to pay all their debts, but as Fisher is not here, and Kilpatrick is worth nothing—it is useless to sue. I think I can get good notes on other men for it in a short time.

The amount of your account with Johnson & Walker is about $700.

I believe it impossible to hire Reuben to any one who will not allow him to hire his own time. I can get 140$ for him from Fisher. He says he will give me good security—but I am satisfied that he intends him to wait on other stores to pay the ballance of his hire.

SAML. P. WALKER

[P.S.] Let me know soon what to do with Reuben.

ALS. DLC–JKP. Addressed to Nashville. AE by Polk, "Rect. for Fisher & Kilpatrick's note for $200. Due to J.K.P. when collected. Note Returned to me—Jany. 7th 1842." The note has not been found.

1. Polk's letter not found.

TO ANDREW JACKSON DONELSON

My Dear Sir Nashville Jany. 8. 1840

The mail of to night brought the first copies of the President's message[1] that arrived. Only those copies came, viz, for the printers, and are contained in the enclosed envelope[2] for you. The printers of course had immediate use for their copies. There was grea[t] [a]nxiety to see the document, and having [no] doubt it was contained in the enc[los]ed[3] envelope to you, I took the liberty to open it for my own & the gratification of several of our friends. We found the message inclosed as we expected, but finding also a note which has not been opened, we put it under cover of this envelope, with this explanation, and will place it to your address in the Post Office.

JAMES K. POLK

ALS. DLC–AJD. Addressed to Nashville.

1. Reference is to Martin Van Buren's Third Annual Message to Congress, which was delivered on December 24, 1839.

2. Enclosure not found.

3. A tear in the manuscript has obliterated parts of four words.

FROM FELIX GRUNDY

Dear Sir Senate Chamber, Jany 13th 1840

White has Just resigned. He read a letter addressed to the Genl. Assembly of Ten, drawn with some ability.[1] He was very respectful—so much so, as not to Justify a reply. I only made a short statement of the course I should pursue. Now elect a successor and I beg my friends to cover the 8 years. The successor should be here immediately as the Independent Treasury bill may [be] in danger in the Senate.[2]

FELIX GRUNDY

ALS. DLC–JKP. Addressed to Nashville and marked "Private."

1. On January 13, 1840, Hugh L. White introduced resolutions from the Tennessee General Assembly instructing its senators to support the Independent Treasury bill; unable to comply with the Assembly's wishes, White resigned from the U.S. Senate.

2. By a vote of twenty-four to eighteen the U.S. Senate approved passage of the Independent Treasury bill on January 23, 1840.

FROM ALBERT T. McNEAL

Dear Sir Coffeeville Mi. January 15th 1840

I acknowledge the receipt of your favour of the 1st Inst. post marked the 4th and also that of the 5th Inst.[1] which came to hand by last nights mail. I wrote to you from Holly Springs early in December[2] and on my return to Coffeeville from that place learned that Charles had come in. I did not advise you of his return learning that Garner had written about that time.[3] And shortly afterwards I visited Bolivar Te. Reached Home again on the 8th Inst. I fear I shall not be able to sell Charles. It is a very unfavourable time for a cash sale. Money is extremely scarce and I have never in my life witnessed "such screwing and twisting" to get it. Charles ought to bring $750 or $800 cash. But few men have money and those who have it, will be disposed to hold on with the expectation of buying negroes low for cash at Sheriffs sales before & at the Spring Term of the approaching circuit courts. In consequence of low waters the planters have not been able to ship their cotton; nor have they found a market at Home. I have not the least doubt but that you might sell Charles for good Mississippi funds in Fayette Co. Te. at a better price than I can get here & as it is probable I may fail to sell him here, you might in the mean time sell him there to some one who may know the boy with the understanding that it shall be no contract in the event of a sale here, which is not probable. I saw Mr. Garner today. All are well at the plantation. Addison however in the woods.[4] Garner as instructed is clearing more land. Your crop of cotton (136 bales) is at Troy, ready for the first rise of the river.

Carroll County lies immediately south of this County and I practice law there. The first time I visit that County I will see Mr. Hamon[5] and get his note with security as desired. Mr. Hamon ought to give you about $400 a year for Harry. Possibly I may be able to get more. A boy of his age and such as you describe ought I think to be worth $1200. The time has been when he would have sold for $2000 here. If Harry be the same black-Smith, who worked at the Caldwell place 5 miles from Columbia,[6] then owned by Uncle Sam Polk. I remember him well (tall &

muscular) though some 18 years have elapsed since I saw him—and my recollection admonishes me that I am fast growing an old bachelor. We have not yet received the Presidents message[7] and from some cause, I know not what, I have not received a number of the tri-weekly Union for 8 or 10 days. I send you a copy of our Governor's message[8] which you will find a sound and interesting document. With McNutt our Governor for about ten years and a Democratic Legislature that would carry out his views, Mississippi might be regenerated &c.

A. T. McNeal

P.S. I will visit the plantation Sunday and probably we may determine to remove the buildings &c. McNeal

ALS. DLC–JKP. Addressed to Nashville. Published in Bassett, *Plantation Overseer*, 136–37.

1. Letters not found.
2. Letter not found.
3. See John J. Garner to Polk, December 25, 1839.
4. Addison, a slave, had been moved to the Mississippi plantation from Fayette County, Tennessee, by Silas M. Caldwell in early 1835.
5. Hamon is not identified.
6. Reference probably is to Samuel Polk's original farm, located on the Nashville Road near Rutherford Creek; Silas M. Caldwell and his wife Lydia Eliza resided on the farm after Samuel Polk moved his family to Columbia in 1817.
7. Martin Van Buren submitted his Third Annual Message to Congress on December 24, 1839.
8. Alexander G. McNutt, a native Virginian, moved to Mississippi in 1824, held a seat in the state Senate in 1835, and by appealing to strong anti-bank sentiment won election as Democratic governor two years later. For two terms he opposed corruption in Mississippi's banking institutions. In his message of January 1840, McNutt detailed abuses in the banking system and recommended repeal of all bank charters.

FROM ADAM HUNTSMAN

D Sir, Jackson Jany 26th 1840

Two days ago I received letters from Senator Coe & Laughlin recommending the Holding of County meetings to appoint delegates to the Nashville convention of the 11th February.[1] So far so good. I am attending to it. They furthermore alledge that it is desirable that I should be one of the delegates from Madison. So far there is nothing wrong in that and can be attended to, but it is further alledged by those Gentlemen that I shall consent for my name to be used as one of the two Candidates selected to Correspond with the two State Senators on their electoral Ticket, or in other words, one of the State electors, seperate and apart from the thirteen to correspond with the congressional districts.[2] To this I have no objection, But delicacy should forbid my attendance upon the convention if it is thought necessary to use my name as a candidate for state elector. Having arranged my private concerns which embarrassed me when I saw you last, I now am ready to do battle for the cause of democracy any where the party may think it advisable for me to fight, either at the head of a division or in the private ranks. If it shall be deemed advisable to nominate me as one of the State electors, It will place it in my power to do (so far as the district is concerned) precisely what I wrote you twelve months ago was the game for us to play in the next presidential election. Instead of selecting men for nomination of great goodness—a Lady Rachel kind of man,[3] select men who are able capable and willing to present and discuss the principles of democracy upon a Stump and to do it if needful. This mode presents two advantages, first a dissemination of truth which is most important. Secondly if the whigs according to their usual custom select the good sort of good-for-nothing men, we will have divers advantages in the coming conflict. If I am selected as a candidate, I will make a speech in every County in the District and invite their good men to the discussion. It will have another effect, by forestalling your dear friend John Bell, for I see no escape for him but to offer for Governor at the next election. The force of circumstances compells him to do it. If you are the nominee for the V.P. at the Baltimore convention we must get the strongest men we can to compete with him. If you are not, the more glory for you in beating him before the people. John Blair of Jonesboro ought to be selected as the other State elector, not only because he can present the questions fully but because more exertions will be required in the ends than in the center of the State where you are allready strong. If Blair will frolick over east Tennessee next spring and summer & make speeches, I have no doubt, it would result in m[uch][4] good. I wrote to him 12 months ago about this. A State Candidate can speak any where. If there is no precedent for this I am willing to make one, so far as I am concerned. The strongest selections should also be made in the Congressional districts who carry out the same views upon a smaller scale. The Harrison nomination has completely enabled us to beat them in the District handsomely. You may rely upon this. Consult our Confidential friends upon this letter and let me hear from you.

A Huntsman

ALS. DLC–JKP. Addressed to Nashville. Published in *THQ*, VI, pp. 345–46.

1. The Democratic State Convention, which convened at Nashville on February 11, 1840, chose Leonard P. Cheatham as its president. Resolutions of the central committee, presented by Andrew J. Donelson and adopted by the convention, called for formation of an electoral ticket in the next presidential election and appointed delegates to the national convention at Baltimore, which was scheduled to meet on May 5, 1840. The Tennessee convention urged the national party to nominate Polk for the vice-presidency.

2. The Democratic ticket for Tennessee's presidential electors consisted of one candidate from each of the thirteen congressional districts and two at-large candidates "corresponding" to the state's two U.S. senators.

3. Reference probably is to Rachel Felix, who by 1840 had become France's most acclaimed actress and had received the amorous attentions of such celebrities as Louis-Désiré Véron and Alfred de Musset, neither of whom was known for his "great goodness." Huntsman repeats below his sarcastic reference to "good" men.

4. A tear in the margin has obliterated part of one word.

FROM JULIUS W. BLACKWELL

Sir, Washington Jan. 28th 1840

After a debate of more than two weeks, upon the subject of Abolition petitions, it has been laid cold in the H. Rep. this evening—unless it is revived by a motion to reconsider—for the present Congress.[1]

The question was sprung in the House, by a proposition to amend the rules, so as to receive Abo. petitions and lay them on the table. After several amendments had been proposed, Mr. W. Cost Johnson of Merilany[2]—a Federalist—obtained the floor and stated that he had an amendment to offer, but would say a few words in a[d]vance; and after making a very lengthly speech strongly opposing the reception of Abolition petitions, and finishing his speech in praise of Harryson and Tyler, and trying to enforce the opinion, that Harrison was no way connected with Abolition—he offered an amendment—the words of which I cannot at this moment give you—to the rules, not to receve the petitions.

The amendment was carried by a vote of 115 to 105, and on the final passage of the Resolutions, the vote stood, I believe 114 Yeas, & 108 Noes. Duncan of Ohio, Howard and three others from Indiana, Bell of Ten. & eleven Democrats from Pennsylvania, & others I do not now recollect, voted in the negative.

The Federal Whigs are trying very hard to bolster up the character of Granny H.[3] and coax their partizans to support him, and I believe they will do it. I differ with Mr. Turney & others as to the relative strength of Clay & Harrison in Tennessee. I think that Harrison, among the great body of voters, will be stronger than Clay. But as the leaders were heart & soul for Clay, I had hoped, that they would kick up against the Nomination of the Harrisburg convention, or at least be lukewarm on the occasion. But, from the best information I have receved from Ten.—particularly from my district—I find the Feds. are going it for Harrison. Anticaucus men in the last Presidential election, how *very concestent* these Gentlemen are, in their support of the Caucus candidate of the Feds. They are concestent, however in one thing. They have said they would vote for the *Devil* rather than for Mr. Van Buren. That is to say, "if I cannot rule, I had rather the *Devil* should seaze the reigns of this Government, and sink it to his lower regions, than that the man who stands in the way of my political advancement, should be elected." The Democrats of Congress seem to be very sanguine of Mr. Van Burens reelection, by a triumphant majority. They seem to be slow, in committing themselves on the Vice Presidency, and will say but little on the subject. They seem rather careless about it, and to wait with patience, the decision of a National convention. I cannot, for my life, determine, who is, or who will be the favourite candidate. Col. Johnson has more friends than I could have imagined, considering the heavy d[r[ead he occasioned during the last canvass. The Col. out of the way, It is my opinion that the nomination will fall on you. Of this, I have scarcely a doubt.

I hardly think that I can, under any circumstances, advocate the claims of the Col. strongly, if he should be run. I know by sad experience, what a dead weight he is upon us, in the south & south west. From all appearance, the Democrats would be glad to drop him, but the manner of doing so, is a delicate matter. I fear the Col. wishes to run. If he would consider all things right, he would decline being a candidate, and thus, in part, cause the cry of Negro wives and Negro children to cease, and rid the Democrats of a heavy load.[4]

J. W. BLACKWELL

ALS. DLC–JKP. Addressed to Nashville.

1. Following the precedent of previous Congresses, the House passed a "gag resolution" on January 28, 1840.

2. A Frederick County, Maryland, lawyer and state legislator, William Cost Johnson won four terms as a Whig in the U.S. House, 1833–35 and 1837–43.

3. William H. Harrison.

4. See J. G. M. Ramsey to Polk, August 20, 1839, and John Catron to Polk, November 5, 1839.

FROM FELIX GRUNDY, ET AL.[1]

Dear Sir. Washington Feb. 3d 1840

In answer to enquiries made by you of some of us, we give the following answer which is the result of the best information within our reach. A National Convention, as recommended by New Hampshire, seems now to be certain. We anticipate no certain good of any kind from that assemblage. We fear, its dissentions, will weaken the Democratic cause, and produce heart-burnings, which may be injurious. If the Vice Presidency should be yielded to the West, Col. Johnson will present Arkansas, Missouri, Illinois, Indiana, Ohio, Michigan, and Kentucky—all claiming his nomination. This will constitute a strong claim which it will be difficult to resist. You have strength in New England, New York, Virginia, North Carolina, and some other states. But whether it can control the vote of those states in the Convention, we can not say. *We consider this very doubtful.* Our impression is, if no convention had been called, and the Electors in the different states had been left to vote *ad-libitum,* your prospects would have been very good, if not certain. The Convention *may* disappoint the wishes of your friends.

We think Members of Congress should have as little to do with the Convention—as members—as possible, although they should act, when it is inconvenient to procure the attendance of others. If the Convention could be dissolved harmoniously, without making nominations at all, it would accord better with our views, than any other course. We speak from the present appearance of things. Further developments may change our views. We were disappointed in Ohio—and the failure of North Carolina to recommend, was not anticipated. If the Convention adopts the rule of the last Convention, that two thirds should be necessary for a choice, it is very likely no nomination can be made, and the whole matter will break up in confusion, which will produce mischief. If a majority shall be deemed sufficient, then much will depend on Virginia, Pennsylvania, and New York, If they concur a majority will be secured—but their concurrence is very questionable.

One thing is very desirable, which is, that *Tennessee should be fully represented in the Baltimore Convention.*

Felix Grundy

LS. DLC–JKP. Addressed to Nashville and marked "*private.*"

1. Signed by Grundy, Abraham McClellan, Harvey M. Watterson, Hopkins L. Turney, Cave Johnson, and Aaron V. Brown.

FROM SAMUEL P. WALKER

Columbia, Tennessee. February 3, 1840

The Maury County Democratic meeting "went off very well." Greenfield presided, and Jonas E. Thomas spoke effectively. Delegates to the state convention were appointed.

ALS. DLC–JKP. Addressed to Nashville.

FROM ALEXANDER O. ANDERSON

Tuesday night

My Dear Sir Near Knoxville Feby 4th 1840

I recd. on last Saturday your favor of the 27th Ult.[1] informing me of the result of the senatorial election, and by the same mail the commission, with an enclosure of the Preamble & resolutions of the Legislature instructing their Senators &c.

In accepting this high & honorable station, I shou'd do great injustice to my feelings if I did not assure you of the weight of obligation which I feel *toward yourself most specially,* and at the same time of the deep sensibility with which I receive this proof of the confidence of our friends. It has been their will to elect me—it will be mine to discharge the trust they have committed to me faithfully & fearlessly.

At the date of my receipt of the commission the Legislature I presume had adjourned. I will forward to you a formal letter of acceptance, addressed, as I suppose it ought to be (in courtesy) to the Legislature. This has been usual, I believe, but it has generally occured, I presume, during the period of their Session. But if any thing is intended for the public, I infer it wou'd be proper to address it to that Body. I will enclose it however to you, & *such disposition* can be made of it as you think proper.

I have also recd. your letter of the 30th Ult.[2] to day. I shall leave here on Thursday or Friday. I have written to Mr Grundy that I will be in Washington by the 18th or 20th. This makes some allowances for the probable failure of the mail, which has repeatedly occured this winter owing to the bad [. . .] on O.[3]

I shou'd have been extremely gratified to have been in the Senate at the passage of the Independent Try. Bill—but we learn by the Globe (Mr Crozier informs me) that it has passed. This does not in the least diminish my anxiety to be there, & shall, therefore, endeavor to reach the City by the 20th.

As soon after my arrival as practicable I will ascertain the true position of things—and no effort of mine, with the best judgement of which I am master, will be left untried in relation to certain things about which I feel the deepest solicitude.[4] I shall not only put forth all my own efforts, but I shall put our friends in motion. I do not know what your information is, but as far as I am informed Mr Calhoun is friendly to the views I entertain upon that subject—at least perfectly practicable.

The truth is our friends must be satisfied of the fact, as it really is, that Tennessee *requires the aid of a strong name.*

Col Laughlin ought, by all means to go to the Baltimore Convention, and if my Brother Pierce can possibly leave his affairs I shou'd like him to go—also, Mr Speaker Thomas—& Mr. Speaker Coe. Col L. writes me that it is possible he may. But this seems uncertain. I want him there—& Thomas there—& Coe—& Pierce, if all this can be done. And I shou'd like them to be there some 10 days in advance. These Gentlemen shou'd all perfectly understand that no *suggestion of any thing Ulterior* shou'd fall from them *remotely, even.*[5] There are many fears wou'd be awakened at Washington. I hear Illinois has nominated Johnson. This will do no harm. The whole Slave holding Country from Virginia round to Louisiana will be right. New York can determine—or Pennsylvania—or Ohio & Massachusetts & so on.

I shou'd be glad to see there my very worthy friend Col Williamson Smith. If you see him tell him whatever can be done for him I shall do with my utmost energy. He ought to send me a Brief on the facts in his case.[6] I shall write him, and address him to Nashville. I dont know his address in Maury.

I wou'd be very much obliged to my friend Dr Young to send me a list of the Democratic members of the Legislature, both Houses, with their address. Let him write to Washington to me.

Present my kind regards to Mrs. Polk; say to her I have made Mrs Anderson very well acquainted with her, so that if they can meet they may be as *old friends.*

A ANDERSON

ALS. DLC–JKP. Addressed to Nashville and marked "Private & Confidential."

1. Letter not found.
2. Letter not found.
3. At least one word has been omitted in the manuscript. Reference is to transportation on the Ohio River.

4. Reference probably is to Anderson's concern to place Polk on the national ticket as the Democratic party's candidate for the vice-presidency.

5. Reference probably is to Polk's presidential ambitions.

6. On October 24, 1837, Williamson Smith contracted with the U.S. government to transport the Cherokee Nation to the west bank of the Mississippi River. Smith claimed that he was not permitted by the government to execute the contract and was forced to sustain considerable monetary loss. On April 17, 1840, the Senate Judiciary Committee rejected Smith's claim; on June 10, 1840, the House Judiciary Committee accepted Attorney General Henry D. Gilpin's opinion that Smith should be indemnified and sent his claim to Secretary of War Joel R. Poinsett for settlement.

FROM AARON V. BROWN

Dear Sir Washington Feby 4th 1840

Last night I forwarded you a joint Letter[1] which one of our friends had prepared & which I thought proper to sign. Forwarded of course to you for your consideration & future expression of opinion to us. I had three weeks before expressd. to you somewhat the same ideas & expect in a few days to receive your answer. In the mean time I beg leave to caution you against the following conclusions: 1st. That we have failed to guard your interest either with less skill or zeal than you expected or 2nd. that we have not faith in your ultimate strength or success in the canvass. We all believe you will be stronger *without than within the convention.* That is to say no convention being held, you can get the strongest electoral vote & be returned, with such assurances of the popular will, as would insure your success to a moral certainty before the Senate. I have conversed freely & confidentially with a good many but with none more so than with Mr Calhoun. *On a full & distinct conversation,* he stated his wishes in your favor—his determination to sustain your pretensions on the score of your *position,* your *abilities* & your *principles.* But he seemed thoroughly convinced that a convention was *inexpedient* & injudicious under present circumstances—unnecessary in reference to your success & calculated to impede rather than benefit *the general cause,* with which he considers you to be inseperably connected. He did all the talking. I had *purposely* brought him into the *neighborhood* of the subject, when he took it up, looked at it in all its bearings, avowed his *predilections,* authorized me to make them known *to you* & to say the subject had been *discussed* by your friends "in the highest places" & the only question was to the most *judicious* mode of action. All this of course between you & I & "that better half"[2] which is so well entitled to know all that concerns you.

I have no news (congressional). The Globe tells you all. I am *buried* in the committee on elections. Tomorrow I think we will go into committee on the Presidents message. Frank Thomas & Dromgoole (two of the impracticables) must come into the fight or they will stand finally seperated from the party. O, Sir, that Speakers business I fear will do us much harm. Our enemies look to it *as boding disunion* & I fear that crimination & recrimination, may effect it. But "nil disperandum"[3] shall be my motto untill I shall have passed the points of personal responsibility. Sir this house is a perfect chaos of confusion & disorder. The Speaker[4] was neither born nor tutord. to command. But no matter, Jupiter himself could not controul such a rebellious host.

Tell Mrs. P. that tomorrow we move down & take possession of her old apartments in the Elliott building.[5] Women I believe allways & every where are pretty much alike. To see & be seen—to hear & be heard is not a *secondary* but I rather think a *primary* nature with them.

Johnson is in very bad health, rarely going to the house & heartily sorry that he consented to be here.

The abolition question is settled—notice it.[6] "The Representative of the Hermitage"[7] declared early, that if no one else did, he would offer a resolution *to receive & to refer* it to the committee on the District of Columbia. Next morning Chinn of La. offerd. such a resolution[8] & it was generally regarded as Mr. B's. Gentry made his maiden speech for it.[9] *All the* rest from Tennessee *refused to receive at all.* This course of B & G. excited great supprise here & *rumor* & appearances say B. & Wise have seperated—time will shew. Excuse all this unrevised faronade[10] & believe me truly . . . .

A V Brown

ALS. DLC–JKP. Addressed to Nashville. AE on the cover states that this letter was answered on February 17, 1840; Polk's reply has not been found.

1. See Felix Grundy et al. to Polk, February 3, 1840.
2. Sarah Childress Polk.
3. Latin motto meaning "never despair."
4. Robert M. T. Hunter.
5. Elliot's Boarding House, Washington, D.C.
6. See Julius W. Blackwell to Polk, January 28, 1840.
7. John Bell.
8. Representative Thomas W. Chinn offered his resolution on December 31, 1839.
9. Meredith P. Gentry of Tennessee spoke in favor of Thomas Chinn's resolution on January 15, 1840.
10. Misspelling of "fanfaronade."

TO JOHN W. CHILDRESS

My Dear Sir Nashville Feby 4th 1840

The Murfreesborough stage did not come in, until an unusually late hour last night, and left this morning before I received your letter of yesterday.[1] I confess my astonishment at the information which you give me. It seems that I was doomed to be censored by one side or the other, no matter what course the Legislature had thot proper to take, upon the question of the removal of the seat of Government. At the time it was thought it *had been removed*, Dr. Jennings in his place upon the floor of the Senate, attributed the removal to the Executive officers, and to myself particularly.[2] I was defended by Yoakum and others and the charge repelled. Still as I understood it continued to be the street talk. And now when the Legislature have rescinded the Resolution of removal I am blamed because it was not removed. The charge on either hand is equally groundless. A statement of the facts will satisfy not only you, but all others when the excitement of the moment passes off, and they become calm, that they are so. Since I have been Governor I have endeavoured, to abstain as far as practicable (occasionally to be sure expressing opinions in relation to public measures, when it was proper to do so) from interfering in the business properly belonging to the Legislature and in relation to the seat of Government I was particularly cautious. As the Governor of the State I thought propriety required, that I should not take an active part, as between different localities having conflicting interests and claims, and whose citizens were my common constituents, nor did I think it a matter of great importance *for the present*, nor until it came to be *located permanently* under the Constitution.[3] Occasionally, but not often in the course of the Session the subject was mentioned in my presence. The night the resolution was taken up, and passed the Senate by one vote, I was at my house. I had no knowledge that it would be taken up, or that it had passed, until the next morning. On that or the next day, it was voted on in the House and passed by one vote. The votes against it, as I understand except four or five, were of the Whig party, and to no one of those four or five of the Democratic party, who voted against it in the House, did I ever speak on the subject. If I possessed the influence which is now attributed to me, by those who would throw the blame upon me, I must have exercised it, with little effect, not to have been able to affect one Democratic voter, and turned him against it, in the first instance. The truth is, I did exercise no such influence. The resolution itself I never saw or heard read, and therefore do not know its precise terms, but it was construed by its friends to require an immediate removal of the public records and offices. This it was seen would as the laws now stand, produce great inconvenience to the public. For example, the law requires the Comptroller to keep his office at the seat of Government, and the Treasurer to deposite all monies received by him, however small the sum in Bank within *three* days, of the time he receives it; so that the Treasurer must either have resided at Nashville (near the Bank) or have been constantly riding between the seat of Government and the Bank to make his deposits according to law. And if he resided at Nashville and the Comptroller at Murfreesboro, as by law no money can be drawn from the State Treasury, but upon a warrant signed, and countersigned, by the Treasurer and Comptroller, it was seen by all that inconvenience must arise, to the public creditors. A sheriff for instance brings a convict to the Penitentiary from one of the extremes of the state. He is entitled to compensation for it. He applies to the Treasurer for his pay, but before he can get it he must ride to Murfreesborough, to get the countersignature of the Comptroller, and then back to the Bank. The same thing would occur with all other public creditors. Another case under the existing law was this. A law had passed at the present Session, devolving certain duties in relation to Internal Improvements, on the Governor, Atto. Genl., and Comptroller, to be *jointly* performed by them. The Atto. Genl. is not required to reside at the seat of Government; the Comptroller is, and the Governor might reside at either place, but would certainly in any case have gone forthwith to the seat of Government and remained there. In this state of the law, a person applies for state Bonds, or to have some other act done in relation to Internal Improvements. He finds the Governor and Comptroller at the seat of Government, but they are not authorized to act without the Atto. Genl. One of two things has to be done; Either the person applying must go to Nashville after the Atto. Genl. and if he cannot come, the Governor and Comptroller, must pack up, the public records (if they can leave other official duties) and go to Nashville to see him, and possibly in their absence some other similar applicant may visit the Seat of Government and find them absent. Some difficulty too was suggested growing out of the electoral law, passed at this session[4] requiring the electors to vote at "Nashville" and not at the seat of Government, which I have not examined. Other cases of inconvenience too I heard stated. These were difficulties not created by me or any one else. They grew out of the existing state of the law. After the Resolution of removal had passed, Col Yoakum and the friends of Removal generally, saw them and attempted to avoid them. It was too late in the session to amend the laws. To avoid them, (except for a very short time) before the meeting of the next session, Col. Yoakum introduced into the Senate, a supplementary Resolution, requiring the removal of the public records and offices, not to take place until a very short time before the next meeting of the Legislature. Had this been thought of, and constituted part of the original Resolution of removal, much of the excitement and trouble which followed would probably have been avoided. This supplementary Resolution passed the Senate, and was rejected in the House by a tie vote. The friends of *removal* in both Houses voted for it, and one or two being absent in the House. The Senate insisted and the House I believe took no further action upon it. For myself, after the Resolution of *removal* had been adopted, I was anxious it should pass, and so expressed myself, for I saw that great public inconvenience would be suffered if it did not. I expressed myself to Mr Fletcher and other members, that the resolution of removal being passed, it would never do to have the state Government in that condition, and that it was indispensible to the public convenience and interest, that the supplementary Resolution should pass. They were as their course shews equally anxious upon the subject. They however failed to pass, and finally an amendment was offered to the appropriation Bill in the Senate and passed, being voted for by Col. Yoakum and all the friends of *removal* in the Senate, making an appropriation for the removal of the public records, and providing that they should be kept at Nashville until a few days before the Session, and this I was anxious should have been concurred in by the House. Instead of a concurrence, without any knowledge or agency of mine, the House amended it by inserting a clause, rescinding the Resolution of *removal*, and this at the last hour of the Session, was concurred in by the Senate. I have thus given you a full, and I believe an accurate history of the question, which has produced as you state, so much feeling in your town.

In regard to some of those of whom you speak, they are perhaps, predisposed from *other causes*, to see me involved and affected by th[is que]stion; I mean the Senatorial and other questi[ons w]hich have been up during the Session, in whic[h their] particular wishes were not gratified.[5] You are right in supposing that I could not have personally, any predilections for a place in which I have been for years, so much calumniated and abused. Whatever opinions I may have entertained in regard to the seat of Government, either temporarily or permanently, I was ready as a public officer, cheerfully to obey the will of the Legislature upon that subject. Col. Yoakum and Mr Fletcher themselves must have thought, that the public interest would have suffered or they would not have introduced their supplementary Resolution. The members who voted against it have the responsibility and not me, and why it should be desired by political friends to cast censure on me, when the attempt must injure both I cannot conceive. The whole Whig party who mainly defeated it, are to be excused, and an attempt made to assail, or if not assail to injuriously affect political friends. When the excitement subsides it cannot be so.

Though this is a long letter, it has been written in great haste, and is *not designed for the public*. I thought it proper to place you in possession of all the facts, that you might, be able to explain them to others. You will therefore regard it as *private*, and for yourself, *and under no circumstances for publication*.

James K. Polk

P.S. You may if you think it necessary shew this to Dr. Rucker and a few personal friends, who can set the matter right so far as I am concerned. J.K.P.

ALS, draft. DLC–JKP. Addressed to Murfreesboro and marked "Copy" on both the cover and the first page of the document.

1. Letter not found.

2. Thomas Reid Jennings, a physician and member of the University of Nashville's medical department, served in the Tennessee Senate as a Whig from 1839 until 1845. On January 29, 1840, the Tennessee House concurred with a Senate resolution to move the seat of government to Murfreesboro; three days later both houses reversed their earlier decision in favor of Murfreesboro and retained the seat of government in Nashville.

3. Tennessee's Constitution of 1834 provided that in 1843 the General Assembly would designate and fix the seat of government.

4. On January 24, 1840, the Tennessee legislature passed an act prescribing the mode of choosing presidential electors.

5. Mutilation of the manuscript renders several words partially illegible.

FROM SAMUEL H. LAUGHLIN

McMinnville, Tennessee. February 6, 1840

Laughlin writes that he has recommended to Young the selection of Armstrong and Donelson as delegates to the national convention. Unsure whether private business will allow him to go to Baltimore, Laughlin suggests that the state convention appoint in his place W. C. Smartt,[1] who will almost certainly decline. By the time of his declination, Laughlin hopes to be able to accept an appointment from a convention committee, which must be created and authorized to fill vacancies. P. B. Anderson should be named to the Baltimore delegation.

Laughlin states, however, that he will not accept a nomination for presidential elector unless it accords with public opinion and party interests. Cheatham should be nominated elector from Polk's district.[2]

ALS. DLC–JKP. Addressed to Nashville and marked "Private."

1. A farmer in Warren County since 1806, Smartt attained the rank of brigadier general in the militia following the War of 1812; he served one term in the Tennessee House, 1817–19, and two terms in the Senate, 1821–23 and 1825–27.

2. Leonard P. Cheatham resided in Tennessee's Seventh Congressional District, which included Davidson and Wilson counties. Polk's "home" district was the ninth.

TO DAVID HUBBARD

My Dear Sir Nashville Feby 7th 1840

Your esteemed favour of the 21st ultimo,[1] came to hand at the moment our Legislature was about to adjourn, and my public duties since have prevented an earlier answer. I have looked on with much solicitude at the unsettled state of things at Washington, and especially in the Ho. Repts. You seem to be without leaders, without concert and without organization as a party. This state of things I have no doubt you attribute to the true causes. None can regret more than I do, the unfortunate division of the party, at the opening of the Session, which prevented the choice of a Speaker. To that is undoubtedly to be traced much of the trouble which you have since had. In regard to the course which any of my friends thought proper to take in that election, I can only say, that so far from being advised by me, if I had been present, I should have exerted all my influence, to have induced *entire union in the party*. I saw with pleasure that *Mr. Lewis Mr Pickens yourself* and others, voted for *Jones*, on the first trials as the regular nominee in caucus, and I regretted his defeat, but when he was dropped, and the body of the party, voted for *Lewis*, it is exceedingly to be regretted that all could not have united and made an election. I expressed to you I believe, when you were here, what my opinions and feelings were upon the subject.

I agree with you that it is madness in us, at this time to agitate the question of the *succession*, and I am much gratified to see that *Mr. Calhoun*, has taken lofty ground, and put that matter to rest, so far as the use of his name had been connected with it. In regard to the currents and undercurrents at Washington, of which you speak, as well as the movements of public men there, and the motives which prompt them, I am so far removed from the scene of action as to know but little of them. In regard to the Vice Presidency, (to which you allude) so far as my name has been mentioned in connexion with it, I have acted a passive part. My course was settled from the beginning. I resolved that, if I should be selected as the candidate of the party, with whom I agree in political sentiment, I should not feel at liberty to decline the nomination, but on the contrary should regard it as a high distinction. This is the only position which I could consent to occupy. The suggestion or rather intimation contained in the Post Script to your letter, that if no regular nomination be made by a convention, and the several persons spoken of, for the Vice Presidency, be run in their respective sections of the Union, we would still have "left all the strength of all the aspirants, in the election to the Presidency," is a position which I could not willingly occupy. If that were the State of the canvass you will at once perceive, that a large proportion of the party might, and probably would regard the present incumbent,[2] by virtue of the *incumbency,* as the regular candidate, and the *odium* of dividing the party would be cast upon the other candidates. As I have had no personal agency in any use which has been made of my name, I can only say that it rests with the party to determine, whether I shall be taken up as their candidate or not. As regards the political principles which I entertain they are not as of yesterday. They were formed upon mature consideration, and have been long acted on. They were boldly and fearlessly avowed every where in my canvass last summer, both orally and in writing. And after the election was over they were deliberately re-iterated, and placed in a durable form, in my Inaugural Address and Message to the Legislature. They are unchanged and I am quite sure, I shall live and die with them, and this too, even though they should prostrate or annihilate me as a public man. I have during my whole course been opposed to a tariff of protection, Internal Improvements by Federal authority, a Bank of the United States, and shall be equally so to large standing armies of any kind, whether of the militia or of regulars.

The course of my old friend *Coles,* upon the abolition question, as you describe it (and of which I was not before apprized) was most unfortunate.[3] Atherton's Resolutions[4] were certainly the best expedient, yet hit upon, to suppress useless and dangerous discussion, and allay agitation upon that delicate and disturbing subject. I see the discussion is running wild in the House.[5] God grant you a safe deliverance from it, and from all your other troubles.

I sincerely thank you for your letter, and hope you will continue to write me as your leisure will permit. Be pleased to make the kind regards of Mrs. P. and myself to Mrs. H.[6] and be assured . . . .

James K. Polk

P.S. *Judge White & Foster* you see are placed at the head of the Harrison electoral ticket. By thus identifying White with Harrison, they expect to make Harrison as strong in the state as White, and in this, the present appearances are they will succeed. All the Whig leaders of any grade are already opened mouthed for Harrison and Tyler, and they will be able to bring in the rank and file of their party. White is to present himself to the people as a martyr to his principles. He will make the tour of the whole state, make speeches &c. We are to have a fierce and bloody battle. Our majority in August was only 2,500 and I have but little doubt we can maintain our ground, unless we have *too much weight to carry.*[7] We will at all events do our duty. J.K.P

ALS. A. Also ALS, draft, in DLC–JKP. Addressed to Washington and marked "Private." EI on cover by Hubbard: "Govr Polk answered that I agreed upon all points except upon the propriety of a convention at Baltimore. That in this crisis I prefered that all should run that we might have the aid of all." See Hubbard to Polk, February 23, 1840.

1. Letter not found.
2. Richard M. Johnson.
3. Walter Coles, a farmer who served several terms in the Virginia House of Delegates, won election as a Democrat to five terms in the U.S. House and served from 1835 until 1845. On December 31, 1839, and again on January 15, 1840, Coles presented resolutions in the House that all abolition petitions be laid on the table without being read, debated, printed, or referred. His version of the gag rule did not touch the question of Congress' power to legislate on the subject. Coles' resolution received a majority vote, but failed for want of the required two-thirds vote to suspend the rules.
4. Charles G. Atherton's resolutions of December 11, 1838, provided for the reception of abolition petitions, but denied them any further consideration on grounds that Congress lacked power to legislate the abolition of slavery, either directly or indirectly.
5. On January 28, 1840, southern Whigs, led by Waddy Thompson and William Cost Johnson, succeeded in passing a gag rule that prohibited the House's receipt of petitions calling for the abolition of slavery.
6. In 1827 Hubbard married Eliza Campbell, daughter of George Washington Campbell.
7. Reference probably is to Richard M. Johnson's vice-presidential candidacy.

FROM A. O. P. NICHOLSON

Dear Sir: Waverly Feby. 8 [1840][1]

I saw Mr. Huntsman yesterday in Huntingdon and had a conversation with him relative to his being an elector for the state. He afterwards shewed me a letter to you which I glanced over & lest I may not have fully understood its purport, I write to you.[2] I had applied to him to know if he would take the field as an elector. He was willing to do so provided his field of labor was confined to the Western District, and because he could not traverse the whole state, he was talking of writing up to decline a nomination. I insisted that he should accept the nomination for the State, and assured him we would be satisfied if he would [give] good battle in the Western District—That we would manage Middle Tennessee without requiring him to cross the river,[3] that if Col. Cahal served as a candidate that I would be at liberty myself to take the field and if it was necessary I would do so. I did not mean thereby that I wished to be an elector, but merely to assure Mr. H. that we privates would take the field in Mid. Ten. if it was necessary. The understanding then was that he was to agree to serve but we would not require him to cross the river. It is important to have him to go all over the district. He is highly excited & I think is resolved to give Crockett a race. In our district Jonas E. Thomas ought to be the elector. I am in great haste. I will write again on my arrival at home.

A. O. P. NICHOLSON

ALS. DLC–JKP. Addressed to Nashville.

1. Year identified through content analysis.
2. See Adam Huntsman to Polk, January 26, 1840.
3. Reference is to the Tennessee River.

FROM FELIX GRUNDY

Dear Sir,

Washington, February 9th 1840

I have no doubt, that a direct or indirect assumption of the State debts, is intended by some of the leaders of the opposition. This you know, would produce a high Tariff &c—which is so much desired by the Capitalists in the North. You will see in my remarks published a few days since in the Globe, that Mr Gentry of Ten, gave notice of a Bill he intended to introduce upon this subject.[1] This is to be the Battle field, rely on it, and our friend Harriss[2] should take a bold start. Gentry would never have ventured on this measure, without a previous arrangement with Bell & others. The Intelligencer in a long article abusing and misrepresenting my report, does not deny the assumption as intended.[3] If his party were against the assumption—It would have said so. We have got the opposition into a difficulty on this subject, from which they will find it difficult to extricate themselves. Tomorrow, the subject will be taken up in the Senate. It is the special order. We are determined to push our adversaries to the Wall and never let them off, without a direct vote on the Resolutions contained in the report.

Your prospects for a nomination at Baltimore are substantially [the same], as stated in our Joint letter,[4] with a little variation for the better.

FELIX GRUNDY

[P.S.] General Anderson has not arrived.

ALS. DLC–JKP. Addressed to Nashville and marked *"private."* AE on the cover states that this letter was answered on March 2, 1840; Polk's reply has not been found.

1. The *Congressional Globe* noted that on January 31, 1840, Grundy spoke in favor of a motion to publish the report from the Senate Select Committee on Federal Assumption of State Debts; in the course of his remarks he noted that Representative Meredith P. Gentry had revealed plans to introduce a bill providing for the assumption of certain state debts by appropriating public land proceeds for that purpose. Gentry had given notice on January 17, 1840, that he would introduce a bill providing for a partial direct assumption, the extent of which he could not then define.

2. J. George Harris.

3. The report of the Senate Select Committee on Federal Assumption of State Debts, printed on February 5, 1840, asserted that reserving public lands or the revenues arising therefrom to finance federal assumption of state debts was unjust, highly inexpedient, and unconstitutional. The Washington *National Intelligencer* of February 8, 1840, denounced the findings of Grundy's report.

4. See Felix Grundy et al. to Polk, February 3, 1840.

FROM ALEXANDER O. ANDERSON

Near Knoxville, Tennessee. February 10, 1840

Anderson reports that the Whig State Convention met in Knoxville this day. Its president, Jefferson Campbell, attacked Anderson verbally, while Addison A. Anderson and Reneau criticized the Independent Treasury scheme.[1] They charged Van Buren with having a plan to establish a standing army. Anderson encloses a letter[2] to the Tennessee legislature accepting his appointment to the U.S. Senate and stating his political sentiments. He requests that Polk arrange for Coe and Thomas[3] to request that the letter be published in the *Nashville Union.*[4] Anderson will travel to Washington by way of Asheville, North Carolina, and expects to arrive in the capital by February 20. Anderson also hopes that Laughlin, Thomas, Coe, and Pierce Anderson have agreed to attend the Democratic convention at Baltimore.

ALS. DLC–JKP. Addressed to Nashville and marked "Private & Confidential."

1. A lawyer, Thomas Jefferson Campbell served numerous terms as clerk of the Tennessee House from 1817 until his election as a Whig to the Tennessee House in 1833. A member of the legislature two terms and a Whig presidential elector in 1840, Campbell won a U.S. House seat in 1841, but held it for only one term. From 1847 until his death in 1850 he served as clerk of the U.S. House of Representatives. A lawyer from Jefferson County and a brother of the writer of this letter, Addison Alexander Anderson served as a Whig in the Tennessee House, 1835–37. A Whig and a lawyer, Lewis Reneau served three terms in the Tennessee House, 1823–27 and 1835–37, and two terms in the Tennessee Senate, 1839–43.

2. Letter not found.

3. Levin H. Coe presided over the Tennessee Senate, and Jonas E. Thomas, over the House.

4. The *Nashville Union* did not publish Anderson's letter; see Anderson to Polk, March 2, 1840.

FROM THEOPHILUS FISK[1]

Sir Richmond Feb. 21. 1840

It is with the most pleasurable emotions that I beg leave to announce that you have this moment been nominated *unanimously* as the candidate for the next Vice Presidency, by the very large democratic convention now assembled at this place. The friends of Mr. Calhoun brought up the matter and although one of the friends of another gentleman[2] made an attempt to substitute the name of R. M. Johnson, the tide of public sentiment set so strongly against him that he was compelled to withdraw his amendment.[3]

Wherever my paper, the Old Dominion, circulates, and it has a very wide one, the people will hear of no candidate but yourself. Indeed Mr. Calhoun and his friends have been exerting their strength in your behalf in every direction. We have resolved to send no delegates to the National Convention, or rather resolved that it is unecessary to hold one, so that Old Virginia is safe any way. Allow me, very respectfully, to congratulate you upon the brilliant destiny which awaits you at the hands of a grateful people.

THEOPHILUS FISK

ALS. DLC–JKP. Addressed to Nashville.

1. Theophilus Fisk and A. F. Cunningham published the Portsmouth and Norfolk *Chronicle and Old Dominion* from 1839 until 1845. Subsequently Cunningham published it by himself for three additional years.

2. Possibly Thomas H. Benton.

3. Newspaper accounts attribute the amendment to "the old Wheelhorse," who is not identified further.

FROM DAVID HUBBARD

My dear Sir Washington 23d Feby 1840

Your last letter[1] was recd. by me and I accord generaly with the views expressed by you but in relation to the Vice Presidency I differ with you wholly and will proceed frankly to state wherein we differ.

In the first place, your ground would be correct so far as relates to our duty to one another as members of a great party but there are times when higher duties are required of us than arises from our obligations to one another. Our country has higher claims upon us than even this. The whole union is in a state of fermentation and effervescence growing out of the derangements produced by paper money. Expansion had produced extravagance & indebtedness. Contraction now produces poverty, ruin and distress and the innocent as well as guilty suffer, the prudent & cautious as well as extravagant & profligate, and the masses finding this state of things likely to continue longer than they expected, are ready to lend a ready and willing ear to the Federalists who are ready to ruin our country to advance their own principles. In this state of things you have nearly one half of the Democrats of the west differing from Whigs in but little except the name. They want a protective Tariff & profuse expenditures for internal Improvements by the General Government, and with this class of politicians the Vice President[2] now acts. He will carry Kentucky, Missouri, Ohio, Indiana & Illinois provided the administration can carry those states of which there is much doubt—but then we hazard the loss of Va. & perhaps one or two other southern states if Johnson should be nominated which he most probably will be if a convention should assemble.

Virginia has as you will see by yesterdays Enquirer nominated you & decided against a convention.[3] I am satisfied that it is bad policy to hold a convention because if *Johnson* is nominated and run against Tyler & Harrison, two of her sons, we lose Virginia and may lose all. Her politicians on our side know this & therefore have acted on the best advice. If we lose this battle, the Federalists, Abolitionists, Bankites, Tariffites & Internal improvement party comes into power & consolidation follows. State debts will be assumed & Democracy will lose its name. There has been no time since our Government was set on foot that we have had equal danger to apprehend. Our people should be advised of the change from a sound to an unsound currency & of the consequent fall in prices & distress created thereby to debtors. Their patriotism should be appealed to, &, the question should be held up as second only to the Revolution itself, and they should be made acquainted with the fact that the foe was within. Monopoly, priveledge, monarchy or aristocracy & all the other forms in which plunderers can be bound together by a common cement (love of power & a desire to enjoy the fruits of labor without undergoing its fatiques) compose his forces & upon all of these questions the people should be advised forewarned & guarded. With all of this now on our hands we will have a terrible conflict. I know it and my desire is that false or mistaken delicacy should be set aside & "every man made to do his duty."[4] Johnson must run to keep the battle hot in Kentucky & the North west & west; You must run to keep strength in Va. & South of that. No one else can do this & a convention would hazard, if it did not destroy all.

These are my deliberate opinions and I think that I have a pretty fair oppertunity of judgeing at least dispassionately. You can & will be run above Johnson into the senate and without doubt would be prefered to any man the Feds could offer.

When I say all of this I seek not to tempt individual ambition, but to save a party, and the principles for which our Revolutionary fathers put all at hazard. We ought to have such men now, and I had hoped & do yet hope to find you one of them. It is not the time to regard too highly our relations to one another. The country requires results, and he who is willing to hazard most in her cause deserves most at her hands.

No nomination will be made unless the convention should be fully attended. This move in Va. will affect other Southern States & also the States of Maine & New Hampshire provided the members here from those states could know in time that you would consent to be run upon a general southern nomination by the states seperately.

David Hubbard

NB: Mrs. Hubbard desires her best respects to Mrs. Polk & yourself. P.S. The fact that Va. the largest of the southern states has refused to attend a convention not only without your advice but against it is sufficient ground for Tennessee to stop the project of convention. Her papers & public men ought to make this act the ground of ceaseing to agitate the question of convention. The getting up a convention could have been of no value but to rule Johnson off, and to do this now is full of hazard & to keep him hazards more, so I conclude that under present circumstances or "as the case stands" that I am right & you wrong & I so make bold to tell you. D Hubbard

ALS. DLC–JKP. Addressed to Nashville and marked "Private." AE on the cover states that this letter was answered by Polk on April 5, 1840.

1. See Polk to David Hubbard, February 7, 1840.
2. Richard M. Johnson.
3. According to the *Richmond Enquirer* of February 24, 1840, the Virginia State Democratic Convention, which had assembled in Richmond on February 20, 1840, unanimously nominated Polk for the vice-presidency, but declined sending delegates to the forthcoming Democratic National Convention.
4. Probably from the quotation, "England expects every man to do his duty." Horatio Nelson, Signal No. 16 at the Battle of Trafalgar, October 21, 1805.

FROM CAVE JOHNSON

Dear Sir, Washington Feby 24th 1840

I recd. yours of the 12th today, informing me of the procedings of the Dem. Convention.[1] It has been well done so far as I am advised. I suppose we shall have a severe struggle but victory with proper management is certain. I hope our friends will be urged to meet Foster upon all occasions. Carter says White will not run—but I dont think so. Rumor says, that Gentry, Crocket & C H Williams have declared they will not again run.

In the Enquirer[2] of this evening I find the [Virginia] Democratic Convention nominated you unanimously for the Vice Presidency but disapprove of a convention at Baltimore. Rely upon it that is our true policy *for your benefit* as well as that of the party. If you all run *I shall look upon your election as certain.* Apart from political considerations we find no man who does not prefer you but the idea which our friends have in the N. West that it is necessary to run old Dick[3] agt. Harrision has such an extended influence that in my opinion, if the Convention decides, it will be given to him & I believe this to be the opinion of most of the M.C.'s with whom I converse. I fear Buckhanon's[4] friends are acting badly—*some of them* declared, they would not vote for Turney or Thomas or any other foes who refused to vote for Lewis, even on a committee (the printing Com). I am glad to learn the prevailing opinion now to be, that we acted correctly and as the party should have acted—& the only proper way for a party ever to act. *If we had yielded,* we would have placed ourselves at the mercy of a few men in every thing and men whose skill or judgment or discretion or prudence is not to be relied on in general.

My health is still bad tho greatly improved & I now attend the

House. I am now convinced that my disease is in the nerves & unless I improve I shall go to Philadelphia & place myself under the care of Chapman.[5] I think it probable that my disease for years has been an aff[l]iction of the nerves rather than rheumatic.

The Com. of Elections is in a strange way—equally divid[ed], (9 men) 4 Demo, 4 Whigs, & one man *equally divided.* If the whigs make a move he votes agt. them. If the Demo make a move he votes against them, and for affirmative action [it] is really no Com. In this State of things they report a resolution to print *certain papers* for the use of the Committee. I happened in my seat & moved to amend—so as to print all the papers.[6] I have never seen such fluttering in the whig ranks. The matter will again come up on Tuesday when I shall modify, so as to direct them to Report to the House all the papers they wish printed & also to report which party had a majority at the elections & all the evidence before them & when the Report comes in it will be followed by a motion to admit the Democrats to their seats leaving the *election* to be enquired into by the Committee. The whole effort of the [Whig] party in the House & in the Committee is to stave off the decision because they know it must be against them—& by staving it off—the clamor in New Jersey & elsewhere agt. the Democrats for keeping N Jersey without Rep. will get worse & worse every day.

An amusing incident took place which the Globe has not noticed, why or wherefore I cannot tell. The appropriation Bill for pensions was up. The whigs moved to amend, to strike out 1st Section & debated four or five days & voted in committee. Bell spoke against it & voted to strike out 1st section in Committee. Well the Bill came into the House[7]—the previous question called. I felt some curiosity to know, how these men who had debated the Bill so many days would vote and called for the Ayes & noes, expressing the wish, that gentlemen who had so long opposed the Bill might have an opportunity of recording their names against the Bill. It was amusing to see, the whigs consulting & moving, pulling on hats & cloaks & moving off. I thought it was a movement designed to defeat the Bill by leaving us without a quorum. Upon the roll being called there was no *No* against the Bill—only 135 voting. When I moved the *Ayes & Noes* I heard Bell saying in an undertone *did you ever see any thing like that.*

I think the whigs are acting upon the settled purpose of preventing us from doing any thing & I shall not be surprised if they do effect their object. Every thing that comes up brings on a debate about the presidential election. The Cumberland Road Bill has occupied [us] in a motion to refer with instructions.[8] The office of Com of Pensions expires in March. A Bill to prolong it is before the House. A motion to reduce

Edwards' Salary from 3,000 to 2,500[9] brought in a general debate as to salaries, extravagance & corruption, defalcations, Wise's Report[10] &c. My proposition to amend in the N. Jersey case comes up on Tuesday & we have determined to keep in & stick to it until it is ended. Write me often.

C. JOHNSON

ALS. DLC–JKP. Addressed to Nashville.

1. Letter not found. Reference is to the Tennessee Democratic Convention.

2. *Richmond Enquirer.*

3. Richard M. Johnson.

4. James Buchanan.

5. Nathaniel Chapman, a renowned clinician at the University of Pennsylvania Medical School at Philadelphia, established the Medical Institute at Philadelphia in 1818. Two years later he founded the *Philadelphia Journal of the Medical and Physical Sciences,* the first permanent medical journal in America. He was named president of the American Medical Association at its founding in 1847.

6. On February 18, 1840, the Committee on Elections sought approval of the House to have printed selected documents relating to the committee's investigation of the New Jersey election. Cave Johnson offered an amendment that would have authorized the printing of all evidence collected by the committee in relation to this election. He resolved further that the committee have papers and documents relating to other contested elections printed by the public printer.

7. The Revolutionary War pensions bill, which came before the House on February 18, 1840, provided for an annual compensation of not more than $1500 for pension agents and provided regulations for the semi-annual distribution of pension funds by such agents.

8. Reference is to a motion of Zadoc Casey to refer the memorial of the National Road Convention, held at Terre Haute, Indiana, to the Committee of Ways and Means, with instructions to report a bill appropriating $150,000 to each of the states of Ohio, Indiana, and Illinois, to be expended on the Cumberland Road; the bill came before the House on February 17, 1840.

9. On February 21, 1840, George H. Profitt, Whig congressman from Indiana, 1839–43, offered an amendment reducing the salary of Commissioner James L. Edwards.

10. On January 17, 1837, the U.S. House created a select committee to inquire into the condition of the several executive departments. Headed by Henry A. Wise, author of the enabling resolution, the committee conducted its investigation and reported at the close of the session on March 3. The majority report found that there was no cause for just complaint about the conduct of the executive departments; the minority report denied that the investigation was sufficiently complete to form a judgment; and Chairman Wise's report protested that President Jackson had obstructed the committee's work.

FROM CAVE JOHNSON

Dear Sir, H of Rep Feby 27th [1840][1]

Brown has recd. a reply to our joint letter[2] which I have not seen, but I understand your views are the same as formerly. Judge Catron has recd. a letter from Genl. Jackson expressing similar views & I write now to be a little more specific as to my views & that you may not draw improper conclusions as to the feelings of your friends here.

If we have a convention you may rely on it that this is the view which will be taken of it. Genl. H[3] is the nominee. Ohio, Ind., Arkansas, Michigan and perhaps Missouri think it essential to the great cause that the present incumbent[4] should *run against him,* whilst Ten., Miss., N.C., Virg., S.C. would no doubt think that you should be the man. Ala. would be for K.[5] or you. Georgia for F[6] or for you. The Northern Democrats will decide it in Convention not upon merits or qualifications or even their own wishes but as matter of policy. The question will be, whether it will be better to risk Ten & other Southern States with R.M.J. on the ticket or risk the five N.W. States with you upon the ticket—& upon this question, in despite of all that can be said or done by your friends the Convention will give it to R.M.J. in my opinion. Va. will not send delegates nor will S.C. It is probable N.C. may—likewise Alabama. In my opinion Penn. & several of the New England States will go for the present incumbent not because they like him better but as a matter of policy. N.Y. will take no stand at present but will stand with the other Northern States upon the policy. In the Convention in my opinion you must be defeated in despite of every effort of your friends. But *if the Convention does not act* & each State is left to run the man they like best—King & F—will be necessarily backed out & in my opinion you might be elected by a majority of the Electors, but if not certainly by the Senate. I must repeat what I have before said that with the Northern Democracy you would have more than 20 to 1 agt. R.M.J. leaving out all questions of policy. You are in my opinion positively popular with them, whilst he is positively unpopular.

In this State of things, they will enquire & they ought to enquire how the presidential election will be affected? That with every body out of Ten. is the great question, to which every thing else will be sacrifised but we must not shew to any party here any disinclination to go into the Convention or be bound by its decision.

I write fairly & truly what I think & I am sure you will give credit for sincerity & I hope disinterestedness & as far as I can learn here the true policy has been adopted by Virginia, all our friends think.

We are trying to sit out the printing of the N. Jersey papers on my motion to amend.[7] I have never seen such a Congress before. I hope never to see such another. The House has just refused to go to the orders of the day & I hope it is indicative of a determination to settle the matter to day.

My health still continues bad but much better than before. I am convinced it is nervous[ness] & unless I improve in 8 or 10 days I will place myself under the care of some distinguished Physician in Philadelphia & let him cure me or kill. My wife[8] is now in better health than usual.

C. JOHNSON

ALS. DLC–JKP. Addressed to Nashville.

1. Year identified through content analysis.
2. See Felix Grundy et al. to Polk, February 3, 1840. Polk's reply to Aaron V. Brown has not been found.
3. William H. Harrison.
4. Richard M. Johnson.
5. William R. King.
6. John Forsyth.
7. See Cave Johnson to Polk, February 24, 1840.
8. Elizabeth Dortch Brunson Johnson.

FROM ALEXANDER O. ANDERSON

Washington City. March 2, 1840

In response to Polk's two letters of the 17th ultimo,[1] Anderson reports on political opinion in Washington about recent developments in the Democratic vice-presidential contest. Polk's nomination by the Virginia convention has produced a favorable impression. New York City's nomination of Johnson "will amount to nothing," for the state will support Polk. Although most congressmen from the Northwest favor Polk, political leaders in Arkansas, Missouri, Illinois, Indiana, and Ohio prefer Johnson. Maryland has nominated Johnson, probably because the Tennessee congressional delegation did not fully support Maryland's candidate for Speaker of the U.S. House, Francis Thomas. Polk's friends agree on the necessity of having a vice-presidential candidate attractive to the South and Southwest, but neither Virginia nor South Carolina will be represented at the Baltimore convention. Thus risking a contest with Johnson at the convention is not safe. Senator Wright suggests that the Democrats avoid a vice-presidential nomination at the convention and run regional candidates in the South and Northwest. Anderson writes that he is satisfied with the decision to withhold publication of his letter to the Tennessee legislature.[2]

ALS. DLC–JKP. Addressed to Nashville and marked "Private & Confidential." AE on the cover states that this letter was answered on March 28, 1840; Polk's reply has not been found.

1. Letters not found.
2. See Alexander O. Anderson to Polk, February 10, 1840.

FROM JOHN J. GARNER

Dear sir Yalobusha Cty. Miss March the 2. 1840

After my respects to you I wil inform you that we have moved on the opposit side of the hill from whare the houses stood to my stables and cribs which wil bee out of my power to move until I lay my crop by or place my self backward in my crop. I have got a large potion of my cotton land ridged up and are getting a long very wel I think. I have sowed some twelve or foretuen acors in oats on the ridgs and have aded to the farm some forty five acors I think. I am aiming to put about two hundred acors in cotton. N.B. I went to Troy yesterday and got a bil of lading for your cotton. It lft Troy a few days cence all in good owder, at the same time and in the same boat, 136 bales weying 57559 lbs, if I have not made a mistake in the calculation of them done in a hurey. I am trying to get a letter to you a mediately as you have fail to come. I would of written to you sooner had it not bin that I was looking for you every hour for some time. I wil now what to dwo in a case of this kind herafter write all the time. Your cotton wil bee in new orleans in a few days from this time, perhaps the last of this weak. It left here in a boat belonging to Minter for Williamses landing[1] and wil bene took from there by a steme boat which wil deliver it there very quick. I shal continue looking for you until you arive here.

JOHN J. GARNER

ALS. DLC–JKP. Addressed to Nashville. Published in Bassett, *Plantation Overseer*, 138.

1. Williams' Landing was situated on the Yalobusha River about twenty miles below Troy, Mississippi.

FROM FELIX GRUNDY

Dear Sir, Washington City, March 2nd 1840

I was glad to receive yours[1] in answer to the Joint letter of the delegation.[2] We shall use our influence, If we have any, discreetly.

I confess I am mortified at some letters I receive upon the subject of your election to the Vicepresidency. They imply without saying it, that we who are here, are not acting as zealously as we should. They also urge the nomination of a Vicepresident by the Baltimore Convention. My own opinion is & has been against such nomination. My original impression was that you could not be nominated by that Convention. Recent circumstances go strongly to confirm my first impression. Virginia & South Carolina will not send delegates. Both these States are decidedly for you. Besides there are other facts within my knowledge, which I am not at liberty to communicate—which go far to satisfy me, that you can be elected, without a Convention & you cannot be nominated by it. I am in an unpleasant situation. If I act as your friends at home wish, I shall assist in defeating you, and also throw our State into difficulties, from which we cannot recover. I will not do a foolish thing knowingly—and therefore my opinion is, that the Ten. delegates should go to Baltimore, and unite in the nomination of the president, then act according to circumstances. And if it is discovered that a nomination will be made, which Ten. cannot sustain herself upon, they should return and not commit the State by any act of theirs &c. A state of things may arise which would change the face of things and of course my views would be changed.

FELIX GRUNDY

ALS. DLC–JKP. Addressed to Nashville and marked "private." AE on the cover states that this letter was answered on March 26, 1840; Polk's reply has not been found.

1. Letter not found.
2. See Felix Grundy et al. to Polk, February 3, 1840.

FROM ANDREW JACKSON DONELSON

Dr. Govr. Washington March 4h 1840

I am here and am busy in tracing the influences which bear on the question of the vice Presidency, though I have not yet seen the prominent actors. Nearly all the friends of the administration with whom I have conversed agree in the main with us in Tennessee in respect to the disadvantage resulting from the position occupied by Col. Johnson. They however think that the best way to harmonize any interest on this subject is to let each section of the union run its own candidate and leave the decision to the electoral colleges or to congress if they fail. The practical effect of the views now prevalent here, will be to reduce the contest to a choice between you & Johnson. The south will be for you—

the west for Johnson—New York & the other northern states holding the ballance. To this suggestion if adopted, it is of course indispensable that there be no nomination by the convention, and if I can be satisfied that such is the determination of the leading friends of the Republican party, as you advocate I do not see that there would be any ground for complaint.

You see that Virginia sends no delegates to the convention. So. Carolina will send none. And one or two of the western states I am informed will send none. So that in all probability the expedient of having no nomination on the subject of the vice Presidency is the only one by which your success can be accomplished. At present the fear is Johnson would be able to get the nomination, or rather be stronger than you.

I will not pursue the subject, however, further at this time. In a day or two you shall know all about it. Our friends here are well and in good spirits.

A J DONELSON

[P.S.] Your conjectures about the views of King & Buchanan are right. The information is that their weight falls to Johnson in Penna—so as to render it almost certain that he will obtain the nomination. This state of things strengthens very much the views I have previously expressed. AJD

ALS. DLC–JKP. Addressed to Nashville and marked "Private" on the cover.

FROM THOMAS P. MOORE

My dear Sir Harrodsburg,[1] March 6. 1840

I have occasionally legged for you, & my recent visit as far North as Boston afforded me many opportunities. I reached Wheeling just before the 8h of Jan Convention at Columbus Ohio,[2] & addressed a letter to Hamer urging him to resist the nomination of Col Johnson, & to secure delegates to the National Convention favorable to you. The enclosed letter[3] is a sign of the times, & hence I send it. The mongrel factions who support Harrison are moving Heaven & earth to get up a hurrah feeling in his favor. My word for it, we will all have as much as we can do. I set out tomorrow for Memphis, Holly Springs, &c, under a cruel necessity, to sacrafice property to meet a probable judgment agst me as one of the sureties of a defaulter. When I return I shall take the stump. At present the pecuniary distress is so pervading that the people cannot be made to think of any thing else.

T P Moore

[P.S.] Regards to Mrs. P. If you chance to see the revered old chief,[4] remember me to him. (Destroy H. letter)

ALS. DLC–JKP. Addressed to Nashville.

1. Harrodsburg, Kentucky.

2. The Ohio State Democratic Convention met on January 8 and 9, 1840, and selected Thomas L. Hamer to chair the meeting, which nominated Wilson Shannon for a second term as governor, supported a call for a national convention, and recommended the reelection of Martin Van Buren and Richard M. Johnson.

3. Moore enclosed a letter from Hamer of January 23, 1840, which had been written as a reply to one from Moore of January 4, 1840. Hamer regretted that the convention had recommended Johnson and explained that as president of the convention he was unable to influence the resolutions committee. Hamer predicted that Johnson would not be nominated at Baltimore and suggested that public support for Polk would continue to increase. ALS. DLC–JKP.

4. Andrew Jackson.

FROM ALEXANDER O. ANDERSON

My Dear Sir Washington City March 9 1840

By the mail which carries this you will receive, probably, the news of the nomination, by the Pennsylvania convention at Harrisburg, of Col. Johnson.[1] This has been done as I believe from the movement of politicians at this place—and in connexion with the north-west line of influence. New York & the East is for you, but they do not wish to be constrained to a nomination in the Convention. My opinion is that Johnson's friends will press a nomination. The true policy is to avoid it. If we do, New York & New Hampshire will hold the balance of power, & will be with us at the poals, as now believed. Some seem to be utterly blind to the fact that Ohio, Indiana & Kentuckey rejected Johnson before.[2] The truth is, the safest part of the Democratic Battle is in the South, for New York (& New Jersey) the former particularly will be closely fought—and some of our friends from Pennsylvania, apprehend that a recent split among the Democrats in the Legislature there, upon the votes as to the Banks, will be injurious. How far, cannot now be told. And it is perfectly certain that you are the most acceptable to the people. And my opinion is, as Virginia & South Carolina are for you, & will not go into Convention at all, that it will be safest not to agree to make any nomination of Vice President. How far it may be best that the delegates should be specifically advised from Tennessee you must judge. But of one thing you may rest assured, we will not compromise your claims. I have examined with unwearied diligence, and my best skill, the whole ground and understand the posture of affairs thoroughly & where the reliance may be placed. New York without a Convention will *unquestionably* cast her vote conformably to the wishes of ______, those in whom she takes the deepest interest. I believe that *Tennessee* has claims upon her, if urged, *from the proper quarter*, uncompromisingly, which cannot be disregarded—and will not be.

Cave Johnson, Brown, Turney & myself have had repeated conferences—and are pressing a line of action in concert.

Buchanan has been wholly neutral between you & Johnson. His choice was King—but he [Buchanan] has been moved out of reach of success, in that matter, in his own State—King recd. 28 votes—& Johnson the remainder.

Our friend Waterson[3] is decidedly earnest in our cause. When the Delegates from Tennessee come here we shall be fully prepared with the best means of information and action. Our friend Judge Grundy expresses a decided solicitude for you—& concurs with us.

You will perceive the propriety of burning this letter *instantly*, and measure the facts. They *impart fully what words can signify*. Write me instantly & freely. My uttermost efforts shall be put forth—and you shall hear from me from time to time.

Major Donelson is here, and I think ought to come to the Convention. I have seen him two or three times.

A ANDERSON

ALS. DLC–JKP. Addressed to Nashville and marked "Private & Confidential." AE on the cover states that this letter was answered on March 28, 1840; Polk's reply has not been found.

1. The Pennsylvania Democratic State Convention met on March 4, 1840, endorsed the reelection of Martin Van Buren and Richard M. Johnson, chose a slate of presidential electors, and selected delegates to the Democratic National Convention.

2. In 1836 the electors from Ohio, Indiana, and Kentucky cast their votes for William H. Harrison for president and for Francis Granger of New York for vice-president.

3. Harvey M. Watterson.

FROM CAVE JOHNSON

Dear Sir, [Washington City] H of Rep 10th March 1840

I am happy to inform you we have to day admitted the Democratic members from N Jersey to their seats by a vote of twenty majority.[1] In haste.

C JOHNSON

ALS. DLC–JKP. Addressed to Nashville.

1. See Harvey M. Watterson to Polk, November 29, 1839.

FROM CAVE JOHNSON

Dear Sir, Washington March 12th 1840

I recd. yours last evening.[1] Every thing I see convinces me that you must loose the nomination at Baltimore if one is made & I am not less satisfied if no nomination is made that you will be the vice pres., & I am now inclined to think that none will be made. I had a conversation today with Gov. L. of Georgia,[2] who is very warmly your friend but at the same time the friend of RMJ & lives with him. I spoke freely to him—that we could not run RMJ in Ten., that it endangered our success etc. He assured me that no nomination would be made—that it was unnecessary etc. Gov. W. of New Jersey[3] intimated as much. I suspect & I regret to do so, that the influence of Col B.[4]—has been adverse to your interests. I also suspect the PM. Genl.[5] & the Globe but have no evidence to warrant more than a bare suspicion. If it be so I will find it out. I have no reason to suppose any others here to be otherwise than friendly. I mention it only as a suspicion & of course you will not receive it or trust it otherwise. I cannot see the causes that should engender such opposition unless it is jealousy which I thought I had taken proper precaution to remove. Buch's[6] influence is also agt. you probably for the same reasons. As far as I can learn the balance of the Northern Democracy are for you if policy does not dictate a different [one]. In my opinion you need make no calculations on Ohio or Pennsylvania or the N.W. states. Virginia has taken the lone ground for us & by it, we ought to stand or fall. Our Legislature should have delayed action on that subject until the result of the deliberations at Harrisburgh were made known.[7] I think I said as much when in Nashville. Balch[8] is made a Florida Judge.

It was known to none of us here until after the nomination & confirmation.

Bell's gag Bill[9] is now the order of the day upon the question of consideration but was postponed to day so as not to loose its place to let Jones take up the Treasury Note Bill.[10] I made that question for fear we should never get a vote upon it any other day. Brown intends making us debate it, if he can get the floor after Bell. I will also if I get well enough to make an effort before the debate closes. I have not been well enough to be in the House any day since I have been here but still I attend & vote.

The New Jersey M.C. are daily expected. A debate has been got up on the motion to print & the squabble between Medil and Reeves[11] on one side & Smith of Con. & Filmore has been revived by Jenifer & Graves[12] who have unnecessarily thrust themselves into the controversy as I think with the determination of getting a fight & by that means to some extent to cover the inequity of the N Jersey transaction. The nullifyers begin to work better than formerly & we are likely to get on better than heretofore.

C. Johnson

ALS. DLC–JKP. Addressed to Nashville and marked "Private." AE on the cover states that this letter was answered on March 30, 1840.

1. Letter not found.

2. Wilson Lumpkin, Democratic governor of Georgia from 1831 until 1835, sat in the U.S. Senate, 1837–41.

3. Garret D. Wall, a New Jersey lawyer, served as clerk of the state Supreme Court, 1812–18, and U.S. district attorney in 1829. In the latter year he was elected governor of New Jersey, but declined to serve. He won election to one term in the U.S. Senate in 1835.

4. Thomas Hart Benton.

5. Amos Kendall.

6. James Buchanan.

7. See Polk to Sarah C. Polk, April 20, 1839.

8. Alfred Balch, a Nashville lawyer, was nominated by Van Buren to a four-year term as judge for the middle district of Florida on March 10, 1840. The Senate confirmed his appointment the following day.

9. On February 10, 1840, Congressman John Bell introduced a bill to secure freedom of elections and prohibit electioneering by employees of the general government. Postponed for one day following March 11, the bill provoked heated debate, including speeches by Tennessee Congressmen Bell, Aaron V. Brown, Meredith P. Gentry, and Harvey M. Watterson. On May 20 the House rejected Bell's "gag bill."

10. Introduced by John W. Jones, Ways and Means Committee chairman, on February 19, 1840, the treasury note bill authorized the Treasury Depart-

ment to issue up to 5 million dollars in treasury notes, including issues outstanding under the act of 1837. All notes issued under authority of this bill were to be redeemed within a year.

11. William Medill and Francis E. Rives. An Ohio lawyer, Medill served as a member and Speaker of the Ohio House, 1835–38, before winning election in 1839 as a Democrat to the first of two terms in the U.S. House. He subsequently held a position in the Post Office Department, 1845, and served as commissioner of Indian affairs, 1845–50. Rives, a Virginia planter who served numerous terms in the state legislature, won election as a Democrat to two terms in the U.S. House and served from 1837 until 1841.

12. Truman Smith, Millard Fillmore, Daniel Jenifer, and William J. Graves. A Yale graduate and lawyer, Smith served several terms in the Connecticut legislature before winning election in 1839 as a Whig to the first of two terms in the U.S. House. Fillmore, a New York congressman, succeeded to the presidency upon the death of Zachary Taylor in 1850. Graves, a Kentucky lawyer, served as a Whig in the U.S. House from 1835 until 1841. On March 11, 1840, John Campbell, chairman of the Committee on Elections, reported all the testimony and proceedings on the New Jersey case to March 5 and moved that the same be printed. Smith, Jenifer, and Graves urged an amendment to include the printing of documents received by the committee since March 5. In the morning hour of March 12 the printing debate continued with Fillmore strongly attacking Campbell's original motion.

FROM LEVIN H. COE

Somerville, Tennessee. March 23, 1840

Coe discusses judicial appointments in the Western District. Before learning that W. C. Dunlap and T. J. Turley would be applicants, Coe had promised to recommend P. T. Scruggs to be judge of the Eleventh Circuit Court; upon sampling public opinion Coe doubts the wisdom of that promise.[1] Also a Whig named Stephens[2] is maneuvering to secure the office of solicitor for Reed's circuit court.[3] W. B. Miller, a former solicitor who defaulted on many thousands of dollars of state funds, is Stephens' brother-in-law.[4] Coe doubts that Stephens would investigate the fraud vigorously.

ALS. DLC–JKP. Addressed to Nashville. AE on the cover states that this letter was answered on March 29, 1840; Polk's reply has not been found.

1. William C. Dunlap, Thomas J. Turley, and Phineas T. Scruggs. Turley, a lawyer, served as attorney general for Shelby County in 1836. Scruggs, a former Methodist Episcopal clergyman, was an active member of the Fayette County bar and later of the Shelby County bar. Dunlap received the appointment of circuit judge of Tennessee's Eleventh District.

2. William H. Stephens, a Whig and early lawyer of Madison County, served at Jackson as clerk of the Supreme Court of Tennessee from 1840 until

1857. An unsuccessful Whig candidate for Congress in 1857, Stephens later served the Confederacy as a colonel and then as a judge.

3. John Read of Jackson served as judge of the Circuit Court for the Tenth District from 1836 until the Civil War.

4. Before he became attorney general, or solicitor, for the Tenth District in 1837, William Blount Miller, son of Pleasant M. Miller, had served in the Tennessee House, 1833–35, and in the Senate, 1836–37. See Polk to Joseph H. Talbot, March 26, 1840.

FROM JAMES WALKER

Dear Sir, Columbia, March 23d 1840

Presuming you are at home, I address you after a long silence. I should have written you on my return from the District, but on no day supposed my letter would have reached before you would leave. I do not like the political signs, and think it is pretty manifest that the Bentonian policy is to run Johnson. If this is so, in addition to the destructive and ruinous course of our Legislature,[1] I very much fear for Tennessee. The Whigs are availing themselves with great dexterity of the distresses of the times, and attribute them all (in part with too much truth) to the destructive effect of Democratic Legislation. I think the position which Virginia has assumed is under all circumstances most fortunate. It is at all events a high complement to be nominated by that state, and as she nominates unconditionally, her attitude will bring the aspirants to the succession to reflection. I do not believe we can carry Johnson, and Benton has not played the game to help his prospects.

We shall be compelled under present circumstances to suspend the work on our road.[2] We cannot build it entirely ourselves. We have already built nearly 12 miles upon entirely our own means (except the interest on the bonds issued). We consider ourselves fairly and legally entitled under the laws to $45000 of bonds which you refuse to issue. In this I think, and we all think, you are wrong, and do us a private wrong, and that its effect is highly injurious to the public in this region. The question whether or not we are entittled to the bonds claimed, narrows down to this: Had this company (prior to the passage of the late law)[3] complied with the former law,[4] so as to entittle them to this issuance of 45000 of bonds. Suppose the late law had not been passed, would we not have been entittled to the bonds under the law as it stood when the certificate of payment by the stockholders was made by the board of Directors on the 9th of March 1839. I need not say that it is manifest that they should have issued, and I recollect that you expressed to me after looking into the law, your surprise that Cannon should have violated so plain and imperative a duty. If I have not always misunderstood your opinion, you (in common with the intelligent of all parties) condemned Cannons conduct as a violation of private rights and of public law, and as an usurpation of Legislative and judicial powers. This point being admitted, what were the rights of this company as they existed, prior to the passage of the late law? If they had done all they were required by law to do, and were entitled to the bonds, their *rights* at this point, and to the amount of this lot of bonds, were *vested rights.* This follows as a necessary consequence: They had complied with the law—nothing remained to be done, and it was the duty of the Governor forthwith to issue the bonds. The right to the bonds being then perfect, it became and was a clear case of *vested rights* and brings this company (so far as this lot of bonds is concerned) within the saving of the last section of the law of 1840. It might be otherwise, if the Stockholders of this or any other company were now to make a payment and apply thereupon for the bonds. But as regards the application and payment of stock before the late law was passed, nothing it seems to me can be clearer. When we simplify the subject, it presents no kind of difficulty or embarrassment. The question of the constitutionality of the late law does not necessarily arise—at least it is not necessarily involved in the decision of this question. The Legislature clearly could not have passed any law which would have properly deprived the Co. of the issuance of this lot of bonds. But the question involving the *power* of the Legislature to pass such a law does not present itself because of the express saving in favor of vested rights of existing companies.

It seems to me that you ought either to issue the bonds we are entitled to, or if you think we are not in good faith complying with the law under which the Co formed, to file a bill against us and let us see wherein there is fraud or wrong on our part. If eminent lawyers were to decide that we are wrong in the views we take of our rights, we would certainly submit quietly, but at present we are dissatisfied and I think we have full and sufficient cause. Your & Mr. Humphrys relationship to the members of this Co. does render the question of the propriety of your action more delicate than usual. To relieve all difficulties, why not let the first legal men in [the][5] state examine the question fully, and decide what is your duty under the laws & the constitution.

I am discouraged, and disgusted with political matters. I have sustained my principles and opinions honestly and fully, at the expense of much time and money. It seems that whenever I have any interest within the power of the general or state government, the very fact of my being interested blights and destroys, plain and fair justice. Others can get justice and obtain their legal & equitable rights. What have I done, that I and all who may be concerned with me should be under the ban, and that too, where our friends have the power, and when the questions are plain and simple and without doubt. Is it not time for me to retire from political excitement. I need not change my principles. This I hope I shall never do—but I can be quiet and possibly may escape the malice of enemies who hate alone for the sake of politics.

JAMES WALKER

ALS. DLC–JKP. Addressed to Nashville. AE on the cover states that this letter was answered on March 29, 1840; Polk's reply has not been found.

1. Reference is to the U.S. Congress.
2. Walker's reference is to the Columbia Central Turnpike Company. See James Walker to Polk, December 30, 1839.
3. See J. G. M. Ramsey to Polk, December 18, 1839.
4. Reference is to the Act of January 19, 1838. See Polk to Benjamin F. Butler, February 6, 1839.
5. A tear in the manuscript has obliterated at least one word.

TO JOSEPH H. TALBOT

My Dear Sir Nashville March 26th 1840

On my arrival at home last night I found numerous letters and strong recommendations from members of the Bar and others in favour of the different applicants for the office of solicitor in the room and stead of Wm B. Miller, who it is represented will shortly resign that office.[1] From a conversation held with you at Bolivar and on our way from thence to Jackson[2] on Saturday last you had reason to calculate that the appointment would be conferred on you. Such was my intention at the time I saw you acting on the information I then had. The recommendations in favour of other applicants I find on reaching home are so numerous and strong as to produce serious doubt in my mind whether I can with propriety overlook them in making the appointment. In regard to your qualifications and fitness for the office I have no doubt, but much is due in deference to the opinions and wishes of the members of the Bar and other citizens residing within the Judicial Circuit where the duties are to be performed. With the kindest feelings personally towards you, as you must know, and with every disposition to gratify your wishes, I have upon reflection serious doubts, whether I ought upon my own personal knowledge of you alone, and without any recommendation or wish expressed by those immediately interested to confer the appointment on you. My first impression on hearing there was likely to be a vacancy, and that you were an applicant, was to appoint you, knowing you to be a lawyer of age & standing and believing you to be well[3] qualified to discharge the duties. The Judge of the Circuit,[4] many members of the bar and other citizens however have recommended other applicants, and it is this which produces embarrassment in my mind. From our long intimacy, I have felt authorized to write you in the spirit of friendship and thus frankly.

Genl. Miller's resignation has not yet been received but I presume will be forwarded shortly.[5] As I understand that no Courts will sit in the Circuit until late in April, no appointment will be made until I have time to hear from you, hoping in the meantime that such an adjustment of the conflicting claims of the different applicants may be effected, as to relieve me from the existing embarrassment.

When at Jackson I was asked the question whether you were an applicant, and of course answered in the affirmative. Some surprize was expressed that you were an applicant, as nothing was known of your intention when you left Jackson a few days before. Under all the circumstances, you will readily see the perplexing embarrassment in which I will be placed, if matters stand as they now are.

I write you with the open frankness and freedom, I am accustomed to use, when addressing known personal friends, & know you will properly appreciate the motives & considerations which induce me to do so.

JAMES K. POLK

ALS, draft. DLC–JKP. Addressed to Jackson and marked "Copy" on both the first page and the cover of the document.

1. On February 14, 1840, Stephen C. Pavatt applied to Polk for an appointment as attorney general of the Tenth District. ALS. T–Governor's Papers. See Levin H. Coe to Polk, March 23, 1840.

2. Having visited his plantation in Mississippi, Polk passed through Bolivar and Jackson en route to Nashville.

3. The words, "and believing you to be well," were written in the left margin of the facing page.

4. John Read.

5. On April 18, 1840, John Read certified to Polk that William B. Miller was residing outside the Tenth Circuit and without the state, in Mississippi. ADS. T–Governor's Papers.

FROM WILLIAMSON SMITH

My Dear Sir. Washington City March [27][1] 1840

I reached here on the 22nd Inst and have thought it might not be un[in]teresting to you to hear some news from Washington. My prospects are by no means flattering for an adjustment of my business. It is yet before the Committee on the Judiciary,[2] and from what I can understand it is very doubtful whether they will report in my favour or against me. M friend Genl. Anderson I think is doing all he can for me, but my old friend Felix[3] I think is letting it shear its own fate, being as I think overly tenacious of taking any responsibility on himself about any thing. I may be mistaken and I hope I am, but things look mightily so to me, more of this hereafter.

I have taken some pains to ascertain how the hang of things are with regard to the Vice Presidency. Your friends here are now in pretty good spirrits much more than they were 3 or 4 weeks ago. The understanding now by your friends is that they will endeavour to prevent a nomination for V. President at the Baltimore Convention since Virginia & South Carolina have refused to send delegates. Some of your friends that you had reason to believe would support you, I understand, you will be decived in. And as I design this letter to be strictly confidential, I will give you such information as I have received. It comes principally through Genl. Anderson, who is doing every thing in his power for your success, and I reckon Grundy is but he [is] mighty lazy. It seems to be understood that Mr. Kendal had an agency in getting Johnson nominated in Pennsylvania and that he is taking a full hand for him. Your friend Allen from Ohio is very strongly suspected. There [are] different opinions with regard to Mr. Benton. Some think he is moving the wires against you; others think not. It is understood here that Mr. Buchannan thinks you are in his way. I understand Mr. Wright of New York takes open ground for you, also Mr Clay of Ala. &c. It is believed if there is no nomination made and you should not be Elected by Electoral votes you will have nothing to fear in the Senate, should it go there. As you have other friends here better informed that will be able to give you information perhaps more correct than I do, I will come a close.

I wish you was here as I think your successor[4] is getting along rather badly.

WILLIAMSON SMITH

ALS. DLC–JKP. Addressed to Nashville. AE on the cover states that this letter was answered on April 5, 1840; Polk's reply has not been found.

1. Date supplied from the letter's postmark.
2. See Alexander O. Anderson to Polk, February 4, 1840.
3. Felix Grundy.
4. Robert M. T. Hunter succeeded Polk as Speaker of the U.S. House.

TO CAVE JOHNSON

My Dear Sir Nashville March 30th 1840

On reaching home after an absence of three weeks I received your several letters. I received also several other letters from friends at Washington, containing similar views with your own. I have addressed two letters to Mr. Grundy in reply,[1] hastily written, and in the midst of official business, which I found on my table on my return, which I requested him to show to you, as you can if you choose show this to him. The course taken by Va seems to have given a new aspect to the Vice Presidential question. If Va. S. Carolina and probably other states shall not be represented in the convention, and that body on that account or for any other reason shall agree to disperse, without a nomination, leaving the selection of the candidate for the Vice Presidency an open question, to be determined by the several States, the question arises, what then should be my course? It has as you know been my fixed purpose from the beginning, as it still is, to act *with* and not *against*, the *majority* of the party, whenever the will of that *majority* can be satisfactorily ascertained. Had a *full* convention of the *whole party*, and from *all the States*, assembled and made a nomination, that would have settled the question. If however a *partial* and not a *full* convention shall assemble, as is now probable & shall disperse without making a nomination, my present impression is, that I should wait a reasonable time, to ascertain what the development of the public opinion of the party was, and be governed by it. If it was ascertained that a clear *majority* of the Democratic party declared an intention to run me on the ticket, that would be one thing, but if otherwise my present impression is, that I ought not and could not consent to be run by a *minority*, against the *majority*, of my own party, and with the certainty that I could not be elected by the people, nor even returned to the Senate as one of the two highest on the list, merely for the purpose, of strengthening the ticket in a few states, in the Presidential election. To be *used* in a few states *merely* for that purpose, would be a sacrifice of myself and of all my future prospects, to which I ought not voluntarily to agree, and which the party ought not to require of me. My friends however and yourself among the number express a confident opinion, that if no nomination be made, I will be stronger than any other Democratic candidate named, and would be generally taken up and run by the party. If that should turn out to be so, it would present an entirely different case, and I should not withdraw my name. With these views I shall await the result at Baltimore on the 5th of May, and be governed in my course after that time, as circumstances and the public opinion of the party, may seem to indicate as proper, always acting cautiously, and taking no step rashly or without the advice of discreet and prudent friends. I cannot consent to play the part, which Judge White did in the Presidential election of 1836, when you rem[em]ber it was one of the grounds, upon which both you and myself successfully attacked him, that he was not run in States enough to elect him, if he had received the votes of all the States where he was run.

All difficulty and embarrassment to the party, may as I confidently believe be avoided by the timely action of our friends. In the present aspect of affairs as I see and understand them, New York and the New England states can settle the matter in a day, by taking a decided and bold stand *at once*. The indications from that quarter I understand are favourable, and such as are not to be mistaken. Without the support of these states, it is certain that Col. J.[2] cannot be nominated or receive the votes of a majority of the party. The delicacy of deciding between common political friends, and the fear of giving offense, I am aware prevents them at present from taking any decided and open stand, but then they must finally take their *position*, and would give no greater offense by taking it *now*, than at a later period when it may be out of their power, to avert the danger which threatens the party. It was the same sort of indecision and fear of giving offense which lost us the Speaker's election in 1834.[3] Instead of waiting for circumstances to occur upon which to base their action, they should by their action and an early avowal of their preference produce the circumstances which they desire to occur.

This State having resolved to be represented in Convention, a full delegation will go on, in time to be at Washington, some days beforehand, so as to have an opportunity for full consultation with our friends there, to learn their views, and communicate the views of our friends here.[4] The present is an important moment, not so much to myself personally, but to the party and its continued ascendancy. We are to have a most active and violent contest, and one that is not without its dangers. A mistaken step may defeat us, whilst at the same time a decided, but prudent course taken *now* by our Northern and Eastern friends would put our success beyond doubt. I have thus frankly but *confidentially*,[5] given you my pre[se]nt impressions and views, but am content for the present to leave the matter so far as I am concerned, to my friends, yourself among the number, having the most entire confidence that I shall be satisfied with whatever you may do.

JAMES K. POLK

ALS, draft. DLC–JKP. Addressed to Washington City and marked "*Private & confidential,*" and "Copy." Three days earlier, on March 27, 1840, Polk had drafted a similar letter to Johnson and had endorsed it, "Not sent, but modified & re-written." Included on the draft was a postscript relating party prospects in the Western District and urging Johnson to push the occupant bill through the Congress during the present session. ALS, draft. DLC–JKP.

1. According to his draft to Johnson of March 27th, Polk wrote to Grundy, "in haste on yesterday," and enclosed a "*private letter*" from Thomas Hamer to Thomas P. Moore, forwarded "*confidentially*" to Polk by Moore, detailing party opinion in the western states. Polk's second letter to Grundy has not been identified. See Moore to Polk, March 6, 1840.

2. Richard M. Johnson.

3. John Bell defeated Polk for the Speakership of the U.S. House on June 2, 1834. See, particularly, Cave Johnson to Polk, September 13, 1834.

4. In his draft to Johnson of March 27, Polk wrote that Jonas E. Thomas and Samuel H. Laughlin had been appointed delegates in the place of others who had declined.

5. Polk suggested in his draft to Johnson of March 27 that Johnson might show the letter to Felix Grundy, Alexander Anderson, and Aaron V. Brown "under the like injunction."

TO SAMUEL H. LAUGHLIN

My Dear Sir Nashville April 1st 1840

The corresponding committee[1] here will meet on tomorrow, and will as I learn appoint yourself and Mr Speaker Thomas as delegates to Baltimore. I learn from a letter recd. from a friend at Columbia that Thomas will certainly accept and go on if you do. T desires to go with you, and makes your acceptance almost a *Sine qua non,* of his own. It is my Dear Sir, an important moment, not so much to myself individually, but to the party and its continued ascendancy. I verily believe that your presence at Baltimore and at Washington a few days beforehand will be more important than that of any other individual in the South West, and I hope nothing may occur to prevent it. Thomas desires to set out by the 10th but would wait for you, until the 12th or 15th if you desired it. Mr Harris has showed me your letter as you requested him. The information from Ohio, accords with that which I had received through another channel. Information reached here by to-night's mail that the Democratic members of the Massachusetts Legislature, and other Democratic citizens have had a State convention,[2] and unanimously made the same nominations as that made by Tennessee and Virginia, and the nominations are placed at the head of the Editorial columns of the Boston Post, the Statesman, Bay-State Democrat,[3] and other Democratic papers in that region. New York now holds the balance of power and can decide the matter in a day, by taking a decided stand *at once*. The delicacy of her relations to the subject, and the fear of giving offence by taking divided ground between common political friends, I am aware prevents her at present from acting, but then she must *finally* take her position, and would give no more offense now, than she would at a later period, when it may be out of her power to avert the danger which threatens the party. But I need not pursue the subject. Let me hear from you, on receipt that you will go on. Take Nashville in your way, as I wish to see you.

James K. Polk

ALS. DLC–JKP. Addressed to McMinnville and marked "*Private & confidential.*" AE by Laughlin reads "Ansd 5 April, accepting appointment; and fixing 14th for meeting at Nashville." Laughlin's reply has not been found. Published in Joseph H. Parks, ed., "Letters from James K. Polk to Samuel H. Laughlin, 1835–1844," *The East Tennessee Historical Society's Publications*, XVIII (1946), 155.

1. See Samuel H. Laughlin to Polk, February 6, 1840, and Polk to Samuel H. Laughlin, April 2, 1840.

2. The Massachusetts State Democratic Convention assembled in Boston on March 14, 1840, and recommended Martin Van Buren and Polk to head the national ticket. The convention also endorsed the call for holding a national convention in Baltimore.

3. Reference is to Boston's three leading Democratic newspapers: the *Boston Morning Post* (1831–1919?), the *Boston Statesman* (1827–81), and the *Bay State Democrat* (1838–44).

TO SAMUEL H. LAUGHLIN

My Dear Sir

Nashville April 2nd 1840

I wrote you a hasty letter last night. Today the Committee here had a meeting and appointed *Mr Speaker Thomas and yourself* Delegates to Baltimore, and I presume will apprise you officially of the fact forthwith. *Col. Keeble* of Murfreesborough will be appointed in place of *McGavock* who declines, & probably *Col. Guild* in place of *Tompkins* of Sumner[1] who declines, and it is believed both will go on. I hope My Dear Sir! you will not decline. Your presence I regard as very important. *Majr Donelson* told me on yesterday he would certainly go on. I think it doubtful whether *Gov. Carroll's* health will enable him to do so. It is suggested here that the Delegates from the Western District and Middle Tennessee, should leave here together between the 12th & 15th of this month. If you concur in this, write to such of them as you know to that effect. The movement of the Democratic portion of the Massachusetts Legislature,[2] which may be regarded as the movement of the Democratic party of all New England, is very important, in this: that it makes it certain that Col. J.[3] cannot get the nomination without the support of both New York and Ohio. From Mr. Hamer's letter to you, of which you speak in your letter to *Mr. Harris,* I do not think it likely that he can get *Ohio. Mr. Hamer* lives near the route as you would go on,[4] is himself a delegate to Baltimore and it might be well to call bye and take him on with you. If New York makes a mistep she may put to hazard the main election, whereas by a prudent but decided course taken *now,* she may put our success beyond all doubt. Our friends at Washington and elsewhere should be early and fully apprised of this. I saw the *Hon. Thomas P. Moore* of Harrodsburg Kentucky at Holly Springs Miss. where he was on business a few days ago; He is of your opinion upon the subject of the Vice Presidency; says Col J. will be an incubus upon the ticket, in *Ohio,* and run in Kentucky, where he represents him as not being the choice of the party. *Moore* is decidedly my friend, and is excited and warm on the subject, not so much for me individually, as for the success of the cause. He has an extensive acquaintance all over the Union, and especially in Ohio & other Western States, and you may write to him safely. Now that the contest is narrowed down between Johnson and myself, our friends *Phelan*[5] and others in Alabama could do much good by taking ground in their newspapers—before the Convention assembles, and this they might do with propriety, since their own citizen[6] is lost sight of in the canvass. Do you know *Col. Nathl. Terry* of Limestone County, *Hon. S. C. Posey* of Florence or *Mr. Woodson* of the Huntsville Democrat.[7] The two former I know to be my warm friends; and the latter I understand is so in his feelings and publications. *Burn this when you have read it.* I write more freely to you than I would to almost any one else, because I know I can do so safely.

James K. Polk

P.S. If Gen. Carroll shall not be able to go to Baltimore, and I think he will not be, our friends here wish to have our friend *Harris* of the Union appointed in his place. The appointment of Mr. H. would be a good one. J.K.P.

ALS. DLC–JKP. Addressed to McMinnville, marked "*Private & confidential.*" AE by Laughlin on the cover reads, "Ansd. Aprl. 5, & fixing 14th of March [April] as day of meeting at Nashville"; Laughlin's reply not found. Published in *ETHSP*, XVIII, pp. 155–56.

1. Joseph Richard A. Tompkins, a prosperous Gallatin merchant and Polk supporter, was postmaster at Gallatin from 1837 until 1841.

2. See Polk to Samuel H. Laughlin, April 1, 1840.

3. Richard M. Johnson.

4. Thomas Lyon Hamer resided in Georgetown, Brown County, Ohio.

5. A lawyer and early editor of the Huntsville *Democrat*, John D. Phelan won election to two terms in the Alabama House, 1834–36 and 1839–41; he presided as Speaker of that body during his latter term. Subsequently, he served as a circuit court judge and as a justice of the Alabama Supreme Court.

6. William R. King.

7. Nathaniel Terry, Sidney C. Posey, and Phillip Woodson. A Limestone County planter, Terry served in the Alabama Senate from 1836 through 1844; he was president of that body for four years. In 1845, he ran unsuccessfully as the Democratic candidate for governor against Joshua L. Martin, an Independent. A Lauderdale County lawyer, Posey sat both in the Alabama House, 1835–36 and 1861, and in the Senate, 1837 and 1844–45. During the interim of his Senate terms, he served as county judge and in 1847 won election as a circuit court judge. Phillip Woodson was the founder, editor, and proprietor of the Huntsville *Democrat*.

TO WILLIAM R. RUCKER

My Dear Sir Nashville April 4th 1840

Your letter of yesterday[1] came to hand today. I communicated to a member of the Committee the fact that Mr Leiper would serve, and herewith enclose to you his appointment.[2] In delivering it to him, as I have a very slight acquaintance with him, it will not be necessary for you to say to him, through what chainnel you received it, and would probably be best not to do so. I would like very much to see him as he goes on, and you may upon your own authority request him to see me when at Nashville. I was surprized to hear that the Col. felt indignant that the appointment was tendered to him. Certainly he must know that no personal disrespect toward himself, or disparagement of his character or standing, either was or could have been intended by the committee. It will not be possible for Gov. Carroll to be at Murfreesborough on Monday. His health was so bad that he could not attend the musters in this County on yesterday and today though *Jones*[3] the Whig elector was there. *Cheatham* went out today to meet *Jones*. Our friends here are excited and say the Governor must resign[4] and let Cheatham or Andrew Ewen[5] be appointed in his place, who are able and willing to go out and do battle in our cause. In haste.

James K. Polk

ALS. DLC–JKP. Addressed to Murfreesboro and marked "*Private.*"

1. Letter not found.

2. Enclosure not found. The appointment may have been that of a delegate to the Democratic National Convention at Baltimore and made contingent upon William Carroll's not attending. Carroll subsequently traveled to Baltimore and presided over the proceedings. Reference probably is to John Leiper, mayor of Murfreesboro, 1847–48.

3. A Whig and farmer from Wilson County, James Chamberlain Jones served in the Tennessee House, 1839–40, and as a Whig presidential elector in 1840. In 1841 and 1843 he defeated Polk in the Tennessee gubernatorial elections. In 1850 Jones moved to Shelby County and became president of the Memphis and Charleston Railroad. He served as a Whig in the U.S. Senate, 1851–57, but supported James Buchanan for president in 1856.

4. On April 17, 1840, Governor Carroll tendered his resignation as Democratic elector from the Seventh Congressional District. A Democratic convention held in that district, however, resolved on May 5 not to accept the resignation.

5. Probably a variant spelling of "Ewing."

TO DAVID HUBBARD

Nashville April 5th 1840

My Dear Sir

On my return home some days ago, after an absence of more than three weeks, I received your letter of the 23rd. Feby, as also letters upon the same subject from several other friends, some of which I have answered.[1] Until the stand taken by Virginia—I had taken it for granted that a *full convention*, from *all the States* would meet and nominate, and in that event I should have regarded the question as settled. The attitude assumed by Virginia, S. Carolina and probably other States, renders it however now certain that the convention will not be *full*, and no nomination could likely be made, that would be satisfactory without estimating the votes of the absent States, or in other words, requiring to make a nomination, a *full* majority, representing a majority of all the electoral votes of the Union. I am informed by my friends that this is not likely to happen and that the probabilities now are, that the convention will meet and disperse without making a nomination. In that event what course should I pursue. It has been my fixed purpose from the beginning as it still is, to act *with* and not *against*, the *majority*, of the political party, with whom I agree generally in political sentiment, and my present impression is that in the event no nomination should be made, I should wait a reasonable time to ascertain what the development of the public sentiment of the majority of the party, in the

Democratic States was, and be governed by it. If it was ascertained that a *clear majority* declared for me, and would run me as their candidate, that would be one thing, but if on the contrary it was clearly seen, that I was to be taken up and run as the *minority* candidate, by a minority of the party, against the declared preference of a *majority*, and that I was to be *used* in a *few States* only, merely for the purpose of strengthening the ticket in the Presidential election in those states, and with the certainty that I could not in any contingency be elected, that is a position which I could not voluntarily consent to occupy, and I think my friends ought not to require me to do so. That was the unenviable position occupied by *Judge White*, in the Presidential election of 1836—when he was *used* only in a *few States* merely to answer a *purpose*, and with the certainty that he could not be elected, even though he received all the votes, in all the States where he was run. His fate is now a matter of history. By permitting himself to be so *used* he was destroyed. I was among those who objected to his position at that time, and made it a chief ground of attack, that he was *used* by a *minority*, to answer a *purpose* merely, and without hope or prospect of his own election. I am aware of the dangers to which you allude, which threaten our principles, as well as the continued ascendancy of the party which holds them, and am ready and willing to do any and every thing to maintain and preserve them, but think my friends ou[gh]t not to require me to sacrifice myself. You express confidence, as do all my friends who have written to me, that a decided majority of the party—are favourable to me, & that in the event of no nomination, that a *clear* and *unquestionable* majority will take me up, as the candidate. Should that turn out to be so, it will remove the embarrassment which I shall otherwise feel. Since you wrote, the Democratic portion of the Massachusetts Legislature have made their nomination,[2] and I am advised that, the same sentiment prevails and that the same course will most likely be taken by the Democratic party in the other New England States. I learn too, that the course of *Ohio* is by no means settled; that her Delegates to Baltimore will not probably consider themselves *instructed* &c. Other Developments may be made before the 5th of May, which may yet possibly put in the power of our friends to settle the matter satisfactorily not only to the South but to the whole party in every part of the Union. My own opinion has been, and is, if an acceptable candidate can be agreed upon, that we will be stronger and fight a stronger battle, with a single candidate, than we can by runing sectional candidates, and the latter should in my judgment be avoided if possible. With these views hastily given I shall await further developments, and be governed accordingly, being now, as I have always been ready and willing to do battle, in our cause, either in the ranks, at the head of a division or any-where that I can be most useful, provided I am not required, to act a part which would sacrifice the little public character, which I have been labouring so many years to make for myself. Finding that I had more time than I expected I have written more fully, than I expected to do when I commenced. I have written you frankly, but *confidentially*, knowing that I could do so, safely with *you*. I shall be pleased to hear from you, again when your leizure will allow. Mrs. Polk joins me in desiring to be kindly presented to Mrs. Hubbard.

JAMES K. POLK

ALS. DLC–GWC. Addressed to Washington City and marked "*Private & confidential.*" Copy, written and signed in the hand of Sarah C. Polk, DLC–JKP.

1. After a copy of his letter had been taken, Polk canceled the following sentence: "I refer you to my answer to Cave Johnson, as containing more fully than I have now the opportunity to express, the impressions and views which I at present entertain." Compare Polk to Cave Johnson, March 30, 1840.
2. See Polk to Samuel H. Laughlin, April 1, 1840.

TO ARTHUR R. CROZIER

My Dear Sir Nashville April 6th 1840

I see the political campaign of the summer has opened in East Tennessee, and from all I learn you will fight the battle with proper spirit. I met Huntsman at Jackson a few days ago. He is more excited than I have ever seen him, and will do his duty. He says in his humourous way, that if brother Ephm.[1] crosses the Tennessee River, and attempts to "poach on his dominions," that he will collar him as he puts his feet on the Western bank, and gallant him through the District; he says he understands that brother Ephm. tells a story about a *Bull calf*, and that it is *funny &c.* Says he wants to hear it. From all I could learn I think we have a decided gain in that part of the State. In middle Tennessee but a few speeches have been made, and the battle is just begining to wax warm. We will do our duty, and our friends need have no fears, but that we will give a good account of ourselves in November. Gov. Carroll though still in feeble health has gone to day, to make a speech at Lebanon. Should Foster go to East Tennessee, Johnson must meet him at every point, and speak wherever he does. He is a feeble adversary, and is easily vanquished by any bold and vigorous competitor. Johnson is greatly his superior in debate. I hope our friends in the 4th District may select an efficient good debater in Rice's place. Our friends everywhere should be active at this moment, as now the impressions are to be made which will last through the canvass. All our candidates should take the field in their respective Districts. Let all do their duty and there is not the slightest danger, the noise and shoutings of the Federalists for Harrison, to the contrary not-withstanding. I have received several letters from my friends in different parts of the state, and was shewn one to day, from you to our friend *Cheatham;* and have only at present to say, that at a proper time I shall avoid neither responsibility or personal labour. Upon suitable occasions and when I can do so with propriety I will be found fighting with my friends to sustain our common principles. But we can confer hereafter upon this point. I take it for granted that you will go on to Baltimore, the committee as I learn having heard nothing to the contrary from you. It is deemed by all our friends here and at Washington to be *very important* that the State should be *fully represented,* in the convention. The recent determination of Virginia not to send Delegates, makes it the more important, that a *full delegation* from this state, should be in attendance. The reasons for this opinion, it is unnecessary I should assign, further than to say, that much as it regards, the result may depend, upon the interest which the state takes in the matter and the earnestness with which she presses her views. Genl. Anderson has doubtless informed you, of the present state of the public opinion there. I hope My Dear Sir! that yourself and your associates from East Tennessee will have it, in your power to go on. The Delegates from this part of the State, will I understand assemble here on the 15th and leave in time to be at Washington some days beforehand, so as to have an opportunity to consult with our friends there, learn their views, and communicate to them, the views of our friends here. I shall be pleased to hear from you when your leizure will allow. Make my respects to Dr. Ramsey.

James K. Polk

ALS. T–JKP. Addressed to Knoxville and marked "*Private.*"
1. Ephraim H. Foster.

FROM SAMUEL H. LAUGHLIN

McMinnville, Tennessee. April 8, 1840

Laughlin writes that he answered Polk's letter of the 4th instant[1] "last Monday."[2] Laughlin plans to arrive in Nashville on the 14th instant en route to Baltimore. He reports that he has "pressed" Terry[3] to write to him and Hubbard at Washington and has informed Hamer that he hopes to see him en route to the City.

ALS. DLC–JKP. Addressed to Nashville.

1. Letter not found.
2. Laughlin's letter to Polk of April 6, 1840, has not been found.
3. See Polk to Samuel H. Laughlin, April 2, 1840.

FROM DANIEL GRAHAM

Jackson, Tennessee. April 9, 1840

Graham writes that the "general opinion" in Jackson, where Graham is attending court, is that Joseph Talbot will be appointed to fill the vacancy.[1]

ALS. DLC–JKP. Addressed to Nashville.

1. Reference is to the attorney generalship of Tennessee's Tenth Judicial District. See Levin H. Coe to Polk, March 23, 1840, and Polk to Joseph H. Talbot, March 26, 1840.

FROM JOSEPHUS C. GUILD

Gallatin, Tennessee. April 9, 1840

In response to Polk's "favor of late date,"[1] Guild writes that Tompkins is arranging to go to Baltimore. Because of legal and personal business Guild will not be able to attend the convention as requested. He believes that Polk is popular and will be supported by Mississippi and Louisiana.

ALS. DLC–JKP. Addressed to Nashville.

1. Letter not found.

FROM WILLIAM H. POLK

Dear Brother, Shelbyville April 9th 1840

Before I left Columbia, I conversed with Mr. Kirk & Cahal[1] on the subject of the sale of your land.[2] They both manifested a disposition to purchase. Cahal was rather out of the notion of making any immediate purchase, as he had made a disposition of the Negroes, for the present year, that he desired to place on the land, if he could have made a purchase at the commencement of the year. I thought it best not to urge, or seem anxious to make a sale—though when I return home I can again broach the subject to him. Mr. Kirk seemed inclined and I thought somewhat anxious to buy the ten acres. I made a proposition to him, that he could have the land for $50 an acre in some shape that it could be made immediately available. He is to give me an answer when I return—when I will write you again.

The note which you let me have when in Nashville, I had discounted in the State Bank at Columbia. It is placed on discount footing and subject to *renewal,* by paying the usual call, when it falls due.

The democrats in this County[3]—as far as I can learn are in fine spirits—and I am informed that considerable dissatisfaction prevails in the Whig ranks, many being unwilling to support Genl. Harrison. I will leave for home in the morning. Write to me on the reception of this letter, relative to your business.

William H. Polk

ALS. DLC–JKP. Addressed to Nashville.

1. John Kirk and Terry H. Cahal. A Columbia merchant and former director of the Columbia Railroad Company, Kirk served as mayor of Columbia in 1837.

2. No sale of Polk's Maury County lands to John Kirk has been identified. However, see James Walker to Polk, May 11, 1840.

3. Bedford County.

FROM WILLIAM R. RUCKER

Murfreesboro, Tennessee. April 10, 1840

The collector of delinquent accounts[1] for the *Nashville Union* is hurting the Democratic cause through a lack of courtesy and proper regard for the feelings of the subscribers. Not a single speech has been made in Murfreesboro by the Democratic electoral candidates, although the Whigs have made many. Rucker fears the Democrats may lose the presidential election in Rutherford County by default. Two or three powerful Democratic debaters should be sent to Murfreesboro to set the Democratic campaign in motion.

ALS. DLC–JKP. Addressed to Nashville.

1. Not identified further.

FROM ALEXANDER O. ANDERSON

My Dear Sir Washington April 14th 1840

I recd. yesterday yours of the 2d Inst.[1] (12 days on its passage) and write immediately, in the hope that this will reach you in 8 days and an answer be returned to me by the 1st day of May.

I have left no effort unassayed, which my best skill and energies cou'd put forth, and I have further surveyed all the ground since receiving your last—and now state to you what I believe to be the true ground upon which the whole case rests. 1st There can be no question that you are the choice of a majority of the Democratic Party. Virginia has continued to persist in not meeting in Convention—South Carolina will not—and the information is *here to day* that Massachusettes will not.[2] These states are decidedly for you, and number 47 votes. I have turned the subject in every possible attitude, & made *every possible effort* to see whether with the loss of the aid of the two first we cou'd effect a nomination. Of this I was doubtful—with them we cou'd—but New York will not consent to be constrained. *This has been tried in all the modes it cou'd be done.* She says if she were to act it wou'd destroy Mr Van Buren, whose election there, and in Pennsylvania, Ohio, & Indiana, they insist is a matter of exciting Contest. Without her decided aid no nomination can be effected—& with the present expected absence of Massachusettes, this wou'd be certain. If the convention separate without a nomination, I have no doubt of what New York will do, relying upon *the faith of our friends,* of which I cannot doubt. Missouiri I think wou'd be for you. *Of this however, no indications show themselves conclusively here.* She has not interfered against you. Indiana, Ohio, Michigan, Arkansas, & Pennsylvania, and New Jersey, Illinois & Maryland are all counted decided for Col Johnson. Now under these circumstances I think it wou'd be exceedingly perilous to risk a nomination by the Convention. As to your being a mere sectional Candidate this cannot be, under any view. Georgia will go into the Convention for Forsyth and *at present she will, it is understood abide by him at all events.* Buchanan & King it is said have given in their a[d]hesion to Col J. Of the electoral votes I think you wou'd get New Hampshire, Maine, New York, Virginia, North Carolina, Soùth Carolina, Alabama, Tennessee & Missippi, & Louisiana—& probably Missouiri. This wou'd be about 140 votes. With the absence, however, of 47 votes—& the non liquet[3] of New York—for it is certain she will not[4] act only so as to *equi-poise* her vote in Convention, it wou'd be wholly impracticable to effect a nomination, to which if we consented it wou'd be equivalent to permitting a minority of the Convention to decide! This is the true view of things here, and I am satisfied you wou'd think so if you were present. The truth is 5 weeks ago, things here had a very unfavorable aspect to Tennessee. They are different now. They are favorable—but without the means of our effecting a nomination. As thus—first we wou'd have 47 friends, from South Carolina, Virginia and Massachusettes who wou'd not be there. New York will *balance* her vote in the Convention, if *compelled now to act.*

This wou'd be equivalent to the absence of 42 more upon which I shou'd count in the electoral college, making in all, as to effect, 89 votes untold—and all in the electoral college for Tennessee—if the faith of man can be trusted. We woud then stand in Convention as follows—

Tennessee	15	Maine	10
Alabama (I think)	6	Vermont	doubtful
Missippi	4	Delaware	"
New Hampshire (We think)	9	North Carolina	15
	34		25
			34
		Total about	59

This you will perceive wou'd hazard much—and I submit it to you whether we shou'd do it. My opinion is we ought not—and if ever I have felt deeply upon any subject, and labored with untiring zeal, & I think with some success, it has been in this. There is as I believe no possible danger of your being the mere Candidate of a few States. Do you not perceive that the very fact of Johnson not being nominated annihilates his prospects—particularly as Mr Van Buren wou'd be? But at all events under the fixed absence of so many of our friends it wou'd be putting at hazard, upon a single vote, the prospects of Tennessee, w[h]ile the hearts of her friends are with her. The votes for Johnson will be to a man in the Convention,

Vermont & Delaware doubtful	from Arkansa		3
Rhode Island—unknown	from Indiana		9
Connecticut is doubtful—but *claimed by Johnson's friends.*	from Ohio		19
	from Pennsylvania		30
	from Michigan		3
	New Jersey (it is said)		8
			72
These two states are claimed positively by J's friend[s].	Illinois	5	
	Maryland	10	15
			87

Here wou'd be a majority for him of the votes then, excepting New York which wou'd certainly take a neutral position. All the votes which Col Johnson can get in the electoral College, he can get in the

Convention—Whereas the very fact he can go no higher is proof that Tennessee cou'd suceed in the College. In the present state of *extreme sensitiveness which prevails here as to the Presidential election it is not practicable to breing the whole Democratic Party to bear.* Our friends look with an anxiety to it particularly as to New York, Ohio, & Indiana, which you can well understand, & which I need not detail. I am of the opinion that if the Convention disperse without a nomination Tennessee succeed—and we cou'd have obtained a nomination if Virginia & South Carolina had come. I think we cou'd have spared Massachusettes.

Judge Grundy entertains these opinions fully—and I have no question of his great solicitude for the choice of Tennessee, & that like myself he has done his best. I think if our friends, & particularly our most esteemed & venerable friends for their experience as to men (as well as age) in Tennessee, were here, they wou'd think as I do upon the subject, and as the rest of your friends think.

Our friend Cave Johnson is sick at Philadelphia. I shall write him tomorrow. He is of the purest & firmest steel—and he & I have specially conferred much, & these opinions were the convictions of his mind at an interview just preceding his departure.

I shall still, however, up to the time leave nothing undone which is proper. Whatever may transpire between this & the Convention I will advise you of, if of any importance.

Upon the receipt of this write me unreservedly. If you say we must risk the trial in the Convention, the best & the ablest shall be done—but it is not my judgement. I wish, however, your full views in answer to this letter—the moment you receive it. I am satisfied we can give Tennessee the Vice President in the electoral colleges, *if the faith of man is to be relied upon*—and I do rely upon it. It is important I get your letter by the 1st or 2d of May—and write decisively.

Present me with the kindest regards to your Lady.

A ANDERSON

P.S. It is now one O'Clock at night—having been out late in confidential conference upon the subject of the Vice Presidency. I have had various, full, and unreserved interviews with Mr Wright. Burn this letter when read.

ALS. DLC–JKP. Addressed to Nashville and marked "Private & Confidential." Enclosed under the same cover is a second letter of the same date from Anderson to Polk; it is essentially repetitious. ALS. DLC–JKP.

1. Letter not found.

2. See Polk to Samuel H. Laughlin, April 1, 1840. Shortly before the national convention met, Massachusetts Democrats attempted to send a delegation to vote against a nomination; only one delegate, Phenias Allen, attended the convention at Baltimore.

3. A legal term used to describe a difficult decision or "a doubtful case." The Latin phrase translates literally, "it is not clear."

4. Anderson wrote "not," but means "now."

FROM M. D. COOPER & CO.

Dear Sir

New Orleans Apl 14th 1840

We Send you by Steamer Red Rover[1] 2 Casks wine, and a letter to you and one to Judge Catron, Containing Invoices of Same, the Costs and Charges of the two Casks $268.24 which is charged to your account.

We received your letter 27th March[2] the day after we sold your Cotton; had we Known your wish previously we would have gratified it, altho contrary to our best judgement then and now. Your Cotton will average a fraction under 7 cents. So soon as we can make out a/c sales we will forward them.

Our Cotton market is active at a slight advance, on qualities from fair to fine, which are scarce and in demand, whilst middlings & inferiors go off heavily.

M. D. Cooper & Co.

LS. DLC–JKP. Addressed to Nashville.

1. A four-hundred-ton steamship built in 1839 expressly for the Nashville and New Orleans trade and owned by Kay, Thomas & Co., *Red Rover* arrived in Nashville on April 23, 1840, from New Orleans.

2. Letter not found.

FROM FELIX GRUNDY

Senate Chamber

Dear Sir,

[Washington City] April 15th 1840

It seems now settled, that Massachusetts will not send delegates to the Baltimore Convention. If a nomination should be made by that body—Colo Johnson will certainly be selected. I do not intend to participate in that result. My convictions ever since my return to this place, have been against that Convention, and I verily beleive there is not one friend of yours in Congress, who differs from me in opinion. Johnson, I think, some weekes ago, would have agreed to dispense with a nomination. In that case, your election would have been certain, unless we are doomed to a general overthrow. He now feels more confident and his views may be different. He is encouraged by a recent letter received by him from Albany which says that altho no nomination for the Vice presidency, was made by the late Democratic State Convention,[1] there was a majority of forty in favor of Johnson. This If true, as it probably is, would I suppose govern the delegates from that State in the Baltimore Convention. Still I have no Idea, that he would get the Electoral vote of that state, were no nomination made. You know, my Judgment has uniformly been against a nomination at Baltimore, and If the Ten. delegation had not been urged from home, to act against their own convictions, the Convention would not have met, or no nomination of Vice president would have been made, and you would have been Vice president, beyond all doubt. It is true, we have not acted against our Judgment, but we have not felt authorised to act, agreeably to it, with that energy with which we might have acted, as it was evident that every letter, newspaper paragraph, &c. from Ten. indicated a different course from the one, we deemed Judicious. Should there be no nomination at Baltimore, you will probably be elected. But the prospect is not as good as it would have been, If the proper steps had been taken, but which seemed to be interdicted by our Constituents. I have at no time in my life, seen my way so clear, as I have on this whole matter, and I have never been so thwarted & vexed by opinions of a contrary character from those who have not the means of Judging, correctly. I waited with great anxiety to hear from Majr Donelson after he got home, and from what he said, I expected to see something in the Union,[2] indicating, different views from those heretofore expressed in that paper—nothing of the kind, has been received. On the contrary, I have recvd a letter ably written, from Genrl. Jackson, urging the propriety of a nomination at Baltimore, and setting forth your claims with great force. To all I have heard upon the subject, I have one answer to make—you cannot be nominated, by that Convention. That I suppose is sufficient.

FELIX GRUNDY

ALS. DLC–JKP. Addressed to Nashville and marked "*private.*" AE on the cover states that this letter was answered on April 28, 1840.

1. The New York State Democratic Convention met in Albany on April 9, 1840, and chose delegates to the Baltimore convention.

2. *Nashville Union.*

FROM FELIX GRUNDY

Dear Sir, Washington April 23rd 1840

I have only time to say, that my present impression is, that no nomination of Vice president will be made at Baltimore. The Tennessee Land Bill has finally passed the Senate.[1] It is precisely a copy of the Bill of Last Session. I could have made out a much better one, and probably have passed it, but I was afraid of accidents. You say I must come home thro East Ten.[2] This I shall probably do. Laughlin & Thomas have not arrived.[3] I hope they will be shortly here.

FELIX GRUNDY

ALS. DLC–JKP. Addressed to Nashville.

1. The U.S. Senate approved the Tennessee land bill on April 23, 1840, and returned the bill to the House for concurrence. See Aaron V. Brown to Polk, March 15, 1839.

2. Polk's communication to Grundy has not been identified. See Polk to Cave Johnson, March 30, 1840.

3. Samuel H. Laughlin and Jonas E. Thomas planned to visit Washington City en route to the Baltimore convention.

FROM SAMUEL H. LAUGHLIN

My dear Sir, Washington City, Wednesday, Apl. 29, 1840

The great matter of our mission here is not yet finally settled. New York alone has the power of preventing the nomination of Johnson at Baltimore. Gov. Clay and Mr. Hubbard are delegates from Alabama, but if three or more others arrive (Bean,[1] a King and Johnson man is here) they will control the delegation, and carry it for a nomination, in which event Clay nor Hubbard will take seats. They are all instructed of course to vote for King in first instance, but he is out of the question himself, and goes in hotly for Johnson and a nomination. The Southern delegates of that state are connexions and immediate friends of King. No two men here take more decided ground than Clay and Hubbard for no nomination, and of course for you, than Clay and Hubbard, it being sure, perfectly so, that no nomination being made, your election is secured. Mr. Calhoun has in the most decided manner, exerted all his powers, and is now exerting them for you. Buchanan and King are at the head of the nomination movement—and carry with them Nicholas of Louisiana,[2] and Walker of Mississippi.

As far as arrangements are matured, Mr. Grundy and Mr. Wright go to Baltimore on Sunday, and meet Gen. Dix from New York,[3] the head of what has been called the Regency.[4] New York will, I am pretty sure defeat the nomination, and it is all she will do; but will, if the faith of politicians is of any value, vote for you in the fall, if the Administration carries the state. The Virginia Election[5] has alarmed the Administration people here, and given uneasiness to the heads of affairs, and operates in our favor in defeating Johnson's nomination. New York wishes to stand uncommitted, and to continue to hold the balance of power.

Our delegation in Congress have exerted themselves in every possible manner, and are doing so. Cave Johnson is sick and has been some weeks in Philadelphia.

From some matter of the Speakership, Frank Thomas is heartily with the Johnsonites; but he is seldom here, being President of a Canal Company,[6] at about $5000 pr. ann. and gives nearly all his time to it.

I have no doubt of the earnest zeal for you on the part of Wright, and this is a sure index to the real (though secret), feelings of the President. Amos[7] is not right, and is, from every indication, a Buchanan man, in counsel and feeling—and of course, wishes you kept back in your political career at present.

These are things I have gathered up here, as I understand matters. Hamer will not be at Baltimore, and is taking the stump at home on all occasions, no doubt laboring to earn an executive appointment—and is neither for you or Johnson, farther than may be for his own advantage. I have no reliance on Allen or Tappan, and Young and Robinson[8] are of the same stripe. Gen. Howard is an Indiana delegate, and of course instructed by his appointment; but Mr. Calhoun, and Gen. Anderson who board with him, have labored him hard. Frank Blair is against nomination honestly—Kendall for it. I will write you tomorrow.

S. H. Laughlin

P.S. Gov. Carroll has not arrived. I have recd yours of 17th with enclosure.[9]

ALS. DLC–JKP. Addressed to Nashville and marked "Private."

1. Jesse Beene, a native Tennessean, moved to Alabama in 1819. A lawyer, he became Dallas County judge in 1821; sat in the state House in 1833; and presided over the state Senate in 1837. Beene was president of the Alabama Democratic Convention in 1839 and was a delegate to the Baltimore convention in 1840.

2. Robert C. Nicholas, a Louisiana sugar planter, won election in 1836 as a Democrat to the U.S. Senate, where he served until 1841.

3. John A. Dix, a New York lawyer, served as adjutant general of the state, 1831–33, and as a member of the state House, 1842. He won election to the U.S. Senate seat vacated by Silas Wright in 1845 and served until 1849. In 1848 Dix ran an unsuccessful race for governor at the head of the Free Soil ticket.

4. The Albany Regency, a group of politicians who led the New York Democracy during Van Buren's extended absences in Washington, controlled party machinery from 1820 until 1854. Azariah C. Flagg and John A. Dix were among the more powerful members of the Regency.

5. The Virginia state elections, held on April 23, 1840, returned a Whig majority to the legislature.

6. Francis Thomas was president of the Chesapeake and Ohio Canal Company in 1839 and 1840.

7. Amos Kendall.

8. William Allen, Benjamin Tappan, Richard M. Young, and John M. Robinson. An Illinois lawyer, Young served in the state House, 1820–22; sat as judge of the Fifth Judicial Circuit, 1825–37; won election as a Democrat to the U.S. Senate in 1836; and went on the bench of the Illinois Supreme Court in 1843. Polk appointed him commissioner of the General Land Office in 1847. Robinson, an Illinois lawyer and general in the state militia, won election in 1830 as a Democrat to the U.S. Senate, where he served until 1841. He sat as a justice of the Illinois Supreme Court for two months prior to his death in 1843.

9. Letter not found.

FROM SAMUEL H. LAUGHLIN

My dear Sir, Washington City, April 29, 1840

Since I wrote you to-day, Gen. Carroll has arrived as I learn, though I have not seen him, his arrival being by the evening cars, and it now being 10 o'clock at night. The House is engaged, in all disorder and confusion, on the appropriation Bill, in Committee of the Whole.[1]

Since I wrote you, I have had a particular conversation with Mr. Jamison,[2] of Missouri, a worthy man, who particularly agrees that in his judgment, no nomination ought to be made—he is a delegate as well as member of Congress. Benton, who is dark, can assuredly secure the determination of Missouri against a nomination. Buchanan and King, however, backed by little Walker, and Nicholas, are the gentlemen who are urging the nomination—and old Dick[3] is stirring heaven and earth, although, to our friends, he has written and declared his acquiescence in the course we propose. He, and those whose hands he is in, however, discover too plainly, that if no nomination is made, he is to be beaten. The speaker (Hunter) is decidedly for you as I most certainly learn; but he is only a man of fine talents, but without any capacity for managing affairs.

Mr. Calhoun, with members of Congress on our side generally, is the most popular Senator from any state (but our own of course) and is clearly acting a more open manly part than any man who has ever heretofore, now, or prospectively aspired to the Presidency. He asks no favors, and acts openly, manly and fairly. The same is the course of Gov. Clay—but Buchanan and Benton, so far as I can perceive, are not acting out like men who have the great cause, more than self, truly at heart. Such creatures as Walker and Sevier, are only fit to do mischief, and Allen is a destructive r[a]dical who soars entirely above common sense. Old Dick keeps a splendid establishment, many members boarding at his House, where a fine set of servants wait, and among the rest, some bea[u]tiful copper colored Circasian chamber maids.[4] Viena, with all its tolerated licentiousness and debauchery, is not worse, in proportion to numbers of population, than this republican Sodom. The very suspicion of a liaison with an interesting woman in the virtuous days of Washington, nearly destroyed Alexander Hamilton;[5] but here, in sight of the capitol, a Vice President of the United States, daily presiding over a grave and sober national Senate, can nightly revel and riot upon the charms of bright eyed mulato. Such is the understanding here among all men who look at the state of public and private affairs below the surface. May God deliver us from the necessity of supporting such a man for office—who, whatever he may profess, and however great his past services, hold[s] no opinion or principle in common with those who are expected to engage in a death struggle for his promotion.

I will see Gov. Carroll in the morning, and write you again. Amos[6] being sick, have not seen him, but distinctly understand his position to be as I wrote to-day.

S. H. LAUGHLIN

ALS. DLC–JKP. Addressed to Nashville and marked "Private."

1. The House passed the general appropriation bill on May 2, 1840.

2. John Jameson, a lawyer, served in the Missouri House, 1830–36, before serving three nonconsecutive terms in the U.S. House as a Democrat: 1839–41, 1843–45, and 1847–49. He had served as Speaker of the Missouri House in 1834 and 1836.

3. Richard Mentor Johnson.

4. See J. G. M. Ramsey to Polk, August 20, 1839, and John Catron to Polk, November 5, 1839.

5. In 1797 allegations of corruption led Alexander Hamilton to confess publicly that in 1791 he had involved himself in an illicit affair with Maria Reynolds and that her husband, James Reynolds of New York, had used the indiscretion to extort money. Republican newspapermen of the period alleged that Hamilton had admitted falsely to the amorous adventure with Maria Reynolds in order to prevent investigation of his and James Reynolds' criminal frauds upon the government.

6. Amos Kendall.

FROM AARON V. BROWN

Dear Sir Washington May 2nd 1840

Up to the present moment no final *agreement* not to make a nomination of V. President has been made—hopes are entertained that it may be in the course of the day. I do not think a nomination can be *forced* by a majority of the delegates in attendance. Ohio will vote for Johnson[1] if one be made—but the Editor of the *Statesman*[2] & the members here, are not disposed to make one. It is understood here that *Duncan* goes for a nomination of J., all the other members from O. against it. N. Jersey (members of Cong.) are against it—& N. York. It is talked here that Buchannon[3] goes for J.s nomination, but I have no evidence of *overt acts. (Confidential)* Allen of Ohio prefers *you* to J. but the powers at home *silence* him here. Benton is very *lofty* on the point. I shall furnish you with all the ascertainable facts—after the Convention is over. Smith of Maine[4] says he likes you better than any other man in the World, but *talks* of the *necessity* of a nomination of somebody. Howard has been laboring amongst his friends "to forbear a nomination"—& he tell me with good success. So today I think no nomination will be made. Edwards of N.C.[5] is here but I have not heard his opinions. I have the promise of some valuable information on the *final resolve* of the Ohio delegation (here) in the morning—which I shall instantly give you. Govr. Shannon is *here in consultation* but won't be at Baltimore from prudential considerations. I give these morning *scraps*. Johnson[6] has returned from Philadelphia improved.

A V Brown

[P.S.] Tell Armstrong that I have paid his $50 order at the risk of not having money to come home upon—so not to *repeat* if he pleases. AVB

ALS. DLC–JKP. Addressed to Nashville.

1. Richard Mentor Johnson.

2. Samuel Medary of the Columbus *Ohio Statesman* was a major power in the Ohio Democracy.

3. James Buchanan.

4. Albert Smith, a lawyer, served as U.S. marshal for Maine, 1830–38, and won election to one term in the U.S. House in 1839.

5. A lawyer and a Democrat, Weldon Nathaniel Edwards served in the North Carolina House, 1814–15; in the U.S. House, 1816–27; and in the North Carolina Senate, 1833–44, and again in 1850 as its president. The Democratic National Convention of 1840 elected him vice-president of their proceedings.

6. Cave Johnson.

FROM SAMUEL H. LAUGHLIN

My dear Sir, Washington City, Saturday, May 2, 1840

Nothing is finally settled here yet. Our Tennessee friends had a meeting at Mr. Grundy's last night, and have agreed upon our course so far as we can see our way clear. W. N. Edwards is here from North Carolina, and takes sides with us, I believe, to defeat Johnsons nomination, by making none. Gov. Hill,[1] representing N. Hampshire, is doing the same. Gov. Shannon is here, and by arrangement he and Medary of the Ohio Statesman, would see the President last night. Grundy and Wright are managing for us—and laboring incessantly by all the appliances and means which you know can be put in operation here. The loss of Virginia in the state election has alarmed many of our friends, and has made the Whigs drunk. Grundy and myself, and most of our delegation go to Baltimore tomorrow. Mr. Wright will be in the neighborhood *incog*, and on tomorrow evening or next morning will meet Gen. Dix—when the final course will be settled. I know confidentially, that a stopper was put on Walker last night; and that this morning Thompson of Mississippi and Brown[2] of the same, are unequivocally against a nomination. Both Grundy and myself saw Bell in close confab with Sevier yesterday, but they cannot, I think, unite in interest—or in any scheme of mischief. I talked with Cuthbert[3] this morning. He thinks that Georgia will go for the administration any how, but that they cannot carry Johnson.

Some of us, if the worst comes to the worst, and they shall, with only the command of a minority of republican electoral votes, determine to force Johnson upon right or wrong, have been considering of the propriety, Alabama and other states joining us, not to go into the Convention and take our seats at all. This can only be settled after Wright, Dix and Grundy meet, and after Parmenter[4] returns from Boston to-day or tomorrow. To aid you, Massachusetts had determined that no Convention was best, or no Vice Presidential nomination at least, after it was determined that Virginia and South Carolina would not be represented. If necessary, he will come back prepared with Hallett[5] and others, to throw in the weight of old Bay State against a V. presidential nomination.

My present impression is, that no nomination will be made, your nomination seeming to be clearly impossible. The conflicts of interests, factions, politicians, and would be leaders, is enough to disgust any man—any rational man—with politics. The spirit of disorganization is abroad—and if a general breaking up can be effected, there are men here I fear, of our own party (not of Tennessee) who hope to build themselves up upon the ruins of the general wreck. I hope providence will prevent the general calamity.

I have seen no Tennessee papers since I left save the Union.[6] It is doing manful battle. Gen. Carroll's health is no better. Gen. Anderson and Mr. Grundy are clear, that in certain contingencies which may happen, we ought not to take our seats; but I do believe, that the prospect of *no nomination* is two to one the strongest. No man can say or ought to say here, but the *Dutch*[7] I doubt not, are for us in this, looking to no other index than Mr. Wrights course and position. Vanderpoel[8] professes to me the clearest opinions and convictions of the necessity of this course.

Our adversaries present the case thus: the convention is called to nominate a President and Vice President. The West (including South and Northwest) gives the nomination of President to the East and North. The East and North then gives to the West the Vice President, and say produce your man or men. We present several. Johnson having the strongest number of supporters *present on the ground*—not regarding the strength that is against him *not on the ground*—claims the right by usage of insisting on the East to give him the nomination, he having the *show* of Western strength. This is flimsy reasoning with those who know all the facts as we do; but it is urged here, and with effect. If everybody, everywhere, had adopted what I understood to be your impressions against any convention, last spring and summer, we would have been free of our present embarrassments, and your election would have been certain. But now, we must do the best we can with a bad business. Whatever may betide, I am, as ever . . . .

S. H. LAUGHLIN

ALS. DLC–JKP. Addressed to Nashville and marked "Private."

1. An ardent Democrat and longtime editor of the *New Hampshire Patriot*, Isaac Hill served as a member in both houses of the New Hampshire legislature; as second comptroller of the U.S. Treasury and member of Jackson's "Kitchen Cabinet," 1829–30; as U.S. Senator, 1831–36; as governor of New Hampshire, 1836–39; and as U.S. subtreasurer at Boston, 1840–41.

2. Jacob Thompson and Albert Gallatin Brown. Brown, a lawyer, served as a member of the Mississippi House, 1835–39; as a Democratic congressman from Mississippi, 1839–41 and 1847–53; as a circuit court judge, 1842–43; as governor of Mississippi, 1844–48; as U.S. Senator, 1854–61; and as CSA Senator, 1861. The reference to Robert J. Walker is not identified further.

3. Alfred Cuthbert served in the Georgia House, 1810–13; in the U.S. House, 1813–16 and 1821–27; in the Georgia Senate, 1817–19; and in the U.S. Senate, 1835–43.

4. William Parmenter, a pioneer in the glass industry and president of the Middlesex Bank, served as a member of the Massachusetts House in 1829 and the Massachusetts Senate in 1836; as a Democratic congressman, 1837–45; and as naval officer at the port of Boston, 1845–49.

5. Benjamin Franklin Hallett, lawyer, editor, and Democratic party manager, merged his *Boston Daily Advocate* with the *Boston Post* in 1838; during the Pierce administration, he served as district attorney of Boston.

6. The *Nashville Union.*

7. Reference is to Van Buren's Democratic organization in New York.

8. Aaron Vanderpoel, a lawyer, served in the New York Assembly, 1826–30; and in the U.S. Congress, 1833–37 and 1839–41; he sat as judge of the Superior Court in New York City from 1842 until 1850.

FROM AARON V. BROWN

Dear Sir Washington Sunday morning [May 3 1840][1]

Grundy left for *the relay* house this morning where he will be joined by other friends & *arrange* things finally.[2] The missing information[3] is that the Ohio delegation determined finally last night against a nomination & that all things have been arranged, if *no treachery* intervenes, which I do not suspect. Little Senator Walker cut some high swells, but Thompson & Brown stood firm & his froth is subsiding.[4] "Aunt Nancy" (K of Ala)[5] tried her best on N.C. but could not alienate her. Buchanan carries his head more *one sided* than usual. The Great *Humbugger, affects* great impartiality—but "all in my eye"[6] depend upon it. Mr. C. . . . . .[7] from the *time I wrote* you[8] has been manly & sincere in his course & won from your friends the kindest regards. Indiana does well—aye very well—she goes against a nomination. I promised myself & you the best *collection* of facts & anecdotes illustrative of the course of the postmaster Genl.[9] which I can collect. *Let the crisis pass* & I mean to comment on the conduct of some of our magnates, as I please—come what may.

A. V. Brown

ALS. DLC–JKP. Addressed to Nashville.

1. Brown dated this letter April 3; however, content analysis and Brown's letter to Polk of May 2, 1840, establish the correct date as May 3, 1840.

2. Felix Grundy was en route to the Democratic National Convention at Baltimore.

3. See Brown to Polk, May 2, 1840.

4. See Samuel H. Laughlin to Polk, May 2, 1840.

5. Reference is to William Rufus King, whose primness, meticulous dress, and formal manners earned him the appellation, "Aunt Nancy."

6. Quotation is from Oliver Goldsmith, *The Good-Natured Man,* act 2 (1768).

7. John C. Calhoun.

8. See Brown to Polk, February 4, 1840.

9. Reference is to Amos Kendall, who resigned as postmaster general effective May 25, 1840.

FROM JOHN J. GARNER

Dear Sir Yalobusha Miss May the 3. 1840

After my respects to you I will inform you that we are all wel with the exception of the girl Matilda.[1] She had a child some ten days agow and is grunting yet—nothing serious. Her child died after some ten or twelve hours, from what caus I dont know. She has not worked more than half her time since you was here. NB. We are getting along very wel with our crop taking the wether in to consideration. It has bin raining near half the time since you left but I am in hopes from the presant apearence we wil have some good wether. I believe I have as good a crop of cotton as I ever saw for the time of year. I wil git over hit with my hoes in a few days. My fored corn[2] is indifernt owing to the wrain, it being on wet low land. I had to plow when the mules wold mier to the nees in places and of corse it cant look wel.

JOHN J. GARNER

ALS. DLC–JKP. Addressed to Nashville. Published in Bassett, *Plantation Overseer*, 139.

1. Reference is to a slave on Polk's Mississippi plantation. Matilda's name appeared on an inventory of property left by Joel Childress in 1820. Polk probably acquired full ownership of her in 1828 from Sarah Polk's brother-in-law, William R. Rucker. See Rucker to Polk, August 26, 1828.
2. "Forward" or "early" planting of corn.

FROM SAMUEL H. LAUGHLIN

My dear Sir, Washington, Sunday, May 3, 1840

I shall go to Baltimore in tomorrow morning's Railway cars with Gen. Anderson. Mr. Grundy went this morning at six. The man who, if not behind the throne, is next to it, will be on the spot, or near hand incog.[1] Tomorrow in Baltimore will be a day of confusion and uproar. Mr. Grundy is to meet Dix to-day. Gov. Shannon has been here with the Ohio delegation, and goes home, not by Baltimore. From Medary, Medill, and Caufman of the Buckeyes,[2] I know all is favorable in that quarter. Allen expressed himself in a new tone yesterday. Our friends of the Senate met in caucus last night—everything now promises, no accident intervening, to result as we wish. Brown tells me he wrote you fully, in schreds and patches, as he could, of the state of matters yesterday.

Shannon, Medary, Edwards (of N.C.) &c. have been *through the White house,*[3] as well as at the Den of *Captain Slick.*[4] Walker and many others have undergone same process. Clay, Hubbard and the Alabama democrats and delegates met last night. I have not seen Clay or Hubbard since, but know, that if King gets them to consent to a nomination, especially of Johnson, he will have to do it over protestations of Clay, Hubbard, and I think, D. H. Lewis.

S. H. LAUGHLIN

ALS. DLC–JKP. Addressed to Nashville and marked "Private."

1. Reference is to Silas Wright. See Laughlin to Polk, May 2, 1840.

2. Samuel Medary, William Medill, and Peter Kaufmann. A native German who immigrated to Pennsylvania and later to Canton, Ohio, Kaufmann was a philosopher and writer whose major views were shaped by the German philosopher, Georg W. F. Hegel. Kaufmann espoused his ideas through *Der Vaterlandsfreund,* a Jacksonian newspaper that he edited and published in Canton for two decades after 1833. He also published numerous almanacs and booklets in German and English. Involved in politics, he became postmaster of Canton in 1837 and attended the Democratic National Conventions of 1836, 1840, and 1844.

3. See Laughlin to Polk, May 2, 1840.

4. Possibly a reference to the residence of Richard M. Johnson; see Laughlin to Polk, April 29, 1840.

FROM A. O. P. NICHOLSON

Columbia, Tennessee. May 3, 1840

Nicholson thinks he may be selected to replace Thomas as a Democratic elector. If so, Nicholson will accept the nomination, but will need documents in order to wage an efficient political war. In a postscript dated May 5, Nicholson adds that he has heard that day of his nomination at Lewisburg and will accept.[1]

The Whigs are attempting to create financial panic in Columbia for political effect. The Democrats must go back to first principles and refight the national bank issue. Democrats in Nashville ought to procure evidence about the operations of the Nashville branch of the Bank of the United States. Also Polk should send him information about price fluctuations from 1826 to 1833 in Nashville and about the exchange rate of the U.S. Bank on notes from Nashville to New Orleans.

Nicholson has seen that the Democrats are doing well in Bedford County and has heard that they are faring well in Giles. Cahal shows no disposition to campaign much for the Whigs in the Ninth Congressional District. Unless Watterson attacks Cahal, there will be little excitement locally.

ALS. DLC–JKP. Addressed to Nashville.

1. Jonas E. Thomas resigned as the Democratic candidate for elector in the Ninth Congressional District because he planned to attend the Democratic National Convention and would not be available to campaign for the ticket. Democrats met in convention at Lewisburg on May 4 and elected A. O. P. Nicholson as Thomas' replacement.

FROM PIERCE B. ANDERSON

Dear Sir Baltimore May 6th 1840

I received your letter[1] a day or two before I left Athens for this City. Coming by the southern Route I reached Washington on the 3rd and from there came on with several of the members of Congress to Baltimore. This evening the convention adjourned. Its proceedings were conducted with great harmony. Martin Vanburen was nominated for President—and a Resolution adopted declaratory of the opinion of the convention that it was most proper under the present circumstances not to nominate a candidate for Vice President. This was accomplished with great difficulty, and I believe that nothing could or would have prevented the nomination of a candidate—but the steady adherence to a course which was calculated to deter the friends of a nomination from urging and insisting on it. The consequences of making a nomination would have been immediate dissension and disunion—as some of the Delegates would not have submitted to the nomination of Col Johnson and would have withdrawn from the convention, when they saw that there was a determination to do so. But I question very much, though some think otherwise, whether there was a majority of states in convention for him. Indeed I am confident that there was not a majority of Delegates for him—for New Jersey and New York were divided, and the personal preferences of the Delegates from other states were divided—though they were instructed by their States to go for Col. Johnson. This was the case with Pa, Ohio and Indiana. The Tennessee Delegation have endeavored to combine firmness and prudence—and I have no doubt that their course has been such as to promote the ultimate triumph of our principles in November. Though our course has been through an ordeal of severe trial—and perhaps it would have been better that this convention had not been held. Yet I think, now that they have adjourned without nominating, the Address and Resolutions[2] & mutual exchange of opinion & feelings among the members will have a good effect—on our friends everywhere. I should have written you before this in reply—but have been travelling night & day to get here in time.

P. B. Anderson

ALS. DLC–JKP. Addressed to Nashville.

1. Letter not found.

2. The Address of the Democratic National Convention was read by Isaac Hill on May 6, 1840; and the text of the same was printed in the Washington *Globe* of May 14, 1840. Delegates also on May 6 adopted a set of nine resolutions setting forth their party's basic principles; and the texts of those resolutions, along with convention proceedings, appeared in the Washington *Globe* on the following evening.

FROM SAMUEL H. LAUGHLIN

3 ocl. P.M.
Baltimore, May 6, 1840

My dear Sir,

The main business of the Convention has just been passed by vote—the nomination of Mr. Van Buren, and a declaration, prudently framed, that it was inexpedient to nominate for Vice President—and complimenting all the persons nominated by States. The vote was 99 for nominating and 132 against nomination. This was the full vote in Committee—and their report was adopted in Convention nem. con. The Committee sat last night, consisting of one from each State, til 12 o'clock, talking the matter over, but did not report til 10 oclock today. Great difficulties had to be overcome. I was on Resolution Committee—of which Gillett was chairman. Our report was adopted nem. con. of resolutions declaring our principles. C. C. Clay was chairman of the great nominating Committee. Isaac Hill of the N.H. was chairman of Com of one from each State, which reported an admirable address to people of U.S.[1]

The men who controlled the matter at last (not mentioning those who are not to be mentioned) was Grundy, Clay, Wright, Dix, and every thing every man from Tennessee could do.

Some men are faithless—but I have no time to write, and will leave for home in morning, and as I pass Nashville will tell you all I know. Thomas says, as I am writing, you will please excuse him. 21 states were represented. Baltimore Republican[2] will contain proceedings at length.

S. H. LAUGHLIN

ALS. DLC–JKP. Addressed to Nashville and marked "Private."

1. See Pierce B. Anderson to Polk, May 6, 1840.

2. The *Baltimore Republican*, a Democratic newspaper, was first published in 1827 by E. W. Reinhart & Company. In 1837 Samuel Harker became proprietor and held an interest in the newspaper until September 1840.

TO M. D. COOPER[1]

Dear Sir Nashville May 7th 1840

I received this evening a letter from your House at New Orleans, giving an acct. sales of my cotton—being $3.128.16 nett.[2] Mr Frierson[3] does not state the precise balance which my crop has failed to meet, but says any arrangement I may make with you in regard to it will be satisfactory. I will be at Columbia, the latter part of next week, when I will arrange it with you, if you know the precise amt. which may be due.

JAMES K. POLK

ALS. T–Cooper Family Papers. Addressed to Columbia.

1. A wealthy Columbia merchant and Polk's political friend, Matthew D. Cooper owned M. D. Cooper & Co., a commission business in New Orleans.
2. Letter not found.
3. Probably Edmund Frierson, an agent for M. D. Cooper & Co.

FROM DAVID HUBBARD

Dear Sir Washington 7th May 1840

Yesterday the Baltimore convention met & nominated Mr Van Buren for President & made no nomination for Vice President. You I have no doubt will hear detailed accounts from your Tennessee friends. I only write to put you in mind of the fact that I advised this course months ago.[1] Had my advice been attended to we would have saved ourselves from any hard feelings among friends but as matters now stand Gov Clay & myself have exposed ourselves to the cencure of all of the disappointed parties who desired a nomination & looked to us as part of the cause of their disappointment. It will not produce any party dissentions, only a few persons will be vexed & this is better than to have to carry such a load as would have been laid upon us had we made the expected nomination from Kentucky.[2] Our party have almost been prostrated by unwise & rash councils, and it remains to be yet seen whether we are to sustain Poinsetts Militia Bill[3] or go down ourselves. I am against it.

DAVID HUBBARD

ALS. DLC–JKP. Addressed to Nashville.

1. See Hubbard to Polk, February 23, 1840.
2. Richard Mentor Johnson.
3. See Cave Johnson to Polk, January 1, 1840.

FROM HOPKINS L. TURNEY

My dear Sir Washington city May the 7th 1840

I presume from the great lenth of time since my last, that you have begun to conclude that I was no longer a correspondant of yours; however without appollogy for past negligence, I will give you a brief account of the convention at Baltimore, which adjourned last evening at 7 O clock. We had our troubles and diffaculties there, and but for the tremendus exertions, and great tack and management of your devoted friend, Mr. Grundy, we would have been defeated. It is due to truth to say that on that occasion, he surpassed himself, and we came off victorious. Johnsons friends so regards it. In fact, it is regarded as a rejection of Johnson. To day I wrode in a hack, to the race, with Genl. Rodgers,[1] a delegate from the Keystone State, & a Johnson man, and he told me, that of their 30 delegates, they were all for you but 4, and that that state was for you—That they voted for a nomination because they were instructed to do so, and that as their state nominee, had been rejected by the national convention, that he would be much weakened by it. I suggested the propriety of their either droping him entirely, or of runing an independant ticket with a pledge to vote for the democratick candidate receiveing the largest vote and thereby to make an election in the electorial collage. He seemed to fall in with the idea.

Johnsons friends are manifestly mortafied though they act prudently. They say that no nomination is tantamount to a rejection of him. Judgeing from all I hear and see, I entertain a strong hope that you will be the strongest democratick candidate. Buckhannon[2] did all in his power against you. Benton did not act as he should have done—he ought to have been with us, but he was coverd in his dignaty and did not speak, and his state, which I regard as the index of his hart, voted against us. J. C. Calhoun, threw off the mask, and took a brod, independant, and a bold, stand for you, for which I like him fifty pr. cent. better than I ever did—the truth is he is worthy of a place in the affections of all patr[i]ots.

You will see Col. Laughlin, on his way home and he will give you all the minusha,[3] in detail. I have writen this in great hast, and it is badly done. I hope you will be enabled, to comprehend me.

H. L. Turney

ALS. DLC–JKP. Addressed to Nashville.

1. William T. Rogers and H. Gold Rogers were delegates from Pennsylvania; reference to "General Rogers" is not further identified.

2. James Buchanan.

3. Misspelling of "minutia."

FROM AARON V. BROWN

Dear Sir Washington May 8th 1840

We are all at our posts. I staid at it all the time, as I believed every thing had been pretty much arranged here before our friends left.[1] Grundy says to me Write to him & say "I am so nearly broke down I cant write for a day or two." All our delegates (in & out of Congress) are very well pleased, under all the circumstances of the case. All persons concur in stating that Grundy did wonders & that Carroll also gave great satisfaction. Our friends here are in *renewed* spirits & beleve all will be well in November. N. Jersey will hold the first State convention I think on the 20th Inst. I shall do my best with her members with whom I am boarding & have some hopes of your nomination.

Van,[2] sends out for his friends to come & see him tomorrow night. Grundy says Keep your flag flying—& all will be well yet.

Hill (of N.H.) wrote the address & Wright of N.Y. is now revising it for greater safety. It [is] said to be a fine paper.[3]

Farewell. I think I shall never have a chance to write you another decent letter.

A. V. Brown

ALS. DLC–JKP. Addressed to Nashville.

1. Brown remained in Washington at his congressional post, while many of his political friends attended the Democratic National Convention at Baltimore.

2. Martin Van Buren.

3. See Pierce B. Anderson to Polk, May 6, 1840.

FROM THOMAS P. MOORE

My dear Sir Harrodsburg May 8th 1840

Your long & interesting confidential letter[1] was recd on my return from Miss—and its content attended to according to my best Judgment. My own opinion is that if a nomination be made you will receive it, but many of our judicious friends think that it is best to make no nomination. *If* their views should prevail, you *must* allow us to use your name. You would get all our N England, N York, Jersey, Md. & Southern vote & of course be so nearly elected by the people as to render your election by the Senate certain. Let me entreat you to be wise upon this subject. Col Johnson will leave us as soon as he is rejected. Mark it!

I perceive that Gustavus Henry[2] is cutting a figure in your State. Make the Union man[3] say that Mr. Henrys course is a very natural one. The Henrys of George Town Ky were all old Federalists & warmly espoused the cause of John Pope when he violated instructions in his vote in favor of rechartering the Bank of the US & *agst* the late War.[4] He removed to Hopkinsville Ky, married a rich & clever woman in Ten., & now seeks to Federalise the state. Regards to Madam P.

T. P. Moore

ALS. DLC–JKP. Addressed to Nashville.

1. Letter not found.

2. A Kentucky lawyer and businessman, Henry served in the Kentucky legislature, 1831–33, before moving to Clarksville, Tennessee. An active Whig, Henry campaigned for Harrison and Tyler in 1840 and won election as a Whig to the electoral college in 1840, 1844, and 1852. He lost bids for a seat in Congress in 1842 and for the governorship in 1853. In 1838 he married Marion McClure, daughter of Hugh McClure of Clarksville.

3. Jeremiah George Harris.

4. A lawyer, John Pope served several terms in the Kentucky House before winning election as a Democrat to one term in the U.S. Senate in 1807. He sat in the Kentucky Senate, 1825–29; went to Arkansas as territorial governor, 1829–35; and served three terms in the U.S. House, 1837–43. On February 20, 1811, Pope voted in the Senate with friends of Treasury Secretary Albert Gallatin, who favored rechartering the first Bank of the United States and avoiding involvement in the Napoleonic Wars.

FROM AARON V. BROWN

Dear Sir [Washington City] H. R. May 9th 1840

You will see in the globe of this morning Forsythe's letter[1]—in bad temper. Let none of our papers say *anything* about it—beyond its mere publication. *Make no great fuss* in Tennessee about the Baltimore proceedings *for a while*. Johnson is *suspected* of having written his letter[2] to the Convention, *in conf*[*id*]*ent* expectation of a nomination & to have intended [it] as a *mere salvo* to his disappointed competitors. I say *wait a little* for developments here but keep your flag *calmly* floating in the breeze. In the mean time look at your *superior chances* over Johnson in any event. Yours is a *certain* capital, his *a doubtful* one. Where ever Harrison *may* succeed it will diminish J's chances & *this run of things* may become so apparent *that the elect*[*i*]*ons* may settle the question, without sending it to the Senate.

A V Brown

ALS. DLC–JKP. Addressed to Nashville.

1. John Forsyth's letter appeared in the Washington *Globe* of May 8, 1840. In his letter the secretary of state withdrew as a vice-presidential candidate, contending that without a national nomination no Democrat could be elected by the electoral college.

2. On April 25, 1840, Richard Mentor Johnson wrote to Linn Boyd and William O. Butler, Kentucky congressmen and delegates to the Democratic National Convention, that a nomination must be made for reasons of party principle, not personal advancement. His letter was read to the convention on May 6, 1840.

FROM ANDREW JACKSON

My dear Sir, Hermitage May 9th 1840

Major A. J. Donelson passed by today to see his little daughter[1] at Wm Donelson['s] who was reported to be sick, & on his way to Nashville, if he could leave her. The Major informed me that Lasley Combs, the chikesaw embasador, was to make a speach in Nashville today.[2] That Mr. Ef. Forster[3] had his agents out all over the county yesterday to drum in hearers to day, I had just now from Mr. Allen who lives near Haysborough.[4]

Your note is recd.[5] I am quite unwell to day, unable to search for papers. I have made the attempt to look over Col Earles[6] file of papers, where I hope all relating to this matter will be found. Two of which I send you,[7] which will be a key to the Chekesaw embasadors visit to Nashville when he made The friendly visit to the Hermitage and Took dinner as a friend with me.[8] Please take care of & return the papers.

You will find from the papers I send you, that after the death of Gov Shelby, Clay &c. by the instrumentality of Thomas Shelby attempted to slander & injure me, on the score of Colbert['s] reserve made in the Chekesaw treaty.[9]

The object of this Chekesaw embassador Lessley Combs['s] visit to Nashville was to obtain evidence to show that I had obtained this reserve for my friends &c &c. This he expected to obtain from Doctor McNairy and thro the influence that Doctor McNairy had over James Jackson.[10] Under this mission he visited me as a friend, dined with me, was very social without every naming his base design—left me very friendly and the next news I had of this scamp, was his attempt to get James Jacksons affidavit—which when he had seen James Jackson in Nashville, & finding that it would not answer his base design, he soon left Nashville, & the first I heard of this scamp was his parthian arrow from the vile sheets of the Lexington press—detailing some base falshoods,[11] which if I could now be able to see this chikesaw embassador I would remind him of his former mission in such a manner that he never would again become the base slanderer of me, or caterer of slander for Thomas Shelby or Henry Clay. But both Shelby & Clay knew he was a fit subject for such employment. How base to approach my house pertake of my hospitality, with the dager of slander in his boosom & leave me without the least hint of his base intentions.

I must close. Search will be made for the papers that unfold this transaction, if got, will be sent you.[12] In haste & great pain with our kind gretings to yr[13]

AL. DLC–JKP. Addressed to Nashville.

1. Rachel Jackson Donelson, born in the White House in 1834, was the fourth child of Andrew Jackson Donelson and his wife, Emily Tennessee Donelson.

2. Leslie Combs, a Kentucky lawyer and soldier, served in the Kentucky volunteers during the War of 1812. Between 1827 and 1859, Combs served several interrupted terms in the Kentucky legislature; he presided over the Kentucky House in 1846. An ardent Whig and friend of Henry Clay, Combs canvassed many states for Harrison during the campaign of 1840. On May 9, 1840, Combs delivered an anti-Jackson speech that was well-received by the Nashville Whigs.

3. Ephraim H. Foster.

4. Allen is not identified.

5. Letter not found.

6. Ralph E. W. Earl, an artist, married Jane Caffery, a niece of Rachel Jackson; following the death of his wife, Earl became a member of the Jackson household. Prior to his own death in 1837, Earl painted several portraits of Jackson.

7. Enclosures not found.

8. Leslie Combs dined at the Hermitage with Jackson on October 11, 1828.

9. Isaac Shelby, Henry Clay, Thomas Shelby, and Levi Colbert. A surveyor, farmer, revolutionary soldier, and Virginia and North Carolina legislator, Isaac Shelby twice won election to the governorship of Kentucky. He gave up that office to lead Kentucky volunteers in support of William H. Harrison during the War of 1812. In 1816 Shelby retired to farming, but returned to public service two years later, when he was commissioned with Andrew Jackson to treat with the Chickasaw Indians. Shelby died on July 18, 1826. Thomas H. Shelby, third son of Isaac Shelby, served as his father's secretary during the Chickasaw negotiations of 1818. He later became a very affluent planter and resided near Lexington, Kentucky. Article 4 of a treaty signed with the Chickasaw Indians on October 19, 1818, reserved a four-mile-square tract, which included a salt lick on the Sandy River, to chieftains

Levi Colbert and James Brown for the use of the nation. The chieftains might in turn lease the reserve to a U.S. citizen in exchange for an annual provision of salt. The reservation went to William B. Lewis for 199 years in exchange for an agreement to pay the Indians 750 bushels of salt annually.

10. Boyd McNairy and James Jackson. Born in Nashville and educated at the University of Pennsylvania, McNairy practiced medicine in Nashville for over forty years after 1815. An early Nashville businessman and associate of Andrew Jackson, James Jackson moved to Florence, Alabama, in the early 1820's and served several terms in the Alabama legislature. After James Jackson and Andrew Jackson broke cordial relations with one another by late 1824, James Jackson became, with Boyd McNairy, an ardent political and personal opponent of Andrew Jackson.

11. In October 1828, the Lexington *Kentucky Reporter* printed an extra edition entitled *Chickasaw Treaty: An Attempt to Obtain the Testimony of James Jackson Esq. to Prove the Connexion of Gen. Andrew Jackson With a Company of Land Speculators, While Acting as United States' Commissioner; and to Sustain the Statement on that Subject, of the Late Governor Shelby.* In that broadside James Shelby attempted to disassociate his father's name from acts of corruption which had been charged against Andrew Jackson by Thomas Shelby in the spring of 1828. Believing that James Jackson, who had held an interest in Colbert's reserve, possessed information "of a private character" concerning Andrew Jackson's conduct in 1818, James Shelby called upon Andrew Jackson to "unseal the lips of James Jackson" on the negotiations. On October 29, 1828, Andrew Jackson wrote to John Coffee at Florence, Alabama, and asked him to "Make James [Jackson] speak on *this*," referring to Jackson's knowledge of the Chickasaw negotiations. Andrew Jackson also requested that Coffee send him a written statement that James Jackson "has never knew of me a dishonest or dishonorable act." See Bassett, ed., *Correspondence of Andrew Jackson,* III, pp. 440–42.

12. See Andrew Jackson to Polk, May 15, 1840.

13. Remainder of the page has been excised.

FROM JAMES WALKER

Dear Sir, Columbia May 11th 1840

Mr. Kirk has paid me $100—30 of which I have paid to Tranum, and send you $70 enclosed. He has not yet taken your note out of Bank, but says he will certainly do so in time or pay the money.[1] When he does I am to deliver him the deed.

Andrew Hays still lingers.[2] He has got up to my House, and if any thing is rather better. Perhaps he appears so, because he is more comfortable. He may die any hour, or the Doctors say he may live a month. I will send a messenger immediately to you should he die before Sam'l[3] returns.

The Senate Journals are going on very rapidly. I am Giffords agent,[4] and I tell Thompson that whenever he fails to have two forms a day, I will put additional hands into the office. I want clear of Thompson badly.[5] We will sell the office to Clayton & Andrew Kerr[6] (a fine boy that can be relied on) and ensure it to be under the editorial controul of Nicholson & myself. They can & will make money by printing it, as they are both, prudent & sensible and good workmen.

I am alarmed about the Presidential election. The result in Virginia looks squally.[7] The hard times and severe distress of the country may beat us. There is no telling what men will do in hopes of averting ruin. Every day convinces me that the destructurs in our last legislature of both parties—I am just sent for to see Andrew who thinks he is worse.

James Walker

ALS. DLC–JKP. Addressed to Nashville.

1. Reference probably is to Polk's note to William H. Polk, sold to the Bank of Tennessee's branch office at Columbia. See William H. Polk to Polk, April 9, 1840.

2. Andrew C. Hays, a first cousin of John B. Hays and James Walker, had been associated with Walker in publishing a Columbia newspaper sometime after 1819. Hays later wrote editorials for Walker's Columbia *Tennessee Democrat* and served as postmaster at Columbia from 1822 until his death on May 14, 1840.

3. Samuel P. Walker.

4. Lawson Gifford had been elected public printer by the Tennessee legislature on October 18, 1839.

5. By deed of trust dated May 23, 1840, Thompson conveyed ownership of the *Tennessee Democrat* to its lien holders, William H. Polk, Samuel P. Walker, and Thomas Madden. Madden's residual interest derived from subscription accounts payable during his previous ownership of the newspaper.

6. Probably David Clayton and Andrew M. Kerr, Jr. Clayton began publishing the *Southern Cultivator*, an agricultural newspaper, in Columbia in 1837. It was probably he whom Walker suggests as a partner for Andrew M. Kerr on the *Democrat*. Kerr was probably a son of Andrew M. Kerr, a Spring Hill wagon maker and farmer.

7. See Samuel H. Laughlin to Polk, April 29, and May 2, 1840.

FROM ERWIN J. FRIERSON

Dear Sir Shelbyville May the 12th 1840

Enclosed is Wisener's receipt for your newspaper subscription.[1] We have had as yet but little political excitement in this county. None of the

Whig orators have paid us a visit. The currency is the only question which is doing us any harm. Our candidates should direct much of their attention to this subject, and show to the people that the Banks are the true culprits. If it is possible to make the State Bank and its branches even partially resume specie payments it would be a great help. It is not the scarcity of money so much as its depreciated value which is injuring our cause. Specie is now selling with us for 10 per cent and a considerable disposition on the part of creditors to demand it, some no doubt for political effect, and a fellow who has sold his property for less than for some years back he has been accustomed to think it worth, to raise money to pay his debts and then has to submit to a further loss of 10 percent is in an excellent condition to be operated upon by a Whig Orator with his one-sided documents to prove that a United States Bank would make all things straight. I am glad to hear that you are ready to do battle whenever your friends may think your aid necessary. I think that Governor Carroll when he returns[2] if his health will permit, could do our cause great service by actively engaging in the canvass throughout middle Tennessee.

E. J. Frierson

ALS. DLC–JKP. Addressed to Nashville.

1. William H. Wisener, a Whig, edited and managed the Shelbyville *Peoples Advocate* which had been established by John H. Laird in 1837.

2. William Carroll had traveled to Baltimore and presided over the Democratic National Convention.

FROM HOPKINS L. TURNEY

Dear Sir, Washington City May the 14th 1840

Since my last[1] I have had a conversation, with both Blair & Rives[2] on the subject of the Vice Presidency, in which I told them, in every point of view prudence would require that they should take not part in the contest between our men both for the good of the cause, as well as for their individual safety—that their interference would drive from them either your or Johnsons friends. In this they bouth fully agreed with me, and solumly pledged themselves to say nothing for nor against either [of] you, but to go for the cause. I hope they will redeem this pledge. I have nothing more than you see in the papers . . . .

H. L. Turney

ALS. DLC–JKP. Addressed to Nashville.

1. See Turney to Polk, May 7, 1840.

2. Francis P. Blair and John Cook Rives edited the Washington *Globe*, 1833–45; Rives reported congressional debates in the *Congressional Globe*, 1833–64.

FROM ANDREW JACKSON

My dear Sir, Hermitage May 15th 1840

Your note of yesterday is this moment recd.[1] The contents duly noted. Your request with regard to the postmaster[2] you will find by the return of your boy duly attended to. My great misfortune is, that with all my care to preserve documents, my friends apply & get them into their possession & never return them. My friend Burton during the canvass for member of Congress got possession of one of my bound vollumes of public documents which he has not returned & Col. Cheatham two others, one of which must contain all about the Chikesaw embassadors[3] visit to Tennessee in 1828. I rode up to Mr. Burtons plantation[4] on wednesday last—met with him—interrogated him on the contents of the bound Book he has. He thought it contained the statement of the Chikesaw embassadors visit & promised to send it down by yesterdays mail—but it did not come. My friends borrow Books but never return them & with all the care I have taken to preserve the documents, *connected*, now when wanted for public good, they cannot be had. Mr. Burton is wrote to by Andrew[5] to send this Book down by tomorrows mail. *If it comes*, I will send it to you.

My ride to meet Burton at his farm on Wednesday last has prostrated me. I have slept but little since, and am much afflicted. With our kind salutations to you & yr lady I bid you adieu,

ANDREW JACKSON

ALS. DLC–JKP. Addressed to Nashville and delivered by return of Polk's slave. Published in Bassett, ed., *Jackson Correspondence*, VI, pp. 60–61.

1. Letter not found.
2. Polk's request is not identified.
3. Reference is to Leslie Combs. See Jackson to Polk, May 9, 1840.
4. Robert M. Burton lived in Lebanon, Tennessee.
5. Andrew Jackson, Jr.

FROM A. O. P. NICHOLSON

Dear Sir: Columbia May 15. 1840

I had the pleasure of receiving your favor[1] yesterday evening. I was unable to see Maj. Lewis[2] until this morning. He informs me that he is of opinion the papers[3] desired are at his house. He speaks with some confidence of being able to furnish them and promises to make the examination tonight. He lives in the country, you know, and will not therefore be able to give me an answer until tomorrow morning which will be too late for this Monday's Union.[4] In relation to visiting Murfreesboro I should cheerfully go at the time you suggest, but for my having to be at Savanah on the 4th Monday of this month. I shall make a speech there on that day and will get Jonas[5] to be at Lewisburg on that day. It will be all I can do to get back from Savanah and be at Shelbyville by the 1st Monday of June, which is the task I have laid out for myself. I am compelled to be at Savanah or I would cheerfully go to Murfreesboro. After my return from Savanah I shall have nothing to prevent me from making speeches at any *reachable* point. I am glad to see that our friends are beginning to call you out from Nashville. We have it [in] contemplation here to ask you to eat something with us shortly. You must not decline. I wish you would have some good documents sent to Francis L. Cooke and Thos. Cooke at Love's X roads[6]—they are said to have bolted and they are all that I hear specified. The standing army[7] ought to be often discussed in the Union. It is made the pretext by some to speak evily of the administration.

You have heard that A. C. Hays is dead—I fear we shall have some trouble in reference to his successor. Already some ill feeling is getting up. There are four applicants[8]—Saml. P. Walker, Jos. Herndon, Will V. Voorhies & E. R. Gunn, all good and true, but the ill feeling is likely to arise from Saml. Walker being an applicant. I have fears that we will be damaged to some extent by this feeling growing up. I hope however for the best. I take no part of course among them—so far from it, I have told them all that I could make no selections & was willing to say that they are all qualified. I agree with you that we can hold fast to the state by doing our duty, and I am also of opinion that any lagging or indifference may defeat us. As far as I can I will attend to the matter when I go.

I am anxious to get complete returns of Harrison's official accounts of the battle at Tippecanoe.[9] The accounts which I have are mere extracts. Can you send it to me immediately? I have all his other official returns in Niles' Register.[10] I am pleased to see the Union doing good service of late. Harris deserves well for his energy. We cannot say any thing for our paper[11] now. We hope to have it in good condition next week. I will write you from Savanah.

A. O. P. NICHOLSON

ALS. DLC–JKP. Addressed to Nashville.

1. Letter not found.

2. Micajah G. Lewis, a Columbia tavern keeper, was Felix K. Zollicoffer's partner in publishing the *Columbia Observer* from 1834 until 1835.

3. Polk wanted to see back issues of the Nashville *Republican Banner* in which Allen A. Hall had attacked Leslie Combs. See Andrew Jackson to Polk, May 9, 1840.

4. *Nashville Union.*

5. Jonas E. Thomas, previously a Democratic presidential elector for the Ninth Congressional District, was a logical choice for the assignment.

6. The 1840 federal census listed Francis L. Cook and Thomas Cooke as residents of Maury County; neither is identified further. Love's Cross Roads was a few miles northwest of Mount Pleasant, Maury County.

7. See Cave Johnson to Polk, January 1, 1840.

8. Joseph Herndon was a lawyer and merchant in Columbia. William V. Voorhies, Jr., a young attorney, formed a legal partnership with William H. Polk in 1844. The other applicant, E. R. Gunn, has not been identified. Samuel P. Walker received the postmaster's appointment at Columbia on May 29, 1840.

9. William Henry Harrison had reported to Secretary of War William Eustis in a letter dated November 18, 1811.

10. Hezekiah Niles, a Baltimore journalist, founded the *Nile's Weekly Register* in 1811 and conducted that newspaper until 1836; his son William Ogden Niles became editor and proprietor in 1838 and changed the masthead to that of *Nile's National Register.*

11. The Columbia *Tennessee Democrat.*

FROM WILLIAM WALLACE

Dear Sir Maryville May 15th 1840

I once took the liberty (although personally unacquainted) to Communicate to you by or through the medium of a letter the views I entertained with regard to the importance of getting up a democratic press at Knoxville,[1] and I have some reason to believe that this small circumstance contributed in some good degree, to bring about the desired object; the success of which has contributed no little to the aid of the democratic cause in E. Ten &c.

I again take the liberty to trouble you, with a few remarks and reflections of my mind with regard to the present contest for the Presidency.

Although I have been much engaged for some time in official business, yet I have been noticing the movements of our whig friends in E Ten and particularly in my own County, and I am clearly of opinion that the whigs are preparing, and are now at work and have been for some time past, to make the most desperate effort that has ever yet been made in our State to regain their lost ground and Carry the whig ticket in Novr. next. Mr. Williams our Member in Congress seems to be doing little else than flood[ing] his district with every doccument Calculated to disceive and mislead the people. He has filled every nook & Corner with the *life of Harrison* as well as many other whig doccuments; and now at this time our County (& I presume the same facts exist in other Counties) are being filled with Copies of the address of the late whig Convention held in Knoxville, a pamphlet containing some 40 odd pages.[2] And a greater number of falsehoods was never embodied in the same number of pages in my opinion. I am told that the whigs are determined that a copy will find its Way to every mans house before the election, about 1000 for our County &c and a like proportion for other Counties in E Ten.

Now Sir these movements are and will do mischief unless they are suitably met and their influence controlled and their deception and fraud exposed; the antidote should at least be continued with the poison or disease. I presume you have noticed that the democrats have it in contemplation to hold a Convention and celebration at Knoxville on the 3rd & 4th of July. I have reflected much as to the most efficient mode or plan for action at that time. I have no doubt but the meeting will be large and respectable but our meeting here will pass off without having any particular influence upon the main body of the people who will remain at home attending to their farms &c. unless we approach them at their own firesides &c. I have therefore thought and it is the opinion of all with whom I have exchanged ideas upon the subject, that it will be all important to send forth an address such as the facts and present position of political parties and men will authorize. I think the whig address should be reviewed and the prominent falsehoods set forth and exposed. The parties from the first formation of our Government down to the present time should be libarly[3] traced so that the plain honest man can see & know for himself that the present whig party is nothing more than the Old Federal party with an accession from the democratic ranks, caused in a great degree by the running of Judge White for President &c. The past and present position of Tennessee should be forceibly brought to bear &c &c. Now Sir I have no doubt that all will be satisfied that an address of some sort will be necessary. Very much will depend upon its fitness to the occasion, a failure in this point would be fatal. My thoughts and Judgment has turned toward yourself as every way the safest and most suitable person to perform this important part for us, at this very interesting and important period. I know it will through[4] upon you some labour, but it is a time when labour must be performed by some person and those important parts should be done by those best fitted for the occasion. You know that the whigs have the advantage of us with regard to men & money. The democratic strength consists of the farmers who are generally in modest Circumstances and are not able nor willing to make sacrifices as to money. The whig strength is with the Banks, merchants, lawyers, Doctors &c. &c. who have money & whose ambitious feelings will prompt them to use it. The City of Knoxville alone is able and willing to flood all E Ten with their doccuments of various kinds to deceive and mislead the people. I have had some confidential talk with some few friends with regard to the application I have here made to yourself and it seems to be considered as the most sure plan & yourself the most suitable person. Mr. Reynolds promised me that he would send to you a copy of the whig address and would also write to you with regard to our affairs &c. If you have as much time as will allow you to do so, I would be glad to hear from you on the subject. Should you find it convenient to prepare an address that fact of course will not and should not be made known. We must have one of the right sort and we look to you with more confidence than any other person &c.

WILL WALLACE

ALS. DLC–JKP. Addressed to Nashville. AE on the cover states that this letter was answered on May 24, 1840; Polk's reply has not been found.

1. Wallace wrote to Polk on October 29, 1838, about establishing a Democratic newspaper at Knoxville. ALS. DLC–JKP.

2. Reference is to a pamphlet entitled, *Address to the People of Tennessee by the Whig Convention* (1840); the Address was delivered at the Whig State Convention held in Knoxville on February 10, 1840. See Alexander O. Anderson to Polk, February 10, 1840.

3. Misspelling of "liberally."

4. Misspelling of "throw."

FROM ROBERT B. REYNOLDS

Dear Sir Knoxville. May 16th 1840

The cause that you and I are engaged in calls for renewed exertions on the part of those who would wish to see them prosper. In East Tennessee the Whigs seem to be driven to desperation and their exertions corespond with their feelings and their depravity. They resort to all kinds of artifices to deceive and mislead the public mind—sparing neither men nor money to regain their lost power.

We have sit quietly by long enough and if we intend to reconquer we must take the field in good earnest. The Democrats will meet in this place in Convention on the 3rd day of July next and put forth an address to spread before the people the principles which govern our party—the principles of the oppositionists and the twistings and turnings of the leaders of the Federal forces in Tennessee. It will require a *Master Workman* to prepare an address of the proper Character to Circulate all over the state, & we have not the man here that has the political experience to draft it. Yet it must be done. A failure now would ensure a defeat in November. Now, sir, I know of but one man in the state that can perform that task well. If it would suit your convenience to do that duty all will be well—otherwise we must have one of a much inferior order. We intend to have 15000 copies for East Tenn alone, to dissipate the errors of the Whig address from the Knoxville convention.[1]

The Whigs have lately announced to the public that they will meet here on the 4th of July & have a Barbacue—& have invited Foster—& will also invite Mr Bell & others—perhaps Clay. We will have a very large Collection of the Democracy here. I hope to see you here on that day & our other friends from the West. The people will rally to see and hear you—all that comes from a distance will attend the Democratic Barbacue to hear you speak. I verrily believe we shall beat the vain glorious boasters 1000 in E Tenn in the fall—but we must meet them & put them down. We must fire our mountains with the address of the 4th of July that will keep the spirit burning hereafter with but little fuel.

I would be glad to hear from you as early as possible upon the receipt of this letter, whether you can draft an address for us. This letter is written you at the request of Gen Wallace & Dr Ramsey. We all concur in the belief that their is no other man in the state capable of performing that duty but yourself.

I would be pleased to see Gen Jackson here also. Bring him if possible—it will augment our forces here largely. Foster & Johnson have met a few times but Foster consumes all the time he can, so as to prevent a reply.

R B REYNOLDS

ALS. DLC–JKP. Addressed to Nashville. AE on the cover states that this letter was answered on May 25, 1840.

1. See Alexander Anderson to Polk, February 10, 1840, and William Wallace to Polk, May 15, 1840.

FROM WEST H. HUMPHREYS

Sir Sommerville Sunday 17th May [1840][1]

I have rode quietly and slowly through the district and have instituted particular enquiries at every step of my progress with regard to the condition of the public mind in reference to the pending presidential election. I am well satisfied that this election will take place at a most unfavorable period for the course of Republican principles—to wit in the midst of a general scarcity of money, and a general fall of prices. This is now increasing the ardor and zeal of the Whigs and damping the energy of the democrats—men who know that the excessive issues of the Banks have brought this state of matters about and acknowledge that it is tracable to the overtrading of individuals say they want *a change.* They are in debt and must have a change right or wrong. They want help. There is a discontented feeling in the popular mind generally and the merchants, specul[at]ors and broken traders have succeeded in convincing many democrats that the distresses of the country are twice as great as they really are—and that some thing must be done.

I do not hear of many positive changes—but many of the Republicans are lukewarm and *ripe for change.*

Also the cry of "Standing army"[2] is having some weight in the counties of Carroll & Madison where the majorities are against us. I believe we have lost strength in those counties. Huntsman is doing nothing as I am informed. He has also let pass all the courts (supreme & Federal, circuit and county) in Madison without making a speech. One man told me that He thought Huntsman could not face up against a majority. Any body would have done better. Coe & Douglas[3] are in McNairy. Coe is acting with much zeal in the canvass—and I think he will probably increase the majority in this range of Border counties.[4] There is no change here against us but some of our friends are uneasy about the condition of things. The times, the times, is the universal cry.

I do not know to what extent this may overate if the delusive idea of a national Bank is brought to bear directly upon the Debtor classes. I fear it.

I write these matters to let you know my impressions about matters in candor as they exist. We must redouble our exertions. I intend to give my humble aid to the colums of the Union[5] upon my return to Nashville. I shall leave here as early as practicable.

There is not the slightest feeling of Respect felt by any portion of the Whigs for Harrison as I verily believe they dispise him and the miserable farce about log cabins, as much as they can do. Their almost entire strength rests upon the condition of the times.

Can not the state Bank[6] do something to relieve the people?

WEST H HUMPHREYS

ALS. DLC–JKP. Addressed to Nashville.

1. Year identified through content analysis.
2. See Cave Johnson to Polk, January 1, 1840.
3. Levin H. Coe and Burchett Douglass. Wilson County elected Douglass to four terms in the Tennessee House during the period from 1821 to 1833; after moving to Fayette County, he won two additional terms in the House, over which he presided when that body was controlled by Whigs, 1837–39 and 1841–42. Douglass also headed the Somerville branch of the Bank of Tennessee and served as a Whig presidential elector in 1840.
4. Shelby, Fayette, Hardeman, and McNairy counties, which comprised part of the Thirteenth Congressional District of Tennessee.
5. The *Nashville Union*.
6. The Bank of Tennessee.

FROM JAMES WALKER

Dr Sir.

Columbia May 18, 1840

In the Post-office case[1] a powerful effort is making by young Voorhies & his friends, aided in all possible ways by the Whigs. On Saturday at Cahal's suggestion an election was gotten up, aided and abetted by Curran Frierson.[2] The election was held by F K Zolicofer, J. B. Alderson & the celebrated Mr. Gillmore.[3] Samuel's[4] friends had nothing to do with it—alledging that it was easy for every person present to put their names to any recomendation they choose and that an election thus got up was one sided, and could not be regarded as a fair expression of public opinion or wishes. At the Court House Esq. Herndon made a furious attack on our family, charging us with grasping at every thing—that our influence was so powerful that nobody else had any chance &c. To this Wm & Knox[5] replied very mildly calling for an instance when any of our family had asked for any office, except yourself, and in that instance only from the people. I think nothing imprudent has been done. The result of the election was for Voorhies 127—for He[r]ndon 40—and 5 of Samls friends without understanding the matter voted for him. It was a thorough Whig affair. Voorhies's recommendations have been got up entirely by Whigs. Those who procured them were, young Akin, the Shaver Stiles & Gallaway[6] at the House of Porter & Partee.[7] The *old feeling* prevails very manifestly. Wm. Voorhies & He[r]ndon are using the Whigs & the Whigs are using them. Let who may be appointed P.M. You will see that Voorhies is a Whig, when he has the right to cast a vote. He is the law student of Wm P. Martin,[8] a very respectable, but decided Whig. Every thing which has been done for him to get the appointment of PM. has been by Whig *Strikers*. He has never yet that I have heard of, avowed any politics. How easy for him to take the other side or profess to be a democrat, and be an enemy in the camp, which would better promote Whig interest, and would be characteristic of his family. I was this morning, very modestly requested to withdraw Sam's pretensions. I asked upon what grounds. The reply was that the influence of his family was so powerful that no one else had a chance against him. To this I replied that if others could proscribe, my sons, it must be so, but that whenever I myself gave into or agreed to it, I would leave the country, and go where every man had an equal right to ask, and to receive office if the appointing power thought proper to bestow it. That this was the first time that me or mine had asked an office, that so far as I knew and believed a majority of our citizens interested had recommended him, that I believed the *weight* of his recommendations here would secure his appointment. The recommendation for Saml is signed by the most respectable portion of our population. I believe by a majority of the town that we know, and such men from the country, as John Miller, Mahan, Kilcrease, Allen &c.[9] It is probable Voorhies signatures are more numerous—but by names that we generally do not know. Knox saw Akins paper—the names were in pencil, and he knew scarcely any of the persons whose signature was there. Whigs do not scruple to manufacture names when it will answer their purposes. The Whig doctrine is, any body but a Walker.

James Walker

ALS. DLC–JKP. Probably addressed to Nashville.

1. See A. O. P. Nicholson to Polk, May 15, 1840.

2. Elias Currin Frierson, member of a large family connection in the Zion community of Maury County, served on the building committee which contracted for a new courthouse in 1845 and assisted in founding the Maury Central Turnpike Company in 1856.

3. Felix K. Zollicoffer, John B. Alderson, and Gillmore. Alderson and Gillmore are not identified.

4. Samuel P. Walker.

5. William H. Polk and J. Knox Walker.

6. Akin, Stiles, and Gallaway are not identified.

7. Elias H. Porter and William B. Partee conducted a successful mercantile business in Columbia between 1830 and 1840.

8. A prominent Columbia lawyer, William P. Martin became judge of the Eighth Judicial Circuit in 1851.

9. John Miller, Thomas J. Mahon, possibly William Kilcrease, and Allen. An early and long-time settler of Maury County, Miller was one of the first justices of the peace of the county. Also an early Maury County settler, Mahon was reputed to be a strong Polk supporter. Kilcrease and Allen are not further identified.

FROM ALEXANDER O. ANDERSON

Washington City. May 22, 1840

In response to Polk's letters of the 10th and 11th instant,[1] Anderson writes that he has been engaged in revising the address of the Baltimore convention.[2] As he had predicted, the convention made no vice-presidential nomination, and Anderson now advises Polk to maintain his position "unaltered in any way." Polk's prospects, Anderson believes, are "decided," and he will "leave nothing undone or *untried* to advance them." Anderson says that Churchwell's appointment[3] has inflicted "very wide and very deep mischief" upon the party; his earlier anti-Jackson speeches will be used against the Democrats in the coming canvass. Polk must avoid even the appearance of any involvement in Churchwell's appointment.

ALS. DLC–JKP. Addressed to Nashville and marked "Private & Confidential."

1. Letters not found.

2. See Pierce B. Anderson to Polk, May 5, 1840.

3. George W. Churchwell, a nullifier who later returned to the Democratic party, received appointment as U.S. attorney for East Tennessee on January 21, 1840.

FROM WEST H. HUMPHREYS

Sommerville, Tennessee. May 23, [1840][1]

Humphreys reports that Huntsman is angry with Polk because Huntsman's partner, T. Scurlock, was not appointed to a state office.[2] Huntsman has done nothing; there is talk he should resign.[3]

Glen and Coe are campaigning well.[4] Humphreys notes, however, that "pride of consistency is all that Holds up many of our friends in the faith under the pressure of the times." Wheatly[5] has suggested that the banks might relieve present financial pressures without retarding specie resumption if they were to issue bills of exchange upon the coming crop; Humphreys believes that the idea is worthy of consideration.

Harrison's committee injures the Whigs greatly.[6] The Whig charge that General Jackson also had a committee[7] avoids the key issue of the different objectives of the two committees. Harris should write an article clarifying this matter.

ALS. DLC–JKP. Addressed to Nashville.

1. Year identified through content analysis.

2. Timothy P. Scurlock wanted to be attorney general for the Tenth Judicial District of Tennessee. Although unsuccessful in 1840, he did fill that office, 1846–50.

3. Adam Huntsman was a Democratic electoral candidate for the state at large.

4. Philip B. Glenn was not an electoral candidate, but was an incumbent Democrat in the Tennessee House. Levin H. Coe was the Democratic electoral candidate for the Thirteenth Congressional District.

5. A lawyer in Shelby County, Seth Wheatley served as mayor of Memphis in 1831.

6. The Whig correspondence committee of Hamilton County, Ohio, answered questions directed to the Whig presidential candidate and managed details of his campaign. Democrats claimed that Harrison's words and actions were controlled by a secret committee; Whigs countered that Harrison simply needed assistance in answering his large volume of mail.

7. Democrats formed a central committee in Nashville in 1827 to defend Jackson against charges that his early relationship with Rachel was improper.

FROM CAVE JOHNSON

Washington City. May 24, 1840

Under separate cover Johnson sends a copy of the life of "Van Buren and Johnson," which is not yet in circulation and which does not identify either its author or publisher.[1] The appearance of the type suggests that the pamphlet may have been printed at the Globe office. Cave Johnson advises that he and others will not promote circulation of the *Extra Globe*,[2] which is expected to support Johnson[3] for vice-president.

Recent political developments are unfavorable to Polk's bid for the vice-presidency. Senator A[llen] of O[hio] has not approached Cave Johnson on that subject lately. New Hampshire voted against Polk's interests at the Baltimore convention. Maryland and New Jersey have nominated [Richard M.] Johnson.[4] State rights men control Georgia and may give her vote to Tyler, even if Van Buren wins the presidential vote.

Johnson notes that Brown and Watterson have made speeches against Bell's gag bill[5] and that Bell will lose ground in Tennessee because of his association with abolitionists.

ALS. DLC–JKP. Addressed to Nashville and marked "private."

1. Not identified further.

2. On May 11, 1840, Amos Kendall had resigned as postmaster general for reasons of health and had become editor of the *Extra Globe*, a national campaign paper which supported Van Buren. On June 9, 1840, Amos Kendall wrote to Cave Johnson, A. V. Brown, H. L. Turney, A. McClellan, and H. M. Watterson, in response to a letter from them, assuring them that none of the vice-presidential candidates stood higher in his estimation than Polk. Kendall's letter was forwarded to Polk; the cover forwarding that letter is in Cave Johnson's hand. ALS. DLC–JKP.

3. Richard M. Johnson.

4. Maryland's delegates met while attending the Democratic National Convention. The New Jersey convention assembled in Trenton on May 20, 1840.

5. Aaron V. Brown addressed the House on May 19 and 20, 1840; Harvey M. Watterson spoke on April 2, 1840. The House rejected John Bell's bill on May 20, 1840. See Cave Johnson to Polk, March 12, 1840.

FROM MINER K. KELLOGG[1]

My dear Friend Cincinnati May 24, 1840

I have delayed writing to you thus long thinking that every day would bring to hand documents you so much desire. Mr. Dawson and others are engaged in procuring them, and if they are to be had, you will receive them immediately. The Senate's Journals, of this State have become very scarce; the Indiana Journals are of more interest and importance in the coming campaign, and will be sent to you, if procured.

In looking over Dawsons late papers, you will, no doubt, be surprized at the mention therein, of Genl Harrison's street brawls![2] But you may rest assured every word is true, and so well known here, that none of the Whig presses have dared deny the Statements. The General is himself a very fair specimen of the Great Whig opposition, violent in language towards the Democracy, without argument and without principle.

Judge Burke[3] has returned from the Balt. Conv. and gives a sad account of the proceedings of the Great Baby Convention of the Federalists.[4] He says their conduct was ridiculous throughout, and disgusting to common sense. He describes one of the Banners, that was paraded through the streets of Baltimore. It represented Mr. Van Buren, prostrate, with the Bank Screws upon his neck, turned by one of the Tippicanoe party so tight, that the Blood is gushing from his eyes, nostrils, ears &c. On *such* representations I need make no comment to *you*, as they are of a piece with all their former conduct and feelings, that have been shewn to the world when they have a feint prospect of getting into power.

The portrait of our beloved General has been opened here for 3 days past, and hundreds have crowded to see it. It is as much admired here, as it was at Nashville. The Committee have granted me permission to take it to Washington before the adjournment of Congress. My object in so doing will be to obtain commissions for copies, which will enable me to make my trip to Europe, with much advantage. I shall go in 2 weeks, if my friends in Washington advise me to this course. You own Portrait will accompany the General's to Washington.[5]

A few days since I recd. by mail, a letter, containing a lock of the Old Hero's hair. My time has not yet permitted me to acknowledge its receipt. Please give my compliments to Mrs. Jackson[6] and thank her for her kindness, if you should see her soon. I shall write to the family ere long. To Genl. Armstrong, Mr Harris, Dr. Ridgely[7] and other friends you will be good enough to remember me.

If your duties will permit you answer this, it would give me exceeding pleasure, together with any advice on my present course that your judgment may deem necessary.

With sentiments of the highest esteem towards yourself and Mrs. Polk, I remain . . . .

MINER K. KELLOGG

ALS. DLC–JKP. Addressed to Nashville.

1. A nineteenth-century American author, traveler, and artist, Kellogg painted portraits of Andrew Jackson, Polk, and Martin Van Buren in 1840.

2. In early May of 1840 Thomas J. Buchanan, member from Clermont County and Speaker of the Ohio House, gave a campaign speech in Cincinnati and argued that the Whig party opposed the interests of the industrial class. Denouncing an 1807 law signed by William H. Harrison, then territorial governor of Indiana, Buchanan alleged that under that legislation poor whites might be whipped and sold into slavery. Harrison confronted both Buchanan and Charles Hale with profane swearing. Published in Moses Dawson's *Cincinnati Advertiser*, news of Harrison's "street brawls" spread throughout the country.

3. William Burke, a delegate to the Democratic National Convention at Baltimore, was postmaster at Cincinnati. He was first appointed to that office by Jackson in 1832.

4. The National Convention of Whig Young Men convened at Baltimore on May 4, 1840, one day before the meeting of the Democratic National Convention.

5. Kellogg's portrait of Andrew Jackson, painted at the Hermitage in the spring of 1840, was first viewed by Robert Armstrong, Andrew J. Donelson, and Polk. Kellogg displayed it in Nashville before showing it in Cincinnati and later Washington. It was during the Nashville showing of Jackson's portrait that Kellogg painted a likeness of Polk.

6. Reference is to Sarah York Jackson, wife of Andrew Jackson, Jr.

7. Robert Armstrong, J. George Harris, and probably James Ridley. Ridley, a Davidson County physician, was the father of Bromfield L. Ridley.

FROM ADAM HUNTSMAN

D Sir

Jackson 25th May 1840

Yours of the 13th Inst.[1] has this moment been recd. I have just closed a circuit of six weeks incessant labour in the Courts and I am now down with the Dysentary.

In relation to the rumor of my intended resignation, there is not the slightest foundation for it. All I have ever said or written was to yourself upon the subject. That was under the supposition (from the many letters I had received) that it was necessary for some one of our party to traverse the state more at large than I have it in my power to do. If my health is sufficiently restored, I shall address the people next Monday at Lauderdale, the following Monday in Haywood at their Court, and I contemplate scouring the counties of Henderson, Carroll & Gibson thoroughly in the months of June & July, also Madison before Eph[2] makes his appearance. Totten[3] & Coe is out actively. Coe & Douglass addresses the people today at Mifflin. They have been in McNairy and Perry. I heard them at Perryville. I intended to make a speech there but Douglass seemed to insist that, as it was a meeting appointed for him and Coe, that I ought not to interfere. Coe handled the subject well. The only fault is the want of a sufficient quantity of *life* and *enthusiasm.* Douglass however has less than Coe. I think we shall hold our own and gain in some places. The greatest difficulty is in Madison. This difficulty originates from the Merchants breaking & suing every body. The Bank[4] suing them and others, and the intense distress in the money market produced by the Bank being located here. Our d—n fool editors broke,[5] run away & Col Street who owns the press or the half of it & who has been on *all sides* has by and through his Brother in law Swan gone over to the Whigs and they are about to issue a Whig paper.[6] All this was done when I was absent on the circuit last week. Street has become so embarressed in his circumstances that he was perfectly in the market. Since I returned three days ago I have not been enabled to go to town to learn the particulars. I am glad to learn that S. D. Rowan[7] has taken ground. He read law in my office, and is a man of talents and can be serviceable. I have a great desire to take a trip to the mountains if possible. The late revulsions here has damaged my pecuniary matters to some extent and I do not yet Know whether I can leave here on that account. It is important that our democratic members of Congress should take ground as soon as they come home, particularly Johnson and Brown in order to keep things strait at home. It seems to be understood here that Eph strikes the District in September. I intend to write to him about the time he gets home (the 1st of July) and propose that we will make appointments through all the Counties and confine ourselves to a two or three hours Speech each. I never did or could make a longer one and talk sense, nor can he. If he chooses to take the whole day then I will make my own appointments and attend them.

I see the Baltimore Convention has made no nomination for the Vice Presidency. This can make no important difference in relation to your course. As this state and others have nominated you, It is not more improper for you to go about and address the [people] than it was for Clay, Webster, White and others to do it when candidates for the Presidency. As many public dinners can be got up as may be necessary but If in your place I should not hesitate one moment to do so even without that pretext. You are certainly right in your suggestions to my last,[8] that all this mighty Whig exirtion in this State is to break you down. You are in the way of Bell, Foster and others and one side must go down. They do not care if Harrison was in purgatory if they can advance them selves. We must all pull together on this rope strongly.

I have recd. an invitation to attend the Gallatin Dinner on the 30th.[9] That together with your letter reached me only today. I am desirous that the answer should reach them and I wish you to see that it is published, as it contradicts the rumour of my intending resignation and other things that the rascally Whigs have circulating as I hear from other quarters and it will offer me a good opportunity to give a flat contradiction thereto. But it will only reach Nashville the same time this reaches you and perhaps may not go on to Gallatin. However I will enclose it to Armstrong with a request to send it.

A Huntsman

ALS. DLC–JKP. Addressed to Nashville. Published in *THQ*, VI, pp. 346–47.

1. Letter not found.

2. Ephraim H. Foster.

3. A successful lawyer in West Tennessee, Archibald W. O. Totten served on the Tennessee Supreme Court, 1850–55.

4. The Union Bank of Tennessee.

5. Reference probably is to Leonard B. Mitchell, who became editor of the Jackson *District Telegraph* in 1839.

6. Henry Swan, a Whig, resided in Jackson. No new Whig press in Jackson has been identified.

7. Reference is to Stokely D. Rowan of Warren County. On May 12, 1840, Polk had received an invitation to a public dinner from Rowan and others. LS. DLC–JKP.

8. The previous extant letter from Huntsman to Polk was dated January 26, 1840.

9. Polk addressed a large gathering at Gallatin on Saturday, May 30, 1840.

TO ROBERT B. REYNOLDS

My Dear Sir Nashville May 25th 1840

I have received your letter of the 16th Instant. My engagements will be such that it will not be in my power to give my personal attention, to the subject mentioned in your letter. If however you will forward to me a copy, of the Address of the East Tennessee Whig Convention, a friend[1] here who is every way competent, will give his attention to it. Send the address without delay, and all shall be done here that can be. In the mean-time, it may not be entirely safe for you to rely, upon the friend to whom I allude here, for something may occur to prevent him, from giving as much time to it as necessary. Let our friends in East Tennessee have an address in a state of preparation, and when they receive what is done here, which will be some days beforehand, they can make out of the two a proper paper.

I have received the invitation to Knoxville for the 4th of July[2] and will answer it shortly. I will accept, and nothing but want of health will prevent me from being present on that occasion. The object of our opponents in having their celebration on the same day, is doubtless with a view, to overwhelm you by their superior numbers in Knox & Jefferson. I presume however that a goodly number of our friends in the adjoining Counties will attend.

The Democracy in this end of the State are firm and unmoved by the senseless noise about "log-cabin & hard cider," made by the Federalists. Our strength in November will be increased, instead of diminished. The State is safe—*absolutely* safe, if we are as vigilent and active as our opponents, *and we must be so.*

James K. Polk

ALS. NHi. Addressed to Knoxville and marked *"Private."*

1. Polk's friend probably was Jeremiah George Harris, who was the editor of the *Nashville Union* and the man most likely to prepare a Democratic address, as requested in Reynolds' letter of May 16. Twelve Democrats, including Harris, issued on July 4, 1840, an anti-Harrison *Address to the Republican People of Tennessee by the Central Corresponding Committee of the State.* For the *Address to the People of Tennessee by the Whig Convention,* see William Wallace to Polk, May 15, 1840.

2. J. G. M. Ramsey was the first of ten signers of the invitation, which was dated May 14, 1840. LS. DLC–JKP.

FROM JAMES WALKER

Dear Sir Columbia May 25. 1840

I have received yours of the 22d.[1] I fear you & Dr. Young will think this Thompson business, very troublesome.[2] It is however on my hands and I wish to get clear of it without any loss myself, and to do as much justice to others as I can. Before I close the business I must have the paper account fully settled. Therefore I will be very much obliged to Dr. Young if he will call upon McEwin & Whiteman (and take a printer with him) and if the paper returned is damaged, pay them the damages. Whatever damages the paper has sustained in coming & going ought to be paid.[3] However in this the paper makers ought not to be very particular, as they charged for what was used nearly or quite 50 pr. cent more than the customary price. It is material however for me to be free from all responsibility on the transaction that I may pay out what is in my hands, to the workmen who have done the work and to Thompson's creditors as agreed on. Dr. Young's receipt says the sum received was $1397. and $.55 This is $100 more than my paper[4] called for, and I supposed it was a mistake, but Thompson says it is so. It has been arranged here that of the sum in my hands, $200 is to be paid W. K. Hill out of a responsibility of $1000 [and] $150 to Frank Butler to pay an execution stayed by him for Thompson.[5] Butler is one of our soundest men, poor and incured this risque for the sake of the cause. Yesterday morning Thompson & myself agreed that $200 should be paid to William[6] & 150 to Butler. But before I had any opportunity to say anything to him on the subject—William went into the office and demanded of Thompson a transfer of his books and accounts to secure him in a responsibility of $510. This Thompson promised and Hill pressing on him he came to me and got my assumpsit, conditionally for that amount to him. Thompson has made a full assignment to Wm. H. Polk & Samuel P. Walker of all books & accounts. Whatever due the office, Judgments &c—to secure them in the sum of $1070. He says the amount due the office is about $3500. I suppose that at least $1000 can be made out of it. The job accounts are generally I suppose good. The amount secured to Sam, is on account of the Bynum debt and is for his benefit & Thos Madden's.[7] An execution that Hill is bound on for about $220 is levied on Thompson's household property and I suppose will be made, or at least good property to its value obtained. Hill will loose about $600—A C Hays estate about $100—of which I have secured a small sum in Type & office fixtures. Others must loose more or less. Thompson is really of no account. You will see that Thompson's estate was fully administered on yesterday, and with the exception of a note that Hill, Wmson Smith, J E. Thomas & Armstrong are bound for [the sum] of $695 pretty fairly divided. Hill done his best to get all he could, and did so. There is no use in trying to keep him up. I have seen that the work for the paper was going on and intend a paper shall be issued next Thursday, announcing the arrangement.[8] It will hereafter be printed by Andrew M Kerr a young man raised in the office of steady, *careful* habits and of good Democratic stock. He may take Clayton into Co-partnership with him. They go in to make living by their labor, which I am satisfied they can do—nothing but perfect worthlessness has heretofore prevented. Nicholson & myself will edit the paper & be responsible for it and put it vigorously into the fight.

James Walker

ALS. DLC–JKP. Addressed to Nashville.

1. Letter not found.

2. See James Walker to Polk, May 11, 1840.

3. On May 18, 1840, Walker had written Polk that 74 reams of paper, valued at $444, remained from the printing of the *Journal* of the Tennessee Senate. By agreement, the surplus stock was returnable to the vendors, McEwen Whiteman & Co. Walker sent the paper by wagon to John S. Young in Nashville. ALS. DLC–JKP.

4. An agreement for settling the expenses of the venture.

5. Possibly Francis Butler, a Columbia undertaker. Neither Butler nor the execution stayed by him for James H. Thompson is identified further.

6. William H. Polk.

7. Chesley P. Bynum and Thomas Madden were both former editors of the *Democrat*.

8. The May 28, 1840, edition of the *Democrat* has not been found.

FROM EZEKIEL P. MCNEAL

Bolivar, Tennessee. May 26, 1840

In response to Polk's letter of the 5th,[1] McNeal writes that he has contacted both General Jones and H. Polk[2] concerning the purchase of Polk's land on Pleasant Run. Jones was "wholly disinclined," and H. Polk will advise McNeal of his decision in a few days. However, McNeal doubts H. Polk's ability to pay. Further, McNeal states that he has failed to rent Polk's 100-acre farm located on the 311-acre tract six miles west of Bolivar. The best plan, McNeal declares, may be to rent the land for five-year terms.

ALS. DLC–JKP. Addressed to Nashville.

1. Letter not found.

2. Calvin Jones and possibly Horace M. Polk. A prominent North Carolina physician and legislator, Jones held several militia offices, including adjutant general, major general, and quartermaster general, before his resignation in 1814. In 1832, Jones retired from medical practice and moved to Bolivar, Tennessee, where he built "Pontine," a large plantation of about 30,000 acres. In 1843 Horace Moore Polk married Ophelia J. Bills, daughter of John H. Bills and niece of Ezekiel P. McNeal. Horace Moore Polk's genealogical line has not been identified.

FROM JAMES WALKER

Dear Sir, Columbia May 26, 1840

The suit commenced against the securiters of Dale for the Bank robbery, creates much sensation and feeling here.[1] The predominant feeling, is pity for the distress & ruin it brings on the securiters, even if no judgement is obtained. The effect is to destroy their credit, and will be to compel them to make an assignment to pay their own debts, and other responsibilities of higher moral obligation. The securiters are, Henry Turney, J B. Johnson, J R Plumner & L H. Duncan.[2] Dale is utterly ruined. His Bank endorsers will have to lose largely by him. The only effect the suit can have on him is to prevent him having the opportunity of making by hard labor, bread for his family. He had concluded in his necessitous condition to again take the cashier's place, if he could get it, and give the security. This is nearly his only chance for a bare support. Now I believe no one can give Security for the situation. Duncan is considered insolvent. Plumner cannot pay more than his own debts, and his indorsement liabilities, if he can do that. I doubt whether Johnson will be able to pay more, if he is pressed and this thing destroys his credit. This would throw it all on Turney and I have no idea that he will pay if he can help it. The impression is that no judgement can or ought to be obtained, but it is clear that the prosecution of the suit will compel the securiters to measures that will be fatal to their future prospets. I do not believe if Judgement is obtained that a cent of the money will ever be made. I understood when I was in Nashville that if the board would say that they did not think the Cashr. ought to be held accountable for the robbery, that would settle it. I think Mr. Nichol ought to come out, and if it is clear that the state cannot recover at law, it would be a pity not to dismiss the suit, and prevent the ruinous consequences on innocent men. It is a great pity of Jack Johnson to loose his all, and still greater upon Plumner, a man of delicate health and a large family to be entirely crushed in his declining years, without fault or imprudence on his own part. I wish you could be here, understand all the facts, and form an opinion what is the duty of the Executive officers to pursue.

JAMES WALKER

ALS. DLC–JKP. Addressed to Nashville.

1. On September 22, 1839, the Columbia Branch of the Bank of Tennessee was robbed of $27,834. The *Columbia Observer* of the following day noted that "many circumstances conspire to confirm the opinion that the miscreant had a familiar knowledge of the Bank, but suspicion we believe has not yet attached to no particular quarter." Edward W. Dale, cashier of the Bank, offered $5,000 reward—one half for the apprehension of the thief or thieves and the other half for the recovery of the money. The suit mentioned by Walker was *James K. Polk Govr. &c. to use of the Bank of Tennessee* v. *Dale, Plummer, Johnson, Duncan, and Turney*. It was heard at the August Term, Maury County Chancery Court on September 5, 1840, and was continued from term to term until March 9, 1843, when a decision was found in favor of the Bank. A $100,000 bond declaration was discharged, and damages were assessed against Turney, Johnson, and Duncan totaling $22,396. The state dropped its suit against Dale, who had committed suicide, and against James R. Plummer, whose plea of bankruptcy had been recognized by the court. See Sarah C. Polk to Polk, July 11, 1840; James Walker to Polk, July 23, 1840; and A. O. P. Nicholson to Polk, July 28, 1840.

2. Henry Turney, John B. Johnson, James R. Plummer, and Lemuel H. Duncan. An early Maury County settler and land owner, Turney was the father-in-law of Edward W. Dale. By 1841, Turney had sold his land and slaves to William Pillow and had moved with his family to Mississippi. Plummer was a Columbia merchant who served several terms as mayor of that town during the 1830's. Another Columbia businessman, Duncan engaged in a general merchandising business with Dale in the early 1830's.

TO FELIX GRUNDY

Dr. Sir Nashville May 27th 1840

The National Democratic Convention lately held at Baltimore, after nominating with perfect unanimity the present Chief Magistrate, for re-election to the station which he has filled with so much honour to himself and advantage to the country, having declined making a nomination for the Vice Presidency, it becomes proper in my judgment, that I should distinctly declare, the position which I occupy before the country, in reference to the use which has been made of my name in connection with that office.

Having been unexpectedly placed in nomination by a portion of my Republican Fellow citizens in some of the States, it was my unalterable determination, often expressed to my friends, from the day that my name first appeared in connection with the Vice Presidency, to be governed by the wishes of the majority of the political party, to which I have been ardently attached during my whole life, whenever the preference of that *majority*, should be ascertained in any satisfactory mode; and in no possible contingency to yield *my own consent*, to the use of my name as a candidate by a *minority* of my own political friends.

If, as was at one time anticipated, a *full convention* of the Democratic party, representing *all the states*, had assembled, and made a nomination, that would have been conclusive, and none would have been more cheerful to abide by the nomination thus made, or to give to the nominee (had the choice fallen upon another) a more cordial and hearty support than myself. It appears however that several of the States were unrepresented in the convention, and the selection of the Democratic candidate for the Vice Presidency, was left open, for the seperate action of the Republican party, of the several states.

I entirely concur with the convention, in the hope expressed by that body that "before the Election shall take place"—the "opinions," of the Republican party "shall become so concentrated as to secure the choice of a Vice President by the electoral colleges."[1]

In times like these when powerful combinations of various sectional interests are acting in extraordinary concert with our old opponents, the *Federalists*, and their allies the *abolitionists*, against the cherished principles of our Republican institutions, personal and sectional preferences between men, of the same political principles are of no importance. The ancient enemies of our long cherished principles with their new recruits and re-inforcements are to be met. The pillars upon which permanently rest our National Independence, and our beautiful fabric of seperate State sovreignties, are to be defended. And as these considerations, are in my judgment, infinitely more important to the country, than the elevation of any individual citizen to this or any other office, I trust I may be permitted to express my sincere desire, *should the further use of my name in connection with the Vice Presidency, be found to interpose the slightest obstacle to the entire and cordial union of the Democratic party, that it may be promptly withdrawn by my friends from before the public.* I can have no desire to be a party to a contest, in which I may be thrown into apparent collision with political friends whom I esteem, and with whom I have acted for a long series of years, and especially if such a position shall have a tendency to weaken the sympathies and energies of the whole Republican party, and hazard the safety and continued ascendancy of their cardinal principles.[2]

The present struggle is a fierce one, and it becomes the duty of every Republican to defend his post manfully. If in my public career I have heretofore evinced any becoming ardour and zeal, in the maintenance of our principles, that ardour is unabated, that zeal is undiminished, and though my position may be that of an individual citizen in the ranks of my party, I shall be found faithfully acting with my political friends and upon all suitable and proper occasions, resolutely exercising my rights as a free *man*, in maintaining the Republican principles of our fathers—and carrying them successfully through the "ordeal of the popular suffrage."[3]

James K. Polk

P.S. Desirous that my position before the people in reference to the Vice Presidency, should be known to my Republican Fellow-Citizens generally, be kind enough to request the Editor[4] of the Globe to publish this letter in his paper. J.K.P.[5]

ALS, draft. DLC–JKP. Addressed to Washington City and marked "Copy." Collation of the ALS, draft, with a copy printed in the Washington *Globe*, June 6, 1840, does not disclose any significant alterations in the text.

1. The quotation is from a resolution written by Clement Comer Clay and adopted by the Democratic National Convention at Baltimore on May 6, 1840.

2. At this point in the draft Polk wrote, and then deleted, the following paragraph: "I should not feel at liberty to deny to my Republican Citizens, the right to use my name, in any manner they may think proper, if it appeared by clear and unequivocal demonstrations of public sentiment that it was done, in accordance with the opinions and wishes of an *undoubted majority* of my Republican friends, but in the absence of such demonstrations, devotion to our common principles and an earnest desire for their preservation, would induce

me so far as my own wishes are respected to withhold my *assent* to the use of my name as a candidate, by a minority of my own party."

3. The source of this quotation has not been identified.
4. Francis P. Blair.
5. This postscript was not published in the Washington *Globe*.

FROM WILLIAM FITZGERALD[1]

Dr Sir Paris May 28 1840

Unparelled exertions are making by the Whig party in the W.D.[2] to carry their candidates for the Presidency. No imaginary means are left untried. The times are appealed to; the indebted people are told that the administration has caused Low prices and scarcity of mony. Every species of deception and imposition is resorted to.

During the Canvass last summer the Branch of the Bank of Tennessee at Trenton was in my opinion used & was a powerful auxiliary to the Whig party in this District. I could not perhaps prove this, but I believe it as firmly as I do my own existence and could adduce facts that would produce the same impression on the mind of any man. If the directin of this Branch is left in the hands of the Whig party we will feel its influence in the Presidential election and I fear we are already losing Ground. It is a matter to us of Great importance that the Directory for the County of Gibson should be of our party as they are the ones who do really all the business of the bank, the directors from the other counties rarely attending as the board is about to be formed at Nashville. I have taken the liberty to make this suggestion to you which is for your own eye.

Wm. Fitzgerald

ALS. DLC–JKP. Addressed to Nashville.

1. Fitzgerald, a lawyer and circuit court clerk of Stewart County, 1822–25, won one term in the Tennessee House, 1825–27; he served as attorney general of the Sixteenth Judicial Circuit before winning election in 1831 to a single term in the U.S. House. Fitzgerald moved to Henry County in the late 1830's and became judge of the Ninth Judicial Circuit in 1841.
2. Reference is to the Western District of Tennessee.

TO A. O. P. NICHOLSON

My Dear Sir Nashville May 28th 1840

The copy of the *Ohio Journal* containing Harrison's vote to sell white-men for fine and costs,[1] taken to you by Dr. Hays is much needed here for a short time. A copy of it was here, but was taken by Mr Gifford to East Tennessee. The Whigs you know deny every thing. The Union in defending *Coe,* published the part of the Journal alluded to, a few days ago, and challenged our opponents to call at the office and see it for themselves.[2] On yesterday one of the leading Whigs called to see it, and unfortunately Harris had permitted Gifford to take it to East Tennessee, he says by mistake, as he intended him to have the Journal of another year. So it was that the Journal was not produced, and we may look out for some notice of the call made for it, in the Banner. Yours is the only copy within reach and you must send it in, *without fail and without delay.* If you think it important for you to have it with you at Shelbyville on monday next *(as I think it will be)* you can send it from that place.

You will receive an invitation from the central Democratic committee here to accompany Mr Foster through middle Tennessee. It is the unanimous wish of your friends, and I hope you will do so. I saw a letter this evening from *Cleveland* in Bradley County giving an account of the meeting at that place between Foster and Johnson.[3] It was from a very intelligent man whom I know,[4] and he says the discussion resulted in a decided victory over Foster by Johnson, that the Democrats were highly delighted, and the Whigs compelled to admit that they had been disappointed in Foster's powers. His anecdotes have become stale—and the writer states were an injury to his cause. We have a decided gain in that part of the state.

I go to Gallatin on tomorrow & will return on sunday. I have accepted an invitation to Knoxville on the 4th of July.

James K. Polk

ALS. NHi–Misc. Mss.; James K. Polk. Addressed to Columbia and marked "*Private.*" Published in Joseph H. Parks, ed., "Letters from James K. Polk to Alfred O. P. Nicholson, 1835–49." *Tennessee Historical Quarterly,* III (March, 1944), 72–73.

1. In the 1820–21 session of the Ohio legislature, William H. Harrison voted for a section of a penal statute that provided for term indentureship of petty larcenists unable to pay the fine and costs of prosecution. See Ohio, *Senate Journal,* 1820–21, pp. 303–5.

2. While campaigning for presidential elector in the Western District, Levin H. Coe charged Harrison with "white slavery" and published his voting record in the Ohio legislature. In the *Nashville Union* of May 21, 1840, Jeremiah Harris defended Coe's charge against Harrison and invited those in doubt to review the Ohio *Senate Journal* deposited at the *Union* office.

3. Ephraim H. Foster and Andrew Johnson, both candidates for elector-at-large, met in Cleveland, Tennessee, on May 15, 1840. Jeremiah Harris published an account of their meeting in the *Nashville Union* of June 4, 1840.

4. Not identified.

FROM A. O. P. NICHOLSON

Columbia, Tennessee. May 29, 1840

In response to Polk's letter of the 28th instant, Nicholson replies that he has the Ohio *Journal* in his possession and will send it from Shelbyville. He will, if his family situation permits, accompany Foster through Middle Tennessee. Nicholson reports that although he had little chance to speak in Savannah, as Shields "eked out the evening & left me only one hour," he has heard good accounts from Coe in McNairy County. Nicholson believes that "with a long & a strong pull," the Democrats can carry the state. The party is suffering most from Poinsett's "infernally foolish" militia plan.[1] Cannot the "eternal cry of standing army" be silenced in Washington, and more Democratic documents be distributed among Tennessee's people?

ALS. DLC–JKP. Addressed to Nashville.

1. See Cave Johnson to Polk, January 1, 1840.

FROM LEVIN H. COE

Dear Sir Somerville May 30, 1840

On my return from a two weeks tour through Perry, Henderson & part of McNairy on yesterday I recd your favor of 19th Inst.[1] As also two copies of the Journals [of the] Ohio Senate.[2] Douglass & myself addressed the people in McNairy—two places in Perry & 4 in Henderson.

There is a decided impression in McNairy—and unless Poinsetts Molitia Bill[3] stops it we will beat them in the county. In Perry as yet little or no change any way. C. H. Williams has his forces as well drilled in Henderson as the Czar of Russia has his cossacks. I suceeded in making such an inroad in one civil District in the county as to break over all his guards. I feel confident we can hold the gain & the fire will continue to spread.

Glenn is here from Tipton. He reports a gain & all our friends firm. Hardeman, Fayette & Shelby are sound. I find my hand bill[4] has produced much excitement in these counteys & more in *North Missi.* It is doing good. The Whigs have very imprudently got mad about it. This enables me to press it the more strongly.

The Molitia Bill is doing much damage. The Whigs are aware of it and talk alone about it & the pressure in the upper counteys.[5] Some of our friends have bolted from us. Others are silent and almost all condemn it. We cant carry it. If Mr Van Buren is fastened down as endorsing the particular plan submitted in Mr Poinsets report 20th March I am thoroughly satisfied we cannot hold up to the vote of last summer. Even if it were sound policy to organise the Molitia, our people hate to muster and will oppose any thing of the kind.

Mr Van Buren is not the cool and cautious "Robin Pollard"[6] both friends & enemies have considered him to permit this new issue to be made at this stage. The m[a]ssive—fall of produce &c give us all we can carry. The sooner the Molitia Bill is buried the better.

I go to Shelby on Sunday next. Adam Huntsman promises shortly to take the field.

Will not the Whigs so manage the Bankrupt Bills[7] as to alarm the debtor part of the community?

Genl Gibbs made a night speech here a few days ago 5 hours long—friends mortified, Democrats amused. Glenn did himself immortal honor in a reply of one hour well suited to the hour & circumstances.

Please say to Dr. J. S. Young his favor is to hand and contents will be promptly attended to.

L. H. Coe

[P.S.] By the Laws of Ohio when Harrison gave his vote were "Misdemeaners" subject to imprisonment, such as fines by a court for contempt, Assault & Battery &c. I[t] would be well for Harriss[8] to publish some sections of the laws showing this.

ALS. DLC–JKP. Addressed to Nashville.

1. Letter not found.
2. See Polk to A. O. P. Nicholson, May 28, 1840.
3. See Cave Johnson to Polk, January 1, 1840.
4. See again, Polk to A. O. P. Nicholson, May 28, 1840.
5. The Thirteenth Congressional District included the upper counties of Tipton, Henderson, and Perry.
6. Not identified.
7. The U.S. Senate passed a bankruptcy bill on June 25, 1840, but the House tabled the bill on July 7. On August 19, 1841, Congress passed a federal bankruptcy act that provided almost every citizen the right to declare voluntary bankruptcy; creditors, of course, might take recovery action against bankrupt traders. Congress repealed the Whig measure in 1846.
8. J. George Harris.

FROM JOHN J. GARNER

Dear sir Yalobusha [County,] Miss June the 1 1840

After my respects to you we are awl wel except marier and Evy.[1] Marier complaning as usiel. She has spels onste a month very bad. Doct Towns is giving her medicin. I dont think her helth ever wil bee restord entierly. Evy has had the rheumatism so she was unable to gow a bout though mutch better at present. She is gowing a bout at this time and I think getting wel fast. NB. My crop on dry land is verry fine. On the lowest wet land it is very indifernt drounded from the unusial cuantaty of wrain we have had this spring. I have bin trying to make arangements with a workman to start the mill and repare the big whele of the gin for instance new cogs and a new band shaft. $100 is the lowest price I can get that work done for. I have bin talking to severl workmen. I got a ginwright to look at the gin stand to swe [see] the work hit needed and the price hit wold cost. Hit wants new saws, the ribs fasing, new wheels, and a new brush, which cost wil bee $125 and perhaps a little more. He says he can make hit as good if not better than when new.

I wish you to write mee whether to employ the work done or what to dwo as the prices apere hye. I wish to [k]now amediately, sow that I can make engagements of that cind in time to bwe sertain of the work. I havent received a letter from your hand sense you left here. They mey bee one there or in the office, I havent bin to town in some time. I have bin cept very bisey, to ceep the gras down in my farm as hit has bin sow constantly wraining. Gras wold not die when cut up.

JOHN. J. GARNER

ALS. DLC–JKP. Addressd to Nashville. Published in Bassett, *Plantation Overseer*, 139–40.

1. "Marier" and "Evy" are variant spellings for the names of Maria and Eve, slaves on Polk's Mississippi plantation.

FROM FELIX GRUNDY

Dear Sir, Washington City, June 1st 1840

Last evening I received yours[1] requesting my opinion on the subject of the Vicepresidency &c. I had delayed writing until I could get some satisfactory information to communicate. These are my impressions and they are pretty strong. If there had been no national Convention, your election would have been certain. At the close of the Convention, between you and Col. Johnson, the chances were rather in your favor, [though] not much. Since that time the developements in favor of Col. Johnson are consideably Stronger, I might say they are almost decisive—not altogether so. The call in the late number of the Union,[2] upon the different States to come out and designate their choice for the Vicepresidency, is operating very prejudicially and will probably produce a premature decision against you. Even, in the City of Newyork, there are several thousands, who prefer Johnson to Vanburen, and the friends of the latter dare not reject the former without the certain loss of the State—so it is in some other States.

What course you shall pursue, is for your own decision. My opinion is, that If you decline, the step would be disastrous—and the best way in doubtful cases, is to stand still. At present there is total silence on the subject of the Vicepresidency, among the member of Congress.

FELIX GRUNDY

ALS. DLC–JKP. Addressed to Nashville and marked *"private."*

1. Polk's letter not found. See Polk to Grundy, May 27, 1840.
2. Reference is to the *Nashville Union* of May 18, 1840.

FROM LEVIN H. COE

Raleigh, Tennessee. June 3, 1840

The Democrats have been too quiet in the campaign, while the Whigs have made every effort. The Whigs have over worked the issue of Harrison's vote, which Coe published; their excesses will damage them.[1] Coe hopes to do well before a large crowd at LaGrange on Saturday; General Polk may bolt and not meet the challenge.[2] Coe hopes C. H. Williams will deny Coe's charge that Williams had announced in his last canvass that he would support Van Buren if the Whigs nominated Harrison.

Coe wants E. M. Ford's name struck from the list of candidates for the directorate of the bank and names his twelve preferences, plus two alternates.[3] Coe advises Polk that a compromising course in appointing the board will damage rather than benefit the Democrats.

ALS. DLC–JKP. Addressed to Nashville. AE on the cover states, "Directors of the Bank at Sommerville."

1. See Polk to A. O. P. Nicholson, May 28, 1840, and Coe to Polk, May 30, 1840.
2. Thomas Gilchrist Polk had challenged Democrats to meet him in debate at LaGrange on Saturday, June 6, 1840. A son of William Polk of Raleigh, North Carolina, Thomas Gilchrist Polk, a lawyer, moved from North Carolina to a plantation near LaGrange in 1838. Formerly a member of the North Carolina House and Senate and a brigadier general in that state's militia, he supported William Henry Harrison in 1840 and Henry Clay in 1844.
3. Coe's list of candidates for the directorate of the Somerville branch of the Bank of Tennessee included John H. Bills, D. Haywood, George H. Taylor, R. B. Daniel, W. A. Jones, William Ruffin, E. Booker, A. H. Browne, James A. Heaslett, Joseph Lenow, John H. Ball, and Thomas Winston; his two alternate choices were Levi Ketchum and John C. Humphreys.

FROM WILLIAM R. HARRIS[1]

Paris, Tennessee. June 3, 1840

Harris writes that he wishes to see the management of the Trenton branch of the state bank placed in the hands of "our political friends." Attributing to the bank the source of considerable Whig strength in his district[2] in the late August election, Harris recommends several Democrats for appointment as bank directors.[3]

ALS. DLC–JKP. Addressed to Nashville.

1. A lawyer from Henry County and an older brother of Isham G. Harris, William R. Harris was judge of the Ninth Judicial Circuit from 1836 until 1845. Six years later, Harris removed to Memphis.

2. Henry County was in the Twelfth Congressional District.

3. Harris proposes the appointment of M. C. Bowles of Henry County, William W. Gleeson of Weakley County, Benjamin Totten of Obion County, Shadrick Flewallen of Carroll County, and Nelson J. Hess, Thomas B. Claiborne, Joseph B. Dibrell, Richard Harvey, James M. Moore, and Lewis Levy of Gibson County. He urges the continuance of Joseph H. Talbot of Madison County.

FROM A. O. P. NICHOLSON

Dear Sir: Columbia June 3 [1840][1]

At Shelbyville I could find no convyance for the Ohio Journal[2] & after bringing it back I am compelled to send it by mail. I must have it back by Monday next, for on Wednesday & Thursday next I have two appointments in Old Bedford when I must have the Journal. I used it with effect at Shelbyville on Monday. Indeed I had a glorious day. It was a Whig appointment but none appeared to speak & I had the field to myself. The crowd was immense & altho I say it myself the fact is I gave Whiggery a raking down which was severly felt. I spoke four hours with a crowd frozen all the time & after all was over there was a great glorious revival among the democrats whilst the Whigs frankly admitted that they were badly whipped. Barri[n]ger was there but he did not venture an answer. I commence on the 22nd in Bedford & spend the week. There is one matter there which is doing us a temporary damage. Th[e]y say the census law requiring the value of all property to be taken down to poultry is designed to ascertain the property so that a tax may [be] laid to support the standing army. If you have a Congress Journal, look & see who made the proposition & if a Whig, send it to me by the first stage & any speech which was made on the measure.[3] As small a matter as it is it must be blowed up & upon its explosion we can make a reaction. You have never sent me a full report of the Tippecanoe battle.

I think we may be satisfied with things in Maury, Marshall & Bedford. If we strike boldly & energetically now we can sweep the State. I have written to Dr. Robertson. See my letter[4] & have such steps taken in making my cause public as you think prudent. I have made one speech in Maury—at Mt. Pleasant, to a large crowd & I think our cause was decidedly benefitted. Coleman[5] answered me, but he admits that he made a failure.

Cahal's health is bad & I doubt whether he can do much for the Whigs. I speak at Charlotte on the 3rd Monday it being Circuit court day. You see, Sir, that I am in the fight & if we fail it shall not be my fault.

A. O. P. NICHOLSON

ALS. DLC–JKP. Addressed to Nashville.

1. Year of the letter is determined through content analysis.
2. See Polk to Nicholson, May 28, 1840, and Nicholson to Polk, May 29, 1840.
3. The Census acts of March 3, 1839, and February 26, 1840, which provided for taking the Sixth Federal Census, contained no property schedule.
4. Enclosure not found.
5. Reference probably is to William White Coleman, deputy sheriff of Maury County in the 1830's and member of the Tennessee House from Shelby County, 1865–67 and 1877–79.

FROM ROBERT B. REYNOLDS

Knoxville, Tennessee. June 3, 1840

In response to Polk's recent request,[1] Reynolds writes that he will help author a Democratic pamphlet to rebut the Address of the Whig Convention being distributed in East Tennessee.[2] Knowing his own "inability to perform the task," Reynolds states that he will "confidently rely" upon Polk's suggestions and the aid of the friend to whom Polk alluded in his letter.[3]

ALS. DLC–JKP. Addressed to Nashville.

1. See Polk to Reynolds, May 25, 1840.
2. See William Wallace to Polk, May 15, 1840.
3. Probably Jeremiah George Harris.

FROM ALEXANDER O. ANDERSON

My Dear Sir

Washington City June 6th 1840

Yours of the 24th Inst[1] I recd three days since & have postponed answering it until to day with a view to be able to communicate to you more satisfactorily than I cou'd at the moment of the receipt. I have uniformly stated to you such views as could be relied upon most fully. They have been of course most highly confidential, as what I now write must also be so considered most specially. You have before this recd. my letter which expressed my opinion generally of the State of the facts.[2]

Judge Grundy has shown me your letter to him[3] intended for publication in the Globe. I think it judicious. It places you upon elevated ground, & so far leaves you without any objection resting upon you, of any kind, which might otherwise be imputed to entire silence. I am of opinion that the letter will not alter, the general action of the states disinclined to support Col. Johnson, & that they will still bestow their suffrages upon you.

I have taken much care to ascertain the true state of things. You are aware that your prominence before the nation excited a feeling of *repellance,* which shaped itself out into action in quarters *unexpected* to you, & to your friends, & which ought never to have manifested itself, under any circumstances.

The following classes of states present themselves, as I think, upon the Vice Presidency, and I speak, not only having the opportunity of knowing with tolerable accuracy, but having particularly availed myself of the means of judgeing. The energy & decision of your friends here arrested the strong current which had been deliberately given to the progress of events, originally, adverse to your interests—and the ground upon which your friends were then placed remains unchanged. But such was *the influence* brought to bear upon New Hampshire & Maine, that if we had come to a vote in the Convention, they wou'd have given it to Johnson. And such is the inclination of their *politicians* now. New York City was for Johnson—is so now—but such is not the feeling & sentiment of the State. The extreme radical Party of the City men [were] put into motion, & [are] to be traced, I think, to several sources. You are, certainly, fully aware of the connexion of New Hampshire & Maine with particular men, who were not friendly to your success under any circumstances. Without mentioning the name of any Individual I apprehend you will understand me. The classes of States to which I refer wou'd be I believe, a true exhibit of positions.

For Col Johnson—certainly.

Arkansas Indiana Ohio & Illinois	doubtful as to the result upon the Presidency
Pennsylvania also Missouri	considered to be debatable, but I count certainly for the Democracy
Maryland & New Jersey	debatable & doubtful as to the Presidency.
Maine & New Hampshire	will go for us [for the Democracy].
Louisiana	doubtful as to the Presidency.

This leaves as you perceive Pennsylvania, Maine, New Hampshire, & Missouri & Arkansas—the only certain States, which will cast their votes for us—and will be given to Col. Johnson.

Pennsylvania	30	
New Hampshire	9	
Maine	10	56.
Missouri	4	
Arkansas	3	

The States for you, I consider certain for us in the Presidential Struggle. to wit:

Virginia	25	
N. Carolina	15	
S. Carolina	11	70.
Tennessee	15	
Missouri	4	

States certain for you	70.
Alabama, if she does not vote for King, votes for you	7.
	77.
New York—I think wou'd give her vote to you	42.
	119.
If Georgia does not cast her vote for Forsyth would give it to you	11.
	130.
The vote which is certain for Col Johnson I have stated at	56.
Add as probable Ohio	21.
Add as debateable Indiana	9.
" " " Illinois	7.
Maryland—doubtful	11.
New Jersey— do.	8.
	102. [*sic*]

This I think is the strongest vote that Col Johnson will get. New York it is understood will give no indication as to what she will do. If the block of the Slave States go for the President she will cast her vote, as I understand the condition of things to be, in the same way. I express the opinion very confidentially that the Votes of Ohio & Indiana, are, to say the least, doubtful. The vote will be unquestionably close.

Your letter I think will do good, and will leave things in their present position, without the least responsibility on your part. I entertain the opinion that Col Johnson cannot, under any circumstances, get a stronger vote than I have set down to him.

The two Democratic Papers of the City of New York[4] represent merely, that Central Point, which took its direction exclusivly, as I think, from *certain politicians*.

I have not been unmindful of your interests here, & when Mr Kendal connected himself with the extra Globe[5] I reminded Mr Blair that there must not be any interference with the Vice Presidency. *To this he pledged himself to me absolutely.*

I will write you again shortly. I think that our papers in Tennessee ought not to alter their present flag—as to the Vice Presidency.

Burn this when read. Your friend Walker was appointed,[6] as you have learnt. Present my kind regard to Mrs. Polk.

A Anderson

P.S. Answer this immediately.

ALS. DLC–JKP. Addressed to Nashville and marked "Private & Confidential."

1. Polk's letter of May 24, 1840, has not been found.
2. See Alexander O. Anderson to Polk, April 14, 1840.
3. See Polk to Felix Grundy, May 27, 1840.
4. Reference probably is to the *New York Herald* and the *New York Evening Post.*
5. See Cave Johnson to Polk, May 24, 1840.
6. See A. O. P. Nicholson to Polk, May 15, 1840.

TO J. G. M. RAMSEY, ET AL[1]

Gentlemen: Nashville June 6th 1840

I have the honour to acknowledge the receipt of your letter of the 14th ultimo,[2] inviting me to unite with my Fellow Citizens of Knox County, and partake with them of a Public Dinner to be given at Knoxville on the approaching anniversary of American Independence. There is perhaps no occasion so well calculated to awaken in my patriotic bosom, an increased attachment to our free institutions, as the annual celebrations of the interesting event which you propose to commemorate. Upon each recurrence of the 4th of July, the mind is naturally thrown back upon the contemplation of first principles, which lie at the foundation of our system of Government, their inestimable value, and the importance of maintaining and preserving them.

If in the humble part I may have borne as a public man, and to which you kindly allude, I may have manifested any becoming ardour and zeal in maintaining the free principles of our ancestors, that ardour is unabated, that zeal is undiminished, and I have an abiding confidence that in the political crisis through which the country is passing, a free, enlightened and patriotic people, will continue to uphold the true Republican principles, upon which the constitution was established.

Be pleased, Gentlemen, to convey to my Fellow Citizens of East Tennessee, in whose behalf you act, my acknowledgements for this renewed evidence of their regard, and to assure them, that it affords me sincere pleasure to accept your invitation to meet them, on an occasion so interesting.

James K. Polk

ALS, draft. DLC–JKP. Addressed to Knoxville and marked "*Copy.*"

1. Inside addressees include Ramsey, William Lyon, Amos Hardin, William Wallace, Julian Frazier, Richard Oliver, James P. H. Porter, Arthur R. Crozier, Samuel P. Roberts, and Wesley Legg, members of a Knox County committee of Democratic citizens.
2. On May 14, 1840, Ramsey and the other members of the Knox County Democratic citizens committee had invited Polk to attend a public dinner at Knoxville on "the 4th July next." LS. DLC–JKP.

FROM JOHN J. GARNER

Yalobusha County, Mississippi. June 7, 1840

Garner is in receipt of Polk's letter of "the seventh of last month,"[1] and states that since the river[2] is very low at Troy, the articles Polk directed to his plantation from New Orleans will probably have to be transported by wagon from Williams' Landing, "some forty miles from here." Despite earlier spring rains and the illnesses of three slaves, Matilda, Maria, and Eve, there are no better crops of cotton and corn "in the contery" than those on Polk's plantation. Garner awaits a reply from Polk concerning repairs needed on the mill and gin stand.[3]

ALS. DLC–JKP. Addressed to Nashville. Published in Bassett, *Plantation Overseer*, 140–42. AE on the cover states that this letter was answered on June 20, 1840; Polk's reply has not been found.

1. Letter not found.
2. Reference is to the Yalobusha River.
3. See Garner to Polk, June 1, 1840.

FROM J. G. M. RAMSEY

My Dear Sir Mecklenburg June 10. 1840

Yours of June 1st[1] did not reach me till Saturday the 6th instant. (The late excessive rains must have detained it one Mail.) That same evening I wrote to Genl. Gamble & Dr. L. W. Jordan[2] that we might expect you to pass through Kingston on the 1st Proximo on your way to our 4th July Barbacue & that the Democratic friends there ought immediately to invite you to address them on that day. I wrote at the same time to J. F. Gillespie Esq. of Madisonville & to Iredell Wright Esq.[3] that after our festival was over the Democrats of the counties through which you would pass on your return should have appointments made & you invited to fill them. I mentioned Madisonville or Philadelphia [for] the 8th. Some point in McMinn the 9th. Vanville the 11th & Pikeville the 13th. Old Dr. Wright[4] happened to be with me that evening & assured me that he would send Iredell right down to have the arrangements made at once. Not knowing any of our prominent friends in the other counties I procured Mr. A. R. Crozier & R. Reynolds to write to their acquaintances to the same effect in Hamilton & Bledsoe. Yesterday I met J. F. Gillespie (our elector) in town & communicated freely on the subject with him. He enters into it with great zeal & determined to set out to day for the lower counties, & he assures me he will see that invitations for these *times* shall be immediately gotten up. The *places* he could not so well decide on till he gets down among our friends. He seems to prefer Philadelphia to Madisonville & some place in McMinn County out of Athens. He promises you shall hear from these several places in a very short time.[5] Old Mr. Martin of Campbells Station wished me to request you to speak at that place the 2nd. If the appointment were made, what you would say would do the Whigs more harm than it would in Knoxville—but it might prevent the attendance of a great many on the 4th. So that I will not advise one way or another. I told him tho that the proper way would be to get Col. Hardin[6] & our other friends around him to invite you & that if you were not too much fatigued &c. &c. perhaps you could accept an invitation—but that they all must be with us the 3rd & 4th. While I think of it allow me to ask how you would prefer to be received at Knoxville? where? & how? It will be the duty of some of us to ascertain that & I hope you will consult your own feelings & good judgment & communicate to me frankly. It shall be executed as you wish. We will have an immense concourse. The Whigs have had their day. They have with their log cabins & cider barrells—&

boyish frivolities—& sophomoric (for they have not given one manly argument) appeals disgusted their sober & considerate friends & have actually run the thing into the ground. Reaction has commenced already in the counties through which Foster & his auxilliaries have passed—& our time comes next. I send you our last Argus.[7] You will see the spirit of our friends is up. In this county *Democracy is gaining.* Fun & anecdote & theatrical bombast are not the materials with which to beat down Tennessee Republicanism. Foster has mistaken our countrymen. Calm & temporate discussion was expected from an ex-U.S. Senator & not puerile vauntings & vulgar witticism. The latter will do for a day but the *sober second thoughts of the people* nauseate & reject them. Read the proceedings of old Blount & Hawkins & Anderson—& compare them with the rhetorical flourish—the vox et preteria nihil[8] of Foster & you can easily decide which side acts most upon the belief that the people are capable of self Government. In his speech here a few days since Foster mentioned you—(with perfect respect however I will do him the justice to add) & read your speech on Gordons(?)[9] bill & compared it with your printed address &c. &c.[10] He done you great injustice as Col. Johnston[11] afterwards fully demonstrated but the Federalists had taken up nearly the whole of the day. The people were tired out—& but few Whigs heard your defense. I have thought it right to give you this information as you may have an opportunity if you think it worthwhile to pay him your respects on the 4th. Indeed if any apology were necessary for you on account of you accepting the invitation of your friends to meet them at the festive boards or even at the hustings an ample one is found in the fact that all the Whig declaimers instead of telling us what their principles are or avowing what policy Genl Harrison will pursue take up a good portion of their time in assailing you not only for your course in Congress, but also your stump efforts in our late glorious revolution & your executive course.

By a strange coincidence I had written myself as have others to Grundy to come down our Southern counties & to Genl A.[12] our Northern on their return from Washington. Your suggestions to the same effect confirm the wisdom of the project. I have not heard from Genl. Jackson in answer to our invitation. If he does not accept I hope not to hear it till the 3rd. All the old Irish & Dutch in E.T. would turn out to see him once more—& every true-hearted patriot in the land will regret his absence. Gillespie gives a very encouraging account in Bradley, McMinn, Monroe, Roane & Blount. He agrees that there is no need of your going to Cleaveland.

If you cannot be my guest the whole of the time you are with us I hope you will find it convenient to be so in part at least. The address of our Convention ought to embody our principles & elucidate & defend our past policy. *What master hand will give it its finish?* We want it to be an able & respectable paper.[13] I am perfectly absorbed & scarcely know what I have written.

J. G. M. Ramsey

ALS. DLC–JKP. Addressed to Nashville.

1. Letter not found.

2. James Gamble and Lewis W. Jordan. A mechanic and farmer, Gamble owned considerable property in Roane County. A physician, Jordan migrated to Roane County from Marion, Virginia. On June 15, 1840, Gamble invited Polk to speak at Kingston on July 1, 1840. ALS. DLC–JKP. In a letter of the same date, Jordan wrote that he looked with pleasure to seeing Polk at Knoxville on July 4. ALS. DLC–JKP.

3. One of the earliest lawyers in Madisonville, Iredell D. Wright was the first postmaster of that town. A Democrat, he won three terms in the Tennessee House, where he served from 1831 until 1837.

4. Not identified further.

5. On June 17, 1840, Polk received an invitation to a public dinner to be given at Madisonville on July 8, 1840. Thomas J. Caldwell et al. to Polk, June 17, 1840. ALS. DLC–JKP.

6. Possibly John G. Hardin, a state militia colonel and successful farmer and stock dealer in Hardin Valley, Knox County.

7. Enclosure not found.

8. Latin phrase meaning "voice and nothing more."

9. The question mark is that of the author.

10. On February 19, 1835, Polk spoke in the U.S. House on an amendment offered by William F. Gordon of Virginia to a bill providing for federal deposits in state banks. Gordon's amendment would have created an Independent Treasury system and required that all receipts and disbursements be made in hard money. Polk opposed the Independent Treasury concept and argued favorably for the administration proposal to place federal deposits in state banks. Four years later, in his "Address to the People of Tennessee," dated April 3, 1839, Polk strenuously supported creation of an Independent Treasury system that was not substantively different from Gordon's proposal in 1835.

11. Reference is to Andrew Johnson.

12. Reference is to Alexander O. Anderson.

13. See Polk to Robert B. Reynolds, May 25, 1840.

FROM LEVIN H. COE

Somerville, Tennessee. June 11, 1840

Coe reports that he and General Polk met in debate at LaGrange last Saturday[1] and that results were favorable to the Democrats. General Polk argued that "a blind enthusiasm had elected General Jackson who possessed not one solitary qualification" to be president. General Polk also "dwelt much upon Abolition & the Missouri question."[2] Coe relates that he linked Harrison to the abolitionists and that the argument was effective with the audience.

ALS. DLC–JKP. Addressed to Nashville.

1. See Coe to Polk, June 3, 1840.

2. Reference is to the Missouri Compromise and the continuing issue of free versus slave states.

FROM HENRY TROTT, JR.[1]

Dear Sir, Woodbury, June 12th 1840

I was thinking last night on retiring to bed, what ought to be done to save this state from the disgrace of supporting a man for the presidency who has lived out his divine lease, who is too old and imbecile to have the liberty to run at large, and whose political principles, to say the least, are "shrouded in mystery"—and I could come to no other conclusion but that you ought again to take the field. You are the head and front of the democracy of our state. The malicious and poisonous arrows of the motley opposition are directed at you: the liberty of speech and the right of self defence will be cheerfully accorded to you by every reasonable and sensible man of all parties, except the infamous defenders of the *Gag*.[2] Therefore, it is hoped you will come forth and make bare your arm of power. Without flatery, you are, in my opinion, the very best public speaker I have heard in my life. You possess the happy art of making every thing look so plain and simple that the most common of our people can understand you: and to this may be attributed your brilliant triumph in 1839. Federalism quakes and trimbles wherever you show your face.

You will reccollect that about 12 months ago I told you at Hillsborough that it was all important that you should make a speech at our town (Woodbury) for the reason that about one third of Cannon was composed of a section taken from Rutherford, & about one fourth taken from Wilson, and consequently an effective speech made here could not help having a favorable bearing on the elections in other counties, particularly on old Rutherford. Well you made a speech here,[3] and what do you think was the result? I will tell you. Two democratic representatives, one senator,[4] 106 majority for yourself in Rutherford—and a loss of about 50 to John Bell & co in the Wilson section. This is not an overwrought picture, no man of sense will or can deny it. Then again I beseech you to come forth. Our rights and liberties are in danger. The country is flooded with Allen A Hall's fell spirit of '76.[5] the *whipers-in*,[6] in the Rutherford section of our county, have visited every mans house and left no. 2[7] with the heads of families, together with other false documents. The Feds boast of great changes in their favor in that section & I believe truly—they were brought over by you in the first place, and if they have gone astray again no man can bring them back but you. If you will consent to address the people here, by request, at such time as may suit your convenience, write me, and we will arrange the correspondence & particulars hereafter. We are too poor & dull spirited to make a dinner parade here. To see, to hear, and to vote according to the best lights before us, is all we can do in the premises. Our people are democratic; and I am sure if you will come up and take the veil from the Prophets face, expose the odious principles of our opponents (if indeed they have any), show the unconstitutionality & inexpediency of a U.S. Bank, place the standing army humbug[8] in its proper position, meet the senseless cry against the reduction of the wages of labor & the destruction of the best currency the world ever had (as the Feds say) and place your self in a proper position in relation to the Independant Treasury Bill, all will be well. This is what they want and this is what they must have, or the probability is that a great many of them will be led off to the support of the certificate Hero.[9] In the absence of something real & tangible there is danger that some of our fellow-citizens will be led astray by the deafening shouts of log cabins, hard cider & gourds, though I make this confession with deep humiliation.

H. Trott, Jr.

P.S. *Private.* On the 18th this inst I see that the Directors of the mother Bank are to make the directors of the Branch Banks.[10] Our county is entitled to one, and when the Whigs had the power at Shelbyville they gave us a good Whig director, viz. Lewis Jetton,[11] who knows about as much about financial matters as a hog does about the 25th day of December. He lives in the Rutherford section of our county and the appointment was made to answer the ends of the Whig leaders about Murfreesboro, who would move heaven and earth to get a majority at the next election. They have had their turn and now I think fair play entitles us to a democratic director this time.

At any rate it is of the highest importance to our friends that this lever should be taken out of the hands of the enemy. They have the post office here which I know is a machine on their side, and now they are making great exertions for the Bank Director. Joseph Ramsey[12] of this place is their man. He is not the choice of the people, and has nothing but Whigery to recommend him. Currin of Murfreesboro will figure for him. Two thirds of our county are democrats and if their voice was consulted in the appointment not one would say aye. Now I know the delicacy of your situation, and therefore will only suggest that justice and right are on the side of a democratic appointment. These are trying times and it behooves every man to do his duty. H.T.

ALS. DLC–JKP. Addressed to Nashville.

1. A farmer and a merchant in Woodbury, Henry Trott served as the first clerk and master of the Chancery Court in Cannon County, 1836–42, and represented that county in the Tennessee House as a Democrat, 1843–47.

2. Reference probably is to John Bell's freedom of elections bill; see Cave Johnson to Polk, March 12, 1840.

3. Polk spoke at Woodbury on June 13, 1839.

4. Reference is to Representatives John D. Fletcher and James S. Smith and to Senator Henderson K. Yoakum. A Rutherford County Democrat, Smith served one term in the Tennessee House, 1839–41.

5. The *Spirit of '76* was a Whig political broadside published in Nashville.

6. Reference probably is to Whig political organizers.

7. Reference probably is to No. 2 of the *Spirit of '76*.

8. See Cave Johnson to Polk, January 1, 1840.

9. Reference probably is to letters from friends and military associates supporting Harrison's honor, bravery, and military competence during the War of 1812. On several occasions during the War of 1812 and again during the 1840 campaign, Harrison's military record was attacked by foes and defended by friends.

10. The Bank of Tennessee.

11. An early settler in Cannon County, Lewis Jetton backed Hugh L. White in 1836 and gained local influence as a Whig leader.

12. Joseph Ramsey was an early merchant in Woodbury.

FROM WILLIAM WALLACE

Dear Sir

Maryville June 12th 1840

I received your letter some ten days ago,[1] and forwarded to you immediately thereafter one of the Whig address. I hope you have received it. I have recently heard from our Knoxville friends and they are depending on the arrangement named between us for our address.[2] I hope therefore that you can procure one, to be prepared suitable for the present Crisis. I know you understand far better than I do, the character of an address to have effect. But I will merely remark, that it is my opinion it should be prepared with a peculiar reference to matters & things in our own state, that is, our present and past political position. My settled opinion long has been, that the division in our own state has been occasioned by the running and defeat of Judge White, and while it will be important that this point should be made [to] appear, yet great Caution will be necessary, especially since the death of Judge White. I Cannot but think that some of the leading Whigs must feel somewhat releaved, now that the old man is off out of the way. Had the Judge lived certainly he and Col Foster Could not have Canvassed together with propriety as electors for the same Whig party. Col Foster has been with us, and taken broad ground against the administration of Genl Jackson generally, he is emphatically for a national Bank &c. Seems to be almost for everything that Judge White had always been against &c. He Called upon the people that if they were for a Bank to go for Harrison and if they were against a Bank to go against him. Now sir this is Coming out for a Bank pretty bold in Tennessee. Mr. Foster having changed he must suppose that every other person & thing has also changed. The Whigs tried to make considerable adv. before, and at the time Col Foster was here. But I do not believe he added strength to their Cause. I think both parties were somewhat disappointed at his effort. It was certainly not what I had expected. Could Col Johnston[3] have had time to have address[ed] the same audience I have no doubt but he would have gotten the decided advantage. He made an appointment for the next day, and a goodly number attended but not so large as on the first. At all costs I am satisfied that we upon the whole held our ground.

As to our Convention and celebration, I am glad that you will be with us, and could it be consistent for Genl Jackson to be there also, it would be of infinnite service; his appearance among us in E Tn would have a more powerfull effect, at this time, in my opinion, than any other event.

It would be also a great advantage should Gov Carroll be with us &c. We are at some loss, as to your passing through our counties on your return. We would be glad to have matters so arranged that you Could be so situated that you Could address the people and at the same time, not by any appointments of your own. This you know would not do, but should Gov Carroll be along it seems that we could properly have appointments for him. You Could, being in Company, and being Called upon address the people also. I am quite anxious that Carroll should be with us, as I have no doubt, he would help our Cause in the East &c. I have understood from our friends that it was probable a meeting would be arranged for you at Madisonville on Wednesday the 8th. It would therefore suit quite well for you to be with us on Monday the 6th. That is the day of our Quarterly County Court, and I have no doubt were it understood that you & Gov Carroll, & Genl Jackson or only one of you, would be here that a great Concourse of people would Turn out. Could we be authorized for instance to give notice that Gov Carroll one of the Candidates for elector, would address the people, our object could be attained &c. I presume from what I have heard that Gov Carroll is still at the east, and perhaps you are not advised wither he will be at Knoxville or not. If you can give me any diffinite understanding about these matters & things before you arrive at Knoxville please do so, and we will try to act for the best according to circumstances. I have written in great haste and have not taken time to look over what I have said, I hope you will be able to read it &c.

WILL WALLACE

ALS DLC–JKP. Addressed to Nashville. AE on the cover states that this letter was answered on June 22, 1840; Polk's reply has not been found.

1. Polk's letter of May 24, 1840, has not been found.
2. See William Wallace to Polk, May 15, 1840; Robert B. Reynolds to Polk, May 16, 1840; and Polk to Robert B. Reynolds, May 25, 1840.
3. Reference is to Andrew Johnson.

FROM J. G. M. RAMSEY

My Dear Sir Mecklenburg T. June 13, 1840

I wrote you on the 10th informing you that our friends below would certainly invite you to a barbacue at Philadelphia or Madisonville on the 8th prox., somewhere in McMinn on the 9th & at Vanville on the 11th (Saturday). Gillespie[1] left town Wednesday for the lower counties & said the arrangement should be made. I will write to Frazier of the Courier at Athens & have written since I opened your letter[2] two hours ago to Col. Shepherd at Vanville suggesting to the *Democrats* there as you could not meet them last summer they ought to invite &c. &c.—on your return from Knoxville. Should he be at home I have no doubt it will all be satisfactorily arranged. I saw yesterday a letter from Genl. Wallace saying to us you must speak at Maryville on Monday the 6th.[3] As that might diminish our company very much on the 4th I lent it no countenance but they will invite you. I hear Dr. Jordan is not in Tennessee[4] & will therefore suggest to a townsman & fellow Democrat of his, Mr. Liggett[5] by this mail to get our friends to meet you on the (1st) Wednesday. I know no one in Bledsoe or Marion—& beside Gillespie thought it might be imposing too much labor on you for you to go there. Therẽ can be no conflicting appointments as I have been particular in every instance about *dates*. Nicholson is invited. I wish he could attend.

J. G. M. RAMSEY

ALS. DLC–JKP. Addressed to Nashville. AE on the cover states that this letter was answered on June 29, 1840; Polk's reply has not been found.

1. John F. Gillespy.
2. See Polk to Ramsey, June 6, 1840.
3. See William Wallace to Polk, June 12, 1840.

4. On June 15, 1840, Lewis W. Jordan wrote Polk that he had returned to Kingston "late this evening from North Carolina." ALS. DLC–JKP.

5. Henry Liggett was a Kingston merchant.

FROM A. O. P. NICHOLSON

Dear Sir: Columbia June 15th 1840

Your favor of the 15th inst.[1] came to hand this evening. I reached here yesterday evening and found my wife[2] on the *straw*. She is very unwell and of course I cannot make any promises about attending my appointments until she has passed safely from her present situation. I was compelled to disappoint our friends in Bedford, but have procured Thomas to go up and fill my appointments in that county. I expect to fill his appointments during next week in this county. I have an aversion to attending Mr. Foster in the terms to which he has subjected Col. Johnson & I think the Central Committee ought to know of him whether he is willing to alternate at his appointments. If he will do so, then I should be happy to attend him, if my family's situation would justify. But to go along & be thrown to the heels of each day, to address exhausted crowds, would be more than I should deem agreeable. My plan would be to propose to Mr. F. that the right of speaking first should be enjoyed alternately. If he will not consent to that, then let the District Electors attend him & do what they can. In the mean time so soon as he makes his appointments let our friends select some two men & make appointments at the same places comme[n]cing a week after F's & going through the same ground. In this way alone can we have both sides fully discussed. I made a speech at Benton on Saturday and I am well pleased with our situation in that democratic section. I made a speech at Charlotte on Monday & was answered by Henry. Our friends were well pleased with my speech altho being limited I did not make a full speech. We are evidently in a strong & unyielding position in Dickson. Our friends are confident of having gained.

A. O. P. NICHOLSON

ALS. DLC–JKP. Addressed to Nashville.

1. Letter not found.

2. Nicholson's wife, Caroline O'Reilly, was the daughter of James C. O'Reilly of Maury County.

TO STOKELY D. ROWAN, ET AL.[1]

Gentlemen, Nashville June 15th 1840

I had the honour shortly after its date, to receive your letter of the 6th ultimo,[2] inviting me on behalf of my "Fellow-Citizens of the County of Warren" to partake with them of a Public Dinner to be given at the Bersheba Springs, and have delayed an answer thus long, that I might be enabled to designate a day, upon which I could certainly be present. Duly sensible of the honour done me, by your invitation, I beg you Gentlemen to be assured, that their are no portion of my Fellow-Citizens, whom it will give me more pleasure to visit, than those of the Republican County of Warren. On Saturday the 18th of July, should that be a day which will suit your convenience, I will be at the Bersheba Springs, when I will be happy to meet yourselves and those in whose behalf you act. That day I learn will suit the convenience of "our illustrious friend—the venerable sage of the Hermitage,"[3] (whom you inform me in your letter you have also invited), should his advanced age and declining health, enable him, to make the journey.

JAMES K. POLK

ALS. DLC–JKP. Addressed to McMinnville and marked "Copy."

1. Polk's letter is addressed to Rowan, Sion S. Read, John W. Ford, L. D. Mercer, William C. Smartt, and Hugh L. W. Hill, members of the Warren County invitation committee.

2. On May 6, 1840, Stokely D. Rowan and other members of the invitation committee extended an open invitation to Polk and Andrew Jackson to attend a public dinner to be held at Beersheba Springs. LS. DLC–JKP.

3. Quotation is from the letter of invitation.

TO JOHN H. BILLS

My Dear Sir Nashville June 18th 1840

The Branch Boards were appointed by the Principal Bank[1] to day, and I apprehend that the re-appointment of Douglass at your Branch,[2] against the strong protestations of *Coe*, *Humphreys*, and others, against it, will give much dissatisfaction, and I fear do mischief. I learn that a letter from you to the Board[3] in his behalf was the leading inducement with some of the members of the Board, to unite with Mr. Nichol and his friends, and thus enable them to appoint him. I know that you could not have intended to do anything, which would dissatisfy our friends, but I fear such may be the effect. You were re-appointed, though I learn you did not desire to be. Mr. Douglass was not placed at the head of the list, but in a subordinate place on the Board, and is therefore not indicated as the choice of the mother Board for President. If he is not re-elected President I hope the mischief, which his appointment as a Director is calculated to produce, may be avoided. I hope you may not find it inconsistent with your sense of duty to support some other for President. I thought it proper to advise you of the feeling of dissatisfaction which I know exists, at his appointment. It is the only mistake of any consequence which was made by the Board. At all the other Branches, I think the appointments will be generally satisfactory.

I start to Knoxville in about a week where I am to be on the 4th of July.[4]

JAMES K. POLK

P.S. The state is safe, absolutely safe, if we are half as active as our opponents. J.K.P.

ALS. T–JKP. Addressed to Bolivar and marked *"Private."*

1. The Bank of Tennessee.
2. The branch office at Somerville.
3. Letter not found.
4. See Polk to Robert B. Reynolds, May 25, 1840.

FROM THOMAS VON ALBADE ANDERSON AND PIERCE B. ANDERSON

Dear Sir, Soldiers Rest [June] 19th 1840[1]

One of us has heretofore addressed you on the subject of the appointment of Mr James W. Deaderick[2] as the Director for the County of Jefferson in the Branch of the Bank of the State of Tennessee at Rogersville.[3] As the time is drawing nigh when this appointment will be made, we again solicit your, favorable consideration of this matter. The appointment of Mr Deaderick will give *general* public satisfaction, & be very acceptable to our Rogersville friends, & very gratifying to us.

One of us was at Rogersville on yesterday, and in conversation with several of our Democratic friends (amongst others Messrs Powell & Fain)[4] understood that Major Robert H Hynds of Dandridge,[5] had been recommended by some of our friends over there, as the Director for Jefferson—but without the knowledge that the appointment wou'd be acceptable to Mr Deaderick whom they wou'd have preferred, and consequently his appointment will be gratifying to them. We will remember with much kindness, your attention & influence in favor of Mr Deadericks appointment.

You will be pleased to learn that the flood tide of popular excitement got up by the British Federal Whig Party, thro' the instrumentality of the empty pageantry of *log cabins* & *hard cider*, & *blue* & *white motto banners* is *already* on the *ebb.* Thus far they have gained *nothing* for their cause, by all their poorly devised exhibitions. There have been it is true some changes—but the *aggregate* gain, is *decidedly* in favor of the Democratic Party. And the Whigs by all their empty pageantry have *disgusted many more,* than they have *pleased.* The Democratic Majority in East Tennessee will be in *November* not *less* than one thousand, & may double that number.

The Whigs say that *Daniel, says* Revolutions never go *backward.*[6] This is as a general rule *most true*—and in the present canvass, in Tennessee they will find, that the *Revolution* affected, mainly by the single arm of *James K Polk*—has *kept* on gaining *strength & vigor*—and will continue until Democratic Principles will be so completely triumphant, that diminished Whiggery, will *forever* hide its head *in everlasting Shame.*

On the subject of the Vice Presidency there is *no voice,* among the Democracy but for *James K Polk* in East Tennessee. Cou'd not a Convention be brought about to meet *exclusively* upon the subject of nominating a Candidate for the Vice Presidency? Or wou'd it be impolitic? Or must we reach unanimity in some other way? And if so—how? In the present state of this question it is one so *ticklish & difficult,* in its leading aspects that *discreet* young Politicians *fear* to say much—and yet they do not like to be *altogether* silent. We wou'd like to know what course our Friends who better understand these things, & have been longer in the field thinke most advisable.

We hope to have the pleasure of seeing you & shaking you by the hand at the Knoxville convention 3d July—and joining with you in the celebration of the 4th.

In the mean time we have the honor to be . . . .

THOS A. ANDERSON
PIERCE B. ANDERSON

LS. DLC–JKP. Addressed to Nashville.

1. Although dated "July 19th," this letter received a postal endorsement that reads, "Cheeks X Road Ten. June 20." Content analysis confirms the earlier date.

2. A son of David Deaderick and cousin of Pierce B. and Thomas A. Anderson, James W. Deaderick was a farmer and store keeper at Cheek's Crossroads, Jefferson County, before entering law practice at Jonesboro in 1844. A Whig, he served one term in the Tennessee Senate, 1851–53. Deaderick married Adeline McDowell, daughter of Ephraim McDowell and granddaughter of Isaac Shelby of Kentucky.

3. On the previous day, June 18, 1840, Pierce B. Anderson had written to Polk, recommending several persons as directors for the Athens branch of the

bank. ALS. DLC–JKP. No previous recommendation of Deaderick by Thomas A. or Pierce B. Anderson has been found.

4. Thomas A. Anderson, George R. Powel, and Nicholas Fain.

5. A Whig lawyer, Hynds won election to one term in the Tennessee Senate where he served from 1835 until 1837. He was a Whig presidential elector in 1844.

6. Reference probably is to Daniel Webster, who campaigned vigorously for the Whigs in the 1840 election. The quotation has not been identified.

FROM LEVIN H. COE

Dear Sir Somerville June 19th 1840

On Saturday last I was at a meeting in the N.W. of this County.[1] On Monday last at Covington [I] had the first speech to a crowded Court House. The Democrats are aroused. Humbug is recoiling upon itself—we will gain in that county.[2] On Tuesday night about midnight I was called upon to speak to expinditures & "Army Bill"[3] at Covington and in doing so took occasion to touch at other things. Newton Cannon was present—stoped to explain when I stated he said Harrison was for a U.S.B. in his speech at Memphis. I put the question to him, what are Harrisons opinions upon a Bank? Ansr. I do not know but the Whigs I believe generally are of the *impression* he will approve a charter if presented. But Harris will get a full account in a few days.[4]

I spent last evening & part of to day with Col. Joseph Watkins[5] of Goochland Cty Va. who has been for more than 20 years a member of the Legislature—author of the expunging Resolutions[6]—decidedly the leader of the party in the Legislature, a gentleman of fine talents & better acquainted with the tone & temper of the people of Va. than any one in the state. He thinks if you take a certain course that state may be lost—that it will not go for Johnson but all is safe if you permit your name to be used. In answer to your objection of a minority candidate, He insists

1st That the party there nominated you as the person most acceptable to them & made public their intention to vote for you and appointed no committee to correspond with you and ask you to accept the nomination.

2nd therefore he doubts whether it is true old fashiond Republicanism for you to say to them you shall not vote for me.

However you may agree about this you will be pleased with him as one of the soundest & best informed politicians of our Country.

I see E. H. Ewing is to make a speech in Nashville justifying Harrisons white slavery vote.[7] Will he try to get off as J. C. Wright[8] in his paper does that it is lighter punishment than working in chains under the 18 sect.[9] on the highways? The Journal[10] shows Hn. voted vs. striking it out. Some Democrat should reply to him & then let his remarks be written out with all care & printed. Depend upon it this vote if pressed firmly will do much. I believe it will carry hundreds in this Congressional District. Particularly in McNairy, Henderson & Perry. I will have this Dist too hot for the Bull Calf hero[11] to make expenses out of. I have about 20 appointments now out for Shelby, Fayette, Hardeman and terminating at the N.E. of McNairy on the 14th July. Thence I will extend into Henderson & Perry say 8 appts. & one or two in Carroll—perhaps a bout in Henry, Gibson & Haywood & down to Tipton by the 8th Augt.

I run against a man of light calibre[12] but all his sense is of the Fox order—cunning & unscrupulous. I tell the people plainly what he is.

L. H. Coe

[P.S.] I wrote to Humphreys to send me a certified copy of Douglass vote against the occupants in '23 (I think) but as usual he has forgotten it. Let it meet me at Bolivar by the fourth July addressed to Care of, W. H. Wood[13] or John H. Bills. It is important I should have it certified by the secretary,[14] under seal of state & in *plain* hand writing.

ALS. DLC–JKP. Addressed to Nashville.

1. Fayette County, Tennessee

2. Tipton County, Tennessee.

3. See Cave Johnson to Polk, January 1, 1840, on Joel R. Poinsett's militia proposals.

4. J. George Harris carried an account of Cannon's speech at Memphis, in the *Nashville Union* of June 29, 1840, but made no reference to Coe.

5. Not further identified.

6. On March 15, 1836, the Virginia legislature instructed its U.S. senators to vote to expunge from the Senate Journal the 1834 censure of Andrew Jackson for removing government deposits from the Bank of the United States.

7. A Nashville lawyer, Edwin Hickman Ewing served as a Whig in the Tennessee House, 1841–43, and in the U.S. House, 1845–47. On numerous occasions he sat as a special judge on the Tennessee Supreme Court. On June 20, 1840, Ewing spoke in Nashville against Coe's charges, endorsed by J. George Harris in the *Nashville Union,* that William Henry Harrison had voted in the Ohio legislature to sell white men into slavery. See Polk to A. O. P. Nicholson, May 28, 1840, and Robert Armstrong to Polk, July 1, 1840.

8. An Ohio lawyer, printer, and politician, John Crafts Wright served in the U. S. House, 1823–29, and on the Ohio Supreme Court, 1831–35. In 1835

he moved from Steubenville to Cincinnati, engaged in newspaper work, and for thirteen years published the *Cincinnati Gazette*, a major Whig newspaper.

9. Reference is to a provision of the Ohio Penal Code.

10. The Ohio *Senate Journal*, 1820–21.

11. During the campaign of 1840, Ephraim H. Foster frequently told a humorous story about a bull calf.

12. Burchett Douglass, the Whig candidate for presidential elector in the Thirteenth Congressional District.

13. In 1834 William Henry Wood married Beniga Polk, the youngest daughter of Ezekiel Polk and his third wife, Sophia Neely Lennard. James K. Polk was some twenty years older than his "Aunt Beniga."

14. John S. Young, Tennessee's secretary of state.

FROM LEWIS P. ROBERTS

My Dear Sir, Knoxville June 19 1840

Enclosed you will receive a letter addressed to you, at this place.[1] Presumeing an immediate answer necessary, I have taken the liberty of forwarding it to you. The Whigs are making a great noise, for effect. It does not appear to affect any thing, as I have heard of no new converts, for some time. Even the *Great Ephraim*[2] did not make a single vote.

The country people are beginning to think for themselves. I have heard a great many express themselves decidedly against the course persued by the Whigs. The standing army humbug is dying away.[3] I do not know what they will invent next.

They (the Whigs) are making great efforts for the 4th, constructing a *Liberty pole* as they are pleased to term it one hundred feet high surmounted with a flag &c.

I hear nothing of log cabbins or any thing of the kind, although I should not be surprised if they did not import some for the upper Whig counties.

I presume the whole of the Whig Electors will be present, as they have all been written to.

I think we have been gaining some few votes in this county since the last election. We are doing our best, exerting our utmost, to defeat the whigs in E Ten, and I hope we shall do it. We have every thing to contend with—hard times, scarcity of money, low prices of produce, standing army humbug, and even the taking of the census the Whigs are attempting to make some political capital of, by representing the President object to lay a direct tax, &c. Notwithstanding all these disadvantages, we still hold our own—no wavering in our ranks—our people firm & stedfast in the faith.

Eastman's list of subscribers is increasing fast. He had orders for 2000 copies of Duncans speech [4] more than he published. He received last night some 500th job type which will enable him to compete with the "Times" which has had every thing in its own way, in that line heretofore.[5]

Hoping to have the pleasure of your company with a host of other good Democrats on the *glorious* 4th . . . .

L P Roberts

ALS. DLC–JKP. Addressed to Nashville.

1. Enclosure not found.
2. Ephraim H. Foster.
3. See Cave Johnson to Polk, January 1, 1840.
4. Alexander Duncan of Ohio made several speeches defending the administration and attacking the Whigs. Reference possibly is to his speech of April 10, 1840, on the general appropriations bill.
5. Reference is to an unidentified font of job type, the use of which will enable the Knoxville *Argus* to compete with the Knoxville *Times* in the printing business.

FROM JAMES WALKER

Dear Sir, Columbia June 20 1840

I have received yours of the 18th.[1] I think the new board will give general satisfaction.[2] We are at least rid of the tyranny of Kenedy[3] and others, and whatever relief the Bank can be fairly and safely made to afford a suffering community, may be afforded. Dr. Polk[4] certainly did wish to be reappointed a director, altho he says he will only serve a week or so, even as a Director. As to the Presidency, I had no feeling whatever. I had supposed it a matter of no consequence either way, that the President would be the mere chairman of the board, and have [no] more influence for good or for evil, than any other member of the board; would of necessity have to attend to the correspondence of the Bank for which a moderate compensation is allowed. I was not aware that any pecuniary responsibility devolved upon the President—he never having charge of the funds. I had made up my mind not to seek the station of President, and to be governed by circumstances whether I would decline positively. You say, however, that "there are other urgent reasons why on your own account, as well other considerations, which you will understand, why you should not accept." This excites my curiosity. If anything occured in relation to the formation of the board, which would make it improper for me *to serve under any circumstances,* I should like to know it. I certainly would not think of giving a bond to the amount required, for the compensation allowed, unless it was clearly ascertained that the bond was only nominal. This itself would be a sufficient reason for declining, if the station should be offered. I am aware of another objection to any one's accepting the Presidency. I do not believe, we will be able to get a Cashier. I am satisfied no one here can give the bond nor do I believe any one will attempt it. If we are without a Cashier, who is to take charge of the funds. I do not believe any member of the board will take the Presidency coupled with such responsibility. *I certainly would not.* My opinion is, that Mr. Dale will be re-elected Cashier by the new board. Sympathy will produce his election, besides a strong wish that his securiters should escape the threatened ruin.[5] But he *cannot* give the security, and I can hardly suppose he will attempt it. Then where are we to get a Cashier. There is no man here but Langtry that will do—and I can hardly suppose the salary would induce him. Indeed I do not believe *he* could give the bond. There is enough that would risque his integrity—but few indeed willing to take the chances of robbery, acciidents, and the insecurity now, of the funds of that Bank. I do not desire the Presidency of the Bank, but I do wish to know if anything has passed which would make it more imprudent in me than any one else, to take it.

The Bank is now fairly in the hands of the Democracy. We are responsible for its usefulness. We can make it useful, if we can get officers. The Presidency is a post of power and with sensible action, much influence. Circumstances might occur that would make it look obstinate to decline—that would make it wrong to do so, unless some fact exists of which I am not apprised. I should like to hear from you *more fully* on this subject. I am satisfied there are a good many bad debts now made. It will require much good judgement, decision and influence over the new board, to get the debts all sound, and to make the Bank as useful to the community as its limited means will allow. I repeat that circumstances may occur that will make it a difficult question to determine what I ought to do. Under no circumstances will I seek the office of President, nor will I be induced to accept it, if the responsibility be greater than merely acting as chairman of the Board, and conducting such correspondence as may be necessary. Nor will I even in this case, if any thing has occurred, that furnishes a good reason for declining under any circumstances. I have just learned from Sam[6] that the new Board is the topic of conversation down town, and that general satisfaction is expressed. Many of the Whigs are pleased. Helm is much pleased, tho' he tries to hide it. So are the Nelson concern.[7]

James Walker

ALS. DLC–JKP. Addressed to Nashville.

1. Letter not found.

2. The Bank of Tennessee appointed Archibald A. Campbell, William Davis, Boling Gordon, Thomas K. Gordon, Meredith Helm, Hillary Langtry, George M. Martin, Pleasant Nelson, William J. Polk, Jesse S. Ross, Samuel Stockard, and James Walker directors of its Columbia branch on June 18, 1840.

3. William E. Kennedy, a Columbia lawyer and cousin of John Bell, was judge of the Sixth Judicial Circuit from 1826 until 1833. He served as a director of the Columbia branch of the bank from 1838 to 1840.

4. William J. Polk, a son of Colonel William Polk of North Carolina, moved to Maury County, Tennessee, in 1836. A physician and farmer, William J. Polk served as president of the Columbia branch of the bank from 1838 to 1840.

5. See James Walker to Polk, May 26, 1840.

6. Samuel P. Walker.

7. Meredith Helm and Pleasant Nelson. An early Maury County settler, Helm established a tannery in Columbia in about 1820. He served nine terms as mayor of Columbia between 1829 and 1852. Nelson, a Columbia hotel keeper, was circuit court clerk from 1840 until 1844.

FROM SAMUEL H. LAUGHLIN

Dear Sir,

McMinnville, June 21, 1840

I have just returned from Jamestown having during the week made speeches in Fentress, Overton and White—at Jamestown on the 15th, Livingston on the 16th, and Taylor's mills (old Isaac's)[1] on the 19th. Every thing is going on well. Bransford will speak at Livingston tomorrow, and will be answered by Col. A. Cullom.[2] I shall address the people at Manchester on tomorrow.

I have seen your letter to our committee agreeing to be at Bersheba on Saturday, 18th proximo.[3] That is not a place where the people from the north, west, and other distant parts of this county, who are busy and throng'd with work can well attend; but we will have a big crowd. If possible I wish it so arranged that you can be in this place on the Monday following which will be the 20th—and then at Woodbery on [the] next day, if you should be homeward bound. Ford had promised to write you.[4] We can have a glorious meeting here on that day—and no public dinner.

Maj. Coe writes me that Huntsman is not, as he is informed, active as he ought to be. Gen. Armstrong and others ought to write & spur him up. Squire Ford will write you.

S. H. LAUGHLIN

P.S. I like and approve your letter to Grundy exceedingly.[5] Coe writes that you must, if possible, not withdraw—and in no event, in haste.

Batey,[6] with whom I spent a night, offers to bet, and swears the Whigs cant give Harrison fifty votes out of 500 in Fentress. He and the Obeds' and Wolf river[7] democrats will attend Fosters meeting,[8] and behave with great decorum, each having a large Hickory, and poke leaf in his hatband.

ALS. DLC–JKP. Addressed to Nashville and marked "Private."

1. One of the early settlers in White County, Isaac Taylor served as sheriff from 1812 to 1814.

2. Thomas Lewis Bransford and Alvin Cullom. Bransford, a merchant and a Whig, represented Jackson County in the Tennessee House, 1839–41. He was a delegate to the Whig National Conventions in 1840 and 1844 and was an unsuccessful Whig candidate for Congress in 1843. Cullom, a lawyer and a Democrat, represented Overton County in the Tennessee House, 1835–37, and served in the U.S. Congress, 1843–47. He was judge of the Fourth Judicial Circuit of Tennessee, 1850–52.

3. See Polk to Stokely D. Rowan et al., June 15, 1840.

4. No such letter from John W. Ford has been found.

5. See Polk to Felix Grundy, May 27, 1840.

6. Not identified further.

7. The Obey and Wolf rivers. The Obey River, formerly called Obids River, rises in Fentress and Overton counties and flows into the Cumberland. The Wolf rises in Fentress County and flows into the Obey.

8. Ephraim H. Foster planned to campaign at Jamestown in Fentress County in early July, while en route to a Whig dinner at Sparta on July 4, 1840.

FROM ISAAC COOPER, ET AL.[1]

Dear Sir Selma, Ala., June 22, 1840

The undersigned, a Committee of the "States Rights Club of Dallas County," appointed for the purpose of inviting the Democratic Electoral Ticket of Alabama, and other distinguished members of the Democratic Party, most respectfully and earnestly solicit your attendance upon the Young Men's Democratic State Convention, to be held in Selma on the 2d Monday of July next; during which a sumptuous Barbacue will be furnished.

As South Alabama may possibly be stubborn in giving up her Federal notions, we hope you will not fail to attend, and contribute to awaken her people to the British character of Federal principles, and the national degradation, and disgrace, and overthrow of our form of government, which must follow the success of the present contending Abolition, Hartford Convention, Fraudulent, Hypocritical, Hard-cider, Granny Harrison, Party.

PL. DLC–JKP. Addressed to Nashville. AE on the cover states that Polk received this letter on July 25, 1840.

1. Attributed to Cooper, William T. Minter, Joseph P. Saffold, James Cantie, V. W. Kinnard, and George R. Evans, none of whom is identified further.

TO SAMUEL H. LAUGHLIN

My Dear Sir: Nashville June 23rd 1840

I wrote you two or three days ago[1] that I would probably be at McMinnville on saturday afternoon. I now think it probable that I may not get further than *Woodbury* or *Bates's*[2] on saturday night, & in that case will be at McMinnville to dinner on sunday. I *must* if possible see *Mr Ford*, and yourself as I go on; I think it important that I should do so, in reference to my movements on my return—as well as *other matters*, which I will communicate, when I see you. I have an invitation to *Jackson Cty*, which I have not answered, and will not until I see you.[3] I do not think it possible that I can spend a day at McMinnville on my return, and hope my friends there will not insist upon it.

James K. Polk

ALS. NjP. Addressed to McMinnville and marked "*Private.*"

1. Polk's letter not found.

2. Possibly a reference to the residence of William Bates, a Woodbury merchant and member of the first Cannon County Court in 1836.

3. On June 3, 1840, Absalom Johnson and four others invited Polk, Andrew Jackson, and William Carroll to attend a public dinner in their honor, given by the Democratic citizens of Jackson County. AE on the cover of the letter states that Polk "accepted and attended" a public dinner in Jackson County on July 21, 1840. LS. DLC–JKP.

FROM J. G. M. RAMSEY

My Dear Sir Mecklenburg June 26, 1840

Yours of the 19th & 21st were both received yesterday.[1] I immediately wrote to Mr. Martin dissuading him & our friends there from insisting upon your meeting them at Campbells Station on the 2nd but urging them to come out on the 4th at Knoxville.[2] I wrote also to Genl. Wallace that if it were deemed important you would meet the citizens of Blount on Monday the 6th if a concourse sufficiently numerous could be got together under Democratic auspices. As he is one of the Comtee. of invitation I expect & so advised him to meet you below town Thursday evening next[3]—when it can better be decided what is most expedient. If Blount turns out well on the 4th & as harvest is upon us—& the season very wet—a large meeting may not be had at Maryville for the 6th. We can know better the 2nd. I saw Capt. Lyon a few days ago & he offered the hospitalities of his house 5 miles below town to yourself & the Comtee. or their friends for the evening of the 2nd. Some of us will meet you between Mrs. Cox[4] & his house Thursday afternoon. Capt. Lyons is the old *Jackson head quarters*—& has been ever since the fall of 1823 & we have so arranged your arrival & reception now. I will write you again at Kingston—especially if any alteration is made. If I cannot meet you the 2nd I will see you Friday Morning early. I fear this may not be in time to find you at Sparta. The Whigs are loosing by their pageantry & we affect nothing of it but are making & doing every thing plain—& without noise or show. We owe no fealty but to our *principles*—& have no standard but the standard of our country.

J. G. M. Ramsey

[P.S.] I have heard nothing further from below. Gillespie had assured me that barbacues should be got up in McMinn, Monroe & Hamilton (Vanville) & invitations forwarded to you at Kingston or Knoxville. At Kingston I do not know whether they will do so. I should say that at Campbell station it would be best not to speak. Our electors have appointed that place certainly as one of their main points.

We have taken rooms for you at Picketts.[5]

ALS. DLC–JKP. Addressed to Sparta, Tennessee.

1. Letters not found.

2. See Ramsey to Polk, June 10, 1840.

3. Ramsey wishes William Wallace to meet Polk on July 2 at Thomas C. Lyon's residence, which is located below Knoxville.

4. In a letter to Polk of June 27, 1840, Ramsey describes Mrs. Cox's residence as "the 10 mile house." ALS. DLC–JKP. Mrs. Cox is not identified further.

5. Reference is to Pickett's hotel or tavern in Knoxville, the owner of which is not identified further.

FROM ALEXANDER O. ANDERSON

My Dear Sir — Washington City June 28th 1840

For some time nothing has transpired in relation to the Vice Presidency, except what has met your observation. The opinion prevails here that the slave holding States will go for the administration, & will cast their votes for the Vice Presidency for you. I think in the present posture of affairs there is no move which you can make that it wou'd place you upon higher ground than that taken in your letter to Mr Grundy.[1] I find that my first impressions upon that subject were correct,[2] & it has been well received by the public, & was in my judgement the very letter you shou'd have written, neither more or less.

I hear that Col Johnson has some thought of returning home *thro' New York*. If this is so, it may be in view of the doubtful aspect which that State presents to his mind, in relation to the Vice Presidency. I shou'd be very much gratified to see you on my return, at some point. I do not know that it will be in my power to go to Nashville. We have a very strong confidence here that we shall carry the Presidency—but the battle has to be fought over every inch of ground, with the strongest unanimity—& no new issues shou'd be made any where, if possible to be avoided. It is in the Creation of new issues that the opposition hope for accessions.

The Bankrupt Bill passed the Senate on last Thursday—by a vote of 21 to 19.[3] Mr Wright voted for it. The Legislature of New York having declared for it unanimously—it was the only proper course left for him to take. The 19 who voted against it were democrats. It is understood Col Johnson was for it, and wou'd have given, in the event of a tie, his casting vote for it. I voted against it, & made a speech against it upon its final passage, which will be published this week.[4]

At one stage it included Banks exclusively owned by the States. Mr. Clay of Alabama moved to strike out the clause containing this provision. I believed to do so wou'd weaken the Bill & being against a measure of Bankruptcy, without knowing more of the opinions of the State [of] Tennessee, I voted for that motion. I entertained the conviction that the measure was unexpected, at least, to the State of Tennessee to pass any Bankrupt law at this Session, and perceiving the very great excitement prevailing, especially in East Tennessee, I had little doubt that it wou'd be seized upon by the whigs there to make a new issue upon, and that they wou'd alledge that I was in favor of the immediate destruction of the Bank of the State, & for going contrary to the inferred will of the Legislature, and for taking the power out of the hands of the legislature in relation to its own money. I was aware they might make capital out of such a state of things, & therefore did not wish to give them the color for it. That the next Session wou'd be a period of better auspices for a calmer action upon the subject. I entertained the confidence that by fighting up to the line on the great issues now depending we wou'd have it in our power to defeat them. Mr. Grundy was opposed to any Bankrupt law whether it included or excluded Banks but did not vote for the motion of Mr Clay of Alabama. My position in East Tennessee was peculiar, and [I] did not believe I cou'd act with too much caution on the subject, particularly as one of the claims they had very much relied upon there, was that we were for the utter destruction of all Banks. In my speech, however, upon the final passage of the Bill I struck the Banks a few hard blows, & ascribed to them the reduction of the price of wages. The Intelligencer as usual made a false report.[5] I think it doubtful whether the Bill will pass the House. If you see General Jackson explain to him these views, & the position of things in East Tennessee. The great Battle was every thing, and I knew they wou'd bring all their metal to bear, particularly in East Tennessee. Several Gentlemen were here from East Tennessee, and I conversed freely with them upon the subject, & they believed it was the safest course for me [to] take in view of the struggle we wou'd have there for the Presidency. Among those who were here was Mr Gammon.

It was also apparent that the vote for the motion of Mr Clay of Alabama, wou'd be very large, & therefore the importance of not allowing to the whigs, particularly in my Section of the State, the opportunity of such an issue, on the very eve of the Presidential election. In the west you know things are different. You are stronger than we are. The forces had been brought up with great care & labor, led on most gallantly by yourself. My letters represented East Tennessee as being greatly excited—and under all circumstances, it seemed to me most desirable to avoid such an issue, in which strong appeals might be made to the people, & there alarm excited for the safety of all their School funds—of which mostly the State Bank had the possession. Whatever investigation therefore had to be made of this question it was safest, at present, to avoid *premature appearances* and action—and to leave the matter of such investigation as might be had under the calmer auspices of the next Session.

If any thing transpires here of interest I will write to you. I have many—very many things to say to you confidentially when we meet. Explain the preceding matter to General Jackson. I know he will perceive at once the great propriety of risking nothing to a new issue, in the state in which things are in East Tennessee. As for myself I go with the opinions of my State—but we must first fight and conquer in this Battle and we have a wily foe to contend with—and they must be allowed no move upon us. This is so now as it was in the late contest. Present my kind regards to Mrs Polk. With my best wishes . . . .

A Anderson

ALS. DLC–JKP. Addressed to Nashville and marked "*Private & Confidential.*"

1. See Polk to Felix Grundy, May 27, 1840.
2. See Anderson to Polk, May 22 and June 6, 1840.
3. See Levin H. Coe to Polk, May 30, 1840.
4. The Washington *Globe* of June 30, 1840, published Anderson's Senate remarks of June 25, 1840.
5. Reference is to Anderson's speech on the bankruptcy bill, which was noticed in the Washington *National Intelligencer* of June 26, 1840.

FROM MINER K. KELLOGG

My dear Sir, Washington City June 30, 1840

The *Sub-Treasury bill*, passed the House of Representatives this day at ½ passed 7 oc. P.M. Ayes 124 nays 107.[1] So you see the Democracy have at length triumphed after a prolonged conflict of 2 years.

The Democratic friends here are in excellent spirits, and will go home with cheerful hearts, after having done their duty, manfully, to their constituents.

The Portrait of Genl Jackson will be opened in one of the Committee rooms of the Capitol tomorrow, when I will invite the President and other distinguished friends to take a view of it.[2] Your kind letter to Mr. Van Buren[3] is not yet delivered. I deemed it more prudent to open the picture, first, that my *work*, might be seen.

Please present my best regards to Mrs Polk, and other friends.

MINER K. KELLOGG

ALS. DLC–JKP. Addressed to Nashville.

1. The Independent Treasury bill had passed the U.S. Senate on January 23, 1840; Van Buren signed the measure into law July 4, 1840.
2. See Kellogg to Polk, May 24, 1840.
3. Letter not found.

FROM ROBERT ARMSTRONG

Dear Sir, Nashville 1 July [18]40

Yesterday old Mr Smith[1] of Jackson County call'd on me, and said that while in the state convention that a peti[ti]on was sent from Jackson [County] praying that a clause be inserted in the constitution for the Emancipation of the Negroes of Tennessee. Those borne after such a time and others at 21 years &c.

I exam'd and found such a peti[ti]on and found it Signed by *Bransford*. I also found the Knox [County] peti[ti]on, gave Harris the names.[2] I recollect the opinions of the Mynatt family[3] on this subject. See Harris letter to the committee sent to day.[4]

Nicholson goes to Nolensville. We will make it a great day. You must try and come by way of Jackson. I know it is important. Declare yourself a Candidate and accept all Invitations.[5] Nicholson is in fine Spirits, and the news from every quarter is good. We have got Ewing in a tight place for his attack upon Coe.[6]

R ARMSTRONG

[P.S.] Say to the committee that I will answer their Invitation by next mail in time for publication. RA[7]

ALS. DLC–JKP. Addressed to Knoxville.

1. James W. Smith represented Jackson County in the Tennessee Constitutional Convention of 1834.

2. On July 13, 1840, J. George Harris published in the *Nashville Union* the abolition petition from the citizens of Jackson County to the delegates of the 1834 Constitutional Convention; Harris attributed the petition to Thomas L. Bransford and others. In the *Union* of August 6, 1840, Harris identified eighteen men by whom he had been called an abolitionist; all eighteen had participated in the Knox County abolition meeting of 1834.

3. Gordon and Joseph Mynatt signed the Knox County abolition petition in 1834. The opinions of the Mynatt family on abolition are not identified further.

4. Harris' letter, probably to the central corresponding committee of the Democratic Party in Tennessee, has not been found.

5. In his Knoxville speech of July 4, 1840, Polk announced he would run for reelection as governor in 1841. After that announcement Polk accepted invitations to speak at many rallies in Tennessee.

6. Speaking in Nashville on June 20, 1840, E. H. Ewing replied to an article in the *Nashville Union* of May 21, 1840, in which Levin H. Coe had alleged that William H. Harrison had voted for the indentureship of persons convicted of minor crimes in the Indiana Territory. See Levin H. Coe to Polk, June 19, 1840. The *Nashville Union* of June 25, 1840, reported that in his Nashville speech Ewing had accused Coe and J. George Harris of lying about Harrison's "white slave" vote; on July 6, 1840, the *Nashville Union* printed a letter by "Looker-On" announcing that Ewing disclaimed the charge of Coe and Harris' lying and that the *Union's* report of Ewing's speech erred in that regard. See Sarah C. Polk to Polk, July 11, 1840.

7. Armstrong wrote his postscript on the inside of his cover sheet. The invitation has not been identified.

FROM JOHN J. GARNER

Dear sir Yalobusha Miss July the 5, 1840

I received you letter of the 7th June[1] on yesterday. The articles which you awderd from Neworleans have arived at williams landing I lerned yesterday. I wil try and make arangements to send my waggon down in a few days. I wold like to send with some other waggon if I can. We are gowing down as the boy has now[2] noledg of the rout.

The negrows have bin very helthey except marier, matilda, Evy. Mariers helth has impruved very mutch since I wrote you before. Though she is better and worse the doct thinks I had better not put her in the farm until her helth is better. Evy has I believe got over the rheumatism and wil make two of her self in a few days. I cwep her out of the farm for fear of some acident. Matilda is sick at this time though considerably on the mend. I thought for some time I shold loose her. Something like the dopsey. She tels mee that she had the dropsey last fawl sow they had to whip her feet and legs with holey busheys to let the water from them. She is of now acount. She hasnt posatively done mee as mutch servis cence she has bin hear as old Ben. Hasnt worked more than half her time at best. I think we wil get her patched up again as she has bin before.

My crop is something better than I cold of expected from the season. It wrained hear awl the time until the last of May, then cuit sudentley. I havent had a good rain cence, though shours. They was a good rain last wensday in the settlement but did not retch mee. Doct Towns rode over my cotton with mee some two weaks a gow, stated he wold give the preference to my crop if any. A gentleman in our conterey past threw the lain a few days a gow, stated he had bin over the contery a good deele, and threw Tallahatchey Cty and that part of my cotton was a little better than he had seen. My late corn is very good and if I can have a few more rains in time I shal make a good crop.

My stock of hogs and catle apere to bwe dwoing wel. It was awl that I cold dwo to make the crop with the mules, owing to the rain in the spring, the hevy plowing and them miering awl the while. Severl of them give out in the spring, part of them two smawl for this contery.

J. J. Garner

ALS. DLC–JKP. Addressed to Nashville. Published in Bassett, *Plantation Overseer*, 142–44.

1. Polk's letter not found.
2. Misspelling of "no."

FROM SAMUEL H. LAUGHLIN

My dear Sir, McMinnville, July 5, 1840

The whigs, I suppose, in their own way, had a big day at Sparta on yesterday. I have seen none from there but whigs. They say *two thousand* persons were there. That is 500 more than White county, even in her old limits, can vote. It is therefore not true. Foster spoke the whole afternoon—they say. He arrived here in the stage this evening, travelling post to Nashville. His wife[1] met him I hear at Sparta, and is going home with him. I have seen him. He is sunbrunt, hoarse, and worn down. He has had at least 40 pounds of whig tallow sweated out of him in East Tennessee. He has need to repeat the prayer of Fallstaff made at Hern's oak, in the Merry Wives of Windsor, while he was waiting for the woman.[2] When the Sparta stage (Jenkin's)[3] delivered him here, it being *Sunday* afternoon, after he had gotten out at Sullivans,[4] the little whiglings, and a few fools, raised a Harrison flag on a Staff on the Stage, and dashed to the post office, and up and down the street two or three times, greatly to the edification of a few idle boys and country negroes, and to the disgust of all religious and soberminded people.

I wrote the day I left you at Lusk's, to Rice, Pope of Bledsoe, Duncan of Liberty, and Gen. Armstrong on the subject of the proposed appointments for you.[5] I think we shall have a real turn out at Bersheba, distant as the place is from the body of our population.

Tomorrow, I shall speak at Woodbury. Foster you see, will not be at Smithville. I have begged Hill to go there any how, but he has married a wife[6] and cant go. From Woodbury, I go to Murfreesboro where Chancery Court will be sitting, and where I must be for two or three days having a suit of my own as well as others. From there, I cut accross to meet Jones in Franklin, where I will be with him at several appointments. Being a whig, he has chosen the most inconvenient time for me, knowing of the Court at Murfreesboro. I will follow him up however, and be with him at Manchester and Hillsborough and Winchester. He will be at Hillsboro on 14th and here on 15th instant—I will then see his movements, and meet you on 18th. I am obliged to be at Winchester on Monday the 20th and have had notice given throughout Franklin. It is Circuit Court day. I had given out the appointment before I heard of Jones invasion. At Bersheba, we will see what is best to be done. God Speed.

S. H. Laughlin

ALS. DLC–JKP. Addressed to Jasper and marked "Private." On the cover Laughlin wrote, "If opportunity permits, will the Postmaster send this by private hand to Vanville by the 11th instant."

1. In 1817 Ephraim H. Foster married Jane Mebane Lytle Dickinson, widow of John Dickinson, under whose guidance Foster had studied law.

2. Reference is to Sir John Falstaff's line, "For me, I am here a Windsor stag; and the fattest, I think, i' the forest: send me a cool rut-time, Jove, or

who can blame me to piss my tallow?" William Shakespeare, *The Merry Wives of Windsor,* act 5, scene 5.

3. James H. Jenkins operated several mail routes, including one from Sparta to McMinnville.

4. Probably C. J. Sullivan, not identified further.

5. Lusk, George W. or William Rice, Jonathan Pope, Thomas H. Duncan, and Robert Armstrong. Lusk is not identified further. George and William Rice were members of the Democratic committee for Marion County. Pope served as postmaster of Mount Airy in Bledsoe County, 1837–43. Duncan headed a DeKalb County committee that on July 16, 1840, invited Polk to a public dinner at Liberty. LS. DLC–JKP.

6. Hugh Lawson White Hill married Virginia Ann Dearing of Lebanon on May 14, 1840.

FROM SARAH C. POLK

Dear Husband Murfreesboro' July 11, 1840

I have not received the first line from you since you left home, and cannot account for it only in one way, that you have directed your letter (if you have written one) to McMinnville or the Springs[1]—supposing I was there. It was our intention to go to the springs the early part of this week, but the bad weather has prevented. It has rained every day since Monday, so much rain here that it would have been madness in any one to travel, and the springs of all other places the worst in damp weather. We have been packed and ready to start every day this week. This being the last day of the week, the time intended to be spent on the mountain, almost expired, we have resolved not to go at all. Though if I knew any thing of your arrangements so that I could flatter myself that I would not be in the way, I might be induced to go in the stage on *monday evening.* But hearing that you had appointments on a different route to Nashville from this, I am at a loss to know how I was to get along in returning, so if I had received any information from you by the mail of to day, I could have made up my mind how to act. At the present moment I have no idea that I will go unless I can learn something from you by Monday afternoon, when the stage leaves for McMinnville. The time is so short there is no possible chance of going up in the carriage. Do write me when you go home; if you come this way I can wait for you, if not, *what day* will you be at home? You see from the want of information I am entirely at a loss what to do.

There is not much political news to be learned at this place. Our friends seem in good spirits. I am told that *Foster* did not brag much as he went through this place. I do not get much news from abrod as I see but few papers. Harris & Ewing had a fight[2] and *E. W. Dale* at Columbia has cut his throat.[3] This is all that I have heard of in the last few days. The Whig newpapers are out on the *traveling Executive* as you are termed, for a long absence and interference—and praying for the adjournment of Congress that John Bell can be at home to meet you on the stump. A poor compliment to their worthies at home. I think that you had better go home without taking to[o] many *little* places in your circuit.

Monday *morning*—I find this morning that it is impossible for me to go, in the carriage or stage. I regret but can not help it. I shall wait here until I hear from you. Nicholson is here and will [. . .][4] to day. You must make an [. . .] for me to Mr. Smart.[5]

SARAH POLK

ALS. DLC–JKP. Addressed to McMinnville or Beersheba Springs.

1. Beersheba Springs.

2. Passing references by J. George Harris in the *Nashville Union* of July 13, 1840, and by Levin H. Coe in the same of August 3, 1840, indicate that Harris and Edwin H. Ewing had a fistfight in Nashville the second week of July. Harris claimed that he used his right arm "to wipe out the stigma" of having been called a liar in the public prints.

3. Dale took his life at his home in Columbia on July 7, 1840; his suicide related to the 1839 "robbery" of the Columbia branch of the Bank of Tennessee. According to newspaper reports Dale left two suicide notes, dated July 3 and July 6, 1840. In the first note, he wrote that he had been done a "flagrant injustice . . . recently by a body of respectable men, occupying an important trust," which was more than he could bear. He denied that he had any knowledge of the identity of the bank's robbers and stated that he found it "exceedingly painful" to leave his endorsers heavily involved on his account. Dale's note of July 6, 1840, has not been found. It is probable that Edward Dale was accused of embezzlement by James Walker and the new Columbia bank directorate when they took control of the branch office in late June and early July 1840. On May 26, 1840, Walker had suggested to Polk that Dale ought to be continued as cashier; on July 23, 1840, Walker expressed a very different opinion of the late cashier. Francis G. Roche was bonded as cashier on July 6, 1840. See particularly James Walker to Polk, July 23, 1840. See also Walker to Polk, May 26, 1840, and A. O. P. Nicholson to Polk, July 28, 1840.

4. A tear on the left margin of the manuscript has obliterated words on two lines of the letter.

5. George R. Smartt, a farmer in Warren County, was one of the founders and owners of a summer resort at Beersheba Springs. A Democrat, he served in the Tennessee House, 1843–45.

FROM JOHN H. BILLS

Bolivar, Tennessee. July 18, 1840

Bills received Polk's "late favour"[1] concerning the organization of the Somerville branch, but did not attend the meeting, as he had declined reappointment as a director. Concerned that the meaning of his letter to Nichol, recommending Douglass, had been "perverted," Bill states that his recommendation was only on the contingency that Douglass was not a candidate for elector. The board was right to appoint Douglass after appointing Gordon, but "Banks & Politics Should be Kept as wide apart as Church & State." Cognizant that he differs with his "political friends" on the management of the Bank of Tennessee, Bills fears that the institution's future is dim and that the party in control will suffer "in reputation." Bills is pleased to learn of Polk's candidacy for reelection.[2]

ALS. DLC–JKP. Addressed to Nashville.

1. See Polk to Bills, June 18, 1840.
2. See Robert Armstrong to Polk, July 1, 1840.

FROM ADAM HUNTSMAN

Dear Sir Jackson 21st of July 1840

I am truly rejoiced to see that you have come out for the relection of Governor.[1] I suggested it to you last fall. I think now we have the game in our hands if we manage it discreetly. I learned from Gibbs when we were out on the canvass week before last that Foster would occupy Middle Tennessee untill the 1st of Sept then strike the District at Perryville canvass the Southern side in that month and the northern side in October. I have written to *Eph*[2] proposing a mutual and friendly canvass through the D, commence Speaking alternately, & each confine himself to a Speech of 2½ or 3 Hours, so that the people can hear us both at the same time and place. From what I can learn from his Terier, F W Parker,[3] he will not accede to it But depends upon playing the same game with me that he did with Johnson in E Tennessee claim the right to speak first and speak all day. Before I will submit to this chicanery I will not attend his appointments at all but make some for myself in his rear and on both of his Flanks as he progresses. If I can get one other hand with Coe and Totton I can do it Completely and read the copy of the letters (2) I have sent him proposing a manly discussion as an excuse to the people for the movement. Now Sir as Cannon is secretly out for Governor and made some Speeches in the District evidently upon that Hook, can you not Strike Henry[4] about the first of September or say the 15 or 20th and take a rapid tour through the counties of the District and head Foster while we are following him in his rear. We can get up any sort of dinners and invitations that may be necessary. His conduct deserves just such a course. Gibbs intends going with him through Tottens District. They cannot affect much for I have been out on a campaign or two & start again tomorrow. My opinion now is that we can hold our own in the District beyond question (to what it was in the August election). If you can in Middle and East Tennessee do the same Old Tip[5] is beat. Gibbs is the most reckless man I have come in contact with—David Crocket[6] not excepted. In fact he is politically a madman. I attended to some of Gibbs appointments in place of Totten. He carried Ash[7] with him to answer me. I made him so sick of it that he notified me if we spoke in Contact again that I should go first so as he could answer me. What do you think of the plan in respect of Foster. In the short days he will Speak untill sunset. What is the news in E Tennessee and on your rout home? Let me hear from you on all these points. Whigism has begun to flag. Now is our time exactly to parellel & press.

A HUNTSMAN

ALS. DLC–JKP. Addressed to Nashville. Published in *THQ*, VI, pp. 348–49.

1. Concerning Polk's announcement for reelection, see Robert Armstrong to Polk, July 1, 1840.
2. Ephraim H. Foster.
3. A lawyer, Felix Parker, Jr., represented Gibson County as a Whig in the Tennessee House, 1835–41 and 1847–49.
4. Henry County.
5. William Henry Harrison.
6. David Crockett.
7. John B. Ashe.

FROM JAMES WALKER

Dear Sir, Columbia July 23d 1840

You will have learned that contrary to your earnest advice, I have accepted the Presidency of the Branch Bank here.[1] I have so much respect for your opinions, and the sincerity of your friendship for all that I hold dear, that it is due both to you & myself that I should give you my reasons for acting contrary to your expectations. *I did not desire the station.* When Langtry resigned, I immediately proposed his re-election, with the view of sustaining him under some difficulties which had occurred with him in the Bank, and with the further view of making him the President. Upon persuasion he consented to serve as a Director upon being unanimously elected upon my motion. It was then proposed to ballot for President, every one voting their choice without any nomination. The result was for me 9, for Langtry 2, one of which was my vote. I do not know who the other voter for Mr. Langtry was. Whoever it was he voted with me my sincere wishes. I insisted upon declining acceptance and urged the election of Mr. Langtry. This he positively refused and all said I must not back out in the difficulty we found ourselves in. We found the Bank was in great confusion, and that Mr. Dale ought not to be continued an hour.[2] I saw that if I accepted the Presidency, we could get Langtry to act temporarily as Cashier, and I was satisfied that to refuse would be to give up the ship, and that all your reasons would not save me from censure, and a just charge of timidity under difficulties.

We all knew that the business of the Bank was in great confusion, and an additional deficiency apparent. A decisive leader was absolutely necessary. Whether I am to gain reputation or loose it by taking the lead, time is to determine. I resolved under the circumstances to try it, and my judgement since has been confirmed that I done right. There is but little difficulty in a sensible directory acquiring fair reputation, following the late board. The incompetency on all hands is glaring. In my station there need be no pecuniary risque or responsiblity. *I am determined there shall be none.* For fairness and impartiality and fidelity to the interest of the state I am willing to be responsible, and hope none of my friends will ever have cause to regret my course. I will see you in a short time and personally give you many explanations which are necessary in forming a judgement on this subject.

You know that Col. Smith has returned bringing with him $75000.[3] This makes a great difference with all concerned in that business.

JAMES WALKER

ALS. DLC–JKP. Addressed to Nashville and marked "Private & confidential."

1. Walker was bonded as president of the Columbia branch of the Bank of Tennessee on July 10, 1840.

2. See Sarah C. Polk to Polk, July 11, 1840, and James Walker to Polk, May 26, 1840.

3. See Alexander O. Anderson to Polk, February 4, 1840.

FROM SAMUEL H. LAUGHLIN

McMinnville, Tennessee. July 24, 1840[1]

Laughlin details political, business, and personal concerns that prevent his accepting an invitation to tour the Western District for the party. He will continue, however, to traverse the Mountain District. If Carroll will speak at Salem, where many of the deceived Whigs are his old companions in arms, the General can gain fifty votes for the Democrats.

ALS. DLC–JKP. Addressed to Nashville and marked "Private." AE on the cover states that Polk answered this letter on July 30, 1840; Polk's reply has not been found.

1. Laughlin dated his letter "Friday, July 25, 1840," but that date in 1840 fell on a Saturday. According to the postmark the letter was mailed on July 24.

FROM WILLIAM FITZGERALD

Dr Sir — Paris July 25, 1840

On the 27 August next the democrats have a festival at this place to which you will be formally invited & my object is to insist that you by all means attend.[1] We are taking Great pains to have an immense collection of people. I dont think we will have less than six or eight thousand. We will also invite various other distinguished Gentlemen of our party, among whom will be Genl. Carroll & I hope his health and business will permit him to come. His presence among the people will do much good. Our opponents in this part of the state are making uncommon exertions to carry the people, and we are resolved if they make any thing it shall be at the point of the bayonett. We will meet them at all points. This county[2] being the most populous in the district and being the strong hold of Democracy in this part of the state has been selected for our general festival at which we hope & expect to do some good. Be sure & come for we have promised the people your presence and we dont wish to forfeit their confidence by disappointing them.[3]

WM. FITZGERALD

ALS. DLC–JKP. Addressed to Nashville.

1. During the summer of 1840, Polk received numerous letters similar to Fitzgerald's, urging his acceptance of campaign invitations.

2. Henry County.

3. When Fitzgerald had received no acceptance from Polk by August 5, 1840, he and A. W. O. Totten wrote to Polk, insisting that he must "by no means omit to be with us." ALS. DLC–JKP.

FROM LEVIN H. COE

Dear Sir

Somerville July 26 1840

Your favor from Bersheba springs came to hand a few days ago.[1] I should have replied immediately but wished to reflect a little upon a part of it. In Tipton, Shelby, Fayette & Hardeman I think but little change can be effected in any way. The Whigs by an early huzza and promises of relief had shaken some of our friends. The smoke has passed off. In Tipton we have recoiled it upon them & are stronger than before. In Shelby it will be about as last year—we may gain a little but the town of Memphis exerts much influence. In this County[2] we will beat them. In Hardeman a gain of 100 votes. I dont think a speech from any person would be of much avail in either of these Countys. In McNairy I have got the ball to rolling finely in different parts of the County and dont think they can by any hook or crook prevent us from carrying the County. Huntsman is now in Henderson & Perry & will I expect write you an account[3] & can tell better than I whether a visit to either of those countys would be a benefit but I am under the impression a speech at Breadstown[4] in N.E. of the County and one at Perryville or Shake rag[5] would be advisable. The impression of many of our friends is that neither Tn or Hn[6] are producing much effect where they go. I have 4 appointments this week—2 in Haywood & 2 in Hardeman. The next several in Shelby & Tipton and the next 5 in McNairy—after which I must recruit[7] a little. My system is now prostrated—breast sore with head ache & fever almost every night. Douglass has put out to mid. Ten & fixed strikers over the Country to meet me.

Our enemies here are many and active. I am pretty well informed of their ways & think it would be imprudent to get as far off as middle Tennessee.

I think I had better remain here and take a tour through the northern Countys of the District in the fall.

By this mail I will write to Huntsman urging him to exchange with Laughlin. L's speaking will do more here than H's can & H's personal popularity will be available in the Mountain District.

The newspapers are asking how many "grants" are lying in the office awaiting the Govr signature whilst you were in E.T. Cant the Union[8] reply by telling how many you found lying in it & how old some of them were—also by some allusion to the Condition in which you found the office. I expect to speak publicly of these things at a meeting in the N.E. of Shelby on the 6th August where they are attempting to urge these complaints against you.

L. H. COE

[P.S.] Aaron V. Brown should promptly make speeches in different parts of Hardin County as soon as he returns. I fear we have sustained some loss there and that Jones cannot react it.

By this mail I have sent an answer to Ewings talk[9] which I have just written out in has[t]e. Examine & alter if you think fit.

ALS. DLC–JKP. Addressed to Nashville.

1. Letter not found.
2. Fayette County.
3. See Adam Huntsman to Polk, August 4, 1840.
4. Beardstown in Perry County.
5. Not identified.
6. A. W. O. Totten and Adam Huntsman.
7. Coe means "to recuperate."
8. The *Nashville Union*.
9. Coe's enclosure not found. The text of his reply to Edwin H. Ewing appeared in the *Nashville Union* of August 3, 1840. For Ewing's Nashville speech, see Coe to Polk, June 19, 1840, and Robert Armstrong to Polk, July 1, 1840.

FROM A. O. P. NICHOLSON

Dear Sir: Columbia July 27. 1840

I am very much embarassed by the appointments made for me in East Tennessee. If they had commenced in Sept. I might have made my arrangements to attend them without much sacrafice, but as things now are if I attend them I must leave three important courts. In my situation, with heavy debts hanging over me, the sacrafice is entirely too great. I assure you that I am grivously embarrassed as to my course. My inclination to go is strong, and I have concluded to take two more days to determine. I will write to you by Thursday's mail what my determination is—in the mean time the appointments through Wilson, Smith, &c. can be made for Trousdale and Carroll & it may be stated that I will probably be along.[1] This is all I can now say. You cannot appreciate the obstacles in my way. I have no idea of following up politics after the election and all that I now do is on account of my anxiety for the success of the cause.

I was much pleased to have so cheering an account from East Tennessee. There surely cannot be any doubt about our success. As to our prospects in the several counties around us here I feel the utmost confidence in saying that all's well. I am greatly deceived if we are not gaining slowly but steadily in almost every neighborhood. The Whig cause is decidedly at a stand, and there is a palpable tendency towards a re-action. We have been in somewhat of a dilemma as to the point of having a dinner. Some are for one general gathering at Lewisburg for the whole district, and others for a separate affair in each county. The latter plan, I believe, would be most acceptable if your arrangements would allow. Say at Websters on the 19th Aug—Lewisburg 21st & Shelbyville 22nd. We will stand still until we hear from you by return mail on this matter.

I wrote to Mrs. Polk in your absence for a volume of the Congress. Debates.[2] Dr. Young wrote to me that he had sent it through Gen. Armstrong. It has never arrived and I fear it has miscarried. We must have it. Thomas stands pledged to prove Harrison's speech in Todds H. Life[3] a forgery & it has to be done by that book. He will need it on the 4th at Lynnville. Please inquire into this & have it sent. If Harris has no further use for the Ohio Journals [4] I should be very glad to have them sent out by the first stage. I had to give my copy to Jones.

Our friends here are in fine spirits and are very active and zealous.

A. O. P. NICHOLSON

ALS. DLC–JKP. Addressed to Nashville.

1. References are to Wilson and Smith counties, William Trousdale, and William Carroll.

2. On July 19, 1840, Nicholson wrote to Sarah C. Polk, requesting loan of the second volume of the *Congressional Debates*, which contained William H. Harrison's speech of March 20, 1826, in answer to John Randolph's charge of Harrison's being a Federalist. ALS. DLC–JKP.

3. In 1840 Charles S. Todd and Benjamin Drake published a campaign biography entitled *Sketches of the Civil and Military Services of William Henry Harrison*. On pages 123–24 the authors include a variant text of Harrison's refutation of John Randolph's charge of federalism in 1826.

4. See Polk to Nicholson, May 28, 1840, and Nicholson to Polk, May 29, 1840.

FROM A. O. P. NICHOLSON

Columbia, Tennessee. July 28, 1840

Nicholson, writing in favor of the sureties of E. W. Dale, urges that their interests would be advanced and those of the state, not injured by disposing of their suit at the appearance term.[1] District Attorney Thomas has no objection to a trial at the August term if he is authorized by the president of the bank[2] and by Polk to appear at that time. Therefore, at the request of Dale's sureties, Nicholson asks Polk to write Thomas and indicate whether or not the case should be tried at the August court.

ALS. DLC–JKP. Addressed to Nashville.

1. See James Walker to Polk, May 26 and July 23, 1840.
2. Reference is to William Nichol, president of the Bank of Tennessee.

FROM ARCHIBALD YELL

My Dear Friend Waxhaws 28th July 1840

I reached home a few days since after an absense of more than three months, making a touer th[r]ough the state, preparatory to the Octr. election; I have now finished my labour and will rest upon my oars until after the election. Mr. Van Buren will receive the vote of this state without question. Judge Cross will be reelected to Congress and we shall have a majority in the Legislature tho. not large, and so fare; my prospect is fare to be the Govr. The Whigs have held their Convention and have made no nomination for Govr. which suited my own Convenience but was no advantage to our party, as we should have been able to have drawn the party lines much stronger if I had an opponant—and they seamed to take that view of the matter, and very prudently made no Nomination. So I shall in all probability be permited to walk over the tract *uncontested*. But theres no telling whos Govr. until after the Election. The Democrats have lost some ground in this state by the Suspension of our Infernal *Banks*. The paper has been from 25 to 40 per Cent discount and not recevable in the Land offices which created no little excitemt against the Banks and their managers who are mostly Democrats. I have had a fare feeler for my *Lo Co Fo Co* notions & they are now the popular doctrine in Arkansas. I shall if elected give a firm & decided Anti Bank message but it wont take withe the Legislature—"Instruct me." If our banks do not resume before the meeting of the Legislature this will force them beyond a doubt—and I shall not be surprised if they commenced winding up. Since the passage of the Independt Treasury Bill[1] our Banks may pro[ba]bly resume which I think most likely. If they can not with the *speicie Clause* they never will. I should like to have your views in relation to the policy of resumption & when and what ground I should assume if elected; I fear my hostility to *Corporations* may lead me astray and I am not disposed knowingly to do wrong. I sent you my circular which if you received would more fully explain the "position I have occupyed." Should the Democratic party have a majority in the next Legislature I presume Gov. Fulton[2] will be reelected to the Senate tho that is not altogether certain. He is sound in politics, but not very popular as a man, tho a worthy good man.

Just before I left home a few days I received your *private* Communication which I read & disposed of, as you sudgested.[3] I was not surprised at your determination tho I then & now think policy would have dictated a diferent course. But it has so turned out as to have placed you on high and enviable ground by your letter to Mr Grundy,[4] perhaps more to your advantage and certainly to the Democratic party much to be preferred. And I hope that you have for yourself & the Nation made a judicious decision. Your letter is of that tone and character as to endear you to the party, and such as the opposition can not in justice condemn. How very diferent is your letter from that Georgia *Aristocrat.*[5] For him I would not vote under any circumstances. I fell out with him the 1st Session I was in Congress and we have been *Introduced* at least a doz times since. We never know each other so we are "put together." I like old *Dick*[6] and at present he is the favorite of my state. But you are more popular with the people & better known here than any prom[ine]nt man now in public life, and with a fare and even start can beat any man, Tom Benton perhaps excepted. Your old Tennessee friends & acquaintances love and admire you.

Well old *Tip*[7] seems to give us no little trouble and it is not altogether certain that he will not beat our man.[8] Still I do not believe. If our Western & southern Banks all resume under the *Sub Treasury* I think it will have a good affect th[r]oughout the West & middle portion of the Country. If the[y] resist and times continue hard & not for the better we shall have an *uphill* business of it. Give me your *private* & *Confidential* oppin[io]n and say how will Ky., N.C. and Georgia go.

Present me to your good Lady most kindly and believe me . . . .

A. YELL

ALS. DLC–JKP. Addressed to Nashville.

1. See Miner K. Kellogg to Polk, June 30, 1840.

2. A Tennessee lawyer and military aide to Andrew Jackson in the 1818 Florida campaign, William S. Fulton moved in 1820 to Florence, Alabama, where he served seven years as county judge until his appointment in 1829 as secretary of the Arkansas Territory. Fulton became governor of that territory in 1835; won election as a Democrat to the U.S. Senate upon Arkansas' admission to statehood in 1836; and gained reelection to the Senate in 1840.

3. Date of Polk's letter is unknown.

4. See Polk to Felix Grundy, May 27, 1840.

5. John Forsyth. See Aaron V. Brown to Polk, May 9, 1840.
6. Richard M. Johnson.
7. William H. Harrison.
8. Martin Van Buren.

FROM MOSES G. REEVES[1]

Dear Sir; Murfreesboro. July 29th 1840

When Mr. Nicholson was here he expressed some doubts as to his trip to East Tennesseee. He told me if you thought it important for him to go he would willingly do so.[2] His speech here[3] was decidedly the best and was listened to with more attention than any other that has been made in the county by any body. I do hope that he will go to E. Ten. and fight manfully. Where ever that man goes he will have a crowd.

Yoakum has gone this morning to Cainsville.[4] Keeble will meet him & Burton on Friday & Saturday up in Cannon. At an election for a magistrate on Saturday last in the Fosterville District where the Feds in August got only 25 votes they only polled 20 for their man, this is one of the Districts that they have boasted about many changes &c. The Democrat candidate got 60 odd. Harris should lash *Hall*, the *Coon* & *Cabbins*. They are sick and tired here of the whole stuff.

M. G. Reeves

ALS. DLC–JKP. Addressed to Nashville.

1. Reeves was named register of Rutherford County in 1826 and served in that post for at least fourteen years.

2. See A. O. P. Nicholson to Polk, July 27, 1840.

3. Exact date of Nicholson's speech in Murfreesboro has not been identified; he left there for Nolensville on July 11, 1840. See Sarah C. Polk to Polk, July 11, 1840.

4. Henderson K. Yoakum wrote to Polk on August 4, 1840, that he had been to Cainsville and Statesville, and had found things "better than I expected at all those places." ALS. DLC–JKP.

FROM JOHN J. GARNER

Dear sir Yalabusha Miss August the 1 1840

I take my pen in hand to let you [k]now how we are getting own. We are awl wel except a little negrow child of Elizabeths[1] which has a bowel complant very bad. Matilda remains in bad helth though she is spinning.

The Dct.[2] says moderate exercise is an advantage to her. Evy has got over the rheumatism and has got a very likely yong negrow daughter. Marier apers to enjoy better helth at presant than cence I have bin here.

My crop is ingering at this time fast for the want of rain. My crop of cotton is shedding hits senars[3] and yong boles very fast. I havent had but one light season cence may. Once and a while a shour so light done very little good. Some neighborhoods they have had plenty of rain. I understand the rope and baling and other articles is at Williamses land-ding. When I got redy to hawl them, catle was dying with the muren[4] so fast in this contery hit so very hot and dry I thought best to let the hawling a lone until I am compeld to have them, or the wether moderats for I am satisfide if I send now I wil perhaps loose a part if not awl of my teem them not dwoing mutch threw the sumer and the wether so very dry and hot though I havent lost arey cow yet.

JOHN J. GARNER

ALS. DLC–JKP. Addressed to Nashville.

1. Elizabeth and her child were slaves.
2. A physician, known only as "Dr. Towns," regularly treated Garner and his charges.
3. Probably "centers."
4. Murrain.

FROM GEORGE W. JONES

[Fayetteville, Tennessee. August 1, 1840][1]

Jones writes that he is resigning his present position, for pecuniary reasons, to run for county court clerk.[2] Should he receive the clerkship, Jones declares that it will not interfere with his canvassing for election.[3] He states that he has been in every county of the district during the last month, and reports that "the good cause is in fine condition" there and that "the Democrats will be Stronger here in November next" than they were in the previous year.

ALS. DLC–JKP. Addressed to Nashville. AE on the cover states that this letter enclosed Jones' resignation from the Tennessee Senate and that his letter was answered on August 6, 1840; Jones' enclosure, dated August 1, 1840, is an ALS and is in T–Governor's Papers; Polk's reply has not been found.

1. Date and place of writing are taken from Jones' enclosed letter of resig-nation.
2. Jones represented Lincoln and Giles counties in the Tennessee Senate in 1839 and 1840; he served as clerk of Lincoln County from 1840 until 1843.
3. Jones ran for Democratic presidential elector in the Tenth Congres-sional District against Ebenezer Shields.

TO SAMUEL H. LAUGHLIN

My Dear Sir Nashville Augt. 2nd 1840

All the forces on both sides are in motion hereabouts. There was a meeting in the County on friday at which A. Ewing & Foster spoke. On yesterday there were three meetings. *Hollingsworth* attended one. Jo. C. Guild was expected to attend the second (I have not heard from them to day) and *Carroll, Cheatham, & A. Ewing* attended the *great one* on the Montgomery line. Little *Davy Dickinson*[1] had three meetings in Williamson last week. He was met by Hollingsworth at two of them & by Nicholson at the third. I have never witnessed such exertions as are making on both sides. I hope you are attending to Gibbs & Jarnigan in your District[2] and will give a good account of them. I will be at Charlotte on Wednesday, return here and be at Dover on the 13th. I will be here during the Federal convention.[3] After that I expect to visit my old District and the other large Counties in Middle Tennessee. I am much pressed to go to *Paris* on the 27th Instant and may have to yield, though my judgment is I could do more nearer home. *Fitzgerald* writes me[4] that it will be the largest collection of people ever held in the District. He calculates that there will be six or eight thousand people present; and he fears unless I go that they will have no foreign speaker. I might go and return immediately back again, but could not at that time attend any other points in the District. By that time *Gibbs & Jarnigan* will probably have left the Mountain District and Turney will be at home. I wish it were possible for you to be at *Paris* on the 27th and proceed from thence to meet appointments at the places of which we spoke. I am satisfied that you could effect more than any half dozen of our ablest men can do elsewhere in the same time. Armstrong and myself have consulted upon the subject, and have concluded, if your professional & private affairs will permit it, that if you will authorize us or either of us to send out the appointments for you, that *Hollingsworth*, will go immediately to your District and speak from day to day in your absence, at such points & times as you may designate as proper for meetings. If Foster goes to the District whilst you are there—as is intimated in the Banner a day or two since, Huntsman & Totten will relieve you of him whilst in their District, so that you could attend your own independent appointments. Huntsman will I have no doubt come to the mountain, between then and November, selecting a time when Foster will not be in the District. *Boling Gordon* and *Jonas E. Thomas Esqr.* will shortly set out on a grand tour through *Lawrence, Wayne, Hardin & Perry*. It is a desperate battle and now is the time to fight. Write me immediately whether you can possibly accede to the proposition to be at *Paris*—and proceed from thence on the tour suggested.[5] If you can and insist upon it I would go with you to *Paris*, though my judgment is, that if *Cheatham* & yourself will go without me (and Cheatham says he will accompany you) that I could do more at the present in *Franklin, Lincoln, Bedford, Marshall, Giles, Maury* & *Lawrence;* and on my return from these in *Wilson, Smith* & *Williamson;* and if need be, go to the District in October. Let me hear from you.

James K. Polk

P.S. Dr. Young has recovered, but Mrs. Y. is yet quite ill.[6] J.K.P.

ALS. PHi–Samuel M. Clements, Jr. Coll. Addressed to McMinnville and marked "Private."

1. David W. Dickinson, a Murfreesboro lawyer, served one term in the Tennessee House, 1831–33, before winning election in 1833 as a Democrat to the U.S. House. In 1843 Dickinson ran as a Whig and won a second term in that body.
2. See Samuel H. Laughlin to Polk, August 3, 1840.
3. Whigs from eleven states assembled in Nashville on August 17, 1840; a campaign address by Henry Clay highlighted the convention program.
4. See William Fitzgerald to Polk, July 25, 1840.
5. See Samuel H. Laughlin to Polk, August 7, 1840.
6. John S. Young's wife is not further identified.

FROM SAMUEL H. LAUGHLIN

My dear Sir, McMinnville, August 3, 1840

I received your favor of July 30th[1] on the day before yesterday, in the evening and hasten to reply to it. I had written to Mr. Huntsman about the 25th ultimo, advising him of my situation and engagements, approving of his arrangements for meeting Foster, and informing him that if he *could* come to the upper part of this district,[2] I hoped much good would result from it. It will be impossible for me, in view of my duties and engagements here, to be in Paris on the 27th instant[3]—but if at any time hereafter, in the course of the canvass, I can make it possible to visit the District, I will do so, even if it is at a late day; and if I find I can do so, I will advise you and Gen. Armstrong, and our friends in the District of it. Gibbs has done nothing up here so far. He has certainly *lost votes*, by causing from seven to five men at least to turn against Harrison and for us at Woodbury. Here, he disgusted many of his old acquaintances—men who had been his former personal friends—and has made them more zealous than ever in our cause. He can do us less harm than any man who could have been sent here. His real business here is to attend to his old private business and lawsuits. He is now at Sparta.

I shall have the pleasure to-day, of addressing a very large collection of the real people of Warren. I shall do so fully, and, I doubt not, with excellent effect, as I shall be heard by those who are willing to hear, and by some who are in doubt. Next Monday is Circuit Court at Smithville. I shall have a good Congregation there. I shall follow up the *poachers*[4] who have been sent up here, through the whole upper part of the district, having most of my appointments at favorable country places. When Turney arrives, we will scour the whole district, and my life for it, we will give an increased majority upon last Summer's election.

I am rejoiced to see that our friends are in proper spirits, and proceeding under proper arrangements in your part of the state; and that Gen. Carroll, Mr. Hollingsworth, Col. Guild, Mr. Cheatham and others are properly "to the fore" as the irish expression has it.

The Log Cabin, empty barrel convention[5] will be a poor affair at Nashville, and however numerously attended, will operate, when properly used, to the detriment of our foes. It will be, in its character and effects, a handsome commentary on the hard times of which they complain—and upon their false pretense of desiring to address and inform the intelligence and judgment of the people. It will be attended by the rich, the dependants of the rich—bank men—merchants and their sons and clerks—by speculators, loafers, and the whole train of your gentlemen of leisure who live from hand to mouth upon credit about the towns. For my part, I am glad to see the parade gotten up. I can and will make votes out of it in my *beat.*

I desire exceedingly, as I mentioned in my last,[6] that you and Gen. Carroll should both visit Franklin. Tell the Gen. that Captain *Barby Collins*[7] and perhaps fifty votes will depend on the circumstance of his making a speech in Salem in that County. Nearly all Bean's Creek[8] have at sometime or other (all the old men) been with him in the army. I mention fifty votes as the lowest computation which he can gain at that point by his personal attendance.

I do hope that you can go to Paris as is desired. *Your* presence, and not mine, is what will do the work.

I hear from Liberty, that your effort there,[9] has gained for us at least twenty-five votes. I learn it from Mr. Savage[10] who was there—has seen the people living there since, and who, himself, lives at Smithville.

I have no certain information, though I expect to hear today, of the approaches and arrangements of our Congressional friends for their short homeward campaign through East Tennessee. When Brown gets home, he or George W. Jones, or both, ought to speak at Murfreesboro—Jones to effect a change among the strong mechanical interest there, which is against us, and Brown to produce effect among his friends, and neutralize the efforts of his kinfolks.

S. H. LAUGHLIN

P.S. I am sorry to hear of the affliction [of] Dr. Young and his family.[11] I hope they are convalescent.

ALS. DLC–JKP. Addressed to Nashville.

1. Letter not found.
2. Tennessee's Fifth Congressional District.
3. The Democracy of Henry County planned to hold a festival on August 27, 1840.
4. Whig politicians Spencer Jarnagin from Athens, Tennessee, and Micah Taul from Winchester, Tennessee, campaigned in Laughlin's district. Taul, formerly from Kentucky, served one term in the U.S. House, 1815–17, before moving to Tennessee.
5. See Polk to Laughlin, August 2, 1840.
6. See Laughlin to Polk, July 24, 1840.
7. Barby Collins served as a captain in the Tennessee militia during the War of 1812; he is not identified further.
8. Reference is to voters in the area of Bean's Creek, a small stream in southwestern Franklin County.
9. In response to an invitation from the citizens of DeKalb County, Polk attended a public dinner at Liberty on July 23, 1840.
10. Reference probably is to one of the brothers John Houston Savage or Abram Monroe Savage, both of whom were Democratic politicians and lawyers in Smithville. John H. served in the U.S. House, 1849–53 and 1855–59, and in the Tennessee House, 1877–79 and 1887. Monroe served in the Tennessee House in 1857.
11. See Polk to Laughlin, August 2, 1840.

FROM LEVIN H. COE

Dear Sir Somerville Augt 4th 1840

By to days mail I barely had time to drop a line to Genl. A.[1] which I suppose you have seen. The Justices will (3) attend at 10 A.M. tomorrow to hear the case.[2] They will be two Whig to one Demo. There is less excitement than could have been expected. This I account for for two reasons. 1st: That I was clarly justifiable and therefore they can not make capital out of it against me. 2 That P. T. S. was pushed on to the attack by others who are behind the curtain and they fear an expose might be made.

A summary of the difficulty is as follows. In the Bolivar paper of the 18th ult. an Editorial article appeared which bore very tight upon him.[3] I learned he charged the authorship of it upon me. This caused me to call on him on the 21st and assure him I had neither written, contributed to or advised it & knew not that the paper would name his name until I saw it in print. Notwithstanding this on the 25th a bitter article signed "Junius"[4] came out in the Somerville paper[5] making a heavy fling at Fentress[6] (not by name) also at "a certain file leader of the party" charging 1st Authorship of Bolivar article, 2nd That in a public speech he had said "he thanked his God he never had been a member of a church & never expected to be," 3rd That in his speeches in 1839[7] he was in the habit of casting contempt upon the ceremonies of religion.

It was rumored in Somerville that Scruggs avowed the authorship of "Junius" and said he alluded to me as the file leader.

On Thursday last I learned he had gone to make a speech in the East of this County. I reached the ground whilst he was speaking & in answer I gave him a reply which told with some effect & mortified him no little. To my questions he admitted in substance our talk of 21st. Refused to admit or deny the authorship of *Junius* or that he had said he alluded to me as the "file leader" &c. I then charged it upon him & pronounced all the assertions as applied to me false. He rose and said he would prove upon me the words "I thank my God" &c. to be true. After some further remarks he said he would meet the people at another time & in an ill natured & threatening manner & Mr Coe elsewhere. I replied yes Sir, wherever you wish to see me.

On my return from home last evening I recd. a letter, quite insulting in its tone enclosing me a certificate signed by 6 little whigs[8] (3 of whom are of the set which manage the printing office here) & that I had made the remark in my speech and in an insulting manner giving me until 10 A.M. to day to apologise &c. This drew from me a cutting letter in which I exhorted him to publish the certificates (I knew well I could get the certificates of double the number that theirs was false).

My letter was handed to him about 8 Oclock. After he read it he came twice into W. A. Jones'[9] store where I was, no notice of the other by either Tho I saw a pistol in his bosom. After he left the 2nd time a friend[10] & myself walked into a yard near the counting room door and sat some time talking. I noticed Scruggs in sight during the time. When we separated I stepped to the Counting room Desk, found paper lying on it and commenced writing a letter. I had just commenced when some person passed me. I did not lift my head to see who. A few moments after (it was Scruggs) I heard him say, Mr. Coe you have insulted me Sir. I looked round. He had a chair lifted over his shoulder & was rushing upon me. I sprang off the stand I was upon, from him as I did so drew & cocked a pistol & in a moment fired—shooting through a slat of the chair & thro the center of his body about 2 inches above the navel, I fear & have but little doubt, a fatal shot.

The evidence will be that he lifted the chair before he spoke & whilst my back was to him—that it was in a striking position & he in 6 feet when I fired. W. A. Jones catching at the chair & W. Burton[11] at my arm. Also that when examined Mr Scruggs had 2 pistols belted round him and a dirk. I will keep this [letter] open until after the trial to morrow. Of my acquital before impartial justices I have no doubt. Neither have jud[g]es W. T. Brown & Austin Miller[12] who are in town. But will not my remaining on the Electoral Ticket do a prejudice? Will not the proper plan for me be to withdraw & publish a calm appeal, in so doing to the people of Tennessee reviewing the past & present position of parties &c? I have heretofore got on well. A fine gain is going on. With the items I can give them others can get on about as well as I can.

I will consult fully with my friends to morrow night, and write further. I wish to pursue that course which will make this unfortunate affair do least damage to the Republican principles I have always venerated.

Augt 6—The trial progressed yesterday so far as to examine the 3 witnesses who saw it.[13] One feeling only prevails that I was justifiable. I will prove positive threats from him before the letters passed between us that he intended to take my life.

I will write you in full by next mail.

L. H. Coe

[P.S.] The old gray headed Democratic farmers all over the Country hearing threats were made by some few hot headed persons to attack me are collected in hast[e] & prepared to repel all things like an attack.

ALS. DLC–JKP. Addressed to Nashville.

1. Robert Armstrong.

2. Coe shot Phineas T. Scruggs on August 3, 1840; the Fayette County Court ruled that Coe acted in self defense; and Scruggs recovered from his injury.

3. Reference probably is to the Bolivar *Sentinel;* no issues of this paper have been found.

4. "Junius" was the pseudonym used by a celebrated Whig polemicist who wrote for the London *Public Advertiser,* 1769–71.

5. Established in 1837, the *Somerville Reporter* was conducted by John C. Reeves from 1838 until 1844.

6. David Fentress, a lawyer in Bolivar, served in the Tennessee House as a Democrat, 1841–43.

7. Reference is to Tennessee's political campaign of 1839.

8. Not identified further.

9. William A. Jones, a farmer and merchant in Somerville, served in the Tennessee House, 1847–49.

10. Not identified further.

11. William Burton of Somerville served as chairman of the Fayette County Court, 1841–44, and as clerk of the Eleventh Circuit Court, 1840–65.

12. William T. Brown and Austin Miller. Brown, formerly a law partner of James P. Grundy in Nashville, served as Sixth Circuit Court judge, 1836–38, before establishing a legal practice in Memphis. Miller practiced law in Bolivar; served as Eleventh Circuit Court judge, 1836–38; and won election as a Democrat to three terms in the Tennessee House, 1843–47 and 1861–63.

13. The third witness, in addition to Jones and Burton, has not been identified.

FROM ADAM HUNTSMAN

Dear Sir Jackson 4th day of Augt. 1840

Your two letters of the 26th ultimo from Nashville and previous one from Bersheba Springs was duly recd.[1] the 2 last on yesterday as I had been absent one week on the canvass and one at Court. In relation to Fosters movements and refusal to meet in fair discussion and some other matters and going to the mountains I refer you to Judge Catrons letter of this date which I requested him to submit to you and Carroll.[2] The time has arrived when I am willing to fight upon any ground that may be chosen for me by my friends. You will see the dose I am preparing for Ephraim[3] when he comes through the District. Whatever determination may be made respecting my Trip to the mountains, I wish to be apprized of it immediately so that I may arrange my business accordingly. I discover we can hold our own in the District. I had just commenced raking the district and had intended to Speak at three or four places in each County and had finished two of them. There is great necessity for a thorough surge in Carroll, Gibson, Henderson, Madison and Haywood and a light blessing upon some of the rest which your aid could be manifestly advantageous and when you can make it convenient you should call if possible upon those counties. But if no person, able and capable, can be got to supply my place I think it of doubtful policy to leave the District. To Foster we might loose more than we would gain by it. If Foster Strikes the District the 1[st] of Sept he will get out about the 16th of October into Wayne, Lawrence &c. I intend to read a copy of my letter to him and his refusal to meet me,[4] every where & my letter to Bell in 1836 also, when I discovered that he was going over to the Federal[i]sts. Mr Fitzgerald informs me that he is greatly anxious that you should fall down on the District at Paris on the 27 Inst. If you could I think it might have a fine effect. I have this moment got Fosters appointments and enclose them to you.[5] I have arranged the Northern District here so that Foster will be followed according to the plan in Judge Catrons letter and will write to Coe this evening with a view to make an arrangement for him in the South. If I go to the mountains I wish by all means for Gov Carroll to go with me. There are very many of his old Soldiers in that quarter.

A. Huntsman

ALS. DLC–JKP. Addressed to Nashville. AE on the cover states that this letter was answered on August 9, 1840; Polk's reply has not been found. Huntsman's letter was published in *THQ*, VI, pp. 349–50.

1. Letters not found.
2. John Catron's letter to Polk and William Carroll was subsequently sent to Samuel H. Laughlin. See Polk to Laughlin, August 9, 1840.
3. Ephraim H. Foster.
4. See Huntsman to Polk, July 21, 1840.
5. Enclosure not found.

FROM WILLIAM S. HAYNES

Dr Sir, Shelbyville Ten. Augst 5th 1840

Upon my arrival at home from Nashville I consulted with several of our political friends with regard to your visiting us, and find them anxious for you to do so; but those who have heretofore been most active in getting up public dinners, I find now unwilling to contribute for that purpose. This change of feelings originates entirely in the recent Bank appointments at this place, and the hardness of the times. One of these two causes are assigned by former active friends for their present apathy. It would be well if you could pay us a visit, so as to heal whatever of dissentions that may have crept in among us, without any thing further than to address, and mingle with, the people. If you will come down, please say so to me by return mail; and it now being Court week here, I can get some hundred or so to a letter of invitation to visit your old constituents and address them. This mode would have a better tendency perhaps, than to get up a public dinner and would give you an opportunity for seeing your old friends and acquaintances and of setting yourself right before them in every point of view. The Feds too, would, by pursuing this course, be deprived of all their sterotype slang against you, of fortifying your self behind a dinner table to prevent discussion. Make the meeting a public one, and the gentlemen could attend and address the people *after you had finished,* provided the people would hear them.

Ex-Gov Cannon addressed the people here on Monday, in reply to Colo. Yoakum, and a most miserable piece of stuff it was. "O faith." He spoke against sense (common), truth, justice, and the Kings english. Each were *badly* murdered by him. Some of his allusions to Genl. Jackson were *ungentlemanly, unmanly,* and *dasterdly mean, and low life,* but all was swallowed by his federal followers in high gusto. He took occasion also to allude to you and your canvass of last summer, the purposes of it &c &c, all of which, I have no doubt, will be *revised, improved* and reported for the Nashville papers, where I doubt not you will see it. Yoakum's address was a weak, pointless affair, and did us no good.[1]

There is no changes taking place in the county of any importance so far as I can learn, but the republicans are acting less in concert than I ever knew them. It requires a strong stimulant, such as you can administer, to get them all at their post as they should be. You should by all means give it [to] them if possible.

The Feds are preparing their county Banner, building their log cabins &c &c, preparatory to a visit to your city on the 17th, to the *Tom foolery* convention.[2] Some two or three hundreds, perhaps more, will attend from this county, headed by the Martins, Armstrongs &c.[3] What an association for men professing republican doctrines!!!

The Banner is preparing by Mr Cooper, of your place, a portrait painter.[4] A fat job that, for a [. . .][5] Federal Whig of another county. The getting up [of] the banner, I learn, has produced some maneuvering in the ranks, and may be productive of good. R. A. Wrench[6] a rank Whig, not yet naturalized, but has always voted, expected the job and failed to get it. I learn from good authority, that *he* curses the party and has left them, and that some of his friends will probably follow. Thus it is that "Coonery," martial parades in politics, an[d] foolish show, has ever operated.

Let me hear from you, if convenient, by next mail so that I may know what course to pursue to meet your feelings and wishes and ever believe me . . . .

WM. SCOTT HAYNES

ALS. DLC–JKP. Addressed to Nashville.

1. On August 4, 1840, Yoakum wrote that he had met Cannon at Shelbyville the previous day. In a speech of three hours, Yoakum examined Harrison's public record and described as "federalists" those who had supported Adams after his Presidential Message of December 1825. ALS. DLC–JKP.

2. See Samuel H. Laughlin to Polk, August 3, 1840.

3. James L. Armstrong and possibly Abram Martin. A Shelbyville physician, Armstrong was an outspoken Whig. Martin was a Shelbyville lawyer.

4. Reference is to Bedford County's standard to be used at the Whig festival in Nashville. W. B. Cooper, a Nashville artist and portrait painter, had sculptured a bust of Andrew Jackson in 1819 and had painted a portrait of Justice John McLean in 1834.

5. A tear in the manuscript has obliterated at least one word.

6. Wrench is not identified further.

FROM SAMUEL H. LAUGHLIN

My dear Sir, McMinnville, August 7, 1840

I have looked carefully over a table of all my courts and engagements here, and find that by missing only one court (Coffee), to which I can depute a friend, I can go to the Western District, or any place our friends may think I can do any good, from the 1st of October up to the day of the Election. I have consulted our friend Ridley, and in full view of my duties, engagements as to time, duty to clients which involves meat and bread with me, and he concurs fully with me in opinion, that I ought to devote my time sedulously to politics and the courts in this District til that time. From that day (1st Oct.) I will, if it is desired, hold myself ready to obey orders, and march to any point, you, Gen. Armstrong, or the Central Committee of Correspondence may designate.

We hold it absolutely necessary, if possible, that you should go to Paris. I do not expect to be at the great Raccoon Show at Nashville.[1] I shall be in Franklin [County] at that time.

Mr. Huntsman, if possible, must be ordered into Overton, Jackson, and White in October—unless he can be better employed in entertaining Foster which I think will be the case. He is assuredly the man of all others to meet and beat Ephe[2] at his own weapons. All in all up in this region—from Fentress to Franklin—and I am well advised—Jones, *Jonakin,*[3] and Gibbs have lost votes to their party—and have made no converts. I shall be in all the upper counties, and in Bledsoe, in the next few weeks. Whig zeal and confidence, both real and affected is dying away here. The Coon Show, I suppose will revive it.

Harris and Coe have really used up all the imprudent, petty fogging efforts of Ewing and others to explain Harrison's approval and votes on selling men for fines and costs.[4] I am very glad to see that the folly of one Ewing, and the run-mad course he is pursuing, has not had any tendency to cool the zeal and useful efforts of his worthy brother.[5]

I must still recur to the necessity of Gen. Carroll going to Franklin—to Salem.

Two of my children are very ill in Nashville.[6] If I do not hear of their being better by next mail, I shall be compelled to come down on Sunday. One of my hard rides, which I can accomplish at any time of emergency, will take me there in a day and night.

S. H. LAUGHLIN

ALS. DLC–JKP. Addressed to Nashville.

1. Reference is to the Whig festival scheduled for Nashville on August 17, 1840. See Laughlin to Polk, August 3, 1840.
2. Ephraim H. Foster.
3. Spencer Jarnagin.
4. See Polk to A. O. P. Nicholson, May 28, 1840; Levin H. Coe to Polk, June 19, 1840; and Robert Armstrong to Polk, July 1, 1840.
5. The "worthy brother" was Andrew Ewing, a Democrat; the Whig brother was Edwin H. Ewing.
6. Neither the children nor the nature of their illness has been identified.

FROM JAMES M. HOWRY[1]

Oxford, Mississippi. August 9, 1840

Howry advises that Mississippi's Democratic electors support Polk's vice-presidential bid. Howry has attended a Whig festival recently and considers the meeting a failure.[2] No "stars" addressed the crowd. Tennessee orators vented "their malignant spleen" upon Polk, but the Democrats will carry Mississippi. Howry adds that in Oxford Harris' energy and ability are acknowledged to be "of the highest order."

ALS. DLC–JKP. Probably addressed to Nashville.

1. Formerly a resident of Hickman County, Tennessee, Howry moved in 1836 to Oxford, Mississippi, where he continued to practice law. In 1840 he lost a special election for judge of the circuit court, but the next year won the regular election for that post.

2. The Whigs met on the state line between Mississippi and Tennessee; exact location and time of the meeting have not been identified.

TO SAMUEL H. LAUGHLIN

My Dear Sir

Nashville Augt. 9th 1840

Your letters of the 3rd and 7th Instant are before me. I have also before me two letters from Huntsman of the 4th Instant—one addressed to myself and the other to a leading political friend here who does not engage actively in politics,[1] and which I am permitted herewith to enclose to you, for your information as to Huntsman's movements. I send also a list of *Foster's* appointments for the District.[2] You will see from Huntsman's letter that he can, if desired enter the mountain District—the last of Augt. or 1st of September, spend a fortnight there, and be back in time to attend to Foster—whose first appointment will be on the 14th of September. Foster's appointments in the District you see extend to the 19th of October—so that if Huntsman does not come to the mountains—the last of the present month he cannot come at all. I regret exceedingly that your engagements—will not permit you to spend two weeks in the District, commencing at the great meeting at Paris on the 27th, and still hope *in view of the great importance of the movement,* that you can so arrange your private affairs, as to enable you to do so. I dislike to be too importunate with friends—who I am aware have already submitted to great sacrifices—and will not I trust be so regarded by you. If however it is still possible for you to go with me to *Paris* (I have determined to go) and be there on *thursday* the 27th Augt.; on *friday* 28th at Huntington[3]; on *saturday* 29th at *Pleasant Exchange* on the line between Henderson & Madison; on *monday* the 31st at *Lexington;* on *tuesday* the 1st Sept. at *Mifflin* in Henderson 15 miles from Lexington; on *wednesday* the 2nd at *Jackson;* on *thursday* the 3rd at *Denmark* in Madison—12 miles from Jackson; on *saturday* the 5th at *Brownsville;* on *monday* the 7th at *Trenton;* on *tuesday* the 8th at *McLemoresville* on the line between Gibson & Carroll; on *Thursday* the 10th at *Camden* in Benton; and on *friday* the 11th at *Waverly* in Humphreys. I am thoroughly satisfied that more good could be done, than by any movement now in our power. At *Waverly* you would be within 2 moderate days ride of Nashville, and could reach home by the 15th. If it be possible for you to do so, advise me of it by the return mail, and I will immediately have hand-bills struck and send the appointments in advance of you. If you will do this I am authorized by Huntsman in his letter to me to make appointments for him in the mountain—commencing on the 31st Augt. & extending to the 10th Sept. and if you can do so, will make the appointments for him, and immediately advise him of it, on receipt of your letter. If you cannot do so, *Huntsman* thinks he cannot safely leave the District. *Totten* I am advised will accompany you, at the appointments suggested for the District, if you can possibly—leave home at that time. *Boling Gordon* and *Barkley Martin* will commence a tour through *Lawrence, Wayne, Hardin* and *Perry* about the 20th Inst. *A. V. Brown* is here in good health and spirits. The Whig story of his having wo[u]nded himself, in a recontre with *Bell* which you have seen in the newspapers,[4] is all sheer fabrication. *Cave Johnson* is at home & in improved health; and will go with us to *Paris*. Great anxiety exists here to hear the particulars of the fight between *Coe & Scruggs*.[5] The fear is that *Scrugg's* wound may be mortal, and that *Coe* may be involved in trouble, though the rumour is, that he acted strictly in self defense.

I have seen Mr. *Kizer*.[6] Your children who were sick are much better.[7] Mr. K. will write you, concerning your visit to the District. All your friends concur in the opinion that it is very important. *Turney* will be at home by the last of the month & he & *Hollingsworth* if necessary, can accompany Huntsman in your District whilst you are gone. I will see that *Carroll* goes with me to *Salem* in Franklin—as you request. We will fix *the day*, before we go to Paris. Write me by return mail as it is important that the arrangement between *Huntsman* and yourself, if made should be made without a moment's delay—so that ample notice may be sent out.

JAMES K. POLK

ALS. DLC–JKP. Addressed to McMinnville and marked "*Private*." On the cover Polk requests the postmaster to deliver this letter upon its arrival. AE on the cover states that this letter was answered on August 11, 1840. Published in *ETHSP*, XVIII, pp. 157–58.

1. On August 4, 1840, Adam Huntsman enclosed letters from John Catron to Polk and William Carroll; Catron's letters, both dated August 4, 1840, have not been found.

2. Second enclosure not found.

3. Misspelling of "Huntingdon."

4. Reprinting a story that originated in the Baltimore *Sun*, the *Nashville Whig* of July 31, 1840, and the Nashville *Republican Banner* of August 1, 1840, reported that Aaron V. Brown wounded himself badly with his own knife in an altercation with John Bell at the Capitol in Washington City.

5. See Levin H. Coe to Polk, August 4, 1840.
6. Timothy Kezer.
7. See Laughlin to Polk, August 7, 1840.

FROM SAMUEL H. LAUGHLIN

My dear Sir, McMinnville, Aug. 11, 1840

Leaving home unwell on yesterday morning early for Smithville, I was compelled to stop at Mountain Creek, ten miles from home at Col. Paris, and get home as best I could. I have had, and now have symtoms of fever, and severe diarrhea, but am getting well—as I hope, by medicine and quiet.

I give up every regard to my private interests—for my personal convenience I have no regard—and will go with you to Paris, and fill the list of appointments you propose in your letter of the 9th, going from Paris to Huntingdon, and ending at Waverly on the 11th of September—and have authorized Mr. Kezer by letter of this date, to have the appointments advertised in handbills and papers, or as may be best. I wrote to him fully by Mr. W. Argo who goes down in the stage—sending other things by him besides the letter.[1] I expect Col. Totten to go with me. Perhaps you will be at Huntingdon. If so, should the notice state it? See Kezer.

I have written to Huntsman that if he does not hear from me again, he must leave home in time to be in the upper part of this district by *Monday, August 31st,* and that if he gets no list of appointments sooner, he will find them with Gen. Armstrong or Col. Harris as he goes up—that I will have a copy left with each of them. I would have them printed instantly, but hope to see Turney in a day or two—and wish them to suit his convenience, unless it should be about the time you will be in Franklin [County]—which I expect it will not be.

When I was prevented from getting to Smithville, our friend Thos. H. Hopkins,[2] a lawyer from Mississippi, lately settled here, went down to make a Speech. He will do so with effect. He has been used to it last canvass in Mississippi, and made a good speech at Newby's[3] in this county on Saturday last. He is a nephew of old Tom Hopkins, and married to Rowan's sister.[4] Gibbs made a total failure at Smithville as Col. Paris called to inform me to day. Hopkins will speak there tomorrow or next day.

I hope the renegade shot by Coe will not die.[5] I am truly rejoiced that Coe stands, as far as we hear, totally justified.

I wish you would drope me a line, or that Kezer would, stating what day you think it best to leave Nashville for Paris. I wish to leave home so as to have a day to remain in Nashville before leaving.

Ford has in type an article upon the cattle man's case about the changes.[6] When some absentees get home, he will make it a case, as to some of the men, of perfect forgery. The trip down compels me to miss three courts—but it will all go in my lifetime—and not be missed from the time in the final account.

S. H. LAUGHLIN

ALS. DLC–JKP. Addressed to Nashville. AE on the cover states that this letter was answered on August 15, 1840.

1. Neither W. Argo nor Laughlin's shipment has been identified further.
2. A lawyer at McMinnville, Hopkins served as a Democrat in the Tennessee House, 1841–43.
3. Not identified further.
4. Eliza Rowan Hopkins, sister of Stokely D. Rowan.
5. See Levin H. Coe to Polk, August 4, 1840. The "renegade" refers to Phineas T. Scruggs.
6. Citing other Tennessee newspapers, the Nashville *Republican Banner* of July 6, 1840, reported that a citizen from Warren County offered to bet a large number of cattle that there had been thirty-five changes from Van Buren to Harrison in a single precinct in Warren County. Immediately below, the *Banner* printed a supporting letter with thirty-five named signers.

FROM HARVEY M. WATTERSON

Dear Sir, Sparta Aug 14th 1840

We landed here to day, after having addressed the people at several points in E Tennessee.[1] Mr Grundy will give you all the particulars. In some counties in that portion of the state we have gained, and in some I fear we have lost. Upon the whole things stand pretty much as they did last August, though many of our leading friends think a change is now going on in favor of the Democratic cause. I am satisfied we are stronger in Sullivan, Washington, Greene and Hawkins than we ever have been.

I see Foster is to speak at Columbia, Lewisburg and Shelbyville. Rely upon it I will attend to *his case*, and if he attempts his Gagery[2] upon me, he will find himself in hot water. I discover also that Henry has an appointment at Lewisburg on the 22d inst. I shall be there on my way to Columbia Court, and will not suffer his speech to go unanswered.

We have a desperate fight on hand, but if all our friends will do their duty, victory is certain. By the by we met with Arnold at several places

& I heard his speeches. Now just such an unprincipled blackguard it has seldom been my misfortune to know. He is without talent too, if the speeches I heard were fair specimens of his powers. At Rutledge he got drunk and he and Brownlow sung Tippecanoe songs[3] in the Bar room at the tavern, loud enough to be heard half a mile. Such things must operate against them.

I should have written to you much oftener from Washington, but I knew you were informed from time to time by other friends, how matters were working there. More of this when I see you.

I am glad to see you actively engaged in the struggle. It is the right move & the Whigs know it, hence the reason why they raise such a hue and cry about "dictation" &c. Your trip to E Tennessee did much good by inspiriting our friends &c. But Foster was like the Devil shearing the hog, "much cry and no wool"[4]—indeed it is thought he injured himself and his party. When I meet him in the 9th District, I am vain enough to think I shall make him sick of the Bull calf, puppy, ground hog, and other such stories.[5]

To morrow Mr Grundy is to speak here, and will be in Nashville some time next week.

H M Watterson

P.S. Mr Grundy and myself spoke here to day to more than I expected considering the short notice &c. Democracy is rising in White *and no mistake*—changes for us—none against us. A good days work to day rely upon it—(O K). Aug 15th 1840. HMW

ALS. DLC–JKP. Addressed to Nashville.

1. Watterson traveled home from Washington City with Felix Grundy and Hopkins L. Turney.

2. During this campaign Ephraim H. Foster frequently insisted upon making the first speech; then he would talk so long that his opponent had no time to reply.

3. Reference is to campaign songs about William Henry Harrison, hero of the Battle of Tippecanoe.

4. Variant quotation from *David and Abigail* by an unknown author.

5. During the 1840 campaign Foster often told an amusing anecdote about a bull calf; see Levin H. Coe to Polk, June 19, 1840. His stories about the puppy and ground hog have not been identified.

TO SAMUEL H. LAUGHLIN

My dear Sir Nashville. Augt. 15th 1840

On my return from *Dover* last night I received your letter of the 11th Inst and have seen one of the same date to Mr Kizer.[1] *Hand-bills* have been struck to day—for your appointments, as also for *Mr Huntsman's* in your District. A large number of those for *Huntsman* will be sent up by Genl. Armstrong by the mail that takes you this addressed to *Mr Ford* or yourself. You will of course see that they are circulated. Copies of the same will be sent to all the Counties, so that if you have made any appointments for *Huntsman* which will conflict with these, you must call them in. I think it probable that *Huntsman* can remain a week longer in the mountain District, and if so, he can pass over from *Lancaster* in Smith—to *Smithville*—and such other places as you may designate. I have written to him and it will be time enough to extend his appointments, if he will agree to it, after he is heard from. *Turney* must *certainly* accompany him, and *Hollingsworth* will do so also, if necessary but perhaps Mr H. might be more usefully engaged elsewhere. *Gov. Carroll* agrees *positively* and *absolutely* to accompany you from *Paris* through *Carroll* and *Henderson* as you will see from the hand bills. From *Lexington* he will come home by easy stages through *Perry, Wayne, Hardin, Lawrence* &c.—where his presence can do more good than in any other part of the State. You must be here ready to start with us to *Paris* on the evening of *Sunday* the 23rd. If it be possible to get a Steam-Boat from this to *Dover*—it would save two days ride on horseback—as *Dover* is only 35 miles from Paris. We will do so if we can. If we cannot we must leave here on the morning of Monday the 24th. You will see that we have made no appointment for you at *Waverly* in *Humphreys* on your way home as was suggested. It can still be done if expedient. Cave Johnson however will be there soon, and it was thought that it might be best for you to return through *Perry* and address the people at *Mount Pleasant* in Maury and in Williamson on your return home, if your arrangements would enable you to do so. This can be settled hereafter.

Nicholson has gone to E. Tenn. My letters from E. Tenn. inform me that *Grundy* is addressing the people with great effect on his way home. I hope he may have a numerous meeting at Sparta. I will return immediately home from *Paris*—and attend *Public occasions* in my old District & the Counties South of it, and if necessary must return to the [Western] District in October.

Clay was at *Tyree's Springs* last night & will be in to day.[2] I am heartily rejoiced that he has come. It must revive old recollections & result in the advancement of our cause. I am rejoiced to learn that *Scruggs* is getting well, & that *Coe* has been fully acquitted & discharged by the examining Court.[3] He will of course continue in the canvass.

James K. Polk

P.S. I have written to *Totten* that he must accompany you from *Paris* & have no doubt he will do so. J.K.P.

ALS. DLC–JKP. Addressed to McMinnville and marked "*Private.*" AE on the cover states that this letter was answered on August 18, 1840, "insisting on our appointments for Huntsman"; Laughlin's reply has not been found. See Laughlin to Polk, August 17, 1840. Polk's letter of August 15, 1840, has been published in *ETHSP*, XVIII, pp. 158–59.

1. Timothy Kezer.
2. See Laughlin to Polk, August 3, 1840.
3. See Levin H. Coe to Polk, August 4, 1840.

TO ALEXANDER O. ANDERSON

My dear Sir Nashville August 16th 1840

I observe in the *Knoxville Times* of the 11th Instant[1] a communication purporting to have been signed [by] about a hundred persons—who represent themselves to be citizens of *Blount*, and friends of mine at the last August election. I have looked over the names and do not recognize one of them as a personal acquaintance, and am satisfied that there has been some fraud or trick in the matter. The communication bears upon its face internal evidence that it was written by some virulent & reckless partizan, and was designed only for political effect. You know how easy it is to obtain signatures to any paper by a plausible misrepresentation of what it contains, and—I have no doubt when the matter comes to be enquired into, it will appear that the paper was prepared by some virulent partizan, and if *signatures* to it be given, that they have been obtained by a fraudulent misrepresentation of its contents. Will you inform me if you can ascertain the fact who got up the paper and circulated it for signitures. Do you know the persons or any of them, and if so did they support my election in August 1839. I would make a publication *over my own signature* in answer to the absurd and silly objections made by my opponents, to my right to the exercise of the "*liberty of Speech,*" which I have yet to learn I do not possess in common with any other citizen—but that it would be a useless job to atempt to answer and expose, the numerous slanders and misrepresentations against me. What is my position in the state? Having succeeded in rejecting the Federal opposition at the last regular election, it became from that moment a leading object with them to prostrate and destroy me. Their presses have kept up an incessant fire upon me. The Presidential canvass opened and all the Federal candidates for election—and stump orators—from one end of the state to the other, attacked me daily by name, and misrepresented me in my absence, and when they knew I could not be present to confute them. My prostration seemed to be their first and main object. It was manifest to all that my re-election would to some extent be affected by the result of the Presidential election in November. We two were intuitively an closely connected. It was under these circumstances that I declared myself a candidate for reelection on the 4th of July at Knoxville. No public duty either has been or will be neglected by me. My most reckless opponents, can not point to a single instance of the kind. There is no law requiring me even to reside at the seat of Government. Several of my predecessors did not do so. Governor Blount[2] resided on his farm in Montgomery and was occasionly at Nashville. Govr *Carroll* whilst the seat of Government was at Murfreesboro *resided* at Nashville. Govenor McMinn[3] was employed to negotiate Indian Treaties whilst in the office, and was for many months absent at Washington. Govenor *Cannon* canvassed the state—and was absent for many weeks at a time last year. In none of these cases were there any complaints, nor would there be any now, but that my opponents wish to place the *Gag* in my mouth, and deny to me a priviledge secured by the constitution to every citizen high and low. I shall disregard their senseless clamour; but at the same time it may be necessary to meet and expose its object and desighn. It is for the purpose of calling your attention to the publication alluded to, that I write you this; that you may ascertain the facts of the case, and cause the proper exposure of them to be made in the Argus.[4]

Our cause is doing well, west of the mountain. I am well satisfied that we are stronger now than we were in August 1839—and that we are gaining. The Federal convention which is to meet here tomorrow[5] is doubtless intended by unceasing *pageants, noise & parade to cover the real issues as far as possible from the people.* They will fail to affect their object. The numbers now here are greatly less than was anticipated. Clay came in yesterday. I am heartily rejoiced that he has come. It can not fail to revive *old recollections,* and must result in the advancement of our cause. *Crittenden* too, the author of the *Gag bill,*[6] was at Gallatin on yesterday and will be here today. What a practical illustration this—holy horror of the Federalist—at Dictation. It is in their estimation all right for these and others of the Federal leaders, to come in to the state and assail me and my principals, but is regarded as an outrage on my part, if I dare to vindicate and defend them. This is the sabbath & whilst I write the *cannon* is fireing, the *Drums beating,* men marching through the streets, whilst, in another part of the town the *church bell* is ringing. The day is thus *desecrated,* but I suppose that nothing which Federal whiggery can do, can be wrong in the eyes of its votaries. *This letter is hastily written; is strictly confidential, and under no circumstances for the press.* I thought it important to call your attention to the communication, purporting to come from *Blount* that you might have it exposed.

James K. Polk

P.S. I prefer to write to you, in preference to any other person, because I know I am safe in doing so. Genl. Wallace of Blount is my fast friend, and will I know willingly aid you, in procuring the information necessary to a full exposure of the publication to which I allude. You can shew this *to him,* if you choose but to *no one else.* A similar publication[7] from persons purporting to be citizens of Anderson County, appeared some time ago; which with the aid of Richd. Oliver Esqr.,[8] it might be well also to expose. I will write you again in a day or two. J.K.P.

LS, copy in hand of Sarah C. Polk. DLC–JKP. Addressed to Knoxville and marked "*Private & confidential.*" Concluding four sentences and postscript in hand of Polk.

1. The *Knoxville Times* of August 11, 1840, has not been found. However, the letter, dated July 28, 1840, was published in the Nashville *Republican Banner* of August 18, 1840. Signed by Samuel Wallace and 116 other Blount County citizens, the letter charged that Polk had abandoned his duties as governor and "assumed the elevated task of a stump orator and itinerant political missionary for a President who cannot find pocket change enough in an annual salary of $25,000, to pay for hemming his dish rags and strainer clothes."
2. Willie Blount served as governor of Tennessee from 1809 until 1815.
3. Joseph McMinn held the governorship of Tennessee from 1815 until 1821. In 1817 he served as a U.S. commissioner to treat with the Cherokee Indians.
4. Knoxville *Argus.*
5. See Samuel H. Laughlin to Polk, August 3, 1840.
6. See Harvey M. Watterson to Polk, November 29, 1839.
7. Not identified further.
8. Richard Oliver served as sheriff of Anderson County from 1834 until 1835.

FROM SAMUEL H. LAUGHLIN

McMinnville, Tennessee. August 17, 1840

Laughlin reports that Grundy, Turney, and Watterson arrived in McMinnville in high spirits. They think prospects in East Tennessee appear favorable to the Democrats. Also, their recent meeting at Sparta produced much good. Laughlin encloses a copy of the appointments Huntsman and Turney must keep in the Mountain District during the period of August 31 through September 12, 1840.[1]

ALS. DLC–JKP. Addressed to Nashville.

1. Laughlin listed some twelve appointments in the five counties of Jackson, Overton, White, DeKalb, and Cannon.

FROM JAMES WALKER

Dear Sir, Columbia Aug. 19. 1840

I have received yours of the 10th.[1] For the last week I have been very much confined at home, and really know, but little what is going on in politics. All that I certainly know is that there has been several changes from Whigs to Democrats, in consequence of the speeches and movements here on Thursday & Friday last. Since Maria returned from Nashville, Leonidas[2] has been unwell—we thought it was teething—he seemed to have got better until about the 7th, when his fever became more violent and alarming. He gradually grew worse, and this morning about 11 oclock died. His disease settled upon the brain, and he went off precisely as did Lazinka,[3] except that he suffered much more.

JAMES WALKER

ALS. DLC–JKP. Addressed to Nashville.

1. Letter not found.

2. Jane Maria Polk Walker and Leonidas Polk Walker. Born in 1839, Leonidas was the sixth son and eleventh child of James Walker and his wife, Jane Maria Polk Walker.

3. Ophelia Lazinka Walker, born in 1837, was James and Jane Walker's tenth child; she died on May 11, 1839.

TO ROBERT M. BURTON

My Dear Sir Nashville August 20th 1840

Governor Carroll has made appointments—commencing in McNairy County—on the 1st day of September cut[t]ing through that County, *Hardin, Perry, Wayne & Lawrence,* and ending on the 12th of that month. He is unable to bear the fatigue of Speaking much and must have some one along to take the labour off his hands. Would it be possible for you to accompany him? If you can I verily believe that more can be done, than in any other part of the State in the same time. The Gov's presence among his old soldiers will effect much, and especially if accompanied by an able debater who can carry the truth home to the people. The Governor, Laughlin & myself will leave here on monday next for *Paris* where we are to be on the 27th Inst. The Governor will accompany Laughlin as far as Lexington where they will be on the 31st Inst. At that point Laughlin turns down through Madison Haywood &c. and *Carroll* through the Counties named. Write to me by the return mail whether you can join him at Lexington on the 31st. The time has come when every man who can speak must go into the fight; & I hope you can spare two weeks—from home—at the time suggested.[1] If you can it will be very important to our cause & I am satisfied would add not less than 1000 votes to our strength.

James K. Polk

ALS. NjMoHP–L. W. Smith Coll. Addressed to Lebanon and marked "*Private.*"

1. See Burton to Polk, September 7, 1840.

FROM PIERCE B. ANDERSON

Dear Sir Athens, Ten Aug 24. 1840

We had a public meeting here on the 21st Inst and appointed a Committee of arrangements for a public dinner here in Oct next. We have, agreably to the instructions of the meeting invited you—Genl. Jackson, Genl. Carroll, Genl. Armstrong—Mr. Grundy, and the letters left by this morning's mail for Nashville.[1] As it is *possible* that these letters may not come to hand, I have thought it best to communicate with you by the next mail on the subject. We request that you and the others invited should make the time mutually convenient. In the letter to Genl. Jackson, we say that we are desirous of having the dinner at such time as will best suit his convenience—and the same desire is expressed in the other letters with the addition that the time may be arranged so as to make it mutually convenient to all of you to attend. The Resolution in regard to the Dinner, after stating that Genl. Jackson yourself &c. should be invited goes on to say that the Committee address a letter to Genl. Jackson to ascertain from him at what time it would suit him to be with us on the occasion. It would be of signal service to the Democratic Cause, if the Old Chief could cross the mountain in September and be here early in October. The Democratic Cause is advancing in this part of East Tennessee. All we want is the distribution of Democratic Documents. The Whigs, I think, have the advantage of us in that respect. We rather lack sufficient concert of action in taking for distribution the Advance Guard and Vidette.[2] The general distribution of those two papers would aid our cause. I am fully persuaded that by proper exertions in the distribution of Democratic papers and Documents in Tennessee and by active and constant discussion through *every neighborhood*, we will carry the State by *ten thousand*. Without this energy of action and diligent and increasing exertion, we may be run very close. I am fully satisfied that with the principles and feelings of the great mass of our citizens in favor of the Democratic Cause nothing but our own remissness can defeat us. Tennessee is Democratic and will sustain Mr. Vanburen agst. the candidate of *Henry Clay* and *Danl. Webster*—if the people are allowed to examine both sides thoroughly. A few of us here are taking upwards of 200 Democratic papers—and I have determined to add 100 more for this County. But I fear that the same course is not taken in other counties. This County and District[3] will not give way. We shall gain on our last vote. But we must afford light to the people. Our friends stand firm—but many of those who voted for Cannon, I find, are willing to read and examine for themselves and some I know have changed and will now support Vanburen. You may rely on this. We may also calculate that influences difficult to counteract in other parts of the State will open to changes against us. Therefore the greater necessity for Exertion and the circulation of Democratic Documents is the best means of affecting the unsteady and warning and undeceiving the deluded. Write me immediately or the committee and let us know when you will be with us in October. We know that this movement will produce a powerful impression in an extensive section of country.

P. B. ANDERSON

ALS. DLC–JKP. Addressed to Nashville.

1. In a letter of August 24, 1840, Pierce B. Anderson, John Crawford, and three other citizens of McMinn County invited Polk to a public dinner to be given near Athens "in the month of October next." LS. DLC–JKP. When Anderson and the invitation committee had received no reply from Polk by September 9, 1840, they wrote and renewed their invitation. LS. DLC–JKP.

2. Reference is to the *Advanced Guard of Democracy* and the *Vedette*. A Democratic campaign paper published in Nashville by J. George Harris, the *Advanced Guard* appeared weekly from April 23, 1840, through the following October. Also a Democratic campaign paper, the *Vedette* was issued in Knoxville, but neither its publisher nor its publication period is identified.

3. Reference is to McMinn County, located in the Fourth Congressional District of Tennessee.

FROM WILLIAM H. POLK

Sir

Columbia Augt 24th 1840

It is the opinion of your friends here that it would be advisable to change your appointment for *Cornersville*—to Tuesday the 8th instead of Monday the 7th. This is deemed advisable from the fact, that on that day the 7th County Court is held at Lewisburg, Pulaski & Columbia, which will necessarily call many persons off to attend Court, and prevent a numerous attendance of the people at Cornersville. In fact many of the committee may be forced to forego the pleasure of hearing your speech. I presume it did not occur to you when making your appointment that the courts would interfere.

The people of Maury have been richly favoured during the last two weeks with heavy showers of Whig slang and denunciation. On Friday last—Mr Henry's appointment. Thomas met him and used him up. He made the best speech he ever made in his life. Made him tacitly acknowledge that he was a zealous supporter of John Quincy Adams, had uniformly opposed Genl Jackson, and the measures and policy which he advocated—and then with a boldness, which he never before evinced, called upon the people to know, if they expected or desired to be taught lessons of Republicanism from this *old Federalist*. He then p[r]oceeded to the discussion of the Whig humbugs of a standing army[1]—the Hooe Case[2]—direct Taxation et cetera—and effectually exposed them. During his speech, Mr Jarnagin challenged him to meet him the next day, at the same place and discuss fully the questions which now agitate the Country—that he Jarnigin would speak one half the day and he should have the other. Thomas accepted the challenge promptly—stating that he had an appointment in another portion of the county, but that he would neglect that appointment—and meet Mr Jarnigin. Saturday come and there was about 100 persons, all told, in attendance. Jarnigain commenced speaking about 11 O'clock and spoke until after six O'clock—giving Thomas no opportunity to answer him. At the close of his speech—Thomas informed the people of the manner in which he had been treated, and appointed Monday the 1st day of County Court to answer the remarks of Jarnigan.

The manner in which Thomas was treated is having its effect. The whigs do not pretend to justify Jarnigans course—that is the reflecting portion of them. I have no doubt, but that there will be a decided gain in Maury County over the last election for Governor. In haste.

William H Polk

ALS. DLC–JKP. Addressed to Nashville.

1. See Cave Johnson to Polk, January 1, 1840.

2. Naval Lieutenant George M. Hooe, court-martialed on charges of insubordination, disobedience of orders, and flogging of two men, was reprimanded in general orders by Secretary of the Navy James K. Paulding and dismissed from the West India squadron in June 1839. Hooe objected at his trial to the admission of testimony of two colored men in proving the charges of flogging against him. When submitted to the U.S. district attorney for an opinion, Hooe's objection was overruled; the testimony of free Negroes was admissible under U.S. law and could be changed only by Congress. Hooe submitted a memorial for review of his case to President Van Buren in December 1839. Upon review, Van Buren found nothing in the proceedings of the trial which required his interference. On June 14, 1840, John M. Botts, Whig congressman from Virginia, called for an investigation of the Hooe case in the U.S. House on grounds that colored persons were not competent witnesses in court. However, attempts in June and July 1840, to alter laws of admissibility of testimony in federal court by Negroes, were unsuccessful. See House Document No. 244, 26 Congress, 1 Session.

FROM ROBERT B. REYNOLDS

Dear Sir, Knoxville August 26th 1840

Col Yoakum reached here last evening on his way to join Nicholson & Johnson at Taz[e]well. He had made several speeches in the counties below. He thinks East Tennessee must decide this contest. He sets West Tennessee down at 2000 Whig majity—Middle Tennessee at 5000 Democratic majity & says E. T. must make a drawn battle &c. I can speak for East Tennessee, as I have just returned from the upper counties—and have seen and conversed with Blair, Kenney, Gammon, Howard, Chester[1] & others—and they all concur, that we shall have increased majorities in Greene & Washington. Powell of Carter,[2] informed me of a small gain there & also in Johnson. Sullivan, you know will do her duty. Hawkins will give a considerably increased majority for our cause.

Claiborne will increase her majority 300 or 400 over last august. Grainger has an infernal disposition to backslide a little—but not much. Johnson warmed them up at Blain's[3] & made votes on the 22nd; Campbell is disposed to play the same game. Our majity will not be so large in Campbell as you recd. We have a great gain in Anderson, Roane, Rhea, Meigs, Monroe & Marion. Blount is looking up again. We thought all was lost there—but Wallace is straining every nerve and will right our losses. Jefferson, Knox, Sevier & Cocke are about as they were when the last vote was taken. Upon the whole E. Tennessee will give a majority of 500 for Van Buren. Bell meets the people to day at Greenville. Gen. Anderson will be with him there & attend him from there to his next & so on thro' all his appointments. I think he is strong enough to meet Bell before the people of those counties.

Nicholson & Johnson are doing the cause good service thus far. We make less noise than the Whigs, but I assure you we are sensibly alive to the importance of the coming contest and are all actively engaged, save G & W[4] who from *indisposition* are doing but little.

ROBT B. REYNOLDS

ALS. DLC–JKP. Addressed to Nashville.

1. John Blair, Daniel Kenney, Nathan Gammon, and John P. Chester. Howard has not been identified.

2. Robert W. Powell, a Carter County lawyer and merchant, served two terms in the Tennessee House from 1841 until 1845. A Democrat, he was a son of Joseph Powell.

3. Reference is to Blain's XRoads in Grainger County.

4. Reference is probably to John F. Gillespy and John E. Wheeler.

FROM EDWIN POLK [1]

Dear Sir

Bolivar August 27th 1840

Having lately seen a vile slander going the rounds of some of the Federal presses of the country against the memory of my father, charging him with being a tory in the Revolutionary war,[2] I deem it proper after reflection to address you a few lines to ask your advice as to the best course to be pursued in the refutation of such a charge. I am aware that the charge is made to affect yourself in a political point of view, but it falls with equal weight upon his own children and I am not disposed to let it pass unrefuted.

It seems to me from the little that I know of my fathers history, that an exposition of facts could be made clearly establishing his position in that struggle and convincing every intelligent mind that he was heart and hand with the Patriots. The Mecklenburg Declaration of Independence together with a Captains commission given him by the State of South Carolina and which Major Bills found among his papers and which he gave to Esq William Polk would be good evidence to disprove the charge if you think it worthy of notice. I confess when I see my father abused for his conduct in that struggle which I had esteemed such at least as to entitle him to the respect of those who knew him, it shakes my confidence if possible still more in the principles, personal and political, of the leaders of that party who not content with slandering the living must attack the characters of the dead to advance their cause. Whatever suggestions you may deem it advisable to make will be satisfactory to our family here.

EDWIN POLK

ALS. DLC–JKP. Addressed to Nashville. AE on the cover states that this letter was answered on September 1, 1840, and that a letter to William Polk of Arkansas was enclosed; neither of Polk's letters has been found.

1. Edwin F. Polk was Polk's uncle. Edwin, the youngest child of Polk's grandfather, Ezekiel Polk, practiced law and farmed in Hardeman County; he was twenty-two years younger than Polk.

2. A farmer and land speculator, Ezekiel Polk led the first white settlers into what became Hardeman County. Early in the Revolutionary War he refused to obey an order to march his patriot company to the Carolina low country; for this refusal he temporarily lost his captain's commission and narrowly escaped a charge of treason. Later, when Lord Cornwallis invaded South Carolina, Ezekiel pledged to the British that he would remain peaceful and cooperate with them if they would spare his property. See A. O. P. Nicholson to Polk, November 15, 1840, and Edwin Polk to Polk, March 30, 1841.

FROM ALBERT T. McNEAL

Dear Sir Coffeeville August 31st 1840

I visited your plantation a few days since and rode over the farm which I found in good condition so far as labour is concerned and I think Garner has worked very faithfully this year. He has done a good deal of repairing. The crop is clear of grass and in good order, but has suffered considerably for the want of rain. Garner thinks he will make as much cotton at least as was made on the place last year. The health of your negroes has been much better this year than heretofore and the Doctor's bill will be small. Garner informs me that as yet there is no account made against you except the Blacksmith's which will be smaller than usual and a note to be executed for the repairs on the Gin &c. In this respect he seems to be getting along much better than Bratton did. Since you left I have heard no complaint from any of the negroes and none of them have run away. The circumstance speaks favourable of his management. I have written this letter at the request of Mr. Garner, who desires to know as early as possible, whether you wish to employ him for another year. When may we expect you in Mississippi?

A. T. MCNEAL

ALS. DLC–JKP. Addressed to Nashville.

TO THOMAS SCOTT, ET AL.[1]

Gentlemen!

Nashville August 31st 1840

I have had the honour to receive your invitation[2] to meet my fellow-citizens at Mr Samuel Adkinson's on Harpith[3] on tomorrow. It would have afforded me sincere pleasure to do so, and I fully intended it, but the state of my health today is such as to prevent it. I beg you Gentlemen to be assured that I regret more than you can the necessity which compels me to decline making the attempt to be present on the occasion.

James K. Polk

ALS, draft. DLC–JKP. Addressed to Davidson County and marked *"Copy."*

1. Polk's letter is addressed to Scott and five other citizens of Davidson County.

2. The invitation to Polk from Thomas Scott et al. to meet "our republican Fellow citizens . . . on the 1st of September" is undated. LS. DLC–JKP.

3. Samuel W. Atkinson lived on the Harpeth River near the mouth of Dog Creek. He is not identified further.

FROM SAMUEL P. WALKER

Dear Uncle

Columbia Aug 31st 1840

The spirit is up and I think we will have a great day on the 4th Sept. The notice for the time for the dinner has been made very general—and our lowest calculation is between 2000 and 3000 people—and I would not be surprised if we had 4 or 5000. Nearly every democrat in the county will be here and a respectable portion of whigs—and probably a great many from Giles, Hickman and Marshall. All accounts that we can hear from every qaurter say they are coming. Our first ca[l]culation was that we would be able to muster some 1500 or 2000 people which you know would be *very respectable* for the short notice, but I now believe that the crowd will be much larger, in fact I would not be surprised at 5000 or 6000. The ladies have been invited and the democratic ladies in town are prepairing to entertain the ladies from the country. In a word—if the weather should be favourable I think the day will be one which will do credit to the democracy of *old Maury*.

We will have no mottoes nor flags unless it be the *Stars and Stripes* to which every citizen may point and say "there is the flag of my country." If you can bring any persons with you from Nashville, you can say to them, they will be welcome and every democrat in our town will open his doores to entertain them. Grundy is expected to be with you—& Carroll if he is at home.

Tell Aunt Sally[1] to come out. She need not be afraid. We will be very glad to see her and I have no doubt but that she will spend the time pleasantly.

SAML P. WALKER

[P.S.] Letters were received this evening from Nicholson. He has been quartering on the enemy ever since he has been in East Tennessee. He thinks *we have lost nothing* but urges his west Tennessee friends not to be idle. S.P.W.

Tuesday morning Sept 1st. I was perhaps too sanguine in my calculations last night—3000 would be about a fair estimate. It may exceed it.

ALS. DLC–JKP. Addressed to Nashville.
1. Sarah C. Polk.

FROM ARTHUR P. BAGBY [1]

My dear Sir, Tuskaloosa Sepr 1st 1840

When we parted last fall I confidently promised myself the pleasure of a visit to your State during the present year. I perceive, however, that it will be impossible without neglecting some duties and incurring risks which, in these times had better be avoided. Indeed I find it extremely difficult to pursue a course which meets the approbation of friends and at the same time to avoid the malignant censure of enemies. The latter, perhaps, is not to be expected and is certainly not much deprecated. Your State has recently, I suppose, been the scene of some of the strongest efforts of which the Whigs are capable. In fact I have been in the habit myself of looking to Tennessee with apprehension and alarm. Not that I ever considered a large majority of her sons as deficient in patriotism and a sincere attachment to sound democratic principles. But it was the misfortune of Tennessee to be misled for a moment by one of her own sons[2] deep in the confidence of her people, and designing men will take advantage of this, to prevent her speedy return to her permanent position in the democratic ranks. You certainly effected a great [feat] last year, but from all accounts you will render to the Republican family a still greater service if you can keep Tennessee erect in the present struggle. North Carolina is I fear, chained to federal idols. My native State too, the old dominion, I consider extremely doubtful. In Alabama although the democratic majority in the Legislature will be reduced to fifteen on joint ballot I have no doubt that Mr. Van Buren will receive a much larger vote than he did in 1836. It will however be a long time before we recover from the effects of that unfortunate heresy, nullification and the subsequent nomination of that deluded old man Judge White, which was but a consequence of nullification. It is but charitable to admit that in theory the nullifiers were ultra democrats. It is a little remarkable however, that when their leader when he attempted to fall back into line with his little spartan band found out that about two thirds of them had deserted to the standard of such men as Preston, Wise, Rives, Waddy Thompson &c. I shall be gratified to receive from you a true account of the actings and doings of the Whig Convention at Nashville.[3] Alabama was represented to be sure, but you know but little reliance is to be placed on expartee statements of such men as generally form the mass of whig Conventions. And unfortunately the press is not always the mirror in which truth [is] the most clearly reflected. Rumor says that twenty States were represented and that there were from fifteen to forty thousand persons.

With fervent wishes for the success of the democratic cause in your State as well as throughout our common Country, and for your individual prosperity & happiness.

A. P. BAGBY

ALS. DLC–JKP. Addressed to Nashville.

1. Arthur Pendleton Bagby, a lawyer, served as governor of Alabama, 1837–41; as U.S. Senator, 1841–48; and as minister to Russia, 1848–49.
2. Hugh Lawson White.
3. See Polk to Samuel H. Laughlin, August 2, 1840.

FROM ROBERT M. BURTON

Gov. Polk Lebanon Sept. 7th 1840

I have only time to say to you that if Gov. Carroll is filling his appointments in the Western District,[1] I will meet him at Mount Pleasant on the 14th and at Spring Hill on the 16th and it would be well if there is time for the notice to have an appointment at some suitable intermediate place on the 15th. Of this you can be the Judge. I will be at Franklin on the 12th. Genl Jackson is here on a visit and will certainly attend the Dinner at Franklin and wishes [you] to inform the Committee as the time is too late for him to write. He will also be at the Dinner at Weaklys Spring in Rutherford[2] the week following. Give notice to this committee also. Craighead & Bodie[3] fought valiantly here last week & they believe we shall have a smart increased vote in this forlorn hope. Keep Bodie and Craighead in action. They can do much good. Bodie makes the best speech for farmers I have heard. If he will go to Smith and Jackson much good can be done. I will take the turn through these counties with him. Every leisure day will be directed to the cause. You must see to the Maury appointments. If they have not been made it is too late to have them made. In great haste.

Robert M. Burton

ALS. DLC–JKP. Addressed to Nashville.

1. See Polk to Burton, August 20, 1840.

2. On August 20, 1840, Robert L. Weakley and a committee of Rutherford County Democrats invited Polk to a barbecue "to be given at R. L. Weakleys Spring—Whenever it may suit your convenience." LS. DLC–JKP. On August 22, 1840, Polk accepted the invitation for September 15, 1840; his reply has not been found.

3. David Craighead and Elijah Boddie. A Sumner County Democrat and lawyer, Boddie served four terms in the Tennessee House, 1827–29, 1831–33, 1835–37, and 1843–45.

FROM SAMUEL WALLACE[1]

Sir Maryville Sept 12th 1840

I have just recd a printed letter signed by your name[2] enclosed to me under cover post paid in which you acknowledge that Messrs Clay & Crittenden have been brought to Nashville upon the invitation of those who affect to condem you. As Mr Clay confessedly came to Nashville upon the invitation of 500 ladies of Nashville; to them of course you must allude as affecting to condemn you. I was aware that a large majority of the gentlemen did condemn you, but was unapprised that the ladies also joined in your condemnation, until you made the confession. Whether it is for polytical or *natural* impotency you are condemned I can not tell, but presume it is the latter from your open failure.

You won my vote by your eloquence in past—but Governor you are *barking* up the wrong tree this time. You have betrayed a soft place in your head by your recent Conduct—which I did not think you possessed.

Sam Wallace

ALS. DLC–JKP. Addressed to Nashville.

1. Samuel Wallace, the brother of William Wallace of Maryville, Tennessee, is not identified further.

2. Polk's letter has not been found. See also Polk to Alexander O. Anderson, August 16, 1840, and Anderson to Polk, September 16, 1840.

TO C. W. NANCE, ET AL.[1]

Gentlemen: Nashville Monday evening Sept. 14th 1840

I have received your letter addressed to me[2] on behalf of the "Whigs of the vicinity" of Jefferson, inviting me to attend a Barbacue at that place on the 16th Instant. In consequence [of] indisposition under which I am now labouring & which has confined me to my house, for the last two days, I have been compeled reluctantly to forego the pleasure which I should otherwise have taken in meeting *my political friends*, at the public barbacue to which *they* had invited me, at Col. Weakley's on tomorrow,[3] and the same cause must necessarily prevent me from attending the Barbacue at Jefferson on the next day, to which *you* have invited me.

JAMES K. POLK

ALS, draft. DLC–JKP. Addressed to Stewartsboro and marked "*Copy.*"

1. Polk's letter is addressed to C. W. Nance and six other members of a corresponding committee of Stewartsboro, Rutherford County.

2. On September 5, 1840, C. W. Nance and the Stewartsboro corresponding committee invited Polk to attend a barbecue at Jefferson "on the 16th Instant." LS. DLC–JKP.

3. See Robert M. Burton to Polk, September 7, 1840.

FROM ALEXANDER O. ANDERSON

At Home. Near Knoxville

My Dear Sir Sept. 16 1840

You have already, inferred that the reason of the long delay to answer your letter of the 16th Ult. was my constant absence from home since my return from Washington, having been engaged, as you know, by the papers, in a political Campaign, the latter part of which was in contact with Mr. Bell. I returned the latter part of last week, & found your letter at hand.

The contents of your letter I have particularly noted, & its object shall be attended to, to the extent of whatever else can be successfully done. I had, already, the moment I saw the letter you refer to[1] put on foot measures, with a view to the object suggested, and when the developements are at an end, the Argus will take an Editorial notice of them &c. &c. in the proper tone, & the next week's paper will take a position of defence & justification of your course &c. &c. You judge rightly in declining any answer to those letters &c &c. They do not deserve it, & no doubt emanated, in their design, from this town. Many of the signers have been utterly deceived &c. &c.[2] Mr. Wallace, the Brother of Genl. Wallace, who heads the list of Blount County, I understand, has taken violent ground against us.[3] But you may rest assured that we have about recovered our former position in Blount, advanced upon our strength, a little, in Anderson, and in Roane. So much for the parade of names &c. &c.

Genl. Wallace is firm and zealous, & I have no doubt of doing as well in Blount as we did before. The Argus will keep a steady & blazing fire to the end—from this time!

You may rest perfectly satisfied that nothing will be permitted to transpire here, affecting you, which will be suffered to pass without full and due attention.

I wrote you from the Cross Roads,[4] where I had just closed the appointments of Mr Bell, as I felt with efficient success. The accounts you see in the papers of the discussions, from our friends, are but meagre statements, and are greatly deficient in detail, and graphic energy. The scenes sometimes were vivid & exciting. *I uniformly commented, line by line, upon his Vauxhall & Hartford speeches*[5]—&c. &c. The particulars would be too tedious and extended for a letter. He sometimes pronounced a high eulogium upon Judge White—to which no one objected, but which all understood. And I never failed to place the Patriot of the Hermitage[6] in full relief, with all his honors, & all his virtues, & all his claims, & all his principles—and the *Contrast of the ingratitude* with which it was now attempted to visit him, for the exaltation of a man who retired from the Battle field of his Country, *at her darkest hour.*

Let me hear from you from time to time, pending the contest. I saw Gifford day before yesterday, & he says our friends in the west can never hear from us. The same applies to them as to ourselves. I think there is not active correspondence enough going on between our Mutual friends of the East here & of the west.

In the acct. of Calculations I sent you, Rhea County is, perhaps, inadvertantly placed under the head of Federalism. If so it should be transferred. Our majority there will be fully equal to what it was. You may rely upon it that the difference in East Tennessee will not exceed 500 votes, unless I am greatly deceived, and I think I am not.

Something was said, by Mr Gifd. about the name of Col Johnson. I dont believe we have any thing at present to expect from taking that position except increased attacks but of this let me hear from you.

At my return home last week I found my Daughter Rosa[7] exceedingly sick of fever. It is now the sixth or seventh day since her attack, & there is no alteration for the better, and I entertain serious fears for the result.

I learn from Dr Paxton this morning, that Mr Bell is in the neighborhood at Addison's—not very well &c.[8] I do not hear what new movements he proposes, or whether any.

The Cumberland Gap Affair[9] was a complete failure. Some of the more rational of the whigs allow, I am told, that there were not more than 3000 persons present. Others think, who are entitled to equal credit, nothing like that. So it was a failure—a complete failure—& has gone off with a blank shot even upon old Claiborne. Our vote in that County will be largely increased, & we shall increase our Vote in Meigs—& hold our vote in Morgan according to the best intelligence last had—or within some 10 or 12 of it.

Write me the true state of things in your section of the Country & of the Western District.

In the hope that the health of my family will be restored in some ten days, & as soon as I have arranged my private affairs which demand my attention, I design to spend the month of October in the field.

In the last Argus of Sept 10th[10] you will perceive the fire upon the opposition editorially & by selection is strongly sustained. I call your attention to the article headed "The newborn Whigs of Tennessee and Genl Jackson." I saw a Harrison man yesterday who after the reading of that Article says he cant stand a party that makes the charge against Genl Jackson of being concerned with Burr & that it was bad policy to bring Clay to Tennessee.

The Charge has been made by that dirty Editor Brownlow but he & his press are not & will not be mentioned, because the Whole Whig Press of Tennessee are answerable, as they have permitted it to be made without *dissent in any expressed,* or to be implied, form. Present my kind regards to Mrs Polk & say to Dr. Young I will write him shortly.

A. ANDERSON

ALS. DLC–JKP. Addressed to Nashville and marked "Private & Confidential."

1. Reference is to a letter from Samuel Wallace et al. to Polk, dated July 28, 1840. See Polk to Alexander O. Anderson, August 16, 1840.

2. On September 3, 1840, the *Nashville Union* carried certificates of sev-

eral Blount County signers who declared the Wallace letter to Polk "scurrilous and contemptible." While some of the signatories declared that they had signed no such letter, nor authorized any person to sign for them, others stated that their signatures had been obtained "by intrigue and false statements."

3. See Samuel Wallace to Polk, September 12, 1840.

4. Reference is probably to Cheek's XRoads in Hawkins County. Anderson's letter has not been found.

5. In his Vauxhall speech, delivered in Nashville on May 23, 1835, John Bell stated that on most points he agreed with Democratic party principles, but declared that if Jackson's policy of proscribing the independent and promoting the subservient continued, the "influence of executive patronage" would soon take complete control of elections. Bell denied that support for Hugh L. White in the 1836 presidential election should be construed as opposition to Jackson. Two and a half years later, on November 22, 1837, in Hartford, Connecticut, Bell charged Jackson and the Democratic party with corruption and abuse. Claiming that he had been "united for years" with New England Federalists in the struggle for Whiggery, Bell declared that the Federal men and Federal measures of Tennessee were allied with those of New England.

6. Andrew Jackson.

7. Anderson's daughter is not identified further.

8. Joseph W. or John Paxton, John Bell, and Addison Anderson. The Paxtons, both physicians, are not identified further.

9. Whigs from Tennessee, Kentucky, and Virginia held a convention at Cumberland Gap on September 10–12, 1840. Addressed by John Bell, John J. Crittenden, and Leslie Combs, the meeting was not so well attended as the Whigs had planned.

10. No issues of the Knoxville *Argus* for September 1840 have been found.

FROM ALEXANDER O. ANDERSON

Knoxville, Tennessee. September 29, 1840

Anderson acknowledges receipt of Polk's letter of September 22 and expresses gratification that Polk has arranged "to have the campaign conducted with energy in every part of the West."[1] Recently obtained information indicates that in East Tennessee the Democrats' greatest losses will be in Blackwell's district and in Sevier, Blount, and Monroe counties. Anderson thinks the difficulty in the eastern section derives from almost exclusive reliance upon documents sent by Democratic members of Congress. Polk must appoint without delay a proxy to represent the state at the next stockholders meeting in Charleston of the Southwestern Railroad Bank.[2] That "meeting is important *here to our friends in many ways.*" Anderson has pledged that Polk will render to Arthur R. Crozier, particularly, a satisfactory explanation of Polk's failure to make such an appointment earlier, in time for the stockholders meeting in North Carolina. "The news from *Maine* is extremely discouraging," but true Democrats in Tennessee must concentrate on victory at home, regardless of what may happen in Maine or Ohio.[3] In a postscript Anderson notes that Major Eaton has been taking a fierce part against Van Buren.[4]

ALS. DLC–JKP. Addressed to Jackson, Tennessee, and marked "*Private & Confidential.*" AE on the cover states that this letter was answered on October 16, 1840; Polk's reply has not been found.

1. Letter not found.
2. See J. G. M. Ramsey to Polk, October 27, 1840, and Anderson to Polk, October 12, 1840.
3. In mid-September, 1840, the Whigs in Maine won the gubernatorial election and a majority of both the congressional and state legislative races. In mid-October Whigs in Ohio also won state and congressional elections.
4. John H. Eaton had just returned to the United States from Spain.

FROM NICHOLAS FAIN

Rogersville, Tennessee. October 1, 1840

Fain reports on the campaign in Hawkins County. Local Democrats do not understand why the party does not announce a vice-presidential candidate. Whig orators "are making a prodigious noise," claiming that Democrats are hiding "something horribly dark & mysterious" in that matter and that Polk's friends are running him for both governor and vice-president, although he can hold but one office. Fain thinks the cause will benefit if Democrats declare a vice-presidential candidate. Wheeler has visited the county, but his health limits his effectiveness in the local campaign.

ALS. DLC–JKP. Addressed to Nashville.

TO SETH M. GATES[1]

Sir Nashville Tenn Oct 2d 1840

I have received through the Post Office a communication under your official frank as a member of Congress, containing certain proceedings of a body of men styling themselves "A convention of the friends of the Negro" assembled from various parts of the world, convened for the purpose of promoting the immediate entire and universal abolition of slavery and the slave trade.[2] This convention it appears was holden at London in the month of June last. The envelope covering the communication which comes to me under your frank is post marked at the City of New York is sealed with a stamp being a pictorial representation of a person in an emploring attitude and encircled with the words "British and Foreign Antislavery Society." The communication itself contains

"An Appeal to the Governor of Tennessee to employ all the influence and power with which Divine Providence has entrusted him to secure immediate and unconditional liberty to the Slave."

The fact is indisputable that you have lent your official Frank to the self styled "World Convention of Abolitionists" as a means of enabling them to send their infamous publications in manuscript through the United States Mails free of expense and the presumption therefore is that you countenance and approve the proceedings which you aid them to circulate. In a postscript to the communication bearing your Frank I am requested to acknowledge its receipt in a letter addressed to the President of the Convention at London. This request I shall disregard. I cannot recognize by any act of mine official or otherwise the right of foreigners to make an attempt in itself so impudent to intermedle or interfere with the domestic institutions of this State. But you, sir, are an American Citizen and by the part you have bourne have made yourself equally criminal and responsible with the foreign agitators and fanatics with whose proceedings you have identified yourself. Were it not for the official station which you occupy I am free to declare that I should treat the part which you have bourne in the dark transactions with the scorn and contempt which I entertain for the proceedings themselves and which I am sure all patriotic citizens ardently attached to the Union and desiring its preservation will pronounce upon your conduct.

It is to be regreted that the affected and hypocritical phylanthropy of British and other foreign abolitionists with whom your official Frank identified you had not been reserved for the sufering subjects of their own dominions whose unremitting trial even . . . .[3] in season of profound peace is in many instances scarcely rewarded with the means of procuring wholesome food and decent raiment. Unacquainted as the convention whose proceedings you endorse and circulate by your Frank seems to have been with the practicable relations of master and slave in the United States their advice is as worthless as it is gratuitous.

The foreigner in extenuation of his crime may plead ignorance of our form of Government but from you Sir his American aider and abettor no such plea is admissible. He may be actuated by a desire to produce insurrection in the heart of a rival nation. But what apology have you sir for lending your official privilege as a member of Congress to aid him in an attempt to produce anarchy and confusion in one of the Constituent sovreignties of your own Government. Have you seriously reflected upon the dangers of the crusade in which you are engaged, a crusade in alliance with foreigners which not only threatens the peace and harmony of the Union but may endanger its existence if the wicked agitation to which you give your countenance is persisted in? Are you so deliberately reckless of consequences as to be willing to lend the aid of your official privilege to countenance and abet foreigners in proceedings calculated if not designed to excite sectional jealousies and heart burnings to divide the states by geographical lines to array one section against another and that too at the imminent perril of producing domestic insurrection and a servile war? Have you yet to be informed that slavery existed in the Colonies long before Independence was achieved? Have you yet to learn that at the adoption of the Constitution the adjustment of the slave question presented one of the chief difficulties to the formation of the Union which had to be encountered and that it was ultimately settled upon principles of mutual concession and compromise? Would you disturb the fundamental compact upon which the Union of the States rests? But I will not argue the question. It is not one which is debatable.

It is a matter of sincere regret that any American Citizen should be guilty of such high treason to the first principles upon which the States became united. Your official Frank covering these proceedings stands up in judgment against you as a witness whose testimony is not [to] be impeached. The only further notice which I shall take of these infamous proceedings of foreigners with whom you stand associated, will be to expose them to the indignant reprobation of the people of Tennessee.

JAMES K. POLK

Copy. T—Governor's Papers, JKP Letterbook, pp. 91–93. Probably addressed to Washington City. Published in Robert H. White, ed., *Messages of the Governors of Tennessee, 1835–1845* (Nashville: Tennessee Historical Commission, 1954), pp. 456–57.

1. A New York lawyer and merchant, Gates won election as an Antislavery Whig to two terms in the U.S. House, 1839–43.

2. The "communication" to which Polk replied included two undated letters from Thomas Clarkson, president of the convention to which Polk refers and also president of the General Anti-Slavery Convention, which met concurrently in London. T–Governor's Papers. Published in White, ed., *Messages of the Governors of Tennessee, 1835–1845*, pp. 453–55.

3. The copyist drew two short lines here, indicating the omission of two words.

TO SAMUEL H. LAUGHLIN

My Dear Sir Nashville Oct. 2nd 1840

From the enclosed notice[1] you will perceive that *Gov. Carroll* has determined to visit East Tennessee. When it was issued it was calculated that either Burton or Hollingsworth could go with him. We had no positive assurance that either *Rowles* or *Blackwell*[2] would meet him, though we took the liberty to put their names in the hand Bill—and have written to them accordingly. Since then we have ascertained that neither Burton or Hollingsworth can go. Will it be possible for either Turney or yourself to join him at Sparta and go over with him. The Governor says, if you think it necessary, he would have no objection to make a speech at Sparta on monday the 12th on his way—provided he could get off by 1 or 2 O'Clock, so as to be able to reach Kingston in time on the morning of the 14th. Should you make the appointment for Sparta—you must notify him of it immediately. Our friends at Kingston, Maryville & Madisonville have been written to, to get up *Free Barbacues*, so as to bring out the whole population, and it will be very important that we should have an able man along to make the main speech at those places—and at Athens where all Hiwassee will come together. Turney or yourself are now our only dependance. It would be better for you to go if you possibly can; but you must arrange it for one or the other to go. Genl. Jackson, Mr Grundy, Cave Johnson, A. V. Brown & myself will be at the great Dinner at Jackson on the 8th.[3] From that point we branch out in four directions, making four speeches at different points—for several successive days, so as to canvass every County in the District in less than a week. The appointments are all made. I have accepted a Dinner at Clarksville on the 19th,[4] at Rutherford on the 23rd[5]—and at Woodbury on the 24th October.[6] I will be back from Jackson on the 15th and if you thought it necessary I could be at a *Barbacue in White*, should one be gotten up on the 26th. Being at Woodbury on the 24th I could easily be at any point in White on monday the 26th, be in Smith on the 28th[7] & Wilson on the 30th[8] and then close the canvass on my part. If Turney and yourself think it necessary and a *Barbacue* is gotten up in Isaac Taylor's neighbourhood, or in any other part of White for the 26th I can attend it. Appointments should be made for Carroll in *Rhea*, *Hamilton*, *Bledsoe* and *Marion* on his return from Athens. I have written to Blackwell and Rowles to do it.[9] Will you write to them and urge them to do it & to let Turney & yourself know the days. *Bledsoe & Marion* especially must be canvassed before the election. Our whole force must be actively in the field every day until the election. Printed tickets should be distributed in every County; Every Democratic voter should be brought to the polls; and leading friends should be at every precinct to guard against fraud and illegal voting. You should organize our leading friends in your District—to attend to these things.[10] As I shall be absent at Jackson, write to Genl. Armstrong informing him whether either Turney or yourself can go with *Carroll*.

James K. Polk

ALS. DLC–JKP. Addressed to McMinnville.

1. Enclosure not found.

2. George W. Rowles and Julius W. Blackwell. A Bradley County lawyer and Democrat, Rowles served two terms in the Tennessee House, 1841–43 and 1857–59. He was a Van Buren elector in 1840.

3. On September 4, 1840, Joseph H. Talbot and a committee of West Tennessee citizens invited Polk to a public dinner to be held at Jackson, Tennessee, on October 8, 1840, in honor of Andrew Jackson. LS. DLC–JKP.

4. On July 28, 1840, H. S. Garland and a committee of Montgomery County citizens invited Polk to partake of a public dinner "at such time as you may select." LS. DLC–JKP. The AE on the cover of that letter states that Polk answered on October 2, 1840, and accepted for Monday, October 19, 1840; Polk's reply has not been found. On October 6, 1840, Garland and the committee wrote a second letter to Polk, in which they acknowledged receipt of Polk's letter of October 2, 1840, and suggested that the dinner be one day later, "wishing not to desecrate the Sabbath by preparations which would necessarily have to be made the day previous." LS. DLC–JKP.

5. On September 28, 1840, Joseph Philips and a committee of Rutherford County Democrats invited Polk to a public dinner to be given in his honor at Claytons Spring on October 23, 1840. LS. DLC–JKP.

6. On August 17, 1840, Henry Trott, Jr., and a committee of Cannon County Democratic citizens invited Polk to a public dinner at Woodbury, to be given at a time convenient to him. LS. DLC–JKP. The AE on the cover of that letter states that Polk answered Trott on October 2, 1840, and accepted for Saturday, October 24, 1840; Polk's reply has not been found. On October 7, 1840, Trott wrote Polk that the public dinner had been canceled, partly because of his own "most severe and unfortunate domestic afflictions" and partly because "it is now too late to make a decent & respectable raly, and . . . the ardor and anxiety have passed away." ALS. DLC–JKP.

7. On October 20, 1840, Grant Allen and a committee of Smith County citizens invited Polk, Jackson, and Carroll to partake of a public dinner "near Majr. Haynes on Peytons Creek" on October 31, 1840. LS. DLC–JKP.

8. Polk received three invitations to visit Wilson County in October 1840. On October 13, 1840, William Williams and citizens of Gainesville invited Polk to a public barbecue "on such a day as may suite youre convenience best." LS. DLC–JKP. The AE on the cover of that letter states that Polk answered on October 17, 1840, and accepted for October 29, 1840; Polk's reply has not been found. On October 20, 1840, R. L. Mason and three other Silver Springs citizens invited Polk to a public dinner to be given in their town "on Saturday next." LS. DLC–JKP. On October 25, 1840, Armistead Moore and a committee of Wilson County citizens invited Polk to a public dinner to be given at the Big Spring on October 30, 1840. LS. DLC–JKP. The AE on the cover of that letter states that Polk "accepted & attended."

9. Letters not found.

10. Reference is to the Fifth Congressional District.

FROM HOPKINS L. TURNEY

My Dear Sir Blackjack Grove Oct. the 2nd 1840

Col Finch informes me that you think that Col Laughlin and myself could render some Service to the cause by canvassing Bledsoe, Marion & Hamilton counties. This I am willing to do provided you will come to this county.[1] You ought to make two Speeches in this county, one in Winchester and the other in Salem. A Speech from you at the latter place would do much good. We have gained there considerably and I do hope that you will address them at that place, at all hazzards, and if you come there it will not do to niglect Winchester. Come be sure.

This is Friday night. Next munday is county court day, and an advertisement is Set up, at every Xroads and groggery in the county that *John Bell* will address the people on that day in Winchester. I had promised friend Brown to be in Fayetteville on that day—but I must attend to Bell at home. I hope Brown under the circumstances will not think hard. It would not do for me to be absent on Such an occasion. I will be at my post and will do my duty. I will not put it in the power of my enemies to Say that I ran from or evaded meeting him. You Shall have an account of the day.

The Mountain District will do its duty in the election. We will give a Small gain over your election, but what the ballance of the State will do I know not—though I fear we are to have a close contest. What Say you to that? Let me have your calculations from the different Sections of the State.

H L TURNEY

ALS. DLC–JKP. Addressed to Nashville.

1. Franklin County.

FROM JOHN J. GARNER

Dear sir Yalobusha Miss. Oct the 4, 1840

I take my pen in hand to write you a few lines. I have nothing strange nor interesting more than I have had the misfortune to loose Elizabeths yongest child. I am unable to say what was the matter with hit. Hit was sick some two months. Matilda is stil complaining yet, but is able to spin. She has not bin in the farm to work, cence early last spring. I am fearful she never wil recover good helth again. Marier apears to enjoy as good helth at present [as] any person. Evy has recoverd entierly from the rheumatism and has got a very likley yong negroe. With the exceptions of them old standing deseses our place cold not bwe beat in point of helth. We have had a cuantaty of rain here in the last two weeks. Hit has defaced our cotton very mutch. If hit dose not continue to rain by the last of this month I shal bwe able to ship some sixty bales. I cant say how maney bales I shal make but I think some where about the last years crop. My corn crop wil bwe short owing to the drouth, but a supply for the place I think. I wil gowown to ship your cotton in the same wey I did last year unles you instruct mee other wise. I think you had better awder your baling and Rope earleyer in the season as our navigation is uncertain sow hit can come to Troy before the water gets down in the spring. Hit gives mee mutch ilconvenience with some expence, having but one waggon, and wanting that awl most constantly at home.

I am fearful I wil bwe pesterd to make my pork this fawl. Owing to the dry sumer my hogs has not done as wel as I wold wish. Grone very little. I have fed them as mutch as my corn wold bare. I indeverd to buy nothing unles nesserly compeeld to have.

J. J. Garner

ALS. DLC–JKP. Addressed to Nashville. Published in Bassett, *Plantation Overseer*, 144–45.

FROM JOHN S. YOUNG

Dear Sir Nashville Oct 11 1840

Nothing of importance has occurred in relation to the office since you left except a demand from the Governor of Alabama for a fugitive from justice here in this county.[1] The agent appointed by the Governor is a Tennessean of White Co. He has gone off uttering a great many complaints about your absence. He has left a lawyer to attend to the business when you return home.[2] I am in hopes you will be able to reach home by the 15th Inst.

The Barbacue to be given to you at Woodbury on the 24th has been declined on account of Maj Trotts difficulties.[3] James M. Brown ran off with Trotts wife a few days since. Mrs Trott is the only Sister of Saml H Laughlin and Mrs Brown the Sister of Trott.[4] It is a most criminal affair and has produced great excitement in Cannon County. Nothing more in the city.

J S Young

ALS. DLC–JKP. Addressed to Columbia.

1. On October 17, 1840, Polk answered Arthur P. Bagby's extradition request of September 29, 1840 (letter not found). Daniel Young of Nashville, accused of slave stealing in Alabama, will be released to that state's agent as soon as a certified copy of John B. Morrow's affidavit of complaint is received. Polk explains that he cannot act on the basis of the uncertified copy accompanying Bagby's request. Copy. T–Governor's Papers.

2. Neither Bagby's agent nor the local lawyer whom the agent retained has been identified.

3. See Polk to Samuel H. Laughlin, October 2, 1840.

4. James M. Brown was an early settler of Cannon County and clerk of the county court, 1839–40. Laura Laughlin married Henry Trott in 1830. Brown's wife is not identified further.

FROM ALEXANDER O. ANDERSON

My Dear Sir Near Knoxville October 12th 1840

I have just returned from an excursion from Blount & Roane, & have ascertained pretty accurately how several precints will vote in each County & the two Counties generally, and *there can be no doubt* that we are improving in these Counties. I leave to-morrow for the Mountain Counties North, & shall be at the Mulberry Gap meeting,[1] & Johnson & myself will regulate our movements from that point according to the most approved views of the state of things. Our heaviest losses will be South of French Broad & Holstein &c. &c. In Grainger we shall get back a considerable portion of our loss. In Claiborne our object is to do better, & [I] think we will—& of Campbell we think things have reacted considerably. In Anderson we are firm & equal to what we were. In Morgan we will beat, but it will be by a very small majority. In Greene & Washington, to the last advice we have improved. The *Great Convention* of the Federalists has just closed in Washington,[2] and we do not know what effect, if any, it has had. My means of information, as to East Tennessee has been very ample, & I think accurate. The Vote in East Tennessee will vary from 500 to 1500 against us. This is a decided improvement upon what things were upon our return from Congress. If the vote had been taken then it wou'd have been almost two to one against us. In Jefferson we shall gain unless there is great *corruption* at the Polls against us.

I wish now to call your attention to the Appointment of a Proxy for the state at Charleston in relation to the SoW.R.R. Bank Stocks.[3] It is important. The meeting at North Carolina failed to make a quorum in consequence of the absence of the late Proxy of Tenn. The Whigs were wrathy about it, but supposed it to be owing to Dr. Ramsay's want of health. But he wou'd have gone if he had recd. it. I wrote you very fully to Jackson.[4] I hope you will appoint Dr. Ramsay immediately upon the receipt of this, if you have not already done it. The meeting takes place in November at Charleston.

There was some disappointment felt by your friends here who had asked the Appointment of Dr Ramsay, for the late meeting at North Carolina. My letter to Jackson, to you, will explain &c.

I write in great haste. If any thing occurs which may be interesting to you to hear, while I am on the closing tour, I will write to you. *I think we shall continue to gain until the day of the election.*

A ANDERSON

ALS. DLC–JKP. Addressed to Nashville and marked *"Private."*

1. The Democrats held a rally at Mulberry Gap in Claiborne County on October 16 and 17, 1840.

2. The Whig rally in Washington County is not identified further.

3. See Anderson to Polk, September 29, 1840, and J. G. M. Ramsey to Polk, October 27, 1840.

4. Anderson to Polk, September 29, 1840.

TO BOLING GORDON

My Dear Sir Nashville Oct. 22nd 1840

I returned from Clarksville last night. I fou[n]d that *Johnson* had orderd no tickets to be printed for his District. On learning this fact I urged him to act in the matter. He accordingly—ordered them to be printed at Clarksville, and would endeavour to distribute them in all the Counties except Hickman. He had neglected it relying upon you to do it. You must not fail to have them printed for Hickman—and distributed to leading men at every precinct. For fear Johnson should not have them distributed for *Humphreys, Dickson & Benton,* I think you had best provide them for those Counties also. *Johnson* was doubting when I left him on yesterday whether he could be at *Waverly* at Court on monday next. My own opinion is, that he will not go. *Henry* will be there, and it is very important I think that you should meet him. I urged *Johnson* to go also to *Benton,* but the situation of his family is such, that he thought he could not.[1] *Benton* I fear has been too much neglected, and *Coe* writes from *Camden* as he passed through the County on the 16th[2]—that it is indispensible that either Johnson or yourself should be at a place called *Unionville* 10 miles from Camden, and at some point in the lower part of the County before the election. *Crockett* has made a speech there lately & it is absolutely necessary.

My impression is, that you should be at *Waverly* on monday. If *Johnson* is there, you & he can understand each other's engagements for the next week. If he should not be there, you should I think, make two appointments in *Benton*. By sending a messenger over from *Waverly*, ample notice could be given in two days.

Fearing that you may not receive this in time by the regular mail—I enclose it to Mr Nicholson & Mr S. P. Walker of Columbia with a request that they will forward it to you.[3]

JAMES K. POLK

P.S. I hope you will urge every Democrat every where to attend the polls. The news from Pennsylvania is good & all will yet be well. J.K.P.

ALS. T–Gordon Papers. Addressed to Hickman County and marked "Private."

1. On October 12, 1840, Cave Johnson wrote Polk, "My wife presented me a fine Son on the 8th & both doing well." ALS. DLC–JKP.
2. Letter not found.
3. Cover letter to A. O. P. Nicholson and Samuel P. Walker not found.

FROM ROBERT B. REYNOLDS

Dear Governor Knoxville October 22nd 1840

Yours of the 18th inst. to Dr Ramsey, Eastman & myself, I this day received.[1] The suggestions & advice are all good & shall be complied with so far as my humble efforts will go. The Federal court has brought intelligent men from every county & I have seen that Tickets have been sent to each. We confidently calculate here, that we will meet you on the mountain[2] with 3000 majity. That majity, coming to our assistance, will settle the question in Tennessee. We are now straining every nerve and we will bring every voter on our side out if we have a good day, (which God send us—) and my honest impression is that we shall not suffer the Federalists to leave our Territory with more than 500 majity. R. M. Woods, U.S. marshal, thinks the Feds will beat us 12 or 1500 votes. He is alarmed about Hawkins & Grainger. I do not think he calculates well this time. It is not, I know necessary, for me to suggest to you the propriety of having middle Tennessee to do her duty. I Know you will have it attended to. The feds here are in a state of lassitude, and we are now aiming to carry every thing by discretion and energetic action. Are you sure of 3000 majity west of the mountains? Please write me—as I am anxious to Know.

I learn that Johnson is now with Senter[3] in the upper counties and is doing us some service. He is our only *man* here & if Nicholson had not been with us perhaps things might be worse for us than they are.

ROB. B. REYNOLDS

P.S. Eastman thinks the Feds are up and a doing and plotting all kind of frauds. We shall watch them.

ALS. DLC–JKP. Addressed to Nashville.

1. Letter not found.

2. Reference is to the Cumberland Mountain of Tennessee.

3. Andrew Johnson and William Tandy Senter. Senter, a Methodist minister and farmer in Hawkins County, was in 1840 the Whig electoral candidate for Tennessee's Second Congressional District, which he represented in the U.S. House, 1843–45.

FROM J. G. M. RAMSEY

My Dear Sir Mecklenburg T. Oct. 27. 1840

Your obliging communication of the 24th inst. inclosing me a commission as proxy for the State of Tennessee at the meeting in Charleston of the L.C.&.C.R.R. Co. has just been received.[1] In undertaking the duties imposed upon me by your appointment I hope to guard the interest as well as maintain the dignity & good faith of Tennessee to the best of my ability. From the first inception of the great enterprise which it has been the object of our Incorporation to accomplish I have viewed it as of most vital importance to Tennessee & the whole West & proud am I that my fellow citizens & my State have by their contributions to its stock from the very commencement of the undertaking done all that could be expected from them & all they promised. Our citizens took more stock in proportion to our wealth than any other community interested in the work. Our Legislature granted a liberal charter to the R. Road Co. & on a further auxilliary, a like liberal charter to the R.R. Bank[2] & made a munificent appropriation to carry on the work when it reached our border. Proud am I that Tennessee & her citizens have done their duty. But yet the enterprise will not be carried through. The road will stop at Columbia.[3] Other communities not less interested in it than we, have failed to meet our exertions in a corresponding spirit. Ohio, Kentucky & N. Carolina have done little—some of them nothing. Generous South Carolina & the infant Hercules Tennessee cannot build the road themselves & if others propose, *we must consent* to abandon it. The proposition will be made at the Charleston Meeting & as the Representative of Tennessee I shall neither compromise her honor nor sacrafice her interest by assenting to it. As in her whole past history she maintains her escutcheon unstained—her good faith unsullied even when she withdraws from a work which her co-terminous States have failed to assist in effecting.

The only loss the State & the private Stockholders will sustain will be the expense of surveys within our own limits. This we cannot refuse to pay, & would not if we could. The Co. will probably retain as much of the State Bonds now in its possession as will liquidate her pro rata portion of that expense & the remainder of the bonds be then returned to the State. I will also apply for the maps & drawings & results of the surveys in Tennessee for future use. This is a general outline of what occurs to me as proper to be done as your proxy.[4] It meets the views of every man to whom I have mentioned it. I hope it may meet your own approbation. If not please write me here till the 7th or at Charleston till the 20th. Nov. I know my conduct or that of any one else you would appoint will be closely & severely scanned. For that reason itself I shall be careful as well of the interests as the reputation of the State. *Private.* Some of your opponents tried to make a little capital out of the circumstance that you had not made a proxy at the Asheville Meeting in Sep. last. Knowing the malignity of their motives I killed it at once by saying (what was literally true) that I had a proxy in my desk & as I was at that time confined by debility from an attack of fever & did not go to Asheville they could make nothing from it & dropped it. Some of them dislike that I am in a specie paying Bank & may be attempting to displace me. It is of little consequence to me if they should but I intend to keep an eye on them.

Our friends are doing what they can. The heavy local majorities against us in this infected region are exerting themselves to diminish our strength—but we hold our own surprisingly. Since your letter to myself & others[5] was received I have written to Cowan, Robeson, Wallace[6] & others to double their exertions. We are gaining wherever we had majorities in 1839. My District gave you 29. We count now from 33 to 35—but have lost a little I fear in the county.[7] Genl. Anderson is out on a campaign among the highlanders in Claibourne &c.—& writes encouragingly. I saw Gillespie to day in town. He is certain that in the lower counties we are continually gaining since the Athens barbacue.[8] Others say so too. Wallace writes me that the Whigs will be much disappointed by the vote in Blount. But the news from Pa.[9] have inspirited us all & I do hope Tenn. is yet safe. Let that be as it may our opponents will drop to pieces after Nov. These log cabin boys will find no money dropping into their pockets from every bush they walk under—& that they must live by the sweat of their brow under every administration—& will then become sane on the subject.

J. G. M. Ramsey

ALS. DLC–JKP. Addressed to Nashville.

1. On October 20, 1840, Ramsey wrote to Polk requesting that a proxy be appointed to represent Tennessee at the annual meeting of the Louisville, Cincinnati and Charleston Railroad Company at Charleston, South Carolina, on November 17, 1840. ALS. DLC–JKP. Polk's reply of October 24, 1840, has not been found.

2. Reference is to the Southwestern Railroad Bank, Knoxville, Tennessee.

3. Columbia, South Carolina.

4. In a letter dated December 10, 1840, Ramsey reported to Polk on the results of the meeting at Charleston. The Railroad Company was to be dissolved; Tennessee's state bonds were to be returned after paying her pro rata expense of the surveys within her borders; and the maps and other results of the Tennessee surveys were to be returned to Tennessee. ALS. T—Governor's Papers.

5. Letter not found; see Robert B. Reynolds to Polk, October 22, 1840.

6. Cowan, Robeson, and William Wallace. Cowan and Robeson are not identified further.

7. Knox County.

8. The Democratic barbecue at Athens probably was held on October 13, 1840. See Pierce B. Anderson to Polk, August 24, 1840, and Polk to Samuel H. Laughlin, October 2, 1840.

9. On October 13, 1840, Pennsylvania held its state and congressional elections; Whigs won majorities in both houses of the legislature; and Democrats succeeded in fifteen of twenty-eight congressional races for a net loss of two U.S. House seats.

FROM JOHN S. YOUNG

Dear Sir

Nashville Oct 27, 1840

Not a single thing has occurred at the office of any importance since you left.

The majority in Pennsylvania is over 15000.[1]

I will not start up until Friday.[2]

Jno S Young

ALS. DLC–JKP. Addressed to Murfreesboro.

1. See James G. M. Ramsey to Polk, October 27, 1840.

2. Young planned to return to his home in Warren County for the presidential election.

FROM JOHN S. YOUNG

Dear Sir [Nashville, Tennessee] At office 29 Oct 1840

You will find herewith enclosed a book of Blanks called *Executive Book*. It contains

1st Pardons for convicts under the act of 1835 Chap 63
2d General form for Pardons
3d Warrant to apprahend fugitives from other states
4th Form & Blk. of Demand for fugitives
5th Proclamations
6th Certificates as to Circuit Judges
7th Do " Justices of peace
8th Do " Notary Publics
9 Blks for Directers in Turnpike Companies
10th A number of Blk leaves signed & sealed.

You will find each set of forms seperated by a Blk leaf of paper. On the certificates as to Judges, Justices of the peace & Notary Publics I am entitled to $1.00. I do not wish you to dun for it but if it is offered I would be glad you would receive it for me. In your internal Improvement drawer I have signed & sealed a number of Blks. I signed at the Bank 40 state bonds. It is hardly probable that you will want to issue any commissions for military officers or Justices of the peace but if you should you will find Blks in the Governors Box in the office. I will return in 10 or 12 days.[1]

JNO S YOUNG

ALS. DLC–JKP. Addressed to "Governor Polk" and hand delivered.

1. See Young to Polk, October 27, 1840.

FROM JOHN J. GARNER

Dear Sir Yalobusha Miss Nov the 1, 1840

I received your letter of the second of last month[1] a few days cence and hav bin trying to find a waggon gowing to memphis to send for the box of shoes. The negroes are needing them very mutch. I am gowing to town tomorrow and wil posably meet with an opportunity to send for them.

You wish to lern how the crop is turning out. I think from what I have getherd of boath cotton and corn, there wil bwe very little difference betwen this crop and last. I have getherd near half of my corn and have to weight until the ground dry some. My waggon mier[ed] down in the fild so that I had to stop. I hav got sixty bales made and wil ship them in a few days if the river is high a nuf. We had the dryest sumer I ever experenced and for the last 5 or 6 weks hit has bin wraining a gradeel [and] wil make me more backword in getting the crop out. I hav had the misfortune to loose the work of three of my negroes cence yesterday three weks. Rhunaway from mee [are] Henry, gilbert, and charls the same boy that was out last fawl so long. I think they hav taken a nother trip to Tennissee.[2] There was now difference in the world betwen myself and two of them. Henry has become so indifernt a bout his duty I was compeld to corect him. He resisted and fought mee. I awdered Charls to take hold of him, being the nearst but [he] refused to dwo so. After Henry and my self [had been] cumbatting some time he got loose from mee and got in to the swamp. Wile I was pursuing him Gilbert, Charls and Perry was runing the other wey. The onley reson was becaus they did not take holt of the other boy when awderd. I concluded that henry wold try to get his cloths while I was weying cotton at night. Got a cople of men to watch for him. While watching for him Pery was slipping up and was awderd to stand but he broke and he shot him in the legs with smawl shot sow I got him, and he is at work. I hav but very little doubt but what they have gone to tennissee likely trying for a free state. I learn that charls told to the negroes that he cold of made his escape before if he has bin a mind two, the ballence of them are wel. Marier thinks henry wil gow to his old master near sumervill Ten.

John J. Garner

ALS. DLC–JKP. Addressed to Nashville. Published in Bassett, *Plantation Overseer*, 145–47.

1. Letter not found.

2. On October 20, 1840, Silas M. Caldwell writes from Dancyville, Haywood County, that Henry has just surrendered himself and has charged that Garner threatened to shoot him, "he says for nothing." Caldwell states that he is informed by Henry that Polk's slave, Perry, was shot in the thigh and could not walk. Henry will remain with Caldwell until instructions are received from Polk. ALS. DLC–JKP.

FROM SAMUEL P. WALKER

Dear Sir Columbia Nov 4 1840

We are *beaten*, badly *beaten*, in spite of every thing we could do we could not rally our people to the polls. The Whig vote is increased but 60 votes whilst our vote falls short upwards of 300. Mooresville, Glens,

Rally Hill and Benton have all voted very thin votes. I do not believe that you have lost any strength but the people could not be *rallied* for Van Buren. Our majority is but 530.

SAML P WALKER

ALS. DLC–JKP. Addressed to Nashville.

FROM A. O. P. NICHOLSON

Dear Sir: Columbia Nov. 6. 1840

It seems that we are badly used up in Mid Ten. and I presume we have met the same fate in the two extremes. I confess this result was wholly unexpected and I hardly know any explanation for it. Indeed it is useless now to look for excuses. We are defeated and our only useful business now is to go to work to retrive our lost fortunes. Now whilst our friends are chagrined and vexed by defeat and by the crowings of our enemies we ought to present at once a declaration of our intention to renew the war for the next summer. The work of organizing should begin at once and we may take many useful lessons from our opponents as to the manner of preparing for the canvass. We are now to be the assailing party and our presses should commence the work boldly and expose all the corruptions of the Federal party and at the same time to keep up a raking fire upon the whole of Harrison's inconsistent and imbecile history. It is unfortunate for us that Harrison's administration (if elected) will not be developed before our Aug. election, but still enough will probably have transpired to present available points of attack. We will go earnestly to work in this county[1] and will have every thing right in a short time. We will first give a new direction to the Ten. Democrat,[2] and here I am at some loss. Maj. Lewis is now with us zealously and under the expectation that Calhoun may be made the most available of our party for the next race. I believe he is willing to take hold of the Democrat. How will this do? You know he is able—but does any objection suggest itself to your mind. Our democratic friends here are exceedingly anxious that I should agree to take the field for Congress or for the Legislature. The sacrifices I have made this summer however forbid me at present from countenancing such an undertaking. I shall however not be inactive, for a triumph we can and will have next summer. We have been calculating that J. E. Thomas would run for sheriff, but I am beginning now to doubt the propriety of withdrawing him from the canvass for the Legislature. I am inclined to think he ought to run for the Senate as Smith does not desire to run, and in the lower house the general understanding is that B. Martin and your brother William will be our ticket. All these matters however I presume William has mentioned to you. Rest assured that notwithstanding our defeat in Maury our strength is but little if any diminished. We can and we will restore it in the next race.

The result of this election makes your position rather gloomy, but still it is not a desparate case by any means. My greatest hope now is that Bell will be your opponent. If so I am well satisfied we will triumph over him. Have you any idea who will probably be the Federal candidate?

Let me hear from you fully immediately.

A. O. P. NICHOLSON

ALS. DLC–JKP. Addressed to Nashville. AE on the cover states that this letter was answered on November 8, 1840.

1. Maury County.
2. Columbia *Tennessee Democrat*.

FROM ROBERT B. REYNOLDS

Dear Sir,

Knoxville Novr 6th 1840

The election in East Tennessee has surprised both parties. The feds have at least 6500 majity. I believe that they have carried but two of our Counties, Campbell & McMinn. Monroe gave us a nominal majity, Hawkins 185, Claiborne 250. They have no doubt carried the state by at least 3000. Our friends many of them have desponded but this will last only for a day or so & reason will resume its empire & then we will go to work again. Knox County has given 1782 majity, Sevier 860, Grainger 645, Blount 558, Anderson 425, Roane 502, Campbell 150, McMinn 128, Jefferson 1670. Frauds have been committed of the most gross character. Virginia will be closely contested. The Log Cabin Cry & the Hard Cider revels have great charms for the Vulgar & it has carried them off to the support of federalism.

ROB. B. REYNOLDS

ALS. DLC–JKP. Addressed to Nashville.

FROM SAMUEL P. WALKER

Dear Sir Columbia Nov. 6th 1840

As soon as the excitement of the present election passes over and we ascertain *how* badly we are beaten in Tennessee—we ought to begin to orga[n]ise for the August Election. It will cost you a great deal of labor but you *can* be reel[e]cted. We have the strength and you can call it out if the county and congressional tickets are made strong. I believe Cahal will be a candidate for Congress in this district—and I fear that Watterson is not strong enough to carry the strength of this County.[1] We must have a ticket that will be an assistance rather than a weight upon you. I dont know Watterson's strength in Bedford but I am satisfied that Nicholson, Martin or Thomas would run a great deal better in this county. I dont object to Watterson myself and under any other circumstances than the present I should be in favour of his running again, but you know that we must have a strong man to contend with Cahal in this county if he should be a candidate. He must be a man for whoom the people will go with enthusiasm. I know that your judgiment is better than mine and my object in writing to you is to inform you, as well as I can, of what our condition is, and to be governed by your opinion. Bill[2] is spoken of for the Legislature. I think he would run well. Our great difficulty will be to get a strong man for Congress without giving offence to some of our friends. Old Tip cant reward all of his friends with my little office[3] and whether in or out I intend if I live, to do my *whole duty* in the next August Election.

SAM P WALKER

ALS. DLC–JKP. Addressed to Nashville and marked "*private.*"

1. Maury County.
2. William H. Polk.
3. Walker was postmaster of Columbia, Tennessee.

TO DAVID BURFORD[1]

My Dear Sir Nashville Nov 7th 1840

We are beaten in the late contest in the state—*beaten* by the superior *organization and industry* of our opponents. Apprehending no danger at the outset, we suffered them to enter actively upon the canvass three months earlier than we did, and thus to give an impulse to public sentiment which it was difficult to resist. In addition to this, we have had a succession of disasters in the elections in the other states, within the last few months, which coming in upon us, in the eve of our election—dispirited and disheartened many of our friends. I am perfectly satisfied that the state is still Democratic, and that by proper *energy and organization* on our part, she will recover herself in August, next. For myself though the majority against us may appear to be large, I am in the field undismayed and unterrified, and if I can be properly sustained by local candidates in each County and District, for the Legislature and for Congress, I have no fears of the result. My opponent has not been announced, but I presume will be, as soon as full returns are received. I shall be prepared to meet him as soon as he is known. Can you not visit Nashville about the 16th or 17th Instant? At that time, some of our members of Congress, and a number of our other leading friends will probably be here; I think it *important* that you should come if you can, and bring my old friend *Col Allen* and also *Col Overton* with you.[2] In the present crisis the state demands the services of all her sons, and it is very desirable that some of her *old public servants*, should be brought forth. I hope it may be convenient for you to be here at the time suggested that we may confer fully together. I will write to *Col Allen*, if I can have time, but lest I should not, if you have an opportunity, request him, as also Col O. to come down with you.

James K. Polk

ALS. Held by Mrs. J. Nash Crump of Montgomery, Alabama. Addressed to Dixon's Springs and marked "*Private.*"

1. A tanner and merchant in Carthage, Burford served as sheriff of Smith County, 1827–29; moving to Dixon's Springs, also in Smith County, he engaged in agriculture and raised blooded stock. He won three terms in the Tennessee Senate, 1829–35, and presided over that body from 1833 to 1835.

2. Robert Allen and Archibald Waller Overton. A lawyer and merchant in Carthage before retiring in 1836 and moving to his farm in Smith County, Overton served in the Tennessee Senate, 1823–25, and in the House, 1829–31. Overton had run unsuccessfully for Congress in 1815 and 1833. Also see Polk's letters of November 7, 1840, to George W. Jones and to A. O. P. Nicholson.

TO GEORGE W. JONES

My Dear Sir Nashville Nov. 7th 1840

We are *beaten* in the state in the late contest, *beaten* by the superior organization and industry of our opponents. Apprehending no danger, we suffered them to commence active operations in the canvass three months earlier than we did, and thus to give an impulse to public sentiment which it was difficult to overcome. I am satisfied that the state is still Democratic, and that with timely and proper organization and exertions on our part, she will recover herself in August. We must not faulter or hesitate, but must "lick the flint and try it again."[1] Our ablest and best men in each County & District, must run for the Legislature and Congress, and the earlier they are announced the better. My opponent has not yet been announced, but I presume will be, as soon as full returns are received. I shall be prepared to meet him. Our members of Congress, will be passing this place for Washington about the 16th or 17th Instant, at which time a number of our other leading friends will probably be here.[2] I hope you can make it convenient to visit Nashville about that time. I think it important that you should do so, if you can.

James K. Polk

ALS. PP–Strouse Coll. of Presidential Letters, Rare Book Department. Addressed to Fayetteville and marked "*Private.*"

1. Quotation not identified.

2. See Polk's letters to David Burford and A. O. P. Nicholson, November 7, 1840.

TO A. O. P. NICHOLSON

My Dear Sir Nashville Nov. 7th 1840

We are *beaten* in the late contest in the state, *beaten* by the superior organization and industry of our opponents. Apprehending no danger, we suffered our opponents to enter actively into the canvass, three months earlier than we did, and thus to give an impulse to public sentiment which it was difficult to resist. I am satisfied that the state is still Democratic—and that with proper *organization and energy* on our part, she will recover herself at the next election. However great the present majority may be, I shall not despond. We must take up courage "lick the flint and try it again."[1] Some of our members of Congress will be passing here on their way to Washington about the 16th or 17th Inst. At that time a number of our other leading friends will be here also.[2] Can you not visit Nashville at that time? I think it *important* that you should do so if you can. Bring *Thomas & Martin* with you if they can come. My opponent has not yet been announced, but I presume will be as soon as the full returns are received. I shall be prepared to meet him as soon as he is known.

James K. Polk

ALS. NHi–Misc. Mss.; James K. Polk. Addressed to Columbia and marked "*Private.*" Published in *THQ*, III, pp. 73–74.

1. Quotation not identified.
2. See Polk to George W. Jones, November 7, 1840.

FROM MINER K. KELLOGG

Dr Sir, Washington City Nov. 8th 1840

New York, Penna and Maine have gone against the administration.[1] This settles the question at present, and all we have to do is to burnish up our armour for the next campaigne, when we shall come up to the battle with renewed strength and zeal from our present defeat and a four years rest.

Mr. Van Buren is at this time sitting for his portrait. He proves himself the *philosopher* as well as the patriot, at this trying moment.

The news instead of depressing my spirits in the great cause of human rights, only serves to nerve them up, and I feel proud to say that I am, this day, a firmer and more uncomprimising *democrat* than ever before.

Virginia still claims the illustrious title of the "Flagship" of Democracy. She has stood true to the faith of her fathers, the founders of our glorious Republic, while the rest of the union has chosen that of Alex. Hamilton.

Remember me kindly to Mrs. Polk and other friends, and may God save our Republic . . . .

MINER K. KELLOGG

[P.S.] Judge Birchard[2] desires me to send his best respects.

ALS. DLC–JKP. Addressed to Nashville.

1. New York, Pennsylvania, and Maine voted majorities for Harrison in the presidential election and returned Whig majorities to Congress. For state elections in Pennsylvania, see J. G. M. Ramsey to Polk, October 27, 1840.
2. Matthew Birchard of Ohio was solicitor of the General Land Office from 1836 until 1840, when Van Buren appointed him solicitor of the Treasury. Birchard subsequently served as a justice of the Ohio Supreme Court.

FROM DAVID LYNCH[1]

Dear Sir, Pittsburgh 8th Nov. 1840

On the morning of the 5 inst. I droped a line informing you that this State was safe for Van Buren.[2] This information was based on a letter from Governor Porter,[3] which arrived only a few minutes previous to my writing, as the Post Master[4] here was kind enough to stop the South-Western Mail til I scratched the few lines I sent.

It is with extreme regret that I now inform you that Pennsylvania in my opinion has sunk under the Bank pressure, low prices, and *dead weight* of our candidate for Vice President.[5] There is a moral feeling against the Col, that nearly overthrew us in 1836, of which I warned our friends at Washington City, immediately after the last Election and pointed out several Counties in this State in which we had been *very much* injured by the Col, but the wise ones their give but little heed to what they call a country politician. I fear we have received a lession that will teach them that a candidate for high office must be pure as well in private as public life. No man admires the Cols Brilliant Exploit at the Thames more than I do, and I have always taken pleasure in listening to his daring bravery on that occassion. His friends promised in 36, as well as 1840, that with him on the ticket they could carry Ohio, Kentucky & Indiana, but the Twenty odd Thousand against us in 36, and the 50,000 in 40, satisfy those short sighted and overzealous politicians of the fallacy of their hopes.

Inclosed is correct returns from this state,[6] which will explain themselves. The Post Master of this city has received a letter from Governor Porter by this days mail in which he gives up the State.

David Lynch

ALS. DLC–JKP. Probably addressed to Nashville.

1. Lynch served as Pittsburgh's postmaster from 1833 until 1840 and as a delegate to the Pennsylvania State Democratic Convention of 1843.

2. Letter not found.

3. An iron manufacturer elected to the Pennsylvania House in 1819, 1820, and 1822 and to the Pennsylvania Senate in 1836, David Rittenhouse Porter served as governor of Pennsylvania from 1839 until 1845.

4. James K. Moorhead held the postmastership from 1840 until 1841.

5. Richard M. Johnson.

6. The enclosure lists the Democratic or Federal majority in each Pennsylvania county for both the congressional election of October 13, 1840, and the presidential election of October 30. Returns from Potter and M'Kean counties were not complete yet, but Lynch estimated that the Democratic majority in those two counties would be about 350 votes and that Harrison would receive a majority of 137 votes in the state. See Miner K. Kellogg to Polk, November 8, 1840.

TO A. O. P. NICHOLSON

My Dear Sir Nashville Nov. 8th 1840

Since I wrote you on yesterday I received your letter of the 6th, and fully concur with you in opinion that this is the moment, to avow our intention, to fight the battle over again in August next. Immediate steps should be taken in each County to effect full and complete organization, by the appointment of County committees, as also committees in each civil District. Let the appointment of these committees be not merely a formal matter, but let the committee men selected be our most active and intelligent friends in every neighbourhood, men who will be able to counteract the movements of our opponents & who will take an interest in the matter. Rutherford is already in motion and will have her organization complete in the course of a few days. Let Maury and every other County do the like. The Candidates for Congress and the Legislature should be brought out as early as practicable. I regret to learn from you, that it may not be convenient for you to run for either; and hope your determination is not irrevocable on the subject. The present is a crisis when the country demands the services of all her sons, and I do not see how yours can be dispensed with, without great detriment to our cause. I hope however to see you here on the 16th or 17th when I can confer more fully with you upon this & other matters. In regard to the Democrat[1] I shall be content with whatever arrangement our friends may think it best to make. I think well of *Majr. Lewis* and have no reason to doubt—that he is my personal friend.[2]

In regard to myself, you may assure all my friends, that I am in the field undismayed & unterrified, and ready to do battle in our cause with renewed vigor and increased energy. If I can be sustained by proper local candidates in each County & District, I have not the shadow of a doubt, but that we shall succeed in August.

James K. Polk

ALS. MH. Addressed to Columbia and marked *"Private."*

1. Columbia *Tennessee Democrat.*
2. See Nicholson to Polk, November 6, 1840.

FROM HOPKINS L. TURNEY

Dear Sir Black Jack Grove Franklin Co. Novr the 12th 1840

I a fiew days since receivd. yours pressing me to take Nashville in my route to Washington.[1] I cannot do so unless the cumberland river should be navagable for Steam boats. It is much better for me to go by way of Charleston, S.C. I shall leave home about the 20th of this month. Will you advise me about the river about that time. I would be gratified to be with you a season to consult about the next summers campaign. We are to have a desperate time of it. The late elections has Shaken my confidence in the *intelligence and independence* of the people. I did not believe they ever could be made to vote for a *mum* but they have done so. I am both mortafied and broke. However as you say we must lick the flint and try it again. I am resolved on victory or death. If I do not see you, you must write me fully and in details about the plan and mode of operation next summer. Assign to me my place and I will do my duty. Let me hear from you. Van I suppose is beaten.

H. L. TURNEY

ALS. DLC–JKP. Addressed to Nashville.

1. Letter not found. See Polk to George W. Jones, November 7, 1840, and Polk to A. O. P. Nicholson, November 7, 1840.

FROM ARCHIBALD WRIGHT

Dear Sir, Pulaski Nov. 13th 1840

I regret that I cannot be in Nashville, about the time designated by you in your letter.[1] I am compelled to attend the Federal Court at Huntsville[2] in a case of some importance & have assigned next week to examine it preparitory to court which sits monday week. Brown & Martin are both absent in Mississippi. I will see Jones & endeavour to see Buford & Buchannon.[3] I assure you, Sir, that although we are beaten in Tennessee for the present, & perhaps in the Union, we are by no means dispirited. We were over-sanguine, had little, or no organization and no one believed, at the out set, not even the whigs themselves, that the people of Tennessee, & elsewhere could be brought to support, in any considerable number, a man of such principles, supported by such disreputable means, as was Genl. Harrison. It is only by defeat, that we can learn to appreciate the full value of our cause & principles. The whigs on the other hand were well & powerfully organized, had the advantage of all the ~~real~~, or imaginary distress & pecuniary pressure of the times, and dealt in the most unrestrained calumny and abuse. We have not had time to counteract it. No man of character, for sense or candor, surely ever before, made such a charge as the one growing out of the Hooe Case.[4] No man deserving the name of a lawyer, could seriously think of censuring the conduct of the president in that case. And yet it was done. By men too, who have sense & information in the whig ranks. What then are we to think of the integrity of such men? So of the standing army "hue and cry"[5] and an innumerable mass of other hobbies equally destitute of truth, or reason. The people will surely come to see how they have been cheated by these pretended patriots &

leaders. In Giles as you will see, the people were not all at the polls, many of our most active friends were sick & unable to be out. I have talked with some of our friends from every district. They say, they know personally we have not lost ground & that the falling off in the vote was because our friends did not all vote. As for our district we mean to give you the same or a stronger vote, than in 1839.

If Harrison should be elected, it is unfortunate for us, that he will be called to do nothing until after our next elections are over. His message, in March, will no doubt, be of a piece with his Dayton[6] & other speeches: it will be upon the non-committal order.

I have much curiosity, as to who your opponent will be; I hope it may be John Bell. I should have great faith, in your success against him. I have heard it said here, but whether it is said elsewhere I cannot say, that if the whigs were fortunate in Tennessee, this time, Foster & Jarnigan, would reserve themselves for the Senate, Bell for the Speakers seat & that some one else, would take the field for Governor; and I have heard Shields & Genl. Caruthers mentioned. My opinion is that our friends will be much better united, & better organized in consequence of our late defeat.

You overcome a majority of 20,000 before and what is there now in the way? My candid opinion is, that when our friends are properly aroused we have a majority in Tennessee. They will not vote for men indirectly so strongly & zealously as for a man who is directly & personally before them.

Our friend Harris of the "Union"[7] has sustained the democratick cause with a zeal and ability un-surpassed elsewhere: I hope, he still feels within him the power to write down, all opposition to our principles in Tennessee. He and Amos Kendal have certainly been the focus of whig abuse in this state, by almost every whig orator and in, perhaps ninety nine, out of every one hundred speeches. An evidence, that the enemy, at least, apprehended danger from them. Write me again.

A. Wright

ALS. DLC–JKP. Addressed to Nashville.

1. Letter not found. See also Polk to George W. Jones, November 7, 1840, and Polk to A. O. P. Nicholson, November 7, 1840.

2. Huntsville, Alabama.

3. John Buchanan.

4. See William H. Polk to Polk, August 24, 1840.

5. See Cave Johnson to Polk, January 1, 1840.

6. A Whig convention convened at Dayton, Ohio, on September 10, 1840, the anniversary of the Battle of Lake Erie. William H. Harrison opened his speech before the convention by reliving scenes of his military command of

1813. Describing himself as "an old soldier and a farmer," Harrison refused to make promises upon particular political issues, but declared Van Buren's "government is now a practical monarchy . . . . It is despotism!"

7. The *Nashville Union*.

FROM DAVID BURFORD

My dear Sir Dixons Springs Tennessee Novr. 14th 1840

Your favor of the 7th Inst. came to hand in due time and would have been answerd sooner but from a hope that I would be able to visit N[ash]ville[1] on the 16 or 17 Inst. and have the pleas[ure] of seeing you and others of our political friends, but sickness amoungst my relatives will deprive me of that pleasure.

You are right in my opinion in ascribing our defeat in this State (and the union too) to their superior organisation, industry, and misrepresentations. When the Whig committee organised at Washington the Democratic members should have organised a similar committee, not composed of such material but of the first men in Congress of our party, and furnished it, them, with money and matter. Every thing taken hold of by the whigs should have been boldly refuted and a true state of the subject made manifest and circulated extensivly throughout the U. States. In addition to which our Candidates for Electors should have taken an early and active part in the canvass, and have met their opponents upon all and every occasion. Your suggestions that we should have strong men for the Legislature and for Congress are correct and deserve verry serious consideration by our friends. It will require powerfull exertions and the most indefatigable industry on our part to bring back the State to her former position. We have delayed for too long; nor have we in [ever]y District or County the proper men; [&] besides we have had men in the field who would have ruined any cause. As for this District[2] I am confident, there is not a Democrat in it who can succeed; nor is there one that can go to the Legislature. Hence I conclude this Dist. and county[3] may well go by default.

These suggestions are made for your consideration and not from a wish that they should have any further influance than they may seem to deserve. As to your success I think it doubtful but I assure you that I shall be found doing all I can as an humble & private individual in your support, and in support of the cause consistant with what I think right, and, with proper aid by meeting your opponant you may and I trust will beat him be he whom he may.

D. BURFORD

ALS. DLC–JKP. Addressed to Nashville and marked *"Private."*

1. A tear in the center of the manuscript has obliterated parts of two words on two lines of both the verso and the recto.

2. Reference is to Tennessee's Sixth Congressional District, which embraced Sumner, Smith, and Jackson counties.

3. Smith County.

FROM HARVEY M. WATTERSON

Dear Sir. Cumberland River Nov. 14. 1840

I called to see you this morning at your House but you were not in. I am now on my way to Washington.

I agree with you that we ought to have a perfect organization of our party in every Civil district in the state, and that immediately. *If we do not,* the thing is out with us to a certainty. *If we do,* I have every confidence that we will triumph next August.

If I were in Bedford I could effect such an organization in that county but I scarcely know who will take the trouble to put the machinery in motion in my absence. You know all our leading men, and if you could see Col Warner, perhaps the matter could be arranged. I will write to several of our friends on the subject, between this and Louisville, and will do all in my power to advance the cause.

Our Democratic paper in Shelbyville[1] should not be discontinued, and although I have spent hundreds of dollars in keeping it up, tell Col Warner that I will contribute fifty dollars more to sustain it. Certainly our Democratic friends in Bedford will make up the balance—not more than a hundred and fifty dollars.

As I said to you last night, Col Warner, Kincaid and Long should constitute our Legislative ticket in Bedford. I wish you would write to Long. You can do so with safety; for he is a man to be relied upon in all things. With such men for the Legislature, we could carry the county in a *"whoop"*.

I determined upon my own course before I left Bedford. Nothing but sickness or death *shall* prevent me from being a candidate for re-election—and I so announced to friends and foes. Such extraordinary efforts have been made by my political opponents in Bedford to destroy me, that I would consider myself totally "used up" to decline a re-election. It has become a pers[onal][2] matter with me. Unless my friends have deceived me, I am stronger with the Democracy of that county than I ever have been. When the Legislative ticket in Maury is formed, I desire it to be made known that I am a candidate for Congress—and when I return home next spring, I will take the field determined to do my duty.

I shall write to you frequently during the Winter, and will be happy to hear from you at any time.

H M WATTERSON

ALS. DLC–JKP. Addressed to Nashville.

1. The Shelbyville *Western Star*.

2. Watterson broke this word at the end of his line and failed to complete its spelling.

FROM A. O. P. NICHOLSON

My Dear Sir: Columbia Nov 15 1840

I hardly think it possible for me to be in Nashville according to your request.[1] My private business is in so much derangement that every moment of my time is essential to my interest here. You may rest assured that whatever measures our friends determine on will receive my hearty co-operation. There seems now to be no further hope of Mr. V.B's election, and of course we will have to contend against immense odds. At no time have I ever felt the chilling effects of poverty so sensibly as I now do. My feelings are strongly enlisted for the coming struggle and yet I see no chance for me to take any other than a very subordinate part in the fight. Whatever I can do however shall be most cheerfully done; and I hope that I may still be of as much service as if I could be in the field as a champion. We have commenced the work of organization here in the right spirit. The democrats in Columbia met last night and made all the preliminary arrangements for a thorough organization in this county. We have our Central Association formed to meet monthly and our Central Committee of five with power to appoint committees in every civil district. In the course of two weeks our county will be fully organized and prepared for vigorous action. We acknowledge ourselves in debt for 1000 majority and we intend to give them. Mark that! You may be assured that the true spirit pervades our friends here. We have yet to make an arrangement for our paper.[2] I have not seen Lewis and if we fail there we shall be much bothered. What think you of a State Convention? I believe we are for it here—at least I am satisfied we could thereby make our organization more complete. If our friends determine on a Convention we will co-operate here. Are measures taking to secure an organization in every county?

I am satisfied that Gen. Caruthers[3] will be your opponent if Cannon can be managed. The Genl is now here among his kin and they already proclaim him the next Governor. The big connexion are now in a fair way in their estimation to rule the state. Caruthers for Governor, Gentry & Cahal in Congress, Judge Caruthers [as] Circuit Judge,[4] Dillahunty to be Supreme Judge and David Looney to be Secretary of State or some other higher office & Dillahunty is taking a rank hold and says he intends to bow his neck in the election. You have a formidable array to contend with but if we can organize well you can beat them all. My opinion is that Cahal will run for Congress, unless Harrison gives him a Foreign Mission which is spoken of by some of his friends. Some of our friends here are very uneasy lest Watterson may be unable to beat Cahal; but I see no cause for alarm myself. I have suggested to Watterson the propriety of his running for the Legislature, but have not requested him to do so.

I regret very much that I cannot be in Nashville for I have some suggestions to make which I cannot well make on paper. My opinion is that in the consultation which takes place now the whole plan of the campaign ought to be arranged, and in that arrangement the most delicate and difficult questions will be in relation to our position on the Currency. We were beaten partly because our Ind. Treas. System promised nothing to the people in the way of aiding them in their difficulties. Our people have become so habituated to look for help and relief from Legislation, that they were not prepared to sanction the negative doctrines of the Sub-Treasury. Whilst we could only point them to their workshops & cotton-fields with the aid of economy for relief, our opponents presented them the more alluring prospect of abounding cash from a National Bank. Our doctrines were certainly correct and if we could have practiced upon them four years longer they would have become popular. So far however as the result of a Presidential election is any evidence the people have decided against the Ind. Treas. System. But in the coming contest in our state can we not so shape the issue as to be able to fight with more prospect of success? This is the important point with me and I throw it out as a mere suggestion for your more mature consideration. Opposition to a National Bank is one of our cardinal doctrines which we can never abandon—but we must do one of two things; either present a system which can come fairly into competition with a U.S. Bank by taking up a plan of pure State Banks—or we must take ground in favor of so amending the constitution as to authorise one U.S. Bank with such checks and restrictions as will best preserve us from its dangers. Sooner than see our opponents establish a U.S. Bank upon their plan, I feel disposed to yield up the Ind. Treas. System for the present as sincerely as I am devoted to it, and to fall back upon a System which shall be composed of one pure State Bank without individual stockholders in each state, whose notes should be receivable in all public dues, with such other modifications as might promise the best result. Think over this suggestion and see if there is any hope of avoiding the catastrophe of a U.S. Bank by taking up another system. In my opinion it will not do to fight the coming struggle without being able to present something promising positive benefit in the way of a currency. The pressure, it is now understood, is to continue, at least until after next August, and it will be continued by the operations of the stock banks. They will undertake so to embarrass the State Bank as to prevent it from giving relief. Can we not take up the necessity of sustaining and strengthening the State Bank, show the oppressive course of the stock banks so as to make them as odious as they ought to be, show that all the advantages of a U.S. Bank can be attained by the State Bank, and that the establishment of a U.S. Bank will be the prostration of the State Bank and inevitable oppression by way of taxation to our people. I again say that I throw out these suggestions without mature deliberation, but that if there is any thing in them you may con them over and make the most of what I have said.

There is a matter in which you are personally concerned to which you will excuse me for alluding. The charge was made last Summer and has been very extensively circulated by way of operating to your prejudice, that your grandfather was a Tory.[5] This will of course be made the theme of much discussion by your enemies. I know nothing of the matter of course, but I am told by some of your friends here that you have conclusive evidence on the subject. To be sure it could not be expected that [you] should undertake to establish the negative until some proof is adduced to sustain the charge; but under all the circumstances I think you ought without delay to have the charge met and the proofs brought forward. I doubt whether any effort will soon be made by regular publications to establish the charge, but there will be found unprincipled men in every section who will urge the charge and who will assert its truth. I am told that we have one such in our Congressional district, who goes so far as to say, that his grandfather was taken by your grandfather and delivered over to the British. I allude to Gen. Barringer. And if the charge is made in that way it becomes important that your friends should be able to meet it with direct proof. If you concur with me in opinion about this matter I will also suggest that it may not be amiss for your defence to come from this county where you were raised. If this meets your approbation I will take great pleasure in attending to the matter. I design spending some of my leisure evenings in preparing an address to be issued by our County Association in which I intend to give a pretty full sketch of your career. I could very conveniently introduce the subject of the charge above alluded to and the proofs into that address. But I will await your answer to this before I do any thing.

It is rumored here that Turney will desire a re-election to Congress and that Judge Greene[6] will resign his seat on the Supreme Bench and run for Congress. In that event Judge Dillahunty is a candidate for Supreme Judge. This rumor I get from Judge Dillahunty. Is it true? I should like to know. I believe it is pretty well understood here that Jonas E. Thomas will be a candidate for Sheriff, and that William[7] will take his place on our ticket for the lower house. No arrangements have been made as to the Senate nor will any be made until Smith returns from Mis.

In making our arrangements for organizing I was made Chairman and John B. Johnson Secretary of the Central Committee for Maury. Be good enough to let the Committee at Nashville know, if they have any occasion to write, to whom they may address.

I shall expect as early an answer as convenient to this letter.

A. O. P. Nicholson

ALS. DLC–JKP. Addressed to Nashville.

1. See Polk to A. O. P. Nicholson, November 7, 1840.
2. See Nicholson to Polk, November 6, 1840.
3. Robert L. Caruthers.
4. Abram Caruthers, a brother of Robert L. Caruthers, was judge of Tennessee's Fourth Judicial Circuit from 1836 until 1847.
5. See Edwin F. Polk to Polk, August 27, 1840.
6. Nathan Green served as chancellor for East Tennessee, 1827–31, and sat on the Tennessee Supreme Court from 1831 until 1853.
7. William H. Polk.

FROM RICHARD WARNER

Chapel Hill, Tennessee. November 15, 1840

Warner regrets that he will be unable to accept Polk's invitation of November 8, 1840,[1] to attend a Democratic meeting in Nashville on November 17.[2] Warner wishes "to retire from the bustle of a political life"; but, if friends need his aid, he will remain at his post "contending for Republican principles."

ALS. DLC–JKP. Addressed to Nashville. AE on the cover states that this letter was answered in November 1840; the specific date in November is illegible; Polk's reply has not been found.

1. Letter not found.
2. See Polk's invitations of November 7, 1840, to David Burford, George W. Jones, and A. O. P. Nicholson.

FROM BOLING GORDON

Dr Sir Cottage Hill,[1] Nov. 16, 1840

I had the pleasure to receive last evening, your favor of the 7th Inst[2] and had I have had the leisure to have visited Nashville at the time, you designated, should not [have] had notice in due time owing to the indirectness of the mail between Nashville and Williamsport. Aside from the inconvenience of leaving home at this time, it would have given me much pleasure to have met in Nashville our political friends from the different quarters of the State who will have been there.

I believe with you that we lost much for the want of an earlier organization; and added to this many of our friends were not sufficiently active during the campaign, and perhaps myself to some extent, among the rest. But my situation at home did not justify me in doing more. But we suffered most from the Capital our opponents made of the embarrasment of the times, and the thousand barefaced slanders heaped upon Mr. Van Buren by men who, from the standing they occupy in society for probity and talents, we had a right to expect more from.

When I review the political course of Mr. Van Buren, the manly and independent manner in which he has discharged his duties, and the frank development of his opinions in answer to the various interrogatories propounded by both parties as contradistinguished from those of his opponents, I can but accord to him even more praise than I otherwise might have done.

In regard to the immediate selection of our candidates both for Congress and the Legislature, I have no doubt of the propriety of its being forthwith done; and I have accordingly taken steps to induce Genl. Allen of Lawrence to take the field for the Senate. He can command considerable Whig support in Lawrence and Wayne, and we can give him all our Democratic weight in Hickman. I think he will be opposed by Kendrick[3] of Wayne, as it is said he is throwing up his clerical calling, to subserve his country in another vocation.

I think it likely I will not be on the turf for any thing, as the peculiar state of my system (somewhat fistulous) will hardly justify me in encountering an animated canvass. Added to this, my pecuniary affairs would greatly suffer by so great an absence from home.

If Walker does not offer for the House, I *may* consent to go in his place, as I should have no opposition.

I recd. a letter from Cave Johnson on yesterday announcing his determination not to run again for Congress. I regret this much, as he has more eminently the confidence of our party than any other person can command; and added to this, he possesses talents worthy of being applied in the service of his country. The contest in our district was so close in the late election, that unless Mr. Van Buren is reelected, it will be very doubtful whether any other candidate of our party can be elected.

Should Harrison be elected, it will give to the candidates of his party at least 10 pr. cent the advantage—they will insist on the people to give his administration a fair trial while the candidate of our party would have to defend the principles of the defeated party.

There is only one way by which I can see that a new member of our party could be made almost certainly to succeed in the regular election; and that would be by the resignation of Mr. Johnson (which I hope will not be the case under any circumstances) so that he could be succeeded under the present administration while the excitement is now up; and which would be the pasport to their confidence in the August elections.

Whether I am in the field as a candidate for any office or not, I shall be found doing service to some extent, and will not spare an adversary candidate from any motive whatever when ever I can come in contact with him.

Relying on the justice of our cause, I can not withold from you the solicitude I feel for your success in the coming election.

B. GORDON

ALS. DLC–JKP. Addressed to Nashville.

1. Cottage Hill was the name of Gordon's plantation, which was located near Gordon's Ferry in Hickman County.

2. Letter not found. See Polk's invitations of November 7, 1840, to David Burford, George W. Jones, and A. O. P. Nicholson.

3. Not identified further.

FROM SAMUEL H. LAUGHLIN

My dear Sir, Near McMinnville, Nov. 17, 1840

I am so bowed down and crushed by the late afflictive dispensation of providence, that I feel almost indifferent to every passing event.[1] I have seen and conversed with no persons save my poor children and immediate family for more than a week past. My deep regret for the public calamity which awaits our common country in Harrison's election is swallowed up in my private sorrows. Since Mr. Kezer's arrival here this morning, and since Dr. Smartt[2] has informed me of a fact communicated to him by Mr. Ford, whom I have not seen for the last fortnight, I have deemed it my duty however to write you a few lines.

Mr. Turney, whom I have not seen, it seems, has written to Mr. Ford, expressing a wish to see me at Winchester where the court sits this week before he leaves for Washington, and stating to Mr. Ford that he (Mr. T.) will be a candidate for re-election to Congress. This is, as I expected. I had supposed if Mr. Van Buren had been re-elected that Mr. T. would have desired to retire on some proper executive appointment, but if Mr. V.B. was defeated, that he would prefer to remain in Congress. This was my own surmise, because I never asked Mr. T. any thing on the subject. Thus you see, whatever my private wishes might have been, in regard to Congress, they are forestalled; but I have no complaints to make, and as I have often said, I do not wish Mr. Turney to forego his own interest on my account. I feel just what I wrote you last on the subject—and if I ever felt any thing of ambition which might be called selfish, I do not feel it now. I have done my duty as a public man and friend by Mr. Turney, as he is well aware, and would do so again if he needed my feeble assistance. This thing being now, I presume, settled, and Mr. V. Buren defeated, I have nothing more to say or to do in the matter. I was willing, for I have no secret reservation in word or act from you, to have served in one Congress, if Mr. T. had chosen, as he had said he would do, to have voluntarily retired—but I never have, nor will I ever, ask him to do so. If he goes to Washington by Nashville, I am willing he should see this letter and my last.[3]

The plough and the bar are open to me, and necessity will compel me to follow both; and myself and my neighbors can and will vote as republicans while the constitution holds the Union together which I fear will not be long. I know of no way in which I can be of any public service except in standing firmly with my friends. The next General Assembly is to be the most important that ever sat in the State. We must look to it as to whom we send to it—and have no conflicts in the pretensions of candidates. Mr. Turney should advise with me, or his other friends here on this subject. It is probable some friend in Franklin is desireing the place I lately filled. I am totally in the dark on this point—while, perhaps, Mr. Turney may know.

If Mr. Turney, to whom I wrote on Monday, comes by here, I will see him. I wrote not a word to him of enquiry as to his intended course, but informed him I had written to you about matters in which he might have an interest. I did not then know he had written to Mr. Ford. I have not seen his letter. Let me hear from you as your convenience may permit. I feel myself to be truly a solitary man, a man broken down by private and domestic griefs, in addition to all the worldly disappointments which I bear in common with our common friends—and in which I bear a multiplied share.

S. H. LAUGHLIN

N.B. Gen. Armstrong must not resign. If he quits his office, he must not *forego* the *honor* of being removed. It will be an honor truly.[4]

ALS. DLC–JKP. Addressed to Nashville and marked "Private."

1. Laughlin mourned the death of Mary C. Bass Laughlin, his wife of twenty-four years. See Laughlin to Polk, November 22, 1840.

2. Thomas C. Smartt, a McMinnville physician, married Laughlin's daughter Sarah Louise. Smartt's father was William C. Smartt, also of Warren County.

3. Letter not found.

4. Laughlin wrote his postscript on the left margin of the third and last page of his letter.

TO ROBERT B. REYNOLDS

My Dear Sir Nashville Nov. 18th 1840

Though *beaten* in the late contest in the State, and in the Union I hope our friends will not for a moment despond. Our defeat must be but temporary. We battle for the ancient & long cherished Republican principles of our fathers, and must ultimately succeed. For myself I am in the field for re-election undismayed & unterrified and with a perfect confidence, that if we can have suitable candidates for the Legislature and for Congress in each County & District, and proper organization, the State will recover herself in August. It is impossible that our people, (when they come calmly to examine them) can ever yield their support to the political principles of Harrison or of the party at the North and East who support him. It is perhaps useless to speculate upon the cause of our defeat; except that we may profit from a knowledge of them for the future. Among them may be noticed the fact, that our opponents had *organization* and we had *none*. They mystified every thing connected with public affairs, and made false issues about comparatively unimportant matters, such as *standing army, the Census, the Hooe-case, gold species & C.*,[1] and thus diverted the public attention from the great principles involved in the contest. They succeeded in getting up a *hurrah*, and in so confusing and exciting the public mind, that many honest men would not investigate or even listen to the truth. This State of things must be temporary and will pass off with the excitement which produced it. Add to this, that we had for several months before the election a succession of disasters, in the result of the elections in the other states coming in upon us, which inspirited our opponents & discouraged our friends, and added hundreds to their strength and especially in their strong Counties. These causes cannot operate in our State election in August next if we will *organize,* and run our ablest and best men for the Legislature and Congress in each County & District. *Organization* is indispensible, to enable us to counteract the movements of our opponents, to refute their misrepresentations & convey the truth to the people. Our friends are already in motion in several of the Counties in the middle-Division, with a view to *organization* & to bring out their candidates. The plan is simple and easy. Let the Democracy of every County, (and it is equally important, whether we are weak or strong in the County) appoint a County Committee, say of five, or some other small number, as also a committee of three in each *Civil District:* and let not this be a *mere matter of form,* but let our most intelligent & efficient friends, compose the committees, let all go to work, and let it be the especial duty of each, by the circulation of sound political Documents & papers and by all fair and honorable means, to refute the misrepresentations of our opponents, and if possible to increase the Democratic strength in *his particular District.* There are upwards of a 1000 civil Districts in the State, and a change of a single vote in each, will make a difference of more than 2000 votes in the final result. The names of the committees with their Post offices, should be furnished to the Central committee here,[2] and to our Democratic members of Congress, so that an important political document could be thrown simultaneously & speedily into every neighbourhood in the State. If we will do this, and bring out our ablest & best men as candidates, our victory in August will not only be *certain* but *triumphant.* The earlier our candidates are announced and especially in our strong Counties the better. We should run candiates in every County & District, if possible. None should be permitted to go by default. I hope our friends in East Tennessee will give early attention to these matters. I hope none of our leading friends will be deterred from becoming candidates, and thus yield the field to our opponents, by apparent heavy majorities against them. None of them can have so large majorities to meet, as I encountered last year, or as that with which I have again to contend. We are engaged in a common cause & must all come up to the work. Though this letter is *confidential,* and was intended when I commenced writing for yourself alone, you can if you choose communicate its views to such *confidential friends,* as you may think it useful to confer with on the subjects. Will not *Genl. Wallace* and *McAmy* of Blount, *Majr. Oliver* of Anderson, *Genl. Frazier* of Grainger, *Dr. Porter* and Majr. Robinson of Cocke, *Hembree* of Roane and Bradshaw of Jefferson co-operate with yourself, our friends *Crozier, Eastman* and others, in affecting proper organization?[3] Will not these gentlemen, or at least some of them agree to run in their respective Counties? If they will not, who will? It will not do for our opponents to have undisputed possession of these strong Whig Counties, for if they do, though we may and *undoubtedly will* beat them in the balance of the State, they may neutralize our majoritys elsewhere by the almost unanimous vote they would throw against us. If we have organization their majorities will be greatly reduced; and if we have candidates their majorities will be reduced still more. In our strong Counties in upper E. Ten., and in *Hiwassee* and Ocoe[e] our friends will have no difficulty, either in organizing or bringing out suitable candidates, but it is important that they should act early. The position of parties will be essentially changed after the 4th of March. Our opponents will then have the *responsibility.* We will see the *Inaugural,* and the political complexion of the new cabinet, and cannot fail to be in a stronger attitude than we were before. I have written to you very freely but *confidentially.* We intend to make a great effort next Summer, but to make it effective we must have the correct and active co-operation of our friends in East Tennessee, as I doubt not we shall have. Let me hear from you soon.

JAMES K. POLK

ALS. NHi. Addressed to Knoxville and marked "*Private.*"

1. See Cave Johnson to Polk, January 1, 1840; Lewis P. Roberts to Polk, June 14, 1840; and William H. Polk to Polk, August 24, 1840, for background on the standing army, the federal census of 1840, and the Hooe case. On the census issue, Whigs argued that new questions in the 1840 enumeration constituted an invasion of the individual citizen's privacy. The gold, specie, and currency issues focused on the administration's support for an Independent Treasury and its opposition to a national bank, the creation of which the Whigs urged as a relief measure.

2. The central corresponding committee of the Democratic party in Tennessee.

3. William Wallace, David McKamy, Richard Oliver, Julian Frazier, George M. Porter, Joel Hembree, Arthur R. Crozier, and E. G. Eastman. Robinson and Bradshaw are not identified further.

FROM WILLIAM H. POLK AND SAMUEL P. WALKER

Dear Sir Columbia Nov. 20 1840

You requested me, if it was thought necessary, for you to visit Columbia relative to the business of organization in this County, to write to you, and you would endeavour to be here on *Monday* next. I have conversed with Mr. Nicholson on the subject of running for the *Senate.* He expresses an unwillingness to run—though my impression is, that if he was urged strenuously by you, and if you could see and converse with him, stating the necessity and the reasons, which should induce and force him to enter into the canvass, that he would enter the *field.* I have not been able to see Thomas,[1] and cannot communicate his views. There can be no doubt, but what it would be advantageous and proper for you to come to Columbia at this particular time. Such is the opinion of some of your immediate *friends.*

WILL HAWKINS POLK

Dear Sir. Bill has shown me his letter on the other page[2] and requests me to join him in urging you to come out. I think [it] *very important.* Nicholson *must run.* Dr. Greenfield & Dr. Thomas[3] are hard to hold off. They will give way to N. Come out if you can on Monday. Sam P. Walker. [P.S.] Bring or send out Michels obligation for rent.[4]

ALS. DLC–JKP. Addressed to Nashville. AE on the cover states that this letter was answered on December 22, 1840; Polk's reply has not been found.

1. Jonas E. Thomas.
2. Walker's note written on verso of William H. Polk's letter.
3. Isaac J. Thomas.
4. Reference in Walker's postscript is to James Mitchell, who rented Polk lands in Maury County.

FROM SAMUEL H. LAUGHLIN

My dear Sir, McMinnville, Nov. 22, 1840

I have received yours of the 19th instant,[1] for which you have my thanks. I have not been from my house, and have scarcely seen any one since I wrote you last.[2] Mr. Kezer is now here, and his activity and prompt interference in my affairs has afforded me the only gleam of comfort or relief which I have felt for the last four weeks. He and his wife[3] insist—and I know not what else to do—that Ellen shall become a mother to my poor orphans—that they will and must take them without seperation in order that they may live and be schooled together, thereby lessening their sense of the loss of their real parent as much as possible—and, at the same time, for I know their generous intentions, to diminish my cares and anxieties as much as is in their power.

You say in your kind letter that you deem it indispensable, if Mr. Turney continues in Congress, that I should try to retain my seat in the state senate. I understand Mr. Turney has expressed a similar sentiment in a letter to a friend here. If he does continue in Congress, it will be possible, though at the loss of money and domestic comfort, for me to be again a candidate, though I seriously do not desire it if things could do as well otherwise. If I am to be a candidate, and an early declaration is necessary, it will be necessary that our friends in Franklin should be moved to call on me to come out. I can have no hand in this. Here, all, I know, will be agreed. You, or perhaps Dr. Young, can write to Col. Finch, Maj. R. Sharpe, the Estills, Capt. P. Calloway at Salem, to Maj. L. Bobo at Manchester, to Col. A. Price [at] Hillsboro, Gen. A. Patton [at] Pelham,[4] suggesting that the good of the cause would, perhaps, be subserved in having me in the senate when so important a matter as the Congressional districts is to be arranged—and suggesting any other consideration. In the late Canvass I neglected Franklin, but I worked elsewhere—and, I know, under my peculiar privations, sacrificed as much as any one. This can be done forthwith when you are *sure* of Mr. Turney's determination. Judge Ridley, Gen. Smartt and others will make the same suggestions to our friends in Franklin from here when the proper time comes. I must avoid opposition of our own family in politics, and early movements will afford the only means of doing it. If I did not hope almost against hope, that new political scenes, interests, and duties, may afford some anodyne and relief to my present depressed and unhappy condition, no temptation of profit or honor—if this place afforded any—would induce me to consent to the course. If Mr. T, *is* a candidate—I leave my friends to do with me as they please. If Dr. Young writes at all, he ought to write at least to all the persons I have named, and to Thos. Howard Esq., Jos. Newman Esq. the sheriff, and to Dr. L. P. Sims.[5] I have written nearly as many letters each day for the last four months until within the last four weeks. He must not think it hard. I will pay him in kind whenever he commands me. If I can avoid democratic opposition, I can attend to my profession, and secure my election against any puny annoyance the whigs can throw in my way.

When my little boy[6] recovers sufficiently to bear travel, I will come down with Kezer's family and my children. I will, likely, be some weeks first. In the meantime, I wish the above to progress. I will write pressingly to Cullom to come out if I do, and as I shall be in Sparta in a week, I will urge upon Sam Turney[7] to offer for the House.

I expect to brake up housekeeping—rent my little place—and board, a painful change after having lived otherwise for the last twenty-four years. Present me respectfully to Mrs Polk to whom I feel all thanks for the kind sympathy she has expressed for my deep distress and irreparable loss. In happiness or sorrow, I can never change from being . . . .

S. H. LAUGHLIN

ALS. DLC–JKP. Addressed to Nashville and marked "Private."

1. Letter not found.

2. See Laughlin to Polk, November 17, 1840.

3. Laughlin's daughter, Ellen, was the wife of Timothy Kezer.

4. Thomas H. Finch, Richard Sharp, William and Wallace Estill, Patrick Calloway, Lecil Bobo, A. Price, and Alexander Patton. Wallace W. and William Estill, brothers, were both prominent physicians in Franklin County. Wallace W. served two terms as a Democrat in the Tennessee House, 1835–37, and 1841–43. Bobo, a farmer, was an early Manchester settler. He held several Coffee County offices before winning one term as a Democrat in the Tennessee House in 1843. Sharp, Calloway, Price, and Patton are not identified further.

5. Thomas Howard, Joseph Newman, and Leonard P. Sims. Newman and Sims are not identified further.

6. Probably Andrew Jackson Laughlin.

7. Samuel Turney, brother of Hopkins L. Turney, served in both the Tennessee House, 1829–35, and the Senate, 1839–47, 1855–57, and 1861–62. A member of the White County bar, he resided in Sparta and developed an extensive practice in the field of land law.

FROM ALEXANDER O. ANDERSON

My Dear Sir At Home Near Knoxville Novr. 30th 1840

I red. your favor,[1] after the election, upon the eve of my leaving for the northern counties. I approve of your views, & shall take, & have taken all the measures necessary to hold up the hand of the Democracy & fight the Battle successfully. I am much gratified to find that your spirit for the contest is unabated, as much depends upon this.

I returned from Athens two days since. I met there many of our friends. We had a consultation, & the spirit infused is decided & will work victory.

You must keep up an active correspondence, but in the present state of the Post office, off of the main lines nothing shou'd be put down which wou'd not bear publication, for my confidence is very shaken in the inviolability of the mails.

Every effort must be made to regain the state. Our great error consisted in not boldly strengthening the State Bank, and going to work to counteract the artificial pressure produced. This must still be done as far as possible, and do not *countenance the least ultraism in our Press at Nashville.*[2] No party can live in this union and carry such a Burthen—and if we loose the next Governor's election, & the Legislature, the state will be gone for a long term of years! *It will be the Doom of Devon goal!*[3] If on the other hand you succeed, and the *state* succeed, I have no doubt you will be the most prominent Democratic man in the nation. For you may rely on it the Ultra school is forever at an end! The clique may drag others down with it as it has the Party, but it never can establish its power. It has been one of the evils under which we have suffered. Upon the old Democratic Platform then, let us plant one standard, & be found contending for the principles which brought our Fathers into power—I mean such men as Jefferson & Madison.

Spence Jarnagin will be pushed by some of his few personal friends, it is thought, for Governor. If he is nominated you can beat him ten thousand votes. Our motto must be "never to give up the ship."[4] We will stand by you here to the last plank—& let nary heart be vexed. Let no cheek blanch—no eye wink—& no step faulter. Let the storm, as it has passed, be looked upon calmly, & we thank one single power.

This letter is very confidential & is for your own eye only. Present me with great Regard to Mrs Polk.

A. ANDERSON

P.S. I take the stage in the morning for Washington.

ALS. DLC–JKP. Addressed to Nashville and marked "Private."

1. Letter not found.

2. Reference is to the radical ideology of the loco foco faction of the Democratic party, which first surfaced in 1835 in opposition to the regular party organization in the state of New York.

3. Probable reference to Devonshire's Dartmoor Prison, in which were confined many U.S. sailors captured during the War of 1812.

4. Variant of the quotation, "Don't give up the ship!" attributed to James Mugford, captain of the schooner *Franklin*. Mugford reportedly gave his order while resisting attack in Boston Harbor, May 19, 1776.

FROM EZEKIEL P. McNEAL

Dear Sir

Bolivar Decr. 2 1840

Your letters of 20 & 28 Untimo have been receaved.[1] I shall use my best efforts to bring the land near this place into market[2] but fear that my exertions will be unavailing. We have a great many more land sellers than buyers, and no person who has land adjoining yours is disposed to enlarge. I hope you may find it convenient to spend one day at least with us, when we will go out & examine the land, and determine what is best to do in the case. If no sale is made by the time you reach here, I hope to be able to report to you more fully than at present the prospects of selling & you can deter[m]ine on the propriety of pressing it into market.

E P McNeal

ALS. DLC–JKP. Addressed to Nashville.

1. Misspelling of "ultimo"; letters not found.

2. In debt to the Bank of Tennessee and the Union Bank, Polk also owed several individuals, including Archibald Yell and John Catron. See William H. Polk to Polk, December 4, 1840.

FROM ROBERT B. REYNOLDS

Dear Sir Knoxville December 2nd 1840

I received yours of the 18th ult. which came to this place during my absence from home. I fully concur with you that we should organize in each county in the state; in the weak as well as the strong democratic counties. I recently visited Wheeler's district. The democrats of Anderson, Morgan & Claiborne are all anxious to wipe out their late defeat. In Campbell & Grainger, whilst we find many good democrats, there are some desponding ones in the ranks. Wheeler's district has given 1100 majty to the feds, & he is somewhat discouraged. We shall have a candidate for the Senate in that District whether he runs or not, and candidates for the lower House also, in each county. We shall certainly carry one in Claiborne. The Senator & the other 3 Representatives, must be put down doubtful. We will endeavor to run candidates in this & Roane. Blount will have a man in the field. Sevier is lost entirely so, unless we can get Cowan[1] out. Doctr. Porter, of Cocke county, I am sorry to say is no more. He died in October. He was an amiable man. I shall confine my operations as much as possible to the counties surrounding this town, leaving our democratic counties to take care of themselves. Jefferson & Cocke will not do much for us next year, but not less than this year. Gen. Frazier will on the first of January leave Grainger & settle in Claiborne. He ought to run for Senator, if Wheeler does not. I go for organising & then fighting for the principles we have ever adhered to. The feds here want any body else than Cannon to run—their first choice is Foster & then they want Jarnagin. Bell will not suit E.T. Caruthers & Henry & "little Davy" are spoken of also.[2] We want Cannon & if he takes the field you can beat him in E. Tennessee. You have already gained on the Harrison vote in this county—some steady men have come out for you. I think with proper exertions on our part we can reduce them to the vote of 1839. Eastman has taken the Argus[3] entirely to himself. He lacks funds to wage this war thro' the summer & I do not know where we shall get them. I wrote Gen. Armstrong about it. We want to borrow $1000 on two or three years time, well secured, interest paid annually and punctually, or we would be glad to borrow, if that way fails, out of the Bk of Tennessee, that amot. We must get money some how or other. He has a large amount due him say $3000, but very little comes in. The feds are striving to break him down. The Athens Courier has breathed its last & it is all important that the Argus be placed on a permanent footing. We have borrowed all the money that is in our reach at present & I have written to Gen. Fain, but have not an answer yet. Gifford acted badly, took all the profits for state printing up home & left us without money in this cursed federal hole. If some capitalist would advance the money in the way first proposed, who is a democrat, I will have it well secured here—by giving Individual security & lean on the office. I shall write you again after we make some progress in organizing our forces.

ROBT. B. REYNOLDS

ALS. DLC–JKP. Addressed to Nashville.

1. Probably Craford Cowan, sheriff of Sevier County, 1833–41.
2. Robert L. Caruthers, Gustavus A. Henry, and John Wesley Crockett.
3. Knoxville *Argus*.

FROM WILLIAM H. POLK

Dear Sir, Columbia Dec 4th 1840

Having been unable to see Genl. Pillow, until to day, I could not answer your letter[1] with the required information concerning Herbert at the time you requested. I conversed with him and Mr Young[2] to day. They looked at Herbert, but would make no definite offer, further than that they would give six hundred dollars cash for him. I informed them that you would not under any circumstances take $600. They then informed me that they would probably give $650 *Cash.* I of course refused it, though that is the price now given for likely negro fellows, until I could write to you, and ascertain what you would do. For cash I do not think he can be sold for more, there being so fiew persons who desire to buy negroes.

The only chance I see to sell your Royal place,[3] for any thing like its value, depends upon circumstances. Mr. S. D. Frierson is endeavouring, so I understand, to purchase Green Lewis's place[4] which ajoins it. If he does he will necessarily want your place. No news. Write me by the next mail.

WILLIAM H POLK

ALS. DLC–JKP. Addressed to Nashville. Published in Bassett, *Plantation Overseer*, 133.

1. Letter not found. Needing cash, Polk evidently wished to sell his slave Herbert. See Ezekiel P. McNeal to Polk, December 2, 1840.

2. Possibly Evan Young or Jacob Young, both residents of Maury County.

3. In 1831 Polk and Samuel H. Laughlin had bought a small farm on the Little Bigby Creek from John Royal. Polk subsequently bought Laughlin's share.

4. Green Lewis is not identified further.

FROM DANIEL GRAHAM

Dear Sir, friday night, 11 Decr [18]40

Grundy is just as you left him.[1] Robertson says that there are favourable symptoms, but not enough to build any opinion on. Bass[2] says that he got through last night indifferently, and that he did not expect, this morning, that he could get through this day. Upon the whole, my decided opinion is for you to remain in Columbia until monday night, when you may expect a decisive opinion. It will be a bad moment for you to return here, if it shall so turn out that you need not. Should a crisis take place before the stage leaves tonight, Bass says he will Convey the intelligence in some way by the mail or passengers. If tomorrow or tomorrow night we will avail of any private conveyance going earlier than mondays mail. I still have no hope of his recovery, but dont return till you hear from us again. Trabue is said to be better this evening.

DANIEL GRAHAM

ALS. DLC–JKP. Addressed to Columbia.

1. Felix Grundy died in Nashville on December 19, 1840. Polk received two additional letters from Graham, dated December 13 and 14, 1840, concerning Grundy's health. ALsS. DLC-JKP.

2. John M. Bass was Felix Grundy's son-in-law.

FROM CAVE JOHNSON

Washington City. December 15, 1840

Johnson says that he probably will not be a candidate for Congress again because of ill health. Although no general announcement should be made at present, he has indicated his retirement plans to potential Democratic candidates and advised them to be prepared for an early election. It is said in many places that Harrison will call a special session of Congress for May of 1841.

Clay's movements suggest that he wishes to repeal the Sub-Treasury without establishing a new national bank. Many think that only when the Whigs are stronger will they take up a new Bank of the United States. Immediate action would sacrifice the support of conservative Democrats. Johnson recounts various rumors about the formation of the new cabinet. He reports that his health is better than it has been for two years and that he hopes for recovery.

ALS. DLC–JKP. Addressed to Nashville.

FROM ANDREW JACKSON

My Dr Sir, Hermitage Decbr. 19th 1840

I received the enclosed letter[1] this evening & agreable to the request of the president, send it to you for perusal.

I received the presidents message[2] with it which I have presented to the Rev. Mr Green as he was desirous to have one. The message is in stile and character as I expected, & as it ought to be, and will have a good effect upon the public mind. It will be a puzzle to his successor and to his whole cabinet—including Webster & Clay.

From the account given of our friend Grundy by Mr. Green I am fearful he is gone. Still I cannot but have hopes of his recovery—& this hope will continue until I hear he is gone.

Tell Genl Armstrong I expected him up—he must be aroused, or his enemies will make it a cause of his removal[3]—bring him up, I would very much like to see you & him here, & converse with you about matters & things. Bring Mrs. Poke with you.

ANDREW JACKSON

[P.S.] This was written before I recd. your note[4] announcing the death of my friend Judge Grundy. A. J.[5]

ALS. DLC–JKP. Addressed to Nashville.

1. Enclosed was an undated letter from Martin Van Buren to Andrew Jackson. Content analysis suggests that Van Buren wrote after December 5, 1840, for he included a copy of his Annual Message of that date. ALS. DLC–JKP.

2. In his Annual Message of December 5, 1840, Van Buren reviewed the economic crisis obtaining at the outset of his term and the "excesses in banking and commerce out of which it arose"; acclaimed the administration's efforts toward extinguishing the national debt; repelled Whig charges of fiscal ex-

travagance; assailed Whig proposals for a new national bank; and urged continuance of the Sub-Treasury.

3. Robert Armstrong was postmaster of Nashville.
4. Letter not found.
5. Jackson wrote his postscript on the cover of his letter.

FROM ANDREW JACKSON

Dr Sir, Hermitage Sunday morning Decbr 20th 1840

I have just received your note,[1] giving me the malancholy information of the death of my friend Judge Grundy, and that he is to be intered this evening.

I sincerely regret that the state of my health and the coldness of the weather prevents me from attending his funeral and of paying this last tribute of respect to the memory of my deceased friend. Please make a tender to Mrs Grundy and all the family and connections, of my sincere condolence on this malancholy occasion. In his death, his family and country have received a sincere loss & great bereavement. Peace to his manes and resignation to his friends—the Lord giveth, and the Lord taketh away & blessed be the name of the Lord.[2]

ANDREW JACKSON

ALS. NHpR–FDR Mss. Probably addressed to Nashville.

1. See Jackson to Polk, December 19, 1840.
2. Variant quotation of Job 1:21.

FROM AARON V. BROWN

Dear Sir Washington Decr. 21st 1840

I yesterday received a letter from Maj Graham from which I fear that our old friend Grunday may now be no more.[1] Most sincerely do I hope that his fears may have been unfounded. In him the Democratic party will have lost one of its ablest defenders & our own state one of its brightest ornaments. I do not see how his place in the Senate Chamber can well be filled by any one else from Tennessee. Genl. Carroll will no doubt be in your eye if bodily infirmity shall not prevent his appointment. But whatever is done, will be done before this can reach you, I therefore make no suggestion as to who shall put on the armor which Achilles so lately wore. My object now is to call up a train of reflections in your own mind in relation to the future positions of affairs in our state. The next contest for your present office is to be certainly arduous & probably doubtful in its issue. If successful you would instantly hold a very conspicuous position *for any thing* your friends might think proper to ask. I repeat it *for any* thing they might desire. If unsuccessful—the consequences might greatly retard if they did not finally defeat purposes in relation to you which I know your friends now contemplate. In this view of matters how would it do *for you* to be returned as Senator by the next *called session* of the Legislature. It is universally expected now that there will be a called session of Congress to meet probably as early as the 1st of June or July. If so Tennessee must have *both* of her senators here & to do that you must convoke the Genl. Assembly. This would place you & your future prospects beyond the uncertainty of a popular election, which must be brought on under very unfavorable circumstances. When here you would be in a situation to counteract cabals against you, which you can never do in a distant position as the Executive of Tennessee. Moving or present objects are the only ones that fix the gaze of & attract the admiration of a restless & intreaguing generation like ours. If such a change of position be practicable is it in other respects adviseable. If *you* were withdrawn in the next canvass—would not a Whig Legislature soon give such *instructions* as would compel you to resign & then throw you in precisely the same situation that you would be in if your beaten for Governor? Or do you hold such position on the great questions of the day & the right of instruction that like Mr Grundy you could defeat by *obedience* the designs of your enemies to get you out of public life all together? Again if such a course was determined on must we in that event let the governorship go by default. I should say no. Let it be competed for by some one else (the strongest in debate &c. [that] we could get) but whose defeat would not so much mar their future views or those of their friends as yours would do. With a pretty good selection such as Johnson or Carroll or perhaps Nicholson Democracy might still make a handsome run & her ascendency in the *Legislature* be possibly preserved, though the *governor* might be lost. You see I go for ulterior results as they relate to yourself as well as the Democratic cause both in Tennessee & elsewhere. I throw out these suggestions for your own mature reflection uninfluenced as I hope it will be by the inclination of my own mind to such a new direction in affairs if our friend shall have departed this life. The nature of these suggestions will show their confidential character between us.

As to the *New Cabinet*—no one *doubts* that Mr Webster will be Sec of State, Crittenden Atto Genl, Sargeant *probably* Sec of Treasury.[2] Mr Bell it is most commonly believed will be Sec of War, Ewing Post Master

Genl,[3] if he will have it. The balance not yet known probably not yet arranged amongst themselves.

Mr. Clay after all will be the master spirit of the coming administration: filling no office himself but having nearly all of them occupied by his warm friends & partizans. Mr. Webster will weald a barren sceptor whilst all the effective *power* will be on Mr. Clay & he must ultimately receive all the benefits of the present organization. I feel of course great concern about all these things as far as the country & my friends are concerned. But for myself seperated as I am from those I am bound to by so many obligations & totally abstracted as I have for some time been from all attention to my private concerns & more than all, disgusted as I am by the low intreagues & profligate appliances by which a nation can be cheated & cajoled out of its most cherished principles—I desire nothing—care for nothing which must be purchased at a price so immeasurably disproportion'd to its intrinsic value. But it is as useless to moralize in this place as it is unnecessary to disclaim any desire for promotions which there is no likelyhood would ever be tender'd to me. If a called session of Congress is to be had at an early day & our elections have to be consequently expedited so as to come on in the spring my friends know my willingness to run again for Congress. If not I have desired Jones to take no definite position until I return—when he must run for one or the other[4]—as the Democracy may signify. I will do nothing to place the District in the least jeopardy nor to weaken you or any other Democrat who may be running for Governor. My Best & Kindest regards to Mrs. Polk. She can simpathize with me better than you can in my "present lonely condition" & more readily account for the gloomy shade of moralizing with which this long letter is concluded.

A V Brown

ALS. DLC–JKP. Addressed to Nashville.

1. See Daniel Graham to Polk, December 11, 1840.

2. John Sergeant, a Philadelphia lawyer, served seven terms in the U.S. House, 1815–23, 1827–29, and 1837–41, as a Federalist, a National Republican, and a Whig, successively. He served as chief legal and political adviser to Nicholas Biddle and the second Bank of the United States. Sergeant declined Harrison's offer of a cabinet position.

3. Thomas Ewing, an Ohio lawyer, sat as a Whig in the U.S. Senate during Jackson's administration, 1831–36, and later, in 1850 and 1851. He served as secretary of the treasury under Harrison in 1841, but resigned in protest of Tyler's opposition to a national bank. Subsequently, Ewing served as secretary of the interior, 1849–50.

4. George W. Jones' choice would be to run for Brown's seat in Congress or for reelection to the Tennessee Senate.

FROM HOPKINS L. TURNEY

Dear Sir Washington City Dec. the 21st 1840

We have this morning received the melancolly intelligence that the life of Mr. Grundy is dispar'd of,[1] most unwelcome news. In him we have lost an honest man, an able Statesman and a pure patriot, but it cannot be help.

This unfortunate event much disorganises and deranges our arrangements in Tenness. and the important question now is how to supply his place so as to prevent a devision among our friends & give satisfaction to the country and stren[g]th to our party if possible. How is this to be done. If Govr Carroll is unable to serve, will there not be a perplexing struggle between Trousdale, Nicholson, Burton, Craighead, and Huntsman. This ought to be avoided if possible. Besides there will be a called Session of Congress, and under the new administration and attempt will be made to change the whole pollicy of the country & to reastablish the old Federal doctrins. In that event we ought to have our full representation in the Senate, which can only be done by convening the Legislature, which in my opinion it would be your duty to do. I think it is to say the least of it doubtful whether you can be reelected Govr. Now Sir I think the best plan is that if there should be a called Session of Congress, that you should convene the legislature for the purpose of electing two Senators, and when convened, that they Should elect you to fill Grundy's place. This in my opinion would fully sustain you, and place you in a far better position for future elevation, than the office you now hold, and at the same time it would prevent that contention and strife in the ranks of our friends which would otherwise be inevitable. Brown concurs with me in opinion, Johnson acquieses. I have consulted no others. If this arrangement could take place, a judicious one as I believe it to be, we could then run either, Carroll, C. Johnson, or Trousdale for Govr. and if they were defeated, the only loss would be the loss of their election, a small matter, compared with the loss in case of your defeat. I have writin plainly and expressed my views freely. It only remains for you to consider and take such course as your better judgement may suggest. I would be pleased to hear from [you].

H L TURNEY

ALS. DLC–JKP. Addressed to Nashville and marked "*Private.*"

1. See Daniel Graham to Polk, December 11, 1840.

FROM A. O. P. NICHOLSON

Dear Sir: Columbia Dec. 23. 1840

Your favor of the 22nd inst[1] tendering to me the appointment of Senator to fill the vacancy occasioned by the death of Mr. Grundy was received this evening, and in compliance with your request I send you an immediate answer. After weighing all the circumstances and consulting with a good many of our friends I have concluded to accept the appointment, provided it will answer to leave Nashville by Sunday the 27th inst. I shall devote myself diligently to preparing for a departure, and if I can get through to-morrow I will be in Nashville on Friday evening, if not on Saturday, and ready to leave on Sunday morning. I learn from Dr. Hays that you are going down the river.[2] If it will suit you to start on Sunday if a boat goes that day or on Saturday if I can get in on Friday, I should be much gratified if we could go together. If it can be so arranged that we can go together I should be glad if you will have the arrangement made. I feel sensibly the honor conferred upon me by the appointment and I shall endeavor so to fulfil the trust that you may not regret the confidence reposed in me.

A. O. P. NICHOLSON

ALS. DLC–JKP. Addressed to Nashville.

1. Letter not found.
2. The Cumberland River.

TO A. O. P. NICHOLSON

Dear Sir Nashville Decr. 24th 1840

Your letter of acceptance[1] of the appointment of Senator was received this ev[en]ing. I shall expect you here by Saturday's stage, when I will issue and deliver to you your commission. I will go down the River by the first Boat after you arrive & of course we will travel together as far as the mouth.[2]

JAMES K. POLK

ALS. NHi. Addressed to Columbia. Published in *THQ*, III, p. 74.

1. See A. O. P. Nicholson to Polk, December 23, 1840.
2. Reference is to the confluence of the Cumberland and Ohio rivers at Smithland, Kentucky.

FROM SARAH C. POLK

Dear Husband

Nashville Dec. 31st 1840

There has nothing occured that is of much consequence since you left. The appointment of Senator[1] as far as I have learned [has] been well received. Letters have come to you from Washington from *Brown*, John[son] & Turney,[2] written before Mr Grundys death but anticipating the event, proposing or I might say suggesting to you that it might be necessary and propper to call the Legislature together for the purpose of electing Senators, for it is almost reduced to a certainty that there *will be* a call Session of Congress in the spring. In which event Brown & Turney both write that *you* should be the person to be elected. I have given you their views written to you privately in as few words as I could express the intention. I do not understand *matters* sufficiently well to form an opinion yet; it does not strike me that it is the right thing for you to do. They all seem to think there will be a call Session of the Congress early in the spring. Johnson wrote that he could not run again, and that it was necessary to have his successor settled on and ready to take the field. This is the Washington news. As to home there has come some letters from Memphis which seem to be of some interest about the Rail R. Directors. One from McLemore[3] & one from Gaines.[4] There appears to be much feeling and excitement on the subject, but I suppose at Memphis you learn[ed] all about it. There are some Sheriff returns which is all that has come to hand. I saw Mr Jerry George[5] last evening but he does not seem to know much about any thing. I have just given Maj G.[6] such letters as you directed me; all he seemed to know was the speculation about the new Cabinet, all of which is to be seen in the papers now and before you left. Now as to *myself* I have been waiting to receive the *meat* before I would leave for Murfreesboro'. This is Thursday and it has not yet come. I sent Elias to the man on Monday. He was not at home so you may see that I am in a state of uncertainty yet. I will go on Saturday, I think, *meat or no meat.* Though I do not know that it will make a man think any more of his *wife* for her to neglect the domestic duties of the house hold, I will riske it at all events. As directed I will write again at Murfreesboro' and hope to hear from you soon.

SARAH POLK

ALS. DLC–JKP. Addressed to Somerville. Published in *THQ* XI, pages 182–83.

1. See A. O. P. Nicholson to Polk, December 23, 1840.

2. See Aaron V. Brown to Polk, December 21, 1840; Cave Johnson to Polk, December 15, 1840; and Hopkins L. Turney to Polk, December 21, 1840.

3. Polk received four letters from John C. McLemore, dated December 14, 21, 23, and 27, 1840, in which it is repeatedly urged that those appointed by the state to the directorate of the LaGrange and Memphis railroad must be persons friendly to the railroad and to the promotion of Ft. Pickering. McLemore also argues for an early and economical completion of the railroad. ALsS. DLC–JKP. Construction of the LaGrange and Memphis railroad, chartered in 1835, did not begin until 1838 and then progressed but very slowly. Never completed, the railroad failed in about 1842.

4. In a letter of December 24, 1840, Pendleton G. Gaines criticizes the present directory's extravagance and its unsatisfactory construction program, which has caused a loss for the railroad of "not less than 20 or 25 per cent per annum on the labor done on account of its unfinished condition." Gaines makes six recommendations for new state directors of the railroad. ALS. DLC–JKP.

5. Jeremiah George Harris.

6. Daniel Graham.

1841

FROM HARVEY M. WATTERSON

Dear Sir, Washington City Jan. 3d [1841][1]

Had I any thing to write about, you should hear from me frequently. Every thing is calm and quiet here on the subject of politics. But little has been done in either branch of Congress—and aside from the appropriation Bill, I think but little will be done during the present Session. It is generally believed that Gen Harrison will call an Extra Session of Congress. How would such a move operate on our Tennessee elections? I fear badly, though it would give us two Senators.[2] When I say badly I mean upon our Congressional elections—for it is more than probable that it would operate favorably upon your election. I have written to Maj Harris at Beech Grove, to Long at Shelbyville, and to the Sheriff of Marshall to send me complete lists of all the voters in the fraction of Coffee, in new Bedford, and in the fraction of Marshall.[3] So far as old Bedford is concerned, I am determined to have a thorough organization of our party. With it we can give the vote of 1839, and if Gen Armstrong is displaced to make room for *John P. Erwin*,[4] it will increase our strength. You have a desperate fight on hand and I might add you have much to gain by a triumph. It would show your strength among the real people and place you very prominently before the American people for any Office within their gift. Your success depends, in my humble opinion, almost entirely upon a proper organization throughout the state, and the ability with which you are sustained by the candidates for Congress and the Legislature on the Democratic ticket.

No doubt you have seen Mr Bentons letter to Moses Dawson Esq recommending Mr Van Buren as the candidate of the Democracy in 1844.[5] With due defference to Mr Bentons better judgment I think this is premature to say the least of it. It occurs to me as our true policy not to show *our hands* for about three years. Then if Mr Van Buren should be pointed out as the man, we will all unite upon him. But I question very much whether the state of Tennessee could ever be carried for him. He was ruined, killed up by Judge Whites popularity in 1836. There are prejudices against him in Tennessee, which, I fear, can never be eradicated—though I do not believe we ever had a President, who stood up with more firmness to his principles and the principles of the Constitution than has Martin Van Buren—and for one I would support him with great pleasure.

I am gratified at the appointment of Nicholson to the Senate. Gen Carroll being out of the way on account of ill health, I do not believe you could have made a better or more popular appointment. Now I presume Thomas will run for the Senate and your brother and Barkly Martin for the House of Representatives.[6]

I learn that Dr. Thomas[7] is a candidate for Congress. Can he not be ruled off? I know his *strength,* still I would much prefer his being out of the way. You have more influence with him than any body else.

I think we will be able to make something out of Harrison's Cabinet. If our people can stand Daniel Webster, and *such Republicans,* they can stand any thing and any body.

The "Spoils principle" is not so odious [to][8] the Whigs at this time, as it was previous to [the el]ection. They say Harrison will turn out every man who has been *medling* in the elections—by which they mean every Democrat. He is expected here in a few days, when he will be annoyed to death by the Office Seekers.

If you know of any thing in particular which I can do either in my own district or out of it to advance the cause in which we are engaged, let me hear from you and if in my power, it shall be attended to.

H M Watterson

ALS. DLC–JKP. Addressed to Nashville.

1. Although Watterson clearly wrote "1840," content analysis identifies the year as 1841.

2. Watterson assumes that Polk will call a special session of the Tennessee Assembly to elect one U.S. Senator to a full six-year term and a second to the remaining four years of Felix Grundy's term. A. O. P. Nicholson's interim appointment to Grundy's seat would expire when the Assembly next met and elected a successor or upon the adjournment of that body. Polk declined calling a special session of the Assembly; and the Twenty-fourth General Assembly failed to fill either place in the U.S. Senate. Tennessee was without representation in the U.S. Senate from February 7, 1842, until October 16, 1843.

3. Harris, Medicus A. Long, and John R. Hill. Harris is not further identified. Hill was sheriff of Marshall County from 1836 until 1842. Upon the

organization of Coffee and Marshall counties in 1836, Bedford County was reduced considerably both in its size and voting strength. The boundaries of the Ninth Congressional District, fixed in 1832, could not be changed until completion of the federal census of 1840.

4. A Nashville lawyer and Whig, John P. Erwin had served as Nashville postmaster from 1826 until 1829. Robert Armstrong succeeded Erwin and held that post until 1845. Erwin also served as mayor of Nashville in 1834.

5. Thomas H. Benton's letter, dated December 6, 1840, was addressed to Moses Dawson, who became editor of the St. Louis *Missouri Argus* in late 1840.

6. Jonas E. Thomas, William H. Polk, and Barkly Martin.

7. Isaac J. Thomas.

8. Manuscript is mutilated here and below.

FROM RICHARD M. WOODS

Dear Sir,

Greeneville 6th Jany 1841

I have seen your letter to Col. Johnson of the 15 November.[1] I am not prepared to believe that Democratic principles have finaly gone down in Tennessee. The large majority against us, was affected by a kind of artificial excitement, *Mobbocracy*, carried on and kept up, with Log cabins, Whisky & cider, coonskins, Tip. songs, roudy conventions, and lies. The Leaders in East Tennessee seem determined to keep the excitement up, with *Jubalees*, drunken feasts, Balls, parties, and conventions, all through the country. I doubt we cannot better it much next August unless we get something new, and tangable, that was not pressed the last race. But we are determined not to give up the Ship. We will give them the best fight we can. We have had a Democratic meeting here and appointed a County Convention, to meet on the 1st Saturday in March next, of Delegates from each Civil District, to nominate a candidate to represent this County in the Legislature, and to recommend suitable candidates for Senate and Floter between us and Washington.[2] Esqr Balch I think will be for the Senate, and Col Johnson for his old place.[3] We have no prominent men for the County, that can do much on the stump, that will be nominated.

Col Johnson does not wish to run for Congress and a majority in this county, are not willing he should. We do not wish to loose his services altogether, and there is no possible chance, to elect him in our District as it now is. We are about ⅓. Neither do I think he could change the parties much. It would appear to be the old race kept up, and the Parties would rally prety much as they did in November.

I have lately been at Jonesborough consulting with some of our friends there, on the subject of candidates most particularly *Congress.* We all agree, that it would be best, to have a candidate if he was strong and able to defend our principles on the stump, effeciently. John Blair, could do more in bringing our old party back to their old Democratic stand than any other man in the District, but I fear he cannot be got out altho he thinks we ought by all means to have a Candidate for Congress—and wants Col Johnson to run. I and a particular friend of Blairs,[4] while at Jonesborough agreed that I should say to you *confidentially,* that you could have more influence over him, than any other person in the state, that if you would press it on him, to permit his name to be used and publish a circular, and send it through the District, & that then perhaps with our call on him, he could be got out. If started he would not suffer himself or his party to be assailed without making resistance. *Will* you *help* us? We had rather have no candidate on our side as to have one who was not able and willing to spend some time and cash to promote the cause, and who was able to do it well. If Blair does not offer I think we will not have any, but try to get up oposition in the Whig ranks and get them divided. A Whig convention which is to meet here the 1st Monday in April, will nominate Thos D Arnold, I think without doubt; our plan (if we have no candidate) will be, to get Genl Brazleton,[5] to oppose him, if *we can,* and elect him. We want to put Arnold on the shelf if possible. I have great confidence in your foresight, skill and ability in arrangeing such things for the best, and would be glad to hear from you when convenient. It appears that D. W. Dickinson will be your opponent.

R. M. Woods

ALS. DLC–JKP. Addressed to Nashville.

1. Polk's letter to Andrew Johnson has not been found.

2. Greene County held one seat in the Tennessee House and shared a second or "floating" seat with neighboring Washington County. In the Senate Greene County shared a seat with Hawkins County.

3. Andrew Johnson, whose "old place" was the "floating" House seat for Greene and Washington counties, won election in 1841 to the Tennessee Senate for Greene and Hawkins counties.

4. Not identified further.

5. William Brazelton.

FROM CAVE J. COUTS[1]

Military Academy West Point N. Y.
January 13, [1841][2]

Dear Sir,

As our Semi-anual examination has just been completed, and knowing the interest which you take in your young friends, I deem it my duty, and which at the same time affords me *great* pleasure, to inform you of the success of our friend Walker,[3] from Columbia, which I know both you and Mrs. Polk, will be happy to hear. He has sustained the reputation of your district, I assure you, and come out with much honor to himself, and his friends.

Near ninety entered in his class last June, and only about fifty got through the examination. And generally, there are as many as one fourth of every class that comes on, discharged at, or before the first Jany. examination, from which you see that you have been very fortunate in your selections—in fact I know of no one, whom you ever appointed, that failed to succeed. I hear from our friend Boyd[4] frequently. He is now in Florida, where he has been ever since a short time after graduating. He was very much surprised, and discouraged, as well as myself, at the result of the elections. Tennessee particularly. Lt. Thomas,[5] is still here. I suppose you will be surprised to hear that he is one of the *warmest whigs,* I nearly ever met with. He Says that he holds his pollitticks next to his religion & that he *glories in the name of Federalist;* he thinks that you are broken down, that you will undoubtedly be beaten for Gov. next summer—and then go to Maury, and be beaten for Congress, as our party will be so split up. I called on him just before your last election, and he was then, one of your strongest pol. supporters. Now he is just the contrary, and says that he has not changed his pollitticks.

I regretted very much to hear of the death of Judge Grundy and of one of my brothers[6] by the same mail.

Young Walker, joins me in love to you and Mrs. Polk.

CADET C. J. COUTS

ALS. DLC–JKP. Addressed to Nashville.

1. A nephew of Cave Johnson, Couts was appointed to the U.S. Military Academy in 1839 and was graduated in 1843. He remained in the Army until 1851, when he resigned and moved to San Diego, California. There he served on frontier duty for two years.

2. Erroneously dated "1840"; year identified through content analysis.

3. Calvin H. Walker left West Point in 1841 and studied at Philadelphia's Jefferson College, from which he was graduated in 1847. Returning to Maury County, he practiced medicine until the Civil War. Walker was killed in battle near Marietta, Georgia, in June 1864.

4. Joseph B. Boyd, a son of Aaron Boyd of Chapel Hill, Tennessee, was graduated from the U.S. Military Academy in 1839; he served two years in the Seminole War in Florida, 1839–41, and returned to Nashville to practice law in 1842.

5. John A. Thomas, a son of Isaac J. Thomas of Columbia, was graduated from the U.S. Military Academy in 1833, remained at the Academy as a pro-

fessor from 1834 until 1841, and served as Commandant from 1842–45. Subsequently, he moved to New York City where he entered the legal profession.

6. Cave Couts' brother is not identified further.

FROM A. O. P. NICHOLSON

Dear Sir: Washington City Jany 13th 1841

After a tedious and uncomfortable trip of fifteen days I reached here on Sunday night inst and took my seat on Monday morning. I could not have arrived at a more propitius time. The discussion on the land question[1] was just fairly under way and altho I have been here but two days I have already heard Mangum, Benton, Crittenden and Calhoun[2] deliver set-speeches. It is manifest that the whole session will be consumed in discussing the land questions and the resolution of Mr. Clay to repeal the Sub-treasury with a distinct understanding that nothing definite is to be done.[3] I was much gratified on my arrival to find that you have the warmest friends here of any man who has ever been here. Great anxiety is manifested as to your success next summer, and I am now better satisfied than ever that you cannot estimate too highly the importance of the contest to you personally. To be plain I shall be disappointed, if your success in this contest does not lead on certainly to your elevation to the Presidency. I have conversed freely with Watterson about the difficulties in his way. I find him as fully bent on running as he can be and I have entirely despaired of inducing him to withdraw. He will however consent to a district convention to rule off Dr. Thomas, but to a convention to rule off both he will not consent. He manifests great feeling about the matter—so much so that I see no chance to arrange the matter but by running him again. The Tennessee Land Bill has passed the Senate in the same shape in which it passed before, and will certainly pass the House of Representatives in a very few days. Our members are fully alive to the importance of its passage and are using the proper exertions to make it soon. The Committee in the House of Rep. have agreed unanimously to recommend its passage. There is now no kind of doubt entertained here but there will be a called session of Congress. It is conceded on all hands by both sides that Gen. Harrison's first movement will be to convene Congress. I have not yet had an opportunity to examine the Statutes of Tennessee to see whether there is any law providing for an election to Congress under the circumstances now presented; but I find that it is a subject which is canvassed here and the impression is, that there is such a statute. Our friend Genl Anderson feels great solicitude about his re-election, but in my opinion he will find it an up-hill business with East Tennessee.

The Cabinet is all formed here except the Treasury & Navy Depts. Webster to be Secty of State, Crittenden Atto Genl, Bell Scty of War, Ewing Post Master Genl, these are certain—doubtless by now. And if we cant make a revolution in Ten. on such a cabinet I shall be deceived. Just think of Webster the anti-war fed, and the two gaggers! But rumor makes another officer which will be still worse. Granger[4] it is said will be Secty of the Navy. This is not certain but highly probable. For the Treasury the question lies between Sergeant & Clayton. Old Tip has not yet come on, but will be here about the 1st of Feby. It is well understood now that an arrangement has been made between Clay, Harrison & Webster by which Webster yields to Clay for the next contest and therefore Harrison gives Clay nothing. So soon as the Cabinet is formed this matter ought to be brought up at every point simultaneously and a storm at once raised. We surely can redeem Ten. with such materials to work upon. I visited Mr. Van Buren yesterday and found him as calm and resigned as if he had met with no defeat. He inquired with much solicitude after you and your prospects. I was exceedingly mortified at the remarks of Mr. Harris in the Union in relation to the appointment of Senator.[5] Many of his remarks I regard as injudicious and indiscreet and one or two of them imprudent and rather unkind. He is certainly deficient in judgment or he would have seen that his remarks were injudicious. I will write you immediately upon the passage of the Ten. Land Bill and enclose a copy of it. I shall expect to hear from you frequently.

A. O. P. Nicholson

P.S. Cave Johnson's health is very good this winter, and I am now disposed to think he can be induced to make another run—but this is not certain. A. O. P. N.

ALS. DLC–JKP. Addressed to Nashville.

1. The Tennessee land bill, introduced in the U.S. Senate by Alexander O. Anderson on December 16, 1840, and passed on February 17, 1841, gave occupants an unconditional right to preempt public lands in the Western District of Tennessee at twelve and a half cents an acre.

2. Willie P. Mangum, Thomas H. Benton, John J. Crittenden, and John C. Calhoun. A North Carolina lawyer, Mangum served in the State House and sat on the Superior Court of North Carolina before winning election to two terms in the U.S. House, 1823–27. Subsequently he won election as a Whig to the U.S. Senate, where he served several terms, 1831–36 and 1840–53.

3. On December 14, 1840, Henry Clay presented a resolution in the Senate calling for the Finance Committee to report a bill for the repeal of the Sub-Treasury system. The resolution was tabled the following day.

4. Francis Granger, a New York lawyer and Whig, served two terms in the U.S. House, 1835–37 and 1839–41, before resigning to accept an appointment

as postmaster general in Harrison's cabinet. He served in that capacity from March until September 1841, when he returned to the House.

5. On December 28, 1840, Jeremiah Harris wrote that the Senatorial appointment had been offered first to William Carroll and George W. Campbell, both of whom declined. Harris described Nicholson as "a much younger gentleman than either Judge Campbell or Governor Carroll . . . of the same school of politics—and is favorably known as a man of extensive political information with more than ordinary talents."

FROM ISAAC H. DISMUKES[1]

Oakachickama P[ost Office] Mis Yal[obusha Co.]
January the 21 1841

Dear Sir

I now take it upon my self to write you a fiew lines to inform you that your cotten left troy the 14 of this month for new orleans. I did not assertain it until the 19 of the month: the remaining part of your cotten is not yet pick out for the weather has bin so unfavourable that I could not have it pict unless picking it weat far wea have not had more than too fair dais since you left hear and they wase too could to pick cotten. I wil pick it as soon as the weather wil omit it. I pick on it one day and the ground was so weat that the hands could scarcely walk through it so if I had of pick it weat it would of bin hear yet for wea have had no sun to dry weat cotten: I have bin mostly engage in the new ground since you left hear when the weather would omit it but their has bin several weat dais and snow togeather so wea could not work. I think that if the weather had not bin so vary bad that I could of had it cleard down to the bridge: the pork that you bought when down hear lost 300 pounds and I saw baker[2] after killing it and wanted him to refun something back but hea would not do it: The hands work finely and keep well so fair: The best estimate that I can make of the hoges that wea wil have to kill a nother year is betwean 60 & 70 heads concludeing piges & all in and sum of them is very poor and I am afraid that I shall loose sum of them as the corn is scarce as you noe: I paide thomas oliver[3] $74 and thare is a balance as yet of $12 for the reparing of the brush wheal. After the first work which you node nothing of the account was presented to mea but I did not pay it as I ware not autherise to doo it: I am making arrangements to have some cloth made as soon as I can: I am geting milk and butter more than I my self make use of. The children have sum occasionly. Wea have noe young calfs as yet nor wea wil not have enny until spring. I had to write a bout all of these little things to make out my letter. Nouthing more but remain . . . .

ISAAC H DISMUKES

ALS. DLC–JKP. Addressed to Nashville. Published in Bassett, *Plantation Overseer*, 148–49.

1. Dismukes managed Polk's Mississippi plantation from 1841 until 1845.
2. Baker is not identified further.
3. Thomas Oliver is not identified further.

FROM E. G. EASTMAN

Dear Sir: Argus office Knoxville, Jan. 21 [18]41

The pecuniary concerns of the Argus office being somewhat embarrassed, I have had serious thoughts of abandoning the enterprise, as I have had, recently, several very flattering offers to remove to other states. At the request of friends, however, I have determined, before finally closing the office, to consult the friends of our cause in Nashville; and, laying before them a fair statement of the concerns of the office, leave them to decide its fate—to sustain it by lending temporary aid, or to let it fail by withholding assistance. I am aware that I ought to make this appeal to some one beside yourself, but as I am totally unacquainted with any one else in Nashville, I must beg of you the favor to hand this to some one who will act promptly, if you think any action necessary on what I have to say.[1]

When I came to Knoxville it was with the expectation—the express promise—that the money necessary to pay for the office was to be loaned for three years without interest. Instead of this, I have had to pay every dollar for the cost of the office out of its earnings; and as, during the first year, these were small, it embarrassed me much to meet those payments. It has been utterly impossible to collect the money the office has earned, owing to the hardness of the times. The office is therefore somewhat in debt, and that, too, to whigs. $800 would completely relieve it from embarrassments, and insure the permanent continuance of the paper. If I could borrow this sum in Nashville, to be paid back in one, two, and three years, with interest, I could give the most unquestioned security for the loan. If I cannot, I shall be obliged to close the office, and force collections. There are now near $5000 due me from subscribers and advertisers, and yet I cannot, in these times, collect more of this than enough to defray the current expenses of the office. But the debts incurred in establishing the office must be paid immediately.

You are aware that the Argus is located in the midst of a population almost exclusively whig. In the strong Democratic neighborhood of

Washington, Sullivan, Greene, and Hawkins, our party have the Sentinel[2] to support, and in the lower part of East Tennessee, where the remaining strength of Democracy lies, they have the Athens Courier. In *my* neighborhood, our party is not only very weak, but very poor. They have not the means to sustain the Argus at this juncture, with every disposition to sustain it. I will not ask favors from our Knoxville Banks, and probably could not get them if I did. This is the reason why I am obliged to look to Nashville, as the only hope. The Democrats here seem to be fully aware of the importance of having a paper devoted to their principles published here, and so far as procuring subscribers is concerned, I have nothing to complain of; but they have no money now, and without it I cannot longer continue here. I have, then, to request a loan from the more wealthy Democrats of Middle Tennessee of $800, which shall be repaid, with interest, in equal proportions, in one, two, and three years, and for the prompt repayment of which I will give the most unquestioned security. If this can be arranged, the Argus can go on its way rejoicing. If not, I shall be forced immediately to discontinue it. Will you have the goodness to write me by return mail whether you think the arrangement can be made; and if it can, tell me what course I must adopt to procure the funds? I shall be very impatient to hear from Nashville, and if you have not time to attend to it will you do me the favor to get some one of the friends of the cause in Nashville to answer this?

E. G. EASTMAN

P.S. We are organizing secretly but efficiently in E.T. In this county, Crozier says we could give you to-day 600 votes. The "hard times" will be much in our favor. If they should not improve before August, there will be an overwhelming revolution here. In our Congressional District there is much ill feeling between the friends of J. L. Williams and A. A. Anderson, rival candidates for Congress. The same division extends to candidates for the Legislature. In Blackwell's district, the Feds are fighting the battle of the Kilkenny cats.[3] Every thing appears to be working right for us, and the prospect is more encouraging than it has ever been before, since I have been acquainted here. You may rest assured that we will do our part towards redeeming the State. Our friends are not in the least disheartened or discouraged. E.

ALS. DLC–JKP. Addressed to Nashville. AEs on the cover state that this letter was answered severally on January 26, 30, and 31, 1841; Polk's replies have not been found.

1. On February 24, 1841, Eastman writes that on this date he has sent Robert Armstrong a promissory note for a loan to be arranged in Nashville and that such an accommodation would place the *Argus* "on a firm and permanent footing." ALS. DLC–JKP.

2. Jonesboro *Tennessee Sentinel.*

3. Allusion is a humorous explanation given for the disappearances of two Kilkenny cats; it is said that they fought each other so ferociously that nothing remained of them but their tails.

TO WILLIAM MOORE

Sir

Nashville Jany 30 1841

I have to request that you will inform me, whether the returns of the strength of the Several Divisions of the militia of the State for the last year have been received by you. The Return of Majr. General Hays[1] of the strength of the 4th Division is here, but none other has come to hand. By the act passed at the last session of the General Assembly (chap. 56 sec. 60) it is made the duty of the Majr. Generals to cause returns of the strength of their respective Divisions to be made to you, "on or before the 15th day of September in *each year.*" If these Returns or any of them, have not been received by you, you will take immediate steps to cause them to be made forthwith, and when received Report them to me without delay. I have received from the U. States the quota of Public arms, to which this state was entitled for the year 1840,[2] which cannot be apportioned among the respective Divisions as directed by law until their strength is ascertained.

James K. Polk

ALS. A. Addressed to Mulberry Post Office, Lincoln County.

1. Samuel Jackson Hays, a nephew of Rachel Jackson, moved to Jackson, Tennessee, about 1830. He became a very wealthy planter and rose to the rank of major general in the militia. Subsequently, he served in the Mexican War.

2. In 1840 the annual allocation of arms to the Tennessee militia was set at 690 muskets. See Senate Document No. 1, 27 Congress, 2 Session, p. 106.

FROM ISAAC H. DISMUKES

Dear Sir

Miss. Yal[obusha] C. Febuary the 1, 1841

According to promise I wil now offer you a fiew lines. Wea are all wel with the exception of sum little complaining. Nouthing though very sereis: I am geting along very smoothly with buisness. I am now ready to starte my ploughs as soon as the ground gets in order for the bisness and would of had a good deal of plough dun if the weather had of bin enny more favouble but wea have had the wettest time since you left hear that I ever sean I believe: I have got all the new ground in order for burning of as soon as it dries so it wil burn. I have not had enny cloth made yet but are makeing evry nesesary arrangement and as soon as I can get sum purson to show one of the wimmin to weave I wil have sum made: I have the balance of your crop of cotten hear yet but as soon as I can get what is due you from Mr Minter I wil send it of immediately.

ISAAC H DISMUKES

ALS. DLC–JKP. Addressed to Nashville. AE on the cover states that this letter was answered on March 17, 1841; Polk's reply has not been found. Dismukes' letter is published in Bassett, *Plantation Overseer,* 149–50.

FROM HARVEY M. WATTERSON

Dear Sir Washington City Feb. 1st 1841

The Treasury Note Bill in the House and the Pre-emption Bill in the Senate have produced much discussion.[1] Both questions will be decided this week. The one will pass almost unanimously—the fate of the other is doubtful. The love of the Whig leaders in Congress for the inmates of Log Cabins has greatly cooled down since the election.

Wise's speech[2] astonished every body. He is against Clays distribution project[3]—against any disturbance of the compromise act[4]—against a called Session of Congress—acknowledged that Harrison's administration could not better the times—said the people must get out of debt by their own industry and economy—and that a National Bank would aggravate the distress of the country when it first went into opperation. The Whigs are much annoyed at his course and many of them are prepared to denounce him. Jennifer[5] stated in reply, that Wise did not speak the sentiments of the first solitary whig in Congress.

As soon as the Treasury note Bill is disposed of, we will take up the Tennessee Land Bill.[6] I do not think there is the smallest doubt of its passage and that by a large majority. Indeed there is no opposition to it—save from Williams and Montgomery of North Carolina.

It is rumored and generally believed here that the Whig Senators held a Caucus the other night, and resolved upon an Extra Session of Congress about the first of June. So you may set it down as absolutely certain, that there will be a called Session—at least such is my decided opinion.

There is no mistake but Webster, Crittendon and Bell will go into the new Cabinet. Will not these appointments greatly strengthen the Democratic cause in Tennessee?

At the next Session the Sub. Treasury Bill or law will be repealed—and the Whigs will endeavor to establish a Bank of the United States. How would it do to fight a National Bank with the State Banks—not stock Banks—but Banks owned solely and exclusively by the States—such Banks for instance, as the Bank of Tenn? I am somewhat inclined to make some such speech as this when I get home: "Now Gentlemen, if the Independent Treasury Bill is repealed—then *as against* a Bank of the United States, I am for making the State Banks the Depositories of the public money and taking their notes in payment of the public dues. This would make the notes of the Bank of Tennessee equal to gold and silver in Philadelphia, New York and Boston &c. Whatever are the profits of the Bank, will lighten your taxes—&c.—&c.—&c."

You see the drift and how will the idea do? It strikes me that I could make such an argument in favor of State Banks when contrasted with a National Bank, as would not fail to convince the people.

Harrison will be here in a few days—but he might as well remain at North Bend. Clay, Webster & Co. will not let him think or act for himself. They have already every thing arranged "cut and dried."

I will write again whenever I have any thing to write about.

H. M. WATTERSON

ALS. DLC–JKP. Addressed to Nashville.

1. The Treasury note bill, authorizing the president to issue up to $5 million in Treasury notes, won approval in both houses by large majorities and received Van Buren's signature on February 15, 1841. The permanent prospective pre-emption bill, introduced by Thomas Hart Benton and known as the "Log Cabin bill," provided settlers the right to purchase at minimum prices 160 acres of public land; the bill further stipulated that owners must cultivate the soil, construct a log cabin, and occupy the property. Benton's bill passed in the Senate on February 2, but failed by a large margin in the House on the last day of the session.

2. Henry A. Wise spoke in the House on January 27, 28, and 29, 1841, in favor of the Treasury note bill.

3. Since the 1820's Henry Clay had advocated distributing to the states those federal revenues raised from the sale of public lands. In June of 1841 such a bill, which also granted settlers preemption rights at minimum prices, was reintroduced in the U.S. House. The preemption-distribution bill became law in September, but Congress repealed the measure the following year.

4. The compromise tariff of 1833 provided for the gradual reduction of rates over a ten-year period and thus helped ease the nullification crisis.

5. Daniel Jenifer.

6. See A. O. P. Nicholson to Polk, January 13, 1841.

TO DAVID BURFORD

My Dear Sir, Nashville Feby. 2, 1841

I received a letter from you some weeks ago,[1] in answer to one which I had addressed to you,[2] in which you expressed a disinclination to enter again upon political life. I hope my Dear Sir, that you will excuse the liberty I take in asking you to reconsider that determination, and attribute it, to the solicitude which I feel for the success of our common principles. The present is a great crisis in public affairs, and I regard the next elections in Tennessee as more important in their consequences, than any which have ever occurred, particularly the Legislative elections, for the reason that the next Legislature will have the Congressional Districts to lay off, to stand for 10 years, the state apportionment to make, two Senators in Congress to elect, as well as the ordinary business of legislation to perform. Since I received your letter I have seen many of our leading political friends from Sumner all of whom concur in the opinion that you can be elected to the Senate, if you will yield your consent. The Revd. H. M. Cryer[3] was here to day, and expressed the same opinion. He informed me that steps had been taken, to call a Convention of our friends to meet at Gallatin on the first day of the Circuit Court, which I believe is on the 3rd Monday of this month, to make a nomination for Senator. I am satisfied if it was known that you would accept that you would be nominated, and I am as well satisfied that you would be elected. I am aware that if you yield your assent, that it may cost you some sacrifice of individual interests, but these we must all make in order to obtain a greater public good. I learn that young *Mr. Allen*, the son of the *Col.*,[4] is an exceedingly worthy and popular man in *Smith*, and could probably be elected to the House. Can he be induced to run? If he can, our ticket would be strengthened in that County. In the approaching contest we will have advantages, which we have not heretofore possessed. Our position will be that of assault and not of defense. We will have no candidate in the field for the Presidency. Our opponents will be in power, and theirs will be the post of responsibility. New issues must necessarily be formed. For example *Webster* and other Federalists will constitute the new Cabinet; and their political character and public conduct cannot be successfully defended before the people of Tennessee. I do not yet know who my opponent is to be, and I suppose will not until our leading opponents meet in a self-constituted convention on the 4th of March and pass the decree. I shall be ready to meet him as soon as he chooses to take the fie[ld].[5] He shall not have a day the start of me [in] the canvass. I have recently passed through the Western

Division of the State; saw *Coe* and others. They are all active in organizing and agreeing upon their candidates. I found that we were already stronger, and in some Counties much stronger than we were in November. I have great confidence in our success, and all I ask of my friends is, that they will organize, and bring out suitable candidates in the different Counties, so as to sustain me reasonably in the canvass. I must again ask you to excuse any importunity in again addressing you, and shall hope to hear from you soon.

James K. Polk

ALS. TU. Addressed to Dixon's Springs, Tennessee, and marked "*Private.*"

1. See David Burford to Polk, November 14, 1840.
2. See Polk to David Burford, November 7, 1840.
3. Hardy M. Cryer, a Sumner County Methodist minister, had been associated frequently with Andrew Jackson in the business of breeding of race horses.
4. The son of Colonel Robert Allen of Smith County is not identified further.
5. A sealing stain in the right margin of the manuscript's third page has obliterated a portion of this word and possibly the whole of another word at the end of the following line.

FROM A. O. P. NICHOLSON

My Dear Sir: Washington City. Feby 2. 1841

Upon an accurate count made this morning by Mr. Calhoun on the question of a U.S. Bank as it will be presented at the next session of Congress, if there is a called session: Mr. Calhoun's count makes 26 in favor of a Bank and 24 against it, leaving Mr. Preston's vote uncertain and one Senator from Tennessee vacant.[1] If the Senate is full from Tennessee it will stand for a Bank 26 and against it 25, with Mr. Preston's vote uncertain. In this point of view the question of a called session of our Legislature becomes exceedingly important. I give you the result of this count that you may have all the lights before you in making up your mind as to a called session of our Legislature.

3½ O'clock

The Log Cabin Bill has this moment passed its third and last reading by a vote of 31 to 19—the Whigs generally voting against it.[2]

A. O. P. Nicholson

ALS. DLC–JKP. Addressed to Nashville.

1. See Harvey M. Watterson to Polk, January 3, 1841.
2. See Harvey M. Watterson to Polk, February 1, 1841.

TO ROBERT B. REYNOLDS

My Dear Sir Nashville Feby. 4th 1841

The meeting of the Whig Convention which is to take place on the 4th of March at Murfreesborough, to nominate my opponent, will probably be the signal for the opening of the next political canvass in the State. Are we ready? For myself I answer in the affirmative. I am not only ready, but I go into the contest confident of success if I can be reasonably sustained by the local candidates, and our friends will *organize* & go actively to work in every County. The Legislative elections are vastly important, even more so than the Gubernatorial or Congressional, for the reason that the next Legislature will have the Congressional Districts to lay off to stand for 10 years, the State apportionment to make, two Senators in Congress to elect, besides other important officers to choose, and the ordinary business of legislation to perform. Our candidates everywhere should be out early and ready to take the field when the Gubernatorial canvass opens, which will probably be shortly after the 4th of March. What has been done in E. Ten.? Who are to be our candidates in the Counties around you? I shall take the liberty of submitting to you such suggestions as occur to me, in relation to the movements in your part of the State, as well as I can judge at this distance. It strikes me then, that *McKamy* in Blount, and *Col. Hembree* in Roane are our strongest men in their Counties, and I think it important that they should run again. *Genl. Julian Frazier*, I think can represent Grainger, or if *Wheeler's* health is such as to compel him to decline for the Senate, *Frazier* might take his place, and let some other, say *John* or *James Lafferty* run for the House in Grainger.[1] In the double Representative District composed of *Campbell, Anderson & Morgan*, I am satisfied that *Majr. Richd. Oliver*, could have been elected in 1839—and I think it probable he can be now. Could not *Oliver & R. A. Dabney Esqr.* of Morgan,[2] or some other whom our friends may select be elected? If they can, it would beyond all doubt secure the Legislature; though I think we may be safe without them. They should however be induced to run if possible. I will not go into further details. It is our true policy, and indeed very important—to run candidates—in every County and District. It is the most effectual way—to bring out our whole strength. I beg you My Dear Sir! to see and write to our friends in every part of East Tennessee, and urge them to bring out their candidates without delay. We must not suffer our opponents to take the start of us, in the next canvass. We lost greatly by suffering them to do so during the last canvass. We must not be discouraged by the apparent majorities against us in November. It was produced by temporary causes, which cannot again be brought to bear upon us. We will have advantages in the next contest, which we have never before possessed. Our position will be that [of] assault and not of defense. We will have no designated candidate for the Presidency in the field, and will not therefore be called upon, to defend *Mr Van Buren* or any other of our prominent men against the personal objections or prejudices, which may be urged against them. Our opponents will be in power & theirs, will be the position of responsibility. New issues must necessarily be formed. For example *Webster* & other federal[ists][3] will form the new Cabinet, & their political character & public conduct cannot be successfully defended before the people of Tennessee. Let our friends be roused, *organize,* bring out suitable *candidates* & go actively to work and our triumph in August will be complete. In the Western Division of the State, through which I have lately passed, our friends are in good spirits, and are actively engaged in organizing and agreeing upon their candidates. They told me that we were stronger & in some Counties much stronger than we were in November. You can if you choose communicate these views to my friends *Dr. Ramsey, A. Crozier* & *E. G. Eastman* Esqr. We here will do our duty & look confidently to our friends in E. Ten. to come up to the good work & aid us. Let me hear from you soon.

JAMES K. POLK

ALS. NHi. Addressed to Knoxville. AE on the cover states that this letter was answered on February 15, 1841.

1. Although he had moved from Grainger to Claiborne County, Frazier remained in the same senatorial district. John and James Lafferty are not identified further.

2. Richard Oliver and Robert A. Dabney. Dabney became court clerk upon the organization of Morgan County in 1817.

3. A sealing stain in the right margin of the manuscript's third page has obliterated a portion of one word.

FROM WILLIAM C. TATE[1]

Morganton, North Carolina. February 6, 1841

William C. Tate states that he has been named guardian of the minor heirs of Marshall T. Polk. Tate sends a certified copy of his appointment[2] and advises that he will send Polk a receipt for all funds received for the children's benefit.

ALS. DLC–JKP. Addressed to Nashville. AE on the cover reads as follows: "Transcript of Record of appointment of Wm. C. Tate guardian in the State of N. Carolina of M. T. Polk's minor children. Ansd. Feby. 15th, 1841." Polk's reply has not been found.

1. William C. Tate, a physician in North Carolina, married Laura Wilson Polk, the widow of Polk's brother and mother of Roxana Eunice Ophelia Polk and Marshall T. Polk, Jr.

2. Tate's enclosure is a certified extract from the official records of the Court of Pleas and Quarter Sessions for Burke County, North Carolina.

FROM ANDREW JACKSON

My dear Sir, Hermitage February 8th 1841

On saturday last I rec'd the inclosed from Mr Nicholson[1] which I hasten to inclose you.

If there should be a call session of congress it will be important to have a full representation in the senate which I believe will give us a republican majority.

If it can be done with propriety, if there is a call session of congress—the Legislature should be convened to give us a full representation in the senate; and to instruct our senators & request our representatives to vote against a high Tarriff, a distribution of the public Lands, against a national Bank of any kind, or deposits in the state Banks and against a repeal of the sub treasury act, and, altho last not least, to pass a law to compell our Banks to resume specie payments or wind up. I do believe that resolutions such as I have suggested by the Legislature would give us a full republican representation. Please think of this. In haste . . . .

Andrew Jackson

P.S. Let me see you soon.

ALS. DLC–JKP. Addressed to Nashville.

1. Enclosure not found.

FROM JOHN F. GILLESPY

My dear Sir, Washington City D. Co[lum]bia Feby 12th 1841

I am now for the first time in the Metropolis of the U States, where I have been "a looker on in Venice"[1] since my arrival on the 24th ult. The monottony of the scene every day repeated of the rolling and tumbling backwards and forward of drays, gocarts, cabs, Hacks, carriages, cars, crowds of men, women, children and negroes, all rushing apparantly under the influence of some powerful motive, and but few of them having any, has made the place to me uninteresting, and somewhat irksome.

The city is at present very much crowded with Strangers. Old Tip[2] arrived here on wednesday last. The day was very unfavourable, but there was much parade. Speculation as to his course is rife, and expectation on tiptoe. Clay and Webster are said to be excessively jealous of each other. Tip is said to favour Webster and his friends most; and Clay is represented to be in a very ill-humour. The Cabinet is said to be formed. Webster is to be Scty of State, Ewing of the Treasury, Bell (it said not of choice, but "en necessitate"[3]) of War, Badger[4] of the Navy. Grainger,[5] if Whittlesey[6] will take under him a subordinate appointment, is to go into the Post office, and Crittenden is to be Atto. Genl.

I am fearful, that our friend and most confident expectant, Spencer Jarnigin[7] will in the confusion of Cabinet appointments, and the organization of the Whig party at Washington be totally forgotten. This will be a most cruel negligence, and a most inexcusable oversight—but "sic transit gloria mundi."[8]

It seems to be well understood, that nothing will be done by Congress during the present Session, except to organize the parties for the next four years canvass for the presidency.

It is confidently said there will be a called Session of Congress early in the month of May next. If so our friends here deem an early call of the Genl. assembly of Tennessee indispensible, which I myself believe would be highly proper not only as a measure of *state*, but of *democratic* policy. There are several reasons, were I not a member of the Legislature, and you the Governor, that I might suggest in favour of such a measure. Should you deem it your duty to convene the Legislature by proclamation I must request the favour of you to notify me of the time fixed on to convene us, as soon as practible at Cannonsburgh Pensylvania, where I shall be on a visit to my sister[9] residing in that place, and from which place I shall upon being notified take the quickest rout to Nashville.

Preston it is said cannot be spared out of the Senate, and will secure no executive appointment. Rives is said to have anounced a determination to support the Virginia doctrines,[10] and some provision it is said will be made for him to get him out of the Senate to make room for a more tractible Whig.

JOHN F. GILLESPY

ALS. DLC–JKP. Addressed to Nashville.

1. William Shakespeare, *Measure for Measure*, act 5, scene 1.

2. William H. Harrison.

3. Variant of the Latin phrase *in necessitate*, meaning "of necessity."

4. A North Carolina lawyer, legislator, and Superior Court judge, George E. Badger served as secretary of the navy under Harrison; he later sat as a Whig in the U.S. Senate from 1846 until 1855.

5. Francis Granger.

6. An Ohio lawyer and one of the founders of the Whig party, Elisha Whittlesey served as a military aide to Harrison during the War of 1812; as a member of the Ohio House, 1820–21; as a U.S. congressman, 1823–38; as sixth auditor of the Treasury, 1841–43; and as first comptroller of the Treasury, 1849–57 and 1861–63.

7. Spencer Jarnagin.

8. Latin quotation from the pontifical coronation liturgy, which translates, "thus passes away the glory of the world."

9. Reference probably is to Ellen Jane Gillespy, who is not identified further.

10. On January 19, 1841, the Virginia House debated a resolution instructing the state's U.S. senators to oppose chartering a new bank. Delegate John F. May, a State Rights Whig, argued that the resolution was unnecessary, since William C. Rives had stated privately in September last that he opposed a national bank on grounds both of expediency and principle. *Richmond Whig and Public Advertiser*, January 22, 1841. Virginia's doctrine of limiting the power of the general government, perhaps best stated in the Virginia Resolutions of 1798, favored a strict construction of the Constitution and opposed institution of a national bank, protective tariffs, and federally financed internal improvements.

FROM A. O. P. NICHOLSON

My Dear Sir: Washington City. Feby 12. 1841

I have deferred writing for several days for the purpose of awaiting the developments as to the Cabinet &c. The Old Hero[1] arrived in a snow storm which detracted much from the *eclat* of his reception. The ceremony however was sufficiently grand and imposing to comport with the Log Cabin simplicity and democracy of the General. No certain developments as to the cabinet were made until this evening, when it became a matter of general notoriety that Gen. Harrison declined selecting his cabinet himself, but submitted the matter to his friends here, deciding however that they must choose three fro the Slave-holding and three from the non-slave holding states. In accordance with this arrangement it is pretty well understood that Webster is to be Secretary of State, Granger Post Master General, and Ewing Secretary of the Treasury, Bell Secretary of War, Crittenden Attorney General, and most probably Preston Secretary of the Navy. About the Navy there is still understood to be some uncertainty. North Carolina is supposed to be entitled to it, and Badger was considered as being selected, but we learn that the Southern Feds have kicked up at Badger's appointment and insisted on having Preston in his place. Mr. Rives and Mr. Tallmadge neither get any thing themselves nor any of their friends. It was rumored here that Talmadge was greatly dissatisfied on yesterday, but the cause is still unknown. He and Rives are standing rather by themselves, neither party showing much disposition to regard them with favor. I shall not be surprised if they stand out for some time on an independent hook until they coerce some concessions from their new allies.[2] What think you now of the Cabinet! I think you may set it down as settled that we are to have an anti-war fed for Secretary State, an abolition fed for Post Master General, a uniform fed for the Treasury, a gag-bill Clay fed for Atto Genl, a gag-bill, no party, White-Whig fed for the War, and a nullification fed for the Navy. Will not this open the eyes of Tennesseans! If not, then may we surrender at discretion. I think you may venture now to call our opponents who can stomach this cabinet *federalists* without giving offence. You will discern that with this Cabinet Mr. Clay will have unbounded control. Mr. Webster will stand alone unless he can carry with him Granger—So that Mr. Clay will be in fact the President; you know his imprudence and rashness too well to doubt for a moment that he will render the administration odious in a very short time. It is rumored that Genl. Harrison will take strong ground in his Inaugural against abolition. I think this probable, as he will ask nothing more; he will in this manner endeavor to break the force of the appointment of Granger. I do not calculate that we will be able to make any capital out of the Inaugural; but the Cabinet will be enough for our purposes, if we use it with skill. I shall endeavor to have such materials connected with the history of the cabinet officers as will be of service to us.

I have heard no doubts expressed for several days on the subject of a called session of Congress. It is spoken of as a matter of course among our friends and not denied or doubted by our opponents. If it is abandoned it will be upon consultation after this time; but I have no idea that Mr. Clay will abandon it, unless he becomes satisfied that a Bank cannot be made without two votes from Tennessee. In that event it may be abandoned, and then our state will be the battle-ground. I regret to be compelled to inform you that the Tennessee Land Bill still hangs in the House, and that its passage is now entirely uncertain.[3] The danger is that the balance of the session will be taken up with the Appropriation bills and that the Land Bill will not be reached at all. Brown is awfully troubled about it.* He is at this moment the worse *hippoed* man in Washington; unless it be some poor devil of a disappointed office hunter. I saw our little Allen Adonis Hall here, but I am unable to find out what he wants. Of course however Mr. Bell will provide for him. Brown has just come in and having recovered a little from his hysterics, he now says the bill will pass, but you know no woman ever yet admitted that she had the hysterics, so that I still doubt what he has written below. I shall write again very soon.

A. O. P. NICHOLSON

*Dont believe a word of this—It will pass. A. V. Brown

ALS. DLC–JKP. Addressed to Nashville.

1. William H. Harrison.

2. William C. Rives and Nathaniel Tallmadge, formerly identified with the conservative wing of the Democratic party, supported Harrison in 1840.

3. See Nicholson to Polk, January 13, 1841.

FROM A. O. P. NICHOLSON

My Dear Sir: Washington City Feby 12/41

I forgot to give you an account of my interview with Watterson in my letter of this date. I read to him your letter[1] and at once appealed to him to agree to settle the difficulty by a District Convention,[2] and to place the matter beyond doubt I urged him forthwith to address a letter to Dr. Thomas proposing to him to submit the case to a Convention. He consented to the proposition and immediately wrote such a letter which I sent to the office myself four days ago. I have no idea myself that Dr. Thomas will accede to the proposition. He is unquestionably encuraged to run by the Whigs, and the same men will advise him not to go into a Convention. I thought it best for Watterson to make the proposition directly to Dr. Thomas, that he might be able to throw him clearly in the wrong if he should decline to accede to a Convention. The understanding with the Tennessee Whigs here is that Cahal will run—at least they are advised that an effort is making to get him in the field. I do not believe he will run, especially if the election comes on in April or May, but I think Dr. Thomas will be very probably the Whig Candidate. Watterson has now done all that could be expected, except that he does not understand himself as agreeing to submit his claims to a convention in competition with any body else than Dr. Thomas. If the election takes place in April or May it will of course have no influence on our other elections, and in that case I have no doubt our best policy is to run him. In relation to my running for the Senate in Maury I am willing that that place shall remain open as it can very well do until I return. If there is no called Congress, then I will run for the Senate if there is nothing more in the way than I now see.

Our friends here express much anxiety on the subject of your convening the Legislature. They are calculating that the vote on a Bank will be so close, that one vote may decide it.[3] But for my own part I should be very reluctant to advise such a step unless the Land Bill shall pass.[4] The situation is exceedingly delicate and responsible. I have asked Brown in whose judgment I have much confidence to turn the matter over in his mind and give you his views. He promises to do so. I now have no doubt about your power to order an election for the Ho. of. Rep.

A. O. P. NICHOLSON

ALS. DLC–JKP. Addressed to Nashville.

1. Letter not found.

2. See Harvey M. Watterson to Polk, January 3, 1841, and Nicholson to Polk, January 13, 1841.

3. See Nicholson to Polk, February 2, 1841.

4. See Nicholson to Polk, January 13, 1841.

FROM JOHN C. McLEMORE

Gentlemen. Memphis 14. Feby 1841

We have been endevouring for the last 12 months to establish a permenant Democratic paper, but the want of funds has defeated us. If you will raise a Cash fund of $1000 for the purchase of a press & $500 a *cash fund* to start with, I will give, or furnish $1000 worth of paper &c. which I think I can negotiate for with the Sumner Mills[1] payable in Fort Pickering lots.[2] Then we might raise here in small sums a further cash fund of say $500 more, making in all a fund of $3000. This done I propose to employ Vanpelt as editor and Grant & Dawson former Editors & proprietors of the "Western World"[3]—Vanpelt to have a half the profits of the paper & Grant & Dawson the other half—all good & faithful democrats and every way qualified to conduct and carry on an able paper. I will do more to place the establishment on a permenant footing. Vanpelt and Dawson are both poor, with each a family to support. I therefore propose (if agreeable to them) to designate a choice lot for each in the new Town Fort Pickering where it is proposed to establish the press; upon which they may build their dwellings, & remain as long as they think it [in] their interest and when they wish to leave will pay them for their improvements, or if the property shou'd rise in value they may keep it & pay me *when they get able*, a *fair* price for their lots, according to present sales & besides I will give them their fire wood for three years free of charge, provided they pay for cuting & hawling it. My wish is to make the establishment permenant. Vanpelt is my choice for editor and if he can be had I am ready to go into the proposed arrangment. Coln. P. G. Gains will also address you on the subject and will explain fully the great importance to our cause, that the above or some other permenant arrangement shou'd be gone into without further delay. He will satisfy you & Mr. Vanpelt of the character & ability of Dawson & Grant to conduct the establishment under the instructions of Vanpelt. This done and then active exertions to procure say a thousand subscribers to the paper at $3 we can with confidence assure you the voice of Democracy will be felt & heard in this the most important portion of the state at the coming election in August. We must organise & push at every point or defeat is the consequence. Union and action with promptness will secure us what we all desire, a Democratic Governor at the next election. Please write Coln. Gains or myself in reply & oblige . . . .

JNO. C. MCLEMORE

ALS. DLC–JKP. Addressed jointly to Polk and Felix Robertson, Nashville.

1. A paper mill built about 1838, Sumner Mills was located three and one-half miles south of Gallatin on the north bank of the Cumberland River. The business was advertised for sale in 1842, and its machinery was offered the following year.

2. In 1840 McLemore laid off Fort Pickering, which he located on his Chickasaw Bluffs tract south of Memphis. He shared his township venture with the La Grange and Memphis Railroad Company, which planned to run a spur from its main line should the speculation prove promising. Memphis Whigs, anxious to protect their control of the river trade and in turn their political hold on the Western District, blocked McLemore's Fort Pickering scheme.

3. Henry Van Pelt, Grant, and Dawson. Van Pelt, who began his editing career with the Franklin *Recorder* in 1821, assumed direction of the Democratic *Memphis Weekly Appeal* on April 21, 1841; the *Appeal* replaced the *Western World and Memphis Banner*. Van Pelt remained with the *Appeal* for some ten years. Grant and Dawson are not identified further.

FROM ROBERT B. REYNOLDS

Dear Governor, Knoxville February [15] 1841[1]

Yours of the 4th inst, was duly received, but our court being in session, so engaged my time, that I could not give it my immediate attention. I have been to several counties recently, and have dilligently enquired for the political movements now going on for the ensuing canvass. In Blount the Whigs have held a county caucus, nominated Dr Hodsden[2] for county member, which by the by has almost ruined them in Blount. They have two candidates in the field now & talk about having another one. McKamy will come out about the 15th of March & Gen Wallace thinks he [McKamy] can succeed in being elected. Things are taking a change for the better for our party; the hard times that were to vanish on the announcement of Harrison's being elected have not been realized; but indeed are twenty times more severe. We never felt the pressure until after the Presidential Election. Now it rages in a fury. These things have put a great number to thinking who were carried off in a storm. Jefferson County is in great distress & the Whigs are much divided; each & every one thinks himself the greatest man in the party. It will do us this much good that they cannot succeed in casting as many illegal votes as they did in November. Sevier County is all over Federal. We cannot get even 100 votes there. Grainger will do better than she did in Novr. Col Wheeler I think will run for the Senate again. The fate of his election depends on whom he has to run against. Frazier cannot be induced to run for the Senate. I believe we can carry the two members in Anderson, Campbell & Morgan. Oliver has given himself up to intemperance; so much so, that I fear that we cannot elect him. He is inclined to run & will do so I expect. I think we shall lose the member from Roane.[3] We shall have a man in the field for this county, so soon as the Campbell Station Fedl. Caucus is over, & we know who the feds put in nomination. I learn from Scott Terry's[4] Senatorial Dist that we have a very fair chance to elect a senator & that Scott has declined to run for the senate & will run for Rep. for Bledsoe. You may rest satisfied that we will gain in East Tennessee—aye, greatly. The Democrats are rousing up & no where that I have heard from, are they desponding. They are determined to give the enemy the best fight they can in august, & altho we enter the field with a fearful odds against us, yet we are united & they, the whigs, are distracted after the spoils, and with the new issues to be presented next summer, I have no doubt that it will enable us to carry the State Elections, if not a majority of the Congressional Districts. I do not believe that it will materially injure us to bring on the Congressional elections, but on the Contrary help us in august: that elections being over would leave us nothing to do but to contend against the Whigs in our state elections & it would carry the federal stump orators off to Washington. The issues would be then mainly upon federal politicks—growing out of the election of Senators, apportionment &c. The Democrats, of East Tennessee are panting for the race. We have concluded it to be best not to run a candidate against J. L. Williams provided the election is brot on in May or June. We do not wish a full vote polled here to count against us in the aggregate. Rest assured, Sir, that we of East Tennessee will meet the opposition at the threshold & battle with them to the last. We fight for principles & must triumph. I go in a few days to Roane & will urge our friends into the contest; I go from there to Anderson & thence to Morgan. I shall spare no pains to organise our forces. Eastman will issue a small paper commencing the first of April for four months, which will place information at every man's door at 75 cents. This will do an essential service. We must have an extra Editor for it. Robt Fraz[i]er has been writen to, to come & edit it. In fact our friends must have information spread before the people, so that we shall not suffer by fedl. misrepresentations. The press—the Argus must be sustained. It is a thorn in the side—& they dread it & would put [it] down if possible. E. is extravagant & we here are few in number & but two or three of those, that have put forth one cent to sustain him. If we had a loan of 7 or $800 it would enable us to carry the war through & place his paper on a permanent footing.[5] The Feds are starting another Journal here to be called the Post,[6] which proves the Jealosies & heart burnings among them. The old Williams party versus the White party. Whilst they are quarrelling about the bone I wish us to take the prize. J. F. Gillespy has gone to Washington City & Dr J. W. Lyde[7] has been nominated for Senator in his stead; G W Rowles & Jas Walker for Representatives; these are good & popular names. We shall have a tight race in Monroe. I fear it. Marion & Hamilton ought to be wheeled into line; certainly we ought to gain a member there.

A question will be sought to be made relative to the Hiwassee Rail Road, & I learn that you are to be forced to come out on the question to be raised—whether you are for a further subscription on the part of the State? and whether you are in favor of Banking privileges being bestowed upon this rotten concern. The feds of the upper counties having got their cue from this town, have declared for the road & opposition to all persons who will not go as far as the farthest for (running the State in debt) the road. I hope the State may comply with her present subscription faithfully. This question has two sides & I think he who comes out for the road right or wrong will make but little.

Another question to be raised is, what shall the State do with the $650,000 subscription to the L.C.&C.R.R. Company?[8] Shall it be withdrawn from East Tenn & the bonds be cancelled? or shall they be preserved for the benefit of East Tennessee? Middle Tennessee & West Tennessee, having already received some State bonds, would it be equitable for East Tennessee to lose her fair proportion of State Capital? Some want a Bank to be founded upon these Bonds, which were subscribed to the L.C.&C.R.R. Company, for the purpose of Cleansing our rivers. Could this be done, I would prefer it, to any other disposition that could be made of them except consuming them with fire. These are the principal issues that now agitate the public mind aside from national politics. Rest assured my dear Sir, that so far as my feeble abilities will go, they shall be exerted in the service of correct principles.

ROBT. B. REYNOLDS

ALS. DLC–JKP. Addressed to Nashville.

1. For letter's dating, see Polk to Reynolds, February 4, 1841.

2. Robert H. Hodsden, a Maryville physician, won election as a Whig to two terms in the Tennessee House and served from 1841 until 1845. In 1844 he moved to Sevier County and subsequently sat for one term as a Union Party member in the Tennessee House, 1861–63.

3. Reference is to Joel Hembree.

4. Terry served as a Democrat in the Tennessee House, 1837–39, and sat in the Senate, 1839–41.

5. See E. G. Eastman to Polk, January 21, 1841.

6. The *Knoxville Post*, a Whig newspaper first issued in April 1841 by James Williams, continued in Knoxville until 1848, when Samuel P. Ivins relocated and published it as the *Athens Post*.

7. John W. Lide is not identified further.

8. Louisville, Cincinnati and Charleston Railroad Company.

FROM ALEXANDER O. ANDERSON

My Dear Sir Washington City Feby. 17th 1841

I duly rec'd your letter of the 1st Inst,[1] & shou'd have answered it earlier, but waited in the expectation of being able to do so more satisfactorily after a little delay, in reference to the progress of things here.

The Tennessee Land Bill which was substituted in the H.R. for that which passed the Senate was finally acted upon today in the Senate, & will be approved to-morrow by the President.[2] I congratulate our friends upon this auspicious result. The provisions of the Bill are substantially such as were contained in the former. The sooner our people get to work under it the better, which, however, requires first the action of the Legislature of Tennessee.

For reasons obvious to you I have forborne to express any opinion to you in favor of your convening the Legislature, in the event of a call Session of Congress. Your letter removes my objections, in part, to the expression of my opinion, by your request to hear what your friends think upon the subject.

I understand your objection to be to a convention of the Legislature under any circumstances. I speak exclusively in regard to what wou'd be the position of things in the event that the President shou'd call an extra Session of Congress. The question as to the Tennessee Land Bill is wholly independent of that, and is one of no small importance to the people of that section of the State, & for the adjustment of which the previous action of the Legislature is necessary, and it may of itself form a very powerful inducement to convene it. Of this, however, of course you will judge when you see the Bill, and weigh all the circumstances, taken in connexion with the great extent of the interest involved, & the wishes of those who are to be affected by it. &c. &c. I refer for the present the whole question to another cause, the extraordinary convention of Congress by the coming administration. It is now understood that General Harrison will call an extra Session, probably, to be held the first week in June.

The first inquiry which presents itself is who is the author of the measure, and upon whom does the responsibility of all the consequences devolve? Not upon the governor! but the President, and his advisers to the extent of the political effects of the act! It is not necessary to reason upon this point! The proposition is identical, and it will strike at once upon the instinct of the public mind.

The next inquiry which presents itself is, under such circumstances, can the Governor of a State avoid the obligation of doing that act which the Constitution has made imperative, by which to provide as far as he has the power, that there shall be a full representation in Congress? As to the Senate he has the Constitutional power of convening the Legislature to supply vacancies & as to the House, there being a law authorising him to fix a day of election at some other period than that regularly assigned, he of course may also do that. If the case stated by you, that a single vacancy, for a short period, cannot justify the convention of the Legislature, be sound as to the duty of the Executive, then the like argument holds for every state in the Union, and applies equally to the assembling of the people to elect members of the H. of R. under this extraordinary exercise of power, as it does to the assembling of the members of the Legislature to elect a Senator, and according to the rule which wou'd excuse the omission to do either, the effect of a vote in either House might be lost on a question of the highest magnitude to the welfare of the Republic. This might affect either our foreign relations, or our domestic interests. A question of high constitutional right or liberty, or a question of peace or war. Besides, a single Senator is half the representation of a whole State, and in this view it is not like counting a unit under ordinary circumstances. Nor will the practical effect be varied from this particular aspect of the case, when the Senate shall be convened at an extra Session. The call presupposes an extraordinary State of things, and the proposition which wou'd leave out the one half of the entire representation of a State in a case of such importance wou'd not be short of surrendering into the hands of others, who may differ widely, the most vital principles to be subject to their control. In the present instance such wou'd be the fact. The vote in the Senate upon one of the greatest questions which can be propounded, that of the Bank of the United States, will be with the full representation of Tennessee precisely equal. The Vice President will give his vote against it as has been ascertained. That measure will surely be attempted, whether it be, or be not recommended by the President.

Such is the understood, and unquestioned object of the leaders of the present dominant Party.[3] The responsibility, therefore, of not carrying out the provisions of the Constitution, by convening the Legislature to make an election, becomes far higher than any which cou'd, indirectly, fall upon the Governor, by the act of doing so. In the one case there exists a positive power and duty united, while the responsibility rests upon the President who created the necessity. In the other there is no consideration of obligation or necessity, but it takes the form of omission, which becomes exceedingly prominent, in proportion as the great questions, which may be agitated in the extra Session of Congress, advance in their magnitude and importance to the vital interests of the Country.

I might go on and enumerate reasons until I shou'd tire your patience, but I think those assigned are sufficient, and I have no doubt when you view the subject in all its bearings no other course will appear to be left.

In regard to our home affairs I have written to Mr Eastman, and given him my views in conformity with those suggested by yourself.[4] He will probably ask for the loan of a few hundred dollars, at the Bank at Nashville,[5] and I hope he will get it. In reference to expenses I have been necessarily very much burthened in a way as to politics not known generally to our friends, but beyond what I have been able fully to meet. Some of my near friends have incurred large expenses and sacrafices to sustain the cause. Dr Anderson went to Jonesboro, specially with all his family, at great expense, to sustain the Editorial Department of the Sentinel, and neither required or received one dollar of compensation. As far as I can I will extend every pecuniary aid in my power to carry on the contest, by the publication, & circulation of the truth, & sound principles amongst our countrymen. Nor have I any doubt we shall be able to sustain the Argus if Eastman takes the course I have suggested to him, and I have no doubt he will.

I will write you again in a few days, and give you whatever information we have as to the movements of the Whigs.

Be pleased to present my kind regards to your Lady.

A ANDERSON

ALS. DLC–JKP. Addressed to Nashville.

1. Letter not found.

2. On January 12, 1841, Anderson wrote that his version of the Tennessee land bill had passed the Senate. ALS. DLC–JKP. See also A. O. P. Nicholson to Polk, January 13, 1841.

3. Reference is to the Whig party.

4. See E. G. Eastman to Polk, January 21, 1841.

5. Reference is to the home office of the Bank of Tennessee.

FROM HOPKINS L. TURNEY

Dear Sir Washington City Feb. the 19th 1841

Yours of the 5th of this month[1] has been received and in answer thereto can only say, that I have consid[er]ed what you suppose would be the arguments of the Feds. in Tennessee in opposition to an extra session of the legislature, and I must confess that they are moore forcible than I had thought them to be. Still I cannot think, under the high party excitement which exist[s] in Tennessee that much if anything could be made out of it. The enclosed Yeas & Nays was marked by Senator King of Alabama, and shows what will be the vote in the senate after the 4th of march next on chartering a bank of the U.S. from which it seems that this question depends on the vote of Preston of South Carolina.[2] If he should resign as some think he will the bank would be defeated but I fear he will not, and I think he has agreed to remain in the senate for the express purpose of voteing for the bill. In this I hope I may be mistaken. Upon the subject of an extra session of the legislature after surveying the whole ground I have arrived at the conclusion that the call of an extra session would perhaps effect us some little in the comeing elections, but that the occasion is one that seems to require a bold and energetic move on the part of the democracy to save the constertution by preventing the establishment of an instertution, which would endanger our republican institutions. To accomplish this, for one I would be willing to hazzard all on the single turn of the die—provided the proper men should be selected for Senators. We are I fear destined to be defeated for Govorner, if not for the legislature. I think however that it is impossible for us to loose both houses of the legislature, and therefore the Feds would not have the power to instruct our senators. If you was senator you could and would contribute moore to revoloutionise the state than you could in any other situation I can concieve of, and to say nothing of your comparrative weight of charactor, with that of the presant incumbant[3] or any other aspirant which I will not do because you might suppose that I was disposed to flatter you, but aside from this what has either of our senators[4] done douring the presant winter? Nothing. When Grundy was here although he was old and fond of ease, still he took charge of the whig districts and sent maney documents to them. He make [made] speeches himself calculated to aid the cause, but now what is it? Nothing. His talant's, energy, and liberality is lost to the cause, and the vacuum created by his death has not been filled. You would moore than fill it by far. Your age, ambition, energy, and tack for leading, to say nothing of your talants, would render you moore conspickuous, and useful than Grundy ever was. I sincearly hope therefore that you will concent to serve if the legislature should elect you, which I have no doubt they would do if you will concent to it. Gillaspie is here and is ripe for it. If however you will not concent, I am opposed to an extra session of the legislature, so that after you are beaten for govorner we may take you up and make you senator if we have the power.

Our friends here are preparing a joint circular[5] which we will send out before we leave the city. The Ten. Senators talk of joining us, but they as I understand are unwilling to commit themselves on the constertutionality of a bank, fearing as I suppose instructions. They are makeing Polaticks a trade. This dont suit me. I believe they are both at hart bank men, and only oppose it for the sake of office. This you know has been my opinion of one of them for some time.[6]

H L TURNEY

ALS. DLC–JKP. Addressed to Nashville and marked "Private."

1. Letter not found.
2. William R. King tallied twenty-six affirmative votes and twenty-five negative votes; he wrote "doubtful" in the "nays" column opposite the name of William C. Preston.
3. Reference is to A. O. P. Nicholson.
4. Nicholson and Alexander O. Anderson.
5. See Cave Johnson to Polk, July 17, 1841.
6. Reference probably is to Nicholson.

FROM JAMES WALKER

Dear Sir,

Columbia, Feb 24. 1841

I have received yours of yesterday.[1] My information is that Martin very much wishes to run for Congress, and there will be some difficulty in preventing him. Dr. Thomas presents rather more trouble. He is so sure that he has directed himself to be announced in the Democrat. *This I have stopped.* The only way we can avoid, the difficulties which our aspiring men seem disposed to produce is to call a convention, and take the ground that the nominations of the convention must be acquiesed in. We must have a convention to nominate for Congress & the county. It is inevitable. I cannot explain to you, the reasons why W. Smith cannot be relied on for the Senate. His pecuniary difficulties is the main cause.[2] In fact, he cannot be considered a citizen, his family having gone to Mississippi and he said to be gone to Washington. Everything in relation to him, rather strange & perplexing.

I will attend the next meeting of the county committee, (unless compelled to be absent at the Federal Court) and will urge the necessity of a county & district convention—at all events, measures to settle existing difficulties—and think the whole matter can be adjusted. Dew is also anxious to come out for Congress. The plan of county & District convention nominations is all that can now prevent confusion & splitting up.

I saw our Cousin Bob Campbell[3] & am to see him again on Monday. He said he could not make the desired trip immediately, but evinced much concern in the matter. Edwin Polk arrived here this morning, and I have arranged it for him to go to Miss and accomplish what we wish with the Alexanders.[4] He will certainly do it, and with very little delay. I have instructed him as fully as I could. This attended to, the only thing material is to see Captain Dobbins.[5] I may be able to get Campbell to go there—if not I think William[6] ought to go. It is certainly in that case a very plain matter and I can counsel with him on the subject. If he is still in Nashville, you had better speak to him on the subject, or write to me who else I had better try to get to go. I cannot leave home & it seems to me that William is the next one on the list that ought to attend to it. It seems to me that what Dobbins can say ought to be procured by some of the decendants of James Knox[7]—or some whose children are interested. Deep interest is a powerful motive to do things well & properly.

JAMES WALKER

ALS. DLC–JKP. Addressed to Nashville.

1. Letter not found.

2. Several financial judgments were brought against Williamson Smith in Maury County Court between September 1839 and May 1840. It is probable that Smith's indebtedness was related to losses he sustained when his 1837 contract with the U.S. government was not honored. See Alexander O. Anderson to Polk, February 4, 1840.

3. Robert Campbell, Jr., was a son of John and Matilda Golden Campbell.

His mother was the eldest daughter of Ezekiel Polk. The "Junior" attached to his name distinguished him from an uncle of the same name.

4. Edwin Polk went to Panola County, Mississippi to obtain a statement from George Alexander denying that Ezekiel Polk was a Tory during the Revolutionary War. See Edwin Polk to Polk, March 30, 1841.

5. David Dobbins of Rowan County, North Carolina, served in the Revolutionary War. Subsequently, he moved to Maury County, Tennessee, where he lived from 1806 until his removal to Graves County, Kentucky, in November 1840.

6. William H. Polk.

7. On April 2, 1841, David Dobbins made deposition that he had served in the Revolution with James Knox, Polk's maternal grandfather. Dobbins declared that he was "well acquainted with Capt. James Knox . . . at the commencement of the war & afterwards." Denying charges of Toryism against Knox, Dobbins stated that he knew Knox to be "as good & true a whig of the Revolution as breathed." Deposition of David Dobbins, April 2, 1841. DS. DLC–JKP. See also Sarah C. Polk to Polk, April 14, 1841.

TO THOMAS L. HAMER

My Dear Sir Nashville Feby. 27th 1841

I see by the authorized annunciation—by the National Intelligencer, that *Mr Ewing* of your State is to be a member of Genl. Harrison's cabinet.[1] I am not familiar with his early political history or principles, and have to request the favour of you to give me, such information, as may be in your possession or at your command, upon the subject. In the old division of parties was he a Federalist or a Republican? In J. Q. Adams's time was he a *National Republican* or a *Democrat?* I know that whilst he was in the Senate of the U. States, he acted with *Clay & Webster* & their party, but I desire information in regard to his earlier opinions & acts. What is his position and opinion upon the subject of Abolition? Has he ever published any opinions upon that subject? If so send me a paper containing them. There is a Document upon another subject which I must trouble you for, if it is in your pow[er][2] to procure it. It is the Volume containing the letters of *Judge Burnett,* addressed I think to the Historical Society of Cincinnati in 1837, and containing the *Address* of the Legislature of the North Western Territory, to *President John Adams* in 1800.[3] This address you will remember was referred to by Genl. Harrison in his speech in the Senate of the U. States, in reply to John Randolph in 1826,[4] as containing sentiments in accordance with his own. I wish the Volume containing it, as it is difficult to make half the people believe any thing that is printed in a newspaper.

We will have a hard & bitter contest in this State during the summer. We have however buoyant hopes that the State will recover herself & resume her old position in the Republican Ranks. To aid in effecting an object so desireable, the information I ask may be important.

JAMES K. POLK

ALS. NjMoHP–L. W. Smith Coll. Addressed to Georgetown, Brown County, Ohio, and marked "*Private.*" AE on the cover states that this letter was received and answered on March 6, 1841.

1. On February 13, 1841, the Washington *National Intelligencer* listed William Henry Harrison's cabinet appointments, including that of Thomas Ewing to be secretary of the treasury.

2. Portion of one word obliterated.

3. A lawyer and banker, Jacob Burnet settled in Cincinnati in 1796 and served as a federal judge in the Northwest Territory before his appointment to several terms on the territorial legislative council, 1799–1802. He served in the Ohio House, 1812–16; on the Ohio Supreme Court, 1821–28; and in the U.S. Senate as a Federalist, 1828–31. Burnet also headed the Cincinnati branch of the U.S. Bank, and in 1839 nominated Harrison for president at the national Whig convention. *Burnet's Letters*, published in the *Transactions of the Historical and Philosophical Society of Ohio*, Vol. I, Pt. 2, appeared in 1839. The Historical Society of Cincinnati, as such, was not founded until 1844. See Hamer to Polk, March 6, 1841.

4. John Randolph "of Roanoke," a states rights Democrat from Virginia, served in the U.S. House, 1799–1813, 1815–17, 1819–25, and 1827–29. He sat in the U.S. Senate, 1825–27, and served briefly as U.S. minister to Russia in 1830. On March 20, 1826, Randolph charged Harrison with having supported "the sedition law and black-cockade administration"; Harrison admitted that he had supported the Adams administration at times, but denied that he had favored adoption of the Sedition Acts.

FROM ANDREW JOHNSON

Dear Sir Greeneville March 4 1841

After so long a time I venture to answer your letter,[1] democracy having met with so signal a defeat in november last. I did not know weather I ever would think about politics again. The wounds received in the last november Conflict haveing measureablely healed up, I at last venture to speak. We have been trying to organise for some time back, and I think we have succeeded very well. The greatest difficulty we have to contend with now, is in our own ranks, in relation to the different candidates that want to run for the Legislature. There is some four or five that wants to run for the County, and to settle all difficulity between the respective claimants, we have called a County Convention, to be composed of deligats chossen from each civil district, which is to set on Saturday next the 6th of this month, and all the would be candidates are well satisfied save Balch & Feezell,[2] and they are protesting most soberly against convention, and sweare they will run if there is five hundred conventions. The truth is the democratic party would like to dispose of them upon good terms, and they know it. They think by takeing ground in advance, that the convention will be driven in to measures, in this they are mistaken.

Balch & Feezell are perfect clogs upon the wheel. The party has to carry them insted of their carring the party. Hawkins County met in convention on the 22 of Feb and ruled Balch off, without decent,[3] which has thrown him in to a furious rage. He is cursing and swaggering about, saying he has done more for *the party* than any man in Tennessee. The truth is we have too many in our ranks that is not willing to make any sacrifice for princable, but are under the entire controll of a sordid disposition. If such men as those are to be placed in the lead, Tennessee can never be reclaimed; if that portion of the democratic party, that has some claime to decency talent & moral worth cant sustain it the debaughers cant. I am for commencing the work of reformation at once in our ranks. Put up the best material we have all over the State, both as respects talents and moral worth, then let's make one more vigorious effort, to redeem the State, and once redeemed, resting upon pure democratic princables, cemented with moral worth, and our over throw will be imposible. I begin to think the State can be carried in august next, if we do our duty. The appointment of Webster and a called session of Congress must be capital for us, if tacched in the propper manner. I am strongly inclined to think that there is a reaction in pub[l]ic sentiment since nove[m]ber last.

The expected change in money matters has fell so far short of promises, the people begin to think soberly about the matter. If there should be a called session of Congress, it will create the necessity for convening the Legislature of this State. (Perhaps in this I am rong.) After the 4 of march we have no members in Congress, and whenever terms expire by limitation the Governor has no power to issue writs of election for members of Congress, in the absenc of law providing for such cases. The same difficulity will present its self in relation to Senators. (Pleas set me right in to this mater.) In your letter you say either Blair or myself must run for Congress. It will be allmost imposible for me to run for Congress. Weather Blair will consent to run or not I do not know. If I thought that I could give you any additional strengh by runing I would be willing to make any sacrifice. It is very uncertain weather I take the field for any thing or not. My friends want me to run for the Senat. What I shall do is uncertain. I intend to do all I can in or out of the canvass. The whig party in this district is likely to blow up. Tom Arnold has taken the field and says he will run, which is contrary to the wishes of the leaders of the whig party. They are to have a convention in this congressional district in April next. The current opinion is now, that R. J. McKinney[4] will receive the nomination if he will accept of it.

And if things turn out as now anticipated, there will be a great deal of angry and vindictive fealing amongst them. The democrats are holding themselvs in a bartering position, to go which ever way they can get most votes for Governor. Some times I think it would be the best policy to run no candidate on the democratic side, for the present. Let them split among themselvs, the democrats holding the balance of power in their own hands, makeing the successful candidate, dependant on them, while they have such an over whelming majority. The runing of a candidate on the democratic side, would prevent a split and make them more closely embodied, (your views on this point). The convention in Hawkins County nominated Nicholas Fain for floater. (Baugh is laid under the table.) Col Philip Critze [for the] County. Wm T Center is the Whig candidate for Congress in McLelland's district.[5] He is the strongest man in the whig ranks and they intend to make a desperate run at McLellan.

Let me know if you intend to canvass the State this summer, and if so, what time you will make your tour through East Tenn. A great manny democrats in this County want to see you here one time more. They are anxious to see you upon the stu[m]p. I think the best policy would be not to open the canvas too early for as the excitement subsides, the reaction is in our favor. I will conclud this incoherant scrawl. Give my best respects to Mr Secretary Young, and accept for your self my bst wishes.

A. Johnson

ALS. DLC–JKP. Probably addressed to Nashville. Published in LeRoy P. Graf and Ralph W. Haskins, eds., *The Papers of Andrew Johnson* (5 vols.; Knoxville, 1967—), I, pp. 30–33.

1. Letter not found.
2. John T. Balch and Samuel Feazel.
3. Misspelling of "dissent."
4. Robert J. McKinney, a Greeneville lawyer, was elected to the Tennessee Supreme Court in 1847 and served until 1861.
5. Philip Critz, William T. Senter, and Abraham McClellan. McClellan was elected from the Second Congressional District.

FROM THOMAS L. HAMER

My dear Sir; Georgetown O. March 6 1841

Your favor of the 27th ult. came this evening & I hasten to give you the information desired. The first office ever held by Thomas Ewing in

Ohio was a seat in the United States Senate. Prior to that he was a practising lawyer & private citizen. Mr. E. is not an old man & could have had no distinct position in politics during the time when the country was divided between the *old Federal & Democratic parties.* He has always been an admirer & friend of Mr Clay & was a warm supporter of John Q. Adams' Administration. In this career he has been consistent & was never suspected of an inclination to what you & I consider democratic doctrines.

I remember to have frequently read, in the papers & elsewhere, the Address of the Territorial legislature that elected W. H. Harrison a delegate to Congress during the Administration of the elder Adams.[1] That address, most distinctly, approved of the leading measures of "the reign of terror."[2] I presume I can obtain it for you, & will do so with pleasure, if practicable. I am a member of the Historical & Philosophical Society of Ohio, and at the last meeting of the society in Decr., we authorised the procurement of a considerable number of Judge Burnet's *book,* for the use of the members. The understanding was that the work was on hand at Cincinnati & could be obtained with facility. So soon as a copy can be had I will forward it.

Is it possible to bring Tennessee back? The event, at this distance, looks too much like the effect of Supernatural interference! Godsend that it may occur; but I have my fears. We are in a deplorable condition in this country. I know that a patriot should never despair of the Republic; but I frankly confess to you that within the last six months I have entertained doubts of the perpetuity of our political Institutions, which never entered my mind before; or if they did so, it was but to be scouted as idle fancies & cowardly dreams. Still I hope for the best, & pray God to save our beloved country from *anarchy, civil strife, & Tyranny*! I have withdrawn from politics almost entirely, and am getting rich by the closest attention to an extensive & profitable practice of the law. My health is excellent, & my mind at ease, comparatively, since I quit Congress. I am actually getting fat! It is not probable that I shall ever be as large as our old friend *Dixon H. Lewis;* but when I pop in upon you some of these times, as I hope to do, I doubt whether you would know me.

Remember me kindly to Mrs. P.

Th. L. Hamer

ALS. DLC–JKP. Addressed to Nashville. AE on the cover reads, "Thos. Ewing. Sec. of Treas. A supporter of 2nd Adams's administration."

1. See Polk to Hamer, February 27, 1841.
2. Reference is to John Adams' administration.

FROM ANDREW JACKSON

My Dear Sir, Hermitage March 6th 1841

I learn by A. Junr.[1] just from Lebanon that the whig convention at Murfreesborough has put forth little Davy Dickeson for Governor.[2] If you cannot beat Davy then, indeed, I will despair of the republic. The wiggs in Wilson have got their candidates for the legislature in the field, Doctor McCorkle, brotherinlaw to James Jones [is] one of them.[3] Therefore I would suppose, Slim Jamy,[4] will surely be up for Congress, if he does not he will soon be forgotton, and never more be heard of as a great man or politician. From Clay & Prestons late speeches in the Senate, and Buchanons reply,[5] I would suppose that Buchannons reply and translation of their speech, which by their silence the[y] admitted, that Genl Armstrong &c. &c. will not be removed.[6] What will become of McNairy, Hall, Erwin & Co. They will surely get Fosters pantaloons to burn Harrison & Clay in effegy.

With proper candidates for the legislature & Congress I have no doubt of sucess at our next election.

I am quite unwell to-day. All my Houshold join me in Kind Salutations to you & Mrs. Polk. Sarah[7] has been unwell, is again up, & intends to pay her personal respects soon to Mrs. Polk. You & Mrs. Polk before you take your circuit must visit us & spend a night with us.

The Election of Blair & Rives printers to the senate[8] has killed Clay. He will either go to England, or die soon with appoplexy. Hea[l]th and respect.

ANDREW JACKSON

Note, When you take the field not to forget, the charges of Bell, Foster, Dickeson & Co against myself & Van Buren, for appointing members of congress. The first move is four members of Congress, & Bell one of them,[9] & accepts thereof. Remember this. A.J.

ALS. DLC–JKP. Probably addressed to Nashville.

1. Andrew Jackson, Jr.

2. Jackson's sarcasm is directed at David W. Dickinson, a prominent Murfreesboro Whig, who withdrew his name from nomination before the Whig Convention at Murfreesboro on March 4, 1841. James C. Jones of Wilson County was unanimously chosen by the convention to oppose Polk for the governorship.

3. Miles B. McCorkle, a Lebanon physician and one-term Whig member of the Tennessee House, 1841–43, married Kittie Ann Munford, sister of Sarah Watson Munford Jones.

4. James C. Jones.

5. Determined to rescind the election of public printer, Henry Clay and William C. Preston each spoke in the Senate on February 19, 1841. Denying the use of proscription by their party, Clay remarked, "I never said that all ought to be turned out who had displeased the Whigs." Preston observed that "the Administration coming into power reject and repudiate the infamous maxim that to the victors belong the spoils." James Buchanan replied that he accepted Clay's and Preston's remarks as a "distinct annunciation of Whig principles" which would "instantly relieve the anxious minds of a very large number of office holders."

6. Robert Armstrong, postmaster of Nashville, served from 1829 until 1845.

7. Sarah York Jackson, wife of Andrew Jackson, Jr.

8. Francis P. Blair and John C. Rives, editors of the Washington *Globe,* were elected to a two-year term as public printers on February 19, 1841.

9. John Bell accepted an appointment as Harrison's secretary of war.

FROM WILLIAM H. POLK

Dear Brother Columbia March 7th 1841

After full and mature consideration, I have determined again to consult you; with regard, to the propriety of my running for a seat in the next Legislature. I discover that much difficulty may be engendered by an open declination, not that my pretensions or claims on the people are of a character to create disatisfaction; but that my claims were presented by the call from Mooresville, which silenced, or prevented the *presentation* of the *claims* of others, who might desire to run. From what I can learn, and I have taken some pains to ascertain, that it is the received and settled opinion with the party, that I will be a Candidate. All contention is now hushed by this opinion. And for me now to decline a canvass, and again throw the party into a State of confusion, by the selection of another person is a matter which I desire to leave to you.

The proposed County Convention which has been sprung and advocated by Col. Dew for some time past, will tend to disorganization, & is founded in selfish purposes. To hold a County Convention, I think would be impolitic, and would only open a field for *designing men* to accomplish their objects—and dissatisfaction would be the result.

I conversed with Joneas E. Thomas a fiew days since relative to the position which he desired to occupy. He seemed entirely disposed to run for the *Senate* but unwilling to run for the House.

There is to be a meeting of the people of Maury at the Court House on next Saturday, to appoint delegates to a District Convention to be holden at Lewisburg on the 3rd or 4th saturday in this month, to select a candidate for Congress. Now if you should think it politic and proper, I will take it upon myself, to see Thomas & Martin, and endeavour to induce them to come forward and anounce themselves, Thomas for the Senate and Martin for the House, and I will also anounce myself for the House.[1] By this course the matter would be immediately settled in a way acceptable to the people of the County.

I am aware that my pecuniary difficulties is the only objection with *you*, to my running. That my affairs are *partially* in a deranged state, I do not pretend to deny; but at the same time I am fully *Confident*, that I can so arrange them, without injury, as to be able to prosecute an uninterupted canvass. To declare myself on Saturday next, I will have from *three* to four weeks, to visit the district and attend to my lands, & place them in a situation to be sold. And by selling my surplus negroes I will *be entirely easy*. I do not say *easy*, without having made a strict calculation, and observed closely my means. I could attend to my District business, before the canvass in the county *properly opened*. Harmony in the county can be established by the course which I suggest. Write me by return mail.

William H. Polk

ALS. DLC–JKP. Addressed to Nashville. AE on the cover states that this letter was answered on March 11, 1841; Polk's reply has not been found.

1. Reference is to the Tennessee General Assembly, not the U.S. Congress.

FROM A. O. P. NICHOLSON

My Dear Sir: Washington March 8. 1841

This day has been spent in discussing the resolution to dismiss Blair & Rives as Printers,[1] and the question was not taken. It is determined however by the federal majority to carry it, altho it is shown to be an outrage scarcely paralleled in the history of proscription. In the course of the discussion to-day Mr. Clay distinctly announced that there will be a called session of Congress between the 15th of May and 1st of June. So that matter is put to rest, and I have just learned the federal plan for defeating us in having a representative in the Senate. I have just seen Capt Armstrong[2] brother of the General who informed me that he had just been in conversation with Gentry, Campbell, Hall and Eaton, and he gave me distinctly to understand that in that conversation it was suggested that if you convened the Legislature the *Federal members might not attend,* and without them there could be no quorum. I get this in a way that would not make it proper to make it public, but I deem it of sufficient consequence to let you know what is going on *here.* You may have noticed that the federal Senators attempted to defeat the nomination of Judge Daniel by withdrawing and reducing us below a quorum.[3] In this they succeeded until one Federal member getting alarmed at so high-handed a measure returned and made a quorum.[4] The example I have no doubt will be followed every where to defeat the action of democratic legislatures. I have no doubt but that the Tennessee members of the Legislature who are federalists will either not attend at Nashville or they will withdraw when the election comes on and defeat an election. Under such circumstances I am fully confirmed in the opinion that you ought not to hesitate to give them a chance to try whether our people are prepared for such revolutionary movements. I think it likely that you will receive the President's Proclamation[5] before I reach Nashville, I must request that you will not issue your proclamation (if you determine to issue any) until I see you. Much depends on the issue of the Call of the Legislature, and I am strongly of opinion that your proclamation ought to specify the objects for which the Legislature is convened, & in specifying these objects I desire to have some consultation with you. I shall go home in company with Judge Catron & we will leave on the 11th and make as quick a trip as we can. Hall will be provided for in some way I learn, but it is not certain how.[6]

A O P NICHOLSON

ALS. DLC–JKP. Addressed to Nashville.

1. On March 4, 1841, Willie P. Mangum submitted a resolution to the U.S. Senate that Blair and Rives be dismissed as printers of the Senate for the 27th Congress. After considerable debate, the resolution passed on March 11, 1841. See also Andrew Jackson to Polk, March 6, 1841.

2. Reference probably is to Robert Armstrong's brother, William, who served as Indian agent for the southern agency of the Western Territory, 1836–39, and, subsequently, as agent for the Choctaws west of the Mississippi River.

3. On February 27, 1841, Peter V. Daniel was nominated associate justice of the U.S. Supreme Court; on March 2, 1841, motion was made to vote on the nomination; but a quorum was not present.

4. Reference is not identified.

5. On March 17, 1841, William H. Harrison called a special session of the U.S. Congress to convene on May 31, 1841, for consideration of "the revenue and finances of the country."

6. See Robert B. Reynolds to Polk, March 28, 1841.

FROM ROBERT M. BURTON

Gov. Polk Murfreesboro. March 9th 1841

In conformity with my promise I write you from this place. I have heard to day from Colo Yoakum that the candidates for this county[1] will be Yoakum for the Senate, Keeble & Smith for the house of Representatives—a strong ticket this. I am delighted with the prospect. I think success will attend the efforts of such talented and valliant champions. The convention of Saturday next will nominate them. The Whigs nominate afterwards. I had an interv[i]ew with Doctr. Sayle the brother in law of Jones on Sunday before I left. He infor[m]ed me that Jones said he will short[l]y go to Nashville and that he w[o]uld propose to you to take the tour of the State togeather. If he should take this course the game will be played as you desire. I fear his advisors will not let him do so. Wait however awhile on him. His nomination I find will not go down here with many of the Whigs; indeed I have heard in my short stay at home several say who had at the last election voted against you that they would now support you. His mane points I learn are your former votes against the subtreasury plan and your subsequent support of the plan and the Instruction Resolutions of the last General Assembly.[2] They would attempt to run him also as the Log Cabin boy taken from the plough—but he never ploughed a day in his life—lives in a fine brick house—owns one third of a large rope and hemp factory—a large store in full opperation—sold his farm for ten thousand Dollars to be paid in state bonds. Made the sale to Genl Anderson who was a large contractor on the Lebanon & Nashville Turnpike. Colo M A Price will support you warmly. I want to get him out for the Assembly. He can be elected. If you see him you might suggest it to him. I will write you from time to time and keep you advised of the movements of your opponent. In great haste . . . .

R M Burton

ALS. DLC–JKP. Addressed to Nashville.

1. Rutherford County.
2. See John Catron to Polk, November 19, 1839.

FROM ISAAC H. DISMUKES

Oakachickama, Mississippi. March 9, 1841

Dismukes writes Polk that plantation work is "geting aloung very smoothly." All except Elizabeth are well. Maria is prepared to weave on the new spinning machine that will soon be delivered to the plantation. Dismukes reports that he will begin planting in a "fiew daies."

ALS. DLC–JKP. Addressed to Nashville. Published in Bassett, *Plantation Overseer*, 150–51.

TO SAMUEL H. LAUGHLIN

My Dear Sir! Nashville March 9th 1841

My opponent you see has been announced.[1] I do not consider him by any means as formidable as *Governor Cannon* would have been much as the leading Whigs seem to object to him. I shall be ready to enter upon the canvass as soon as I receive the official announcement of the Cabinet & the Inaugural Speech;[2] though I will not do so, for some three weeks to come unless my competitor shall move sooner than that time, in which event I will be with him. My present purpose is (though this I shall not make public until I can learn the movements of my opponent) to be at Jackson at the meeting of the Federal & Supreme Courts on the 1st monday in April, and open the canvass at that time. From Jackson I would return immediately here, and thence to Athens in E. Ten. by the most direct route. Should this be the case I would desire to make speeches on my way at *Woodbury*, and some point in Warren that you might designate. Would McMinnville be the point, or would some other be better? Or had I better go by the way of *Smithville* and omit *Woodbury*, until my return from E. Tennessee. I can delay but little on the way as my object is to canvass every County in E. Tennessee by the 20th of May. Should my competitor however go into another part of the State I will go with him.

I see from the last *Gazette* that you are announced for the Senate—and intend soon to take the field. This is right. We must not allow our opponents to take start of us in the canvass, as they did last year. I see too in the same paper that two candidates are announced for the House in Warren,[3] and that a County meeting is called for the 20th. I do most sincerely hope that the Democracy of the County may be able to harmonize & that there may be no divisions in our ranks. Do affect this if possible. The Candidates in *Franklin* should be announced immediately. Why do they delay? Who will they be? Will you see or write to our friends in that County? *Saml. Turney* Esqr. I learn will run for the House in *White*. This is right. Why does he not announce himself? You may rely upon it, that it is our true policy to be out early & take the start of our opponents, rather than suffer them to take it of us.

My letters from Washington up to the 26th ultimo, express doubts whether there will be a *called Session of Congress* or not. I think Genl. Harrison's advisers are beginning to be alarmed, lest such a step might do them great harm. Let me hear from you.

JAMES K. POLK

ALS. MHi. Addressed to McMinnville and marked *"Private."* Published in "Letters of Three Presidents," *Massachusetts Historical Society Proceedings*, LXIII, pp. 80–81.

1. See Andrew Jackson to Polk, March 6, 1841.

2. In his Inaugural Address of March 4, 1841, William H. Harrison pledged himself to one term in office, declared that he would not encroach on legislative power by use of the veto, or assume undue power by the use of federal patronage, particularly in the Treasury Department. Harrison urged that Congress not become involved in the slavery question. Control of the currency system, however, did belong in the hands of Congress.

3. No copies of the McMinnville *Central Gazette* for 1841 have been found. However, Polk's reference probably is to Hugh L. W. Hill and Thomas H. Hopkins, both of whom won seats in the Tennessee House from Warren County.

FROM A. O. P. NICHOLSON

My Dear Sir: Washington March 9th 1841

The debate on the resolution to dismiss Blair and Rives has been continued to-day without being brought to a close.[1] It has become exceedingly angry and personal, and out of the discussion to-day a challenge is understood to have passed from Mr. King of Ala. to Mr. Clay of Ky. The circumstances are these. On yesterday Mr. Clay said in his speech that Francis P. Blair was an *infamous* man and therefore ought to be removed. This morning Mr. King in reply said, that he believed Mr. Blair's private character was as fair as that of any man in the community. Mr. Clay considered this remark as placing Blair on an equality with himself, and therefore pronounced it false and *cowardly.* Mr. King rose and said, he had no reply to make to that remark! He sat down, instantly wrote a letter, took out Dr. Linn and in a few moments the Senate adjourned, when Dr. Linn is understood to have delivered the letter. So that a fight is inevitable unless Mr. Clay makes an unconditional back-out. This is all that has transpired. Our friends rely confidently on King's nerve and his resolution to bring the matter to an immediate issue. From all that I have seen of Mr. Clay I am very much inclined to believe, that he will avoid a fight. He cannot do it by denying to King the character of a gentleman, for in giving the insult he distinctly stated that he recognized him as responsible. How it will terminate we shall probably know tomorrow. It will be utterly impossible to get along here without fighting. Clay's insolence is insufferable, and it will not be borne. Never have I seen power so tyranically used as the new Senate are now using it, and every federal senator bows servilely to the arrogant dictation of Clay. I have heard nothing to-day of the Extra-session. No other nominations have been made. I think it probable we may adjourn to-morrow.

A. O. P. NICHOLSON.

ALS. DLC–JKP. Addressed to Nashville.

1. See Nicholson to Polk, March 8, 1841.

FROM A. O. P. NICHOLSON

My Dear Sir: Washington City March 10. [1841][1]

The affair of King and Clay of Ky is still pending.[2] After King had sent his note by Dr. Linn and before Clay had given any answer, they were both arrested upon the information of our newly made Federal Sergeant at arms[3] and bound in $5000 to keep the peace. This proceeding operates over the District and has suspended the matter until the adjournment, when the two gentlemen are expected to settle the matter out of the district. I have learned that it was upon the suggestion of Mr. Wise that our Sergeant acted. Dr. Linn and Mr. Sevier are the friends of Col. King in the affair. I have seen some signs of an attempt at reconciliation, but that can only take place I think upon an unconditional withdrawal by Clay of his insulting remark. I believe it will probably come to that and that there will be no fight. I have no idea that Mr. Clay wishes to fight. On account of a severe snow storm which has raged all this day we have deferred starting until the 13th.[4] The Senate is still in session. We acted to-day on several small nominations, none of consequence.

A. O. P. NICHOLSON

ALS. DLC–JKP. Addressed to Nashville.

1. Year determined through content analysis.

2. See Nicholson to Polk, March 9, 1841.

3. Edward Dyer was elected sergeant at arms and doorkeeper of the U.S. Senate on March 8, 1841.

4. Nicholson and John Catron planned to travel together on their return trip to Tennessee.

FROM JAMES WALKER

Dear Sir, Columbia March 10 1841

I return your draft & note endorsed as requested.[1] We have nothing new here. The Whig nomination excites very little attention. On my return home, I was frequently asked the news, I think with the expectation that I would mention Jones's nomination as a matter of importance. I invariably replied *nothing new* &c. I think the best way is to affect at least, to treat the matter as of no importance. But at the same time I think every nerve should be strained to accomplish a victory.

William could not certainly have received your letter on Monday,[2] as he made regular sett speeches and every exertion to prevent the call of a county convention. I thought our political power in this county to some extent at hazard, and was obliged to oppose his views directly & openly. This was disagreeable & I confess I am at a loss to understand his motives. If he is really determined to run for the Legislature I think he can get the nomination, if he wishes it—and if he was to run upon the nomination of the county, *it could do nobody else any harm.* The question was postponed on Sam's[3] Suggestion until Saturday night, when we expect a much fuller meeting. The county convention will certainly be called. It is very popular with all our friends, except William, and he must for general good be overruled.

I think it will be best for you, neither to write, or say any thing to him on the subject. I will accomplish what I think will strengthen us in this county, without any heart burning with him. At least I will give him no just cause for dissatisfaction with me. Him and me differ as to the course we think ought to be pursued. He advances his opinions. I advance mine. The meeting decides. If they decide according to his views, I shall of course acquiesce. Let this matter work its own way, without interference. *It will work right.*

JAMES WALKER

[P.S.] Maria[4] is worse than she was last week. I now am apprehensive of a long & certainly very painful confinement. J.W.

ALS. DLC–JKP. Addressed to Nashville.

1. Walker enclosed a draft dated March 18, 1841, made in his favor by Polk in the amount of $1,143, and drawn on Polk's account with M. D. Cooper & Co. of New Orleans. Walker endorsed the verso of the draft. DS. DLC–JKP.

2. Polk's letter to his brother, William, has not been found.

3. Samuel P. Walker.

4. Jane Maria Polk Walker.

TO JAMES C. JONES

Sir

Nashville March 15th 1841

In the Nashville Banner of this date, I find a correspondence between yourself and a number of gentlemen acting as a committee of a Convention of Citizens recently assembled at Murfreesborough, from which it appears that you were nominated by that Convention as a candidate for Governor of this State, and that you have accepted the nomination. In the same paper I find a list of appointments of times and places, at which it is stated you will address the people, published I presume by your authority. It is probably known to you, that I am a candidate for re-election to the office of Governor, and the object of this communication is to inform you, that it is my intention to observe the usual custom of addressing the people throughout the State, so far as my official duties may permit and that I expect to be with you at most if not all the appointments which you have made. Your first appointment I perceive is at Smithville, in DeKalb County on friday the 2nd day of April. I have made several appointments in Rutherford Wilson and Smith Counties for the week preceeding that time, a list of which I send you herewith, and at which I respectfully invite you to attend. That as candidates we may stand before our fellow citizens, on terms of perfect equality, I have to assure you that the usages heretofore observed, respecting the division of time, by which each may be allowed an equal space with the other, on every occasion and each make the leading or opening address on each alternate day, will be intirely agreeable to me, as I have no doubt it will be to you. This courtesy I believe has been always observed by competing candidates in the State. It was observed by my competitor and myself two years ago, whenever we met at an appointment, whether made by him or by me, and its perfect fairness both for the speakers and hearers is so manifest that I cannot doubt your readiness to observe it whenever I may attend your appointments, as I shall cheerfully do, whenever you shall attend mine. In this mode of conducting the canvass, the people can have an opportunity, to hear the discussions on both sides of every public question, upon which we may differ in opinion, and be the better able to decide between us. If any of the political principles or opinions which I hold are erroneous or unsound, I am willing to have them publickly exposed when standing face to face, before the people, and if any of yours may be so, I cannot doubt but that you will be willing to have [them exposed][1] in like manner.

Had I known that you intended to make the appointments, which were published in the Banner of to day, I should have been pleased to have conferred with you, in relation to them.[2] I will however endeavour to make it convenient to attend them with you. I have to request the favour of an answer.

JAMES K. POLK

P.S. The following are the appointments which I have made, viz—At Murfreesborough, in Rutherford on Saturday the 27th of March
At Lebanon in Wilson on Monday 29th March
At the Big Spring in Wilson on Tuesday 30th Do.
At Rome in Smith on wednesday—31st Do. J.K.P.

ALS, draft. DLC–JKP. Addressed to Lebanon and marked *"Copy."*

1. A tear in the manuscript has obliterated at least two words.

2. Polk canceled the following words: "As however I knew nothing of them, until they appeared in the paper of this morning."

FROM JAMES C. JONES

Sir Lebanon March 18th 1841

Yours of the 15th Instant has been receivd; and I beg leave to assure you; that your proposition as to the manner in which you desire the canvass between us should be conducted is entirely acceptable to me. They are just such as I myself would have proposed; had I felt it my duty to have made propositions at all.

I should have sought an interview with you before making my appointments; if I had thought it was desired on your part; I was in Nashville for several days and recevd no intimation from you of a desire or willingness on your part to make mutual arrangements for the canvass.

You had been in the field for several months and of course I had supposed you had canvassed such portions of the State as were most conducive to your interest. I thought it but just that I should have the privilege of travelling over the ground that you had so recently occupied. The spirit of liberality manifested in your letter I assure is properly appreciated and fully reciprocated on my part.

It will afford me pleasure to have you with me at all my appointments and you may rest satisfied that you shall have an equal division of time. I ask no advantage. I desire an open field and a fair fight leaving the final decision in the hands of our fellow citizens whose province it is to determine between us. I await that decision with the greatest composure. I shall avail myself of your invitation to attend your appointments.

JAMES C JONES

ALS. DLC–JKP. Addressed to Nashville.

FROM JAMES WALKER

Dear Sir, Columbia March 18, 1841

There is still no visible improvement in Maria's health. I cannot ascertain from her physicians, whether any progress is making in eradicating the disease. She suffers, with what seems short intervals, the most excrutiating pain. Her life is not considered in danger, but it seems almost certain that she has yet to suffer much pain & misery. I furnish Dr. Dickinson with a regular dairy [diary] of her condition [and] symptoms, and he can at any time inform you from the information I give him, whether she is better or worse, better than I can with my knowledge judge. It is indeed almost as bad a case as can be where life is not immediately threatened [and] much worse than I apprehended when I saw you.

The political symptoms in this county are very favorable, so far as I can judge. A great many whigs will undoubedly vote for you and all seems to work well, except one single difficulty, which to me is annoying. William[1] is decidedly opposed to the calling [of] a county convention. He put it off as long as he could, and when it was determined on by the Democratic association, made a furious speech, insulting to the meeting, and seeming purposely to misconceive the measure adopted. To-day before the Democrat was published, he took me aside and made efforts to get me to have withheld the call for another week stating it as Jonas E. Thomas request, and that Thomas would not run as a *convention candidate* &c. I resisted his importunity, and told him it must be as determined on. That it was particularly due to you & your relations that the convention system should be adopted—that I did not know of a single one of our friends except himself, who was not warmly and decidedly in favor of a convention nomination. The determination to settle conflicting aspirations, seems to have hushed up all the great men (except Wm.) and so far as I can learn they are all agreed to work where the people choose to put them. I do not fully understand William. If he has aspirations at present (& I believe he has) his present course, if it was generally known, is well calculated to defeat his views. If he wishes to run for the Legislature against all the dictates of common sense, why not refer his claims to the convention, and if *they* choose to nominate him among others, it cannot be said that *Gov. Polks* kin run & controul the country & all such slang.

You are almost always, in my judgement, very prudent. But with William, I do not think you are so. You *command him too much*, & have too little patience with him. My advice is, that you write him a *kind letter,* and inform him what you think will promote your success in the great contest we are now entering upon. It is a struggle for life, with our party and all minor and *personal* considerations must be yielded. I know he is ambitous, but it is without judgement & in writing to him, you must not give him a hint that you know his course & are dissatisfied with it. Give him your views as to the course you think *we all* here ought to pursue—and if he does not take it, we must make the best of it, we have no time now for reproaches.

Marsh.[2] has just returned from old man Haily's,[3] to purchase a horse for you, pr. order. He reports that Haily's is a fine young Horse, three years old this spring, never been worked, but very gentle—price $85, but can probably be got for less. He will bring him in for me to see on Saterday. I sent Phill[4] with him, supposing his judgement more to be relied on than Marshall's. Phill says he is a *very fine,* strong, young horse, larger and if possible Stronger than my horse John. He thinks he will do. Phill says he can break him to harness in a week, and as he is well disposed I suppose so. Perhaps if you think he will do, you had better send Elias out for him & let him make a business of training him until you want him. I have no doubt he can be had for $80 Christmas hay. Phill says he is *mighty cheap.*

I should like to hear from you how the Jones nomination works, as far as you are advised. I wish also to know when Van Pelt returns from Memphis & the result of his trip.[5] I see that Hogan[6] is *well employed* at Murfreesboro. If Van Pelt is engaged at Memphis, we will employ a young man by the name of Dickinson,[7] as editor of the Democrat & *assist him.*

I have just received yours of the 17th.[8]

James Walker

ALS. DLC–JKP. Addressed to Nashville.

1. William H. Polk.
2. Marshall, one of Walker's slaves, is not identified further.
3. Hailey is not identified further.
4. Phill, one of Walker's slaves, is not identified further.
5. See John C. McLemore to Polk, February 14, 1841.
6. In 1841 Thomas Hogan became editor of the Murfreesboro *Weekly Times,* a Democratic newspaper published by James M. Johnston and James H. Harrison.
7. C. J. Dickerson, a Columbia lawyer, was secured to edit the Columbia *Tennessee Democrat* in March 1841; he replaced Andrew M. Kerr, Jr., as publisher of the paper on June 2, 1842.
8. Letter not found.

TO ROBERT J. CHESTER

My Dear Sir Nashville March 19th 1841

I expected when you were here that I would be at Jackson at the Supreme Court. My opponent however has made a list of appointments for East Tennessee commencing before that time and I *must be with him.*[1] This I regret. Many of our leading friends will probably be at Court. *Candidates must be brought out in every County where it is practicable. Coe* will be there, and I must rely—*him, Huntsman, yourself* and others to attend to this. Do not neglect it. I will be in the District before the canvass is over.

James K. Polk

P.S. I enter the canvass at Murfreesboro', on the 27th in buoyant spirits & confident of success, if I can only be reasonably sustained by the local candidates. J.K.P.

ALS. THi–JKP. Addressed to Jackson and marked "*Private.*"

1. See Polk to James C. Jones, March 15, 1841, and Jones to Polk, March 18, 1841.

FROM EDWIN CROSWELL[1]

Albany, New York. March 19, 1841

Croswell writes Polk that Francis Granger, son of Democrat Gideon Granger,[2] "has been a Clintonian, a federalist, an anti-mason, an abolitionist (in fact), & a whig—but never for a moment a democrat."

ALS. DLC–JKP. Probably addressed to Nashville.

1. Croswell was editor of the *Albany Argus* from 1823 until 1854.

2. A lawyer and political writer, Granger served as U.S. postmaster general from 1801 until 1814, when President Madison forced his resignation.

FROM ANDREW JACKSON

My Dear Sir, Hermitage March 20th 1841

I see from the Union that you are about to enter upon your political campaign.[1] Mr. Jones (I cannot call him Major for he never was a corporal) is your competitor. This is well for the Democratic cause. I have no fear of your Success, but recollecting the falshoods propagated by Bell, Foster, Jones, and Col Caruthers in their addresses to the people I wish you to remember in your address at Lebanon These things and have with you the debates in the late congress on the Subject of the appropriation of $6000 for the furniture of the presidents House in addition to the present furniture[2] in with the report of the commissioner of the public buildings &c. &c. &c.[3] These are full evidence of the falshood of the charge of extravagance charged against Mr. Van Buren, & a falshood by Bell Foster &c. &c. wilfully, wickedly and knowingly by them pronounced, because Bell knew & so did Foster that it was a wicked falshood known by them when they pronounced it. This even in wilson will damn them—for it can be well enquired of the audience How a moral people can have any confidence in men who will wilfully slander his neighbour & that for the sake of office or party purposes. Mr. Bell was working for a place in the cabinet; and you can further add, that if I had given him the place of Secretary of War when recommended by Judge White, he would never have sold himself to the blue light Federalists of the East. This was the cause of his apostacy & he will make another somerset, abandon his present party if a prospect opens to agrandise himself. Can, you may ask, any moral and christian people have any confidence in such office seekers & corrupt politicians as these. If necessary you can give me as the author of his application for the war department on the recommendation of Judge White. Mr. Burton has Judge Whites letter recommending Bell. Health & respect, & success to you.

ANDREW JACKSON

ALS. DLC–JKP. Addressed to Nashville and delivered by Andrew Jackson, Jr. Published in Bassett, ed., *Jackson Correspondence*, VI, pp. 95–96.

1. The *Nashville Union* of March 18, 1841, announced that on March 27 Polk would start a short campaign trip to the eastward and would speak in Rutherford, Wilson, and Smith counties.

2. In House debates of April 14 and 16 on the 1840 civil appropriation bill, Charles Ogle, a Pennsylvania Whig opposed inclusion of a $3,665 item for the alteration and repair of the President's House and furniture and for maintenance of the mansion's grounds. Ogle charged that in 1838 Van Buren had spent over $6,000 on luxurious furnishings and that such extravagance belied the president's profession of republican principles. Ogle's arguments circulated widely during the presidential campaign of 1840. See also Robert B. Reynolds to Polk, March 28, 1841.

3. William Noland's annual reports and treasury accounts as commissioner of public buildings did not itemize expenditures on the President's House; however, the July 21, 1840, report of the House Committee on Expenditures on the Public Buildings did disclose in detail expenditures for 1837 through 1839. The House did not order the report printed until 1842; see House Report No. 552, 27 Congress, 2 Session.

FROM JAMES WALKER

Dear Sir, Columbia, March 21, 1841

Maria was much better on Friday & yesterday, than she has been since her illness commenced.[1] She was pretty free from pain, cheerful and in good spirits. She continued so up to 8 P.M. yesterday, when pain & uneasiness manifested itself. She slept however until 3 A.M. and from that time grew worse, until about 8 to 9 [when] she became frantic with pain, and obtained but little relief, until 12 to 1—when she became easy enough to sleep, & now (4 P.M.) she is tolerably easy. I cannot ascertain from her Physicians whether any progress is making in eradicating the disease or not. It is most painful & discouraging.

Hailey brought in his horse yesterday.[2] He is cheap enough but I do not think he will answer your purpose. He is too young, and scarcely bridle wise. I think if broke, he would be too young to *endure* the service you would wish him to perform. I think you had better get a tried horse at Nashville as I know of none here that I think would suit you.

William says he cannot go to see Captain Dobbins.[3] He is obliged he says to attend the called Circuit Court that commences to-morrow. Samuel[4] cannot go, principally on account of his quarterly return, which he must prepare in person 1st of April.

I *believe* William is determined to run for the Legislature. He will probably try for the nomination. If he does not get that, I am not sure he can be restrained any how. I think his running in any way will loose you some votes—but if he runs against the convention nominees he is certainly ruined & hurts you here very much. I do not know that I am correct in my opinions, but think I am. I give you my thoughts that you may shape your letters to him *for effect*. Be sure that you do not let him know you are informed on the subject. I think he ought not to be a candidate for any thing or under any circumstances, in this great trial contest.

I do not know who can be got to go to Captain Dobbins. William I do not think will go at all. You know I cannot, and Sam. cannot well go. If you think James[5] would do, I think it probable he would go, if you would write to himself & particularly request it. I think he would do.

JAMES WALKER

ALS. DLC–JKP. Addressed to Nashville.

1. See James Walker to Polk, March 10 and 18, 1841.
2. See James Walker to Polk, March 18, 1841.
3. William H. Polk. See James Walker to Polk, February 24, 1841, and Sarah C. Polk to Polk, April 14, 1841.

4. Samuel P. Walker.
5. James H. Walker was the second son of James Walker.

FROM ROBERT ARMSTRONG

Sunday Evening
Nashville [March 28, 1841][1]

Gover.

The Proclamation is here Convening Congress for 31 May.[2] I sent some to Doct Rucker by the mail last. I hope you have continued on to Lebanon and will return here some time on Monday night or Tuesday morning. The official paper was rec'd last night by Mrs. Polk. Fletcher & myself prepared the writs; they are now printing. Jesse Thomas[3] is takeing four Copies of your Proclamation. I will have it mentioned in the Union in the morning that the Proclamation is here & that you will be here on monday & your Proclamation & the writs of Election will be issued on Tuesday morning.[4]

I Send this to Donelson's. If he has gone the Carrier Foster[5] will go on to Lebanon. In haste.

R. Armstrong

[P.S.] Say to Burton I will send the addresses[6] for Wilson[7] in the Stage in the morning.

ALS. DLC–JKP. Addressed to Lebanon.

1. Date of the letter identified through content analysis. Armstrong clearly, but incorrectly wrote "Nashville 27th"; he designated neither the month nor year.

2. See A. O. P. Nicholson to Polk, March 8, 1841.

3. Not identified further.

4. Canceling his speaking engagement in Lebanon for Monday, March 29, 1841, Polk returned to Nashville on Sunday evening, March 28. The following morning he issued a gubernatorial proclamation authorizing a special congressional election to be held on the first Thursday in May 1841. Writs authorizing the same were issued to the sheriffs of the several counties. Also on March 29, Polk wrote "A Letter to the Public," published in the *Nashville Union* of April 1, 1841, in which he explained his reasons for not calling an extra session of the Tennessee General Assembly.

5. Not identified further.

6. Polk's "Address to the People of Tennessee," the first installment of which was published in the *Nashville Union* on March 29, 1841, sketched his public career and outlined his political philosophy. Printed in a forty-page pamphlet, the "Address" was distributed throughout Tennessee during the 1841 gubernatorial campaign.

7. Wilson County.

FROM SARAH C. POLK

Dear Husband Sunday, March 28, 1841

Fearing that you had left Murfreesboro before the mail got in this morning, I thought it best and safe to send a letter to Majr. Donelson to take to you. The Proclamation[1] came to hand last night both in the news papers, & the *Official* from the *Department of State.* I think you had better come part of the way tomorrow night if you can not come all. Your absence and the Proclamation will or has been swallowed up in the all prevailing topic of today the Union Bank robbery[2]—so you need not think that your absense will make any impression as they have something else to talk about. I look a little for you this evening, but could not rest satisfied without sending a messenger to Majr. Donelson who I knew was going to Lebanon tomorrow.

SARAH POLK

ALS. DLC–JKP. Addressed to Lebanon.

1. See A. O. P. Nicholson to Polk, March 8, 1841, and Robert Armstrong to Polk, March 28, 1841.

2. On March 29, 1841, the Nashville *Republican Banner* reported that rumors of embezzlement of Union Bank funds had circulated for several days. Examination of bank ledgers showed that discrepancies existed back to 1839. Missing were two packages of bills amounting to $18,500. Authorities arrested bank clerk Thomas L. Budd, who confessed to making false ledger entries.

FROM ROBERT B. REYNOLDS

Dear Sir, Knoxville March 28th, 1841

I have delayed writing you until now for the purpose of gleaning something that would be important to communicate to you. I believe that there are no wavering Democrats in East Tennessee, but I do Know of many persons who voted for Harrison, who will now Support you. In many Counties, I learn that changes are going on in behalf of democratic principles. It is impossible to effect a proper organization of our party at the present time. We are in great want of men, who are capable of transacting the business necessary to be done in organising our forces. In some counties, I fear we shall not be able to run candidates for the Legislature, altho' its importance is conceded. I have endeavored to have things arranged as well as possible in this respect, but I have not succeeded as well as I wished to do. McKamy, will I understand, be a candidate for re-election. He has two Whig opponents and with proper exertions will succeed. I have no doubt, Col. Hembree of Roane is true as ever, and will Shortly be in the field for re-election. He will have two, if not three Whig opponents. The Col. is much Stronger than Mr VanBuren was in Novr. I learn that Harrison has issued his proclamation, for an Extra Session of Congress. I suppose it will be necessary to fix upon some day for an election for members of the H. Rep's. I hope it will be put off as long as possible. I am afraid it would injure us much, in our State elections for Govr. & members to the Legislature, to call the Legislature together to fill the vacancy in the Senate. It would seem like we have no confidence in carrying the elections in August. Justice and right, perhaps would demand that it Should be done, but I fear that it would have a tendency to injure us. Gen. Anderson, I learn, is in favor of the immediate call of the Legislature for that special purpose, and urges as an argument in behalf of his proposition, that by so doing a bank charter will be defeated. I am decidedly opposed to a bank, under any set of circumstances whatever, but as we are to have a hard contested field, for the August election, I hope we will So manage it, as to not increase our difficulties. But I need not argue this question to you.

We are determined to carry the August election if possible, and will give you every assistance in our power. We hope to put Tennessee once more upon the republican tack. The policy of Mr Jones in relation to the tipling law[1] will have a powerful bearing in East Tennessee & this question alone, in our division of the State, will injure him greatly, if prudently managed by our candidates for the Legislature. His internal improvement policy[2] will be of no advantage to him in East Tennessee. These things will bear heavily upon him, and we are placing them in the mouths of the people. There are many persons who are strongly in favor of the present law, against retailers of Spiritous liquors; but we will manage it so as [to] retain all our democrats and make more. At our last term of the Circuit Court here, there were a great many Indictments made against retailers &c. and consequently much excitement was roused in opposition to the present law. It will effect much in the Gubernatorial election. But the appointment of Webster, the rewarding of Allen A. Hall,[3] and the appointment of Members of Congress to office must help us. The expense of a call session & a farther appropriation for the President's House,[4] must Show the people what kind of economists these federalists are. I have great confidence in the result of the next election. I think we have gotten entirely clear of Hard cider & log cabin shows. The people must by this time, have become sober, & consequently disgusted with the riotous scenes of last year. The elections which have taken place in N. Hampshire & which will shortly take place in Virginia will encourage our friends. Your visit to East Tennessee will be of vast service to us, and especially to Blackwell & McClellan. The Senatorial election in Terry's old District must be revolutionized. If we can have the proper man out—Frazier,[5] the Federal Candidate, must be defeated. If we can but succeed in August, the claims of Tennessee upon the whole union, I mean the Democratic portion of the union, will be great; but [there] is time enough to speculate on that matter, after we fight the battle of the 5th of August. We want the Legislature, but we must carry the election for Govr in the first place. It will exalt us more abroad to defeat Jones, than to have a majority in the Legislature. But if we Succeed in the one, there can be no doubt of the other. I fear some trouble in the Greenville[6] & Hawkins Senatorial District. Balch says he is determined to run against Johnson. It will only injure us in the Election for Govr if he should do so, because Johnson can beat him & a whig to boot. I fear we Shall not be able to carry Wheeler's District. He has injured himself, & I fear an attempt to reelect him would fail. Frazier[7] could carry the District, but is in pecuniary distress & says he cannot run. Monroe is debateable ground and we will have a close contest in that county. Walker is opposed by a popular whig, and I greatly fear he is to be beaten. Nothing but the party vote can possibly save him. His vote upon the Common School bill for Monroe, McMinn, Bradley & Polk will greatly injure him.[8]

I have written much about East Tennessee. Our friends in the west may rely upon us making a breach upon the enemy's ranks. We are determined to roll back the tide of Federal Whiggery to where it was in 1839. It is true we have a heavy majority now against us, but that can be reduced if not totally neutralized. The opportunity to poll illegal votes, will not be half so great as in Novr. last. In all the Strong federal counties there will be two or more candidates of their own party running, thereby, making it their interest not to poll illegal votes.

I trust I Shall See you on the 22nd of April in good health & spirits. Until then no more.

R. B. Reynolds

ALS. DLC–JKP. Addressed to Sparta.

1. James C. Jones supported the Tippling House Act of 1838, which provided that persons convicted of retailing spiritous liquors in quantities of less than a quart could be fined at the discretion of the court and that fines would be reserved for the use of the common schools.

2. Jones regarded the 1837 Internal Improvements Act as impolitic and inadequate. Desiring a better regulated system, he argued for selectivity in the allocation of state bonds.

3. Allen A. Hall went to Venezuela as chargé d'affaires.

4. See Andrew Jackson to Polk, March 20, 1841. On February 24, 1841, Whig members of the U.S. House amended the civil appropriations bill by adding $6,000 for the purchase of furniture for the President's House.

5. Thomas N. Frazier served as chancery court clerk at Pikeville, 1836–37, and as deputy sheriff of Bledsoe County, 1839, before running unsuccessfully for a seat in the Tennessee Senate against Richard G. Waterhouse, a large landholder in Rhea County.

6. Greeneville, Tennessee.

7. Reference is to Julian Frazier of Grainger County.

8. James Walker of McMinn County won reelection to the Tennessee House by defeating Levi Trewhitt, a Bradley County lawyer. Walker voted against the 1841 common school bill for Monroe, McMinn, Bradley, and Polk counties.

FROM ARCHIBALD YELL

My dear Friend — Little Rock 28th March 1841

For the last few months we seem mutually, to drop our correspondence, without cause, save the cause of state; I have leasure and am determind to renew our acquaintance. Well we were badly beaten in the last contest—and it was brought about not from any malfeasence of the President—but produced by the *Stock Jober, Broker, and Banks.* A panic was produced & the screws put to the people while our currency was never in a more reched condition, from which the people were induced to desire a cha[n]ge & as things seemed to be at their worst any cha[n]ge would be for the better, and so we were beaten. They have now a difficult task to perform. They will have to produce a cha[n]ge for the better & visibly so or all's lost with them; a N. Bank with a capital of *one or two* hundred million may save them for the present—they must have money & better than what we now have. Can they charter a bank at all? If they do not the "Jig is up."[1] Will they not pass a "Protective Tariff" to enable them to retain their strength in the N. England state[s] and to carry on their wild and visionary schemes of Internal Improvement & the Assumption of the state debts.

I have more fears for their system of Assumption than any other; the state[s] are overwhelmed in debt & a majority of them will willingly accept the proposit[io]n of Distribut[io]n & Assumpt[io]n, & tho I believe it to be the *entering wedge* to a final disolution of this Union, yet I believe if the Whigs have a majority in the next Congress that Clay will pass it in some shape, which will terminate in a National Debt. By Fund[i]ng the money arising from the sale of the Pub. Land the States will be relieved for the present from Taxation—tho it may ultimately involve us in a war with Grate Brittain or produce Separation and Disolut[io]n at Home.

My only hope now is that we shall have a War & that speedily—that will Settle the *Interest account* withe our foreign Stockholders until the close of the War. It might & would most likely ensure the Charter of a Bank—but that's less dangerous in my estimat[io]n than the Bill of Assumption. Still I have no Idea that the Admn. can be kicked into a War—on her part—she is now in a position however that the attack will come from G. Brittan. I have a *presentiment* that we shall succeed at the next election come what may—the Federal party never has been longer than one term in power. We shall be better organized & act withe more harmony than we did in the late election. We want only one candidate & he a *full blood* & no matter who he may be. The called Session will drive off many of the Whig party. Disappointment in getting office will thin their ranks a hundred thousand. The Bank & Tariff will drive many Southern Whigs from them.

When you find leasure sit down & give me your views fully & freely. Tell me how your prospect is in Tennessee. Can you beat *Jones* and how many members of Congress will we elect & what is the prospect as to the Legislature? These are all subjects about which an old Tennessean feels a deep interest.

Arkansas is safe. Rely on that!!! Your old friends and acquaintances are well. I have appointed your old friend A. Whiney Insptr Genl of the state with the rank of Brigd Genl.

I have not sold any of your land & until times change there will be but little hope.[2]

Be so good as to present me to your good lady and accept for yourself the best wishes of your old friend.

A. YELL

ALS. DLC–JKP. Addressed to Nashville.

1. An eighteenth-century American colloquialism meaning "All is over."

2. See Ezekiel P. McNeal to Polk, December 2, 1840, and William H. Polk to Polk, December 4, 1840.

FROM EDWIN POLK

Sir Bolivar March 30, 1841

Enclosed I send you a statement given by George Alexander of Panola County Miss with respect to the character of my father during the Revolutionary war.[1] Having understood that George Alexander and his sister an old maid were living in Panola County Miss and that they were formerly residents of Mecklenburgh County N.C., and that their testimony might be material in fixing the true position of my father in the Revolutionary contest. I paid them a visit at their residence in Panola, from which I have just returned. I found him a hale man in his seventy eight year, and was a resident of Mecklenburgh County during the Revolutionary war. His sister was several years younger and of course her recollections more indistinct concerning the incidents of the war so much so that I deemed it unnecessary to question her, though her recollections of my father seemed to be of a pleasing nature. The old man, George Alexander, is a strong supporter of the *new* Administration having learned which previously to my going to his house, I was prepared to act with some caution. He told me that sometime previous to the late Presidential election he received a letter from Gen Thomas Polk of La Grange calling upon him to give his testimony as to the true position of Col William Polk during the Revolutionary war whose character he stated had been calumniated by being charged with toryism in that contest. He of course returned the proper answer. I then asked him to state to me candidly what he knew concerning the history of my father in the early part of his life. He then frankly communicated to me what he knew, concerning my father's position during the Revolutionary war, and related some other circumstances concerning him of some interest to me; but unconnected with the subject, concerning which I wished his evidence. He stated two circumstances concerning my father which are worthy of some attention as they do not accord with the tradition which has come down to us; first, that he removed, (as you see in his statement) to Mecklenburgh from South Carolina in or about the year 1778 and secondly, that he was *not* according to his understanding a Signer of the Mecklenburgh Declaration of Independence, which I did not deem necessary to write down in his Statement, as it would have been a negative statement and wholly uncalled for in a general narration of facts. Besides if it were *true* that he removed to Mecklenburgh in 1778 he could not have signed it unless he had been there on a visit. I inquired concerning the origin of the title of Colonel which he bore. He said that he had it when he came to Mecklenburgh and he did not know, how he obtained it. The fact of my father, removing his property, on Cornwallis's second return from the South and a part of it being taken by Cornwallis' troops, in crossing the river Yadkin, corroborates a statement previously made by an old negro now living, and who belonged to my father at that time, and who says also that my father did not get it back during the war. He told me also that he was a cousin of my father. He is a strong Whig and labors under political prejudices and seemed to be aware that the charge was made by partisans of his own Political creed, yet though it made him cautious he seemed to spurn the idea that Col Ezekiel Polk ever acted in any wise for or with the British.

I should have had this testimony taken in the form of an affidavit, and have procured the County seal but for the reason that I was unacquainted then with the *nature* of *protections*, and was fearful that the fact of getting the evidence legally authenticated would seem an admission that my father did take a protection.[2] If the slander should be renewed and you should think that this evidence would be material I shall take pleasure in getting it legally authenticated either by going down myself or sending it to him by mail as he told me he would make affidavit of the facts as g[iven][3] once I should send it. My desire is to place my fathers position during that contest in its true character, and from all the evidence which I have as yet been able to obtain, I have no doubt that he was a Republican in every sense of the word.

EDWIN POLK
March 31st 1841

[P.S.] I wrote the enclosed copy in a great hurry in order to get it in last nights mail, but did not do so. If you think the evidence material I can get the original Statement properly certified and send it to you. No person here knows the object of my visit to Miss; indeed the affair is not thought of, at least not spoken of. E. Polk

ALS. DLC–JKP. Addressed to Nashville and forwarded to Polk at Athens by Sarah C. Polk on April 9, 1841. ALS. DLC–JKP.

1. Enclosure not found. Alexander's statement, dated March 25, 1841, at Panola County, Mississippi, exonerated Ezekiel Polk from charges of Toryism. Copy. DLC–JKP. AEI by Polk states that "The above [statement] is a true copy from the original furnished to me by *Edwin Polk Esqr* of Bolivar Tennessee July 21st 1844." See also, Edwin Polk to Polk, August 27, 1840, and James Walker to Polk, February 24, 1841.

2. "Taking protection" from the British required a promise of nonresistance to and cooperation with the occupying military forces.

3. Seal of the letter has obliterated a portion of one word.

FROM ISAAC H. DISMUKES

Gov J K Polk Miss. Oake[1] Aprile the 1, 1841

I will now write you a fiew lines that you may hear from us. Wea are all well. I have got all of my ould ground courn planted and it is cummin up but on the last saderday and sunday in this munth wea had a tremenderous rain which overflowed and wash up a great deal of it and I expect to have most all of it to plant over again unless it cumup better than I expect it will.

I was at a lost to noe what to write to you. I have commence planting of cotten. I commence to day as it is the first of April. I have noe diffeyculty with my boys.

Mr. bobit[2] was down to sea mea the other day for the first time and I have not heard from you since you left: you must write. Nuthing more.

ISAAC H. DISMUKES

ALS. DLC–JKP. Addressed to Nashville. Published in Bassett, *Plantation Overseer*, 151.

1. Oakachickama, Mississippi.
2. William Bobbitt served as Polk's agent in Coffeeville.

FROM ROBERT ARMSTRONG

Dear Govr. [Nashville] 5 Apl [1841][1]

I am in some what better spirits than I was a few days ago, when I wrote you.[2] I find a stiring and moving of our friends and trust good may come of it. Letters from every part of the state say that our cause is gaining. Col. Chester writes [we] will do great good by coming out [even] if he should not succed. He thinks he may be elected,[3] and speaks of Pavatts[4] Improving prospects with some confidence. Make every arrangement in the counties to insure a majority in the Legislature. This is the great front for I feel confident that you will beat Jones with ease. Foster is very uneasy and I have no doubts he thot their party cannot be kept to geather. Their is great disatisfaction in their ranks.

I have appointed the 19th for you to address the people of this County.[5] Have had hand bill[s] issued and such and sending them to every civil Dist. I have and will write our friends to come in. Harris is doing so, and I hope we may have a good meeting.

You say your addresses have not reached East Tenss. I hav sent 700 to Knoxville, 700 to Ford. Told them at both places where to send. I send Ford to day 500 more to send over to Marion McMinn Rhea &c &c. You will meet them there & can dispose of them. I sent 900 to Jackson for Distribution, 500 to Cave Johnton,[6] 800 to Walker at Columbia, 300 to Guild &c for Campbell's District, and others in every direction that I could send out by our friends. Hall[7] is out against Caruthers. Can do nothing.

We may get out candidates in this County but I fear it. Virginia doing well for members [of the] Legislature; Kentucky better than we expected.[8]

Mrs. Polk well. Young up and doing, and I am yet in *Office*.[9]

R ARMSTRONG

ALS. DLC–JKP. Addressed to McMinnville.

1. Year identified through content analysis.

2. On April 2, 1841, Armstrong wrote that J. George Harris was slow in publishing Polk's "Address to the People of Tennessee" and his "Letter to the Public," in which the governor had announced his decision not to call a special session of the General Assembly. ALS. DLC–JKP. See also Armstrong to Polk, March 28, 1841.

3. Robert J. Chester's name did not appear in returns from Madison County for either the congressional race in May or the state legislative races in August.

4. A lawyer from Huntingdon, Stephen C. Pavatt served as a Democrat in the Tennessee House, 1833–37, and in the state Senate, 1851–53. He ran unsuccessfully for Congress as a Democrat in 1839, 1841, 1843, and 1853. Pavatt moved from Huntingdon to Camden in 1846.

5. Polk spoke at the courthouse in Nashville on May 19, 1841.

6. Cave Johnson.

7. John Hall, a Lebanon lawyer, served in the Tennessee House, 1835–37. Hall was a supporter of Hugh Lawson White and became a Whig. In 1841, however, Hall was running for Congress as a Democrat.

8. In Virginia's legislative elections Democrats gained three seats in the House, but lost one in the Senate; the Whigs won a majority of one in the Senate and two in the House. In Kentucky's congressional races only, Democrats claimed victory in four of thirteen contests.

9. Armstrong probably expected to be removed as Nashville's postmaster early in Harrison's administration of the general government.

FROM SARAH C. POLK

Dear Husband Nashville April 8th 1841

There is not as yet any business to call your attention, no letter from Jackson by last nights mail.[1] But a letter from the President and directors of the Lagrange & Memphis railroad company, asking for bonds to the amount of 37,000, and asking immediate attention to it.[2] And also stating that James Rembert[3] was dead, and that the board had that day unanimously recommended Ge[n]l. Thomas G. Polk to fill the vacancy. I will enclose a leter from Knoxville,[4] on the same subject of road commissioners, something which you could attend to where you are. A letter of invitation to a Dinner given to A. V. Brown at *Savannah* on the 22nd, which is about all that has come since I wrote last. If you wish me to send letters or newspapers to you write.

The Banner was out on you a few days ago, on your reasons for not calling the Legislature together, the article said to be written by *Allen Hall, a Office Holder.*[5] The Union of this morning charged it upon him,[6] and also had some good articles relative to your prospects. The Banner of to day has two letters from *Big Spring* & *Sparta* telling what an extraordinary man Jones proves himself to be and that he uses you up so. Thus they (I suppose Jones traveling companions or puffers) think that you will leave them by the 15th with an excuse to attend to Executive business.

There is rather a calm here on politics and every thing else. There is not much said, only what appears in the papers. I do not think it likely that the Democrats will get out any candidates in this county.[7] There seems to be no prospects of doing so. I can not gather much news as I see but few persons to talk to. I have written all I [k]now at present. You must write where to direct my letters to. I am not at all discouraged at any thing I see in the papers or hear from any quarter, but when I think of the labour and fatigue you have to undergo, I feel *sad* and melancholy, and conclude that *success* is not worth the labour. Dr. Young is yet in his room but attends to his business *that I send* him faithfully. If *Jones* does frighten you home by the 15th you may tell him your wife will be glad to see you.

SARAH POLK

[P.S.] Since writing I have received the Columbia *Observer* which has changed Editors from Zolly to two Roseboroughs,[8] & An[c]d Barkley Martin candidate, for the Senate. *William* & Dew, for the House of Representatives.[9]

ALS. DLC–JKP. Addressed to Athens. Published in *THQ*, XI, pp. 183–84.

1. The judges of the Tennessee Supreme Court at Jackson, Tennessee, requested Polk to appoint a special judge to hear a case in which one of the judges was an interested party. Nathan Green, W. B. Reese, and William B. Turley to Polk, April 5, 1841. LS. T–Governor's Papers. AE by Polk states that on April 14, 1841, he appointed William Fitzgerald to be the special judge.

2. Reference is to a letter of April 1, 1841, from the company president, Eastin Morris, and six directors, John J. Potts, George Anderson, E. W. Harris, David Johnson, David Jernigan, and R. J. Yancy. LS. T–Governor's Papers.

3. A planter from Shelby County and a Democrat, James Rembert had been appointed by Polk to the LaGrange and Memphis Railroad's board as one of the state's directors.

4. William Lyon wrote from Knoxville that upon reconsideration he was unable to accept Polk's appointment as a commissioner of the Hiwassee Railroad Company. Lyon to Polk, April 1, 1841. ALS. T–Governor's Papers. AE by Polk states that he received Lyon's letter at Athens on April 15, 1841; Polk appointed James Berry to the post on April 17, 1841.

5. The Nashville *Republican Banner* of April 5, 1841, carried an unsigned editorial entitled "Gov. Polk's Address."

6. The *Nashville Union* of April 8, 1841, identified the author of the *Banner*'s article as "an office holder." Reference was to Allen A. Hall, frequent critic of the spoils system and newly appointed chargé d'affaires to Venezuela.

7. Davidson County.

8. Felix K. Zollicoffer, A. M. Rosborough, and J. B. Rosborough. The new editors continued the *Observer*'s tradition of supporting the Whig party.

9. William H. Polk and John H. Dew, candidates for the Tennessee House.

FROM SARAH C. POLK

Dear Husband Nashville April 10th 1841

The application for a special Judge at Jackson did not come until last night.[1] Genl. Armstrong attended to procuring some person to go with it, according to your directions. I suppose the appointment will reach there in time as I understand that it is likely the Court will hold four weeks. I had written to you by the mail yesterday morning and sent some papers, which I could have sent by the messenger if I had then known that one would be sent. The Banner & Whig of yesterday give you a touch. Their attacks amount to but little and only proves to me they are uneasy. Allen Hall is here writing for the Banner. And the Whig is not severe. The article yesterday was a rally to the Whig candidates for the Legislature, saying that to you a defeat would be nothing, if the Legislature was Democrattic. Your ambition now was the Senate of W.[2] In my last I wrote you that *Jones* letter writers had appeared in the Banner representing you as used up by Jones &c. &c. I do not believe any thing they put in the papers will have any affect, so you need not be uneasy. *I am not troubled* at any thing that has yet appeared. *Old Tip* is dangerously ill, so it is understood from the mails of last night. I believe that I wrote you all the business in my last letter, directed to Athens.

Sarah Polk

[P.S.] Genl. Armstrong found great difficulty in getting a competent person to go, which delayed the starting of a messenger.[3]

ALS. DLC–JKP. Probably addressed to Athens and delivered by messenger. Published in *THQ*, XI, pp. 184–85.

1. See Sarah C. Polk to Polk, April 8, 1841.
2. Reference is to the U.S. Senate in Washington.
3. On April 10, 1841, Robert Armstrong writes that he will dispatch a confidential messenger, "Mr. Penticost," to return to Nashville with Polk's appointment of a special judge. Armstrong will then mail the commission to Jackson, where it will be received on April 19th. ALS. DLC–JKP. John S. Young writes on April 21, 1841, that he mailed the commission earlier in the evening. ALS. DLC–JKP.

TO SARAH C. POLK

My Dear Wife Cleveland April 11th 1841

Since I wrote you from *Jasper*[1] I have been gradually recovering from my cold, & am now less fatigued than I was a week ago. Since I left Jasper I have made speeches at *Chatanooga*, at *Harrison*, and at this point. All the counties through which I have passed, until I reached this point, gave majorities against me, in 1839, as also majorities for Harrison during the last year. I am satisfied that I maintain my full strength of 1839, every where I have been, and in most of the counties have increased that strength. The Democracey are every where active, and doing their duty. I hear of many Whigs who declare their intention to support me; though great ifforts are making by the leaders of that party, to bind the mass of their party down to *old party lines*. I do not think they can do so, to the full extent.

Jones has his nephew (Mr Hart), a young man about the age of Thomas Claiborne, travelling with him.[2] He has also a man by the name of *Patterson*, who was formerly the Editor of a *Whig paper* at Gallatin, with him.[3] Patterson's business I have no doubt is to write letters back to the Whig papers. I gave Mr Harris a hint of this from Sparta.[4] The letters that appear in the Nashville Whig papers, will I have no doubt contain internal evidence that they came from the same hand. My friends every where that we have met say, that I have had decidedly the advantage of *Jones* in the discussions, and that I have made votes at most of them. Still I have no doubt that many falsehoods, will be written back with a view to effect, by this *hireling* letterwriter. I wish you to see *Mr Harris* and request him to watch the Whig letters which appear, and to expose *Patterson*, if he shall think it necessary.

I have not seen a single Nashville paper of later date, than the day of my departure from Nashville, and do not therefore know what is going on West of the mountain. Not a copy of my *Address* has reached this county[5] or *Hamilton*. This is unaccountable. Will you see *Mr Harris* & *Genl. Armstrong*, and urge them to take means to have them sent on.[6]

I hope that you as well as my friends will make full communications to me to Knoxville where I will be on the 22nd Instant.

JAMES K. POLK

ALS. DLC–JKP. Addressed to Nashville and forwarded to Columbia.

1. Letter not found.

2. Possibly Henry William Hart and Thomas Burwell Claiborne. Hart, a Smith County farmer, served one term in the Tennessee House as a Whig, 1853–55. Claiborne, son of Thomas Claiborne of Nashville, traveled with Polk in the 1841 campaign, joined the Nashville bar in 1843, but removed that same year to Trenton to edit the *True American*.

3. Patterson is not identified further. The Gallatin *Republican Sentinel and Sumner, Smith and Jackson Intelligencer* supported the Whig Party in 1840 and ceased publication within a year.

4. Letter not found.

5. Bradley County.

6. See Robert Armstrong to Polk, April 5, 1841.

FROM SARAH C. POLK

Dear Husband Nashville April 14th 1841

I enclose you a communication given me this morning by Mr. Walker, from David Dobbins.[1] Mr. Walker said he retained a copy and requested me to send you this. There is nothing since I last wrote you that is worth writing. The *Whigs* I am told are in a good deal of concern since the death of their President,[2] not knowing what *Tyler* will do, &c. &c. According to my judgement the same powers will controul, *Clay*, &c. The Banner is still harping on your two addresses.[3] In their articles *now*, they award to you, what they never did before that you are able talented and a great leader, and that the Whigs are in danger of another defeat. I am told that they have become *here*, very uneasy fearing that there will be a Democratic Legislature. They say in their articles you are a *wily* and *a dangerous foe* so I think that they will level all their artilery against you. Their [they] are more respectful toward you, then they were in former times. They make no new charges, and all they have said does not amount to much in *my* judgement. I have felt some uneasiness since you wrote me from *Jasper* that you were not well,[4] and seeing in the papers that you declined speaking on some occasion because you were unwell.[5] I hope to hear from you tomorrow and hear that you are well again. Success is not worth the trouble, much less ruining ones health by it and do take care of yourself.

Thursday April 15th. I was much disappointed that I did not hear from you to day. If I do not hear in a day or two I shall be uneasy, as the last I heard [was] that you were sick. I have a letter from the Overseer in Miss. dated the first of April. All was well.[6] He had planted corn and commenced planting cotton on that day. Nothing more at present.

SARAH POLK

ALS. DLC–JKP. Addressed to Knoxville. Published in *THQ*, XI, p. 185.

1. Enclosure probably was the affidavit of David Dobbins made in Graves County, Kentucky, on April 2, 1841. See James Walker to Polk, February 24 and March 21, 1841.

2. William H. Harrison died of pneumonia on April 4, 1841. Vice-President John Tyler of Virginia succeeded to the presidency.

3. Reference is to Polk's "Letter to the Public," published in the *Nashville Union* of March 29, 1841, and his "Address to the People of Tennessee," also published on March 29, 1841. See Robert Armstrong to Polk, March 28, 1841.

4. Letter not found.

5. The Nashville *Republican Banner* of April 14, 1841, reported that because of illness Polk declined his turn to speak first at a meeting in Jasper on April 7. Polk gave a reply to Jones' speech, but was not expected to keep the joint appointment at Chattanooga for the following day.

6. See Isaac H. Dismukes to Polk, April 1, 1841.

TO SARAH C. POLK

My Dear Wife Athens April 16th 1841

After having delivered a speech every day, for the last two weeks (Sundays excepted) I reached here last night. I am in good health except the effects of a bad cold under which I have been labouring during my whole tour. I shall continue to attend *Jones's* appointments, up to the period of the special election for members of Congress (6th of May), when I will cross over from *Jonesboro'* or *Elizabethton*, to Sullivan, and make speeches on my way to Nashville, at *Rogersville*, *Bean's Station*, *Campbell's Station*, *Van Buren C.H.*, *McMinnville* & *Woodbury*. This will enable me to reach home on the 13th or 14th of May. My calculation will be to issue the commissions to the members of Congress, who may be elected, and join *Jones* again at his appointment in *Fentress*.

In regard to my prospects, in East Tennessee, I think them as good as they were in 1839, as far as I have gone, if not better. For the last four days we have been in the strong Democratic Counties of *Bradley*, *Polk*, *Rhea* & *Meigs*. In those Counties I will have an increased vote. In this County *(McMinn)* the parties are very equally divided. In the Presidential election the Whigs have a majority of 125 votes. My friends are now confident that I will carry a majority. A large crowd is expected here tomorrow, and something may depend on the speeches. I expect to make a full & a long one. I will write to you again from Knoxville, where I will be on the 22nd.

James K. Polk

P.S. Enclosed is a letter to Mr Harris[1] which you will of course read & deliver it to him. J.K.P.

ALS. DLC–JKP. Addressed to Nashville.

1. Letter not found.

TO SARAH C. POLK

My Dear Wife Dandridge, Saturday, Apl. 24th 1841

I should have written to you from Knoxville, but had not a moments leisure. I reached here this afternoon & will rest until Monday. My health is good, though the fatigue during the past week has been very great. I refer you to the enclosed letter which I send open for an account of prospects since I wrote you last.[1] I will have *Jones* at Rheatown in Greene on the 1st May, and will address the people on my return home at the following times and places, viz—

At Rogersville—in Hawkins on the	3rd May	Monday
″ Bean's Station in Grainger—	4th Do.	Tuesday
″ Taz[e]well in Claiborne—	5th Do.	Wednesday
″ Jacksborough in Campbell—	6th Do.	Thursday
″ Clinton in Anderson—	7th Do.	Friday
″ Campbell's Station in Knox—	8th Do.	Saturday
″ Kingston in Roane—	10th Do.	Monday
″ Van Buren Court House	12th Do.	Wednesday
″ McMinnville in Warren—	13th Do.	Thursday
″ Woodbury in Cannon—	14th Do.	Friday

And from thence home on Saturday the 15th. My present calculation is to remain at Nashville, four or five days, and join Jones again at Montgomery in Morgan County on the 24th of May.

I informed Jones at Knoxville of these appointments & invited him to attend them. He, much more fatigued than I am, is anxious to return home, & I think it likely he will accompany me. I will write to you, as soon as I learn whether he will do so or not.

As I will be at home on the 17th, 18th & 19th, you can say to Genl. Armstrong & Mr Harris, that I can attend a meeting, anywhere in Davidson County on Wednesday the 19th, if they shall think it necessary to make one.

I receivd. two letters from you, at Knoxville[2] but none from any one else. Why do my friends not write. Tell Genl. Armstrong & Mr. Harris to write me, addressed to *Campbell's Station* or *Kingston* where I will receive their letters on my return. I shall expect a letter from you at one or both of those points.

James K. Polk

ALS. DLC–JKP. Addressed to Nashville.

1. Enclosure not found. The *Nashville Union* of May 3, 1841, carried an article detailing Polk's campaign activities for the week preceding April 24. The *Union* did not identify its source of information.

2. See Sarah C. Polk to Polk, April 14, 1841. Only one letter addressed by Sarah C. Polk to Polk at Knoxville has been found.

TO CAVE JOHNSON

[Dear Sir,] [Dandridge, Tennessee] April 25, 1841

I am, as you see, in the stronghold of the Whig party in East Tennessee. As to my prospects I have not time to give you details. It is certain that I have gained over the vote of November, in every County through which I have passed; and I think will fully maintain my vote of 1839. This I think [I] will do, even in the *Flag County* of *Sevier*. In *Blount* I may not quite reach it, but in other Counties I will exceed it. I find the *Whigs*, (except the leaders) calm and unexcited and ready to hear. Many of them dislike the Cabinet, whilst the ardour of others is cooled by the death of Harrison. Many are doubting and many declaring boldly that they will vote for me.

I will be compelled to return to Nashville to issue the commissions to the members of Congress, who may be elected on the 6th of May. I will attend *Jones's* appointments to *Rheatown in Greene* on the 1st of May; will cross over to Hawkins and make speeches—every day on my return journey (except Sundays and one other day), and will reach Nashville on the evening of the 15th May. I will remain there until the 20th and on the latter day, leave for Morgan City,[1] where I must be on the 24th May. I will send *Duplicates* of your commissions to Washington to meet you there, and thus guard against the possible failure of the *originals* to reach you before you leave. I am exceedingly anxious to see you. Can you not meet me at Nashville on the night of the 15th of May? You will then have full time to get on.

I will be at Kingston on my way to Nashville on the 10th May, and if when you receive this, you think, there is time for a letter to reach me, write me to that point. Is *Dortch* a candidate in Montgomery?[2] Who are the candidates in the other Counties of your District? What are their prospects of election? If you cannot meet me at Nashville, write me to that place.

P.S. Major Jones informed me today that he had some idea of abandoning some of his appointments in East Tennessee and returning with me. He is much more fatigued than I am, and I think the probabilities are that he will return to Middle Tennessee with me.

April 26th, 1841. Ascertaining that the mail would not leave until tomorrow, I kept this letter open [until][3] this evening. We addressed about 500 [?] here to day. My few friends here, think [I will] more than maintain my vote of 1839 in this County.

Copy. In St. George L. Sioussat, ed., "Letters of James K. Polk to Cave Johnson, 1833–1848," *Tennessee Historical Magazine*, I (1915), pp. 227–28. Addressed to Clarksville.

1. Polk intended to meet James C. Jones at Montgomery in Morgan County. See Polk to Sarah C. Polk, April 24, 1841.

2. James N. Dortch, brother-in-law of Cave Johnson, ran against Peter C. Buck for a seat in the Tennessee House from Montgomery County; Dortch lost to his Whig opponent.

3. Bracketed emendation here and below made by copyist with notation that the manuscript was torn at these places.

FROM SARAH C. POLK

My dear Husband, Nashville April 25th 1841

I have just returned from Columbia, where I have been during the last week. Sister Walker I left some better and her family in fine spirits with the hope that she will now recover. Though when I was sent for a week ago she was not expected to live. I think that she may get well but it will be a great while before she is entirely restored, so think her Physicians.[1] S. P. Walker promised me to write you all concerning the politics of that county.[2] As far as I could learn all would go on well. *Cahal* is a candidate, but no one thinks of him being elected. *Waterson*[3] was there. As to you they think that you will get as good a vote as you ever did. There is no enthusiasm for *Jones* there, here, or any where else that I hear from, but rather an indifference. *Here* I am told nobody seems to care or to be uneasy but *E. H. Foster*. He is mightily troubled about your address and the Legislature.[4] About once a week he has several colums in the *Banner*[5] headed Gov. Polks address. The articles are weak and feeble and does not amount to any thing. They can not hurt you any where. I have not seen Harris since I returned from Columbia. Indeed I have seen but few persons. I have not seen Young, because he is sick again.[6] (I suppose he has *over eat* himself). He attends to the business faithfully as far as I know. I hear no complaints on your absense. Only such as *your wife makes* and I confess that I feel much anxiety for your *health,* and I do not know how you are to stand the fatigue of the campaign. It makes me unhappy to think of what you must suffer, and for what? You can not be honoured by success, nor dishonoured by defeat, so I have not much to stimulate me. I received since I got home *Thomas*[7] letter from Madisonville. Tell him I am much obliged to him for his kindness in writing me. I wrote to you at Knoxville and enclosed a paper from David Dobbins which I suppose you received.[8] I learned when at Columbia that *Williams* nomination was well received and he would probably get a better vote than any one of them, so you need not be uneasy about him.[9] I have nothing more. Nashville is dull and quiet on every thing.

SARAH POLK

[P.S.]Tell Thomas all are well at his Fathers.[10]

ALS. DLC–JKP. Addressed to Jonesboro, Published in *THQ*, XI, pp. 185–86.

1. See James Walker to Polk, March 10, 18, and 21, 1841.
2. In a letter dated April 19, 1841, Samuel P. Walker wrote to Polk about Maury County politics and about his mother's illness. ALS. DLC–JKP.
3. Harvey M. Watterson.
4. See Robert Armstrong to Polk, March 28, 1841.
5. Nashville *Republican Banner*.
6. On John S. Young's sickness, see Robert Armstrong to Polk, April 5, 1841, and Sarah C. Polk to Polk, April 8, 1841.
7. Thomas Burwell Claiborne.
8. See James Walker to Polk, February 24, 1841, and Sarah C. Polk to Polk, April 14, 1841.
9. William H. Polk won his 1841 bid for a seat in the Tennessee House and sat in that body a total of three terms, 1841–45 and 1857–59. He also served as U.S. minister to Naples, 1845–47, and as a member of the U.S. House, 1851–53.
10. Thomas Claiborne, Polk's neighbor in Nashville.

TO SARAH C. POLK

My Dear Wife — Near Rheatown May 2nd 1841

I receivd on yesterday, your letter addressed to me at Jonesboro'.[1] I was much gratified to learn that there was a fair prospect of the recovery of Sister Walker.[2]

From this point I turn my face homeward. I will be at McMinnville on thursday the 13th & had made an appointment at Woodbury for friday the 14th. At Greenville however I received President Tyler's Proclamation recommending that friday the 14th should be observed as a day of fasting and prayer throughout the U. States,[3] and as it would be manifestly improper for me to address the people *any-where*, on that day, I have written to Ford of McMinnville & Col. Keeble of Rutherford, to countermand the notice of the appointment. If Mr Harris has published the appointment for Woodbury on the 14th will you request him to give notice that it will not take place, and to assign the reason which will prevent it.

I am in the midst of friends in this Democratic Region. They are all in fine spirits & the prospects good. I am now in excellent health.

James K. Polk

ALS. DLC–JKP. Addressed to Nashville.

1. See Sarah C. Polk to Polk, April 25, 1841.

2. See James Walker to Polk, March 10, 18, and 21, 1841.

3. On April 13, 1841, John Tyler issued a proclamation recommending that Friday, May 14th, be observed as "a day of fasting and prayer by such religious services as may be suitable" to commemorate the death of William H. Harrison.

FROM SARAH C. POLK

Dear Husband, Nashville Sunday May the 2, 1841

I write because you requested me to do so,[1] not that I have any thing to say of consequence. As far as you are concerned every thing is quiet, nothing in the Whig papers for the last week or two. No business come into the office requiring your attention, and nothing said about your absense. Mr Harris promised me to attend to your appointments; they will appear in the Union tomorrow morning. I suppose that you have seen that John Hall of Wilson is a candidate for Congress.[2] He spoke here on Thursday and Caruthers will speak tomorrow. I see so few Gentlemen that I do not have much chance to pick up news. *Coe*, I am told, is running for Congress in the District. If I can pick up any thing tomorrow or next day I will write to Kingston again. But to night I know nothing to write about. So you must excuse me for I know that it will be a tax on your time to read a long letter containing *nothing*. I hope soon to see you.

Sarah Polk

[P.S.] A letter came to night from Middleburgh, Hardeman County,[3] inviting you to a dinner any time, that will suit your convenience signed by a committee—also one from Mason's Grove, Madison County[4] inviting you and your Competitor to *address* them when it may suit you &c. These I suppose will come under consideration when you make your appointments. The Memphis *Appeal* came with *L. H. Coe's* circular letter declaring himself a candidate.[5] It is long; I have not read it. As it is sunday night, I will only write to my husband. Your Wife.

ALS. DLC–JKP. Addressed to Campbell's Station. Published in *THQ*, XI, pp. 186–87.

1. See Polk to Sarah C. Polk, April 24, 1841.
2. See Robert Armstrong to Polk, April 5, 1841.
3. On April 29, 1841, Andrew Taylor and a committee of Hardeman County citizens invited Polk to a public dinner to be held at his convenience. LS. DLC–JKP.
4. On April 24, 1841, E. B. Mason and a committee invited Polk to visit Madison County. LS. DLC–JKP.
5. On April 26, 1841, Coe wrote that he had met Christopher H. Williams in Memphis and had entered the race against him. Coe issued a circular in which he attacked Williams and "chronicled all his sins." ALS. DLC–JKP.

FROM JAMES WALKER

Dear Sir Columbia May 7th 1841

I did not receive yours from Dandridge[1] in time to reply to it at Kingston, and prefered waiting until I could inform you the result of our election for Congress.[2] That result, when we take into view all the circumstances is most cheering. It proves beyond all doubt the durable strength and stability of the Democracy of Maury. Cahal and his friends, no doubt calculated much on his personal popularity in this county. He is undoubtedly the strongest man of their party among [them] and Watterson is undoubtedly personally unpopular with us, and many of the firmest Democrats have great repugnance to his private character. Watterson has scarcely been here since his return from Washington and then only long enough to put out a circular[3] and push off. If under the circumstances Cahall has received a smaller vote than any Whig candidate since the regular division of parties among us, is it not evidence of the great strength of our party. If Watterson can beat Cahall 427 votes in Maury, you can beat Jones from 10. to 1200. The change of men even if party lines are strictly drawn will make a vast difference. In the late election from 7. to 1000 did not vote—not a particle of excitement could be got up on either side. Of those who did not vote, a very small [percentage] are Whigs. This is proved by the fact so often proven, that we have in our county about 1200 anti-Polk & Anti Jackson voters. This is made up of persons who choose to indulge personal & envious feelings; and it is not reasonable that such feelings would allow them to abstain from any opportunity of striking, where they had. From my knowledge of the county I am satisfied that the Whig strength has been acted out to nearly its full extent & the delinquent vote is from indifference and sluggishness of Democrats, many of whom had strong personal objections to Watterson, *as you know I have over & over told you.* I am exceedingly pleased ith the indications given in the result of this election. In our county the political strength has been very stationary & immovable for the last 5 or 6 years. I believe we have recently gained, and the election of yesterday proves it.

In this contest there was a piece of generalship of the Whigs that is rather amusing. Some 10 days ago it was observed that the Whig leaders from every part of the county was here. We supposed the object was to bring out candidates for the Representative Branch of the Legislature. This was a mistake. The result of the late election proves conclusively, that the principal object of the Whigs was to obtain as large a majority as possible at the Columbia precinct. In this they had two objects. First to gratify Cahal's pride in having it to say he was popular at home; 2nd that Gov. Polk was extremely weak at his own precinct. I think the movement of a small importance, but it must be explained. I think it now probable that Gordon[4] will decline & that we shall have no Whig candidates for the Legislature.

The vote yesterday was:

	W.	C.	V.B.	H.
Glenn's	119	10	114	16
Mooresville	107	21	118	27
Cedar Spring	90	48	118	41
Greshams	52	54	50	51
Whitakers	18	20	14	32
Hines	129	30	151	26
Bigbyville	35	73	49	95
Knotts	11	68	11	45
Columbia	144	351	187	344
Hansen's	9	41	7	49
Worthams	39	43	42	59
Mt Pleasant	119	127	145	139
Buckners	40	11	47	23
Blockers	76	41	92	36

Askews	61	44	82	[. . .][5]
Johnsons	53	18	65	26
Crosby's	45	15	62	22
Benton	170	36	172	61
Campbell's	47	12	55	11
Porter's	80	24	64	33
Beaucamp	55	26	69	46
Spring Hill	89	86	106	119
Lockridges	24	16	44	22
Folsom's	43	41	46	55
Rally Hill	105	41	115	40

Whole no. of votes 3013. Watterson's majority 427. Bedford not yet heard from [at] 5 P.M. Maria is slowly recovering.

JAMES WALKER

ALS. DLC–JKP. Addressed to McMinnville.

1. Letter not found.

2. A special election for members of Congress was held on May 6, 1841.

3. According to the *Nashville Union* of April 29, 1841, Harvey M. Watterson returned to Tennessee about April 24, 1841. His circular is not further identified.

4. George W. Gordon, a Columbia lawyer, did run, although unsuccessfully, against Barkly Martin for a seat in the Tennessee Senate.

5. Figure obliterated by sealing stain.

TO SARAH C. POLK

Sunday Morning

My Dear Wife — Campbell's Station May 9th 1841

I received your letter addressed to me at this place on yesterday.[1] I have had an unusually hard week's service, but am in better health than usual. I will be at home on Saturday night next.

I wish you to see *Major Graham*, and remind him, that I wish him to have all the writing done, relating to the Internal Improvement cases, which may be ready for my action.[2] Tell him that he *must* examine and decide upon the application of the *Columbia Central Turnpike Company* especially. There are *reasons* why *he* should examine & decide that case,[3] & I wish it done, before I reach Nashville. Tell him he must not neglect or omit to do so.

I wish you to see *Dr. Young* and tell him to have the Congressional

Commissions ready,[4] & to have all other writing prepared in relation to business, which may require my action.

I shall have but a short time to remain at home, & wish every thing which may require my official action to be in a state of preparation & forwardness.

The prospects, since I wrote to you, are good. I have received but partial returns from *McClellan's* & *Blackwell's* Districts, but have no doubt, they are both elected. Jones returns home with me.

JAMES K. POLK

ALS. DLC–JKP. Addressed to Nashville.

1. See Sarah C. Polk to Polk, May 2, 1841.

2. In letters dated May 2, 4, and 10, 1841, Daniel Graham reported to Polk about requests for state aid submitted by internal improvement companies in Columbia, Gallatin, Charlotte, Franklin, LaGrange, and Pulaski. ALsS. DLC–JKP.

3. Polk probably declined involvement in the Columbia Central Turnpike application because his family connection had an interest in the company. See James Walker to Polk, May 2, 1838, and March 23, 1840.

4. Reference is to the preparation of commissions certifying the results of the May congressional elections.

FROM SAMUEL H. LAUGHLIN

My dear Sir, McMinnville, May 10, 1841

I was over in Meigs County the week before the election, passing through Rhea and Bledsoe, and seeing many of our friends at the Court in Decatur. Every thing in that quarter seems to be highly flattering. We will loose nothing in the Assembly by any possibility, and I am fully persuaded we will gain Waterhouse[1] in the place of Terry. Col. Cox in Meigs[2] thinks your vote will be increased over the vote of 1839. Waterhouse thinks the same result will take place in Rhea, and in regard to Bledsoe, Mr. Spring[3] and others expect the same. The Congressional election here, and in this district, gives indications of a clear increase of our strength.

I regret that I cannot be with you at Spencer and McMinnville. Many of our friends however will meet you. I go off to-day through Cannon, and will give the full explanation, as I did in the last Gazette, of the reason why you will not speak at Woodbury.[4] I am obliged to go to Nashville on two accounts, and our court sitting here next week makes *this week* the only time I can have to spare. Harris & Humphreys have both desired my advice and assistance in the cases against Foster[5]—or rather Harris has applied to me on the suggestion of Mr. Humphreys. I suggested the propriety of consulting Fulton, and have written to him. The Court comes on in Davidson this month. I go to Nashville to consult on the matter, and give such advice as I think the present state of facts may require. I think it possible, that as Harris is not prosecutor—never advised or set the prosecution on foot—is no party to the proceeding in any form—and as things may be so *packed* as to ensure an acquittal before a Nashville jury and Nashville Judge, it may become the part of prudence for Harris to stand aloof and disclaim any agency in the proceeding. It may be, that the Fosters can prove *anything,* and however much falsehood may be borne down by the superior weight of truth in the eyes of honest and impartial men, yet upon the doctrine of *reasonable doubts* &c. and by foregone determinations of a partizan judge, and the prejudices of a party jury, an acquittal will be the certain result. If these conjectures are true, what ought Harris to do? I think it probable, that he had better, on every account, public and private, stand aloof, and refuse to involve himself in any form.[6] If you do not get to Nashville before I leave; I will meet you on the road. I wish much for your opinion in regard to this and other matters, which can only be given, and ought only to be given, face to face, and under the strict seal of confidence.

In addition to the above, I am sued in the Circuit Court of Davidson for a debt or account of Smith & Nesbit,[7] unjustly and dishonestly, and must prepare a defence. I think the most vile rascal I ever knew, is old Scotch Jim Smith. Through his conduct and others, I have never received a cent of about $6000 which was due the Union office when I left it, and which was covenanted to be collected as far as practicable and paid to me and creditors whom I have had to pay otherwise—and to some of whom I am yet indebted.

Hoping to meet you on the road, at Murfreesboro, or in Nashville, I will say no more. No one here, except Dr. Smartt knows any thing of my business except that I have gone in haste to Nashville. I have requested Mr. Campbell to write *instanter* to Harris a brief and pointed account of the meetings at Spencer & this place.

S. H. Laughlin

ALS. DLC–JKP. Addressed to Spencer and marked "Private."

1. Richard G. Waterhouse, a large landholder in Rhea County, was a justice of the peace, 1836, before winning election as a Democrat to one term in the Tennessee Senate in 1841.

2. Cox is not identified further.

3. Valentine Spring, a Bledsoe County Democrat, is not identified further.

4. No 1841 issue of the McMinnville *Central Gazette* has been found. For

cancellation of the Woodbury engagement, see Polk to Sarah C. Polk, May 2, 1841; also Polk to James C. Jones, May 17, 1841.

5. On January 11, 1841, J. George Harris was shot at the Nashville Inn in an altercation with Robert C. Foster III and William L. Foster, sons of Ephraim H. Foster. The case of *State v. Robert C. Foster and William L. Foster* came before the Davidson County Circuit Court on June 1, 1841; Thomas Maney presided and West H. Humphreys prosecuted for the state. On the fourth day of the trial the Foster brothers won an acquittal from a jury composed of nine Whigs and three Democrats.

6. Harris, summoned as a witness for the prosecution, refused to testify for the state and was held in contempt of court.

7. James Smith and Robert Nesbit purchased Laughlin's interest in the *Nashville Union* in 1837; they subsequently sold the newspaper to Joel M. Smith. The suit against Laughlin is not identified further.

FROM LEVIN H. COE

Somerville, Tennessee. May 11, 1841

Coe reports that he lost a short, but furious congressional race. A wet day and an expectation that C. H. Williams would win kept more Democrats than Whigs from the polls. Prospects are favorable for Polk and other Democrats in the coming state elections.

ALS. DLC–JKP. Addressed to Nashville.

FROM ALEXANDER O. ANDERSON

Knoxville, Tennessee. May 12, 1841

Anderson has sent Robert Armstrong a note for $6,000 to be discounted. Creditors are pursuing Anderson because his business partners were "inefficient collectors."[1] At present Anderson's "attention is necessarily divided"; but as soon as he can arrange his pecuniary affairs, he will attend to Democratic political organization in East Tennessee.

ALS. DLC–JKP. Addressed to Nashville.

1. Anderson's business partners are not identified further.

TO JAMES C. JONES

Dr. Sir Nashville May 17th 1841

When I reached Woodbury on saturday, I found a number of persons assembled who had not learned that the proposed meeting for that day had been postponed.[1] I declined to address them, but at the request of some of those who were present, I appointed Saturday the 5th of June as a day on which I would meet & address the people at that place.

Since my return I learn that it is the general expectation that I will address the people of this County at this place on wednesday next and that, I cannot with propriety, postpone the meeting to a later day in the canvass, as I desired to have done. I hope it may be convenient for you, to attend the meeting at this place, as also, that at Woodbury, on the 5th of June. I propose to address the people of Wilson at Lebanon on monday the 31st of the present month.

JAMES K. POLK

ALS, draft. DLC–JKP. Addressed to Lebanon and marked *"Copy."*

1. See Polk to Sarah C. Polk, May 2, 1841.

FROM ISAAC H. DISMUKES

Dear sir June the 1 1841

According to promise I wil now offer you a fiew lines to inform you wea are still geting aloung as well as wea possible can. When I wrote to you before I wrote you word that my courn and cotten look very well.[1] But in a fiew dais after that my cotten commense diing out and it continued to dye utill the stand is not very good. My stand is though principlie as good as this neighbourhood wil afourd. Standes is generally very bad in this sexion of cuntry. This spring sum has ploud up ther cotten and has planted courn. My courn still lookes very well. Sir I have not got my negrows clothen yet. I have sent to troy too or three times to sea wheather it had got thare or noe, but it has not cum.

AL. DLC–JKP. Addressed to Nashville. AE on the cover reads, "Dismukes—overseer." Extract published in Bassett, *Plantation Overseer*, 152.

1. Letter not found. See Dismukes to Polk, September 1, 1841.

TO SARAH C. POLK

My Dear Wife Shelbyville June 7th 1841

We had a fine day at Woodbury & I am here in good health. I have but a moment to write & devote that moment to say, that I wish you to send to Lawrenceburg with my documents a bound volume which I brought from Genl. Jackson's entitled "*U.S. Telegraph Extra*"[1]; I left it on the mantle piece in the parlour below stairs. You will find also among my bundles of papers, in the top of the smaller trunk in my office, several numbers of the "National Intelligencer" & "Globe,"[2] with a manuscript endorsement written on them—of Mr Clay's course towards the occupants, whom he called "Squatters." Send them also to Lawrenceburg.

JAMES K. POLK

ALS. DLC–JKP. Addressed to Nashville.

1. A campaign edition of the Washington *United States Telegraph*, the Washington *United States Telegraph Extra*, was issued in 1828 and 1836. Both the regular *Telegraph* and the *Extra* were edited by Duff Green, who supported Andrew Jackson in 1828 and Hugh Lawson White in 1836.

2. Washington *National Intelligencer* and Washington *Globe*.

FROM DANIEL GRAHAM

Dear Sir, Nashville, Tenne. 10 June 1841

I have just finished a set of papers for demanding Hiram Baker from Alabama, and will take them to Young for his signature & then to Bass, who is waiting for them at the Bank.[1] I have kept Copies of every thing, so that you need only sign. The chain of Circumstances is very clear that a *part* of the money at least, got to Bakers hands, after it had been taken by Budd from the Bank.

Young had an operation performed, fundamentally by Jennings[2] on monday last, and now thinks he will recover. I also think it most probably. He would hear to no proposition but for Frank Campbell[3] to keep the key & report to me ever & anon as Customers come in. Campbell is faithful to his trust, but the outer door is, you know, very insecure—to be opened only by a kick. The Message pleases nor displeases Whig nor Demo. Historically noncommittal.[4] Ed Childress has not got his paper fixed about the Charlotte turnpike gate.[5] It will probably meet you at Lawrence, where also you will meet the Gallatin Bonds.[6] They sent down their document yesterday amended to order, and I had the Bank[7] this morning filling up the $22.000. The York Whigs broke up their long session in great discontent, and the Demos there are buoyant.[8] Mrs. P and Mrs. G ride out every day to Willo: Williams', Ibbeys &c &c &c.[9]

GRAHAM

ALS. DLC–JKP. Addressed to Fayetteville.

1. Graham's reference is to Polk's signing extradition papers on Hiram

Baker, who allegedly was implicated in Thomas L. Budd's embezzlement fraud on the Union Bank in Nashville. See Sarah C. Polk to Polk, March 28, 1841.

2. Thomas Reid Jennings, a Nashville physician, held an appointment in the medical department of the University of Nashville; he served as a Whig member of the Tennessee Senate from 1839 until 1845.

3. Francis Campbell, probably a clerk in the office of Secretary of State John S. Young, is not identified further.

4. John Tyler submitted his first congressional message on June 1, 1841.

5. Ed H. Childress of Nashville became a director of the Nashville and Charlotte Turnpike Company upon its organization in 1838; he also served as treasurer of the company.

6. See Polk to Sarah C. Polk, June 15 and 25, 1841.

7. Bank of Tennessee.

8. In 1841 the New York legislature, dominated by a Whig majority, held a lengthy session of 142 days; in the fall elections Democrats won control of the legislature.

9. Sarah C. Polk, Maria M'Iver Graham, and Willoughby Williams. Maria M'Iver of Murfreesboro married Daniel Graham in 1823. Willoughby Williams, a Nashville lawyer and former sheriff of Davidson County, served briefly in 1837 as president of the Union Bank of Tennessee and owned a plantation in the Arkansas Territory. Reference to "Ibbeys" is not identified further.

FROM AARON V. BROWN

Dear Sir Washington June 12th 1841

Mr. Wise nearly fainted on yesterday in an animated argument, against the astounding doctrines of Mr. Adams in favor of abolition.[1] He was borne from the Hall—is better today but the debate lies over until monday (this being saturday). The whole South is alarmed at the *vote* by which his doctrines were sustained.[2] With one or two exceptions such as Jno. M Botts[3] The Southern Whigs, now discover when I fear it is too late, that they are standing on a burning volcano, which every hour may destroy them. Marshall of Kentucky made an eloquent but discursive argument against Mr. Adams, but was evidently *too mellow* & at times too extravagantly eulogistic of him, for his Speech to produce much valuable effect.[4] He is the *equal* of our old friend Mimms[5] in genius & fancy, but far below him in dignity of manner & purity of style.

Mr. Adams first threw his fire brand into our deliberations & he & his friends will keep it there the balance of the session. Even at this moment, abolition petitions have just been presented & a general excitement prevails on all sides of the house, on the question of what shall be done with them (the old rule having been rejected). Mr. Campbell of

S. Carolina, seeing that they will be *forced* on the house by an unrelenting majority moves an adjournment but what *good* will *that* do? Without our old rule[6] every single case stands for *seperate argument* & must lead to the most *fiery* discussions. Look at the structure of the committees—many, very many distinguished abolitionist[s] placed at the *head* of the committees—Such as Fillmore, Giddens, Salstanstall, Adams, James of Pa., Wm. B. Calhoun &c. &c.[7] (*2. Ock.* the excitement still continues. Gilmer of Va.[8] is trying an adjournment again, in order to avoid the *reception & reference* of one of these horrid missil[e]s of disunion & insurrection. You could know the *exultation* of the abolitionist[s] by hearing Slade & Gates & Jno C. Clark's voice,[9] bold & loud above all others, as they answer the call of the clerk.) Where or how all this is to end, time only can shew; but if the South does not *as one man* break off from all political concert of action with the Northern Whig party, who now hold the majority in this house, her institutions are gone forever. He is a madman or a traitor to the South, who after this, can doubt on the subject. I send you an extract from the American & Foreign Anti-Slavery reporter[10] of a correspondence between Mr. Adams & certain free negroes (on[e] half of them no doubt fugitives from their masters) shewing to what that old man has come to on that fanatical subject.

I send you a Madisonian whose Editorial on the subject of a *Fiscal Agency,* is thought to contain something *official.*[11] At all events the idea has gained ground rapidly that the President will positively veto Mr Clays Bank,[12] which is expected to resemble the old one pretty much & which he seems *determined* to press through with insolent willfulness—consulting very little the opinions of Reeves, Wise[13] & others who *demur* to his project & who are supposed to have the largest share of the Presidents confidence. If *Tylers project* shall be presented in such form as will enable *the Democrats proper* to fall into its support, *as against Clays,* it will enable the minority to be sufficiently strong to encourage the President to venture on a veto. Otherwise *his own party proper* would be too weak for the occasion.

I write you in the midst of the uproar of a saturday nights session, & will only add that Buchanon & Calhoun gave Webster a terrible castigation, for his *tameness* in not repelling *the threat* contained in Mr. Foxes letter.[14] "Mr President (said Mr. B.) when I read these words, I could not but ask myself, what would be the emotions of that venerable man, now living on the Banks of the Cumberland & whom Mr. Jefferson called the noblest Roman of them all,[15] what would be *his* emotions, when he should hear that this threat of the British nation was hanging over his country & the American Secretary of State had not the boldness to repel it."[16] Boyd of K. comes to me at this moment (4 Ock.) & says Mr.

Ewings "Fiscal Bank" project is in the Senate. Capital of 30 millions; U.S. to hold one fifth.

Wednesday [June] 16

This far I had written in the confusion of the scene. It was so inadequate a sketch that I concluded not to send it, but to wait untill the *conclusion* of this struggle & then give you a calm & distinct summary of it. But it is not over yet. The vote adopting the resolution *excluding* the 21st rule was yesterday reconsidered & as it was under that rule that the house was organized the Speaker inclined to the opinion that all done under it was set aside & so the house was *not yet organized.* So seemed to think & to say most of the leading Whigs & yesterday & to day have never been surpassed in tumult & violent crimination & recrimination. Wise, Mallory & it is thought Rayner[17] & others are consider'd *as gone finally* from the Whigs & to compose what was here publicly charged in debate "the Tyler portion" of the Whig party. If Gilmer goes with that portion & some of the Georgia delegation which is now thought probable, *it may* make a serious impression on their majority. It is not yet known how far the President & his friends *distinctively* approve the Bank project which I now send you—for consideration.[18] No development of Northern opinion about it so you must look to the newspapers themselves hereafter. The extent of the *discord* in the Whig ranks on *this* subject, not yet well ascertained, but there is no doubt it is *very considerable.*

The messenger waits & I am obliged to send off this which is intended only for your own eye on account of its imperfections.

A V Brown

ALS. DLC–JKP. Addressed to Nashville.

1. On May 31, 1841, Henry A. Wise moved that the rules of the previous House be adopted temporarily; John Quincy Adams offered an amendment rescinding the previous House's 21st rule, which prohibited reception of abolition petitions. See J. George Harris to Polk, June 18, 1841.

2. On June 7, 1841, Wise's Resolution, as amended by Adams, passed by a vote of 125 to 91; three days later the House voted 113 to 107 not to reconsider its decision.

3. A Virginia lawyer, Botts served three terms as a Whig in the U.S. House, 1839–43 and 1847–49.

4. Thomas F. Marshall, a Kentucky lawyer, served in the U.S. House from 1841 until 1843. On June 10, 1841, he addressed the House in opposition to Adams' amendment to abolish the House's 21st rule.

5. Mimms is not identified further.

6. Reference is to the 21st rule, popularly known as the "gag rule."

7. Millard Fillmore, Joshua R. Giddings, Leverett Saltonstall, John Quincy Adams, Francis James, and William B. Calhoun. Fillmore, Whig congressman

from New York, chaired the House Ways and Means Committee; Giddings of Ohio, the Committee of Claims; Saltonstall of Massachusetts, the Committee on Manufactures; Adams, the Committee on Indian Affairs; James, a Pennsylvania Whig, the Committee on Revisal and Unfinished Business; and Calhoun of Massachusetts, Committee on Naval Affairs.

8. Thomas W. Gilmer served several terms in the Virginia House before being elected governor in 1840. A year later Gilmer resigned the governorship to serve as a Whig in the U.S. House. Gilmer won reelection to the House as a Democrat in 1843 and served until February of 1844, when he became secretary of the navy. He died in an explosion aboard the U.S.S. *Princeton* on February 28, 1844.

9. William Slade, Seth M. Gates, and John C. Clark. Slade, a Whig from Vermont served in the U.S. House from 1831 until 1843. A New York lawyer and merchant, Gates won election as an Anti-Slavery Whig to two terms in the U.S. House, 1839–43. Also a New York lawyer, Clark served two terms as a Democrat in the U.S. House, 1827–29 and 1837–39. Opposed to Van Buren's Sub-Treasury system, Clark became a Whig and served two additional terms in the House, 1839–43.

10. Enclosure not found. *The American and Foreign Anti-Slavery Reporter*, a publication of the American and Foreign Anti-Slavery Society, first appeared in July 1840. Led by Arthur and Lewis Tappan, the society represented that wing of the abolitionist movement not controlled by William Lloyd Garrison.

11. Enclosed copies of the Washington *Madisonian* not found. On June 3, 1841, Treasury Secretary Thomas Ewing sent to the U.S. House a report recommending the repeal of the Independent Treasury Act and the creation of a fiscal agent of the United States. As reported to the Senate on June 12, Ewing's "Fiscal Bank" scheme provided for a central bank in the District of Columbia with branches, or offices of discount and deposit, located in the several states whose legislatures did not object. Ewing's plan received the endorsement of Tyler, who had objected to the creation of a national bank on constitutional grounds; Ewing's plan removed those objections. Tyler urged, but failed to receive, Henry Clay's support. See A. O. P. Nicholson to Polk, June 14, 1841.

12. Henry Clay's bill, reported in the U.S. Senate on June 21, 1841, also provided for a central bank in the District of Columbia, but did not admit state authority over the establishment of the branches. Unable to gain sufficient support, Clay amended his bill on July 27 by giving legislatures authority to disallow the establishment of branches in their states. By August 6 Clay's bill had passed both houses of Congress; Tyler vetoed the bill, arguing that power over the branches belonged to the states and could not be given or denied by Congress.

13. William C. Rives and Henry A. Wise.

14. The correspondence between Daniel Webster, U.S. secretary of state, and British Minister Henry S. Fox related to the arrest and imprisonment of a Canadian, Alexander McLeod. The state of New York had charged McLeod

with murder in the capture and destruction of the steamboat *Caroline* on December 29, 1837. Fox wrote Webster on March 12, 1841, that his government considered the attack on the *Caroline* to be an act of public force done by national authority. The question should be settled by the two governments, not by the courts of an individual state. Fox renewed Great Britain's demand for McLeod's release.

15. Reference is to Andrew Jackson.

16. According to the *Congressional Globe,* James Buchanan spoke in the Senate on June 10, 1841, and said of Fox's letter, "I imagined I saw that man whom Mr. Jefferson truly denominated the old Roman, as President, sitting in his apartment and reading this letter for the first time. When he came to this sentence, what would be his feelings? What indignant emotions would it arouse in his breast? . . . Would he not have resolved never to make any explanation under such a threat? Would he not have required it to be withdrawn or explained before any answer whatever to Mr. Fox's demand? In this possibly he might have gone too far. Our Secretary, however, has passed over this threat without adverting to it in any manner whatever."

17. Henry A. Wise, Francis Mallory, and Kenneth Rayner. Rayner, a North Carolina Whig, served three terms in the House, 1839–45.

18. Enclosure not found.

TO SARAH C. POLK

My Dear Wife Fayetteville June 13th 1841

I send enclosed a letter to Mr Harris.[1] Will you send for him & deliver it? I send by this mail a letter containing a Proclamation to Dr Young, to be published in the Union.[2] Request Mr Harris to call on Young, procure it & publish it in his paper. I would write to Graham, but think it likely he has started to Knoxville. Prospects are fine & improving in the Democratic Counties where I have been during the past week.

Why have not the candidates in Davidson announced? If you see Genl. Armstrong, urge him to have them out. It is a matter of great importance.

JAMES K. POLK

P.S. I have some cold, but am in very fine health. J.K.P

N.B. If you can find the paper containing *Mr Clay's* speech,[3] mentioned in the enclosed letter to Mr Harris, send it to me to *Bolivar, without fail.* J.K.P.

ALS. DLC–JKP. Addressed to Nashville.

1. Polk's letter to J. George Harris has not been found, but see Harris to Polk, June 18, 1841.

2. On June 21, 1841, the *Nashville Union* carried a proclamation, issued by Polk on June 12, for the apprehension of Frederick Benson for murder.

3. Henry Clay's speech is not identified further.

FROM A. O. P. NICHOLSON

My Dear Sir: Washington City. June 14th 1841

We have at length a full development of the measures which are to be acted on and consummated at the Extra Session. The repeal of the Sub-Treasury is certain—the bill has already passed the Senate.[1] Until yesterday we had some hopes that Mr. Tyler would save the country from the curse of another U.S. Bank; but on yesterday all hope was snatched from us, and we now regard it as settled and certain, that a Bank will be chartered and sanctioned. In obedience to a call Mr. Ewing submitted a plan of a Bank prepared in detail which is regarded as the Cabinet plan and as having the sanction of Mr. Tyler.[2] It appeases Mr. Tyler's conscience by its location in the District of Columbia and requiring the assent of the States for the introduction of branches into them. In all other respects the same objections rest against it which were urged against the late Bank. Its Capital is to be $30,000,000, of which the Federal and State Governments are to have one half and individual stockholders the balance. Foreigners are *not* excluded from taking stock!! The stock of the U.S. and of the States is to be raised by creating a public debt. The bonds of the U.S. to be issued at fifteen years for the amount of the stock to be owned by the U.S. and the States. There are to be seven directers, two be appointed by the President and five by the individual stockholders. Such is a mere sketch of the prominent features, and I have no doubt of its passage. Now I submit to you this question: Are you not satisfied that if this U.S. Bank question was out of the issue in Tennessee that your way would be easy to success? If this is your opinion, I submit this suggestion for your consideration: Is it better for you to surrender the question and admit that a Bank will certainly be made, and thereby withdraw that issue from the contest, and make the deciding point turn on *distribution*,[3] or can you make more by holding up the objections to the plan as it is now presented! For myself I am satisfied that a bank will be made and I am satisfied that the Bank question is the great point which holds up and binds together the federal party in Tennessee. If you can make *distribution* of the public land revenues the leading issue I believe you will find our opponents far less united on it. W. B. Campbell is out against it and will speak against it at this session. Turn these suggestions over in your mind. There is some doubt still hanging over the question of distribution. What is to be done in the Tariff question has not yet transpired, and this will probably depend on the fate of the distribution bill. Besides the fifteen millions for the bank there will be probably a further debt of eight or ten millions contracted to supply the pretended deficiency in the Treasury.

Mr. Clay is carrying every thing by storm—his will is the [la]w[4] of Congress. His Speaker in the House has made the most outrageous arra[n]gement of Committees. He has made *five* known Abolitionists Chairmen of important committees.[5] In fact the Abolitionists now seem to hold the balance of power in the House.

It is the design of Mr. Clay to apply the gag very freely and to have but little discussion. He made a bold attempt yesterday to cut off all enquiries into the conduct of the departments; but some of his friends flinched.

There is some division in the federal ranks, but not enough to enable us to defeat their measures.

A. O. P. Nicholson

ALS. DLC–JKP. Addressed to Raleigh, Tennessee.

1. Henry Clay introduced in the Senate on June 4, 1841, a bill to repeal the Independent Treasury; the amended bill passed in the Senate on June 9.

2. See Aaron V. Brown to Polk, June 12, 1841.

3. See Harvey M. Watterson to Polk, February 1, 1841.

4. Manuscript torn.

5. In his letter of June 12, 1841, Aaron V. Brown refers to Speaker John White's appointment of abolitionists to head important congressional committees. White, a lawyer, served in the Kentucky House in 1832 and as a Whig in the U.S. House from 1835 until 1845, during which period he was elected Speaker of the House for the Twenty-seventh Congress.

TO SARAH C. POLK

Tuesday evening

My Dear Wife Lawrenceburg June 15th 1841

I send this letter by Knox Walker to [be] mailed at Columbia. Send for Mr Harris & deliver the enclosed to him, immediately.[1]

I am much distressed that Graham did not send the papers (I want the Report of the Commissioners & the last return of the company—shewing that their capital stock had been increased) with the Gallatin Bonds.[2] See Graham as soon as you can & urge him to do it—by mail—to the nearest point it will reach. If he does so I will employ a messenger to take the Bonds to Nashville. I cannot act on *faith* & without seeing the papers. Humphreys & Graham I have no doubt decided right, but still I must see the papers, to judge for myself.

JAMES K. POLK

ALS. DLC–JKP. Addressed to Nashville.

1. Enclosure not found.

2. See Daniel Graham to Polk, June 10, 1841, and Polk to Sarah C. Polk, June 25, 1841.

FROM J. GEORGE HARRIS

My Dear Sir, Nashville June 18, 1841

I shall publish in next Union the certificate of those Wilson gentlemen[1]—a good opportunity to do so has not before offered. I have just rec'd a letter from Knox Walker detailing your meeting at Pulaski—it will also appear.[2] I have also several letters from Nicholson (Junius) and Watterson in addition to those which appear in last Union.[3] I send you accompanying the National Intelligencer cont'g Adams's Incendiary Remarks, just from hand of Nicholson.[4] I send you also a copy of a letter rec'd last night from N.[5]—enclosed in Nat. Int. I have just opened two letters from Washington dated 10th—they state that great confusion prevails.[6] An attempt was made on the 10th to reconsider the vote whereby the 21st rule was rescinded but failed 110 to 116.[7] Abolition stalks forth in the Halls of Congress unpunished—nay, as an idol of whig worship! Great God! what may we not expect. The *crisis* is come.

Hollingsworth has consented to run for the Senate—I shall announce in next Union.[8] Doubtful whether candidates for the Ho: can be got out. These faltering fellows deserve the worst.

You will have seen that I have *speared* Jones—the Whig floundered awfully about it.[9]

If Tennessee is not an abolition State she cannot stand this Incendiary movement of the whig party in Congress. If she is not hitched fast to the car of Ultra Federalism she can not support a party which nurses as a darling in its bosom the Archbishop of British Interest Danl Webster.

I will cut to the core from this out.

J GEO HARRIS

[P.S.] Mrs. Polk informs me that She forwards you the paper for which you wrote me in your last.[10]

ALS. DLC–JKP. Addressed to Somerville.

1. In the *Nashville Union* of June 21, 1841, Harris published statements by Jonas Swingley, Jesse A. Grigg and R. D. Curd, G. C. Matlock, and Jesse A. Grigg and Lewis Lindsay, all of Wilson County, that in 1839 James C. Jones had proposed making state bonds redeemable in sterling. During the 1841 gubernatorial race Jones attacked Polk for making a similar proposal.

2. No newspaper account of the meeting has been found. The gubernatorial candidates spoke at Pulaski on June 14, 1841.

3. The *Nashville Union* of June 17, 1841, carried two letters from "Junius," written from Washington and dated June 3 and 7, and one letter from "O.I.O. of Ohio," written from Washington and dated June 7. On June 21 the *Nashville Union* published three "Junius" letters, dated June 9, 10, and 11, and one "O.I.O. of Ohio" letter, dated June 10, 1841.

4. Enclosure not found. Harris refers to John Q. Adams' remarks in the U.S. House on June 9, 1841, as reported in the Washington *National Intelligencer* of June 10. Adams had suggested that Congress might intervene in the event of a slave insurrection in the South.

5. Enclosure not found; reference probably is to A. O. P. Nicholson's "Junius" letter of June 9, 1841.

6. Reference probably is to A. O. P. Nicholson's "Junius" letter of June 10, 1841, and to Harvey M. Watterson's "O.I.O. of Ohio" letter of June 10, 1841.

7. A. O. P. Nicholson stated in his "Junius" letter of June 10, 1841, that the House had rejected by a vote of 116 to 110 a motion to reconsider its revocation of its gag rule against abolition petitions. Nicholson, a member of the Senate, erred in his report of the voting. On June 10 the House approved by vote of 116 to 100 a motion to end debate on the motion to reconsider; by vote of 113 to 107 the House refused to reconsider its June 7th vote on the gag rule.

8. Henry Hollingsworth announced his candidacy for the Tennessee Senate from Davidson County in the *Nashville Union* of June 21, 1841.

9. The *Nashville Whig* of June 11, 1841, devoted two columns to defending James C. Jones against charges made in the "Loco Foco press." Harris had charged in the *Nashville Union* of June 7 that Jones had favored John J. Crittenden's gag bill, had ignored frauds upon Tennessee's public school fund, had advocated soft-money policies, and had defended Henry Clay's "corrupt bargain."

10. See Polk to Sarah C. Polk, June 13, 1841.

FROM SARAH C. POLK

My dear Husband Nashville June 18th 1841

Your letters from Lawrenceburg[1] I have received and will try to impress on your friends the necessity of attending to your requests contained in them. Any business you wish attended through Genl.

Armstrong I know will be faithfully and immediately done, for he seems willing and alive to the canvass, but *Harris* is *wild* and *crazed* about the widow or her fortune.[2] I saw Genl A. to day and he says that he (Harris) is a common subject of remark, and can do nothing with him and can not even get to see him to converse with. I do not wish to give you uneasiness of mind, but he is no account. *Him* and paper has been so much abused that I do not think that it can do any good, so in my opinion you do not loose much from the ineficiency of his paper. *Hollingsworth* will be a candidate in opposition to *Jennings* and it is understood that he is out, but not yet announced in the paper.[3] I *understand* there has been some money made up for him and he takes the field. They can not get any one for the *House* to run. The Whigs are not in good spirits here; they I am told, think or fear that they will loose the Legislature. Foster is dispirited and is sick again with the wound, had three Doctors to go out to probe it for the *knife blade.*[4] I expect it is half pretence. Judge Catron told me he had in a few instances in his tour in the District intimated to some of the Whigs, that Judge Green would be a more suitable candidate for the Senate than Foster, a broken down hackneyed politician and it took well. I suppose you get the Washington news through the papers. If you desire me to send you the Globe[5] & other papers that you file here write me so. I do not send them more frequently, because I thought you wished the files kept. I believe that I have written all I can think of now.

I have kept my letter open for the mail this evening. You had no letters to come, and I of course have no information. I send you the last papers. I had scarcely time to look at the Globe or Inteligencer,[6] but supposing they contained the Abolition & repeal of the Sub-Treasury I send them. I saw Harris to day and give him your letter from Lawrencburg.[7] He promised to have all attended to & in the Union of Monday.[8] Hollingsworth *is a candidate*, and *Mrs. Walker*[9] (from whom you know that I get a good deal of news) says it makes some sensation among the *whigs*. Dr. McNairy will vote for him, & Joe Norvell[10] thinks he will be elected. This of course is *womens* gossip and not worth much. This is rather a long conclusion to my letter.

SARAH POLK

ALS. DLC–JKP. Addressed to Brownsville and forwarded to Somerville. Published in *THQ*, XI, pp. 187–88.

1. See Polk to Sarah C. Polk, June 15, 1841.

2. A letter from Daniel Graham of June 12, 1841, states that the woman's last name was Wynn; she is not identified further. ALS. DLC–JKP.

3. See J. George Harris to Polk, June 18, 1841.

4. In May of 1841 James Brown, probably a Nashvillian, but not identified

further, stabbed Ephraim H. Foster in the right side in an altercation arising from personal misunderstandings.

5. The Washington *Globe*.

6. The Washington *National Intelligencer*.

7. Letter not found.

8. The *Nashville Union* of Monday, June 21, carried a lengthy letter from an unnamed resident of Lawrenceburg, who wrote a detailed account of Polk's June 15th debate with his gubernatorial opponent, James C. Jones.

9. Mary Norvell Walker, the wife of James Walker, resided near the Polks. She was the sister of Caleb C. Norvell, editor of the *Nashville Whig*.

10. Joseph Norvell, Nashville businessman and publisher, was the brother of Mary Norvell Walker and Caleb C. Norvell.

TO SARAH C. POLK

My Dear Wife Somerville June 25th 1841

I received Graham's communication causing the Gallatin papers directed to this place.[1] In his letter to me at Lawrenceburg he stated that Humphreys had been so much engaged about other matters, that he had been unable to procure his *personal attendance* at the Secretary's office, to *sign the accord.*[2] In his letter to me at this place he does not inform me, whether *Humphreys* had yet signed it or not. I presume he has, but still he may have neglected it. Upon the whole I conclude that it is safest not to sign the Bonds, until my return which will only be three weeks. The Gallatin Company are my friends, and will not probably object to this course. If any thing should be said in the newspapers, see *Mr Harris & Genl. Armstrong,* and have the proper explanations made, *viz,* that it was necessary for the comptroller & atto. to concur,[3] and that the information that they had acted on their part, had not been forwarded to me; and the further fact should be stated that before I left Nashville, the case was considered by the Board & the papers returned to the Company for amendment. At that time they had not brought themselves within the law & cannot therefore complain of the delay because it was their own fault. I do not anticipate that there will be any complaint, but if there should be any danger of it, *Genl Armstrong* can stop it by seeing B. Watkins[4] Esqr. (who is my friend) the Secretary of the Company.

Say to Genl. Armstrong I will write to him from Raleigh; & I will write to you again from that point.

Political prospects stand here about as I expected. The party lines are tightly drawn & but little is to be effected by speaking. My friends are very firm & active.

James K. Polk

ALS. DLC–JKP. Addressed to Nashville.

1. On June 17, 1841, Daniel Graham wrote to Polk at Somerville and enclosed the papers of the Gallatin Turnpike Company. ALS. DLC–JKP. See Daniel Graham to Polk, June 10, 1841, and Polk to Sarah C. Polk, June 15, 1841.

2. On June 12, 1841, Graham, comptroller of the treasury, wrote that he had been trying for three days to draw the attention of West H. Humphreys, attorney general, to the Gallatin papers. ALS. DLC–JKP. John S. Young, secretary of state, could not attend the business of his office because of illness; his duties required that he sign and issue all bonds warranted by the governor to pay for the state's part-ownership of internal improvement companies qualifying under the terms of the 1838 Internal Improvements Act.

3. By Act of January 25, 1841, the Tennessee General Assembly created an Internal Improvement Board, consisting of the governor, comptroller, and attorney general, and gave that board power to revise applications for bonds from improvement companies in which the state had invested prior to 1840.

4. Not identified further.

FROM SARAH C. POLK

Dear Husband Nashville June 25th 1841

I have been absent for a few days in Murfreesboro' [and] returned last night, when I received your letter from Savannah.[1] I found Dr. Young anxious to learn some thing about the Bonds sent to you.[2] Graham left, I suppose without giving Young any information concerning them. Graham I presume did send them & papers to you, and they have not had time to be returned of course, and I have so informed him.

You can see by the Union (which I send you by this mail) that Hollingsworth is a candidate[3] and I have just seen Donelson & Dr. Esselman who says his chances for success is pretty good. They can not get any one out for the House and think it will be an advantage to have none. Ewing & Campbell[4] will not take the field an[d] discuss, if they have no opposition and *Jennings* is unpopular, so you may see that they have a hope of electing their man Hollingsworth. You may discover that the last *Union*[5] is better filled than usual. I am in hopes that Harris will do better in future. I learn no news since I come home but that Genl. Jackson has been dangerously ill, but now *much* better. The *knife blade* has been cut from E. H. Fosters side and he is well.[6] Genl. Anderson is here from Knoxville, gives a flattering account of the prospects in E. Tennessee, says that you will increase your vote of '39, [and] told me of many counties he had been in and traveled through. His account is flattering. In Rutherford the Democrats seem to be sure of success. The removal of the Post Master[7] at that place will do good. Henderson being a poor Methodist preacher, the Whigs will loose some vote where ever the towns have no influence. There is a good deal of excitement in the *little* place about the removal. There comes to you now, but few letters and &c. Young says there is no business in the office. Sister Walker is here and much improved in health and intends going to the springs.[8] I hope that you will take care of yourself. I think some times that it is impossible for you to stand the fatigue until August but I pray that you may have health which is more than success. The mail of this evening brought you a letter from A V Brown which I send you.[9] Nothing else come.

SARAH POLK

ALS. DLC–JKP. Addressed to Trenton. Published in *THQ* XI, pp. 188–89.

1. Letter not found. Polk's schedule called for him to speak in Savannah on Friday, June 18, 1841.

2. See Daniel Graham to Polk, June 10, 1841.

3. See J. George Harris to Polk, June 18, 1841.

4. Formerly from Franklin County, James Campbell had served in the Tennessee House, 1827–29, and in the Senate, 1829–31, before moving to Nashville in 1835. A lawyer, he won election to the Tennessee House as a Whig in 1841 and served one term.

5. Reference is to the *Nashville Union* of June 24.

6. See Sarah C. Polk to Polk, June 18, 1841.

7. David D. Wendel replaced Greenville T. Henderson as U.S. postmaster at Murfreesboro on June 4, 1841.

8. Jane Maria Polk Walker probably planned to visit Tyree's Springs, twenty miles north of Nashville. See James Walker to Polk, March 10, 18, and 21, 1841, for references to Maria's illness. Also see Sarah C. Polk to Polk, April 25, 1841.

9. See Aaron V. Brown to Polk, June 12, 1841.

FROM SARAH C. POLK

Dear Husband Nashville June 30th [1841][1]

I do not write because I have any thing to communicate, on the contrary I know nothing and have heard nothing since I wrote you last. Every thing as far as I can learn is quiet, *remarkably* so at this place. The Whig papers have not noticed nor denied the charges against Jones as published in the Union.[2] All the Democratic papers has the cirtificate and comments in them, yet I have not heard or seen a single denial in the papers. Harris's two or three last papers are more spirited and I think probably his senses are returning for he appeared more rational when I last saw him.[3] I am a little surprised not to have heard from you before this. E. P. McNeal was kind enough to write me how you were at Bolivar, which is all that I have heard from you in ten days. But I hope to hear from you this evening.

SARAH POLK

ALS. DLC–JKP. Addressed to Paris. Published in *THQ*, XI, p. 189.
1. Year identified through content analysis.
2. See J. George Harris to Polk, June 18, 1841.
3. See Sarah C. Polk to Polk, June 18, 1841.

TO SARAH C. POLK

My Dear Wife, Dyer County July 1st 1841

On yesterday morning I was taken with an affection of the bowels, such as frequently happens with me. The attack was rather more violent than usual, and I deemed it imprudent to speak at *Dyersburg* on yesterday. I lost but little by this, for *Jones* was nearly broken down, and made an apology for not speaking, rather than a speech to the people. *Dr Purcell*[1] (who was the Representative in the last Legislature from this County) thought it prudent that I should take a simple doze of medicine, which I did. I addressed a letter of apology to the people of *Obion Cty.* for not meeting my appointment at *Troy* to day and sent Thos. *Claiborne* up with it. This morning I rode out 10 miles to *Mr Richard Henderson's*,[2] formerly of Maury County, where I now am. I feel well except the debility produced by the attack, and the operation of medicine. I will remain quiet to day (writing some letters to different parts of the state) and will go tomorrow to an appointment at *Yorkville*, 10 miles from here, made by the citizens, and will resume my regular appointment at *Trenton* on the 3d Inst. I have made up my mind to go to East Tennessee, immediately after my return to middle Tennessee, and be there at the election. I expect to forward my appointments from *Trenton* or *Paris*. I wish you to meet me at Columbia on my return, as I shall probably not have a day to remain at home after my return.

In the Counties of *McNairy, Hardeman, Haywood, Fayette, Shelby, Tipton, Lauderdale & Dyer,* which I have visited in this Division of the State, the party lines are tightly drawn; still I find that I will get a few Whig votes in every County, and will I think more than maintain my vote of 1839. I apprehend that the Whig papers, every where, on hearing of my slight indisposition, will endeavour to make the impression that I am very ill, or have broken down. I wish you to see *Mr Harris* immediately and inform him of the facts, that he may be able to counteract it, if such an attempt should be made. The contest in the State may be close, but I am satisfied that, if my friends will be reasonably active that I will be elected.

JAMES K. POLK

P.S. Since writing the above I conclude to write to Mr Harris & herewith enclose my letter to him,[3] which you will deliver. Will you send for Genl. Armstrong & urge upon him the importance of getting all my friends to write letters to their acquaintances in different parts of the State, urging them to bring every Democratic voter to the polls, as suggested in my letter to Mr Harris. J.K.P.

ALS. DLC–JKP. Addressed to Nashville.

1. A physician from Dyer County, Osborne Purcell served one term, 1839–41, as a Democrat in the Tennessee House.

2. Not identified further.

3. Letter not found. The *Nashville Union* of July 8, 1841, reported that when Polk spoke at Dresden on July 5th, he was "in fine health and spirits. From exposure to inclement weather he had been compelled to omit his appointments in Dyer and Obion, to recruit. Our informant states, however, that he was never in better condition for public service than on the 5th at Dresden."

FROM ALEXANDER O. ANDERSON

Nashville, Tennessee. July 5, 1841

Anderson writes that he believes the Democrats are gaining in East Tennessee and that he expects Polk to receive a vote there equal to that in his race against Cannon. Anderson suggests that Polk campaign in the counties of upper East Tennessee. Congress' $25,000 appropriation to Harrison's widow[1] will not be well received, when so many soldiers' widows receive no pension.

ALS. DLC–JKP. Addressed to Huntingdon, marked "Private," and probably enclosed in Sarah C. Polk to Polk, July 5, 1841.

1. By Act of June 30, 1841, the U.S. Congress appropriated $25,000 to Anna Symmes Harrison, daughter of John Cleves Symmes.

FROM SARAH C. POLK

My dear Husband Nashville July 5, 1841

I am afraid that you will think me troublesome in imposing on you the necessity of reading my letters which in truth contain nothing. For I assure you that I know nothing to write and have a poor opportunity of learning any thing. Sister Walker[1] being here has confined me at home for the last two weeks, and I know but little that is going on, only from the papers, which you see. There is as far as I can learn no excitement, and very little interest in Politics. I send you the Union of to day.[2] I think of late that *Harris* seems to give more attention to his paper and it is more spirited. The Whig papers say but little about the election, do not abuse you, nor do they praise Jones, nor defend him. If any thing I think the Democrats are more active and spirited here than the Whigs. But I hear so much less of Politics here than I ever did before that I am at a loss what to think of prospects. Let the result be what it may, so you do not destroy your health or kill yourself with fatigue; I shall not greive, but be thankful. You have scarcely any letters of any sort, and there is no business in the office. *Young* is going about. I have heard nothing of the *bonds.*[3] Indeed everything as far as I know is quiet. I will not close my letter until the mail of this evening comes in. I received no letter from you nor any thing else. You need not be alarmed when I inform you that there is an addition of ten to our family this evening: Mr. & Mrs Walker, Majr. Bills, Mr. McDowel, Jane, Sally, Andrew &c. &c.[4] Do you think I am lonesome.

SARAH POLK

ALS. DLC–JKP. Addressed to Jackson. Published in *THQ*, XI, pp. 189–90.

1. Jane Maria Polk Walker.

2. Enclosed copy of the *Nashville Union* not found.

3. See Daniel Graham to Polk, June 10, 1841, and Polk to Sarah C. Polk, June 15 and 25, 1841.

4. James Walker, Jane Maria Polk Walker, John H. Bills, Samuel McDowell, Jane Clarissa Walker, Sarah Naomi Walker, and Andrew Jackson Walker. McDowell, a former resident of Maury County, was clerk of the Hardeman County Court, 1840–44. Jane Clarissa, Sarah Naomi, and Andrew Jackson were children of James Walker and his wife Jane Maria Polk Walker.

FROM ROBERT ARMSTRONG

My dear Sir, Nashville 6th July 41

We are going on here better than when you left, in better hopes and spirits. Hollingsworth made his first speech to day. The signs are right. I believe he will succeed. Jennings did not answer, makes light of the opposition. [. . .][1] opposition in this county. All as it should be. Our friends are doing and the accounts from all quarters are good & Cheering.

I have now under way written Letters for every county in the State to be signd by Doct. R.[2] One or two to a county to rouse our friends. I send you a Whig *marked.*[3] They are Whiped; see their calcu[l]ations. Foster is not out yet; the Knife *blade* is.[4]

No news. Harris is doing but little and will do less. He wont take hold. Write him.

My voice is still for East Tenss.[5] Drop down at Greenville. Sweep round our strong counties. Come in by Fraziers District &c &c. You will have 10 days speaking. I doubt if Jones will go, they are so confident. Genl. Anderson is here & has been for the last two weeks. Money affairs.[6] I told him to write you on the East Tennessee matter. I enclos'd his letter to Jackson.[7] This I expect to reach you at Huntingdon. Write. You will have a great affair at Mount Pleat.[8] All looks well.

No news but what you see. The Whigs will get no Bank This session. If they [do] not now they never will. The old Genl has nearly gone and I thought he would leave us on the 4th. He is now better and Improving.[9]

Mrs. P. well & writes you to Jackson.[10]

R. A.

ALI. DLC–JKP. Addressed to Huntingdon.

1. Manuscript torn.

2. The *Nashville Union* of July 26, 1841, published Felix Robertson's July 12th campaign letter rallying Democrats for the August election. Robertson was chairman of the Central Corresponding Committee of Tennessee.

3. Enclosed copy of the *Nashville Whig* not found.

4. See Sarah C. Polk to Polk, June 18 and 25, 1841.

5. See Polk to Sarah C. Polk, July 1, 1841.

6. See Alexander O. Anderson to Polk, May 12 and July 8, 1841.

7. See Alexander O. Anderson to Polk, July 5, 1841.

8. Polk planned to speak at Mt. Pleasant on July 15, 1841.

9. Reference is to Andrew Jackson. See also Sarah C. Polk to Polk, June 25, 1841.

10. See Sarah C. Polk to Polk, July 5, 1841.

TO SARAH C. POLK

Tuesday evening
Gibson County July 6th 1841

My Dear Wife

I remained at Trenton all day on yesterday. The town is situated on low ground bordering on the Forked-Deer swamp & is an exceedingly hot place, being wholly unprotected by shadetrees. In addition to this, it is Court week & I found it impossible to keep my room from being crowded with people. This morning I resolved to leave, and accordingly came out 10 miles towards Hundingdon,[1] to the house of an old Virginian,[2] where I now am, and where I am as comfortable as it is possible for me to be anywhere, unless it were *at my wife's house.* I am I think entirely well, but am considerably debilitated by the disease and the medicine I have taken.[3] I am resolved to take care of myself, and will particularly guard against exposure or over-fatigue. I will remain here until morning, and in the cool part of the day, employing the morning & evening, will go to Huntingdon tomorrow night, when I have but little doubt I shall be able to meet my appointment at Huntingdon on thursday, and then pursue my appointments until I reach home. You need have no apprehension concerning my health. I know my situation and know how to take care of myself. Jones's nephew (Mr Hart) was taken sick on saturday, f[r]om the same cause probably which produced my attack & I left him at Trenton this morning. Some cases of sickness are occurring in the lower part of the District. I am now through the most sickly portion of it, and glad that I will soon be out of it. I saw many of my friends from different parts of the District at Trenton. The lawyers from Jackson, Paris &c. were there. They all say that as I was so unfortunate as to be sick, it was fortunate that it happened whilst the appointments were going on in the Democratic Counties in the Northern part of the District. FitzGerald, McMeans & Judge Harris[4] say that my absence in Weakley, Henry & Benton will not loose me a vote.

It is very important that I should be in good consti[tu]tion at Jackson, and therefore I will make but a moderate effort at Huntingdon on thursday.

James K. Polk

P.S. Mr Jetton[5] reached Trenton last night & brought me direct information from home. He left the Documents, you gave him, at *Camden.*[6] Thos. Claiborne will bring them to me to Huntingdon. J.K.P.

ALS. DLC–JKP. Addressed to Nashville.

1. Huntingdon, seat of Carroll County.
2. Not identified further.
3. See Polk to Sarah C. Polk, July 1, 1841.
4. William Fitzgerald, James R. McMeans, and William R. Harris. A Paris lawyer, McMeans served several terms in the Tennessee Senate, 1819, 1825–29, and 1833–35. He was attorney general of the Ninth Judicial Circuit from 1836 until 1841.
5. Reference possibly is to Isaac L. Jetton, a pioneer settler of Gibson County and owner of a farm a few miles west of Trenton.
6. Documents not identified further.

FROM ALEXANDER O. ANDERSON

My Dear Sir Nashville July 8th 1841

I have delayed leaving here until now, under some reasonable expectation that I wou'd be able to get some money here from the State Bank.[1] They had the money but they wou'd not lend me any of it. The President[2] seemed to think they wou'd find Bills on orleans a good investment at Athens, & wou'd therefore do them there. But they wont discount upon any terms there. I saw my Brother Pierce as I came by, & he told me such was the fact. He is a Director & understands what they will do. I wanted to get five thousand Dollars on a note here. Failing in this I am utterly disappointed. Tho' some of the Directors intimated that a note for $2500 might be had.

I will send a note here endorsed by James W. Deaderick & Pierce B. Anderson for that sum. I will enclose it to Dr Robertson—and hope it may reach here by the time you get here. At any rate I will be obliged if you will speak to him & some of our friends, and with your aid I have no doubt I can get it. It is important to me to succeed in this matter—& hope you will impress some of our friends upon this subject to whom you can speak freely. I leave in the morning in the Stage.

A Anderson

[P.S.] The difficulty chiefly in that Board I learn is to get Govr Carrol[l] & Mr Nichol to agree—so that neither takes in any one case the exclusive responsibility &c. I think the Board acted harshly with me & with unnecessary fastidiousness. I need the money & unless I get at least $2500 of the Bank there I shall be in considerable difficulty. They have the money & will be cashing Alabama Bills I have no doubt. This is Irregular when they are a[l]lowed to distribute it without state. This is guess work—*in part only.*

ALS. DLC–JKP. Addressed to Nashville and marked "Private & Confidential."

1. See Alexander O. Anderson to Polk, May 12, 1841.
2. William Nichol.

FROM JAMES WALKER

Columbia, Tennessee. July 14, 1841

Walker states that he must go to Marshall County on business, but expresses hope that he can return the following evening. That failing, he will meet Polk at Spring Hill. Walker observes that Powhatan Gordon has ignored the county convention and is running as a Democrat "under Whig auspices."[1] Greenfield and Keeble[2] are also in the field. Walker urges that William "must now run the race out." Many of the Whigs, Walker contends, will support both of the Polk brothers.

ALS. DLC–JKP. Probably addressed locally.

1. Powhatan Gordon, brother of Boling Gordon, won election to two terms in the Tennessee House, 1843–47; however he failed to defeat Barkly Martin for the Tennessee Senate in 1841.

2. Gerrard T. Greenfield and probably John G. Keeble. Greenfield, a Columbia physician, and Keeble, a Columbia merchant, ran against William H. Polk and John H. Dew for Maury County's two seats in the Tennessee Houise.

FROM CAVE JOHNSON

Dear Sir, Washington July 17th 1841

Knowing your continued absence from home & the uncertainty of a letter reaching you at any of your appointments I have omitted writing tho much has occurred every day which would amuse and interest you. Without attempting an outline of everything that has occurred I shall c[on]tent[1] myself for the present in giving you the present aspect of business & politics, as they appear to a looker on, who is not in the confidence of either of the belligerents of the Whig party. The Pres. sets up for himself & I believe will play the game out. He is backed by Reeves, Archer, Preston, Merrick certainly and probably by Choat, Bates & *Barrow*, the two first footstep followers of Webster & the latter attending closely to the interests of Washington B., who goes as charge to Portugal.[2] Clay you know must be the *Senate*, Government & all or his proud spirit would fight omnipotence herself. Tyler & *friends denounce*, rather secretly yet, Clay & his friends, as enemies and the latter you know will repay in kind & with interest. Webster & Grainger[3] goes thoroughly with the Pres. whilst Ewing & Bell go with him nominally but are at heart with Clay & have been or will be caught. Rumor says B.[4] has already been detected in communicating cabinet secrets to Clay. In this state of the Case, Clay's Bank Bill[5] will be if it has not been already defeated. They took up the loan Bill[6] on yesterday—& Sargeants Com.[7] had a meeting for the first time in two weeks and took up Clays Bank Bill & will probably report it to the House on tuesday, adding to it the Bill to repeal the subtreasury. Thus it will pass the House, probably during the ensuing week. With their amended rules, they have the previous question substantially in Com. & use it upon all occasions & it is conjectured that no further steps will be taken in the

Senate until our Bill gets there—& in the mean time, the public opinion of Maryland will be brought upon Merrick & if possible send the Bill to Tyler, so as to compel him to veto the Bank & the repeal together. This he will probably do—his friends say certainly. The democrats in the House have stood by, been kicked & cuffed & gaged & run over, by the Speaker,[8] & the majority without the slightest regard to the *rules* or parliamentary Law & with a committee on Rules ever ready to make a rule to suit the emergency authorised to Report *at all times.* We have borne it long enough to disgrace us almost. Yet as we knew the fight was going on between Whigs it seemed most prudent to stand by—look on quietly knowing that when rogues fall out honest men will get their rights.

In the Senate the Dem. have fought a noble battle—and are keeping it up with great spirit. The world never saw a debate so ably & so well managed as on the Bank Bill. Clay has threatened the gag but he cannot inforce it. It would produce open war—rebellion. They would resist it in blood. I think Clay will be deterred. The loan Bill will pass—& probably the Land Bill.[9] We think the fortification Bill[10] will be rejected and the home squadron.[11] The Democrats were amused this morning on Arnolds motion to re-consider.[12] He came out in the most furious manner, saying that he had been informed from a high source *almost certain*, that all the great measures of relief were defeated & that we had better go home &c &c (his authority is said to have been J.Q.A.).[13] The decision of the S.C. of NY on McClouds case[14] prostrates Websters letter & in New York, Penn. & Maine no doubt is entertained of the complete overthrow of the Whigs this faul. *Gov. Everett goes to England*—Jenifer to Austria—Pendleton to Russia—Todd to Naples—& Wash B. to Portugal—good heavens![15] What a batch of Ministers & little Allen A. to S.A.![16] McKay thinks there is no honesty or sense in this world and that nothing is wanting but impudence & insolence to ensure success. Ten or twelve Clerks were dismissed from the Treasury today. I expect no democrat will be left save McClintock Young.[17] I luckily caught them this morning. Davis[18] of Ky wanted to know all persons employed by the different departments with a view to retrenchment and offered *his resolution* which was recd. I *got the floor* & offered mine as an amendment calling for all the names of those dismissed & appointed. You never saw such confusion, such consultation & manouivers & tricks to evade it but they were compelled at last to the vote & we passed it, with an amendment of Botts calling for all from 1829.

I think T. J. Campbell is the bitterest Whig in the House, much worse than any Boston Blue light. Mr G[19] is not muc[h] behind him. The balance seem more rational except T. D. A.,[20] who is never counted. We lack democratic leaders in the House more than we ever did.

We have heard but little of your election upon which we can rely & are almost ready to give it up as lost from the Whig news. We hope our documents will do some good. We scattered them as well as we could—not having recd any lists except for a few counties. We sent about 12.000 circulars.[21] We managed among ourselves to get a democratic name in each county upon which we thought we could rely & sent to him for distribution—generally to the democrat candidates. Philadelphia is pressing Old Ironsides[22] & your name suggested with his as Vice President. The Democrats were never in better spirits or the Whigs in greater confusion.

My health is better than usual tho I occasionally feel my old complaint worse for a day or two past than before but not to confine me or prevent business. My respects to Mrs. P.

C. JOHNSON

ALS. DLC–JKP. Addressed to Nashville and marked "*Private.*"

1. An ink blot has obscured part of this word.

2. William C. Rives, William S. Archer, William C. Preston, William D. Merrick, Rufus Choate, Isaac C. Bates, and Washington Barrow. After several terms in the Virginia House of Delegates, Archer, a lawyer, served in the U.S. House, 1820–35, and in the U.S. Senate, 1841–47. After single terms in the Massachusetts House and Senate, Choate, a lawyer, served as a Whig in the U.S. House, 1831–34, in the U.S. Senate, 1841–45, and as attorney general of Massachusetts in 1853. After a term in the Massachusetts House, Bates, also a lawyer, served in the U.S. House, 1827–35, and in the U.S. Senate as a Whig, 1841–45. A lawyer from Tennessee and briefly from Mississippi, Barrow served as U.S. chargé d'affaires to Portugal, 1841–44; edited the Nashville *Republican Banner*, 1845–47; and sat in the U.S. House as a Whig, 1847–49.

3. Francis Granger.

4. John Bell.

5. See Aaron V. Brown to Polk, June 12, 1841.

6. By Act of July 21, 1841, Congress authorized the president to issue up to $12 million in U.S. Treasury notes.

7. U.S. House Committee on the Currency.

8. John White of Kentucky.

9. Reference is to the distribution and preemption bill. See Harvey M. Watterson to Polk, February 1, 1841.

10. By Act of September 9, 1841, Congress appropriated $2.4 million for military fortifications. Johnson argued against commencing any new works on the grounds that revenues were insufficient. He also argued that the War Department had a sum of unexpended appropriations larger than the average annual expenditure and therefore should not need more money.

11. An appropriation for eight naval vessels and contingent expenses received the president's approval on August 1, 1841.

12. Thomas D. Arnold moved that the House reconsider its vote of the previous day to stop committee debate on the fortification bill; the House voted 103 to 89 to reconsider. The resolution to terminate committee debate was withdrawn.

13. John Quincy Adams.

14. Reference is to the case of Alexander McLeod of Upper Canada; see Aaron V. Brown to Polk, June 12, 1841. In July of 1841 the New York Supreme Court refused to grant a writ of habeas corpus to McLeod, who based his appeal on a letter of instructions from Webster to U.S. Attorney General John J. Crittenden, March 15, 1841. Webster had argued that McLeod should be discharged from the state courts because at the time of his alleged participation in the border incident he was acting as an agent of a foreign government, not as a private individual.

15. Edward Everett, Daniel Jenifer, John S. Pendleton, Charles S. Todd, and Washington Barrow. Everett, a Harvard professor and an editor, sat as an Independent in the U.S. House, 1825–35; served as Whig governor of Massachusetts, 1836–39; went to Great Britain as U.S. minister, 1841–45; presided as president of Harvard College, 1846–49; served as U.S. secretary of state, 1852–53; and sat in the U.S. Senate, 1853–54. Pendleton, a lawyer, won several terms in the Virginia House of Delegates; went to Chile as U.S. chargé d'affaires, 1841–44; sat as a Whig in the U.S. House, 1845–49; and served as U.S. chargé to the Argentine Confederation, 1851–54. Todd, also a lawyer, served on William H. Harrison's staff during the War of 1812; sat in the Kentucky legislature, 1817–18; went to Colombia as a U.S. diplomatic agent, 1820–23; collaborated on a Harrison campaign biography; published the *Cincinnati Republican* during the 1840 contest; and went to Russia as U.S. minister, 1841–45.

16. Allen A. Hall went to Venezuela as U.S. chargé.

17. McClintock Young, first appointed by Andrew Jackson to be chief clerk in the office of the secretary of the treasury, held his post into Zachary Taylor's presidency.

18. Garrett Davis, a lawyer, served one term in the Kentucky House, 1833–35; sat as a Whig in the U.S. House, 1839–47; and won election to the U.S. Senate as a Whig in 1861 and as a Democrat in 1867.

19. Reference probably is to Meredith P. Gentry of Tennessee.

20. Thomas D. Arnold.

21. The six Democratic congressmen from Tennessee distributed to their constituents a circular letter dated March 1, 1841. Their twenty-eight page pamphlet favored economy in public expenditures, an Independent Treasury system, and popular sovereignty; it opposed relief measures advocated by the new Whig administration.

22. Charles Stewart achieved a distinguished record while commanding the U.S.S. *Constitution* during the War of 1812; both he and his frigate earned the nickname, "Old Ironsides." George M. Dallas of Philadelphia backed Stewart for the presidency in 1844 as well as earlier.

FROM SILAS M. CALDWELL

Dr. Sir Dancyville July 23d 1841

Your Boy Addison has run away from your farm and is at my house.[1] From the wounds that are on his neck & arms it appears that the Overseer intended to kill Him. The wounds are well. He says the overseer says he will kill him and is afraid to stay there. You will please write to me what to do with him. He has been runaway about four weeks. I have hired him in the neighborhood until I hear from you. Your prospects are as good in this County as they were in '39. Saml. is sick.[2] Rest Well.

S. M. Caldwell

ALS. DLC–JKP. Addressed to Nashville. AE on the cover states that this letter was answered on August 11, 1841; Polk's reply has not been found. Published in Bassett, *Plantation Overseer*, 153–54.

1. On July 16, 1841, William Bobbitt also informed Polk of Addison's disappearance and advised him that if he replaced the slave he "would have the most agreeable set of negroes with which I am acquainted." ALS. DLC–JKP.

2. Samuel Polk Caldwell was the eldest son of Silas M. Caldwell and Lydia Eliza Polk Caldwell, Polk's sister.

TO SARAH C. POLK

Sunday morning

My Dear Wife Bean's Station July 25th 1841

I am here in the Stage, on my way to a meeting for tomorrow made by the Citizens for Kingsport or the Boat Yard.[1] I have met the people at Kingston & Blain's XRoads,[2] and find my health improving daily. I enclose a short letter to Genl. Armstrong,[3] which I send under cover to you lest it might be delayed on the way, if directed directly to him. Send for him & explain to him why it was enclosed to you.

James K. Polk

ALS. DLC–JKP. Addressed to Nashville.

1. Situated in Sullivan County on the north side of the Holston River and one mile above its northern fork, Kingsport was first known as "the Boat Yard," for it was the shipping point for the King's Salt Works in Virginia. Polk had planned to speak in Sullivan County at Blountville; however, on July 8, 1841, Nicholas Fain wrote that it would be best for the governor to speak at Kingsport, "the stronghold of Whigery in that County." ALS. DLC–JKP.

2. Polk spoke at Kingston, Roane County, on July 22, 1841, and at Blain's XRoads, Grainger County, on July 24, 1841.

3. Enclosure not found.

FROM SARAH C. POLK

My Dear Husband, Nashville July 25th [1841][1]

I am distressed that I know nothing, nor have learned nothing since you left to write you. As far as I know there is yet a calm and quietness in politics. Though I confess to you the truth that I have had no opportunity of learning much. The house full of *kin*[2] that I have had ever since you left, and indeed *all the summer* has made *me* nothing more than a servant and a senseless round in my house keeps me at home and keeps away such company as I might gather some information from. So you can perceive that I have no means to learn anything to write you, which I offer as an excuse. I sent you the Banner containing *Jones* letter to the people in the Clarksville District.[3] I directed it to Blountsville. As far as I can learn it made no impression here, for nothing is said about it. And there has been nothing said in the papers. I regret that I have nothing to write you; the truth is, I know nothing, I hear nothing, and of course to read a long letter from me would be a loss of time. So I will leave off.

SARAH POLK

ALS. DLC–JKP. Addressed to Jonesboro. Published in *THQ*, XI, p. 190.

1. Year identified through content analysis.

2. See Sarah C. Polk to Polk, July 5, 1841.

3. On July 19, 1841, James C. Jones addressed a circular letter to the citizens of Sumner, Robertson, Stewart, Montgomery, Dickson, Humphreys, and Hickman counties in which he explained that he had canceled his speaking engagements in each of those counties in order to follow Polk to East Tennessee during the period immediately before the election of August 5. Jones' letter was published in the *Nashville Whig* of July 23, 1841. It probably was published in the Nashville *Republican Banner* of July 21, 1841; no complete copy of that paper has been found.

FROM SARAH C. POLK

Dear Husband, Nashville July 29, 1841

I have not heard from you since you left McMinnville,[1] but hope to hear to day. I am told that there is more interest and I may say excitement within the last few days on the subject of the Election. The Whigs it is said are uneasy. The Democrats in good spirits. I learn from Mr

Currin that there has been many changes in Williamson since you were there,[2] among them old *Beaufort* who interogated you at the speaking.[3] But whether there can be changes enough to elect, you next *Thursday* is another question, but I shall have philosophy to stand it and think that I can be as happy with my husband *at home,* defeated candidate, as to have a successful one always from me. And you have now character enough in the country to stand a defeat, temporary as it must be, without injury to your future prospects. The Banner[4] of this day has two articles rallying the Whigs, and urgeing them not to let *personal* considerations induce them to vote against their principles at this important time. If you can get through the canvass, health unimpaired and at home safely once more, I will be content. Let the result be what it may, but hope for the best in all things.

SARAH POLK

ALS. DLC–JKP. Addressed to Knoxville. Published in *THQ*, XI, pp. 190–91.

1. Letter not found.
2. Polk and Jones spoke at Franklin, Williamson County, on July 17, 1841. No account of that engagement has been found.
3. Beaufort is not identified further.
4. Nashville *Republican Banner*.

TO ROBERT ARMSTRONG

My Dear Sir Jonesborough Augt. 2nd 1841

I think I may have a small gain over my vote of 1839 in *Sullivan, Johnson, Carter & Washington*. The gain in these Counties will I think balance the probable loss in *Granger & Hawkins*. I have good news from *Cocke*. Before I reached East Tennessee, there had been a manifest falling off from my strength from what it was when I was here in the spring, as more properly speaking, our friends seemed to have lost confidence of our success, & were therefore not making the proper exertions. Since my arrival here they have taken fresh courage & in this part of E. Tennessee are very active. The proceedings at Washington too, are producing a decided re-action in our favour, but the time is so short before the election that it is difficult to say to what extent they may operate.[1] Upon the whole my opinion is that I may be beaten something in E. Tennessee, say from 2 to 3 thousand votes. It cannot be worse than this. If I maintain my old strength in the *West* I will be re-elected. But it is needless to speculate on the result, as before this reaches you, the contest will be over. I will reach *Sparta* on Saturday night after the election.[2] Drop me a line to that point giving me the vote of Davidson. We expect an immense crowd here to day.

I enclose this to my wife, as my hand-writing is known & I have reason to think that my correspondence is closely watched.[3] In haste.

JAMES K. POLK

P.S. Tomorrow I will meet a very large crowd as it is said, in the lower part of *Greene* adjoining Hawkins. J.K.P.

ALS. DLC–AJ. Addressed to Nashville and marked "*Private.*"

1. Reference is to the deliberations of the special session of the U.S. Congress and to Whig divisions on the national bank question.

2. Polk planned to reach Sparta on August 7, 1841, on his return to Nashville from East Tennessee.

3. Polk directed political letters through Sarah C. Polk on more than one occasion. See Polk to Sarah C. Polk, July 25, 1841.

FROM ISAAC H. DISMUKES

Dear sir August the 2 1841

I wil now oifer you a fiew lines to inform you sumthing of our heath and bisness. I shall not bea very particular as I expect you down sum time in the course of this month. Wea are all wel at the preasent time. My crop of cotten lookes very well. My corn is sorrey. My cattle have stop dying. I lost nine of them. Thare is nuthing else of importance. The money wich you left with mea have given out sum time since for I had to pay freait on the bagen and rope to the amount of 42.62½. I have plide to magour bobit[1] and hea has not got eny money by him. I stand in neade of a niew waggon for this has past repairing.

ISAAC H. DISMUKES

ALS. DLC–JKP. Addressed to Nashville. Published in Bassett, *Plantation Overseer*, 154.

1. William Bobbitt.

FROM AARON V. BROWN

Dear Sir Washington August 8th 1841

I suppose you to be now slowly returning from E. Tennessee where you closed your arduous campaign. Your Friends here have evinced the liveliest interest in your behalf. I do not refer to the Tennessee Delegation alone, but to your distant friends who have not ceased to look on the mighty struggles in which you have been engaged with the highest solicitude. Your friends in the Delegation, have received but few letters—none from you & are left to form their opinions chiefly from the newspaper statements. From these we have gloomy forbodings of the result as to your election. We commonly conclude that you have most probably been beaten by 5 or 6 thousand. We hope ardently without a single exception that it may have been otherwise, but fear that the time was too short for you to receive that benefit from the recent movements here, which they were calculated to give on longer period. Of the Legislature we have more hopes—but of course not without some *apprehension* that *that* may have been lost too. In that event, our discomfiture is complete. All will have been lost but the consciousness of having done our duty. We of the Dem. delegation, have done not only *what* but *all* we thought would be likely to be of any service. We have kept the public press apprised of the earliest movements in the Capital & have sent out to our friends who were candidates, private letters & public Documents, best calculated to advance the course throughout the State. Our joint circular[1] was written in a calm tone, that it might gain more credence & might not subject us to any imputation of *dictating* to the people. It was a *delicate* point sometimes to settle, how far the introduction of *new topics* might injure you & our friends generally, or what particular ones might prove serviceable. But we have done the best we could, amidst the unsettled state of the great questions here. It was not considered here the best policy to make a run at *Webster* who was understood to be standing by & sustaining Tyler against the Clay party in the Cabinet.[2] But our policy on Tennessee I knew to be different & on that account I made the McC[l]eod speech[3] to bring down "Websters strong English predilections" from the last War to the present time. I had 1500 copies in pamplet struck off, distributed 1000 myself & gave the other 500 to my colleagues who sent them & *others* of their own off to the State about the 12, 13 and 14 July, perhaps a day or two later than that. I have received no news of their arrival or whether they seemed likely to do any good. The Union has not *noticed* the simple fact of my having made a speech on the subject. He publishs Nicholsons speech made on the same day,[4] publishd in the same Globe & does not notice my speech at all. He must not only have seen it in the Globe, & Herald but must have seen it in pamplet for I sent him one.[5] Continued & oft repeated slights like this, a very remarkable one you will remember in the regular session of the last Congress,[6] has induced me to believe that that paper has taken some strange aversion to me, which no conduct on my part, could ever have provoked. My colle[a]gu[e]s here hurr[i]ed me in the publication & transmission of that speech before the elections should come on & yet our favorite organ would not spare three lines to notice *the fact* of a speech having been made, although he was writing paragraphs constantly on the McCleod case. On the Bank Bill, I made another speech,[7] but as it could not get home in time for the elections It will not appear in the Globe for some time on account of the press of business in the office. I shall send you a copy pamplet in a day or two, hoping my friends will have no occasion to disown it. If we should all be disappointed here[8] & you shall have been successful, It will of course be a blasting result to our adversaries at home. If the contrary should be the fact & the Legislature shall have been gained, it will become a matter for your consideration, whether satisfactory arrangements could not be made for your being returned as Senator. Such a thing would be gratifying to your friends *abroad* & I hope it might be effected without the loss of any at home. Whatever was thought likely to take place on that subject, should not of course be announced too soon after the close of the canvass.

Now if a veto should come in on Tuesday morning next,[9] an absolute & full one—Will not *that* & other considerations soon break up the present Cabinet or at least the Clay portion of it? If so will "He of the War"[10] retire & then make a hard push for the Senate? If they get the Legislature, will not this bring up collision between him & Foster? Some of our Whig Colleagues, insist that Foster will be sure to try & return to the Senate if he possibly can.

But about the veto, all is as uncertain today as it was the first day of the Session. *No one knows*, the President either having been prudently silent or spoken out imprudently both ways. I do not doubt that he will veto but I fear it will not be full enough so as to stop the matter this session—but may be obviated by a slight amendment & then be passed. Old John Q.,[11] the great sinner of the age, voted against it. So did Marshall, Clays own Representative; he was very *severe* against the compromise & in his conversations out of the house *denounces* Mr. Clay severely. But he has been in "a state of Hilarity" all the time & sober second thoughts may *right up* matters again with him.

It was *suspected* that Mr. Clay did not wish to give Tyler the chance of putting a veto on the Bank, as that might instantly make him a rival of decided pretensions & that therefore he desired the Bill to be sent back to the Senate, there to be put in Tyler trim or rejected altogether but the strong vote of his friends against all amendments finally renderd this conjecture probably erroneous.

In the way of undercurrents—it is said Benton wanted it sent back to the Senate where he thought it would fail because *he* did not wish Tyler to have the Acclaim of its defeat. I expect there is something in that two. Nothing of the sort is intimated against Calhoun.

You will have noticed Vanderpoels speech at the great Park meeting in N. York[12] in which he said in reference to Tyler "Veto or no Veto the Democratic party, would never reach him with a forty foot pole," or some such balderdash as that—bad in time, place & sentiment. But you know him well enough. The Democrats make no overtures—or assurances but wait *respectfully* & patiently for *results*. Wise, Gilmer & Hunter, are in decided favor & say he will undoubtedly veto & if necessary will break entirely with the Whigs if they denounce him for standing up to what *they knew* were his principles before they elected him. Wise, Gilmer, Hunter, Mallory act decidedly with us. Proffit & a few others are said to be waiting for the veto & will come when it comes.

With the struggle in Tennessee, now final one way or the other, so far as my exertions could be available, my inclination to be in public life, now terminates. The close of my present term in Congress will terminate the Bank, the Distribution & other great questions at lea[s]t for the present & then if not sooner by resignation I shall go back to my private pursuits, with more pleasure than I left them—not from disappointment for I have been personally gratified but from a conviction, that there is nothing in public life or rather in political life, which can fairly compensate the most fortunate, for the anxieties & cares which they must necessarily endure. Each individual has some peculiarity of condition & disposition, qualifying or disqualifying them for public pursuits. Mine are of the latter class & I shall hasten to get back into private life now that I have done all the good in my power for my friends & the advancement of those great principles, which I have not simply professed as party designations, but cherished with a sincere & hearty devotion.

A V Brown

ALS. DLC–JKP. Probably addressed to Nashville.

1. See Cave Johnson to Polk, July 17, 1841.

2. All members of Tyler's inherited cabinet, except Daniel Webster and Postmaster General Francis Granger, were Clay partisans. They included Secretary of the Treasury Thomas Ewing, Secretary of War John Bell, Secretary of the Navy George E. Badger, and Attorney General John J. Crittenden.

3. On July 9, 1841, Brown spoke in the U.S. House concerning the case of Alexander McLeod. Brown denounced Webster's failure to repel Great Britain's "degrading threat" and declared that the secretary "should have stopped all negotiation at once—instantly to have stopped it—until that menace was withdrawn." Brown thus considered McLeod's case as "one of peace and of war" between the U.S. and Great Britain. See A. V. Brown to Polk, June 12, 1841.

4. References are to the *Nashville Union* of July 22, 1841, and its editor, J. George Harris. On July 9, 1841, A. O. P. Nicholson spoke in the U.S. Senate in

favor of an amendment to the Fiscal Bank bill that would have required the central bank to disclose publicly all orders issued to its branch offices.

5. Brown's and Nicholson's speeches were published in the *Congressional Globe* of July 14, 1841; in the Washington *Globe* of July 10, 1841; and in the *New York Herald* of July 12, 1841. On August 9, 1841, the *Nashville Union* printed Brown's speech in full.

6. Harris' earlier slight of Brown is not identified further.

7. On August 4, 1841, Brown spoke in the U.S. House against the Fiscal Bank bill. Brown supported Tyler's argument that although the people decided against the Sub-Treasury in the late presidential election, they did not decide for a U.S. Bank; least of all did they register support for a bank modeled on the second Bank of the U.S. Brown objected to the Fiscal Bank bill on constitutional grounds.

8. Brown's point of reference was the gloomy election prediction made by Polk's friends in Washington.

9. Tyler did not send Congress his veto message on the Fiscal Bank bill until August 16, 1841. See A. V. Brown to Polk, June 12, 1841.

10. Reference is to John Bell, secretary of war.

11. John Quincy Adams.

12. On July 15, 1841, Democrats rallied in the park in front of City Hall in New York to demonstrate against Congress' chartering a new national bank; Vanderpoel was one of several speakers at the rally.

FROM HOPKINS L. TURNEY

Dear Sir Washington. Aug. the 12th 1841

I have not heard a word from the elections in Tennessee, but suppose that you are for the first time, defeated and by a decided vote. I entertain Strong hopes that we have a majority in the Legislature and If so it is fortunate for you that you are beaten. If you could be here I believe your chance for a nomination for the Presidency, would be better than any other mans. The feeling among the members from Pennsylvania, New York, and in fact, from a large majority of the States, is so far as I have been enabled to assertain it, decidedly in your favour even over Benton, mainly for the reason as I believe of private character. If therefore we have the legislature, I shall not grieve much at your defeat for Govr. All now agree that Tyler will veto the bank bill; that will kill him with the Whigs and also distroy the Whig party.[1] He differs with us on the Sub Treasury and also on maney other eaquilly important measures, and besides he is a *Judas to* and *renegade from* all parties. Our party therefore will not toutch him with a ten foot pole. He will be in the way of no body. Benton, Buchannan[2] and Calhoun all say they will not run under any circumstances. The field is open, and your chance at least eaquil and if you were here greatly best of any man now spoken here.

H. L. Turney

ALS. DLC–JKP. Addressed to Nashville.

1. See Aaron V. Brown to Polk, June 12 and August 8, 1841.

2. James Buchanan.

FROM LEVIN H. COE

Dear Sir Somerville Augt 13, 1841

It seems that we have met the enemy and we are theirs.[1] Though we still have hopes of a Democratic majority in the Legislature on joint ballott. If so you must go into the Senate.

If Douglass had been left out of the Directory here in 1840[2] he would have been beaten at the late Election. The soft headed Democratic Directors who voted for him deserve the fate that awaits them.

Douglass must be beaten for Speaker of the House.[3] The Democrats united can do it with the aid of one or two Whigs. This can easily be done if the pegs are set before a *caucus* fastens all down to Douglass.

In fact a proper management of this and the course of the Democrats in selecting between Whig candidates for Clerks—Door Keepers &c. may secure some Whig votes upon many questions such as laying off Districts &c. I see little chance of laying off Congressional Districts as the Legislature stands. I am perfectly willing to see the state makes nothing—13 on one side or the other.

L. H. Coe

ALS. DLC–JKP. Addressed to Nashville.

1. Variant of quotation from Oliver H. Perry's dispatch to William H. Harrison, September 10, 1813. Perry wrote, "we have met the enemy, and they are ours."

2. Burchett Douglass was reappointed to the directorate of the Somerville branch of the Bank of Tennessee in 1840.

3. A Whig banker and legislator, Douglass served five terms in the Tennessee House; he presided over that body for two terms, 1837–38 and 1841–42.

FROM CAVE JOHNSON

Sunday evening

Dear Sir, Washington 15th Augt 1841

The news we have as yet recd is very limited & induces us to believe that you have been defeated. I never believed so until I got the Banner of the 6th,[1] tho the impression has been general, that such would be the result. I did not suppose it possible that Tennessee ever could give her support to such men as now administer the Government or such principles as they act on. Really such things are enough to make us yield to the old Federal doctrine, that the people are not capable of self-government. We suppose that we have lost the Legislature too. Rumor is that we have lost Rutherford & Montgomery. If so I give up & you will have to retire for the next two years. I think you had best setle in the 11th Congressional District (in Hickman) and I will resign & you can take my place. We need your services in the House & I should do better at home with my wife & boy.

Every thing here is in a state [of] uncertainty painful in the extreme to some of us. We have expected the Veto to the Bank Bill[2] every day since Thursday; yet none has come. Now tomorrow it is to be certain. Every power is brought to bear on Tyler. Clayton of Delaware has been here.[3] Thurlow Weed.[4] Counssellers from N.Y. & Philadelphia, begging his signature. Whigs surround him by day & by night crying & entreating. Clay threatens demolition & ruin. Threats are given out from the populace that he will be mobbed.[5] He was to have visited the Delaware,[6] lying off Annapolis, the other day. He was deterred from going by the advice of friends. Yet I believe he will remain firm backed as he is by Wise & Gilmore.[7] In my opinion Wise is de facto Pres. of U.S. We may rely upon one thing for comfort in our Ten[nessee] misfortunes. The Cabinet will be blown sky high & J.B.[8] will go into a state of retiracy. Mrs. B.[9] says if the Bank is vetoed & B. does not resign, she will never sleep with him again. Under *such a threat* he must of course retire. B. & our Whig colleagues hold a caucus to night (we have learned by accident) to settle upon the victims in Tennessee in anticipation of a dissolution of the Cabinet the present week. Armstrong, Marshall,—Chester,—Majr. Bills & Some few others are the supposed victims—but I think they cannot succeed.[10] I intend to call on Tyler in the morning & will say to him what I have heard & what I think. The Whigs are most outrageous agt. Tyler but agreed in caucus the other night to smother their indignation even if a veto comes, hoping still to control him hereafter. The Bankrupt Bill in the House—The New Tariff & the Land Bill in the Senate are delayed,[11] with threats of defeating all if there comes a veto, so as to throw the odium of the defeat of all these measures upon Tyler & rally the friends of these measures in opposition to him hereafter. The Veto was expected on Thursday. The Whigs fixed upon Friday at 2 oclock to take the Bankrupt Bill out of Committee. The veto did not come. On Friday morning the Whigs rescended the order & the Bill is yet in Committee & will there remain until the Pres. acts on the Bank

Bill. Talmadge[12] is the selected Champion for the assault on the veto & will be followed up by Clay & others. We shall probably adjourn in a few days after the veto & do nothing else. Madam rumor has not yet setled upon the successors of the cabinet. It is thought, Everetts nomination as Minister to England will be withdrawn (or it will be defeated) & Webster nominated in his place & Tazwell or Reeves[13] go in to the State Department. Silas Wright or Gov. Marcy[14] into the Treasury. Cushing to the Navy—& Horace Binney Atto. Genl. & Gov. Polk of Tennessee into the War department & Gov. Shanon P.M. Genl.[15] We have another cast of the cabinet more talked of than thought off—Reeves Sec of State, Wise Sec of War, B. Peyton[16] Atto. Genl., Stanly in the Navy, Graves P.M. Genl., Cushing Sec. of Treasury. The Whigs have commenced caricaturing Tyler. They have him siting at the table, chin upon his hand, quill in his hand, in deep thought & saying, "to sign or not to sign—that is the question." Drawn by Stanberry & hawked about the House.[17] In these embarrassments which surround the Pres. it might be supposed that the Democrats take an active part in fomenting & keeping them up—but not so & I am proud to say it. They stand aloof, make no promises, further than to sustain him or any other man who acts upon our principles—and unite with one voice, *to repeal* all their measures Bank & all. I have heard of but one exception (Watterson), who will go *agt. Repeal of the Bank.*

The Cabinet except Ewing visited the Delaware on Saturday. Webster got lordly drunk & went to bed on board. Bell & Badger[18] had *a sufficiency.* Badger boasted of the Ship & talked of building 100 such & having 600 Steamers so as to master the British &c. There never was before collected together so *much talent* & so *little principle* or *honesty* as is to be found in the present Cabinet.

Bela Badger has been rejected by the Senate una voce.[19] I suppose many others will share the same fate.

I fear I shall weary you with such details or I would give you some acct. of Mr. Speaker White—the over bearing domineering course of Clay & the White Charleys[20] in both Houses but I must desist. The day of adjournment will not be fixed until the veto comes in & I suppose will depend upon that. If it covers *all the ground,* we shall break up in a row & come immediately home. If it be like the inaugural, half & half, we may be detained to try another financial scheme. I suspect Tyler will fall back on Jacksons Bank or his message in 1831.[21] My health is better than usual. My respects to Mrs. Polk.

C JOHNSON

ALS. DLC–JKP. Probably addressed to Nashville. Marked "*Private.*"

1. The Nashville *Republican Banner* of August 6 carried unofficial election returns that indicated Whig victories in Davidson, Rutherford, and Sumner counties.

2. See Aaron V. Brown to Polk, June 12, 1841.

3. John Middleton Clayton, a lawyer, sat in the Delaware House in 1824; served as Delaware's secretary of state, 1826–28; sat in the U.S. Senate as a National Republican, 1829–36, and as a Whig, 1845–49 and 1853–56; served as chief justice of Delaware, 1937–39; and negotiated the Clayton-Bulwer Treaty with Great Britain during his tenure as U.S. secretary of state, 1849–50.

4. A newspaper editor and an adroit party manager, Thurlow Weed contributed significantly to Whig victories in New York, beginning with the 1838 election of William Henry Seward to the governorship. In 1841 Weed edited the *Albany Evening Journal.*

5. Early in the morning of August 18, 1841, a crowd did demonstrate at the President's House against the veto. The next evening Tyler was burned in effigy.

6. The third U.S.S. *Delaware*, a ship of the line, was launched in Norfolk in 1820. From August 4 to September 29, 1841, the ship performed local operations at Annapolis under the command of Capt. Charles S. McCauley.

7. Thomas W. Gilmer.

8. John Bell.

9. Jane Erwin Yeatman Bell.

10. Robert Armstrong and John H. Bills were U.S. postmasters at Nashville and Bolivar, respectively. Samuel B. Marshall and Robert J. Chester were U.S. marshals for Middle and West Tennessee, respectively. None was replaced in 1841, but Bills and Marshall resigned the following year.

11. By Act of August 19, 1841, Congress established a uniform system of bankruptcy throughout the United States. A new tariff measure, imposing a tariff of not less than twenty per cent ad valorem on all imported articles not specifically excluded from the duty, became law on September 11, 1841. See Harvey M. Watterson to Polk, February 1, 1841, for a summary of the Land Act of 1841.

12. Nathaniel P. Tallmadge.

13. Littleton Waller Tazewell and William C. Rives. Tazewell, a lawyer, served in the Virginia House of Delegates, 1796–1800 and 1816; in the U.S. House, 1800–1801; in the U.S. Senate, 1824–32; and in the Virginia governorship, 1834–36.

14. William Learned Marcy, a lawyer and member of the Albany Regency, served as New York comptroller, 1823–29; justice of the New York Supreme Court, 1829–31; U.S. senator, 1831–32; governor of New York, 1833–38; secretary of war, 1845–49; and secretary of state, 1853–57.

15. Caleb Cushing, Horace Binney, and Wilson Shannon. Cushing, a lawyer, won election to several terms in both the Massachusetts House and Senate; sat in the U.S. Congress as a Whig, 1835–43; traveled to China as U.S. minister, 1843–45; served as U.S. attorney general, 1853–57; and went

to Spain as U.S. minister, 1874–77. Binney, a legal scholar, won election to the U.S. House in 1832 as an anti-Jackson candidate; previously he had served one term in the Pennsylvania legislature and had sat as a director of the first Bank of the United States.

16. Balie Peyton, a lawyer from Gallatin, Tennessee, sat as a Whig in the U.S. House, 1833–37; declined appointment as secretary of war under Tyler; became U.S. district attorney for eastern Louisiana in 1841; served as aide-de-camp for General W. J. Worth during the Mexican War; went to Chile as U.S. minister, 1849–53; and sat in the Tennessee Senate, 1869–70.

17. Variant of quotation for William Shakespeare's *Hamlet*, act 3, scene 1, line 56. Stanberry is not identified further.

18. George Edmund Badger, secretary of the navy in 1841.

19. Tyler nominated Bela Badger as naval officer for the district of Philadelphia on June 16, 1841. On July 22 the Senate postponed consideration of the nomination and in September formally rejected the appointment.

20. "Charley" is a slang expression meaning "watchman." "The White Charleys" refers to Speaker John White's followers.

21. In his Annual Message of December 6, 1831, Jackson declined taking a firm stand on the bank question and left it "to the investigation of an enlightened people and their representatives."

FROM A. O. P. NICHOLSON

My Dear Sir: Washington City. Augt 15. [1841][1]

The mail to-day brought news *entirely satisfactory* as to our fate in Tennessee. We seem to be essentially licked, with very little to comfort us in the fall. I submit myself, just as I know you will, with all becoming resignation to the will of the people. My eye is now *law-ward*—Blackstone, Espinasse &c. &c.[2] have been running in my head for the last hour. As the play runs: "This is a d—d bad world we live in—it will be burnt up one of these days—there is some comfort in that."[3]

There are others in as much trouble as we are. The Whigs here are in all sorts of difficulties. They have just found out that they "caught a Tartar"[4] in Tyler, and they are pouring out the bitterest wrath upon his head. He will veto the bank bill; it will be sent in to-morrow. The Cabinet is to be blown up; that is considered certain. So that Bell goes home to take up Blackstone too. What say you to a partnership with him!

I will write again to-morrow.[5]

A. O. P. Nicholson

ALS. DLC–JKP. Addressed to Nashville.

1. Year identified through content analysis.

2. Nicholson's allusion is to a return to the practice of law and to the works of Sir William Blackstone and Isaac Espinasse, noted English and French legal scholars.

3. Quotation not identified.

4. Variant of the quotation, "Ha—what a devil have I caught—a Tartar?" Aphra Behn, *Feign'd Courtezans*, act 4, scene 2.

5. On August 16, 1841, Nicholson wrote that Tyler's Fiscal Bank bill veto had been received by the Congress "amidst a tremendous excitement." ALS. DLC–JKP.

TO ROBERT B. REYNOLDS

My Dear Sir Nashville Augt. 19th 1841

In consequence of the lamented death of *Judge Powell*[1] it may become my duty to make a temporary appointment, before the Legislature shall meet. Will you be good enough to inform me at what time the first Court in that Circuit will be holden, and advise with me in reference to a suitable person to be appointed, should it become my duty to make an appointment. I will mention that the name of the *Hon. John Kennedy* formerly of Jonesborough, now of Polk County, has been presented to me.[2] *Judge Kennedy* has age, experience and undoubted qualifications to recommend him, and personally it would give me sincere pleasure to confer the appointment upon him, unless his residence at so great a distance from the Circuit, should constitute an objection. Give me your opinion in reference to this. Will there be any aspirants residing within the Circuit? If any of the Courts come on, before the meeting of the Legislature, it is possible that *Judge Anderson* would agree to hold them & thus supersede the necessity of an appointment.[3] Give me your views *confidentially*. They will be for *my own consideration alone.*[4]

In regard to the election, you know the result. It is now perfectly manifest, that we had the power to succeed, if we had known our own strength & the weakness of our opponents. Our friends however in many parts of the State gave up the contest in advance. They could not be convinced that there was any hope of my success, and such was the apathy prevailing in some of the Counties, that hundreds of them did not attend the polls. Now that they see that it was in our power to have succeeded I am receiving daily, letters expressing unavailing regrets that the writers had not known it in time. The large Counties in the Middle Division of the State could alone have saved the election. Now that it is too late, the proper spirit is up, and if the election were to come on tomorrow there could not be a doubt of the result. The State is now Democratic and before two years shall roll round I do not doubt, will be overwhelmingly so. So far as I am personally concerned, I feel that I have more cause to be satisfied than our leading opponents. I have performed a hard summer's labour, and boldly and honestly maintained my principles. I have fought a good fight, and in many parts of the State, as you know, almost single-handed unaided and alone. I yield to the result cheerfully and without a regret—so far as my own agency in the contest has been concerned. "The will of the people be done" is now as it has ever been my motto, though in the late contest it is manifest that a full expression of that will has not been given. We must keep on our armour & continue to do battle for our principles. I am glad to see that *Eastman* has "nailed his flag to the mast."[5] All our presses should do the same thing. Now is the time [to][6] make a permanent and lasting impr[essio]n. Let the ruinous course of the present Federal administration be fearlessly exposed & kept constantly before the people.

Hardwicke of Dickson writes that *Marable* (the Whig Representative elect from the Democratic Counties of Humphreys & Benton)[7] stands pledged to his constituents from the stump, faithfully and truly to obey their wishes, and that our leading friends are already engaged in getting up *instructions*, which will be signed by every Democrat in the two Counties, who compose near two thirds of his constituents. He thinks there is no doubt but that he will be forced to vote & act with the Democratic party, in the Election of Senators &c. If this be so, the Legislature will be *tied* on joint ballot.

James K. Polk

P.S. After conferring *confidentially*, with *Genl. Anderson, Dr. Ramsey & Arthur Crozier*, I shall be pleased to hear from you, at your earliest convenience in reference to the judgship. J.K.P.

ALS. NHi. Addressed to Knoxville and marked "*Private & confidential.*"

1. Samuel Powel, judge of the First Judicial Circuit, died on August 2, 1841.

2. A lawyer, John Kennedy earlier had served two terms in the Tennessee House, 1803–7, and sat two terms in the Senate, 1807–9 and 1811–13. On August 9, 1841, Kennedy applied for an appointment as judge of the First Circuit. ALS. DLC–JKP.

3. On August 21, 1841, Polk wrote to Robert M. Anderson, requesting him to meet Powel's court in the First Judicial Circuit until the General Assembly could meet and elect a judge. ALS, copy. T–Governor's Papers, JKP Letterbook. On August 28, 1841, Anderson replied that a heavy court schedule and debilitating health would prevent his complying with Polk's request. ALS. DLC–JKP.

4. On September 6, 1841, Reynolds stated in reply to Polk's inquiry concerning the appointment of Kennedy, "I do not think he would do at all."

Reynolds informed Polk that "Robt. J. McKinney Esqr of Greenville would be the most popular appointment that could be made." ALS. DLC–JKP.

5. In an editorial in the Knoxville *Argus* of August 11, 1841, E. G. Eastman upheld the principles of the Democracy and praised Polk's exertions in the late election. The title of the editorial, "Flag Nailed to the Mast," was probably a variant of the quotation, "Stood for his country's glory fast, And nail'd her colors to the mast!" Sir Walter Scott, *Marmion*, canto I, introduction. See Alexander O. Anderson to Polk, August 20, 1841.

6. A tear in the manuscript here and one line below has obliterated parts of at least two words.

7. Henry H. Marable, a Humphreys County physician and farmer, won election to a single term in the Tennessee House in 1841. In 1865, Marable returned to that body for a year as a member of the Reconstruction General Assembly.

FROM ALEXANDER O. ANDERSON

My Dear Sir At Home Near Knoxville Augt 20th 1841

By reference to the 1st number of the Argus, after the election you will find the *"flag nailed to the mast,"*[1] and the Democracy cheered on. So in the next paper the leading Article headed "Democracy—the progress of the Revolution" &c.[2] These articles I hastily prepared to keep up the tone of our Party, & will have another for the next. I mention this for two reasons, first that you may know that I feel that we are not conquered—and secondly to say that the same tone ought to be maintained in our papers, & particularly the Union.[3] I hope that a spirited conduct of all our papers will distinguish the present state of our contest. It is necessary—and will ensure success.

I was not much deceived in the election in East Tennessee. Not at all as to the Legislature. We shou'd have carried Frazier's District,[4] but that he was *without means* in certain particulars. Our friends at Nashville, considering our position here, & the value which their aid would have been, I think, to say the least, were not liberal. I have not spared myself in this contest *in any way*—and we never shall present in East Tennessee a more disciplined front than we did in this canvass, altho' in the next we will carry the majority here. I do not calculate by any rule of animal temperament at the moment. I have a perfect knowledge of the State of things here and am confident that the majority will be with us.

It is important that the next Legislature shall check-mate the Governor[5] as to the monied power—and if the nominations for the Bank[6] are acted upon separately by the respective Houses he may be counteracted.

I must congratulate you upon the honor with which you have maintained & closed this struggle, tho' defeated. I believe you are the more popular now than you were on the day of the election.

The Whigs here, and it is intimated that Jones gave origin to it, said when they supposed we wou'd have the Legislature upon joint ballot, & they the Senate, that they wou'd not permit us to hold an election for Senators, because the popular vote was with them. But this affair is reversed—and we think here, from some calculations, that the popular Vote is with us. First, if the whole had been polled we believe you wou'd have had the majority—& secondly, we believe the Senatorial district votes will be found to have cast a majority for us, fully equal to the representation of one in the Senate. If so we are entitled at least to the same right of checking them, that they claimed to check us.

I perceive that some of the Whigs wish to elect Cannon instead of Foster, & that some of our Democratic friends prefer this. I think that it is always one of the most skilful modes of weakening a Party, if you can prevent it, when it is triumphant, from putting its favorite Leaders into office—into the official Lead. Such a man, at present, would distract and humble them, from the Governor down. It is believed here that Foster, Jones & Jarnagin, agreed, or understood each other, before the election. But if there are 4 or 5 Whigs who want Cannon, they must not be indulged except upon the condition that they will give us one of the Senators. This they will do—because all the moves are now that way—I mean with a Tendency to severance amongst the Whigs. Tyler will veto the Bank Bill[7]—on three days p[. . .][8] from the 7th when it passed.—and Mr Clay will be enraged in the line of action, and this of itself will confound the Whig Counsels at our Legislature. And if they really want Cannon they will give us a Senator. This can be accomplished—and the end of it wou'd be the total prostration of the Whig Party in Tennessee, forever. This is worth turning over in the mind—and worth execution too. And the end of it all wou'd be a President of our own choice, and a Vice President from Tennessee. And we then occupy the ground to look in *advance to the position* we have, (I mean some of us) held in view, for Tennessee—hereafter. Let me hear from you.

A ANDERSON

[P.S.] We want Eastman here, to be appointed Clerk of the Federal Court. Their Clerk is Post Master.[9] Will you speak to Catron.

ALS. DLC–JKP. Addressed to Nashville.

1. See Polk to Robert B. Reynolds, August 19, 1841.

2. The editorial which appeared in the Knoxville *Argus* on August 18, 1841, was entitled "Democracy—the Progress of the Revolution—Final

Triumph Certain." Upholding the principles of the Democracy, this article called Democrats to "look forward with a determined purpose of success."

3. The *Nashville Union*.

4. Julian Frazier lost his race for a seat in the Tennessee Senate to William Williams. Frazier's senatorial district included the East Tennessee counties of Anderson, Campbell, Claiborne, Grainger, and Morgan.

5. James C. Jones.

6. The Bank of Tennessee.

7. See Aaron V. Brown to Polk, June 12 and August 8, 1841.

8. Portion of one word obliterated, probably the word *past*.

9. James W. Campbell was postmaster of Knoxville from March 1841 until January 1845.

FROM ISAAC WRIGHT[1]

Mount Pisgah, Tennessee. August 20, 1841

Wright states that Brown of Roane County favors Polk's election as U.S. Senator from the western half of the state. Wright then observes that Brown is his own choice for the East Tennessee Senate seat. Brown can give Polk the Whig vote in the East and with Democrat support can defeat any of the Whigs "hunting for office."

ALS. DLC–JKP. Addressed to Nashville.

1. An early settler of Blount County, Wright engaged in the Holston River trade and practiced medicine in the vicinity of Mount Pisgah and Louisville, Tennessee. In 1833 he published a book of cures called *Wright's Family Medicine or System of Domestic Practices*.

TO SAMUEL H. LAUGHLIN

My Dear Sir. Nashville Augt. 24th 1841

We have no *Bank veto* yet.[1] Nicholson writes under date of the 15th that there would certainly be one, and in that event he thinks there will be a blow up in the Cabinet. *Quere de hoc*.[2] I know Mr Tyler and the influences which will be brought to bear upon him, and have doubted from the beginning whether he would have the moral courage to take an independant stand upon his old principles. Whether there be a *veto* or not, the party in power have no common principles to bind them together, and every day furnishes new evidence that they must soon dissolve into their original factions.

In reference to our State affairs, the result of the late election proves beyond cavil or doubt, that had there been a full attendance at the polls we would have succeeded. I am now in the receipt of letters from my friends almost daily, expressing their unavailing regrets, that they had not known in time that it was *possible* for us to have overcome the majority cast against us in November. All now see and know, that with ordinary exertions we could have done so. So far as I am personally concerned I yield to the result cheerfully and without complaint. My motto is now as it has always been, "the will of the people be done," though it is manifest that in the late contest there has not been a full expression of that will. From the evidences before me I have not a remaining doubt, but that the State is at this moment Democratic, and still less do I doubt, that she will be overwhelmingly so before two years shall roll round. We must not cease our exertions, but on the contrary keep on our armour & continue to do battle in the cause of sound principles. I see *Eastman* of the *Knoxville Argus*, has "nailed his flag to the mast."[3] This is the proper spirit. I hope all our presses will do the same thing. Now is the time to make a lasting impression on the public mind. The ruinous course of the present Federal Administration should be boldly exposed & kept constantly before the people.

We learn from a source to be relied on, that *Dr. Marable* (the Whig Representative elect, from the Democratic Counties of Humphreys & Benton) pledged himself publickly to his constituents previous to the Election truly & faithfully to represent the *majority*. We learn further that *instructions*[4] are being gotten up, which will be signed by *two-thirds* of all the voters; and no reasonable doubt seems to be entertained, but that he will be forced to vote & act with the Democratic party in the Election of Senators &c. &c. If this be so, the parties will be equally divided in joint ballot. We have a rumour here that the Representative elect from White,[5] was supported by the body of the Democrats in that County, & may probably act with the Democratic party in the Legislature. Have you any information upon this point? Have you seen or heard from *Saml. Turney Esqr.* since the election?[6] Should *Tyler* veto, the Bank Bill, it is I think very probable, that there will be several *Tyler-Whigs*, in the Legislature. We have fortunately, the majority in the Senate, and in [that][7] body is lodged the conservative power to preven[t] mischief, even though they may be unable to affect any positive good. It is of the greatest importance that every Democratic Senator should be here at least four or five days before the meeting of the Legislature. You will I know see and appreciate the importance of this, and I hope you *will*, if you have not done so, write immediately to your colleagues of the Senate, urging its importance upon them. The failure of a single Senator to attend in time might be disastrous to us. It is important too, that the members of the House should all be here some days before the meeting. I have not had time, to write to *Ford*. You can shew him this letter, that he may see that though beaten, "my voice is still for war."[8]

JAMES K. POLK

P.S. Wm. G. Childress Esqr. will be a candidate for the Principal Clerkship of the Senate. Without designing to interfere as between friends: I think you could not have a better man. *Hogan* of the Times[9] would make an excellent assistant. I throw out these suggestions for your consideration. J.K.P.

ALS. MH. Addressed to McMinnville and marked "*Private*." AE on the cover states that this letter was answered by Laughlin on September 1, 1841.

1. See Aaron V. Brown to Polk, June 12 and August 8, 1841, and A. O. P. Nicholson to Polk, August 15, 1841.

2. Latin phrase meaning "ask about this," or "look into this."

3. See Polk to Robert B. Reynolds, August 19, 1841, and Alexander O. Anderson to Polk, August 20, 1841.

4. On August 26, 1841, Jonathan P. Hardwicke wrote that the Whigs "have sent a deputy to confer with Marable upon the subject of his pledges and says he will be d—d if he do'nt stand up to them if properly instructed, but flatters himself no Instructions will be given." ALS. DLC–JKP.

5. John England, a White County farmer and horse-breeder, served a single term as a Whig in the Tennessee House, 1841–43.

6. Polk received several letters indicating he might be supported by England and Samuel Turney. On August 24, 1841, H. D. Rogers wrote that England "has pledged himself to vote for you," for Senator. ALS. DLC–JKP. Three days later, on August 27, 1841, Alvin Cullom also wrote that England would vote for Polk. ALS. DLC–JKP. Finally, on August 30, 1841, Robert A. Campbell wrote that Polk was England and Turney's first choice. ALS. DLC–JKP.

7. Manuscript mutilated here and one line below.

8. Quotation from Joseph Addison, *Cato*, act 2, scene 1.

9. Thomas Hogan was editor of the Murfreesboro *Weekly Times*.

FROM HOPKINS L. TURNEY

Dear Sir Washington Aug. the 24th 1841

I this day received yours of the 15th of this month[1] giving me the result of the Tennessee elections, and I am free to confess that you have made a much better run than I thought was possible for any man to make under the circumstances, and I now agree with you that we can and will carry the State two years hence. But the question now is how to elect democratick Senators, or at least how to elect one of each party makeing you one of them. Johnson says he will attend to that man in his district.[2] S. Turney will vote for the democrats. No mistake. I know all about him and the supposed pledge, and I have a verry Strong hope that England will go with him, and I have reason to believe that he made private pledges to that effect before the election.[3] His feelings I believe are with us. He I think voted for you and for myself in our late elections, however I will do all I can, and will this knight write to my brother on the subject, suggesting and urging him to Secure his vote if possible.

I saw Tyler this morning. His whig friends has or will abandon him at the close of the present session, and will openly denounce him. He will dismiss his cabinett, &c. His feelings are with us and [he] desires to know if there are no States wrights whigs elected to our legislature and who can be made to unite with us. He would give us any aid in his power. I fear however he can do us no good. Wise will write to Jennings and Peyton,[4] but I know not the effect it will have. There will be no other removals made in Tennessee, and in future democrats will be appointed. There will be no bank, but a second veto of a charter by the President. I yet hope that all will turnout for the best.

H. L. TURNEY

ALS. DLC–JKP. Addressed to Nashville.

1. Letter not found.

2. Reference is to Henry H. Marable. See Polk to Cave Johnson, September 21, 1841.

3. See Polk to Samuel H. Laughlin, August 24, 1841.

4. John H. Peyton, a Sumner County physician and Whig, served one term in the Tennessee Senate, 1841–43, before winning election to a single term in the U.S. House in 1843.

FROM J. G. M. RAMSEY

My Dear Sir Mecklenburg T. Aug. 25. 1841

Contrary to our wishes but certainly not to any just ground of expectation the election has terminated in favor of Mr. Jones. The triumph is yours. Your vote is more than we could have rationally calculated from the posture of things—& the nature of the ground on which the late battle was fought. Every thing was against you. The note of triumph had scarcely sounded in our ears last Nov. when flushed with their recent victory the Federal party throughout the U.S. & especially in Tennessee marked you for its next victim. The trumpeters were abroad. The tocsin was sounded. The people weary with agitation & desirous of repose were summoned again to the contest. Fresh excitants were added to the gross delusions so successfully practised last year. The avalanche of feeling that had hurried them away was kept in motion.

Lights not less illusory & deceptive than those that mislead & deceived during the Tippecanoe excitement were still held out by your opponents & it is matter of boasting to your friends that under all these circumstances formidable & disheartening as they were you have been able to diminish the Whig vote 4000. I repeat it, the victory is yours. You have not crouched to power—you have not sacrificed an iota of principle—but with a lofty moral courage you have spurned a compromise with venality & corruption & defied the influences of office & station. Could the Democracy of Tennessee have believed it in the range of possibility—it would have placed you again in the Executive chair. As it is the admiration of your friends for your briliant services especially in the late campaign remains unabated—continues to increase. I have just returned from a visit to the upper counties. An admirable spirit prevails in our ranks. We feel assured that a revolution has commenced & knowing that revolutions never go backward we are harnassed again, already for another fight. Democracy must again be in the ascendant & you either upon the *same* theatre or a *higher* must be our leader. The Whigs crow not over their success—another such will anihilate them. The "Post"[1] you see is driving Wester[2] into our ranks. In some questions he will be available to us—impracticable to them. A majority of his voters was clearly Democratic. He knows it to be so & acknowledges it—Pate[3] tho elected by a majority of Whigs clearly owes his election to us. At this precinct he got not only the same number of votes with you but the identical voters themselves. He will never offer again & will therefore act independently. The first choice of both is Williams for Senator & after that I think they will act as they please. Ought not the Legislature to give us at least one Senator & let the Districts remain as they are? It is said Cannon is to run as well as Foster. We feel disposed to prevent the election of Foster—on the same principle that we went against Humes & Graves. They sung Tipecanoe songs—& F. set the woods on fire. Are we right? Some of your friends say you ought to go to the Senate—& that it will subserve our wishes 3 years hence. I still believe Providence will come to the deliverance of Tennessee (in other words that we will have a majority)—as it did signally interpose to deliver the U.S. from Harrison's reign. While I write I hear the cannon in Knoxville. I know what it means. A hot Whig just passed my door who brings news from town that T. has vetoed the Bank. He lives in Jefferson County & I asked him what "Little Massachusetts"[4] would think of the veto. He said it will kill us dead as a door nail. We spoke yesterday in town of meeting to approve the veto if T. gave it. I have not seen the veto but if he takes the proper ground—it may be right for us while *we distinctly withold our adhesion to* the present administration—its cabinet &c. &c., yet to approve of his checking *quoad hoc*[5] the Federal measures & policy of Mr. Clay & his subalterns.

Col Gadsden Prest. L.C.&C.R.R. Co.[6] writes me that he has forwarded to you the proceedings of the Co.[7]—proposing to surrender the State Bonds—on the payment by the State of $2.40 on each 100 dollars subscribed by the State—her proportion of the expense of the survey. The Legislature should appropriate at once that amount $15,600 & the interest now due & unpaid on that much of the Bonds—which Mr. Nicholl refused to pay. Good faith to a noble sister State requires it. Will this come from your message or Mr. Jones before the Legislature? Is my *official* report in your Department. I believe for I kept no copy that I explained the whole matter in the report to you from myself as the State proxy.[8] Your elasticity will not allow an apparent reverse of fortune to discourage you. Your country needs & expects higher & other services.

J. G. M. RAMSEY

P.S. I have just seen the veto. Our Whigs are in a perfect storm. They say the cabinet will resign—that you & Calhoun will be called to it—that Bell shall be made Senator. In short they are in perfect confusion. J.G.M.R.

Post scriptum et sigillatum[9]

Wester will adhere to his pledge to go first for Williams—then for Jarnagin & after that I believe will go as he pleases. How would making him Speaker operate? It will disaffect his Whig friends—conciliate himself with the Democrats—& make him go for Democratic Senators. The veto will I think influence him & others in our favor. I will see him & Pate in a day or two.

ALS. DLC–JKP. Addressed to Nashville.

1. Reference is to the Knoxville *Post.*

2. John W. Wester, a Roane County physician, served two terms as a Whig in the Tennessee House, 1841–43 and 1847–49, and sat two terms in the Senate, 1849–51 and 1861–63.

3. John F. Pate, a Knox County Whig, won election to a single term in the Tennessee House in 1841.

4. Reference is to Jefferson County, which was as staunchly Whig as the state of Massachusetts.

5. *Quoad hoc,* a Latin phrase meaning "as to this."

6. James Gadsden was president of the Louisville, Cincinnati and Charleston Railroad Company and its successor, the South Carolina Railroad Company, from 1840 until 1850. Gadsden strongly advocated construction of a southern transcontinental railroad, and his diplomatic negotiations with Mexico led to the Gadsden Purchase in 1853–54.

7. On March 11, 1841, James Gadsden wrote and enclosed the proceedings

of the L.C.&C.R.R. stockholders' meeting at Charleston "in February last." The stockholders were "forced under circumstances beyond the control of this company to suspend all operations on the Road for the present, beyond the limits of this state. . . ." ALS. T–Governor's Papers.

8. See Ramsey to Polk, October 27, 1840.

9. "Post scriptum et sigillatum," a Latin phrase meaning "written after and sealed."

FROM ALEXANDER O. ANDERSON

My Dear Sir At Home Near Knoxville Augt 30th 1841

When I reached home last night I had the pleasure to receive yours[1] acknowledging the receipt of my last.[2] The opinions you express are strictly true in regard to the recent election.[3] With the exception of the Candidates for the Legislature there were but very few of our leading men who took an active part in the Contest. I had occasion to know this, having surveyed the ground thoroughly. I must however except, to some extent, the broad Democracy south of this. I found many willing hearts & hands who, at being moved upon, readily moved themselves. I have never myself made greater efforts in all the modes essential to success.

In regard to any appointment you may be called upon to make in the place of our much lamented friend Judge Powel having been requested by you to give you my advice *confidentially,* I shall do it in the spirit of frankness as an attached friend. In reference to the Gentleman of whom you speak[4] I entertain the kindest feelings, but whether it wou'd not be in your case too specially marked to pass beyond the limits of the Circuit,[5] without good cause existing as to the character of the Bar, is worthy your grave consideration. I shou'd be extremely gratified to see that Gentleman placed in that position, but if it is done it must be at your responsibility to such an extent as is scarcely justified by the very temporary tenure of the Appointment. It certainly wou'd not strengthen him in a poll before the Legislature—and to that he might more successfully appeal without having had such an Appointment. As to yourself—(a matter to be looked to as connected with our public affairs)—I fear it wou'd do you mischief at a future day. Your position at this moment is most advantagious before the American Public—but it is specially desirable that it shou'd be maintained in the admirable relations you now sustain to the state. The latter is auxilliary to the former, in connection with the favorable & very strong impression your presence at Washington made upon our public men generally. In this view, the question recurs, ought you to jeopardize your present vantage ground in East Tennessee? For it is here that you have recently had to struggle against the effect of your presence in the late Presidential election. That is now obliterated forever—& you *are this day stronger* in East Tennessee than you have ever been. I fear this appointment wou'd give cause for one of those *humbugs* at which the Whigs have shewn themselves such perfect masters. I presume but one or two courts wou'd be held until the Legislature cou'd supply the vacancy, & it is probable your safest plan might be to confine yourself to the Circuit. I suppose this has been the practice—and if so the burthen of choosing from amongst them is by no means inconsiderable. If you have any inquiry to make upon the subject touching any of these I will answer it, at any time, with pleasure.

I am exceedingly anxious that we shou'd preserve our power in the State *as you perceive that at Washington things will take such a direction, if the Democrats are wise & conciliatory,* as will sever forever, the Whig forces. Our position here then, from this very moment until the next three years is highly important. The Union in Nashville shou'd hold up Mr. Tylers hand manfully—& while it is being done, *sprinkle no cold water in his face.* You may rely upon it, say my confidential correspondents at Washington, that Mr. Bell, Mr. Crittenden, & Mr. Ewing go out of Office by the commencement of the next session, or soon after—& Mr. Webster will have in the end to go. Mr. Tyler is anxious to get clear of them all—Grainger & crew. And I am informed that the most *extraordinary* efforts *& means were* [made] use of upon Mr. Tyler to force him to sign the Bk Bill—such as have never been made before upon any President. But to his lasting honor he has resisted them. In Athens they threaten to burn him in effigee.

I will not neglect to attend to the matter as to our Senators & other members passing early to Nashville. I will urge it immediately.

You did not answer me very definitely as to some parts of my letter. Was my conjecture as to Cannon right, as far as the Democrats are concerned? If so, in the present confused condition of the Whig Party the move I suggested wou'd be a master stroke of policy. It wou'd destroy them forever—& send the greetings of political death to meet Mr. Bell as he retires, wrathy & dismayed from the War office. This must be thought of, and our Senate must on *no slight ground* consent to an election.

A ANDERSON

P.S. Burn this letter when read &c.

ALS. DLC–JKP. Probably addressed to Nashville. Marked "*Private & Confidential.*"

1. Letter not found.

2. See Alexander O. Anderson to Polk, August 20, 1841.

3. For Polk's views on the recent election, see Polk to Robert B. Reynolds, August 19, 1841, and Polk to Samuel H. Laughlin, August 24, 1841.

4. Reference probably is to John Kennedy. See Polk to Robert B. Reynolds, August 19, 1841.

5. John Kennedy resided in Polk County, which was not part of the First Judicial Circuit.

TO ELIJAH BODDIE, ET AL.[1]

Gentlemen: Nashville, August 31st 1841

It is with no ordinary pleasure I assure you, that I acknowledge the receipt of the kind invitation of the Republican citizens of the County of Sumner,[2] which in their behalf you have done me the honour to convey to me, to partake with them of a public dinner. For the terms in which they have been pleased to express their approbation of my public course, as contained in the proceedings of their public meeting held at Gallatin on the 23rd Instant, a copy of which accompanies your letter, I am deeply grateful. At no former period of my public life could such a testimonial of respect, voluntarily emanating from the body of my Fellow-citizens have been more highly valued. For near twenty years, it has been my fortune to have been in the service of the people. During that period, I have borne an humble part, in most, if not all the public questions, which have agitated and divided the country. It has been my constant aim to promote and advance the public interest, and thereby to deserve the public approbation. In taking a retrospect of the past, I have seen no sufficient reason to convince me of error, or to change the political principles, upon which I set out in public life, and which have uniformly guided me in my course. To have been consistent in maintaining these principles, unchanged (unless convinced of error) was a duty which as an honest man, I owed to myself, as well as to those whose public servant I was.

I concur fully in the sentiment expressed by the meeting of Republicans in Sumner, that "a majority of the people of Tennessee are Republicans, that they will not long be found in the leading strings of their political enemies," who by an artful and cautious concealment of their *real principles and designs,* seduced them, into their support and that the State will ere long "assume her ancient Republican position amongst her sister States." The developments of the last few months cannot fail ultimately to expose the false pretences, by which the party now in power were enabled to induce thousands of honest Republicans to yield to them their support. The ruinous course of policy of the present Federal Administration, must soon convince all Republicans, that prominent leading men of the ruling party, have only "held the word of promise to the ear,"[3] that they might deceive and betray them. That the preponderating majority of the party in power are "Federalists," acting under the "cloak of a new name," is abundantly demonstrated, not only by the composition of the Cabinet, but by the measures brought forward and advocated by them, in the Congress of the United States now in Session. That this majority have "dictated" and will continue to "dictate," the public policy, during their continuance in power, is certain. In the prophetic language of Mr Jefferson,[4]—"The Federalists must not have the passions of other men if after getting thus into the seat of power, they suffer themselves to be governed by the minority." The deceived and betrayed "minority," of Republicans, by whose aid they have been enabled to grasp the reins of Government, must soon "quit them and draw the seat from under them." It is true that all the "venal," who have obtained or hope to obtain official places, "will have become associated with them," and will add to their numbers, but the unbought masses, the body of Republicans who have for a short period been seduced into their support, must abandon them and return and cling to their ancient and long cherished principles. "The Republican branch of the Whig party," now that they are undeceived, must speedily return to the old land marks, which seperated the Federalists from the Republicans, early after the Government was organized, and thus leave the former in that minority in the country, to which they have ever been destined, when their *real principles*, have been aroused & known.[5]

Already are these divisions apparent in Congress & the country. And in the midst of the downward and consolidating tendencies of the Government, as now made manifest by the leading policy of the ruling party, one bright ray of hope is found, in the firmness and independence of the acting President in seperating himself from his advisers, in arresting one of their measures,[6] which did manifest violence to the Constitution. If he shall adhere to the lofty position he has assumed, and thus save the Country from the arrogant & corrupting power of a monied aristocracy, not dependant on the people and irresponsible to them, it may lead to the "sober second thought"[7] on other measures recently acted on, and now in progress, & it is to be hoped to a speedy return of the "Republican branch of the Whig party," to the old land marks, which seperated the Federalists from the Republicans, early after the Government was organized, and thus leave the former in that minority in the country, to which they have ever been destined, when their *real principles* have been aroused and known. In the recent political canvass in the State to which you have alluded, I could not with my convictions and opinions, give to the leading measures of the present administration my support. To have done so would have been to renounce and abandon, all the leading political principles of my life; and sooner than do this, I am free to declare, as I have often done, that I regard "a private station as the post of honour."[8] It is gratifying to perceive that the recent demonstrations of public sentiment at Washington & in many parts of the Union give assurance, that the days of their ascendancy and power are numbered, and will in all human probability be limited to a single Presidential term. We should take fresh courage at the brightening prospect before us. We should not cease our exertions, but on the contrary keep on our armour & continue to do battle in the cause of sound principles.

In accepting the invitation which you have tendered, I have to return to yourselves, and the citizens in whose behalf you act, my acknowledgements for the honour done me, and to add that Saturday the 11th of September, the day suggested in the personal interview, which I had the honour to have with you at the time it was delivered, will be a day, on which it will give me sincere pleasure to meet my Fellow-Citizens of Sumner at Gallatin.

James K. Polk

ALS, draft. DLC–JKP. Addressed to Gallatin and marked *"Copy."*

1. Polk's letter is addressed to Boddie and ten other Sumner County citizens.

2. On August 25, 1841, Elijah Boddie and a ten-member committee of Sumner County Republicans invited Polk to a public dinner to be given in his honor at Gallatin. LS. DLC–JKP.

3. Variant quotation of William Shakespeare, *Macbeth,* act 5, scene 7, line 48.

4. Quotation not identified further.

5. Here Polk deleted twelve lines, the substance of which he included in the paragraph following.

6. Reference is to John Tyler's veto of the Fiscal Bank bill on August 16, 1841.

7. Variant quotation from a 1788 speech by Fisher Ames, who said, "I consider biennial elections as a security that the sober, second thought of the people shall be law."

8. Variant quotation of Joseph Addison, *Cato,* act 1, scene 4.

FROM SACKFIELD MACLIN

Seclusa Near LaGrange Tennessee
August 31st 1841

My dear Sir,

Yours of the 19th and 24th inst. was duly recd.,[1] and would have had a much earlier acknowledgment had I not been absent from home.

The leading Whigs in this division of the state upon the reception of the veto message[2] seemed perfectly astonished—as much disconcerted, as a maiden girl of fourteen would be, by being caught in the most awkward predicament immaginable by her lover. They stamp and swell, and declare, that they wished Tyler had died before he signed the message. Some declare, that they are willing to take their guns, and go to Washington and dislodge Tyler. In sober truth, I have never witnessed as much dissatisfaction before in relation to the action of the government. This is confined however, to town politicians and desperate partisans. Among the great mass of the people in the country there is no excitement—for left to their own unbiased judgments, nine out of ten are opposed to the Bank of the United States. In fact, all those great questions of *plunder* and *power* now advocated by Clay and his party in Congress have alarmed to a considerable extent the honest of all parties. Many of those who voted against you and myself at the last election, told me, that they were satisfied something was wrong at Washington, but they would vote the Whig ticket this time.

I must bear testimony also to the fact, that it was the unpardonable apathy of our friends that produced the late result. It was carried to such an extent in this senatorial district, that I had to visit them at their houses, and get them to promise that they would go to the elections. And I was told in hundreds of instances, that neither you or myself stood any chance under the sun; *and this by Democrats.* I made speeches not only in every civil district, but in every neighbourhood in the three counties[3]—and after all, hundreds of Democrats did not turn out. But they are now convinced, that the s[t]ate of Tennessee is democratic, and our friends will bring more energy in the field, in the next contest, than they have ever done. And I entertain no doubt of our success.

I will be at Nashville at least four days before the meeting of the Legislature—and I will also procure the attendance of Gardener of Dresden.[4]

I am for you going to the Senate—and unless there should be a compromise so as to give us one Senator I will be uncompromisingly opposed to going into the election during the session. *I can bear my part of the responsibility*—provided the constitution does not command absolutely to go into the election which I think it does not.

One of the last speeches Douglass made during the canvass, he declared his opposition to a bank charter that authorised Foreners to hold stock—and that would force branc[h]es into the states without their consent. If he upon calculation conclude, that it would be to his interest to go for Tyler, he will do so, and not otherwise. I have no great confidence in his political principles. Douglass will calculate on being made Speaker of the House of Representatives. *This must not be done;* we must not give him more character than he has already got—for either Coe or myself will have him to beat for congress. If Coes health will allow it he will have to run against him—and he is very hard to beat.

I will write you again in a few days who to appoint Director in the Railroad Company in place of James Trezevant.[5]

SACKFIELD MACLIN

ALS. DLC–JKP. Addressed to Nashville.

1. Letters not found.

2. Reference is to John Tyler's veto of the Fiscal Bank bill, August 16, 1841.

3. Reference is to Fayette, Hardeman, and Shelby counties.

4. John A. Gardner, a Weakley County lawyer, served three terms as a Democrat in the Tennessee Senate, 1841–47, and sat a single term in the House, 1879–81.

5. Trezevant was appointed a director on behalf of the state in the La Grange and Memphis Railroad Company on January 26, 1841. On July 5, 1841, he tendered Polk his resignation for reasons of ill health. ALS. T–Governor's Papers. AE on the cover of this letter states that Polk appointed Seth Wallard in Trezevant's place on September 25, 1841.

FROM JULIUS W. BLACKWELL

Dear Sir, Athens Ten. Sept. 1st 1841

Yours of the 21st ulto.[1] was recd. last night. I agree with you that, the cause of our defeat has been throug the neglect of the Democrats to go to the poles. Most of our leading friends were negligent, and inactive, believeing your chance was hopeless. I did not, myself, dispair, but I had at times, doubts which I could not resist.

My defeat was caused in may last, by Gen. Stone continueing on the tract. The Whigs every where, were singing out—"Blackwells election is certain, it is not worth while to strugle, Campbell cannot possibly be elected." This they said *publickly*—while at the same time, they sent *secretly*, ageants all over the District to urge the Whigs out. It is very certain that Stone got as many Democratic votes as Whig votes, and now, there is upwards of 400 ma[jo]rity for you in this Dist. By a comparison of others on our side, the average majority is over 400.

I am sorry to inform you that the Courier Printing Office will go down, and that shortly. Eastman has made propositions to Williams which he is about to accept.[2] But few of the Democrats are able to pay out money to sustain the paper, and the few that are able, are not willing. As to myself, I am utterly prostrated and at this time entirely out of business, and scarcely able to support my family, as all my debts—or nearly all, are given up to my creditors. My enemies commenced on me soon after my election in 1839, and did not cease untill they broke me up. I have never as yet, been sued by a Democrat. Had I been elected to this Congress, I could have held up. They the Whigs have accomplished two things which they most earnestly desired; that is, they have broke me *up* in my private business, and have broke me *down* as a politition for the present. They have, however, learned one thing, and that is, whether they break me *up* or *down* they cannot cause me to flag and faulter in my political energy, while I have a tongue to wag, or a hand to hold a pen; and I flatter myself that I have done some good to the cause since my defeat. I have wrode, I have spoken and I have written on suitable occasions. Mr. Williams has no Editor and, I have had to scribble for the Courier, altho I am utterly incompetent to the task, as I never received more than an A.B.C. education. During the summers campaign, I took several trips to Hamilton, Bradley and Polk, and thus I became thoroughly convinced, that I was defeated in my election, not by the strength of the Whigs, but by the neglect of the Democrats to turn out and vote.

Notwithstanding the backwardness in our friends to spend their money to desiminate their principles, yet they are wide awake, and in admirable spirits, and confident in the belief, that the star of Democracy is rising higher, and shining brighter every day. The Democrats feel a small degree of hope that, J. K. Polk may be elected to the U.S. Senate. They also feel a simpathy for Nicholson, but believe that he will cheerfully give way, and that some Whig may possible be induced to vote for you as Senator, that would not vote for Nicholson. If by any luckey turn, you could be elected Senator, the Democrats would feel that they had gained at least two thirds of the victory. Rowles has sustained the Democratic cause most nobly. Though thought by the Whigs to be unpopular, he has proved to all, that he has talents to carry him through, in peace or in War. The Whigs here have almost gone mad on the Bank question. The veto has almost vetoed some of them. I see the Madisonian & Intelligencer[3] are quarreling; Clay & Archer of Va. are quarreling; Wise and Adams are quarreling; Wise and Nisbet of Ga. are quarreling.[4] "Those whom the Gods intend to distroy, they first make mad."[5] Give the mongrel party rope, and they will hang each other. The bank question however, will have to be fought over again in 1843. When striped of log cabins and hard cider; gourds and red pepper; moonshine and live Bears, I am willing to meet the question, either as a candidate, or as a voter. I will comply with your request and try to see the gentlemen you named. I would take great pleasure in paying a visit to

Nashville, but it will be almost impossible to "raise the wind." The times in this section of the State, are truly distressing, money is very scarce, and the people complainin of the Whigs for not redeeming their promises. I must close this lenghey epistle, as I know you will be worried in reading.

J. W. BLACKWELL

P.S. I should have writen to you and sent to Kingston, as requested by Doctr. Jordan, but did not get the news of the votes even in this Co. untill late in the evening of friday after the election, and from the adjoining counties untill nearly night. On Saturday morning I left home for Jefferson Co. and was absent from home nearly two weeks or I would have written to you at Nashville. J.W.B.

ALS. DLC–JKP. Addressed to Nashville.

1. Letter not found.

2. Williams had been associated with the Athens *Courier* since 1839; he is not identified further. E. G. Eastman's propositions for the *Courier* are not identified further.

3. The Washington *Madisonian* and the Washington *National Intelligencer*.

4. Reference is to in-fighting among various leaders of the Whig Party, including Henry Clay, William S. Archer, Henry A. Wise, John Q. Adams, and Eugenius A. Nisbet. A Morgan County, Georgia, lawyer, Nisbet served several terms in the state legislature before winning election as a Whig to the U.S. House, where he served from 1839 until his resignation in October 1841. He subsequently sat as an associate justice on the Georgia Supreme Court, 1845–53.

5. Probably a variant of the quotation: "Whom the gods destroy, they first make mad," attributed by James Boswell, *Life of Johnson* (1783), to Euripedes, *Fragment*.

FROM ISAAC H. DISMUKES

Dear sir. Oakachickima P.[1] September the 1 1841

I wil once more endeaver to write you a fiew lines that you may hear from us. Wea are all well at the preasent time hopeing that thes fiew lines may finde you and your family well. I have nuthing of consequence to write to you. I am now goen own geatherin of the crop. I think that I shall make corn anuff to doo the fairm another year. I shall make as much or more, I think than was made hear last year and my cotten crop cant bea beaten by the neighbourhood. Adderson and gilburt got hear a fiew dais since.[2] Gilburt left mea a bout the last of july that you new nuthing of. Hea got to tennessee the day that the doctor[3] ware about starteing of Adderson and hea stade there three dais and was sent back with adderson and when hea got hear hea stade hear too nightes and one day and hea left again without one lik or a short word. The ware not sent according to your request. I should of whip them as soon as the landed had it not of bin your request that mr bobit[4] should bin preasant though I think that if I had of taken them and of whip them as soon as the got hear that gilburt would not of run away again soon which I should of dun if I had not thought that you would of thought that I would of whip them too much though that is what I neaver have dun since I have bin dooing of bisness and it is what I would not doo as to disenable them from work one our. My fealinges would not suffer mea to gone as fair as that. You ware complaining in your letter to mr bobit[5] of my not writing to you though I have written to you the first or the second day of eavry month since hear I bin and started the letter to the post office. Wheather Charles carrid them or noe I am not able to say. I doant expect hea did though, had [he] you would of got them. I wrote to you about the thinges that I got from new orleans I got. The thinges [for] the mill I have not got nor heard of since mr. pearse left here.[6] Mr lea[7] has taken a gin and sum other thinges from mempris and wea cannot join in sending up as the understanding ware batwean you and him: I wrote you word that I neaded a new waggon hear and that soon you could send a waggon down the rivver to memffris. I could then send for the waggon and mill bourth at the same time.

Clothing for the negrows wea hav anuff with the exception of a fiew yardes which mr bobit sas his wife wil furnish on the best turms. I wil just say to you that I learn hear a from the negroes that gilburt should say that doctor Colwell wantes to buy him and I expect that hea is gone back to him again but doo not sell him, if you whish to brake them from running away for they had reather bea sould twice than to bea whip once. If hea getes back thane have him iron and send him to mea if you please. I wil not inger him by whiping him. I beleave that they balieve that tennessee is a place of parridise and the all want to gow back to tennessee. So stop them by ironing them and send them back again and they wil soon stop cumming to tennessee.[8]

ISAAC DISMUKES

ALS. DLC–JKP. Addressed to Nashville. Published in Bassett, *Plantation Overseer*, 157–59.

1. Oakachickama Post Office, Mississippi.
2. See Silas M. Caldwell to Polk, July 23, 1841.
3. Reference is to Silas M. Caldwell.
4. Reference is to William Bobbitt.
5. Letter not found.

6. On November 10, 1840, John Pearce, Jr., wrote that he had shipped the mill to Memphis on October 7. Pearce wished Polk to forward a draft for $175 to Memphis. ALS. DLC–JKP.

7. John T. Leigh.

8. Polk probably agreed to the correction of his runaway slaves, for William Bobbitt wrote on August 29, 1841, that he approved of Polk's "determination to put a stop to it, by making examples of the offenders in every instance, that is by correcting instead of selling." ALS. DLC–JKP.

FROM SAMUEL H. LAUGHLIN

My dear Sir, McMinnville, Sept 1, 1841

I have been absent at Van Buren Court, and at Bersheba Springs with our friend Long who is unwell, about ten days, and on returning to this place late last night, found your letter of the 24th ultimo, in the post office. I have not time to reply to it in detail, but will say, that the Democracy of this District are undismayed by the mortification we all feel at your defeat—and are determined to prosecute the war with new vigor. For one, I feel confident of our being able in the approaching Genl. Assembly, to elect you to the Senate of the U.S. I have it from Farmer Dibrell's mouth, that England of White is pledged not to vote for any man, Whig or democrat, against you—that he is for you, owing his election to his personal friends among the Whigs of White, and to the unanimous support of our growing party in that county. In addition, I have had a sure friend at work on him, fastening and securing him to his promise.

I have seen Sam Turney. He considers England's vote sure.[1] Therefore, let Marable be pressed with instructions,[2] and the day is our own, and instead of being beaten, we will triumph. I have heretofore said to both Anderson and Nicholson, that your claims are paramount to all others, regardless of locality of residence. Now will be the time to test the sincerity of friends—and who are your true friends, and who are your friends as a means of helping themselves. The test will show the difference between cold blooded and warm blooded men; and I am glad such an occasion has arisen, though I regret deeply the cause which has produced it.

Make my respects to Mrs. Polk, and assure her that it was a true saying of a certain Roman Consul more than two thousand years ago, that a wife never gives up the ship where her husband or his friends are concerned.

S. H. LAUGHLIN

ALS. DLC–JKP. Addressed to Nashville and marked "Private."

1. See Polk to Samuel H. Laughlin, August 24, 1841, and H. L. Turney to Polk, August 24, 1841.

2. See Polk to Samuel H. Laughlin, August 24, 1841.

TO SAMUEL H. LAUGHLIN

My Dear Sir Nashville Sept. 2nd 1841

I will take a *Public Dinner* at Gallatin in Sumner on Saturday the 11th Instant,[1] when I should be much pleased to meet you. Can you not be there, and bring with you your Representatives, *Hopkins & Hill?* It is intended I understand to be a *great affair*, and will be the occasion of "putting the ball in motion," and signifying to the public, that we have still our armour on & intend to continue to do battle in the cause of sound principles. *B. Martin* and *Col. Dew* of Maury, *Hardwicke* of Dickson and probably several other Democratic members of the Legislature are expected to be there.

The *Whigs* here are becoming exceedingly alarmed about the Legislature, and particularly so, in reference to the course which rumour has said [the] Representative from *White* will take.[2] All their power and influence will be put in motion in that direction. Yourself and other friends in your quarter must look to it. *Marable* we understand will be, if he has not already been, *instructed*, by not less than 300 of a majority of his constituents, and avows his intention unconditionally to *obey*. This being so, with the aid of one vote more we will have a majority on joint ballot.

The information here renders it probable, almost certain, that President Tyler, will veto the *"kite-flying fiscality,"* which has passed the Ho. Rept. & is now before the Senate.[3]

JAMES K. POLK

ALS. CU. Addressed to McMinnville and marked *"Private."* AE by Laughlin on the cover reads: "Ansd. Sept 12, second day after coming from Decatur, Meigs Co. & wrote about England, Terrell, &c. prospects."

1. See Polk to Elijah Boddie et al., August 31, 1841.

2. Reference is to the selection of U.S. senators and the vote of John England. See Polk to Samuel H. Laughlin, August 24, 1841, and Laughlin to Polk, September 1, 1841.

3. Polk's reference is to the Fiscal Corporation bill introduced in the House of Representatives on August 20, 1841, by John Sergeant and passed in that body, three days later. The Fiscal Corporation bill differed from the vetoed Fiscal Bank bill in that the proposed corporation would require a smaller capital, establish agencies in lieu of branches, and deal in bills of exchange

rather than discounts. See Aaron V. Brown to Polk, June 12, 1841. On August 24, 1841, James Buchanan remarked to the U.S. Senate that if the proposed Fiscal Corporation "had derived its name from its nature, it ought to be called *The Kite Flying Fiscality.*"

FROM GEORGE W. SMITH[1]

Dr Sir Memphis Sept 2nd 1841

When I saw you last I was certain of spending the winter with you in Nashville, but have been a little disappointed in my calculations; personally it was & is a matter of indifference. It is for the cause, for the triumph of true principles of self Government, in which I am disappointed. My election like yours went by *default.* The Democrats to my certain knowledge did not vote their strength in this county by 100 or 120 votes. I was defeated by 24 votes, and yourself by less than 100. I had thought you would have been elected. I thought Tenn still would have stood firm to your standard, *the Standard of Democracy.* In this too I have been disappointed, and was mortified that the people should have placed James C. Jones at the head of my native State. A man with whom I am intimately acquainted, and whom I know, to say *nothing* of his qualifications!!! to be perfectly devoid of *moral and political honesty.* Still, under all the circumstances, so soon after the political tornado of Harrison, the Coon & hard Cider, and our strength which did not come to the polls, I do not think *you ought to complain.* I believe it is *the proudest victory you ever achieved*—one which was won, by the display of more talent, more independence & moral courage on your part than you ever before developed to the people of your native State & the U States and one too which in after times will tell upon them as sure as there is a God in heaven! Many, many were convinced that they had been misled, yet had not the courage immediately to acknowledge it to the world. If you have confidence in me as a friend, & I know you have no better, for with my present opinions and feelings there is no office in the gift of the American people, which I would not bestow upon you, that a laudable ambition would prompt you to aspire to. I should like to know something of your future course. It is due to yourself to give to your friends some intimation at least that they may vindicate you before the public, for you are uppermost in the minds of your enemies as well as friends. If you will allow me to suggest altho' I do not know your sentiments, I do not think you ought to suffer your name to go before the

Legislature for U.S. Senator, if for no other reason the possibility of defeat I should think a sufficient one.

Though there are other reasons. The Feds slandering you, said you were running for that office, and you said you asked office *from the people.* I make these suggestions, having no fears at all upon the subject, and at the same time believing even with the present Complexion of our Legislature, the Democrats if they will manage well, can defeat the objects of the *Whigs* & elect at least one Democratic *Senator,* though I would not like to see you managed into the U.S. Senate. When you go, let it be by the force of your qualifications & the clear expression of the people.

We intend to give you a public Dinner at Memphis. I have spoken of it to some of your friends, when ever it will suit your convenience and views. Will you be so good as to intimate *to me,* some where about the time it would soot you. You have never spoken in Memphis. There are many here who have never heard you. Our Town is rapidly increasing in population, & will soon be a City, and it will take great talents & industry, owing to the Commerce of the place to keep it from being a *Bank City.*

Tylers veto[2] was received here I suppose about like it was received at Nashville & other points in the State, and I think my Dr Sir, has effectually disbanded the whig party. The old Federalists will take up Clay, but the Democrats will all come back. The Federal Leaders, The political Jugglers and Gamblers, have been playing with a marked deck of cards, and got beat at their own game. What do you think of Clays next movement, together with his Cabinet, which I think will be a Bank of deposit for the safe keeping &c of public revenue & authorised to purchase & sell Bills of *Exchange.*[3] We can repeal the thing if they establish it, though I am opposed to it from the start. Clays object will be to make it a Bank of discount hereafter. Do you think Tyler is looking to the next presidency, or will he retire to private life? The whigs will not have him, and he wont suit us—though we sustain him when he does right. If you have leisure I should be pleased to hear from you.

GEO. W. SMITH

ALS. DLC–JKP. Addressed to Nashville and marked "*Confidential.*"

1. A young Shelby County lawyer, Smith lost his bid for a seat in the Tennessee House to Adam R. Alexander in 1841.

2. Reference is to John Tyler's veto of the Fiscal Bank bill on August 16, 1841.

3. Reference is to the proposed Fiscal Corporation of the United States. See Polk to Samuel H. Laughlin, September 2, 1841.

FROM J. GEORGE HARRIS

My Dear Sir Washington Sept. 3, 1841

The speed with which I hurled on to Washington by stage prevented me from writing you before I reached here, and the two days I have been here have been more than occupied with friends from whom I could not well break away to write, thankful for time to witness the Senatorial Debates of yesterday. I have a thousand things to write, and scarcely know where to begin. I have just concluded a letter to Armstrong which contains a few current notes of the times and which may or may not be worth your examination.

Our friends here consider that the contest from which we have just emerged in Tenn. has resulted in a signal victory to our arms, and every body seems to be at prayer that *straight work* may be made of electing two demo. Senators.

Never were partisan leaders so much dismayed as they are at Washington *now*. I heard it as the saying of a *whig* yesterday, "The Lord took our president—the demos have taken our Vice President—and the Devil will take our party."[1] Well said, (thought I) for a whig. Divine Justice is working out its legitimate ends in its dealings with whiggery. There are ten thousand rumors about. The rumors that the Cabinet was to break up, that you was to be offered the War Office, that Bailie Peyton, now here, was to be offered it, &c. &c. are rife but I cannot say reliable. Indeed one member, at this moment scarcely knows what is the opinion of the man that sits next [to] him. That Ty will give a second veto,[2] and mayhap (not probable) a *third* (say the Land Bill), is reduced almost to a certainty.[3] In that case what course will demo members take? What course will whig members take? What will be popular sentiment? Calhoun says "he shall not want my support"—speech yesterday. Buchanan eulogises, and says such a course will command his sanction & support. Such indeed seems to be the tone of leading Senators. Clay says if he vetoes the second, he will be a "traitor to his party"—yet he qualifies the saying away on being *triced* up by Rives. A stormy day yesterday—more stormy will be to-day.

I am told that Wise has a powerful influence with the President. Some say that he is *the* power behind the Throne. He is evidently anti-Clay, and I am told that he confers with democrats exclusively. Turney is said to be thick with him.

It is a matter of doubt & speculation whether if the Cabinet breaks up the new one will be made up of moderate whigs or democrats. Indeed, there seems to [be] a thick cloud of mystery over coming events which I am satisfied no man, not even Tyler himself, can see through.

I have not time to write a letter to the Union. Mr. Nicholson has done so, and will continue until my return. Give my respects to all, and especially to Bro: Hogan who I perceive is doing good duty at my post. I will reserve the remainder of this page for to-night.

Evening. The Fiscality passed the Senate this aft. All the whigs voting for it, except Rives. *Veto* sure.[4] I will write you again in a day or two.

J GEO HARRIS

ALS. DLC–JKP. Addressed to Nashville.

1. Quotation not identified further.
2. Reference is to John Tyler's veto of the Fiscal Corporation bill, which was returned to Congress on September 9, 1841. See Polk to Samuel H. Laughlin, September 2, 1841.
3. See A. O. P. Nicholson to Polk, June 14, 1841, and Cave Johnson to Polk, July 17, 1841. John Tyler signed the distribution bill on September 4, 1841.
4. Reference is to the passage of the Fiscal Corporation bill in the Senate on September 3, 1841.

FROM ANN S. JOHNSON[1]

Sir: Columbia Tennessee Sept. the 7th 1841

I have been informed that it is your intention to return to Columbia. I desire therefore to know whether you will wish to occupy your dwelling-house[2] and if so at what time you will want me to remove. If you will rent the house I will engage it for the ensuing year on the same terms that I have this. Be pleased to give me information on these matters as early as possible, in order that I may know how to make my arrangements. I have an opportunity of shortly obtaining a house but do not wish to remove if I can remain here.

ANN S. JOHNSON

ALS. DLC–JKP. Addressed to Nashville. AE on the cover states that this letter was answered on September 15, 1841; Polk's reply has not been found.

1. Ann Street Johnson, a widow, married John P. Spindle, a physician, in 1845 and resided in Columbia until her death in 1894.
2. See Nathan Vaught to Polk, September 10, 1841.

FROM A. O. P. NICHOLSON

My Dear Sir: Washington City Sept 7th 1841

The new Fiscal Corporation has been three days in the hands of "Capt Tyler"[1] and it is supposed will continue there for one or two days more. It will be returned with a veto[2]—so say all sides—but we are very apprehensive that it will be such a veto as will be entirely unsatisfactory to democracy. We have some intimations that it will be a suit of half & half, wishy washy, affair, to which the Whigs will accede, and on which his cabinet may be retained.[3] This is now the fear rather than the impression of our friends. I write that you may not expect too much of Mr. Tyler. The Whigs are making great efforts to compromise with him.

A O P Nicholson

P.S. I think we will adjourn by the 13th inst.

ALS. DLC–JKP. Addressed to Nashville.

1. Captain John Tyler's company, organized in 1813 for the defense of Richmond, saw no active combat in the War of 1812. Some Tyler detractors used the president's military title as a sarcasm.

2. See Polk to Samuel H. Laughlin, September 2, 1841.

3. On September 11, 1841, all members of Tyler's cabinet, except Webster, resigned in protest to the president's veto of the Fiscal Corporation bill.

FROM WILLIAM H. POLK

Columbia, Tennessee. September 7, 1841

William acknowledges receipt of Polk's letter of September 3, 1841.[1] Boling Gordon has agreed to visit Perry County and inquire of Graham what course he may take in the election of U.S. Senators.[2] William suggests that voting instructions to Marable be kept secret; otherwise the Whigs may counteract such efforts by instructing Turney and Hembree.

ALS. DLC–JKP. Addressed to Nashville.

1. Letter not found.

2. Charles Graham represented Perry County as a Whig in the Tennessee House, 1839–43. See Alexander O. Anderson to Polk, August 20, 1841; Polk to Samuel H. Laughlin, August 24 and September 2, 1841; Laughlin to Polk, September 1, 1841; Hopkins L. Turney to Polk, August 24, 1841; and Sackfield Maclin to Polk, August 31, 1841.

FROM BROMFIELD L. RIDLEY

Livingston, Tennessee. September 7, 1841

Ridley has interviewed John England, representative-elect from White County, and has received assurances of his support for Polk for U.S. Senator.[1] Contrary to rumor, Ridley doubts that Sherrell[2] has declared for Polk and asks on what basis fellow Democrats calculate the support of the member from Benton and Humphreys counties.[3]

ALS. DLC–JKP. Addressed to Nashville.

1. See William H. Polk to Polk, September 7, 1841.
2. Cravens Sherrell, a farmer, represented Bledsoe County as a Whig in the Tennessee House, 1841–45 and 1851–53.
3. Henry H. Marable.

FROM NATHAN VAUGHT[1]

Columbia, Tennessee. September 10, 1841

Vaught states that he is prepared to begin the renovation of Polk's house in Columbia, if Polk has decided to make the improvement.[2] Vaught encloses a draft of the proposed work and offers advice about style and materials. He asks Polk to determine quickly what is to be done, so that the buildings may be closed before bad weather commences.

ALS. DLC–JKP. Addressed to Nashville.

1. Vaught, a Columbia carpenter, began the practice of his trade in 1810.
2. See Ann S. Johnson to Polk, September 7, 1841.

FROM SAMUEL H. LAUGHLIN

My dear Sir, McMinnville, September 12, 1841

Evening before last, at night, I returned home from Decatur, Meigs Co. and found yours of the 2nd. instant in the Post office, marked on the back *missent*, without explanation of when or where. It ought to have been here about the time I left home. I also found a letter of invitation to the Gallatin Dinner, which I am sorry I did not receive in time either to attend or forward a suitable answer to the Committee before the festival. I have no doubt it was a grand affair, as our Sumner friends never do things by halves. I have, however, been busy in another portion of the vineyard.

I have seen and conferred with Waterhouse, Rowles, Wan and Walker.[1] All things over the Mountain are working together for good. I will not go into detail, but we have *more* than a fair and equal prospect of getting Sherrell's vote.[2] The chief minister in this good work is Old Billy Wan. Waterhouse and myself have projected some of the ways and means, but Wan is the Executor. I will state a few things, leaving you to put them together as you may. Sherrell has been an indulgent sheriff, loving popularity, and is about broke. Wan has money and credit, and is his best friend. He is going to move to Missouri, where democracy abounds, and where one James K. Polk is a very popular man—as much so, perhaps, as any man in the Union, living out of the state. Sherrell wants to become popular in his new home, and is a republican at heart. He owes his present election to the unanimous vote of the democracy of Bledsoe, united with the votes of his personal friends, and he beat Terry, Bridgeman,[3] and the entire Foster and Bell whig party proper of the County. He hates them and they hate him. If he goes to Missouri, well recommended by letters, to the proper men, as the man who elected the aforesaid James K. Polk to the Senate, he is a made man at once. But apart from all these things, he hates *Jonakin*,[4] and will vote for the said Polk, if the friends of said Polk will join him and Dr. Wester in electing one Tom Williams or Tom Brown to the Senate from East Tennessee. He will be ruled by no caucus, and will come to Nashville at a late hour, in company with the said Billy Wan, and will be fixed in a mess with him. Now put all this together, and something may and will be made out of it.

Again, Mr. England of White, has expressly authorized Judge Ridley to say to you, to me, and your friends, that he will vote for you, and for no man in the State against you. He is fully to be relied on. I told you in my last,[5] that this matter was in proper train and in proper hands. Besides this, we have the chance for Marable.[6] I saw two of his constituents the other day in East Tennessee. They say he was elected on the tippling law question as a repealer,[7] and that hundreds of good democrats voted for him on that ground, and on his pledge connected with it, to vote for democratic Senator. One thing you will please observe in the matter of Sherrell and England is, that we have no hope of either of them voting for any democrat but yourself. They will not run any risks for any other man. This will test your friend Nicholson. If he does not unite [he]art,[8] hand, and soul with us, in our just [en]deavors to promote the good of the party by promoting you, I am not the only man by some twenty that will be found determined to be off from *him* at least.

A new thing under the Sun! Sam Turney intends *pollin* for Speaker. If so, the whigs may, and I doubt not will, elect him—as the price of his vote for one whig Senator as they will think, but in which I am confident they will be deceived. I hope his brother will be home and at Nashville at our meeting. Mischief must be prevented. Myself, Hill, Hopkins, Waterhouse, Rowles, Walker, Miller and Torbett[9] will be in Nashville on the Tuesday and Wednesday before the session commences; and I have written to Estill and Howard to be there also. Long has promised me to be there also. My respects to Madam, and remind her again of the saying of the Roman Consuls wife, that a lady never gives up the ship when her husband is on board.

S. H. LAUGHLIN

ALS. DLC–JKP. Addressed to Nashville and marked "Private."

1. Richard G. Waterhouse, George W. Rowles, William Wann, and James Walker of McMinn County.
2. See Bromfield L. Ridley to Polk, September 7, 1841.
3. Scott Terry and Bridgeman. Bridgeman, possibly a son of John Bridgeman, Bledsoe County member of the Tennessee House, 1819–21, is not identified further.
4. Reference is to Spencer Jarnagin.
5. See Laughlin to Polk, September 1, 1841.
6. See Polk to Robert B. Reynolds, August 19, 1841, and Polk to Samuel H. Laughlin, August 24, 1841.
7. Reference is to the repeal of Tennessee's 1838 "quart law," which prohibited the retailing of spiritous liquors in quantities of less than one quart. The "quart law" served as a ban on tippling houses or taverns.
8. A tear in the manuscript has obliterated part of this word and part of one word on the line following.
9. Hugh L. W. Hill, Thomas H. Hopkins, Richard G. Waterhouse, George W. Rowles, James Walker, John Miller, and Granville C. Torbett. A McMinn County farmer, Miller served two terms in the Tennessee House, 1829–31 and 1835–37, and sat one term in the Senate, 1841–43. A Monroe County lawyer, Torbett served one term as a Democrat in the Tennessee House, 1841–43, and sat two terms in the Senate, 1843–47. In 1852 Torbett moved to Nashville where he practiced law and published with E. G. Eastman the *Nashville American*.

FROM ADAM HUNTSMAN

Jackson, Tennessee. September 15, 1841

Huntsman informs Polk that Marable has been instructed and will vote the Democratic ticket for senators.[1] Alexander, Goodall, Standifer, Sherrell, and Graham are other Whigs who might be susceptible to Democratic influence in the senatorial contest.[2] While at court in Perry County, Huntsman will try to influence Graham. Democrats must not allow a tie vote and thereby prevent an election. Any U.S. Senator from a western state, even a Whig, ought to vote against a tariff and other "abominations" that Congress is likely to act upon soon; would not one Democrat and one Whig from Tennessee be better than no Senator at all? Anderson ought to be able to secure a vote or two from East Tennessee's Whig delegation to the legislature.

ALS. DLC–JKP. Addressed to Nashville. Published in *THQ*, VI, pp. 352–53.

1. See William H. Polk to Polk, September 7, 1841.

2. Adam R. Alexander, Isaac Goodall, William Standifer, Cravens Sherrell, and Charles Graham. Alexander, a farmer, represented Maury County in the Tennessee Senate, 1815–19; served in the U.S. House as a Federalist from Madison County, 1823–27; and represented Shelby County as a Whig in the Tennessee House, 1841–45. Goodall, also a farmer, represented Smith County as a Whig in the Tennessee House, 1837–39 and 1841–44.

FROM DAVID HUBBARD

Dear Sir Washington 17th Sept 1841

Before this can reach you, you will hear the news from your own friends having better opportunities than I of knowing correctly the tale of things here. Wise hates Clay because he Clay repudiated his Quaker Mistress (Philadelphia) and has transfered his affections to a New Paramour (New York). This is the foundation of the split in the Whig Ranks. Mr Tyler desires to profit by it & intends running for the Presidency & expects to so shape his course as to compell our party as a choice of evils to take him up.

We require or should require of him *works faithfully performed in advancing* our principles before we confide in him. I have so told him in the plainest language. His power added to our numbers could stand against and defy all opposition. Our numbers must not be added without our principles are advanced. This will hurt the feelings of many of Mr. Tylers Republican Whig friends but as the leaders are few, and high spirited men, their own self respect must induce them to submit to this concession to the multitudes, rather than to the degradation of turning back & becomeing the "whipt dogs" of their former party & finaly be cast out altogether. They *cannot* get back with honor as equals. They *will* not get back as hirelings for any little honors that Clays party from motives of policy may hereafter offer. They are *men* & men remember injuries longer than favors. They hate stronger than they love & whenever the feelings have been once trampled upon they reqire more than merely saying I wont do so again. They require attonement for injuries which they know have been wantonly inflicted. Clay & his men wont do this. They are mad & intoxicated with power & the split is therefore final.

Bell has not sold his furniture; in fact I learn [he] refused to sell expecting to come back as Senator. It is said he too hates Clay more than he hates Tyler, but that Clay forced him out by his influence upon the delegation. It must have gone hard with him to quit. Give us Tyler, Antibank, Antidistribution, Antitariff Whigs for Congress if whigs we must have. I hope however that you can send us Democrats.

David Hubbard

NB. My respects to Mrs. Polk. D.H.

ALS. DLC–JKP. Addressed to Nashville.

TO CAVE JOHNSON

[Dear Sir,] [Nashville, Tennessee] September 21, 1841

I hear from the Stage contractor (Hough)[1] that your trunk has arrived here, and that you probably left the stage at *Benton's*[2] and are now at home. If this be so, I congratulate you, upon your safe return, after your *warm* and arduous labours.

I have only time now to address you hastily upon matters requiring immediate attention. We have ascertained *with certainty*, that the Legislature will be *tied* on joint ballot, so far at least as one of the Senators is concerned without *Marable's* vote, and that his vote can decide the election for us. When I saw *Hardwicke* two weeks ago, he considered *Marable's* vote as certain as his own. He informed me that he had been *instructed* by a majority of all his *constituents*, and would *obey*, that he had so repeatedly declared, and that he (Hardwicke) had no doubt he would act with us.[3] Within a day or two a gentleman[4] who had just passed through his District and saw and conversed with him, brings information that he denies having made pledges, or that he is bound in any way to obey instructions, and considers his course doubtful. I have not conversed with the gentleman who brings the information, but learn that it may be relied on as correct. I have no doubt *Marable* has been powerfully operated upon from here, and as little doubt that the leaders here will prevent him from *obeying instructions*, if they can. These operations must be counteracted, and I know of no way, in which it can be so well done, as by getting as many of our leading friends in his District as can possibly come, to be here at the opening of the Session.[5]

Can you not have this done? It is a matter of great importance and I suggest to you, to write to them and send a messenger down m-mediately. We learn here, that the calculation is that *Bell* will return and be adopted by East Tennessee, and elected to the Senate. I have no doubt he will be here before the meeting of the Legislature.

All the Democratic members elect are expected to be here by *Tuesday* or *Wednesday* next, at which time I hope it may be in your power to be here also. Everything will depend upon harmonious action at the opening of the Session, and I know you could do much good in effecting this if you were here. Besides I wish to consult you about my message[6] and other matters. You must not fail to come up by the middle of the week, if you possibly can.

P.S. I am not sure that *Cherry* of Stuart[7] has been written to, to be here by *Tuesday* or *Wednesday*. Will you write to him? None of your colleagues have reached here from Washington.

Copy. In *THM*, I, pp. 228–29. Addressed to Clarksville and marked "*Private.*"

1. Joseph H. Hough was a Nashville stage contractor and coach builder.

2. Not identified further.

3. See Polk to Robert B. Reynolds, August 19, 1841; Polk to Samuel H. Laughlin, August 24, 1841; and Laughlin to Polk, September 12, 1841.

4. Not identified further.

5. Henry H. Marable sat in the Tennessee House for Humphreys and Benton counties. Johnson wrote Polk on September 30, 1841, that he had had no opportunity to carry out Polk's wish; however, it was the "opinion of all that I have seen that instructions *will be obeyed. I do not think so.* He talks of going to Arkansas & if so, he will probably disregard public opinion." Johnson adds that he will come to Nashville in a few days. ALS. DLC–JKP.

6. Polk transmitted his valedictory message to the Tennessee legislature on October 7, 1841. The governor reviewed in detail his administration of the state government during the previous two years. He analyzed Tennessee's banking problems and again recommended compulsory resumption of specie payments; he surveyed the state's financial investments in its internal improvement system and the construction progress thereon; and he urged reforms in the management of the Lunatic Hospital and the penal system.

7. William B. Cherry, a Stewart County farmer, was sheriff of that county, 1837–40, before serving three terms as a Democrat in the Tennessee House, 1839–45.

FROM N. S. ANDERSON[1]

Nashville, Tennessee. September 24, 1841

Acting upon instructions from the Cumberland Lodge, Anderson invites Polk to attend, with members of the legislature and other state officers, Governor Cannon's funeral sermon, which will be held at the Methodist Episcopal Church on October 3.[2]

ALS. DLC–JKP. Addressed locally.

1. Anderson was the secretary of Cumberland Lodge No. 8 of the Masonic Order.

2. Newton Cannon died in Nashville on September 16, 1841.

TO WILLIAM MOORE

My Dear Sir: Nashville Sept. 24th 1841

I desire to see you here some days before the meeting of the Legislature, if you can come, with any convenience. I desire to see you *first* in reference to matters connected with your office of Adjutant General, to which it may be proper to have reference in my message;[1] and *secondly* because your presence here at that time may do good in advancing our common cause. All the Democratic members of the Legislature are expected to be here by *tuesday* or *wednesday* next; & I hope it may be in your power to be here by *thursday* or *friday*. Every thing will depend upon harmonious action among our friends at the opening of the Session, and I am sure, if you are here you can do much good in affecting that object, by preventing collisions among friends. The Senatorial elections will probably be brought on within the first days of the Session. The rumour here is, that *Bell* will return in a few days with the expectation that he is to be adopted by *East Tennessee* & elected as her Senator. This can & must be prevented. I have written to your Senator (Ross)[2] that we will expect the delegation from "Old Lincoln" to be here early. In the expectation that I will certainly see you here, I must postpone much that I would be pleased to say to you, until we meet.

James K. Polk

ALS. T–JKP. Addressed to Mulberry P.O., Lincoln County, and marked "*Private.*"

1. See Polk to Cave Johnson, September 21, 1841.

2. Letter not found. William T. Ross, a Fayetteville criminal lawyer, served single terms as a Democrat in the Tennessee Senate, 1841–43, and in the House, 1843–45.

FROM ISAAC H. DISMUKES

Dear sir [Oakachickama, Mississippi][1] September 27th 1841

I received your letter on the 23 of this munth.[2] You requested mea to write to you as soon as I got your letter. Wea are All well at the present time. I am gowen own geatharen the crop as fast as posible. I have got 10 bails of cotten in troy. I had my first thare the 14 of the month. I should of had more pick and pack if the weather had not of bin so unfaverable. Wea hav had a great deal of rain hear this faul which has kep our cotten from opening.

I saw majer babit the other day. Hea had just received your letter.[3] Hea said that you ware vary much parplext about your negrows runing a way and gown to tennessee. You will finde that you wil have to bea the man that wil have to stop that amoungst your negrows for you noe that you have had men hear of different ages and sizes and the runaway from all. I think though the plan that you have faulen own now will brake them if you will keep it up for a time or too. Try it for an example though as I w[r]ote you adderson[4] ware not sent down accorden to your request. Had that of bin dun gilbert would not of left the second time. Send him as soon as you hear from him[5] for I neade him hear for I have got my hands ful to save my crop as fast as it neades it. I doo not noe wheather or not you want mea or noe for I have not heard for the next year and I should like to noe as places are filing up hear very fast indeed that I may have a chance to get sum of them if you doo not want mea and as I have lived hear for small wages this year I shall ask you $500 for the next. Let mea hear from you soon if you doo not cum down next month.

I expect that the mill is at memfris at this time and I want to noe wheather or not you are goin to send a waggon down to memfris or noe that I may send for boath under one. You wil want sum plowes on the farm for another year and I think you had best get them in memfris too. It wil take half dozen one horse ploughes.

Isaac H Dismukes

ALS. DLC–JKP. Addressed to Nashville. Published in Bassett, *Plantation Overseer,* 159–60, under date of September 17, 1841.

1. Dismukes' address identified by the place of cancellation.
2. Letter not found.
3. Polk's letter to William Bobbitt has not been found.
4. Addison, a slave.
5. David B. Molloy wrote on September 30, 1841, that Polk's slave, Gilbert, had been found in northern Mississippi. On October 20, 1841, Molloy advised Polk that Dismukes had recovered Gilbert, who had been jailed in Holly Springs, Mississippi. ALsS. DLC–JKP.

FROM ROBERT B. REYNOLDS

My dear Sir, Knoxville September 27th 1841

Permit me, Sir, to trespass for a moment upon your time, in giving you my view in regard to the election of U.S. Senators. It is a question of much delicacy and out of which no little soil is likely to grow. Equally ballanced as I believe the parties to be in the next General Assembly, their must be an abandonment of principle somewhere if Senators are made at all during the approaching Session. I do not believe that there is a single democrat elected who will prove the traitor to democratic principles. Therefore I set it down as certain that no whig can be elected to the Senate unless by a compromise. What then Shall be done? Shall we compromise and elect one of each party to the Senate? Against this policy, I enter my most solemn protest. Against "bargain & intrigue" I have ever set my face, and I am sure it will ruin the man who is elevated, by so traitorous a policy. If upon going into an election, some of the Whig party, prefer the Democratic candidate to the federal, without any reciprocal arrangement having been made, I, for one say Amen to it; but upon no other principle, whatever. I trust that our party may so manage it as to elect two democrats to the Senate, without compromising one single principle for which we have ever contended. I am sure, that if one Democrat & one Whig are elected to the Senate, it will be fastened down upon the public mind that it was done by an arrangement to effect it. It would be far better to refer the election back to the people, at least one of the Senators. I have seen several of the East Tennessee members, and there is not one of them that will vote for a Whig under any set of circumstances. I have conversed with many of our best Democrats upon this subject and they fully concur with me in the foregoing views. The Whig party is crumbling to pieces throughout the land, and we must not give them any capital to go upon. But I have my fears that something evil is to grow out of the election of Senators. I feel confident that it wants but one more campaign to be fought under your lead, to redeem the State permanently from federal thraldom. We must act discreetly. A few mischief makers may do us a lasting injury. I turn my eyes to you, Sir, to settle this matter at once, and let us await the coming day to give them battle once more, and proud will that day be for you, for the Democracy & for your humble Servant . . . .

ROBERT B. REYNOLDS

ALS. DLC–JKP. Addressed to Nashville.

FROM ALEXANDER O. ANDERSON

My Dear Sir At Home Near Knoxville September 28th 1841

I had expected an answer to my last letter,[1] and regret, for several reasons, that I recd. none. Since then events have taken place at Washington which, it seems to me, if properly managed ought to bring to our ranks, at least, an accession of two or three Whigs, in the Legislature.

One of my objects, however, in writing at this time was in reference to the election of Senators. If we are to have but a single Senator, and you have any views of that kind yourself, you are sufficiently confident of my friendship to feel assured, that as far as I am personally concerned it will have my approval—and you must regard me, in this particular, with the assurance, that you have no friend, who has more devoted and disinterested attachment. If, however, you shall not have your attention directed in that way by our friends, then I confide, in the event we are to have but a single Senator, my claims, whatever they may be thought to be, to your hands. I must say, if you have any wishes for yourself upon that subject, I know of no one who has such claims upon his friends as you have, and it wou'd be my wish to aid your views, if I were upon the ground. If this, however,is not your case I do not feel that there is any other to whom I ought to concede. To you I do, as I wou'd to an older Brother, an older friend, as one having hig[h]er claims, not only freely, but with sincere pleasure. I repeat, I do not say this in regard to any other person. So far as I know there is in relation to myself but one feeling in East Tennessee, among the people, and I am informed, with the members also. But, I, also, write to say that I understand *G. W. Churchwell is a Candidate*—and has busied himself extremely. The result of which is, it is said, Mr Torbitt[2] of Monroe is for him—and this is all. I make no comments upon this—except to say that the *project originated in the quarters of the enemy, as I have reason to believe.*

My impression, however, is if we can elect one, we can elect two—and we ought to do it. And if we are to be beaten, the question had better lie over to the decision of the people, upon the fact that the Whig Party, by the publication of their recent address,[3] have now taken ground publicly, & the people will be better prepared to decide. They have divorced Mr Tyler—and if they now get Senators they will hold on for at least four years, for there can be no U.S. Bank question till after his administration—and no instructions can reach them, which wou'd compel their retirement.

If, however, they shall beat us it wou'd be better that they vacate the Supreme Bench. Or if they have one & we have one—the Democrat (if such shou'd be the case) ought to be the six years man. In any such event if Reese's position on the Supreme Bench shou'd be vacated, it wou'd be better than the election of Jarnagin—because that position wou'd be open to us then in East Tennessee, pending the period, at least, for which our opponent wou'd be in the Senate.[4] But I am of the opinion it wou'd be the best policy for us either to effect the election of both Senators, or not to permit the election, upon the avowed ground that the issues have not, until now, been fairly made before the people, that a new state of things has arisen—and that several counties—Humphreys & Benton, & Dyer & Obion are not represented, in conformity with their political character. As to what may be said of Roane & other Counties—our men were elected upon a full knowledge of their politicks, and can be elected again, in single handed races. Besides, another ground is that we have a new Census, & new apportionment to make. East Tennessee, will have a change of members, as will Middle & West Tennessee, giving in all probability a fair representation of the people.

I have now given you my views frankly, & confidentially, and shou'd be glad to hear from you—and inform me if you think I had better visit Nashville. Write me immediately upon receipt of this—and let me know your views. They shall be kept perfectly confidential.

I hope my friends will not permit me to be affected by any pretentions, from East Tennessee, on the part of those who have kept the shade & the purse, while my line of action has been wholly different. I feel great delicacy in writing to any members of the Legislature upon this subject—confiding in the consciousness of having done my duty whether in peril or in safety—in defeat or prosperity.

A ANDERSON

ALS. DLC–JKP. Addressed to Nashville and marked "Confidential."

1. Reference possibly is to a letter from Anderson to Polk, dated September 2, 1841, in which Anderson advised Polk of senatorial hopefuls in East Tennessee as well as of recent confidences on the extra session of Congress. AL, fragment. DLC–JKP.

2. Granville C. Torbett.

3. Whig members of the 27th Congress met in Washington on September 11, 1841, and appointed a committee of three Senators and three Representatives to prepare an exposition of the prominent proceedings of the extra session of Congress, including those measures that failed as well as those that passed. The committee's report not only summarized the legislative proceedings, but deplored John Tyler's vetoing the Fiscal Bank bill and the Fiscal Corporation bill. The report also called for limiting the president's veto power, restricting the chief executive to a single term of office, granting Congress authority to appoint the treasury secretary, establishing a fiscal agency under congressional control, and retrenching the cost of administering the general government. The full text of the committee's report was printed in the Washington *National Intelligencer* of September 15, 1841.

4. Anderson's calculation is that if the legislature should elect a Whig to

East Tennessee's seat in the U.S. Senate, the choice should fall on William B. Reese and thereby vacate East Tennessee's seat on the Supreme Court. The six-year term to be filled by the legislature belonged to East Tennessee; the four-year term, to Middle Tennessee. Reese held East Tennessee's seat on the Supreme Court from 1835 until 1847.

FROM ALEXANDER O. ANDERSON

My Dear Sir Near Knoxville Sept 29th 1841

I have already written to you a long letter by this mail,[1] in which I have said it will give me pleasure to see you placed in the Senate of the U.S., and if a single Democratic Senator only can be elected that I consider your claims as paramount to those of any other. Since writing that letter my attention has been called by a leading democratic friend to the expressed wish in the Union, in a late article, headed "U.S. Senators" that *Mr Nicholson's name shou'd be added to yours.* The paper is dated the 21st of September.[2] I shall make no comment upon it. I am satisfied you will not, nor any of our discreet friends approve it. You will find the sentiment expressed in the latter part of the article. It has certainly been expressed in no kindness to me. Nor cou'd the writer understand the great difficulties with which we have had to contend here. If in a series of years I had not been compelled to make sacrafices of such magnitude as have deranged, materially, my private affairs, I might look upon this attempt to hold up Mr Nicholson, under the circumstances, with more indifference. But I am not aware of *any paramount claims of faith,* or *sacrafices, in the hours of need, thro' a long series of years, which he can set up.* The attempted conjunction of his name with yours is not justifiable—if such, upon reflection, be the serious purpose of the present Editor of the Union.[3] In relation to your own Claims they stand, in my estimation, upon a wholly different footing, not to mention the age of Mr Nicholson, which has nothing to loose by postponement. You have been in the breach from the first—& beheld but a few faithful hands to uphold you in the gallant struggle which you made to redeem the democracy, and you have higher claims than all other men, & such as touch our state character abroad—hence, while I have the most decided approbation to extend in favor of your occupation of any station, within our gift, I cannot acquiesce in the sentiment which conjoins Mr Nicholson to yourself, to the exclusion of older soldiers than he is, & who have been severe sufferers from all our defeats.

Of course, I believe, the Democracy ought to have both the Senators. But I have no question that we can elect you by honorable compromise—making it a drawn Battle. In that event I have stated to you who ought to be the man of the opposition, and I have given you my reasons.[4] They are sound—and if it is to be made a drawn Battle they are reasons which ought to govern, for they can be made available to us, I think, in East Tennessee—if our friends cou'd be rallied to a man, as doubtless they cou'd, in the election of a Supreme Judge.

In the letter which I wrote to you, which was on yesterday, I stated it as my opinion that the wisest possible move wou'd be to have either both Senators or to postpone the election for the decision of the people—and I stated the ground. You perceive that we are advancing every where—and an election now may defeat us against the actual will of the people. Virginia has done so heretofore. So has Delaware. And it is now certain that nothing in the shape of a United States Bank will be brought before Congress, during Mr Tylers Administration. The Whigs have disowned him in the most denunciatory terms, & Mr Clay, in substance, has said that he intends the Sub Treasury under a new form &c &c. But if it be thought best to compromise for a drawn Battle, and we are to have but a single Senator, I consider your claims as paramount.

In these two letters I have written you of course for your own eye.

A ANDERSON

ALS. DLC–JKP. Addressed to Nashville and marked "*Private & Confidential.*"

1. See Alexander O. Anderson to Polk, September 28, 1841.

2. The September 21, 1841, issue of the *Nashville Union* has not been found.

3. J. George Harris.

4. William B. Reese. See Alexander O. Anderson to Polk, September 28, 1841.

FROM JOHN F. GILLESPY

Dear Sir, Maryville, Tennessee [October 1][1] 1841

Since my return home I have seen and conversed with many of our democratic friends on the propriety and policy of your election to the Senate of the U.S. I mentioned the prospect of your consenting to allow your name to be run as extremely problematical, but told them I knew you would be strongly urged by your friends West of the Mountain. I have found none, but most heartily concur with me in approving the measure, Except our friend Reynolds of Knoxville.[2] He seems to intertain some doubts of the policy of such a course. The more I have reflected upon the subject, the more thoroughly I am convinced you ought not to hesitate in yielding your consent provided you ascertain you can certainly be elected. I have not had an opportunity of seeing any of the democratic members before they went on except Torbet.[3] He will do any thing that is *right.* Reynolds informs me, that Johnston, Campbell and Critz,[4] when they passed through Knoxville, were decidedly in favour of running Nicholson. Jarnigin[5] informs me, that Judge Reese is in the field and electioneering for the office, and that he Jarnigin is unwilling to yield his pretentions for a seat on the Supreme bench. His friends here predicate his claims upon the great, extraordinary and efficient services he performed for *the party.* Jarnigin told me he did not think it was right to take sides either for or against Tyler upon the Bank question merely, for it was impossible to foresee what great and absorbing questions might arise during the present administration, nor on what side the ballance would fall. His is a mill dam case. He talks of moving to Mobile. I think it would be wrong to embarrass him in his laudable purpose by imposing any public restraints upon him. Judge Williams, Genl Carter and Maj Tom Brown are also talked of for Senators. Brown & Carter will do us least harm and Brown I think with a little coaxing might be made a tolerably good democrat.

Since the last veto[6] Whiggery in this quarter seems to be in a state of despondency, and democracy walking with her head erect. New life and zeal seems to animate our party, and I doubt not that two years hence there will be a total rout of the whigs in Tennessee.

My father[7] informs me, that it will not be in his power to be at Nashville at the commencement of the Session, but will be there shortly thereafter. Jarnigin informed me, that he had recd. a letter from Marable since the election, that he had no fears of his voting against whig Senators, that when Embree[8] failed to give the whig vote of his county Marable would feel himself at equal liberty to decline giving the democratic vote of his District. If Jarnigin is not elected Senator, he is to become a democrat; no very desirable accession.

JOHN F. GILLESPY

ALS. DLC–JKP. Addressed to Nashville.

1. Erroneously dated, "Sept. 31st."
2. See Robert B. Reynolds to Polk, September 27, 1841.
3. Granville C. Torbett.
4. Andrew Johnson, Brookins Campbell, and Philip Critz.
5. Spencer Jarnagin.
6. Reference is to Tyler's veto of the Fiscal Corporation bill. See Polk to Samuel H. Laughlin, September 2, 1841.
7. James Gillespy.
8. Joel Hembree.

FROM ALEXANDER O. ANDERSON

My Dear Sir At Home Near Knoxville Oct 6th 1841

I have not had the pleasure of hearing from you in reply to the several letters which I have written to you[1] since the receipt of yours upon the subject of the Judgeship of the upper circuit.[2] I have had some apprehension that my letters may have been suppressed in the passage.

Upon the subject of the election of Senators you have my views fully, so that if you have recd. them, so far as you are concerned you will be perfectly satisfied. I hope there is a fair prospect of the election of two Democratic Senators. If there is not, and they are to have a Whig for this end of the State, who will it be? If Reese or Williams it will vacate the Supreme Bench or the Chancery Court. In this event, and we are cut off from a Democratic Senator, I wou'd like to occupy the vacated seat, at least during the Whig reign—temporarily until we cou'd make our triumph complete. But I hope we may have Democratic Senators.

While I think of it let me remind you that any attempt of ours now to nominate a Candidate for the Presidency, wou'd weaken us materially, & probably produce reunion among the Whigs. Besides, I know Tennessee was not dealt with, in relation to the Vice Presidency, at the last term, as she ought to have been. So if we are to make any nominations, and we shall want a Vice President, when the proper time arrives, we can make our own nomination for Vice President, & have the nomination for President open to a general arrangement. Tennessee is the fifth State in the Union.

The Chief object of this letter, however, is to call your attention to a matter of great private interest to me. I am obliged to raise about five thousand Dollars—and the Bank at Nashville, can lend it if they will.[3] I can make as good paper for that amount as can be made in the State—and I want the aid of your influence to get the money. The following are the facts: I am liable for about that amount as a partner—Tho' I have not been the acting Partner. The Debts have been sued for, and I am *made the object of attack*. The judgment, will be had at our federal court early in this month,[4] and I am informed by a friend, that the counsel intend to press them fiercely, and that the object is to injure me as deeply as possible. That to my door is laid a large share of the sins of the Argus,[5] and other political sins—and that with this Instrument they will take revenge. I have no doubt that such is the fact, and that my informant is not mistaken. All I want is the money for some twelve months, paying in the interval the usual curtailments. I want the money temporarily so that I may have time to sell some property.

I have negroes and other valuable personal property which I can part with without any great inconvenience, if I can have a little time, which will enable me to realize, at reduced prices, more than five thousand Dollars. But to do this I must have a little time. The money I cannot get here. The object of my enemies is to sell this property under execution. They are full of gall & bitterness. The truth is I have been so long involved in politics, and under peculiar circumstances, which have cost me large sacrafices, that notwithstanding I have large means & property I have necessarily suffered great losses &c &c.

I have given you the facts. Write me what chance there is to get the money. Surely I can—with strong paper such as I can make in East Tennessee—& particularly as I need the money for a very limited period. Be pleased to write me upon the receipt of this.

It is very important to elect a Democrat for Judge in the upper circuit. If you do not—it will be mischievous. Burn this letter when read.

A ANDERSON

ALS. DLC–JKP. Addressed to Nashville and marked "Private & Confidential."

1. See Anderson to Polk, September 28 and 29, 1841.
2. Letter not found. See Polk to Robert B. Reynolds, August 19, 1841.
3. See Anderson to Polk, May 12 and July 8, 1841.
4. Case not reported.
5. The *Knoxville Argus*.

TO ANDREW JACKSON DONELSON

Nashville

My Dear Sir: Wednesday morning October [13]th[1] 1841

We will entertain the Legislature and other friends at my house on friday evening next, and Mrs. P. & myself, request the pleasure of your presence on the occasion. The Inauguration of the Governor elect[2] takes place tomorrow.

I have written a note to Genl. Jackson, and am anxious that he should do us the honour of being present on the occasion. I hope his health may be such as to enable him to come down.[3] I have written to him to invite also Mr & Mrs. Jackson,[4] whom we will be much pleased to see.

JAMES K. POLK

ALS. DLC–AJD. Addressed to Davidson County.

1. Erroneously dated "Oct. 12th."

2. James C. Jones.

3. Andrew Jackson declined because of poor health. See Andrew Jackson to Polk, October 14, 1841.

4. Letter not found. Reference is to Sarah York and Andrew Jackson, Jr.

FROM ANDREW JACKSON

My dear Sir, Hermitage Octbr. 14th 1841

Your kind note of invitation to Spend tomorrow evening with, & pertake of your festival,[1] came safe to hand & should have been replied to this morning, but I was so unwell I could not write. Was I able, nothing would afford me more gratification than to comply with your polite invitation, particularly as it would afford me the pleasure of becoming acquainted with the members of the Legislature, and conversing with them on the politics of the day; but my dear Sir, I have not the strength to comply, and sickness of our dear little children are such that Sarah cannot leave them at night.[2]

Present our kind regards to Mrs. Polk and accept for yourself our kindest wishes, and believe me your friend sincerely.

ANDREW JACKSON

ALS. DLC–JKP. Addressed to Nashville and delivered by George, probably a slave.

1. Letter not found. See Polk to Andrew J. Donelson, October 13, 1841.

2. Reference is to the children of Sarah York and Andrew Jackson, Jr.

TO J. P. HARDWICKE, G. W. CAMPBELL, ET AL.[1]

Gentlemen: Nashville, October 18, 1841

I have received with lively sensibility the renewed expression of my "past public course," conveyed to me in your letter of the 16th inst.,[2] inviting me on behalf "of the democratic members of the General Assembly, now in session in this city, and of the citizens of Nashville and Davidson county," to partake with them of a public dinner at the Nashville Inn, at such early day as may best suit my convenience." Such a manifestation of personal regard, emenating from such a source, cannot be otherwise than gratifying.

Through a long course of public service I have endeavored to make principle my guide and the public good my aim. And in retiring to private life I carry with me my principles unchanged, and shall ever take a proper interest in whatever may be calculated to advance and promote the prosperity and happiness of the people, whose honored public servant I have been.

I have never received office but at the hands of the people, save when chosen by their immediate representatives to preside over the deliberations of the popular branch of Congress. To the people I have been at all times amenable. My public conduct has been constantly before them, and been subject to the searching examination and scrutiny as well of those who differed with me in sentiment as of those with whom I agreed. If I have not been as able an advocate of their rights as I would have desired to be, none I think can justly charge that my labors have not been honestly exerted to promote their interests. I yield to their late decision—though made by a diminished popular vote without complaint. It is a maxim with me now, as it has ever been, "the will of the people be done."

The day is not far distant gentlemen, when our common principles must again be in the ascendant, not only in Tennessee, but in the Union. The astounding strides which have been made, during the late memorable Extra Session of Congress, to consolidate power in the Federal head, and to trench on the reserved rights of the States and the people; the ruinous measures of policy brought forward by a dominant majority in Congress, which in the short period of *one hundred days* have developed themselves, have roused up the whole country to a sense of danger, and the people, uncontrolled by politicians or the monied power, everywhere that they have spoken, are re-asserting their rights. State after State has returned to the Republican fold, from which they had been temporarily estranged in the maddened political contest of 1840. Will Tennessee follow their example? The evidences of public opinion around us are too palpable to doubt it. At the August election the policy of the ruling party at Washington was but partially known. Enough however was seen to create many doubts in the public mind. Many honest men were brought to pause, but were induced yet a little longer to act with the party with whom they had been associated, upon assurances everywhere made by leading men that they were mistaken. Time has now been afforded for calm reflection and more full development, and they see that all their apprehensions were well founded. "Truth is mighty and will prevail."

Tendering to you gentlemen, and through you to the Democratic members of the General Assembly and the citizens whom you represent, my acknowledgments for the distinguished honor you have done me, it gives me sincere pleasure to accept your invitation for Saturday next the 23d instant.

James K. Polk

Copy. In the *Nashville Union*, October 20, 1841. Addressed locally.

1. Polk's letter is addressed to Jonathan P. Hardwicke, George W. Campbell, and eighteen other Democratic members of the Tennessee General Assembly and Democratic citizens of Nashville and Davidson County.

2. Letter not found.

FROM HARVEY M. WATTERSON

Dear Sir. Washington City Oct. 19th 1841

To day I called to see the President and Secretary of War,[1] and requested them to suspend for the present any action in regard to the appointment of Agent for the Chickasaw Indians.[2] With the President I talked freely upon the subject, and *all is right.*

Bostick of Williamson County[3] is here, the most anxious man to be Marshall of Middle Tennessee that you ever saw. I thought at one time that he would get the appointment. It is now doubtful. He *professes* to be a devoted friend to Tyler.

On last Thursday I received a few lines from the President stating that he desired to see me immediately. I called and he read me a letter from you recommending Wm G Childres Esq for the Office of Marshall,[4] also letters from Gen Jackson and others urging the claims of Col Claiborne. He said he did not know how he was to get round Gen Jackson's recommendation and spoke of the Old Chief in very complimentary terms. Indeed he seemed to be highly gratified that Gen Jackson had written to him as well as yourself. Taking into consideration Col Claiborne's states rights, anti-Proclamation,[5] virginia notions, my own impression is, (founded on the President's conversation) that his prospects of success are good. The probability is that the appointment will not be made for some weeks.[6]

The President is willing to do any thing in his power to prevent the election of two "*White Charlies*" to the Senate from Tennessee. He would infinitely prefer you to either Bell, Foster or any of their company. In fact he stated so to me himself.

He told Gov Branch and myself and swore to it, that the Whigs would get no Bank whilst he was President. With the result of the elections in Maryland, Georgia, Maine, Ohio and Pennsylvania he is well pleased.[7]

I think his Message will be pretty thoroughly Democratic.[8] He knows that if he dont take the Democratic track, he is a "used up man." Still he keeps around him some of the most mercenary and corrupt members of the Whig party. They are doubtless always flattering him and he regards them as his best friends.

I have just finished reading your message.[9] It is good—very good.

H. M. WATTERSON

ALS. DLC–JKP. Addressed to Nashville.

1. John C. Spencer, former New York legislator, congressman, and secretary of state of New York, served as U.S. secretary of war from October 12, 1841, until March 3, 1843, when he became secretary of the treasury. He remained in that post until his resignation on May 2, 1844.

2. A. M. M. Upshaw, first appointed Agent for the Chickasaw Indians on March 4, 1840, remained in his post and was re-appointed by Tyler for a second term of four years, beginning March 4, 1844.

3. Richard W. H. Bostick, a Williamson County lawyer and farmer, served two terms as a Whig in the Tennessee House, 1841–43 and 1845–47, and a single term in the Senate, 1849–51. Bostick married Rebecca L. Cannon, daughter of Newton Cannon.

4. Letter not found.

5. Reference is to Andrew Jackson's Proclamation to the People of South Carolina, issued December 10, 1832.

6. On January 18, 1842, Tyler nominated Thomas Claiborne to be U.S. marshal for the Middle District of Tennessee; the Senate rejected the nomination on March 9, 1842. Tyler later nominated Benjamin H. Sheppard, who was confirmed on August 6, 1842.

7. Each of these states returned Democratic majorities to their legislatures.

8. Reference is to Tyler's First Annual Message to Congress, subsequently communicated on December 7, 1841.

9. Reference is to Polk's Valedictory Address to the Tennessee legislature of October 7, 1841. See Polk to Cave Johnson, September 21, 1841.

FROM LEVIN H. COE

Dear Sir Somerville Tennessee Oct 26. 1841

A failure to forward as I had directed prevented the recpt of your favor of the 11th[1] until the 21st when I received it at Covington. I hurried home and on my arrival on the 23rd learned from report that both houses had agreed to go into the election of Senators on the 23rd.

I considered therefore that so far as the election of Senators was concerned I could be of no service. I have reason to believe the *man* you allude to[2] entertains for me the kindest feelings. He gave me many evidences of it towards the close of the last Session and if I had been aware in time of the situation of matters would have dropped my buisiness at Covington and gone up from Raleigh Court. If you think I can be of service write me and I will come up—but I do not wish to miss the Chancery Court here, three weeks hence if I can well avoid it.

I have thought often of the propriety of your accepting the office of Senator if tendered you—and upon the whole I had settled down into the opinion that you should accept the *office made vacant* by *Mr Grundys decease.*[3] Your enemies would at once raise a hugh & cry against you but so far as my information extends I do not know one Democrat who will not prefer you to any other man in the state. In fact they would feel mortified at your refusal to accept. The office would place you in a prominent position before the public. They would be constantly hearing from you upon the great questions which will agitate the country for the next two years. I think the influence you would thus exercise will more than counterbalance all the damage your enemies could do you by having accepted the office.

These are my impressions as to the effect in the region of Country *south of Hatchee* & north of Mississippi. Of the other parts of the State you can form a much more correct opinion than I can. If you decline our friends here tho they will feel regret will not be the less united & firm at the next election.

I fear Col. S.T.[4] bargained with the whigs for office. They count here with confidence on his voting for Foster. His committees look a little suspicious.

The Banks must be made to resume specie payments. Let them make their paper good and Democracy will carry the Country with a whirlwind in 1843.

If you, Mr President Nichol and others think it is necessary to give the control asked for by Nichol over the Branches of the Bank of Tennessee—all that we here want is to be put upon our own bottom. Step mother never was more illiberal to an orphan child than Nichol has been to the Branch here. He envies us our cotton Bales & wants the Bills based upon them for the benefit of the mother Bank & E. Ten. branches. This we dont intend to submit to. We are willing to be reorganized so as to stand independent of the Principal Bank and be directly accountable to the Legislature. But it is not our intrest to have our people ground down to afford Exchange for Middle & E. Ten. We are willing to let the Bank stand as it is. If it must be changed give us the priviledge of walking without leading strings held by a middle Ten. Directory.

Judging from what I know of the tone of feeling in the Legislature I think the best plan is to let the Bank stand as now organised.

Concentration of Branches wont go down. The centrifugal force is the one to be dreaded. The danger is that the Bank will be split into

County agencies. We barely prevented it two years ago by letting the Clarksville Branch stand & giving one to the Mountain region. If we had not done this the Bank would have been split into agencies in 1839.

L. H. Coe

ALS. DLC–JKP. Addressed to Nashville.

1. Letter not found.
2. Probably Isaac Goodall of Smith County.
3. Polk had appointed A. O. P. Nicholson to fill the U.S. Senate seat vacated by the death of Felix Grundy. Nicholson served from January 11, 1841, until February 7, 1842.
4. Samuel Turney, Speaker of the Tennessee Senate in the Twenty-fourth General Assembly.

TO ANDREW JACKSON

My Dear Sir! Nashville Oct. 30th. 1841

I have the pleasure to make known to you my friend the *Revd. Mr Connor*[1] who calls to pay his respects to you. *Mr Connor* is a citizen of Haywood County and feels some anxiety, as I do myself, for the appointment of *Charles P. Taliaferro* of Brownsville[2] as Post Master at that place, in the room & stead of the former incumbent resigned.[3] My friend *Dr. Haywood* writes to me in behalf of *Mr Taliaferro*[4] and I learn that it is the wish of our friends in Haywood generally that he should be appointed. *Mr Taliaferro* is known to me personally and I know him to be well qualified for the office. I think a letter from you to the President would have much weight in procuring the appointment for him. Will you do me the favour to write a letter to the President—and send it down by *Mr Connor.*

The news of the appointment of *Claiborne*[5] to be Marshall of Middle Tennessee seems to operate among the Federalists here, as a *third veto.*[6]

James K. Polk

P.S. Perhaps it will be better for you to address your letter to Mr Wickliffe the Post-Master General, instead of to the President as suggested in the foregoing letter.[7] You know Mr Wickliffe personally—and he would no doubt feel complimented to receive a letter from you. J.K.P.

ALS. DLC–AJ. Addressed to the Hermitage and delivered by Champ C. Connor.

1. Champ C. Connor was a young Baptist minister from Brownsville.

2. Charles P. Taliaferro, brother of Polk's inspector general, John E. Taliaferro, served numerous terms as clerk of Haywood County, 1852–65 and 1875–76. Charles Taliaferro received the appointment as Brownsville postmaster on December 14, 1841.

3. William E. Owen was postmaster of Brownsville from 1838 until 1841.

4. Egbert Haywood, a Brownsville physician, recommended Charles P. Taliaferro to Polk for the Brownsville postmastership in a letter dated October 23, 1841. ALS. DLC–JKP.

5. See Harvey M. Watterson to Polk, October 19, 1841.

6. Reference is to Whig reactions to John Tyler's vetoing the Fiscal Bank bill and the Fiscal Corporation bill.

7. On October 31, 1841, Jackson replied that he had addressed a note to Charles Wickliffe and requested Polk to forward it, if he thought it "serviceable to the object in view." ALS. DLC–JKP.

TO WILLIAM C. TATE

Dr. Sir Nashville Nov. 1st 1841

In the early part of the present year I received a letter from you,[1] enclosing a transcript of the record of the Court of Burke County N.C., shewing that you had been appointed Guardian of the two minor children[2] of my brother Marshall T. Polk, deceased. In your letter you informed me that you were ready to receive any money belonging to the children, which might come into my hands as their guardian in this State. I accordingly enclose to you herewith a check of *Five hundred dollars*, from the Bank of Tennessee on the Philade[l]phia Bank at Philadelphia, and have to request that you will forward to me a receipt for the same by return mail. I think it probable that I will be able to remit to you an equal amount between the middle and the last of the next year.

I was gratified to learn from you that the children were promising. *Eunice* is now of the proper age to be at school, and if you think it necessary, & will so advise me, I will from time to time, make such advance of my own funds as I can conveniently spare for that purpose.

Remember me kindly to the children, and most especially to your good lady.[3]

JAMES K. POLK

[Certification][4] I Robert Armstrong Post Master at Nashville Tenn.— do certify that James K. Polk did this day deposite in the Post office at Nashville Ten. a letter addressed to *Dr. William C. Tate Morganton, Burke County N. Carolina,* of which the foregoing is a copy; Which letter contained enclosed a check from the Bank of Tennessee for

$500.00, on the Philadelphia Bank at Philadelphia of which check the following is a copy viz.[5]

ALS. DLC–JKP. Addressed to Morganton, North Carolina, and marked "*Copy.*"

1. See William C. Tate to Polk, February 6, 1841.
2. Roxana Eunice Ophelia Polk and Marshall Tate Polk, Jr.
3. Laura Wilson Polk Tate, widow of Marshall Tate Polk and wife of William C. Tate.
4. The text of the certification statement was written in Polk's hand.
5. Here followed the text of Polk's check, written in Polk's hand, and the further endorsement, written by Armstrong, "Given under my hand at Nashville on this the 1st day of November 1841. R. Armstrong P.M."

FROM J. G. M. RAMSEY

My Dear Sir Mecklenburg Nov. 9, 1841

I received a few days since a letter from which the accompanying extract is taken. It is written by a gentleman[1] of the first character in Charleston. Tho not a politician by profession he is now & has been since 1827 & 1828 a leader of the leaders in S.C., gave the strongest impulse at that time to the cause of Gen Jackson, stuck to him through the nullification war but never (such is the consideration in which all parties held him) became estranged from the dominant party of S.C. He is perfectly familiar with public opinion at home—in N.C., in Ga., Alabama & the South generally. He is a shrewd, sagacious, honorable gentleman & one in whose good faith every confidence can be placed, & in whose calculation there is nothing visionary or Eutopian—a true lover of his country & identified by his rank, his connections & his wealth with all its interests. What he says he means & what he asserts he knows. He is just now taking an active part in politics. Was in Georgia during the late election & is said to have assisted essentially in effecting there the late revolution. I have extracted all that part of his letter bearing on politics. What is it intended for & how shall I reply to it? I wish I could see you one hour. My answer will be used prudently & confidentially & *skillfully* in at least three states. It ought to be given therefore if not with caution at least with great discretion. It is a delicate subject to bring to your attention especially by letter. Still it is due to you that you should know what your friends are doing & propose to do with & for you. Will you therefore write me early (yourself or some friend—Humphries?)[2] & let me hear so much at least as will keep me from doing you an injury, or will aid me in serving you & Tennessee & the country. I give you my own views. Van Buren ought not to be taken up again. Benton nor Buchanan will not do. If Calhoun is not taken up you are decidedly the strongest man in the party & I believe would be his choice. If he is taken up your name must be associated with him or he cannot be elected. Your vote on the Force Bill[3] will neutralise the objection to his nullification. And then on the score of *talents, long experience, profound statesmanship, disinterested patriotism, enlarged & liberal views, purity, & private virtue* what a ticket would be presented to the country, to say nothing of your respective locations, which are the most favorable imaginable. But can Calhoun even with your aid succeed? You know I am some thing of a nullifier myself. Still I fear there will be a difficulty in making the people believe that there is not something of *disunion* implied in the doctrine. I believe Mr. C. would make the best President we ever had, except Jackson & in some respects as good or better than he. He cannot be elected without you are associated with him, while you cannot be defeated if he is not a candidate & will give you his support & influence.

These are the views I honestly entertain & upon them would my answer be predicated, subject however to such modification as your superior judgment might suggest. My correspondent as you see expects an answer early. Your inaugural must be republished, can you furnish me a copy? If you were now before us you would beat Jones 5000 votes in E. T. We have several Tyler Whigs made so by the vetos.[4] Did you notice how Jones butchered our Carolina partnership?[5] Would not Tennessee be disgraced to let S.C. pay the expense of surveys in her boundaries? & yet he intimates as much by his silence about our appropriation &c &c. Oh he must be beaten in 43 & you can do it, & go the year after to Washington too.

J. G. M. RAMSEY

P.S. I thank you for your notice of our financiering.[6]

Extract from a letter from a gentleman in Charleston S.C. to a friend in Tennessee[7]

"We hope to see the union between the South & West consumated by the union of the democratic party in support of Mr. Calhoun & Mr. Polk for the first & second offices in the government. We feel here that Mr. Calhoun occupies a position higher than the presidency & we can do him no honor by conferring that office upon him, but we consider him at the same time as the great expositor & stay of the Constitution & the party supporting it & if the democracy should unite upon him it would be considered a high complyment to S.C. But if they should select another in good faith & sincerity we are ready to go our death for him. Mr. C. is however our first choice beyond all question. Mr. Polk stands well with us & with the whole democratic party & we should rejoice to see him taken up by the party. *The time is come now when it is necessary that the movement be made.* The nomination should be made first in the papers, by county or town meetings, by Legislatures & lastly by Convention of the whole party. Pray keep the iron hot by striking. *Tennessee is a good point from whence to give the signal.* Let me hear from you on this point. I am going to N.C. in a few days to be absent a fortnight & will see how the land lies there. From what I see I fear Van Buren may be brought in the field again. The interest of the party can not be advanced or even maintained by him. He wants personal popularity & commanding influence. Calhoun, Buchanan, Cass[8] or Forsyth would either of them unite the party better & the last two are out of the question. Even Polk as young as he is were better than Van Buren for the first office & the time is not yet quite come for that. What does Polk think or say of it himself? Do you know? It is quite possible I may be at the Legislature of both Georgia & S. Carolina & should be pleased to hear from you previously.

ALS. DLC–JKP. Addressed to Nashville and forwarded to Coffeeville, Mississippi. AE on the cover states that this letter was answered on December 29, 1841; Polk's reply has not been found.

1. Not identified further.

2. West H. Humphreys.

3. A response to South Carolina's nullification threat, the Force Act of 1833 authorized the president to use military force to secure compliance with U.S. revenue laws.

4. Reference is to the vetoes of the Fiscal Bank bill and the Fiscal Corporation bill. See A. V. Brown to Polk, June 12, 1841, and Polk to Samuel H. Laughlin, September 2, 1841.

5. Reference is to the dissolution of the Louisville, Cincinnati and Charleston Railroad Company and the disposition of the company's surveys in Tennessee. See Ramsey to Polk, October 27, 1840.

6. In his Valedictory Message of October 7, 1841, Polk noted favorably the continuance of specie payments by the Southwestern Railroad Bank, of which Ramsey was president.

7. Extract in Ramsey's hand.

8. Lewis Cass, lawyer and Democrat, served as governor of the Michigan Territory, 1813–31; U.S. secretary of war, 1831–36; U.S. minister to France, 1836–42; U.S. Senator from Michigan, 1845–48 and 1851–57; and U.S. secretary of state, 1857–60. In 1848 Cass ran unsuccessfully as the Democratic candidate for president.

FROM JONATHAN P. HARDWICKE

My Dear Sir, Nashville Nov 12th 1841

Your friendly favour from Jackson[1] reached me by the mail of to day. I am much obliged to you for the inclosed as well the suggestions in your kind letter; they will be duly considered before I determine on the matter.

Things are about as when you left, at a dead stand, to all appearance. Maj Brown & H. L. Turney are both gone home. Tho our sky is not as clear as it might be, I have not dispared. When all human efforts fail we have another source to look to. I mean the same kind hand that did interpose for our Fathers in the first struggle for independence and more recently arrested the country from the hands of the spoilers.

There is a mighty fluttering in the Whig camps, and as Jack Dow[n]ing used to say, a tarn'd sight of hard thinkin amongst them.[2] Brown will shower down on Wester a long list of Instructions in a short time. Genl. Graham from Perry is on the fence & goes to morrow to see and spend a night with Genl. Jackson. The old chief is apprised of his coming & the object in view. Goodall says earnestly he hopes we may elect two Democratic Senators.

Mr Bell is hourly expected. A city meeting has been had and 100 managers appointed to prepare & receive him at this place & a similar arrangement at Lebanon all of which only tends to make Ephraim[3] more uneasy. Our boys stands firm and on all occasions presents an undivided front. Barclay Martin read a letter in my room a few evenings ago from our friend A. O. P.[4] to several persons present, H.L.T.[5] amongst the number. He is bitter as you please & makes heavy threats, charges heavily using his own words. You know who, without giving names.[6] You will find it necessary to keep an eye on that man, and that is all you have to do. If any thing occurs, I will write you immediately.

J. P. Hardwicke

ALS. DLC–JKP. Addressed to Coffeeville, Mississippi.

1. Letter not found. Polk was en route from Nashville to his plantation in Yalobusha County, Mississippi.

2. Quotation not identified further. "Major Jack Downing" was a fictitious character created in the early 1830's by Seba Smith, founder of the Portland (Maine) *Daily Courier*. Downing was a "Down East Yankee" whose rustic speech and political humor won considerable popular acclaim.

3. Ephraim H. Foster.

4. A. O. P. Nicholson.
5. Hopkins L. Turney.
6. Reference is to A. O. P. Nicholson. See Samuel H. Laughlin to Polk, November 24, 1841, and Hopkins L. Turney to Polk, December 26, 1841.

FROM SAMUEL H. LAUGHLIN

Nashville, Tennessee. November 13, 1841

Laughlin advises that the election contest for U.S. Senator remains much as it was when Polk left.[1] Democrats in the upper house stand firm and expect to send down separate nominations, first for Turney and then for Brown. Before leaving town, Brown wrote an ungrammatical paper in answer to the Democratic interrogatories.[2] Democratic members must try to correct his rather confused answers, for the Whigs will try to make him look ridiculous. Laughlin discusses legal and financial problems stemming from his former service as editor of the *Nashville Union.*[3] If political friends, such as Cave Johnson, unite with the Whigs in oppressing him financially, he may "seek a new home" or "give up at once."

ALS. DLC–JKP. Addressed to Coffeeville, Mississippi, and marked "Private." AE on the cover states that this letter was answered on December 29, 1841.

1. Polk left Nashville for Mississippi the first week of November.
2. The thirteen Democrats in the Tennessee Senate addressed a circular letter to the U.S. senatorial candidates asking their views on the principal issues raised at the special session of the U.S. Congress. The "Immortal Thirteen" inquired especially if the candidate admitted the right of the legislature to instruct U.S. Senators and whether the candidate would obey instructions or resign.
3. See Laughlin to Polk, January 11, 1839.

FROM SAMUEL H. LAUGHLIN

My dear Sir, Nashville, Nov. 24th 1841

On saturday last the "13"[1] were safe against the world, and the whigs considered themselves as beaten. Guess then, what our astonishment was, when coming into the Senate on Monday morning, Sam Turney announced that he had changed his mind, and would call up and vote for his own resolutions to bring on the Senatorial election at an early day on joint vote in Convention.[2] He said he had been written to by his constituents—whigs who voted for him—that made it necessary to do so. This was all a lie. Any letters he might have received were from persons of the same party who had previously instructed him,[3] and whom in his speeches he had again and again pronounced to be a minority. The true secret is, his brother[4] had left for Washington, and Sam had concluded he could not be elected, and that no Senators would be elected, and that thereby he would incur some responsibility. Now, without a price, Sam can encounter nothing. Besides this, John Nelson had abused and bullied him in the chair[5] until he was afraid to call his life his own.

Because the Senate was not full the resolution was laid on table & has not yet been called up. Gardner has a resolution on the table, with an excellent preamble, appointing H. L. Turney and Tom Brown Senators,[6] which Sam is now pledged to pass for us by his vote, and send it to the House for concurrence,[7] before his own resolution shall be taken up or passed.[8] Half an hour ago, we were ready to pass Gardner's resolution, when Bob Foster communicated to Turney that he had a proposition to make confidentially to him, in re[gard][9] to compromise to-night. Upon the m[atter] being communicated to us by him, we have laid Gardner's Resolution until tomorrow.

Now, Sir, what shall we do? Supp[ose] the proposition to Turney is to elect Foster and any democrat we please—or what is more likely, H. L. Turney? Ought we to agree to it?

Before these things can be properly decided, you must know that John Bell is here, and that although he declares his approval of the nominations of Foster & Jarnagin in his letter to the dinner Committee,[10] yet he does it with most apparent reluctance—and many whigs prefer him to Foster or Jonakin.[11] Some of them are at work for him. Now, Sir, to prevent *his* election I would take Foster as the lesser evil and as less capable of mischief. But no one can tell what a day may bring forth.

Judge Catron I am advised, advised Sam Turney, on last saturday evening, that it would be better to suffer the temporary evils of the election of whigs, than to adopt the untried expedient of elections by choosing seperately by the Houses in their organized capacities, and defeating a choice. That it was doubtful whether the people would approve the seeming innovation—and if they were to condemn it, our party would sustain great damage.

Now, I have no fears of what the people would have done. I mention the fact as connected with Turney's course. I only hear the fact from Gen. Armstrong that the Judge so advised. Turney told me casually on Monday that he had not seen Judge Catron. If he had seen him, that was not true. He may have forgotten.

S. H. LAUGHLIN

ALS. DLC–JKP. Addressed to Bolivar and marked "Private."

1. Reference is to the thirteen Democratic members of the Tennessee Senate. The Democratic delegation held a majority of one in that body.

2. On November 22, 1841, Samuel Turney moved that the Senate consider his resolution of October 28, 1841, which proposed that the Senate and House meet in convention to elect a Senator to the United States Congress for a six-year term from the 4th of March last. The motion was tabled.

3. On October 28, 1841, some 934 citizens of Jackson County petitioned the Tennessee Senate in behalf of the election of Whigs to Tennessee's two vacant seats in the U.S. Senate.

4. Hopkins L. Turney.

5. Samuel Turney was Speaker of the Tennessee Senate.

6. On November 22, 1841, John A. Gardner proposed that Thomas Brown and H. L. Turney be chosen U.S. Senators, the former for six years from and after the 4th of March last, to succeed Alexander O. Anderson; the latter to fill the unexpired term of Felix Grundy. The preamble of Gardner's resolution passed on November 23, 1841.

7. Gardner's resolution was never adopted. On November 29, 1841, Robert W. Powell moved that H. L. Turney be appointed to fill Grundy's seat. Powell's resolution was passed in lieu of Gardner's. On December 1, 1841, the House rejected Powell's resolution.

8. On December 2, 1841, the legislature finally approved Samuel Turney's resolutions calling for a joint convention to choose two U.S. Senators. The six-year seat would be filled on December 2; the four-year seat, on December 3.

9. Manuscript mutilated here and at ends of two lines following.

10. Bell addressed his letter of November 22, 1841, to S. V. D. Stout and seven other Whig citizens of Nashville and Davidson County who had invited him to partake of a public dinner. Text is printed in the Nashville *Republican Banner* of November 23, 1841.

11. Ephraim H. Foster and Spencer Jarnagin.

FROM J. GEORGE HARRIS

Dear Sir, Nashville Dec. 13th 1841

I have just learned from your brother[1] that you are at Columbia on Saturday, and desired me to send you a copy of the message[2] by the morrow morning stage—which it gives me pleasure to do.

I wish you would sit down in moment of leisure after reading Mr. Tyler's message and give a few of your conclusions with reference thereto. It strikes me upon a hurried glance that the Captain goes in for a double-refined Sub Treasury.[3] But we shall see when the Sec. of the treas. submits "the plan of finance."[4] How do you like the name? I have run over it in such a hurry that I am unable to speak of it *as a whole.*

No senators yet[5]—and no prospect—unless the old switzer of E. Tenn.[6] should run in upon a resolution, which though improbable is not impossible. Thank God & the immortal thirteen, Ephraim's fiddle is broke.[7] No more will its dulcet strains minister to the desponding faculties of faction. He has committed the unpardonable sin, and must bear the mark of the first-born.[8] I call the sin unpardonable, for it is an offence against a confiding people which the humblest of their number will discover and never forgive. How any public man can expect to succeed before the masses under the *dumb* flag is perfectly inexplicable. There is no policy under Heaven half so short-sighted.

I think there is a broad and deep gulf opening between Bell and Foster.[9] Bell is heard to murmur about as if he would like to be honered with a call for his opinions by "the thirteen." My judgment is rather against it, but perhaps it is not essential. The Banner is cold towards Mr. Bell—the whig is still colder—and both are evidently Fosterian.[10] Meantime Mr. Bell is invited to a public Dinner in Wilson which he declines,[11] and the correspondence is published in the *Lebanon Chronicle*[12]—copied into the Banner of this morning, but not even noticed by the Whig. The inferences from these "straws" are strengthened by the jaw apparent among whig members of the Legislature.

Mr. Jarnagin has fallen back into his appropriate sphere because he happened to have hold of Ephraim's coat tail at the time that the snapping and cracking of fiddle strings took place. He went back to E. Tenn. as a punished spaniel goes back to his kennel.

You know that the downfall of the dummies fills my cup of joy to the brim. That fiddle made a noi̇se that annoyed me sorely at one time.[13] Thank Heaven it is past repair. What a pity, that after entertaining the members of the legislature so often and so liberally, it should now be unstrung, destroyed! As Donnelson said when Old Tip[14] went off to the climacteric of those that were, "I have unbounded faith in the Lord God Almighty."

But a single word upon another theme. I have lately discovered one of the reasons, probably, why I received so many little overtures from Calhoun while at Washington. I learn from no questionable source that his friends in So: Caro. are ploughing with some of your friends in E. Tenn. to strike a "Calhoun & Polk" flag for the next presidential contest. There is no doubt in my mind that the effort is being made. It will do no harm, perhaps, as it will awaken northern men to the fact that the south shall not be neglected. But that *crumb* should not satisfy us, when a larger portion of the loaf is within our reach. We have too much northern capital of which Calhoun could never avail himself, to waste words with seriousness and in a public manner upon such a proposition at this juncture. But the day is so early the mere agitation of such an idea in the right quarter may do no harm. Pardon these random thoughts. But they are honest ones.

I cannot tell you any local news, as no doubt your brother told you all. *It strikes me* that as a U.S. Senator—one at least—is almost indispensable; as there is no doubt that Brown will act with us—as he is a rejected whig—as he is pledged to obey and resign[15]—as he has answered and the fiddler[16] has not—to elect him now by democratic votes if possible, would strengthen our position as a party, conciliate E. Tennessee, more effectually destroy the fiddler, and make our position more easily defensible. What do you think? My best respects to Mrs. Polk and all our friends.

J. GEO. HARRIS

[P.S.][17] That art. in the Observer looks awful![18] Mr. Bell's fate should teach a lesson to those who adventure against "bank proof batteries."

ALS. DLC–JKP. Addressed to Columbia and marked "A private scrap."

1. William H. Polk.

2. Reference is to John Tyler's First Annual Message, transmitted to Congress on December 7, 1841.

3. Tyler's "plan of finance" called for the establishment of a Board of Exchequer at Washington with agencies at prominent commercial points or elsewhere, as Congress might direct. Public creditors would hold the option of receiving payment in Treasury notes or in specie; note issues in excess of $15 million would be made only with express legislative sanction; and notes would be convertible to specie only at their place of issue. The board and its agencies would receive private deposits of specie, issue certificates of deposit thereon, and sell domestic bills of deposit, redeemable at the place of issue. Although the board and its agencies could buy and sell bills of exchange, neither could deal in discounts or accommodations.

4. On December 15, 1841, Caleb Cushing moved that the secretary of the treasury be requested to submit Tyler's plan of finance to the House. On December 21, 1841, Secretary of the Treasury Walter Forward submitted the draft of a bill to establish a Board of Exchequer at the seat of government, with agencies, etc. See House Document No. 20, 27 Congress, 2 Session. Forward, a lawyer from Pennsylvania and former member of the U.S. House, 1822–25, advocated a high tariff and frequently differed with Tyler in economic and political affairs. He headed the Treasury Department for two years.

5. The Tennessee legislature failed to elect U.S. Senators in joint convention. On December 2 twelve of the Senate's Democratic members refused to attend the convention, which could not proceed to an election for want of a quorum in both houses. On the following day the Senate voted against attending the convention. See Samuel H. Laughlin to Polk, November 24, 1841.

6. Reference is to Thomas Brown, an East Tennessee Whig whom some Democrats had encouraged to run.

7. Ephraim H. Foster and Spencer Jarnagin declined to answer interrogatories submitted to them by the Tennessee legislature. Democrats charged them with disrespect for the legislature and defiance of the right of instruction by that body.

8. Reference is to the marking of Cain, eldest son of Adam and Eve. Genesis 4:15.

9. See Samuel H. Laughlin to Polk, November 24, 1841.

10. The Nashville *Republican Banner* and the *Nashville Whig*.

11. John Bell's declination, published in the Nashville *Republican Banner*, was dated November 29, 1841, and addressed to Jordan Stokes and others.

12. Edited by William Polk McClain, the *Lebanon Chronicle* began publication in 1839 and ran until 1846; the issue of the *Chronicle* to which Harris refers has not been found.

13. See Samuel H. Laughlin to Polk, May 10, 1841.

14. Andrew Jackson Donelson and William H. Harrison.

15. Reference is to the Democratic interrogatories to which Thomas Brown had replied.

16. Ephraim H. Foster.

17. Harris' postscript is written in the left margin of his first page.

18. The issue of the *Columbia Observer* to which Harris refers has not been found.

FROM JONATHAN P. HARDWICKE

My Dear Sir, Nashville Dec. 15th 1841

Yours the 14th Inst[1] is at hand. For answer I will say we are at a point from which, one bad move would or might do much harm. Some of [our] own men have become refractory by the intefearance of others. In a word Sir, with[out] you we cant get on at all.

From all I can see or learn, we will be forced into an election soon, by Fosters friends making use of Sam Turney, for that purpose. If they choose to meet us upon our terms we cant prevent it. They have a majority in the Ho. & Sam in the Senate, clinches the nail. They would have done it long since but for an internal dificulity. Jarnigan[2] has been all the time an incubus upon the party having some 4 or 5 fast friends who would not let the machine move without he was in it, & without them Foster could not move. The conventional farce played off[3] was to effect two objects: to cast if posible odium on our party, but above all to get rid of Jarnigan, which is effected. Now if Bell dont take his place & divide them again the scene will be over soon. Of that I think it most probable he is straining every nerve, to bring him self into notice & favour with his party. Foster speaks of him as an enemy. Bell says on the streets, he will answer interogatories,[4] and do it respectfully. Some of our friends are clearly in favour of addressing him, without delay. I have hitherto, advised such to consider well before they determined upon that course. It might produce some good & much harm. Hence I have indeavoured to keep the whole matter open til you could come. I might say some of our party have acted badly & sewed the seeds of discord in our own ranks. It comes from a quarter that renders it certain none but your self can stop the current. Sir it comes from Murry,[5] and I assure you it is all important that you come without delay. No one here can control M. & D.[6] They have and still are, acting badly. Something must be done to obliterate, what they have done before the final action or all is lost. D. told me he had proposed to Foster, the compromise and assured him, the Democrats would unite & elect him & Nicholson, and that was to be the result. M. has poisoned Johnson of Greene & he said to me the other day he believed Hop Turney was as mean as Sam and that, there was intreaguing to raise one man & put down another much more worthy &c &c. All this is for your own eye & breast.

J. P. HARDWICKE

ALS. DLC–JKP. Addressed to Columbia.

1. Letter not found.
2. Spencer Jarnagin.
3. See J. George Harris to Polk, December 13, 1841.
4. See Samuel H. Laughlin to Polk, November 13, 1841.
5. Maury County.
6. Barkly Martin and John H. Dew of Maury County promoted A. O. P. Nicholson for one of the two U.S. Senate seats. In advancing Nicholson, Martin and Dew opposed Hopkins L. Turney, another Democratic candidate for the Senate.

FROM J. GEORGE HARRIS

My Dear Sir, Nashville Dec. 15. 1841

We are in the midst of schemers of all sorts, and at the suggestion and in the presence of our mutual friend Armstrong, I have a word or two for your ear. We have an eighteen months campaign before us upon which you know every thing hangs. Our party in the Legislature occupy a fair and equal ground with their opponents, at least. They have laid Foster and Jarnigan on the shelf where they may be kept in quiet by proper caution.[1] But another head springs from the hydra of Whiggism. Bell, supremely selfish as he is, exults at Foster's downfall, denounces his main course and endeavors to worm himself in to the place whence Foster has fallen. The tricks, the intrigues, the appliances, and the serpentine windings through which he is finding his way into some of our most reliable counsels are numberless and astonishing. And I fear that he finds one or more of our counsel who are as selfish as he is, and like him would *bargain* upon any terms for self-aggrandisement. The whigs hold caucuses nightly, while it seems to me that most of our friends are sleeping in fancied security, as if all had been accomplished.

You know my eternal hostility to Foster, and my hostility to Bell should be as endless as that—for no man could be sent to the Senate from this State who would devote half so much of his time and influence to heading you in all your hopes as Bell. I consider Bell and Foster *pas nobile fratrum,*[2] and with an ounce of timely caution they may both be consigned to oblivion. Bell should not be interrogated.[3] Let him remain under implied silence as adopting the non-instruction doctrine of the National Intelligencer, and he goes with Foster into retirement.[4]

But there are deep schemes that smack of bargain & corruption in which Bell is proposed to be advanced. The workers are like moles under soil. *There is one movement* that will prevent all that we fear, defeat both Foster and Bell, relieve our party from the imputation of preventing Tennessee from having any representation in the Senate, show that while we resist dumb whig candidates[5] we are yet willing to elect by our own votes a reputed whig rather than have our State without a representative in the U.S. Senate—thus more effectually disarming the dumb candidates whom I understand have mutually agreed to take the stump in the gubernatorial canvass, if no Senators are elected—and placing our party on higher and better ground, more easily defended, and in itself full of advantages. *That movement* is the election of Tom Brown to fill either of the vacancies forthwith, and that by resolution under the independent action of each House. I believe this can be done. It would increase your own strength in East Tennessee. It would keep Bell from the heart of the Union where he itches to get that he may affect your prospects. It would at once upset all the deep schemes now laid by might to cripple the party in this State, blast the prospects of both Bell and Foster forever, and secure to us a more glorious triumph than that of '39. And what is better than all would give us, *in fact,* a democratic senator, at least one whom we can instruct out if we choose.[6]

We want your counsel. We want your presence. We want the voice of the chief—at this moment, as we believe, more than ever. A bold push for Brown would throw dismay into the opposition ranks and completely frustrate all their insidious designs. An *attack* of this kind would *surprise* and discomfit them, and I think your voice could accomplish it.

The General[7] joins in insisting that if it be possible for you to make us a visit of a few days *immediately,* say Saturday that you have a quiet hour for conference, that you will do so.

J. Geo. Harris

ALS. DLC–JKP. Addressed to Columbia.

1. See Harris to Polk, December 13, 1841.
2. A mixture of French and Latin that translates "Not noble brothers."
3. See Samuel H. Laughlin to Polk, November 13, 1841.
4. On November 8 and 13, 1841, the Washington *National Intelligencer* carried articles opposing the right of state legislatures to instruct those whom they elect to the U.S. Senate.
5. Reference is to those candidates refusing to answer interrogatories asked by the legislature.
6. See Samuel H. Laughlin to Polk, November 13, 1841.
7. Robert Armstrong.

FROM HOPKINS L. TURNEY

My dear Sir Washington Dec. the 26th 1841

I have just received yours of the 14th Inst.[1] and am glad to learn you are at home and are before now in Nashville as I hope and believe you can and will be of great service to our friends, as they in the presant position of things need aid and assistance.[2]

I do not believe Bell has any possible chance to be elected as in the presant state of parties in the legislature, no man can be elected who cannot unite the entire strength of one or the other party. Bell cannot. He could not get more than a dozen whigs, and I know He cannot get five democrats. So I regard him as out of the question. Foster can unite the whigs, and with one democratick senator can be elected. This he can only obtain by a compromise with the democrats. Tho. Brown could unite the democrats if he could bring Wester & Sherrald[3] to the support of their man. He is the only whig in the State who could unite the democrats, & Foster the only whig who could unite the whigs, and therefore if a compromise is made it must be with either one of these men. I have writen a private letter to Brown, and also a letter to Maj Hardwicke on this subject, and urged Brown to go to Nashville and again to try his hand on Wester. Wester surely will fall into this plan when he sees that it is to result in a compromise, and that too in the selection of both from west of the mountain.

I regret the necessity which forced our friends into their presant position. It is unfortunate because it draws public attention to it, and to some extent diverts it from the odious measures of the extra session, but I do think the meriets of the issues thus formed at Nashville are with us, and that the people of the State will sustain our friends in their course. They present two facts that are unanswerable. 1st. Marrable,[4] without whose vote no whig could be elected. 2. the people will never again support *mum* candidates, and I might add a third: The attempt to make an election in the absence of a corum of the senate.

I shall write to my old friend R. B. Moore[5] this day in which I will not only give him facts but will also freely express my opinions in relation to A.O.P.N. which you know are of long standing, and I do it with the belief that it will make Nicholson my uncompromiseing enemy for life. For that however I dont *care a button.*

I saw a letter from M. A. Long to Waterson[6] in which he says that Carroll & Nicholson are spoken of as senators, and that propositions of compromise are makeing &c. I will not stand in the way of an adjustment of our diffaculties, but I must be premitted to say, that to if I am made to stand aside in order to make place for N. it would to say the least of it, be bad treatment, as no good reason could be assigned, except to make room for him. If any other good and true man is selected in my sted I have not aught to Say against it.

You have seen the message.[7] The fiscal project[8] has no advocates in congress except the Tyler & Webster Whigs. The *White Charleys*[9] are understood to be opposed to it. The democrats are also opposed to it, and will in a fiew days make open war on it in the senate. This I fear is bad policy. If the Clay men were 1st to make war on the measure, we would have an oppertunaty of compromiseing with the Tyler men, and of substituteing our own plan, and thereby produce a union between us and them on this great question, which would enable us to controle the house and perhaps to reorganise it. However there never can be a reunion between the friends of Clay and Webster & Tyler.

I would be glad to hear from you at all times, and when anything occurs worthy of communication I will write.

H. L. TURNEY

ALS. DLC–JKP. Addressed to Columbia,

1. Letter not found.
2. Reference is to the delay and confusion in the election of U.S. senators from Tennessee. See William H. Polk to Polk, September 7, 1841.
3. John W. Wester and Cravens Sherrell.
4. Henry H. Marable.
5. Possibly Richard B. Moore of Maury County, not identified further.
6. Harvey M. Watterson.
7. President Tyler's First Annual Message, December 7, 1841.
8. See J. George Harris to Polk, December 13, 1841.
9. Reference is to the followers of John White, Speaker of the U.S. House of Representatives.

TO SAMUEL H. LAUGHLIN

My Dear Sir: Columbia Decr. 29th 1841

I have received no letter from Nashville since I left, and presume from that circumstance that the Senatorial question[1] rests in *statu quo.*[2] When will your resolutions be taken up?[3] I hope the Democracy of both Houses may be united in their support. Great pains should be taken to see the few who have doubts, and to convince them if possible, of the great importance of uniting with the body of their friends & presenting an undivided front. If this can be affected, I think it probable that *Brown* at least may be chosen. This done, the State will not be wholly unrepresented in the Senate, and our attitude before the people will be much strengthened. If we have one Senator & should fail to have another the people will be better satisfied. *Brown* we know is not the individual choice of our friends, but he admits the right of instructions, has answered interrogatories,[4] whilst others of his party have refused, upon some subjects he agrees with us, and our doubting friends should remember that he is voted for, only on principles of concession & compromise. They cannot elect whom they will & must take whom they can. I hope there may at last be entire union on this point.

It is due to candour that I should say to you, that within the last few days, some [of] our plain & honest friends from the country have come to me & expressed their fears that if no Senators were chosen we would be weakened in the State. To such I have pointed to your Resolutions of compromise & endeavoured to allay their apprehensions. Do let me hear what is doing & your opinions of the prospects ahead.

When I was at Nashville I failed as I had intended to have done, to have a conversation with you, in relation to your private affairs concerning which you wrote me, when I was at my plantation in Mississippi. I cannot do otherwise than feel an interest in your behalf in the matter, to which you refer & still hope that our friend Johnson will do as Mr Grundy, Majr. Donaldson[5] & myself did. I will do any and every thing in my power to bring about such a result. Indeed not having heard of it for a long time, I supposed the matter had been understood between you and him. If Majr. Donelson would give his views to *Johnson* also; they would probably have weight. He is a reasonable and an honourable man, & will I know listen kindly to views and opinions of his friends. No man appreciats more properly than I do, your sufferings & sacrafices in our cause, & I hope that you may be relieved from the embarrassing difficulty to which you refer. I do not know what further I can say. You know what I have borne; & now that I have leizure to take a survey of my private affairs, I find them in a condition to require all my attention & energies to avoid pecuniary embarrassments, to which I have not heretofore been accustomed.[6]

JAMES K. POLK

ALS. DLC–JKP. Addressed to Nashville and marked *"Private."*

1. See William H. Polk to Polk, September 7, 1841.
2. The ablative case of the noun in the Latin expression, "status quo."
3. On December 20, 1841, Laughlin introduced in the Tennessee Senate resolutions that the legislature should choose two U.S. senators and that those senators should be Hopkins L. Turney and Thomas Brown. The resolutions passed in the Senate on December 31, 1841, but failed in the Tennessee House on January 5, 1842.
4. See Laughlin to Polk, November 13, 1841.
5. Andrew Jackson Donelson.
6. See Ezekiel P. McNeal to Polk, December 2, 1840.

FROM JONATHAN P. HARDWICKE

My Dear Sir, Nashville Decr. 31st 1841

I am glad to say our Senatorial preamble & Resolutions passed the Senate to day, the vote was 13–12, a street[1] party matter from which circumstance, I think there is but little hope the House will concur.[2] Now Sir, if this move of ours dont alarm and kick away the only prop, from the gentry, I begin to think we wont make an election this session, not with standing Ephraim[3] is now telling our Democratic friends he does now and all ways intended answering our interogateries.[4]

I hope this move will place the whole matter in a fair point of view before the country, and the blame upon those who, ought to bare it. Please to let me know what you done with the package I directed to Dillard Hardwicke [in] Mi.[5] I have not herd from him nor did I think to enquire of you when here.

J. P. HARDWICKE

P.S. C. Johnson says the parties are standing with swords drawn, but no move yet. Turney thinks Capt Tyler will take sides with the Democrats, and lead off on the plain old Republican tract.

ALS. DLC–JKP. Addressed to Columbia.

1. Misspelling of "straight."
2. See Polk to Samuel H. Laughlin, December 29, 1841.
3. Ephraim H. Foster.
4. See Samuel H. Laughlin to Polk, November 13, 1841.
5. Probably a relative residing in Mississippi, Dillard Hardwicke is not identified further.

TO ANDREW JACKSON

Dear Sir: Columbia Decr. 31st 1841

Your opinion that a Bank of the United States chartered by Congress, was unconstitutional, and that such an institution possessed a power, which in the hands of ambitious or corrupt men, would make it dangerous to the public liberty, has been often expressed in the most solemn forms. Your settled opposition to the late Bank of the United States, was well known by your friends, before your election to the Presidency. That opposition rested, not *alone* upon any objections, (strong as these were,) to the peculiar provisions in the charter of that Bank, but also, upon the higher ground of the unconstitutionality and inexpediency of that or any similar institution. Notwithstanding these, are known to have been your opinions, not only previously to your election, but during the whole period of your Presidency, and since that time, you have no doubt observed that certain general and detached passages, contained in some of your messages to Congress, have been seperated from their context, & often quoted and referred to by the advocates of a National Bank, for the purpose of invoking (unjustly I know) the weight of your opinion as authority in favour of the establishment of *some Bank*, similar to the late one, but with suitable & proper restrictions and modifications of its charter. Sometimes they insist, that your opposition to the late Bank, had no other or higher object than the establishment of "another Bank" (of discount & deposite) "upon its ruins, based on the revenue and credit of the Government." Those who attribute to you such a motive or object do you, I am sure great injustice.

The frequency and boldness with which the passages of your messages to which I refer, have been quoted and relied on, and especially of late, by those who I am persuaded either misunderstood their meaning, or would misrepresent your opinions, as inferred from them, to the public, induces me to call your attention to them,[1] and to ask that you will state more distinctly and fully than you have done in the passages themselves, the character of the fiscal agency, which you suggested to Congress as a practicable substitute for the late Bank of the United States, and which would avoid the Constitutional & other objections to which in your judgment, that or any similar institution was subject. It would not I know be necessary to trouble you, by asking such a statement, in order to satisfy candid men, to whatever political party they may belong, who are willing to do you justice, much less those who have been familiar with what your real opinions have at all times been, but it may be important that you should do so, that in aftertimes there may be a refutation coming directly from yourself of the *false inferences* which have been drawn from the general ph[r]aseology, employed in the passages referred to, as also of the *false opinions* which have been, and which may again be attributed to you.

The passages referred to, are contained in your annual messages to Congress, of December 1829, of December 1830, and in your veto message of the 10th of July 1832, returning to Congress, with your objections to the same, the "Bill to modify and continue the act entitled an act to incorporate the subscribers to the Bank of the United States." In your message of December 1829, you expressed the opinion that "Both the Constitutionality and the Expediency of the law creating this Bank" (the late Bank of the United States) "are *well questioned* by a large portion of our fellow-citizens; and it must be admitted by all that it has failed in the great end of establishing a uniform & sound currency. Under these circumstances, *if* such an institution is deemed *essential to the fiscal operations of the government,* I submit to the wisdom of the Legislature whether a national one, founded upon the credit of the Government and its revenues, might not be devised, which would avoid all constitutional difficulties, and at the same time secure all the advantages to the Government and country which were expected to result from the present Bank."

In your message of December 1830 you again call the attention of Congress to "the importance of the principles involved in the inquiry whether it will be proper to recharter the Bank of the United States." In that message you say, "Nothing has occurred to lessen in any degree the dangers, which many of our citizens apprehend from that institution as at present organized. In the spirit of improvement, and compromise which distinguishes our country and its institutions, it becomes us to enquire whether it be not possible to secure the advantages afforded by the present Bank, through the agency of a Bank of the United States, so modified in its *principles & structure* as to obviate constitutional and other objections." In the paragraph immediately following you give the outline of the "*principles and structure*" of the institution which you supposed it practicable to substitute for the late Bank of the United States. You say "It is thought practicable to organize such a Bank with the necessary officers as *a branch of the Treasury Department,* based on the public and individual deposites, *without power to make loans or purchase property, which shall remit the funds of the government,* and the expense of which may be paid if thought adviseable, by allowing its officers to *sell bills of exchange* to private individuals at a moderate premium. Not being a corporate body, having *no stockholders, debtor, or property,* and but few officers, it would not be obnoxious to the constitutional objections which are urged against the present Bank; and having no means to operate on the hopes, fears and interests of large masses of the community, it would be shorn of the influence which makes that Bank formidable. The States would be strengthened by having in their hands, the means of furnishing the local paper currency through their own Banks; while the Bank of the United States, *though issuing no paper* would check the issues of the State Banks, by taking their notes in deposite & for exchange, only so long as they continue to be redeemed with specie." You conclude your notice of the subject by saying, "*These* suggestions are made *not so much as a recommendation,* as with a view of calling the attention of Congress to the possible modifications of a system which cannot continue to exist in its present form, without occasional collisions with the local authorities, and perpetual apprehensions and discontent on the part of the States and the people."

In your veto message of July 10th 1832, after having made an argument against the Constitutionality and expediency of an incorporated National Bank, and referring probably to the same description of fiscal agency which you had suggested in your Message of December 1830, you say, "That a Bank of the United States, *competent to all the duties which may be required by the Government,* might be so organized as not to infringe on our own delegated powers, and the reserved rights of the States I do not entertain a doubt. Had the Executive been called upon to furnish the project of such an institution, the duty would have been cheerfully performed."

In the general ph[r]aseology employed, in these passages, the term *Bank* is used; but no one who will carefully examine them, with an honest view of arriving at truth, can believe that it was used in the ordinary acceptation of that term, as commonly understood & applied to the business of Banking in this country. It is clear that you did not mean to be understood as expressing an opinion favourable to the establishment of an incorporated Bank of the United States, in which private Stockholders should own a part or the whole of the shares, for in your message of 1830, you expressly state, that the fiscal agency which you suggest, as a substitute for the late Bank of the United States, would have "*no stockholders, debtors or property,*" and in all your messages when you speak of such a Bank and especially in your veto message you declare it be unconstitutional, and "*dangerous to the Government & country.*" It is clear that you did not mean a Bank of discount, for you say, that the fiscal agency suggested would be "*without power to make loans or purchase property.*" No power was proposed to be given to it, *to purchase* Bills of Exchange from individuals, for that would have been to discount their paper and loan them money. It is clear that you did not mean a Bank of paper issues, for you say, that "*though issuing no paper,* it would check the issues of the State Banks." The fiscal agency suggested was proposed to be *"a branch of the Treasury Department,"* and its duties were defined to be *"to remit the funds of the Government."* Its officers who were probably intended to be officers of the customs, it being *"a branch of the Treasury Department,"* it was suggested might "if thought adviseable," be clothed with authority to "sell Bills of Exchange to private individuals at a moderate premium," in order to meet "the expense," of such Government remittance.

The fiscal agency therefore which in your messages, you suggested by the use of the term *Bank*, seems to have been in fact, when taken in connection with your own description of its character, its object & its duties, divested of many of the most essential attributes and functions of a Bank, as these are generally understood in this country, and to have been a simple institution connected with the Treasury Department, designed to afford facilities to the Government in effecting remittances of the public money from the points of collection to the points where it was needed for disbursement. In doing this it was proposed to accomodate trade to the extent of the Government remittances, by raising deposites from individuals, at the points of disbursement and selling to them Bills of Exchange, for the amounts deposited on points where the funds of the Government were, and where individuals making the deposite wished to use their money. By this operation the Government would effect the remittance of its funds, and the individual his "at a moderate premium." The fiscal agency, which you sugested, may have been and probably was designed to be, (though you said nothing distinctly on that point), the keeper of the money of the Government, from the period of collection until the period of disbursement.

These are the conclusions, to which an examination of your messages, and especially that of 1830, would seem to lead. You will be able I doubt not, to place your own views, as you entertained them, at the several periods, when your messages, referred to, were communicated to Congress, in so clear a light as to prevent them hereafter from being misunderstood or misrepresented.

JAMES K. POLK

ALS. NNPM–Autographs, Presidents of the U.S. Addressed to the Hermitage. ALS, copy, in DLC–JKP. Andrew Jackson penned the following endorsement at the end of the ALS: "Note—the word *Bank*, when applied to mony, its meaning is where mony is kept. The government to convay their funds have the power to buy a bill for that purpose. Say a merchant has mony at St Lou[i]s and wants funds in philadelphia, the keeper of the public mony at St Leous should be authorised to receive the merchants mony and give him a draft upon the keeper of public mony or Banker at Philadelphia or should the government want mony at St Lewis or elsewhere, and a merchant in Newyork had funds there the government wanting mony at that place, might buy a bill of exchange from the merchant to transfers its fund to the point where the mony is wanted. This is a power that the Genl government possesses, which does not infringe the constitution and when the true signification of the word Bank is looked into the word Bank as used in my messages referred to must be considered as excluding all kinds of incorporated Banks, and merely as the keeper of the deposits of the funds of the Government and its fiscal agent."

1. Polk's letter to Andrew Jackson was occasioned by recent press suggestions that John Tyler's banking views were similar to those of Jackson. On January 4, 1842, Polk wrote Andrew Jackson Donelson, "I see it insisted upon in some of the newspapers, that the Bank he suggested in some of his messages, was similar to Mr Tyler's Exchequer Bank." ALS. DLC–AJD.

INDEX

Smith, Parker, and Cutler

WAYNE CUTLER is associate professor of American history at Vanderbilt University, where he has taught since 1975. He earned his bachelor's degree at Lamar University and his master's and doctor's degree from the University of Texas at Austin.

Professor Cutler became director of the Polk Project in 1975 and served as associate editor of the fourth volume of the correspondence. He began his professional career in 1966 as an editorial associate of the *Southwestern Historical Quarterly* and moved to the assistant editorship of the Henry Clay Project in 1970.

EARL J. SMITH, associate editor of the Polk Project, received his bachelor's degree from Haverford College and his master's and doctor's degrees from Vanderbilt University. He came to the Polk Project in 1975 on a postdoctoral fellowship sponsored by the National Historical Publications and Records Commission.

CARESE M. PARKER, associate editor of the Polk Project, took her bachelor's and master's degrees from Auburn University. Before joining the Polk staff in 1976 she taught at Columbia Community College and served as a research assistant for the Andrew Jackson Project.

S U M N E R
W I L S O N
R U T H E R F O R D
B E D F O R D
L I N C O L N
W H I T E
H A M I L T O N
C H E R O K E E
G E O R